FROM INQUIRY
TO ACADEMIC
WRITING

A Text and Reader

Stuart Greene

University of Notre Dame

April Lidinsky

Indiana University South Bend

Bedford/St. Martin's   BOSTON ■ NEW YORK

For Bedford/St. Martin's

Executive Editors: Leasa Burton and Stephen A. Scipione
Senior Production Editor: Lori Chong Roncka
Senior Production Supervisor: Nancy Myers
Senior Marketing Manager: Karita dos Santos
Editorial Assistant: Marisa Feinstein
Production Assistants: Lidia MacDonald-Carr and Lindsay DiGianvittorio
Copyeditor: Barbara Bell
Text Design: Linda M. Robertson
Art Director: Donna Lee Dennison
Cover Art: Lucio del Pezzo, *Casellario*, 1988. Painted wood.
        © Berardinelli Arte, Verona, Italy.
Composition: Stratford/TexTech
Printing and Binding: R. R. Donnelley & Sons Company

President: Joan E. Feinberg
Editorial Director: Denise B. Wydra
Editor in Chief: Karen S. Henry
Director of Marketing: Karen Melton Soeltz
Director of Editing, Design, and Production: Marcia Cohen
Managing Editor: Elizabeth M. Schaaf

Library of Congress Control Number: 2007934301

Manufactured in the United States of America.

1   2   3   4   5   14   13   12   11   10

For information, write: Bedford/St. Martin's, 75 Arlington Street, Boston, MA 02116 (617–399–4000)

ISBN-10: 0–312–66778–7   ISBN-13: 978–0–312–66778–8
ISBN-10: 0–312–38767–9   ISBN-13: 978–0–312–38767–9 (high school edition)

Acknowledgments

Jean Anyon. "The Economic Is Political." From *Radical Possibilities: Public Policy, Urban Education and a New Social Movement* by Jean Anyon. Copyright © 2005 by Taylor & Francis Group LLC. Reprinted by permission of Routledge, an imprint of Taylor & Francis Group.
Kwame Anthony Appiah. "Moral Disagreement." From *Cosmopolitanism: Ethics in a World of Strangers* by Kwame Anthony Appiah. Copyright © 2006 Kwame Anthony Appiah. Used by permission of W. W. Norton & Company, Inc.

Acknowledgments and copyrights are continued at the back of the book on pages 829–31, which constitute an extension of the copyright page. It is a violation of the law to reproduce these selections by any means whatsoever without the written permission of the copyright holder.

Preface for Instructors

From Inquiry to Academic Writing: A Text and Reader is a rhetoric and reader that introduces students to college-level reading, thinking, inquiry, analysis, and argument. It is based on a first-year composition course that we have taught over the years in which we guide students through the writing process to produce essays that use evidence and sources in increasingly complex ways. Throughout, we present academic writing as conversational — as a collegial exchange of ideas, undertaken in a spirit of collaboration in the pursuit of new knowledge. On the one hand, we want students to see that academic writing is a social act in which they are expected to work responsibly with the ideas of others. On the other hand, we encourage students to see themselves as makers of knowledge — as writers who use sources in a variety of ways to develop and advance arguments that make new contributions to ongoing conversations about ideas and issues. Thus, the first part of the book introduces the habits of mind and core skills students will need to enter multidisciplinary conversations of ideas, and the second part of the book presents several multidisciplinary conversations, forums in which students can use those habits and skills to enter.

We aim to demystify cross-curricular thinking, reading, and writing by breaking down their processes into a series of manageable habits and skills that students can learn and practice. Because academic writing involves complex and overlapping skills, we use a sequenced pedagogy to clarify (without oversimplifying) the various skills involved. That is, the text portion of the book — the rhetoric in Part One — offers a "step-by-step" approach to developing academic arguments. For example, we explain that students must learn to make inquiries (by asking questions to discover and explore issues) and value complexity (by avoiding binary thinking and engaging with multiple perspectives); and then we provide activities to help students practice and develop those habits of mind.

The second part of the book is built around multidisciplinary conversations of ideas that are as important in the academy as they are in the culture at large. Because these conversations are complex and rich, the readings we have chosen are complex and rich. They include substantial texts both by academics (such as Mary Louise Pratt, Henry A. Giroux, and Cynthia L. Selfe) and by public intellectuals (such as Jonathan Kozol, Malcolm Gladwell, and Barbara Ehrenreich). Although the readings tend to be lengthy and challenging, they are also (if the responses of our students are any indication) engaging and bursting with ideas and perspectives that students can adapt and use in their own thinking and writing. Further, students are likely to have a stake — and some expertise — in these particular conversations, which focus on higher education, globalization, race and class, gender, and popular culture. Additionally, the questions and assignments in the reader support students by reinforcing the skills and strategies (how to read rhetorically, make connections among ideas, and pursue a line of research to develop an academic argument) presented in the text.

We now take a detailed chapter-by-chapter look at what's in the text, and what's in the reader.

■ Organization of the Text

Although you can teach the chapters in Part One, "A Text for Moving from Inquiry to Academic Writing," in any order, adapting them to suit the needs of your course and your students, the arc of the text follows an incremental and cumulative sequence that begins with academic thinking and proceeds to academic reading, academic research, and finally to academic writing. That said, we hasten to add that we constantly emphasize the recursive and overlapping nature of these skills (especially the connection between reading and writing) and the centrality of the writing process. Indeed, we assume students will be writing throughout the semester, and so punctuate every chapter with short readings and activities designed to get students to pause and try out the kinds of writing they will need to practice through the various stages of developing their papers.

We begin with an introduction for students, in which we explain what academic writing is, and how the book is designed to help them develop as academic thinkers, readers, and writers. Part One, "A Text for Moving from Inquiry to Academic Writing," opens with an overview of academic writing as a process motivated by inquiry, and is followed by chapters that offer strategies for reading critically and working with other writers' ideas. Inevitably, reading and writing processes are intertwined. Thus in Chapter 2 we encourage students to practice "writerly reading" — reading texts as writers analyzing the decisions other writers make (whether those writers are scholars or peers) — so that they can implement the most appropriate strategies given their own purpose for writing. Although Chapters 2 through 5 address the nuts and bolts of starting to write, from how to mark a text to forming questions and developing a working thesis, we recognize that this process is rarely linear and that it benefits from conversation with invested readers. Chapters 6 and 7 help students develop and support their theses by providing a range of strategies for finding and working with sources — for example, showing students the ways they can paraphrase, summarize, and synthesize in the service of their writing. In Chapters 8 and 9 we link writerly reading with the ability to practice "readerly writing," or writing that is self-conscious of readers' needs.

Chapter 10 presents revision in the context of peer groups. The responses of their classmates can help students shape more effective research questions, for example, or identify areas in a draft where more evidence is needed to support an argument. The materials for and about peer workshops foster productive group interaction at every stage of writing, from reading, collecting, and planning to developing, researching (for some assignments), and revising. These materials emphasize both the spirit of inquiry that should guide peer editing and the conversational aspect of writing that should be evident in peer workshops and on the page as a writer engages the ideas of others. Finally, in Chapter 11, we describe strategies for conducting original research that build on earlier discussions of using personal experience and writing a researched argument.

As we noted earlier, although the process of developing an academic argument can be messy and unruly at times, the structured step-by-step pedagogy in Part One should support students during each stage of the process. Throughout we use short readings to reinforce the skills students need to enter a conversation of ideas. Most of these readings are followed by questions ("For Analysis and Discussion") that send students back into the readings to identify and internalize the writers' rhetorical strategies. In every chapter, "Steps to . . ." boxes summarize the major points about each stage of reading, thinking, and writing, quick references that bring the most salient information into focus for students to review and practice. And "Practice Sequences" in each chapter ask students to try out and build on the strategies we have explained or demonstrated. In places we also provide intermittent templates, formulas, and worksheets that students can use as heuristics or to organize information as they read and write. Your students should feel further supported and encouraged by seeing the many examples of student writing we've included in Part One, side by side with examples of professional writing.

■ Organization of the Reader

Part Two, "A Reader for Entering the Conversation of Ideas," includes thirty selections that approximate the kinds of reading and writing college students are expected to do in most of their classes. Although the selections are generally longer and more complex than those found in most other first-year composition readers, students who have had some practice with the reading and writing strategies in the first part of the book are generally more than up to the task of working with these readings. Moreover our students are usually exhilarated by what they discover in the readings — the kind of "big thinking" they came to college to experience.

As you would expect in a book that emphasizes cross-curricular writing, many of the readings are taken from journals and publications intended for scholarly audiences, and so model what would traditionally be considered academic writing. They are written by academics like Robert Scholes, Ann duCille, Judith Lorber, and Henry Jenkins, scholars whose texts are influential among their peers and whose ideas are respected and admired by those outside the academy. But other selections are drawn from thought-provoking and engaging books on recent *New York Times* best sellers' lists, many of them required reading on college campuses. The authors of these books — Thomas L. Friedman, Thomas Frank, Deborah Tannen, and Eric Schlosser, to name only a few — are intellectuals who use the same strategies of research and analysis that academic writers do. And, like academic writers, they use those strategies and their skills to take on big ideas, frame them in interesting new ways, and offer striking examples that capture the interest of readers.

Although all of these readings are researched essays — texts that build on ideas others have written about — they also provide students with a wide range of rhetorical styles to use as models. Some readings take a journalistic approach, objective and matter-of-fact. Some offer autobiographical details, the authors using personal anecdotes to explain their interest in an issue or illustrate a point. And some take a more formal tone, relying on research and expertise to build their arguments. We chose these selections in part because of the many different strategies they use to make many different kinds of connections — from the personal to the scholarly, from the individual experiences to the larger social patterns. This multileveled inquiry is at the heart of the reading and thinking and writing we invite students to learn in this book.

We have divided the readings into five chapters, each focused on a range of inquiries into a central topic. The readings in Chapter 12, "Conventional and Unconventional Wisdom," ask "What does it mean to be educated, and who decides?" The authors in this chapter ask us to question common assumptions about how classrooms operate, from the dynamics between teacher and student to the material that has been designated "important knowledge." These readings will help students see their past and present educational experiences through fresh eyes, and help them consider the relationship between education and social power and envision alternatives to standard educational practices and goals.

Chapter 13, "A World of Difference/A Shrinking World," contains readings that ask "Who are 'we' in relation to 'others'?" These authors offer models for making sense of the nationalism and globalization that together shape our daily lives. What do failed civilizations, the game of soccer, and the "tipping point" of cross-cultural behaviors help us see about present-day politics and economics?

The readings in Chapter 14, "'Check All the Boxes That Apply': Unstable Identities in the United States," raise the question "How do we experience the daily effects of race and class assumptions?" The authors in this chapter provide new ways of analyzing the social categories that shape our lives, from the way we do (or don't) see ourselves reflected in the toys we buy, to our awareness of class barriers in America. How have seemingly stable categories of race changed over time, and why? How do ethnic identities become "hot" or "cold" commodities?

The selections in Chapter 15, "Acting 'Naturally': The Practices of Gender," ask "How do we learn to think and behave as gendered people?" These authors question how and why we act in female and male roles. They ask us to consider how cultural practices and institutions — like sports, children's films, advertisements, and even preschool — create and support gender divisions, sometimes with quite damaging results. These readings here offer new lenses for seeing gendered behaviors and their implications in ways that may be surprising and possibly transforming.

Chapter 16, "Indoctrination or Revolution? Technologies of Popular Culture," contains readings that ask "How does popular culture reinforce or unsettle social standards?" These authors shine a light on popular pastimes — playing video games, surfing the Web, eating fast food, reading fantasy novels — often contesting the widespread belief that they are bad for us. Indeed, author Steven Johnson proclaims as much in his provocative title, *Everything Bad Is Good for You*. Although the dangers of popular culture have been debated for years, these readings offer arguments and perspectives that are likely to be new and thought provoking.

Every reading is introduced by a headnote that provides biographical and contextual information, as well as some suggestions for what students might pay attention to as they read it. And every reading is followed by three kinds of questions: "Reading Rhetorically," "Inquiring Further," and "Framing Conversations." "Reading Rhetorically" questions ask students to consider the stylistic decisions the writer makes in crafting the piece. "Inquiring Further" questions use the essay as a launching point for further inquiry, research, and discovery about an issue raised in the text. "Framing Conversations" questions suggest topics for writing essays in response to the ideas of two or sometimes three authors, asking students to use framing strategies to develop their ideas on the issue at hand.

Finally, the book concludes with assignment sequences for instructors to implement or adapt to their specific needs. They define a subject for inquiry and offer a sequential path through readings and several writing assignments that build on one another. Assignment sequences give students the opportunity to engage in intellectual inquiry that lasts longer than one assignment. Instead of writing a paper and then moving on to a completely new topic, each paper in a sequence helps students develop ideas for the next paper, to consider an issue from many perspectives, and with a range of sources. In other words, these assignment sequences invite students to read, research, and write with the habits of mind and practices of academic writers, writers who are in conversation with other thinkers, and who bring scholarly analysis to experiences beyond the classroom.

■ The Text Is Available Separately

If you are interested in assigning the text chapters only (Chapters 1 through 11), they are available separately, without the accompanying readings in Part Two, as *From Inquiry to Academic Writing: A Practical Guide.*

■ Additional Resources

We have prepared an instructor's manual, *Resources for Teaching FROM INQUIRY TO ACADEMIC WRITING: A TEXT AND READER.* The first part of the manual addresses every step of the process of academic writing we set forth in Part One, with additional comments on the readings integrated in the text chapters. Not only do we discuss many of the issues involved in taking our rhetorical approach to academic argument — problems and questions students and instructors may have — we also suggest background readings on the research informing our approach. The second part of the manual provides concrete strategies for teaching the selections in Part Two of the book; it is based on our own experiences working with these readings. We also suggest possible responses to the questions that follow the readings in Part Two.

The instructor's manual is available as a bound volume; but it also can be downloaded from the companion Web site, **www.bedfordstmartins .com/frominquiry**. Additional resources on the Web site include downloadable templates, worksheets, and summary boxes for students; TopLinks that supplement the readings in the book; and connections to the suite of online resources offered by Bedford/St. Martin's, including *Re: Writing.*

■ Acknowledgments

We would first like to thank the many reviewers who commented on the proposal and the manuscript. Their comments were invariably useful, and frequently cheering as well. The list of reviewers includes Angela Adams, Loyola University Chicago; Steve Adkison, Idaho State University; Teresa Fernandez Arab, University of Kansas; Yesho Atil, Asheville-Buncombe Technical Community College; Paula Bacon, Pace University–Pleasantville; Susan Bailor, Front Range Community College; Mary Ellen Bertolini, Middlebury College; Laurel Bollinger, University of Alabama–Huntsville; Margaret Bonesteel, Syracuse University; Laurie Britt-Smith, St. Louis University; Lise Buranen, California State University, Los Angeles; Marie

Coffey, San Antonio College; Carolyn Cole, Oklahoma Baptist University; Tami Comstock-Peavy, Arapahoe Community College; Emily Cosper, Delgado Community College; Ryan Crider, Missouri State University; Calum Cunningham, Fanshawe College–London; J. Madison Davis, University of Oklahoma–Norman; Erin Denney, Community College of San Francisco; Jason DePolo, North Carolina A&T State University; Brock Dethier, Utah State University; Lisa Egan, Brown University; Ed Eleazer, Francis Marion University; Elaine Fredericksen, University of Texas–El Paso; Rhoda Greenstone, Long Beach City College; Rima Gulshan, George Mason University; Sinceree Gunn, University of Alabama–Huntsville; Ann Hartney, Fort Lewis College; Virginia Scott Hendrickson, Missouri State University; Zachery Hickman, University of Miami; Monica Hogan, Johnson County Community College; Karen Keaton Jackson, North Carolina Central University; Margaret Johnson, Idaho State University; Laura Katsaros, Monmouth University; Howard Kerner, Polk Community College; Jeff Klausman, Whatcom Community College; Tamara Kuzmenkov, Tacoma Community College; Erin Lebacqz, University of New Mexico; Lindsay Lewan, Arapahoe Community College; April Lewandowski, Front Range Community College–Westminster; Renee Major, Louisiana State University; Mark McBeth, John Jay College; Timothy McGinn, Northwest Arkansas Community College; Erica Messenger, Bowling Green State University–Main; Alyce Miller, Indiana University; Whitney Myers, University of New Mexico; Teddy Norris, St. Charles Community College; Lolly J. Ockerstrom, Park University; Jill Onega, University of Alabama–Huntsville; Robert Peltier, Trinity College; Jeanette Pierce, San Antonio College; Mary Jo Reiff, University of Tennessee; Mary Roma, New York University; David Ryan, University of San Francisco; Daniel Schenker, University of Alabama–Huntsville; Roy Stamper, North Carolina State University; Scott Stevens, Western Washington University; Sarah Stone, University of California–Berkeley; Joseph Sullivan, Marietta College; Gretchen Treadwell, Fort Lewis College; Charles Warren, Salem State College; Patricia Webb, Arizona State University; Susan Garrett Weiss, Goucher College; Worth Weller, Indiana University–Purdue University Fort Wayne; and Jackie White, Lewis University.

We are also grateful to many people at Bedford/St. Martin's, starting with president Joan E. Feinberg, editorial director Denise B. Wydra, and editor-in-chief Karen S. Henry. We would especially like to thank executive editor Leasa Burton, who believed in this project early on and told us to be prepared to revise — revise a lot. (And we have!) Steve Scipione has been a terrific editor: he read our work carefully and offered sage advice at every stage of the process. We could not have completed this project without Leasa and Steve and their tireless assistants, Sarah Guariglia and Marisa Feinstein. In the marketing department, we thank marketing director Karen M. Soeltz, and are especially grateful to marketing manager Karita dos Santos and her assistant Jessica Chesnutt. The talented production department conscientiously steered the manuscript through a demanding schedule to create the book you hold. We thank managing editor Elizabeth M. Schaaf; assistant managing editor John Amburg; Lori Chong Roncka, the book's patient and scrupulous production editor; and their assistant Lidia McDonald-Carr. Barbara Bell provided exceptionally alert and constructive copyediting, while Sandy Schechter and Warren Drabek negotiated the complicated process of acquiring permissions. Anna Palchik oversaw the design of the book, and Donna Dennison designed the cover.

A note from Stuart Greene: I want to thank the many students and faculty with whom I've worked over the years. Specifically, I would like to thank Kelly Kinney, Stephen Fox, Rebecca Nowacek, and Katherine Weese, who served as my assistant directors in the past and who taught me a great deal about the teaching of writing. I also would like to thank Robert Kachur, who made important contributions to early iterations of this book. And I will always appreciate the many discussions I have had with John Duffy over these many years and with Connie Mick, a tireless and innovative teacher of writing. A special thanks to Mike Palmquist with whom I taught writing as "conversation" more than twenty years ago and who gave this book direction. Finally, very special thanks to Denise Della Rossa, who has listened to me rehearse these ideas for years. I dedicate this book to her.

A note from April Lidinsky: I am grateful for the superb pedagogical training I received from Lou Kelly at the University of Iowa and Kurt Spellmeyer and Hugh English at Rutgers, the State University of New Jersey, who demonstrated the deep pleasures of theorizing and practicing a hermeneutical approach to writing. Ron Christ, also at Rutgers, taught me the ropes of classical rhetoric and the connected delights of close reading and "close writing." My colleagues and graduate student instructors at the University of Notre Dame, especially Julie Bruneau, Connie Mick, Marion C. Rohrleitner, Misty Schieberle, and Scott T. Smith, inspired me with their energy and vision. Without students to test and sharpen our ideas, this book would not be possible; my teaching has deepened through interactions with many wonderful students over the years. More personally, I am indebted to JoElla Hunter and Tom Lidinsky, my parents, for their model of lifelong reading and learning, and to Ken Smith for his talent for crafting sentences as well as a life of meaning. My thinking, writing, and daily life are immeasurably richer for his partnership.

Contents

Preface for Instructors   iii

Introduction: What Is Academic Writing?   1

PART ONE
A Text for Moving from Inquiry to Academic Writing   9

1 Starting with Inquiry:
   Habits of Mind of Academic Writers   11

   Academic Writers Make Inquiries   13
   - *Steps to Inquiry   14*
   - *A Practice Sequence: Inquiring   14*

   Academic Writers Seek and Value Complexity   16
   - *Steps to Seeking and Valuing Complexity   17*
   - *A Practice Sequence: Seeking and Valuing Complexity   17*

   Academic Writers See Writing as a Conversation   18
   - *Steps to Joining an Academic Conversation   20*
   - *A Practice Sequence: Joining an Academic Conversation   20*

Academic Writers Understand That Writing Is a Process   *21*

Collect Information and Material   *22*

■ *Steps to Collecting Information and Material   22*

Draft, and Draft Again   *22*

■ *Steps to Drafting   23*

Revise Significantly   *23*

■ *Steps to Revising   24*

2   **From Reading as a Writer
to Writing as a Reader   25**

Reading as an Act of Composing: Annotating   25

■ *A Practice Sequence: Annotating   28*

Reading as a Writer: Analyzing a Text Rhetorically   29

E. D. HIRSCH JR., **Preface to *Cultural Literacy*   29**

Identify the Situation   *33*

Identify the Writer's Purpose   *33*

Identify the Writer's Claims   *34*

Identify the Writer's Audience   *34*

■ *Steps to Analyzing a Text Rhetorically   35*

■ *A Practice Sequence: Reading Rhetorically   35*

Writing as a Reader: Composing a Rhetorical Analysis   38

Write a Rhetorical Analysis of a Paragraph   *39*

ADA MARÍA ISASI-DÍAZ, **Hispanic in America:
Starting Points   40**

■ *A Practice Sequence: Rhetorically Analyzing a Paragraph   42*

Write a Rhetorical Analysis of an Essay   *43*

BARBARA EHRENREICH, **Cultural Baggage   *43***

■ *A Practice Sequence: Rhetorically Analyzing an Essay   46*

3   **From Identifying Claims to Analyzing Arguments   47**

Identifying Types of Claims   47

MYRA SADKER and DAVID SADKER, **Hidden Lessons   *48***

Identify Claims of Fact   *51*

Identify Claims of Value   *52*

Identify Claims of Policy   *52*

■ *Steps to Identifying Claims   53*

■ *A Practice Sequence: Identifying Claims   53*

Analyzing Arguments *53*

Analyze the Reasons Used to Support a Claim *54*

Identify Concessions *56*

Identify Counterarguments *57*

■ *Steps to Analyzing an Argument* *58*

Analyze a Sample Student Argument *59*

RYAN METHENY *(student writer),* ***from* The Problems and Dangers of Assimilatory Policies** *59*

■ *A Practice Sequence: Analyzing an Argument* *64*

4 From Identifying Issues to Forming Questions 65

Identifying Issues *67*

Draw on Your Personal Experience *67*

Identify What Is Open to Dispute *68*

Resist Binary Thinking *68*

Build On and Extend the Ideas of Others *69*

Read to Discover a Writer's Frame *71*

Consider the Constraints of the Situation *72*

■ *Steps to Identifying Issues* *73*

Identify Issues in an Essay *74*

ANNA QUINDLEN, **No Place Like Home** *74*

■ *A Practice Sequence: Identifying Issues* *76*

Formulating Issue-Based Questions *77*

Refine Your Topic *78*

Explain Your Interest in the Topic *79*

Identify an Issue *79*

Formulate Your Topic as a Question *80*

Acknowledge Your Audience *80*

■ *Steps to Formulating an Issue-Based Question* *81*

■ *A Practice Sequence: Formulating an Issue-Based Question* *81*

5 From Formulating to Developing a Thesis 83

Working Versus Definitive Theses *84*

Developing a Working Thesis: Three Models *85*

The Correcting-Misinterpretations Model *85*

The Filling-the-Gap Model *86*

The Modifying-What-Others-Have-Said Model *87*

■ *Steps to Formulating a Working Thesis: Three Models*   87

■ *A Practice Sequence: Identifying Types of Theses*   88

Establishing a Context for a Thesis   89

JENNY ECK *(student writer)*, **from *Nuestra Clase:* Making the Classroom a Welcoming Place for English Language Learners   89**

Establish That the Issue Is Current and Relevant   92

Briefly Present What Others Have Said   92

Explain What You See as the Problem   93

State Your Thesis   94

■ *Steps to Establishing a Context for a Thesis*   94

Analyze the Context of a Thesis   95

SHIRLEY BRICE HEATH, ***from*** Protean Shapes in Literacy Events: Ever-Shifting Oral and Literate Traditions   95

Analyze a Student Argument   98

JESSIE POTISH *(student writer),* **AIDS in Women: A Growing Educational Concern   98**

■ *A Practice Sequence: Building a Thesis*   103

6   From Finding to Evaluating Sources   105

Identifying Sources   *106*

Consult Experts Who Can Guide Your Research   *106*

Develop a Working Knowledge of Standard Sources   *107*

Distinguish Between Primary and Secondary Sources   *107*

Distinguish Between Popular and Scholarly Sources   *111*

■ *Steps to Identifying Sources   113*

■ *A Practice Sequence: Identifying Sources   113*

Searching for Sources   *114*

Perform a Keyword Search   *115*

Try Browsing   *116*

Perform a Journal or Newspaper Title Search   *117*

■ *Steps to Searching for Sources   118*

■ *A Practice Sequence: Searching for Sources   118*

Evaluating Library Sources   *118*

Read the Introductory Sections   *119*

Examine the Table of Contents and Index   *120*

Check the Notes and Bibliographic References   *120*

Skim Deeper   *120*

■ *Steps to Evaluating Library Sources   121*

■ *A Practice Sequence: Evaluating Library Sources   121*

Evaluating Internet Sources   *122*

Evaluate the Author of the Site   *122*

Evaluate the Organization That Supports the Site   *122*

Evaluate the Purpose of the Site   *123*

Evaluate the Information on the Site   *123*

■ *Steps to Evaluating Internet Sources   124*

■ *A Practice Sequence: Evaluating Internet Sources   124*

7   From Summarizing to Documenting Sources   125

Summaries, Paraphrases, and Quotations   *125*

Writing a Paraphrase   *126*

■ *Steps to Writing a Paraphrase   129*

■ *A Practice Sequence: Paraphrasing   130*

Writing a Summary   *130*

STEVEN F. LAWSON, *from* **Debating the Civil Rights Movement: The View from the Nation   131**

Describe the Key Claims of the Text   *132*

Select Examples to Illustrate the Author's Argument   *133*

Present the Gist of the Author's Argument   *134*

Contextualize What You Summarize   *135*

■ *Steps to Writing a Summary   137*

■ *A Practice Sequence: Summarizing   137*

Synthesis Versus Summary   *138*

Writing a Synthesis   *139*

CHARLES PAYNE, *from* **Debating the Civil Rights Movement: The View from the Trenches   139**

RONALD TAKAKI, **Policies: Strategies and Solutions   142**

Make Connections Between Different Texts   *145*

Decide What Those Connections Mean   *146*

Formulate the Gist of What You've Read   *148*

■ *Steps to Writing a Synthesis   149*

■ *A Practice Sequence: Writing a Synthesis   149*

Avoiding Plagiarism   *150*

■ *Steps to Avoiding Plagiarism   151*

Integrating Quotations into Your Writing   *152*

Take an Active Stance   *152*

Explain the Quotations   *153*

Attach Short Quotations to Your Own Sentences   *155*

■ *Steps to Integrating Quotations into Your Writing*   *156*

■ *A Practice Sequence: Integrating Quotations*   *156*

Citing and Documenting Sources   *156*

The Basics of MLA Style   *159*

■ *Steps to Compiling an MLA List of Works Cited*   *160*

The Basics of APA Style   *162*

■ *Steps to Compiling an APA List of References*   *163*

**8   From Ethos to Logos:
Appealing to Your Readers   167**

Connecting with Readers: A Sample Argument   *168*

JAMES W. LOEWEN, **The Land of Opportunity**   *168*

Appealing to Ethos   *173*

Establish That You Have Good Judgment   *173*

Convey to Readers That You Are Knowledgeable   *174*

Show That You Understand the
Complexity of a Given Issue   *175*

■ *Steps to Appealing to Ethos*   *175*

Appealing to Pathos   *175*

Show That You Know What Your Readers Value   *176*

Use Illustrations and Examples That Appeal to
Readers' Emotions   *176*

Consider How Your Tone May Affect
Your Audience   *177*

■ *Steps to Appealing to Pathos*   *178*

■ *A Practice Sequence: Appealing to Ethos and Pathos*   *179*

**Appealing to Logos: Using Reason and Evidence to
Fit the Situation   *181***

State the Premises of Your Argument   *183*

Use Credible Evidence   *184*

Demonstrate That the Conclusion Follows from
the Premises   *184*

■ *Steps to Appealing to Logos*   *185*

Recognizing Logical Fallacies   *186*

Analyzing the Appeals in a Text   *190*

JEAN ANYON, **The Economic Is Political**   *190*

■ *A Practice Sequence: Analyzing the Appeals in a Text*   *199*

9 From Introductions to Conclusions: Drafting an Essay 201

Drafting Introductions *201*

The Inverted-Triangle Introduction *202*

The Narrative Introduction *203*

The Interrogative Introduction *204*

The Paradoxical Introduction *205*

The Minding-the-Gap Introduction *206*

■ *Strategies for Drafting Introductions 207*

■ *A Practice Sequence: Drafting an Introduction 207*

Developing Paragraphs *208*

ELIZABETH MARTÍNEZ, *from* Reinventing "America": Call for a New National Identity *209*

Use Topic Sentences to Focus Your Paragraphs *213*

Create Unity in Your Paragraphs *214*

Use Critical Strategies to Develop Your Paragraphs *216*

■ *Steps to Developing Paragraphs 219*

■ *A Practice Sequence: Working with Paragraphs 220*

Drafting Conclusions *220*

Echo the Introduction *222*

Challenge the Reader *223*

Look to the Future *223*

Pose Questions *224*

Conclude with a Quotation *224*

■ *Steps to Drafting Conclusions 225*

■ *A Practice Sequence: Drafting a Conclusion 226*

10 From Revising to Editing: Working with Peer Groups 227

Revising Versus Editing *227*

The Peer Editing Process *228*

■ *Steps in the Peer Editing Process 229*

Peer Groups in Action: A Sample Session *230*

BRETT PREACHER *(student writer),* **Representing Poverty in *Million Dollar Baby* 231**

Working with Early Drafts *233*

Consider the Writer's Responsibilities *233*

Consider the Reader's Responsibilities   *234*

Analyze an Early Draft   *235*

TASHA TAYLOR *(student writer),* **Memory Through Photography**   *235*

Working with Later Drafts   *237*

Consider the Writer's Responsibilities   *237*

Consider the Reader's Responsibilities   *238*

Analyze a Later Draft   *239*

TASHA TAYLOR *(student writer),* **Memory Through Photography**   *239*

Working with Final Drafts   *242*

Consider the Writer's Responsibilities   *242*

Consider the Reader's Responsibilities   *242*

Analyze a Near-Final Draft   *243*

TASHA TAYLOR *(student writer),* **Memory Through Photography**   *243*

Further Suggestions for Peer Editing Groups   *248*

11 Other Methods of Inquiry: Interviews and Focus Groups   249

Why Do Original Research?   *250*

Getting Started: Writing a Proposal   *251*

Describe Your Purpose   *252*

Define Your Method   *252*

Discuss Your Implications   *253*

Include Additional Materials That Support Your Research   *253*

Establish a Timeline   *256*

■ *Steps to Writing a Proposal*   *256*

Analyzing a Proposal   *257*

MARY RONAN *(student writer),* **Research Paper Proposal: A Case Study of One Homeless Child's Education and Lifestyle**   *257*

Interviewing   *261*

Plan the Interview   *262*

Prepare Your Script   *262*

Conduct the Interview   *263*

Make Sense of the Interview   *264*

Turn Your Interview into an Essay   *264*

■ *Steps to Interviewing*   *265*

Using Focus Groups   *265*

> Select Participants for the Focus Group   *266*
>
> Plan the Focus Group   *266*
>
> Prepare Your Script   *267*
>
> Conduct the Focus Group   *269*
>
> Interpret the Data from the Focus Group   *269*
>
> ■ *Steps for Conducting Focus Groups*   *270*

PART TWO
A Reader for Entering the Conversation of Ideas   273

12 Conventional and Unconventional Wisdom
What does it mean to be educated, and who decides?   275

MARK EDMUNDSON, **On the Uses of a Liberal Education**   *277*

> A professor of English argues that higher education caters too much to the consumerist tendencies of students.

bell hooks, ***from* Teaching to Transgress: Education as the Practice of Freedom**   *293*

> "Engaged pedagogy does not seek simply to empower students," claims this well-known cultural critic and teacher. "Any classroom that employs a holistic model of learning will also be a place where teachers grow, and are empowered by the process."

JONATHAN KOZOL, **Still Separate, Still Unequal: America's Educational Apartheid**   *308*

> An eminent writer and social critic make the case that even "if it takes people marching in the streets," it is "well past the time" for inequity in public schools to be eliminated.

JAMES W. LOEWEN, ***from* Lies My Teacher Told Me: Everything Your American History Textbook Got Wrong**   *332*

> A professor of sociology asserts that current practices of teaching history leave most high school seniors "hamstrung in their efforts to analyze controversial issues in our society."

MARY LOUISE PRATT, **Arts of the Contact Zone**   *354*

> A professor of comparative literature sets forth her influential idea of contact zones — "social spaces where cultures meet, clash, and grapple with each other, often in contexts of highly asymmetrical relations of power."

ROBERT SCHOLES, **On Reading a Video Text**   *370*

> Through his analysis of a Budweiser commercial, a literary theorist demonstrates how much Americans can glean about the nature of their beliefs by reading the world as closely as they read written language.

13 A World of Difference/A Shrinking World
Who are "we" in relation to "others"?   377

KWAME ANTHONY APPIAH, **Moral Disagreement**   *378*

A professor of philosophy explores the challenges of acting ethically in a shrinking world that is increasingly characterized by "clashing civilizations."

JARED DIAMOND, **Why Do Some Societies Make Disastrous Decisions?**   *390*

An evolutionary biologist and cultural geographer examines ancient and modern societies that have flourished or collapsed based on their ability or inability to discern impending disasters.

FRANKLIN FOER, *from* **How Soccer Explains the World: An Unlikely Theory of Globalization**   *406*

Reflecting on his childhood experiences playing soccer, the editor of *The New Republic* uses the fans, politics, economics, and metaphors of the sport to advance his thoughts on the American culture wars.

THOMAS L. FRIEDMAN, **While I Was Sleeping**   *417*

A visit to India leads a Pulitzer Prize–winning journalist to a surprising economic and political hypothesis: "The global competitive playing field was being leveled. The world was being flattened."

MALCOLM GLADWELL, *from* **The Tipping Point: How Little Things Can Make a Big Difference**   *432*

This selection from a best-selling study of mass behavior presents a theory of how certain trends emerge and become wildly popular: "Think of them as epidemics. Ideas and products and messages and behaviors spread just like viruses do."

MICHAEL S. KIMMEL, **Gender, Class, and Terrorism**   *448*

A professor of sociology analyzes how social scripts of masculinity may have contributed to the events of September 11, 2001: "Someone else — some 'other' — had to be held responsible for the terrorists' downward mobility and failures."

14 "Check All the Boxes That Apply": Unstable Identities in the United States
How do we experience the daily effects of race and class assumptions?   457

ANN duCILLE, **Dyes and Dolls: Multicultural Barbie and the Merchandising of Difference**   *458*

Toys and games "play crucial roles in helping children determine what is valuable in and around them," writes a professor of African American studies. She asks, "What did it mean for me that I was nowhere in the toys I played with?"

BARBARA EHRENREICH, **Maid to Order:**
The Politics of Other Women's Work   *479*

Drawing on her research working as a maid for minimum wage, a
cultural critic weighs the moral losses such labor entails: "Almost
everything we buy, after all, is the product of some other person's
suffering and miserably underpaid labor."

THOMAS FRANK, **The Two Nations**   *497*

In this chapter from his best-selling *What's the Matter with Kansas?
How Conservatives Won the Heart of America,* a journalist analyzes the
red-blue divide in American politics.

NOEL IGNATIEV, **Immigrants and Whites**   *512*

An historian and the editor of the journal *Race Traitor* examines
the construction of race in America, arguing that "to the extent the
immigrants became 'white' they abandoned the possibility of becoming
fully American."

PEGGY McINTOSH, **White Privilege and Male Privilege: A Personal**
Account of Coming to See Correspondences Through Work in
Women's Studies   *520*

A feminist scholar analyzes "white privilege," which she characterizes as
"an invisible weightless knapsack of special provisions, assurances, tools,
maps, guides, codebooks, passports, visas, clothes, compass, emergency
gear, and blank checks."

HÉCTOR TOBAR, *from* **Americanismo: City of Peasants**   *533*

A Pulitzer Prize–winning journalist reflects on the complex and thriving
culture of Spanish-speaking Los Angeles, examining the inner workings
of the city to peek through the window of the nation's future.

15 Acting "Naturally": The Practices of Gender
How do we learn to think and behave as gendered people?   549

SHARI L. DWORKIN and MICHAEL A. MESSNER, **Just Do . . . What? Sport,**
Bodies, Gender   *551*

A professor of behavioral medicine and a professor of sociology examine
the ways notions of masculinity and femininity are tested, exhibited, and
enforced through watching and participating in sports.

HENRY A. GIROUX, **Children's Culture and Disney's**
Animated Films   *567*

A professor of education and culture studies argues that, beyond simply
entertaining us, Disney films function as "teaching machines," making
stereotypes about race and gender seem like fantasy and fun.

JEAN KILBOURNE, **"Two Ways a Woman Can Get Hurt":**
Advertising and Violence   *592*

A media educator takes aim at sex in advertising, which she claims
is "more about disconnection and distance than connection and
closeness . . . more often about power than passion, about violence
than violins."

JUDITH LORBER, **"Night to His Day":**
The Social Construction of Gender   *617*

A professor of sociology and women's studies examines the implications
of gender's being "so much the routine ground of everyday activities that
questioning its taken-for-granted assumptions and presuppositions is like
thinking about whether the sun will come up."

KARIN A. MARTIN, **Becoming a Gendered Body:**
Practices of Preschools   *632*

A sociologist analyzes the "hidden curriculum" of preschools, a
curriculum that "turn[s] kids who are similar in bodily comportment,
movement, and practice into girls and boys, children whose bodily
practices are different."

DEBORAH TANNEN, **Talking Up Close:**
Status and Connection   *654*

A linguist explores office communication dynamics in this selection
from her best-selling *Talking from 9 to 5: How Women's and Men's
Conversational Styles Affect Who Gets Ahead, Who Gets Credit, and What
Gets Done at Work.*

16 Indoctrination or Revolution? Technologies of Popular Culture

*How does popular culture reinforce or unsettle
social standards?*   677

MARGUERITE HELMERS, **Media, Discourse, and the Public Sphere:**
Electronic Memorials to Diana, Princess of Wales   *679*

A professor of composition and visual literacy examines Internet
memorial sites to discover the ways their authors "reinvent Diana" as
they invent themselves.

HENRY JENKINS, **"Complete Freedom of Movement":**
Video Games as Gendered Play Spaces   *700*

A professor of media studies analyzes the cultural geography and cultural
work of video games: "Video games did not make backyard play spaces
disappear; rather, they offer children some way to respond to domestic
confinement."

STEVEN JOHNSON, ***from* Everything Bad Is Good for You:**
How Today's Popular Culture Is Actually Making Us Smarter   *730*

A cultural critic takes on conventional wisdom about popular culture in
the Internet era: "For decades, we've worked under the assumption that
mass culture follows a steadily declining path toward lowest-common-
denominator standards. . . . But in fact, the exact opposite is happening."

ERIC SCHLOSSER, **Your Trusted Friends**   *754*

In this chapter from *Fast Food Nation: The Dark Side of the All-American
Meal,* a journalist compares the origins and marketing practices of two
iconic corporations, McDonald's and Disney.

CYNTHIA L. SELFE, **Lest We Think the Revolution Is a Revolution:
Images of Technology and the Nature of Change**   *783*

A professor of composition traces the "contradictory impulses" in several
"powerful narratives" we tell ourselves about what we find promising and
terrifying about computer technology.

ELIZABETH TEARE, **Harry Potter and the Technology of Magic**   *800*

A literary scholar examines the Harry Potter series and asks, "What is it
that makes these books . . . not only an international phenomenon
among children and parents and teachers but also a topic of compelling
interest to literary, social, and cultural critics?"

Assignment Sequences   817

Index of Authors, Titles, and Key Terms   833

Introduction:
What Is Academic Writing?

In the strictest sense, *academic writing* is what scholars do to communicate with other scholars in their fields of study, their disciplines. It's the research report a biologist writes, the interpretive essay a literary scholar composes, the media analysis a film scholar produces. At the same time, *academic writing* is what you have to learn so that you can participate in the different disciplinary conversations that take place in your courses. You have to learn to *think* like an academic, *read* like an academic, *do research* like an academic, and *write* like an academic — even if you have no plans to continue your education and become a scholar yourself. Learning these skills is what this book is about.

Fair warning: It isn't easy. In fact, initially you may well be perplexed by the vocabulary and sentence structure of many of the academic essays you read. Scholars often use specialized language to capture the complexity of an issue or to introduce specific ideas from their discipline. Every discipline has its own vocabulary. You probably can think of words and phrases that are not used every day but that are necessary, nevertheless, to express certain ideas precisely. For example, consider the terms *centrifugal force*, *Oedipus complex*, and *onomatopoeia*. These terms carry with them a history of study; when you learn to use them, you also are learning to use the ideas they represent. Terms like these help us describe the world specifically rather than generally; they help us better understand how things work and how to make better decisions about what matters to us.

Sentence structure presents another challenge. The sentences in academic writing are often longer and more intricate than the sentences in popular magazines. Academics want to go beyond what is quick, obvious, and general. They want to ask questions based on studying a subject from multiple points of view, to make surprising, interesting connections that would not occur to someone who has not analyzed the subject carefully. It follows that academic writers are accustomed to extensive reading that prepares them to examine an issue, knowledgeably, from many different perspectives, and to make interesting intellectual use of what they discover in their research. To become an adept academic writer, you have to learn these practices as well.

Academic writing will challenge you, no doubt. But hang in there. Any initial difficulty you have with academic writing will pay off when you discover new ways of looking at the world and of making sense of it. Moreover, the habits of mind and core skills of academic writing are highly valued in the world outside the academy.

At base, academic writing entails making an **argument** — text crafted to persuade an audience — often in the service of changing people's minds and behaviors. When you write an academic essay, then, you have to

- define a situation that calls for some response in writing;
- demonstrate the timeliness of your argument;
- establish a personal investment;
- appeal to readers whose minds you want to change by understanding what they think, believe, and value;
- support your argument with good reasons;
- anticipate and address readers' reasons for disagreeing with you, while encouraging them to adopt your position.

From this list you can see that an academic argument is not about shouting down an opponent. Instead, it is the careful expression of an idea or perspective based on reasoning and the insights garnered from a close examination of the arguments others have made on the issue.

MOVING FROM INQUIRY TO ACADEMIC WRITING

The chapters in the first part of this book introduce you to the habits of mind and core skills of academic writing. By **habits of mind**, we mean the patterns of thought that lead you to question assumptions and opinions, explore alternative opinions, anticipate opposing arguments, compare one type of experience to another, and identify the causes and consequences of ideas and events. These forms of **critical thinking** demand an inquiring mind that welcomes complexities and seeks out and weighs many different points of view, a mind willing to enter complex conversations both in and out of the academy. We discuss academic habits of mind in Chapter 1 and refer to them throughout the rest of the text.

Core skills are the specific steps and strategies needed to develop habits of mind into strong, persuasive writing. The core skills of academic writers manifest in specific reading, writing, and research practices. Many students fantasize about having a "Eureka!" moment, a sudden flash of insight that allows them to write a brilliant paper at a blazing pace in a single draft — and just in time to turn in the assignment. In fact, good academic writing has far less to do with a writer's luck or brilliance than it does with the effective practice of specific core skills that anyone can learn. To help you develop those core skills, we include many opportunities to practice them throughout this book. Chapter by chapter, you will hone your abilities to

- read as a writer and write as a reader;
- analyze arguments;
- discover issues;
- develop an academic thesis;
- use sources;
- write an academic essay.

Read as a writer, and write as a reader.   Writers read to gather ideas; they also read to discover the strategies other writers use to persuade (and even entertain) readers. In other words, writers analyze not only *what* other writers say but also *how* they say it. When you study how writers influence readers through language, you are analyzing the **rhetoric** (the available means of persuasion) of what you read. In practice, this means you consider how the writer's choices are shaped by his or her perspectives, motives, and values, and then infer the effect these choices have on how the issue is presented. As you read, think about the strategies that are most persuasive: lively language, detailed descriptions, clear organization, occasional humor, provocative examples, a passion for the issue. Then, use those strategies in your own writing.

Reading is also the first step in the writing process. When you mark up a text as you read — an activity we see as essential — you begin to put your own ideas on paper. The passages you underline, the comments you scribble in the margins, the connections you make to other texts you have read are the sketchy prelude to the argument you will eventually make in your essay. We focus on the connection between reading and writing in Chapter 2.

Analyze arguments.   When you read an academic essay, you need to understand the argument the writer is making, what the writer wants to persuade you to believe. To a great extent, an argument is a chain of **claims** — assertions, some supported by evidence, some not, that advance the argument. To evaluate an argument, then, you need to recognize and analyze the kinds of claims the writer is making. We show you how to do this in Chapter 3.

Discover issues.   All academic writing begins with curiosity about an issue. An **issue** is a question that presents a fundamental tension within a topic that can be explored and debated. A writer makes an inquiry into a topic, reading what others have said until a particular issue becomes apparent. Consider, for example, the topic of homelessness. At issue for some is that not enough is being done to address the roots of the problem (What can city governments do to remedy the causes of homelessness?). For others, the issue is economic (Where do cities find the money to build adequate shelters?). For still others, the issue is that solutions can generate problems for other groups (What effect will a new homeless shelter have on nearby businesses?). In Chapter 4 we discuss the process of exploring a topic to identify an issue and then shape it into a question that can be debated.

Develop an academic thesis.   A **thesis** is a writer's main claim, the assertion that crystallizes the writer's argument on a given issue. The thesis in an effective piece of academic writing is a central argument that is evident at the beginning of the essay and threads through every paragraph thereafter. As you read more and more academic writing in your classes, you will discover many different strategies for building an argument. In fact, you may be surprised to find that the thesis in a piece of academic writing often does not fit tidily into a single sentence that always appears at the end of a single introductory paragraph. In Chapter 5, we discuss how you can develop an academic thesis that acknowledges the conversation in which you are participating, recognizes the needs and assumptions of your readers, and advances your own fresh perspective on an issue.

Use sources.   All academic writing responds to **sources** — texts that convey the ideas of others — even if the sources are not quoted in the body of the essay. Academic writers do more than gather and repeat the ideas of others. They use sources in a variety of ways but always to advance an argument that contributes to the ongoing conversation about an issue. That is, academic writing is researched; it makes use of sources to advance the writer's own argument. In Chapters 6 and 7, we show you how to find and evaluate sources and then use them effectively in your writing.

Write an academic essay.   In your own essays, you need to present yourself and your argument in a way that will win your readers' minds and hearts. In Chapter 8 we examine the kinds of appeals that can help you do that. You also need to structure your essays so that they lead your readers where you want to them to be: in agreement with, or at least respectful of, your point of view on an issue. Chapter 9 shows you a number of ways to shape your essays to these ends. And because the academic writing process is inherently collaborative, and because it is enormously useful to develop your ideas within the context of peer review, we devote Chapter 10 to describing strategies for working with your classmates to improve your writing and theirs. Finally, in Chapter 11, we discuss another kind of research — primary, or field, research — and the methods that can help you explore an issue beyond the pages of texts.

WRITING IN AND OUT OF THE ACADEMY: ENTERING THE CONVERSATION OF IDEAS

Earlier we claimed that the habits of mind and core skills of academic writing are highly valued in the world outside the academy. In fact, if we count as "academic" any argument that draws on the habits of mind and core skills we present throughout this book, academic writing is common-place outside the academy — to disseminate and debate ideas, to help people look at the world differently and, perhaps, to change their lives. This kind of writing can alter the way issues are discussed in the culture at large and even the direction of events in that culture.

One example is Martin Luther King Jr.'s famous "Letter from Birmingham Jail," a text that has become an icon of American culture and the civil rights movement. (If you haven't read "Letter from Birmingham Jail," you can easily find a copy on a number of Web sites.) King composed the letter on April 16, 1963, writing in the margins of the *Birmingham News* and on paper that a sympathetic jailer gave him. In prison because he had dared to challenge the status quo, King was critical of "liberal-minded" people who failed to act on behalf of social justice. A jailhouse is certainly not a place where academic writing would be expected to occur, and King did not cite the sources he alludes to in his letter, as he would were he writing for publication in an academic journal. Still, the habits of mind and rhetorical strategies of one trained in academic thinking and writing (King earned a doctorate in theology from Boston University) are very much in evidence in "Letter from Birmingham Jail."

King's letter is characteristically academic in its questioning of conventional assumptions and opinions, in its exploration of alternative opinions, in its anticipation of opposing arguments, and in its use of what he had read in the service of making an argument. Responding to a recently published statement, "White Clergymen Urge Local Negroes to Withdraw from Demonstrations," King's letter sharply criticizes those who argue that his protests against segregation are misplaced and ill timed, interweaving ideas about justice and moral action from a wide range of sources with which educated readers would be familiar. His assertion is clear and focused, and he uses evidence to support his argument that nonviolent protest that challenges unjust laws is both timely and necessary. He is appealing to an audience of white moderates who are sympathetic to his cause but not his actions. To help them see the need for civil disobedience, he draws a parallel between the blacks' struggle for civil rights and the American patriots' struggle for independence from Britain.

In his effort to distinguish between just and unjust laws, King was in conversation with historical and contemporary thinkers; and, like an academic, he drew on his knowledge of different disciplines — specifically, law, philosophy, and theology — to advance his argument about ethics, justice, and moral action. In doing so, he attributed his definitions of justice to venerated thinkers and writers, among them Socrates, St. Augustine, Thomas Aquinas, Martin Buber, and Reinhold Niebuhr. In this way, King used what he had read to explain how many different thinkers in history thought and acted in ways consistent with what he argues in his letter.

It's probably safe to say you are not (yet) at the center of a major conversation of ideas, as Martin Luther King Jr. was. Still, our assumption is that you will have to participate in any number of such conversations during your college career, and, indeed, that you may find yourself compelled and even eager to enter such conversations — either as a trained academic or an educated citizen — when college is behind you. The examples we present in Part One of the book and the readings we have compiled in Part Two give you the flavor of the conversations taking place in and out of the academy. The readings, which range widely in subject and style, have been chosen because they explore ideas that capture the imaginations and consciences of our students as well as those of the larger reading public. Many of the selections here originally appeared in academic journals, but many others have spent weeks on the *New York Times* best-sellers' list. They have been required reading for incoming students on many campuses, but they also have intrigued and engaged general readers. In fact, you may have encountered some of these texts on tables at the front of your local bookstore or been exposed to the writers themselves on talk radio or television. Writers like Jared Diamond, Barbara Ehrenreich, Thomas Friedman, and Malcolm Gladwell are intellectuals who use their academic research and analytical skills to write texts that take on big ideas, to frame them in interesting new ways, and to offer striking examples that make readers think outside the box.

The big ideas the readings explore — what we think is important to learn, the individual's place in a shrinking world, the slippery categories of social identity, the social effects of gender, the intersections of technology and popular culture, for example — raise questions that resist easy answers. Some of the readings grapple with frustrating classroom dynamics or examine the commercial and political contexts of educational institutions. Some take on the marketing of children's toys or Disney films. Others inquire into the ways cyber technologies shape our communication with one another, our understanding of the astounding success of the Harry Potter series or other cultural events, or the tipping point of some behaviors or products that turn mundane practices or objects into social epidemics.

Although all of these selections are researched essays, they do not read like dry research papers. Instead their authors employ a wide range of rhetorical styles to interest their readers. Some take a journalistic approach that may remind you of in-depth news analysis. Some make use of autobiographical details, the authors sharing personal anecdotes to explain their interest in an issue or offer an example. Others employ a more formal tone, relying on research and expertise to build their arguments. Like your own writing, then, these readings use many different strategies to make many different kinds of connections — from the personal to the scholarly, from the individual experience to a larger social pattern. This multileveled inquiry is at the heart of the thinking and writing we invite you to try throughout this book.

All the readings we have included in Part Two are substantial, and many are quite challenging; they are not skim-it-once-and-you've-got-it pieces. You will need to return to them more than once, probably more than twice, with your pen in hand, asking questions in the margins and forging links to other readings and ideas. These readings are also typical of other texts you will read in college that embrace complexity rather than shy away from it. The premise of most of the college-level writing you will read and write yourself is this: "Things are more complex and interesting than you may think: Let me teach you how."

We do not ask you to face the challenging readings in Part Two without guidance. The headnotes that introduce each reading suggest some of the rhetorical and thematic features you should look for as you read. The questions that follow every reading will help you focus on specific aspects of the text, to help you gain the fullest understanding of the reading through different perspectives. Reading Rhetorically questions ask you to look at the stylistic decisions a writer makes in crafting an essay. Inquiring Further questions use each essay as a launching point for further thinking, research, and discovery about an issue raised in the text. Framing Conversations questions provide the starting point for writing your own essays in response to two or three readings. All of these questions are meant to help you increase your mastery of the habits of mind and core skills we present in Part One.

Finally, the assignment sequences at the end of the book define a subject for extended inquiry, offering a sequential path through the readings via writing assignments that build on one another. Topics for these sequences include media representations of American education, the challenges of researching other people, and the tensions between individual and group identities. Instead of asking you to write an essay and then move on to a new topic, we present each essay as an opportunity to develop a frame or lens through which to consider subsequent readings. As you draw on different combinations of resources over a series of compositions, and contribute your own research from the library and from data you've gathered in the field, your ideas about the issues you write about will become richer and more complex. You will be reading, research-ing, and writing like an academic writer, taking part in conversations with other academic writers. Furthermore, these assignments may help you see the world around you — from everyday happenings to special events — in unexpected and illuminating ways.

PART ONE

A Text for Moving from Inquiry to Academic Writing

1

Starting with Inquiry: Habits of Mind of Academic Writers

A t the center of all academic writing is a curiosity about how the world works and a desire to understand it in its full complexity. To discover and make sense of that complexity, academic writers apply rigorous **habits of mind**, patterns of thought that lead them to question assumptions, explore alternatives, anticipate opposing arguments, compare experiences, and identify the causes and consequences of ideas and events. Habits of mind are especially important today, when we are bombarded with appeals to buy this or that product and with information that may or may not be true. For example, in "106 Science Claims and a Truckful of Baloney" (*The Best American Science and Nature Writing*, 2005), William Speed Weed illustrates the extent to which the claims of science vie for our attention alongside the claims of advertising. He notes that advertisers often package their claims as science, but wonders whether a box of Cheerios really can reduce cholesterol. As readers we have a responsibility to test the claims of both science and advertising in order to decide what to believe and act upon. Weed found that "very few of the 100 claims" he evaluated "proved completely true" and that "a good number were patently false." Testing the truth of claims — learning to consider information carefully and critically, and to weigh competing points of view before making our own judgments — gives us power over our own lives.

The habits of mind and practices valued by academic writers are probably ones you already share. You are behaving "academically" when you comparison-shop, a process that entails learning about the product in magazines and on the Internet and then looking at the choices firsthand before you decide which one you will purchase. You employ these same habits of mind when you deliberate over casting a vote in an election. You inform yourself about the issues that are most pressing; you learn about the candidates' positions on these issues; you consider other arguments for and against both issues and candidates; and you weigh those arguments and your own understanding to determine which candidate you will support.

Fundamentally, academic habits of mind are analytical. When you consider a variety of factors — the quality and functionality of the item you plan to buy, how it meets your needs, how it compares to similar items before making a shopping choice, you are conducting an **analysis**. That is, you are pausing to examine the reasons why you should buy something, instead of simply handing over your cash and saying, "I want one of those." To a certain extent, analysis involves breaking something down into its various parts and reflecting on how the parts do or don't work together. For example, when you deliberate over your vote, you may consult one of those charts that newspapers often run around election time: A list of candidates appears across the top of the chart, and a list of issues appears on the side. You can scan the columns to see where each candidate stands on the issues, and you can scan the rows to see how the candidates compare on a particular issue. The newspaper editors have performed a preliminary analysis for you. They've asked, "Who are the candidates?" "What are the issues?" and "Where does each candidate stand on the issues?"; and they have presented the answers to you in a format that can help you make your decision. But you still have to perform your own analysis of the information before you cast your ballot. Suppose no candidate holds your position on every issue. Who do you vote for? Which issues are most important to you? Or suppose two candidates hold your position on every issue. Which one do you vote for? What characteristics or experience are you looking for in an elected official? And you may want to investigate further by visiting the candidates' Web sites or by talking with your friends to gather their thoughts on the election.

As you can see, analysis involves more than simply disassembling or dissecting something. It is a process of continually asking questions and looking for answers. Analysis reflects, in the best sense of the word, a *skeptical* habit of mind, an unwillingness to settle for obvious answers in the quest to understand why things are the way they are and how they might be different.

This book will help you develop the questioning, evaluating, and conversational skills you already have into strategies that will improve your ability to make careful, informed judgments about the often conflicting and confusing information you are confronted with every day in your classes, in the news, in advertising, in all of your interactions. With these strategies, you will be in a position to use your writing skills to create change where you feel it is most needed.

The first steps in developing these skills are to recognize the key academic habits of mind and then to refine your practice of them. We explore four key habits of mind in the rest of this chapter: (1) inquiring, (2) seeking and valuing complexity, (3) understanding that academic writing is a conversation, and (4) understanding that writing is a process.

ACADEMIC WRITERS MAKE INQUIRIES

Academic writers usually study a body of information so closely and from so many different perspectives that they can ask questions that may not occur to people who are just scanning the information. That is, academic writers learn to make **inquiries**. Every piece of academic writing begins with a question about the way the world works, and the best questions lead to rich, complex insights that others can learn from and build on. You will find that the ability to ask good questions is equally valuable in your daily life. Asking thoughtful questions about politics, popular culture, work, or anything else — questions like How has violence become so commonplace in our schools? What exactly did that candidate mean by "Family values are values for all of us," anyway? What is lost and gained by bringing Tolkien's *Lord of the Rings* trilogy to the screen? What does it take to move ahead in this company? Are those practices ethical? — is the first step in understanding how the world works and how it can be changed.

Inquiry typically begins with **observation**, a careful noting of phenomena or behaviors that puzzle you or challenge your beliefs and values (in a text or in the real world), which prompts an attempt to understand them by **asking questions** (Why does this exist? Why is this happening? Do things have to be this way?) and **examining alternatives** (Maybe this doesn't need to exist. Maybe this could happen another way instead.). For example, Mark Edmundson, a professor of English at the University of Virginia, *observes* that his students seem to prefer classes they consider "fun" over those that push them to work hard. This prompts him to *ask* how the consumer culture — especially the entertainment culture — has altered the college experience. In his essay "On the Uses of a Liberal Education," he wonders what it means that colleges increasingly see students as customers they need to please with Club Med–style exercise facilities that look "like a retirement spread for the young" more than as minds to be educated. He further *asks* what will happen if we don't change course — if entertaining students and making them feel good about themselves continue to be higher priorities than challenging students to stretch themselves with difficult ideas. Finally, he considers alternatives to entertainment-style education and *examines those alternatives* to see what they would offer students.

In her reading on the American civil rights movement of the 1950s and 1960s, one of our students *observed* that the difficulties many immigrant groups experienced when they first arrived in the United States are not acknowledged as struggles for civil rights. This student of Asian descent *wondered why* the difficulties Asians faced in assimilating into American culture are not seen as analogous to the efforts of African Americans to gain civil rights (Why are things this way?). In doing so, she *asked* a number of relevant questions: What do we leave out when we tell stories about ourselves? Why reduce the struggle for civil rights to black-and-white terms? How can we represent the multiple struggles of people who have contributed to building our nation? Then she *examined alternatives* — different ways of presenting the history of a nation that prides itself on justice and the protection of its people's civil rights (Maybe this doesn't need to exist. Maybe this could happen another way.). The academic writing you will read — and write yourself — starts with questions and seeks to find rich answers.

Steps to Inquiry

1 Observe. Note phenomena or behaviors that puzzle you or challenge your beliefs and values.

2 Ask questions. Consider why things are the way they are.

3 Examine alternatives. Explore how things could be different.

A Practice Sequence: Inquiring

The activities below will help you practice the strategies of observing, asking questions, and examining alternatives.

1 Find an advertisement for a political campaign (you can find many political ads on the Internet), and write down anything about what you observe in the ad that puzzles you or that challenges your beliefs and values. Next, write down questions you might have (Do things have to be this way?). Finally, write down other ways you think the ad could persuade you to vote for this particular candidate (Maybe this could happen another way instead.).

2 Locate and analyze data about the students at your school. For example, you might research the available majors and determine which departments have the highest and lowest enrollments. (Some schools have fact books that can be accessed online; and typically the registrar maintains a database with this information.) Is there anything that puzzles you? Write down any questions you have (Why are things the way they are?). What alternative explanations can you provide to account for differences in the popularity of the subjects students major in?

3 Read the following passage about school choice that appeared on the Civil Rights Project Web site in 2002. The Civil Rights Project is a leading research center on civil rights, with a particular interest in education reform. Since its founding in 1996, the project has

convened dozens of national conferences and roundtables; commissioned more than 400 new research and policy studies; and produced major reports on desegregation, student diversity, school discipline, special education, dropouts, and Title I programs.

After you read the passage, write down what puzzles you or challenges your beliefs and values. Next, write down any questions you might have. Finally, write down what you see as alternative ways to look at the problem the writer identifies. When you complete this exercise, share your responses with one of your classmates.

School choice has been viewed as a remedy to improve the quality of local schools and empower inner-city and lower-income parents by offering parents the freedom to choose the kind of education their children would receive.

In the realm of public school education, school choice has taken the form of magnet schools, charter schools, and other test-based or specially tracked schools. Parents and students have the option to choose schools other than neighborhood schools that generally have a similar racial, ethnic, and socio-economic makeup to their local area. Private school choice, on the other hand, is a measure that some states have adopted to give lower-income students the opportunity to attend private schools they otherwise could not afford. This comes in the form of a voucher that parents can use toward the cost of private or religious school tuition for their children.

Though advocates of school choice claim that it is the best way to enable students in failing public schools to get a better education, the issue of school choice raises some troubling questions about the impacts of individual "choice" on a society that aims to provide all of its citizens with equal access to educational opportunities.

Educators have found that choice programs are likely to increase the segregation of students by race, social class, and educational background. Greater choice in public education is also unlikely, on its own, to increase either the number of programs offered or the overall performance of schools.

While school choice may allow such *informed* families and communities to make significant decisions about their children's education, it is important to understand that not all families are equally informed. Better-educated parents who are more likely to be involved closely with their children's schooling, for example, have consistently been prone to participate in choice programs. While those children in families that are aware of school options and have the means to actively choose them may benefit from a greater range of opportunities, those that are not aware of options will not. The lack of resources and information for families living in largely minority areas of high poverty means that not everyone will benefit equally from school choice. Those students that are able to make informed school decisions will leave those that are not in their neighborhood schools. Thus, school choice will further segregate schools along racial, ethnic, socio-economic, and educational backgrounds.

ACADEMIC WRITERS SEEK AND VALUE COMPLEXITY

Seeking and valuing complexity are what inquiry is all about. As you read academic arguments (for example, about school choice), observe how the media work to influence your opinions (for example, in political ads), or analyze data (for example, about major subjects), you will explore reasons why things are the way they are and how they might be different. When you do so, we encourage you not to settle for simple either/or reasons. Instead, look for multiple explanations.

When we rely on **binary thinking** — imagining there are only two sides to an issue — we tend to ignore information that does not fall tidily into one side or the other. Think of the sound-bite assertions you hear bandied about on talk shows on the pretext of "discussing" a hot-button issue like stem-cell research or abortion: "It's just wrong/right because it is!" Real-world questions — How has the Internet changed our sense of what it means to be an author? What are the global repercussions of fast food? How do we make sense of terrorism? — don't have easy for-or-against answers. Remember that an **issue** is a subject that can be explored and debated. Issue-based questions, then, need to be approached with a mind open to complex possibilities. (We say more about identifying issues and formulating issue-based questions in Chapter 4.)

If we take as an example the issue of terrorism, we would discover that scholars of religion, economics, ethics, and politics tend to ask very different questions about terrorism, and to propose very different approaches for addressing this worldwide problem. This doesn't mean that one approach is right and the others are wrong; it means that complex issues are likely to have multiple explanations, rather than a simple choice between A and B.

In her attempt to explain the popularity of the Harry Potter books and movies, Elizabeth Teare, a professor of English, provides a window on the steps we can take to examine the complexity of a topic. She begins her essay "Harry Potter and the Technology of Magic" with the observations that author J. K. Rowling is one of the ten most influential people in publishing, and that her books have "transformed both the technologies of reading and the way we understand those technologies." Motivated by a sense of curiosity, if not puzzlement, Teare formulates a guiding question: "What is it that makes these books — about a lonely boy whose first act on learning he is a wizard is to go shopping for a wand — not only an international phenomenon among children and parents and teachers but also a topic of compelling interest to literary, social, and cultural critics?" Notice that in doing so, she indicates that she will examine this question from the multiple perspectives of literary, social, and cultural critics. To find answers to this question, Teare explores a range of perspectives from a variety of sources, including publishers' Web sites, trade journals, academic studies, and works of fiction for young readers.

One of our students was curious about why a well-known musician, Eminem, was at once so widely popular and so bitterly reviled, a phenomenon he observed in discussions with friends and in reviews of Eminem's music. He set out to understand these conflicting responses by examining the differing perspectives of music critics, politicians, religious evangelists, and his peers; and then he formulated an issue-based question: "How can we explain Eminem's popularity given the ways people criticize Eminem personally and his music?" In looking at this issue, the student opened himself to complexity by resisting simple answers to his question about why Eminem and his music evoked such different and conflicting responses.

Steps to Seeking and Valuing Complexity

1 **Reflect on what you observe.** Clarify your initial interest in a phenomenon or behavior by focusing on its particular details. Then reflect on what is most interesting and least interesting to you about these details, and why.

2 **Examine issues from multiple points of view.** Imagine more than two sides to the issue, and recognize that there may well be other points of view too.

3 **Ask issue-based questions.** Try to put into words questions that will help you explore why things are the way they are.

A Practice Sequence: Seeking and Valuing Complexity

These activities build on the previous exercises we asked you to complete.

1 Look again at the political ad. Think about other perspectives that would complicate your understanding of how the ad might persuade voters.

2 Imagine other perspectives on the data you found on the students in your school. Let's say, for example, that you've looked at data on student majors. How did you explain the popularity of certain majors and the unpopularity of others? How do you think other students would explain these discrepancies? What explanations would faculty members offer?

3 Consider your responses to the excerpt on school choice that you shared with one of your classmates. In addition to the explanations each of you provided, what are some other ways you could look at the issue of school choice? What would parents argue? What about administrators? Teachers? Students?

ACADEMIC WRITERS SEE WRITING
AS A CONVERSATION

Another habit of mind at the heart of academic writing is the understanding that ideas always build on and respond to other ideas, just as they do in the best kind of conversations. Of course, conversations in academic writing happen on the page; they are not spoken. Still, these conversations are quite similar to the conversations you have through e-mail and instant messaging: You are responding to something someone else has written (or said) and are writing back in anticipation of future responses. Academic writing also places a high value on the belief that good, thoughtful ideas come from conversations with others, *many* others. As your exposure to other viewpoints increases, as you take more and different points of view into consideration and build on them, your own ideas will develop more fully and fairly. You already know that to get a full picture of something, often you have to ask for multiple perspectives. When you want to find out what "really" happened at an event when your friends are telling you different stories, you listen to all of them and then evaluate the evidence to draw conclusions you can stand behind — just as academic writers do.

Theologian Martin Marty starts a conversation about hospitality in his book *When Faiths Collide* (2004). *Hospitality* is a word he uses to describe a human behavior that has the potential to bring about real understanding among people who do not share a common faith or culture. As Marty points out, finding common ground is an especially important and timely concern "in a world where strangers meet strangers with gunfire, barrier walls, spiritually land-mined paths, and the spirit of revenge." He believes that people need opportunities to share their stories, their values, and their beliefs; in doing so, they feel less threatened by ideas they do not understand or identify with.

Yet Marty anticipates the possibility that the notion of hospitality will be met with skepticism or incomprehension by those who find the term "dainty." After all, he observes, that there are hospitality suites and hospitality industries suggests current usage of the term is different from historical usage, particularly in the Bible. To counter the incredulity or incomprehension of those who do not immediately understand his use of the term *hospitality*, Marty gives his readers entré to a conversation with other scholars who understand the complexity and power of the kind of hospitality shown by people who welcome a stranger into their world. The stranger he has in mind may simply be the person who moves in next door; but that person could also be an immigrant, an exile, or a refugee. Marty brings another scholar, Darrell Fasching, into the conversation to explain that hospitality entails welcoming "the stranger . . . [which] inevitably involves us in a sympathetic passing over into the other's life and stories" (cited in Marty, p. 132). And John Koenig, another scholar Marty cites, traces the biblical sources of the term in an effort to show the value of understanding those we fear. That understanding, Marty argues, might lead to peace among warring factions. The conversation Marty begins on the page helps us see that his views on bringing about peace have their source in other people's ideas. In turn, the fact that he draws on multiple sources gives strength to Marty's argument.

The characteristics that make for effective oral conversation are also in play in effective academic conversation: empathy, respect, and a willingness to exchange and revise ideas. **Empathy** is the ability to understand the perspectives that shape what people think, believe, and value. To express both empathy and respect for the positions of all people involved in the conversation, academic writers try to understand the conditions under which each opinion might be true and then to represent the strengths of that position accurately. For example, imagine that your firm commitment to protecting the environment is challenged by those who see the value of developing land rich with oil and other resources. In challenging their position, it would serve you well to understand their motives, both economic (lower gas prices, new jobs that will create a demand for new houses) and political (less dependence on foreign oil). If you can demonstrate your knowledge of these factors, those committed to developing resources in protected areas will listen to you. To convey empathy and respect while presenting your own point of view, you might introduce your argument by saying:

> Although it is important to develop untapped resources in remote areas of the United States both to lower gas prices and create new jobs, and to eliminate our dependence on other countries' resources, it is in everyone's interest to use alternative sources of power and protect our natural resources.

As you demonstrate your knowledge and a sense of shared values, you could also describe the conditions under which you might change your own position.

People engaging in productive conversation try to create change by listening and responding to one another rather than dominating one another. Instead of trying to win an argument, they focus on reaching a mutual understanding. This does not mean that effective communicators do not take strong positions; more often than not they do. However, they are more likely to achieve their goals by persuading others instead of ignoring them and their points of view. Similarly, writers come to every issue with an agenda. But they realize that they may have to compromise on certain points to carry those that mean the most to them. More important, they understand that their perceptions and opinions may be flawed or limited, and they are willing to revise them when valid new perspectives are introduced.

In an academic community, ideas develop through give-and-take, through a conversation that builds on what has come before and grows stronger from multiple perspectives. You will find this dynamic at work in your classes, when you discuss your ideas: You will build on other people's insights, and they will build on yours. As a habit of mind, paying attention to academic conversations can improve the thinking and writing you do in every class you take.

Steps to Joining an Academic Conversation

1 **Be receptive to the ideas of others.** Listen carefully and empathetically to what others have to say.

2 **Be respectful of the ideas of others.** When you refer to the opinions of others, be respectful.

3 **Engage with the ideas of others.** Try to understand how people have arrived at their feelings and beliefs.

4 **Be flexible in your thinking about the ideas of others.** Be willing to exchange ideas and to revise your own opinions.

A Practice Sequence: Joining an Academic Conversation

The following excerpt is taken from Thomas Patterson's *The Vanishing Voter* (2002), an examination of voter apathy. Read the excerpt and then complete the exercises that follow.

> Does a diminished appetite for voting affect the health of American politics? Is society harmed when the voting rate is low or in decline? As the *Chicago Tribune* said in an editorial, it may be "humiliating" that the United States, the oldest continuous democracy, has nearly the lowest voting rate in the world. But does it have any practical significance? . . .
>
> The increasing number of nonvoters could be a danger to democracy. Although high participation by itself does not trigger radical change, a flood of new voters into the electorate could possibly do it. It's difficult to imagine a crisis big and divisive enough to prompt millions of new voters to suddenly flock to the polls, especially in light of Americans' aversion to political extremism. Nevertheless, citizens who are outside the electorate are less attached to the existing system. As the sociologist Seymour Martin Lipset observed, a society of nonvoters "is potentially more explosive than one in which most citizens are *regularly* involved in activities which give them some sense of participation in decisions which affect their lives."
>
> Voting can strengthen citizenship in other ways, too. When people vote, they are more attentive to politics and are better informed about issues affecting them. Voting also deepens community involvement, as the philosopher John Stuart Mill theorized a century ago. Studies indicate that voters are more active in community affairs than nonvoters are. Of course, this association says more about the type of person who votes as opposed to the effect of voting. But recent evidence, as Harvard University's Robert Putnam notes, "suggests that the act of voting itself encourages volunteering and other forms of government citizenship."

1 In this excerpt, Patterson presents two arguments: that increasing voter apathy is a danger to democracy and that voting strengthens citizenship. With which of these arguments do you sympathize more? Why? Can you imagine reasons that another person might not agree with you? Write them down. Now do the same exercise with the argument you find less compelling.

2   Your instructor will divide the class into four groups and assign each group a position — pro or con — on one of Patterson's arguments. Brainstorm with the members of your group to come up with examples or reasons why your group's position is valid. Make a list of those examples or reasons, and be prepared to present them to the class.

3   Your instructor will now break up the groups into new groups, each with at least one representative of the original groups. In turn with the other members of your new group, take a few moments to articulate your position and the reasons for it. Remember to be civil and as persuasive as possible.

4   Finally, with the other members of your new group, talk about the merits of the various points of view. Try to find common ground ("I understand what you are saying; in fact, it's not unlike the point I was making about . . ."). The point of this discussion is not to pronounce a winner (who made the best case for his or her perspective) but to explore common ground, exchange and revise ideas, and imagine compromises.

ACADEMIC WRITERS UNDERSTAND THAT WRITING IS A PROCESS

Academic writing is a process of defining issues, formulating questions, and developing sound arguments. This view of writing counters a number of popular myths: that writing depends on inspiration, that writing should happen quickly, that learning to write in one context prepares you to write in other contexts, and that revision is the same as editing. The writing process addresses these myths. First, choosing an idea that matters to you is one way to make your writing matter. And, there's a better chance that writing you care about will contribute in a meaningful way to the conversation going on about a given issue in the academic community. Second, writers who invest time in developing and revising their ideas will improve both the quality of their ideas and their language — their ability to be specific and express complexity.

There are three main stages to the writing process: collecting information, drafting, and revising. We introduce them here and expand on them throughout this book.

■ Collect Information and Material

Always begin the process of writing an essay by collecting *in writing* the material — the information, ideas, and evidence — from which you will shape your own argument. Once you have read and marked the pages of a text, you have begun the process of building your own argument. The important point here is that you start to put your ideas on paper. Good writing comes from returning to your ideas on your own and with your classmates, reconsidering them, and revising them as your thinking develops. This is not something you can do with any specificity unless you have written down your ideas. The box below shows the steps for gathering information from your reading, the first stage in the process of writing an academic essay. (In Chapter 2, these steps are illustrated and discussed in more detail.)

Steps to Collecting Information and Material

1 **Mark your texts as you read.** Note key terms; ask questions in the margins; indicate connections to other texts.

2 **List quotations you find interesting and provocative.** You might even write short notes to yourself about what you find significant about the quotes.

3 **List your own ideas in response to the reading or readings.** Include what you've observed about the way the author or authors make their arguments.

4 **Sketch out the similarities and differences among the authors whose work you plan to use in your essay.** Where would they agree or disagree? How would each respond to the others' arguments and evidence?

■ Draft, and Draft Again

The next stage in the writing process begins when you are ready to think about your focus and how to arrange the ideas you have gathered in the collecting stage. Writers often find that writing a first draft is an act of discovery, that their ultimate focus emerges during this initial drafting process. Sometimes it is only at the end of a four-page draft that a writer says, "Aha! This is what I really want to talk about in this essay!" Later revisions of an essay, then, are not simply editing or cleaning up the grammar of a first draft. Instead, they truly involve *re*vision, seeing the first draft again to establish the clearest possible argument and the most persuasive evidence. This means that you do not have to stick with the way a draft turns out the first time. You can — and must! — be willing to rewrite a substantial amount of a first draft if the focus of the argument changes, or if in the process of writing new ideas emerge that enrich the essay. This is why it's important not to agonize over wording in a first draft: It's difficult to toss out a paragraph you've sweated over for hours. Use the first draft to get your ideas down on paper so that you and your peers can discuss what you see there, with the knowledge that you (like your peers) will need to stay open to the possibility of changing an aspect of your focus or argument.

Steps to Drafting

1 **Look through the materials** you have collected to see what interests you most and what you have the most to say about.

2 **Identify what is at issue,** what is open to dispute.

3 **Formulate a question** that your essay will respond to.

4 **Select the material you will include,** and decide what is outside your focus.

5 **Consider the types of readers** who might be most interested in what you have to say.

6 **Gather more material** once you've decided on your purpose — what you want to teach your readers.

7 **Formulate a working thesis** that conveys the point you want to make.

8 **Consider possible arguments** against your position and your response to them.

■ Revise Significantly

The final stage, revising, might involve several different drafts as you continue to sharpen your insights and the organization of what you have written. As we discuss in Chapter 10, you and your peers will be reading one another's drafts, offering feedback as you move from the larger issues to the smaller ones. It should be clear by now that academic writing is done in a community of thinkers: That is, people read other people's drafts and make suggestions for further clarification, further development of ideas, and sometimes further research. This is quite different from simply editing someone's writing for grammatical errors and typos. Instead, drafting and revising with real readers, as we discuss in Chapter 7, allow you to participate in the collaborative spirit of the academy, in which knowledge making is a group activity that comes out of the conversation of ideas. Importantly, this process approach to writing in the company of real readers mirrors the conversation of ideas carried on in the pages of academic books and journals.

Steps to Revising

1 **Draft and revise the introduction and conclusion.**

2 **Clarify any obscure or confusing passages** your peers have pointed out.

3 **Provide details and textual evidence** where your peers have asked for new or more information.

4 **Check to be sure you have included opposing points of view** and have addressed them fairly.

5 **Consider reorganization.**

6 **Check to be sure every paragraph contributes clearly to your thesis or main claim,** and that you have included signposts along the way, phrases that help a reader understand your purpose ("Here I turn to an example from current movies to show how this issue is alive and well in pop culture").

7 **Consider using strategies you have found effective in other reading** you have done for class (repeating words or phrases for effect, asking rhetorical questions, varying your sentence length).

The four academic habits of mind we have discussed throughout this chapter — making inquiries, seeking and valuing complexity, understanding writing as a conversation, and understanding writing as a process — are fundamental patterns of thought you will need to cultivate as an academic writer. The core skills we discuss through the rest of the book build on these habits of mind.

2

From Reading as a Writer
to Writing as a Reader

Reading for class and then writing an essay might seem to be separate tasks, but reading is actually the first step in the writing process. In this chapter we present the small steps and specific practices that will help you read more effectively and move from reading to writing strategies as you compose your own college essays. These steps and practices will lead you to understand a writer's purpose in responding to a situation, the motivation for asserting a claim in an essay and entering a particular conversation with a particular audience.

READING AS AN ACT OF COMPOSING: ANNOTATING

Leaving your mark on the page — **annotating** — is your first act of composing. When you mark up the pages of a text, you are reading critically, engaging with the ideas of others, questioning and testing those ideas, and inquiring into their significance. **Critical reading** is sometimes called *active reading* to distinguish it from memorization, when you just read for the main idea so that you can "spit it back out on a test." When you read actively and critically, you bring your knowledge, experiences, and interests to a text, so that you can respond to the writer, continuing the conversation the writer has begun.

Experienced college readers don't try to memorize a text or assume they must understand it completely before they respond to it. Instead they read strategically, looking for the writer's claims, for the writer's key ideas and terms, and for connections with key ideas and terms in other texts they have read. They also read to discern what conversation the writer has entered, and how the writer's own argument is connected to those he or she makes reference to.

When you annotate a text, your notes in the margins might address the following questions:

- What arguments is this author responding to?
- Is the issue relevant or significant?
- How do I know that what the author says is true?
- Is the author's evidence legitimate? Sufficient?
- Can I think of an exception to the author's argument?
- What would the counterarguments be?

Good readers ask the same kinds of questions of every text they read, considering not just *what* a writer says (the content), but *how* he or she says it given the writer's purpose and audience.

The marks you leave on a page might indicate your own ideas and questions, patterns you see emerging, links to other texts, even your gut response to the writer's argument — agreement, disgust, enthusiasm, confusion. They reveal your own thought processes as you read and signal that you are entering the conversation. In effect, they are traces of your own responding voice.

Developing your own system of marking or annotating pages can help you feel confident when you sit down with a new reading for your classes. Based on our students' experiences, we offer this practical tip: Although wide-tipped highlighters have their place in some classes, it is more useful to read with a pen or pencil in your hand, so that you can do more than draw a bar of color through words or sentences you find important. Experienced readers write their responses to a text in the margins, using personal codes (boxing key words, for example), writing out definitions of words they have looked up, drawing lines to connect ideas on facing pages, or writing notes to themselves ("Connect this to Scholes on video texts"; "Hirsch would disagree big time — see his ideas on memorization in primary grades"; "You call THIS evidence?!"). These notes will help you get started on your own writing assignments, and you cannot make them with a highlighter.

Marking or annotating your readings benefits you twice. First, it is easier to participate in class discussions if you have already noted passages that are important, confusing, or linked to specific passages in other texts you have read. It's a sure way to avoid that sinking feeling you get when you return to pages you read the night before but now can't remember at all. Second, by marking key ideas in a text, noting your ideas about them, and making connections to key ideas in other texts, you have begun the process of writing an essay. When you start writing the first draft of your essay, you can quote the passages you have already marked and explain what you find significant about them based on the notes you have already made to yourself. You can make the connections to other texts in the paragraphs of your own essay that you have already begun to make on the pages of your textbook. If you mark your texts effectively, you'll never be at a loss when you sit down to write the first draft of an essay.

Let's take a look at how one of our students marked several paragraphs of Douglas Massey and Nancy Denton's *American Apartheid: Segregation and the Making of the Underclass* (1993). In the excerpt below, the student underlines what she believes is important information and begins to create an outline of the authors' main points.

1. racist attitudes

2. private behaviors

3. & institutional practices lead to ghettos (authors' claim?)

Ghetto = multi-story, high-density housing projects. Post-1950

I remember this happening where I grew up, but I didn't know the government was responsible. Is this what happened in There Are No Children Here?

The spatial isolation of black Americans was achieved by a conjunction of <u>racist attitudes</u>, <u>private behaviors</u>, and institutional <u>practices</u> that disenfranchised blacks from urban housing markets and led to the creation of the <u>ghetto</u>. Discrimination in employment exacerbated black poverty and limited the economic potential for integration, and black residential mobility was systematically blocked by pervasive discrimination and white avoidance of neighborhoods containing blacks. <u>The walls of the ghetto were buttressed after 1950</u> by government programs that promoted slum clearance and <u>relocated displaced ghetto residents into multi-story, high-density housing projects.</u>   *1*

In theory, this self-reinforcing cycle of prejudice, discrimination, and segregation was broken during the 1960s by a growing rejection of racist sentiments by whites and a series of court decisions and federal laws that banned discrimination in public life. (1) <u>The Civil Rights Act of 1964 outlawed racial discrimination in employment, (2) the Fair Housing Act of 1968 banned discrimination in housing, and</u>   *2*

Authors say situation of "spatial isolation" remains despite court decisions. Does it?

(3) the <u>*Gautreaux* and *Shannon* court decisions prohibited public authorities from placing housing projects</u> exclusively in black neighborhoods. Despite these changes, however, the <u>nation's largest black communities remained as segregated as ever in 1980.</u> Indeed, many urban areas displayed a pattern of intense racial isolation that could only be described as <u>hypersegregation</u>.

Although the racial climate of the United States improved outwardly during the 1970s, <u>racism still restricted the residential freedom of black Americans</u>; it just did so in

Subtler racism, not on public record.

less blatant ways. In the aftermath of the civil rights revolution, few whites voiced openly racist sentiments; realtors no longer refused outright to rent or sell to blacks; and few

Lack of enforcement of Civil Rights Act? Fair Housing Act? Gautreaux and Shannon? Why? Why not?

local governments went on record to oppose public housing projects because they would contain blacks. This lack of overt racism, however, did not mean that prejudice and discrimination had ended.

Notice that this student underlines information that helps her understand the argument the authors make. In her annotations, she numbers the three key factors (racist attitudes, private behaviors, and institutional practices) that influenced the formation of ghettos in the United States. She also identifies the situation that motivates the authors' analysis: the extent to which "the spatial isolation of black Americans" still exists despite laws and court decisions designed to end residential segregation. And she makes connections to her own experience and to another book she has read. By understanding the authors' arguments and making these connections, she begins the writing process. She also sets the stage for her own research, for examining the authors' claim that residential segregation still exists.

A Practice Sequence: Annotating

1 Take a few minutes to read and mark what you find significant in the paragraph below from Massey and Denton's *American Apartheid*. Notice how many different kinds of marks you make (circling, boxing, underlining, asking questions, noting your responses and connections to other texts you've read, and the like).

> Economic arguments can be invoked to explain why levels of black-white segregation changed so little during the 1970s. After decades of steady improvement, black economic progress stalled in 1973, bringing about a rise in black poverty and an increase in income inequality. As the black income distribution bifurcated, middle-class families experienced downward mobility and fewer households possessed the socioeconomic resources necessary to sustain residential mobility and, hence, integration. If the economic progress of the 1950s and 1960s had been sustained into the 1970s, segregation levels might have fallen more significantly. William Clark estimates that 30%–70% of racial segregation is attributable to economic factors, which, together with urban structure and neighborhood preferences, "bear much of the explanatory weight for present residential patterns."

2 Now, move into a small group with three or four other students and compare your annotated texts. What do you make of the similarities and differences you see? What strategies can you borrow from one another?

READING AS A WRITER: ANALYZING A TEXT RHETORICALLY

When you identify a writer's purpose for responding to a situation by composing an essay that puts forth claims meant to sway a particular audience, you are performing **rhetorical analysis** — separating out the parts of an argument to better understand how the argument works as a whole. We discuss each of these elements — situation, purpose, claims, and audience — as we analyze the following preface from E. D. Hirsch's book *Cultural Literacy: What Every American Needs to Know* (1987). Formerly a professor of English, Hirsch has long been interested in educational reform. That interest developed from his (and others') perception that today's students do not know as much as students did in the past. Although he wrote this book more than twenty years ago, many observers still believe that the contemporary problems of illiteracy and poverty can be traced to a lack of cultural literacy. Read the preface. You may want to mark it up with your own questions and responses, and then consider them in light of our analysis (following the preface) of Hirsch's rhetorical situation, purpose, claims, and audience.

ABOUT THE READING

E. D. Hirsch Jr., a retired English professor, is the author of many acclaimed books, including *The Schools We Need and Why We Don't Have Them* (1996) and *The Knowledge Deficit* (2006). His book *Cultural Literacy* was a best seller in 1987 and had a profound effect on the focus of education in the late 1980s and 1990s.

E. D. HIRSCH JR.

Preface to *Cultural Literacy*

Rousseau points out the facility with which children lend themselves to our false methods: . . . "The apparent ease with which children learn is their ruin."
—JOHN DEWEY

There is no matter what children should learn first, any more than what leg you should put into your breeches first. Sir, you may stand disputing which is best to put in first, but in the meantime your backside is bare. Sir, while you stand considering which of two things you should teach your child first, another boy has learn't 'em both.
—SAMUEL JOHNSON

To be culturally literate is to possess the basic information needed to thrive in the modern world. The breadth of that information is great, extending over the major domains of human activity from sports

1

to science. It is by no means confined to "culture" narrowly understood as an acquaintance with the arts. Nor is it confined to one social class. Quite the contrary. Cultural literacy constitutes the only sure avenue of opportunity for disadvantaged children, the only reliable way of combating the social determinism that now condemns them to remain in the same social and educational condition as their parents. That children from poor and illiterate homes tend to remain poor and illiterate is an unacceptable failure of our schools, one which has occurred not because our teachers are inept but chiefly because they are compelled to teach a fragmented curriculum based on faulty educational theories. Some say that our schools by themselves are powerless to change the cycle of poverty and illiteracy. I do not agree. They *can* break the cycle, but only if they themselves break fundamentally with some of the theories and practices that education professors and school administrators have followed over the past fifty years.

Although the chief beneficiaries of the educational reforms advocated in this book will be disadvantaged children, these same reforms will also enhance the literacy of children from middle-class homes. The educational goal advocated is that of mature literacy for *all* our citizens.   2

The connection between mature literacy and cultural literacy may already be familiar to those who have closely followed recent discussions of education. Shortly after the publication of my essay "Cultural Literacy," Dr. William Bennett, then chairman of the National Endowment for the Humanities and subsequently secretary of education in President Ronald Reagan's second administration, championed its ideas. This endorsement from an influential person of conservative views gave my ideas some currency, but such an endorsement was not likely to recommend the concept to liberal thinkers, and in fact the idea of cultural literacy has been attacked by some liberals on the assumption that I must be advocating a list of great books that every child in the land should be forced to read.   3

But those who examine the Appendix to this book will be able to judge for themselves how thoroughly mistaken such an assumption is. Very few specific titles appear on the list, and they usually appear as words, not works, because they represent writings that culturally literate people have read about but haven't read. *Das Kapital* is a good example. Cultural literacy is represented not by a *prescriptive* list of books but rather by a *descriptive* list of the information actually possessed by literate Americans. My aim in this book is to contribute to making that information the possession of all Americans.   4

The importance of such widely shared information can best be understood if I explain briefly how the idea of cultural literacy relates to currently prevailing theories of education. The theories that have dominated American education for the past fifty years stem ultimately from   5

Jean Jacques Rousseau, who believed that we should encourage the natural development of young children and not impose adult ideas upon them before they can truly understand them. Rousseau's conception of education as a process of natural development was an abstract generalization meant to apply to all children in any time or place: to French children of the eighteenth century or to Japanese or American children of the twentieth century. He thought that a child's intellectual and social skills would develop naturally without regard to the specific content of education. His content-neutral conception of educational development has long been triumphant in American schools of education and has long dominated the "developmental," content-neutral curricula of our elementary schools.

In the first decades of this century, Rousseau's ideas powerfully influ-   6
enced the educational conceptions of John Dewey, the writer who has the most deeply affected modern American educational theory and practice. Dewey's clearest and, in his time, most widely read book on education, *Schools of Tomorrow*, acknowledges Rousseau as the chief source of his educational principles. The first chapter of Dewey's book carries the telling title "Education as Natural Development" and is sprinkled with quotations from Rousseau. In it Dewey strongly seconds Rousseau's opposition to the mere accumulation of information.

> Development emphasizes the need of intimate and extensive personal acquaintance with a small number of typical situations with a view to mastering the way of dealing with the problems of experience, not the piling up of information.

Believing that a few direct experiences would suffice to develop the   7
skills that children require, Dewey assumed that early education need not be tied to specific content. He mistook a half-truth for the whole. He placed too much faith in children's ability to learn general skills from a few typical experiences and too hastily rejected "the piling up of information." Only by piling up specific, communally shared information can children learn to participate in complex cooperative activities with other members of their community.

This old truth, recently rediscovered, requires a countervailing theory   8
of education that once again stresses the importance of specific information in early and late schooling. The corrective theory might be described as an anthropological theory of education, because it is based on the anthropological observation that all human communities are founded upon specific shared information. Americans are different from Germans, who in turn are different from Japanese, because each group possesses specifically different cultural knowledge. In an anthropological perspective, the basic goal of education in a human community is acculturation, the transmission to children of the specific information shared by the adults of the group or polis.

Plato, that other great educational theorist, believed that the specific   *9*
contents transmitted to children are by far the most important elements
of education. In *The Republic* he makes Socrates ask rhetorically, "Shall
we carelessly allow children to hear any casual tales which may be
devised by casual persons, and to receive into their minds ideas for the
most part the very opposite of those which we shall wish them to have
when they are grown up?" Plato offered good reasons for being concerned with the specific contents of schooling, one of them ethical: "For
great is the issue at stake, greater than appears — whether a person is to
be good or bad."

Time has shown that there is much truth in the durable educational   *10*
theories of both Rousseau and Plato. But even the greatest thinkers, being
human, see mainly in one direction at a time, and no thinkers, however
profound, can foresee the future implications of their ideas when they are
translated into social policy. The great test of social ideas is the crucible of
history, which, after a time, usually discloses a one-sidedness in the best
of human generalizations. History, not superior wisdom, shows us that
neither the content-neutral curriculum of Rousseau and Dewey nor the
narrowly specified curriculum of Plato is adequate to the needs of a modern nation.

Plato rightly believed that it is natural for children to learn an adult   *11*
culture, but too confidently assumed that philosophy could devise the
one best culture. (Nonetheless, we should concede to Plato that within
our culture we have an obligation to choose and promote our best traditions.) On the other side, Rousseau and Dewey wrongly believed that
adult culture is "unnatural" to young children. Rousseau, Dewey, and
their present-day disciples have not shown an adequate appreciation of
the need for transmission of specific cultural information.

In contrast to the theories of Plato and Rousseau, an anthropological   *12*
theory of education accepts the naturalness as well as the relativity of
human cultures. It deems it neither wrong nor unnatural to teach young
children adult information before they fully understand it. The anthropological view stresses the universal fact that a human group must have
effective communications to function effectively, that effective communications require shared culture, and that shared culture requires transmission of specific information to children. Literacy, an essential aim of
education in the modern world, is no autonomous, empty skill but
depends upon literate culture. Like any other aspect of acculturation, literacy requires the early and continued transmission of specific information. Dewey was deeply mistaken to disdain "accumulating information
in the form of symbols." Only by accumulating shared symbols, and the
shared information that the symbols represent, can we learn to communicate effectively with one another in our national community.

■ Identify the Situation

The **situation** is what motivates you to write. Suppose you want to respond to the government's attempts to limit music downloads from the Internet. The *situation* is that the music industry has long believed it has been losing sales of CDs and other music products because of downloading, so industry leaders lobbied lawmakers in Washington, D.C., and persuaded them to restrict people's ability to take what the industry argues is its property. Discovering the range of perspectives here — for instance, of the music industry and its lobbyists, of legislators, of copyright lawyers, of consumer groups, of consumers who download music — will take some research, which is why we call writing a form of inquiry — it often begins with learning to identify the situation. Learning to identify the situation in a piece of writing, the conversations and issues that motivated the author to respond in writing, will help you figure out how to respond in your own writing.

To understand what motivated Hirsch to write, we need look no further than the situation he identifies in the first paragraph of the preface: "the social determinism that now condemns [disadvantaged children] to remain in the same social and educational condition as their parents." Hirsch wants to make sure his readers are aware of the problem so that they will be motivated to read his argument (and take action). He presents as an urgent problem the situation of disadvantaged children, an indication of what is at stake for the writer and for the readers of the argument. For Hirsch, this situation needs to change.

The urgency of a writer's argument is not always triggered by a single situation; often it is multifaceted. Again in the first paragraph, Hirsch identifies a second concern when he states that poverty and illiteracy reflect "an unacceptable failure of our schools, one which has occurred not because our teachers are inept but chiefly because they are compelled to teach a fragmented curriculum based on faulty educational theories." When he introduces a second problem, Hirsch helps us see the interconnected and complex nature of the situations authors confront in academic writing.

■ Identify the Writer's Purpose

The **purpose** for writing an essay may be to respond to a particular situation; it also can be what a writer is trying to accomplish. Specifically, what does the writer want readers to do? Does the writer want us to think about an issue, to change our opinions? Does the writer want to make us aware of a problem that we may not have recognized? Does the writer advocate for some type of change? Or is some combination of all three at work?

Hirsch's overall purpose is to promote educational reforms that will produce a higher degree of literacy for all citizens. He begins his argument with a broad statement about the importance of cultural literacy: "Cultural literacy constitutes the only sure avenue of opportunity for disadvantaged children, the only reliable way of combating the social determinism that now condemns them to remain in the same social and educational condition as their parents" (para. 1). As his argument unfolds, his purpose continues to unfold as well. He identifies the schools as a source of the problem and suggests how they must change to promote literacy:

> Some say that our schools by themselves are powerless to change the cycle of poverty and illiteracy. I do not agree. They *can* break the cycle, but only if they themselves break fundamentally with some of the theories and practices that education professors and school administrators have followed over the past fifty years. (para. 1)

The "educational goal," Hirsch says at the end of paragraph 2, is "mature literacy for *all* our citizens." To reach that goal, he insists, education must break with the past. In paragraphs 5 through 11, he cites the influence of Jean-Jacques Rousseau, John Dewey, and Plato, tracing what he sees as the educational legacies of the past. Finally, in the last paragraph of the excerpt, Hirsch describes an "anthropological view, . . . the universal fact that a human group must have effective communications to function effectively, that effective communications require shared culture, and that shared culture requires transmission of specific information to children." It is here, Hirsch argues, in the "transmission of specific information" to children, that schools must do a better job.

■ Identify the Writer's Claims

Claims are assertions that authors must justify and support with evidence and good reasons. The **thesis**, or **main claim**, is the controlling idea that crystallizes a writer's main point, helping readers track the idea as it develops throughout the essay. A writer's purpose clearly influences the way he or she crafts the main claim of an argument, the way he or she presents all assertions and evidence.

Hirsch's main claim is that "cultural literacy constitutes the only sure avenue of opportunity for disadvantaged children, the only reliable way of combating the social determinism that now condemns them to remain in the same social and educational condition as their parents" (para. 1). Notice that his thesis also points to a solution: making cultural literacy the core of public school curricula. Here we distinguish the main claim, or thesis, from the other claims or assertions that Hirsch makes. For example, at the very outset, Hirsch states that "to be culturally literate is to possess the basic information needed to thrive in the modern world." Although this is an assertion that requires support, it is a **minor claim**; it does not shape what Hirsch writes in the remainder of his essay. His main claim, or thesis, is really his call for reform.

■ Identify the Writer's Audience

A writer's language can help us identify his or her **audience**, the readers whose opinions and actions the writer hopes to influence or change. In

Hirsch's text, words and phrases like *social determinism, cycle of poverty and illiteracy, educational reforms, prescriptive,* and *anthropological* indicate that Hirsch believes his audience is well educated. References to Plato, Socrates, Rousseau, and Dewey also indicate the level of knowledge Hirsch expects of his readers. Finally, the way the preface unfolds suggests that Hirsch is writing for an audience that is familiar with a certain **genre**, or type, of writing: the formal argument. Notice how the author begins with a statement of the situation and then asserts his position. The very fact that he includes a preface speaks to the formality of his argument. Hirsch's language, his references, the structure of the document, all suggest that he is very much in conversation with people who are experienced and well-educated readers.

More specifically, the audience Hirsch invokes is made up of people who are concerned about illiteracy in the United States and the kind of social determinism that appears to condemn the educationally disadvantaged to poverty. Hirsch also acknowledges directly "those who have closely followed recent discussions of education," including the conservative William Bennett and liberal thinkers who might be provoked by Bennett's advocacy of Hirsch's ideas (para. 3). Moreover, he appears to assume his readers have achieved "mature literacy," even if they are not actually "culturally literate." He is writing for an audience that not only is well educated but also is deeply interested in issues of education as they relate to social policy.

Steps to Analyzing a Text Rhetorically

1 **Identify the situation.** What motivates the writer to write?

2 **Identify the writer's purpose.** What does the writer want readers to do or think about?

3 **Identify the writer's claims.** What is the writer's main claim? What minor claims does he or she make?

4 **Identify the writer's audience.** What do you know about the writer's audience? What does the writer's language imply about the readers? What about the writer's references? The structure of the essay?

A Practice Sequence: Reading Rhetorically

This exercise asks you to work your way through a series of paragraphs, identifying in turn the key elements of rhetorical analysis: situation, purpose, claim, and audience.

1 Begin by identifying the situation. Read the following passage from a student essay titled "Overcoming Social Stratification in

America." As you read, identify the specific words and phrases that suggest the situation that motivated the writer to compose the essay. Then describe the situation in one or two sentences.

> The social stratification encompassing American society today has placed African Americans and other minority groups at a disadvantage: Limited social mobility is preventing them from achieving higher social status. In his article "What Every American Needs to Know," E. D. Hirsch suggests that minority groups are disadvantaged as a result of a major decline in communication among Americans caused by the current educational system's failure to teach "cultural literacy." Hirsch contends that cultural literacy acts as a social equalizer, creating an American identity based on shared knowledge among all individuals independent of their social stratum. However, Hirsch's theory ignores race's inherent ability to define all social constructions in America. JanMohamed and Lloyd, in their article "Toward a Theory of Minority Discourse: What Is to Be Done?" propose that a schism separating minorities from the majority has been evolving since the colonial period. E. B. Higginbotham alludes to the effect of this deep separation and a broad antagonism toward the majority, claiming they have turned the idea of race into what she calls in her article "African-American Women's History and the Metalanguage of Race," a "metalanguage." Because of race, Hirsch's notion of cultural literacy has little relevance to attempts to eradicate social stratification in America. For minorities to achieve higher status, they must overcome the metalanguage, which has turned the term *minority* into a reference to a person of inferior political status instead of a group of people comprising a smaller population in society.

2 Identify the writer's purpose. Read the passage below from a student essay titled "Education Today: From Cultural Literacy to Multicultural Contact." What words and phrases suggest the student's purpose for writing? In a few sentences, describe the writer's purpose.

> The telephone as we know it today was invented exactly 125 years ago. The first wireless telephone was first used some 45 years later. The development of the Internet took place in the late sixties. Today, handheld devices can transmit real-time video via satellite. These and other technological advances have allowed the world to expand at an ever-increasing pace. Nowadays, the world is a place of continuous progress, a constantly changing environment in which adaptation is the only key to success. While some sectors of society were able to perform a smooth transition from the national to the global level of thinking, others had a more difficult time. One particular component that failed to adapt properly is the educational system. The emphasis on test taking and short-term memorization, which was introduced during the early 1900s, is outdated but still maintained in the teaching style today. I propose that education should be more multifaceted.

3 Identify the writer's claim. Read the passage below from a student essay titled "'Writing' the Wrong: The Dilemma of the Minority Author." Identify and write down the writer's main claim, or thesis.

> Literature, because of its ability to convey a set of values and ideals to a particular audience, has been a significant medium for shaping revolutionary events in America. For minority authors of various ethnic backgrounds, literature is a means by which they can encourage an end to the subordination of minority groups. Yet the goal of minority literature goes beyond achieving reform. Minority authors also hope to convey a piece of their own unique identity through the text that fills their pages. Unfortunately, however, because of the marginalization of minority texts by Western culture, many minority authors have found it difficult to achieve the twofold purpose of their writing. To move their works toward the forefront of society and so disseminate their message of societal reform to a larger audience that includes European Americans, minority authors have found that they must risk a portion of their own unique identity. An unwillingness to do so, in fact, can leave them powerless to effect any form of societal revolution that could end the overshadowing of minorities by the dominant culture. Although it is unfortunate that minority authors must initially sacrifice a piece of their identity to reach a larger audience, doing so gives them "insider" status and thus greater influence on societal change.

4 Identify the writer's audience. Read the following excerpt from "The Problems and Dangers of Assimilatory Policies." Admittedly, the essay was written in response to a classroom assignment, so the student's instructor and classmates would be part of the writer's audience. But what sort of generalizations can you make about the audience that would read this essay outside the classroom environment?

> American society considers itself to be in an age of enlightenment. Racism has been denounced, and cultural colorblindness in all things is encouraged. Economic opportunities are available for everyone, and equal consideration before the law is provided for each citizen. American society considers itself the embodiment of liberty, equality, and justice for all.
>
> In a society like the one described, it follows that one's background and culture [do] not have any influence on one's socioeconomic status; theoretically, the two should be completely disconnected. Yet, as we all know, this is not the case. The people of the highest status in America are almost uniformly white males. Sadly, America, the place of equality and liberty, is still very much a stratified society, not only by socioeconomic class/status, but minority cultures much more often fill the ranks of the lower classes. Fortunately for those of minority cultures, the country's policymakers now accept, at least in

speech, the basic equality and potential of all cultures to rise out of poverty; unfortunately, they still refuse to recognize the validity of differences in these cultures from what they, the policymakers, view as American.

5 Share your analysis. Working with two or three of your classmates, come to a consensus on the (1) situation, (2) purpose, (3) main claim, and (4) audience of the excerpts. Then choose a spokesperson to report your group's thoughts to the rest of the class.

WRITING AS A READER: COMPOSING A RHETORICAL ANALYSIS

One of our favorite exercises is to ask our students to choose a single paragraph from a text they have read and to write a rhetorical analysis of it. Once you are able to identify how writers make their arguments, you are better able to make use of their strategies in your own writing. You may be amazed by how much you can say or write about a single paragraph in an essay once you begin to consider such factors as purpose and audience.

For example, one of our students wrote a rhetorical analysis of the third paragraph of Ada María Isasi-Díaz's essay "Hispanic in America: Starting Points." Here is the paragraph from Isasi-Díaz's work:

> A preliminary note about terminology. What to call ourselves is an issue hotly debated in some segments of our communities. I use the term "Hispanic" because the majority of the communities I deal with include themselves in that term, though each and every one of us refers to ourselves according to our country of origin: Cubans, Puerto Ricans, Mexican Americans, etc. What I do wish to emphasize is that "Latina/o" does not have a more politicized or radical connotation than "Hispanic" among the majority of our communities. In my experience it is most often those outside our communities who insist on giving Latina/o such a connotation. The contrary, however, is true of the appellation "Chicana/o," which does indicate a certain consciousness and political stance different from but not necessarily contrary to those who call themselves Mexican Americans.

Now here is the student's analysis of the paragraph, which she wrote after she read Isasi-Díaz's whole essay and identified (1) the situation that Isasi-Díaz responded to, (2) her purpose, (3) her claim, and (4) her intended audience (through the use of language). Our annotations highlight some of the rhetorical strategies the student made use of in her analysis.

The student focuses on the author's language as a way to grasp the situation.

Isasi-Díaz is obviously concerned about the words she uses to set   *1*
out her argument: She begins this early paragraph with "a preliminary note about terminology." She wants us to know that there is
an argument about the label *Hispanic* within Hispanic communities, and she uses *our* repeatedly in this paragraph to remind us

The student notes that the author uses personal experience as evidence.

that she is part of those communities. She assumes that we might
be outside those communities and that we need this terminology
clarified (in my case, she's right!). Isasi-Díaz uses personal experience to show us that she knows what she is talking about: "In my
experience it is most often those outside our communities who

The student also considers how what she reads might apply to her own writing. The student identifies those parts of the essay that could affect readers, using her own response as an example.

insist . . ." She walks us through the different terms (*Latina/o,
Chicana/o, Mexican American*) and offers not exactly definitions
but connotations, telling us which label indicates what kind of
political position. I like the way she wants to clear up all these
different terms, and I think I might try in my own essay to have a
paragraph early on that clarifies the definitions and connotations
of the key words I am using.

It is interesting that Isasi-Díaz makes a big deal of being   *2*
inside her communities, and blames those "outside" her communities for "insist[ing]" on giving what she sees as the wrong connotation to words. As an outsider myself, this might have turned me
off a bit, but she does make clear that there is a wide range of
experiences (suggested by her long list of countries of origin) and
opinions within "our communities" (the fact that *communities* is
plural rather than singular suggests this, too), so she is doing
something more complicated than "us versus them" here. It makes

The student makes a connection to other essays she has read.

me think of Gloria Anzaldúa's essay, where she also shows how
many different perspectives are embedded in the very words a
person uses, particularly on the border between Mexico and the
United States. It also reminded me of Mary Louise Pratt's idea of
"transculturation," where people struggle to retain and adapt
their cultural identities in "contact zones."

■ Write a Rhetorical Analysis of a Paragraph

Now we'd like you to try the same exercise. First, read the excerpt from
Ada María Isasi-Díaz's essay that follows. As you read, underline where the
writer makes the following points explicit:

- The situation to which she is responding
- The purpose of her essay
- Her main claim, or thesis
- Words and phrases that suggest who she believes is her audience

---

ABOUT THE READING

Ada María Isasi-Díaz is a professor of theology and ethics at the Theological School, Drew University. A political refugee from Cuba, she came to the United States in 1960 and entered an Ursuline convent. She later spent three years as a missionary in Lima, Peru, where she worked with the poor and the oppressed, joining them in their struggle for justice. In her book *Mujerista Theology* (1996), she provides what she calls a comprehensive introduction to Hispanic feminist theology, which seeks to create a valid voice for Latinas and challenges theological understandings, church teachings, and religious practices that oppress Latinas. "Hispanic in America: Starting Points" was originally published in the May 13, 1991, issue of *Christianity in Crisis*.

ADA MARÍA ISASI-DÍAZ

Hispanic in America: Starting Points

The twenty-first century is rapidly approaching and with it comes a definitive increase in the Hispanic population of the United States. We will soon be the most numerous ethnic "minority" — a minority that seems greatly problematic because a significant number of us, some of us would say the majority, behave differently from other immigrant groups in the United States.

Our unwillingness to jump into the melting pot; our insistence on maintaining our own language; our ongoing links with our countries of origin — due mostly to their geographic proximity and to the continuous flow of more Hispanics into the United States; and the fact that the largest groups of Hispanics, Mexican Americans and Puerto Ricans are geographically and politically an integral part of this country: These factors, among others, make us different. And the acceptance of that difference, which does not make us better or worse than other groups but simply different, has to be the starting point for understanding us. What follows is a kind of working paper, a guide toward reaching that starting point.

A preliminary note about terminology. What to call ourselves is an issue hotly debated in some segments of our communities. I use the term "Hispanic" because the majority of the communities I deal with include themselves in that term, though each and every one of us refers to ourselves according to our country of origin: Cubans, Puerto Ricans, Mexican Americans, etc. What I do wish to emphasize is that "Latina/o" does not have a more politicized or radical connotation than "Hispanic" among the majority of our communities. In my experience it is most often those outside our communities who insist on giving Latina/o such a connotation. The contrary, however, is true of the appellation "Chicana/o," which does indicate a certain consciousness and political stance different from but not necessarily contrary to those who call themselves Mexican Americans.

The way Hispanics participate in this society has to do not only with 4 us, but also with U.S. history, economics, politics, and society. Hispanics are in this country to begin with mostly because of U.S. policies and interests. Great numbers of Mexican Americans never moved to the United States. Instead, the border crossed *them* in 1846 when Mexico had to give up today's Southwest in the Treaty of Guadalupe-Hidalgo. The spoils of the Spanish American War at the end of the nineteenth century included Puerto Rico, where the United States had both military and economic interests. Without having any say, that nation was annexed by the United States.

Cuba suffered a somewhat similar fate. The United States sent troops to 5 Cuba in the midst of its War of Independence against Spain. When Spain surrendered, the United States occupied Cuba as a military protectorate. And though Cuba became a free republic in 1902, the United States continued to maintain economic control and repeatedly intervened in Cuba's political affairs. It was, therefore, only reasonable that when Cubans had to leave their country, they felt they could and should find refuge here. The United States government accepted the Cuban refugees of the Castro regime, giving them economic aid and passing a special law making it easy for them to become residents and citizens.

As for more recent Hispanic immigrants, what can be said in a few lines 6 about the constant manipulation by the United States of the economies and political processes of the different countries of Central America? The United States, therefore, has the moral responsibility to accept Salvadorans, Guatemalans, Hondurans, and other Central Americans who have to leave their countries because of political persecution or hunger. In short, the reasons Hispanics are in the United States are different from those of the earlier European immigrants, and the responsibility the United States has for our being here is vastly greater.

In spite of this difference, many people believe we Hispanics could 7 have become as successful as the European immigrants. So why haven't we? For one thing, by the time Hispanics grew in numbers in the United States, the economy was no longer labor-intensive. Hispanics have lacked not "a strong back and a willingness to work," but the opportunity to capitalize on them. Then, unlike the European immigrants who went west and were able to buy land, Hispanics arrived here after homesteading had passed. But a more fundamental reason exists: racism. Hispanics are considered a nonwhite race, regardless of the fact that many of us are of the white race. Our ethnic difference has been officially construed as a racial difference: In government, businesses, and school forms, "Hispanic" is one of the choices under the category *race*.

No possibility exists of understanding Hispanics and being in dialogue   *8*
with us unless the short exposition presented is studied and analyzed.
The starting point for all dialogue is a profound respect for the other, and
respect cannot flourish if the other is not known. A commitment to study
the history of Hispanics in the United States — from the perspective of
Hispanics and not only from the perspective presented in the standard
textbooks of American history — must be the starting point in any
attempt to understand Hispanics.

A second obstacle to dialogue is the prevalent insistence in this coun-   *9*
try that one American Way of Life exists, and it is the best way of life for
everybody in the world. The melting pot concept has provided a framework in which assimilation is a must, and plurality of cultures an impos-
sibility. Hispanic culture is not seen as an enrichment but as a threat. Few
understand that Hispanic culture provides for us, as other cultures do for
other peoples, guidelines for conduct and relationships, a system of values, and institutions and power structures that allow us to function at our
best. Our culture has been formed and will continue to be shaped by the
historical happenings and the constant actions of our communities —
communities in the United States that are influenced by what happens
here as well as in our countries of origin.

It is only within our own culture that Hispanics can acquire a sense of   *10*
belonging, of security, of dignity, and of participation. The ongoing
attempts to minimize or to make our culture disappear will only create
problems for the United States. They engender a low sense of identity that
can lead us to nonhealthy extremes in our search for some self-esteem.
For us, language is the main means of identification here in the United
States. To speak Spanish, in public as well as in private, is a political act, a
means of asserting who we are, an important way of struggling against
assimilation. The different state laws that forbid speaking Spanish in official situations, or militate against bilingual education, function as an
oppressive internal colonialism that ends up hurting U.S. society.

A Practice Sequence: Rhetorically Analyzing a Paragraph

1 Review your annotations and write a paragraph in which you
describe the rhetorical situation and the writer's purpose, main
claim, and audience.

2 Now write an analysis of a paragraph in Isasi-Díaz's essay. Choose
a substantial paragraph (not paragraph 3!) that you find especially
interesting either for what the author writes or how she writes it.
Using quotations from the text, write a one-page essay in which
you consider the situation Isasi-Díaz is responding to, her purpose
as a writer, or her audience.

■ Write a Rhetorical Analysis of an Essay

By now you should be developing a strong sense of what is involved in analyzing a paragraph rhetorically. You should be ready to take the next steps: performing a rhetorical analysis of a complete text and then sharing your analysis and the strategies you've learned with your classmates.

Read the next text, "Cultural Baggage" by Barbara Ehrenreich, annotating it to help you identify her situation, purpose, thesis, and audience. As you read, also make a separate set of annotations — possibly with a different color pen or pencil, circled, or keyed with asterisks — in which you comment on or evaluate the effectiveness of her essay. What do you like or dislike about it? Why? Does Ehrenreich persuade you to accept her point of view? What impressions do you have of her as a person? Would you like to be in a conversation with her?

ABOUT THE READING

Barbara Ehrenreich is a social critic, activist, and political essayist. Her book *Nickel and Dimed: On (Not) Getting By in America* (2001) describes her attempt to live on low-wage jobs; it became a national best seller in the United States. Her most recent book, *Bait and Switch: The (Futile) Pursuit of the American Dream* (2005), explores the shadowy world of the white-collar unemployed. Ehrenreich has also written for *Mother Jones, The Atlantic, Ms., The New Republic, In These Times,* Salon.com, and other publications. "Cultural Baggage" was originally published in the *New York Times Magazine* in 1992.

BARBARA EHRENREICH

Cultural Baggage

An acquaintance was telling me about the joys of rediscovering her ethnic and religious heritage. "I know exactly what my ancestors were doing 2,000 years ago," she said, eyes gleaming with enthusiasm, "and *I can do the same things now.*" Then she leaned forward and inquired politely, "And what is your ethnic background, if I may ask?"

"None," I said, that being the first word in line to get out of my mouth. Well, not "none," I backtracked. Scottish, English, Irish — that was something, I supposed. Too much Irish to qualify as a WASP; too much of the hated English to warrant a "Kiss Me, I'm Irish" button; plus there are a number of dead ends in the family tree due to adoptions, missing records, failing memories and the like. I was blushing by this time. Did "none" mean I was rejecting my heritage out of Anglo-Celtic self-hate? Or was I revealing a hidden ethnic chauvinism in which the Britannically derived serve as a kind of neutral standard compared with the ethnic "others"?

Throughout the 1960s and 70s, I watched one group after another — *African Americans, Latinos, Native Americans — stand up and proudly reclaim their roots while I just sank back ever deeper into my seat. All this excitement over ethnicity stemmed, I uneasily sensed, from a past in which *their* ancestors had been trampled upon by *my* ancestors, or at least by people who looked very much like them. In addition, it had begun to seem almost un-American not to have some sort of hyphen at hand, linking one to more venerable times and locales. *3*

But the truth is, I was raised with none. We'd eaten ethnic foods in my childhood home, but these were all borrowed, like the pasties, or Cornish meat pies, my father had picked up from his fellow miners in Butte, Montana. If my mother had one rule, it was militant ecumenism in all manners of food and experience. "Try new things," she would say, meaning anything from sweetbreads to clams, with an emphasis on the "new." *4*

As a child, I briefly nourished a craving for tradition and roots. I immersed myself in the works of Sir Walter Scott. I pretended to believe that the bagpipe was a musical instrument. I was fascinated to learn from a grandmother that we were descended from certain Highland clans and longed for a pleated skirt in one of their distinctive tartans. *5*

But in *Ivanhoe,* it was the dark-eyed "Jewess" Rebecca I identified with, not the flaxen-haired bimbo Rowena. As for clans: Why not call them "tribes," those bands of half-clad peasants and warriors whose idea of cuisine was stuffed sheep gut washed down with whiskey? And then there was the sting of Disraeli's remark — which I came across in my early teens — to the effect that his ancestors had been leading orderly, literate lives when my ancestors were still rampaging through the Highlands daubing themselves with blue paint. *6*

Motherhood put the screws on me, ethnicity-wise. I had hoped that by marrying a man of Eastern European Jewish ancestry I would acquire for my descendants the ethnic genes that my own forebears so sadly lacked. At one point, I even subjected the children to a seder of my own design, including a little talk about the flight from Egypt and its relevance to modern social issues. But the kids insisted on buttering their matzos and snickering through my talk. "Give me a break, Mom," the older one said. "You don't even believe in God." *7*

After the tiny pagans had been put to bed, I sat down to brood over Elijah's wine. What had I been thinking? The kids knew that their Jewish grandparents were secular folks who didn't hold seders themselves. And if ethnicity eluded me, how could I expect it to take root in my children, who are not only Scottish English Irish, but Hungarian Polish Russian to boot? *8*

But, then, on the fumes of Manischewitz, a great insight took form in my mind. It was true, as the kids said, that I didn't "believe in God." But *9* this could be taken as something very different from an accusation — a reminder of a genuine heritage. My parents had not believed in God either, nor had my grandparents or any other progenitors going back to the great-great level. They had become disillusioned with Christianity generations ago — just as, on the in-law side, my children's other ancestors had shaken their Orthodox Judaism. This insight did not exactly furnish me with an "identity," but it was at least something to work with: We are the kind of people, I realized — whatever our distant ancestors' religions — who do *not* believe, who do not carry on traditions, who do not do things just because someone has done them before.

The epiphany went on: I recalled that my mother never introduced a   10
procedure for cooking or cleaning by telling me, "Grandma did it this way." What did Grandma know, living in the days before vacuum cleaners and disposable toilet mops? In my parents' general view, new things were better than old, and the very fact that some ritual had been performed in the past was a good reason for abandoning it now. Because what was the past, as our forebears knew it? Nothing but poverty, superstition and grief. "Think for yourself," Dad used to say. "Always ask why."

In fact, this may have been the ideal cultural heritage for my particular   11
ethnic strain — bounced as it was from the Highlands of Scotland across the sea, out to the Rockies, down into the mines and finally spewed out into high-tech, suburban America. What better philosophy, for a race of migrants, than "Think for yourself"? What better maxim, for a people whose whole world was rudely inverted every thirty years or so, than "Try new things"?

The more tradition-minded, the newly enthusiastic celebrants of   12
Purim and Kwanzaa and Solstice, may see little point to survival if the survivors carry no cultural freight — religion, for example, or ethnic tradition. To which I would say that skepticism, curiosity and wide-eyed ecumenical tolerance are also worthy elements of the human tradition and are at least as old as such notions as "Serbian" or "Croatian," "Scottish" or "Jewish." I make no claims for my personal line of progenitors except that they remained loyal to the values that may have induced all of our ancestors, long, long ago, to climb down from the trees and make their way into the open plains.

A few weeks ago, I cleared my throat and asked the children, now   13
mostly grown and fearsomely smart, whether they felt any stirrings of ethnic or religious identity, etc., which might have been, ahem, insufficiently nourished at home. "None," they said, adding firmly, "and the world would be a better place if nobody else did, either." My chest swelled with pride, as would my mother's, to know that the race of "none" marches on.

A Practice Sequence: Rhetorically Analyzing an Essay

1 Write a brief rhetorical analysis of Barbara Ehrenreich's essay, referring to your notes and citing passages where she indicates her situation, purpose, main claim, and audience.

2 An option for group work: As a class, divide into three or more groups. Each group should answer the following questions in response to their reading of Ehrenreich's essay "Cultural Baggage":

Group 1: Identify the situation(s) motivating Ehrenreich to write. Then evaluate: How well does her argument function as a conversation with other authors who have written on the same topic?

Group 2: Analyze the audience's identity, perspectives, and conventional expectations. Then evaluate: How well does the argument function as a conversation with the audience?

Group 3: Analyze the writer's purpose. Then evaluate: Do you believe Ehrenreich achieves her purpose in this essay? Why or why not?

Then, as a class, share your observations:

- To what extent does the author's ability as a conversationalist — that is, her ability to enter into a conversation with other authors and her audience — affect your evaluation of whether she achieves her purpose in this essay?

- If you were to meet this writer, what suggestions or advice would you give her for making her argument more persuasive?

Much if not all of the writing you do in college will be based on what you have read. This is the case, for example, when you summarize a philosopher's theory, analyze the significance of an experiment in psychology, or, perhaps, synthesize different and conflicting points of view in making an argument about race and academic achievement in sociology. As we maintain throughout this book, writing and reading are inextricably linked to each other. Good academic writers are also good critical readers: They leave their mark on what they read, identifying issues, making judgments about the truth of what writers tell them, and evaluating the adequacy of the evidence in support of an argument. This is where writing and inquiry begin: understanding our own position relative to the scholarly conversations that we want to enter. Moreover, critical readers try to understand the strategies that writers use to persuade them to agree with them. At times, these are strategies that we can adapt in advancing our arguments. In the next chapter, we provide some strategies for identifying and evaluating the adequacy of a writer's claims.

3

From Identifying Claims
to Analyzing Arguments

A **claim** is an assertion of fact or belief that needs to be supported with **evidence** — the information that backs up a claim. A main claim, or thesis, summarizes the writer's position on a situation and answers the question(s) the writer addresses. It also encompasses all of the minor claims and their supporting evidence that the writer makes throughout the argument. As readers, we need to identify a writer's main claim because it helps us organize our own understanding of the writer's argument. It acts as a signpost that tells us, "This is what the essay is about," "This is what I want you to pay attention to," and "This is how I want you to think, change, or act." When you evaluate a claim, whether it is an argument's main claim or a minor claim, it is helpful to identify the type of claim it is: a claim of fact, a claim of value, or a claim of policy. You also need to evaluate the reasons for and the evidence that supports the claim. Because academic argument should acknowledge multiple points of view, you also should be prepared to identify what, if any, concessions a writer offers his or her readers, and what counterarguments he or she anticipates from others in the conversation.

IDENTIFYING TYPES OF CLAIMS

To illustrate how to identify a writer's claims, let's take a look at a text by educators Myra and David Sadker that examines gender bias in schools. The text is followed by our analyses of the types of claims (fact, value, and policy) and then, in the next section, of the nature of the arguments (evidence, concessions, and counterarguments) the authors present.

ABOUT THE READING

Myra Sadker was a professor of education at American University until 1995, the year she died. Dr. Sadker coauthored *Sexism in School and Society*, the first book on gender bias in America's schools in 1973, and became a leading advocate for equal educational opportunities.

David Sadker is a professor at American University and has taught at the elementary, middle school, and high school levels. David Sadker and his late wife earned a national reputation for their groundbreaking work in confronting gender bias and sexual harassment. "Hidden Lessons" is an excerpt from their book *Failing at Fairness: How Our Schools Cheat Girls* (1994).

MYRA SADKER AND DAVID SADKER

Hidden Lessons

Sitting in the same classroom, reading the same textbook, listening to the same teacher, boys and girls receive very different educations. From grade school through graduate school female students are more likely to be invisible members of classrooms. Teachers interact with males more frequently, ask them better questions, and give them more precise and helpful feedback. Over the course of years the uneven distribution of teacher time, energy, attention, and talent, with boys getting the lion's share, takes its toll on girls. Since gender bias is not a noisy problem, most people are unaware of the secret sexist lessons and the quiet losses they engender.

Girls are the majority of our nation's schoolchildren, yet they are second-class educational citizens. The problems they face — loss of self-esteem, decline in achievement, and elimination of career options — are at the heart of the educational process. Until educational sexism is eradicated, more than half our children will be shortchanged and their gifts lost to society.

Award-winning author Susan Faludi discovered that backlash "is most powerful when it goes private, when it lodges inside a woman's mind and turns her vision inward, until she imagines the pressure is all in her head, until she begins to enforce the backlash too — on herself."* Psychological backlash internalized by adult women is a frightening concept, but what is even more terrifying is a curriculum of sexist school lessons becoming secret mind games played against female children, our daughters, and tomorrow's women.

---

*Editor's note: Journalist Faludi's book *Backlash: The Undeclared War Against American Women* (1991) was a response to the antifeminist backlash against the women's movement.

After almost two decades of research grants and thousands of hours of classroom observation, we remain amazed at the stubborn persistence of these hidden sexist lessons. When we began our investigation of gender bias, we looked first in the classrooms of one of Washington, D.C.'s elite and expensive private schools. Uncertain of exactly what to look for, we wrote nothing down; we just observed. The classroom was a whirlwind of activity so fast paced we could easily miss the quick but vital phrase or gesture, the insidious incident, the tiny inequity that held a world of meaning. As we watched, we had to push ourselves beyond the blind spots of socialization and gradually focus on the nature of the interaction between teacher and student. On the second day we saw our first example of sexism, a quick, jarring flash within the hectic pace of the school day:

> Two second-graders are kneeling beside a large box. They whisper excitedly to each other as they pull out wooden blocks, colored balls, counting sticks. So absorbed are these two small children in examining and sorting the materials, they are visibly startled by the teacher's impatient voice as she hovers over them. "Ann! Julia! Get your cottonpickin' hands out of the math box. Move over so the boys can get in there and do their work."

Isolated here on the page of a book, this incident is not difficult to interpret. It becomes even more disturbing if you think of it with the teacher making a racial distinction. Picture Ann and Julia as African-American children moved away so white children can gain access to the math materials. If Ann and Julia's parents had observed this exchange, they might justifiably wonder whether their tuition dollars were well spent. But few parents actually watch teachers in action, and fewer still have learned to interpret the meaning behind fast-paced classroom events.

The incident unsettles, but it must be considered within the context of numerous interactions this harried teacher had that day. While she talked to the two girls, she was also keeping a wary eye on fourteen other active children. Unless you actually shadowed the teacher, stood right next to her as we did, you might not have seen or heard the event. After all, it lasted only a few seconds.

It took us almost a year to develop an observation system that would register the hundreds of daily classroom interactions, teasing out the gender bias embedded in them. Trained raters coded classrooms in math, reading, English, and social studies. They observed students from different racial and ethnic backgrounds. They saw lessons taught by women and by men, by teachers of different races. In short, they analyzed America's classrooms. By the end of the year we had thousands of observation sheets, and after another year of statistical analysis, we discovered a syntax of sexism so elusive that most teachers and students were completely unaware of its influence.

Recently a producer of NBC's *Dateline* contacted us to learn more about our discovery that girls don't receive their fair share of education. Jane Pauley, the show's anchorwoman, wanted to visit classrooms, capture these covert sexist lessons on videotape, and expose them before a television audience. The task was to extricate sound bites of sexism from a fifth-grade classroom where the teacher, chosen to be the subject of the exposé, was aware she was being scrutinized for sex bias.

Dateline had been taping in her class for two days when we received a concerned phone call. "This is a fair teacher," the producer said. "How can we show sexism on our show when there's no gender bias in this teacher's class?" We drove to the NBC studio in Washington, D.C., and found two *Dateline* staffers, intelligent women concerned about fair treatment in school, sitting on the floor in a darkened room staring at the videotape of a fifth-grade class. "We've been playing this over and over. The teacher is terrific. There's no bias in her teaching. Come watch."   9

After about twenty minutes of viewing, we realized it was a case of déjà vu: The episodal sexist themes and recurring incidents were all too familiar. The teacher was terrific, but she was more effective for half of the students than she was for the other. She was, in fact, a classic example of the hundreds of skillful well-intentioned professionals we have seen who inadvertently teach boys better than girls.   10

We had forgotten how difficult it was to recognize subtle sexism before you learn how to look. It was as if the *Dateline* staff members were wearing blinders. We halted the tape, pointed out the sexist behaviors, related them to incidents in our research, and played the tape again. There is a classic "aha!" effect in education when people finally "get it." Once the hidden lessons of unconscious bias are understood, classrooms never look the same again to the trained observer.   11

Much of the unintentional gender bias in that fifth-grade class could not be shown in the short time allowed by television, but the sound bites of sexism were also there. *Dateline* chose to show a segregated math group: boys sitting on the teacher's right side and girls on her left. After giving the math book to a girl to hold open at the page of examples, the teacher turned her back to the girls and focused on the boys, teaching them actively and directly. Occasionally she turned to the girls' side, but only to read the examples in the book. This teacher, although aware that she was being observed for sexism, had unwittingly transformed the girls into passive spectators, an audience for the boys. All but one, that is: The girl holding the math book had become a prop.   12

Dateline also showed a lively discussion in the school library. With both girls' hands and boys' hands waving for attention, the librarian chose boy after boy to speak. In one interaction she peered through the forest of girls' hands waving directly in front of her to acknowledge the raised hand of a boy in the back of the room. Startled by the teacher's attention, the boy muttered, "I was just stretching."   13

The next day we discussed the show with future teachers, our students at The American University. They were bewildered. "Those teachers really were sexist. They didn't mean to be, but they were. How could that   14 happen — with the cameras and everyone watching?" When we took those students into classrooms to discover the hidden lessons for themselves, they began to understand. It is difficult to detect sexism unless you know precisely how to observe. And if a lifetime of socialization makes it difficult to spot gender bias even when you're looking for it, how much harder it is to avoid the traps when you are the one doing the teaching.

■ Identify Claims of Fact

Claims of fact are assertions (or arguments) that a condition has existed, exists, or will exist. Claims of fact are made by individuals who believe that something is true; but claims are never simply facts, and some claims are more objective, and so easier to verify, than others. For example, "It's raining in Boston today" is a "factual" claim of fact; it's easily verified. But consider the argument some make that the steel and automotive industries in the United States have depleted our natural resources and left us at a crisis point. This is an assertion that a condition exists. A careful reader must examine the basis for this kind of claim: Are we truly facing a crisis? And if so, are the steel and automotive industries truly responsible? A number of politicians counter this claim of fact by insisting that if the government would harness the vast natural resources in Alaska, there would be no "crisis." This is also a claim of fact, in this case an assertion that a condition will exist in the future. Again, it is based on evidence, evidence gathered from various sources that indicates sufficient resources in Alaska to keep up with our increasing demands for resources and to allay a potential crisis.

Our point is that most claims of fact are debatable. They may be based on factual information, but they are not necessarily true. Most claims of fact present **interpretations** of evidence derived from **inferences**. That is, a writer will examine evidence (for example, about the quantity of natural resources in Alaska and the rate that industries harness those resources and process them into goods), draw a conclusion based on reasoning (an inference), and offer an explanation based on that conclusion (an interpretation). So, for example, an academic writer will study the evidence on the quantity of natural resources in Alaska and the rate that industries harness those resources and process them into goods; only after the writer makes an informed decision on whether Alaska's resources are sufficient to keep pace with the demand for them will he or she take a position on the issue.

In the first paragraph of their essay, the Sadkers make the claims of fact that female students are "more likely to be invisible members of classrooms," and that teachers interact differently with female students than they do with male students. The careful reader will want to see how the Sadkers support these claims of fact throughout the essay. Can they convincingly present their argument about "the secret sexist lessons and the quiet losses they engender" in the paragraphs that follow?

■ Identify Claims of Value

A claim of fact is different from a **claim of value**, which expresses an evaluation of a condition that has existed, exists, or will exist. Is a condition good or bad? Is it important or inconsequential? An argument that developing the wilderness in Alaska would irreversibly mar the beauty of the land indicates that the writer values the beauty of the land over the possible benefits of development. A claim of value presents a judgment, which is sometimes signaled by a value-laden word like *ugly, beautiful,* or *immoral,* but may also be conveyed more subtly by the writer's tone and attitude.

Sadker and Sadker make a claim of value when they suggest that a "majority of our nation's schoolchildren" have become "second-class educational citizens" and point out that the consequences of treating girls differently from boys in school has resulted in a "loss of self-esteem, decline in achievement, and elimination of career options" for girls (para. 2). Of course, the critical reader's task is to question these evaluations: Does gender bias in the classroom affect self-esteem, achievement, and career options? Both of these statements are minor claims, but they make assertions that require support. After all, how do the Sadkers know these things? Whether or not readers are persuaded by these claims depends on the evidence or reasons that the authors use to support them. We discuss the nature of evidence and what constitutes "good reasons" later in this chapter.

■ Identify Claims of Policy

A **claim of policy** is an argument for what should be the case; it is a call for change. Two recent controversies on college campuses center on claims of policy. One has activists arguing that universities and colleges should have a policy that all workers on campus earn a living wage. The other has activists arguing that universities and colleges should have a policy that prevents them from investing in countries where the government ignores human rights. Claims of policy are often signaled by words like *should* and *must*: "For public universities to live up to their democratic mission, they *must* provide all their workers with a living wage." Myra and David Sadker make a claim of policy when they assert that "educational sexism" must be eradicated; otherwise, they point out, "more than half our children will be shortchanged and their gifts lost to society" (para. 2).

Not all writers make their claims as explicitly as the Sadkers do; nor does every argument include all three types of claims. But you should be able to identify the three different types of claims. Moreover, you should keep in mind what the situation is and what kind of argument can best address what you see as a problem. Ask yourself: Does the situation involve a question of fact? Does the situation involve a question of value? Does the situation require a change in policy? Or is some combination at work?

> ## Steps to Identifying Claims
>
> **1** **Ask:** Does the argument assert that a condition has existed, exists, or will exist? If so, it's a claim of fact.
>
> **2** **Ask:** Does the argument express an evaluation of a condition that has existed, exists, or will exist? If so, it's a claim of value.
>
> **3** **Ask:** Does the argument call for change, and is it directed at some future action? If so, it's a claim of policy.

A Practice Sequence: Identifying Claims

What follows is a series of claims. Identify each one as a claim of fact, value, or policy. Be prepared to justify your categorizations.

1 Taxing the use of fossil fuels will end the energy crisis.

2 We should reform the welfare system to ensure that people who receive support from the government also work.

3 Images of violence in the media create a culture of violence in schools.

4 The increase in homelessness is a deplorable situation that contradicts the whole idea of democracy.

5 Distributing property taxes is the one sure way to end poverty and illiteracy.

6 Individual votes don't really count.

7 Despite the 20 percent increase in the number of females in the workforce over the past forty years, women are still not treated equitably.

8 Affirmative action is a policy that has outlived its usefulness.

9 There are a disproportionate number of black males in American prisons.

10 The media are biased, which means we cannot count on newspapers or television news for the truth.

ANALYZING ARGUMENTS

Analyzing an argument involves identifying the writer's main and minor claims and then examining (1) the reasons and evidence given in support of each claim, (2) the writer's concessions, and (3) the writer's attempts to handle counterarguments.

■ Analyze the Reasons Used to Support a Claim

Stating a claim is one thing; supporting that claim is another. As a critical reader, you need to evaluate whether a writer has provided *good reasons* to support his or her position. Specifically, you will need to decide whether the support for a claim is recent, relevant, reliable, and accurate. As a writer, you will need to use the same criteria when you support your claims.

Is the source recent?   Knowledgeable readers of your written arguments not only will be aware of classic studies that you should cite as "intellectual touchstones"; they will also expect you to cite recent evidence, evidence published within five years of when you are writing. Of course, older research can be valuable. For example, in a paper about molecular biology, you might very well cite James Watson and Francis Crick's groundbreaking 1953 study in which they describe the structure of DNA. That study is an intellectual touchstone that changed the life sciences in a fundamental way, much as Einstein's theory of relativity changed how physicists think about the universe. Or if you were writing about educational reform, you might very well mention Hirsch's 1987 book *Cultural Literacy*. Hirsch's book did not change the way people think about curricular reform as profoundly as Watson and Crick's study changed the way scientists think about biology, but his term *cultural literacy* continues to serve as useful shorthand for a particular way of thinking about curricular reform that remains influential to this day.

Although citing Hirsch is an effective way to suggest you have studied the history of an educational problem, it will not convince your readers that there is a crisis in education today. To establish that, you would need to use as evidence studies published over the past few years to show, for example, that there has been a steady decline in test scores since Hirsch wrote his book. And you would need to support your claim that curricular reform is the one sure way to bring an end to illiteracy and poverty with data that are much more current than those available to Hirsch in the 1980s. No one would accept the judgment that our schools are in crisis if your most recent citation is more than twenty years old.

Is the source relevant?   Evidence that is relevant must have real bearing on your issue and also depends greatly on what your readers expect. Suppose two of your friends complain that they were unable to sell their condominiums for the price they asked. You can claim there is a crisis in the housing market, but your argument won't convince most readers if your only evidence is personal anecdote. Such anecdotal evidence may alert you to a possible topic and help you connect with your readers, but you will need to test the **relevance** of your friends' experience — Is it pertinent? Is it typical of a larger situation or condition? — if you want your readers to take your argument seriously. At the very least, you should scan real estate listings to see what the asking prices are for properties comparable to your friends' properties. By comparing listings, you are defining the grounds for your argument. If your friends are disappointed that their one-bedroom condominiums sold for less than a three-bedroom condominium with deeded parking in the same neighborhood, it may will be that their expectations were too high. If you aren't comparing like things, your argument is going to be seriously flawed. If your friends' definition of what constitutes a "reasonable price" differs dramatically from everyone else's, their experience is probably irrelevant to the larger question of whether the local housing market is depressed.

Is the source reliable?   You also need to evaluate whether the data you are using to support your argument are reliable. After all, some researchers present findings based on a very small sample of people that can also be rather selective. For example, a researcher might argue that 67 percent of the people he cited believe that school and residential integration are important concerns. But how many people did this person interview? More important, who responded to the researcher's questions? A reliable claim cannot be based on a few of the researcher's friends.

Let's return to the real estate example. You have confirmed that your friends listed their condominiums at prices that were not out of line with the market. Now what? You need to seek out reliable sources to continue testing your argument. For example, you might search the real estate or business section of your local newspaper to see if there are any recent stories about a softening of the market; and you might talk with several local real estate agents to get their opinions on the subject. In consulting your local newspapers and local agents, you are looking for **authoritative sources** against which to test your anecdotal evidence — the confirmation of experts who report on, study, evaluate, and have an informed opinion on local real estate. Local real estate agents are a source of **expert testimony**, firsthand confirmation of the information you have discovered. You would probably not want to rely on the testimony of a single real estate agent, who may have a bias; instead, talk with several agents to see if a consensus emerges.

Is the source accurate?   To determine the accuracy of a study that you want to use to support your argument, you have to do a little digging to find out who else has made a similar claim. For instance, if you want to cite authoritative research that compares the dropout rate for white students with the rate for students of color, you could look at research conducted by the Civil Rights Project. Of course, you don't need to stop your search there. You could also check the resources available through the National Center for Education Statistics. You want to show your readers that you have done a relatively thorough search to make your argument as persuasive as possible.

The accuracy of **statistics** — factual information presented numerically or graphically (for example, in a pie or bar chart) — is difficult to verify. To a certain extent, then, their veracity has to be taken on faith. Often the best you can do is assure yourself that the source of your statistical information is authoritative and reliable — government and major research universities generally are "safe" sources — and that whoever is interpreting the statistical information is not distorting it. Returning again to our real estate example, let's say you've read a newspaper article that cites statistical information about the condition of the local real estate market (for example, the average price of property and volume of sales this year in comparison to last year). Presumably the author of the article is an expert, but he or she may be interpreting rather than simply reporting on the statistics. To reassure yourself one way or the other, you may want to check the sources of the author's statistics — go right to your source's sources — which a responsible author will cite. That will allow you to look over the raw data and come to your own conclusions. A further step you could take would be to discuss the article with other experts — local real estate agents — to find out what they think of the article and the information it presents.

Now, let's go back to Myra and David Sadker's essay. How do they develop their assertion that girls are treated differently from boys in classrooms from "grade school through graduate school"? First, they tell us (in paragraph 4) that they have been conducting research continuously for "almost two decades" and that they have accumulated "thousands of hours of classroom observation." This information suggests that their research is both recent and relevant. But are their studies reliable and accurate? That their research meets the reliability criterion is confirmed by the grants they received over the years: Granting institutions (experts) have assessed their work and determined that it deserved to be funded. Grants confer authority on research. In addition, the Sadkers explain that they observed and refined their analyses over time to achieve accuracy: "As we watched, we had to push ourselves beyond the blind spots of socialization and gradually focus on the nature of the interaction between teacher and student."

In paragraph 7, the authors provide more evidence that the observations that support their claim are accurate. Not only have they observed many instances of gender bias in classrooms; so have trained "raters." The raters add objectivity to the findings because they did not share the Sadkers' interest in drawing a specific conclusion about whether gender bias exists in classrooms. Also the raters observed a wide cross-section of students and teachers from "different racial and ethnic backgrounds." At the end of their study, the Sadkers had collected thousands of pieces of data and could feel quite confident about their conclusion — that they had "discovered a syntax of sexism so elusive that most teachers and students were completely unaware of its influence."

■ Identify Concessions

Part of the strategy of developing a main claim supported with good reasons is to offer a **concession**, an acknowledgment that readers may not agree with every point the writer is making. A concession is a writer's way of saying, "Okay, I can see that there may be another way of looking at the issue or another way to interpret the evidence used to support the argument I am making." For example, you may not want your energy costs to go up, but after examining the reasons why it may be necessary to increase taxes on gasoline — to lower usage and conserve fossil fuels — you might concede that a tax increase on gasoline could be useful. The willingness to make concessions is valued in academic writing because it acknowledges both complexity and the importance of multiple perspectives. It also acknowledges the fact that information can always be interpreted in different ways.

The Sadkers make a concession when they acknowledge in the last paragraph of the excerpt that "it is difficult to detect sexism unless you know precisely how to observe." And, they explain, "if a lifetime of socialization makes it difficult to spot gender bias even when you're looking for it, how much harder it is to avoid the traps when you are the one doing the teaching." Notice that these concessions do not weaken their argument. The authors' evidence appears overwhelmingly to support their thesis. The lesson here is that conceding a point in your argument shows that you have acknowledged there are other ways of seeing things, other interpretations. This is an important part of what it means to enter a conversation of ideas.

Often a writer will signal a concession with a variation of the phrase "It is true that . . ." (for example, "I agree with X that Y is an important factor to consider" or "Some studies have convincingly shown that . . ."). Generally, the writer will then go on to address the concession, explaining how it needs to be modified or abandoned in the light of new evidence or the writer's perspective on the issue.

■ Identify Counterarguments

As the term suggests, a **counterargument** is an argument raised in response to another argument. You want to be aware of and acknowledge what your readers may object to in your argument. Anticipating readers' objections is an important part of developing a conversational argument. For example, if you were arguing in support of universal health care, you would have to acknowledge that the approach departs dramatically from the traditional role the federal government has played in providing health insurance. That is, most people's access to health insurance has depended on their individual ability to afford and purchase this kind of insurance. You would have to anticipate how readers would respond to your proposal, especially readers who do not feel that the federal government should ever play a role in what has heretofore been an individual responsibility. Anticipating readers' objections demonstrates that you understand the complexity of the issue and are willing at least to entertain different and conflicting opinions.

In the excerpt from "Hidden Lessons," the Sadkers describe the initial response of *Dateline* staffers to what they observed in the classroom they were videotaping: "This is a fair teacher. . . . [T]here's no gender bias in this teacher's class." Two women whom the Sadkers describe as "intelligent" and "concerned about fair treatment in school" agreed: "We've been playing this over and over. The teacher is terrific. There's no bias in her teaching. Come watch" (para. 9).

Notice the Sadkers' acknowledgment that even intelligent, concerned people may not see the problems that the Sadkers spent more than twenty years studying. In addressing the counterargument — that sexism does not exist — the authors are both empathetic to and respectful of what any reasonable person might or might not see. This is in keeping with what we would call a conversational argument: that writers listen to different points of view, that they respect arguments that diverge from their own, and that they be willing to exchange ideas and revise their own points of view.

In an argument that is more conversational than confrontational, writers often establish areas of common ground, both to convey to readers that they are understood and to acknowledge the conditions under which readers' views are valid. Writers do this by making concessions and anticipating and responding to counterarguments. This conversational approach is what many people call a **Rogerian approach to argument**, based on psychologist Carl Rogers's approach to psychotherapy. The objective of a Rogerian strategy is to reduce listeners' sense of threat so that they are open to alternatives. For academic writers, it involves four steps:

1. Conveying to readers that they are understood
2. Acknowledging conditions under which readers' views are valid
3. Helping readers see that the writer shares common ground with them
4. Creating mutually acceptable solutions to agreed-on problems

The structure of an argument, according to the Rogerian approach, grows out of the give-and-take of conversation between two people and the topic under discussion. In a written conversation, the give-and-take of face-to-face conversation takes the form of anticipating readers' counterarguments and uses language that is both empathetic and respectful to put the readers at ease.

Steps to Analyzing an Argument

1 **Identify the type of claim.** A claim of fact? Value? Policy?

2 **Analyze the reasons used to support the claim.** Are they recent? Relevant? Reliable? Accurate?

3 **Identify concessions.** Is there another argument that even the author acknowledges is legitimate?

4 **Identify counterarguments.** What arguments contradict or challenge the author's position?

■ Analyze a Sample Student Argument

Read the excerpt from a student essay that follows with pen or pencil in hand, noting the writer's claims, reasons, concessions, and responses to counterarguments. The essay is an example of a **researched argument**: The writer uses evidence to advance an argument that contributes to the ongoing conversation about an issue. (Notice how the author cites and documents his research; we have more to say about citation and documentation in Chapter 7.) The author, Ryan Metheny, was writing at a time when anti-immigrant attitudes in the United States were running high. In this essay, which was selected from a pool of exceptional student essays to be published in a campus magazine that was required reading for all first-year students at his school, Metheny addresses what he sees as a fundamental tension between democratic principles of equality and the exclusionary nature of the English-only movement. Specifically, he responds to the marginalization of Ebonics (also known as African American Vernacular English) in schools. His purpose is to make policymakers and educators aware of the problem. He also explains to a broader audience the ways in which race and power, not grammatical correctness, determine which language practices gain legitimacy and which do not.

Metheny 1

Ryan Metheny
Professor Klein
English 1020
May 16, 20--

The Problems and Dangers of Assimilatory Policies

American society considers itself to be in an age of enlightenment. Racism has been denounced and cultural colorblindness in all
things is encouraged. Economic opportunities are available for everyone, and equal consideration before the law is provided for each citizen. American society considers itself the embodiment of liberty,
equality, and justice for all.

In a society such as the one described, it follows that one's
background and culture do not have any influence on one's
socioeconomic status; theoretically, the two should be completely
disconnected. Yet, as we all know, this is not the case. The people
of the highest status in America are almost uniformly white males.
Sadly, America, the place of equality and liberty, is still very much a

1

2

Metheny 2

stratified society, not only by socioeconomic class/status, but because minority cultures much more often fill the ranks of the lower classes. Fortunately for those of minority cultures, the country's policymakers now accept, at least in speech, the basic equality and potential of all cultures to rise out of poverty; unfortunately, they still refuse to recognize the validity of differences in these cultures from what they, the policymakers, view as American (Labov i–iii).

3

The most obvious example of this is the stubborn grasp the country holds on what it calls "standard English" — the dialect used by the intellectual and social elite of America. Standard English is considered to be the one and only conduit through which people of status exchange information — and therefore the one and only conduit through which power can be attained. It is seen as the American method of communication. Historically, the various groups that come to America have had to adopt this method as their own in order to receive their piece of the American socioeconomic pie — and, indeed, many groups have — Germans, Irish, Italians. These groups, however, are white. Assimilation for non-white groups has been agonizingly slow, especially for historically oppressed peoples such as African Americans (Smitherman 167–200). We consider adoption of standard English to be the price one pays for entrance into the all-inclusive society. But, of course, this is not only contradictory (an inclusive society should accept all cultural differences as valid), but it is also an unfair policy for non-white groups. We have set up standard English as the holy grail of communication. If we wish to avoid hypocrisy, we should live up to the virtues of inclusiveness we claim to have.

4

Implementation of more inclusiveness should begin by decreasing our fervor in support of standard English. The reasons for this are many. On the technical, linguistic level, standard English should certainly not be esteemed so highly because it is a superior language — it is not. Standard English is just as flexible and changing as any other language. It is ironic that the cultural dialects that many minorities utilize, such as Ebonics, have a heavy hand in changing the standard English that we demand they adopt. Even the slaves brought to America, the lowest of the low socioeconomically during the period in which they were enslaved, had a heavy hand in changing American standard English. Joseph Holloway and Winifred

Voss pointed out in 1993 that nearly 200 place names in nine Southern states are of African origin. They also [point] out the African origins of many other terms now used in standard English — even the beloved name "Bambi" of Walt Disney's cartoon has its origins in the Bantu word "mubambi," a word which means "one who lies down in order to hide" (Holloway and Voss 57, 227–229). This flexibility of standard English seems to point toward another hypocrisy of America — we play down the importance of the non-standard Ebonics dialect, while accepting parts of that dialect as our own. Certainly this suggests that standard English is not inherently more "civilized" than other dialects.

Conversely, is Ebonics then not accepted because it is inherently "uncivilized"? No. Ebonics can be just as expressive and meaningful, if not more so, than standard English (Smitherman 167–200). Ebonics as a language fosters important verbal reasoning and logical skills, just as any language does. Its nuances of grammar and intonation are highly communicative combinations of English vocabulary and grammar with African mechanics. Anyone who has ever heard a bout of the "dozens" will readily admit that Ebonics can indeed be a fast-paced, inventive dialect that requires quick thinking. The ability to express an impromptu "yo mama" joke on the spur of the moment is a kind of genius all its own. Such verbal skills should not be discouraged. To do so invalidates the experiences of African Americans. A people's experiences cannot be denied, especially in the land of equality and justice. If Ebonics remains unrecognized despite its clear validity as a mode of communication, and despite standard English's lack of any kind of superiority to it, what ideologies are truly behind its continuing lack of recognition? Actually, the lack of recognition of Ebonics may well be rooted in mere class-related bigotry (Smitherman). The upper class views such a mode of speech as unintelligent, a mockery of the "true" language. What such a view is in fact indicative of is not only a blatant case of ethnocentrism . . . but also a feeling of superiority that native standard English speakers feel over the lower classes. This sense of superiority fuels the demand that speakers of other dialects and languages adopt standard English in order to join the successful mainstream. Such an attitude supports the dominance of the upper classes. This must surely be considered wrong in a land

5

Metheny 4

where every person, regardless of income and status, is equal before the law.

Ebonics is not inferior: oppression of Ebonics could well be a case of bigotry. Therefore, acceptance of Ebonics as a valid form of communication should be strongly considered. To implement such an acceptance, we must begin with the schools, for that is where society first exerts influence upon the individual. So far, any kind of acceptance here has been rare, and when present, it has often been implemented inappropriately. Baugh pointed out in 1999 several cases in which Ebonics and Ebonics-related problems were not addressed appropriately. In one case, two native Ebonics speakers were placed in special education based on verbal aptitude tests given in standard English — a dialect they were not familiar with. In another case, a math teacher gave his inner-city students word problems that he thought were being culturally sensitive, but which in fact could be considered racist. One problem asked, "If you were a pimp and had knocked up seven hos, and had twenty-three hos total, how many hos would still need to be knocked up?" while another asked, "If you had a half-pound of heroin, and want to make twenty percent more profit, how much cut would you need?" These are extreme examples, true, but they illustrate the lack of success that many educators have had when it comes to addressing the problems inherent in educating Ebonics speakers.

Such problems are further frustrated by the aforementioned stratified nature of American society. Baugh illustrates this using a graph in which five theoretical socioeconomic groups, and their corresponding dialects, are arrayed vertically from upper to lower classes. The children in the uppermost group are capable of going even higher socioeconomically than their parents, shown by a line slanting up, or slightly lower, shown by a line slanting down. The next group down is similarly capable of a certain amount of increase or decrease in status.

This graph shows two things: first, that each socioeconomic group is normally only capable of a certain range of change in status; and second, that there is very little overlap in range between groups. This implies that the lower classes most minorities are still a part of cannot advance their status very quickly in succeeding generations. Baugh goes on to claim that this is due to the manner in which

children are educated from a very early age, both in schools and at
home. Inner-city schools are often poorly funded and fail to teach
their students adequately. Similarly, the home life of poorer students
often does not foster learning in important ways, such as the reading
of parents to children at an early age. Which is not to say, of course,
that Ebonics as a language does not support learning — rather, low
socioeconomic status often does not support learning. Ebonics speakers, since they more often fill lower socioeconomic groups, are often at
an unfair disadvantage when compared to native standard English
speakers.

    As the inclusive society, we must address this economic
unfairness. Arguments in favor of using standard English as the only
valid form of communication in the United States have not done this.
E. D. Hirsch argues that cultural literacy focused around a single
standard dialect is necessary for a society to operate efficiently. Com-
plementing Hirsch's ideas, Richard Rodriguez argues that knowing the
"public language" is needed for one to have a public identity. These
scholars make logical points in support of the efficiency of having
one language per society. Efficiency, however, should not come at the
expense of the marginalization of economically disadvantaged non-
standard English speakers. Standard English proponents have no solution to the problem of assimilation other than telling the
marginalized to bite the bullet and join the mainstream, so to speak.
What ever happened to equality and inclusiveness? Assimilation
should not even be necessary — rather, differences should be
accepted. Pragmatists may respond that joining the mainstream is
vital in order to advance economically, whether doing so at the
expense of one's identity is right or not. Of course, in the current
state of American society, they are largely correct. I propose, however, that living up to reasonable standards of inclusiveness as a
country will correct the join-the-mainstream-or-fail dilemma. We
should not simply accept the hard reality, but rather work to change.

9

Metheny 6

Works Cited

Baugh, John. *Out of the Mouths of Slaves: African American Language and Educational Malpractice.* Austin: University of Texas Press, 1999. 1–39. Print.

Hirsch, E. D. *Cultural Literacy: What Every American Needs to Know.* New York: Vintage Books, 1988. 1–32. Print.

Holloway, Joseph E., and Winifred K. Voss. *The African Heritage of American English.* Bloomington: Indiana UP, 1993. Print.

Labov, William. Foreword. In *Out of the Mouths of Slaves: African American Language and Educational Malpractice* by John Baugh, i–iii. Austin: University of Texas Press, 1999. Print.

Rodriguez, Richard. *Hunger of Memory: The Education of Richard Rodriguez.* New York: Bantam Books, 1983. Print.

Smitherman, Geneva. *Talkin and Testifyin: The Language of Black America.* Detroit: Wayne State UP, 1977. 167–200. Print.

A Practice Sequence: Analyzing an Argument

Now that you have annotated Ryan Metheny's essay, we would like you to work in four groups to consider the strategies this writer uses to advance his argument. That is, analyze the way the writer states his main claim and develops his argument in drawing the conclusions he does.

Group 1: What type of claim does Metheny make? What reasons does he use to support his argument?

Group 2: To what extent are you persuaded by the reasons the writer gives to support his argument that Ebonics should be given legitimacy? Point to specific words and phrases you found persuasive.

Group 3: How effective is the writer in anticipating his readers' responses? Does he make any concessions to readers or anticipate possible counterarguments?

Group 4: Make an outline in which you include your own counterargument to this writer's position.

4

From Identifying Issues
to Forming Questions

Remember that inquiry is central to the process of composing. As you read and begin to write an essay, you will find that the real work of writing is figuring out the answers to the following questions:

- What have these authors been talking about?
- What are the relevant concerns of those whose work I have been reading?
- What are the situations motivating these people to write?
- What frames do these writers use to construct their arguments?
- Who will be interested in reading what I have to say?
- How can I connect with readers who may be both sympathetic and antagonistic toward my argument?
- What is at stake in my own argument? (What if things change? What if things stay the same?) For whom?
- What kinds of evidence might persuade my readers?
- What objections are my readers likely to raise?

To answer these questions, you must read in the role of writer, with an eye toward *identifying an issue* (an idea or statement that is open to dispute) that compels you to respond in writing, *understanding the situation* (the factors that give rise to the issue and shape your response), and *formulating a question* (what you intend to answer in response to the issue). In Table 4.1, we identify a series of situations and one of the issues and questions that derive from each of them. Notice that the question you ask is a tool that defines the area of inquiry as you read; it also can help you

TABLE 4.1   A Series of Situations with Related Issues and Questions

SITUATION	ISSUE	QUESTION
Congress plans to pass legislation that prohibits music downloads.	You feel that this piece of legislation would challenge your freedom as a consumer.	To what extent can Congress pass legislation that compromises the freedoms of individual consumers?
Different state legislatures are passing legislation to prevent Spanish-speaking students from using their own language in schools.	Your understanding of research on learning contradicts the idea that students should be prevented from using their own language in the process of learning a new language.	Under what conditions should students be allowed to use their own language while they learn English?
A manufacturing company has plans to move to your city with the promise of creating new jobs in a period of high unemployment.	You feel that this company will compromise the quality of life for the surrounding community because the manufacturing process will pollute the air.	What would persuade the city to prevent this company from moving in even though the company will provide much-needed jobs?
Your school has made an agreement with a local company to supply vending machines that sell drinks and food. The school plans to use its share of the profit to improve the library and purchase a new scoreboard for the football field.	You see that the school has much to gain from this arrangement, but you also know that obesity is a growing problem at the school.	Is there another way for the school to generate needed revenue without putting students' health at risk?
An increasing number of homeless people are seeking shelter on your college campus.	Campus security has stepped up its efforts to remove the homeless even though the shelters off campus are overcrowded.	How can you persuade the school to shelter the homeless and to provide funds to support the needs of the homeless in your city?

formulate your working thesis, the statement that answers your question. (We say more about developing a thesis in Chapter 5.) In this chapter, in addition to further discussing the importance of situation, we look at how you can identify issues and formulate questions to guide your reading and writing.

IDENTIFYING ISSUES

Below we present several steps to identifying an issue. You don't have to follow them in this particular order, of course; in fact, you may find yourself going back and forth among them as you try to bring an issue into focus. Keep in mind that issues do not simply exist in the world well formed. Instead, writers construct what they see as issues from the situations they observe. For example, consider legislation to limit music downloads from the Internet. If this kind of law conflicts with your own practices and sense of freedom, you may have begun to identify an issue: the clash of values over what constitutes fair use and what does not. Be aware that others may not understand your issue, and that in your writing you will have to explain carefully what is at stake.

■ Draw on Your Personal Experience

Writing begins with critical reading, identifying what is at issue for *you*. After all, the issue typically is what motivates people to write. You may have been taught that formal writing is objective, that you must keep a dispassionate distance from your subject, and that you should not use *I* in a college-level paper. The fact is, however, that our personal experiences influence how we read, what we pay attention to, and what inferences we draw. It makes sense, then, to begin with you — where you are and what you think and believe. We all use personal experience to make arguments in our everyday lives, to urge the people around us to act or think in certain ways. In an academic context, the challenge is to use personal experience to argue a point, to illustrate something, or to illuminate a connection between theories and the sense we make of our daily experience. You don't want simply to tell your story; but you do want your story to strengthen your argument.

In his book *Cultural Literacy*, E. D. Hirsch personalizes his interest in reversing the cycle of illiteracy in America's cities. To establish the nature of the problem in the situation he describes, he cites research showing that student performance on standardized tests in the United States is falling. But he also reflects on his own teaching in the 1970s, when he first perceived "the widening knowledge gap [that] caused me to recognize the connection between specific background knowledge and mature literacy." And he injects anecdotal evidence from conversations with his son, a teacher. Those stories heighten readers' awareness that school-aged children do not know much about literature, history, or government. (For example, his son mentions a student who challenged his claim that Latin is a "dead language" by demanding, "What do they speak in Latin America?") Hirsch's use of his son's testimony makes him vulnerable to criticism, as readers might question whether Hirsch can legitimately use his son's experience to make generalizations about education. But in fact, Hirsch is using personal testimony — his own and his son's — to augment and put a human face on the research he cites. He presents his issue, that schools must teach cultural literacy, both as something personal and as something with which we should all be concerned. The personal note helps readers see Hirsch as someone who has long been concerned with education and who has even raised a son who is an educator.

In "Dyes and Dolls: Multicultural Barbie and the Merchandising of Difference," author Ann duCille reveals how a personal experience drives her argument about the cultural significance of children's toys. She explains that although Barbie as icon seems harmless, her own examination reveals that "toys and games play crucial roles in helping children determine what is valuable in and around them." The questions she raises not only grow out of her statement of the issue, but also motivate the concerns she addresses in her essay: "More than simple instruments of pleasure and amusement, toys and games play crucial roles in helping children determine what is valuable in and around them." The issue she seizes on is the role toys play in shaping cultural attitudes; but her personal stake in the issue — what may have attracted her to it in the first place — was her own experience playing with dolls that did not reflect her ethnicity.

■ Identify What Is Open to Dispute

We have said that an issue is something that is open to dispute. Sometimes the way to clarify an issue is to think of it as a fundamental tension between two or more conflicting points of view. If you can identify conflicting points of view, an issue may become clear. Consider E. D. Hirsch, who believes that the best approach to educational reform (the subject he writes about) is to change the curriculum in schools. His position: A curriculum based on cultural literacy is the one sure way to reverse the cycle of poverty and illiteracy in urban areas. What is the issue? Hirsch's issue emerges in the presence of an alternative position. Jonathan Kozol, a social activist who has written extensively about educational reform, believes that policymakers need to address reform by providing the necessary resources that all students need to learn. Kozol points out how students in many inner-city schools are reading textbooks that were published twenty years ago, and that the dilapidated conditions in these schools — windows that won't close, for example — make it impossible for students to learn. In tension are two different views of the reform that can reverse illiteracy: Hirsch's view that educational reform should occur through curricular changes, and Kozol's view that educational reform demands socioeconomic resources.

■ Resist Binary Thinking

As you begin to define what is at issue, try to tease out complexities that may not be immediately apparent. That is, try to resist the either/or mindset that signals binary thinking. Looking at what Hirsch and Kozol have to say, it would be easy to characterize the problems facing our schools as either curricular or socioeconomic. But it may be that the real issue combines these arguments with a third or even a fourth, that neither curricular nor socioeconomic changes by themselves can resolve the problems with American schools.

After reading essays by both Hirsch and Kozol, one of our students pointed out that both Hirsch's focus on curriculum and Kozol's socioeconomic focus ignore another concern. She went on to describe her school experience in racial terms. In the excerpt below, notice how this writer uses personal experience (in a new school, she is not treated as she had expected to be treated) to formulate an issue.

> Moving to Tallahassee from Colorado Springs, Colorado, I was immediately struck by the differences apparent in local home life, school life, and community unity, or lack thereof. Ripped from my sheltered world at a small Catholic school characterized by racial harmony, I, both bewildered and unprepared, was thrown into a large public school where outward prejudice from classmates and teachers and "race wars" were common and tolerated. . . .
>
> In a school where students and teachers had the power and free reign to abuse anyone different from them, I was constantly abused. As the only black student in English honors, I was commonly belittled in front of my "peers" by my all-knowing teacher. If I developed courage enough to ask a question, I was always answered with the use of improper grammar and such words as "ain't" as my teacher attempted to simplify the material to "my level" and to give me what he called "a little learning." After discussing several subjects he often turned to me, singling me out of a sea of white faces, and asked, "Do *you* understand, Mila?" When asking my opinion of a subject, he frequently questioned, "What do *your* people think about this?" Although he insisted on including such subjects as Martin Luther King's "I Have a Dream" speech in the curriculum, the speech's themes of tolerance and equity did not accompany his lesson.

Through her reading, this student discovered that few prominent scholars have confronted the issue of racism in schools directly. Although she grants that curricular reform and increased funding may be necessary to improve education, she argues that scholars also need to address race in their studies of teaching and learning.

Our point in using this example is to emphasize that issues may be more complex than you first think they are. For this student, the issue wasn't one of two positions — reform the curriculum or provide more funding. Instead it combined a number of different positions, including race ("prejudice" and "race wars") and the relationship between student and teacher ("Do *you* understand, Mila?") in a classroom. In this passage, the writer uses her experience to challenge binary thinking. Like the student writer, you should examine issues from different perspectives, avoiding either/or propositions that oversimplify the world.

■ Build On and Extend the Ideas of Others

Academic writing builds on and even extends the ideas of others. As an academic writer, you will find that by extending other people's ideas, you will extend your own. You may begin in a familiar place; but as you read more and pursue connections to other readings, you may well end up at an unexpected destination. For example, one of our students was troubled when he read Melissa Stormont-Spurgin's description of homeless children. The student uses details from her work (giving credit, of course) in his own:

> The children . . . went to school after less than three hours of sleep. They wore the same wrinkled clothes that they had worn the day before. What will their teachers think when they fall asleep in class? How will they get food for lunch? What will their peers think? What could these homeless children talk about with their peers? They have had to grow up too fast. Their worries are not the same as other children's worries. They are worried about their next meal and where they will seek shelter. Their needs, however, are the same. They need a home and all of the securities that come with it. They also need an education (Stormont-Spurgin 156).

Initially the student was troubled by his own access to quality schools, and the contrast between his life and the lives of the children Stormont-Spurgin describes. Initially, then, his issue was the fundamental tension between his own privileged status, something he had taken for granted, and the struggle that homeless children face every day. However, as he read further and grew to understand homelessness as a concern in a number of studies, he connected his personal response to a larger conversation about democracy, fairness, and education:

> Melissa Stormont-Spurgin, an author of several articles on educational studies, addresses a very real and important, yet avoided issue in education today. Statistics show that a very high percentage of children who are born into homeless families will remain homeless, or in poverty, for the rest of their lives. How can this be, if everyone actually does have the same educational opportunities? There must be significant educational disadvantages for children without homes. In a democratic society, I feel that we must pay close attention to these disadvantages and do everything in our power to replace them with equality.

Ultimately, the student refined his sense of what was at issue: *Although all people should have access to public education in a democratic society, not everyone has the opportunity to attend quality schools in order to achieve personal success.* In turn, his definition of the issue began to shape his argument:

> Parents, teachers, homeless shelters and the citizens of the United States who fund [homeless] shelters must address the educational needs of homeless children, while steering them away from any more financial or psychological struggles. Without this emphasis on education, the current trend upward in the number of homeless families will inevitably continue in the future of American society.

The student has shifted away from a personal issue — the difference between his status and that of homeless children — to an issue of clashing values: the principle of egalitarian democracy on the one hand and the social reality of citizens in a democracy living in abject poverty on the other. When he started to read about homeless children, he could not have made the claim he ends up making, that policymakers must make education a basic human right. This student offers us an important lesson about the role of inquiry and the value of resisting easy answers. He has built on and extended his own ideas — and the ideas of others — after repeating the process of reading, raising questions, writing, and seeing problems a number of times.

■ Read to Discover a Writer's Frame

A more specialized strategy of building on and extending the ideas of others involves reading to discover a writer's **frame**, the perspective through which a writer presents his or her arguments. Writers want us to see the world a certain way, so they frame their arguments much the same way photographers and artists frame their pictures. For example, if you were to take a picture of friends in front of the football stadium on campus, you would focus on what you would most like to remember — your friends' faces — blurring the images of the people walking behind your friends. Setting up the picture, or framing it, might require using light and shade to make some details stand out more than others. Writers do the same with language.

E. D. Hirsch uses the term *cultural literacy* to frame his argument for curricular reform. For Hirsch, the term is a benchmark, a standard: People who are culturally literate are familiar with the body of information that every educated citizen should know. Hirsch's implication, of course, is that people who are not culturally literate are not well educated. But that is not necessarily true. In fact, a number of educators insist that literacy is simply a means to an end — reading to complete an assignment, for example, or to understand the ramifications of a decision — not an end in itself. By defining and using *cultural literacy* as the goal of education, Hirsch is framing his argument; he is bringing his ideas into focus.

When writers use framing strategies, they also call attention to the specific conversations that set up the situation for their arguments. Framing often entails quoting specific theories and ideas from other authors, and then using those quotations as a perspective, or lens, through which to examine other material. In his memoir *Hunger of Memory: The Education of Richard Rodriguez* (1982), Richard Rodriguez uses this method to examine his situation as a nonnative speaker of English desperate to enter the mainstream culture, even if it means sacrificing his identity as the son of Mexican immigrants. Reflecting on his life as a student, Rodriguez comes across Richard Hoggart's book *The Uses of Literacy* (1957). Hoggart's description of "the scholarship boy" presents a lens through which Rodriguez can see his own experience. Hoggart writes:

> With his family, the boy has the intense pleasure of intimacy, the family's consolation in feeling public alienation. Lavish emotions texture home life.

Then, at school, the instruction bids him to trust lonely reason primarily. Immediate needs set the pace of his parents' lives. From his mother and father the boy learns to trust spontaneity and nonrational ways of knowing. *Then*, at school, there is mental calm. Teachers emphasize the value of a reflectiveness that opens a space between thinking and immediate action.

Years of schooling must pass before the boy will be able to sketch the cultural differences in his day as abstractly as this. But he senses those differences early. Perhaps as early as the night he brings home an assignment from school and finds the house too noisy for study. He has to be more and more alone, if he is going to "get on." He will have, probably unconsciously, to oppose the ethos of the hearth, the intense gregariousness of the working-class family group. . . . The boy has to cut himself off mentally, so as to do his homework, as well as he can.

Here is Rodriguez's response to Hoggart's description of the scholarship boy:

For weeks I read, speed-read, books by modern educational theorists, only to find infrequent and slight mention of students like me. . . . Then one day, leafing through Richard Hoggart's *The Uses of Literacy*, I found, in his description of the scholarship boy, myself. For the first time I realized that there were other students like me, and so I was able to frame the meaning of my academic success, its consequent price — the loss.

Notice how Rodriguez introduces ideas from Hoggart "to frame" his own ideas: "I found, in his description of the scholarship boy, myself. For the first time I realized that there were other students like me, and so I was able to frame the meaning of my academic success, its consequent price — the loss." Hoggart's scholarship boy enables Rodriguez to revisit his own experience with a new perspective. Hoggart's words and idea advance Rodriguez's understanding of the problem he identifies in his life: his inability to find solace at home and within his working-class roots. Hoggart's discription of the scholarship boy's moving between cultural extremes — spontaneity at home and reflection at school — helps Rodriguez bring his own youthful discontent into focus.

Rodriguez's response to Hoggart's text shows how another writer's lens can help frame an issue. If you were using Hoggart's term *scholarship boy* as a lens through which to clarify an issue in education, you might ask how the term illuminates new aspects of another writer's examples or your own. And then you might ask, "To what extent does Hirsch's cultural literacy throw a more positive light on what Rodriguez and Hoggart describe?" or "How do my experiences challenge, extend, or complicate the scholarship-boy concept?"

■ Consider the Constraints of the Situation

In identifying an issue, you have to understand the situation that gives rise to the issue, including the contexts in which it is raised and debated. One of the contexts is the audience. In thinking about your issue, you must consider the extent to which your potential readers are involved in the dialogue you want to enter, and what they know and need to know. In a sense, audience functions as both context and **constraint**, a factor that narrows the choices you can make in responding to an issue. An understanding of your potential readers will help you choose the depth of the discussion; it will also determine the kind of evidence you can present and the language you can use.

Another constraint on your response to an issue is the form that response takes. For example, if you decide to make an issue of government-imposed limits on the music you can download from the Internet, your response in writing might take the form of an editorial or a letter to a legislator. In this situation, length is an obvious constraint: Newspapers limit the word count of editorials, and the best letters to legislators tend to be brief and very selective about the evidence they cite. A few personal examples and a few statistics may be all you can include to support your claim about the issue. By contrast, if you were making your case in an academic journal, a very different set of constraints would apply. You would have more space for illustrations and support, for example.

Finally, the situation itself can function as a major constraint. For instance, suppose your topic is the decline of educational standards. It's difficult to imagine any writer making the case for accelerating that decline or any audience being receptive to any argument that a decline in standards is a good thing.

Steps to Identifying Issues

1. **Draw on your personal experience.** Start with your own sense of what's important, what puzzles you, or what you are curious about. (Then build your argument by moving on to other sources to support your point of view.)

2. **Identify what is open to dispute.** Identify a phenomenon or some idea in a written argument that challenges what you think or believe.

3. **Resist binary thinking.** Think about the issue from multiple perspectives.

4. **Build on and extend the ideas of others.** As you read, be open to new ways of looking at the issue. The issue you finally write about may be very different from what you set out to write about.

5. **Read to discover a writer's frame.** What theories or ideas shape the writer's focus? How can these theories or ideas help you frame your argument?

6. **Consider the constraints of the situation.** Craft your argument to meet the needs of and constraints imposed by your audience and form.

■ Identify Issues in an Essay

Consider the situation of writer Anna Quindlen, who in 1992 published an editorial in the *New York Times* addressing the issue of homelessness. At the time, New Yorkers seemed to have accepted homelessness as something that could be studied but not remedied. As you read Quindlen's "No Place Like Home," note the words and phrases Quindlen uses to identify both the situation and her audience. Is her main claim one of fact, value, or policy? Finally, answer the questions that follow the essay to see if you can discern how Quindlen locates, defines, and advances her issue.

ABOUT THE READING

Anna Quindlen is the best-selling author of novels (including *Blessings, Black and Blue, One True Thing,* and *Object Lessons*) and nonfiction books (including *A Short Guide to a Happy Life, Living Out Loud, Thinking Out Loud,* and *How Reading Changed My Life*). She has also written children's books (including *The Tree That Came to Stay* and *Happily Ever After*). She won the Pulitzer Prize in 1992 for her *New York Times* column, "Public & Private." Since 1999 she has been writing a biweekly column for *Newsweek.*

ANNA QUINDLEN

No Place Like Home

Homeless is like the government wanting you locked up
And the people in America do not like you.
They look at you and say Beast!
I wish the people would help the homeless
And stop their talking.

—FRANK S. RICE, *The Rio Times*

The building is beautiful, white and beige and oak, the colors of yuppies. The rehab of the Rio came in $700,000 under budget, two months ahead of schedule. The tenants say they will not mess it up, no, no, no. "When you don't have a place and you get a good place, the last thing you want to do is lose it," said one man who slept in shelters for seven years, seven years during which time you might have gotten married, or lost a loved one, or struck it rich, but all this guy did was live on the streets.

Mayor David Dinkins has announced that he will study parts of the study he commissioned from a commission on the homeless, the newest in a long line of studies.

One study, done in 1981, was called "Private Lives, Public Spaces." It was researched by Ellen Baxter, who now runs the nonprofit company that has brought us the Rio and four other buildings that provide permanent housing for the homeless in Washington Heights.

Another study, done in 1987, was called "A Shelter Is Not a Home" and   *4*
was produced by the Manhattan Borough President David Dinkins, who now runs the City of New York. At the time, the Koch administration said it would study Mr. Dinkins's study, which must have taught Mr. Dinkins something.

Robert Hayes, one of the founding fathers of the movement to help the   *5*
homeless, once told me there were three answers to the problem: housing, housing, housing. It was an overly simplistic answer, and it was essentially correct.

Despite our obsessions with pathology and addiction, Ms. Baxter has   *6*
renovated one apartment building after another and filled them with people. At the Rio, what was once a burnt-out eyesore is now, with its curving facade and bright lobby, the handsomest building on the block; what were once armory transients with dirt etched in the creases of hands and face are now tenants. The building needed people; the people needed a home. The city provided the rehab money; Columbia University provides social service support.

Some of the tenants need to spend time in drug treatment and some go   *7*
to Alcoholics Anonymous and some of them lapse into pretty pronounced fugue states from time to time. So what? How would you behave if you'd lived on the streets for seven years? What is better: to leave them out there while we lament the emptying of the mental hospitals and the demise of jobs? Or to provide a roof over their heads and then get them psychiatric care and job training?

What is better: to spend nearly $20,000 each year to have them   *8*
sleep on cots at night and wander the streets by day? Or to make a one-time investment of $38,000 a unit, as they did in the single rooms with kitchens and baths in the Rio, for permanent homes for people who will pay rent from their future wages or from entitlement benefits?

Years ago I became cynical enough to envision a game plan in which   *9*
politicians, tussling over government stuff like demonstration projects and agency jurisdiction and commission studies, ignored this problem until it went away.

And, in a sense, it has. We have become so accustomed to people sleeping   *10*
on sidewalks and in subway stations that recumbent bodies have become small landmarks in our neighborhoods. Mary Brosnahan, executive director of the Coalition for the Homeless, says she was stunned, talking to students, at their assumption that people always had and always would be living on the streets. My children call by pet names — "the man with the cup," "the lady with the falling-down pants" — the homeless people around their school.

And when a problem becomes that rooted in our everyday perceptions,   *11*
it is understood to be without solution. Nonprofit groups like the one that

renovated the Rio prove that this is not so. The cots in the armory are poison; drug programs and job training are icing. A place to shut the door, to sleep without one eye open, to be warm, to be safe — that's the cake. There's no place like home. You didn't need a study to figure that out, did you?

For Analysis and Discussion

1. Can you find evidence of Quindlen's personal responses and experiences?
2. What phenomenon has challenged what Quindlen thinks and believes about homelessness? How has she made it into an issue?
3. Where does she indicate that she has considered the issue from multiple perspectives and is placing her ideas in conversation with those of others?
4. What sort of lens does Quindlen seem to be using to frame her argument?
5. What constraints seem to be in play in the essay?

A Practice Sequence: Identifying Issues

This sequence of activities will give you practice in identifying and clarifying issues based on your own choice of reading and collaboration with your classmates.

1 Draw on your personal experience. Reflect on your own responses to what you have been reading in this or in other classes, or issues that writers have posed in the media. What concerns you most? Choose a story that supports or challenges the claims people are making in what you have read or listened to. What questions do you have? Make some notes in response to these questions, explaining your personal stake in the issues and questions you formulate.

2 Identify what is open to dispute. Take what you have written and formulate your ideas as an issue, using the structure we used in our example of Hirsch's and Kozol's competing arguments:

- Part 1: Your view of a given topic
- Part 2: At least one view that is in tension with your own

If you need to, read further to understand what others have to say about this issue.

3 Resist binary thinking. Share your statement of the issue with one or more peers and ask them if they see other ways to formulate the issue that you may not have thought about. What objections, if any, do they make to your statement in part 1? Write these objections down in part 2 so that you begin to look at the issue from multiple perspectives.

4   Build on and extend the ideas of others. Now that you have formulated an issue from different perspectives, explaining your personal stake in the issue, connect what you think to a broader conversation in what you are reading. Then try making a claim using this structure: "Although some people would argue _____, I think that _____."

5   Read to discover a writer's frame. As an experiment in trying out multiple perspectives, revise the claim you make in exercise 4 by introducing the frame, or lens, through which you want readers to understand your argument. You can employ the same sentence structure. For example, here is a claim framed in terms of race: "Although people should have access to public education, recent policies have exacerbated racial inequalities in public schools." In contrast, here is a claim that focuses on economics: "Although people should have access to public education, the unequal distribution of tax money has created what some would call an 'economy of education.'" The lens may come from reading you have done in other courses or from conversations with your classmates, and you may want to attribute the lens to a particular author or classmate: "Although some people would argue_____, I use E. D. Hirsch's notion of cultural literacy to show_____."

6   Consider the constraints of the situation. Building on these exercises, develop an argument in the form of an editorial for your local newspaper. This means that you will need to limit your argument to about 250 words. You also will need to consider the extent to which your potential readers are involved in the conversation. What do they know? What do they need to know? What kind of evidence do you need to use to persuade readers?

FORMULATING ISSUE-BASED QUESTIONS

When you identify an issue, you need to understand it in the context of its situation. Ideally, the situation and the issue will be both recent and relevant, which will make your task of connecting to your audience that much easier when you write about the issue. For example, the student writer who was concerned about long-standing issues of homelessness and lack of educational opportunity connected to his readers by citing recent statistics and giving the problem of homelessness a face: "The children . . . went to school after less than three hours of sleep. They wore the same wrinkled clothes that they had worn the day before." If your issue does not immediately meet the criteria of timeliness and relevance, you will need to take that into consideration as you continue your reading and research. Ask yourself: What is on people's minds these days? What do they need to know about? Think about why the issue matters to you, and imagine why it might matter to others. By the time you write, you should be prepared to make the issue relevant for your readers.

In addition to understanding the situation and defining the issue that you feel is most timely and relevant, you can formulate an **issue-based question** to help you think through your subject. This question should be specific enough to guide your inquiry into what others have written. An issue-based question should help you

- clarify what you know about the issue and what you still need to learn.
- clearly guide your inquiry.
- organize your inquiry.
- develop an argument — a more complex task than simply collecting information by asking how, why, should, or the extent to which something is true or not.
- consider who your audience is.
- determine what resources you have so that you can ask a question that you have the resources to answer.

A good question develops out of an issue, some fundamental tension that you identify within a conversation. For Anna Quindlen in "No Place Like Home," the tension exists between what she sees as an unacceptable situation in New York and the city's ongoing failure to do something about it. Implicit is a question of how she can change people's attitudes, especially those of city leaders, who seem willing to "spend nearly $20,000 each year to have [homeless people] sleep on cots at night and wander the streets by day" rather than "make a one-time investment of $38,000 a unit" for housing. By identifying what is at issue, you should begin to understand for whom it is an issue — for whom you are answering the question. In turn, the answer to your question will help you craft your thesis.

In the following paragraphs, we trace the steps one of our students took to formulate an issue-based question on the broad topic of language diversity. Although we present the steps in sequence, be aware that they are guidelines only: The steps often overlap, and there is a good deal of room for rethinking and refining along the way.

■ Refine Your Topic

Generally speaking, a **topic** is the subject you want to write about. For example, homelessness, tests, and violence are all topics. So are urban homelessness, standardized tests, and video game violence. And so are homelessness in New York City, aptitude tests versus achievement tests, and mayhem in the video game Grand Theft Auto. As our list suggests, even a specific topic needs refining into an issue before it can be explored effectively in writing.

The topic our student wanted to focus on was language diversity, a subject her linguistics class had been discussing. She was fascinated by the extraordinary range of languages spoken in the United States, not just by immigrant groups but by native speakers whose dialects and varieties of English are considered nonstandard. She herself had relatives for whom English was not a first language. She began refining her topic by putting her thoughts into words:

> I want to describe the experience of being raised in a home where non–Standard English is spoken.
>
> I'd like to know the benefits and liabilities of growing up bilingual.
>
> I am curious to know what it's like to live in a community of nonnative speakers of English while trying to make a living in a country where the dominant language is English.

Although she had yet to identify an issue, her attempts to articulate what interested her about the topic were moving her toward the situation of people in the United States who don't speak Standard English or don't have English as their first language.

■ Explain Your Interest in the Topic

At this point, the student encountered E. D. Hirsch's *Cultural Literacy* in her reading, which had both a provocative and a clarifying effect on her thinking. She began to build on and extend Hirsch's ideas. Reacting to Hirsch's assumption that students should acquire the same base of knowledge and write in Standard Written English, her first, somewhat mischievous thought was, "I wonder what Hirsch would think about cultural literacy being taught in a bilingual classroom?" But then her thinking took another turn, and she began to contemplate the effect of Hirsch's cultural-literacy agenda on speakers whose English is not standard or for whom English is not a first language. She used a demographic fact that she had learned in her linguistics class in her explanation of her interest in the topic: "I'm curious about the consequences of limiting language diversity when the presence of ethnic minorities in our educational system is growing."

■ Identify an Issue

The more she thought about Hirsch's ideas, and the more she read about language diversity, the more concerned our student grew. It seemed to her that Hirsch's interest in producing students who all share the same base of knowledge and all write in Standard Written English was in tension with her sense that this kind of approach places a burden on people whose first language is not English. That tension clarified the issue for her. In identifying the issue, she wrote:

> Hirsch's book actually sets some priorities, most notably through his list of words and phrases that form the foundations of what it means to be "American." However, this list certainly overlooks several crucial influences in American culture. Most oversights generally come at the expense of the minority populations.

These two concerns — with inclusion and with exclusion — helped focus the student's inquiry.

■ Formulate Your Topic as a Question

To further define her inquiry, the student formulated her topic as a question that pointed toward an argument: "To what extent can E. D. Hirsch's notion of 'cultural literacy' coexist with our country's principles of democracy and inclusion?" Notice that her choice of the phrase *To what extent* implies that both goals do not go hand in hand. If she had asked, "Can common culture coexist with pluralism?" her phrasing would imply that a yes or no answer would suffice, possibly foreclosing avenues of inquiry and certainly ignoring the complexity of the issue.

Instead, despite her misgivings about the implications of Hirsch's agenda, the student suspended judgment, opening the way to genuine inquiry. She acknowledged the usefulness and value of sharing a common language and conceded that Hirsch's points were well taken. She wrote:

> Some sort of unification is necessary. Language, . . . on the most fundamental level of human interaction, demands some compromise and chosen guidelines. . . . How can we learn from one another if we cannot even say hello to each other?

Suspending judgment led her to recognize the complexity of the issue, and her willingness to examine the issue from different perspectives indicated the empathy that is a central component of developing a conversational argument.

■ Acknowledge Your Audience

This student's question ("To what extent can E. D. Hirsch's notion of 'cultural literacy' coexist with our country's principles of democracy and inclusion?") also acknowledged an audience. By invoking cultural literacy, she assumed an audience of readers who are familiar with Hirsch's ideas, probably including policymakers and educational administrators. In gesturing toward democracy, she cast her net very wide: Most Americans probably admire the "principles of democracy." But in specifying inclusion as a democratic principle, she wisely linked all Americans who believe in democratic principles, including the parents of schoolchildren, with all people who have reason to feel excluded by Hirsch's ideas, especially nonnative speakers of English, among them immigrants from Mexico and speakers of African American Vernacular English. Thus this student was acknowledging an audience of policymakers, administrators, parents (both mainstream and marginalized), and those who knew about and perhaps supported cultural literacy.

Steps to Formulating an Issue-Based Question

1 **Refine your topic.** Examine your topic from different perspectives. For example, what are the causes of homelessness? What are its consequences?

2 **Explain your interest in the topic.** Explore the source of your interest in this topic and what you want to learn.

3 **Identify an issue.** Consider what is open to dispute.

4 **Formulate your topic as a question.** Use your question to focus your inquiry.

5 **Acknowledge your audience.** Reflect on what readers may know about the issue, why they may be interested, and what you would like to teach them.

A Practice Sequence: Formulating an Issue-Based Question

As you start developing your own issue-based question, it might be useful to practice a five-step process that begins with a topic, a word or phrase that describes the focus of your interests. Here, apply the process to the one-word topic homelessness.

1 Expand your topic into a phrase. "I am interested in the *consequences* of homelessness," "I want to *describe* what it means to be homeless," or "I am interested in discussing the *cause* of homelessness."

2 Explain your interest in this topic. "I am interested in the consequences of homelessness because it challenges democratic principles of fairness."

3 Identify an issue. "The persistence of homelessness contradicts my belief in social justice."

4 Formulate your topic as a question. "To what extent can we allow homelessness to persist in a democratic nation that prides itself on providing equal opportunity to all?"

5 Acknowledge your audience. "I am interested in the consequences of homelessness because I want people who believe in democracy to understand that we need to work harder to make sure that everyone has access to food, shelter, and employment."

The answer to the question you formulate in step 4 should lead to an assertion, your main claim, or *thesis*. For example, you could state your main claim this way: "Although homelessness persists as a widespread problem in our nation, we must develop policies that eliminate homelessness, ensuring that everyone has access to food, shelter, and employment. This is especially important in a democracy that embraces social justice and equality."

The thesis introduces a problem and makes an assertion that you will need to support: "We must develop policies that eliminate homelessness, ensuring that everyone has access to food, shelter, and employment." What is at issue? Not everyone would agree that policies must be implemented to solve the problem. In fact, many would argue that homelessness is an individual problem, that individuals must take responsibility for lifting themselves out of poverty, homelessness, and unemployment. Of course, you would need to read quite a bit to reach this final stage of formulating your thesis.

Try using the five-step process we describe above to formulate your own topic as a question, or try formulating the following topics as questions:

- Downloading music
- Violence in video games
- Gender and employment
- The popularity of a cultural phenomenon (a book, a film, a performer, an icon)
- Standardized tests
- Civil rights
- Town-gown relationships
- Media and representation
- Government and religion
- Affirmative action

5

From Formulating to Developing a Thesis

Academic writing explores complex issues that grow out of relevant, timely conversations in which something is at stake. An academic writer reads as a writer to understand the issues, situations, and questions that lead other writers to make claims. Readers expect academic writers to take a clear, specific, logical stand on an issue, and they evaluate how writers support their claims and anticipate counterarguments. The logical stand is the **thesis**, an assertion that academic writers make at the beginning of what they write and then support with evidence throughout their essay. The illustrations and examples that a writer includes must relate to and support the thesis. Thus, a thesis encompasses all of the information writers use to further their arguments; it is not simply a single assertion at the beginning of an essay.

One of our students aptly described the thesis using the metaphor of a shish kebab: The thesis penetrates every paragraph, holding the paragraphs together, just as a skewer penetrates and holds the ingredients of a shish kebab together. Moreover, the thesis serves as a signpost throughout an essay, reminding readers what the argument is and why the writer has included evidence — examples, illustrations, quotations — relevant to that argument.

An academic thesis

- makes an assertion that is clearly defined, focused, and supported.

- reflects an awareness of the conversation from which the writer has taken up the issue.

- is placed at the beginning of the essay.

- penetrates every paragraph like the skewer in a shish kebab.
- acknowledges points of view that differ from the writer's own, reflecting the complexity of the issue.
- demonstrates an awareness of the readers' assumptions and anticipates possible counterarguments.
- conveys a significant fresh perspective.

It is a myth is that writers first come up with a thesis and then write their essays. The reality is that writers use issue-based questions to read, learn, and develop a thesis throughout the process of writing. Through revising and discussing their ideas, writers hone their thesis, making sure that it threads through every paragraph of the final draft. The position writers ultimately take in writing — their thesis — comes at the end of the writing process, after not one draft but many.

WORKING VERSUS DEFINITIVE THESES

Writers are continually challenged by the need to establish their purpose and to make a clear and specific assertion of it. To reach that assertion, you must first engage in a prolonged process of inquiry, aided by a well-formulated question. The question serves as a tool for inquiry that will help you formulate your **working thesis**, your first attempt at an assertion of your position. A working thesis is valuable in the early stages of writing because it helps you read selectively, in the same way that your issue-based question guides your inquiry. Reading raises questions, helping you see what you know and need to know, and challenging you to read on. Never accept your working thesis as your final position. Instead, continue testing your assertion as you read and write, and modify your working thesis as necessary. A more definitive thesis will come once you are satisfied that you have examined the issue from multiple perspectives.

For example, one of our students wanted to study representations of femininity in the media. In particular, she focused on why the Barbie doll has become an icon of femininity despite what many cultural critics consider Barbie's "outrageous and ultimately unattainable physical characteristics." Our student's working thesis suggested she would develop an argument about the need for change:

The harmful implications of ongoing exposure to these unattainable ideals,
such as low self-esteem, eating disorders, unhealthy body image, and acceptance
of violence, make urgent the need for change.

The student assumed that her research would lead her to argue that Barbie's unattainable proportions have a damaging effect on women's self-image and that something needs to be done about it. However, as she read scholarly research to support her tentative thesis, she realized that a more compelling project would be less Barbie-centric. Instead, she chose to examine the broader phenomenon of how the idea of femininity is created and reinforced by society. That is, her personal interest in Barbie was supplanted by her discoveries about cultural norms of beauty and the power they have to influence self-perception and behavior. In her final draft, this was her definitive thesis:

> Although evidence may be provided to argue that gender is an innate characteristic, I will show that it is actually the result of one's actions, which are then labeled *masculine* or *feminine* according to society's definitions of ideal gender. Furthermore, I will discuss the communication of such definitions through the media, specifically in music videos, on TV, and in magazines, and the harmful implications of being exposed to these ideals.

Instead of arguing for change, the student chose to show her readers how they were being manipulated, leaving it to them to decide what actions they might want to take.

DEVELOPING A WORKING THESIS: THREE MODELS

What are some ways to develop a working thesis? We suggest three models that may help you organize the information you gather in response to the question guiding your inquiry.

■ The Correcting-Misinterpretations Model

This model is used to correct writers whose arguments you believe have misconstrued one or more important aspects of an issue. The thesis typically takes the form of a factual claim. Consider this example and the words we have underlined:

> <u>Although scholars have addressed curriculum</u> to explain low achievement in schools, <u>they have failed to fully</u> appreciate the impact of <u>limited resources</u> to fund up-to-date textbooks, quality teachers, and computers. Therefore, reform in schools must focus on economic need as well as curriculum.

The clause beginning with "Although" lays out the assumption that many scholars make, that curriculum explains low educational achievement; the clause beginning with "they have failed" identifies the error those scholars have made by ignoring the economic reasons for low achievement in schools. Notice that the structure of the sentence reinforces the author's position. He offers the faulty assumption in a subordinate clause, reserving the main clause for his own position. The two clauses also reinforce that there are conflicting opinions here. One more thing: Although it is a common myth that a thesis must be phrased in a single sentence, this example shows that a thesis can be written in two (or more) sentences.

■ The Filling-the-Gap Model

The gap model points to what other writers may have overlooked or ignored in discussing a given issue. The gap model typically makes a claim of value. Consider this student's argument that discussions of cultural diversity in the United States are often framed in terms of black and white. Our underlining indicates the gap the writer has identified:

> If America is truly a "melting pot" of cultures, as it is often called, then why is it that stories and events seem only to be in black and white? Why is it that when history courses are taught about the period of the civil rights movement, only the memoirs of African Americans are read, like those of Melba Pattillo Beals and Ida Mae Holland? Where are the works of Maxine Hong Kingston, who tells the story of alienation and segregation in schools through the eyes of a Chinese child? African Americans were denied the right to vote, and many other citizenship rights; but Chinese Americans were denied even the opportunity to become citizens. I am not diminishing the issue of discrimination against African Americans, nor belittling the struggles they went through. I simply want to call attention to discrimination against other minority groups and their often-overlooked struggles to achieve equality.

In the student's thesis, the gap in people's knowledge stems from their limited understanding of history — that many minority groups were denied their rights.

A variation on the gap model also occurs when a writer suggests that although something might appear to be the case, a closer look reveals something different. For example: "Although it would *appear* that women and people of color have achieved equality in the workplace, their paychecks suggest that this is not true." One of our students examined two poems by the same author that appeared to contradict each other. She noticed a gap others had not seen:

> In both "The Albatross" and "Beauty," Charles Baudelaire chooses to explore the plight of the poet. Interestingly, despite their common author, the two poems' portrayals of the poet's struggles appear contradictory. "The Albatross" seems to give a somewhat sympathetic glimpse into the exile of the

poet — the "winged voyager" so awkward in the ordinary world. "Beauty" takes what appears to be a less forgiving stance: The poet here is docile, simply a mirror. Although both pieces depict the poet's struggles, a closer examination demonstrates how the portrayals differ.

In stating her thesis, the student indicates that although readers might expect Baudelaire's images of poets to be similar, a closer examination of his words would prove them wrong.

■ The Modifying-What-Others-Have-Said Model

The modification model of thesis writing is premised on the possibility of mutual understanding. For example, in proposing a change in policy, one student asserts:

Although scholars have claimed that the only sure way to reverse the cycle of homelessness in America is to provide an adequate education, we need to build on this work, providing school-to-work programs that ensure graduates have access to employment.

Here the writer seeks to modify other writers' claims, suggesting that education alone does not solve the problem of homelessness; the challenge he sets for himself is to understand the complexity of the problem by building on and extending the ideas of others. In effect, he is in a constructive conversation with those whose work he wants to build on, helping readers see that he shares common ground with the other writers and hopes to find a mutually acceptable solution to the agreed-on problem.

Steps to Formulating a Working Thesis: Three Models

1 **Misinterpretations model:** "Although many scholars have argued about X and Y, a careful examination suggests Z."

2 **Gap model:** "Although scholars have noted X and Y, they have missed the importance of Z."

3 **Modification model:** "Although I agree with the X and Y ideas of other writers, it is important to extend/refine/limit their ideas with Z."

A Practice Sequence: Identifying Types of Theses

Below is a series of working theses. Read each one and then identify the model — misinterpretations, gap, or modification — it represents.

1 A number of studies indicate that violence on television has a detrimental effect on adolescent behavior. However, few researchers have examined key environmental factors like peer pressure, music, and home life. In fact, I would argue that many researchers have oversimplified the problem.

2 Although research indicates that an increasing number of African American and Hispanic students are dropping out of high school, researchers have failed to fully grasp the reasons why this has occurred.

3 I want to argue that studies supporting single-sex education are relatively sound. However, we don't really know the long-term effects of single-sex education, particularly on young women's career paths.

4 Although recent studies of voting patterns in the United States indicate that young people between the ages of 18 and 24 are apathetic, I want to suggest that not all of the reasons these studies provide are valid.

5 Indeed, it's not surprising that students are majoring in fields that will enable them to get a job after graduation. But students may not be as pragmatic as we think. Many students choose majors because they feel that learning is an important end in itself.

6 Although good teachers are essential to learning, we cannot ignore the roles that race and class play in students' access to a quality education.

7 It is clear that cities need to clean up the dilapidated housing projects that were built over half a century ago; but few, if any, studies have examined the effects of doing so on the life chances of those people who are being displaced.

8 In addition to its efforts to advance the cause of social justice in the new global economy, the university must make a commitment to ending poverty on the edge of campus.

9 Although the writer offers evidence to explain the sources of illiteracy in America, he overstates his case when he ignores other factors, among them history, culture, and economic well-being. Therefore, I will argue that we place the discussion in a broader context.

10 More and more policymakers argue that English should be the national language in the United States. Although I agree that English is important, we should not limit people's right to maintain their own linguistic and cultural identity.

ESTABLISHING A CONTEXT FOR A THESIS

In addition to defining the purpose and focus of an essay, a thesis must set up a **context** for the writer's claim. The process of establishing a background for understanding an issue typically involves four steps:

1. Establish that the topic of conversation, the issue, is current and relevant — that it is on people's minds or should be.

2. Briefly summarize what others have said to show that you are familiar with the topic or issue.

3. Explain what you see as the problem — a misinterpretation, gap, or a modification that needs to be made in how others have addressed the topic or issue — perhaps by raising the questions you believe need to be answered.

4. State your thesis, suggesting that your view on the issue may present readers with something new to think about as it builds on and extends what others have argued.

You need not follow these steps in this order as long as your readers come away from the first part of your essay knowing why you are discussing a given issue and what your argument is.

We trace these four steps below in our analysis of the opening paragraphs of one of our student's essays. She was writing in response to what many call the English-only movement. Specifically, she responds to the effects of Proposition 227 in California, a piece of legislation that prevents non-English-speaking students from using their first language in school. Our discussion of how she provides a context for her thesis follows the excerpt.

Nuestra Clase   1

Jenny Eck
Professor Walters
English 200
March 18, 20--

Nuestra Clase: Making the Classroom a Welcoming Place
for English Language Learners

With the Latino population growing exponentially and Spanish quickly becoming one of the most widely spoken languages in the United States, the question arises of how the American educational system is meeting the needs of a growing Hispanic population. What does our educational system do to address the needs of students whose primary language is not English?

Nuestra Clase 2

In 1998, the state of California passed Proposition 227, which prohibited bilingual instruction in public schools. Ron Unz, a former Republican gubernatorial candidate and software developer, launched the initiative under the name "English for the Children." Unz argued that the initiative would help Latinos and other recent immigrants free themselves from bilingual education, which he avowed would hinder the ability of immigrants to assimilate into American culture (Stritikus, 2002). Supporters of Proposition 227 assert that bilingual education has failed English language learners (ELLs) because it does not adequately equip them with the English language skills essential to success in school. Eradicating bilingual education, they believe, will help students learn English more effectively and consequently achieve more in their educational careers.

Since its passage, Proposition 227 has been hotly debated. Many researchers claim that its strictures have stunted the education of Spanish-speaking students (Halcón, 2001; Stritikus, 2002). Many studies have indicated the harmful effects of what Gutiérrez and her colleagues describe as "backlash pedagogy" (Gutiérrez, Asato, Santos & Gotanda, 2002), which prohibits the use of students' complete linguistic, sociocultural, and academic repertoire. In essence, they claim that Proposition 227's backlash pedagogy, in attempting to emphasize "colorblindness" in education, has instead eradicated differences that are crucial to students' efforts to become educated. They argue that by devaluing these differences, the educational system devalues the very students it is attempting to help.

A sociocultural theory of learning, with its emphasis on the significant impact that factors such as language, culture, family, and community have on a student's potential for educational success (Halcón, 2001), calls attention to growing concerns that schools may not be meeting the needs of ELLs. Russian psychologist Lev Vygotsky (1978) introduced this viewpoint to educators when he proposed that development and learning are firmly embedded in and influenced by society and culture. With Vygotsky's theory in mind, other researchers have embraced the idea that the failure of minority students is more often than not a systematic failure, rather than an individual failure (Trueba, 1989). Sociocultural theory posits that learning needs to be understood not only in the broader context of the sociocultural lives

Nuestra Clase   3

of students, teachers, and schools, but also in their sociopolitical lives. A sociocultural context takes a student's culture, race, religion, language, family, community, and other similar factors into consideration, while a sociopolitical context takes into account the inherent ideologies and prejudices that exist in society today. In order for teaching to be effective, both sociocultural and sociopolitical factors must be identified and addressed.

Many educators seem to dismiss sociocultural and sociopolitical factors, perhaps not realizing that by ignoring these factors, they are inadvertently privileging the students in their classrooms for whom English is a first language (Larson, 2003). Such a dismissive attitude does not reckon with other studies that have shown how important it is for English language learners to explore and express their bilingual/bicultural identities (McCarthey, García, López-Velásquez, Lin & Guo, 2004). Some of these other studies have even proposed that schooling acts as a "subtractive process" for minority students, not only denying them opportunities to express their identities, but also divesting them of important social and cultural resources, which ultimately leaves them vulnerable to academic failure (Valenzuela, 1999). These other studies convincingly show that sociocultural factors are essential to the educational success of English language learners. Therefore, although many educators believe they know the best way to teach these students, I will argue that the educational system, by not taking into account factors that sociocultural theory emphasizes, has mostly failed to create classrooms that embrace cultural differences, and by so doing has failed to create optimal conditions for teaching and learning.

Nuestra Clase   9

References

Gutiérrez, K., Asato, J., Santos, M. & Gotanda, N. (2002). Backlash pedagogy: Language and culture and the politics of reform. *The review of education, pedagogy, and cultural studies, 24,* 335–351.

Nuestra Clase   10

Halcón, J. J. (2001). Mainstream ideology and literacy instructions for Spanish-speaking children. In M. Reyes & J. J. Halcón (Eds.), *The best for our children: Critical perspectives on literacy for Latino students* (pp. 65–77). New York, NY: Teacher's College Press.

Larson, J. (2003). Negotiating Race in Classroom Research: Tensions and Possibilities. In S. Greene & D. Abt-Perkins (Eds.), *Making race visible: Literacy research for cultural understanding* (pp. 89–106). New York, NY: Teacher's College Press.

McCarthey, S. J., López-Velásquez, A. M., García, G. E., Lin, S., & Guo, Y. (2004). Understanding writing contexts for English language learners. *Research in the teaching of English, 38,* 351–394.

Stritikus, T. (2002). *Immigrant children and the politics of English-only: Views from the classroom.* New York, NY: LFB Scholarly Publishing LLC.

Trueba, H. T. (1989). *Raising silent voices: Educating the linguistic minorities for the 21st century.* Cambridge, MA: Newbury House.

Valenzuela, A. (1999). *Subtractive schooling: U.S. Mexican youth and the politics of caring.* Albany, NY: State University of New York Press.

Vygotsky, L. S. (1978). *Thought and language.* Cambridge, MA: MIT Press.

■ Establish That the Issue Is Current and Relevant

Ideally, you should convey to readers that the issue you are discussing is both current (what's on people's minds) and relevant (of sufficient importance to have generated some discussion and written conversation). In the first sentence, Eck tells readers of a trend she feels they need to be aware of, the dramatic growth of the Hispanic population in the United States. Her issue is what the schools are doing to meet the needs of a growing population of students "whose primary language is not English." At the beginning of the third paragraph, she signals the relevance of the issue when she observes that the passage of Proposition 227 has been "hotly debated."

■ Briefly Present What Others Have Said

It is important to introduce who has said what in the conversation you are entering. After all, you are interrupting that conversation to make your contribution, and those who are already in that conversation expect you to have done your homework and acknowledge those who have already made important contributions. (For more on presenting the ideas of others, see Chapter 7.)

In the second paragraph, Eck sets the stage for her review with a brief history of Proposition 227. Here she describes what was at issue for supporters of the law and what they hoped the law would accomplish. Starting with paragraph 3, Eck acknowledges the researchers who have participated in the debate surrounding Proposition 227 and reviews a number of studies that challenge the premises on which Proposition 227 rested. Notice that she introduces the frame of sociocultural theory to help her readers see that denying students the use of their native language in the classroom is a problem.

By pointing out the ways that researchers on language learning challenge the assumptions underlying the English-only movement, Eck is doing more than listing sources. She is establishing that a problem, or issue, exists. Moreover, her review gives readers intellectual touchstones, the scholars who need to be cited in any academic conversation about bilingual education. A review is not a catchall for anyone writing on a topic; instead, it should reflect a writer's selection of the most relevant participants in the conversation. Eck's choice of sources, and how she presents them, conveys that she is knowledgeable about her subject. (Of course, it is her readers' responsibility to read further to determine whether she has reviewed the most relevant work and has presented the ideas of others accurately. If she has, readers will trust her whether or not they end up agreeing with her on the issue.)

■ Explain What You See as the Problem

If a review indicates a problem, as Eck's review does, the problem can often be couched in terms of the models we discussed earlier: misinterpretations, gap, or modification. In paragraph 5, Eck identifies what she concludes is a misunderstanding of how students learn a new language. She suggests that the misunderstanding stems from a gap in knowledge (notice our underlining):

> Many educators seem to dismiss sociocultural and sociopolitical factors, perhaps not realizing that by ignoring these factors, they are inadvertently privileging the students in their classrooms for whom English is a first language (Larson, 2003). Such a dismissive attitude does not reckon with other studies that have shown how important it is for English language learners to explore and express their bilingual/bicultural identities (McCarthey, García, López-Velásquez, Lin & Guo, 2004). Some of these other studies have even proposed that schooling acts as a "subtractive process" for minority students, not only denying them opportunities to express their identities, but also divesting them of important social and

cultural resources, which ultimately leaves them vulnerable to academic failure (Valenzuela, 1999).

While Eck concedes that efforts to understand the problems of language learning have been extensive and multifaceted, her review of the research culminates with her assertion that ignoring students' language practices could have devastating results — that educators, by denying students "important social and cultural resources," may be leaving those students "vulnerable to academic failure."

■ State Your Thesis

An effective thesis statement helps readers see the reasoning behind the author's claim; it also signals what readers should look for in the remainder of the essay. Eck closes paragraph 5 with a statement that speaks to both the purpose and the substance of her writing:

> Therefore, although many educators believe they know the best way to teach ELL students, I will argue that the educational system, by not taking into account factors that sociocultural theory emphasizes, has mostly failed to create classrooms that embrace cultural differences, and by so doing has failed to create optimal conditions for teaching and learning.

In your own writing, you can make use of the strategies that Eck uses in her essay. Words like *although* and *though* can set up problem statements: "Although [though] some people think that nonnative speakers of English can best learn English by not using their first language, the issue is more complex than most people realize." Words like *but, however,* and *yet* can serve the same purpose: "One might argue that nonnative speakers of English can best learn English by not using their first language; but [however, yet] the issue is more complex than most people realize."

Steps to Establishing a Context for a Thesis

1 **Establish that the issue is current and relevant.** Point out the extent to which others have recognized the problem, issue, or question that you are writing about.

2 **Briefly review what others have said.** Explain how others have addressed the problem, issue, or question you are focusing on.

3 **Explain what you see as the problem.** Identify what is open to dispute.

4 **State your thesis.** Help readers see your purpose and how you intend to achieve it — by correcting a misconception, filling a gap, or modifying a claim others have accepted.

■ Analyze the Context of a Thesis

In "Protean Shapes in Literacy Events," cultural anthropologist and linguist Shirley Brice Heath argues that communities of practice shape the ways in which people use reading and writing. Heath points out the problem of holding up a standard of literacy from one community to measure the extent to which another community is or is not literate. Her essay, originally published in 1982, is addressed to a community of scholars who study literacy. As you read the excerpt that follows, you will likely find yourself puzzled by Heath's vocabulary and possibly even excluded from the conversation at times. Our point in reprinting this excerpt is not to initiate you into Heath's academic community but to show, through our annotations, how Heath has applied the strategies we have been discussing in this chapter. As you read, feel free to make your own annotations, and then try to answer the questions — which may involve some careful rereading — that we pose after the excerpt. In particular, watch for signpost words (*but, few, little, however*) that signal the ideas the writer is challenging.

SHIRLEY BRICE HEATH

From Protean Shapes in Literacy Events: Ever-Shifting Oral and Literate Traditions

The first sentence establishes that the issue that interests Heath has been discussed for more than a few years, helping us see the continuing relevance of the area of study.

From the sentence that begins "Much of this research" to the end of the paragraph, Heath reviews some of the relevant literature and points to a problem: that previous work has seen literate and oral cultures as somehow opposed to one another. The author gives us more than a list of sources.

Since the mid-1970s, anthropologists, linguists, historians, and psychologists have turned with new tools of analysis to the study of oral and literate societies. They have used discourse analysis, econometrics, theories of schemata and frames, and proposals of developmental performance to consider the possible links between oral and written language, and between literacy and its individual and societal consequences. Much of this research is predicated on a dichotomous view of oral and literate traditions, usually attributed to researchers active in the 1960s. Repeatedly, Goody and Watt (1963), Ong (1967), Goody (1968), and Havelock (1963) are cited as having suggested a dichotomous view of oral and literate societies and as having asserted certain cognitive, social, and linguistic effects of literacy on both the society and the individual. Survey research tracing the invention and diffusion of writing systems across numerous societies (Kroeber, 1948) and positing the effects of the spread of literacy on social and individual

1

memory (Goody and Watt, 1963; Havelock, 1963, 1976) is cited as supporting a contrastive view of oral and literate social groups. Research which examined oral performance in particular groups is said to support the notion that as members of a society increasingly participate in literacy, they lose habits associated with the oral tradition (Lord, 1965).

In short, existing scholarship makes it easy to interpret a picture which depicts societies existing along a continuum of development from an oral tradition to a literate one, with some societies having a restricted literacy, and others having reached a full development of literacy (Goody, 1968:11). One also finds in this research specific characterizations of oral and written language associated with these traditions.

2

But a close reading of these scholars, especially Goody (1968) and Goody and Watt (1963), leaves some room for questioning such a picture of consistent and universal processes or products—individual or societal—of literacy. Goody pointed out that in any traditional society, factors such as secrecy, religious ideology, limited social mobility, lack of access to writing materials and alphabetic scripts could lead to restricted literacy. Furthermore, Goody warned that the advent of a writing system did not amount to technological determinism or to sufficient cause of certain changes in either the individual or the society. Goody went on to propose exploring the concrete context of written communication (1968:4) to determine how the potentialities of literacy developed in traditional societies. He brought together a collection of essays based on the ethnography of literacy in traditional societies to illustrate the wide variety of ways in which *traditional*, i.e., pre-industrial but not necessarily pre-literate, societies played out their uses of oral and literate traditions.

3

In the first sentence in this paragraph, Heath suggests that a close reading would raise some important unanswered questions about the relationship between orality and literacy.

Few researchers in the 1970s have, however, heeded Goody's warning about the possible wide-ranging effects of societal and cultural factors on literacy and its uses. In particular, little attention has been given in *modern* complex industrial societies to the social and cultural correlates of literacy or to the work experiences adults have which may affect the

4

The previous paragraph sets up the problem and the gap that Heath believes her research — indicated in the first two sentences of this paragraph — should address.

maintenance and retention of literacy skills acquired in formal schooling. The public media today give much attention to the decline of literacy skills as measured in school settings and the failure of students to acquire certain levels of literacy. However, the media pay little attention to occasions for literacy retention—to the actual uses of literacy in work settings, daily interactions in religious, economic, and legal institutions, and family habits of socializing the young into uses of literacy. In the clamor over the need to increase the teaching of basic skills, there is much emphasis on the positive effects extensive and critical reading can have on improving oral language. Yet there are scarcely any data comparing the forms and functions of oral language with those of written language produced and used by members of social groups within a complex society. One of the most appropriate sources of data for informing discussions of these issues is that which Goody proposed for traditional societies: the concrete context of written communication. Where, when, how, for whom, and with what results are individuals in different social groups of today's highly industrialized society using reading and writing skills? How have the potentialities of the literacy skills learned in school developed in the lives of today's adults? Does modern society contain certain conditions which restrict literacy just as some traditional societies do? If so, what are these factors, and are groups with restricted literacy denied benefits widely attributed to full literacy, such as upward socioeconomic mobility, the development of logical reasoning, and access to the information necessary to make well-informed political judgments?

The underlined sentence indicates the gap: The media focus on one set of concerns when they should be attending to a very different set of issues.

Heath elaborates on what she sees as a troubling gap between what educators know and what they need to know.

In the last four sentences of the excerpt, Heath raises the questions that she wants readers to consider and that guide her own research.

For Analysis and Discussion

1. What specific places can you point to in the selection that illustrate what is at issue for Heath?

2. How does Heath use her review to set up her argument?

3. What specific words and phrases does Heath use to establish what she sees as the problem? Is she correcting misinterpretations, filling a gap, or modifying what others have said?

4. What would you say is Heath's thesis? What specifics can you point to in the text to support your answer?

5. What would you say are the arguments Heath wants you to avoid? Again, what specific details can you point to in the text to support your answer?

■ Analyze a Student Argument

Now, drawing on the lessons of this chapter, try your own analysis of the following student essay. Read through it with pen or pencil in hand, looking for (1) the author's thesis, (2) the gap it addresses, (3) the problem or issue she sees, (4) evidence of her audience, and (5) her use of sources. Then answer the questions that follow the essay.

Potish 1

Jessie Potish
Professor Riley
English 1020
April 5, 20--

AIDS in Women: A Growing Educational Concern

Due to the fervent efforts of health educators, young people today have a very intimate knowledge of HIV and AIDS. These students were born in the early eighties at the beginning of the AIDS epidemic. Teachers guided students through years of health classes in their junior high and high school years and informed students about the destructive nature of the AIDS virus and ways in which it can and cannot be contracted. Health educators made sure that students were well informed about HIV and presented the topic as being gender-neutral. Although pop culture and the media claimed that homosexual males were responsible for the epidemic, this idea was never presented in the classroom. Though I am grateful for this aspect of AIDS education, it seems that there was an important aspect missing from the curriculum: the more numerous negative effects that the disease has on women. Health education needs to present the effects of AIDS on women and encourage them to be more concerned about contracting and living with the disease.

In spite of this need for reform, health educators may feel uneasy about changing their curriculum and argue that there are a number of reasons to keep the HIV and AIDS curriculum the same.

1

2

One reason that they might have for maintaining the current curriculum is that they fear that presenting HIV as more of a woman's issue could decrease awareness of the disease in men. However, this probably will not happen. Many people, though not necessarily health educators, already view HIV as more of a man's disease. In fact, according to Allen E. Carrier of AIDS Project Los Angeles, gay men ages 17 to 24 are at very high risk for HIV infection and realize the dangers of unsafe sex, but continue to engage in high-risk behavior (quoted in DeNoon and Key, "National"). In other words, most men are aware and informed, but some are choosing to ignore some of the education that they have received. In reality, men need to make as many changes as women in order to stop the AIDS epidemic. Peter Piot, the executive director of the Joint United Nations Program on HIV/AIDS, says that "men have a crucial role to play in bringing about this radical change" (Henderson). Therefore, the new AIDS curriculum would be encouraging both men and women to change their attitudes and actions in order to bring about changes.

Health educators might also claim that by focusing more on HIV education, they will have to ignore other important health topics. However, few other health topics today are as important or as relevant to young people as HIV; it is a worldwide epidemic that is constantly affecting them. In addition, it is one of the few diseases that can be controlled with sufficient knowledge and responsible behavior. Teachers should not feel as though they are ignoring more important topics; they are merely focusing on an issue of growing prevalence. Health educators might also argue that they should not be the only ones responsible for making young women more aware of this issue. They could say that parent education and community programs could be used in lieu of education in the classroom. I would argue, though, that while education in the home and through the community could certainly be useful as well, many students do not have a strong support system at home or access to a wealth of materials about health subjects. Therefore, health education in the schools is surely the most effective way to reach young people, and this is where HIV and AIDS education should have the strongest presence.

One of the most important points missing from current AIDS education is the fact that women are, for the most part, more susceptible to the disease. Heterosexual contact is the chief mode of

3

4

transmission for women infected with the disease, followed by intra-venous drug use. Women should be especially concerned about con-tracting this disease through sexual contact because, according to Saglio, Kurtzman, and Radner's article in *American Family Physician*, the sexual transmissibility of the virus from men to women is much greater, up to 19 times more likely than the transmission from women to men. This figure is quite astounding, and I felt concerned that I had never before heard it when learning about HIV. Though abstinence and safe sex were repeatedly taught and encouraged in the classroom, teachers never fully explained how important it is for women to protect themselves. To make this clear to students, health educators should empower young women and encourage them to have more control over their sexuality. C. W. Henderson, editor-in-chief of *AIDS Weekly*, states that social expectations limit a woman's access to materials about sexual matters. He also claims that high-risk sexual behaviors are more common and socially acceptable in males, who can in turn transmit the infection to their partners. These social norms should not be acceptable. Women should not feel uneasy about getting information or asking about their partner's sex-ual history. Young women need to be taught this in the classroom.

Young women should also be told about the numerous physi-cal conditions that can afflict them if they contract HIV or AIDS. These effects include some that are unique to women in addition to the tragic course that AIDS normally takes on the body. Disease pro-gression in both men and women is similar, and treatment methods are the same; but, according to a study published in the December 28, 1994, issue of the *Journal of the American Medical Association*, women have lower survival rates than men (cited in DeNoon and Key, "At Last"). In addition, women have complications, mainly gynecol-ogical disorders due to HIV or AIDS, that can have very adverse effects. Pelvic inflammatory disease and vaginal candidiasis are par-ticularly common and difficult to treat in infected women. Also, infected women with herpes require long-term treatment to keep outbreaks under control. There is even an increased frequency of abnormal cervical cells and cervical cancer in HIV-infected women (Saglio et al.). These are definitely very serious health conditions for a woman to consider, as they can do a lot of damage to her

5

Potish   4

reproductive system and even lead to death. In health classes, I learned very clearly the risks of gynecological diseases and the adverse permanent effects that they can have. However, I never once heard that HIV could worsen the effects of these pelvic disorders or that they were in any way connected. This is a very important topic that should be stressed among young women. Perhaps health educators should consider discussing this important health connection that until now has been ignored in the classroom.

In addition, a woman must consider the ramifications of being infected with HIV and carrying a child. Many young women probably do not see how much of an effect this disease can have on their decision to have children. An estimated 84 percent of infected women are between the ages of 15 and 44, the prime childbearing years. Nearly 2,000 babies are born each year in the United States infected with HIV, and 90 percent of children under the age of 15 acquire the disease through vertical transmission (Saglio et al.). That is, they acquire it from their infected mother while in the womb, during the birth process, or through breast-feeding. There are drugs, namely zidovudine, that can help decrease the chance of vertical transmission, but nothing is completely effective. Also, the side effects of the use of the drug are not fully understood in the mother or the child (Bianco). There needs to be increased awareness about HIV among pregnant women and more encouragement for women to be tested for the disease prior to conception or during the first trimester of pregnancy. Many young women are not planning on having children for several years, and they may not be prepared to think that far ahead. This is when the educator should step in and explain the adverse effects that AIDS can have on a pregnancy. Health educators need to help young women understand the effects that HIV can have on their unborn children and encourage them to think more about their futures.

The changes in AIDS education that I am suggesting are necessary and relatively simple to make. Although the current curriculum in high school health classes is helpful and informative, it simply does not pertain to young women as much as it should. AIDS is killing women at an alarming rate, and many people do not realize this. According to Daniel DeNoon and Keith Key, AIDS is one of the

6

7

Potish 5

six leading causes of death among women ages 18 to 45, and women "bear the brunt of the worldwide AIDS epidemic." For this reason, DeNoon and Key argue, women are one of the most important new populations that are contracting HIV at a high rate. Young women need to be better informed about AIDS and their link to the disease, or many new cases may develop. As the epidemic continues to spread, women need to realize that they can stop the spread of the disease and protect themselves from infection and a number of related complications. It is the responsibility of health educators to present this to young women and inform them of the powerful choices that they can make.

Potish 6

Works Cited

Bianco, Mabel. "Women, Vulnerability and HIV/AIDS — A Human Rights Perspective (Part 22 of 37)." *Women, Vulnerability and HIV/AIDS — A Human Rights Perspective*. 1998. *Contemporary Women's Issues*. WebSPIRS. Web. 5 October 2000.

DeNoon, Daniel J., and Keith K. Key. "At Last, a Sex-Based Study of HIV Disease." *Infectious Disease Weekly* 16 January 1995: 5–7. *Academic Search Elite*. Ebsco Publishing. Web. 22 October 2000.

———. "National Model Launched in HIV/AIDS Prevention." *AIDS Weekly Plus* 8 July 1996: 16. *Academic Search Elite*. Ebsco Publishing. Web. 22 October 2000.

Henderson, C. W. "Gender Is Crucial Issue in Slowing the Spread of HIV." *AIDS Weekly* 10 July 2000: 12–14. *Academic Search Elite*. Ebsco Publishing. Web. 22 October 2000.

Saglio, Stephen Dower, James Todd Kurtzman, and Allen Bruce Radner. "HIV Infection in Women: An Escalating Health Concern." *American Family Physician,* 54.5, October 1996: 1541–1549. *Academic Search Elite*. Ebsco Publishing. Web. 5 October 2000.

For Analysis and Discussion

1. What is Potish's thesis? Which sentences spell out her argument most clearly?

2. In what way does Potish's thesis address a misinterpretation, a gap, or the need for a modification?

3. Who do you think Potish's audience is? What passages suggest this?

4. How does Potish use what she has read to define a problem or issue?

5. How does Potish use what she has read to establish the conversation she wants to enter?

A Practice Sequence: Building a Thesis

We would like you to practice some of the strategies we have covered in this chapter. If you have already started working on an essay, exercises 1 through 4 present an opportunity to take stock of your progress, a chance to sort through what you've discovered, identify what you still need to discover, and move toward refining your thesis. Jot down your answer to each of the questions below and make lists of what you know and what you need to learn.

1 Have you established that your issue is current and relevant, that it is or should be on people's minds? What information would you need to do so?

2 Can you summarize briefly what others have said in the past to show that you are familiar with how others have addressed the issue? List some of the key texts you have read and the key points they make.

3 Have you identified any misunderstandings or gaps in how others have addressed the issue? Describe them. Do you have any ideas or information that would address these misunderstandings or help fill these gaps? Where might you find the information you need? Can you think of any sources you should reread to learn more? (For example, have you looked at the works cited or bibliographies in the texts you've already read?)

4 At this point, what is your take on the issue? Try drafting a working thesis statement that will present readers with something new to think about, building on and extending what others have argued. In drafting your thesis statement, try out the three models discussed in this chapter and see if one is an especially good fit:

- *Misinterpretations model*: "Although many scholars have argued about X and Y, a careful examination suggests Z."
- *Gap model*: "Although scholars have noted X and Y, they have missed the importance of Z."

> • *Modification model*: "Although I agree with X and Y ideas of other writers, it is important to extend/refine/limit their ideas with Z."

5 If you haven't chosen a topic yet, try a group exercise. Sit down with a few of your classmates and choose one of the following topics to brainstorm about as a group. Choose a topic that everyone in the group finds interesting, and work through exercises 1 through 4 in this practice sequence. Here are some suggestions:

- The moral obligation to vote
- The causes or consequences of poverty
- The limits of academic freedom
- Equity in education
- The popularity of _____
- The causes or consequences of teen violence
- Gender stereotypes in the media
- Linguistic diversity
- On the uses of a liberal education
- Journalism and truth

We cannot overstate the role your working thesis statement plays in helping you organize your evidence, illustrations, and quotations from other texts. Remember that the writing you do should begin with reading, identifying issues, formulating questions, and reading again before you try to state your thesis. Accept that you may have to write a few drafts of your essay before you actually decide on your thesis. An academic thesis statement is complex: It must help readers understand what is at issue, what the writer thinks is true, and what will follow in the essay itself. In this way, the thesis statement is as important for you as a writer as it is for your readers. Readers need signposts to grasp the meaning of what you write, to follow your ideas through every paragraph, and to understand how every paragraph contributes to your argument. The ability to write a good thesis statement is essential to persuading your readers to see your issue through fresh eyes — through your eyes as a writer.

6

From Finding
to Evaluating Sources

I n this chapter, we look at strategies for expanding the base of sources you work with to support your argument. The habits and skills of close reading and analysis that we have discussed and that you have practiced are essential for evaluating the sources you find. Once you find sources, you will need to assess the claims the writers make, the extent to which they provide evidence in support of those claims, and the recency, relevance, accuracy, and reliability of the evidence. The specific strategies we discuss here are those you will use to find and evaluate the sources you find in your library's electronic catalog or on the Internet. These strategies are core skills for developing a researched academic argument. They are also essential to avoid being overwhelmed by the torrent of information unleashed at the click of a computer mouse.

Finding sources is not difficult; finding and identifying good sources is challenging. You know how simple it is to look up a subject in an encyclopedia or to use a search engine like Google or Yahoo! to discover basic information on a subject or topic. Unfortunately, this kind of research will only take you so far. What if the information you find doesn't really address your question? True, we have emphasized the importance of thinking about an issue from multiple perspectives — and finding multiple perspectives is easy when you search the Internet. But how do you know whether a perspective is authoritative or trustworthy or even legitimate? Without knowing how to find and identify good sources, you can waste a lot of time reading material that will not contribute to your essay. Our goal is to help you use your time wisely to collect the sources you need to support your argument.

IDENTIFYING SOURCES

We assume that by the time you visit the library or log on to the Internet to find sources, you are not flying blind. At the very least, you will have chosen a topic to explore (something in general you want to write about), possibly identified an issue (a question or problem about the topic that is arguable), and perhaps even have a working thesis (a main claim that you want to test against other sources) in mind. Let's say you are already interested in the topic of mad cow disease. Perhaps you have identified an issue: Is mad cow disease a significant threat in the United States given the massive scale of factory farming? And maybe you have drafted a working thesis: "Although factory farming is rightly criticized for its often unsanitary practices and lapses in quality control, the danger of an epidemic of mad cow disease in the United States is minimal." The closer you are to having a working thesis, the more purposeful your research will be. With the working thesis above, instead of trying to sift through hundreds of articles about mad cow disease, you can probably home in on materials that examine mad cow disease in relation to epidemiology and agribusiness.

Once you start expanding your research, however, even a working thesis is just a place to begin. As you digest all the perspectives your research yields, you may discover that your thesis, issue, and perhaps even interest in the topic will shift significantly. Maybe you'll end up writing about factory farming rather than mad cow disease. This kind of shift happens more often than you may think. What is important is to follow what interests you and to keep in mind what is going to matter to your readers.

■ Consult Experts Who Can Guide Your Research

Before you embark on a systematic hunt for sources, you may want to consult with experts who can help guide your research. The following experts are nearer to hand and more approachable than you may think.

Your Writing Instructor.   Your first and best expert is likely to be your writing instructor, who can help you define the limits of your research and the kinds of sources that would prove most helpful. Your writing instructor can probably advise you on whether your topic is too broad or too narrow, help you identify your issue, and perhaps even point you to specific reference works or readings you should consult. He or she can also help you figure out whether you should concentrate mainly on popular or scholarly sources (for more about popular and scholarly sources, see pp. 111–12).

Librarians at Your Campus or Local Library.   In all likelihood, there is no better repository of research material than your campus or local library, and no better guide to those resources than the librarians who work there. Their job is to help you find what you need (although it's up to you to make the most of what you find). Librarians can give you a map or tour of the library, and provide you with booklets or other handouts that instruct you in the specific resources available and their uses. They can explain the catalog system and reference system. And, time allowing, most librarians are willing to give you personal help in finding and using specific sources, from books and journals to indexes and databases.

Experts in Other Fields.   Perhaps the idea for your paper originated outside your writing course, in response to a reading assigned in, say, your psychology or economics course. If so, you may want to discuss your topic or issue with the instructor in that course, who can probably point you to other readings or journals you should consult. If your topic originated outside the classroom, you can still seek out an expert in the appropriate field. If so, you may want to read the advice on interviewing we present in Chapter 11.

Manuals, Handbooks, and Dedicated Web Sites.   These exist in abundance, for general research as well as for discipline-specific research. They are especially helpful in identifying a wide range of authoritative search tools and resources, although they also offer practical advice on how to use and cite them. Indeed, your writing instructor may assign one of these manuals or handbooks, or recommend a Web site, at the beginning of the course. If not, he or she can probably point you to the one that is best suited to your research.

■ Develop a Working Knowledge of Standard Sources

As you start your hunt for sources, it helps to know broadly what kinds of sources are available and what they can help you accomplish. Table 6.1 lists a number of the resources you are likely to rely on when you are looking for material, the purpose and limitations of each type of resource, and some well-known examples. Although it may not help you pinpoint specific resources that are most appropriate for your research, the table does provide a basis for finding sources in any discipline. And familiarizing yourself with the types of resources here should make your conversations with the experts more productive.

■ Distinguish Between Primary and Secondary Sources

As you define the research task before you, you will need to understand the difference between primary and secondary sources, and figure out which you will need to answer your question. Your instructor may specify which he or she prefers, but chances are you will have to make the decision

TABLE 6.1   Standard Types of Sources for Doing Research

SOURCE	TYPE OF INFORMATION	PURPOSE	LIMITATIONS	EXAMPLES
Abstract	Brief summary of a text and the bibliographic information needed to locate the complete text	To help researchers decide whether or not they want to read the entire source		*Biological Abstracts* *Historical Abstracts* *New Testament Abstracts* *Reference Sources in History: An Introductory Guide*
Bibliography	List of works, usually by subject and author, with full publication information	For an overview of what has been published in a field and who the principal researchers in the field are	Difficult to distinguish the best sources and the most prominent researchers	*Bibliography of the History of Art* *MLA International Bibliography*
Biography	Story of an individual's life and the historical, cultural, or social context in which he or she lived	For background on a person of importance	Lengthy and reflects the author's bias	Biography and Genealogy Master Index Biography Resource Center Biography .com Literature Resource Center *Oxford Dictionary of National Biography*
Book review	Description and usually an evaluation of a recently published book	To help readers stay current with research and thought in their field and to evaluate scholarship	Reflects the reviewer's bias	ALA *Booklist* *Book Review Digest* Book Review Index *Books in Print* with Book Reviews on Disc

Source	Type of Information	Purpose	Limitations	Examples
Database, index	Large collection of citations and abstracts from books, journals, and digests, often updated daily	To give researchers access to a wide range of current sources	Lacks evaluative information	Education Resources Information Center (ERIC) Humanities International Index Index to Scientific & Technical Proceedings United Nations Bibliographic Information System
Data, statistics	Measurements derived from studies or surveys	To help researchers identify important trends (e.g., in voting, housing, residential segregation)	Requires a great deal of scrutiny and interpretation	American FactFinder American National Election Studies Current Index to Statistics Current Population Survey *Statistical Abstract of the United States*
Dictionary	Alphabetical list of words and their definitions	To explain key terms and how they are used		*Merriam-Webster's Collegiate Dictionary* *Oxford English Dictionary*
Encyclopedia	Concise articles about people, places, concepts, and things	A starting point for very basic information	Lack of in-depth information	*The CQ Researcher* Encyclopedia Brittanica Online *Information Please Almanac*

(*continued on next page*)

TABLE 6.1   *(continued)*

Source	Type of Information	Purpose	Limitations	Examples
				McGraw-Hill Encyclopedia of Science & Technology
Internet search engine	Web site that locates online information by keyword or search term	For quickly locating a broad array of current resources	Reliability of information open to question	Google Yahoo!
Newspaper, other news sources	Up-to-date information	To locate timely information	May reflect reporter's or medium's bias	America's Historical Newspapers LexisNexis Academic Newspaper Source ProQuest Historical Newspapers World News Connection
Thesaurus	Alphabetical list of words and their synonyms	For alternative search terms		*Roget's II: The New Thesaurus*

yourself. A **primary source** is a firsthand, or eyewitness, account, the kind of account you find in letters or newspapers or research reports in which the researcher explains his or her impressions of a particular phenomenon. For example, "Hidden Lessons," the Sadkers' study of gender bias in schools, is a primary source. The authors report their own experiences of the phenomenon in the classroom. A **secondary source** is an analysis of information reported in a primary source. For example, even though it may cite the Sadkers' primary research, an essay that analyzes the Sadker's findings along with other studies of gender dynamics in the classroom would be considered a secondary source.

If you were exploring issues of language diversity and the English-only movement, you would draw on both primary and secondary sources. You would be interested in researchers' firsthand (primary) accounts of language learning and use by diverse learners for examples of the challenges nonnative speakers face in learning a standard language. And you would also want to know from secondary sources what others think about whether national unity and individuality can and should coexist in communities and homes as well as in schools. You will find that you are often expected to use both primary and secondary sources in your research.

■ Distinguish Between Popular and Scholarly Sources

To determine the type of information to use, you also need to decide whether you should look for popular or scholarly books and articles. **Popular sources** of information — newspapers like *USA Today* and *The Chronicle of Higher Education,* and large-circulation magazines like *Newsweek* and *Field & Stream* — are written for a general audience. This is not to say that popular sources cannot be specialized: *The Chronicle of Higher Education* is read mostly by academics; *Field & Stream,* by people who love the outdoors. But they are written so that any educated reader can understand them. **Scholarly sources**, by contrast, are written for experts in a particular field. *The New England Journal of Medicine* may be read by people who are not physicians, but they are not the journal's primary audience. In a manner of speaking, these readers are eavesdropping on the journal's conversation of ideas; they are not expected to contribute to it (and in fact would be hard pressed to do so). The articles in scholarly journals undergo **peer review**. That is, they do not get published until they have been carefully evaluated by the author's peers, other experts in the academic conversation being conducted in the journal. Reviewers may comment at length about an article's level of research and writing, and an author may have to revise an article several times before it sees print. And if the reviewers cannot reach a consensus that the research makes an important contribution to the academic conversation, the article will not be published.

When you begin your research, you may find that popular sources provide helpful information about a topic or issue — the results of a national poll, for example. Later, however, you will want to use scholarly sources to advance your argument. You can see from Table 6.2 that popular magazines and scholarly journals can be distinguished by a number of characteristics. Does the source contain advertisements? If so, what kinds of advertisements? For commercial products? Or for academic events and resources? How do the advertisements appear? If you find ads and glossy pictures and illustrations, you are probably looking at a popular magazine. This is in contrast to the tables, charts, and diagrams you are likely to find in an education, psychology, or microbiology journal. Given your experience with rhetorical analyses, you should also be able to determine the makeup of your audience — specialists or nonspecialists — and the level of language you need to use in your writing.

TABLE 6.2   Popular Magazines Versus Scholarly Journals

Criteria	Popular Magazines	Scholarly Journals
Advertisements	Numerous full-page color ads	Few if any ads
Appearance	Eye-catching; glossy; pictures and illustrations	Plain; black-and-white graphics, tables, charts, and diagrams
Audience	General	Professors, researchers, and college students
Author	Journalists	Professionals in an academic field or discipline
Bibliography	Occasional and brief	Extensive bibliography at the end of each article; footnotes and other documentation
Content	General articles to inform, update, or introduce a contemporary issue	Research projects, methodology, and theory
Examples	*Newsweek, National Review, PC World, Psychology Today*	*International Journal of Applied Engineering Research, New England Journal of Medicine*
Language	Nontechnical, simple vocabulary	Specialized vocabulary
Publisher	Commercial publisher	Professional organization, university, research institute, or scholarly press

SOURCE: Adapted from materials at the Hessburg Library, University of Notre Dame.

Again, as you define your task for yourself, it is important to consider why you would use one source or another. Do you want facts? Opinions? News reports? Research studies? Analyses? Personal reflections? The extent to which the information can help you make your argument will serve as your basis for determining whether or not a source of information is of value.

Steps to Identifying Sources

1 **Consult experts who can guide your research.** Talk to people who can help you formulate issues and questions.

2 **Develop a working knowledge of standard sources.** Identify the different kinds of information that different types of sources provide.

3 **Distinguish between primary and secondary sources.** Decide what type of information can best help you answer your research question.

4 **Distinguish between popular and scholarly sources.** Determine what kind of information will persuade your readers.

A Practice Sequence: Identifying Sources

We would now like you to practice using some of the strategies we have discussed so far: talking with experts, deciding what sources of information you should use, and determining what types of information can best help you develop your paper and persuade your readers. We assume you have chosen a topic for your paper, identified an issue, and perhaps formulated a working thesis. If not, think back to some of the topics mentioned in earlier chapters. Have any of them piqued your interest? If not, here are five very broad topics you might work with:

- The civil rights movement
- The media and gender
- Global health
- Science and religion
- Immigration

Once you've decided on a topic, talk to experts and decide which types of sources you should use: primary or secondary, popular or scholarly. Consult with your classmates to evaluate the strengths and weaknesses of different sources of information and the appropriateness of using different types of information. Here are the steps to follow:

1 Talk to a librarian about the sources you might use to get information about your topic (for example, databases, abstracts, or bibliographies). Be sure to take notes.

2 Talk to an expert who can provide you with some ideas about current issues in the field of interest. Be sure to take detailed notes.

3 Decide whether you should use primary or secondary sources. What type of information would help you develop your argument?

4 Decide whether you should use popular or scholarly sources. What type of information would your readers find compelling?

SEARCHING FOR SOURCES

Once you've decided on the types of sources you want to use — primary or secondary, popular or scholarly — you can take steps to locate the information you need. You might begin with a tour of your university or local library, so that you know where the library keeps newspapers, government documents, books, journals, and other sources of information. Notice where the reference desk is: This is where you should head to ask a librarian for help if you get stuck. You also want to find a computer where you can log on to your library's catalog to start your search. Once you have located your sources in the library, you can begin to look through them for the information you need.

You may be tempted to rely on the Internet and a search engine like Google or Yahoo! But keep in mind that the information you retrieve from the Internet may not be trustworthy: Anyone can post his or her thoughts on a Web site. Of course, you can also find excellent scholarly sources on the Internet. (For example, Johns Hopkins University Press manages Project MUSE, a collection of 300-plus academic journals that can be accessed online through institutional subscription.) School libraries also offer efficient access to government records and other sources essential to scholarly writing.

Let's say you are about to start researching a paper on language diversity and the English-only movement. When you log on to the library's site, you find a menu of choices: Catalog, Electronic Resources, Virtual Reference Desk, and Services & Collections. (The wording may vary slightly from library to library, but the means of locating information will be the same.) When you click on Catalog, another menu of search choices appears: Keyword, Title, Author, and Subject (Figure 6.1). The hunt is on.

Search type:

Keyword Anywhere
Title begins with...
Title Keyword
Author (last name first)
Author Keyword
Subject begins with...
Subject Keyword
Call Number begins with...

More Search Options

FIGURE 6.1   Menu of Basic Search Strategies

■ Perform a Keyword Search

A **keyword** is essentially your topic: It defines the topic of your search. To run a keyword search, you can look up information by author, title, or subject. You would search by author to locate all the works a particular author has written on a subject. So, for example, if you know that Paul Lang is an expert on the consequences of the English-only movement, you might begin with an author search. You can use the title search to locate all works with a key word or phrase in the title. The search results are likely to include a number of irrelevant titles, but you should end up with a list of authors, titles, and subject headings to guide another search.

A search by subject is particularly helpful as you begin your research, while you are still formulating your thesis. You want to start by thinking of as many words as possible that relate to your topic. (A thesaurus can help you come up with different words you can use in a keyword search.) Suppose you type in the phrase "English only." A number of different sources appear on the screen, but the most promising is Paul Lang's book *The English Language Debate: One Nation, One Language?* You click on this record, and another screen appears with some valuable pieces of information, including the call number (which tells you where in the library you can find the book) and an indication that the book has a bibliography, something you can make use of once you find the book (Figure 6.2). Notice that the subject listings — *Language policy, English language – Political aspects, English-only movement, Bilingual education* — also give

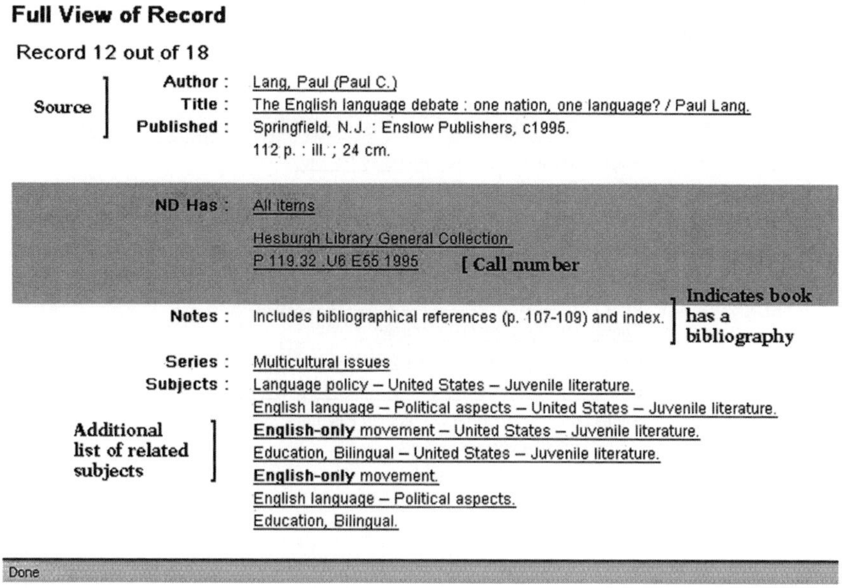

FIGURE 6.2   Full-View Bibliographic Entry

you additional keywords to use in finding relevant information. The lesson here is that it is important to generate keywords to get initial information and then to look at that information carefully for more keywords and to determine if the source has a bibliography. Even if this particular source isn't relevant, it may lead you to other sources that are.

■ Try Browsing

Browse is a headings search; it appears in the menu of choices in Figure 6.1 as "Subject begins with . . ." This type of search allows you to scroll through an alphabetical index. Some of the indexes available are the Author Index, the Title Index, and the Library of Congress Subject Headings, a subject index. Browse

- displays an alphabetical list of entries;
- shows the number of records for each entry;
- indicates whether or not there are cross-references for each entry.

What appears in the window is "Browse List: Choose a field, enter a phrase and click the 'go' button." Figure 6.3 shows the results of a preliminary browse when the words "English-only" are entered. Notice that a list of headings or titles appears on the screen. This is not a list of books, and not all of the entries are relevant. But you can use the list to determine which headings are relevant to your topic, issue, or question.

For your paper on the English-only movement, the first two headings seem relevant: *English-only debate* and *English-only movement.* A further

Browse List: Subjects

No. of Recs	Entry
	English one-act plays - [LC Authority Record]
	See: One-act plays, English
	English-only debate - [LC Authority Record]
	See: English-only movement
4	English-only movement - [LC Authority Record]
1	English-only movement — California — Case studies
1	English-only movement — Colorado
4	English-only movement — United States
1	English-only movement — United States — Juvenile literature
	English-only question - [LC Authority Record]
	See: English-only movement
1	English — Ontario — Correspondence
1	English oration

FIGURE 6.3   Preliminary Browse of "English-only" Subject Heading

click would reveal the title of a relevant book and a new list of subject headings (Figure 6.4) that differs from those of your initial search. This list gives you a new bibliography from which you can gather new leads and a list of subject headings to investigate.

We suggest that you do a keyword search first and then a browse search to home in on a subject. Especially when you don't know the exact subject, you can do a quick keyword search, retrieve many sets of results, and then begin looking at the subjects that correspond to each title. Once you find a subject that fits your needs, you can click on the direct subject (found in each bibliographic record) and execute a new search that will yield more-relevant results.

■ Perform a Journal or Newspaper Title Search

Finally, you can search by journal or newspaper title. For this kind of search, you will need exact information. You can take the name of a journal, magazine, or newspaper cited in your keyword or browse search. The journal or newspaper title search will tell you if your library subscribes to the publication and in what format — print, microform or -film, or electronic.

Suppose you want to continue your search in the *New York Times* for information on the English-only movement by searching for articles in the *New York Times*. You would run a basic search under the category "Periodicals": "Periodical Title begins with . . ." That would give you access to a limited number of articles that focused on the debate surrounding the English-only movement. To find more recent articles, you could go to the *New York Times* Web site (nytimes.com) where you could find many potentially useful listings. Recent newspaper articles will lack the depth and complexity of more scholarly studies, but they are undeniably useful in helping you establish the timeliness and relevance of your research. To see the full text of the articles, you must subscribe or pay a nominal fee,

#	Year	Author	Title
1	☐ 2006	United States.	**English as the official language : hearing before the Subcommittee on Education Reform of the Co** <Book> Click for ONLINE ACCESS (Text version:) Documents Center Owned: 1 Checked Out: 0 Display full record
2	☐ 1996	United States.	**S. 356—Language of Government Act of 1995 : hearings before the Committee on Governmental Affai** <Book> Documents Center Display full record
3	☐ 1996	United States.	**Hearing on English as the common language : hearing before the Subcommittee on Early Childhood,** <Book> Documents Center Display full record
4	☐ 1995	United States.	**Hearing on English as a common language : hearing before the Subcommittee on Early Childhood, Yo** <Book> Documents Center Display full record

Done

FIGURE 6.4   **Results of Browsing Deeper: A New List of Sources**

although you can usually preview the articles because the Web site will include a few sentences describing the content of each article.

Steps to Searching for Sources

1 **Perform a keyword search.** Choose a word or phrase that best describes your topic.

2 **Try browsing.** Search an alphabetical list by subject.

3 **Perform a journal or newspaper title search.** Find relevant citations by identifying the exact title of a journal or newspaper, or by subject.

A Practice Sequence: Searching for Sources

If you tried the practice sequence on identifying sources (p. 113), explore your topic further by practicing the types of searches discussed in this section: a keyword search; a browse; and a journal or newspaper title search (or a subject search).

EVALUATING LIBRARY SOURCES

The information you collect can and will vary in terms of its relevance and overall quality. You will want to evaluate this information as systematically as possible to be sure that you are using the most appropriate sources to develop your argument. Once you have obtained at least some of the sources you located by searching your library's catalog, you should evaluate the material as you read it. In particular, you want to evaluate the following information for each article or book:

- the author's background and credentials (What is the author's educational background? What has he or she written about in the past? Is this person an expert in the field?)
- the writer's purpose
- the topic of discussion
- the audience the writer invokes and whether you are a member of that audience
- the nature of the conversation (How have others addressed the problem?)
- what the author identifies as a misinterpretation or a gap in knowledge, or an argument that needs modifying

- what the author's own view is
- how the author supports his or her argument (that is, with primary or secondary sources, with facts or opinions)
- the accuracy of the author's evidence (can you find similar information elsewhere?)

If your topic is current and relevant, chances are your searches are going to turn up a large number of possible sources. How do you go about choosing which sources to rely on in your writing? Of course, if time were not an issue, you would read them all from start to finish. But in the real world, assignments come with due dates. To decide whether a library source merits a close reading and evaluation, begin by skimming each book or article. **Skimming** — briefly examining the material to get a sense of the information it offers — involves four steps:

1. Read the introductory sections.
2. Examine the table of contents and index.
3. Check the notes and bibliographic references.
4. Skim deeper.

■ Read the Introductory Sections

Turn to the introductory sections of the text first. Many authors use a preface or introduction to explain the themes they focus on in a book. An **abstract** serves a similar purpose, but article abstracts are usually only 250 words long. In the introductory sections, writers typically describe the issue that motivated them to write, whether or not they believe the work corrects a misconception, fills a gap, or builds on and extends the research of others. For example, in the preface to her book *Learning and Not Learning English: Latino Students in American Schools* (2001), Guadalupe Valdés explains that even after two years of language instruction, many students remain at a low level of language competence. In this passage, Valdés makes clear the purpose of her work:

> This book examines the learning of English in American schools by immigrant children. It focuses on the realities that such youngsters face in trying to acquire English in settings in which they interact exclusively with other non-English-speaking youngsters the entire school day. It is designed to fill a gap in the existing literature on non-English-background youngsters by offering a glimpse of the challenges and difficulties faced by four middle-school students enrolled in the United States for the first time when they were 12 or 13 years old. It is my purpose here to use these youngsters' lives and experiences as a lens through which to examine the policy and instructional dilemmas that now surround the education of immigrant children in this country. (p. 2)

If you were looking for sources for a paper on the English-only movement, in particular the consequences of that movement for young students, you might very well find Valdés's words compelling and decide the book is worth a closer reading.

■ Examine the Table of Contents and Index

After reading the introductory sections, it is useful to analyze the table of contents to see how much emphasis the writer gives to topics that are relevant to your own research. For example, the table of contents to *Learning and Not Learning English* includes several headings that may relate to your interest: "Educating English-Language Learners," "Challenges and Realities," "Implications for Policy and Practice," and the "Politics of Teaching English." You also should turn to the back of the book to examine the **index**, an alphabetical list of the important and likely to be repeated concepts in a book, and the page numbers on which they appear. An index also would include the names of authors cited in the book. In the index to Valdés's book, you would find references to "English-language abilities and instruction" with specific page numbers where you can read what the author has to say on this subject. You would also find references to "English-only instruction," "equal educational opportunities," and "sheltered instruction."

■ Check the Notes and Bibliographic References

Especially in the initial stages of writing, you should look closely at writers' notes and bibliographies to discern who they feel are the important voices in the field. Frequent citation of a particular researcher's work may indicate that the individual is considered to be an expert in the field you are studying. Notes usually provide brief references to people, concepts, or context; the bibliography includes a long list of related works. Mining Valdés's bibliography, you would find such titles as "Perspectives on Official English," "Language Policy in Schools," "Not Only English," "Language and Power," and "The Cultural Politics of English."

■ Skim Deeper

Skimming a book or article entails briefly looking over the elements we have discussed so far: the preface or abstract, the table of contents and the index, and the notes and bibliography. Skimming also can mean reading chapter titles, headings, and the first sentence of each paragraph to determine the relevance of a book or article.

Skimming the first chapter of *Learning and Not Learning English*, several topic sentences reveal the writer's purpose:

> "In this book, then, I examine and describe different expressions that both learning and not-learning English took among four youngsters."

> "In the chapters that follow . . ."

> "What I hope to suggest . . ."

These are the types of phrases you should look for to get a sense of what the writer is trying to accomplish and whether the writer's work will be of use to you.

If after you've taken these steps, a source still seems promising, you should read it closely, from start to finish, to determine how effectively it can help you answer your research question. Keep in mind all you've learned about critical reading. Those skills are what you'll rely on most as you work through the texts and choose the ones you should use in your paper. Remember the steps of rhetorical analysis: identifying the writer's situation, purpose, claims, and audience. And remember how to identify claims and evaluate the reasons used to support the claims: Is the evidence recent, relevant, accurate, and reliable?

Steps to Evaluating Library Sources

1 **Read the introductory section(s).** Get an overview of the researcher's argument.

2 **Examine the table of contents and index.** Consider the most relevant chapters to your topic and the list of relevant subjects.

3 **Check the notes and bibliographic references.** Identify the authors a researcher refers to (do the names come up in many different books?) and the titles of both books and articles.

4 **Skim deeper.** Read chapter titles and headings and topic sentences to determine the relevance of what you are reading for your own research.

A Practice Sequence: Evaluating Library Sources

For this exercise, we would like you to choose a specific book or article to examine in order to practice these strategies. If you are far along on your own research, use a book or article you have identified as potentially useful.

1 Read the introductory section(s). What issue is the author responding to? What is the writer's purpose? To correct a misconception? To fill a gap? To build on or extend the work of others?

2 Examine the table of contents and index. What key words or phrases are related to your own research? Which topics does the author focus on? Are you intending to give these topics similar emphasis? (Will you give more or less?)

3 Check the notes and bibliographic references. Make a list of the sources you think you want to look up for your own research. Do certain sources seem more important than others?

4 Skim deeper. What is the writer's focus? Is that focus relevant to your own topic, issue, question, or working thesis?

EVALUATING INTERNET SOURCES

Without question, the World Wide Web has revolutionized how research is conducted. It has been a particular boon to experienced researchers who have a clear sense of what they are looking for, giving them access to more information more quickly than ever before. But the Internet is rife with pitfalls for inexperienced researchers. That is, sites that appear accurate and reliable may prove not to be. The sources you find on the Internet outside your school library's catalog pose problems because anyone can post anything he or she wants. Unfortunately, there is no way to monitor the accuracy of what is published on the Internet. Although Internet sources can be useful, particularly because they are current, you must take steps to evaluate them before using information from them.

■ Evaluate the Author of the Site

If an author's name appears on a Web site, ask: Who is this person? What is this person's background? Can I contact this person?

One of our students googled "English only" and clicked on the first result, "Language Policy — English Only Movement," which eventually led her to James Crawford's Language Policy Web Site & Emporium. On the site, Crawford explains that he is "a writer and lecturer — formerly the Washington editor of *Education Week* — who specializes in the politics of language."* He notes that "since 1985, I have been reporting on the English Only movement, English Plus, bilingual education, Native American language revitalization, and language rights in the U.S.A." Between 2004 and 2006, he served as executive director of the National Association for Bilingual Education. Perhaps most important, Crawford has authored four books and a number of articles, and has testified before Congress on "Official English Legislation." From this biographical sketch, the student inferred that Crawford is credentialed to write about the English-only movement.

Less certain, however, are the credentials of the writer who penned an article titled "Should the National Anthem Be Sung in English Only?" which appeared on another Web site our student visited. Why? Because the writer's name never appears on the site. An anonymous posting is the first clue that you want to move on to a more legitimate source of information.

■ Evaluate the Organization That Supports the Site

You have probably noticed that Internet addresses usually end in with a suffix: .edu, .gov, .org, or .com. The .edu suffix means the site is associated

---

Education Week has been published since 1981 by Editorial Projects in Education, a nonprofit organization that was founded with the help of a Carnegie grant. The publication covers issues related to primary and secondary education. If you are not familiar with a publication and are uncertain about its legitimacy, you can always ask your instructor, a librarian, or another expert to vouch for its reliability.

with a university or college, which gives it credibility. The same holds true for .gov, which indicates a government agency. Both types of sites have a regulatory body that oversees their content. The suffix .org indicates a nonprofit organization; .com, a commercial organization. You will need to approach these Web sites with a degree of skepticism because you cannot be sure that they are as carefully monitored by a credentialed regulatory body. (In fact, even .edu sites may turn out to be postings by a student at a college or university.)

Our student was intrigued by James Crawford's site because he appears to be a credible source on the English-only movement. She was less sure about the reference to the Institute for Language and Education Policy. Is the institute a regulatory body that oversees what appears on the site? How long has the institute existed? Who belongs to the institute? Who sits on its board of directors? As a critical thinker, the student had to ask these questions.

■ Evaluate the Purpose of the Site

Information is never objective, so whenever you evaluate a book, an article, or a Web site, you should consider the point of view the writer or sponsor is taking. It's especially important to ask if there is a particular bias among members of the group that sponsors the site. Can you tell what the sponsors of the site advocate? Are they hoping to sell or promote a product, or to influence opinion?

Not all Web sites provide easy answers to these questions. However, James Crawford's Language Policy Web Site & Emporium is quite explicit. In fact, Crawford writes that "the site is designed to encourage discussion of language policy issues, expose misguided school 'reforms,'" and, among other goals, "promote [his] own publications." (Notice "Emporium" in the name of the site.) He is candid about his self-interest, which does raise a question about his degree of objectivity.

What about a site like Wikipedia ("The Free Encyclopedia")? The site appears to exist to convey basic information. Although the popularity of Wikipedia recommends it as a basic resource, you should approach the site with caution because it is not clear whether and how information posted on the site is regulated. It is prudent to confirm information from Wikipedia by checking on sites that are regulated more transparently rather than take Wikipedia as an authoritative source.

■ Evaluate the Information on the Site

In addition to assessing the purpose of a Web site like Wikipedia, you need to evaluate the extent to which the information is recent, accurate, and consistent with information you find in print sources and clearly regulated sites. For example, clicking on "The modern English-only movement" on Wikipedia takes you to a timeline of sorts with a number of links to other sites. But again, what is the source of this information? What is included?

What is left out? You should check further into some of these links, reading the sources cited and keeping in mind the four criteria for evaluating a claim — recency, relevance, accuracy, and reliability. Because you cannot be certain that Internet sources are reviewed or monitored, you need to be scrupulous about examining the claims they make: How much and what kind of evidence supports the writer's (or site's) argument? Can you offer counterarguments?

In the last analysis, it comes down to whether the information you find stands up to the criteria you've learned to apply as a critical reader and writer. If not, move on to other sources. In a Web-based world of information, there is no shortage of material, but you have to train yourself not to settle for the information that is most readily available if it is clearly not credible.

Steps to Evaluating Internet Sources

1 **Evaluate the author of the site.** Determine whether or not the author is an expert.

2 **Evaluate the organization that supports the site.** Find out what the organization stands for and the extent of its credibility.

3 **Evaluate the purpose of the site.** What interests are represented on the site? What is the site trying to do? Provide access to legitimate statistics and information? Advance an argument? Spread propaganda?

4 **Evaluate the information on the site.** Identify the type of information on the site and the extent to which the information is recent, relevant, accurate, and reliable.

A Practice Sequence: Evaluating Internet Sources

For this exercise, we would like you to work in groups on a common topic. The class can choose its own topic or use one of the topics we suggest on page 113. Then google the topic and agree on a Web site to analyze:

> *Group 1:* Evaluate the author of the site.
>
> *Group 2:* Evaluate the organization that supports the site.
>
> *Group 3:* Evaluate the purpose of the site.
>
> *Group 4:* Evaluate the information on the site.

Next, each group should share its evaluation. The goal is to determine the extent to which you believe you could use the information on this site in writing an academic essay.

7

From Summarizing to
Documenting Sources

When you start to use sources to build your argument, there are certain strategies for working with the words and ideas of others that you will need to learn. Often you can quote the words of an author directly; but just as often you will restate and condense the arguments of others (paraphrasing and summarizing) or make comparisons to the ideas of others in the process of developing your own argument (synthesizing). We walk you through these more challenging strategies in this chapter. We also briefly discuss plagiarism and ways to avoid it. Finally, we provide some guidelines for quoting, citing, and documenting sources in your writing.

SUMMARIES, PARAPHRASES, AND QUOTATIONS

In contrast to quotations, which involve using another writer's exact words, paraphrases and summaries are both restatements of another writer's ideas in your own words. The key difference: A paraphrase is usually about the same length as the original passage; a summary generally condenses a significantly longer text, conveying the argument not only of a few sentences, but also of entire paragraphs, essays, or books. In your own writing, you might paraphrase a few sentences or even a few paragraphs, but you certainly would not paraphrase a whole essay (much less a whole book). In constructing your arguments, however, you will often have to summarize the main points of the lengthy texts with which you are in conversation.

Both paraphrasing and summarizing are means to inquiry. That is, the act of recasting someone else's words or ideas into your own language, to suit your argument and reach your readers, forces you to think critically: What does this passage really mean? What is most important about it for my argument? How can I best present it to my readers? It requires making choices, not least of which is the best way to present the information — through paraphrase, summary, or direct quotation. In general, the following rules apply:

- *Paraphrase* when all the information in the passage is important, but the language may be difficult for your readers to understand.

- *Summarize* when you need to present only the key ideas of a passage (or essay or book) to advance your argument.

- *Quote* when the passage is so effective — so clear, so concise, so authoritative, so memorable — that you would find it difficult to improve on.

WRITING A PARAPHRASE

A **paraphrase** is a restatement of all the information in a passage in your own words, using your own sentence structure and composed with your own audience in mind to advance your argument. When you paraphrase a passage, start by identifying key words and phrases and substituting synonyms for them. A dictionary or thesaurus can help, but you may also have to reread what led up to the passage to remind yourself of the context. For example, did the writer define terms earlier that he or she uses in the passage and now expects you to know? Continue by experimenting with word order and sentence structure, combining and recombining phrases to convey what the writer says without replicating his or her style, in the best sequence for your readers. As you shuffle words and phrases, you should begin arriving at a much better understanding of what the writer is saying. By thinking critically, then, you are clarifying the passage for yourself as much as for your readers.

Let's look at a paraphrase of a passage from science fiction writer and scholar James Gunn's essay "Harry Potter as Schooldays Novel"*:

ORIGINAL PASSAGE

The situation and portrayal of Harry as an ordinary child with an extraordinary talent make him interesting. He elicits our sympathy at every turn. He plays a Cinderella-like role as the abused child of mean-spirited foster parents who favor other, less-worthy children, and also fits another fantasy role, that

---

*Gunn's essay appears in *Mapping the World of Harry Potter: An Unauthorized Exploration of the Bestselling Fantasy Series of All Time*, edited by Mercedes Lackey (Dallas: BenBella, 2006), p. 145.

of changeling. Millions of children have nursed the notion that they cannot be the offspring of such unremarkable parents; in the Harry Potter books, the metaphor is often literal truth.

PARAPHRASE

According to James Gunn, the circumstances and depiction of Harry Potter as a normal boy with special abilities captivate us by playing on our empathy. Gunn observes that, like Cinderella, Harry is scorned by his guardians, who treat him far worse than they treat his less-admirable peers. And like another fairy-tale figure, the changeling, Harry embodies the fantasies of children who refuse to believe that they were born of their undistinguished parents (146).

In this paraphrase, synonyms have replaced main words (*circumstances and depiction* for "situation and portrayal," *guardians* for "foster parents"), and the structure of the original sentences has been rearranged. But the paraphrase is about the same length as the original and says essentially the same things as Gunn's original.

Now, compare the paraphrase with this summary:

SUMMARY

James Gunn observes that Harry Potter's character is compelling because readers empathize with Harry's fairy tale–like plight as an orphan whose gifts are ignored by his foster parents (144–45).

The summary condenses the passage, conveying Gunn's main point without restating the details. Notice how both the paraphrase and the summary indicate that the ideas are James Gunn's, not the writer's — "According to James Gunn," "James Gunn observes" — and signal, with page references, where Gunn's ideas end. *It is essential that you acknowledge your sources,* a subject we come back to in our discussion of plagiarism on page 150. The point we want to make here is that borrowing from the work of others is not always intentional. Many students stumble into plagiarism, especially when they are attempting to paraphrase. Remember that it's not enough to change the words in a paraphrase; you also must change the structure of the sentences. The only sure way to protect yourself is to cite your source.

You may be wondering: If paraphrasing is so tricky, why bother? What does it add? I can see how the summary of Gunn's paragraph presents information more concisely and efficiently than the original, but the paraphrase doesn't seem to be all that different from the source, and doesn't seem to add anything to it. Why not simply quote the original or summarize it? Good questions. The answer is that you paraphrase when the ideas in a passage are important but are conveyed in language your readers may have difficulty understanding. When academics write for their peers, they draw on the specialized vocabulary of their disciplines to make their arguments. By paraphrasing, you may be helping your readers, providing a translation of sorts for those who do not speak the language.

Consider this paragraph by George Lipsitz from his academic book *Time Passages: Collective Memory and American Popular Culture*, 1990), and compare the paraphrase that follows it:

ORIGINAL PASSAGE

The transformations in behavior and collective memory fueled by the contradictions of the nineteenth century have passed through three major stages in the United States. The first involved the establishment and codification of commercialized leisure from the invention of the telegraph to the 1890s. The second involved the transition from Victorian to consumer-hedonist values between 1890 and 1945. The third and most important stage, from World War II to the present, involved extraordinary expansion in both the distribution of consumer purchasing power and in both the reach and scope of electronic mass media. The dislocations of urban renewal, suburbanization, and deindustrialization accelerated the demise of tradition in America, while the worldwide pace of change undermined stability elsewhere. The period from World War II to the present marks the final triumph of commercialized leisure, and with it an augmented crisis over the loss of connection to the past.

PARAPHRASE

Historian George Lipsitz argues that Americans' sense of the past is rooted in cultural changes dating from the 1800s, and has evolved through three stages. In the first stage, technological innovations of the nineteenth century gave rise to widespread commercial entertainment. In the second stage, dating from the 1890s to about 1945, attitudes toward the consumption of goods and services changed. Since 1945, in the third stage, increased consumer spending and the growth of the mass media have led to a crisis in which Americans find themselves cut off from their traditions and the memories that give meaning to them (12).

Notice that the paraphrase is not a word-for-word translation of the original. Instead, the writer has made choices that resulted in a slightly briefer and more accessible restatement of Lipsitz's thinking. (Although this paraphrase is shorter than the original passage, a paraphrase can also be a little longer than the original if extra words are needed to help readers understand the original.) Notice too that several specialized terms and phrases from the original passage — "the codification of commercialized leisure," "the transition from Victorian to consumer-hedonist values," "the dislocations of urban renewal, suburbanization, and deindustrialization" — have disappeared. The writer not only looked up these terms and phrases in the dictionary, but also reread the several pages that preceded the original passage to understand what Lipsitz meant by them. The paraphrase is not an improvement on the original passage — in fact, historians would probably prefer what Lipsitz wrote — but it may help readers who do not share Lipsitz's expertise understand his point without distorting his argument.

Now compare this summary to the paraphrase:

SUMMARY

Historian George Lipsitz argues that technological, social, and economic changes dating from the nineteenth century have culminated in what he calls a "crisis over the loss of connection to the past," in which Americans find themselves cut off from the memories of their traditions (12).

Which is better, the paraphrase or the summary? Neither is better or worse in and of itself. Their correctness and appropriateness depend on how the restatements are used in a given argument. That is, the decision to paraphrase or summarize depends entirely on the information you need to convey. Would the details in the paraphrase strengthen your argument? Or is a summary sufficient? In this case, if you plan to focus your argument on the causes of America's loss of cultural memory (the rise of commercial entertainment, changes in spending habits, globalization), then a paraphrase might be more helpful. But if you plan to define *loss of cultural memory,* then a summary may provide enough context for the next stage of your argument.

Steps to Writing a Paraphrase

1 Decide whether to paraphrase. If your readers don't need all the information in the passage, consider summarizing it or presenting the key points as part of a summary of a longer passage. If a passage is clear, concise, and memorable as originally written, consider quoting instead of paraphrasing. Otherwise, and especially if the original was written for an academic audience, you may want to paraphrase the original to make its substance more accessible to your readers.

2 Understand the passage. Start by identifying key words, phrases, and ideas. If necessary, reread the pages leading up to the passage, to place it in context.

3 Draft your paraphrase. Replace key words and phrases with synonyms and alternative phrases (possibly gleaned from the context provided by the surrounding text). Experiment with word order and sentence structure until the paraphrase captures your understanding of the passage, in your own language, for your readers.

4 Acknowledge your source. That's the only sure way to protect yourself from a charge of plagiarism.

A Practice Sequence: Paraphrasing

1 In one of the sources you've located in your research, find a sentence of some length and complexity, and paraphrase it. Share the original and your paraphrase of it with a classmate, and discuss the effectiveness of your restatement. Is the meaning clear to your reader? Is the paraphrase written in your own language, using your own sentence structure?

2 Repeat the activity using a short paragraph from the same source. You and your classmate may want to attempt to paraphrase the same paragraph and then compare results. What differences do you detect?

WRITING A SUMMARY

As you have seen, a **summary** condenses a body of information, presenting the key ideas and acknowledging their source. Summarizing is not an active way to make an argument, but summaries do provide a common ground of information for readers so that you can make your argument more effectively. You can summarize a paragraph, several paragraphs, an essay, a chapter in a book, or even an entire book, depending on the use you plan to make of the information in your argument.

We suggest a method of summarizing that involves (1) describing the author's key claims, (2) selecting examples to illustrate the author's argument, (3) presenting the gist of the author's argument, and (4) contextualizing what you summarize. We demonstrate these steps following the excerpt from "Debating the Civil Rights Movement: The View from the Nation," by Steven F. Lawson. Read Lawson's essay, and then follow along as we write a summary of it.

ABOUT THE READING

A professor of history at Rutgers University, Steven F. Lawson's main area of research is the history of the civil rights movement, especially the expansion of black voting rights and black politics. His major publications include *Black Ballots: Voting Rights in the South, 1944–1969* (1976); *In Pursuit of Power: Southern Blacks and Electoral Politics, 1965–1982* (1985); and *Running for Freedom: Civil Rights and Black Politics in America Since 1941* (1990). The following excerpt is from *Debating the Civil Rights Movement: 1945–1968*, where it appeared with Charles Payne's essay (see p. 139) in 1998.

STEVEN F. LAWSON

From Debating the Civil Rights Movement: The View from the Nation

The federal government played an indispensable role in shaping the fortunes of the civil rights revolution. It is impossible to understand how Blacks achieved first-class citizenship rights in the South without concentrating on what national leaders in Washington, D.C., did to influence the course of events leading to the extension of racial equality. Powerful presidents, congressional lawmakers, and members of the Supreme Court provided the legal instruments to challenge racial segregation and disfranchisement. Without their crucial support, the struggle against white supremacy in the South still would have taken place but would have lacked the power and authority to defeat state governments intent on keeping Blacks in subservient positions.

Along with national officials, the fate of the civil rights movement depended on the presence of national organizations. Groups such as the National Association for the Advancement of Colored People (NAACP), founded in 1901, drew on financial resources and legal talent from all over the country to press the case for equal rights in Congress and the courts. In similar fashion, Dr. Martin Luther King, Jr., and the Southern Christian Leadership Conference (SCLC), established in the mid-1950s, focused their attention on spotlighting white southern racism before a national audience to mobilize support for their side. Even if white Americans outside the South had wanted to ignore the plight of southern Blacks, NAACP lawyers and lobbyists, SCLC protesters, and their like-minded allies made that choice impossible. They could do what Black residents of local communities could not do alone: turn the civil rights struggle into a national cause for concern and prod the federal government into throwing its considerable power to overturn the entrenched system of white domination that had prevailed for centuries in the South.

Historical accounts that center on the national state in Washington and the operations of national organizations take on a particular narrative. The story begins with World War II, which stimulated Black protests against racism, and winds its way through the presidencies of Franklin D. Roosevelt, Harry S. Truman, Dwight D. Eisenhower, John F. Kennedy, and Lyndon B. Johnson. This period witnessed significant presidential executive orders promulgating desegregation in the military and in housing, five pieces of pioneering civil rights legislation, and landmark Supreme Court rulings toppling segregationist practices and extending the right to vote. The familiar geographical signposts of civil rights demonstrations — Montgomery, Birmingham, Selma, Albany, Little Rock — derive their greatest importance as places that molded the critical national debate on ending racial discrimination.

Overall, a nuanced account of the Black freedom struggle requires an   *4*
interconnected approach. A balanced portrayal acknowledges that Black
activists had important internal resources at their disposal, derived from
religious, economic, educational, and civic institutions, with which to
make their demands. But it does not belittle African-American creativity
and determination to conclude that given existing power relationships
heavily favoring whites, southern Blacks could not possibly eliminate
racial inequality without outside federal assistance. Furthermore, Washington officials had to protect African Americans from intimidation
and violence to allow them to carry out their challenges to discrimination. Without this room for maneuvering, civil rights advocates would
encounter insurmountable hurdles in confronting white power.

At the same time, the federal government could shape the direction of   *5*
the struggle by choosing whether and when to respond to Black protest
and by deciding on whom to bestow its support within Black communities. Although united around the struggle against white supremacy,
African Americans were not monolithic in their outlook and held various
shades of opinion on how best to combat racial bias. By allocating precious resources and conferring recognition on particular elements within
local Black communities, national leaders could accelerate or slow down
the pace of racial change.

■ Describe the Key Claims of the Text

As you read through a text with an eye to summarizing it, you want to recognize how the author develops his or her argument. You can do this by
"chunking," grouping related material together into the argument's key
claims. Here are two strategies to try:

Pay Attention to the Beginnings and Endings of Paragraphs.   Often,
underlining the first and last sentences of paragraphs will alert you to the
shape and direction of an author's argument. For example, consider the
first and last sentences of Lawson's opening paragraphs:

> *Paragraph 1:* The federal government played an indispensable role in shaping
> the fortunes of the civil rights revolution. . . . Without their crucial support,
> the struggle against white supremacy in the South still would have taken
> place but would have lacked the power and authority to defeat state govern-
> ments intent on keeping Blacks in subservient positions.

> *Paragraph 2:* Along with national officials, the fate of the civil rights movement
> depended on the presence of national organizations. . . . They could do what
> Black residents of local communities could not do alone: turn the civil rights
> struggle into a national cause for concern and prod the federal government
> into throwing its considerable power to overturn the entrenched system of
> white domination that had prevailed for centuries in the South.

Right away you can see that Lawson has introduced a topic in each paragraph — the federal government in the first, and national civil rights organizations in the second — and has indicated a connection between them. How will Lawson elaborate on this connection? What major points does he seem to be developing?

Notice the Author's Point of View and Use of Transitions. Another strategy for identifying major points is to pay attention to descriptive words and transitions. Notice the words Lawson uses to describe how the federal government advanced the cause of civil rights: *indispensable, significant, pioneering, landmark,* and *precious.* His word choices suggest an aspect of Lawson's point of view: that he highly values government action. Once you identify an author's point of view, you will start noticing contrasts and oppositions in the argument — instances where the words are less positive, or neutral, or even negative — which often are signaled by how the writer uses transitions.

For example, Lawson begins his fourth paragraph with two neutral-sounding sentences: "Overall, a nuanced account of the Black freedom struggle requires an interconnected approach. A balanced portrayal acknowledges that Black activists had important internal resources . . . with which to make their demands." However, in the next two sentences (the sentences that begin with the transition words *But* and *Furthermore*) Lawson signals that he is not neutral on what he believes was most important to the "Black freedom struggle": help from federal institutions.

These strategies can help you recognize the main points of an essay and describe them in a few sentences. For example, you could describe the key claims of Lawson's essay this way:

1. The civil rights movement would have failed without the support of the federal government.

2. Certainly the activism of national organizations with a local presence in the South was vital to making the struggle for civil rights a national cause.

3. But the primary importance of local activism was providing the executive, legislative, and judicial branches of the federal government with choices of where best to throw the weight of their support for racial equality in the nation.

■ Select Examples to Illustrate the Author's Argument

A summary should be succinct, which means you should limit the number of examples or illustrations you use. As you distill the major points of the argument, try to choose one or two examples to illustrate each major point. Here are the examples you might use to support Lawson's main points:

1. The civil rights movement would have failed without the support of the federal government. *Examples of federal support: Desegregation in*

the military and in housing; Supreme Court rulings toppling segrega-
tionist practices and extending the right to vote (para. 3).

2. Certainly the activism of national organizations with a local presence
    in the South was vital to making the struggle for civil rights a national
    cause. *Examples of activism: NAACP drew on nationwide resources to*
    press the case for equal rights; SCLC spotlighted white southern racism
    (para. 2).

3. But the primary importance of local activism was providing the execu-
    tive, legislative, and judicial branches of the federal government with
    choices of where best to throw the weight of their support for racial
    equality in the nation. *Examples of events prompting federal support:*
    Local struggles in Montgomery, Birmingham, Selma, Albany, and Little
    Rock (para. 3).

A single concrete example may be sufficient to clarify the point you want
to make about an author's argument. In his five paragraphs, Lawson cites
numerous examples to support his argument, but the most concrete, specific
instance of federal involvement appears in paragraph 3, where he cites the
series of presidential orders that mandated desegregation. This one example
may be sufficient for the purposes of a summary of Lawson's passage.

■ Present the Gist of the Author's Argument

When you present the **gist of an argument**, you are expressing the
author's central idea in a sentence or two. The gist of an argument is not
the same thing as the author's thesis statement; it is your formulation of
the author's main idea, written with the needs of your own argument in
mind. Certainly you need to understand the author's thesis when you formulate the gist. Lawson's first sentence — "The federal government played
an indispensable role in shaping the fortunes of the civil rights movement" — is his thesis statement: It clearly expresses his central idea. But in
formulating the gist of his argument, you want to do more than paraphrase
Lawson. You want to use his position to support your own. For example,
suppose you want to expand on how the three branches of the federal government each played an important role in the civil rights movement. You
would want to mention each branch when you describe the gist of Lawson's argument:

GIST

In his essay, "Debating the Civil Rights Movement: The View from the Nation,"
Steven Lawson argues that actions taken by the president, Congress, and the Supreme Court were all vital to advancing the struggle for civil rights.

Notice that this gist could not have been written based only on Lawson's
thesis statement. It reflects a knowledge of Lawson's major points and his
examples (of executive orders, legislation, and judicial rulings).

■ Contextualize What You Summarize

Your summary should help readers understand the context of the conversation:

- Who is the author?
- What is the author's expertise?
- What is the title of the work?
- Where did the work appear?
- What was the occasion of the work's publication? What prompted the author to write the work?
- What are the issues?
- Who else is taking part in the conversation, and what are their perspectives on the issues?

Again, because a summary must be concise, you must make decisions about how much of the conversation your readers need to know. If your assignment is to practice summarizing, it may be sufficient to include only information about the author and the source. However, if you are using the summary to build your own argument, you may need to provide more context. Your practice summary of Lawson's essay should mention that he is an historian and should cite the title of and page references to his essay. Depending on what else your argument needs, you may want to mention that this piece appeared as one of two essays, each of which sets the stage for a series of primary documents focusing on the roots of the civil rights movement. You also may want to include information about Lawson's audience (historians, other academics, policymakers, general readers); publication information (publisher, date); and what led to the work's publication. Was it published in response to another essay or book, or to commemorate an important event?

We compiled our notes on Lawson's essay (key claims, examples, gist, context) in a worksheet (Figure 7.1). All of our notes in the worksheet constitute a type of prewriting, our preparation for writing the summary. Creating a worksheet like this can help you track your thoughts as you plan to write a summary. (You can download a template of this worksheet at bedfordstmartins.com/frominquiry.)

FIGURE 7.1 Worksheet for Writing a Summary

Key Claims (by paragraph)	Examples (by key claim)	Gist	Context
1. The civil rights movement would have failed without the support of the federal government.	Desegregation in the military and in housing; Supreme Court rulings toppling segregationist practices and extending the right to vote (para. 3).	In his essay, "Debating the Civil Rights Movement: The View from the Nation," Steven Lawson argues that actions taken by the president, Congress, and the Supreme Court were all vital to advancing the struggle for civil rights.	Lawson is a historian. His essay "Debating the Civil Rights Movement: The View from the Nation" appeared in *Debating the Civil Rights Movement, 1945–1968* by Lawson and Charles Payne (Lanham, MD: Rowman & Littlefield, 1998). Lawson's essay runs from pages 3 to 42; under consideration are his opening paragraphs on pages 3 to 5.
2. Certainly the activism of national organizations with a local presence in the South was vital to making the struggle for civil rights a national cause.	NAACP drew on nationwide resources to press the case for equal rights; SCLC spotlighted white southern racism (para. 2).		
3. But the primary importance of local activism was providing the executive, legislative, and judicial branches of the federal government with choices of where best to throw the weight of their support for racial equality in the nation.	Local struggles in Montgomery, Birmingham, Selma, Albany, and Little Rock (para. 3).		

Here is our summary of Lawson's essay:

The gist of Lawson's argument, with supporting examples.

In his essay "Debating the Civil Rights Movement: The View from the Nation," historian Steven Lawson argues that actions taken by the president, Congress, and the Supreme Court were all vital to advancing the struggle for civil rights. Lawson's emphasis on the role the federal government played in the civil rights movement comes at a time when other historians are challenging that thinking.

Sentence places Lawson's argument in context, explaining the larger conversation.

Many of these historians believe that the success of the movement rested on activists' participation in the struggle to create change and achieve equality. Although Lawson

Lawson's main point.

recognizes the value of black activism in the South, he also makes clear that desegregation could only have occurred as a result of the federal government's intervention (3–5).

Steps to Writing a Summary

1 **Describe the key claims of the text.** To understand the shape and direction of the argument, study how paragraphs begin and end, and pay attention to the author's point of view and use of transitions. Then combine what you have learned into a few sentences describing the key claims.

2 **Select examples to illustrate the author's argument.** Find one or two examples to support each key claim. You may need only one example when you write your summary.

3 **Present the gist of the author's argument.** Describe the author's central idea in your own language with an eye to where you expect your argument to go.

4 **Contextualize what you summarize.** Cue your readers into the conversation. Who is the author? Where and when did the text appear? Why was the author writing? Who else is in the conversation?

A Practice Sequence: Summarizing

1 Summarize a text that you have been studying for research or for one of your other classes. You may want to limit yourself to an excerpt of just a few paragraphs or a few pages. Follow the four steps we've described, using a summary worksheet for notes, and write a summary of the text. Then share the excerpt and your summary of it with two of your peers. Be prepared to justify your choices in composing the summary. Do your peers agree that your summary captures what is important in the original?

2 With a classmate, choose a brief text of about three pages. Each of you use the method we describe above to write a summary of the text. Exchange your summaries and worksheets, and discuss the effectiveness of your summaries. Each of you should be prepared to discuss your choice of key claims and examples and your wording of the gist. Did you set forth the context effectively?

SYNTHESIS VERSUS SUMMARY

A **synthesis** is a discussion that forges connections between the arguments of two or more authors. Like a summary, a synthesis requires you to understand the key claims of each author's argument, including his or her use of supporting examples and evidence. Also like a summary, a synthesis requires you to present a central idea, a *gist*, to your readers. But in contrast to a summary, which explains the context of a source, a synthesis creates a context for your own argument. That is, when you write a synthesis comparing two or more sources, you demonstrate that you are aware of the larger conversation about the issue, and begin to claim your own place in that conversation. Most academic arguments begin with a synthesis that sets the stage for the argument that follows. By comparing what others have written on a given issue, writers position themselves in relation to what has come before them, acknowledging the contributions of their predecessors as they advance their own points of view.

Like a summary, a synthesis requires analysis: You have to break down arguments and categorize their parts to see how they work together. In our summary of Lawson's passage (p. 137), the parts we looked at were the key claims, the examples and evidence that supported them, the central idea (conveyed in the gist), and the context. But in a synthesis, your main purpose is not simply to report what another author has said. Rather, you must think critically about how multiple points of view intersect on your issue, and decide what those intersections mean.

Comparing different points of view prompts you to ask why they differ. It also makes you more aware of *counterarguments* — passages where claims conflict ("writer X says this, but writer Y asserts just the opposite") or at least differ ("writer X interprets this information this way, while writer Y sees it differently"). And it starts you formulating your own counterarguments: "Neither X nor Y has taken this into account. What if they had?"

Keep in mind that the purpose of a synthesis is not merely to list the similarities and differences you find in different sources, nor to assert your agreement with one source as opposed to others. Instead, it sets up your argument. Once you discover connections between texts, you have to decide what those connections mean to you and your readers. What bearing do they have on your own thinking? How can you make use of them in your argument?

WRITING A SYNTHESIS

To compose an effective synthesis, you must (1) make connections between ideas in different texts, (2) decide what those connections mean, and (3) formulate the gist of what you've read, much like you did when you wrote a summary. The difference is that in a synthesis, your gist should be a succinct statement that brings into focus not the central idea of one text but the relationship among different ideas in multiple texts.

To help you grasp the strategies of writing a synthesis, read the essays below by historians Charles Payne and Ronald Takaki which, like Steven Lawson's essay, deal with race in America. You will see that we have annotated the Payne and Takaki readings not only to comment on their ideas, but also to connect their ideas with those of Lawson. Annotating your texts in this manner is a useful first step in writing a synthesis.

Following the Payne and Takaki selections, we explain how annotating contributes to writing a synthesis. Then we show how you can use a worksheet to organize your thinking on the way to formulating the gist of your synthesis. Finally, we present our own synthesis based on the texts of Lawson, Payne, and Takaki.

ABOUT THE READING

Charles Payne is a professor of history and African American studies at Duke University, where his current research focuses on urban education, the civil rights movement, social change, and social inequality. He is the principal investigator in an ethnographic study of the most improved low-income schools in Chicago. The following selection on the civil rights movement appears with Steven Lawson's essay in *Debating the Civil Rights Movement, 1945–1968*.

CHARLES PAYNE

From Debating the Civil Rights Movement: The View from the Trenches

Point of paragraph seems to be that the language used to describe the civil rights movement distorts the actual goals and results of the movement. Is this Payne's main claim?

The [civil rights] movement continues to exercise a considerable hold on the American imagination. Our understanding of social change, our conceptions of leadership, our understanding of the possibilities of interracial cooperation are all affected by how we remember the movement. Even much of the language that we use to discuss social issues derives from movement days. We think of the movement as a movement for "civil rights" and against "segregation." Even those seemingly innocuous terms carry their own historical baggage.

1

"Segregation" became the accepted way to describe the South's racial system among both Blacks and whites. In its denotative meaning, suggesting separation between Blacks and whites, it is not a very accurate term to describe that system. The system involved plenty of integration; it just had to be on terms acceptable to white people. Indeed, the agricultural economy of the early-twentieth-century South probably afforded a good deal more interracial contact than the modern urban ghetto. "White supremacy" is a more accurate description of what the system was about. "Segregation" is the way apologists for the South liked to think of it. It implies, "We're not doing anything to Black people: we just want to keep them separate from us." It was the most innocent face one could put on that system. When we use the term as a summary term for what was going on in the South, we are unconsciously adopting the preferred euphemism of nineteenth-century white supremacist leadership.

2

Supports the claim that "movement" language hides or distorts reality.

If "segregation" is a poor way to describe the problem, "integration" may not tell us much about the solution. It is not at all clear what proportion of the Black population was interested in "integration" as a general goal. African Americans have wanted access to the privileges that white people have enjoyed and have been interested in integration as a possible avenue to those privileges, but that view is different from seeing integration as important in and of itself. Even in the 1950s, it was clear that school integration, while it would potentially put more resources into the education of Black children, also potentially meant the loss of thousands of teaching jobs for Black teachers and the destruction of schools to which Black communities often felt deeply attached, however resource-poor they were. There was also something potentially demeaning in the idea that Black children had to be sitting next to white children to learn. The first Black children to integrate the schools in a given community often found themselves in a strange position, especially if they were

3

Payne talks about African Americans' preferring "privileges" and "resources" to "integration."

Integration might lead to fewer resources — what's gained economically on the one hand would be lost on the other.

teenagers. While some Black people thought of them as endangering themselves for the greater good of the community, others saw them as turning their backs on that community and what it had to offer. It is probably safest to say that only a segment of the Black community had anything like an ideological commitment to "integration," while most Black people were willing to give it a try to see if it really did lead to a better life.

We might also ask how "civil rights" came to be commonly used as a summary term for the struggle of African Americans. In the late 1960s, after several civil rights bills had been passed, a certain part of white America seemed not to understand why Black Americans were still angry about their collective status. "You have your civil rights. Now what's the problem?" In part, the problem was that "civil rights" was always a narrow way to conceptualize the larger struggle. For African Americans, the struggle has always been about forging a decent place for themselves within this society, which has been understood to involve the thorny issues of economic participation and self-assertion as well as civil rights. Indeed, in the 1940s, Gunnar Myrdal had demonstrated that economic issues were the ones that Black Americans ranked first in priority. At the 1963 March on Washington — which was initially conceived as a march for jobs — [the Student Nonviolent Coordinating Committee's] John Lewis wanted to point out that SNCC was not sure it could support what became the Civil Rights Act of 1964 partly because it did not have an economic component:

> What is in the bill that will protect the homeless and starving people of this nation? What is there in this bill to insure the equality of a maid who earns $5.00 a week in the home of a family whose income is $100,000 a year?

One hypothesis, of course, would be that "civil rights" becomes so popular precisely because it is so narrow, precisely because it does not suggest that distribution of privilege is a part of the problem.

Is this "segment" the activists Lawson refers to? Are Lawson and Payne on the same page about the black community's not being "monolithic" (Lawson, para. 5) in its approach to civil rights?

Lawson, by contrast, emphasizes that civil rights were vital to the struggle for equality.

Payne's examples suggest that economic equality, not legal rights, is what the civil rights movement was about.

Payne's main point — that the language of civil rights is limited because it ignores economic factors.

4

5

ABOUT THE READING

Ronald Takaki is a professor of ethnic studies at the University of California, Berkeley. An adviser to the ethnic studies PhD program, he was instrumental in establishing Berkeley's American cultures graduation requirement. Takaki is a prolific writer with several award-winning books to his credit, including *A Pro-Slavery Crusade* (1971), a study of the South's ideological defense of slavery; *Violence in the Black Imagination* (1972), an examination of nineteenth-century black novelists; the Pulitzer Prize–nominated *Strangers from a Different Shore: A History of Asian Americans* (1989); and *A Different Mirror: A History of Multicultural America* (1993). The essay that follows is from a collection he edited, *Debating Diversity: Clashing Perspectives on Race and Ethnicity in America* (2002), and is his response to the Los Angeles riots of April 29, 1992.

RONALD TAKAKI

Policies: Strategies and Solutions

What dream? Civil rights? Economic equality?

What happens, asked black poet Langston Hughes, to a "dream deferred?" Does it "dry up like a raisin in the sun," or "does it explode?" An answer was hurled at America during the bloody and destructive 1992 Los Angeles race riot. On April 29, a California jury announced its not-guilty verdict in the trial of four white police officers charged with beating Rodney King, an African American who had been stopped for a traffic violation. Videotaped images of King being brutally clubbed had been repeatedly beamed across the country. The jury's shocking decision ignited an explosion of fury and violence in the inner city of Los Angeles. During the days of rage, scores of people were killed, over 2,000 injured, 12,000 arrested, and almost a billion dollars in property destroyed.

Business Week links the riots to economic inequality.

"It took a brutal beating, an unexpected jury verdict, and the sudden rampage of rioting, looting, and indiscriminate violence to bring this crisis [of urban America] back to the forefront," *Business Week* reported. "Racism surely explains some of the carnage in Los Angeles. But the day-to-day living conditions with which many of America's urban poor must contend is an equally compelling story — a tale of economic injustice." This usually conservative

1

2

The dream is not only deferred; it seems to be moving further away!

magazine pointed out that "the poverty rate, which fell as low as 11 percent in the 1970s, moved higher in the Reagan years and jumped during the last couple of years. Last year [1991], an estimated 36 million people — or about 14.7 percent of the total population — were living in poverty."

The explosion unshrouded the terrible conditions   3
and the anger of poor African Americans trapped in inner cities. "South Central Los Angeles is a Third World country," declared Krashaun Scott, a former member of the Los Angeles Crips gang. "There's a South Central in every city, in every state." Describing the desperate conditions in his community, he continued: "What we got is inadequate housing and inferior education. I wish someone would tell me the difference between Guatemala and South Central." This comparison graphically illustrated the squalor and poverty present within one of America's wealthiest and most modern cities. A gang member known as Bone commented that the recent violence was "not a riot — it was a class struggle. When Rodney King asked, 'Can we get along?' it ain't just about Rodney King. He was the lighter and it blew up."

More recent examples of economic inequality than Payne's. Decades after the civil rights movement, economic inequality remains an issue.

What exploded was anguish born of despair.   4
Plants and factories had been moved out of central Los Angeles into the suburbs, as well as across the border into Mexico and overseas to countries like South Korea. The Firestone factory, which had employed many of the parents of these young blacks, was boarded up, like a tomb. In terms of manufacturing jobs, South Central Los Angeles had become a wasteland. Many young black men and women nervously peered down the corridor of their futures and saw no possibility of full-time employment paying above minimum wage, or any jobs at all. The unemployment rate in this area was 59 percent — higher than the national rate during the Great Depression.

More examples of increasing economic inequality.

"Once again, young blacks are taking to the   5
streets to express their outrage at perceived injustice," *Newsweek* reported, "and once again, whites are fearful that The Fire Next Time will consume them." But

In a multiethnic America, do Payne's and Lawson's focus on black-and-white civil rights still apply?

this time, the magazine noticed, the situation was different from the 1965 Watts riot: "The nation is rapidly moving toward a multiethnic future in which Asians, Hispanics, Caribbean islanders, and many other immigrant groups compose a diverse and changing social mosaic that cannot be described by the old vocabulary of race relations in America." The terms "black" and "white," *Newsweek* concluded, no longer "depict the American social reality."

At the street level, African American community organizer Ted Watkins observed: "This riot was deeper and more dangerous. More ethnic groups were involved." Watkins had witnessed the Watts fury; since then, he had watched the influx of Hispanics and Koreans into South Central Los Angeles. Shortly after the terrible turmoil, social critic Richard Rodriguez reflected on the significance of these changes: "The Rodney King riots were appropriately multiracial in this multicultural capital of America. We cannot settle for black and white conclusions when one of the most important conflicts the riots revealed was the tension between Koreans and African Americans." He also noted that "the majority of looters who were arrested . . . turned out to be Hispanic."

Another comment on the new multicultural — black versus white — reality.

Out of the ashes emerged a more complex awareness of our society's racial crisis. "I think good will come of [the riot]," stated Janet Harris, a chaplain at Central Juvenile Hall. "People need to take off their rose-colored glasses," she added, "and take a hard look at what they've been doing. They've been living in invisible cages. And they've shut out that world. And maybe the world came crashing in on them and now people will be moved to do something." A black minister called for cross-cultural understanding between African Americans and Korean Americans: "If we could appreciate and affirm each other's histories, there wouldn't be generalizations and stigmatizations, and we could see that we have more in common." The fires of the riot illuminated the harsh reality of class inequality. "At first I didn't notice," a Korean shopkeeper said, "but I slowly realized the

Like Payne, Takaki emphasizes the importance of economic factors — rich versus poor.

6

7

looters were very poor. The riot happened because of the gap between rich and poor." Executive director of the Asian Pacific American Legal Center, Steward Kwoh direly predicted that "the economic polarization between the 'haves' and 'have nots' would be the main ingredient for future calamities."

During the 1992 calamity, Rodney King pleaded: "We all can get along. I mean, we're stuck here for a while. Let's try to work it out." But we find ourselves wondering, how can we get along and how can we work it out? Is "the Negro today," as Irving Kristol contends, "like the immigrant yesterday," or do "race and class" intersect in the black community? Should there be limits on immigration from Mexico, or are these immigrants scapegoats for our nation's problems? What should we do and not do about crime? What should be the future of affirmative action? Have American blacks, Nathan Glazer admits, turned out to be "not like the immigrants of yesterday"?

8

■ Make Connections Between Different Texts

The texts by Lawson, Payne, and Takaki all deal with race in America, but race is such a large topic that you cannot assume that connections are going to leap off the page at you. In fact, each text deals with a main issue that does not immediately connect with those of the others:

- Lawson emphasizes the importance of federal actions for advancing the cause of civil rights.
- Payne contends that the terms we use to talk about the civil rights movement distort its goals and accomplishments.
- Takaki writes about the 1992 Los Angeles riots, arguing that desperate economic circumstances led to an outburst of multicultural violence.

But closer reading does suggest connections. Both Lawson and Payne are writing about the civil rights movement. They seem to agree that civil rights activists were a crucial minority in the black community, but they seem to disagree on the importance of legislation versus economic factors.

Notice how our annotations call out these connections: "Payne talks about African Americans' preferring 'privileges' and 'resources' to 'integration.'" "Are Lawson and Payne on the same page about the black community's not being 'monolithic' . . . in its approach to civil rights?" "Lawson, by contrast, emphasizes that civil rights were vital to the struggle for equality." "Payne's examples suggest that economic equality, not legal rights, is what the civil rights movement was about."

Turning to Takaki, we notice that he is also writing about economic inequality and race, but in the 1990s, not the 1950s and 1960s: "More recent examples of economic inequality than Payne's. Decades after the civil rights movement, economic inequality remains an issue." But Takaki adds another factor: economic inequality in an increasingly multicultural America. Our comment: "In a multiethnic America, do Payne's and Lawson's focus on black-and-white civil rights still apply?"

With these annotations, we are starting to think critically about the ideas in the essays, speculating about what they mean. Notice, however, that not all of the annotations make connections. Some try to get at the gist of the arguments: "Is this Payne's main claim?" Some note examples: "More examples of increasing economic inequality." Some offer impromptu opinions and reactions: "The dream is not only deferred; it seems to be moving further away!" You should not expect every annotation to contribute to your synthesis. Instead, use them to record your responses and spur your thinking too.

■ Decide What Those Connections Mean

Having annotated the selections, we filled out the worksheet in Figure 7.2, making notes in the grid to help us see the three texts in relation to one another. Our worksheet included columns for

- author and source information,
- the gist of each author's arguments,
- supporting examples and illustrations,
- counterarguments,
- our own thoughts.

A worksheet like this one can help you concentrate on similarities and differences in the texts to determine what the connections between texts mean. (You can download a template for this worksheet at bedfordst martins.com/frominquiry.) Of course, you can design your own worksheet as well, tailoring it to your needs and preferences. If you want to take very detailed notes about your authors and sources, for example, you may want to have separate columns for each.

Once you start noticing connections, including points of agreement and disagreement, you can start identifying counterarguments in the readings — for example, Payne countering Lawson's position that equality can be legislated. Identifying counterarguments gives you a sense of what is at issue for each author. And determining what the authors think in relation to one another can help you realize what may be at issue for you. Suppose

	FIGURE 7.2	Worksheet for Writing a Synthesis			
AUTHOR AND SOURCE	GIST OF ARGUMENT	EXAMPLES/ ILLUSTRATIONS	COUNTER-ARGUMENTS	WHAT I THINK
Historian Steven F. Lawson, from "Debating the Civil Rights Movement: The View from the Nation"	Actions taken by the president, Congress, and the Supreme Court were all vital to advancing the struggle for civil rights.	The executive orders, the legislation, and the court decisions that promoted desegregation	Desegregation cannot be legislated. The struggle was not simply about civil rights; it also was about achieving economic equality.	I'm not convinced by Lawson's argument.
Historian Charles Payne, from "Debating the Civil Rights Movement: The View from the Trenches"	By granting African Americans their civil rights, the Supreme Court did not — and could not — guarantee access to economic equality.	Continued inequalities between rich and poor	The executive orders, legislation, and Court rulings that promoted desegregation indicate that there was some attempt to achieve equality.	An interesting argument, but I'm not sure Payne took the best approach by working with definitions.
Ethnic historian Ronald Takaki, "Policies: Strategies and Solutions"	Economic inequality persists in urban areas where ethnic minorities live in poverty and squalor.	Inadequate housing, schools, and employment	Racial equality has been legislated; so poverty is an individual problem, not a systemic one.	The multiethnic connection makes me want to look into his issue more deeply.

you are struck by Payne's argument that the term *civil rights* obscures an equally important issue in African Americans' struggle for equality: economic equality. Suppose you connect Payne's point about economic inequality with Takaki's more-recent examples of racial inequality in the areas of housing, education, and employment. Turning these ideas around in your mind, you may decide that race-based economic inequality in a multicultural society is a topic you want to explore and develop.

■ Formulate the Gist of What You've Read

Remember that your gist should bring into focus the relationship among different ideas in multiple texts. Looking at the information juxtaposed on the worksheet, you can begin to construct the gist of your synthesis:

- The first writer, Lawson, believes that the civil rights movement owes its success to the federal government.
- The second writer, Payne, believes that blacks' struggle for economic equality was not addressed by the actions of the federal government.
- The third writer, Takaki, seems to support Payne when he claims that poverty still exists for African Americans. But he broadens the issue of economic inequality, extending it to people of different racial backgrounds.

How do you formulate this information into a gist? You can use a transition word (we've used *although*) to connect the ideas these authors bring together while conveying their differences (Lawson's emphasis on civil rights versus Payne and Takaki's emphasis on economic inequality). Thus a gist about these essays might read:

GIST OF A SYNTHESIS

Although historian Steven Lawson argues that the federal government played a crucial role in extending civil rights to African Americans, other scholars, among them Charles Payne and Ronald Takaki, point out that the focus on civil rights ignored the devastating economic inequality that persists among people of color today.

Having drafted this gist, we returned to our notes on the worksheet and complete the synthesis, presenting examples and using transitions to signal the relationships among the texts and their ideas. It's a good idea in a synthesis to use at least one illustration from each author's text to support the point you want to make, and to use transition words and phrases to lead your readers through the larger argument you want to make.

Here is our brief synthesis of the three texts:

The gist of our synthesis. "Although" signals that Lawson's argument is qualified or countered later in the sentence.

Although historian Steven Lawson argues that the federal government played a crucial role in extending civil rights to African Americans, other scholars, among them Charles Payne and Ronald Takaki, point out that the focus on civil rights ignored the devastating economic inequality that persists among people of color today. Indeed, Lawson illustrates the extent to which presidents, lawmakers,

Transition: Lawson claims one thing, but ignores something else.

and judges brought an end to legal segregation, but he largely ignores the economic component of racial discrimination. Unfortunately, integration is still what Langston Hughes would call a "dream deferred" (quoted in Takaki). A historian, Charles Payne also observes that by granting

African Americans their civil rights, the federal government did not — and could not — guarantee their access to economic equality. Ronald Takaki, an ethnic historian, supports Payne's argument, demonstrating through a number of examples that economic inequality persists in urban areas where ethnic minorities live in poverty and squalor. Takaki also makes the important point that the problem of economic inequality is no longer a black-white problem, as it was during the civil rights movement. Today's multiracial society complicates our understanding of the problem of inequality and of a possible solution.

Example that backs up the gist: Both Payne and Takaki argue that the negative effects of economic inequality outweigh the positive effects of civil rights protections.

Sets up argument to follow

Writing a synthesis, like writing a summary, is principally a strategy for framing your own argument. In writing a synthesis, you are conveying to your readers how various points of view in a conversation intersect and diverge. The larger point of this exercise is to find your own issue — your own position in the conversation — and make your argument for it.

Steps to Writing a Synthesis

1 Make connections between different texts. Annotate the texts you are working with with an eye to comparing them. As you would for a summary, note major points in the texts, choose relevant examples, and formulate the gist of each text.

2 Decide what those connections mean. Fill out a worksheet to compare your notes on the different texts, track counterarguments, and record your thoughts. Decide what the similarities and differences mean to you and what they might mean to your readers.

3 Formulate the gist of what you've read. Identify an overarching idea that brings together the ideas you've noted, and write a synthesis that forges connections and makes use of the examples you've noted. Use transitions to signal the direction of your synthesis.

A Practice Sequence: Writing a Synthesis

1 Choose at least three texts you expect to work with in your researched argument, read them closely, and fill out a synthesis worksheet to organize your information about them. With the worksheet in hand, write down any similarities and differences you find. Are the ideas weighted in one direction or the other, as they are in our readings? On what points do the authors agree? Formulate the gist of the works, and then write the synthesis, incorporating examples and using transitions to signal the relationships among ideas and authors. Does the synthesis suggest the direction of your argument?

2 As a class, choose three or more texts to synthesize. Then break up into small groups, each group working with the same texts. Within each group, work through the steps in synthesizing. One person in each group should take notes in a format like our worksheet. After you complete the worksheet, identify similarities and differences among the ideas. Are they weighted in one direction or the other? Are there points of agreement among the authors? Your answers to these questions should help you formulate the gist of the synthesis. After you formulate the gist, share what you've written with the other groups. Be sure to explain how you arrived at the gist you formulated. Did each group construct the same gist? What was similar? What was different?

AVOIDING PLAGIARISM

Whether you paraphrase, summarize, or synthesize, it is essential that you acknowledge your sources. Academic writing requires you to use and document sources appropriately, making clear to readers the boundaries between your words and ideas and those of other writers. Setting boundaries can be a challenge because so much of academic writing involves interweaving the ideas of others into your own argument. Still, no matter how difficult, you must acknowledge your sources. It's only fair. Imagine how you would feel if you were reading a text and discovered that the writer had incorporated a passage from one of your papers, something you slaved over, without giving you credit. You would see yourself as a victim of plagiarism, and you would be justified in feeling very angry indeed.

In fact, **plagiarism** — the unacknowledged use of another's work, passed off as one's own — is a most serious breach of academic integrity, and colleges and universities deal with it severely. If you are caught plagiarizing in your work for a class, you can expect to fail that class and may even be expelled from your college or university. Furthermore, although a failing grade on a paper or in a course, honestly come by, is unlikely to deter an employer from hiring you, the stigma of plagiarism can come back to haunt you when you apply for a job. Any violation of the principles set forth in Table 7.1 could have serious consequences for your academic and professional career.

Even if you know what plagiarism is and wouldn't think about doing it, you can still plagiarize unintentionally. Again, paraphrasing can be especially tricky: Attempting to restate a passage without using the original words and sentence structure is, to a certain extent, an invitation to plagiarism. If you remember that your paper is *your* argument, and understand

TABLE 7.1   Principles Governing Plagiarism

1. All written work submitted for any purpose is accepted as your own work. This means it must not have been written even in part by another person.

2. The wording of any written work you submit is assumed to be your own. This means you must not submit work that has been copied, wholly or partially, from a book, article, essay, newspaper, another student's paper or notebook, or any other source. Another writer's phrases, sentences, or paragraphs can be included only if they are presented as quotations and the source acknowledged.

3. The ideas expressed in a paper or report are assumed to originate with you, the writer. Written work that paraphrases a source without acknowledgment must not be submitted for credit. Ideas from the work of others can be incorporated in your work as starting points, governing issues, illustrations, and the like, but in every instance the source must be cited.

4. Remember that any online materials you use to gather information for a paper are also governed by the rules for avoiding plagiarism. You need to learn to cite electronic sources as well as printed and other sources.

5. You may correct and revise your writing with the aid of reference books. You also may discuss your writing with your peers in a writing group or with peer tutors at your campus writing center. However, you may not submit writing that has been revised substantially by another person.

that any paraphrasing, summarizing, or synthesizing should reflect *your* voice and style, you will be less likely to have problems with plagiarism. Your paper should sound like you. And, again, the surest way to protect yourself is to cite your sources.

Steps to Avoiding Plagiarism

1 **Always cite the source.** Signal that you are paraphrasing, summarizing, or synthesizing by identifying your source at the outset — "According to James Gunn," "Steven Lawson argues," "Charles Payne and Ronald Takaki . . . point out." And if possible, indicate the end of the paraphrase, summary, or synthesis with relevant page references to the source. If you cite a source several times in your paper, don't assume your first citation has you covered; acknowledge the source as often as you use it.

2 **Provide a full citation in your bibliography.** It's not enough to cite a source in your paper; you must also provide a full citation for every source you use in the list of sources at the end of your paper.

INTEGRATING QUOTATIONS INTO YOUR WRITING

When you integrate quotations into your writing, bear in mind a piece of advice we've given you about writing the rest of your paper: Take your readers by the hand and lead them step-by-step. When you quote other authors to develop your argument — using their words to support your thinking or to address a counterargument — discuss and analyze the words you quote, showing readers how the specific language of each quotation contributes to the larger point you are making in your essay. When you integrate quotations, then, there are three basic things you want to do: (1) Take an active stance, (2) explain the quotations, and (3) attach short quotations to your own sentences.

■ Take an Active Stance

Critical reading demands that you adopt an active stance toward what you read — that you raise questions in response to a text that is telling you not only what the author thinks but also what you should think. You should be no less active when you are using other authors' texts to develop your own argument. Certainly taking an active stance when you are quoting means knowing when to quote. Don't use a quote when a paraphrase or summary can convey the information from a source more effectively and efficiently. (Don't forget to acknowledge your source!) More important, however, it means you have to make fair and wise decisions about what and how much you should quote to make your researched argument:

- It's not fair (or wise) to quote selectively — choosing only passages that support your argument — when you know you are distorting or misrepresenting the argument of the writer you are quoting. Ideally, you want to demonstrate that you understand the writer's argument and that you want to make evenhanded use of it in your own argument, whether you agree or disagree, in whole or in part, with what the other writer has written.

- It's not wise (or fair to yourself) to flesh out your paper with an overwhelming number of quotations that could make readers think that you either do not know your topic well or do not have your own ideas. Don't allow quotations to take over your paragraphs and shape your own words about the topic. In structuring your paragraphs, remember that your ideas and argument — your thesis — are what is most important to the readers and what justifies a quotation's being included at all.

Above all, taking an active stance when you quote means taking control of your own writing. You want to establish your own argument and guide your readers through it, allowing sources to contribute to but not dictate its direction. You are responsible for plotting and pacing your essay. Always keep in mind that your thesis is the skewer that runs through every paragraph, holding all of the ideas together. When you use quotations, then, you must organize them to enrich, substantiate, illustrate, and help support your central claim or thesis.

■ Explain the Quotations

When you quote an author to support or advance your argument, you must be sure that readers know exactly what they should learn from the quotation. Read the excerpt below from one student's early draft of an argument that focuses on the value of service learning in high schools as a means for creating change. The student reviews several relevant studies — but then simply drops in a quotation, expecting readers to know what they should pay attention to in the quotation.

> Other research emphasizes community service as an integral and integrated part of moral identity. In this understanding, community service activities are not isolated events but are woven into the context of students' everyday lives (Yates, 1995); the personal, the moral, and the civic become "inseparable" (Colby, Ehrlich, Beaumont, & Stephens, 2003, p. 15). In their study of minority high schoolers at an urban Catholic school who volunteered at a soup kitchen for the homeless as part of a class assignment, Youniss and Yates (1999) found that the students underwent significant identity changes, coming to perceive themselves as lifelong activists. The researchers' findings are worth quoting at length here because they depict the dramatic nature of the students' changed viewpoints. Youniss and Yates write:
>
>> Many students abandoned an initially negative view of homeless people and a disinterest in homelessness by gaining appreciation of the humanity of homeless people and by showing concern for homelessness in relation to poverty, job training, low-cost housing, prison reform, drug and alcohol rehabilitation, care for the mentally ill, quality urban education, and welfare policy. Several students also altered perceptions of themselves from politically impotent teenagers to involved citizens who now and in the future could use their talent and power to correct social problems. They projected articulated pictures of themselves as adult citizens who could affect housing policies, education for minorities, and government programs within a clear framework of social justice. (p. 362)

The student's introduction to the quoted passage provided a rationale for quoting Youniss and Yates at length; but it did not help her readers see what was important about the research in relation to the student's own argument. Our student needed to frame the quotation for her readers. Instead of introducing the quotation by saying "Youniss and Yates write," she should have made explicit that the study supports the argument that community service can create change. A more appropriate frame for the quotation might have been a summary like this one:

Frames the quotation, explaining it in the context of the student's argument.

One particular study underscores my argument that service can motivate change, particularly when that change begins within the students who are involved in service. Youniss and Yates (1999) write that over the course of their research, the students developed both an "appreciation of the humanity of homeless people" and a sense that they would someday be able to "use their talent and power to correct social problems" (p. 362).

In the following example, notice that the student writer uses Derrick Bell's text to say something about the ways the effects of desegregation have been muted by political manipulation.* The writer shapes what he wants readers to focus on, leaving nothing to chance.

The effectiveness with which the meaning of *Brown v. Board of Education* has been manipulated, Derrick Bell argues, is also evidenced by the way in which such thinking has actually been embraced by minority groups. Bell claims that a black school board member's asking "But of what value is it to teach black children to read in all-black schools?" indicates this unthinking acceptance that whiteness is an essential ingredient to effective schooling for blacks. Bell continues:

> The assumption that even the attaining of academic skills is worthless unless those skills are acquired in the presence of white students illustrates dramatically how a legal precedent, namely the Supreme Court's decision in *Brown v. Board of Education*, has been so constricted even by advocates that its goal — equal educational opportunity — is rendered inaccessible, even unwanted, unless it can be obtained through racial balancing of the school population. (p. 255)

Bell's argument is extremely compelling, particularly when one considers the extent to which "racial balancing" has come to be defined in terms of large white majority populations and small nonwhite minority populations.

Notice how the student's last sentence helps readers understand what the quoted material suggests and why it's important by embedding and extending Bell's notion of racial balancing into his explanation.

In sum, you should always explain the information that you quote so that your readers can see how the quotation relates to your own argument. ("Take your readers by the hand . . . ") As you read other people's writing, keep an eye open to the ways writers introduce and explain the sources they use to build their arguments.

---

*This quotation is from Derrick Bell's *Silent Covenants: Brown v. Board of Education and the Unfulfilled Hopes for Racial Reform* (Oxford UP, 2005).

▪ Attach Short Quotations to Your Own Sentences

The quotations we discussed above are **block quotations,** lengthy quotations, generally of more than five lines, that are set off from the text of a paper with indention. Make shorter quotations part of your own sentences so your readers can understand how the quotations connect to your argument and can follow along easily. How do you make a quotation part of your own sentences? There are two main methods:

- Integrate quotations within the grammar of your writing.
- Attach quotations with punctuation.

If possible, use both to make your integration of quotations more interesting and varied.

Integrate Quotations within the Grammar of a Sentence.   When you integrate a quotation into a sentence, the quotation must make grammatical sense and read as if it is part of the sentence:

> Fine, Weiss, and Powell (1998) expanded upon what others call "equal status contact theory" by using a "framework that draws on three traditionally independent literatures — those on community, difference, and democracy" (p. 37).

If you add words to the quotation, use square brackets around them to let readers know that the words are not original to the quotation:

> Smith and Wellner (2002) asserted that they "are not alone [in believing] that the facts have been incorrectly interpreted by Mancini" (p. 24).

If you omit any words in the middle of a quotation, use an **ellipsis,** three periods with spaces between them, to indicate the omission:

> Riquelme argues that "Eliot tries . . . to provide a definition by negations, which he also turns into positive terms that are meant to correct misconceptions" (156).

If you omit a sentence or more, make sure to put a period before the ellipsis points:

> Eagleton writes, "What Eliot was in fact assaulting was the whole ideology of middle-class liberalism. . . . Eliot's own solution is an extreme right-wing authoritarianism: men and women must sacrifice their petty 'personalities' and opinions to an impersonal order" (39).

Whatever you add (using square brackets) or omit (using ellipses), the sentence must read grammatically. And, of course, your additions and omissions must not distort the author's meaning.

Attach Quotations with Punctuation.   You also can attach a quotation to a sentence by using punctuation. For example, this passage attaches the run-in quotation with a colon:

> For these researchers, there needs to be recognition of differences in a way that will include and accept all students. Specifically, they ask: "Within multiracial settings,

when are young people invited to discuss, voice, critique, and re-view the very notions of race that feel so fixed, so hierarchical, so damaging, and so accepted in the broader culture?" (p. 132).

In conclusion, if you don't connect quotations to your argument, your readers may not understand why you've included them. You need to explain some significant point that each quotation reveals as you introduce or end it. This strategy helps readers know what to pay attention to in a quotation, particularly if the quotation is lengthy.

Steps to Integrating Quotations into Your Writing

1 **Take an active stance.** Your sources should contribute to your argument, not dictate its direction.

2 **Explain the quotations.** Explain what you quote so your readers understand how each quotation relates to your argument.

3 **Attach short quotations to your own sentences.** Integrate short quotations within the grammar of your own sentences, or attach them with appropriate punctuation.

A Practice Sequence: Integrating Quotations

1 Using several of the sources you are working with in developing your paper, try integrating quotations into your essay. Be sure you are controlling your sources. Carefully read the paragraphs where you've used quotations. Will your readers clearly understand why the quotations are there — the points the quotations support? Do the sentences with quotations read smoothly? Are they grammatically correct?

2 Working in a small group, agree on a substantial paragraph or passage (from this book or some other source) to write about. Each member should read the passage and take a position on the ideas, and then draft a page that quotes the passage using both strategies for integrating these quotations. Compare what you've written, examining similarities and differences in the use of quotations.

CITING AND DOCUMENTING SOURCES

You must provide a brief citation in the text of your paper for every quotation or idea taken from another writer, and you must list complete information at the end of your paper for the sources you use. This information is essential for readers who want to read the source to understand a quotation or idea in its original context. How you cite sources in the body of your paper and document them at the end of your paper varies from discipline to discipline, so it is important to ask your instructor what documentation style he or she prefers.

Even within academic disciplines, documentation styles can vary. Specific academic journals within disciplines will sometimes have their own set of style guidelines. The important thing is to adhere faithfully to your chosen (or assigned) style throughout your paper, observing all the niceties of form prescribed by the style. You may have noticed small differences in the citation styles in the examples throughout this chapter. That's because the examples are taken from the work of a variety of writers, both professionals and students, who had to conform to the documentation requirements of their publication or of their teachers.

Here we briefly introduce two common documentation styles that may be useful in your college career: the Modern Language Association (MLA) for listing bibliographic information in the humanities, and the American Psychological Association (APA), in the social sciences. The information is basic, for use when you begin drafting your paper. In the final stages of writing, you should consult either the *MLA Handbook for Writers of Research Papers* (7th ed.) or the *Publication Manual of the American Psychological Association* (6th ed.). Although you'll need the manuals for complete style information, both the MLA (http://www.mlahandbook.org) and the APA (http://www.apastyle.org) maintain Web sites for frequently asked questions. Again, before you start your research, check with your instructor to find out whether you should use either of these styles or if there's another style he or she prefers.

MLA and APA styles have many similarities — for example, both require short citations in the body of an essay linked to a list of sources at the end of the essay. But it is their differences, though subtle, that are crucial. To a great extent, these differences reflect the assumptions writers in the humanities and in the social sciences bring to working with sources. In particular, you should understand each style's treatment of the source's author, publication date, and page numbers in in-text citations, and verb use in referring to sources.

Author.   MLA style requires you give the author's full name on first mention in your paper; APA style uses last names throughout. The humanities emphasize "the human element" — the individual as creative force — so the MLA uses the complete name at first mention to imply the author's importance. Because the social sciences emphasize the primacy of data in studies of human activity, in APA style last names are deemed sufficient.

Publication Date.   In-text citations using MLA style leave out the date of publication. The assumption: that the insights of the past may be as useful as those of the present. By contrast, APA style gives the date of the study after the author's name, reflecting a belief in the progress of research, that recent findings may supersede earlier ones.

Page Numbers.   The MLA requires page numbers be included with paraphrases and summaries as well as quotations (the written text is so important, a reader may want to check the exact language of the original). By contrast, the APA requires attribution but not page numbers for paraphrases and summaries (it is the findings, not how they are described, that are most important).

Verb Use.   The MLA uses the present tense of verbs ("Writer X claims") to introduce cited material, assuming the cited text's timelessness, whether written last week or centuries ago. By contrast, the verbs introducing citations in APA style acknowledge the "pastness" of research ("Writer X claimed" or "Writer Y has claimed") on the assumption that new data may emerge to challenge older research.

Although it is useful to understand that different citation styles reflect different attitudes toward inquiry and research in different disciplines, for the purposes of your writing it is mainly important to know the style you have to follow in your paper, and to stick to it scrupulously. Whenever you consult a source — even if you don't end up using it in your paper — write down complete citation information so you can cite it fully and accurately if you need to. Table 7.2 shows the basic information needed to cite books, chapters in books, journal articles, and online sources. You also should note any other information that could be relevant — a translator's name,

TABLE 7.2   Basic Information Needed for Citing Sources

BOOKS	CHAPTERS IN BOOKS	JOURNAL ARTICLES	ONLINE SOURCES
Author(s) or editor(s)	Author(s)	Author(s)	Author(s)
Title and subtitle	Chapter title and subtitle	Article title and subtitle	Document title and subtitle
Edition information	Book editor(s)	Journal title	Print publication information, if any
Place of publication	Book title	Volume and series number	Site sponsor
Publisher	Edition information	Date of publication	Site title
Year of publication	Place of publication	Page numbers	Year of publication
	Publisher		Date accessed
	Year of publication		URL
	Page numbers		

for example, or a series title and editor. Ideally, you want to be able to cite a source fully without having to go back to it to get more information.

■ The Basics of MLA Style

In-Text Citations.   In MLA style, you must provide a brief citation in the body of your essay (1) when you quote directly from a source, (2) when you paraphrase or summarize what someone else has written, and (3) even when you use an idea or concept that originated with someone else. In the excerpt below, the citation tells readers that the student writer's argument about the evolution of Ebonics is rooted in a well-established source of information. Because the writer does not mention the author in the paraphrase of her source in the text, she gives the author's name in the citation:

> The evolution of US Ebonics can be traced from the year 1557 to the present day. In times of great oppression, such as the beginning of the slave codes in 1661, the language of the black community was at its most "ebonified" levels; whereas, in times of racial progress, for example during the abolitionist movement, the language as a source of community identity was forsaken for greater assimilation (Smitherman 119).

The parenthetical citation refers to page 119 of Geneva Smitherman's book *Talkin and Testifyin: The Language of Black America* (1977). Smitherman is a recognized authority on Ebonics. Had the student mentioned Smitherman's name in her introduction to the paraphrase, she would not have had to repeat it in the citation. Notice that there is no punctuation within the parentheses and no *p.* before the page number. Also notice that the citation is considered part of the sentence in which it appears, so the period ending the sentence follows the closing parenthesis.

By contrast, in the example that follows, the student quotes directly from Richard Rodriguez's book *Hunger of Memory: The Education of Richard Rodriguez* (1982):

> Many minority cultures in today's society feel that it is more important to maintain cultural bonds than to extend themselves into the larger community. People who do not speak English may feel a similar sense of community and consequently lose some of the individuality and cultural ties that come with speaking their native or home language. This shared language within a home or community also adds to the unity of the community. Richard Rodriguez attests to this fact in his essay "Aria." He then goes on to say that "it is not healthy to distinguish public words from private sounds so easily" (183).

Because the student mentions Rodriguez in her text right before the quotation ("Richard Rodriguez attests"), she does not need to include his name in the citation; the page number is sufficient.

Works Cited.   At the end of your researched essay, and starting on a new page, you must provide a list of works cited, a list of all the sources you have used (leaving out sources you consulted but did not cite). Entries should be listed alphabetically by author's last name or by title if no author is identified. Figure 7.3 is a sample works cited page in MLA style that illustrates a few (very few) of the basic types of documentation.

Steps to Compiling an MLA List of Works Cited

1 Begin your list of works cited on a new page at the end of your paper.

2 Put your last name and page number in the upper-right corner.

3 Double-space throughout.

4 Center the heading ("Works Cited") on the page.

5 Arrange the list of sources alphabetically by author's last name or by title if no author is identified.

6 Begin the first line of each source flush left; second and subsequent lines should be indented 1/2 inch.

7 Invert the author's name, last name first. In the case of multiple authors, only the first author's name is inverted.

8 Italicize the titles of books, journals, magazines, and newspapers. Put the titles of book chapters and articles in quotation marks. Capitalize each word in all titles except for articles, short prepositions, and conjunctions.

9 For books, list the place of publication and the name of the publisher, and the year of publication. For chapters, list the editors of the book and the book title, and the publication information. For articles, list the journal title, volume and series numbers, and the date of publication.

10 List the relevant page numbers.

11 List the medium of publication.

The steps outlined here for compiling a list of works cited apply to printed sources. MLA formats for citing online sources vary, but this is an example of the basic format:

Author. "Document Title." *Name of Site.* Site Sponsor, Date posted/revised.
    Medium of publication. Date you accessed the site.

FIGURE 7.3   Sample List of Works Cited, MLA Format

Eck 10

Works Cited

Gutierrez, Kris. "'English for the Children': The New Literacy of the Old
World Order." *Bilingual Research Journal,* in press. Print.

Online article,   "History of Bilingual Education." *Rethinking Schools*. Rethinking Schools,
no author   2010. Web. Retrieved on 8 Apr. 1998.

Lanehart, Sonja L. "African American Vernacular English and Education."
Article in a   *Journal of English Linguistics* 26 (1998): 122–37. Print.
scholarly   Pompa, Delia. "Bilingual Success: Why Two-Language Education Is Critical
journal   for Latinos." *Hispanic* 13 (1996): 96. Print.
Article in a
magazine   Rawls, John. *Political Liberalism*. New York: Columbia UP, 1993.

---. "Social Unity and Primary Goods." *Utilitarianism and Beyond*. Ed.
Essay in an   Amartya Sen and Bernard Williams. Cambridge, Eng.: Cambridge UP,
edited collec-   1982. 159–85. Print.
tion; second
source by   Rodriguez, Richard. "Aria." *Hunger of Memory: The Education of Richard*
same writer   *Rodriguez*. New York: Bantam, 1982. 11–40. Print.

Schrag, Peter. "Language Barrier." *New Republic* 9 Mar. 1998: 14–15. Print.

Smitherman, Geneva. Talkin and Testifyin: *The Language of Black America*.
A book   Detroit: Wayne State UP, 1977. Print.

Willis, Arlette. "Reading the World of School Literacy: Contextualizing the
Experience of a Young American Male." *Harvard Educational Review*.
65 (1996): 30–49. Print.

Things to remember:

- Invert the author's name or the first author's name.
- Italicize the name of the site.
- MLA accepts both day-month-year and month-day-year formats for dates. Just be consistent.
- If the site sponsor — usually an institution or organization — isn't clear, check the copyright notice at the bottom of the Web page.
- If there is no sponsor, use the abbreviation "n.p." for "no publisher."
- If there is no date of publication, use "n.d." for "no date."

In addition to online sources, you will likely use other nonprint sources in researching your papers. Our students, for example, regularly analyze films, recordings, television and radio programs, paintings, and photographs. For details on how to format these sources, consult the *MLA Handbook* or go to Purdue University's Online Writing Lab (OWL) site (http://owl.english.purdue.edu/owl/resource/557/01/).

■ The Basics of APA Style

In-Text Citations.   In APA style, in-text citations identify the author or authors of a source and the publication date. If the author or authors are mentioned in the text, only the publication date is needed:

> Feingold (1992) documented the fact that males perform much better than females do in math and science and other "masculine" areas.

Notice that the in-text citation does not include a page number. Because Feingold is only cited, not quoted, no page reference is necessary. If the source is quoted directly, a page number is added in parentheses following the quote:

> Feingold (1992) argued that "men scored significantly higher than women in situations designed to test aptitude in mathematics and hard sciences" (p. 92).

APA style uses the abbreviation *p.* or *pp.* before page numbers, which MLA style does not. If the author is not identified with a signal phrase, the name, year, and page number would be noted parenthetically after the quotation:

> One study found that "men scored significantly higher than women in situations designed to test aptitude in mathematics and hard sciences" (Feingold, 1992, p. 92).

Many studies in the social sciences have multiple authors. In a work with two authors, cite both authors every time:

> Dlugos and Friedlander (2000) wrote that "sustaining passionate commitment to work as a psychotherapist reflects passionate commitment in other areas of life" (p. 298).

Here, too, if you do not identify the authors in a signal phrase, include their names, the year the source was published, and the relevant page number parenthetically after the quotation — but use an ampersand (&) instead of the word *and* between the authors' names:

> Some believe that "sustaining passionate commitment to work as a psychotherapist reflects passionate commitment in other areas of life" (Dlugos & Friedlander, 2000, p. 298).

Use the same principles the first time you cite a work with three to five authors:

Booth-Butterfield, Anderson, and Williams (2000) tested . . .
(Booth-Butterfield, Anderson, & Williams, 2000, p. 5)

Thereafter, you can use the name of the first author followed by the abbreviation *et al.* (Latin for "and others") in roman type:

Booth-Butterfield et al. (2000) tested . . .
(Booth-Butterfield et al., 2000, p. 5)

For a work with six or more authors, use et al. from the first mention.

These are only some of the most basic examples of APA in-text citation. Consult the APA manual for other guidelines.

References.   APA style, like MLA style, requires a separate list of sources at the end of a research paper. This list is called "References," not "Works Cited." The list of references starts on a new page at the end of your paper and lists sources alphabetically by author (or title if no author is identified). Figure 7.4 shows a sample list of references with sources cited in APA style.

Steps to Compiling an APA List of References

1 Begin your list of references on a new page at the end of your paper.

2 Put a shortened version of the paper's title (not your last name) and the page number in the upper-right corner.

3 Double-space throughout.

4 Center the heading ("References") on the page.

5 Arrange the list of sources alphabetically by author's last name or by title if no author is identified.

6 Begin the first line of each source flush left; second and subsequent lines should be indented ½ inch.

7 Invert all authors' names. If a source has more than one author, use an ampersand (not *and*) before the last name.

8 Insert the date in parentheses after the last author's name.

9 Italicize the titles of books, capitalizing only the first letter of the title and subtitle and proper nouns.

10 Follow the same capitalization for the titles of book chapters and articles. Do not use quotation marks around chapter and article titles.

11 Italicize the titles of journals, magazines, and newspapers, capitalizing the initial letters of all key words.

 For books, list the place of publication and the name of the pub-
lisher. For chapters, list the book editor(s), the book title, the rele-
vant page numbers, and the place of publication and the name of
the publisher. For articles, list the journal title, the volume number, and the relevant pages.

FIGURE 7.4   Sample References, APA Format

Gender and Teaching 15

References

Campbell, R. J. (1969). Co-education: Attitudes and self-concepts of
girls at three schools. *British Journal of Educational Psychology,
39,* 87.

Journal article, seven authors
Coleman, J., Campbell, E., Hobson, C., McPartland, J., Mood, A.,
Weinfeld, F., & York, R. (1966). *Equality of educational opportu-
nity (The Coleman report).* Washington, DC: U.S. Government
Printing Office.

Feingold, A. (1992, Spring). Sex differences in variability in intellectual abilities: A new look at an old controversy. *Review of Educational Research, 62,* 61–84.

Online source
Haig, P. (2004). K-12 single-sex education: What does the research
say? Retrieved from
http://www.ericdigests.org/2001-2/sex.html

Hallinan, M. T. (1994). Tracking: From theory to practice. *Sociology of
Education, 67,* 79–84.

Hanson, S. L. (1994). Lost talent: Unrealized educational aspirations
and expectations among U.S. youth. *Sociology of Education, 67,*
159–183.

Jovanovic, J., & King, S. S. (1998, Fall). Boys and girls in the
performance-based science classroom: Who's doing the performing? *American Educational Research Journal, 35,* 477–496.

Lee, V. E., & Marks, H. M. (1990). Sustained effects of the single-sex
secondary school experience on attitudes, behaviors, and values
in college. *Journal of Educational Psychology, 82,* 578–592.

Mickelson, R. A. (1989). Why does Jane read and write so well? The
anomaly of women's achievement. *Sociology of Education, 62,*
47–63.

Scholarly book
Rosenberg, M. (1965). *Society and the adolescent self-image.* Princeton, NJ: Princeton University Press.

Schneider, F. W., & Coutts, L. M. (1982). The high school environment: A comparison of coeducational and single-sex schools.
Journal of Educational Psychology, 74, 898–906.

*Essay
in edited
collection*

Spade, J. Z. (2000). Gender education in the United States. In J. H.
Ballantine & J. Z. Spade (Eds.). (2001). *Schools and society: A
sociological approach to education* (pp. 270–278). Belmont, CA:
Wadsworth/Thomson Learning.

Streitmatter, J. L. (1999). *For girls ONLY: Making a case for single-sex
schooling.* Albany: State University of New York Press.

*Microfilm
source*

Winslow, M. A. (1995). *Where the boys are: The educational aspirations and future expectations of working-class girls in an all-
female high school.* Ann Arbor, MI: University Microfilms,
Dissertation Services. Internet.

The *APA Manual* is your best resource for formatting online sources, but here is an example of a basic reference to an online source:

Author. (Date posted/revised). Document title. *Name of site.* Retrieved day-month-
year, from URL

- If no author is identified, alphabetize the entry under the document title followed by the date in parentheses.
- Capitalize an online document title like an article title, and don't enclose it in quotes.
- Use the same initial-capital-only style for the site name, but italicize it.
- Notice that there is no end punctuation after the URL.
- APA style asks you to break lengthy URLs after a slash or before a period, again being sure that your program doesn't insert a hyphen at the line break.

The *APA Manual* is also your best resource for formatting references to other nonprint sources. You should know that certain nonprint sources you are likely to rely on in your research in the social sciences — interviews and focus groups, for example — do not have to be included in your list of references. Instead you would cite the person you interviewed or the focus group you conducted in the text of your paper. For example:

(Long, J., interview, April 7, 2007)

▨ ▨ ▨

Throughout this chapter we have emphasized two key points: that academic writing is researched — which means it is connected to a broader conversation — and that you should use sources strategically to develop your own thesis. The decisions you make about how to use the ideas of others matter: Will you paraphrase or summarize? Should you orchestrate a comparison of ideas in a synthesis? Should you use a direct quotation? Have you taken an active stance in using direct quotations? Have you analyzed the information in ways that clarify for readers why you are paraphrasing, summarizing, or quoting? Does the evidence you use support your thesis? Ultimately, sources should enhance and enrich the ideas you have developed through research, giving you the best chance of persuading your readers to listen to you, learn from you, and perhaps change their minds about an issue that is important to you.

8

From Ethos to Logos: Appealing to Your Readers

Who you believe your readers are influences how you see a particular situation, define an issue, explain the ongoing conversation surrounding that issue, and formulate a question. You may need to read widely to understand how different writers have dealt with the issue you address. And you will need to anticipate how others might respond to your argument — whether they will be sympathetic or antagonistic — and to compose your essay so that readers will "listen" whether or not they agree with you. To achieve these goals, you will no doubt use reason in the form of evidence to sway readers. But you can also use other means of persuasion: That is, you can use your own character, by presenting yourself as someone who is knowledgeable, fair, and just; and you can appeal to your readers' emotions. Although you may believe that reason alone should provide the means for changing people's minds, people's emotions also color the way they see the world.

Your audience is more than your immediate reader, your instructor or a peer. Your audience encompasses those you cite in writing about a particular issue and those you anticipate responding to your argument. This is true no matter what you write about, from an interpretation of the novels of a particular author, or an analysis of the cultural work of horror films, to the ethics of treating boys and girls differently in schools, or the moral issues surrounding homelessness in America. In this chapter we discuss different ways of engaging your readers, centering on three kinds of appeals: **ethos**, appeals from character; **pathos**, appeals to emotion; and **logos**, appeals to reason. *Ethos, pathos,* and *logos* are terms derived from ancient Greek writers, but they are still of great value today when considering how to persuade your audience. Readers will judge your argument on whether or not you present an argument that is fair and just, one that creates a sense of goodwill. All three appeals rely on these qualities. You want your argument to convey that you are reasonable and value fairness, justice, and goodwill, that you trust that your readers are reasonable and value these qualities too; and that your argument makes reasonable use of evidence that appeals to your readers' sense of fairness, justice, and goodwill. Your task as a writer is to decide the proper balance of these different appeals in your argument, based on your thesis, the circumstances, and your audience.

CONNECTING WITH READERS: A SAMPLE ARGUMENT

To consider how an author connects with his audience, read the excerpt below from James W. Loewen's book *Lies My Teacher Told Me: Everything Your American History Textbook Got Wrong*. As you read the excerpt, note Loewen's main points, and select key examples that illustrate his argument. As a class, test the claims he makes — To what extent do you believe that what Loewen argues is true? This may entail recalling your own experiences in high school history classes or locating one or more of the books that Loewen mentions.

ABOUT THE READING

In addition to *Lies My Teacher Told Me* (1995), James Loewen, who holds a PhD in sociology, has written several other books, including *Lies Across America: What Our Historic Sites Get Wrong* (1999) and *Sundown Towns: A Hidden Dimension of American Racism* (2005). As the titles of these books suggest, Loewen is a writer who questions the assumptions about history that many people take for granted. This is especially true of the excerpt below, from a chapter in which Loewen challenges a common American belief — that everyone has an equal chance in what he calls the "land of opportunity" — by arguing that we live in a class system that privileges some people and raises barriers for others. History textbook writers, he points out, are guilty of complicity in this class system because they leave a great deal of history out of their textbooks.

JAMES W. LOEWEN

The Land of Opportunity

High school students have eyes, ears, and television sets (all too many have their own TV sets), so they know a lot about relative privilege in America. They measure their family's social position against

1

that of other families, and their community's position against other communities. Middle-class students, especially, know little about how the American class structure works, however, and nothing at all about how it has changed over time. These students do not leave high school merely ignorant of the workings of the class structure; they come out as terrible sociologists. "Why are people poor?" I have asked first-year college students. Or, if their own class position is one of relative privilege, "Why is your family well off?" The answers I've received, to characterize them charitably, are half-formed and naïve. The students blame the poor for not being successful. They have no understanding of the ways that opportunity is not equal in America and no notion that social structure pushes people around, influencing the ideas they hold and the lives they fashion.

High school history textbooks can take some of the credit for this state of affairs. Some textbooks cover certain high points of labor history, such as the 1894 Pullman strike near Chicago that President Cleveland broke with federal troops, or the 1911 Triangle Shirtwaist fire that killed 146 women in New York City, but the most recent event mentioned in most books is the Taft-Hartley Act of fifty years ago. No book mentions the Hormel meat-packers' strike in the mid-1980s or the air traffic controllers' strike broken by President Reagan. Nor do textbooks describe any continuing issues facing labor, such as the growth of multinational corporations and their exporting of jobs overseas. With such omissions, textbook authors can construe labor history as something that happened long ago, like slavery, and that, like slavery, was corrected long ago. It logically follows that unions appear anachronistic. The idea that they might be necessary in order for workers to have a voice in the workplace goes unstated.

Textbooks' treatments of events in labor history are never anchored in any analysis of social class. This amounts to delivering the footnotes instead of the lecture! Six of the dozen high school American history textbooks I examined contain no index listing at all for "social class," "social stratification," "class structure," "income distribution," "inequality," or any conceivably related topic. Not one book lists "upper class," "working class," or "lower class." Two of the textbooks list "middle class," but only to assure students that America is a middle-class country. "Except for slaves, most of the colonists were members of the 'middling ranks,'" says *Land of Promise,* and nails home the point that we are a middle-class country by asking students to "Describe three 'middle-class' values that united free Americans of all classes." Several of the textbooks note the explosion of middle-class suburbs after World War II. Talking about the middle class is hardly equivalent to discussing social stratification, however; in fact, as Gregory Mantsios has pointed out, "such references appear to be acceptable precisely because they mute class differences."

Stressing how middle-class we all are is particularly problematic today, because the proportion of households earning between 75 percent and 125 percent of the median income has fallen steadily since 1967. The Reagan-Bush administrations accelerated this shrink-age of the middle class, and most families who left its ranks fell rather than rose. This is the kind of historical trend one would think history books would take as appropriate subject matter, but only four of the twelve books in my sample provide any analysis of social stratification in the United States. Even these fragmentary analyses are set mostly in colonial America. *Land of Promise* lives up to its reassuring title by heading its discussion of social class "Social Mobility." "One great difference between colonial and European society was that the colonists had more social mobility," echoes *The American Tradition*. "In contrast with contemporary Europe, eighteenth-century America was a shining land of equality and opportunity — with the notorious exception of slavery," chimes in *The American Pageant*. Although *The Challenge of Freedom* identifies three social classes — upper, middle, and lower — among whites in colonial society, compared to Europe "there was greater *social mobility*."

Never mind that the most violent class conflicts in American history — Bacon's Rebellion and Shays's Rebellion — took place in and just after colonial times. Textbooks still say that colonial society was rel-atively classless and marked by upward mobility. And things have got-ten rosier since. "By 1815," *The Challenge of Freedom* assures us, two classes had withered away and "America was a country of middle class people and of middle class goals." This book returns repeatedly, at inter-vals of every fifty years or so, to the theme of how open opportunity is in America. "In the years after 1945, *social mobility* — movement from one social class to another — became more widespread in America," *Challenge* concludes. "This meant that people had a better chance to move upward in society." The stress on upward mobility is striking. There is almost nothing in any of these textbooks about class inequali-ties or barriers of any kind to social mobility. "What conditions made it possible for poor white immigrants to become richer in the colonies?" *Land of Promise* asks. "What conditions made/make it difficult?" goes unasked. Textbook authors thus present an America in which, as preach-ers were fond of saying in the nineteenth century, men start from "humble origins" and attain "the most elevated positions."

Social class is probably the single most important variable in society. From womb to tomb, it correlates with almost all other social charac-teristics of people that we can measure. Affluent expectant mothers are more likely to get prenatal care, receive current medical advice, and enjoy general health, fitness, and nutrition. Many poor and working-class mothers-to-be first contact the medical profession in the last month, sometimes the last hours, of their pregnancies. Rich babies come out healthier and weighing more than poor babies. The infants go home to very different situations. Poor babies are more likely to have high levels of poisonous lead in their environments and their bodies. Rich babies get more time and verbal interaction with their parents and higher quality day care when not with their parents. When they enter kindergarten, and through the twelve years that follow, rich children benefit from suburban schools that spend two to three times as much money per student as schools in inner cities or impoverished rural areas. Poor children are taught in classes that are often 50 percent larger than the classes of affluent children. Differences such as these help account for the higher school-dropout rate among poor children.

Even when poor children are fortunate enough to attend the same school as rich children, they encounter teachers who expect only children of affluent families to know the right answers. Social science research shows that teachers are often surprised and even distressed when poor children excel. Teachers and counselors believe they can predict who is "college material." Since many working-class children give off the wrong signals, even in first grade, they end up in the "general education" track in high school. "If you are the child of low-income parents, the chances are good that you will receive limited and often careless attention from adults in your high school," in the words of Theodore Sizer's best-selling study of American high schools, *Horace's Compromise*. "If you are the child of upper-middle-income parents, the chances are good that you will receive substantial and careful attention." Researcher Reba Page has provided vivid accounts of how high school American history courses use rote learning to turn off lower-class students. Thus schools have put into practice Woodrow Wilson's recommendation: "We want one class of persons to have a liberal education, and we want another class of persons, a very much larger class of necessity in every society, to forgo the privilege of a liberal education and fit themselves to perform specific difficult manual tasks."

As if this unequal home and school life were not enough, rich teenagers then enroll in the Princeton Review or other coaching sessions for the Scholastic Aptitude Test. Even without coaching, affluent children are advantaged because their background is similar to that of the test-makers, so they are comfortable with the vocabulary and subtle subcultural assumptions of the test. To no one's surprise, social class correlates strongly with SAT scores.

All these are among the reasons why social class predicts the rate of college attendance and the type of college chosen more effectively than does any other factor, including intellectual ability, however measured. After college, most affluent children get white-collar jobs, most working-class children get blue-collar jobs, and the class differences continue. As adults, rich people are more likely to have hired an attorney and to be a member of formal organizations that increase their civic power. Poor people are more likely to watch TV. Because affluent families can save some money while poor families must spend what they make, wealth differences are ten times larger than income differences. Therefore most poor and working-class families cannot accumulate the down payment required to buy a house, which in turn shuts them out from our most important tax shelter, the write-off of home mortgage interest. Working-class parents cannot afford to live in elite subdivisions or hire high-quality day care, so the process of educational inequality replicates itself in the next generation. Finally, affluent Americans also have longer life expectancies than lower- and working-class people, the largest single cause of which is better access to health care. Echoing the results of Helen Keller's study of blindness, research has determined that poor health is not distributed randomly about the social structure but is concentrated in the lower class. Social Security then becomes a huge transfer system, using monies contributed by all Americans to pay benefits disproportionately to longer-lived affluent Americans.

Ultimately, social class determines how people think about social   10
class. When asked if poverty in America is the fault of the poor or the fault of the system, 57 percent of business leaders blamed the poor; just 9 percent blamed the system. Labor leaders showed sharply reversed choices: only 15 percent said the poor were at fault while 56 percent blamed the system. (Some replied "don't know" or chose a middle position.) The largest single difference between our two main political parties lies in how their members think about social class: 55 percent of Republicans blamed the poor for their poverty, while only 13 percent blamed the system for it; 68 percent of Democrats, on the other hand, blamed the system, while only 5 percent blamed the poor.

Few of these statements are news, I know, which is why I have not   11
documented most of them, but the majority of high school students do not know or understand these ideas. Moreover, the processes have changed over time, for the class structure in America today is not the same as it was in 1890, let alone in colonial America. Yet in *Land of Promise*, for example, social class goes unmentioned after 1670.

For Analysis and Discussion

1. List what you think are Loewen's main points. What appeals does he seem to draw on most when he makes those points: appeals based on his own character (ethos), on the emotions of his reader (pathos), or on the reasonableness of his evidence (logos)? Are the appeals obvious or difficult to tease out? Does he combine them? Discuss your answers with your classmates.

2. Identify what you think is the main claim of Loewen's argument, and choose key examples to support your answer. Compare your chosen claim and examples to those chosen by your classmates. Do they differ significantly? Can you agree on Loewen's gist and his key examples?

3. As a class, test the claims Loewen makes by thinking about your own experiences in high school history classes. Do you remember finding out that

something you were taught from an American history textbook was not true? Did you discover on your own what you considered to be misrepresentations in or important omissions from your textbook? If so, did these misrepresentations or omissions tend to support or contradict the claims about history textbooks that Loewen makes?

APPEALING TO ETHOS

Although we like to believe that our decisions and beliefs are based on reason and logic, in fact often they are based on what amounts to character judgments. That is, if a person you trust makes a reasonable argument for one choice, and a person you distrust makes a reasonable argument for the opposite choice, you are more likely to be swayed by the argument of the person you trust. Similarly, the audience for your argument will be more disposed to agree with you if its members believe you are a fair, just person who is knowledgeable and has good judgment. Even the most well developed argument will fall short if you do not leave this kind of impression on your readers. Thus it is not surprising that ethos may be the most important component of your argument.

There are three strategies for evoking a sense of ethos: (1) Establish that you have good judgment; (2) convey to readers that you are knowledgeable; and (3) show that you understand the complexity of the issue. These strategies are interrelated: A writer who demonstrates good judgment is more often than not someone who is both knowledgeable about an issue and who acknowledges the complexity of it by weighing the strengths *and* weaknesses of different arguments. However, keep in mind that these characteristics do not exist apart from what readers think and believe.

■ Establish That You Have Good Judgment

Most readers of academic writing expect writers to demonstrate good judgment by identifying a problem that readers agree is worth addressing. In turn, good judgment gives writers credibility. Loewen crafts his introduction to capture the attention of educators as well as concerned citizens when he claims that students leave high school unaware of class structure and as a consequence "have no understanding of the ways that opportunity is not equal in America and no notion that social structure pushes people around, influencing the ideas they hold and the lives they may fashion" (para. 1). Loewen does not blame students, or even instructors, for this lack of awareness. Instead, he writes, "textbooks can take some of the credit for this state of affairs" (para. 2) because, among other shortcomings, they leave out important events in "labor history" and relegate issues facing labor to the past. Whether or not an educator — or a general reader for that matter — will ultimately agree with Loewen's case is, at this point, up for grabs, but certainly the possibility that high schools in general, and history textbooks in particular, are failing students by leaving them vulnerable to class-based manipulation would be recognized as a problem by readers who believe America should be a society that offers equal opportunity for all. At this point, Loewen's readers are likely to agree that the problem of omission he identifies may be significant if its consequences are as serious as he believes them to be.

One could also argue that writers establish good judgment by conveying to readers that that they are fair-minded, just, and have the best interests of readers in mind. Loewen is particularly concerned that students understand the persistence of poverty and inequality in the United States and the historical circumstances of the poor, which they cannot do unless textbook writers take a more inclusive approach to addressing labor history, especially "the growth of multinational corporations and their exporting of jobs overseas" (para. 2). It's not fair to deny this important information to students, and it's not fair to the poor to leave them out of official histories of the United States. Loewen further demonstrates that he is fair and just when he calls attention in paragraph 6 to the inequality between rich and poor children in schools, a problem that persists despite our forebears' belief that class would not determine the fate of citizens of the United States.

■ Convey to Readers That You Are Knowledgeable

Being thoughtful about a subject goes hand in hand with being knowledgeable about the subject. Loewen demonstrates his knowledge of class issues and their absence from textbooks in a number of ways (not the least of which is his awareness that a problem exists — many people, including educators, may not be aware of this problem). In paragraph 3, Loewen makes a bold claim: "Textbooks' treatments of events in labor history are never anchored in any analysis of social class." As readers, we cannot help wondering: How does the author know this? How will he support this claim? Loewen anticipates these questions by demonstrating that he has studied the subject through a systematic examination of American history textbooks. He observes that six of the twelve textbooks he examined "contain no index listing at all for 'social class,' 'social stratification,' 'class structure,' 'income distribution,' 'inequality,' or any conceivably related topic; and that "not one book lists 'upper class,' 'working class,' or 'lower class.'" Loewen also demonstrates his grasp of class issues in American history, from — the "violent class conflicts" that "took place in and just after colonial times" (para. 5), which contradict textbook writers' assertions that class conflicts did not exist during this period, to the more recent conflicts in the 1980s and early 1990s (paras. 2 and 4). Moreover, Loewen backs up his own study of textbooks with references to a number of studies from the social sciences to illustrate that "social class is probably the single most important variable in society" (para. 6). Witness the statistics and findings he cites in paragraphs 6 through 10. The breadth of Loewen's historical knowledge and the range of his reading should convince readers that he is knowledgeable, and his trenchant analysis contributes to the authority he brings to the issue and to his credibility.

▪ Show That You Understand the Complexity of a Given Issue

Recognizing the complexity of an issue helps readers see the extent to which authors know that any issue can be understood in a number of different ways. Academic readers value writing that displays inquisitiveness and curiosity. Loewen acknowledges that most of the history he recounts is "not news" (para. 11) to his educated readers, who by implication "know" and "understand" his references to historical events and trends. What may be news to his readers, he explains, is the extent to which class structure in the United States has changed over time. With the steady erosion of middle-class households since 1967, "class inequalities" and "barriers . . . to social mobility" (para. 5) are limiting more and more Americans' access to even the most fundamental of opportunities in a democratic society — health care and education.

Still, even though Loewen has introduced new thinking about the nature of class in the United States and has demonstrated a provocative play of mind by examining an overlooked body of data (high school history textbooks) that may influence the way class is perceived in America, there are still levels of complexity he hasn't addressed explicitly. Most important, perhaps, is the question of why history textbooks continue to ignore issues of class when there is so much research that indicates its importance in shaping the events history textbooks purport to explain.

Steps to Appealing to Ethos

1 **Establish that you have good judgment.** Identify an issue your readers will agree is worth addressing, and demonstrate that you are fair-minded and have the best interests of your readers in mind when you address it.

2 **Convey to readers that you are knowledgeable.** Support your claims with credible evidence that shows you have read widely, thought about, and understand the issue.

3 **Show that you understand the complexity of the issue.** Demonstrate that you understand the variety of viewpoints your readers may bring — or may not be able to bring — to the issue.

APPEALING TO PATHOS

An appeal to pathos recognizes that people are moved to action by their emotions as well as by reasonable arguments. In fact, pathos is a vital part of argument that can predispose readers one way or another. Do you want to arouse readers' sympathy? Anger? Passion? You can do that by knowing what readers value. Appeals to pathos are typically indirect. You can appeal to pathos by using examples or illustrations that you believe will arouse the appropriate emotions, and by presenting them using an appropriate tone.

To acknowledge that writers play on readers' emotions is not to endorse manipulative writing. Rather, it is to acknowledge that effective writers use all available means of persuasion to move readers to agree with them. After all, if your thoughtful reading and careful research have led you to believe that you must weigh in with a useful insight on an important issue, it stands to reason that you would want your argument to convince your readers to believe as strongly in what you assert as you do. For example, if you genuinely believe that the conditions some families are living in are abysmal and unfair, you want your readers to believe it too. And an effective way to persuade them to believe as you do, in addition to convincing them of the reasonableness of your argument and of your own good character and judgment, is to establish a kind of emotional common ground in your writing — the common ground of pathos.

■ Show That You Know What Your Readers Value

Let's consider some of the ways James Loewen signals that he knows what his readers value. In the first place, Loewen assumes that readers feel the same way he does: Educated people should know that the United States has a class structure despite the democratic principles that the nation was founded on. He also expects readers to identify with his unwillingness to accept the injustice that results from that class structure. He believes that women living in poverty should have access to appropriate health care, that children living in poverty should have a chance to attend college, and that certain classes of people should not be written off to "perform specific difficult manual tasks" (para. 7). Time and again, Loewen cites examples that reveal that the poor are discriminated against by the class structure in the United States not for lack of ability, lack of desire, lack of ambition, or lack of morality, but for no better reason than lack of money — and that such discrimination has been going on for a long time. He expects his readers also will find such discrimination an unacceptable affront to their values of fair play and democracy, and that they will experience the same sense of outrage that he does.

■ Use Illustrations and Examples That Appeal to Readers' Emotions

You can appeal to readers' emotions indirectly through the illustrations and examples you use to support your argument. In paragraph 2, Loewen contends that textbook writers share responsibility for high school students' not knowing about the continued relevance of class issues in American life.

Loewen's readers — parents, educators, historians — may very well be angered by the omissions he points out. Certainly he would expect them to be angry when they read about the effects of economic class on the health care expectant mothers and then their children receive (para. 6) and on their children's access to quality education (paras. 6–8). In citing the fact that social class "correlates strongly with SAT scores" (para. 8) and so "predicts the rate of collage attendance and the type of college chosen" (para. 9), Loewen forces his readers to acknowledge that the educational playing field is far from level. Finally, he calls attention to the fact that accumulated wealth accounts for deep class divisions in our society — that their inability to save prevents the poor from hiring legal counsel, purchasing a home, or taking advantage of tax shelters. The result, Loewen observes, is that "educational inequality replicates itself in the next generation" (para. 9). Together, these examples strengthen both Loewen's argument and what he hopes will be readers' outrage that history textbooks do not address class issues. Without that information, Americans cannot fully understand or act to change the existing class structure.

■ Consider How Your Tone May Affect Your Audience

The **tone** of your writing is your use of language that communicates your attitude toward yourself, your material, and your readers. Of course, your tone is important in everything you write, but it is particularly crucial when you are appealing to pathos. When you are appealing to your readers' emotions, it is tempting to use loaded, exaggerated, and even intemperate language to convey how you feel (and hope your readers will feel) about an issue. Consider these sentences: "The Republican Party has devised the most ignominious means of filling the pockets of corporations." "These wretched children suffer heartrending agonies that can barely be imagined, much less described." "The ethereal beauty of the Brandenburg concertos thrill one to the deepest core of one's being." All of these sentences express strong and probably sincere beliefs and emotions, but some readers might find them overwrought and coercive, and question the writer's reasonableness.

Some writers rely on irony or sarcasm to set the tone of their work. **Irony** is the use of language to say one thing while meaning quite another. **Sarcasm** is the use of heavy-handed irony to ridicule or attack someone or something. Although irony and sarcasm can make for vivid and entertaining writing, they also can backfire and end up alienating readers. The sentence "Liberals will be pleased to hear that the new budget will be making liberal use of their hard-earned dollars" may entertain some readers with its irony and wordplay, but others may assume that the writer's attitude toward liberals is likely to result in an unfairly slanted argument. And the sentence "In my opinion, there's no reason why Christians and Muslims shouldn't rejoice together over the common ground of their both being deluded about the existence of a God" may please some readers, but it risks alienating those who are uncomfortable with breezy comments about religious beliefs. Again, think of your readers and what they value, and weigh the benefits of a clever sentence against its potential to detract from your argument or offend your audience.

You often find colorful wording and irony in op-ed and opinion pieces, where a writer may not have the space to build a compelling argument using evidence and has to resort to shortcuts to readers' emotions. However, in academic writing, where the careful accumulation and presentation of evidence and telling examples are highly valued, the frequent use of loaded language, exaggeration, and sarcasm is looked on with distrust.

Consider Loewen's excerpt. Although his outrage comes through clearly, he never resorts to hectoring. For example, in paragraph 1, he writes that students are "ignorant of the workings of the class structure" and that their opinions are "half-formed and naïve." But he does not imply that students are ignoramuses or that their opinions are foolish. What they lack, he contends, is understanding. They need to be taught something about class structure that they are not now being taught. And paragraph 1 is about as close to name-calling as Loewen comes. Even textbook writers, who are the target of his anger, are not vilified. True, Loewen occasionally makes use of irony, for example in paragraph 5, where he points out inconsistencies and omissions in textbooks: "Never mind that the most violent class conflicts in American history — Bacon's Rebellion and Shays's Rebellion — took place in and just after colonial times. Textbooks still say that colonial society was relatively classless and marked by upward mobility. And things have gotten rosier since." But he doesn't resort to ridicule. Instead, he relies on examples and illustrations to connect with his readers' sense of values and appeal to their emotions.

Steps to Appealing to Pathos

1 **Show that you know what your readers value.** Start from your own values and imagine what assumptions and principles would appeal to your readers. What common ground can you imagine between your values and theirs? How will it need to be adjusted for different kinds of readers?

2 **Use illustrations and examples that appeal to readers' emotions.** Again, start from your own emotional position. What examples and illustrations resonate most with you? How can you present them to have the most emotional impact on your readers? How would you adjust them for different kinds of readers?

3 **Consider how your tone may affect your audience.** Be wary of using loaded, exaggerated, and intemperate language that may put off your readers; and be careful in your use of irony and sarcasm.

A Practice Sequence: Appealing to Ethos and Pathos

Discuss the language and strategies the writers use in the passages below to connect with their audience, in particular their appeals to both ethos and pathos. As you consider each excerpt, discuss who you think the implied audience is and whether you think the strategies the writers use to connect with their readers are effective or not.

1 Almost a half century after the U.S. Supreme Court concluded that Southern school segregation was unconstitutional and "inherently unequal," new statistics from the 1998–99 school year show that segregation continued to intensify throughout the 1990s, a period in which there were three major Supreme Court decisions authorizing a return to segregated neighborhood schools and limiting the reach and duration of desegregation orders. For African American students, this trend is particularly apparent in the South, where most blacks live and where the 2000 Census shows a continuing return from the North. From 1988 to 1998, most of the progress of the previous two decades in increasing integration in the region was lost. The South is still much more integrated than it was before the civil rights revolution, but it is moving backward at an accelerating rate.

—GARY ORFIELD, "Schools More Separate:
Consequences of a Decade of Resegregation"
(http://www.civilrightsproject.ucla.edu/research/deseg/
Schools_More_Separate.pdf)

2 No issue has been more saturated with dishonesty than the issue of racial quotas and preferences, which is now being examined by the Supreme Court of the United States. Many defenders of affirmative action are not even honest enough to admit that they are talking about quotas and preferences, even though everyone knows that that is what affirmative action amounts to in practice.

Despite all the gushing about the mystical benefits of "diversity" in higher education, a recent study by respected academic scholars found that "college diversity programs fail to raise standards" and that "a majority of faculty members and administrators recognize this when speaking anonymously."

This study by Stanley Rothman, Seymour Martin Lipset, and Neil Nevitte found that "of those who think that preferences have some impact on academic standards those believing it negative exceed those believing it positive by 15 to 1."

Poll after poll over the years has shown that most faculty members and most students are opposed to double standards in college admissions. Yet professors who will come out publicly and say what they say privately in these polls are as rare as hens' teeth.

Such two-faced talk is pervasive in academia and elsewhere. A few years ago, in Berkeley, there was a big fight over whether a faculty vote on affirmative action would be by secret ballot or open vote. Both sides knew that the result of a secret ballot would be the direct opposite of the result in a public vote at a faculty meeting.

—THOMAS SOWELL, "The Grand Fraud:
Affirmative Action for Blacks"
(http://www.capmag.com/article.asp?ID=2637)

3 When the judgment day comes for every high school student — that day when a final transcript is issued and sent to the finest institutions, with every sin of class selection written as with a burning chisel on stone — on that day a great cry will go up throughout the land, and there will be weeping, wailing, gnashing of teeth, and considerable grumbling against guidance counselors, and the cry of a certain senior might be, "WHY did no one tell me that Introduction to Social Poker wasn't a solid academic class?" At another, perhaps less wealthy school, a frustrated and under-nurtured sculptress will wonder, "Why can't I read, and why don't I care?" The reason for both of these oversights, as they may eventually discover, is that the idea of the elective course has been seriously mauled, mistreated, and abused under the current middle-class high school system. A significant amount of the blame for producing students who are stunted, both cognitively and morally, can be traced back to this pervasive fact. Elective courses, as shoddily planned and poorly funded as they may be, constitute the only formation that many students get in their own special types of intelligences. Following the model of Howard Gardner, these may be spatial, musical, or something else. A lack of stimulation to a student's own intelligence directly causes a lack of identification with the intelligence of others. Instead of becoming moderately interested in a subject by noticing the pleasure other people receive from it, the student will be bitter, jealous, and without empathy. These are the common ingredients in many types of tragedy, violent or benign. Schools must take responsibility for speaking in some way to each of the general types of intelligences. Failure to do so will result in students who lack skills, and also the inspiration to comfort, admire, emulate, and aid their fellow humans.

"All tasks that really call upon the power of attention are interesting for the same reason and to an almost equal degree," wrote Simone Weil in her *Reflections on Love and Faith*, her editor having defined attention as "a suspension of one's own self as a center of the world and making oneself available to the reality of another being." In Parker Palmer's *The Courage to Teach*, modern scientific theorist David Bohm describes "a holistic underlying implicate order whose information unfolds into the explicate order of particular fields." Rilke's euphemism for this "holistic . . . implicate order," which Palmer borrows, is "the grace of great things." Weil's term would be "God." However, both agree that eventual perception of this singular grace, or God, is accessible through education of a specific sort, and for both it is doubtless the most necessary experience of a lifetime. Realizing that this contention is raining down from different theorists, and keeping in mind that the most necessary experience of a lifetime should not be wholly irrelevant to the school system, educators should therefore reach the conclusion that this is a matter worth looking into. I assert that the most fruitful and practical results of their attention will be a wider range of electives coupled with a new acknowledgment and handling of them, one that treats each one seriously.

—ERIN MEYERS,
"The Educational Smorgasbord as Saving Grace"

APPEALING TO LOGOS: USING REASON AND EVIDENCE TO FIT THE SITUATION

To make an argument persuasive, you need to be in dialogue with your readers, using your own character (ethos) to demonstrate that you are a reasonable, credible, fair person and appealing to your readers' emotions (pathos), particularly their sense of right and wrong. Each type of appeal goes hand in hand with an appeal to logos, using converging pieces of evidence — statistics, facts, observations — to advance your claim. Remember that the type of evidence you use is determined by the issue, problem, situation, and readers' expectations. As an author, you should try to anticipate and address readers' beliefs and values. Ethos and pathos are concerned with the content of your argument; logos addresses both form and content.

An argument begins with one or more premises and ends with a conclusion. A **premise** is an assumption that you expect your readers to agree with, a statement that is either true or false — for example, "Alaska is cold in the winter" — that is offered in support of a claim. That claim is the **conclusion** you want your readers to draw from your premises. The conclusion is also a sentence that is either true or false. For instance, Loewen's major premise is that class is a key factor in Americans' access to health care, education, and wealth. Loewen also offers a second, more specific premise: that textbook writers provide little discussion of the ways class matters. Loewen crafts his argument to help readers draw the following conclusion: "We live in a class system that runs counter to the democratic principles that underlie the founding of the United States, and history textbooks must tell this story. Without this knowledge, citizens will be uninformed." Whether or not readers accept this as true depends on how Loewen moves from his initial premises to reach his conclusion — that is, whether or not we draw the same kinds of inferences, or reasoned judgments, that he does. He must do so in a way that meets readers' expectations of what constitutes relevant and persuasive evidence and guides them one step at a time toward his conclusion.

There are two main forms of argument: deductive and inductive. A **deductive argument** is an argument in which the premises support (or appear to support) the conclusion. If you join two premises to produce a conclusion that is taken to be true, you are stating a **syllogism.** This is the classic example of deductive reasoning through a syllogism:

1. All men are mortal. (First premise)
2. Socrates is a man. (Second premise)
3. Therefore, Socrates is mortal. (Conclusion)

In a deductive argument, it is impossible for both premises to be true and the conclusion to be false. That is, the truth of the premises means that the conclusion must also be true.

By contrast, an **inductive argument** relies on evidence and observation to reach a conclusion. Although readers may accept a writer's premises as true, it is possible for them to reject the writer's conclusion. Let's consider this for a moment in the context of Loewen's argument. Loewen introduces the premise that class matters, then offers the more specific premise that textbook writers leave class issues out of their narratives of American history, and finally draws the conclusion that citizens need to be informed of this body of knowledge in order to create change:

1. Although class is a key factor in Americans' access to health care, education, and wealth, students know very little about the social structure in the United States.
2. Textbook writers do not address the issue of class in their textbooks, an issue that people need to know about.
3. Therefore, if people had this knowledge, they would understand that poverty cannot be blamed on the poor.

Notice that Loewen's premises are not necessarily true. For example, readers could challenge the premise that "textbook writers do not address issues of class in their textbooks." After all, Loewen examined just twelve textbooks. What if he had examined a different set of textbooks? Would he have drawn the same conclusion? And even if Loewen's evidence convinces us that the two premises are true, we do not have to accept that the conclusion is true.

The conclusion in an inductive argument is never definitive. That is the nature of any argument that deals with human emotions and actions. Moreover, we have seen throughout history that people tend to disagree much more on the terms of an argument than on its form. Do we agree that Israel's leaders practice apartheid? (What do we mean by *apartheid* in this case?) Do we agree with the need to grant women reproductive rights? (When does life begin?) Do we agree that all people should be treated equally? (Would equality mean equal access to resources or to outcomes?)

Deductive arguments are conclusive. In a deductive argument, the premises are universal truths — laws of nature, if you will — and the conclusion must follow from those premises. That is, a^2 plus b^2 always equals c^2, and humans are always mortal. By contrast, an inductive argument is never conclusive. The premises may or may not be true; and even if they are true, the conclusion may be false. We might accept that class matters and that high school history textbooks don't address the issue of class structure in the United States; but we still would not know that students who have studied social stratification in America will necessarily understand the nature of poverty. It may be that social class is only one reason for poverty; or it may be that textbooks are only one source of information about social stratification in the United States, that textbook omissions are simply not as serious as Loewen claims. That the premises of an argument are true only establishes that the conclusion is probably true and, perhaps, only for some readers.

Inductive argument is the basis of academic writing; it is also the basis of any appeal to logos. The process of constructing an inductive argument involves three steps:

1. State the premises of your argument.
2. Use credible evidence to show readers that your argument has merit.
3. Demonstrate that the conclusion follows from the premises.

In following these three steps, you will want to determine the truth of your premises, help readers understand whether or not the inferences you draw are justified, and use word signals to help readers fully grasp the connections between your premises and conclusion.

■ State the Premises of Your Argument

Stating a premise establishes what you have found to be true and what you want to persuade readers to accept as truth as well. Let's return to Loewen, who asserts his premise at the very outset of the excerpt: "Middle-class students . . . know little about how the American class structure works . . . and nothing at all about how it has changed over time." Loewen elaborates on this initial premise a few sentences later, arguing that students "have no understanding of the ways that opportunity is not equal in America and no notion that the social structure pushes people around, influencing the ideas they hold and the lives they fashion." Implicit here is the point that class matters. Loewen makes this point explicit several paragraphs on, where he states that "social class is probably the single most important variable in society" (para. 6). He states his second, more specific premise in paragraph 2: "High school history textbooks can take some of the credit for this state of affairs." The burden of demonstrating that these premises are true is on Loewen. If readers find that either of the premises is not true, it will be difficult, if not impossible, for them to accept his conclusion that with more knowledge, people will understand that poverty is not the fault of the poor (para. 10).

■ Use Credible Evidence

The validity of your argument depends on whether or not the inferences you draw are justified, and whether or not you can expect a reasonable person to draw the same conclusion from those premises. Loewen has to demonstrate throughout (1) that students do not have much, if any, knowledge about the class structure that exists in the United States and (2) that textbook writers are in large part to blame for this lack of knowledge. He also must help readers understand how this lack of knowledge contributes to (3) his conclusion that greater knowledge would lead Americans to understand that poor people are not responsible for poverty. He can help readers with the order in which he states his premises and by choosing the type and amount of evidence that will enable readers to draw the inferences that he does.

Interestingly, Loewen seems to assume that one group of readers — educators — will accept his first premise as true. He does not elaborate on what students know or do not know. Instead, he moves right to his second premise, which involves first acknowledging what high school history textbooks typically cover, then identifying what he believes are the important events that textbook writers exclude, and ultimately asserting that "treatments of events in labor history are never anchored in any analysis of social class" (para. 3). He supports this point with his own study of twelve textbooks (paras. 3–5) before returning to his premise that "social class is probably the single most important variable in society" (para. 6). What follows is a series of observations about the rich and references to researchers' findings on inequality (paras. 7–9). Finally, he asserts that "social class determines how people think about social class" (para. 10), implying that fuller knowledge would lead business leaders and conservative voters to think differently about the source of poverty. The question to explore is whether or not Loewen supports this conclusion.

■ Demonstrate That the Conclusion Follows from the Premises

Authors signal their conclusion with words like *consequently, finally, in sum, in the end, subsequently, therefore, thus, ultimately,* and *as a result.* Here is how this looks in the structure of Loewen's argument:

1. Although class is a key factor in Americans' access to health care, education, and wealth, students know very little about the social structure in the United States.

2. Textbook writers do not address the issue of class in their textbooks, an issue that people need to know about.

3. Ultimately, if people had this knowledge, they would understand poverty cannot be blamed on the poor.

We've reprinted much of paragraph 9 of Loewen's excerpt below. Notice how Loewen pulls together what he has been discussing. He again underscores the importance of class and achievement ("All these are among the reasons."). And he points out that access to certain types of colleges puts people in a position to accumulate and sustain wealth. Of course, this is not true of the poor "because affluent families can save some money while poor families must spend what they make." This causal relationship ("Because") heightens readers' awareness of the class structure that exists in the United States.

> <u>All these are among the reasons</u> why social class predicts the rate of college attendance and the type of college chosen more effectively than does any other factor, including intellectual ability, however measured. After college, most affluent children get white-collar jobs, most working-class children get blue-collar jobs, and the class differences continue. As adults, rich people are more likely to have hired an attorney and to be a member of formal organizations that increase their civic power. Poor people are more likely to watch TV. <u>Because</u> affluent families can save some money while poor families must spend what they make, wealth differences are ten times larger than income differences. <u>Therefore</u> most poor and working-class families cannot accumulate the down payment required to buy a house, which in turn shuts them out from our most important tax shelter, the write-off of home mortgage interest. Working-class parents cannot afford to live in elite subdivisions or hire high-quality day care, so the process of educational inequality replicates itself in the next generation. <u>Finally,</u> affluent Americans also have longer life expectancies than lower- and working-class people, the largest single cause of which is better access to health care. . . .

Once Loewen establishes this causal relationship, he concludes ("Therefore," "Finally") with the argument that poverty persists from one generation to the next.

In paragraph 10, Loewen uses the transition word *ultimately* to make the point that social class matters, so much so that it limits the ways in which people see the world, that it even "determines how people think about social class." (We discuss how to write conclusions in Chapter 9.)

Steps to Appealing to Logos

1 **State the premises of your argument.** Establish what you have found to be true and what you want readers to accept as well.

2 **Use credible evidence.** Lead your readers from one premise to the next, making sure your evidence is sufficient and convincing and your inferences are logical and correct.

3 **Demonstrate that the conclusion follows from the premises.** In particular, use the right words to signal to your readers how the evidence and inferences lead to your conclusion.

RECOGNIZING LOGICAL FALLACIES

We turn now to **logical fallacies**, flaws in the chain of reasoning that lead to a conclusion that does not necessarily follow from the premises, or evidence. Logical fallacies are common in inductive arguments for two reasons: Inductive arguments rely on reasoning about probability, not certainty; and they derive from human beliefs and values, not facts or laws of nature.

Here we list fifteen logical fallacies. In examining them, think about how to guard against the sometimes-faulty logic behind statements you might hear from politicians, advertisers, and the like. That should help you examine the premises on which you base your own assumptions and the logic you use to help readers reach the same conclusions you do.

1. *Erroneous Appeal to Authority.* An authority is someone with expertise in a given subject. An *erroneous authority* is an author who claims to be an authority but is not, or someone an author cites as an authority who is not. In this type of fallacy, the claim might be true, but the fact that an unqualified person is making the claim means there is no reason for readers to accept the claim as true. Because the issue here is the legitimacy of authority, your concern should be to prove to yourself and your readers that you or the people you are citing have expertise in the subject. An awareness of this type of fallacy has become increasingly important as celebrities offer support for candidates running for office or act as spokespeople for curbing global warming or some other cause. The candidate may be the best person for the office, and there may be very good reasons to attack global warming; but we need to question the legitimacy of a nonexpert endorsement.

2. *Ad Hominem.* An ad hominem argument focuses on the person making a claim instead of on the claim itself. (*Ad hominem* is Latin for "to the person.") In most cases, an ad hominem argument does not have a bearing on the truth or the quality of a claim. Keep in mind that it is always important to address the claim or the reasoning behind it, rather than the person making the claim. "Of course Senator Wiley supports oil drilling in Alaska — he's in the pocket of the oil companies!" is an example of an ad hominem argument. Senator Wiley may have good reasons for supporting oil drilling in Alaska that have nothing to do with his alleged attachment to the oil industry. However, if an individual's character is relevant to the argument, then an ad hominem argument can be valid. If Senator Wiley has been found guilty of accepting bribes from an oil company, it makes sense to question both his credibility and his claims.

3. *Shifting the Issue.* This type of fallacy occurs when an author draws attention away from the issue instead of offering evidence that will enable people to draw their own conclusions about the soundness of an argument. For example:

> Affirmative action proponents accuse me of opposing equal opportunity in the workforce. I think my positions on military expenditures, education, and public health speak for themselves.

The author of this statement does not provide a chain of reasoning that would enable readers to judge his or her stance on the issue of affirmative action.

4. *Either/Or Fallacy.* At times, an author will take two extreme positions to force readers to make a choice between two seemingly contradictory positions. For example:

> Either you support the war in Iraq, or you are against it.

Although the author has set up an either/or condition, in reality one position does not exclude the other. Many people support the troops in Iraq even though they do not support the reasons for starting the war.

5. *Sweeping Generalizations.* When an author attempts to draw a conclusion without providing sufficient evidence to support the conclusion or examining possible counterarguments, he or she may be making sweeping generalizations. For example:

> Despite the women's movement in the 1960s and 1970s, women still do not receive equal pay for equal work. Obviously, any attempt to change the status quo for women is doomed to failure.

As is the case with many fallacies, the author's position may be reasonable, but we cannot accept the argument at face value. Reading critically entails testing assumptions like this one — that any attempt to create change is doomed to failure because women do not receive equal pay for equal work. We could ask, for example, whether inequities persist in the public sector. And we could point to other areas where the women's movement has had measurable success. Title IX, for example, has reduced the dropout rate among teenage girls; it has also increased the rate at which women earn college and graduate degrees.

6. *Bandwagon.* This is a fairly common mode of argument in advertising when, for example, a commercial attempts to persuade us to buy a certain product because it's popular.

> Because Harvard, Stanford, and Berkeley have all added a multicultural component to their graduation requirements, other institutions should do so as well.

The growing popularity of an idea is not sufficient reason to accept that it is true.

7. *Begging the Question.* This fallacy entails advancing a circular argument that asks readers to accept a premise that is also the conclusion readers are expected to draw:

> We could improve the undergraduate experience with coed dorms because both men and women benefit from living with members of the opposite gender.

Here readers are being asked to accept that the conclusion is true despite the fact that the premises — men benefit from living with women, and women benefit from living with men — are essentially the same as the conclusion.

Without evidence that a shift in dorm policy could improve on the under-graduate experience, we cannot accept the conclusion as true. Indeed, the conclusion does not necessarily follow from the premise.

8. *False Analogy.* Authors (and others) often try to persuade us that something is true by using a comparison. This approach is not in and of itself a problem, as long as the comparison is reasonable. For example:

> It is ridiculous to have a Gay and Lesbian Program and a Department of African American Culture. We don't have a Straight Studies Program or a Department of Caucasian Culture.

Here the author is urging readers to rethink the need for two academic departments by saying that the school doesn't have two other departments. That, of course, is not a reason for or against the new departments. What's needed is an analysis that compares the costs (economic and otherwise) of starting up and operating the new departments versus the contributions (economic and otherwise) of the new departments.

9. *Technical Jargon.* If you've ever had a salesperson try to persuade you to purchase a television or stereo with capabilities you absolutely *must* have — even if you don't understand a word the salesperson was saying about alternating currents and circuit splicers — then you're familiar with this type of fallacy. We found this passage in one of our student's papers:

> You should use this drug because it has been clinically proven that it inhibits the reuptake of serotonin and enhances the dopamine levels of the body's neu-rotransmitters.

The student's argument may very well be true, but he hasn't presented any substantive evidence to demonstrate that the premises are true and that the conclusion follows from the premises.

10. *Confusing Cause and Effect.* It is challenging to establish that one factor causes another. For example, how can we know for certain that eco-nomic class predicts, or is a factor in, academic achievement? How do we know that a new president's policies are the cause of a country's economic well-being? Authors often assume cause and effect when two factors are simply associated with each other:

> The current recession came right after President Bush was elected.

This fallacy states a fact; but it does not prove that the president's election caused the recession.

11. *Appeal to Fear.* One type of logical fallacy makes an appeal to read-ers' irrational fears and prejudices, preventing them from dealing squarely with a given issue and often confusing cause and effect:

> We should use whatever means possible to avoid further attack.

The reasoning here is something like this: "If we are soft on defense, we will never end the threat of terrorism." But we need to consider whether there is indeed a threat, and, if so, whether the presence of a threat should lead to action, and, if so, whether that action should include "whatever means possible." (Think of companies that sell alarm systems by pointing to people's vulnerability to harm and property damage.)

12. *Fallacy of Division.* A fallacy of division suggests that what is true of the whole must also be true of its parts:

> Conservatives have always voted against raising the minimum wage, against stem cell research, and for defense spending. Therefore, we can assume that conservative Senator Harrison will vote this way.

The author is urging readers to accept the premise without providing evidence of how the senator has actually voted on the three issues.

13. *Hasty Generalization.* This fallacy is committed when a person draws a conclusion about a group based on a sample that is too small to be representative. Consider this statement:

> Seventy-five percent of the seniors surveyed at the university study just 10 hours a week. We can conclude, then, that students at the university are not studying enough.

What you need to know is how many students were actually surveyed. Seventy-five percent may seem high, but not if the researcher surveyed just 400 of the 2,400 graduating seniors. This sample of students from a total population of 9,600 students at the university is too small to draw the conclusion that students in general are not studying enough.

14. *The Straw Man Argument.* A straw man fallacy makes a generalization about what a group believes without actually citing a specific writer or work:

> Democrats are more interested in running than in trying to win the war on terrorism.

Here the fallacy is that the author simply ignores a person's actual position and substitutes a distorted, exaggerated, or misrepresented version of that position. This kind of fallacy often goes hand in hand with assuming that what is true of the group is true of the individual, what we call the fallacy of division.

15. *Fallacy of the Middle Ground.* The fallacy of the middle ground assumes that the middle position between two extreme positions must be correct. Although the middle ground may be true, the author must justify this position with evidence.

> E. D. Hirsch argues that cultural literacy is the only sure way to increase test scores, and Jonathan Kozol believes schools will improve only if state legislators increase funding; but I would argue that school reform will occur if we change the curriculum *and* provide more funding.

This fallacy draws its power from the fact that a moderate or middle position is often the correct one. Again, however, the claim that the moderate or middle position is correct must be supported by legitimate reasoning.

ANALYZING THE APPEALS IN A TEXT

Now that you have studied the variety of appeals you can make to connect with your audience, we would like you to read a chapter from a study of education by Jean Anyon and analyze her strategies for appealing to her readers. The chapter is quite long and carefully argued, so we suggest you take detailed notes about her use of appeals to ethos, pathos, and logos as you read. You may want to refer to the Practice Sequence questions on p. 199 to help focus your reading. Ideally, you should work through the text with your classmates, in groups of three or four, appointing one student to record and share each group's analysis of Anyon's argument.

ABOUT THE READING

Jean Anyon teaches educational policy in the doctoral program in urban education at the City University of New York. Her articles on cities, race, social class, and schools have been reprinted in more than forty edited collections and translated into several languages. This chapter appears in her book *Radical Possibilities: Public Policy, Urban Education, and a New Social Movement* (2005).

JEAN ANYON

The Economic Is Political

It is widely acknowledged that one of the most important causes of poorly funded, staffed, and resourced schools is the poverty of the families and neighborhoods in which the schools are located. What is rarely acknowledged, however, is the proactive role of the federal government in maintaining this poverty and therefore poverty education.

All economies depend on government regulations in order to function. Capitalism would not be capitalism without constitutional and other federal provisions that make legal the private ownership of property, the right of business to charge more for products than the cost of producing them, or the right of corporations to keep those profits rather than sharing them with workers or employees. The 14th Amendment to the Constitution, passed in 1867, turns corporations into "persons" so they will be free from government "interference." Because economies are maintained by rules made by governments, economic institutions are inescapably political; they function according to determinative macroeconomic policies.

This chapter demonstrates that the poverty of U.S. families is considerably more widespread than commonly believed — and is catastrophic in low-income urban neighborhoods of color. I demonstrate that the basic reason people are poor is that there are not enough jobs paying decent wages. In cities, the harsh economic realities of poverty shape the lives of parents of school children, and therefore the lives of their children as well. Neighborhood poverty also impacts the education students receive by contributing to low school funding levels, poorly paid teachers, and a lack of resources.

First, I provide an overview of national poverty as a backdrop to the   *4*
situation in urban America. I then focus specifically on urban families of color. . . .

Income

Almost three-fourths (70%) of all American employees saw their wages   *5*
fall between 1973 and 1995 (in constant dollars — that is, adjusted for inflation); even with the boom of the late 1990s, a majority of workers made less in 2000 than they had in 1973. New college graduates earned $1.10 less per hour in 1995 than their counterparts did in 1973. The earnings of the average American family did improve slightly over this period, but only through a dramatic increase in the number of hours worked and the share of families in which both parents worked (Lafer, 2002, p. 45; Mishel, Bernstein, and Boushey, 2003, p. 162).

Some of the largest long-term wage declines have been among entry-   *6*
level workers (those with up to five years' work experience) with a high school education. Average wages for male entry-level high school graduates were 28% lower in 1997 than two decades earlier. The decline for comparable women was 18% (Economic Policy Institute, Feb. 17, 1999, p. 1).

Low wages are an important cause of poverty. Low-wage workers are   *7*
those whose hourly wage is less than the earnings necessary to lift a family above the official poverty line — in 2004, $15,670 or less for a family of three, and $18,850 for a family of four.

The percentage of people who work full-time, year-round yet are poor   *8*
is staggering. In 2000, at the height of a booming economy, almost a fifth of all men (19.5%), and almost a third of all women (33.1%) earned poverty-level wages working full-time, year-round. In the same year, over one in four Black men (26.3%), over one in three Black women (36.5%) and Hispanic men (37.6%), and almost half of Hispanic women (49.3%) earned poverty wages working full-time, year-round (Mishel, Bernstein, and Schmitt, 2001, pp. 137–139).

I analyzed figures provided by the Economic Policy Institute to calcu-   *9*
late the overall percentage of people who work full-time, year-round, yet make *poverty-zone* wages. Poverty zone is defined here as wages up to 125% of the official poverty threshold needed to support a family of four at the poverty level (ibid., p. 133). The analysis demonstrates that in 1999, during the strong economy, almost half of people at work in the

U.S. (41.3%) earned poverty-zone wages — in 1999, $10.24/hour ($21,299/year) or less, working full-time, year-round (ibid., Table 2.10, p. 130). Two years later, in 2001, 38.4 earned poverty-zone wages working full-time, year-round (in 2001, 125% of the poverty line was a $10.88 hourly wage) (ibid., p. 134). These figures indicate that even in "good times" the U.S. pyramid of wages sits squarely on the shoulders of almost half of U.S. employees, who are the working poor.

In 2000, more than half (59.5%) of the working poor were women. Over 60% were White (60.4%). Thirty-five percent were Black or Latino (ibid., p. 353). Over 61.8% had a high school degree or less, while a quarter (24.2%) had some college, and 8% had a bachelor's degree (ibid., p. 353). This last figure indicates that *almost one in ten of the working poor is a college graduate.*

Seventy percent of the working poor had jobs in services or retail trade and 10% worked in manufacturing (ibid., p. 353). The vast majority (93.3%) were not in unions. More than half (57.7%) were under the age of 35 (ibid., p. 353). It is important to note that these workers are poor by official standards. As we will see below, a more realistic measure of poverty would literally double the amount of income under which people are defined as poor.

Moving up the income scale in the U.S. is more difficult than in other countries. As *Business Week* pointed out several years ago, economic mobility in the U.S. declined after the 1960s. Because most young people earn less than their parents, mobility here is second worst among similar countries recently studied — only Canada is worse (Dreier, Swanstrom, and Mollenkopf, 2001, pp. 18, 47). Low-wage workers in the U.S. are more likely to remain in the low-wage labor market longer than workers in Germany, France, Italy, the UK, Denmark, Finland, Sweden, and Canada (Mishel, Bernstein, and Schmitt, 2001, p. 12).

Relatively few U.S. individuals or families make high incomes. In 2000, only 7.8% of women and 16% of men earned at least three times the official poverty level (Mishel, Bernstein, and Boushey, 2003, p. 133). In 2001, only 19% of *families* earned more than $94,000, and only 4% made more than $164,000 (in 2001 dollars) (ibid., p. 56).

In the last two decades, income has skyrocketed at the tip of the distributional pyramid. The top one percent of tax filers, the 2.1 million people earning $700,000 a year or more, had after-tax income that jumped 31% in the last few years, while the after-tax income of the bottom 90% of tax filers rose only 3.4% (Mishel, Bernstein, and Schmitt, 2001, p. 83).

While employee pay has lagged, CEO pay has skyrocketed. And the ratio of CEO to worker pay has increased dramatically: In the 1960s and '70s, the ratio was between 26% and 37%. In the 1990s, it was between 102% and 310%. By 2001, the ratio had grown to 245% (Mishel, Bernstein, and Boushey, 2003, p. 215). In other words, in 2001, a CEO earned more in one workday (there are 260 in a year) than an average worker earned in 52 weeks (Economic Policy Institute, July 24, 2002, p. 1). In recent years, the average ratio of CEO pay to worker pay in all other advanced countries was considerably lower — 18.1 to 1 (Mishel, Bernstein, and Boushey, 2003, p. 216).

Jobs

What job opportunities are available for Americans? For two decades,   *16* numerous politicians, educators, and corporate spokespeople have been arguing that the U.S. must improve education because people need advanced skills in order to get a job. This is a myth, however. Most job openings in the next 10 years will not require either sophisticated skills or a college degree. Seventy-seven percent of new and projected jobs will be low-paying. Only a quarter of the new and projected jobs are expected to pay over $26,000 a year (Department of Labor, 2002, Chart 9; see also Economic Policy Institute, July 21, 2004).

Most will require on-the-job training only, and will not require a col-   *17* lege education; most will be in service and retail, where poverty-zone wages are the norm. Only 12.6% of new jobs will require a bachelor's degree. Of the 20 occupations expected to grow the fastest, only six require college — these six are in computer systems and information technology (Department of Labor, 2002, Chart 8), and there are relatively few of these jobs.

The typical job of the future is not in information technology. Most   *18* job openings will be in food preparation and service and in fast-food restaurants, as telephone customer service representatives, and as cashiers (Department of Labor, 2002, Chart 9). In the next decade, about 5 million new jobs will be created for food workers, including waiters and waitresses. Another 4 million will be for cashiers and retail salespersons, and 3 million for clerks. Over 2 million will be for packagers, laborers, and truck drivers. Managerial and professional occupations will also need more workers, but their numbers pale compared with openings requiring less education.

Indeed, a typical job of the future is retail sales at Wal-Mart. The aver-   *19* age pay at Wal-Mart, which employs over a million people and is the largest private employer in the world, was $20,030 in 2000. According to *Business Week*, half of Wal-Mart's full-time employees are eligible for food stamps (households earning up to 130% of the official poverty line are eligible) (March 13, 2000, p. 78).

A main determinant of whether one is poor or not is whether or not   *20* one has a decently paying job. The assertion that jobs are plentiful — if only workers were qualified to fill them — has been a central tenet of federal policy for 20 years. In 1982, the Reagan administration eliminated the Comprehensive Employment and Training Administration

(CETA), which by 1978 had created almost 2 million full-time jobs, and substituted a major federal job training program (Job Partnership Training Act) (Lafer, 2002, pp. 1–2). Since then, and continuing today, job training has been the centerpiece of federal and state efforts to solve both the unemployment problem and the poverty problem. For almost all of this time, however, the federal government has not collected data on job availability (vacancies). If they had, and if they had consulted studies that had been carried out, they would have found that all the evidence demonstrates that at any given time there are far more unemployed people than there are job openings (ibid., p. 23; see also Pigeon and Wray, 1999, among others). The federal government has spent $85 billion on job training since the Reagan years, claiming all the while that there are jobs for those who want them (Lafer, 2002, p. 19).

In an exhaustive analysis, labor economist Gordon Lafer demonstrates that "over the period 1984 to 1996 — at the height of an alleged labor shortage — the number of people in need of work exceeded the total number of job openings by an average of five to one. In 1996, for example, the country would have needed 14.4 million jobs in order for all low-income people to work their way out of poverty. However, there were at most 2.4 million job openings available to meet this need; of these, only one million were in full-time, non-managerial positions" (ibid., 3, pp. 29–44). Thus, "there simply are not enough decently paying jobs for the number of people who need them — no matter how well trained they are" — and therefore job training programs cannot hope to address more than a small fraction of either the unemployment or poverty problems (ibid., 3, pp. 88–123; see also Jargowsky, 1998; and Eisenhower Foundation, 1998).   21

Lafer also demonstrates that throughout the 1984 to 1996 period, the total number of vacancies in jobs that paid above poverty wage was never more than one-seventh the number of people who needed those jobs, and "the gap between jobs needed and decently paying jobs available was never less than 16 million" (2002, pp. 34–35).   22

In the last 15 years or so, corporate pronouncements and federal economic policies (regarding expansion of visas for foreign workers, for example) have often been premised on the assumption that there has been a U.S. shortage of highly skilled computer technicians. And employers report that scientific and technical positions are often hard to fill (ibid., p. 54). Large corporations have argued that there are no skilled workers at home as a rationale for transferring computer-based operations to other countries. Although there are some shortages (nursing, for example), the evidence suggests that there is no actual shortage of programmers or systems analysts. "Rather, technology companies have hired lower-wage foreign programmers while thousands of more experienced (and more expensive) American programmers remained unemployed" (ibid., p. 54; see also Lardner, 1998).   23

Even in occupations such as nursing where there have been shortages, most technical professions are quite small as a share of the overall workforce, and therefore the total number of such jobs going begging has never been a significant source of job openings. For example, "the combined total of jobs for mathematicians, computer scientists, computer programmers, numerical control tool programmers, science technicians, electrical and electronic technicians, health technicians, and health assessment and treating occupations amounted to only 4.1% of the total workforce in 1984. After twenty years of unprecedented growth, this share is projected to grow to only 6.4 by the year 2006" (Lafer, 2002, p. 54; see also Galbraith, 1998; and Mishel, Bernstein, and Boushey, 2003).

Furthermore, as the technology has been adapted by business, "computer work" has been highly differentiated, with technical knowledge used by a relatively small group of well-paid specialists, and the vast majority of daily computer operators carrying out tasks in relatively low-wage occupations with few educational requirements (social workers, secretaries, credit card and computer call center operators, etc.) (Lafer, 2002, p. 56; see also Frenkel, Korczynski, Shire, and Tam, 1999; Galbraith, 1998; and Osterman, 2001).

To make the case for terminating the job-creation programs of CETA in 1982, Ronald Reagan argued that "if you look at the want ads, you see lots of available jobs" (Lafer, 2002, p. 44). As Lafer points out, however, "A look at the want ads in the newspapers shows that there are, indeed jobs, but only for the number of people the ads specify; and this illusion masks a deeper truth, which is that for large numbers of the poor there are NO decently paying jobs, no matter how hard they work or what training programs they enroll in" (ibid., p. 44).

A report in the *New York Times* in 1999 offered on-the-ground confirmation of the lack of jobs for workers who need them; Journalist Amy Waldman reported that at the height of the "full economy" in 1999, about 5,000 lined up for a job fair in the Bronx, New York. More than 40 employers were inside the Bronx County Building, trying to fill positions from sales clerk to registered nurse. Many of the people in line, who had been waiting for over three hours, said they had been looking for work, most often entry-level clerical positions, for months. Many of the people in line were on public assistance and were trying to get off it. "There is a huge pool of people with entry-level skills and not enough jobs for them," said Lucy Mayo, an employment specialist. "Most of the jobs that were available," she said, "offered low pay and no benefits. For example, Barnes and Noble, which was scheduled to open a new bookstore at Bay Plaza in the Bronx, had 50–75 jobs to fill. The jobs pay $7.25 an hour, are part-time with no benefits. Some of the large corporations there, however (Montefiore Medical Centers and the Correctional Services Corporation), offered benefits after six months. One man, aged 25, said he had left his last manufacturing job in Chatham,

NJ [a suburb of New York City], because the transportation was eating up half of his $7 hourly pay. With two children to support, he had been looking for work for six months. . . . There were 2,600 jobs created in the Bronx last year [1998], mostly in retail and construction. Still, 250,000 Bronx residents work outside the borough" (Waldman, Oct. 20, 1999).

Compounding the problem for entry-level workers, college-educated persons may be crowding them out. Research by Richard Murnane and Frank Levy shows that controlling for a person's mathematics or reading skill while a high school senior eliminates a substantial portion of the growth in the college-to-high school wage premium in a later period (for women essentially all, and for men about one-third). This suggests that it is basic high school–level skills that are increasingly in demand by employers, who are relying more and more on college completion as a screen to get the people who are more likely to have them (Murnane and Levy, 1996, p. 29; see also Pigeon and Wray, 1999).   *28*

That employers hire college-educated workers for jobs that require high school skills helps to explain why a more highly educated workforce does not necessarily earn higher wages. As entry-level employees obtain more education, employers merely ratchet up the requirements (see Galbraith, 1998; and Moss and Tilly, 2001).   *29*

Poverty

One consequence of a predominance of low-wage work and too few jobs in the U.S. is the numbers of poor people that approach the figures of 1959 before massive urban poverty became a national issue. Although the percentages are lower now, the numbers are still staggering: There were about as many people officially poor in 1993 (39.2 million) as in 1959 (39.4 million) — three years before Michael Harrington galvanized the nation's conscience, and ultimately a "war on poverty," by demonstrating that upwards of 40 million people were poor (Harrington, 1963, p. 9). (In 2003, almost 36 million — 35.8 million — were officially poor.)   *30*

Most poverty today is urban poverty. Demographic researcher Myron Orfield analyzed the distribution of poverty populations in the 25 largest metropolitan areas in the U.S. and found (confirmed by the 2000 Census) that about two-thirds of the U.S. poor today live in central cities and "urbanized," financially distressed suburbs.   *31*

As has been the case since the mid-1960s, most of the urban poor are Black or Latino. . . . The concentration of Black and Latino poor in low-income urban areas is due not only to a lack of jobs with decent pay (and insufficient income to support a move out if desired) but to the lack of federal and state implementation of antiracial discrimination laws, the lack of affordable housing outside of urban areas, and state-enabled local zoning exclusions based on social class (income).   *32*

The figures on poverty presented so far in this chapter are based on fed-   *33*
eral guidelines, and they underestimate the number of people who are
actually poor. The federal poverty formula in 1998 — during the height of
the '90s boom — determined that 13% of U.S. households (families and
unattached individuals) were poor. A single mother with two children was
officially poor if she earned $13,133 or less in that year. In 2003, a single
mother of two children was officially poor if she earned $15,260 or less.

Many social scientists have come to believe that these amounts are   *34*
too low, and that individuals and families with incomes up to 200% of
government thresholds are poor. The official formula for figuring
poverty — designed by federal employee Molly Orshansky in 1963 and
used in the war on poverty — utilized data collected in the 1950s. The
formula Orshansky devised was based on the price of a minimal food
budget (as determined by the Department of Agriculture). She multiplied the cost of food by three, to cover housing and health-care costs.
This figure, adjusted for family size, was the level below which families
and individuals were designated as poor.

Research in the 1950s showed that families spent about a third of   *35*
their budget on food. Since that time, however, the costs of housing and
health care have skyrocketed. Thus, most families today spend only
about a fifth of their income on food, and considerably more on housing
and health care (Bernstein, Brocht, and Spade-Aguilar, 2000, pp. 12–13;
see also Short, Iceland, and Garner, 1999; and recommendations by the
National Research Council, reported in Citro and Michael, 1995).

A recent national assessment of working families concluded that twice   *36*
the official poverty line is a more realistic measure of those who face critical and serious hardships in the U.S. This research documents that
working families with income up to 200% of the poverty line "experience
as many hardships" as families who are officially poor (Boushey,
Brocht, Gundersen, and Bernstein, 2001, p. 2).

A calculation of the individuals who earned less than 200% of the   *37*
poverty level in 2001 demonstrates a much larger percentage of poor
employees than is commonly acknowledged: 84.3% of Hispanic workers,
80% of Black workers, and 64.3% of White workers made wages at or
under 200% of the official poverty line (Mishel, Bernstein, and Schmitt,
2001, pp. 130–139). A calculation of *families* living with earnings up to
200% of the poverty line reveals that Black and Latino families face the
greatest financial hurdles. Over 50% of Black and Latino families earn
less than 200% of the poverty level, compared to only 20.3% of White
families, even though White families make up the majority (50.5%) of
families that fall below 200% of the poverty level (ibid., p. 12).

Families headed by a worker with less than a high school education   *38*
are the most likely to fall below 200% (68.6%), but over three-fourths of
families who fall below are headed by a worker with a high school education or more. An indication of the failure of higher education to
secure good wages is the fact that over a third (33.6%) are headed by a

worker with some college or a college degree (ibid., p. 13). And an indictment of the failure of full-time work to provide a decent living is the fact that a full half (50.0%) of families falling below 200% of the poverty line have a *full-time, year-round worker* (ibid., p. 15).

The statistics in this chapter relate in a fairly staid manner what is   *39* actually a potentially inflammatory political situation. A humane reckoning of poverty reveals that the vast majority of African Americans and Latinos who have jobs, and more than two-thirds of employed Whites, do not earn enough to live on. This outrages me, as the experience must anger those who live it. But the situation is not immutable. Economies are indeed political, regulated by officials elected and appointed who formulate legislation, legal decisions, and other policy. These officials, and their mandates, can be changed — but only if all of us who are incensed by the policies' indecency stand together.

In order for injustice to create an outrage that can ultimately be   *40* channeled into public demands, knowledge of the facts is necessary, and an appreciation of the consequences must be clear. I hope this chapter clarifies the situation regarding poverty. It is also extremely important . . . that people who are poor come to see their situation not as a result of their own failure but as a result of systemic causes. That is, if governments created enough jobs, and if businesses paid higher wages, workers would not be poor.

And knowledge is crucial to an accurate understanding of what   *41* plagues urban education. We must know where the problem lies in order to identify workable solutions. We can win the war against poverty and poor schools only if we know where the poverty originates. The next chapter describes one important source, federal policies that maintain low-wage work and unemployment in urban areas, and ways these can set up failure for the families and schools there.

BIBLIOGRAPHY

Bernstein, Jared, Brocht, Chauna, and Spade-Aguilar, Maggie. (2000). *How much is enough? Basic family budgets for working families.* Washington, DC: Economic Policy Institute.
Boushey, Heather, Brocht, Chauna, Gundersen, Betheny, and Bernstein, Jared. (2001). *Hardships in America: The real story of working families.* Washington, DC: Economic Policy Institute.
Citro, Constance, and Michael, Robert (Eds.). (1995). *Measuring poverty: A new approach.* Washington, DC: National Academy Press.
Department of Labor. (2002). *Occupation projections to 2010.* Washington, DC.
Economic Policy Institute. (1999, Feb. 17). *Entry-level workers face lower wages.* Washington, DC.
Economic Policy Institute. (2002, July 24). *Economic snapshots.* Washington, DC.
Economic Policy Institute. (2004, July 21). *Jobs in the future: No boom in the need for college graduates.* Washington, DC.
Eisenhower Foundation. (1998). *Background report.* Washington DC.

Frenkel, Stephen, Korczynski, Maretk, Shire, Karen, and Tam, May. (1999). *On the front line: Organization of work in the information economy.* Ithaca, NY: Cornell University Press.

Galbraith, James K. (1998). *Created unequal: The crisis in American pay.* Twentieth Century Fund Book. New York: Free Press, Simon and Schuster.

Harrington, Michael. (1963). *The other America: Poverty in the United States.* Baltimore, MD: Penguin.

Jargowsky, Paul. (1998). *Poverty and place: Ghettos, barrios, and the American city.* New York: Russell Sage.

Lafer, Gordon. (2002). *The job training charade.* Ithaca, NY: Cornell University Press.

Lardner, James. (1998, March 16). Too old to write code? *U.S. News & World Report.* Cited in Lafer, 2002 (p. 250).

Mishel, Lawrence, Bernstein, Jared, and Boushey, Heather. (2003). *The state of working America: 2002/2003.* Ithaca, NY: Cornell University Press.

Mishel, Lawrence, Bernstein, Jared, and Schmitt, John. (2001). *The state of working America: 2000/2001.* Ithaca, NY: Cornell University Press.

Moss, Philip, and Tilly, Chris. (2001). *Stories employers tell: Race, skill, and hiring in America.* New York: Russell Sage.

Murnane, Richard, and Levy, Frank. (1996). *Teaching the new basic skills: Principles for educating children to thrive in a changing economy.* New York: Free Press.

Orfield, Myron. (1997). *Metropolitics: A regional agenda for community and stability.* Washington, DC: Brookings Institute.

Osterman, Paul. (2001). *Working in America: A blueprint for the new labor market.* Cambridge, MA: MIT Press.

Pigeon, Marc-Andre, and Wray, Randall. (1999). Down and out in the United States: An inside look at the out of the labor force population. Public Policy Brief No. 54. Annandale-on-Hudson, NY: The Jerome Levy Economics Institute of Bard College.

Short, Kathleen, Iceland, John, and Garner, Thesia. (1999). *Experimental poverty measures.* Washington, DC: U.S. Census Bureau.

Waldman, Amy. (1999, Oct. 20). Long line in the Bronx, but for jobs, not the Yankees. *New York Times.*

A Practice Sequence: Analyzing the Appeals in a Text

1 Make a list of the major premises that inform Anyon's argument, and examine the evidence she uses to support them. To what extent do you find her evidence credible? Do you generally agree or disagree with the conclusions she draws? Be prepared to explain your responses to your class or peer group.

2 Note instances where Anyon appeals to ethos, pathos, and logos. How would you describe the ways she makes these three types of appeals? How does she present herself? What does she seem to assume? How does she help you understand the chain of reasoning by which she moves from premises to conclusion?

3 Working in groups of three or four, compose a letter to Anyon in which you take issue with her argument. This does not mean your group has to disagree with her entire argument, although of course you may. Rather, present your group's own contribution to the conversation in which she is participating. You may want to ask her to further explain one or more of her points, or suggest what she might be leaving out, or add your own take or evidence to her argument. As a group, you will have to agree on your focus. In the letter, include a summary of Anyon's argument or the part of it on which your group is focusing. Pay close attention to your own strategies for appealing to her — how you present yourselves, how you appeal to her values and emotions, and how you present your reasons for your own premises and conclusion.

9

From Introductions to Conclusions: Drafting an Essay

In this chapter, we describe strategies for crafting introductions that set up your argument. We then describe the characteristics of well-formulated paragraphs that will help you build your argument. Finally, we provide you with some strategies for writing conclusions that reinforce what is new about your argument, what is at stake, and what readers should do with the knowledge you convey.

DRAFTING INTRODUCTIONS

The introduction is where you set up your argument. It's where you identify a widely held assumption, challenge that assumption, and state your thesis. Writers use a number of strategies to set up their arguments. In this section we look at five of them:

- Moving from a general topic to a specific thesis (inverted-triangle introduction)
- Introducing the topic with a story (narrative introduction)
- Beginning with a question (interrogative introduction)
- Capturing readers' attention with something unexpected (paradoxical introduction)
- Identifying a gap in knowledge (minding-the-gap introduction)

Remember that an introduction need not be limited to a single paragraph. It may take several paragraphs to effectively set up your argument.

Keep in mind that you have to make these strategies your own. That is, we can suggest models, but you must make them work for your own argument. You must imagine your readers and what will engage them. What tone do you want to take? Playful? Serious? Formal? Urgent? The attitude you want to convey will depend on your purpose, your argument, and the needs of your audience.

■ The Inverted-Triangle Introduction

An **inverted-triangle introduction**, like an upside-down triangle, is broad at the top and pointed at the base. It begins with a general statement of the topic and then narrows its focus, ending with the point of the paragraph (and the triangle), the writer's thesis. We can see this strategy at work in the introduction from a student's essay below. The student writer (1) begins with a broad description of the problem she will address, (2) then focuses on a set of widely held but troublesome assumptions, and (3) finally, responding to what she sees as a pervasive problem, presents her thesis.

The student begins with a general set of assumptions about education that she believes people readily accept.

She then cites author bell hooks, to identify an approach that makes use of these assumptions — the "banking system" of education, a term hooks borrows from educator Paulo Freire.

The student then points to the banking system as the problem. This sets up her thesis about the "true purpose" of education.

In today's world, many believe that education's sole purpose is to communicate information for students to store and draw on as necessary. By storing this information, students hope to perform well on tests. Good test scores assure good grades. Good grades eventually lead to acceptances into good colleges, which ultimately guarantee good jobs. Many teachers and students, convinced that education exists as a tool to secure good jobs, rely on the *banking system*. In her essay "Teaching to Transgress," bell hooks defines the *banking system* as an "approach to learning that is rooted in the notion that all students need to do is consume information fed to them by a professor and be able to memorize and store it" (185). Through the banking system, students focus solely on facts, missing the important themes and life lessons available in classes and school materials. The banking system misdirects the fundamental goals of education. Education's true purpose is to prepare students for the real world by allowing them access to pertinent life knowledge available in their studies. Education should then entice students to apply this pertinent life knowledge to daily life struggles through praxis. In addition to her definition of the banking system, hooks offers the idea of praxis from the work of Paulo Freire. When incorporated into education, *praxis*, or "action and reflection upon the world in order to change it" (185), offers an advantageous educational tool that enhances the true purpose of education and overcomes the banking system.

The strategy of writing an introduction as an inverted triangle entails first identifying an idea, argument, or concept that people appear to accept as true; next, pointing out the problems with that idea, argument, or concept; and then, in a few sentences, setting out a thesis — how those problems can be resolved.

■ The Narrative Introduction

Opening with a short **narrative**, or story, is a strategy many writers use successfully to draw readers into a topic. A narrative introduction relates a sequence of events and can be especially effective if you think you need to coax indifferent or reluctant readers into taking an interest in the topic. Of course, a narrative introduction delays the declaration of your argument, so it's wise to choose a short story that clearly connects to your argument, and get to the thesis as quickly as possible (within a few paragraphs) before your readers start wondering "What's the point of this story?"

Notice how the student writer uses a narrative introduction to her argument in her essay titled "Throwing a Punch at Gender Roles: How Women's Boxing at Notre Dame Empowers Women."

The student's entire first paragraph is a narrative that takes us into the world of women's boxing and foreshadows her thesis.

Glancing at my watch, I ran into the gym, noting to myself that being late to the first day of boxing practice was not the right way to make a good first impression. I flew down the stairs into the basement, to the room the boxers have lovingly dubbed "The Pit." What greeted me when I got there was more than I could ever have imagined. Picture a room filled with boxing gloves of all sizes covering an entire wall, a mirror covering another, a boxing ring in a corner, and an awesome collection of framed newspaper and magazine articles chronicling the boxers whose pictures were hanging on every wall. Now picture that room with seventy-plus girls on the floor doing push-ups, sweat dripping down their faces. I was immediately struck by the discipline this sport would take from me, but I had no idea I would take so much more from it.

With her narrative as a backdrop, the student identifies a problem, using the transition word yet to mark her challenge to the conditions she observes in the university's women's boxing program.

The university offers the only nonmilitary-based college-level women's boxing program in America, and it also offers women the chance to push their physical limits in a regulated environment. Yet the program is plagued with disappointments. I have experienced for myself the stereotypes female boxers face and have dealt with the harsh reality that boxing is still widely recognized as only a men's sport. This paper will show that the women's boxing program at ND serves as a much-needed outlet for females to come face-to-face with aspects of themselves they would not typically get a chance to explore. It will

The writer then states her thesis (what her paper "will show"): Despite the problems of stereotyping, women's boxing offers women significant opportunities for growth.

also examine how viewing this sport as a positive opportunity for women at ND indicates that there is growing hope that very soon more activities similar to women's boxing may be better received by society in general. I will accomplish these goals by analyzing scholarly journals, old *Observer* [the school newspaper] articles, and survey questions answered by the captains of the 2003 women's boxing team of ND.

The student writer uses a visually descriptive narrative to introduce us to the world of women's college boxing; then, in the second paragraph, she steers us toward the purpose of the paper and the methods she will use to develop her argument about what women's boxing offers to young women and to the changing world of sports.

■ The Interrogative Introduction

An **interrogative introduction** invites readers into the conversation of your essay by asking one or more questions, which the essay goes on to answer. You want to think of a question that will pique your readers' interest, enticing them to read on to discover how your insights shed light on the issue. Notice the question Daphne Spain, a professor of urban and environmental planning, uses to open her essay "Spatial Segregation and Gender Stratification in the Workplace."

Spain sets up her argument by asking a question and then tentatively answering it with a reference to a published study.

In the third sentence she states her thesis — that men and women have very little contact in the workplace.

Finally, she outlines the effects that this lack of contact has on women.

To what extent do women and men who work in different occupations also work in different space? Baran and Teegarden propose that occupational segregation in the insurance industry is "tantamount to spatial segregation by gender" since managers are overwhelmingly male and clerical staff are predominantly female. This essay examines the spatial conditions of women's work and men's work and proposes that working women and men come into daily contact with one another very infrequently. Further, women's jobs can be classified as "open floor," but men's jobs are more likely to be "closed door." That is, women work in a more public environment with less control of their space than men. This lack of spatial control both reflects and contributes to women's lower occupational status by limiting opportunities for the transfer of knowledge from men to women.

By the end of this introductory paragraph, Spain has explained some of the terms she will use in her essay (*open floor* and *closed door*) and has offered in her final sentence a clear statement of her thesis.

In "Harry Potter and the Technology of Magic," literature scholar Elizabeth Teare begins by contextualizing the Harry Potter publishing phenomenon. Then she raises a question about what is fueling this success story.

In her first four sentences, Teare describes something she is curious about and she hopes readers will be curious about — the growing popularity of the Harry Potter books.

The July/August 2001 issue of *Book* lists J. K. Rowling as one of the ten most influential people in publishing. She shares space on this list with John Grisham and Oprah Winfrey, along with less famous but equally powerful insiders in the book industry. What these industry leaders have in common is an almost magical power to make books succeed in the marketplace, and this magic, in addition to that performed with wands, Rowling's novels appear to practice. Opening weekend sales charted like those of a blockbuster movie (not to mention the blockbuster movie itself), the reconstruction of the venerable *New York Times* bestseller lists, the creation of a new nation's worth of web sites in the territory of cyberspace, and of course the legendary inspiration of tens of millions of child readers — the Harry Potter books have transformed both the technologies of reading and the way we

In the fifth sentence, Teare asks the question she will try to answer in the rest of the essay.

understand those technologies. What is it that makes these books — about a lonely boy whose first act on learning he is a wizard is to go shopping for a wand — not only an international phenomenon among children and parents and teachers but also a topic of compelling interest to literary, social,

Finally, in the last sentence, Teare offers a partial answer to her question — her thesis.

and cultural critics? I will argue that the stories the books tell, as well as the stories we're telling about them, enact both our fantasies and our fears of children's literature and publishing in the context of twenty-first-century commercial and technological culture.

In the final two sentences of the introduction, Teare raises her question about the root of this "international phenomenon" and then offers her thesis. By the end of the opening paragraph, then, the reader knows exactly what question is driving Teare's essay and the answer she proposes to explain throughout the essay.

■ The Paradoxical Introduction

A **paradoxical introduction** appeals to readers' curiosity by pointing out an aspect of the topic that runs counter to their expectations. Just as an interrogative introduction draws readers in by asking a question, a paradoxical introduction draws readers in by saying, in effect, "Here's something completely surprising and unlikely about this issue, but my essay will go on to show you how it is true." In this passage from "'Holding Back': Negotiating a Glass Ceiling on Women's Muscular

Strength," sociologist Shari L. Dworkin points to a paradox in our commonsense understanding of bodies as the product of biology, not culture.

In the first sentence, Dworkin quotes from a study to identify the thinking that she is going to challenge.

Notice how Dworkin signals her own position (however) relative to commonly held assumptions.

Dworkin ends by stating her thesis, noting a paradox that will surprise readers.

Current work in gender studies points to how "when examined closely, much of what we take for granted about gender and its causes and effects either does not hold up, or can be explained differently." These arguments become especially contentious when confronting nature/culture debates on gendered *bodies*. After all, "common sense" frequently tells us that flesh and blood bodies are about biology. However, bodies are also shaped and constrained through cumulative social practices, structures of opportunity, wider cultural meanings, and more. Paradoxically, then, when we think that we are "really seeing" naturally sexed bodies, perhaps we are seeing the effect of internalizing gender ideologies — carrying out social practices — and this constructs our vision of "sexed" bodies.

Dworkin's strategy in the first three sentences is to describe common practice, the understanding that bodies are biological. Then, in the sentences beginning "However" and "Paradoxically," she advances the surprising idea that our bodies — not just the clothes we wear, for example — carry cultural gender markers. Her essay then goes on to examine women's weight lifting, and the complex motives driving many women to create a body that is perceived as muscular but not masculine.

■ The Minding-the-Gap Introduction

This type of introduction takes its name from the British train system, the voice on the loudspeaker that intones "Mind the gap!" at every stop, to call riders' attention to the gap between the train car and the platform. In a **minding-the-gap introduction**, a writer calls readers' attention to a gap in the research on an issue, and then uses the rest of the essay to fill in the "gap." A minding-the-gap introduction says, in effect, "Wait a minute. There's something missing from this conversation, and my research and ideas will fill in this gap."

For example, in the introductory paragraphs to their book *Men's Lives*, Michael S. Kimmel and Michael A. Messner explain how the book is different from other books that discuss men's lives, and how it serves a different purpose.

The authors begin with an assumption and then challenge it. A transition word (but) signals the challenge.

This is a book about men. But, unlike other books about men, which line countless library shelves, this is a book about men as men. It is a book in which men's experiences are not taken for granted as we explore the "real" and significant accomplishments of men, but a book in which those experiences are treated as significant and important in themselves.

The authors follow with a question that provokes readers' interest and points to the gap they summarize in the last sentence.

But what does it mean to examine men "as men"? Most courses in a college curriculum are about men, aren't they? But these courses routinely deal with men only in their public roles, so we come to know and understand men as scientists, politicians, military figures, writers, and philosophers. Rarely, if ever, are men understood through the prism of gender.

Kimmel and Messner use these opening paragraphs to highlight both what they find problematic about the existing literature on men and to introduce readers to their own approach.

Strategies for Drafting Introductions

1 **Use an inverted triangle.** Begin with a broad situation, concept, or idea, and narrow the focus to your thesis.

2 **Begin with a narrative.** Capture readers' imagination and interest with a story that sets the stage for your argument.

3 **Ask a question that you will answer.** Provoke readers' interest with a question, and then use your thesis to answer the question.

4 **Present a paradox.** Begin with an assumption that readers accept as true and formulate a thesis that not only challenges that assumption but may very well seem paradoxical.

5 **Mind the gap.** Identify what readers know and then what they don't know (or what you believe they need to know).

A Practice Sequence: Drafting an Introduction

1 Write or rewrite your introduction (which, as you've seen, may involve more than one paragraph), using one of the strategies described above. Then share your introduction with one of your peers and ask the following questions:

- To what extent did the strategy compel you to want to read further?
- To what extent is my thesis clear?
- How effectively do I draw a distinction between what I believe others assume to be true and my own approach?
- Is there another way that I might have made my introduction more compelling?

After listening to the responses, try a second strategy and then ask your peer which introduction is more effective.

2 If you do not have your own introduction to work on, revise the introduction below from one of our students' essays, combining two of the strategies we describe above.

> News correspondent Pauline Frederick once commented, "When a man gets up to speak people listen then look. When a woman gets up, people look; then, if they like what they see, they listen." Ironically, the harsh reality of this statement is given life by the ongoing controversy over America's most recognizable and sometimes notorious toy, Barbie. Celebrating her 40th birthday this year, Barbie has become this nation's most beleaguered soldier (a woman no less) of idolatry who has been to the front lines and back more times than the average "Joe." This doll, a piece of plastic, a toy, incurs both criticism and praise spanning both ends of the ideological spectrum. Barbie's curvaceous and basically unrealistic body piques the ire of both liberals and conservatives, each contending that Barbie stands for the distinct view of the other. One hundred and eighty degrees south, others praise Barbie's (curves and all) ability to unlock youthful imagination and potential. M. G. Lord explains Barbie best: "To study Barbie, one sometimes has to hold seemingly contradictory ideas in one's head at the same time. . . . The doll functions like a Rorschach test: people project wildly dissimilar and often opposing meanings on it. . . . And her meaning, like her face, has not been static over time." In spite of the extreme polarity, a sole unconscious consensus manifests itself about Barbie. Barbie is "the icon" of womanhood and the twentieth century. She is the American dream. Barbie is "us." The question is always the same: What message does Barbie send? Barbie is a toy. She is the image of what we see.

DEVELOPING PARAGRAPHS

In your introduction, you set forth your thesis. Then, in subsequent paragraphs, you have to develop your argument. Remember our metaphor: If your thesis, or main claim, is the skewer that runs through each paragraph in your essay, then these paragraphs are the "meat" of your argument. The paragraphs that follow your introduction carry the burden of evidence in your argument. After all, a claim cannot stand on its own without supporting evidence. Generally speaking, each paragraph should include a topic sentence that brings the main idea of the paragraph into focus, be unified around the main idea of the topic sentence, and adequately develop the idea. At the same time, a paragraph does not stand on its own; as part of your overall argument, it can refer to what you've said earlier, gesture toward where you are heading, and connect to the larger conversation to which you are contributing.

We now ask you to read an excerpt from "Reinventing 'America': Call for a New National Identity," by Elizabeth Martínez, and answer some questions about how you think the author develops her argument, paragraph by paragraph. Then we discuss her work in the context of the three key elements of paragraphs: *topic sentences*, *unity*, and *adequate development*. As you read, pay attention to how, sentence by sentence, Martínez develops her paragraphs. We also ask that you consider how she makes her argument provocative, impassioned, and urgent for her audience.

┌─ **ABOUT THE READING** ───────────────────────────────────

Elizabeth Martínez is a Chicana activist who since 1960 has worked in and documented different movements for change, including the civil rights, women's, and Chicano movements. She is the author of six books and numerous articles. Her best-known work is *500 Years of Chicano History in Pictures* (1991), which became the basis of a two-part video she scripted and codirected. Her latest book is *De Colores Means All of Us: Latina Views for a Multi-Colored Century* (1998). In "Reinventing 'America,'" Martínez argues that Americans' willingness to accept a "myth" as "the basis for [the] nation's self-defined identity" has brought the country to a crisis.

└───

ELIZABETH MARTÍNEZ

From Reinventing "America": Call for a New National Identity

For some fifteen years, starting in 1940, 85 percent of all U.S. elementary schools used the Dick and Jane series to teach children how to read. The series starred Dick, Jane, their white middle-class parents, their dog Spot and their life together in a home with a white picket fence.   1

"Look, Jane, look! See Spot run!" chirped the two kids. It was a house full of glorious family values, where Mom cooked while Daddy went to work in a suit and mowed the lawn on weekends. The Dick and Jane books also taught that you should do your job and help others. All this affirmed an equation of middle-class whiteness with virtue.   2

In the mid-1990s, museums, libraries and eighty Public Broadcasting Service (PBS) stations across the country had exhibits and programs commemorating the series. At one museum, an attendant commented, "When you hear someone crying, you know they are looking at the Dick   3 and Jane books." It seems nostalgia runs rampant among many Euro-Americans: a nostalgia for the days of unchallenged White Supremacy — both moral and material — when life was "simple."

We've seen that nostalgia before in the nation's history. But today it signifies a problem reaching a new intensity. It suggests a national identity crisis that promises to bring in its wake an unprecedented nervous breakdown for the dominant society's psyche.   *4*

Nowhere is this more apparent than in California, which has long been on the cutting edge of the nation's present and future reality. Warning sirens have sounded repeatedly in the 1990s, such as the fierce battle over new history textbooks for public schools, Proposition 187's ugly denial of human rights to immigrants, the 1996 assault on affirmative action that culminated in Proposition 209, and the 1997 move to abolish bilingual education. Attempts to copycat these reactionary measures have been seen in other states.   *5*

The attack on affirmative action isn't really about affirmative action. Essentially it is another tactic in today's war on the gains of the 1960s, a tactic rooted in Anglo resentment and fear. A major source of that fear: the fact that California will almost surely have a majority of people of color in 20 to 30 years at most, with the nation as a whole not far behind.   *6*

Check out the February 3, 1992, issue of *Sports Illustrated* with its double-spread ad for *Time* magazine. The ad showed hundreds of newborn babies in their hospital cribs, all of them Black or brown except for a rare white face here and there. The headline says, "Hey, whitey! It's your turn at the back of the bus!" The ad then tells you, read *Time* magazine to keep up with today's hot issues. That manipulative image could have been published today; its implication of shifting power appears to be the recurrent nightmare of too many potential Anglo allies.   *7*

Euro-American anxiety often focuses on the sense of a vanishing national identity. Behind the attacks on immigrants, affirmative action and multiculturalism, behind the demand for "English Only" laws and the rejection of bilingual education, lies the question: with all these new people, languages and cultures, what will it mean to be an American? If that question once seemed, to many people, to have an obvious, universally applicable answer, today new definitions must be found. But too often Americans, with supposed scholars in the lead, refuse to face that need and instead nurse a nostalgia for some bygone clarity. They remain trapped in denial.   *8*

An array of such ostriches, heads in the sand, began flapping their feathers noisily with the publication of Allan Bloom's 1987 best-selling book, *The Closing of the American Mind*. Bloom bemoaned the decline of our "common values" as a society, meaning the decline of Euro-American cultural centricity (shall we just call it cultural imperialism?). Since then we have seen constant sniping at "diversity" goals across the land. The assault has often focused on how U.S. history is taught. And with reason,   *9* for this country's identity rests on a particular narrative about the historical origins of the United States as a nation.

The Great White Origin Myth

Every society has an origin narrative that explains that society to itself *10*
and the world with a set of stories and symbols. The origin myth, as scholar-activist Roxanne Dunbar Ortiz has termed it, defines how a society understands its place in the world and its history. The myth provides the basis for a nation's self-defined identity. Most origin narratives can be called myths because they usually present only the most flattering view of a nation's history; they are not distinguished by honesty.

Ours begins with Columbus "discovering" a hemisphere where some 80 *11*
million people already lived but didn't really count (in what became the United States, they were just buffalo-chasing "savages" with no grasp of real estate values and therefore doomed to perish). It continues with the brave Pilgrims, a revolution by independence-loving colonists against a decadent English aristocracy and the birth of an energetic young republic that promised democracy and equality (that is, to white male landowners). In the 1840s, the new nation expanded its size by almost one-third, thanks to a victory over that backward land of little brown people called Mexico. Such has been the basic account of how the nation called the United States of America came into being as presently configured.

The myth's omissions are grotesque. It ignores three major pillars of *12*
our nationhood: genocide, enslavement and imperialist expansion (such nasty words, who wants to hear them? — but that's the problem). The massive extermination of indigenous peoples provided our land base; the enslavement of African labor made our economic growth possible; and the seizure of half of Mexico by war (or threat of renewed war) extended this nation's boundaries north to the Pacific and south to the Rio Grande. Such are the foundation stones of the United States, within an economic system that made this country the first in world history to be born capitalist. . . .

Racism as Linchpin of the U.S. National Identity

A crucial embellishment of the origin myth and key element of the *13*
national identity has been the myth of the frontier, analyzed in Richard Slotkin's *Gunfighter Nation*, the last volume of a fascinating trilogy. He describes Theodore Roosevelt's belief that the West was won thanks to American arms, "the means by which progress and nationality will be achieved." That success, Roosevelt continued, "depends on the heroism of men who impose on the course of events the latent virtues of their

'race.' " Roosevelt saw conflict on the frontier producing a series of virile "fighters and breeders" who would eventually generate a new leadership class. Militarism thus went hand in hand with the racialization of history's protagonists. . . .

The frontier myth embodied the nineteenth-century concept of Manifest Destiny, a doctrine that served to justify expansionist violence by means of intrinsic racial superiority. Manifest Destiny was Yankee conquest as the inevitable result of a confrontation between enterprise and progress (white) versus passivity and backwardness (Indian, Mexican). "Manifest" meant "God-given," and the whole doctrine is profoundly rooted in religious conviction going back to the earliest colonial times. In his short, powerful book *Manifest Destiny: American Expansion and the Empire of Right*, Professor Anders Stephanson tells how the Puritans reinvented the Jewish notion of chosenness and applied it to this hemisphere so that territorial expansion became God's will. . . .   *14*

Manifest Destiny Dies Hard

The concept of Manifest Destiny, with its assertion of racial superiority sustained by military power, has defined U.S. identity for 150 years. . . .   *15*

Today's origin myth and the resulting concept of national identity make for an intellectual prison where it is dangerous to ask big questions about this society's superiority. When otherwise decent people are trapped in such a powerful desire not to feel guilty, self-deception becomes unavoidable. To cease our present falsification of collective memory should, and could, open the doors of that prison. When together we cease equating whiteness with Americanness, a new day can dawn. As David Roediger, the social historian, has said, "[Whiteness] is the empty and therefore terrifying attempt to build an identity on what one isn't, and on whom one can hold back."   *16*

Redefining the U.S. origin narrative, and with it this country's national identity, could prove liberating for our collective psyche. It does not mean Euro-Americans should wallow individually in guilt. It does mean accepting collective responsibility to deal with the implications of our real origin. A few apologies, for example, might be a step in the right direction. In 1997, the idea was floated in Congress to apologize for slavery; it encountered opposition from all sides. But to reject the notion because corrective action, not an apology, is needed misses the point. Having defined itself as the all-time best country in the world, the United States fiercely denies the need to make a serious official apology for anything. . . . To press for any serious, official apology does imply a new origin narrative, a new self-image, an ideological sea-change.   *17*

Accepting the implications of a different narrative could also shed light on today's struggles. In the affirmative-action struggle, for example,   *18* opponents have said that that policy is no longer needed because racism ended with the Civil Rights Movement. But if we look at slavery as a fundamental pillar of this nation, going back centuries, it becomes obvious that racism could not have been ended by 30 years of mild reforms. If we see how the myth of the frontier idealized the white male adventurer as the central hero of national history, with the woman as sunbonneted helpmate, then we might better understand the dehumanized ways in which women have continued to be treated. A more truthful origin narrative could also help break down divisions among peoples of color by revealing common experiences and histories of cooperation.

For Analysis and Discussion

1. To what extent does the narrative Martínez begins with make you want to read further?
2. How does she connect this narrative to the rest of her argument?
3. How does she use repetition to create unity in her essay?
4. What assumptions does Martínez challenge?
5. How does she use questions to engage her readers?

■ Use Topic Sentences to Focus Your Paragraphs

The **topic sentence** states the main point of a paragraph. It should

- provide a partial answer to the question motivating the writer.
- act as an extension of the writer's thesis and the question motivating the writer's argument.
- serve as a guidepost, telling readers what the paragraph is about.
- help create unity and coherence both within the paragraph and within the essay.

Elizabeth Martínez begins by describing how elementary schools in the 1940s and 1950s used the Dick and Jane series not only to teach reading but also to foster a particular set of values — values that she believes do not serve all children enrolled in America's schools. In paragraph 4, she states her thesis, explaining that nostalgia in the United States has created "a national identity crisis that promises to bring in its wake an unprecedented nervous breakdown for the dominant society's psyche." This is a point that builds on an observation she makes in paragraph 3: "It seems nostalgia runs rampant among many Euro-Americans: a nostalgia for the days of unchallenged White Supremacy — both moral and material — when life was 'simple.'" Martínez often returns to this notion of nostalgia for a past that seems "simple" to explain what she sees as an impending crisis.

Consider the first sentence of paragraph 5 as a topic sentence. With Martínez's key points in mind, notice how she uses the sentence to make her thesis more specific. Notice too, how she ties in the crisis and break-down she alludes to in paragraph 4. Essentially, Martínez tells her readers that they can see these problems at play in California, an indicator of the "nation's present and future reality."

> *Nowhere is this more apparent than in California, which has long been on the cutting edge of the nation's present and future reality.* Warning sirens have sounded repeatedly in the 1990s, such as the fierce battle over new history textbooks for public schools, Proposition 187's ugly denial of human rights to immigrants, the 1996 assault on affirmative action that culminated in Proposition 209, and the 1997 move to abolish bilingual education. *Attempts to copycat these reactionary measures have been seen in other states.*

The final sentence of paragraph 5 sets up the remainder of the essay.

As readers, we expect each subsequent paragraph to respond in some way to the issue Martínez has raised. She meets that expectation by formulating a topic sentence that appears at the beginning of the paragraph. The topic sentence is what helps create unity and coherence in the essay.

■ Create Unity in Your Paragraphs

Each paragraph in an essay should focus on the subject suggested by the topic sentence. If a paragraph begins with one focus or major point of discussion, it should not end with another. Several strategies can contribute to the unity of each paragraph:

Use details that follow logically from your topic sentence and maintain a single focus — a focus that is clearly an extension of your thesis. For example, in paragraph 5, Martínez's topic sentence ("Nowhere is this more apparent than in California, which has long been on the cutting edge of the nation's present and future reality") helps to create unity because it refers back to her thesis (*this* refers to the "national identity crisis" mentioned in paragraph 4) and limits the focus of what she includes in the paragraph to "the fierce battle over new history textbooks" and recent pieces of legislation in California that follow directly from and support the claim of the topic sentence.

Repeat key words to guide your readers.   A second strategy for creating unity is to repeat (or use synonyms for) key words within a given paragraph. You can see this at work in paragraph 12 (notice the words we've underscored), where Martínez explains that America's origin narrative omits significant details:

> The myth's omissions are grotesque. It ignores three major pillars of our nationhood: <u>genocide</u>, <u>enslavement</u> and <u>imperialist expansion</u> (such nasty words, who wants to hear them? — but that's the problem). The massive <u>extermination</u> of indigenous peoples provided our land base; the <u>enslavement</u> of African labor made our economic growth possible; and

the seizure of half of Mexico by war (or threat of renewed war) extended this nation's boundaries north to the Pacific and south to the Rio Grande. Such are the foundation stones of the United States, within an economic system that made this country the first in world history to be born capitalist. . . .

Specifically, Martínez tells us that the origin narrative ignores "three major pillars of our nationhood: genocide, enslavement and imperialist expansion." She then substitutes *extermination* for "genocide," repeats *enslavement*, and substitutes *seizure* for "imperialist expansionist." By connecting words in a paragraph, as Martínez does here, you help readers understand that the details you provide are all relevant to the point you want to make.

Use transition words to link ideas from different sentences.   A third strategy for creating unity within paragraphs is to establish a clear relationship among different ideas by using **transition words** or phrases. Transition words or phrases signal to your readers the direction your ideas are taking. Table 9.1 lists common transition words and phrases grouped by function — that is, for adding a new idea, presenting a contrasting idea, or drawing a conclusion about an idea.

Martínez uses transition words and phrases throughout the excerpt here. In several places, she uses the word *but* to make a contrast — to draw a distinction between an idea that many people accept as true and an alternative idea that she wants to pursue. Notice in paragraph 17 how she signals the importance of an official apology for slavery — and by implication genocide and the seizure of land from Mexico:

> . . . A few apologies, for example, might be a step in the right direction. In 1997, the idea was floated in Congress to apologize for slavery; it encountered opposition from all sides. But to reject the notion because corrective action, not an apology, is needed misses the point. Having defined itself as the all-time best country in the world, the United States fiercely denies the need to make a serious official apology for anything. . . . To press for any serious, official apology does imply a new origin narrative, a new self-image, an ideological sea-change.

TABLE 9.1   Common Transition Words and Phrases

Adding an Idea	Presenting a Contrasting Idea	Drawing a Logical Conclusion
also, and, further, moreover, in addition to, in support of, similarly	although, alternatively, as an alternative, but, by way of contrast, despite, even though, however, in contrast to, nevertheless, nonetheless, rather than, yet	as a result, because of, consequently, finally, in sum, in the end, subsequently, therefore, thus

Similarly, in the last paragraph, Martínez counters the argument that affirmative action is not necessary because racism no longer exists:

> . . . In the affirmative-action struggle, for example, opponents have said that that policy is no longer needed because racism ended with the Civil Rights Movement. But if we look at slavery as a fundamental pillar of this nation, going back centuries, it becomes obvious that racism could not have been ended by 30 years of mild reforms. . . .

There are a number of ways to rephrase what Martínez is saying in paragraph 18. We could substitute *however* for "but." Or, we could combine the two sentences into one to point to the relationship between the two competing ideas: *Although some people oppose affirmative action, believing that racism no longer exists, I would argue that racism remains a fundamental pillar of this nation.* Or we could pull together Martínez's different points to draw a logical conclusion using a transition word like *therefore.* Martínez observes that our country is in crisis as a result of increased immigration. *Therefore, we need to reassess our conceptions of national identity to account for the diversity that increased immigration has created.* We can substitute any of the transition words in Table 9.1 for drawing a logical conclusion.

The list of transition words and phrases in Table 9.1 is hardly exhaustive, but it gives you a sense of the ways to connect ideas so that readers understand how the ideas you write about are related. Are they similar ideas? Do they build on or support one another? Are you challenging accepted ideas? Or are you drawing a logical connection from a number of different ideas?

■ Use Critical Strategies to Develop Your Paragraphs

To develop a paragraph, you can use a range of strategies, depending on what you want to accomplish and what you believe your readers will need to be persuaded by what you argue. Among these strategies are using examples and illustrations; citing data (facts, statistics, evidence, details); analyzing texts; telling a story or anecdote; defining terms; making comparisons; and examining causes and evaluating consequences.

Use examples and illustrations.   Examples make abstract ideas concrete through illustration. Using examples is probably the most common way to develop a piece of writing. Of course, Martínez's essay is full of examples. In fact she begins with an example of a series of books — the Dick and Jane books — to show how a generation of school children were exposed to white middle-class values. She also uses examples in paragraph 5, where she lists several pieces of legislation (Propositions 187 and 209) to develop the claim in her topic sentence.

Cite data.   **Data** are factual pieces of information. They function in an essay as the bases of propositions. In the first few paragraphs of the excerpt, Martínez cites statistics ("85 percent of all U.S. elementary schools used the Dick and Jane series to teach children how to read") and facts ("In the mid-1990s, museums, libraries and eighty Public Broadcasting Service . . . stations across the country had exhibits and programs commemorating the series") to back up her claim about the popularity of the Dick and Jane series and the nostalgia the books evoke.

Analyze texts.   Analysis is the process of breaking something down into its elements to understand how they work together. When you analyze a text, you point out parts of the text that have particular significance to your argument and explain what they mean. By *texts,* we mean both verbal and visual texts. In paragraph 7, Martínez analyzes a visual text, an advertisement that appeared in *Sports Illustrated,* to reveal "its implication of shifting power" — a demographic power shift from Anglos to people of color.

Tell narratives or anecdotes.   Put simply, a narrative is an account of something that happened. More technically, a narrative relates a sequence of events that are connected in time; and an **anecdote** is a short narrative that recounts a particular incident. An anecdote, like an example, can bring an abstraction into focus. Consider Martínez's third paragraph, where the anecdote about the museum attendant brings her point about racially charged nostalgia among white Americans into memorable focus: The tears of the museum-goers indicate just how profound their nostalgia is. By contrast, a longer narrative, in setting out its sequence of events, often opens up possibilities for analysis. Why did these events occur? Why did they occur in this sequence? What might they lead to? What are the implications? What is missing? In paragraph 11, for example, Martínez relates several key events in the origin myth of America. Then, in the next paragraph, she explains what is omitted from the myth, or narrative, and builds her argument about the implications and consequences of those omissions.

Define terms.   A definition is an explanation of what something is and, by implication, what it is not. The simplest kind of definition is a synonym, but for the purpose of developing your argument, a one-word definition is rarely enough. When you define your terms, you are setting forth meanings that you want your readers to agree on, so that you can continue to build your argument on the foundation of that agreement. You may have to stipulate that your definition is part of a larger whole to develop your argument. For example: "Nostalgia is a bittersweet longing for things of the past; but for the purposes of my essay, I focus on white middle-class nostalgia, which combines a longing for a past that never existed with a hostile anxiety about the present."

In paragraph 10, Martínez defines the term *origin narrative* — a myth that explains "how a society understands its place in the world and its history . . . the basis for a nation's self-defined identity." The "Great White

Origin Myth" is an important concept in her developing argument about a national crisis of identity.

Make comparisons.   Technically, a **comparison** shows the similarities between two or more things, and a **contrast** shows the differences. In practice, however, it is very difficult, if not impossible, to develop a comparison that does not make use of contrast. Therefore, we use the term *comparison* to describe the strategy of comparing *and* contrasting. Doubtless you have written paragraphs or even whole essays that take as a starting point a version of this sentence: "X and Y are similar in some respects and different in others." This neutral formulation is seldom helpful when you are developing an argument. Usually, in making your comparison — in setting forth the points of similarity and difference — you have to take an evaluative or argumentative stance. Consider the comparison in this passage:

> Although there are similarities between the current nostalgias for Dick and Jane
> books and for rhythm and blues music of the same era — in both cases, the object
> of nostalgia can move people to tears — the nostalgias spring from emotional
> responses that are quite different and even contradictory. I will argue that the Dick
> and Jane books evoke a longing for a past that is colored by a fear of the present, a
> time when white middle-class values were dominant and unquestioned as they no
> longer are. By contrast, the nostalgia for R&B music may indicate a yearning for a
> past when multicultural musicians provided a sweaty release on the dance floor from
> those very same white-bread values of the time.

The writer does more than list similarities and differences; he offers an analysis of what they mean and is prepared to argue for his interpretation.

Certainly Elizabeth Martínez takes an evaluative stance when she compares versions of American history in paragraphs 11 and 12. In paragraph 11, she angrily relates the sanitized story of American history, setting up a contrast in paragraph 12 with the story that does not appear in history textbooks, a story of "genocide, enslavement and imperialist expansion." Her evaluative stance comes through clearly: She finds the first version repugnant and harmful, its omissions "grotesque."

Examine causes and evaluate consequences.   In any academic discipline, questions of cause and consequence are central. Whether you are analyzing the latest election results in a political science course, reading about the causes of the Vietnam War in a history course, or speculating about the long-term consequences of global warming in a science course, questions of why things happened, happen, or will happen are inescapable. Examining causes and consequences usually involves identifying a phenomenon and asking questions about it until you gather enough information to begin analyzing the relationships among its parts and deciding which are most significant. You can then begin to set forth your own analysis of what happened and why.

Of course, this kind of analysis is rarely straightforward, and any phenomenon worthy of academic study is bound to generate a variety of conversations about its causes and consequences. In your own thinking and research, avoid jumping to conclusions and continue to sift evidence until plausible connections present themselves. Be prepared to revise your thinking — perhaps several times — in light of new evidence.

In your writing, you also want to avoid oversimplifying. A claim like this — "The answer to curbing unemployment in the United States is to restrict immigration" — does not take into account corporate outsourcing of jobs overseas or the many other possible causes of unemployment. At the very least, you may need to explain the basis and specifics of your analysis, and qualify your claim: "Recent studies of patterns of immigration and unemployment in the United States suggest that unrestricted immigration is a major factor in the loss of blue-collar job opportunities in the Southwest." Certainly this sentence is less forceful and provocative than the other one, but it does suggest that you have done significant and focused research and respect the complexity of the issue.

Throughout her essay, Martínez analyzes causes and consequences. In paragraph 8, for example, she speculates that the *cause* of "attacks on immigrants, affirmative action and multiculturalism" is "Euro-American anxiety," "the sense of a vanishing national identity." In paragraph 13, she concludes that a *consequence* of Theodore Roosevelt's beliefs about race and war was a "militarism [that] went hand in hand with the racialization of history's protagonists." In paragraph 16, the topic sentence itself is a statement about causes and consequences: "Today's origin myth and the resulting concept of national identity make for an intellectual prison where it is dangerous to ask big questions about this society's superiority."

Having shown where and how Martínez uses critical strategies to develop her paragraphs, we must hasten to add that these critical strategies usually work in combination. Although you can easily develop an entire paragraph (or even an entire essay) using comparison, it is almost impossible to do so without relying on one or more of the other strategies. What if you need to tell an anecdote about the two authors you are comparing? What if you have to cite data about different rates of economic growth to clarify the main claim of your comparison? What if you are comparing different causes and consequences? Our point is that the strategies described here are methods for exploring your issue in writing. How you make use of them, individually or in combination, depends on which can help you best communicate your argument to your readers.

Steps to Developing Paragraphs

1 **Use topic sentences to focus your paragraphs.** Remember that a topic sentence partially answers the question motivating you to write; acts as an extension of your thesis; indicates to your readers

what the paragraph is about; and helps create unity both within the paragraph and within the essay.

2 **Create unity in your paragraphs.** The details in your paragraph should follow logically from your topic sentence and maintain a single focus, one tied clearly to your thesis. Repetition and transition words also help create unity in paragraphs.

3 **Use critical strategies to develop your paragraphs.** Use examples and illustrations; cite data; analyze texts; tell stories or anecdotes; define terms; make comparisons; and examine causes and evaluate consequences.

A Practice Sequence: Working with Paragraphs

We would like you to work in pairs on paragraphing. The objective of this exercise is to gauge the effectiveness of your topic sentences and the degree to which your paragraphs are unified and fully developed.

Make a copy of your essay and cut it up into paragraphs. Shuffle the paragraphs to be sure they are no longer in the original order, and then exchange cut-up drafts with your partner. The challenge is to put your partner's essay back together again. When you both have finished, compare your reorderings with the original drafts. Were you able to reproduce the original organization exactly? If not, do the variations make sense? If one or the other of you had trouble putting the essay back together, talk about the adequacy of your topic sentences, ways to revise topic sentences in keeping with the details in a given paragraph, and strategies for making paragraphs more unified and coherent.

DRAFTING CONCLUSIONS

In writing a conclusion to your essay, you are making a final appeal to your audience. You want to convince readers that what you have written is a relevant, meaningful interpretation of a shared issue. You also want to remind them that your argument is reasonable. Rather than summarize all of the points you've made in the essay — assume your readers have carefully read what you've written — pull together the key components of your argument in the service of answering the question "So what?" Establish why your argument is important: What will happen if things stay the same? What will happen if things change? How effective your conclusion is depends on whether or not readers feel you have adequately addressed "So what?" — that you have made clear what is significant and of value.

In building on the specific details of your argument, you can also place what you have written in a broader context. What are the sociological implications of your argument? How far reaching are they? Are there political implications? Economic implications? Finally, explain again how your ideas contribute something new to the conversation by building on, extending, or even challenging what others have argued.

In her concluding paragraph, Elizabeth Martínez brings together her main points, puts her essay in a broader context, indicates what's new in her argument, and answers the question "So what?":

> Accepting the implications of a different narrative could also shed light on today's struggles. In the affirmative-action struggle, for example, opponents have said that that policy is no longer needed because racism ended with the Civil Rights Movement. But if we look at slavery as a fundamental pillar of this nation, going back centuries, it becomes obvious that racism could not have been ended by 30 years of mild reforms. If we see how the myth of the frontier idealized the white male adventurer as the central hero of national history, with the woman as sunbonneted helpmate, then we might better understand the dehumanized ways in which women have continued to be treated. A more truthful origin narrative could also help break down divisions among peoples of color by revealing common experiences and histories of cooperation.

Although Martínez refers back to important events and ideas she has discussed, she does not merely summarize. Instead, she suggests the implications of those important events and ideas in her first sentence (the topic sentence), which crystallizes the main point of her essay: Americans need a different origin narrative. Then she puts those implications in the broader context of contemporary racial and gender issues. She signals what's new in her argument with the word *if* (if we look at slavery in a new way, if we look at the frontier myth in a new way). Finally, her answers to "So what?" — important new insights into racial and gender issues — culminate in the last sentence, which also connects and extends the claim of her topic sentence, by asserting that a "more truthful origin narrative" could help heal divisions among peoples of color who have been misrepresented by the old origin myth. Clearly, she believes the implications of her argument matter: A new national identity has the potential to heal a country in crisis, a country on the verge of a "nervous breakdown" (para. 4).

Martínez also does something else in the last sentence of the concluding paragraph: She looks to the future, suggesting what the future implications of her argument could be. Looking to the future is one of five strategies for shaping a conclusion. The others we discuss are echoing the introduction, challenging the reader, posing questions, and concluding with a quotation. Each of these strategies appeals to readers in different ways; therefore, we suggest you try them all out in writing your own conclusions. Also, remember that some of these strategies can be combined. For example, you can write an introduction that challenges readers, poses a question, looks to the future, and ends with a quotation.

■ Echo the Introduction

Echoing the introduction in your conclusion helps readers come full circle. It helps them see how you have developed your idea from beginning to end. In the example below, the student writer begins with a voice speaking from behind an Islamic veil, revealing the ways that Western culture misunderstands the symbolic value of wearing the veil. The writer repeats this visual image in her conclusion, quoting from the Koran: "Speak to them from behind a curtain."

Notice that the author begins with "a voice from behind the shrouds of an Islamic veil" and then echoes this quotation in her conclusion: "Speak to them from behind a curtain."

Introduction: A voice from behind the shrouds of an Islamic veil exclaims: "I often wonder whether people see me as a radical, fundamentalist Muslim terrorist packing an AK-47 assault rifle inside my jean jacket. Or maybe they see me as the poster girl for oppressed womanhood everywhere." In American culture where shameless public exposure, particularly of females, epitomizes ultimate freedom, the head-to-toe covering of a Muslim woman seems inherently oppressive. Driven by an autonomous national attitude, the inhabitants of the "land of the free" are quick to equate the veil with indisputable persecution. Yet Muslim women reveal the enslaving hijab as a symbolic display of the Islamic ideals — honor, modesty, and stability. Because of an unfair American assessment, the aura of hijab mystery cannot be removed until the customs and ethics of Muslim culture are genuinely explored. It is this form of enigmatic seclusion that forms the feminist controversy between Western liberals, who perceive the veil as an inhibiting factor against free will, and Islamic disciples, who conceptualize the veil as a sacred symbol of utmost morality.

Conclusion: By improperly judging an alien religion, the veil becomes a symbol of oppression and devastation, instead of a representation of pride and piety. Despite Western images, the hijab is a daily revitalization and reminder of the Islamic societal and religious ideals, thereby upholding the conduct and attitudes of the Muslim community. Americans share these ideals yet fail to recognize them in the context of a different culture. By sincerely exploring the custom of Islamic veiling, one will realize the vital role the hijab plays in shaping Muslim culture by sheltering women, and consequently society, from the perils that erupt from indecency.

Notice how the conclusion echoes the introduction in its reference to a voice speaking from behind a curtain.

The principles implored in the Koran of modesty, honor, and stability construct a unifying and moral view of the Islamic Middle Eastern society when properly investigated. As it was transcribed from Allah, "Speak to them from behind a curtain. This is purer for your hearts and their hearts."

■ Challenge the Reader

By issuing a challenge to your readers, you create a sense of urgency, provoking them to act to change the status quo. In this example, the student writer explains the unacceptable consequences of preventing young women from educating themselves about AIDS and the spread of a disease that has already reached epidemic proportions.

Here the author cites a final piece of research to emphasize the extent of the problem.

Here she begins her explicit challenge to readers about what they have to do to protect themselves or their students from infection.

The changes in AIDS education that I am suggesting are necessary and relatively simple to make. Although the current curriculum in high school health classes is helpful and informative, it simply does not pertain to young women as much as it should. AIDS is killing women at an alarming rate, and many people do not realize this. According to Daniel DeNoon, AIDS is one of the six leading causes of death among women aged 18–45, and women "bear the brunt of the worldwide AIDS epidemic." For this reason, DeNoon argues, women are one of the most important new populations that are contracting HIV at a high rate. I challenge young women to be more well-informed about AIDS and their link to the disease; otherwise, many new cases may develop. As the epidemic continues to spread, women need to realize that they can stop the spread of the disease and protect themselves from infection and a number of related complications. It is the responsibility of health educators to present this to young women and inform them of the powerful choices that they can make.

■ Look to the Future

Looking to the future is particularly relevant when you are asking readers to take action. To move readers to action, you must establish the persistence of a problem and the consequences of letting a situation continue unchanged. In the concluding paragraph below, the student author points out a number of things that teachers need to do to involve parents in their children's education. She identifies a range of options before identifying what she believes is perhaps the most important action teachers can take.

The second through fifth sentences present an array of options.

First and foremost, teachers must recognize the ways in which some parents are positively contributing to their children's academic endeavors. Teachers must recognize nontraditional methods of participation as legitimate and work toward supporting parents in these tasks. For instance, teachers might send home suggestions for local after-school tutoring programs. Teachers must also try to make urban parents feel welcome and respected in their school. Teachers might call parents to ask their opinion about a certain difficulty their child is having, or invite them to talk about something of interest to them. One parent, for instance, spoke highly of the previous superintendent who had let him use his work as a film producer to help with a show for students during homeroom. If teachers can develop innovative ways to utilize parents' talents and interests rather than just inviting them to be passively involved in an already-in-place curriculum, more parents might respond. Perhaps, most importantly, if teachers want parents to be involved in their students' educations, they must make the parents feel as though their opinions and concerns have real weight. When parents such as those interviewed for this study voice concerns and questions over their child's progress, it is imperative that teachers acknowledge and answer them.

In the last two sentences, the writer looks to the future with her recommendations.

■ Pose Questions

Posing questions stimulates readers to think about the implications of your argument and to apply what you argue to other situations. This is the case in the paragraph below, in which the student writer focuses on immigration and then shifts readers' attention to racism and the possibility of hate crimes. It's useful to extrapolate from your argument, to raise questions that test whether what you write can be applied to different situations. These questions can help readers understand what is at issue.

Also, my research may apply to a broader spectrum of sociological topics. There has been recent discussion about the increasing trend of immigration. Much of this discussion has involved the distribution of resources to immigrants. Should immigrants have equal access to certain economic and educational resources in America? The decision is split. But, it will be interesting to see how this debate will play out. If immigrants are granted more resources, will certain Americans mobilize against the distribution of these resources? Will we see another rise in racist groups such as the Ku Klux Klan in order to prevent immigrants from obtaining more resources? My research can also be used to understand global conflict or war. In general, groups mobilize when their established resources are threatened by an external force. Moreover, groups use framing processes to justify their collective action to others.

The first question.

Other speculative questions follow from possible responses to the writer's first question.

■ Conclude with a Quotation

A quotation can add authority to your argument, indicating that others in positions of power and prestige support your stance. A quotation also can add poignancy to your argument, as it does in the excerpt below, in which the quotation amplifies the idea that people use Barbie to advance their own interests.

> The question still remains, what does Barbie mean? Is she the spokeswoman for the empowerment of women or rather is she performing the dirty work of conservative patriarchy? I do not think we will ever know the answer. Rather, Barbie is the undeniable "American Icon." She is a toy, and she is what we want her to be. A test performed by Albert M. Magro at Fairmont State College titled "Why Barbie Is Perceived as Beautiful" shows that Barbie is the epitome of what we as humans find beautiful. The test sought to find human preferences on evolutionary changes in the human body. Subjects were shown a series of photos comparing different human body parts, such as the size and shape of the eyes, and asked to decide which feature they preferred: the primitive or derived (more evolved traits). The test revealed that the subjects preferred the derived body traits. Ironically, it is these preferred evolutionary features that are utilized on the body of Barbie. Barbie is truly an extension of what we are and what we perceive.

The writer quotes an authority to amplify the idea that individually and collectively, we project significance on toys.

> Juel Best concludes his discourse on Barbie with these words: "Toys do not embody violence or sexism or occult meanings. People must assign toys their meanings." Barbie is whoever we make her out to be. Barbie grabs hold of our imaginations and lets us go wild.

Steps to Drafting Conclusions

1 **Pull together the main claims of your essay.** Don't simply repeat points you make in the paper. Instead, show readers how the points you make fit together.

2 **Answer the question "So What?"** Show your readers why your stand on the issue is significant.

3 **Place your argument in a larger context.** Discuss the specifics of your argument, but also indicate its broader implications.

4 **Show readers what is new.** As you synthesize the key points of your argument, explain how what you argue builds on, extends, or challenges the thinking of others.

5 **Decide on the best strategy for writing your conclusion.** Will you echo the introduction? Challenge the reader? Look to the future? Pose questions? Conclude with a quotation? Choose the best strategy or strategies to appeal to your readers.

A Practice Sequence: Drafting a Conclusion

1 Write your conclusion, using one of the strategies described in this section. Then share your conclusion with a classmate. Ask this person to address the following questions:

- Did I pull together the key points of the argument?
- Did I answer "So what?" adequately?
- Are the implications I want readers to draw from the essay clear?

After listening to the responses, try a second strategy, and then ask your classmate which conclusion is more effective.

2 If you do not have a conclusion of your own, analyze each example conclusion above to see how well each appears to (1) pull together the main claim of the essay, (2) answer "So what?" (3) place the argument in a larger context, and (4) show readers what is new.

10

From Revising to Editing: Working with Peer Groups

Academic writing is a collaborative enterprise. By reading and commenting on your drafts, your peers can support your work as a writer. And you can support the work of your peers by reading their drafts with a critical but constructive eye. As a critical reader of your peers' writing, you bring your knowledge, experiences, and interests to bear on what you read, and your responses to their texts can help other writers continue the conversations they have joined. The questions you raise may reveal what is missing from a writer's argument, motivating the writer to revise his or her work. It is easier to see problems in other people's writing than in our own because we have a critical distance from their work that we don't have from our own. At the same time, as you read other work critically, you will begin to internalize the questions that will help you revise your own arguments.

In this chapter, we set out the differences between revising and editing, discuss the peer editing process in terms of the composition pyramid, present a model peer editing session, and then explain the writer's and reader's responsibilities through early drafts, later drafts, and final drafts, providing opportunities for you to practice peer response on three drafts of a student paper.

REVISING VERSUS EDITING

We make a distinction between revising and editing. By **revising**, we mean making changes to a paper to reflect new thinking or conceptualizing. If a reader finds that the real focus of your essay comes at the end of your draft, you need to revise the paper with this new focus in mind. Revising differs from **editing**, which involves minor changes to what will be the final draft of a paper — replacing a word here and there, correcting misspellings, or substituting dashes for commas to create emphasis, for example. When you're reading a first or second draft, the niceties of style, spelling, and punctuation are not priorities. After all, if the writer had to change the focus of his or her argument, significant changes to words, phrases, and punctuation would be inevitable. Concentrating on editing errors early on, when the writer is still trying to develop an argument with evidence, organize information logically, and anticipate counterarguments, is inefficient and even counterproductive.

Here are some characteristics of revising and editing that can guide how you read your own writing and the comments you offer to other writers:

REVISING	EDITING
Treats writing as a work in progress	Treats writing as an almost-finished product
Focuses on new possibilities both within and beyond the text	Addresses obvious errors and deficiencies
Focuses on new questions or goals	Focuses on the text alone
Considers both purpose and readers' needs	Considers grammar, punctuation, spelling, and style
Encourages further discovery	Polishes up the essay

You should understand that writing is a process, and that revising is an integral part of that process. Your best writing will happen in the context of real readers' responding to your drafts. Look at the acknowledgments in any academic book, and you will see many people credited with having improved the book through their reading and discussion of drafts and ideas. All academic writers rely on conversations with others to strengthen their work.

THE PEER EDITING PROCESS

In sharing writing with others, you need to be clear about your responsibilities. You may find that you assume one role when you read a peer's early draft, trying to encourage and support the writer to find ways to strengthen his or her argument. Although you will need to be critical, asking probing questions, you also will need to be sure that your conversation is constructive, that you encourage your peer to continue writing. You play a very different role when the writer tells you, "This is it. It's finished."

We emphasize that the different stages of writing — early, later, and final — call for different work from both readers and writers because writers' needs vary with each successive draft. These stages correspond to what has been called the composition pyramid (Figure 10.1).* The

---

*We thank Susannah Brietz-Monta and Anthony Monta for this idea.

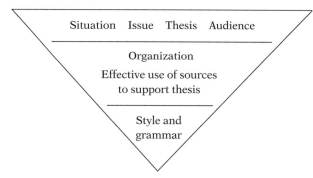

Figure 10.1   The Composition Pyramid

composition pyramid represents elements of writing that can help you decide what to pay attention to at different stages of writing.

The top of this inverted pyramid corresponds to the early stages of writing. At this point, members of the writing group should identify the situation the writer is responding to (for example, homelessness, inequality, or air pollution), the issue the writer has defined (for example, the economic versus the social costs of homelessness), the thesis or argument the writer advances, and the extent to which the writer addresses a given audience appropriately. The middle portion of the pyramid corresponds to a later stage of the writing process, the point at which members of the group should move on to discuss the extent to which the writer has organized the argument logically and used sources effectively to support the thesis. Has the writer integrated quotations smoothly into the paper? Is the evidence relevant, recent, and credible? Finally, the bottom of the pyramid corresponds to the final stages of drafting. As the writer's focus shifts to grammar and style, so should the group's. Questions to ask: Is this specific language appropriate to the intended audience? Has the writer presented the argument in ways that will compel readers — even those who disagree — to listen?

Steps in the Peer Editing Process

1 The writer distributes copies of the draft to each member of the writing group. (Ideally, the group should not exceed four students.)

2 The writer distributes a cover letter, setting an agenda for each member of the group.

3 The members read the cover letter.

4 The writer then reads the draft aloud, while members follow along, underlining passages and making notes to prepare themselves to discuss the draft.

> 5 Members ask questions that help the writer identify concepts that need further elaboration or clarification.
>
> 6 Discussion focuses on the strengths and weaknesses of the draft appropriate to the stage of writing and the writer's concerns. (Even in the early stage, readers and writer should sustain discussion for at least ten minutes before the next student takes a turn as writer.)

PEER GROUPS IN ACTION: A SAMPLE SESSION

Let's take a look at one writing group in action to see the potential of this approach to writing. One student, Brett Preacher, worked collaboratively with three other students for several weeks on plans for and drafts of his paper. The assignment was to argue whether the movie *Million Dollar Baby* accurately portrays poverty. Brett explained to his group that he had struggled to find ways to advance his argument at the same time that he was trying to synthesize different authors' points of view. Moreover, he was worried that he didn't do the assignment:

> BRETT: That was the assignment, to argue whether the movie portrays poverty justly or unjustly. That was the assignment, what we were supposed to do, and I didn't do that at all.
>
> CAITLIN: Well, I didn't do that either, but I used hooks's "Seeing and Making Culture: Representing the Poor" and Freedman's *From Cradle to Grave: The Human Face of Poverty in America.*
>
> BRETT: Yeah, well, I kind of quit. I strayed off the movie at the end. I basically quit talking about the movie about halfway through the paper, so the whole second half of my paper, so basically the whole second half of my paper is the weak part. I just kind of quit talking about *Million Dollar Baby.*

Brett restated his understanding of the assignment before reading his draft aloud. This is a valuable starting point because a writer's interpretation of the assignment — the task, the purpose, the audience — helps the peer readers understand why the writer is taking a particular approach. If the readers disagree with the writer's interpretation, they should discuss their differences before the writer shares the draft, to determine an appropriate response to the assignment.

As you read the excerpt Brett shared with his group, we would like you to analyze the extent to which he formulated an argument that synthesizes his reading:

- Highlight Brett's key claim(s).
- Note the connections he makes to different readings.
- Decide what those connections mean.

Preacher 1

Brett Preacher
Professor Tindall
English 200
October 10, 20--

Representing Poverty in *Million Dollar Baby*

In "Seeing and Making Culture: Representing the Poor," bell
hooks discusses the extent to which the media describes the poor as
all nihilistic and longing for material worth. This image is slightly
expressed in the movie *Million Dollar Baby* through Maggie's family.
In the only scenes her family makes an appearance, they present
themselves as white trash by worrying that their welfare will be taken
away and trying to make an easy dollar off a crippled Maggie.
Jonathan Friedman, however, seems to capture the essence of the
movie much more accurately in a chapter out of his book, *From
Cradle to Grave*, called "The Human Face of Poverty in America." In
this chapter, Freedman presents many stories that support his argument that perseverance can help people rise from a life of poverty.
This argument is portrayed perfectly by Maggie throughout the
movie.

In the movie, Maggie strives to become a professional boxer
to support herself rather than succumb to a life of poverty as her
family did. Through drive and determination, Maggie strives to rise
out of poverty despite all the doubt and negativity directed towards
her. With nothing more than her wages and tips from her waitressing
job, she saves her money, sacrificing much along the way to pay for
her trainer. Her family, however, represents the other side of the
spectrum and looks for nothing more than an easy way out of their
welfare sustained lifestyle. Rather than working to better themselves,
they depend on welfare, and after putting Maggie down repeatedly
about her career, they try to sign her savings over to themselves
when she gets injured. Through her hard work and determination,
Maggie achieves her dream in the end, helping to support the argument Friedman makes. Jonathan Freedman catches the face of
poverty precisely by arguing that perseverance can put anyone out of
a life of poverty. Most people, however, cannot fathom this idea until
they have witnessed something similar.

1

2

Preacher 2

3

In her essay, hooks describes the generalizations that the media have of the poor, which convey stereotypes. Friedman observes that it takes money, organization, and laws to maintain a social structure, but none of it works if there are not opportunities for people to meet and help each other along the way. For example, he tells the story of about Nitza, a young homeless mother with four children. She is forced to put her children into foster care for three years until she works her way out of poverty and can support her family. Friedman's point is that that there is not enough opportunity to maintain the social structure that we desire. At the same time, we see that Nitza succeeds because she is motivated to change her circumstances.

Unable to identify Brett's key claim, his writing group members asked a number of questions that they hoped would guide Brett toward making an explicit claim about whether or not the film *Million Dollar Baby* represents poverty in a fair way:

CAITLIN: So what you are saying is that the film does and doesn't support hooks's argument that the media misrepresent the poor?

MEGHAN: You give a lot of examples here, like about Maggie. You could expand those into a paper. But what point do you want to make?

BRETT: Yeah, each example could be in a different paragraph.

CAITLIN: Those could be your main points, you know?

Caitlin believed that Brett's point may have been more implicit than explicit, that the film *Million Dollar Baby* "does and doesn't support hooks's argument that the media misrepresent the poor." Caitlin's suggestion underscores the complexity of what Brett was trying to argue — that the film does and doesn't represent poverty in a fair way — and poses a challenge that Meghan appeared to understand. Meghan suggested to Brett that he formulate different paragraphs to advance the point that *Million Dollar Baby* offers a contradictory image of poverty that is at once realistic and unrealistic. Caitlin agreed when she said that "those could be your main points." (Actually, that's just one key claim.)

However, Daimon, the fourth member of the group, recognized that Brett was going to have to develop his discussion of *Million Dollar Baby* before it became clear whether or not the film offers two conflicting images of poverty:

> DAIMON: It's just you don't talk about *Million Dollar Baby* enough, and I think that's what the essay is supposed to be about. Not so much about the other two. You can use the other two, but not so much as you did.
>
> BRETT: Just tie in *Million Dollar Baby* a little more, you think?
>
> CAITLIN: Well, because you talk a lot, it does fit with your paper, but it doesn't . . . it's supposed to be about *Million Dollar Baby*. . . . Do you think the film portrays poverty in a realistic way?
>
> MEGHAN: Yeah, give examples of the way the film describes Maggie's family. It's like they depend on her to get themselves out of poverty.

And then Caitlin steered Brett back to the point she made earlier — that Brett could revise his paper to address the complicated way the film represents poverty:

> CAITLIN: That could be the issue. There are contradictory images of poverty and how people deal.
>
> BRETT: Yeah, well, I don't know. I'm going to have to think about that.

Brett's draft reflects his first attempt to get his ideas down. It's fine for a first draft to be exploratory. When writers formulate a working thesis or when they fail to formulate a thesis, readers in a peer group can offer support, noting strengths or pointing to places of greatest interest in an effort to sustain the writer's energy for writing. Caitlin helped Brett generate a plan for taking the next step by pointing out how he could define the issue — "There are contradictory images of poverty and how people deal."

A peer group can also ask questions to help a writer set new goals. A good strategy is to paraphrase particular parts of the draft so that the writer can hear how you, the reader, have understood what he or she is trying to say. This is what Caitlin did when she said, "So what you are saying is that the film does and doesn't support hooks's argument that the media misrepresent the poor?"

WORKING WITH EARLY DRAFTS

■ Consider the Writer's Responsibilities

When you present an early draft of your essay to your writing group, you want the group to focus on top-level pyramid concerns — situation, purpose, issue, thesis, and audience. You should explain this and any other concerns you have in a cover letter. Use the template in Figure 10.2 as a model for what needs explaining in the letter to your readers.

During the session it's important to be open to suggestions. Although you don't have to incorporate every suggestion your group makes when you revise your draft, be sure you at least understand the members' comments and concerns. If you don't understand what the members are saying about your draft, ask them to clarify or give you an example.

Finally, if you decide not to take someone's suggestion, have a good reason for doing so. It's fine to say no to a suggested change in the purpose or intended audience of your essay if that change means you won't be addressing the terms of the assignment or that you would no longer be interested in the issue.

FIGURE 10.2   The Writer's Cover Letter: Early Drafts

1. What is your question (or assignment)?
2. What is the issue motivating you to write?
3. How have published writers addressed the issue about which you are writing?
4. What is your working thesis?
5. Who is your audience, and what kind of response do you want from your readers?
6. What do you think is working best?
7. What specific aspect of the essay are you least satisfied with at this time?
8. What kind of feedback do you especially want today?

■ Consider the Reader's Responsibilities

Your task as a reader is to follow along as the early draft is read, paying special attention to the concerns the writer has explained in the cover letter and focusing on the top of the pyramid: situation, issue, thesis, and audience. Take notes directly on the draft copy, circling or underlining sections you find confusing or have questions about, so that you can refer to them specifically in the discussion.

When it's your turn to talk, have a conversation about your reactions to the draft — where the draft amused, confused, or persuaded you, for example. Don't just jump in and start telling the writer what he or she should be doing in the paper. Your role as a reader is to give the writer a live audience: Your responses can help the writer decide what parts of the paper are working and what parts need serious revision. There are times, however, when you should play the role of *deferring reader*, putting off certain comments. You don't want to overwhelm the writer with problems no matter how many questions the essay raises.

Offer both positive and negative remarks. Start by pointing out what is working well in the paper, so the writer knows where he or she is on the right track. This also leaves the writer more open to constructive criticism. But don't shy away from telling the writer what should be working better. It's your job as a reader to offer honest and specific responses to the draft, so the writer can develop it into an effective piece of writing. Figure 10.3 lists key questions you should ask as a reader of an early draft.

FIGURE 10.3   A Reader's Questions: Early Drafts

1. Are the questions and issues that motivate the writer clear?
2. Has the writer effectively related the conversation that published writers are engaged in?
3. What is at issue?
4. What is the writer's thesis?
5. Is the writer addressing the audience's concerns effectively?
6. What passages of the draft are most effective?
7. What passages of the draft are least effective?

■ Analyze an Early Draft

Keep these questions in mind as you read the following excerpt from a student's early draft. After reading a number of scholarly articles on the civil rights movement, Tasha Taylor decided to address what she sees as the difference between scholars' understanding of the movement and more popular treatments in textbooks and photographs. She also tries to tie in the larger question of historical memory to her analysis of southern blacks' struggle for equality — what people remember about the past and what they forget. In fact, she begins her essay with a quotation she believes summarizes what she wants to argue ("The struggle of man against power is the struggle of memory against forgetting").

As you read Taylor's essay, take detailed notes, and underline passages that concern you. Then write a paragraph or two explaining what she could do to strengthen the draft. Keep in mind that this is an early draft, so focus on the top level of the pyramid: the situation or assignment; the issue; the thesis; and the audience.

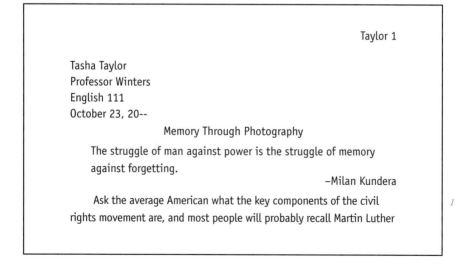

Taylor 1

Tasha Taylor
Professor Winters
English 111
October 23, 20--

Memory Through Photography

The struggle of man against power is the struggle of memory against forgetting.

–Milan Kundera

Ask the average American what the key components of the civil rights movement are, and most people will probably recall Martin Luther

Taylor 2

King, Jr. speaking of a dream in front of the Lincoln Memorial, Rosa Parks riding a bus, a few court decisions, and perhaps a photograph of Elizabeth Eckford cowering before an angry mob in front of Central High School in Little Rock. Few people are aware A. Philip Randolph planned the march on Washington. Few could describe Rosa Parks's connection to the civil rights movement (for example, the fact that she had been a member of the NAACP since 1943) before her legendary refusal to give up her seat in December 1955, which led to the Montgomery Bus Boycott. Few recognize the years of struggle that existed between the *Brown v. Board of Education* decision and the actual desegregation of schools. Few consider the fate of Elizabeth Eckford after the federal troops were sent to protect her and the other members of the Little Rock Nine had left Central High or the months of abuse (physical and emotional) that they endured in the name of integration. What most people know is limited to textbooks they read in school or the captions under photographs that describe where a particular event occurred.

Why is it that textbooks exclusively feature the stories of larger than life figures like Martin Luther King? Why is it that we remember things the way we do? Historical events "have little meaning without human interpretation, without our speaking about them within the contexts of our lives and our culture, without giving them names and meanings" (Kolker xix). Each person experiencing the exact same event will carry a different memory from that event. Trying to decipher what memories reveal about each person is a fascinating yet difficult endeavor, because each retelling of a memory and each additional memory alters existing ones.   2

The story that photographs and textbooks tell us does not even begin to describe the depth of the movement or the thousands who risked their lives and the lives of their families to make equality a reality. Embracing this selective memory as a nation prevents understanding and acknowledgement of the harsh reality of other images from the civil rights movement (demonstrators being plowed down by fire hoses, beatings, and the charred bodies of bombing victims) which are key aspects of understanding who we are as a society. The question therefore is why. Why is it that textbook writers and   3

Taylor 3

publishers have allowed so much of this history to be skewed and forgotten? How can it be that barely 50 years after these events so many have been forgotten or diluted?

For Analysis and Discussion

1. What is working well in Taylor's draft?
2. What is Taylor's thesis or argument?
3. To what extent does she connect her analysis of the civil rights movement and historical memory?
4. What parts of her analysis could Taylor explain further? (What do you still need to know?)
5. What would you suggest Taylor do next?

WORKING WITH LATER DRAFTS

■ Consider the Writer's Responsibilities

At a later stage, after you've had the opportunity to take readers' suggestions and do further research, you should be able to state your thesis more definitively than you did in your earlier draft. You also should be able to support your thesis with evidence, anticipating possible counterarguments. Ideally, your readers will still provide constructive criticism, offering their support, as in the first draft, but they will also question and challenge more than before.

Here, too, you want to help readers focus on your main concerns, which you should explain in a cover letter. You may still need to work on one or two top-level pyramid concerns; but your focus will likely be midlevel concerns — organization and the effective use of sources. Use the list of questions in Figure 10.4 to help you write your cover letter.

FIGURE 10.4   The Writer's Cover Letter: Later Drafts

1. What is your research question?
2. What is the issue motivating you to write?
3. What is your thesis?
4. How do you go about identifying a gap in readers' knowledge, modifying others' ideas, or trying to correct readers' misunderstandings?

(continued on next page)

FIGURE 10.4   (Continued)

---

5. To what extent do you distinguish your argument from the information you quote, summarize, or paraphrase from the sources you have read?

6. To what extent have you organized your ideas in ways that will help readers follow the logic of your argument?

7. To what extent have you anticipated potential counterarguments to your thesis?

8. What do you think is working best?

9. What specific aspect of the essay are you least satisfied with at this time?

■ Consider the Reader's Responsibilities

In a later draft, your focus as reader should be on midlevel concerns in the composition pyramid: places in the writer's text that are confusing, that require better transitions, or that could use sources more effectively. You can challenge writers at this stage of the composing process, perhaps playing the role of *naive reader*, suggesting places in the draft where the writer has left something out or isn't clear. The naive reader's comments tend to take the form of questions: "Do you mean to suggest that everyone who learns to write well succeeds in life? What kind of success are you talking about?" Closely related to the naive reader is the *devil's advocate reader*. This reader's comments also challenge the writer, often taking the form of a question like this: "But why couldn't this be attributed to the effects of socialization rather than heredity?" Figure 10.5 offers questions for reading later drafts.

FIGURE 10.5   A Reader's Questions: Later Drafts

---

1. To what extent is it clear what questions and issues motivate the writer?

2. What is the writer's thesis?

3. How effectively does the writer establish the conversation — identity a gap in people's knowledge, attempt to modify an existing argument, or try to correct some misunderstanding?

4. How effectively does the writer distinguish between his or her ideas and the ideas he or she summarizes, paraphrases, or quotes?

5. How well does the writer help you follow the logic of his or her argument?

6. To what extent are you persuaded by the writer's argument?

7. To what extent does the writer anticipate possible counterarguments?

8. To what extent does the writer make clear how he or she wants readers to respond?

9. What do you think is working best? Explain by pointing to specific passages in the writer's draft.

10. What specific aspect of the draft is least effective? Explain by pointing to a specific passage in the writer's draft.

■ Analyze a Later Draft

Now read the following excerpt from Taylor's second draft. You will see that she begins with her discussion of historical memory. She also has included an analysis of a book of photographs that Nobel Prize–winning author Toni Morrison compiled. Take notes as you read the draft and write a paragraph in which you describe what you see as some of the strengths of what Taylor has written and what she can do to make other elements stronger. In particular, focus on the middle level of the composition pyramid — on organization and the effective use of sources and evidence to support her thesis.

Taylor 1

Tasha Taylor
Professor Winters
English 111
November 14, 20--

Memory Through Photography

> The struggle of man against power is the struggle of memory against forgetting.
>
> –Milan Kundera

Memory is such an integral part of what it is to be human, yet is *1* something so often taken for granted: people assume that their memories are accurate to protect themselves from the harsh realities of the atrocities committed by ordinary people. Even the pictures used to represent the much-celebrated civil rights movement give us a false sense of security and innocence. For example, the Ku Klux Klan is most often depicted by covered faces and burning crosses; the masks allow us to remove ourselves from responsibility. Few could describe Rosa Parks's connection to the civil rights movement (for example, the fact that she had been a member of the NAACP since 1943) before her legendary refusal to give up her seat in December 1955, which led to the Montgomery Bus Boycott. Few recognize the years of struggle that existed between the *Brown v. Board of Education* decision and the actual desegregation of schools. Few consider the fate of Elizabeth Eckford after the federal troops were sent to protect her and the other members of the Little Rock Nine had left Central High or the months of abuse (physical and emotional) that they endured in the name of integration. What most people know is limited to textbooks they read in school or the captions under photographs that describe where a particular event occurred.

Taylor 2

It is important, therefore, to analyze what is remembered and even
more importantly to recognize what it is forgotten: to question why it
is that it is forgotten, what that says about society today, how far it has
come and how much it has unwittingly fallen back into old patterns
such as prejudice and ignorance. The discrepancies in cultural memory
are due more to a society's desire to remember itself in the best light
and protect itself from the reality of its brutality and responsibility.
Such selective memory only temporarily heals the wounds of society;
lack of awareness does not cause healing. Although there have been
many recent moves to increase awareness, they are tainted by unavoidable biases and therefore continue to perpetuate a distorted memory.

Images play a central role in the formation of cultural memory
because people can point to photographs and claim them as concrete
evidence: "Images entrance us because they provide a powerful illusion of owning reality. If we can photograph reality or paint or copy
it, we have exercised an important kind of power" (Kolker 3). A picture of black and white children sitting at a table together is used to
reinforce the cultural perception that the problems of racism are
over, that it has all been fixed.

In her book *Remember*, Toni Morrison strives to revitalize the
memory of school integration through photographs. The book is dedicated to Denise McNair, Carole Robertson, Addie Mae Collins, and
Cynthia Wesley, the four girls killed in the 16th Street Baptist Church
bombing in 1963. Morrison writes, "Things are better now. Much,
much better. But remember why and please remember us" (Morrison
72). The pictures are of black and white children happily eating
together, solemnly saluting the flag together, and holding hands. The
photographs of the four murdered girls show them peacefully and
innocently smiling as if everything really is better now. In reality,
according to the Bureau of Alcohol, Tobacco and Firearms, between
1995 and 1997 there were 162 incidents of arson or bombing in
African American houses of worship (*ATF Online*). There are a few
images of people protesting integration, but they are also consistent
with the cultural memory (protesters are shown simply holding signs
and yelling, not beating and killing innocent children). Finally, the
captions are written in a child's voice. Yet it is not a child's voice at
all it is merely a top down view of children that serves to perpetuate
a distorted cultural memory.

Taylor 3

The photographs used to suggest how things are much, much better now are misleading. For example, the last photograph is of a black girl and a white girl holding hands through a bus window, which was transporting them to an integrated school. The caption reads: "Anything can happen. Anything at all. See?" (71). It is a very powerful image of how the evil of Jim Crow and segregation exist in a distant past and the nation has come together and healed. However, Morrison neglects to point out that the picture was taken in Boston, Massachusetts, not the deep south, the heart of racism. Children holding hands in Boston is much less significant than if they were in Birmingham where that action would be concrete evidence of how far we as a nation have come.

Morrison also glorifies of Martin Luther King, Jr. and Rosa Parks pointing to them as epitomizing the movement. Unfortunately, she perpetuates the story that one needs to be special or somehow larger than life to affect change. Paul Rogat Loeb writes in *Soul of a Citizen*:

> Once we enshrine our heroes, it becomes hard for mere mortals to measure up in our eyes . . . in our collective amnesia we lose the mechanisms through which grassroots social movements of the past successfully shifted public sentiment and challenged entrenched institutional power. Equally lost are the means by which their participants managed to keep on, sustaining their hope and eventually prevailing in circumstances at least as difficult as those we face today. (Loeb 38/36)

Placing a select few on pedestals and claiming them as next to divine heroes of the movement does society a disservice; people fail to realize that ordinary people can serve as agents of change.

Morrison's book ignores the thousand of ordinary people who risked their lives for the cause to bring about equality. The caption besides the picture of Rosa Parks in *Remember* reads "because if I ever feel helpless or lonely I just have to remember that all it takes is one person" (Morrison 62). Ironically, Morrison gives credit for the Montgomery Bus Boycott to one person, ignoring the months of planning and involved dozens of planners. Even the photograph presents Rosa Parks in a position of power. It is a low-angle shot up at Parks that makes her appear larger than life and authoritative. The photographs of Martin Luther King, Jr. also further the impression of power with a

5

6

7

Taylor 4

close up shot of his face as he stands above thousands of participants in the March on Washington. Although these photographs were selected to perpetuate the hero illusion, it is more inspiring to remember the ordinary people who took a stand and were able to accomplish extraordinary feats because of their dedication and persistence rather than glorify extraordinary people who were destined for greatness.

For Discussion and Analysis

1. What is Taylor's thesis or argument?
2. How well does she help you follow the logic of her argument with transitions?
3. How effectively does she distinguish between her ideas and the ideas she summarizes, paraphrases, or quotes?
4. To what extent are you persuaded by her argument?
5. What should Taylor do next?

WORKING WITH FINAL DRAFTS

■ Consider the Writer's Responsibilities

Your final draft should require editing, not revising. At this stage, readers should focus on errors in style and grammar in the text, not on the substance of your work. Here, too, indicate your main concerns in a cover letter (Figure 10.6).

FIGURE 10.6   The Writer's Cover Letter: Final Drafts

1. What is your unique perspective on your issue?
2. To what extent do the words and phrases you use reflect who you believe your readers are?
3. Does your style of citation reflect accepted conventions for academic writing?
4. What do you think is working best?
5. What specific aspect of the essay are you least satisfied with at this time?

■ Consider the Reader's Responsibilities

Once a writer's ideas are developed and in place, readers should turn their attention to the bottom level of the composition pyramid, to matters of style and grammar. At this stage, details are important: Is this the best word to use? Would this sentence be easier to follow if it was broken into two sentences? Which spelling is correct — *Freedman* or *Friedman*? Are citations handled consistently? Should this question mark precede or follow the quotation mark? The *grammatically correct reader* evaluates and makes judgments about the writer's work. This reader may simply indicate with a mark of some sort that there's a problem in a sentence or paragraph, or may even correct the writer's work. Figure 10.7 is a list of questions a reader should ask of a final draft.

FIGURE 10.7   A Reader's Questions: Final Drafts

1. How does the writer go about contributing a unique perspective on the issue?
2. To what extent does the writer use words and phrases that are appropriate for the intended audience?
3. To what extent does the style of citation reflect accepted conventions for academic writing?
4. What do you think is working best?
5. What specific aspect of the essay are you least satisfied with at this time?

■ Analyze a Near-Final Draft

Now read Taylor's near-final draft and write a paragraph detailing what she can do to strengthen it. Again, you will see that Taylor has made substantial changes. She compares Morrison's book of photographs to a Spike Lee documentary that she watched with her class. As you read the essay, focus on the bottom level of the composition pyramid: Does the writer use appropriate language? Does she adhere to appropriate conventions for using and citing sources? (See Chapter 7 for information on MLA and APA formats.)

Taylor 1

Tasha Taylor
Professor Winters
English 111
December 5, 20--

Memory Through Photography

    Memory is such an integral part of what it is to be human, yet it is something so often taken for granted: people assume that their memories are accurate to protect themselves from the harsh realities of the atrocities committed by ordinary people. Even the pictures

1

Taylor 2

used to represent the much-celebrated civil rights movement give us a false sense of security and innocence. For example, the Ku Klux Klan is most often depicted by covered faces and burning crosses; the masks allow us to remove ourselves from responsibility. Few could describe Rosa Parks's connection to the civil rights movement before her legendary refusal to give up her seat in December 1955, which led to the Montgomery Bus Boycott (for example, the fact that she had been a member of the NAACP since 1943). Few recognize the years of struggle that existed between the 1954 *Brown v. Board of Education* decision and the actual desegregation of schools. Few consider the fate of Elizabeth Eckford after the federal troops sent to protect her and the other members of the Little Rock Nine had left Central High or the months of abuse (physical and emotional) that they endured in the name of integration. What most people know is limited to the textbooks they read in school or the captions under photographs that describe where a particular event occurred.

It is important, then, to analyze what is remembered, and even *2* more important to recognize what is forgotten: to question why it is that it is forgotten, what that says about society today, how far it has come and how much it has unwittingly fallen back into old patterns of prejudice and ignorance. The discrepancies in cultural memory are due more to society's desire to remember itself in the best light and protect itself from the reality of its brutality and responsibility. Such selective memory only temporarily heals the wounds of society; lack of awareness does not cause healing. Although there have been many recent moves to increase awareness, they are tainted by unavoidable biases and therefore continue to perpetuate a distorted memory.

Images play a central role in the formation of cultural memory *3* because people can point to photographs and claim them as concrete evidence: "Images entrance us because they provide a powerful illusion of owning reality. If we can photograph reality or paint or copy it, we have exercised an important kind of power" (Kolker 3). A picture of black and white children sitting at a table together is used to reinforce the cultural perception that the problems of racism are over, that they have all been fixed.

In her book *Remember*, Toni Morrison strives to revitalize the *4* memory of school integration through photographs. The book is

Taylor 3

dedicated to Denise McNair, Carole Robertson, Addie Mae Collins, and Cynthia Wesley, the four girls killed in the 16th Street Baptist Church bombing in 1963. Morrison writes: "Things are better now. Much, much better. But remember why and please remember us" (72). The pictures are of black and white children happily eating together, solemnly saluting the flag together, and holding hands. The photographs of the four murdered girls show them peacefully and innocently smiling as if everything really is better now. In reality, according to the Bureau of Alcohol, Tobacco, Firearms and Explosives, between 1995 and 1997 there were 162 incidents of arson or bombing in African American houses of worship (*ATF Online*). There are a few images of people protesting integration, but they are also consistent with the cultural memory (protesters are shown simply holding signs and yelling, not beating and killing innocent children). Finally, the captions are written in a child's voice. Yet it is not a child's voice at all; it is merely a top-down view of children that serves to perpetuate a distorted cultural memory.

The photographs used to suggest how things are much, much better now are misleading. For example, the last photograph, taken through a bus window, is of a black girl and a white girl holding hands; the bus was transporting them to an integrated school. The caption reads: "Anything can happen. Anything at all. See?" (71). It is a very powerful image of how the evil of Jim Crow and segregation exist in a distant past and the nation has come together and healed. However, Morrison neglects to point out that the picture was taken in Boston, not in the Deep South, the heart of racism. Children holding hands in Boston is much less significant than if they were in Birmingham, where that action would be concrete evidence of how far we as a nation have come.

Morrison also glorifies Martin Luther King Jr. and Rosa Parks, pointing to them as epitomizing the movement. Unfortunately, she perpetuates the story that one needs to be special or somehow larger than life to effect change. Paul Rogat Loeb writes in *Soul of a Citizen*:

> Once we enshrine our heroes, it becomes hard for mere mortals to measure up in our eyes. . . . In our collective amnesia we lose the mechanisms through which grassroots social movements of the past successfully shifted public sentiment and challenged entrenched institutional power. Equally lost are the means by

5

6

which their participants managed to keep on, sustaining their hope and eventually prevailing in circumstances at least as difficult as those we face today. (38/36)

Placing a select few on pedestals and claiming them as next-to-divine heroes of the movement does society a disservice; people fail to realize that ordinary people can serve as agents of change.

Morrison's book ignores the thousands of ordinary people who risked their lives for the cause to bring about equality. The caption beside the picture of Rosa Parks in *Remember* reads "Because if I ever feel helpless or lonely I just have to remember that all it takes is one person" (Morrison 62). Ironically, Morrison gives credit for the Montgomery Bus Boycott to one person, ignoring the months of planning that involved dozens of planners. Even the photograph presents Rosa Parks in a position of power. It is a low-angle shot up at Parks that makes her appear larger than life and authoritative. The photographs of Martin Luther King Jr. also further the impression of power with a close-up shot of his face as he stands above thousands of participants in the March on Washington. Although these photographs were selected to perpetuate the hero illusion, it is more inspiring to remember the ordinary people who took a stand and were able to accomplish extraordinary feats because of their dedication and persistence rather than to glorify extraordinary people who were destined for greatness.

In contrast, Spike Lee's 1998 documentary titled *4 Little Girls* is a stirring depiction of the lives and deaths of the girls who died in the 1963 16th Street Baptist Church bombing. In his film, Spike Lee looks behind what some would call "societal amnesia" to disclose the harsh realities of the civil rights movement. Lee interviews family members and friends of the murdered girls, revealing the pain and anger that they grapple with more than forty years after the tragedy. Lee not only includes images of the bombed church but also the charred and nearly unrecognizable bodies of the murdered girls. These disturbing images underscore the reality of their deaths without appearing sensationalist. The film does an exceptional job of reminding the viewer of the suffering and mindless hate that were prevalent during the civil rights movement.

However, the documentary is also biased. For instance, the girls were not little; they were fourteen, not really little girls. Lee chose to describe them as little to elicit emotion and sympathy for their tragic deaths. They were victims. They had not marched through the streets demanding equality; instead, Denise McNair, Carole Robertson, Addie Mae Collins, and Cynthia Wesley were simply attending Sunday school and were ruthlessly murdered. Victimizing Denise, Carole, Addie Mae, and Cynthia is not detrimental to the cultural memory in and of itself. The problem is that the victimization of the four girls is expanded to encompass the entire black community, undermining the power and achievement of the average black citizen. We need to remember the people who struggled to gain employment for blacks in the labor movement of the 1940s and 1950s that initiated the civil rights movement.

One can argue that despite the presence of misleading images in Spike Lee's film and Toni Morrison's book, at least some of the story is preserved. Still, it is easy to fall victim to the cliché: those who do not remember history are doomed to repeat it. Just because a portion of the story is remembered, it does not mean that society is immune to falling back into its old habits. This cultural amnesia not only perpetuates the injustices of the time but leaves open the possibility that these atrocities can occur again. If people believe the government can simply grant black equality, then they may believe that it can also take it away. In essence memory is about power: "The struggle of man against power is the struggle of memory against forgetting." Those who are remembered hold power over the forgotten. Their legacy is lost and so is their ability to inspire future generations through their memory.

10

Works Cited

ATF Online. Bureau of Alcohol, Tobacco, Firearms and Explosives, U.S. Department of Justice. Web. Dec. 2004.

Kolker, Robert. *Film, Form, and Culture*. New York: McGraw Hill, 1998. Print.

Kundera, Milan. *The Columbia World of Quotations*. New York: Columbia UP, 1996. Web. Dec. 2004.

Loeb, Paul Rogat. *Soul of a Citizen*. New York: St. Martin's/Griffin, 1999. Print.

Morrison, Toni. *Remember*. Boston: Houghton, 2004. Print.

For Analysis and Discussion

1. What would you say is Taylor's argument?

2. To what extent does she provide transitions to help you understand how her analysis supports her argument?

3. To what extent does she integrate quotations appropriately into the text of her argument?

4. To what extent does the style of citation reflect accepted conventions for academic writing?

5. If Taylor had more time to revise, what would you suggest she do?

FURTHER SUGGESTIONS FOR PEER EDITING GROUPS

Monitoring your own writing group can help ensure that the group is both providing and receiving the kinds of responses the members need. Here is a list of questions you might ask of one another after a session:

- What topics were discussed?
- Were most questions and comments directed at the level of ideas? Structure? Language?
- Were topics always brought up with a question or a comment?
- Who initiated talk more frequently — the writer or the readers?
- What roles did different group members play?
- Did each author open with specific questions or concerns?
- Did the readers begin by giving specific reactions?

After answering these questions, identify two things that are working well in your group. Then identify two things that you could improve. How would you go about making those improvements?

When we asked our students what they thought contributed to effective conversation in their writing groups, here is what they told us:

- Honest and spontaneous expression
- Free interaction among members
- High levels of personal involvement
- Members' commitment to insight and change
- The sense that self-disclosure is safe and highly valued
- Members' willingness to take responsibility for the group's effectiveness
- Members' belief that the group is important
- Members' belief that they are primary agents of help for one another
- Members' focus on communication within the group over other discussions

11

Other Methods of Inquiry: Interviews and Focus Groups

Sometimes to advance your argument you may need to do original research. By **original research**, we mean using primary sources of evidence you gather yourself. (Another common term for this type of investigation is *field research*.) Remember that primary sources of evidence include firsthand or eyewitness accounts like those found in letters or newspapers, or in research reports in which the researcher explains his or her impressions of a particular phenomenon — for example, gender relations in classroom interactions. (In contrast, a secondary source is an analysis of information contained in primary sources.)

The type of original research we discuss in this chapter relies on people — interviewees and members of focus groups — as primary sources of information. To inquire into gender dynamics in college science classrooms, then, you might conduct interviews with young women to understand their perceptions of how gender affects teaching. Or you might convene a focus group to put a variety of perspectives into play on questions about gendered teaching practices. The pages that follow present strategies for conducting interviews and setting up focus groups that can generate multiple responses to your research questions.

When you conduct research, keep in mind that you are not setting out to prove anything; instead, the process of inquiry will enable you to answer the questions *you* ask, address problems, and move readers to rethink their positions. Good critical readers know that the arguments they produce as writers are influenced by what they choose to discuss and how they construe the evidence they provide.

Although there is really no way to avoid the limitations of writing from one point of view, writers can provide readers with multiple sources of information, so that they can make their own judgments about what to believe or not believe. In fact, this is the argument we make above in studying inequities in education. Relying on a single source of data will inevitably limit your field of vision. Multiple sources of information add complexity and texture to your analysis, conveying to readers the thoroughness of your approach.

WHY DO ORIGINAL RESEARCH?

We can think of four reasons (all of which overlap to some extent) why you might do original research for a writing class.

To Increase Your Ability to Read Critically.   When you do original research, you learn, at a basic and pragmatic level, how the studies you consult in a researched argument come into being — you're on the ground floor of knowledge making. As a critical reader, you know it's important to ask questions like these: What is the source of the author's claim? Why should I believe the author? What is the source of the author's authority? What are the possible counterarguments? When you are doing original research, you are in the position of that author, with a real stake in establishing your own authority. By coming to understand what it takes to establish your own authority, you are in a better position to evaluate how effectively other researchers establish theirs.

Let's say your research question concerns gender differences in math education. You might read a study that asserts that girls and young women are being shortchanged in math classes, impeding their ability to go into math-related fields. You would want to ask about the nature of the data used to support this claim. If the author of the study states that 56 percent of the female students interviewed said they were discouraged from going into math-related fields, you might wonder where the figure of 56 percent came from. How many girls and young women were interviewed? How was this sample selected? What were the students asked? Questions like these inform your own use of interviews and focus groups.

To Increase Your Own Research Skills.   Doing original research broadens your own range of research methods. By developing a repertoire of research methods, you will be better able to explore questions that may be too complex to answer by examining texts alone. One scholar put it this way: "I couldn't see what a text was doing without looking at the worlds in which these texts served as significant activities."* After all, it is one thing to read a research report and understand its purpose, its intended

---

*Bazerman, C. (1988). *Shaping written knowledge: The genre and activity of the scientific article in science.* Madison: University of Wisconsin Press, p. 4.

audience, the nature of its claims, and the like. But it is quite another to watch scientists at work and begin to understand how they have come to know what they know. The discovery of DNA, for example, was the result of an arduous process that involved much risk, collaboration, chance, error, and competition. The neat structure of a scientific report could mislead you into thinking that science is a linear process that begins with a question, moves on to an experiment, and ends with an answer. Real research is messier than that. Original research takes us behind the words we read, introducing levels of complexity.

To Broaden Your Scope of Inquiry.   Doing original research may also broaden the scope of your inquiry. First, it is useful to use different research methods than the ones you are accustomed to using. Learning to interview and run focus groups, at the very least, can give you insight and practice for nonacademic applications — market research, for example. Second, it can make you aware of how people outside your field address the questions you raise. Consider, for example, the different perspectives an educator, a sociologist, and an economist would bring to the question of educational inequities. An educator might study educational inequities as a curricular problem, and so analyze the content of different curricula within and across schools. A sociologist might visit students' homes, noting the presence or absence of books or asking parents how they go about preparing their children for school. An economist might examine income levels in both wealthy and impoverished neighborhoods. The point is that each field brings its own perspective to a problem, adding complexity and richness to your own discussion of that problem.

To Make a Unique Contribution to a Conversation of Ideas.   Finally, doing original research affords you the opportunity to make a unique contribution to a conversation of ideas. Instead of relying exclusively on texts others have written as evidence for your claims, you can offer your own data to address a question or problem, data that others do not have available. For instance, if you wanted to examine claims that primary school teachers pay more attention to boys in class than to girls, you could review the relevant literature and then add to that literature a study that systematically analyzes the ways in which teachers in different classrooms treat boys and girls.

GETTING STARTED: WRITING A PROPOSAL

A **proposal** is a formal plan that outlines your objectives for conducting a research project, specifies the methods you intend to use, and describes what you expect the implications of the work to be. The proposal is a tool that helps guide you through various stages of the project. The most immediate benefit of writing a proposal is that through the act of writing — by setting forth an outline of your project — your thinking will become more precise.

At a minimum, a research proposal should include three sections: purpose, method, and discussion and implications. You may also want to include additional sections with materials that provide concrete support for your proposal — some of the tools that will help you get the job done. You should arrange your plan and use headings so that readers can find information quickly.

■ Describe Your Purpose

In the purpose section of your proposal, formulate the question that is motivating your study. Inquiry begins with a good question.

- A good question can help you think through the issue you want to write about.
- It is specific enough to guide your inquiry and to be answered with the tools and resources you have available and have decided to use.
- It does not limit the answer to yes, no, or either/or.
- It asks how, why, should, or the extent to which.
- It conveys a clear idea of who you are answering the question for — your audience.

In your purpose section (usually the introduction), you should summarize the issue and explain how it has led to the question driving your research. You also should explain why you are interested in this issue area, why it is important, and what is at stake. Ask yourself why others should be interested in your effort to answer the question.

■ Define Your Method

In the method section, you list and describe the tools and strategies you will use to conduct your research. Some of the tools and strategies of original research are

- conducting interviews or focus groups,
- taking notes,
- recording on audio- or videotape a particular activity or activities,
- doing background, historical, or archival work,
- observing and coming to terms with your own impressions.

In addition to identifying your method, you need to discuss the appropriateness of your tools and strategies, why they are the best means for answering your research question. Given the objectives you have set for yourself and the constraints of doing the research, are some methods better than others?

■ Discuss Your Implications

It may seem a little premature to talk about what you hope to find in your study, but it is important to address "So what?" — to explain what you believe is the significance of your study. Place your argument in the context of the conversation you want to join and explain how your study can contribute to that conversation. Write about how your study will build on, challenge, or extend other studies in your area of research. And, finally, identify what you believe is going to be new about your findings.

■ Include Additional Materials That Support Your Research

Depending on your instructor and the level of formality of your proposal, you may be asked to include additional materials that reveal other dimensions of your research. Those materials may include (1) an annotated bibliography, (2) scripts of the questions you are planning to ask in interviews and focus groups, and (3) the consent forms you will ask interviewees or participants in your focus groups to sign.

Annotated bibliography.   An **annotated bibliography** is a list of sources (arranged alphabetically by author) that you plan to consult and make use of in your research paper. Typically you provide a citation (author, date, title of source, and publication information) and a short summary of the source. You can present all your sources in one long list or organize them by type of source (books, journals, and so forth). An excerpt from a student's annotated bibliography is shown in Figure 11.1.

FIGURE 11.1   An Excerpt from a Student's Annotated Bibliography

Bibliography

Books

Dupper, D. R. (2003). *School social work: Skills and interventions for effective practice.* Hoboken, NJ: John Wiley & Sons.

> This book provides a general overview of the duties and responsibilities of school social workers. It explains various social problems that many students encounter, and evaluates intervention and prevention programs.

Kryder-Coe, J. H., Salamon, L. H., & Molnar, J. M. (Eds.). (1991). *Homeless children and youth: A new American dilemma.* New Brunswick, NJ: Transaction.

> This book examines the impact of child homelessness on society, the causes of child homelessness, and society's

---

(continued on next page)

FIGURE 11.1   (Continued)

---

response to child homelessness. Part of the book focuses on
the developmental and educational consequences of homelessness on children.

Vostanis, P., & Cumella, S. (Eds.). (1999). *Homeless children:
Problems and needs.* London: Jessica Kingsley.

This book is a collection of articles examining the various
aspects of life for homeless children. One article focuses
specifically on problems surrounding education for homeless
youth.

Journal Articles

All of the following journal articles focus on the educational and
developmental needs of homeless youth. They relate this issue to the
effectiveness of the McKinney-Vento Homeless Assistance Act (1987),
to the current and future work of school counselors and social workers, and to the development of community programs.

Markward, M. J., & Biros, E. (2001, July). McKinney revisited: Implications for school social work. *Children & Schools, 23*(3).
Retrieved from
http://web11.epnet.com.lib-proxy.nd.edu/

This article examines the extent to which the McKinney-Vento
Act has affected homeless children and youth. It discusses
the implications the act has had for school social work.

Moroz, K. J., & Segal, E. A. (1990, January). Homeless children:
Intervention strategies for school social workers. *Social Work in
Education, 12*(2). Retrieved from
http://web11.epnet.com.lib-proxy.nd.edu/

This article investigates the various effects of homelessness
on children. The authors propose a model for intervention for
school social workers that would connect them with community services.

Questions You Plan to Ask.   Including a list (or lists) of the questions
you expect to ask those you plan to interview or survey will help you focus
your thinking. What personal information do you need to know? What
information about your issue? What opinions and recommendations
would be helpful? Each list should include at least five good questions, but
can include many more. A sample set of questions to ask the parents of
homeless children appears in Figure 11.2.

FIGURE 11.2　Sample Interview Questions

Parent(s)

1. a. Describe your current living and family situation (parents, siblings, how long homeless, where living, where child attends school).
   b. Describe your child.
   c. Describe your relationship with your child.

2. a. Do you think homelessness is affecting your child's schooling?
   b. If so, tell me how (grades, friends, attendance, transportation).

3. Tell me about enrolling your child in school. What was the process like? Were there any problems? Conditions? Challenges?

4. a. Do you feel that your child's right to an education has been recognized?
   b. Why or why not? What experiences can you point to to support your answer?

5. Describe the relationship between your child and his or her teachers.

6. a. What types of support services is your child currently being offered in school and in the community?
   b. How effective are those services?
   c. How supportive of your child's educational and developmental growth do you feel your child's school has been?
   d. What about the Center for the Homeless?
   e. Do you have any recommendations for these sources of help or requests for other types of help or services for your child that are not currently offered?

7. How do you envision your child's future?

Consent Forms.　Whenever you plan to solicit information in an interview or focus group, you need to get the interviewee's or participants' permission to make use of that information in your research paper. We have included a sample consent form for an interview in Figure 11.3.

FIGURE 11.3　Sample Interview Consent Form

You are invited to participate in a study of homelessness and education conducted by Mary Ronan, an undergraduate at the University of Notre Dame, during the next few months. If you decide to participate, you will

1. provide up to two interviews with the researcher,
2. allow the researcher to use excerpts from the interviews in publications about research with the understanding that your identity will not be revealed at any time.

   Participation is completely voluntary. You may choose to stop participating at any time prior to completion of the project. Should you have any questions at any time, you are welcome to contact the researcher by phone or e-mail. Your decision to participate will have no effect on or prejudice your future relationship with the University of Notre Dame. One possible benefit of participating in the

---

(continued on next page)

FIGURE 11.3   (Continued)

study is that you will have the opportunity to learn about the implications of homelessness on education.

If you are willing to participate in this research, please read and sign the consent form below. You will be given a copy of this form to keep.

CONSENT FORM
I agree to participate in all of the procedures above. I understand that my identity will be protected during the study and that others will not have access to the interviews I provide. I also understand that my name will not be revealed when data from the research are presented in publications. I have read the above and give the researcher, Mary Ronan, permission to use excerpts from transcripts of tapes without identifying me as the writer or speaker.

_____   _____
Date   *Signature*

                                          _____
                                          Signature of Researcher
                                          [Telephone number]/[E-mail address]

■ Establish a Timeline

To write a proposal, you'll need to draw up a schedule for your research. This timeline should include the dates when you expect to finish the proposal, when you will conduct interviews and focus groups, when you hope to have a draft, and when you will complete the project. As you develop your timeline, you need to be realistic about when you can actually complete the different stages of collecting your data and writing. You can anticipate that events will prevent everything from going as planned. People cannot always meet you when you would like them to, and you may have to change your own schedule. Therefore, be sure to contact participants well in advance of the time you would like to speak with them in interviews or focus groups.

Steps to Writing a Proposal

1 **Describe your purpose.** Summarize your issue, describing how it has led you to the question motivating your research.

2 **Define your method.** What tools and strategies are you planning to use? Why are they appropriate and sufficient for your purposes?

3 **Discuss your implications.** What is the context of the conversation you are entering? What significant information do you expect your study to uncover?

4 **Include additional materials that support your research.** These may include an annotated bibliography, a series of interview questions, and blank consent forms.

ANALYZING A PROPOSAL

Our student Mary Ronan submitted a formal proposal for a study of the education of a homeless child. Ronan's proposal was exceptionally well prepared, thorough, and thoughtful; and she included a number of additional materials — an annotated bibliography; sample questions for the teachers, students, and parents she planned to interview; and sample consent forms. We reprint only the main part of her proposal, the part that includes her purpose, methods, and discussion and implications sections, for you to consider as a model for proposal writing. Notice how Ronan summarizes her issue and explains how it led to her research, and how she makes her readers understand why her research is important.

Ronan 1

Research Paper Proposal:
A Case Study of One Homeless Child's Education and Lifestyle
Mary Ronan

In 2000, the Urban Institute estimated that 1.35 million children experience homelessness over the course of a year (Urban Institute, 2000). The U.S. Department of Education estimated that the number of children and youth in homeless situations increased from approximately 841,700 to 930,000 in 2000 (U.S. Department of Education, 2000). It also determined that preschool and elementary-aged children make up the largest numbers of children experiencing homelessness (U.S. Department of Education, 2000). Homelessness as experienced by school-aged children is clearly increasing. *1*

Homeless children and youth are defined as "those individuals who lack a fixed, regular, and adequate nighttime residence" (McKinney-Vento Homeless Assistance Act, 1987). This includes children who live in shelters, cars, motels, and numerous other inadequate housing situations. The McKinney-Vento Act states that each child of a homeless individual and each homeless youth must have equal access to the same free, appropriate public education as provided to other children. It states specifically that homelessness alone is not a sufficient reason to separate these students from the mainstream school environment. *2*

Homelessness has serious implications for children's developmental and academic growth. Developmental problems include *3*

Ronan 2

withdrawal, aggression, short attention span, sleep disorders, speech delays, regressive behaviors, immature motor behavior, immature peer interaction, and inappropriate social interaction with adults (Baumohl, 1996; Pawlas, 1994). These developmental problems lead to academic problems, which are especially evident in reading and math. The majority of homeless students read below grade level and score below grade level in mathematics (Pawlas, 1994; Stormont-Spurgin & De Reus, 1995; Walsh & Buckley, 1994; Ziesemer & Marcoux, 1992). Homeless students have higher rates of school transfer, special education services, and grade retention (Baumohl, 1996; Walsh & Buckley, 1994). Homeless students face barriers to school enrollment and attendance. These students often do not have the documents required for school enrollment; as a result, many children are turned away from attending school until this issue is resolved (U.S. Department of Education, 2000). Transportation to and from school is the biggest problem for homeless youth (U.S. Department of Education, 2000). These barriers directly and negatively affect the success of homeless students in school.

A stable lifestyle for these children is crucial to their mental, emotional, physical, and social well-being. "Stability is central to children's growth and development, and times of transition are times of risk" (Baumohl, 1996, p. 118). Homelessness creates great risks for the developmental and academic growth of youth; these risks need to be confronted. "Children who have lost their homes live the experience of having, as they describe it, 'nowhere to go'" (Walsh & Buckley, 1994, p. 2).

Communities need to examine how they are reacting and responding to the struggles and needs of homeless students. Despite the obstacles that homeless students face, schools are an ideal setting for developing and organizing the educational and social services they need (Wall, 1996). Comprehensive services including both educators and social workers can be done both within and outside the school system (Wall, 1996). If these homeless children's lives are to improve, they will require the help of schools and social agencies, both working as parts of a community that is sensitive and responsive to these students' needs. It is clear that society understands the importance of caring for homeless students, but to what extent have schools and social service agencies carried out their suggestions or plans?

The McKinney-Vento Homeless Assistance Act defines homeless youth and explains the rights of students facing homelessness. It
provides specific guidelines for how schools and social service agencies are to care for homeless students' educational needs. Yet,
Congress has not adequately funded state or local efforts to implement this legislation. In 2003, Congress appropriated $55 million for
educational programs under the McKinney-Vento Act. However, this is
$15 million less than the authorized amount of $70 million (National
Coalition for the Homeless, 2004). Is the country doing everything it
can to ensure the rights of homeless children as stated in the
McKinney-Vento Homeless Assistance Act?

6

The question this research is attempting to answer is "To
what extent are schools and social service agencies, working as
parts of larger communities, creating a stable lifestyle that will
improve homeless students' developmental and educational growth?"
There has not been much research examining how effectively schools
and social service agencies are creating stability in homeless students' lives. In order to better the lives of these children, research
must be done investigating and evaluating the current services
offered.

7

The developmental and academic lives of students are threatened by the lack of stability resulting from homelessness. This issue
is a very important one as the numbers of homeless children continue
to increase each year. Answering this question will provide valuable
information to both schools and social agencies about how to better
care for the specific needs and rights of homeless students. Moreover,
this research will lead to a greater sense of community caring for
those who live in poverty. It may inspire future research and the
creation of programs that better aid homeless students.

8

Methods

I will take a case study approach in order to better understand this issue and attempt to answer my research question. My
case study will focus on one child from the South Bend Center for the
Homeless. I will interview the child, his or her parents, teacher,
school social worker, and others who play a role in creating stability
in this child's life. I will take notes as well as audio-record the interviews. These interviews will allow me to explore the connections

9

Ronan 4

between homelessness and education as explained by the voices of those who witness or are affected by homelessness every day.

I will also be using archival information, including both journal articles and books, from the library. I will explore what other researchers have contributed to this issue and what they are currently saying about it. I will also examine present-day statistics involving homelessness, youth, and education, and will study the plans of various government and community programs and policies, particularly the McKinney-Vento Homeless Assistance Act. This will help me to further develop and answer my own questions about homelessness and education.

Utilizing these various methods will provide me with a broad range of information and resources that will aid me in completing my research. Directly discussing this education issue with participants will hopefully lead to an honest and realistic perspective. It is the true stories of those who are faced with the issue of homelessness on a daily basis that will bring this important issue to the surface.

Discussion and Implications

In America, over 800,000 children are homeless. In South Bend, over 300 children live in one of three homeless shelters. It is believed that 50 percent of these local children will grow up to be homeless. Many homeless children do not attend school regularly. Studies have found that those who do attend school do not perform as well as their peers and have difficulties socializing with others. A school should be a permanent safe-haven for these students. A school should be one place that these students might be able to consider their home. Why then do problems involving homeless youth and education continue to exist?

Homelessness traps the young in a vicious cycle from which they may never be able to escape. If they are continuously moving from shelter to shelter, they are continuously moving from school to school. As a result, their attendance may drop; their performance may not be at grade level; they may be stereotyped and labeled by others based on their temporary lifestyle. Without the psychological, social, and mental benefits a strong formal education imparts, the homeless child seems to be left to the fate of his or her parents. The cycle of homelessness continues for another generation.

10

11

12

13

Ronan 5

Clearly, this issue is an important one. When we think of the   *14*
homeless, we might imagine a disheveled man sleeping on the street
or a woman holding a cardboard sign begging for food. But what
about the children who, instead of going home to a three-bedroom
house in a residential neighborhood, go to a large dormitory at a
shelter? The issue of homelessness and its effects on education need
to be examined.

The need for school social workers is great. It seems that   *15*
much more can be offered to those students who face such grave
realities every day. Communities need to work with both schools and
social agencies to ensure that these children are cared for. Homelessness impairs the ability of the individual to receive a good education,
something to which every child has a right.

Perhaps as a result of this study there will be more community   *16*
and school action and involvement to support homeless students.
Perhaps there will be better busing systems so that these students
can remain enrolled in the same school for longer periods. Perhaps
school social workers can work toward finding more permanent living
arrangements for their homeless students. Perhaps more mentoring
and tutoring programs can be formed to aid homeless students. Much
can be done and should be done to better the lives of these students.

For Analysis and Discussion

1. How would you describe the conversation Ronan wants to contribute to in
   her study of homeless children?
2. What is the gap or issue that she identifies?
3. What is at stake in addressing this problem?
4. To what extent do you think Ronan's proposed research is compelling?
5. To what extent do you think the author can answer her question by using
   the research methods she describes?

INTERVIEWING

An **interview** is a face-to-face conversation in which you ask questions to
collect information or opinions that relate to your research question. It's
certainly possible to conduct an interview by phone, especially if the

interviewee is not local, but a face-to-face conversation, in which you can note physical details and body language, is preferable.

The ways writers incorporate interviews into their writing appears almost seamless; but keep in mind that a finished text hides the process involved in conducting a successful interview. What you don't see is the planning that occurs. Writers have to make appointments with each of the people they interview; they have to develop a script, or list of questions, before actually conducting the interview; and they have to test the questions to be sure they work — that is, that the answers give them the information they are looking for. In other words, the key to a successful interview is preparation. The following information should help you plan for your interview and prepare you for writing down your results.

■ Plan the Interview

You'll want to do some preliminary research to identify people who can help you understand more about your subject: What kind of expertise or experience do they have? Then you have to contact them to find out if they are willing to be interviewed. Begin by explaining your project and why you want to interview them (you may want to send them a copy of your proposal). Let them know about how much of their time you are requesting: Half an hour? An hour? (More than an hour is probably excessive.) If you are planning to record the interview — always a wise idea — make sure the person consents to being recorded. Then make the necessary arrangements. For example, you may need to reserve a room where you can conduct your interview without being disturbed.

Obviously it is crucial to find out in your first contact whether your candidates actually have expertise in an area relevant to your study. If they lack that expertise, consider asking if they can recommend someone who has it.

It's important to set up appointments with people early on. To keep on schedule, list the names of people who have agreed to be interviewed:

Interviewee 1: _____ Contacted? _____(y/n)

Interviewee 2: _____ Contacted? _____(y/n)

■ Prepare Your Script

You should now begin to work on your script in earnest. If you submitted a series of questions with your proposal, you may have received some response to them from your instructor or classmates. Perhaps they suggested refinements or proposed additional questions. If you agree with their suggestions, now is the time to incorporate them. As you work on your script, keep the following points in mind:

Try to Establish Common Ground.   In any conversation, you want to establish common ground, and an interview is no different. Do you have any interests in common with the person that may ease you into the interview? Order your questions so that you begin by establishing common ground and then move on to the issues you want to learn more about.

Start with Nonthreatening Questions.   For example, "How long have you been working at the homeless shelter?" "What prompted you to work at a homeless shelter?" "What role do you play with the children at the homeless shelter?"

Ask Filter Questions.   Filter questions help you determine what the person you are interviewing knows or has experienced. For instance, you might ask a worker at a homeless shelter if he or she works with children. If not, does he or she work with parents? Of course, if you've done your homework, you will know where to start the interview.

Beware of Yes/No Questions.   Try not to ask questions that encourage simple yes or no responses. Work on rephrasing yes/no questions in your script so that you're more likely to get an enlightening answer. For example, don't ask "Do you think that the children at the homeless shelter can overcome the obstacles they face?" Instead, ask something like this: "How do you think children at the homeless shelter can overcome the obstacles they face?"

Try Funneling.   *Funneling* means moving from more-general questions — "What challenges have you faced as an educator in the homeless shelter?" — to more-specific ones — "How did you respond to those challenges?"

Rehearse and Then Revise the Script.   After you've reworked your script, rehearse it with your writing group or some friends to see how it works. You want to develop a sense of how an interviewee is going to respond to your questions. Is the wording clear? Are you getting the information you need? If not, what other questions should you ask? How did the order and pacing of the questions make your stand-in interviewees feel? How long did the interview take? After the rehearsal, revise the script to improve the content, order, and pacing of your questions.

■ Conduct the Interview

On the day of an interview, contact your interviewee again to make sure he or she remembers the time of the interview and knows how to find the location where it will take place. See to it that your tape recorder or video camera is charged and functioning, and has sufficient recording capacity for the interview. Be on time. Start by having the person sign a simple consent form (see Figure 11.3). It should specify how you will use the material and should indicate that the interviewee knows you will be recording the interview and agrees to let you use quotes from the interview in your paper.

Once you begin asking questions, if at all possible, take notes and record the conversation. Be flexible with the script as you go. Pursue new questions that are raised by what the interviewee tells you. If the interviewee's answers are vague, evasive, or misdirected, try rephrasing your questions to be more specific about the information you need. If you think the interviewee is implying something that is of special interest to you, ask for clarification. This kind of reflective query may shake loose some interesting new material.

Toward the end of the interview, check your script for important questions you may have forgotten to ask. If there are several, try to ask only the most important ones in the time remaining.

▪ Make Sense of the Interview

Conducting an interview is only part of the challenge; you then have to make sense of what was said. That process involves four steps:

1. *Familiarize yourself with the conversation.* If you recorded the interview, listen to or watch it a couple of times to become really familiar with what was said. Read through your notes several times too.

2. *Transcribe the interview.* Being familiar with the conversation will make it easier to transcribe. Keep in mind that transcription takes more time than you think, and plan accordingly. An hour interview usually takes about three hours to transcribe.

3. *Analyze the interview.* Read through the interview again. Look for answers to the questions motivating your research, and look for recurring patterns or themes. Make a list of those ideas relevant to the issues you intend to focus on, especially evidence that might support your argument.

4. *Find one good source.* Using the themes you identify in your analysis as a guide, find one good source that relates to your interview in some way. Maybe your subject's story fits into an educational debate (for example, public versus private education). Or maybe your subject's story counters a common conception about education (that inner-city schools are hopelessly inadequate). You're looking for a source you can link to your interview in an interesting and effective way.

▪ Turn Your Interview into an Essay

Try to lay out on paper, in paragraphs, the material you've collected that pertains to the focus of your paper. In a first draft, you might take these steps:

1. State your argument, or the purpose of your essay. What do you want to teach your readers?

2. Begin writing your supporting evidence for your thesis. What examples from your reading, observations, or interviews do you want to offer your readers? How do those examples illuminate your claim?

3. Place quotations from more than one source in as many paragraphs as you can, so that you can play the quotations off against one another. What is significant about the ways you see specific quotations "in conversation" with one another? How do these conversations between quotations help you build your own point?

4. Consider possible counterarguments to the point you want to make.

5. Help readers understand what is at stake in adopting your position.

Steps to Interviewing

1 **Plan the interview.** After you've identified candidates through research, contact them to explain your project and set up appointments if they are willing to participate.

2 **Prepare your script.** Draft your questions, rehearse them with your classmates or friends, and then make revisions based on their responses.

3 **Conduct the interview.** Be flexible with your script as you go, making sure to take good notes even if you are recording the interview.

4 **Make sense of the interview.** Review the recording and your notes of the interview, transcribe the interview, analyze the transcript, and connect the conversation to at least one good source.

5 **Turn your interview into an essay.** State your argument, organize your evidence, use quotes to make your point, consider counterarguments, and help your readers understand what's at stake.

USING FOCUS GROUPS

Focus groups can provide you with an original source of evidence to complement (or complicate, contradict, or extend) the evidence you find in books and articles. Conducting a focus group is much like conducting an interview. According to Bruce L. Berg, in *Qualitative Research Methods for the Social Sciences*, a **focus group** "may be defined as an interview style designed for small groups . . . addressing a particular topic of interest or relevance to the group and the researcher." College administrators often speak with groups of students to understand the nature of a problem — for instance, whether writing instruction is as effective as it should be beyond a first-year writing course, or whether technology is used to best effect in classes across the curriculum. One advantage of a focus group, as opposed to an interview, is that once one person starts talking, others join in. It is generally easier to get a conversation going in a focus group than to get an interview started with a single person.

A typical focus group session is guided by a facilitator, or moderator. The moderator's job is much like the interviewer's: to draw out information from the participants on topics of importance to a given investigation. The informal atmosphere of the focus group is intended to encourage participants to speak freely and completely about their behaviors, attitudes, and opinions. Interaction among group members often takes the form of brainstorming, generating a larger number of ideas, issues, topics, and even solutions to problems than could be produced through individual conversations.

What follow are several basic tasks necessary to orchestrating a focus group.

■ Select Participants for the Focus Group

Focus groups should consist of five to seven participants, in addition to you, the moderator. Think carefully about the range of participants you'll need to gather the information you're hoping to gather. Depending on your issue, you might choose participants based on gender, ethnicity, major, year in school, living situation, or some other factor. Do you want a wide range of participants? Or do you want to control the focus of the conversation by looking at just one particular group of people? For instance, if you wanted to find out if technology is serving students' needs, would you talk only to people in the sciences? Or would you want a cross-section of disciplines represented? Or if your question is whether colleges and universities should take race and ethnicity into consideration when selecting students from the applicant pool, would you limit participation to the admissions staff? Where should you look for input on the purpose of giving preference to minority students or the advantages of a diverse campus?

■ Plan the Focus Group

Planning is as important for a focus group as it is for an interview. Make specific arrangements with participants about the time and place of the focus group session, and be clear about how much time it will take, usually 30 minutes. You should tape-record or videotape the session, in addition to any notes you take. Jot down important information during the session, and allow yourself time to make more extensive notes as soon as it is over. You will need to get permission from respondents to use the information they give you and ensure their anonymity. (In your essay, you can refer to participants by letter, number, or some other designation.) Make a sheet with your signature that spells this out clearly, and make sure all your participants sign it before the session. You should include a statement pointing out that people have the right not to participate. We have included sample consent forms in Figures 11.4 and 11.5.

FIGURE 11.4   Sample Consent Form for a Focus Group

You are invited to participate in a study of academic writing at the university over the next four years. You were selected from a random sample of all first-year students. If you decide to participate, you will

1. provide the researcher with copies of the writing you complete for every class and the assignment, when available;

2. attend up to four focus group sessions during a given academic year;

3. allow the researcher to use excerpts from the writing you complete and the focus group sessions in publications about research with the understanding that your identity will not be revealed at any time.

In all, out-of-class participation will take no more than four hours during an academic year.

Participation is completely voluntary; you may stop participating at any time prior to completion of the project. Should you have any questions at any time, you are welcome to contact the researcher at the address below or via e-mail. Your decision to participate or not will have no effect on your grade in any course or prejudice your future relationship with the university. One benefit of participating in the study is that you will have the opportunity to learn important information about writing.

If you are willing to participate in this research, please read and sign the consent form below. You will be given a copy of this form to keep.

CONSENT FORM

I agree to participate in all of the procedures above. I understand that my identity will be protected during the study and that instructors will not have access to the statements I make in focus group sessions. I also understand that my name will not be revealed when data from the research are presented in publications. (Tapes from this study will be kept for five years and then destroyed.) I have read the above and give the researcher, Stuart Greene, and his coauthors permission to use excerpts from what I write or transcripts of tapes without identifying me as the writer or speaker.

_____   _____
Date   *Signature*

                                                _____
                                                Signature of Researcher
                                                [Telephone number]/[E-mail address]

◼ Prepare Your Script

Many of the guidelines for designing interview questions (see p. 262) apply equally well to focus group questions. So, for example, you might start by establishing common ground or with a couple of nonthreatening questions. For variety, and to keep the discussion moving, use both open and closed (yes/no answer) questions. Consider asking participants for definitions,

---

FIGURE 11.5   Sample Consent Form for a Focus Group

Should colleges and universities take race and ethnicity into consideration when selecting new freshmen from the applicant pool? What is the purpose of giving preference to minority status in admissions? What does a diverse campus offer its students? These are some of the issues I want to discuss in today's focus group. But before we start, let me tell you about the assignment and your involvement.

The focus group is an interview style designed for small groups of five to seven participants. Focus group interviews are guided discussions that address a particular topic of interest or relevance to the group and the researcher. The informality of the focus group structure is intended to encourage participants to speak freely about their behaviors, attitudes, and opinions. For the purposes of my research, focus groups are a way to include multiple perspectives in my paper.

This session will be recorded so that I can prove my research. No names will be used in any drafts or in my final paper; instead, I will use letters (A, B, C) to identify different speakers. Two focus groups — one for minority students at Notre Dame and another for nonminority students — are being held so that I can obtain opinions and viewpoints from both sides of the issue and discuss their similarities and differences in my report. Some things to keep in mind during the session:

- Because I need to transcribe the dialogue, try not to talk over another person.
- Feel free to agree or disagree with a question, statement, or another person's answer.
- Focus on the discussion, not the question.
- Avoid going off on tangents.
- Be open and honest in all your responses.

Thank you for taking the time to be involved in my research. By signing below you give me permission to use the comments you provide for my paper. You understand that in no way will your identity be revealed, except by your minority or nonminority status. If you would like a copy of the results of the focus groups, please include your e-mail address, and the documents will be sent to you.

Name _____   Male Female (circle one)
Ethnicity _____   Class of _____
E-mail address _____

---

impressions, examples, their ideas of others' perceptions, and the like. Also, consider quoting from key passages in the scholarly research you will be using and asking for the group's responses to these "expert" theories. Not only will this be interesting; it also will help you organize and integrate your focus group evidence with evidence from library sources in your essay. Ask a wider range of questions than you think you might need, so that you can explore side issues if they arise.

■ Conduct the Focus Group

On the day you conduct the focus group, contact those who have agreed to participate to remind them of when and where it will happen. Show up ahead of time to make sure that your tape recorder or video camera is in good working order and that the room has sufficient seating for the participants. And don't forget your script. Here are three other guidelines:

Ask Questions That Draw People Out.   During the focus group, be ready to draw out participants with follow-up questions ("Can you offer an example?" "Where do you think this impression comes from?"). Encourage all participants to speak; don't allow one member to dominate the discussion. (You may need to ask a facilitating question like "Do the rest of you agree with X's statement?" or "How would you extend what X has said?" or "Has anyone had a different experience?")

Limit the Time of a Focus Group Session.   It's a good idea to limit the session to twenty to thirty minutes. When deciding how long the session should last, remember that it will take approximately three times longer to transcribe it. You must transcribe the session so that you can read through the participants' comments and quote them accurately.

Notice Nonverbal Interactions.   The tape recorder or video camera will give you a record of what was said, but be sure to notice nonverbal interactions and responses in your session, taking notes of body language, reluctance or eagerness to speak, and dynamics between group members that either open up or shut down conversation. These responses should be part of the data you analyze.

■ Interpret the Data from the Focus Group

Once you transcribe your focus group session, decide how you will refer anonymously to your participants. You then need to interpret the significance of the way participants talk about issues, as well as the information they relate. Interpret the nonverbal communication in the group as well as the verbal communication.

In making claims based on focus group data, remember that data from focus group interviews are not the same as data from individual interviews. They reflect collective thinking, ideas shared and negotiated by the group. Also, although you might speculate that data from a focus group are indicative of larger trends, be careful about the kinds of claims you make. One first-year student's idea is not necessarily every first-year student's idea.

The principal aim of doing original research is to make a contribution to a conversation using primary material as evidence to support your

Steps for Conducting Focus Groups

1 **Select participants for the focus group.** Identify the range of your five to seven participants. Are you looking for diverse perspectives or a more specialized group?

2 **Plan the focus group.** Make sure you have a specified time and place, and that your participants are willing to sign consent forms.

3 **Prepare your script.** Prepare a variety of open and closed questions; consider quoting research you are interested in using in your paper to get participants' responses; and try to rehearse and revise.

4 **Conduct the focus group.** Record the session; ask questions that draw people out; limit the time of the session; and notice nonverbal interactions. And don't forget the consent forms.

5 **Interpret the data from the focus group.** Transcribe and analyze the data, including nonverbal communications; draw conclusions, but be careful not to overgeneralize from your small sample.

argument. For instance, when you conduct interviews or focus group discussions, you are collecting information (or data) that can offer a unique perspective. And doing original research also can enable you to test others' claims or assumptions and broaden your scope of inquiry beyond secondary materials. An effective piece of original research still relies on secondary materials, particularly as you find ways to locate what you discover in the context of what other authors have observed and argued. Moreover, there is the value of using multiple sources of information to support your claims — using your observations and the findings of others to say something about your subject. Also important, the research method(s) you choose depends on the question you ask. A focus on the types of educational opportunities available to the homeless lends itself more to close observation, interviews, and perhaps focus groups.

Finally, we want to end with an ethical reminder: *Be fair to your sources.* Throughout this chapter, we have included a number of forms on which you can base your own consent forms when you conduct interviews and focus groups. When people give you their consent to use their words, it is incumbent on you — really it is essential — that you represent as faithfully as possible what people have said. As a researcher, you are given a kind of power over the people you interview and write about, using what they tell you for your own purposes. You cannot abuse the trust they place in you when they consent to be part of your research. It is important that they understand why you're doing the research, and how your theories and assumptions will likely figure into your interpretation of the information you gather. You must also be aware of how their words will be construed by those who read what you write.

PART TWO

A Reader for Entering the Conversation of Ideas

12

Conventional and Unconventional Wisdom

What does it mean to be educated, and who decides?

Students don't always get a chance to step back and reflect on the many elements that shape the educational system — elements that at this very moment are shaping you. The readings in this chapter take a range of inventive approaches to two central questions: What does it mean to be educated? And who decides?

Some of these authors invite you to reflect on your own primary and secondary educational experiences, both good and bad. For example, Mary Louise Pratt brings up the seemingly arbitrary rules that often govern education, and the ways students, like her own young son, sometimes see right through teachers' authority and the game playing that is part of many assignments and tests. Pratt argues for a clear-eyed assessment of the power dynamics of education, noting that altering uneven power relationships, which she calls *contact zones*, can lead to exciting learning if teachers are willing to take risks right along with their students.

Jonathan Kozol and bell hooks also draw on specific examples of early education to demonstrate the ways teachers can offer skills that empower or disempower their students. They also describe political and social contexts that help us make sense of classroom dynamics, particularly in their depictions of segregated education in the United States in the 1950s and of what Kozol provocatively calls the "educational apartheid" of the present. Although public education is widely thought to be the most crucial element of a democracy, clearly public education in the United States is not truly equal. These writers use personal experiences and interviews with students to argue that many American schools fall far short of their democratic potential. What do you think it means for learning to be a form of revolution? Kozol and hooks offer ways to think about this big idea.

James W. Loewen turns his eye toward high school education, focusing on the teaching of history, which he claims is designed not only to bore students but often to teach them lies. Loewen's central complaint is that many of the facts and dates that bloat most history textbooks are incorrect; more important, they ignore the sometimes unpleasant truths of this nation's founding and development. Many adults lament how little today's students know about history, but Loewen blames teachers and textbook writers for students' lack of knowledge and inability to ask critical questions about the past and present, claiming, "We've got to do better."

Mark Edmundson takes on what he calls the "lite" college education experience. He also blames instructors for learning environments that pander to the student consumer. He suggests something is wrong when college students expect to enjoy their classes more than be challenged by them. You may find yourself disagreeing with his assertion that campuses look "more and more like a retirement spread for the young," but we bet he will get you thinking about the ways students "shop" for classes or praise professors for being "fun." Edmundson, like the other writers in this chapter, challenges instructors to create demanding courses that stretch students beyond their comfort zones. What is education for, these writers wonder, if not to change us?

Although these writers have plenty of criticism for what is being taught in our educational institutions at every level, they acknowledge the challenge of educating students in complex political times and in a world shaped by communications technology. What new literacies should we foster in school? Robert Scholes proposes that we should teach students to analyze video texts as carefully as other texts, while Edmundson warns us that we risk losing the values of canonical greats if we focus too much on popular culture in our classrooms.

All of the writers in this chapter push us to ask what it means in contemporary culture to be educated. Several also ask who has access to education, and why. These readings invite you to question common assumptions about how classrooms operate, from teacher-student dynamics to the material that has been designated "important knowledge." These readings will help you see your past and present educational experiences through fresh eyes, to consider the relationship between education and social power, and to ask an important question: What is education — *your* education — for?

■ MARK EDMUNDSON

On the Uses of a Liberal Education

Mark Edmundson is a professor of English at the University of Virginia. He has published many scholarly articles on literary and cultural criticism, and he has written several scholarly books, including *Why Read?: On the Uses of Great Writing* (2004), in which he defends the teaching of "great" poetry. Although Edmundson is a scholar, he is best known for writing for broader audiences on the topic of modern education. Edmundson's popular-press books on the business of teaching and learning include the acclaimed *Teacher: The One Who Made the Difference* (2003), about a quirky high school philosophy teacher who inspired Edmundson, a self-described jock, to become a teacher. Edmundson's strongly held ideas about education — in particular, liberal arts education in modern universities — have been published in *The New Republic*, *The Nation*, and the *New York Times Magazine*.

The following essay was published in 1997 in *Harper's*, where Edmundson is a contributing editor. In this piece, you can hear his distinctive voice, which can be funny as well as sharply critical. As you read, consider both his argument that higher education caters too much to consumers — students and their parents — and the way he makes this argument, drawing on examples of himself, his students, and his campus. In particular, notice how Edmundson depicts himself and his students in the opening paragraphs. Is he on target about student culture? When you and your friends talk about "good" versus "bad" professors, do you talk in terms of those who are fun or boring? Edmundson challenges our expectation to be pleased by whatever we pay for. Do you think you should simply enjoy your education? Or do you think education should challenge and change you (and if so, how?), as Edmundson suggests in paragraph 6? Discuss with your classmates his characterization of today's students. Do you agree that they are eager not to offend or be offended? That they are "decent" despite volunteering simply for "a stripe on their résumés" (para. 17)?

Because this is an article for a general readership, Edmundson does not quote other scholars at length or cite them in a bibliography. However, he does make a number of literary and historical references; and he assumes his readers know what he means when he refers to Adorno and Horkheimer (para. 48), or lists Lenin, Trotsky, Freud, and Blake (para. 52). As a reader, how does it feel to be expected to know these names? Do you usually look up names and words you don't know? How might your willingness to do this "extra" work be connected to Edmundson's argument?

In paragraph 53, we get a hint of the larger conversation Edmundson has joined with this essay:

> The aim of a good liberal-arts education was once, to adapt an observation by the scholar Walter Jackson Bate, to see that "we need not be the passive victims of what we deterministically call 'circumstances' (social, cultural, or reductively psychological-personal), but that by linking ourselves through what Keats calls an 'immortal free-masonry' with the great we can become freer — freer to be ourselves, to be what we most want and value."

By the time Edmundson wrote this essay, many people had already chimed in on this debate, among them E. D. Hirsch, Robert K. Carlson, W. B. Carnochan, and Robert Bates Graber; and the conversation has continued since in books and articles by James O. Freedman, Meira Levinson, and many others.

Much of Edmundson's evidence comes from his personal observations and exchanges with students. As you read, weigh the strengths and weaknesses of these kinds of examples. Which of them draw you in and make you think about your own school experiences? Which do you find least convincing, and why? As you assess your educational highs and lows, consider how much his concluding challenges to students might apply to you. Many of us tend to react to criticism with a shrug and a muttered "Whatever," but Edmundson hopes to get under our skin so that our response will be much more self-challenging and far more passionate.

▪ ▪ ▪

Today is evaluation day in my Freud class, and everything has changed. *1* The class meets twice a week, late in the afternoon, and the clientele, about fifty undergraduates, tends to drag in and slump, looking disconsolate and a little lost, waiting for a jump start. To get the discussion moving, they usually require a joke, an anecdote, an off-the-wall question — When you were a kid, were your Halloween getups ego costumes, id costumes, or superego costumes? That sort of thing. But today, as soon as I flourish the forms, a buzz rises in the room. Today they write their assessments of the course, their assessments of *me*, and they are without a doubt wide-awake. "What is your evaluation of the instructor?" asks question number eight, entreating them to circle a number between five (excellent) and one (poor). Whatever interpretive subtlety they've acquired during the term is now out the window. Edmundson: one to five, stand and shoot.

And they do. As I retreat through the door — I never stay around for *2* this phase of the ritual — I look over my shoulder and see them toiling away like the devil's auditors. They're pitched into high writing gear, even the ones who struggle to squeeze out their journal entries word by word, stoked on a procedure they have by now supremely mastered. They're playing the informed consumer, letting the provider know where he's come through and where he's not quite up to snuff.

But why am I so distressed, bolting like a refugee out of my own class- *3* room, where I usually hold easy sway? Chances are the evaluations will be much like what they've been in the past — they'll be just fine. It's likely that I'll be commended for being "interesting" (and I am commended, many times over), that I'll be cited for my relaxed and tolerant ways (that happens, too), that my sense of humor and capacity to connect the arcana of the subject matter with current culture will come in for some praise (yup). I've been hassled this term, finishing a manuscript, and so haven't given their journals the attention I should have, and for that I'm called — quite civilly, though — to account. Overall, I get off pretty well.

Yet I have to admit that I do not much like the image of myself that *4* emerges from these forms, the image of knowledgeable, humorous detachment and bland tolerance. I do not like the forms themselves, with their number ratings, reminiscent of the sheets circulated after the TV pilot has just played to its sample audience in Burbank. Most of all I dislike the attitude of calm consumer expertise that pervades the responses. I'm disturbed by the serene belief that my function — and, more important, Freud's, or Shakespeare's, or Blake's — is to divert, entertain, and interest. Observes one respondent, not at all unrepresentative: "Edmundson has done a fantastic job of presenting this difficult, important & controversial material in an enjoyable and approachable way."

Thanks but no thanks. I don't teach to amuse, to divert, or even, for ⁵ that matter, to be merely interesting. When someone says she "enjoyed" the course — and that word crops up again and again in my evaluations — somewhere at the edge of my immediate complacency I feel encroaching self-dislike. That is not at all what I had in mind. The off-the-wall questions and the sidebar jokes are meant as lead-ins to stronger stuff — in the case of the Freud course, to a complexly tragic view of life. But the affability and the one-liners often seem to be all that land with the students; their journals and evaluations leave me little doubt.

I want some of them to say that they've been changed by the course. ⁶ I want them to measure themselves against what they've read. It's said that some time ago a Columbia University instructor used to issue a harsh two-part question. One: What book did you most dislike in the course? Two: What intellectual or characterological flaws in you does that dislike point to? The hand that framed that question was surely heavy. But at least it compels one to see intellectual work as a confrontation between two people, student and author, where the stakes matter. Those Columbia students were being asked to relate the quality of an *encounter*, not rate the action as though it had unfolded on the big screen.

Why are my students describing the Oedipus complex and the death ⁷ drive as being interesting and enjoyable to contemplate? And why am I coming across as an urbane, mildly ironic, endlessly affable guide to this intellectual territory, operating without intensity, generous, funny, and loose?

Because that's what works. On evaluation day, I reap the rewards of my ⁸ partial compliance with the culture of my students and, too, with the culture of the university as it now operates. It's a culture that's gotten little exploration. Current critics tend to think that liberal-arts education is in crisis because universities have been invaded by professors with peculiar ideas: deconstruction, Lacanianism, feminism, queer theory. They believe that genius and tradition are out and that P.C., multiculturalism, and identity politics are in because of an invasion by tribes of tenured radicals, the late millennial equivalents of the Visigoth hordes that cracked Rome's walls.

But mulling over my evaluations and then trying to take a hard, ⁹ extended look at campus life both here at the University of Virginia and around the country eventually led me to some different conclusions. To me, liberal-arts education is as ineffective as it is now not chiefly because there are a lot of strange theories in the air. (Used well, those theories *can* be illuminating.) Rather, it's that university culture, like American culture writ large, is, to put it crudely, ever more devoted to consumption and entertainment, to the using and using up of goods and images. For someone growing up in America now, there are few available alternatives to the cool consumer worldview. My students didn't ask for that view, much less create it, but they bring a consumer weltanschauung to school, where it exerts a powerful, and largely unacknowledged, influence. If we want to understand current universities, with their multiple woes, we might try leaving the realms of expert debate and fine ideas and turning to the classrooms and campuses, where a new kind of weather is gathering.

From time to time I bump into a colleague in the corridor and we have   *10* what I've come to think of as a Joon Lee fest. Joon Lee is one of the best students I've taught. He's endlessly curious, has read a small library's worth, seen every movie, and knows all about showbiz and entertainment. For a class of mine he wrote an essay using Nietzsche's Apollo and Dionysus to analyze the pop group The Supremes. A trite, cultural-studies bonbon? Not at all. He said striking things about conceptions of race in America and about how they shape our ideas of beauty. When I talk with one of his other teachers, we run on about the general splendors of his work and presence. But what inevitably follows a JL fest is a mournful reprise about the divide that separates him and a few other remarkable students from their contemporaries. It's not that some aren't nearly as bright — in terms of intellectual ability, my students are all that I could ask for. Instead, it's that Joon Lee has decided to follow his interests and let them make him into a singular and rather eccentric man; in his charming way, he doesn't mind being at odds with most anyone.

It's his capacity for enthusiasm that sets Joon apart from what I've   *11* come to think of as the reigning generational style. Whether the students are sorority/fraternity types, grunge aficionados, piercer/tattooers, black or white, rich or middle class (alas, I teach almost no students from truly poor backgrounds), they are, nearly across the board, very, very self-contained. On good days they display a light, appealing glow; on bad days, shuffling disgruntlement. But there's little fire, little passion to be found.

This point came home to me a few weeks ago when I was wandering   *12* across the university grounds. There, beneath a classically cast portico, were two students, male and female, having a rip-roaring argument. They were incensed, bellowing at each other, headstrong, confident, and wild. It struck me how rarely I see this kind of full-out feeling in students anymore. Strong emotional display is forbidden. When conflicts arise, it's generally understood that one of the parties will say something sarcastically propitiating ("whatever" often does it) and slouch away.

How did my students reach this peculiar state in which all passion   *13* seems to be spent? I think that many of them have imbibed their sense of self from consumer culture in general and from the tube in particular. They're the progeny of 100 cable channels and omnipresent Blockbuster outlets. TV, Marshall McLuhan famously said, is a cool medium. Those who play best on it are low-key and nonassertive; they blend in. Enthusiasm, à la Joon Lee, quickly looks absurd. The form of character that's most appealing on TV is calmly self-interested though never greedy, attuned to the conventions, and ironic. Judicious timing is preferred to sudden self-assertion. The TV medium is inhospitable to inspiration, improvisation, failures, slipups. All must run perfectly.

Naturally, a cool youth culture is a marketing bonanza for producers *14* of the right products, who do all they can to enlarge that culture and keep it grinding. The Internet, TV, and magazines now teem with what I call persona ads, ads for Nikes and Reeboks and Jeeps and Blazers that don't so much endorse the capacities of the product per se as show you what sort of person you will be once you've acquired it. The Jeep ad that features hip, outdoorsy kids whipping a Frisbee from mountaintop to mountaintop isn't so much about what Jeeps can do as it is about the kind of people who own them. Buy a Jeep and be one with them. The ad is of little consequence in itself, but expand its message exponentially and you have the central thrust of current consumer culture — buy in order to be.

Most of my students seem desperate to blend in, to look right, not to *15* make a spectacle of themselves. (Do I have to tell you that those two students having the argument under the portico turned out to be acting in a role-playing game?) The specter of the uncool creates a subtle tyranny. It's apparently an easy standard to subscribe to, this Letterman-like, Tarantino-like cool, but once committed to it, you discover that matters are rather different. You're inhibited, except on ordained occasions, from showing emotion, stifled from trying to achieve anything original. You're made to feel that even the slightest departure from the reigning code will get you genially ostracized. This is a culture tensely committed to a laid-back norm.

Am I coming off like something of a crank here? Maybe. Oscar Wilde, *16* who is almost never wrong, suggested that it is perilous to promiscuously contradict people who are much younger than yourself. Point taken. But one of the lessons that consumer hype tries to insinuate is that we must never rebel against the new, never even question it. If it's new — a new need, a new product, a new show, a new style, a new generation — it must be good. So maybe, even at the risk of winning the withered, brown laurels of crankdom, it pays to resist newness-worship and cast a colder eye.

Praise for my students? I have some of that too. What my students are, *17* at their best, is decent. They are potent believers in equality. They help out at the soup kitchen and volunteer to tutor poor kids to get a stripe on their résumés, sure. But they also want other people to have a fair shot. And in their commitment to fairness they are discerning; there you see them at their intellectual best. If I were on trial and innocent, I'd want them on the jury.

What they will not generally do, though, is indict the current system. *18* They won't talk about how the exigencies of capitalism lead to a reserve army of the unemployed and nearly inevitable misery. That would be getting too loud, too brash. For the pervading view is the cool consumer perspective, where passion and strong admiration are forbidden. "To stand in awe of nothing, Numicus, is perhaps the one and only thing that can make a man happy and keep him so," says Horace in the *Epistles*, and I fear that his lines ought to hang as a motto over the university in this era of high consumer capitalism.

It's easy to mount one's high horse and blame the students for this   *19* state of affairs. But they didn't create the present culture of consumption. (It was largely my own generation, that of the Sixties, that let the counter-culture search for pleasure devolve into a quest for commodities.) And they weren't the ones responsible, when they were six and seven and eight years old, for unplugging the TV set from time to time or for hauling off and kicking a hole through it. It's my generation of parents who sheltered these students, kept them away from the hard knocks of everyday life, making them cautious and overfragile, who demanded that their teachers, from grade school on, flatter them endlessly so that the kids are shocked if their college profs don't reflexively suck up to them.

Of course, the current generational style isn't simply derived from   *20* culture and environment. It's also about dollars. Students worry that taking too many chances with their educations will sabotage their future prospects. They're aware of the fact that a drop that looks more and more like one wall of the Grand Canyon separates the top economic tenth from the rest of the population. There's a sentiment currently abroad that if you step aside for a moment, to write, to travel, to fall too hard in love, you might lose position permanently. We may be on a conveyor belt, but it's worse down there on the filth-strewn floor. So don't sound off, don't blow your chance.

But wait. I teach at the famously conservative University of Virginia.   *21* Can I extend my view from Charlottesville to encompass the whole coun-try, a whole generation of college students? I can only say that I hear com-parable stories about classroom life from colleagues everywhere in America. When I visit other schools to lecture, I see a similar scene unfolding. There are, of course, terrific students everywhere. And they're all the better for the way they've had to strive against the existing conformity. At some of the small liberal-arts colleges, the tradition of strong engagement persists. But overall, the students strike me as being sweet and sad, hovering in a nearly suspended animation.

Too often now the pedagogical challenge is to make a lot from a little.   *22* Teaching Wordsworth's "Tintern Abbey," you ask for comments. No one responds. So you call on Stephen. Stephen: "The sound, this poem really flows." You: "Stephen seems interested in the music of the poem. We might extend his comment to ask if the poem's music coheres with its argument. Are they consistent? Or is there an emotional pain submerged here that's contrary to the poem's appealing melody!" All right, it's not usually that bad. But close. One friend describes it as rebound teaching: they proffer a weightless comment, you hit it back for all you're worth, then it comes dribbling out again. Occasionally a professor will try to explain away this intellectual timidity by describing the students as perpetrators of postmodern irony, a highly sophisticated mode. Everything's a slick counter-feit, a simulacrum, so by no means should any phenomenon be taken seri-ously. But the students don't have the urbane, Oscar Wilde–type demeanor that should go with this view. Oscar was cheerful, funny, confident, strange. (Wilde, mortally ill, living in a Paris flophouse: "My wallpaper and I are fighting a duel to the death. One or the other of us has to go.") This genera-tion's style is considerate, easy to please, and a touch depressed.

Granted, you might say, the kids come to school immersed in a con-   23
sumer mentality — they're good Americans, after all — but then the uni-versity and the professors do everything in their power to fight that dreary mind-set in the interest of higher ideals, right? So it should be. But let us look at what is actually coming to pass.

Over the past few years, the physical layout of my university has been   24
changing. To put it a little indecorously, the place is looking more and more like a retirement spread for the young. Our funds go to construction, into new dorms, into renovating the student union. We have a new aquat-ics center and ever-improving gyms, stocked with StairMasters and Nau-tilus machines. Engraved on the wall in the gleaming aquatics building is a line by our founder, Thomas Jefferson, declaring that everyone ought to get about two hours' exercise a day. Clearly even the author of the Declara-tion of Independence endorses the turning of his university into a sports-and-fitness emporium.

But such improvements shouldn't be surprising. Universities need to   25
attract the best (that is, the smartest *and* the richest) students in order to survive in an ever more competitive market. Schools want kids whose par-ents can pay the full freight, not the ones who need scholarships or want to bargain down the tuition costs. If the marketing surveys say that the kids require sports centers, then, trustees willing, they shall have them. In fact, as I began looking around, I came to see that more and more of what's going on in the university is customer driven. The consumer pressures that beset me on evaluation day are only a part of an overall trend.

From the start, the contemporary university's relationship with stu-   26
dents has a solicitous, nearly servile tone. As soon as someone enters his junior year in high school, and especially if he's living in a prosperous zip code, the informational material — the advertising — comes flooding in. Pictures, testimonials, videocassettes, and CD ROMs (some bidden, some not) arrive at the door from colleges across the country, all trying to cap-ture the student and his tuition cash. The freshman-to-be sees photos of well-appointed dorm rooms; of elaborate phys-ed facilities; of fine dining rooms; of expertly kept sports fields; of orchestras and drama troupes; of students working alone (no overbearing grown-ups in range), peering with high seriousness into computers and microscopes; or of students arrayed outdoors in attractive conversational garlands.

Occasionally — but only occasionally, for we usually photograph rather   27
badly; in appearance we tend at best to be styleless — there's a professor

teaching a class. (The college catalogues I received, by my request only, in the late Sixties were austere affairs full of professors' credentials and course descriptions; it was clear on whose terms the enterprise was going to unfold.) A college financial officer recently put matters to me in concise, if slightly melodramatic, terms: "Colleges don't have admissions offices anymore, they have marketing departments." Is it surprising that someone who has been approached with photos and tapes, bells and whistles, might come in thinking that the Freud and Shakespeare she had signed up to study were also going to be agreeable treats?

How did we reach this point? In part the answer is a matter of demo- 28 graphics and (surprise) of money. Aided by the G.I. bill, the college-going population in America dramatically increased after the Second World War. Then came the baby boomers, and to accommodate them, schools continued to grow. Universities expand easily enough, but with tenure locking faculty in for lifetime jobs, and with the general reluctance of administrators to eliminate their own slots, it's not easy for a university to contract. So after the baby boomers had passed through — like a fat meal digested by a boa constrictor — the colleges turned to energetic promotional strategies to fill the empty chairs. And suddenly college became a buyer's market. What students and their parents wanted had to be taken more and more into account. That usually meant creating more comfortable, less challenging environments, places where almost no one failed, everything was enjoyable, and everyone was nice.

Just as universities must compete with one another for students, so 29 must the individual departments. At a time of rank economic anxiety, the English and history majors have to contend for students against the more success-insuring branches, such as the sciences and the commerce school. In 1968, more than 21 percent of all the bachelor's degrees conferred in America were in the humanities; by 1993, that number had fallen to about 13 percent. The humanities now must struggle to attract students, many of whose parents devoutly wish they would study something else.

One of the ways we've tried to stay attractive is by loosening up. We 30 grade much more softly than our colleagues in science. In English, we don't give many Ds, or Cs for that matter. (The rigors of Chem 101 create almost as many English majors per year as do the splendors of Shakespeare.) A professor at Stanford recently explained grade inflation in the humanities by observing that the undergraduates were getting smarter every year; the higher grades simply recorded how much better they were than their predecessors. Sure.

Along with softening the grades, many humanities departments have 31 relaxed major requirements. There are some good reasons for introducing more choice into curricula and requiring fewer standard courses. But the move, like many others in the university now, jibes with a tendency to serve — and not challenge — the students. Students can also float in and out of classes during the first two weeks of each term without making any commitment. The common name for this time span — shopping period — speaks volumes about the consumer mentality that's now in play. Usually, too, the kids can drop courses up until the last month with only an innocuous "W" on their transcripts. Does a course look too challenging? No problem. Take it pass-fail. A happy consumer is, by definition, one with multiple options, one who can always have what he wants. And since a course is something the students and their parents have bought and paid for, why can't they do with it pretty much as they please?

A sure result of the university's widening elective leeway is to give students   32
more power over their teachers. Those who don't like you can simply avoid you. If the clientele dislikes you en masse, you can be left without students, period. My first term teaching I walked into my introduction to poetry course and found it inhabited by one student, the gloriously named Bambi Lynn Dean. Bambi and I chatted amiably awhile, but for all that she and the pleasure of her name could offer, I was fast on the way to meltdown. It was all a mistake, luckily, a problem with the scheduling book. Everyone was waiting for me next door. But in a dozen years of teaching I haven't forgotten that feeling of being ignominiously marooned. For it happens to others, and not always because of scheduling glitches. I've seen older colleagues go through hot embarrassment at not having enough students sign up for their courses: they graded too hard, demanded too much, had beliefs too far out of keeping with the existing disposition. It takes only a few such instances to draw other members of the professoriat further into line.

And if what's called tenure reform — which generally just means the   33
abolition of tenure — is broadly enacted, professors will be yet more vulnerable to the whims of their customer-students. Teach what pulls the kids in, or walk. What about entire departments that don't deliver? If the kids say no to Latin and Greek, is it time to dissolve classics? Such questions are being entertained more and more seriously by university administrators.

How does one prosper with the present clientele? Many of the most   34
successful professors now are the ones who have "decentered" their classrooms. There's a new emphasis on group projects and on computer-generated exchanges among the students. What they seem to want most is to talk to one another. A classroom now is frequently an "environment," a place highly conducive to the exchange of existing ideas, the students' ideas. Listening to one another, students sometimes change their opinions. But what they generally can't do is acquire a new vocabulary, a new perspective, that will cast issues in a fresh light.

The Socratic method — the animated, sometimes impolite give-and-   35
take between student and teacher — seems too jagged for current sensibilities. Students frequently come to my office to tell me how intimidated they feel in class; the thought of being embarrassed in front of the group fills them with dread. I remember a student telling me how humiliating it was to be corrected by the teacher, by me. So I asked the logical question: "Should I let a major factual error go by so as to save discomfort?"

The student — a good student, smart and earnest — said that was a tough question. He'd need to think about it.

Disturbing? Sure. But I wonder, are we really getting students ready *36* for Socratic exchange with professors when we push them off into vast lecture rooms, two and three hundred to a class, sometimes face them with only grad students until their third year, and signal in our myriad professorial ways that we often have much better things to do than sit in our offices and talk with them? How bad will the student-faculty ratios have to become, how teeming the lecture courses, before we hear students righteously complaining, as they did thirty years ago, about the impersonality of their schools, about their decline into knowledge factories? "This is a firm," said Mario Savio at Berkeley during the Free Speech protests of the Sixties, "and if the Board of Regents are the board of directors. . . . then . . . the faculty are a bunch of employees and we're the raw material. But we're a bunch of raw material that don't mean . . . to be made into any product."

Teachers who really do confront students, who provide significant *37* challenges to what they believe, *can* be very successful, granted. But sometimes such professors generate more than a little trouble for themselves. A controversial teacher can send students hurrying to the deans and the counselors, claiming to have been offended. ("Offensive" is the preferred term of repugnance today, just as "enjoyable" is the summit of praise.) Colleges have brought in hordes of counselors and deans to make sure that everything is smooth, serene, unflustered, that everyone has a good time. To the counselor, to the dean, and to the university legal squad, that which is normal, healthy, and prudent is best.

An air of caution and deference is everywhere. When my students *38* come to talk with me in my office, they often exhibit a Franciscan humility. "Do you have a moment?" "I know you're busy. I won't take up much of your time." Their presences tend to be very light; they almost never change the temperature of the room. The dress is nondescript: clothes are in earth tones; shoes are practical — cross-trainers, hiking boots, work shoes, Dr. Martens, with now and then a stylish pair of raised-sole boots on one of the young women. Many, male and female both, peep from beneath the bills of monogrammed baseball caps. Quite a few wear sports, or even corporate, logos, sometimes on one piece of clothing but occasionally (and disconcertingly) on more. The walk is slow; speech is careful, sweet, a bit weary, and without strong inflection. (After the first lively week of the term, most seem far in debt to sleep.) They are almost unfailingly polite. They don't want to offend me; I could hurt them, savage their grades.

Naturally, there are exceptions, kids I chat animatedly with, who offer *39* a joke, or go on about this or that new CD (almost never a book, no). But most of the traffic is genially sleepwalking. I have to admit that I'm a touch wary, too. I tend to hold back. An unguarded remark, a joke that's taken to be off-color, or simply an uncomprehended comment can lead to difficulties. I keep it literal. They scare me a little, these kind and melancholy students, who themselves seem rather frightened of their own lives.

Before they arrive, we ply the students with luscious ads, guaranteeing *40*
them a cross between summer camp and lotusland. When they get here,
flattery and nonstop entertainment are available, if that's what they want.
And when they leave? How do we send our students out into the world?
More and more, our administrators call the booking agents and line up
one or another celebrity to usher the graduates into the millennium. This
past spring, Kermit the Frog won himself an honorary degree at Southamp-
ton College on Long Island; Bruce Willis and Yogi Berra took credentials
away at Montclair State; Arnold Schwarzenegger scored at the University
of Wisconsin–Superior. At Wellesley, Oprah Winfrey gave the commence-
ment address. (*Wellesley* — one of the most rigorous academic colleges in
the nation.) At the University of Vermont, Whoopi Goldberg laid down the
word. But why should a worthy administrator contract the likes of Susan
Sontag, Christopher Hitchens, or Robert Hughes — someone who might
actually say something, something disturbing, something "offensive" —
when he can get what the parents and kids apparently want and what the
newspapers will softly commend — more lite entertainment, more TV?

Is it a surprise, then, that this generation of students — steeped in *41*
consumer culture before going off to school, treated as potent customers
by the university well before their date of arrival, then pandered to from
day one until the morning of the final kiss-off from Kermit or one of
his kin — are inclined to see the books they read as a string of entertainments to be placidly enjoyed or languidly cast down? Given the way universities are now administered (which is more and more to say, given the
way that they are currently marketed), is it a shock that the kids don't
come to school hot to learn, unable to bear their own ignorance? For some
measure of self-dislike, or self-discontent — which is much different than
simple depression — seems to me to be a prerequisite for getting an education that matters. My students, alas, usually lack the confidence to acknowledge what would be their most precious asset for learning: their ignorance.

Not long ago, I asked my Freud class a question that, however hoary, never *42*
fails to solicit intriguing responses: Who are your heroes? Whom do you
admire? After one remarkable answer, featuring T. S. Eliot as hero, a series
of generic replies rolled in, one gray wave after the next: my father, my best
friend, a doctor who lives in our town, my high school history teacher. Virtually all the heroes were people my students had known personally,
people who had done something local, specific, and practical, and had
done it for them. They were good people, unselfish people, these heroes,
but most of all they were people who had delivered the goods.

My students' answers didn't exhibit any philosophical resistance to the *43*
idea of greatness. It's not that they had been primed by their professors
with complex arguments to combat genius. For the truth is that these students don't need debunking theories. Long before college, skepticism
became their habitual mode. They are the progeny of Bart Simpson and
David Letterman, and the hyper-cool ethos of the box. It's inane to say that

theorizing professors have created them, as many conservative critics like to do. Rather, they have substantially created a university environment in which facile skepticism can thrive without being substantially contested.

Skeptical approaches have *potential* value. If you have no all- 44 encompassing religious faith, no faith in historical destiny, the future of the West, or anything comparably grand, you need to acquire your vision of the world somewhere. If it's from literature, then the various visions literature offers have to be inquired into skeptically. Surely it matters that women are denigrated in Milton and in Pope, that some novelistic voices assume an overbearing godlike authority, that the poor are, in this or that writer, inevitably cast as clowns. You can't buy all of literature wholesale if it's going to help draw your patterns of belief.

But demystifying theories are now overused, applied mechanically. It's 45 all logocentrism, patriarchy, ideology. And in this the student environment — laid-back, skeptical, knowing — is, I believe, central. Full-out debunking is what plays with this clientele. Some have been doing it nearly as long as, if more crudely than, their deconstructionist teachers. In the context of the contemporary university, and cool consumer culture, a useful intellectual skepticism has become exaggerated into a fundamentalist caricature of itself. The teachers have buckled to their students' views.

At its best, multiculturalism can be attractive as well-deployed theory. 46 What could be more valuable than encountering the best work of far-flung cultures and becoming a citizen of the world? But in the current consumer environment, where flattery plays so well, the urge to encounter the other can devolve into the urge to find others who embody and celebrate the right ethnic origins. So we put aside the African novelist Chinua Achebe's abrasive, troubling *Things Fall Apart* and gravitate toward hymns on Africa, cradle of all civilizations.

What about the phenomenon called political correctness? Raising the 47 standard of civility and tolerance in the university has been — who can deny it? — a very good thing. Yet this admirable impulse has expanded to the point where one is enjoined to speak well — and only well — of women, blacks, gays, the disabled, in fact of virtually everyone. And we can owe this expansion in many ways to the student culture. Students now do not wish to be criticized, not in any form. (The culture of consumption never criticizes them, at least not *overtly*.) In the current university, the movement for urbane tolerance has devolved into an imperative against critical reaction, turning much of the intellectual life into a dreary Sargasso Sea. At a certain point, professors stopped being usefully sensitive and became more like careful retailers who have it as a cardinal point of doctrine never to piss the customers off.

To some professors, the solution lies in the movement called cultural 48 studies. What students need, they believe, is to form a critical perspective on pop culture. It's a fine idea, no doubt. Students should be able to run a critical commentary against the stream of consumer stimulations in which they're immersed. But cultural-studies programs rarely work, because no matter what you propose by way of analysis, things tend to bolt downhill toward an uncritical discussion of students' tastes, into what they like and don't like. If you want to do a Frankfurt School–style analysis of *Braveheart*, you can be pretty sure that by mid-class Adorno and Horkheimer will be consigned to the junk heap of history and you'll be collectively weighing the charms of Mel Gibson. One sometimes wonders if cultural studies hasn't prospered because, under the guise of serious intellectual analysis, it gives the customers what they most want — easy pleasure, more TV. Cultural studies becomes nothing better than what its detractors claim it is — Madonna studies — when students kick loose from the critical perspective and groove to the product, and that, in my experience teaching film and pop culture, happens plenty.

On the issue of genius, as on multiculturalism and political correct- 49 ness, we professors of the humanities have, I think, also failed to press back against our students' consumer tastes. Here we tend to nurse a pair of — to put it charitably — disparate views. In one mode, we're inclined to a programmatic debunking criticism. We call the concept of genius into question. But in our professional lives per se, we aren't usually disposed against the idea of distinguished achievement. We argue animatedly about the caliber of potential colleagues. We support a star system, in which some professors are far better paid, teach less, and under better conditions than the rest. In our own profession, we are creating a system that is the mirror image of the one we're dismantling in the curriculum. Ask a professor what she thinks of the work of Stephen Greenblatt, a leading critic of Shakespeare, and you'll hear it for an hour. Ask her what her views are on Shakespeare's genius and she's likely to begin questioning the term along with the whole "discourse of evaluation." This dual sensibility may be intellectually incoherent. But in its awareness of what plays with students, it's conducive to good classroom evaluations and, in its awareness of where and how the professional bread is buttered, to self-advancement as well.

My overall point is this: It's not that a left-wing professorial coup has 50 taken over the university. It's that at American universities, left-liberal politics have collided with the ethos of consumerism. The consumer ethos is winning.

Then how do those who at least occasionally promote genius and high lit- 51 erary ideals look to current students? How do we appear, those of us who take teaching to be something of a performance art and who imagine that if you give yourself over completely to your subject you'll be rewarded with insight beyond what you individually command?

I'm reminded of an old piece of newsreel footage I saw once. The 52 speaker (perhaps it was Lenin, maybe Trotsky) was haranguing a large crowd. He was expostulating, arm waving, carrying on. Whether it was flawed technology or the man himself, I'm not sure, but the orator looked like an intricate mechanical device that had sprung into fast-forward. To my students, who mistrust enthusiasm in every form, that's me when

I start riffing about Freud or Blake. But more and more, as my evaluations showed, I've been replacing enthusiasm and intellectual animation with stand-up routines, keeping it all at arm's length, praising under the cover of irony.

It's too bad that the idea of genius has been denigrated so far, because 53 it actually offers a live alternative to the demoralizing culture of hip in which most of my students are mired. By embracing the works and lives of extraordinary people, you can adapt new ideals to revise those that came courtesy of your parents, your neighborhood, your clan — or the tube. The aim of a good liberal-arts education was once, to adapt an observation by the scholar Walter Jackson Bate, to see that "we need not be the passive victims of what we deterministically call 'circumstances' (social, cultural, or reductively psychological-personal), but that by linking ourselves through what Keats calls an 'immortal free-masonry' with the great we can become freer — freer to be ourselves, to be what we most want and value."

But genius isn't just a personal standard; genius can also have political 54 effect. To me, one of the best things about democratic thinking is the conviction that genius can spring up anywhere. Walt Whitman is born into the working class and thirty-six years later we have a poetic image of America that gives a passionate dimension to the legalistic brilliance of the Constitution. A democracy needs to constantly develop, and to do so it requires the most powerful visionary minds to interpret the present and to propose possible shapes for the future. By continuing to notice and praise genius, we create a culture in which the kind of poetic gamble that Whitman made — a gamble in which failure would have entailed rank humiliation, depression, maybe suicide — still takes place. By rebelling against established ways of seeing and saying things, genius helps us to apprehend how malleable the present is and how promising and fraught with danger is the future. If we teachers do not endorse genius and self-overcoming, can we be surprised when our students find their ideal images in TV's latest persona ads?

A world uninterested in genius is a despondent place, whose sad 55 denizens drift from coffee bar to Prozac dispensary, unfired by ideals, by the glowing image of the self that one might become. As Northrop Frye says in a beautiful and now dramatically unfashionable sentence, "The artist who uses the same energy and genius that Homer and Isaiah had will find that he not only lives in the same palace of art as Homer and Isaiah, but lives in it at the same time." We ought not to deny the existence of such a place simply because we, or those we care for, find the demands it makes intimidating, the rent too high.

What happens if we keep trudging along this bleak course? What hap- 56 pens if our most intelligent students never learn to strive to overcome what they are? What if genius, and the imitation of genius, become silly, outmoded ideas? What you're likely to get are more and more one-dimensional men and women. These will be people who live for easy pleasures, for comfort and prosperity, who think of money first, then second, and third, who hug the status quo; people who believe in God as a sort of insurance policy (cover your bets); people who are never surprised. They will be people so pleased with themselves (when they're not in despair at the general pointlessness of their lives) that they cannot imagine humanity could do better. They'll think it their highest duty to clone themselves as frequently as possible. They'll claim to be happy, and they'll live a long time.

It is probably time now to offer a spate of inspiring solutions. Here 57 ought to come a list of reforms, with due notations about a core curriculum and various requirements. What the traditionalists who offer such solutions miss is that no matter what our current students are given to read, many of them will simply translate it into melodrama, with flat characters and predictable morals. (The unabated capitalist culture that conservative critics so often endorse has put students in a position to do little else.) One can't simply wave a curricular wand and reverse acculturation.

Perhaps it would be a good idea to try firing the counselors and send- 58 ing half the deans back into their classrooms, dismantling the football team and making the stadium into a playground for local kids, emptying the fraternities, and boarding up the student-activities office. Such measures would convey the message that American colleges are not northern outposts of Club Med. A willingness on the part of the faculty to defy student conviction and affront them occasionally — to be usefully offensive — also might not be a bad thing. We professors talk a lot about subversion, which generally means subverting the views of people who never hear us talk or read our work. But to subvert the views of our students, our customers, that would be something else again.

Ultimately, though, it is up to individuals — and individual students 59 in particular — to make their own way against the current sludgy tide. There's still the library, still the museum, there's still the occasional teacher who lives to find things greater than herself to admire. There are still fellow students who have not been cowed. Universities are inefficient, cluttered, archaic places, with many unguarded corners where one can open a book or gaze out onto the larger world and construe it freely. Those who do as much, trusting themselves against the weight of current opinion, will have contributed something to bringing this sad dispensation to an end. As for myself, I'm canning my low-key one-liners; when the kids' TV-based tastes come to the fore, I'll aim and shoot. And when it's time to praise genius, I'll try to do it in the right style, full-out, with faith that finer artistic spirits (maybe not Homer and Isaiah quite, but close, close), still alive somewhere in the ether, will help me out when my invention flags, the students doze, or the dean mutters into the phone. I'm getting back to a more exuberant style; I'll be expostulating and arm waving straight into the millennium, yes I will.

■ ■ ■

Reading Rhetorically

1. How would you describe Edmundson's ethos, or self-representation, in this essay? How would you describe his tone and attitude? Find three passages

that you think best illustrate the author's character, and discuss how his character contributes to, or detracts from, the argument he makes in this essay.

2. What is the relationship between university culture and the examples from advertising and television that Edmundson offers in this essay? What point is he making, exactly, about higher education and "the cool consumer world view" (para. 9)? Find specific passages to illustrate your responses.

3. Edmundson spends a lot of time describing what he thinks is wrong with university culture, but he also makes recommendations for change. What does he want students and professors to do differently? What do his recommendations have to do with the idea of genius that he brings up at the end of the essay? How practical do you find Edmundson's suggestions? Do you agree with them? Why or why not?

Inquiring Further

4. How unique is Edmundson's complaint about the commercialization of higher education? Use your library's electronic databases (EBSCOhost, for example) to search for other writers' ideas on this issue. How does Edmundson's characterization of the problems and possible solutions compare to others you find? Where do you stand in this conversation about the commercialization of higher education?

5. How well do Edmundson's descriptions of college students align with behaviors you have seen? Look particularly at passages where he depicts student-teacher interactions in class. How do you account for the similarities and differences between what Edmundson describes and what you have seen?

6. Do an Edmundson-style analysis of the role consumer culture plays on your own campus. For example, you might consider the images and sales pitch in the brochures the admissions office sends to prospective students. Or analyze the physical layout of your campus. Edmundson claims his campus looks "like a retirement spread for the young" (para. 24). What would he conclude about your campus? What do you conclude?

Framing Conversations

7. The college students Edmundson analyzes may seem at first to have little in common with the primary and secondary school children Jonathan Kozol describes (p. 308). But both authors address the goals of education and the methods that work best to meet those goals. Write an essay in which you draw on the authors' arguments about educational goals and methods to take your own position on these issues. Feel free to draw on examples from your own educational experience in developing your argument.

8. Like Edmundson, Robert Scholes (p. 370) analyzes the cultural messages embedded in advertising. What issues does each author bring up about advertising on television and our responses to the messages we see there? Write an essay in which you compare the two authors' ideas — where would they agree and disagree? — to argue a point you would like to make about the messages we see on television. You might take notes on a television

commercial or two, and include your Edmundson-style and Scholes-style analyses of the commercials as part of the evidence for your argument. Be sure to explain why this type of cultural analysis is important. In other words, anticipate an antagonistic reader who might say, "Who cares? It's just a commercial."

9. How do our educational systems work to preserve or undo class and race divisions? Draw on the ideas in Edmundson's essay and connect them to concepts in one or two essays by the following authors: bell hooks (below), Jonathan Kozol (p. 308), Noel Ignatiev (p. 512), Peggy McIntosh (p. 520), and Cynthia Selfe (p. 783). Write an essay in which you use the works to build an argument about what American education accomplishes in relation to class and race differences — and, perhaps, what you think it should accomplish. Be sure to use and analyze specific examples from the texts and, if you want, your own experiences.

BELL HOOKS

From Teaching to Transgress: Education as the Practice of Freedom

bell hooks is the pen name of Gloria Watkins, a cultural critic, scholar, and prolific writer. She has taught at many schools, including Oberlin College and the City College of New York. hooks has a wide range of intellectual interests, and that is reflected in her long list of articles and books. Her book *Feminist Theory: From Margin to Center* (revised 2000) has been very influential in the field of gender politics, and her many books on race, gender, and politics are taught frequently in both undergraduate and graduate courses. With Cornel West, hooks edited *Breaking Bread: Insurgent Black Intellectual Life* (1991). She is well known for her collaborations with people from many different intellectual backgrounds, from politics to religion to activism. Her most recent project was coediting a collection of essays on the aftermath of Hurricane Katrina, *What Lies Beneath: Katrina, Race, and the State of the Nation* (2007). The selection here is taken from *Teaching to Transgress: Education as the Practice of Freedom* (1994).

Despite her publishing success, some scholars have criticized hooks for refusing to follow the "rules" of academic publishing. For example, although she quotes and engages with numerous scholars in her writing, she does not use footnotes in her work because she believes many readers find them off-putting, and she is interested in making her ideas accessible to people outside the academy, people who may be less educated but are still very interested in the topics she explores. In this selection, she makes mention of a related writing strategy: She believes teachers and writers should foster the ability to "speak differently to diverse audiences" (para. 26), as most of us do in our daily lives. (Think for a moment about how you speak with your teachers as opposed to how you speak — or blog or e-mail — with friends.) As you read pay attention to the different levels of formality in hooks's language. Where does she sound like a scholar?

Where does she sound like a friend? What effect do these linguistic shifts have on your experience as a reader? How are they connected to the larger argument about education she makes in this piece?

The second section of the excerpt here is titled "Engaged Pedagogy." *Pedagogy* means the art or profession of teaching, and this piece was written for an audience of teachers (although hooks does include her own experiences as a student). What does it feel like to be "listening in" on a conversation among teachers? As you read, notice the student-teacher dynamics she describes. How do you think your experiences as a student might be transformed in the kind of classroom hooks argues for — where education is "the practice of freedom" (para. 14) and learning is pleasurable and exciting (para. 16)?

Like some of the other writers in this collection, hooks reflects on her own experiences in her discussion of teaching and learning. She begins by describing her experiences as a professor about to earn tenure; then she takes us back to her positive experiences in an all-black grade school. Follow the way hooks uses her early memories of school to lay the groundwork for her argument about "learning as revolution" (para. 3). How do her examples of being a student and then a professor work in the different sections of this piece? Which examples interest you most? Why?

hooks is a practicing Buddhist, and she draws on the language of spirituality in her argument. She believes that teaching is "sacred, . . . that our work is not merely to share information but to share in the intellectual and spiritual growth of our students" (para. 30). As you read her discussion of "engaged pedagogy" — teaching that empowers students to become self-actualized — consider your own experiences as a student. Has your education led you toward self-actualization? Or have you simply been learning how to play the game of school?

bell hooks envisions education as a revolutionary experience for both teachers and students. Given all the discussion today about No Child Left Behind, magnet and charter schools, and private and sex-segregated schools, where do hooks's ideas fit? Most people agree that education is crucial to a healthy democracy. But this piece reveals how divided we are on the best way to educate . . . and even on what it means to say we believe that education is "the practice of freedom."

Introduction

In the weeks before the English Department at Oberlin College was about to decide whether or not I would be granted tenure, I was haunted by dreams of running away — of disappearing — yes, even of dying. These dreams were not a response to fear that I would not be granted tenure. They were a response to the reality that I *would* be granted tenure. I was afraid that I *would* be trapped in the academy forever.

Instead of feeling elated when I received tenure, I fell into a deep, life-threatening depression. Since everyone around me believed that I should be relieved, thrilled, proud, I felt "guilty" about my "real" feelings and could not share them with anyone. The lecture circuit took me to sunny California and the New Age world of my sister's house in Laguna Beach where I was able to chill out for a month. When I shared my feelings with my sister (she's a therapist), she reassured me that they were entirely appropriate because, she said, "You never wanted to be a teacher. Since we were little, all you ever wanted to do was write." She was right. It was always assumed by everyone else that I would become a teacher. In the apartheid South, black girls from working-class backgrounds had three career choices. We could marry. We could work as maids. We could become school teachers. And since, according to the sexist thinking of the time, men did not really desire "smart" women, it was assumed that signs of intelligence sealed one's fate. From grade school on, I was destined to become a teacher.

But the dream of becoming a writer was always present within me. 3 From childhood, I believed that I would teach *and* write. Writing would be the serious work, teaching would be the not-so-serious-I-need-to-make-a-living "job." Writing, I believed then, was all about private longing and personal glory, but teaching was about service, giving back to one's community. For black folks teaching — educating — was fundamentally political because it was rooted in antiracist struggle. Indeed, my all-black grade schools became the location where I experienced learning as revolution.

Almost all our teachers at Booker T. Washington were black women. 4 They were committed to nurturing intellect so that we could become scholars, thinkers, and cultural workers — black folks who used our "minds." We learned early that our devotion to learning, to a life of the mind, was a counter-hegemonic act, a fundamental way to resist every strategy of white racist colonization. Though they did not define or articulate these practices in theoretical terms, my teachers were enacting a revolutionary pedagogy of resistance that was profoundly anticolonial. Within these segregated schools, black children who were deemed exceptional, gifted, were given special care. Teachers worked with and for us to ensure that we would fulfill our intellectual destiny and by so doing uplift the race. My teachers were on a mission.

To fulfill that mission, my teachers made sure they "knew" us. They 5 knew our parents, our economic status, where we worshiped, what our homes were like, and how we were treated in the family. I went to school at a historical moment where I was being taught by the same teachers who had taught my mother, her sisters, and brothers. My effort and ability to learn were always contextualized within the framework of generational family experience. Certain behaviors, gestures, habits of being were traced back.

Attending school then was sheer joy. I loved being a student. I loved 6 learning. School was the place of ecstasy — pleasure and danger. To be changed by ideas was pure pleasure. But to learn ideas that ran counter to values and beliefs learned at home was to place oneself at risk, to enter the danger zone. Home was the place where I was forced to conform to someone else's image of who and what I should be. School was the place where I could forget that self and, through ideas, reinvent myself.

School changed utterly with racial integration. Gone was the mes- *7* sianic zeal to transform our minds and beings that had characterized teachers and their pedagogical practices in our all-black schools. Knowledge was suddenly about information only. It had no relation to how one lived, behaved. It was no longer connected to antiracist struggle. Bussed to white schools, we soon learned that obedience, and not a zealous will to learn, was what was expected of us. Too much eagerness to learn could easily be seen as a threat to white authority.

When we entered racist, desegregated, white schools we left a world *8* where teachers believed that to educate black children rightly would require a political commitment. Now, we were mainly taught by white teachers whose lessons reinforced racist stereotypes. For black children, education was no longer about the practice of freedom. Realizing this, I lost my love of school. The classroom was no longer a place of pleasure or ecstasy. School was still a political place, since we were always having to counter white racist assumptions that we were genetically inferior, never as capable as white peers, even unable to learn. Yet, the politics were no longer counter-hegemonic. We were always and only responding and reacting to white folks.

That shift from beloved, all-black schools to white schools where black *9* students were always seen as interlopers, as not really belonging, taught me the difference between education as the practice of freedom and education that merely strives to reinforce domination. The rare white teacher who dared to resist, who would not allow racist biases to determine how we were taught, sustained the belief that learning at its most powerful could indeed liberate. A few black teachers had joined us in the desegregation process. And, although it was more difficult, they continued to nurture black students even as their efforts were constrained by the suspicion they were favoring their own race.

Despite intensely negative experiences, I graduated from school still *10* believing that education was enabling, that it enhanced our capacity to be free. When I began undergraduate work at Stanford University, I was enthralled with the process of becoming an insurgent black intellectual. It surprised and shocked me to sit in classes where professors were not excited about teaching, where they did not seem to have a clue that education was about the practice of freedom. During college, the primary lesson was reinforced: we were to learn obedience to authority.

In graduate school the classroom became a place I hated, yet a place *11* where I struggled to claim and maintain the right to be an independent thinker. The university and the classroom began to feel more like a prison, a place of punishment and confinement rather than a place of promise and possibility. I wrote my first book during those undergraduate years, even though it was not published until years later. I was writing; but more importantly I was preparing to become a teacher.

Accepting the teaching profession as my destiny, I was tormented by *12* the classroom reality I had known both as an undergraduate and a graduate student. The vast majority of our professors lacked basic communication skills, they were not self-actualized, and they often used the classroom to enact rituals of control that were about domination and the unjust exercise of power. In these settings I learned a lot about the kind of teacher I did not want to become.

In graduate school I found that I was often bored in classes. The banking system of education (based on the assumption that memorizing information and regurgitating it represented gaining knowledge that could be deposited, stored, and used at a later date) did not interest me. I wanted to become a critical thinker. Yet that longing was often seen as a threat to authority. Individual white male students who were seen as "exceptional," were often allowed to chart their intellectual journeys, but the rest of us (and particularly those from marginal groups) were always expected to conform. Nonconformity on our part was viewed with suspicion, as empty gestures of defiance aimed at masking inferiority or substandard work. In those days, those of us from marginal groups who were allowed to enter prestigious, predominantly white colleges were made to feel that we were there not to learn but to prove that we were the equal of whites. We were there to prove this by showing how well we could become clones of our peers. As we constantly confronted biases, an undercurrent of stress diminished our learning experience.

My reaction to this stress and to the ever-present boredom and apathy *14* that pervaded my classes was to imagine ways that teaching and the learning experience could be different. When I discovered the work of the Brazilian thinker Paulo Freire, my first introduction to critical pedagogy, I found a mentor and a guide, someone who understood that learning could be liberatory. With his teachings and my growing understanding of the ways in which the education I had received in all-black Southern schools had been empowering, I began to develop a blueprint for my own pedagogical practice. Already deeply engaged with feminist thinking, I had no difficulty bringing that critique to Freire's work. Significantly, I felt that this mentor and guide, whom I had never seen in the flesh, would encourage and support my challenge to his ideas if he was truly committed to education as the practice of freedom. At the same time, I used his pedagogical paradigms to critique the limitations of feminist classrooms.

During my undergraduate and graduate school years, only white *15* women professors were involved in developing Women's Studies programs. And even though I taught my first class as a graduate student on black women writers from a feminist perspective, it was in the context of a Black Studies program. At that time, I found, white women professors were not eager to nurture any interest in feminist thinking and scholarship on the part of black female students if that interest included critical challenge. Yet their lack of interest did not discourage me from involvement with feminist ideas or participation in the feminist classroom. Those classrooms were the one space where pedagogical practices were interrogated, where it was assumed that the knowledge offered students would empower them to be better scholars, to live more fully in the world beyond academe. The feminist classroom was the one space where students could raise critical questions about pedagogical process. These critiques were not always encouraged or well received, but they were allowed. That small acceptance of critical interrogation was a crucial challenge inviting us as students to think seriously about pedagogy in relation to the practice of freedom.

When I entered my first undergraduate classroom to teach, I relied on *16* the example of those inspired black women teachers in my grade school, on Freire's work, and on feminist thinking about radical pedagogy. I longed passionately to teach differently from the way I had been taught since high school. The first paradigm that shaped my pedagogy was the idea that the classroom should be an exciting place, never boring. And if boredom should prevail, then pedagogical strategies were needed that would intervene, alter, even disrupt the atmosphere. Neither Freire's work nor feminist pedagogy examined the notion of pleasure in the classroom. The idea that learning should be exciting, sometimes even "fun," was the subject of critical discussion by educators writing about pedagogical practices in grade schools, and sometimes even high schools. But there seemed to be no interest among either traditional or radical educators in discussing the role of excitement in higher education.

Excitement in higher education was viewed as potentially disruptive of *17* the atmosphere of seriousness assumed to be essential to the learning process. To enter classroom settings in colleges and universities with the will to share the desire to encourage excitement was to transgress. Not only did it require movement beyond accepted boundaries, but excitement could not be generated without a full recognition of the fact that there could never be an absolute set agenda governing teaching practices. Agendas had to be flexible, had to allow for spontaneous shifts in direction. Students had to be seen in their particularity as individuals (I drew on the strategies my grade-school teachers used to get to know us) and interacted with according to their needs (here Freire was useful). Critical reflection on my experience as a student in unexciting classrooms enabled me not only to imagine that the classroom could be exciting but that this excitement could co-exist with and even stimulate serious intellectual and/or academic engagement.

But excitement about ideas was not sufficient to create an exciting *18* learning process. As a classroom community, our capacity to generate excitement is deeply affected by our interest in one another, in hearing one another's voices, in recognizing one another's presence. Since the vast majority of students learn through conservative, traditional educational practices and concern themselves only with the presence of the professor, any radical pedagogy must insist that everyone's presence is acknowledged. That insistence cannot be simply stated. It has to be demonstrated through pedagogical practices. To begin, the professor must genuinely *value* everyone's presence. There must be an ongoing recognition that everyone influences the classroom dynamic, that everyone contributes. These contributions are resources. Used constructively they enhance the capacity of any class to create an open learning community. Often before this process can begin there has to be some deconstruction of the traditional notion that only the professor is responsible for classroom dynamics. That responsibility is relative to status. Indeed, the professor will always be more responsible because the larger institutional structures will always ensure that accountability for what happens in the classroom rests with the teacher. It is rare that any professor, no matter how eloquent a lecturer, can generate through his or her actions enough excitement to create an exciting classroom. Excitement is generated through collective effort.

Seeing the classroom always as a communal place enhances the likelihood of collective effort in creating and sustaining a learning community. One semester, I had a very difficult class, one that completely failed on the communal level. Throughout the term, I thought that the major drawback inhibiting the development of a learning community was that the class was scheduled in the early morning, before nine. Almost always between a third and a half of the class was not fully awake. This, coupled with the tensions of "differences," was impossible to overcome. Every now and then we had an exciting session, but mostly it was a dull class. I came to hate this class so much that I had a tremendous fear that I would not awaken to attend it; the night before (despite alarm clocks, wake-up calls, and the experiential knowledge that I had never forgotten to attend class) I still could not sleep. Rather than making me arrive sleepy, I tended to arrive wired, full of an energy few students mirrored. 19

Time was just one of the factors that prevented this class from becoming a learning community. For reasons I cannot explain it was also full of "resisting" students who did not want to learn new pedagogical processes, who did not want to be in a classroom that differed in any way from the norm. To these students, transgressing boundaries was frightening. And though they were not the majority, their spirit of rigid resistance seemed always to be more powerful than any will to intellectual openness and pleasure in learning. More than any other class I had taught, this one compelled me to abandon the sense that the professor could, by sheer strength of will and desire, make the classroom an exciting, learning community. 20

Before this class, I considered that *Teaching to Transgress: Education as the Practice of Freedom* would be a book of essays mostly directed to teachers. After the class ended, I began writing with the understanding that I was speaking to and with both students and professors. The scholarly field of writing on critical pedagogy and/or feminist pedagogy continues to be primarily a discourse engaged by white women and men. Freire, too, in conversation with me, as in much of his written work, has always acknowledged that he occupies the location of white maleness, particularly in this country. But the work of various thinkers on radical pedagogy 21

(I use this term to include critical and/or feminist perspectives) has in recent years truly included a recognition of differences — those determined by class, race, sexual practice, nationality, and so on. Yet this movement forward does not seem to coincide with any significant increase in black or other nonwhite voices joining discussions about radical pedagogical practices.

My pedagogical practices have emerged from the mutually illuminating interplay of anticolonial, critical, and feminist pedagogies. This complex and unique blending of multiple perspectives has been an engaging and powerful standpoint from which to work. Expanding beyond boundaries, it has made it possible for me to imagine and enact pedagogical practices that engage directly both the concern for interrogating biases in curricula that reinscribe systems of domination (such as racism and sexism) while simultaneously providing new ways to teach diverse groups of students.   22

In this book I want to share insights, strategies, and critical reflections on pedagogical practice. I intend these essays to be an intervention — countering the devaluation of teaching even as they address the urgent need for changes in teaching practices. They are meant to serve as constructive commentary. Hopeful and exuberant, they convey the pleasure and joy I experience teaching; these essays are celebratory! To emphasize that the pleasure of teaching is an act of resistance countering the overwhelming boredom, uninterest, and apathy that so often characterize the way professors and students feel about teaching and learning, about the classroom experience.   23

Each essay addresses common themes that surface again and again in discussions of pedagogy, offering ways to rethink teaching practices and constructive strategies to enhance learning. Written separately for a variety of contexts there is unavoidably some degree of overlap; ideas are repeated, key phrases used again and again. Even though I share strategies, these works do not offer blueprints for ways to make the classroom an exciting place for learning. To do so would undermine the insistence that engaged pedagogy recognize each classroom as different, that strategies must constantly be changed, invented, reconceptualized to address each new teaching experience.   24

Teaching is a performative act. And it is that aspect of our work that offers the space for change, invention, spontaneous shifts, that can serve as a catalyst drawing out the unique elements in each classroom. To embrace the performative aspect of teaching we are compelled to engage "audiences," to consider issues of reciprocity. Teachers are not performers in the traditional sense of the word in that our work is not meant to be a spectacle. Yet it is meant to serve as a catalyst that calls everyone to become more and more engaged, to become active participants in learning.   25

Just as the way we perform changes, so should our sense of "voice." In our everyday lives we speak differently to diverse audiences. We communicate best by choosing that way of speaking that is informed by the   26 particularity and uniqueness of whom we are speaking to and with. In keeping with this spirit, these essays do not all sound alike. They reflect my effort to use language in ways that speak to specific contexts, as well as my desire to communicate with a diverse audience. To teach in varied communities not only our paradigms must shift but also the way we think, write, speak. The engaged voice must never be fixed and absolute but always changing, always evolving in dialogue with a world beyond itself.

These essays reflect my experience of critical discussions with teach- *27* ers, students, and individuals who have entered my classes to observe. Multilayered, then, these essays are meant to stand as testimony, bearing witness to education as the practice of freedom. Long before a public ever recognized me as a thinker or writer, I was recognized in the classroom by students — seen by them as a teacher who worked hard to create a dynamic learning experience for all of us. Nowadays, I am recognized more for insurgent intellectual practice. Indeed, the academic public that I encounter at my lectures always shows surprise when I speak intimately and deeply about the classroom. That public seemed particularly surprised when I said that I was working on a collection of essays about teaching. This surprise is a sad reminder of the way teaching is seen as a duller, less valuable aspect of the academic profession. This perspective on teaching is a common one. Yet it must be challenged if we are to meet the needs of our students, if we are to restore to education and the classroom excitement about ideas and the will to learn.

There is a serious crisis in education. Students often do not want to *28* learn and teachers do not want to teach. More than ever before in the recent history of this nation, educators are compelled to confront the biases that have shaped teaching practices in our society and to create new ways of knowing, different strategies for the sharing of knowledge. We cannot address this crisis if progressive critical thinkers and social critics act as though teaching is not a subject worthy of our regard.

The classroom remains the most radical space of possibility in the *29* academy. For years it has been a place where education has been undermined by teachers and students alike who seek to use it as a platform for opportunistic concerns rather than as a place to learn. With these essays, I add my voice to the collective call for renewal and rejuvenation in our teaching practices. Urging all of us to open our minds and hearts so that we can know beyond the boundaries of what is acceptable, so that we can think and rethink, so that we can create new visions, I celebrate teaching that enables transgressions — a movement against and beyond boundaries. It is that movement which makes education the practice of freedom.

Engaged Pedagogy

To educate as the practice of freedom is a way of teaching that anyone can *30* learn. That learning process comes easiest to those of us who teach who also believe that there is an aspect of our vocation that is sacred; who believe that our work is not merely to share information but to share in the intellectual and spiritual growth of our students. To teach in a manner that respects and cares for the souls of our students is essential if we are to provide the necessary conditions where learning can most deeply and intimately begin.

Throughout my years as student and professor, I have been most *31* inspired by those teachers who have had the courage to transgress those boundaries that would confine each pupil to a rote, assembly-line approach to learning. Such teachers approach students with the will and desire to respond to our unique beings, even if the situation does not allow the full emergence of a relationship based on mutual recognition. Yet the possibility of such recognition is always present.

Paulo Freire and the Vietnamese Buddhist monk Thich Nhat Hanh are *32* two of the "teachers" who have touched me deeply with their work. When I first began college, Freire's thought gave me the support I needed to challenge the "banking system" of education, that approach to learning that is rooted in the notion that all students need to do is consume information fed to them by a professor and be able to memorize and store it. Early on, it was Freire's insistence that education could be the practice of freedom that encouraged me to create strategies for what he called "conscientization" in the classroom. Translating that term to critical awareness and engagement, I entered the classrooms with the conviction that it was crucial for me and every other student to be an active participant, not a passive consumer. Education as the practice of freedom was continually undermined by professors who were actively hostile to the notion of student participation. Freire's work affirmed that education can only be liberatory when everyone claims knowledge as a field in which we all labor. That notion of mutual labor was affirmed by Thich Nhat Hanh's philosophy of engaged Buddhism, the focus on practice in conjunction with contemplation. His philosophy was similar to Freire's emphasis on "praxis" — action and reflection upon the world in order to change it.

In his work Thich Nhat Hanh always speaks of the teacher as a healer. *33* Like Freire, his approach to knowledge called on students to be active participants, to link awareness with practice. Whereas Freire was primarily concerned with the mind, Thich Nhat Hanh offered a way of thinking about pedagogy which emphasized wholeness, a union of mind, body, and spirit. His focus on a holistic approach to learning and spiritual practice enabled me to overcome years of socialization that had taught me to believe a classroom was diminished if students and professors regarded one another as "whole" human beings, striving not just for knowledge in books, but knowledge about how to live in the world.

During my twenty years of teaching, I have witnessed a grave sense of *34* dis-ease among professors (irrespective of their politics) when students want us to see them as whole human beings with complex lives and experiences rather than simply as seekers after compartmentalized bits of knowledge. When I was an undergraduate, Women's Studies was just finding a place in the academy. Those classrooms were the one space where teachers were willing to acknowledge a connection between ideas learned in university settings and those learned in life practices. And, despite those times when students abused that freedom in the classroom by only wanting to dwell on personal experience, feminist classrooms were, on the whole, one location where I witnessed professors striving to create participatory spaces for the sharing of knowledge. Nowadays, most women's studies professors are not as committed to exploring new pedagogical strategies. Despite this shift, many students still seek to enter feminist classrooms because they continue to believe that there, more than in any other place in the academy, they will have an opportunity to experience education as the practice of freedom.

Progressive, holistic education, "engaged pedagogy" is more demanding than conventional critical or feminist pedagogy. For, unlike these two teaching practices, it emphasizes well-being. That means that teachers must be actively committed to a process of self-actualization that promotes their own well-being if they are to teach in a manner that empowers students. Thich Nhat Hanh emphasized that "the practice of a healer, therapist, teacher or any helping professional should be directed toward his or herself first, because if the helper is unhappy, he or she cannot help many people." In the United States it is rare that anyone talks about teachers in university settings as healers. And it is even more rare to hear anyone suggest that teachers have any responsibility to be self-actualized individuals.   35

Learning about the work of intellectuals and academics primarily from nineteenth-century fiction and nonfiction during my pre-college years, I was certain that the task for those of us who chose this vocation was to be holistically questing for self-actualization. It was the actual experience of college that disrupted this image. It was there that I was made to feel as though I was terribly naive about "the profession." I learned that far from being self-actualized, the university was seen more as a haven for those who are smart in book knowledge but who might be otherwise unfit for social interaction. Luckily, during my undergraduate years I began to make a distinction between the practice of being an intellectual/teacher and one's role as a member of the academic profession.   36

It was difficult to maintain fidelity to the idea of the intellectual as someone who sought to be whole — well-grounded in a context where there was little emphasis on spiritual well-being, on care of the soul. Indeed, the objectification of the teacher within bourgeois educational structures seemed to denigrate notions of wholeness and uphold the idea of a mind/body split, one that promotes and supports compartmentalization.   37

This support reinforces the dualistic separation of public and private, encouraging teachers and students to see no connection between life practices, habits of being, and the roles of professors. The idea of the intellectual questing for a union of mind, body, and spirit had been replaced with notions that being smart meant that one was inherently emotionally   38 unstable and that the best in oneself emerged in one's academic work. This meant that whether academics were drug addicts, alcoholics, batterers, or sexual abusers, the only important aspect of our identity was whether or not our minds functioned, whether we were able to do our jobs in the classroom. The self was presumably emptied out the moment the threshold was crossed, leaving in place only an objective mind — free of experiences and biases. There was fear that the conditions of that self would interfere with the teaching process. Part of the luxury and privilege of the role of teacher/professor today is the absence of any requirement that we be self-actualized. Not surprisingly, professors who are not concerned with inner well-being are the most threatened by the demand on the part of students for liberatory education, for pedagogical processes that will aid them in their own struggle for self-actualization.

Certainly it was naive for me to imagine during high school that I 39 would find spiritual and intellectual guidance in university settings from writers, thinkers, scholars. To have found this would have been to stumble across a rare treasure. I learned, along with other students, to consider myself fortunate if I found an interesting professor who talked in a compelling way. Most of my professors were not the slightest bit interested in enlightenment. More than anything they seemed enthralled by the exercise of power and authority within their mini-kingdom, the classroom.

This is not to say that there were not compelling, benevolent dictators, 40 but it is true to my memory that it was rare — absolutely, astonishingly rare — to encounter professors who were deeply committed to progressive pedagogical practices. I was dismayed by this; most of my professors were not individuals whose teaching styles I wanted to emulate.

My commitment to learning kept me attending classes. Yet, even so, 41 because I did not conform — would not be an unquestioning, passive student — some professors treated me with contempt. I was slowly becoming estranged from education. Finding Freire in the midst of that estrangement was crucial to my survival as a student. His work offered both a way for me to understand the limitations of the type of education I was receiving and to discover alternative strategies for learning and teaching. It was particularly disappointing to encounter white male professors who claimed to follow Freire's model even as their pedagogical practices were mired in structures of domination, mirroring the styles of conservative professors even as they approached subjects from a more progressive standpoint.

When I first encountered Paulo Freire, I was eager to see if his style of 42 teaching would embody the pedagogical practices he described so eloquently in his work. During the short time I studied with him, I was deeply moved by his presence, by the way in which his manner of teaching exemplified his pedagogical theory. (Not all students interested in Freire have had a similar experience.) My experience with him restored my faith in liberatory education. I had never wanted to surrender the conviction that one could teach without reinforcing existing systems of domination. I needed to know that professors did not have to be dictators in the classroom.

While I wanted teaching to be my career, I believed that personal success   *43*
was intimately linked with self-actualization. My passion for this quest led
me to interrogate constantly the mind/body split that was so often taken to
be a given. Most professors were often deeply antagonistic toward, even
scornful of, any approach to learning emerging from a philosophical
standpoint emphasizing the union of mind, body, and spirit, rather than
the separation of these elements. Like many of the students I now teach,
I was often told by powerful academics that I was misguided to seek such a
perspective in the academy. Throughout my student years I felt deep inner
anguish. Memory of that pain returns as I listen to students express the
concern that they will not succeed in academic professions if they want to
be well, if they eschew dysfunctional behavior or participation in coercive
hierarchies. These students are often fearful, as I was, that there are no
spaces in the academy where the will to be self-actualized can be affirmed.

This fear is present because many professors have intensely hostile   *44*
responses to the vision of liberatory education that connects the will to
know with the will to become. Within professorial circles, individuals often
complain bitterly that students want classes to be "encounter groups."
While it is utterly unreasonable for students to expect classrooms to be
therapy sessions, it is appropriate for them to hope that the knowledge
received in these settings will enrich and enhance them.

Currently, the students I encounter seem far more uncertain about the   *45*
project of self-actualization than my peers and I were twenty years ago.
They feel that there are no clear ethical guidelines shaping actions. Yet,
while they despair, they are also adamant that education should be liberatory. They want and demand more from professors than my generation
did. There are times when I walk into classrooms overflowing with students who feel terribly wounded in their psyches (many of them see thera-
pists), yet I do not think that they want therapy from me. They do want an
education that is healing to the uninformed, unknowing spirit. They do
want knowledge that is meaningful. They rightfully expect that my colleagues and I will not offer them information without addressing the connection between what they are learning and their overall life experiences.

This demand on the students' part does not mean that they will always   *46*
accept our guidance. This is one of the joys of education as the practice of
freedom, for it allows students to assume responsibility for their choices.
Writing about our teacher/student relationship in a piece for the *Village
Voice*, "How to Run the Yard: Off-Line and into the Margins at Yale," one of
my students, Gary Dauphin, shares the joys of working with me as well as
the tensions that surfaced between us as he began to devote his time to
pledging a fraternity rather than cultivating his writing:

> People think academics like Gloria [my given name] are all about difference:
> but what I learned from her was mostly about sameness, about what I had
> in common as a black man to people of color; to women and gays and
> lesbians and the poor and anyone else who wanted in. I did some of this
> learning by reading but most of it came from hanging out on the fringes of

> her life. I lived like that for a while, shuttling between high points in
> my classes and low points outside. Gloria was a safe haven. . . . Pledging a
> fraternity is about as far away as you can get from her classroom, from the
> yellow kitchen where she used to share her lunch with students in need of
> various forms of sustenance.

This is Gary writing about the joy. The tension arose as we discussed his reason for wanting to join a fraternity and my disdain for that decision. Gary comments, "They represented a vision of black manhood that she abhorred, one where violence and abuse were primary ciphers of bonding and identity." Describing his assertion of autonomy from my influence he writes, "But she must have also known the limits of even her influence on my life, the limits of books and teachers."

Ultimately, Gary felt that the decision he had made to join a fraternity   47
was not constructive, that I "had taught him openness" where the fraternity had encouraged one-dimensional allegiance. Our interchange both during and after this experience was an example of engaged pedagogy.

Through critical thinking — a process he learned by reading theory   48
and actively analyzing texts — Gary experienced education as the practice of freedom. His final comments about me: "Gloria had only mentioned the entire episode once after it was over, and this to tell me simply that there are many kinds of choices, many kinds of logic. I could make those events mean whatever I wanted as long as I was honest." I have quoted his writing at length because it is testimony affirming engaged pedagogy. It means that my voice is not the only account of what happens in the classroom.

Engaged pedagogy necessarily values student expression. In her essay,   49
"Interrupting the Calls for Student Voice in Liberatory Education: A Feminist Poststructuralist Perspective," Mimi Orner employs a Foucauldian framework to suggest that

> regulatory and punitive means and uses of the confession bring to mind curricular and pedagogical practices which call for students to publicly reveal, even confess, information about their lives and cultures in the presence of authority figures such as teachers.

When education is the practice of freedom, students are not the only ones who are asked to share, to confess. Engaged pedagogy does not seek simply to empower students. Any classroom that employs a holistic model of learning will also be a place where teachers grow, and are empowered by the process. That empowerment cannot happen if we refuse to be vulnerable while encouraging students to take risks. Professors who expect students to share confessional narratives but who are themselves unwilling to share are exercising power in a manner that could be coercive. In my classrooms, I do not expect students to take any risks that I would not take, to share in any way that I would not share. When professors bring narratives of their experiences into classroom discussions it eliminates the possibility that we can function as all-knowing, silent interrogators. It is often productive if professors take the first risk, linking confessional narratives to academic discussions so as to show how experience can illuminate and enhance our understanding of academic material. But most professors must practice being vulnerable in the classroom, being wholly present in mind, body, and spirit.

■   ■   ■

Reading Rhetorically

1. hooks includes many personal anecdotes and insights in this selection. Use a pen or highlighter to bracket all the places where she makes use of personal experiences. Discuss with your classmates the relationship between these personal experiences and the larger point she is making about education. What do you notice about the structure of the work? What conclusions can you draw about effective strategies for using personal experiences in scholarly writing?

2. Who is hooks's audience? How can you tell? Be prepared to explain to the class (by pointing to specific passages in the text) whether or not you see yourself as her intended audience and the effect on you as a reader of being or not being part of her intended audience.

3. Circle a number of the key phrases hooks uses in this work — for example, "banking system of education" (para. 13), "engaged pedagogy" (para. 14), and "self-actualization" (para. 35) — and list them on the class chalkboard. Working in small groups, develop a clear definition and explanation of one phrase and present them to the rest of the class.

Inquiring Further

4. In paragraph 14 and elsewhere, hooks refers to the work of Brazilian scholar Paulo Freire and his notion of critical pedagogy. Look at two or three of the official Web sites devoted to Freire's work, including the Instituto Paulo Freire (http://www.paulofreire.org/) and the Paulo Freire Institute at UCLA (http://www.paulofreireinstitute.org/). Be prepared to share with the class several key ideas you learn about Freire and his followers from the sites. How has this additional information helped you understand the appeal of Freire's work to hooks?

5. Prepare a summary of hooks's key points, including the concept of education as "the practice of freedom" (para. 8). Discuss hooks's ideas with two K–12 teachers or two professors on your campus who train K–12 teachers. What do they think about her ideas, given their understanding of local educational structures and issues? Discuss your findings with your class.

6. In the second section here, "Engaged Pedagogy," hooks refers several times to "the union of mind, body, and spirit" when she talks about her educational ideal. In small groups, discuss the implications of this kind of spiritual language. What are the advantages of applying spirituality to teaching and learning situations? What are the disadvantages? You might compare experiences your classmates have had in public and parochial schools before you draw conclusions about hooks's language and claims.

Framing Conversations

7. In paragraph 6, hooks writes:

> School was the place of ecstasy — pleasure and danger. To be changed by ideas was pure pleasure. But to learn ideas that ran counter to values and beliefs learned at home was to place oneself at risk, to enter the danger zone. Home was the place where I was forced to conform to someone else's image of who and what I should be. School was the place where I could forget that self, and, through ideas, reinvent myself.

Write an essay in which you place the ideas in this passage in conversation with the ideas Mary Louise Pratt sets forth about contact zones in "Arts of the Contact Zone" (p. 354). Drawing on specific passages in Pratt's work, describe the role you think contact zones should play in education.

8. hooks's text picks up on class issues that are also evident in Barbara Ehrenreich's "Maid to Order" (p. 479) and Héctor Tobar's "Americanismo: City of Peasants" (p. 533). Write an essay in which you explore the ideas about class, education, and social power that are evident in the examples and arguments of these three texts. What conclusions can you draw?

9. While hooks argues for improving educational practices along the specific lines of engaged pedagogy, she doesn't let us forget the complex role race plays in current educational issues. Write an essay in which you imagine a conversation among bell hooks, Jonathan Kozol (below), and Peggy McIntosh (p. 520) about race relations and education in the United States and what we all — both inside and outside the classroom — ought to do about them. Draw on your own experiences as well, as you add your voice to the conversation.

■ JONATHAN KOZOL

Still Separate, Still Unequal: America's Educational Apartheid

Jonathan Kozol is an award-winning writer and lecturer who focuses on social injustice in the United States, an interest that began in the 1960s, when he taught in the Boston public school system. That first exposure to inner-city schools, to poor and undereducated youngsters, led him to investigate and write extensively about what he calls social and educational apartheid in the United States, the racial segregation that keeps many people in a cycle of poverty that he believes is nearly impossible to break. In 1967 he documented his experience in Boston in his first book, *Death at an Early Age*. His goal was to help readers get to know and care about his subjects deeply enough to consider the changes in social policy necessary for all Americans to realize the democratic dream. It is a strategy he has adhered to in his work since. For example, in *Rachel and Her Children: Homeless Families in America* (1987), Kozol brings readers into the difficult lives of the homeless; in *Amazing Grace: The Lives of Children and the Conscience of a Nation* (1995) and *Ordinary Resurrections: Children in the Years of Hope* (2000), he takes readers to an impoverished neighborhood in the South Bronx. An Internet search of Kozol's name demonstrates how widely he is quoted and how often he appears in the media as an expert on social inequality.

The essay here, published in *Harper's* in September 2005, was adapted from *The Shame of the Nation: The Restoration of Apartheid Schooling in America* (2005). Notice that Kozol uses many different sources to support his argument; but, in the style of magazine journalism, he does not cite them. You might keep track of all the different kinds of sources in this piece, though, to see what connections you can make between Kozol's central argument and the voices he includes here. As a reporter, Kozol wants us to hear the voice of the schoolchild who asks, "We do not have the things you have. . . . Can you help us?" (paras. 18–19) as well as the voice of the president insisting his educational program is "making a difference" (para. 108). Kozol makes his case in part by juxtaposing the words of the powerless and the powerful, adding context with statistics and facts that demonstrate what he believes is a profoundly unjust system of keeping the haves and have-nots separated through a variety of policies and belief systems.

You no doubt are aware that all schools in the United States are not equal. But as you read Kozol's piece, consider how the statistics and information he includes shape what you thought you knew about this issue. How does Kozol use numbers to make his point? How does he use a reporter's eye to help readers understand what life is like inside an underfunded, undersupported school? What visual details do you find most persuasive, and why? Where does he appeal to emotion in support of his argument, and what do you think of this strategy?

Before you read, consider what you know about the No Child Left Behind Act (2001), which plays a role in Kozol's examination of urban school systems. Research the arguments of — and the emotions expressed by — supporters and opponents of the law so that you have a sense of the high stakes of this conversation. Also keep your own school experiences in mind. When did you first realize, for example, that some children have more than others? Kozol taps into a discussion about education that is linked to almost every other kind of social division in our country. What does he hope to illuminate? What solutions does he propose? And perhaps most important, where do you place yourself in this conversation on what it means to learn and grow as an American?

■ ■ ■

Many Americans who live far from our major cities and who have no firsthand knowledge of the realities to be found in urban public schools seem to have the rather vague and general impression that the great extremes of racial isolation that were matters of grave national significance some thirty-five or forty years ago have gradually but steadily diminished in more recent years. The truth, unhappily, is that the trend, for well over a decade now, has been precisely the reverse. Schools that were already deeply segregated twenty-five or thirty years ago are no less segregated now, while thousands of other schools around the country that had been integrated either voluntarily or by the force of law have since been rapidly resegregating.

In Chicago, by the academic year 2002–2003, 87 percent of public-   2
school enrollment was black or Hispanic; less than 10 percent of children in the schools were white. In Washington, D.C., 94 percent of children were black or Hispanic; less than 5 percent were white. In St. Louis, 82 percent of the student population were black or Hispanic; in Philadel-phia and Cleveland, 79 percent; in Los Angeles, 84 percent; in Detroit, 96 percent; in Baltimore, 89 percent. In New York City, nearly three quarters of the students were black or Hispanic.

Even these statistics, as stark as they are, cannot begin to convey how   3
deeply isolated children in the poorest and most segregated sections of these cities have become. In the typically colossal high schools of the Bronx, for instance, more than 90 percent of students (in most cases, more than 95 percent) are black or Hispanic. At John F. Kennedy High School in 2003, 93 percent of the enrollment of more than 4,000 students were black and Hispanic; only 3.5 percent of students at the school were white. At Harry S. Truman High School, black and Hispanic students represented 96 percent of the enrollment of 2,700 students; 2 percent were white. At Adlai Stevenson High School, which enrolls 3,400 students, blacks and Hispanics made up 97 percent of the student population; a mere eight tenths of 1 percent were white.

A teacher at P.S. 65 in the South Bronx once pointed out to me one of   4
the two white children I had ever seen there. His presence in her class was something of a wonderment to the teacher and to the other pupils. I asked how many white kids she had taught in the South Bronx in her career. "I've been at this school for eighteen years," she said. "This is the first white stu-dent I have ever taught."

One of the most disheartening experiences for those who grew up in   5
the years when Martin Luther King Jr. and Thurgood Marshall were alive is to visit public schools today that bear their names, or names of other honored leaders of the integration struggles that produced the temporary progress that took place in the three decades after *Brown v. Board of Edu-cation*, and to find out how many of these schools are bastions of contem-porary segregation. It is even more disheartening when schools like these are not in deeply segregated inner-city neighborhoods but in racially mixed areas where the integration of a public school would seem to be most natural, and where, indeed, it takes a conscious effort on the part of parents or school officials in these districts to avoid the integration option that is often right at their front door.

In a Seattle neighborhood that I visited in 2002, for instance, where   6
approximately half the families were Caucasian, 95 percent of students at the Thurgood Marshall Elementary School were black, Hispanic, Native

American, or of Asian origin. An African-American teacher at the school told me — not with bitterness but wistfully — of seeing clusters of white parents and their children each morning on the corner of a street close to the school, waiting for a bus that took the children to a predominantly white school.

"At Thurgood Marshall," according to a big wall poster in the school's   7
lobby, "the dream is alive." But school-assignment practices and federal court decisions that have countermanded long-established policies that previously fostered integration in Seattle's schools make the realization of the dream identified with Justice Marshall all but unattainable today. In San Diego there is a school that bears the name of Rosa Parks in which 86 percent of students are black and Hispanic and only some 2 percent are white. In Los Angeles there is a school that bears the name of Dr. King that is 99 percent black and Hispanic, and another in Milwaukee in which black and Hispanic children also make up 99 percent of the enrollment. There is a high school in Cleveland that is named for Dr. King in which black students make up 97 percent of the student body, and the graduation rate is only 35 percent. In Philadelphia, 98 percent of children at a high school named for Dr. King are black. At a middle school named for Dr. King in Boston, black and Hispanic children make up 98 percent of the enrollment.

In New York City there is a primary school named for Langston Hughes   8
(99 percent black and Hispanic), a middle school named for Jackie Robinson (96 percent black and Hispanic), and a high school named for Fannie Lou Hamer, one of the great heroes of the integration movement in the South, in which 98 percent of students are black or Hispanic. In Harlem there is yet another segregated Thurgood Marshall School (also 98 percent black and Hispanic), and in the South Bronx dozens of children I have known went to a segregated middle school named in honor of Paul Robeson in which less than half of 1 percent of the enrollment was Caucasian.

There is a well-known high school named for Martin Luther King Jr. in   9
New York City too. This school, which I've visited repeatedly in recent years, is located in an upper-middle-class white neighborhood, where it was built in the belief — or hope — that it would draw large numbers of white students by permitting them to walk to school, while only their black and Hispanic classmates would be asked to ride the bus or come by train. When the school was opened in 1975, less than a block from Lincoln Center in Manhattan, "it was seen," according to the *New York Times*, "as a promising effort to integrate white, black and Hispanic students in a thriving neighborhood that held one of the city's cultural gems." Even from the start, however, parents in the neighborhood showed great reluctance to permit their children to enroll at Martin Luther King, and, despite "its prime location and its name, which itself creates the highest of expectations," notes the *Times*, the school before long came to be a destination for black and Hispanic students who could not obtain admission into more successful schools. It stands today as one of the nation's most visible

and problematic symbols of an expectation rapidly receding and a legacy substantially betrayed.

Perhaps most damaging to any serious effort to address racial segrega-   10
tion openly is the refusal of most of the major arbiters of culture in our northern cities to confront or even clearly name an obvious reality they would have castigated with a passionate determination in another section of the nation fifty years before — and which, moreover, they still castigate today in retrospective writings that assign it to a comfortably distant and allegedly concluded era of the past. There is, indeed, a seemingly agreed-upon convention in much of the media today not even to use an accurate descriptor like "racial segregation" in a narrative description of a segregated school. Linguistic sweeteners, semantic somersaults, and surrogate vocabularies are repeatedly employed. Schools in which as few as 3 or 4 percent of students may be white or Southeast Asian or of Middle Eastern origin, for instance — and where every other child in the building is black or Hispanic — are referred to as "diverse." Visitors to schools like these discover quickly the eviscerated meaning of the word, which is no longer a proper adjective but a euphemism for a plainer word that has apparently become unspeakable.

School systems themselves repeatedly employ this euphemism in   11
describing the composition of their student populations. In a school I visited in the fall of 2004 in Kansas City, Missouri, for example, a document distributed to visitors reports that the school's curriculum "addresses the needs of children from diverse backgrounds." But as I went from class to class, I did not encounter any children who were white or Asian — or Hispanic, for that matter — and when I was later provided with precise statistics for the demographics of the school, I learned that 99.6 percent of students there were African American. In a similar document, the school board of another district, this one in New York State, referred to "the diversity" of its student population and "the rich variations of ethnic backgrounds." But when I looked at the racial numbers that the district had reported to the state, I learned that there were 2,800 black and Hispanic children in the system, 1 Asian child, and 3 whites. Words, in these cases, cease to have real meaning; or, rather, they mean the opposite of what they say.

High school students whom I talk with in deeply segregated neighbor-   12
hoods and public schools seem far less circumspect than their elders and far more open in their willingness to confront these issues. "It's more like being hidden," said a fifteen-year-old girl named Isabel[1] I met some years ago in Harlem, in attempting to explain to me the ways in which she and her classmates understood the racial segregation of their neighborhoods and schools. "It's as if you have been put in a garage where, if they don't have room for something but aren't sure if they should throw it out, they put it there where they don't need to think of it again."

[1]The names of children mentioned in this article have been changed to protect their privacy.

I asked her if she thought America truly did not "have room" for her or *13*
other children of her race. "Think of it this way," said a sixteen-year-old
girl sitting beside her. "If people in New York woke up one day and learned
that we were gone, that we had simply died or left for somewhere else, how
would they feel?"

"How do you think they'd feel?" I asked. *14*

"I think they'd be relieved," this very solemn girl replied. *15*

Many educators make the argument today that given the demographics *16*
of large cities like New York and their suburban areas, our only realistic
goal should be the nurturing of strong, empowered, and well-funded
schools in segregated neighborhoods. Black school officials in these situations have sometimes conveyed to me a bitter and clear-sighted recognition that they're being asked, essentially, to mediate and render functional
an uncontested separation between children of their race and children of
white people living sometimes in a distant section of their town and sometimes in almost their own immediate communities. Implicit in this mediation is a willingness to set aside the promises of *Brown* and — though
never stating this or even thinking of it clearly in these terms — to settle
for the promise made more than a century ago in *Plessy v. Ferguson*, the
1896 Supreme Court ruling in which "separate but equal" was accepted as
a tolerable rationale for the perpetuation of a dual system in American
society.

Equality itself — equality alone — is now, it seems, the article of faith *17*
to which most of the principals of inner-city public schools subscribe. And
some who are perhaps most realistic do not even dare to ask for, or expect,
complete equality, which seems beyond the realm of probability for many
years to come, but look instead for only a sufficiency of means — "adequacy"
is the legal term most often used today — by which to win those practical
and finite victories that appear to be within their reach. Higher standards,
higher expectations, are repeatedly demanded of these urban principals,
and of the teachers and students in their schools, but far lower standards —
certainly in ethical respects — appear to be expected of the dominant society that isolates these children in unequal institutions.

"Dear Mr. Kozol," wrote the eight-year-old, "we do not have the things *18*
you have. You have Clean things. We do not have. You have a clean bathroom. We do not have that. You have Parks and we do not have Parks. You
have all the thing and we do not have all the thing. Can you help us?"

The letter, from a child named Alliyah, came in a fat envelope of *19*
twenty-seven letters from a class of third-grade children in the Bronx.
Other letters that the students in Alliyah's classroom sent me registered
some of the same complaints. "We don't have no gardens," "no Music or
Art," and "no fun places to play," one child said. "Is there a way to fix this
Problem?" Another noted a concern one hears from many children in such
overcrowded schools: "We have a gym but it is for lining up. I think it is not
fair." Yet another of Alliyah's classmates asked me, with a sweet mis-
spelling, if I knew the way to make her school into a "good" school — "like

the other kings have" — and ended with the hope that I would do my best to make it possible for "all the kings" to have good schools.

The letter that affected me the most, however, had been written by a *20* child named Elizabeth. "It is not fair that other kids have a garden and new things. But we don't have that," said Elizabeth. "I wish that this school was the most beautiful school in the whole why world."

"The whole why world" stayed in my thoughts for days. When I later *21* met Elizabeth, I brought her letter with me, thinking I might see whether, in reading it aloud, she'd change the "why" to "wide" or leave it as it was. My visit to her class, however, proved to be so pleasant, and the children seemed so eager to bombard me with their questions about where I lived, and why I lived there rather than in New York, and who I lived with, and how many dogs I had, and other interesting questions of that sort, that I decided not to interrupt the nice reception they had given me with questions about usages and spelling. I left "the whole why world" to float around unedited and unrevised in my mind. The letter itself soon found a resting place on the wall above my desk.

In the years before I met Elizabeth, I had visited many other schools in *22* the South Bronx and in one northern district of the Bronx as well. I had made repeated visits to a high school where a stream of water flowed down one of the main stairwells on a rainy afternoon and where green fungus molds were growing in the office where the students went for counseling. A large blue barrel was positioned to collect rainwater coming through the ceiling. In one makeshift elementary school housed in a former skating rink next to a funeral establishment in yet another nearly all-black-and-Hispanic section of the Bronx, class size rose to thirty-four and more; four kindergarten classes and a sixth-grade class were packed into a single room that had no windows. The air was stifling in many rooms, and the children had no place for recess because there was no outdoor playground and no indoor gym.

In another elementary school, which had been built to hold 1,000 chil- *23* dren but was packed to bursting with some 1,500, the principal poured out his feelings to me in a room in which a plastic garbage bag had been attached somehow to cover part of the collapsing ceiling. "This," he told me, pointing to the garbage bag, then gesturing around him at the other indications of decay and disrepair one sees in ghetto schools much like it elsewhere, "would not happen to white children."

Libraries, once one of the glories of the New York City school system, *24* were either nonexistent or, at best, vestigial in large numbers of the elementary schools. Art and music programs had also for the most part disappeared. "When I began to teach in 1969," the principal of an elementary school in the South Bronx reported to me, "every school had a full-time licensed art and music teacher and librarian." During the subsequent decades, he recalled, "I saw all of that destroyed."

School physicians also were removed from elementary schools during *25* these years. In 1970, when substantial numbers of white children still attended New York City's public schools, 400 doctors had been present to address the health needs of the children. By 1993 the number of doctors had been cut to 23, most of them part-time — a cutback that affected most severely children in the city's poorest neighborhoods, where medical facilities were most deficient and health problems faced by children most extreme. Teachers told me of asthmatic children who came into class with chronic wheezing and who at any moment of the day might undergo more serious attacks, but in the schools I visited there were no doctors to attend to them.

In explaining these steep declines in services, political leaders in New   26
York tended to point to shifting economic factors, like a serious budget crisis in the middle 1970s, rather than to the changing racial demographics of the student population. But the fact of economic ups and downs from year to year, or from one decade to the next, could not convincingly explain the permanent shortchanging of the city's students, which took place routinely in good economic times and bad. The bad times were seized upon politically to justify the cuts, and the money was never restored once the crisis years were past.

"If you close your eyes to the changing racial composition of the   27
schools and look only at budget actions and political events," says Noreen Connell, the director of the nonprofit Educational Priorities Panel in New York, "you're missing the assumptions that are underlying these decisions." When minority parents ask for something better for their kids, she says, "the assumption is that these are parents who can be discounted. These are kids who just don't count — children we don't value."

This, then, is the accusation that Alliyah and her classmates send our   28
way: "You have . . . We do not have." Are they right or are they wrong? Is this a case of naive and simplistic juvenile exaggeration? What does a third-grader know about these big-time questions of fairness and justice? Physical appearances apart, how in any case do you begin to measure something so diffuse and vast and seemingly abstract as having more, or having less, or not having at all?

Around the time I met Alliyah in the school year 1997–1998, New   29
York's Board of Education spent about $8,000 yearly on the education of a third-grade child in a New York City public school. If you could have scooped Alliyah up out of the neighborhood where she was born and plunked her down in a fairly typical white suburb of New York, she would have received a public education worth about $12,000 a year. If you were to lift her up once more and set her down in one of the wealthiest white suburbs of New York, she would have received as much as $18,000 worth of public education every year and would likely have had a third-grade teacher paid approximately $30,000 more than her teacher in the Bronx was paid.

The dollars on both sides of the equation have increased since then,   30
but the discrepancies between them have remained. The present per-pupil spending level in the New York City schools is $11,700, which may be compared with a per-pupil spending level in excess of $22,000 in the well-to-do

suburban district of Manhasset, Long Island. The present New York City level is, indeed, almost exactly what Manhasset spent per pupil eighteen years ago, in 1987, when that sum of money bought a great deal more in services and salaries than it can buy today. In dollars adjusted for inflation, New York City has not yet caught up to where its wealthiest suburbs were a quarter-century ago.

Gross discrepancies in teacher salaries between the city and its afflu- 31 ent white suburbs have remained persistent as well. In 1997 the median salary for teachers in Alliyah's neighborhood was $43,000, as compared with $74,000 in suburban Rye, $77,000 in Manhasset, and $81,000 in the town of Scarsdale, which is only about eleven miles from Alliyah's school. Five years later, in 2002, salary scales for New York City's teachers rose to levels that approximated those within the lower-spending districts in the suburbs, but salary scales do not reflect the actual salaries that teachers typically receive, which are dependent upon years of service and advanced degrees. Salaries for first-year teachers in the city were higher than they'd been four years before, but the differences in median pay between the city and its upper-middle-income suburbs had remained extreme. The overall figure for New York City in 2002–2003 was $53,000, while it had climbed to $87,000 in Manhasset and exceeded $95,000 in Scarsdale.

"There are expensive children and there are cheap children," writes 32 Marina Warner, an essayist and novelist who has written many books for children, "just as there are expensive women and cheap women." The governmentally administered diminishment in value of the children of the poor begins even before the age of five or six, when they begin their years of formal education in the public schools. It starts during their infant and toddler years, when hundreds of thousands of children of the very poor in much of the United States are locked out of the opportunity for preschool education for no reason but the accident of birth and budgetary choices of the government, while children of the privileged are often given veritable feasts of rich developmental early education.

In New York City, for example, affluent parents pay surprisingly large 33 sums of money to enroll their youngsters, beginning at the age of two or three, in extraordinary early-education programs that give them social competence and rudimentary pedagogic skills unknown to children of the same age in the city's poorer neighborhoods. The most exclusive of the private preschools in New York, which are known to those who can afford them as "Baby Ivies," cost as much as $24,000 for a full-day program. Competition for admission to these pre-K schools is so extreme that private counselors are frequently retained, at fees as high as $300 an hour, to guide the parents through the application process.

At the opposite extreme along the economic spectrum in New York are 34 thousands of children who receive no preschool opportunity at all. Exactly how many thousands are denied this opportunity in New York City and in other major cities is almost impossible to know. Numbers that originate in governmental agencies in many states are incomplete and imprecise and do not always differentiate with clarity between authentic pre-K programs that have educative and developmental substance and those less expensive child-care arrangements that do not. But even where states do compile numbers that refer specifically to educative preschool programs, it is difficult to know how many of the children who are served are of low income, since admissions to some of the state-supported programs aren't determined by low income or they are determined by a complicated set of factors of which poverty is only one.

There are remarkable exceptions to this pattern in some sections 35 of the nation. In Milwaukee, for example, virtually every four-year-old is now enrolled in a preliminary kindergarten program, which amounts to a full year of preschool education, prior to a second kindergarten year for five-year-olds. More commonly in urban neighborhoods, large numbers of low-income children are denied these opportunities and come into their kindergarten year without the minimal social skills that children need in order to participate in class activities and without even such very modest early-learning skills as knowing how to hold a crayon or a pencil, identify perhaps a couple of shapes and colors, or recognize that printed pages go from left to right.

Three years later, in third grade, these children are introduced to what 36 are known as "high-stakes tests," which in many urban systems now determine whether students can or cannot be promoted. Children who have been in programs like those offered by the "Baby Ivies" since the age of two have, by now, received the benefits of six or seven years of education, nearly twice as many as the children who have been denied these opportunities; yet all are required to take, and will be measured by, the same examinations. Which of these children will receive the highest scores? The ones who spent the years from two to four in lovely little Montessori programs and in other pastel-painted settings in which tender and attentive and well-trained instructors read to them from beautiful storybooks and introduced them very gently for the first time to the world of numbers and the shapes of letters, and the sizes and varieties of solid objects, and perhaps taught them to sort things into groups or to arrange them in a sequence, or to do those many other interesting things that early childhood specialists refer to as pre-numeracy skills? Or the ones who spent those years at home in front of a TV or sitting by the window of a slum apartment gazing down into the street? There is something deeply hypocritical about a society that holds an eight-year-old inner-city child "accountable" for her performance on a high-stakes standardized exam but does not hold the high officials of our government accountable for robbing her of what they gave their own kids six or seven years earlier.

Perhaps in order to deflect these recognitions, or to soften them some- 37 what, many people, even while they do nor doubt the benefit of making very large investments in the education of their own children, somehow — paradoxical as it may seem — appear to be attracted to the argument that money may not really matter that much at all. No matter with what regularity such doubts about the worth of spending money on a child's education are advanced, it is obvious that those who have the money, and who spend it lavishly to benefit their own kids, do not do it for no reason. Yet shockingly large numbers of well-educated and sophisticated people whom I talk with nowadays dismiss such challenges with a surprising ease. "Is the answer really to throw money into these dysfunctional and failing schools?" I'm often asked. "Don't we have some better ways to make them 'work'?" The question is posed in a variety of forms. "Yes, of course, it's not a perfectly fair system as it stands. But money alone is surely not the sole response. The values of the parents and the kids themselves must have a role in this as well you know, housing, health conditions, social factors." "Other factors" — a term of overall reprieve one often hears — "have got to be considered, too." These latter points are obviously true but always seem to have the odd effect of substituting things we know we cannot change in the short run for obvious solutions like cutting class size and constructing new school buildings or providing universal preschool that we actually could put in place right now if we were so inclined.

Frequently these arguments are posed as questions that do not invite 38 an answer because the answer seems to be decided in advance. "Can you really buy your way to better education for these children?" "Do we know enough to be quite sure that we will see an actual return on the investment that we make?" "Is it even clear that this is the right starting point to get to where we'd like to go? It doesn't always seem to work, as I am sure that you already know," or similar questions that somehow assume I will agree with those who ask them.

Some people who ask these questions, although they live in wealthy 39 districts where the schools are funded at high levels, don't even send their children to these public schools but choose instead to send them to expensive private day schools. At some of the well-known private prep schools in the New York City area, tuition and associated costs are typically more than $20,000 a year. During their children's teenage years, they sometimes send them off to very fine New England schools like Andover or Exeter or Groton, where tuition, boarding, and additional expenses rise to more than $30,000. Often a family has two teenage children in these schools at the same time, so they may be spending more than $60,000 on their children's education every year. Yet here I am one night, a guest within their home, and dinner has been served and we are having coffee now; and this entirely likable, and generally sensible, and beautifully refined and thoughtful person looks me in the eyes and asks me whether you can really buy your way to better education for the children of the poor.

As racial isolation deepens and the inequalities of education finance 40 remain unabated and take on new and more innovative forms, the principals of many inner-city schools are making choices that few principals in public schools that serve white children in the mainstream of the nation ever need to contemplate. Many have been dedicating vast amounts of time and effort to create an architecture of adaptive strategies that promise incremental gains within the limits inequality allows.

New vocabularies of stentorian determination, new systems of incentive, 41
and new modes of castigation, which are termed "rewards and sanctions,"
have emerged. Curriculum materials that are alleged to be aligned with
governmentally established goals and standards and particularly suited to
what are regarded as "the special needs and learning styles" of low-income
urban children have been introduced. Relentless emphasis on raising test
scores, rigid policies of nonpromotion and nongraduation, a new empiri-
cism and the imposition of unusually detailed lists of named and numbered
"outcomes" for each isolated parcel of instruction, an oftentimes fanatical
insistence upon uniformity of teachers in their management of time, an
openly conceded emulation of the rigorous approaches of the military and
a frequent use of terminology that comes out of the world of industry and
commerce — these are just a few of the familiar aspects of these new adaptive strategies.

Although generically described as "school reform," most of these prac- 42
tices and policies are targeted primarily at poor children of color; and
although most educators speak of these agendas in broad language that
sounds applicable to all, it is understood that they are valued chiefly as
responses to perceived catastrophe in deeply segregated and unequal
schools.

"If you do what I tell you to do, how I tell you to do it, when I tell you to 43
do it, you'll get it right," said a determined South Bronx principal observed
by a reporter for the *New York Times.* She was laying out a memorizing
rule for math to an assembly of her students. "If you don't, you'll get it
wrong." This is the voice, this is the tone, this is the rhythm and didactic
certitude one hears today in inner-city schools that have embraced a pedagogy of direct command and absolute control. "Taking their inspiration
from the ideas of B. F. Skinner . . . ," says the *Times,* proponents of scripted
rote-and-drill curricula articulate their aim as the establishment of "fault-
less communication" between "the teacher, who is the stimulus," and "the
students, who respond."

The introduction of Skinnerian approaches (which are commonly 44
employed in penal institutions and drug-rehabilitation programs), as a
way of altering the attitudes and learning styles of black and Hispanic children, is provocative, and it has stirred some outcries from respected scholars. To actually go into a school where you know some of the children very,
very well and see the way that these approaches can affect their daily lives
and thinking processes is even more provocative.

On a chilly November day four years ago in the South Bronx, I entered 45
P.S. 65, a school I had been visiting since 1993. There had been major
changes since I'd been there last. Silent lunches had been instituted in the
cafeteria, and on days when children misbehaved, silent recess had been
introduced as well. On those days the students were obliged to sit in rows
and maintain perfect silence on the floor of a small indoor room instead
of going out to play. The words SUCCESS FOR ALL, the brand name
of a scripted curriculum — better known by its acronym, SFA — were
prominently posted at the top of the main stairway and, as I would later

find, in almost every room. Also frequently displayed within the halls and classrooms were a number of administrative memos that were worded with unusual didactic absoluteness. "Authentic Writing," read a document called "Principles of Learning" that was posted in the corridor close to the principal's office, "is driven by curriculum and instruction." I didn't know what this expression meant. Like many other undefined and arbitrary phrases posted in the school, it seemed to be a dictum that invited no interrogation.

I entered the fourth grade of a teacher I will call Mr. Endicott, a man in   *46* his midthirties who had arrived here without training as a teacher, one of about a dozen teachers in the building who were sent into this school after a single summer of short-order preparation. Now in his second year, he had developed a considerable sense of confidence and held the class under a tight control.

As I found a place to sit in a far corner of the room, the teacher and his   *47* young assistant, who was in her first year as a teacher, were beginning a math lesson about building airport runways, a lesson that provided children with an opportunity for measuring perimeters. On the wall behind the teacher, in large letters, was written: "Portfolio Protocols: 1. You are responsible for the selection of [your] work that enters your portfolio. 2. As your skills become more sophisticated this year, you will want to revise, amend, supplement, and possibly replace items in your portfolio to reflect your intellectual growth." On the left side of the room: "Performance Standards Mathematics Curriculum: M-5 Problem Solving and Reasoning. M-6 Mathematical Skills and Tools . . ."

My attention was distracted by some whispering among the children   *48* sitting to the right of me. The teacher's response to this distraction was immediate: his arm shot out and up in a diagonal in front of him, his hand straight up, his fingers flat. The young co-teacher did this, too. When they saw their teachers do this, all the children in the classroom did it, too.

"Zero noise," the teacher said, but this instruction proved to be   *49* unneeded. The strange salute the class and teachers gave each other, which turned out to be one of a number of such silent signals teachers in the school were trained to use, and children to obey, had done the job of silencing the class.

"Active listening!" said Mr. Endicott. "Heads up! Tractor beams!"   *50* which meant "Every eye on me."

On the front wall of the classroom, in handwritten words that must   *51* have taken Mr. Endicott long hours to transcribe, was a list of terms that could be used to praise or criticize a student's work in mathematics. At Level Four, the highest of four levels of success, a child's "problem-solving strategies" could be described, according to this list, as "systematic, complete, efficient, and possibly elegant," while the student's capability to draw conclusions from the work she had completed could be termed "insightful" or "comprehensive." At Level Two, the child's capability to draw conclusions was to be described as "logically unsound"; at Level One, "not present." Approximately 50 separate categories of proficiency, or lack of such, were detailed in this wall-sized tabulation.

A well-educated man, Mr. Endicott later spoke to me about the form of classroom management that he was using as an adaptation from a model of industrial efficiency. "It's a kind of 'Taylorism' in the classroom," he explained, referring to a set of theories about the management of factory employees introduced by Frederick Taylor in the early 1900s. "Primitive utilitarianism" is another term he used when we met some months later to discuss these management techniques with other teachers from the school. His reservations were, however, not apparent in the classroom. Within the terms of what he had been asked to do, he had, indeed, become a master of control. It is one of the few classrooms I had visited up to that time in which almost nothing even hinting at spontaneous emotion in the children or the teacher surfaced while I was there.

The teacher gave the "zero noise" salute again when someone whispered to another child at his table. "In two minutes you will have a chance to talk and share this with your partner." Communication between children in the class was not prohibited but was afforded time slots and, remarkably enough, was formalized in an expression that I found included in a memo that was posted on the wall beside the door: "An opportunity . . . to engage in Accountable Talk."

Even the teacher's words of praise were framed in terms consistent with the lists that had been posted on the wall. "That's a Level Four suggestion," said the teacher when a child made an observation other teachers might have praised as simply "pretty good" or "interesting" or "mature." There was, it seemed, a formal name for every cognitive event within this school: "Authentic Writing," "Active Listening," "Accountable Talk." The ardor to assign all items of instruction or behavior a specific name was unsettling me. The adjectives had the odd effect of hyping every item of endeavor. "Authentic Writing" was, it seemed, a more important act than what the children in a writing class in any ordinary school might try to do. "Accountable Talk" was something more self-conscious and significant than merely useful conversation.

Since that day at P.S. 65, I have visited nine other schools in six different cities where the same Skinnerian curriculum is used. The signs on the walls, the silent signals, the curious salute, the same insistent naming of all cognitive particulars, became familiar as I went from one school to the next.

"Meaningful Sentences," began one of the many listings of proficiencies expected of the children in the fourth grade of an inner-city elementary school in Hartford (90 percent black, 10 percent Hispanic) that I visited a short time later. "Noteworthy Questions," "Active Listening," and other designations like these had been posted elsewhere in the room. Here, too, the teacher gave the kids her outstretched arm, with hand held up, to reestablish order when they grew a little noisy, but I noticed that she tried to soften the effect of this by opening her fingers and bending her elbow slightly so it did not look quite as forbidding as the gesture Mr. Endicott had used. A warm and interesting woman, she later told me she disliked the regimen intensely.

Over her desk, I read a "Mission Statement," which established the *57* priorities and values for the school. Among the missions of the school, according to the printed statement, which was posted also in some other classrooms of the school, was "to develop productive citizens" who have the skills that will be needed "for successful global competition," a message that was reinforced by other posters in the room. Over the heads of a group of children at their desks, a sign anointed them BEST WORKERS OF 2002.

Another signal now was given by the teacher, this one not for silence *58* but in order to achieve some other form of class behavior, which I could not quite identify. The students gave exactly the same signal in response. Whatever the function of this signal, it was done as I had seen it done in the South Bronx and would see it done in other schools in months to come. Suddenly, with a seeming surge of restlessness and irritation — with herself, as it appeared, and with her own effective use of all the tricks that she had learned — she turned to me and said, "I can do this with my dog."

"There's something crystal clear about a number," says a top adviser to *59* the U.S. Senate committee that has jurisdiction over public education, a point of view that is reinforced repeatedly in statements coming from the office of the U.S. education secretary and the White House. "I want to change the face of reading instruction across the United States from an art to a science," said an assistant to Rod Paige, the former education secretary, in the winter of 2002. This is a popular position among advocates for rigidly sequential systems of instruction, but the longing to turn art into science doesn't stop with reading methodologies alone. In many schools it now extends to almost every aspect of the operation of the school and of the lives that children lead within it. In some schools even such ordinary acts as children filing to lunch or recess in the hallways or the stairwells are subjected to the same determined emphasis upon empirical precision.

"Rubric For Filing" is the printed heading of a lengthy list of num- *60* bered categories by which teachers are supposed to grade their students on the way they march along the corridors in another inner-city district I have visited. Someone, in this instance, did a lot of work to fit the filing proficiencies of children into no more and no less than thirty-two specific slots:

"Line leader confidently leads the class. . . . Line is straight. . . . Spac- *61* ing is right. . . . The class is stepping together. . . . Everyone shows pride, their shoulders high . . . no slumping," according to the strict criteria for filing at Level Four.

"Line is straight, but one or two people [are] not quite in line," accord- *62* ing to the box for Level Three. "Line leader leads the class," and "almost everyone shows pride."

"Several are slumping. . . . Little pride is showing," says the box for *63* Level Two. "Spacing is uneven. . . . Some are talking and whispering."

"Line leader is paying no attention," says the box for Level One. 64 "Heads are turning every way. . . . Hands are touching. . . . The line is not straight. . . . There is no pride."

The teacher who handed me this document believed at first that it was 65 written as a joke by someone who had simply come to be fed up with all the numbers and accounting rituals that clutter up the day in many over-regulated schools. Alas, it turned out that it was no joke but had been printed in a handbook of instructions for the teachers in the city where she taught.

In some inner-city districts, even the most pleasant and old-fashioned 66 class activities of elementary schools have now been overtaken by these ordering requirements. A student teacher in California, for example, wanted to bring a pumpkin to her class on Halloween but knew it had no ascertainable connection to the California standards. She therefore had developed what she called "The Multi-Modal Pumpkin Unit" to teach science (seeds), arithmetic (the size and shape of pumpkins, I believe — this detail wasn't clear), and certain items she adapted out of language arts, in order to position "pumpkins" in a frame of state proficiencies. Even with her multi-modal pumpkin, as her faculty adviser told me, she was still afraid she would be criticized because she knew the pumpkin would not really help her children to achieve expected goals on state exams.

Why, I asked a group of educators at a seminar in Sacramento, was a 67 teacher being placed in a position where she'd need to do preposterous curricular gymnastics to enjoy a bit of seasonal amusement with her kids on Halloween? How much injury to state-determined "purpose" would it do to let the children of poor people have a pumpkin party once a year for no other reason than because it's something fun that other children get to do on autumn days in public schools across most of America?

"Forcing an absurdity on teachers does teach something," said an 68 African-American professor. "It teaches acquiescence. It breaks down the will to thumb your nose at pointless protocols — to call absurdity 'absurd.'" Writing out the standards with the proper numbers on the chalkboard has a similar effect, he said; and doing this is "terribly important" to the principals in many of these schools. "You *have* to post the standards, and the way you know the children know the standards is by asking them to *state* the standards. And they *do* it — and you want to be quite certain that they do it if you want to keep on working at that school."

In speaking of the drill-based program in effect at P.S. 65, Mr. Endicott 69 told me he tended to be sympathetic to the school administrators, more so at least than the other teachers I had talked with seemed to be. He said he believed his principal had little choice about the implementation of this program, which had been mandated for all elementary schools in New York City that had had rock-bottom academic records over a long period of time. "This puts me into a dilemma," he went on, "because I love the kids at P.S. 65." And even while, he said, "I know that my teaching SFA is a charade . . . if I don't do it I won't be permitted to teach these children."

Mr. Endicott, like all but two of the new recruits at P.S. 65 — there   70
were about fifteen in all — was a white person, as were the principal and
most of the administrators at the school. As a result, most of these neo-
phyte instructors had had little or no prior contact with the children of an
inner-city neighborhood; but, like the others I met, and despite the distancing between the children and their teachers that resulted from the scripted
method of instruction, he had developed close attachments to his students
and did not want to abandon them. At the same time, the class- and race-
specific implementation of this program obviously troubled him. "There's
an expression now," he said. "'The rich get richer, and the poor get SFA.'"
He said he was still trying to figure out his "professional ethics" on the
problem that this posed for him.

White children made up "only about one percent" of students in the   71
New York City schools in which this scripted teaching system was imposed,
according to the *New York Times*, which also said that "the prepackaged
lessons" were intended "to ensure that all teachers — even novices or the
most inept" would be able to teach reading.[2] As seemingly pragmatic and
hardheaded as such arguments may be, they are desperation strategies
that come out of the acceptance of inequity. If we did not have a deeply
segregated system in which more experienced instructors teach the children
of the privileged and the least experienced are sent to teach the children of
minorities, these practices would not be needed and could not be so convincingly defended. They are confections of apartheid, and no matter by
what arguments of urgency or practicality they have been justified, they
cannot fail to further deepen the divisions of society.

There is no misery index for the children of apartheid education.   72
There ought to be; we measure almost everything else that happens to
them in their schools. Do kids who go to schools like these enjoy the days
they spend in them? Is school, for most of them, a happy place to be? You
do not find the answers to these questions in reports about achievement
levels, scientific methods of accountability, or structural revisions in the
modes of governance. Documents like these don't speak of happiness. You
have to go back to the schools themselves to find an answer to these questions. You have to sit down in the little chairs in first and second grade, or
on the reading rug with kindergarten kids, and listen to the things they
actually say to one another and the dialogue between them and their
teachers. You have to go down to the basement with the children when it's

[2]SFA has since been discontinued in the New York City public schools, though it is
still being used in 1,300 U.S. schools, serving as many as 650,000 children. Similar
scripted systems are used in schools (overwhelmingly minority in population) serving
several million children.

EDITORS' NOTE: The article Kozol cites is titled "Fearing a Class System in the
Classroom; A Strict Curriculum, but Only for Failing Schools, Mostly in Poor Areas of
New York"; it was written by Abby Goodnough and appeared in the January 19, 2003,
edition of the *Times*.

time for lunch and to the playground with them, if they have a playground, when it's time for recess, if they still have recess at their school. You have to walk into the children's bathrooms in these buildings. You have to do what children do and breathe the air the children breathe. I don't think that there is any other way to find out what the lives that children lead in school are really like.

High school students, when I first meet them, are often more reluctant 73 than the younger children to open up and express their personal concerns; but hesitation on the part of students did not prove to be a problem when I visited a tenth-grade class at Fremont High School in Los Angeles. The students were told that I was a writer, and they took no time in getting down to matters that were on their minds.

"Can we talk about the bathrooms?" asked a soft-spoken student 74 named Mireya.

In almost any classroom there are certain students who, by the force 75 of their directness or the unusual sophistication of their way of speaking, tend to capture your attention from the start. Mireya later spoke insightfully about some of the serious academic problems that were common in the school, but her observations on the physical and personal embarrassments she and her schoolmates had to undergo cut to the heart of questions of essential dignity that kids in squalid schools like this one have to deal with all over the nation.

Fremont High School, as court papers filed in a lawsuit against the 76 state of California document, has fifteen fewer bathrooms than the law requires. Of the limited number of bathrooms that are working in the school, "only one or two . . . are open and unlocked for girls to use." Long lines of girls are "waiting to use the bathrooms," which are generally "unclean" and "lack basic supplies," including toilet paper. Some of the classrooms, as court papers also document, "do not have air conditioning," so that students, who attend school on a three-track schedule that runs year-round, "become red-faced and unable to concentrate" during "the extreme heat of summer." The school's maintenance records report that rats were found in eleven classrooms. Rat droppings were found "in the bins and drawers" of the high school's kitchen, and school records note that "hamburger buns" were being "eaten off [the] bread-delivery rack."

No matter how many tawdry details like these I've read in legal briefs 77 or depositions through the years, I'm always shocked again to learn how often these unsanitary physical conditions are permitted to continue in the schools that serve our poorest students — even after they have been vividly described in the media. But hearing of these conditions in Mireya's words was even more unsettling, in part because this student seemed so fragile and because the need even to speak of these indignities in front of me and all the other students was an additional indignity.

"The problem is this," she carefully explained. "You're not allowed to 78 use the bathroom during lunch, which is a thirty-minute period. The only time that you're allowed to use it is between your classes." But "this is a huge building," she went on. "It has long corridors. If you have one class at one end of the building and your next class happens to be way down at the other end, you don't have time to use the bathroom and still get to class before it starts. So you go to your class and then you ask permission from your teacher to go to the bathroom and the teacher tells you, 'No. You had your chance between the periods . . .'

"I feel embarrassed when I have to stand there and explain it to a 79 teacher."

"This is the question," said a wiry-looking boy named Edward, leaning 80 forward in his chair. "Students are not animals, but even animals need to relieve themselves sometimes. We're here for eight hours. What do they think we're supposed to do?"

"It humiliates you," said Mireya, who went on to make the interesting 81 statement that "the school provides solutions that don't actually work," and this idea was taken up by several other students in describing course requirements within the school. A tall black student, for example, told me that she hoped to be a social worker or a doctor but was programmed into "Sewing Class" this year. She also had to take another course, called "Life Skills," which she told me was a very basic course — "a retarded class," to use her words — that "teaches things like the six continents," which she said she'd learned in elementary school.

When I asked her why she had to take these courses, she replied that 82 she'd been told they were required, which as I later learned was not exactly so. What was required was that high school students take two courses in an area of study called "The Technical Arts," and which the Los Angeles Board of Education terms "Applied Technology." At schools that served the middle class or upper-middle class, this requirement was likely to be met by courses that had academic substance and, perhaps, some relevance to college preparation. At Beverly Hills High School, for example, the technical-arts requirement could be fulfilled by taking subjects like residential architecture, the designing of commercial structures, broadcast journalism, advanced computer graphics, a sophisticated course in furniture design, carving and sculpture, or an honors course in engineering research and design. At Fremont High, in contrast, this requirement was far more often met by courses that were basically vocational and also obviously keyed to low-paying levels of employment.

Mireya, for example, who had plans to go to college, told me that she 83 had to take a sewing class last year and now was told she'd been assigned to take a class in hairdressing as well. When I asked her teacher why Mireya could not skip these subjects and enroll in classes that would help her to pursue her college aspirations, she replied, "It isn't a question of what students want. It's what the school may have available. If all the other elective classes that a student wants to take are full, she has to take one of these classes if she wants to graduate."

A very small girl named Obie, who had big blue-tinted glasses 84 tilted up across her hair, interrupted then to tell me with a kind of wild gusto that she'd taken hairdressing *twice*! When I expressed surprise that this was possible, she said there were two levels of hairdressing offered here at Fremont High. "One is in hairstyling," she said. "The other is in braiding."

Mireya stared hard at this student for a moment and then suddenly began to cry. "I don't *want* to take hairdressing. I did not need sewing either. I knew how to sew. My mother is a seamstress in a factory. I'm trying to go to college. I don't need to sew to go to college. My mother sews. I hoped for something else." 85

"What would you rather take?" I asked. 86

"I wanted to take an AP class," she answered. 87

Mireya's sudden tears elicited a strong reaction from one of the boys who had been silent up till now: a thin, dark-eyed student named Fortino, who had long hair down to his shoulders. He suddenly turned directly to Mireya and spoke into the silence that followed her last words. 88

"Listen to me," he said. "The owners of the sewing factories need laborers. Correct?" 89

"I guess they do," Mireya said. 90

"It's not going to be their own kids. Right?" 91

"Why not?" another student said. 92

"So they can grow beyond themselves," Mireya answered quietly. "But we remain the same." 93

"You're ghetto," said Fortino, "so we send you to the factory." He sat low in his desk chair, leaning on one elbow, his voice and dark eyes loaded with a cynical intelligence. "You're ghetto — so you sew!" 94

"There are higher positions than these," said a student named Samantha. 95

"You're ghetto," said Fortino unrelentingly. "So sew!" 96

Admittedly, the economic needs of a society are bound to be reflected to some rational degree within the policies and purposes of public schools. But, even so, there must be *something* more to life as it is lived by six-year-olds or ten-year-olds, or by teenagers, for that matter, than concerns about "successful global competition." Childhood is not merely basic training for utilitarian adulthood. It should have some claims upon our mercy, not for its future value to the economic interests of competitive societies but for its present value as a perishable piece of life itself. 97

Very few people who are not involved with inner-city schools have any real idea of the extremes to which the mercantile distortion of the purposes and character of education have been taken or how unabashedly proponents of these practices are willing to defend them. The head of a Chicago school, for instance, who was criticized by some for emphasizing rote instruction that, his critics said, was turning children into "robots," found no reason to dispute the charge. "Did you ever stop to think that these robots will never burglarize your home?" he asked, and "will never snatch your pocketbooks. . . . These robots are going to be producing taxes." 98

Corporate leaders, when they speak of education, sometimes pay *99*
lip-service to the notion of "good critical and analytic skills," but it is reasonable to ask whether they have in mind the critical analysis of *their* priorities. In principle, perhaps some do; but, if so, this is not a principle that
seems to have been honored widely in the schools I have been visiting. In
all the various business-driven inner-city classrooms I have observed in the
past five years, plastered as they are with corporation brand names and
managerial vocabularies, I have yet to see the two words "labor unions." Is
this an oversight? How is that possible? Teachers and principals themselves, who are almost always members of a union, seem to be so beaten
down that they rarely even question this omission.

It is not at all unusual these days to come into an urban school in *100*
which the principal prefers to call himself or herself "building CEO" or
"building manager." In some of the same schools teachers are described as
"classroom managers."[3] I have never been in a suburban district in which
principals were asked to view themselves or teachers in this way. These ter-
minologies remind us of how wide the distance has become between two
very separate worlds of education.

It has been more than a decade now since drill-based literacy methods *101*
like Success for All began to proliferate in our urban schools. It has been
three and a half years since the systems of assessment that determine the
effectiveness of these and similar practices were codified in the federal legislation, No Child Left Behind, that President Bush signed into law in
2002. Since the enactment of this bill, the number of standardized exams
children must take has more than doubled. It will probably increase again
after the year 2006, when standardized tests, which are now required in
grades three through eight, may be required in Head Start programs and,
as President Bush has now proposed, in ninth, tenth, and eleventh grades
as well.

---

[3]A school I visited three years ago in Columbus, Ohio, was littered with "Help
Wanted" signs. Starting in kindergarten, children in the school were being asked to think
about the jobs that they might choose when they grew up. In one classroom there was a
poster that displayed the names of several retail stores: J. C. Penney, Wal-Mart, Kmart,
Sears, and a few others. "It's like working in a store," a classroom aide explained. "The
children are learning to pretend they're cashiers." At another school in the same district,
children were encouraged to apply for jobs in their classrooms. Among the job positions
open to the children in this school, there was an "Absence Manager" and a "Behavior
Chart Manager," a "Form Collector Manager," a "Paper Passer Outer Manager," a "Paper
Collecting Manager," a "Paper Returning Manager," an "Exit Ticket Manager," even a
"Learning Manager," a "Reading Corner Manager," and a "Score Keeper Manager."
I asked the principal if there was a special reason why those two words "management"
and "manager" kept popping up throughout the school. "We want every child to be working as a manager while he or she is in this school," the principal explained. "We want to
make them understand that, in this country, companies will give you opportunities to
work, to prove yourself, no matter what you've done." I wasn't sure what she meant by "no
matter what you've done," and asked her if she could explain it. "Even if you have a felony
arrest," she said, "we want you to understand that you can be a manager someday."

The elements of strict accountability, in short, are solidly in place; and *102* in many states where the present federal policies are simply reinforcements of accountability requirements that were established long before the passage of the federal law, the same regimen has been in place since 1995 or even earlier. The "tests-and-standards" partisans have had things very much their way for an extended period of time, and those who were convinced that they had ascertained "what works" in schools that serve minorities and children of the poor have had ample opportunity to prove that they were right.

What, then, it is reasonable to ask, are the results? *103*

The achievement gap between black and white children, which nar- *104* rowed for three decades up until the late years of the 1980s — the period in which school segregation steadily decreased — started to widen once more in the early 1990s when the federal courts began the process of re-segregation by dismantling the mandates of the *Brown* decision. From that point on, the gap continued to widen or remained essentially unchanged; and while recently there has been a modest narrowing of the gap in reading scores for fourth-grade children, the gap in secondary school remains as wide as ever.

The media inevitably celebrate the periodic upticks that a set of scores *105* may seem to indicate in one year or another in achievement levels of black and Hispanic children in their elementary schools. But if these upticks were not merely temporary "testing gains" achieved by test-prep regimens and were instead authentic education gains, they would carry over into middle school and high school. Children who know how to read — and read with comprehension — do not suddenly become nonreaders and hopelessly disabled writers when they enter secondary school. False gains evaporate; real gains endure. Yet hundreds of thousands of the inner-city children who have made what many districts claim to be dramatic gains in elementary school, and whose principals and teachers have adjusted almost every aspect of their school days and school calendars, forfeiting recess, canceling or cutting back on all the so-called frills (art, music, even social sciences) in order to comply with state demands those students, now in secondary school, are sitting in subject-matter classes where they cannot comprehend the texts and cannot set down their ideas in the kind of sentences expected of most fourth- and fifth-grade students in the suburbs. Students in this painful situation, not surprisingly, tend to be most likely to drop out of school.

In 48 percent of high schools in the nation's 100 largest districts, *106* which are those in which the highest concentrations of black and Hispanic students tend to be enrolled, less than half the entering ninth-graders graduate in four years. Nationwide, from 1993 to 2002, the number of high schools graduating less than half their ninth-grade class in four years has increased by 75 percent. In the 94 percent of districts in New York State where white children make up the majority, nearly 80 percent of students graduate from high school in four years. In the 6 percent of districts where black and Hispanic students make up the majority, only 40 percent do so. There are 120 high schools in New York, enrolling nearly 200,000 minority students, where less than 60 percent of entering ninth-graders even make it to twelfth grade.

The promulgation of new and expanded inventories of "what works," no matter the enthusiasm with which they're elaborated, is not going to change this. The use of hortatory slogans chanted by the students in our segregated schools is not going to change this. Desperate historical revisionism that romanticizes the segregation of an older order (this is a common theme of many separatists today) is not going to change this. Skinnerian instructional approaches, which decapitate a child's capability for critical reflection, are not going to change this. Posters about "global competition" will certainly not change this. Turning six-year-olds into examination soldiers and denying eight-year-olds their time for play at recess will not change this.

107

"I went to Washington to challenge the soft bigotry of low expectations," said President Bush in his campaign for reelection in September 2004. "It's working. It's making a difference." Here we have one of those deadly lies that by sheer repetition is at length accepted by surprisingly large numbers of Americans. But it is not the truth; and it is not an innocent misstatement of the facts. It is a devious appeasement of the heartache of the parents of the black and brown and poor, and if it is not forcefully resisted it will lead us further in a very dangerous direction.

108

Whether the issue is inequity alone or deepening resegregation or the labyrinthine intertwining of the two, it is well past the time for us to start the work that it will take to change this. If it takes people marching in the streets and other forms of adamant disruption of the governing civilities, if it takes more than litigation, more than legislation, and much more than resolutions introduced by members of Congress, these are prices we should be prepared to pay. "We do not have the things you have," Alliyah told me when she wrote to ask if I would come and visit her school in the South Bronx. "Can you help us?" America owes that little girl and millions like her a more honorable answer than they have received.

109

■ ■ ■

Reading Rhetorically

1. How would you describe Kozol's relationship to the people who are the subject of his essay? How does this relationship work to his advantage, or disadvantage, as he builds his argument? Be prepared to point to and explain several passages that support your responses to these questions.

2. How do the direct quotations from his subjects contribute to Kozol's essay? Locate at least three examples and his analysis of them, and be ready to discuss the function they serve in the essay. You might consider, for example, how Kozol plays the voices of the students against the voices of teachers, administrators, and others.

3. Who is Kozol's audience? How can you tell? Identify specific passages that indicate who Kozol is targeting and why. You might find it helpful to look for the counterarguments Kozol addresses, the kinds of sources and references he uses to make his argument, and the examples he uses to illustrate his points.

Inquiring Further

4. Kozol describes the educational methods he witnesses in the city schools as "Skinnerian" (para. 44), referring to the ideas of behaviorist B. F. Skinner. Do some research on Skinner to find out what his principal theories were. Do you think Kozol's description of the educational methods as Skinnerian is accurate or fair? Why or why not? Is all education to some extent Skinnerian? What do you think a non-Skinnerian education would look like?

5. What effect has No Child Left Behind had on local schools? Interview at least two specialists in primary and secondary education at your university or in the local school system to learn what your area's experts believe about the impact of the policy. What do you conclude, based on their responses and Kozol's claims?

6. Kozol refers to two historical court cases as he builds his argument about what is troubling inner-city schools: *Plessy v. Ferguson* (1896) and *Brown v. Board of Education* (1954). Brainstorm in class to discover what you already know — and don't know — about these significant court rulings. Then split into groups to research one of the cases. Each group's assignment: to bring at least three new pieces of information about the ruling to the class. Why do you think Kozol draws on these cases in this article?

Framing Conversations

7. Kozol and bell hooks (p. 293) both describe teacher-student dynamics in racially segregated schools. Write an essay in which you analyze the similarities and differences in the points they raise and the conclusions they draw about the problems and potential of education in America. Where do you stand on the issues they raise?

8. In his essay, Kozol notes that certain school districts claim a diverse population, but he reveals what he calls the "eviscerated meaning of the word" (para. 10). Ann duCille (p. 458) is also interested in the ways that terms related to multiculturalism and diversity are often euphemisms for something else. Drawing on both Kozol's and duCille's points about how the language of diversity and multiculturalism is used and misused, write an essay in which you consider the significance of this dynamic in the contemporary United States. Include your own analysis of Kozol's and duCille's examples and any other examples that can help you make your point.

9. Like Kozol, Noel Ignatiev (p. 512) is interested in changing assumptions about race in the United States. Write an essay in which you use several of Ignatiev's insights about the history of racial categories in America as a tool for analyzing the dynamics Kozol finds in inner-city schools today.

What significance do you see in the intersection between education and race in these institutions?

■ JAMES W. LOEWEN ────────────────────────────

From Lies My Teacher Told Me: Everything Your American History Textbook Got Wrong

James W. Loewen was a professor of sociology at the University of Vermont for twenty years; today he continues his research and teaching in Washington, D.C., where his academic focus is on the history and the sociology of U.S. race relations. He is the recipient of many awards, including the American Book Award (for *Lies My Teacher Told Me*) and the Oliver Cromwell Cox Award for Distinguished Anti-Racist Scholarship. Loewen's commitment to applying his research to real people's lives is evident in his serving as an expert witness in more than fifty civil rights, voting rights, and employment lawsuits. He is also a popular campus lecturer, as you can tell from a quick Internet search of his name. Loewen is an expert at surprising his readers and audiences with historical facts most of us never learned and teaching us what history books get wrong and why we should care.

Loewen is the author of *Lies Across America: What our Historic Sites Get Wrong* (1999), an ironic look at the many mistakes etched on historical markers across the United States. He considers the absurdity of many of the claims historical sites make, and leads readers to consider the implications of those often self-interested versions of history. Another one of his award-winning books is *Sundown Towns: A Hidden Dimension of American Racism* (2005), an examination of the 3,000 to 15,000 independent towns in the United States between 1890 and 1930 that Loewen believes adopted all-white policies to keep blacks out of town in the evenings. He coedited (with Nathaniel May and Clint Willis) the book *We Are the People: Voices from the Other Side of American History* (2003), a collection of letters, personal accounts, and essays from those whose stories are largely left out of U.S. history textbooks — slaves, women, Native Americans, and the poor. The fact that one of his books, *Mississippi: Conflict and Change* (1974), which won the Lillian Smith Award for Best Southern Nonfiction, was rejected by Mississippi for use in the public schools should alert us to the high stakes involved in deciding which version of history to tell. The situation led to an important First Amendment case, *Loewen v. Turnipseed* (1980) and to the eventual adoption of the book by Mississippi.

The reading here is drawn from Loewen's best-known book, *Lies My Teacher Told Me: Everything Your American History Textbook Got Wrong* (1996). The epigraphs leading into the introduction give you a sense of his tone, as he moves from serious quotations to his own twist on a familiar saying: "Those who don't remember the past are condemned to repeat the eleventh grade." As a writer, Loewen is very sensitive to his readers: Notice, for example, the empathy he shows bored high school students in the first paragraph. As you read, pay particular attention to the ways he anticipates readers who might be skeptical, and consider why he might offer such extensive and detailed footnotes to support his claims.

Although Loewen is troubled by most American students' lack of knowledge about U.S. history and their lack of curiosity, he does not blame the students themselves. Rather, he examines the ways textbooks present half-truths (and even untruths) as if they were the whole story, so that students rarely consider asking what might lie underneath claims that America was first settled in 1620, for example. While you read, keep in mind how and what you learned about American history, from Thanksgiving-themed crafts in primary school to your high school history survey classes. What do you find especially surprising in Loewen's new look at old "facts"? And do you agree with Loewen's reasons why the truth matters?

Introduction: Something Has Gone Very Wrong

It would be better not to know so many things than to know so many things that are not so.

— Felix Okoye[1]

American history is longer, larger, more various, more beautiful, and more terrible than anything anyone has ever said about it.

— James Baldwin[2]

Concealment of the historical truth is a crime against the people.

— Gen. Petro G. Grigorenko,
Samizdat letter to a history journal, c. 1975, USSR[3]

Those who don't remember the past are condemned to repeat the eleventh grade.

— James W. Loewen

High school students hate history. When they list their favorite sub-jects, history invariably comes in last: Students consider history "the most irrelevant" of twenty-one subjects commonly taught in high school. *Bor-r-ring* is the adjective they apply to it. When students can, they avoid it, even though most students get higher grades in history than in math,

[1]Felix Okoye, *The American Image of Africa: Myth and Reality* (Buffalo, N.Y.: Black Academy Press, 1971), 3.

[2]James Baldwin, "A Talk to Teachers," *Saturday Review*, December 21, 1963, reprinted in Rick Simonson and Scott Walker, eds., *Multicultural Literacy* (St. Paul, Minn.: Graywolf Press, 1988), 11.

[3]Gen. Petro G. Grigorenko, quoted in Robert Slusser, "History and the Democratic Opposition," in Rudolf L. Tökés, ed., *Dissent in the USSR* (Baltimore: Johns Hopkins University Press, 1975), 329–53.

science, or English.[4] Even when they are forced to take classes in history, they repress what they learn, so every year or two another study decries what our seventeen-year-olds don't know.[5]

African American, Native American, and Latino students view history 2 with a special dislike. They also learn history especially poorly. Students of color do only slightly worse than white students in mathematics. If you'll pardon my grammar, nonwhite students do more worse in English and most worse in history.[6] Something intriguing is going on here: surely history is not more difficult for minorities than trigonometry or Faulkner. Students don't even know they are alienated, only that they "don't *like* social studies" or "aren't any good at history." In college, most students of color give history departments a wide berth.

Many history teachers perceive the low morale in their classrooms. If 3 they have a lot of time, light domestic responsibilities, sufficient resources, and a flexible principal, some teachers respond by abandoning the over-stuffed textbooks and reinventing their American history courses. All too many teachers grow disheartened and settle for less. At least dimly aware that their students are not requiting their own love of history, these teachers withdraw some of their energy from their courses. Gradually they end up going through the motions, staying ahead of their students in the textbooks, covering only material that will appear on the next test.

College teachers in most disciplines are happy when their students 4 have had significant exposure to the subject before college. Not teachers in history. History professors in college routinely put down high school history courses. A colleague of mine calls his survey of American history "Iconoclasm I and II," because he sees his job as disabusing his charges of what they learned in high school. In no other field does this happen. Mathematics professors, for instance, know that non-Euclidean geometry is rarely taught in high school, but they don't assume that Euclidean geometry was *mistaught.* Professors of English literature don't presume that

---

[4]I use the term *history* as encompassing social studies, as do most researchers and students. When the distinction is important, I will make it. Robert Reinhold, Harris Poll, reported in *New York Times*, July 3, 1971, and quoted in Herbert Aptheker, *The Unfolding Drama* (New York: International, 1978), 146; Terry Borton, *The Weekly Reader National Survey on Education* (Middletown, Conn.: Field Publications, 1985), 14, 16; Mark Schug, Robert Todd, and R. Beery, "Why Kids Don't Like Social Studies," *Social Education* 48 (May 1984): 382–87; Albert Shanker, "The 'Efficient' Diploma Mill," paid column in *New York Times*, February 14, 1988; Joan M. Shaughnessy and Thomas M. Haladyna, "Research on Student Attitudes Toward Social Studies," *Social Education* 49 (November 1985): 692–95. National grade averages in *1992 ACT Assessment Results, Summary Report, Mississippi* (Iowa City: ACT, 1993), 7.

[5]Diane Ravitch and Chester E. Finn, Jr., *What Do Our 17-Year-Olds Know?* (New York: Harper and Row, 1987); National Geographic Society, *Geography: An International Gallup Survey* (Washington, D.C.: National Geographic Society, 1988).

[6]Richard L. Sawyer, "College Student Profiles: Norms for the ACT Assessment, 1980–81" (Iowa City: ACT, 1980). Sawyer finds larger differences by race and income in social studies than in English, mathematics, and the natural sciences.

Romeo and Juliet was misunderstood in high school. Indeed, history is the only field in which the more courses students take, the stupider they become.

Perhaps I do not need to convince you that American history is impor- [5] tant. More than any other topic, it is about *us*. Whether one deems our present society wondrous or awful or both, history reveals how we arrived at this point. Understanding our past is central to our ability to understand ourselves and the world around us. We need to know our history, and according to C. Wright Mills, we know we do.[7]

Outside of school, Americans show great interest in history. Historical [6] novels, whether by Gore Vidal (*Lincoln, Burr,* et al.) or Dana Fuller Ross (*Idaho!, Utah!, Nebraska!, Oregon!, Missouri!,* and on! and on!) often become bestsellers. The National Museum of American History is one of the three big draws of the Smithsonian Institution. The series "The Civil War" attracted new audiences to public television. Movies based on historical incidents or themes are a continuing source of fascination, from *Birth of a Nation* through *Gone with the Wind* to *Dances with Wolves* and *JFK*.

Our situation is this: American history is full of fantastic and impor- [7] tant stories. These stories have the power to spellbind audiences, even audiences of difficult seventh-graders. These same stories show what America has been about and are directly relevant to our present society. American audiences, even young ones, need and want to know about their national past. Yet they sleep through the classes that present it.

What has gone wrong? [8]

We begin to get a handle on this question by noting that the teaching [9] of history, more than any other discipline, is dominated by textbooks.[8] And students are right: the books are boring.[9] The stories that history textbooks tell are predictable; every problem has already been solved or is about to be solved. Textbooks exclude conflict or real suspense. They leave out anything that might reflect badly upon our national character. When they try for drama, they achieve only melodrama, because readers know that everything will turn out fine in the end. "Despite setbacks, the United States overcame these challenges," in the words of one textbook. Most

---

[7]Years ago Mills discerned that Americans feel a need to locate themselves in social structure in order to understand the forces that shape their society and themselves. See C. Wright Mills, *The Sociological Imagination* (New York: Oxford University Press, 1959), 3–20.

[8]Paul Goldstein, *Changing the American Schoolbook* (Lexington, Mass.: D. C. Heath, 1978). Goldstein says textbooks are the organizing principle for more than 75 percent of classroom time. In history, the proportion is even higher.

[9]Mel Gabler's right-wing textbook critics and I concur that textbooks are boring. Mrs. W. Kelley Haralson writes, "The censoring of emotionalism from history texts during the last half century has resulted in history textbooks which are boring to students." "Objections [to *The American Adventure*]" (Longview, Tex.: Educational Research Analysts, n.d.), 4. We part company in our proposed solutions, however, for the only emotion that Gabler and his allies seem to want to add is pride.

authors of history textbooks don't even try for melodrama. Instead, they write in a tone that if heard aloud might be described as "mumbling lecturer." No wonder students lose interest.

Textbooks almost never use the present to illuminate the past. They *10* might ask students to consider gender roles in contemporary society as a means of prompting students to think about what women did and did not achieve in the suffrage movement or in the more recent women's movement. They might ask students to prepare household budgets for the families of a janitor and a stockbroker as a means of prompting thinking about labor unions and social classes in the past and present. They might, but they don't. The present is not a source of information for writers of history textbooks.

Conversely, textbooks seldom use the past to illuminate the present. *11* They portray the past as a simple-minded morality play. "Be a good citizen" is the message that textbooks extract from the past. "You have a proud heritage. Be all that you can be. After all, look at what the United States has accomplished." While there is nothing wrong with optimism, it can become something of a burden for students of color, children of working-class parents, girls who notice the dearth of female historical figures, or members of any group that has not achieved socioeconomic success. The optimistic approach prevents any understanding of failure other than blaming the victim. No wonder children of color are alienated. Even for male children from affluent white families, bland optimism gets pretty boring after eight hundred pages.

Textbooks in American history stand in sharp contrast to other teach- *12* ing materials. Why are history textbooks so bad? Nationalism is one of the culprits. Textbooks are often muddled by the conflicting desires to promote inquiry and to indoctrinate blind patriotism. "Take a look in your history book, and you'll see why we should be proud," goes an anthem often sung by high school glee clubs. But we need not even look inside.[10] The titles themselves tell the story: *The Great Republic, The American Way, Land of Promise, Rise of the American Nation.*[11] Such titles differ from the titles of all other textbooks students read in high school or college. Chemistry books, for example, are called *Chemistry* or *Principles of Chemistry,* not *Rise of the Molecule.* And you can tell history textbooks just from their covers, graced as they are with American flags, bald eagles, the Statue of Liberty.

Between the glossy covers, American history textbooks are full of *13* information — overly full. These books are huge. The specimens in my collection of a dozen of the most popular textbooks average four and a half pounds in weight and 888 pages in length. No publisher wants to lose an

---

[10]"It's a Great Country," sung with pride by a high school choir from Webster Groves, Missouri, in a CBS News videotape, *Sixteen in Webster Groves* (New York: Carousel Films, 1966).

[11]In the aftermath of the Vietnam War, Harcourt Brace renamed this last one *Triumph of the American Nation.* This is the Rambo approach to history: We may have lost the war in Southeast Asia, but we'll win it on the book jackets!

adoption because a book has left out a detail of concern to a particular geographical area or a particular group. Textbook authors seem compelled to include a paragraph about every U.S. president, even Chester A. Arthur and Millard Fillmore. Then there are the review pages at the end of each chapter. *Land of Promise*, to take one example, enumerates 444 chapter-closing "Main Ideas." In addition, the book lists literally thousands of "Skill Activities," "Key Terms," "Matching" items, "Fill in the Blanks," "Thinking Critically" questions, and "Review Identifications," as well as still more "Main Ideas" at the ends of the various sections within each chapter. At year's end, no student can remember 444 main ideas, not to mention 624 key terms and countless other "factoids." So students and teachers fall back on one main idea: to memorize the terms for the test following each chapter, then forget them to clear the synapses for the next chapter. No wonder so many high school graduates cannot remember in which century the Civil War was fought![12]

None of the facts is remembered, because they are presented simply as *14* one damn thing after another. While textbook authors tend to include most of the trees and all too many twigs, they neglect to give readers even a glimpse of what they might find memorable: the forests. Textbooks stifle meaning by suppressing causation. Students exit history textbooks without having developed the ability to think coherently about social life.

Even though the books bulge with detail, even though the courses are *15* so busy they rarely reach 1960, our teachers and our textbooks still leave out most of what we need to know about the American past. Some of the factoids they present are flatly wrong or unverifiable. In sum, startling errors of omission and distortion mar American histories.

Errors in history textbooks often go uncorrected, partly because the his- *16* tory profession does not bother to review textbooks. Occasionally outsiders do: Frances FitzGerald's 1979 study, *America Revised*, was a bestseller, but it made no impact on the industry. In pointing out how textbooks ignored or distorted the Spanish impact on Latin America and the colonial United States, FitzGerald predicted, "Text publishers may now be on the verge of rewriting history." But she was wrong — the books have not changed.[13]

History can be imagined as a pyramid. At its base are the millions of *17* primary sources — the plantation records, city directories, speeches, songs, photographs, newspaper articles, diaries, and letters that document times past. Based on these primary materials, historians write secondary works — books and articles on subjects ranging from deafness on Martha's Vineyard to Grant's tactics at Vicksburg. Historians produce hundreds of these works every year, many of them splendid. In theory, a few historians, working individually or in teams, then synthesize the secondary literature into tertiary works — textbooks covering all phases of U.S. history.

In practice, however, it doesn't happen that way. Instead, history *18* textbooks are clones of each other. The first thing editors do when

---

[12]Ravitch and Finn, *What Do Our 17-Year-Olds Know?*, 49.
[13]Frances FitzGerald, *America Revised* (New York: Vintage, 1980 [1979]), 93–97.

recruiting new authors is to send them a half-dozen examples of the competition. Often a textbook is written not by the authors whose names grace its cover, but by minions deep in the bowels of the publisher's offices. When historians do write textbooks, they risk snickers from their colleagues — tinged with envy, but snickers nonetheless: "Why are you devoting time to pedagogy rather than original research?"

The result is not happy for textbook scholarship. Many history text-   *19* books list up-to-the-minute secondary sources in their bibliographies, yet the narratives remain totally traditional — unaffected by recent research.[14]

What would we think of a course in poetry in which students never   *20* read a poem? The editor's voice in an English literature textbook might be as dull as the voice in a history textbook, but at least in the English textbook the voice stills when the book presents original works of literature. The omniscient narrator's voice of history textbooks insulates students from the raw materials of history. Rarely do authors quote speeches, songs, diaries, or letters. Students need not be protected from this material. They can just as well read one paragraph from William Jennings Bryan's "Cross of Gold" speech as read *American Adventures*'s two paragraphs *about* it.

Textbooks also keep students in the dark about the nature of history.   *21* History is furious debate informed by evidence and reason. Textbooks encourage students to believe that history is facts to be learned. "We have not avoided controversial issues," announces one set of textbook authors; "instead, we have tried to offer reasoned judgments" on them — thus removing the controversy! Because textbooks employ such a godlike tone, it never occurs to most students to question them. "In retrospect I ask myself, why *didn't* I think to ask, for example, who *were* the original inhabitants of the Americas, what was *their* life like, and how did it change when Columbus arrived," wrote a student of mine in 1991. "However, back then everything was presented as if it were the full picture," she continued, "so I never thought to doubt that it was."

As a result of all this, most high school seniors are hamstrung in their   *22* efforts to analyze controversial issues in our society. (I know because I encounter these students the next year as college freshmen.) We've got to do better. Five-sixths of all Americans never take a course in American history beyond high school. What our citizens "learn" in high school forms much of what they know about our past. . . .

The Truth about the First Thanksgiving

Considering that virtually none of the standard fare surrounding Thanksgiving contains an ounce of authenticity, historical accuracy, or cross-cultural

[14]James Axtell, "Europeans, Indians, and the Age of Discovery in American History Textbooks," *American Historical Review* 92 (1987): 627. Essays such as Axtell's, which review college-level textbooks, rarely appear in history journals. Almost never are high school textbooks reviewed.

perception, why is it so apparently ingrained? Is it necessary to the American psyche to perpetually exploit and debase its victims in order to justify its history?

— Michael Dorris[15]

European explorers and invaders discovered an inhabited land. Had it been pristine wilderness then, it would possibly be so still, for neither the technology nor the social organization of Europe in the 16th and 17th centuries had the capacity to maintain, of its own resources, outpost colonies thousands of miles from home.

— Francis Jennings[16]

The Europeans were able to conquer America not because of their military genius, or their religious motivation, or their ambition, or their greed. They conquered it by waging unpremeditated biological warfare.

— Howard Simpson[17]

It is painful to advert to these things. But our forefathers, though wise, pious, and sincere, were nevertheless, in respect to Christian charity, under a cloud; and, in history, truth should be held sacred, at whatever cost . . . especially against the narrow and futile patriotism, which, instead of pressing forward in pursuit of truth, takes pride in walking backwards to cover the slightest nakedness of our forefathers.

— Col. Thomas Aspinwall[18]

Over the last few years, I have asked hundreds of college students, "When was the country we now know as the United States first settled?" This is a generous way of phrasing the question; surely "we now know as" implies that the original settlement antedated the founding of the United States. I initially believed — certainly I had hoped — that students would suggest 30,000 B.C., or some other pre-Columbian date.   23

They did not. Their consensus answer was "1620."   24

Obviously, my students' heads have been filled with America's origin myth, the story of the first Thanksgiving. Textbooks are among the retailers of this primal legend.   25

Part of the problem is the word *settle*. "Settlers" were white, a student once pointed out to me. "Indians" didn't settle. Students are not the only people misled by *settle*. The film that introduces visitors to Plimoth Plantation tells how "they went about the work of civilizing a hostile wilderness." One recent Thanksgiving weekend I listened as a guide at the Statue of Liberty talked about European immigrants "populating a wild   26

[15]Michael Dorris, "Why I'm Not Thankful for Thanksgiving" (New York: Council on Interracial Books for Children *Bulletin* 9, no. 7, 1978): 7.

[16]Francis Jennings, *The Invasion of America: Indians, Colonialism, and the Cant of Conquest* (Chapel Hill: University of North Carolina Press, 1975), 15.

[17]Howard Simpson, *Invisible Armies: The Impact of Disease on American History* (Indianapolis: Bobbs-Merrill, 1980), 2.

[18]Col. Thomas Aspinwall, quoted in Jennings, *The Invasion of America*, 175.

East Coast." As we shall see, however, if Indians hadn't already settled New England, Europeans would have had a much tougher job of it.

Starting the story of America's settlement with the Pilgrims leaves out 27 not only the Indians but also the Spanish. The very first non-Native settlers in "the country we now know as the United States" were African slaves left in South Carolina in 1526 by Spaniards who abandoned a settlement attempt. In 1565 the Spanish massacred the French Protestants who had settled briefly at St. Augustine, Florida, and established their own fort there. Some later Spanish settlers were our first pilgrims, seeking regions new to them to secure religious liberty: these were Spanish Jews, who settled in New Mexico in the late 1500s.[19] Few Americans know that one-third of the United States, from San Francisco to Arkansas to Natchez to Florida, has been Spanish longer than it has been "American," and that Hispanic Americans lived here before the first ancestor of the Daughters of the American Revolution ever left England. Moreover, Spanish culture left an indelible mark on the American West. The Spanish introduced horses, cattle, sheep, pigs, and the basic elements of cowboy culture, including its vocabulary: *mustang, bronco, rodeo, lariat,* and so on.[20] Horses that escaped from the Spanish and propagated triggered the rapid flowering of a new culture among the Plains Indians. "How refreshing it would be," wrote James Axtell, "to find a textbook that began on the West Coast before treating the traditional eastern colonies."[21]

Beginning the story in 1620 also omits the Dutch, who were living in 28 what is now Albany by 1614. Indeed, 1620 is not even the date of the first permanent British settlement, for in 1607, the London Company sent settlers to Jamestown, Virginia.

No matter. The *mythic* origin of "the country we now know as the 29 United States" is at Plymouth Rock, and the year is 1620. Here is a representative account from *The American Tradition:*

> After some exploring, the Pilgrims chose the land around Plymouth Harbor for their settlement. Unfortunately, they had arrived in December and were not prepared for the New England winter. However, they were aided by friendly Indians, who gave them food and showed them how to grow corn. When warm weather came, the colonists planted, fished, hunted, and prepared themselves for the next winter. After harvesting their first crop, they and their Indian friends celebrated the first Thanksgiving.[22]

[19]Kathleen Teltsch. "Scholars and Descendants Uncover Hidden Legacy of Jews in Southwest," *New York Times,* November 11, 1990, A30: "Hidden Jews of the Southwest," *Groundrock,* Spring 1992.

[20]Alfred W. Crosby, Jr., *The Columbian Exchange: Biological and Cultural Consequences of 1492* (Westport, Conn.: Greenwood, 1972), 83. Our cowboy culture's Spanish origin explains why it is so similar to the gaucho tradition of Argentina.

[21]James Axtell, "Europeans, Indians, and the Age of Discovery in American History Textbooks," 630.

[22]The passage is basically accurate, although the winter of 1620–21 was not particularly harsh and probably did not surprise the British, and Indians did not assist them until spring.

My students also remember that the Pilgrims had been persecuted in *30*
England for their religious beliefs, so they had moved to Holland. They
sailed on the *Mayflower* to America and wrote the Mayflower Compact, the
forerunner to our Constitution, according to my students. Times were
rough, until they met Squanto, who taught them how to put a small fish as
fertilizer in each little cornhill, ensuring a bountiful harvest. But when I
ask my students about the plague, they just stare back at me. "What plague?
The Black Plague?" No, I sigh, that was three centuries earlier. . . .

About the plagues the textbooks tell even less. Only three of the twelve *31*
textbooks even mention Indian disease as a factor at Plymouth or anywhere in New England.[23] *Life and Liberty* does quite a good job. *The
American Way* is the only book that draws the appropriate geopolitical
inference about the Plymouth outbreak, but it doesn't discuss any of the
other plagues that beset Indians throughout the hemisphere. According to
Triumph of the American Nation: "If the Pilgrims had arrived at Plymouth a
few years earlier, they would have found a busy Indian village surrounded
by farmland. As it was, an epidemic had wiped out most of the Indians.
Those who survived had abandoned the village." "Fortunately for the
Pilgrims," *Triumph* goes on, "the cleared fields remained, and a brook of
fresh water flowed into the harbor." These four sentences exemplify what
Michael W. Apple and Linda K. Christian-Smith call dominance through
mentioning.[24] The passage can hardly offend Pilgrim descendants, yet it
gives the publisher deniability — *Triumph* cannot be accused of omitting
the plague. But the sentences bury the plague within a description of the
beautiful harbor at Plymouth. Therefore, even though gory details of disease and death are exactly the kinds of things that high school students
remember best, the plague won't "stick." I know, because I never remembered the plague, and my college textbook mentioned it — in a fourteen-
word passage nestled within a paragraph about the Pilgrims' belief in
God.[25]

In colonial times, everyone knew about the plague. Even before the *32*
Mayflower sailed, King James of England gave thanks to "Almighty God in
his great goodness and bounty towards us" for sending "this wonderful
plague among the salvages [*sic*]."[26] Two hundred years later the oldest
American history in my collection — J. W. Barber's *Interesting Events in
the History of the United States*, published in 1829 — still recalled the
plague.

> A few years before the arrival of the Plymouth settlers, a very mortal sickness
> raged with great violence among the Indians inhabiting the eastern parts of

[23]A paragraph in *The American Pageant* does tell of the 90 percent toll throughout
the hemisphere but leaves out any mention of the plague at Plymouth.

[24]Michael W. Apple and Linda K. Christian-Smith, *The Politics of the Textbook* (New
York: Routledge, 1991), 66.

[25]Richard Hofstadter, William Miller, and Daniel Aaron, *The American Republic*
(Englewood Cliffs, N.J.: Prentice-Hall, 1959), 47–48.

[26]Quoted in Ziner, *Squanto*, 147.

New England. "Whole towns were depopulated. The living were not able to bury the dead; and their bodies were found lying above ground, many years after. The Massachusetts Indians are said to have been reduced from 30,000 to 300 fighting men. In 1633, the small pox swept off great numbers."[27]

Today it is no surprise that not one in a hundred of my college students has ever heard of the plague. Unless they have read *Life and Liberty,* students could scarcely come away from these books thinking of Indians as people who made an impact on North America, who lived here in considerable numbers, who *settled,* in short, and were then killed by disease or arms. Textbook authors have retreated from the candor of Barber. Treatments like that in *Triumph* guarantee our collective amnesia.

Having mistreated the plague, the textbooks proceed to mistreat the [33] Pilgrims. Their arrival in Massachusetts poses another historical controversy that textbook authors take pains to duck. The textbooks say the Pilgrims intended to go to Virginia, where there existed a British settlement already. But "the little party on the *Mayflower,*" explains *American History,* "never reached Virginia. On November 9, they sighted land on Cape Cod." How did the Pilgrims wind up in Massachusetts when they set out for Virginia? "Violent storms blew their ship off course," according to some textbooks; others blame an "error in navigation." Both explanations may be wrong. Some historians believe the Dutch bribed the captain of the *Mayflower* to sail north so the Pilgrims would not settle near New Amsterdam. Others hold that the Pilgrims went to Cape Cod on purpose.[28]

Bear in mind that the Pilgrims numbered only about 35 of the 102 [34] settlers aboard the *Mayflower;* the rest were ordinary folk seeking their fortunes in the new Virginia colony. George Willison has argued that the Pilgrim leaders, wanting to be far from Anglican control, never planned to settle in Virginia. They had debated the relative merits of Guiana, in South America, versus the Massachusetts coast, and, according to Willison, they intended a hijacking.

Certainly the Pilgrims already knew quite a bit about what Massa- [35] chusetts could offer them, from the fine fishing along Cape Cod to that "wonderful plague," which offered an unusual opportunity for British

---

[27]J. W. Barber, *Interesting Events in the History of the United States* (New Haven: Barber, 1829), 30. Barber does not cite the authority he quotes.

[28]Even though "Virginia" then included most of New Jersey, the *Mayflower* nonetheless landed hundreds of miles northeast. Historians who support the "on purpose" theory include George F. Willison, *Saints and Strangers* (New York: Reynal and Hitchcock, 1945); Lincoln Kinnicutt, "The Settlement at Plymouth Contemplated before 1620," *Publications of the American Historical Association,* 1920, 211–21; and Neal Salisbury, *Manitou and Providence* (New York: Oxford University Press, 1982), 109, 270. Leon Clark Hills, *History and Genealogy of the Mayflower Planters* (Baltimore: Genealogical Publ. Co., 1975), and Francis R. Stoddard, *The Truth about the Pilgrims* (New York: Society of Mayflower Descendants, 1952), 19–20, support the "Dutch bribe" theory, based on primary source material by Nathanial Morton. Historians at Plimoth Plantation support the theories of pilot error or storm.

settlement. According to some historians, Squanto, an Indian from the village of Patuxet, Massachusetts, had provided Ferdinando Gorges, a leader of the Plymouth Company in England, with a detailed description of the area. Gorges may even have sent Squanto and Capt. Thomas Dermer as advance men to wait for the Pilgrims, although Dermer sailed away when the Pilgrims were delayed in England. In any event, the Pilgrims were familiar with the area's topography. Recently published maps that Samuel de Champlain had drawn when he had toured the area in 1605 supplemented the information that had been passed on by sixteenth-century explorers. John Smith had studied the region and named it "New England" in 1614, and he even offered to guide the Pilgrim leaders. They rejected his services as too expensive and carried his guidebook along instead.[29]

These considerations prompt me to believe that the Pilgrim leaders *36* probably ended up in Massachusetts on purpose. But evidence for any conclusion is soft. Some historians believe Gorges took credit for landing in Massachusetts after the fact. Indeed, the *Mayflower* may have had no specific destination. Readers might be fascinated if textbook authors presented two or more of the various possibilities, but, as usual, exposing students to historical controversy is taboo. Each textbook picks just one reason and presents it as fact.

Only one of the twelve textbooks adheres to the hijacking possibility. *37* "The New England landing came as a rude surprise for the bedraggled and tired [non-Pilgrim] majority on board the *Mayflower*," says *Land of Promise*. "[They] had joined the expedition seeking economic opportunity in the Virginia tobacco plantations." Obviously, these passengers were not happy at having been taken elsewhere, especially to a shore with no prior English settlement to join. "Rumors of mutiny spread quickly." *Promise* then ties this unrest to the Mayflower Compact, giving its readers a fresh interpretation of why the colonists adopted the agreement and why it was so democratic: "To avoid rebellion, the Pilgrim leaders made a remarkable concession to the other colonists. They issued a call for every male on board, regardless of religion or economic status, to join in the creation of a 'civil body politic.'" The compact achieved its purpose: the majority acquiesced.

Actually, the hijacking hypothesis does not show the Pilgrims in such a *38* bad light. The compact provided a graceful solution to an awkward problem. Although hijacking and false representation doubtless were felonies then as now, the colony did survive with a lower death rate than Virginia, so no permanent harm was done. The whole story places the Pilgrims in a somewhat dishonorable light, however, which may explain why only one textbook selects it.

[29]Ziner, *Squanto*, 147; Kinnicutt, "The Settlement at Plymouth Contemplated before 1620"; Almon W. Lauber, *Indian Slavery in Colonial Times within the Present Limits of the United States* (Williamstown, Mass.: Corner House, 1970 [1913]), 156–59; Stoddard, *The Truth about the Pilgrims*, 16.

The "navigation error" story lacks plausibility: the one parameter of   *39*
ocean travel that sailors could and did measure accurately in that era was
latitude — distance north or south from the equator. The "storms" excuse
is perhaps still less plausible, for if a storm blew them off course, when the
weather cleared they could have turned southward again, sailing out to sea
to bypass any shoals. They had plenty of food and beer, after all.[30] But
storms and pilot error leave the Pilgrims pure of heart, which may explain
why the other eleven textbooks choose one of the two.

Regardless of motive, the Mayflower Compact provided a democratic   *40*
basis for the Plymouth colony. Since the framers of our Constitution in
fact paid the compact little heed, however, it hardly deserves the attention
textbook authors lavish on it. But textbook authors clearly want to package the Pilgrims as a pious and moral band who laid the antecedents of
our democratic traditions. Nowhere is this motive more embarrassingly
obvious than in John Garraty's *American History*. "So far as any record
shows, this was the first time in human history that a group of people
consciously created a government where none had existed before." Here
Garraty paraphrases a Forefathers' Day speech, delivered in Plymouth in
1802, in which John Adams celebrated "the only instance in human history of that positive, original social compact." George Willison has dryly
noted that Adams was "blinking several salient facts — above all, the circumstances that prompted the compact, which was plainly an instrument
of minority rule."[31] Of course, Garraty's paraphrase also exposes his ignorance of the Republic of Iceland, the Iroquois Confederacy, and countless
other polities antedating 1620. Such an account simply invites students to
become ethnocentric.

In their pious treatment of the Pilgrims, history textbooks introduce   *41*
the archetype of American exceptionalism. According to *The American
Pageant*, "This rare opportunity for a great social and political experiment
may never come again." *The American Way* declares, "The American
people have created a unique nation." How is America exceptional? Surely
we're exceptionally *good*. As Woodrow Wilson put it, "America is the only
idealistic nation in the world."[32] And the goodness started at Plymouth
Rock, according to our textbooks, which view the Pilgrims as Christian,
sober, democratic, generous to the Indians, God-thanking. Such a happy
portrait can be painted only by omitting the facts about the plague, the
possible hijacking, and the Indian relations.

---

[30]The *Mayflower* sailed south for half a day, until encountering "dangerous shoals,"
according to several of our textbooks. Then the captain and the Pilgrim leadership
insisted on returning to Provincetown and eventually New Plymouth. Conspiracy theorists take this to be a charade to dissuade the majority from insisting on Virginia. See
Willison, *Saints and Strangers*, 145, 466; Kinnicutt, "The Settlement at Plymouth Contemplated before 1620"; and Salisbury, *Manitou and Providence*, 109, 270.

[31]Willison, *Saints and Strangers*, 421–22.

[32]Speech in Sioux Falls, September 8, 1919, in *Addresses of President Wilson*
(Washington, D.C.: Government Printing Office, 1919), 86.

For that matter, our culture and our textbooks underplay or omit *42* Jamestown and the sixteenth-century Spanish settlements in favor of Plymouth Rock as the archetypal birthplace of the United States. Virginia, according to T. H. Breen, "ill-served later historians in search of the mythic origins of American culture."[33] Historians could hardly tout Virginia as moral in intent; in the words of the first history of Virginia written by a Virginian: "The chief Design of all Parties concern'd was to fetch away the Treasure from thence, aiming more at sudden Gain, than to form any regular Colony."[34] The Virginians' relations with the Indians were particularly unsavory: in contrast to Squanto, a volunteer, the British in Virginia took Indian prisoners and forced them to teach colonists how to farm.[35] In 1623 the British indulged in the first use of chemical warfare in the colonies when negotiating a treaty with tribes near the Potomac River, headed by Chiskiack. The British offered a toast "symbolizing eternal friendship," whereupon the chief, his family, advisors, and two hundred followers dropped dead of poison.[36] Besides, the early Virginians engaged in bickering, sloth, even cannibalism. They spent their early days digging random holes in the ground, haplessly looking for gold instead of planting crops. Soon they were starving and digging up putrid Indian corpses to eat or renting themselves out to Indian families as servants — hardly the heroic founders that a great nation requires.[37]

Textbooks indeed cover the Virginia colony, and they at least mention *43* the Spanish settlements, but they devote 50 percent more space to Massachusetts. As a result, and due also to Thanksgiving, of course, students are much more likely to remember the Pilgrims as our founders.[38] They are then embarrassed when I remind them of Virginia and the Spanish, for when prompted students do recall having heard of both. But neither our culture nor our textbooks give Virginia the same archetypal status as Massachusetts. That is why almost all my students know the name of the Pilgrims' ship, while almost no students remember the names of the three ships that brought the British to Jamestown. (For the next time you're on *Jeopardy*, they were the *Susan Constant*, the *Discovery*, and the *Goodspeed*.)

Despite having ended up many miles from other European enclaves, the *44* Pilgrims hardly "started from scratch" in a "wilderness." Throughout southern New England, Native Americans had repeatedly burned the underbrush,

---

[33]T. H. Breen, "Right Man, Wrong Place," *New York Review of Books,* November 20, 1986, 50.

[34]Written by Robert Beverley in 1705 and quoted in Wesley Frank Craven. *The Legend of the Founding Fathers* (Westport, Conn.: Greenwood, 1983 [1956]), 5–8.

[35]Axtell, *The European and the Indian,* 292–95.

[36]J. Leitch Wright, Jr., *The Only Land They Knew* (New York: Free Press, 1981), 78.

[37]Kupperman, *Settling with the Indians,* 173; James Truslow Adams, *The March of Democracy,* vol. 1 (New York: Scribner's, 1933), 12.

[38]I encountered most of these students in New England, but many of them came from suburbs of Philadelphia. Washington, D.C., and New Jersey. I suspect that replies from the rest of the United States would be similar, except perhaps the Far West.

creating a parklike environment. After landing at Provincetown, the Pilgrims assembled a boat for exploring and began looking around for their new home. They chose Plymouth because of its beautiful cleared fields, recently planted in corn, and its useful harbor and "brook of fresh water." It was a lovely site for a town. Indeed, until the plague, it had been a town, for "New Plimoth" was none other than Squanto's village of Patuxet! The invaders followed a pattern: throughout the hemisphere Europeans pitched camp right in the middle of Native populations — Cuzco, Mexico City, Natchez, Chicago. Throughout New England, colonists appropriated Indian cornfields for their initial settlements, avoiding the backbreaking labor of clearing the land of forest and rock.[39] (This explains why, to this day, the names of so many towns throughout the region — Marshfield, Springfield, Deerfield — end in *field*.) "Errand into the wilderness" may have made a lively sermon title in 1650, a popular book title in 1950, and an archetypal textbook phrase in 1990, but it was never accurate. The new settlers encountered no wilderness: "In this bay wherein we live," one colonist noted in 1622, "in former time hath lived about two thousand Indians."[40]

Moreover, not all the Native inhabitants had perished, and the survivors now facilitated British settlement. The Pilgrims began receiving Indian assistance on their second full day in Massachusetts. A colonist's journal tells of sailors discovering two Indian houses:

> Having their guns and hearing nobody, they entered the houses and found the people were gone. The sailors took some things but didn't dare stay. . . . We had meant to have left some beads and other things in the houses as a sign of peace and to show we meant to trade with them. But we didn't do it because we left in such haste. But as soon as we can meet with the Indians, we will pay them well for what we took.

It wasn't only houses that the Pilgrims robbed. Our eyewitness resumes his story:

> We marched to the place we called Cornhill, where we had found the corn before. At another place we had seen before, we dug and found some more corn, two or three baskets full, and a bag of beans. . . . In all we had about ten bushels, which will be enough for seed. It was with God's help that we found this corn, for how else could we have done it, without meeting some Indians who might trouble us.

From the start, the Pilgrims thanked God, not the Indians, for assistance that the latter had (inadvertently) provided — setting a pattern for later thanksgivings. Our journalist continues:

> The next morning, we found a place like a grave. We decided to dig it up. We found first a mat, and under that a fine bow. . . . We also found bowls, trays,

---

[39]Gary Nash, *Red, White, and Black* (Englewood Cliffs, N.J.: Prentice-Hall, 1974), 139, describes the same process in Pennsylvania.

[40]Emmanuel Altham letter quoted in Sydney V. James, ed., *Three Visitors to Early Plymouth* (Plymouth: Plimoth Plantation, 1963), 29.

dishes, and things like that. We took several of the prettiest things to carry away with us, and covered the body up again.[41]

A place "like a grave"!

Although Karen Kupperman says the Pilgrims continued to rob graves for years,[42] more help came from a live Indian, Squanto. Here my students return to familiar turf, for they have all learned the Squanto legend. *Land of Promise* provides a typical account:

> Squanto had learned their language, he explained, from English fishermen who ventured into the New England waters each summer. Squanto taught the Pilgrims how to plant corn, squash, and pumpkins. Would the small band of settlers have survived without Squanto's help? We cannot say. But by the fall of 1621, colonists and Indians could sit down to several days of feast and thanksgiving to God (later celebrated as the first Thanksgiving).

What do the books leave out about Squanto? First, how he learned English. According to Ferdinando Gorges, around 1605 a British captain stole Squanto, who was then still a boy, along with four Penobscots, and took them to England. There Squanto spent nine years, three in the employ of Gorges. At length, Gorges helped Squanto arrange passage back to Massachusetts. Some historians doubt that Squanto was among the five Indians stolen in 1605.[43] All sources agree, however, that in 1614 a British slave raider seized Squanto and two dozen fellow Indians and sold them into slavery in Málaga, Spain. What happened next makes Ulysses look like a homebody. Squanto escaped from slavery, escaped from Spain, and made his way back to England. After trying to get home via Newfoundland, in 1619 he talked Thomas Dermer into taking him along on his next trip to Cape Cod.

It happens that Squanto's fabulous odyssey provides a "hook" into the plague story, a hook that our textbooks choose not to use. For now Squanto set foot again on Massachusetts soil and walked to his home village of Patuxet, only to make the horrifying discovery that "he was the sole member of his village still alive. All the others had perished in the

---

[41]Could there be a fairy tale parallel to this Pilgrim incident? Like Goldilocks, the Pilgrims broke-and-entered, trespassed, vandalized, and stole, and like Goldilocks, educators forgive them because they are Aryan. The Goldilocks tale makes her victims less than human, and the shadowy way our histories represent Indians makes the Pilgrims' victims also less than human. My thanks to Toni Cade Bambara for this analysis of Goldilocks.

[42]Kupperman, *Settling with the Indians.* 125.

[43]All five had names other than Squanto or Tisquantum, but Indians sometimes went by different names in different tribes. Squanto's biographer, Feenie Ziner, believes he was one of the five. Ferdinando Gorges stated in 1658 that Squanto was among those abducted in 1605 and lived with him in England for three years, which convinced Lincoln Kinnicutt ("The Settlement at Plymouth Contemplated before 1620," 212–13) but not historians at Plimoth Plantation or Salisbury (*Manitou and Providence,* 265–66), although Salisbury seems more positive in "Squanto: Last of the Patuxets." See also Lauber, *Indian Slavery in Colonial Times,* 156–59.

epidemic two years before."[44] No wonder Squanto threw in his lot with the Pilgrims.

Now *that* is a story worth telling! Compare the pallid account in *Land of Promise:* "He had learned their language from English fishermen."   50

As translator, ambassador, and technical advisor, Squanto was essential to the survival of Plymouth in its first two years. Like other Europeans in America, the Pilgrims had no idea what to eat or how to raise or find it until Indians showed them. William Bradford called Squanto "a special instrument sent of God for their good beyond their expectation. He directed them how to set their corn, where to take fish, and to procure other commodities, and was also their pilot to bring them to unknown places for their profit." Squanto was not the Pilgrims' only aide: in the summer of 1621 Massasoit sent another Indian, Hobomok, to live among the Pilgrims for several years as guide and ambassador.[45]   51

"Their profit" was the primary reason most *Mayflower* colonists made the trip. As Robert Moore has pointed out, "Textbooks neglect to analyze the profit motive underlying much of our history."[46] Profit too came from the Indians, by way of the fur trade, without which Plymouth would never have paid for itself. Hobomok helped Plymouth set up fur trading posts at the mouth of the Penobscot and Kennebec rivers in Maine; in Aptucxet, Massachusetts; and in Windsor, Connecticut.[47] Europeans had neither the skill nor the desire to "go boldly where none dared go before." They went to the Indians.[48]   52

All this brings us to Thanksgiving. Throughout the nation every fall, elementary school children reenact a little morality play, *The First Thanksgiving,* as our national origin myth, complete with Pilgrim hats made out of construction paper and Indian braves with feathers in their hair: Thanksgiving is the occasion on which we give thanks to God as a nation for the blessings that He [*sic*] hath bestowed upon us. More than any other celebration, more even than such overtly patriotic holidays as Independence Day and Memorial Day, Thanksgiving celebrates our ethnocentrism. We have seen, for example, how King James and the early Pilgrim leaders gave thanks for the plague, which proved to them that God was on their   53

---

[44]Simpson, *Invisible Armies,* 6.

[45]William Bradford, *Of Plimouth Plantation,* 99. See also, inter alia, Salisbury, "Squanto: Last of the Patuxets," 228–46.

[46]Robert Moore, *Stereotypes, Distortions. and Omissions in U.S. History Textbooks* (New York: CIBC, 1977), 19.

[47]Robert M. Bartlett, *The Pilgrim Way* (Philadelphia: Pilgrim Press, 1971), 265; and Loeb, *Meet the Real Pilgrims,* 65.

[48]Charles Hudson et al., "The Tristan de Luna Expeditions, 1559–61," in Jerald T. Milanich and Susan Milbrath, eds., *First Encounters* (Gainesville: University of Florida Press, 1989), 119–34, supplies a vivid illustration of European dependence on Indians for food. They tell of the little-known second Spanish expedition (after De Soto) into what is now the southeastern United States. Because the Indians retreated from them and burned their crops, the Europeans almost starved.

side. The archetypes associated with Thanksgiving — God on our side, civilization wrested from wilderness, order from disorder, through hard work and good Pilgrim character traits — continue to radiate from our history textbooks. More than sixty years ago, in an analysis of how American history was taught in the 1920s, Bessie Pierce pointed out the political uses to which Thanksgiving is put: "For these unexcelled blessings, the pupil is urged to follow in the footsteps of his forbears, to offer unquestioning obedience to the law of the land, and to carry on the work begun."[49]

Thanksgiving dinner is a ritual, with all the characteristics that Mircea 54 Eliade assigns to the ritual observances of origin myths:

1. It constitutes the history of the acts of the founders, the Supernaturals.
2. It is considered to be true.
3. It tells how an institution came into existence.
4. In performing the ritual associated with the myth, one "'experiences' knowledge of the origin" and claims one's patriarchy.
5. Thus one "lives" the myth, as a religion.[50]

My Random House dictionary lists as its main heading for the Plymouth colonists not *Pilgrims* but *Pilgrim Fathers*. The Library of Congress similarly catalogs its holdings for Plymouth under *Pilgrim Fathers*, and of course *fathers* is capitalized, meaning "fathers of our country," not of Pilgrim children. Thanksgiving has thus moved from history into the field of religion, "civil religion," as Robert Bellah has called it. To Bellah, civil religions hold society together. Plymouth Rock achieved iconographic status around 1880, when some enterprising residents of the town rejoined its two pieces on the waterfront and built a Greek templet around it. The templet became a shrine, the Mayflower Compact became a sacred text, and our textbooks began to play the same function as the Anglican *Book of Common Prayer,* teaching us the meaning behind the civil rite of Thanksgiving.[51]

The religious character of Pilgrim history shines forth in an introduc- 55 tion by Valerian Paget to William Bradford's famous chronicle *Of Plimoth Plantation:* "The eyes of Europe were upon this little English handful of unconscious heroes and saints, taking courage from them step by step. For their children's children the same ideals of Freedom burned so clear and strong that . . . the little episode we have just been contemplating, resulted

---

[49]Bessie L. Pierce, *Public Opinion and the Teaching of History in the United States* (New York: Alfred A. Knopf, 1926), 113–14. See also Alice B. Kehoe, "'In fourteen hundred and ninety two, Columbus sailed . . . : The Primacy of the National Myth in U.S. Schools," in Peter Stone and Robert MacKenzie, eds., *The Excluded Past* (London: Unwin Hyman, 1990), 207.

[50]Mircea Eliade, *Myth and Reality* (New York: Harper and Row, 1963), 18–19.

[51]Robert N. Bellah, "Civil Religion in America," *Daedalus,* winter 1967, 1–21. See Hugh Brogan, *The Pelican History of the U.S.A.* (Harmondsworth, Eng.: Penguin, 1986), 37, re Plymouth Rock. See also Michael Kammen, *Mystic Chords of Memory* (New York: Alfred A. Knopf, 1991), 207–10.

in the birth of the United States of America, and, above all, of the establishment of the humanitarian ideals it typifies, and for which the Pilgrims offered their sacrifice upon the altar of the Sonship of Man."[52] In this invocation, the Pilgrims supply not only the origin of the United States, but also the inspiration for democracy in Europe and perhaps for all goodness in the world today! I suspect that the original colonists, Separatists and Anglicans alike, would have been amused.

The civil ritual we practice marginalizes Indians. Our archetypal image of the first Thanksgiving portrays the groaning boards in the woods, with the Pilgrims in their starched Sunday best next to their almost naked Indian guests. As a holiday greeting card puts it, "I is for the Indians we invited to share our food." The silliness of all this reaches its zenith in the handouts that schoolchildren have carried home for decades, complete with captions such as, "They served pumpkins and turkeys and corn and squash. The Indians had never seen such a feast!" When the Native American novelist Michael Dorris's son brought home this "information" from his New Hampshire elementary school, Dorris pointed out that "the *Pilgrims* had literally never seen 'such a feast,' since all foods mentioned are exclusively indigenous to the Americas and had been provided *by* [or with the aid of] the local tribe."[53]

This notion that "we" advanced peoples provided for the Indians, exactly the converse of the truth, is not benign. It reemerges time and again in our history to complicate race relations. For example, we are told that white plantation owners furnished food and medical care for their slaves, yet every shred of food, shelter, and clothing on the plantations was raised, built, woven, or paid for by black labor. Today Americans believe as part of our political understanding of the world that we are the most generous nation on earth in terms of foreign aid, overlooking the fact that the net dollar flow from almost every Third World nation runs *toward* the United States.

The true history of Thanksgiving reveals embarrassing facts. The Pilgrims did not introduce the tradition; Eastern Indians had observed autumnal harvest celebrations for centuries. Although George Washington did set aside days for national thanksgiving, our modern celebrations date back only to 1863. During the Civil War, when the Union needed all the patriotism that such an observance might muster, Abraham Lincoln proclaimed Thanksgiving a national holiday. The Pilgrims had nothing to do with it; not until the 1890s did they even get included in the tradition. For that matter, no one used the term *Pilgrims* until the 1870s.[54]

---

[52]Valerian Paget, introduction to *Bradford's History of the Plymouth Settlement, 1608–1650* (New York: McBride, 1909), xvii.

[53]Dorris, "Why I'm Not Thankful for Thanksgiving," 9. The addition is mine, in the interest of accuracy.

[54]Plimoth Plantation: "The American Thanksgiving Tradition, or How Thanksgiving Stole the Pilgrims" (Plymouth, Mass.: n.d., photocopy); Stoddard, *The Truth about the Pilgrims*, 13.

The ideological meaning American history has ascribed to Thanksgiv- *59* ing compounds the embarrassment. The Thanksgiving legend makes Americans ethnocentric. After all, if our culture has God on its side, why should we consider other cultures seriously? This ethnocentrism intensified in the middle of the last century. In *Race and Manifest Destiny*, Reginald Horsman has shown how the idea of "God on our side" was used to legitimate the open expression of Anglo-Saxon superiority vis-à-vis Mexicans, Native Americans, peoples of the Pacific, Jews, and even Catholics.[55] Today, when textbooks promote this ethnocentrism with their Pilgrim stories, they leave students less able to learn from and deal with people from other cultures.

On occasion, we pay a more direct cost: censorship. In 1970, for *60* example, the Massachusetts Department of Commerce asked the Wampanoags to select a speaker to mark the 350th anniversary of the Pilgrims' landing. Frank James "was selected, but first he had to show a copy of his speech to the white people in charge of the ceremony. When they saw what he had written, they would not allow him to read it."[56] James had written:

> Today is a time of celebrating for you . . . but it is not a time of celebrating for me. It is with heavy heart that I look back upon what happened to my People. . . . The Pilgrims had hardly explored the shores of Cape Cod four days before they had robbed the graves of my ancestors, and stolen their corn, wheat, and beans. . . . Massasoit, the great leader of the Wampanoag, knew these facts; yet he and his People welcomed and befriended the settlers. . . . little knowing that . . . before 50 years were to pass, the Wampanoags . . . and other Indians living near the settlers would be killed by their guns or dead from diseases that we caught from them. . . . Although our way of life is almost gone and our language is almost extinct, we the Wampanoags still walk the lands of Massachusetts. . . . What has happened cannot be changed, but today we work toward a better America, a more Indian America where people and nature once again are important.[57]

What the Massachusetts Department of Commerce censored was not *61* some incendiary falsehood but historical truth. Nothing James would have said, had he been allowed to speak, was false, excepting the word *wheat*. Our textbooks also omit the facts about grave robbing, Indian enslavement, the plague, and so on, even though they were common knowledge in colonial New England. For at least a century Puritan ministers thundered their interpretation of the meaning of the plague from New England pulpits. Thus our popular history of the Pilgrims has not been a process of

---

[55]Reginald Horsman, *Race and Manifest Destiny* (Cambridge, Mass.: Harvard University Press, 1981), 5.

[56]Arlene Hitshfelder and Jane Califf, "Celebration or Mourning? It's All in the Point of View" (New York: Council on Interracial Books for Children *Bulletin* 10, no. 6, 1979), 9.

[57]Frank James, "Frank James' Speech" (New York: Council on Interracial Books for Children *Bulletin* 10, no. 6, 1979), 13.

gaining perspective but of deliberate forgetting. Instead of these important facts, textbooks supply the feel-good minutiae of Squanto's helpfulness, his name, the fish in the cornhills, sometimes even the menu and the number of Indians who attended the prototypical first Thanksgiving.

I have focused here on untoward detail only because our histories have 62 suppressed everything awkward for so long. The Pilgrims' courage in setting forth in the late fall to make their way on a continent new to them remains unsurpassed. In their first year the Pilgrims, like the Indians, suffered from diseases, including scurvy and pneumonia; half of them died. It was not immoral of the Pilgrims to have taken over Patuxet. They did not cause the plague and were as baffled as to its origin as the stricken Indian villagers. Massasoit was happy that the Pilgrims were using the bay, for the Patuxet, being dead, had no more need for the site. Pilgrim-Indian relations started reasonably positively. Plymouth, unlike many other colonies, usually paid the Indians for the land it took. In some instances Europeans settled in Indian towns because Indians had *invited* them, as protection against another tribe or a nearby competing European power.[58] In sum, U.S. history is no more violent and oppressive than the history of England, Russia, Indonesia, or Burundi — but neither is it exceptionally less violent.

The antidote to feel-good history is not feel-bad history but honest and 63 inclusive history. If textbook authors feel compelled to give moral instruction, the way origin myths have always done, they could accomplish this aim by allowing students to learn both the "good" and the "bad" sides of the Pilgrim tale. Conflict would then become part of the story, and students might discover that the knowledge they gain has implications for their lives today. Correctly taught, the issues of the era of the first Thanksgiving could help Americans grow more thoughtful and more tolerant, rather than more ethnocentric.

Origin myths do not come cheaply. To glorify the Pilgrims is danger- 64 ous. The genial omissions and the invented details with which our textbooks retail the Pilgrim archetype are close cousins of the overt censorship practiced by the Massachusetts Department of Commerce in denying Frank James the right to speak. Surely, in history, "truth should be held sacred, at whatever cost."

■ ■ ■

Reading Rhetorically

1. Select several specific passages to help you describe Loewen's ethos, or self-representation, in this text. How do you think he represents students? How are these characterizations important to the point he makes in the selection?

---

[58]Willison, *Saints and Strangers;* Salisbury, *Manitou and Providence,* 114–17; Wright, *The Only Land They Knew,* 220. Salisbury, *Manitou and Providence,* 120–25, tells of the militaristic and coercive nature of Plymouth's dealings with the Indians, however, right from the first.

2. How are the ideas Loewen sets up in the first section of the reading ("Introduction: Something Has Gone Very Wrong") illustrated in the second section "The Truth about the First Thanksgiving"? Locate several specific passages that demonstrate the connection, and be prepared to explain your ideas to a small group or the class.

3. How and where does Loewen anticipate counterarguments? How effectively do you think he addresses the concerns of readers who might disagree with him? What conclusions can you draw from Loewen's writing about addressing resistant readers in your own writing?

Inquiring Further

4. Choose a specific event in U.S. history and trace it through several history textbooks. Then do a Loewen-style analysis of the material you find. Look for textbooks from different periods (your library may have some on the shelf). What does the language of each textbook suggest about the author's perspective? What kind of story about the United States is being told? Share your findings with the class.

5. Interview a college history professor about the strengths and weaknesses of current approaches to teaching history. What does your interviewee think about the key ideas Loewen raises in his text? Be prepared to tell your classmates what you discover.

    Alternatively, search the Web for teaching advice for instructors of history. How does that advice seem to respond to Loewen's criticisms of the way American history is taught? (The *Journal of American History* has a site called Textbooks and Teaching [http://www.indiana.edu/~jah/textbooks/] that could be a useful resource.)

6. Do a basic Google search for "Squanto" and compare the images, language, and sounds on the first five Web sites listed. How does what you find there conform to Loewen's description of the myths and truths about this historical figure? What conclusions can you draw?

Framing Conversations

7. How do popular films tell the story of early encounters between the Puritans and the Native Americans? Choose a film to analyze — perhaps Disney's *Pocahontas* or a more recent film like *The New World* — using insights from Loewen and Henry Giroux (p. 567) as your tools. Given these scholars' insights on the significance of the way this story is told to popular audiences, what can you say about the film? Be sure to include specific examples of the language and visual aspects of the film in your argument.

8. How do Mary Louise Pratt's (p. 354) concepts of contact zones and transculturation help you analyze the power dynamics Loewen describes? Write an essay in which you use Pratt's concepts to analyze specific examples in Loewen's text. Be sure to consider both the power dynamics Loewen describes in textbooks and the act of writing he is engaged in himself. What conclusions can you draw?

9. Although they each point to different kinds of evidence, both Loewen and Héctor Tobar (p. 533) are interested in what it means to be American. Write an essay in which you place in conversation the ideas and examples each author presents to build your own argument about being American. You can also include evidence from your own experience.

■ MARY LOUISE PRATT ──────────────────────────────────

Arts of the Contact Zone

Mary Louise Pratt is a professor of comparative literature, Spanish, and Portuguese. She taught at Stanford University from 1976 to 2003, and joined the faculty of New York University in 2003, where she is affiliated with the Hemispheric Institute of Performance and Politics. She is best known as a scholar of postcolonial Latin American literature, but she also has written on travel literature and modern fiction. She is the author of many essays and reviews, and has published several books, including *Imperial Eyes: Travel Writing and Transculturation* (1992). In 2003, she served as president of the Modern Language Association (MLA), a professional organization for professors of literature, and her numerous fellowships include funding from the Guggenheim Foundation and the National Endowment for the Humanities.

This essay, "Arts of the Contact Zone," was the keynote address at the second Modern Language Association Literacy Conference, held in Pittsburgh in 1990. As you read, "listen" for clues that the paper was being delivered to a live audience, and consider how effectively the speech translates to the written page. Throughout the essay, Pratt offers her listeners/readers indications of what her larger point is and where she is going. Pay close attention to sentences like "I propose immediately to head back several centuries to a text that has a few points in common with baseball cards" (para. 5) and "I propose to say a few more words about this erstwhile unreadable text, in order to lay out some thoughts about writing and literacy in what I like to call the *contact zones*" (para. 7), where she clearly signals how she is structuring her argument and why. Think about how you might use similar strategies in your own writing.

At Stanford, Pratt advocated for replacing traditional Western civilization courses with a multicultural alternative. That work has made her instrumental to administrative conversations about multicultural curricula at many universities. In a related move, she coined the term *contact zones* to describe "social spaces where cultures meet, clash, and grapple with each other, often in contexts of highly asymmetrical relations of power, such as colonialism, slavery, or their aftermaths" (para. 7). A wide range of scholars have used the concept of contact zones to analyze the ways literacy and power interact in contexts ranging from the Spanish conquest of the Incas in the sixteenth century to the culture of any classroom in which college freshmen are introduced to the language and customs of discussion, research, and writing at the college level.

It is fitting that a paper that began as a speech for the MLA uses MLA citation style. You can see from Pratt's list of works cited that she draws on scholars who work directly with the primary texts by Guaman Poma and Inca Garcilaso that Pratt herself analyzes in the essay. She also applies ideas from Benedict Anderson, who theorizes more broadly about the way nationalist identity hinges on what he calls imagined communities. And Pratt weaves into the essay a number of concepts from other scholars, including the idea of transculturation, invented in the 1940s by Cuban sociologist Fernando Ortiz "to describe processes whereby members of subordinated or marginal groups select and invent from materials transmitted by a dominant or metropolitan culture" (para. 13). Pratt's essay helped repopularize the concept, and scholars in many fields have since used the analytical insights of transculturation to make sense of hybrid cultural practices from jazz to rap, to Indian "Bollywood films," just to name a few examples.

As you read, notice the way Pratt balances her close analysis of centuries-old texts and images with lively modern examples of literacy drawn from one son's enthusiasm for baseball to another's frustration with unimaginative teachers. Remember that Pratt's essay was delivered to a live audience. Notice the ways she anticipates her audience's potential exhaustion or boredom. How and when does she cut between past and present examples, both to hold her listeners' interest and to help them (and us, as readers) make connections between clashing cultures of long ago and those of today?

Whenever the subject of literacy comes up, what often pops first into my mind is a conversation I overheard eight years ago between my son Sam and his best friend, Willie, aged six and seven, respectively: "Why don't you trade me Many Trails for Carl Yats . . . Yesits . . . Yastrum-scrum." "That's not how you say it, dummy. It's Carl Yes . . . Yes . . . oh, I don't know." Sam and Willie had just discovered baseball cards. Many Trails was their decoding, with the help of first-grade English phonics, of the name Manny Trillo. The name they were quite rightly stumped on was Carl Yastrzemski. That was the first time I remembered seeing them put their incipient literacy to their own use, and I was of course thrilled.

Sam and Willie learned a lot about phonics that year by trying to decipher surnames on baseball cards, and a lot about cities, states, heights, weights, places of birth, stages of life. In the years that followed, I watched Sam apply his arithmetic skills to working out batting averages and subtracting retirement years from rookie years; I watched him develop senses of patterning and order by arranging and rearranging his cards for hours on end, and aesthetic judgment by comparing different photos, different series, layouts, and color schemes. American geography and history took shape in his mind through baseball cards. Much of his social life revolved around trading them, and he learned about exchange, fairness, trust, the importance of processes as opposed to results, what it means to get cheated, taken advantage of, even robbed. Baseball cards were the medium of his economic life too. Nowhere better to learn the power and arbitrariness of money, the absolute divorce between use value and exchange value, notions of long- and short-term investment, the possibility of personal values that are independent of market values.

Baseball cards meant baseball card shows, where there was much to   3
be learned about adult worlds as well. And baseball cards opened the door to baseball books, shelves and shelves of encyclopedias, magazines, histories, biographies, novels, books of jokes, anecdotes, cartoons, even poems. Sam learned the history of American racism and the struggle against it through baseball; he saw the depression and two world wars from behind home plate. He learned the meaning of commodified labor, what it means for one's body and talents to be owned and dispensed by another. He knows something about Japan, Taiwan, Cuba, and Central America and how men and boys do things there. Through the history and experience of baseball stadiums he thought about architecture, light, wind, topography, meteorology, the dynamics of public space. He learned the meaning of expertise, of knowing about something well enough that you can start a conversation with a stranger and feel sure of holding your own. Even with an adult — especially with an adult. Throughout his preadolescent years, baseball history was Sam's luminous point of contact with grown-ups, his lifeline to caring. And, of course, all this time he was also playing baseball, struggling his way through the stages of the local Little League system, lucky enough to be a pretty good player, loving the game and coming to know deeply his strengths and weaknesses.

Literacy began for Sam with the newly pronounceable names on the   4
picture cards and brought him what has been easily the broadest, most varied, most enduring, and most integrated experience of his thirteen-year life. Like many parents, I was delighted to see schooling give Sam the tools with which to find and open all these doors. At the same time I found it unforgivable that schooling itself gave him nothing remotely as meaningful to do, let alone anything that would actually take him beyond the referential, masculinist ethos of baseball and its lore.

However, I was not invited here to speak as a parent, nor as an expert   5
on literacy. I was asked to speak as an MLA member working in the elite academy. In that capacity my contribution is undoubtedly supposed to be abstract, irrelevant, and anchored outside the real world. I wouldn't dream of disappointing anyone. I propose immediately to head back several centuries to a text that has a few points in common with baseball cards and raises thoughts about what Tony Sarmiento, in his comments to the conference, called new visions of literacy. In 1908 a Peruvianist named Richard Pietschmann was exploring in the Danish Royal Archive in Copenhagen and came across a manuscript. It was dated in the city of Cuzco in Peru, in the year 1613, some forty years after the final fall of the Inca empire to the Spanish and signed with an unmistakably Andean indigenous name: Felipe Guaman Poma de Ayala. Written in a mixture of Quechua and ungrammatical, expressive Spanish, the manuscript was a

letter addressed by an unknown but apparently literate Andean to King Philip III of Spain. What stunned Pietschmann was that the letter was twelve hundred pages long. There were almost eight hundred pages of written text and four hundred of captioned line drawings. It was titled *The First New Chronicle and Good Government.* No one knew (or knows) how the manuscript got to the library in Copenhagen or how long it had been there. No one, it appeared, had ever bothered to read it or figured out how. Quechua was not thought of as a written language in 1908, nor Andean culture as a literate culture.

Pietschmann prepared a paper on his find, which he presented in 6 London in 1912, a year after the rediscovery of Machu Picchu by Hiram Bingham. Reception, by an international congress of Americanists, was apparently confused. It took twenty-five years for a facsimile edition of the work to appear, in Paris. It was not till the late 1970s, as positivist reading habits gave way to interpretive studies and colonial elitisms to postcolonial pluralisms, that Western scholars found ways of reading Guaman Poma's *New Chronicle and Good Government* as the extraordinary intercultural tour de force that it was. The letter got there, only 350 years too late, a miracle and a terrible tragedy.

I propose to say a few more words about this erstwhile unreadable 7 text, in order to lay out some thoughts about writing and literacy in what I like to call the *contact zones.* I use this term to refer to social spaces where cultures meet, clash, and grapple with each other, often in contexts of highly asymmetrical relations of power, such as colonialism, slavery, or their aftermaths as they are lived out in many parts of the world today. Eventually I will use the term to reconsider the models of community that many of us rely on in teaching and theorizing and that are under challenge today. But first a little more about Guaman Poma's giant letter to Philip III.

Insofar as anything is known about him at all, Guaman Poma exem- 8 plified the sociocultural complexities produced by conquest and empire. He was an indigenous Andean who claimed noble Inca descent and who had adopted (at least in some sense) Christianity. He may have worked in the Spanish colonial administration as an interpreter, scribe, or assistant to a Spanish tax collector — as a mediator, in short. He says he learned to write from his half brother, a mestizo whose Spanish father had given him access to religious education.

Guaman Poma's letter to the king is written in two languages (Spanish 9 and Quechua) and two parts. The first is called the *Nueva corónica* ("New Chronicle"). The title is important. The chronicle of course was the main writing apparatus through which the Spanish represented their American conquests to themselves. It constituted one of the main official discourses. In writing a "new chronicle," Guaman Poma took over the official Spanish genre for his own ends. Those ends were, roughly, to construct a new picture of the world, a picture of a Christian world with Andean rather than European peoples at the center of it — Cuzco, not Jerusalem. In the *New Chronicle* Guaman Poma begins by rewriting the Christian history of the world from Adam and Eve (Figure 1), incorporating the Amerindians into it as offspring of one of the sons of Noah. He identifies five ages of Christian history that he links in parallel with the five ages of canonical Andean history — separate but equal trajectories that diverge with Noah and reintersect not with Columbus but with Saint Bartholomew, claimed to have preceded Columbus in the Americas. In a couple of hundred pages, Guaman Poma constructs a veritable encyclopedia of Inca and pre-Inca history, customs, laws, social forms, public offices, and dynastic leaders. The depictions resemble European manners and customs description, but also reproduce the meticulous detail with which knowledge in Inca society was stored on *quipus* and in the oral memories of elders.

Guaman Poma's *New Chronicle* is an instance of what I have proposed   *10* to call an *autoethnographic* text, by which I mean a text in which people undertake to describe themselves in ways that engage with representations others have made of them. Thus if ethnographic texts are those in which European metropolitan subjects represent to themselves their others (usually

FIGURE 1   Adam and Eve.

their conquered others), autoethnographic texts are representations that the so-defined others construct *in response to* or in dialogue with those texts. Autoethnographic texts are not, then, what are usually thought of as autochthonous forms of expression or self-representation (as the Andean *quipus* were). Rather they involve a selective collaboration with and appropriation of idioms of the metropolis or the conqueror. These are merged or infiltrated to varying degrees with indigenous idioms to create self-representations intended to intervene in metropolitan modes of understanding. Autoethnographic works are often addressed to both metropolitan audiences and the speaker's own community. Their reception is thus highly indeterminate. Such texts often constitute a marginalized group's point of entry into the dominant circuits of print culture. It is interesting to think, for example, of American slave autobiography in its autoethnographic dimensions, which in some respects distinguish it from Euramerican autobiographical tradition. The concept might help explain why some of the earliest published writing by Chicanas took the form of folkloric manners and customs sketches written in English and published in English-language newspapers or folklore magazines (see Treviño). Autoethnographic representation often involves concrete collaborations between people, as between literate ex-slaves and abolitionist intellectuals, or between Guaman Poma and the Inca elders who were his informants. Often, as in Guaman Poma, it involves more than one language. In recent decades autoethnography, critique, and resistance have reconnected with writing in a contemporary creation of the contact zone, the *testimonio*.

Guaman Poma's *New Chronicle* ends with a revisionist account of 11 the Spanish conquest, which, he argues, should have been a peaceful encounter of equals with the potential for benefiting both, but for the mindless greed of the Spanish. He parodies Spanish history. Following contact with the Incas, he writes, "In all Castille, there was a great commotion. All day and at night in their dreams the Spaniards were saying 'Yndias, yndias, oro, plata, oro, plata del Piru'" ("Indies, indies, gold, silver, gold, silver from Peru") (Figure 2). The Spanish, he writes, brought nothing of value to share with the Andeans, nothing "but armor and guns con la codicia de oro, plata, oro y plata, yndias, a las Yndias, Piru" ("with the lust for gold, silver, gold and silver, Indies, the Indies, Peru") (372). I quote these words as an example of a conquered subject using the conqueror's language to construct a parodic, oppositional representation of the conqueror's own speech. Guaman Poma mirrors back to the Spanish (in their language, which is alien to him) an image of themselves that they often suppress and will therefore surely recognize. Such are the dynamics of language, writing, and representation in contact zones.

The second half of the epistle continues the critique. It is titled *Buen* 12 *gobierno y justicia* ("Good Government and Justice") and combines a description of colonial society in the Andean region with a passionate denunciation of Spanish exploitation and abuse. (These, at the time he was writing, were decimating the population of the Andes at a genocidal

FIGURE 2   Conquista. Meeting of Spaniard and Inca. The Inca says in Quechua, "You eat this gold?" Spaniard replies in Spanish, "We eat this gold."

rate. In fact, the potential loss of the labor force became a main cause for reform of the system.) Guaman Poma's most implacable hostility is invoked by the clergy, followed by the dreaded *corregidores*, or colonial overseers (Figure 3). He also praises good works, Christian habits, and just men where he finds them, and offers at length his views as to what constitutes "good government and justice." The Indies, he argues, should be administered through a collaboration of Inca and Spanish elites. The epistle ends with an imaginary question-and-answer session in which, in a reversal of hierarchy, the king is depicted asking Guaman Poma questions about how to reform the empire — a dialogue imagined across the many lines that divide the Andean scribe from the imperial monarch, and in which the subordinated subject single-handedly gives himself authority in the colonizer's language and verbal repertoire. In a way, it worked — this extraordinary text did get written — but in a way it did not, for the letter never reached its addressee.

FIGURE 3   Corregidor de minas. Catalog of Spanish abuses of indigenous labor force.

To grasp the import of Guaman Poma's project, one needs to keep in mind that the Incas had no system of writing. Their huge empire is said to be the only known instance of a full-blown bureaucratic state society built and administered without writing. Guaman Poma constructs his text by appropriating and adapting pieces of the representational repertoire of the invaders. He does not simply imitate or reproduce it: he selects and adapts it along Andean lines to express (bilingually, mind you) Andean interests and aspirations. Ethnographers have used the term *transculturation* to describe processes whereby members of subordinated or marginal groups select and invent from materials transmitted by a dominant or metropolitan culture. The term, originally coined by Cuban sociologist Fernando Ortiz in the 1940s, aimed to replace overly reductive concepts of acculturation and assimilation used to characterize culture under conquest. While subordinate peoples do not usually control what emanates from the dominant culture, they do determine to varying extents what gets absorbed into

their own and what it gets used for. Transculturation, like autoethnography, is a phenomenon of the contact zone.

As scholars have realized only relatively recently, the transcultural
character of Guaman Poma's text is intricately apparent in its visual as
well as its written component. The genre of the four hundred line drawings is European — there seems to have been no tradition of representational drawing among the Incas — but in their execution they deploy
specifically Andean systems of spatial symbolism that express Andean values and aspirations.[1]

In Figure 1, for instance, Adam is depicted on the left-hand side below
the sun, while Eve is on the right-hand side below the moon, and slightly
lower than Adam. The two are divided by the diagonal of Adam's digging
stick. In Andean spatial symbolism, the diagonal descending from the sun
marks the basic line of power and authority dividing upper from lower,
male from female, dominant from subordinate. In Figure 2, the Inca
appears in the same position as Adam, with the Spaniard opposite, the two
at the same height. In Figure 3, depicting Spanish abuses of power, the
symbolic pattern is reversed. The Spaniard is in a high position indicating
dominance, but on the "wrong" (right-hand) side. The diagonals of his
lance and that of the servant doing the flogging mark a line of illegitimate,
though real, power. The Andean figures continue to occupy the left-hand
side of the picture, but clearly as victims. Guaman Poma wrote that the
Spanish conquest had produced "un mundo al reves," the world in reverse.

In sum, Guaman Poma's text is truly a product of the contact zone. If
one thinks of cultures, or literatures, as discrete, coherently structured,
monolingual edifices, Guaman Poma's text, and indeed any autoethnographic world appears anomalous or chaotic — as it apparently did to the
European scholars Pietschmann spoke to in 1912. If one does not think of
cultures this way, then Guaman Poma's text is simply heterogeneous, as
the Andean region views itself and remains today. Such a text is heterogeneous at the reception end as well as the production end: it will read very
differently to people in different positions in the contact zone. Because it
deploys European and Andean systems of meaning making, the letter necessarily means differently to bilingual Spanish-Quechua speakers and to
monolingual speakers in either language; the drawings mean differently
to monocultural readers, Spanish or Andean, and to bicultural readers
responding to the Andean symbolic structures embodied in European
genres.

In the Andes in the early 1600s there existed a literate public with considerable intercultural competence and degrees of bilingualism. Unfortunately,
such a community did not exist in the Spanish court with which Guaman

---

[1]For an introduction in English to these and other aspects of Guaman Poma's work,
see Rolena Adorno. Adorno and Mercedes Lopez-Baralt pioneered the study of Andean
symbolic systems in Guaman Poma.

Poma was trying to make contact. It is interesting to note that in the same year Guaman Poma sent off his letter, a text by another Peruvian was adopted in official circles in Spain as the canonical Christian mediation between the Spanish conquest and Inca history. It was another huge encyclopedic work, titled the *Royal Commentaries of the Incas,* written, tellingly, by a mestizo, Inca Garcilaso de la Vega. Like the mestizo half brother who taught Guaman Poma to read and write, Inca Garcilaso was the son of an Inca princess and a Spanish official, and had lived in Spain since he was seventeen. Though he too spoke Quechua, his book is written in eloquent, standard Spanish, without illustrations. While Guaman Poma's life's work sat somewhere unread, the *Royal Commentaries* was edited and reedited in Spain and the New World, a mediation that coded the Andean past and present in ways thought unthreatening to colonial hierarchy.[2] The textual hierarchy persists: the *Royal Commentaries* today remains a staple item on PhD reading lists in Spanish, while the *New Chronicle and Good Government,* despite the ready availability of several fine editions, is not. However, though Guaman Poma's text did not reach its destination, the transcultural currents of expression it exemplifies continued to evolve in the Andes, as they still do, less in writing than in storytelling, ritual, song, dance-drama, painting and sculpture, dress, textile art, forms of governance, religious belief, and many other vernacular art forms. All express the effects of long-term contact and intractable, unequal conflict.

Autoethnography, transculturation, critique, collaboration, bilingualism, mediation, parody, denunciation, imaginary dialogue, vernacular expression — these are some of the literate arts of the contact zone. Miscomprehension, incomprehension, dead letters, unread masterpieces, absolute heterogeneity of meaning — these are some of the perils of writing in the contact zone. They all live among us today in the transnationalized metropolis of the United States and are becoming more widely visible, more pressing, and, like Guaman Poma's text, more decipherable to those who once would have ignored them in defense of a stable, centered sense of knowledge and reality.   *18*

Contact and Community

The idea of the contact zone is intended in part to contrast with ideas   *19*
of community that underlie much of the thinking about language,

---

[2]It is far from clear that the *Royal Commentaries* was as benign as the Spanish seemed to assume. The book certainly played a role in maintaining the identity and aspirations of indigenous elites in the Andes. In the mid-eighteenth century, a new edition of the *Royal Commentaries* was suppressed by Spanish authorities because its preface included a prophecy by Sir Walter Raleigh that the English would invade Peru and restore [the] Inca monarchy.

communication, and culture that gets done in the academy. A couple of years ago, thinking about the linguistic theories I knew, I tried to make sense of a utopian quality that often seemed to characterize social analyses of language by the academy. Languages were seen as living in "speech communities," and these tended to be theorized as discrete, self-defined, coherent entities, held together by a homogeneous competence or grammar shared identically and equally among all the members. This abstract idea of the speech community seemed to reflect, among other things, the utopian way modern nations conceive of themselves as what Benedict Anderson calls "imagined communities."[3] In a book of that title. Anderson observes that with the possible exception of what he calls "primordial villages," human communities exist as *imagined* entities in which people "will never know most of their fellow-members, meet them or even hear of them, yet in the minds of each lives the images of their communion." "Communities are distinguished," he goes on to say, "not by their falsity/ genuineness, but by *the style in which they are imagined*" (15; emphasis mine). Anderson proposes three features that characterize the style in which the modern nation is imagined. First, it is imagined as *limited*, by "finite, if elastic, boundaries"; second, it is imagined as *sovereign;* and, third, it is imagined as *fraternal*, "a deep, horizontal comradeship" for which millions of people are prepared "not so much to kill as willingly to die" (15). As the image suggests, the nation-community is embodied metonymically in the finite, sovereign, fraternal figure of the citizen-soldier.

Anderson argues that European bourgeoisies were distinguished by their ability to "achieve solidarity on an essentially imagined basis" (74) on a scale far greater than that of elites of other times and places. Writing and literacy play a central role in this argument. Anderson maintains, as have others, that the main instrument that made bourgeois nation-building projects possible was print capitalism. The commercial circulation of books in the various European vernaculars, he argues, was what first created the invisible networks that would eventually constitute the literate elites and those they ruled as nations. (Estimates are that 180 million books were put into circulation in Europe between the years 1500 and 1600 alone.) 20

Now obviously this style of imagining of modern nations, as Anderson describes it, is strongly utopian, embodying values like equality, fraternity, liberty, which the societies often profess but systematically fail to realize. The prototype of the modern nation as imagined community was, it seemed to me, mirrored in ways people thought about language and the speech community. Many commentators have pointed out how modern views of language as code and competence assume a unified and homogeneous social world in which language exists as a shared patrimony — as a device, pre- 21

---

[3]The discussion of community here is summarized from my essay "Linguistic Utopias."

cisely, for imagining community. An image of a universally shared literacy is also part of the picture. The prototypical manifestation of language is generally taken to be the speech of individual adult native speakers face-to-face (as in Saussure's famous diagram) in monolingual, even monodialectal situations — in short, the most homogeneous case linguistically and socially. The same goes for written communication. Now one could certainly imagine a theory that assumed different things — that argued, for instance, that the most revealing speech situation for understanding language was one involving a gathering of people each of whom spoke two languages and understood a third and held only one language in common with any of the others. It depends on what workings of language you want to see or want to see first, on what you choose to define as normative.

In keeping with autonomous, fraternal models of community, analy- 22 ses of language use commonly assume that principles of cooperation and shared understanding are normally in effect. Descriptions of interactions between people in conversation, classrooms, medical and bureaucratic settings, readily take it for granted that the situation is governed by a single set of rules or norms shared by all participants. The analysis focuses then on how those rules produce or fail to produce an orderly, coherent exchange. Models involving games and moves are often used to describe interactions. Despite whatever conflicts or systematic social differences might be in play, it is assumed that all participants are engaged in the same game and that the game is the same for all players. Often it is. But of course it often is not, as, for example, when speakers are from different classes or cultures, or one party is exercising authority and another is submitting to it or questioning it. Last year one of my children moved to a new elementary school that had more open classrooms and more flexible curricula than the conventional school he started out in. A few days into the term, we asked him what it was like at the new school. "Well," he said "they're a lot nicer, and they have a lot less rules. But know *why* they're nicer?" "Why?" I asked. "So you'll obey all the rules they don't have," he replied. This is a very coherent analysis with considerable elegance and explanatory power, but probably not the one his teacher would have given.

When linguistic (or literate) interaction is described in terms of order- 23 liness, games, moves, or scripts, usually only legitimate moves are actually named as part of the system, where legitimacy is defined from the point of view of the party in authority — regardless of what other parties might see themselves as doing. Teacher-pupil language, for example, tends to be described almost entirely from the point of view of the teacher and teaching, not from the point of view of pupils and pupiling (the word doesn't even exist, though the thing certainly does). If the classroom is analyzed as a social world unified and homogenized with respect to the teacher, whatever students do other than what the teacher specifies is invisible or anomalous to the analysis. This can be true in practice as well. On several occasions my fourth grader, the one busy obeying all the rules they didn't have, was given writing assignments that took the form of answering a series of questions to build up a paragraph. These questions often asked him to identify with the interests of those with power over him — parents, teachers, doctors, public authorities. He invariably sought ways to resist or subvert these assignments. One assignment, for instance, called for imagining "a helpful invention." The students were asked to write single-sentence responses to the following questions:

What kind of invention would help you?

How would it help you?

Why would you need it?

What would it look like?

Would other people be able to use it also?

What would be an invention to help your teacher?

What would be an invention to help your parents?

Manuel's reply read as follows:

A grate adventchin

Some inventchins are GRATE!!!!!!!!!!! My inventchin would be a shot that would put every thing you learn at school in your brain. It would help me by letting me graduate right now!! I would need it because it would let me play with my friends, go on vacachin and, do fun a lot more. It would look like a regular shot. Ather people would use to. This inventchin would help my teacher parents get away from a lot of work. I think a shot like this would be GRATE!

Despite the spelling, the assignment received the usual star to indicate the task had been fulfilled in an acceptable way. No recognition was available, however, of the humor, the attempt to be critical or contestatory, to parody the structures of authority. On that score, Manuel's luck was only slightly better than Guaman Poma's. What is the place of unsolicited oppositional discourse, parody, resistance, critique in the imagined classroom community? Are teachers supposed to feel that their teaching has been most successful when they have eliminated such things and unified the social world, probably in their own image? Who wins when we do that? Who loses?

Such questions may be hypothetical, because in the United States in the 1990s, many teachers find themselves less and less able to do that even if they want to. The composition of the national collectivity is changing and so are the styles, as Anderson put it, in which it is being imagined. In the 1980s in many nation-states, imagined national syntheses that had retained hegemonic force began to dissolve. Internal social groups with histories and lifeways different from the official ones began insisting on those histories and lifeways *as part of their citizenship*, as the very mode of their membership in the national collectivity. In their dialogues with dominant institutions, many groups began asserting a rhetoric of belonging that made demands beyond those of representation and basic rights granted from above. In universities we started to hear. "I don't just want you to let me be here; I want to belong here; this institution should belong to me as much as it does to anyone else." Institutions have responded with, among other things, rhetorics of diversity and multiculturalism whose import at this moment is up for grabs across the ideological spectrum.

These shifts are being lived out by everyone working in education 25
today and everyone is challenged by them in one way or another. Those of us committed to educational democracy are particularly challenged as that notion finds itself besieged on the public agenda. Many of those who govern us display, openly, their interest in a quiescent, ignorant, manipulable electorate. Even as an ideal, the concept of an enlightened citizenry seems to have disappeared from the national imagination. A couple of years ago the university where I work went through an intense and wrenching debate over a narrowly defined Western-Culture requirement that had been instituted there in 1980. It kept boiling down to a debate over the ideas of national patrimony, cultural citizenship, and imagined community. In the end, the requirement was transformed into a much more broadly defined course called Cultures, Ideas, Values.[4] In the context of the change, a new course was designed that centered on the Americas and the multiple cultural histories (including European ones) that have intersected here. As you can imagine, the course attracted a very diverse student body. The classroom functioned not like a homogeneous community or a horizontal alliance but like a contact zone. Every single text we read stood in specific historical relationships to the students in the class, but the range and variety of historical relationships in play were enormous. Everybody had a stake in nearly everything we read, but the range and kind of stakes varied widely.

It was the most exciting teaching we had ever done, and also the hard- 26
est. We were struck, for example, at how anomalous the formal lecture became in a contact zone (who can forget Atahualpa throwing down the Bible because it would not speak to him?). The lecturer's traditional (imagined) task — unifying the world in the class's eyes by means of a monologue that rings equally coherent, revealing, and true for all, forging an ad hoc community, homogeneous with respect to one's own words — this task became not only impossible but anomalous and unimaginable. Instead, one had to work in the knowledge that whatever one said was going to be systematically received in radically heterogeneous ways that we were neither able nor entitled to prescribe.

The very nature of the course put ideas and identities on the line. All the 27
students in the class had the experience, for example, of hearing their culture discussed and objectified in ways that horrified them; all the students saw their roots traced back to legacies of both glory and shame; all the students experienced face-to-face the ignorance and incomprehension, and

---

[4]For information about this program and the contents of courses taught in it, write Program in Cultures, Ideas, Values (CIV), Stanford Univ., Stanford, CA 94305.

occasionally the hostility, of others. In the absence of community values and the hope of synthesis, it was easy to forget the positives; the fact, for instance, that kinds of marginalization once taken for granted were gone. Virtually every student was having the experience of seeing the world described with him or her in it. Along with rage, incomprehension, and pain there were exhilarating moments of wonder and revelation, mutual understanding, and new wisdom — the joys of the contact zone. The sufferings and revelations were, at different moments to be sure, experienced by every student. No one was excluded, and no one was safe.

The fact that no one was safe made all of us involved in the course appreciate the importance of what we came to call "safe houses." We used the term to refer to social and intellectual spaces where groups can constitute themselves as horizontal, homogeneous, sovereign communities with high degrees of trust, shared understandings, temporary protection from legacies of oppression. This is why, as we realized, multicultural curricula should not seek to replace ethnic or women's studies, for example. Where there are legacies of subordination, groups need places for healing and mutual recognition, safe houses in which to construct shared understandings, knowledges, claims on the world that they can then bring into the contact zone.

Meanwhile, our job in the Americas course remains to figure out how to make that crossroads the best site for learning that it can be. We are looking for the pedagogical arts of the contact zone. These will include, we are sure, exercises in storytelling and in identifying with the ideas, interests, histories, and attitudes of others; experiments in transculturation and collaborative work and in the arts of critique, parody, and comparison (including unseemly comparisons between elite and vernacular cultural forms); the redemption of the oral; ways for people to engage with suppressed aspects of history (including their own histories); ways to move *into and out of* rhetorics of authenticity; ground rules for communication across lines of difference and hierarchy that go beyond politeness but maintain mutual respect; a systematic approach to the all-important concept of *cultural mediation*. These arts were in play in every room at the extraordinary Pittsburgh conference on literacy. I learned a lot about them there, and I am thankful.

WORKS CITED

Adorno, Rolena. *Guaman Poma de Ayala: Writing and Resistance in Colonial Peru.* Austin: U of Texas P, 1986.

Anderson, Benedict. *Imagined Communities: Reflections on the Origins and Spread of Nationalism.* London: Verso, 1984.

Garcilaso de la Vega, El Inca. *Royal Commentaries of the Incas.* 1613. Austin: U of Texas P, 1966.

Guaman Poma de Ayala, Felipe. *El primer nueva corónica y buen gobierno.* Manuscript. Ed. John Murra and Rolena Adorno. Mexico: Siglo XXI, 1980.

Pratt, Mary Louise. "Linguistic Utopias." *The Linguistics of Writing.* Ed. Nigel Fabb et al. Manchester: Manchester UP, 1987. 48–66.

Treviño, Gloria. "Cultural Ambivalence in Early Chicano Prose Fiction." Diss. Stanford U, 1985.

■ ■ ■

Reading Rhetorically

1. Pratt's statement in paragraph 5 that she "was asked to speak as an MLA member working in the elite academy" reveals that this essay was written as a speech that was delivered to a group of professors at a literature conference. What other words and phrases in the essay suggest to you that Pratt is shaping her argument to be heard by this particular audience? How does knowing Pratt's target audience affect the way you respond to the essay as a student reader?

2. What can you say about the way Pratt structures her piece? You might look in particular at the opening paragraphs about her son and baseball. What is the effect of starting this way? How does this anecdote relate to the other parts of the essay? How are all the parts related to the title?

3. How would you paraphrase Pratt's central argument? What key phrases in the essay clarify her argument for you? Make a list of the kinds of examples — personal anecdotes, quotations from other texts, images, and the like — that she uses to support her argument. How effective do you find these different examples?

Inquiring Further

4. Pratt opens with a reference to literacy ("Whenever the subject of literacy comes up . . ."). How do each of the two sections of the essay relate to literacy? What does *literacy* mean in each section? How do these definitions tie into Pratt's notion of the contact zone?

5. What distinctions does Pratt draw between the texts of Guaman Poma and Inca Garcilaso? How does each text illustrate her ideas about the "literate arts" and the "perils" of the contact zone (para. 18)? What other examples of contact zone texts (written or visual) can you think of that would demonstrate Pratt's ideas? Share your ideas with the class.

6. Pratt opens the second section of the essay ("Contact and Community") with a discussion of Benedict Anderson's imagined communities. Working in groups, define *imagined communities* in your own words. Then explain the traits and practices of imagined communities in the various examples Pratt uses in her essay and in examples drawn from your own experiences.

Framing Conversations

7. Given her argument, what do you think Pratt would say are the goals of education? Write an essay in which you consider how Pratt would evaluate the goals of education articulated in the essays by bell hooks (p. 293), Jonathan Kozol (p. 308), and James Loewen (p. 332). How do you think those authors would evaluate Pratt's educational goals?

8. Clearly, Pratt is interested in what happens when different groups of people connect with one another in what she calls a contact zone. One of the "arts of the contact zone" that she identifies is transculturation, which she defines as the "processes whereby members of subordinated or marginal groups select and invent from materials transmitted by a dominant or metropolitan culture" (para. 13). Write an essay in which you consider

how transculturation works in one or two other essays in this book. The selections by Ann duCille (p. 458), Noel Ignatiev (p. 512), and Héctor Tobar (p. 533) would be particularly good choices for this assignment.

9. Pratt analyzes visual texts to understand both the artist's thoughts and cultural ideas at the time the artwork was produced. In what ways is this similar to the visual analysis in the essays by Jean Kilbourne (p. 592), Henry Jenkins (p. 700), and Cynthia Selfe (p. 783)? Write an essay in which you draw on the strategies of at least two of these authors to analyze a visual text of your choice — for example, an advertisement, a painting, or a film poster — to consider what it says about cultural beliefs. In what way does the image make an argument about those beliefs?

■ ROBERT SCHOLES

On Reading a Video Text

Robert Scholes is a research professor at Brown University in the Department of Modern Culture and Media. He has been the recipient of many awards for literary study and has been president of the Modern Language Association of America. Scholes retired from full-time teaching in 1999, but he continues to teach and publish on many aspects of reading and writing, and contemporary literary studies. He has written, cowritten, and edited more than two dozen books and many journal articles, and has developed digital collections. He is perhaps best known for his books *Textual Power* (1985), on the subject of literary theory, and *Protocols of Reading* (1989), from which this piece is excerpted. In this text, Scholes demonstrates how much we can glean about the nature of our beliefs by "reading" the world as closely as we read written language. As you will see in this short but well-argued piece, Scholes finds meaning everywhere, including the "text" of a Budweiser commercial.

Scholes is part of a widening group of scholars that sees popular culture as an important source of information. He situates himself in a heated scholarly conversation about what students should be learning. In "On Reading a Video Text," he takes on critics like William Bennett (editor of the best-selling *Book of Virtues* series) and E. D. Hirsch — two scholars who lament what they see as the decline in cultural literacy among students today, who are learning less and less about classical literature. Scholes rebuts this claim, saying that "many Americans are not without culture; they simply have a different culture from that of Bennett and Hirsch" (para. 7). Scholes doesn't let his readers off the hook easily, though. He doesn't want us to assume that because we can quote from our favorite television shows and commercials that we are culturally literate. Instead, he points out, "What [Americans] really lack, for the most part, is any way of analyzing and criticizing the power of a text like the Budweiser commercial — not its power to sell beer, which is easily resisted, especially once you have tasted better beer — but its power to sell America" (para. 7). In this quotation you can see a number of Scholes's concerns.

One is how best to teach Americans to resist video culture when it is so tempting to "surrender" to the pleasure of simply watching. Another is the way the seemingly harmless stories embedded in commercials teach a view of America that can distort important truths, often hiding history and other information we need to make informed ethical decisions.

Just as the ancient Greeks shared rituals and collective cultural knowledge that allowed them to catch the nuances of plays by Aeschylus and Sophocles, Scholes believes we can — and must — teach contemporary students to discern and analyze the messages in video texts that reinforce myths that can be harmful. The Budweiser commercial Scholes describes is no longer playing on television, but you should be able to think of several current commercials that contain miniature narratives built on myths about what it means to be American. How easy is it to resist the simple pleasures of watching video images? Scholes urges us not to surrender to that pleasure, but instead to think critically about images and stories and how they compare to the reality of life in the United States. Critical thinking, he says, is the mark of the "greatest patriots" (para. 8). Read the piece carefully, and see if you agree.

The moments of surrender proposed to us by video texts come in many forms, but all involve a complex dynamic of power and pleasure. We are, for instance, offered a kind of power through the enhancement of our vision. Close-ups position us where we could never stand. Slow motion allows us an extraordinary penetration into the mechanics of movement, and, combined with music, lends a balletic grace to ordinary forms of locomotion. Filters and other devices cause us to see the world through jaundiced or rose-colored optics, coloring events with emotion more effectively than verbal pathetic fallacy and less obtrusively. These derangements of normal visual processing can be seen as either constraints or extensions of visual power — that is, as power over the viewer or as extensions of the viewer's own optical power, or both. Either way they offer us what is perhaps the greatest single virtue of art: change from the normal, a defense against the ever-present threat of boredom. Video texts, like all except the most utilitarian forms of textuality, are constructed upon a base of boredom, from which they promise us relief.

Visual fascination — and I have mentioned only a few of its obvious forms — is just one of the matrices of power and pleasure that are organized by video texts. Others include narrativity and what I should like to call, at least tentatively, cultural reinforcement. By narrativity, of course, I mean the pleasures and powers associated with the reception of stories presented in video texts. By cultural reinforcement, I mean the process through which video texts confirm viewers in their ideological positions and reassure them as to their membership in a collective cultural body. This function, which operates in the ethical-political realm, is an extremely important element of video textuality and, indeed, an extremely important dimension of all the mass media. This is a function performed throughout much of human history by literature and the other arts, but now, as the arts have become more estranged from their own culture and even opposed to it, the mass media have come to perform this role. What the epic poem did for ancient cultures, the romance for feudalism, and the novel for bourgeois society, the media — and especially television — now do for the commodified, bureaucratized world that is our present environment.

It is time, now, to look at these processes as they operate in some   3
specific texts. Let us begin with a well-known Budweiser commercial, which tells — most frequently in a format of twenty-eight seconds, though a longer version also exists — the life story of a black man pursuing a career as a baseball umpire. In this brief period of time, we are given enough information to construct an entire life story — provided we have the cultural knowledge upon which this construction depends. The story we construct is that of a young man from the provinces, who gets his "big break," his chance to make it in the big city, to rise to the top of his profession. We see him working hard in the small-time, small-town atmosphere of the minor leagues, where the pace of events is slower and more relaxed than it is "at the top." He gets his chance for success — the voice-over narrator says, "In the minors you got to make all the calls, and then one day you *get* the call" — after which we see him face his first real test. He must call an important and "close" play correctly and then withstand the pressure of dispute, neither giving ground by changing his mind (which would be fatal) nor reacting too vigorously to the challenge of his call by an offended manager. His passing of this test and being accepted is presented through a later scene in a bar, in which the manager who had staged the protest "toasts" the umpire with a bottle of Budweiser beer, with a chorus in the background singing, "You keep America working. This Bud's for you." From this scene we conclude that the ump has now "made it" and will live happily ever after. From a few scenes, then, aided by the voice-over narration and a music track, we construct an entire life. How do we do this? We draw upon a storehouse of cultural information that extends from fairy tales and other basic narrative structures to knowledge about the game and business of baseball.

In processing a narrative text we actually construct the story, bringing   4
a vast repertory of cultural knowledge to bear upon the text that we are contemplating. Our pleasure in the narrative is to some extent a constructive pleasure, based upon the sense of accomplishment we achieve by successfully completing this task. By "getting" the story, we prove our competence and demonstrate our membership in a cultural community. And what is the story that we "get"? It is the myth of America itself, of the racial melting pot, of upward mobility, of justice done without fear or favor. The corporate structure of baseball, with minor leagues offering a path for the talented to the celebrity and financial rewards of the majors,

embodies values that we all possess, we Americans, as one of the deepest parts of our cultural heritage or ideology. It is, of course, on the playing field that talent triumphs most easily over racial or social barriers. Every year in baseball new faces arrive. Young men, having proved themselves in the minors, get their chance to perform at the highest level. Yale graduates and high-school dropouts who speak little or no English are judged equally by how well they hit, run, throw, and react to game situations. If baseball is still the national pastime, it is because in it our cherished myths materialize — or appear to materialize.

The commercial we are considering is especially interesting because it 5 shows us a black man competing not with his body but with his mind, his judgment, and his emotions, in a cruelly testing public arena. Americans who attend to sports are aware that black athletes are just beginning to find acceptance at certain "leadership" positions, such as quarterback in professional football, and that there is still an active scandal over the slender representation of blacks at baseball's managerial and corporate levels. The case of the black umpire reminds viewers of these problems, even as it suggests that here, too, talent will finally prevail. The system works, America works. We can take pride in this. The narrative reduces its story to the absolutely bare essentials, making a career turn, or seem to turn, on a single decision. The ump must make a close call, which will be fiercely contested by a manager who is deliberately testing him. This is a story of initiation, in that respect, an ordeal that the ump must meet successfully. The text ensures that we know this is a test, by showing us the manager plotting in his dugout, and it gives us a manager with one of those baseball faces (Irish? German?) that have the history of the game written on them. This is not just partisan versus impartial judge, it is old man against youth, and white against black. We root for the umpire because we want the system to work — not just baseball but the whole thing: America. For this story to work, of course, the ump must make the right call, and we must know it to be right. Here, the close-up and slow motion come into play — just as they would in a real instant replay — to let us see both how close the call is and that the umpire has indeed made the right call. The runner is out. The manager's charge from the dugout is classic baseball protest, and the ump's self-control and slow walk away from the angry manager are gestures in a ritual we all know. That's right, we think, that's the way it's done. We know these moves the way the contemporaries of Aeschylus and Sophocles knew the myths upon which the Greek tragedies were based. Baseball is already a ritual, and a ritual we partake of mostly through the medium of television. The commercial has only to organize these images in a certain way to create a powerful narrative.

At the bar after the game, we are off stage, outside that ritual of base- 6 ball, but we are still in the world of myth. The manager salutes the ump with his tilted bottle of beer; the old man acknowledges that youth has passed its test. The sword on the shoulder of knighthood, the laying on of hands, the tilted Bud — all these are ritual gestures in the same narrative structure of initiation. To the extent that we have wanted this to happen we are gratified by this closing scene of the narrative text, and many things, as I have suggested, conspire to make us want this ending. We are dealing with an archetypal narrative that has been adjusted for maximum effect within a particular political and social context, and all this has been deployed with a technical skill in casting, directing, acting, photographing, and editing that is of a high order. It is very hard to resist the pleasure of this text, and we cannot accept the pleasure without, for the bewildering minute at least, also accepting the ideology that is so richly and closely entangled with the story that we construct from the video text. To accept the pleasure of this text is to believe that America works; and this is a comforting belief, itself a pleasure of an even higher order — for as long as we can maintain it. Does the text also sell Budweiser? This is something only market research (if you believe it) can tell. But it surely sells the American way first and then seeks to sell its brand of beer by establishing a metonymic connection between the product and the nation: a national beer for the national pastime.

An audience that can understand this commercial, successfully constructing the ump's story from the scenes represented in the text and the comments of the narrative voice, is an audience that understands narrative structure and has a significant amount of cultural knowledge as well, including both data (how baseball leagues are organized, for instance, and how the game is played) and myth (what constitutes success, for example, and what initiation is). At a time when critics such as William Bennett and E. D. Hirsch are bewailing our ignorance of culture, it is important to realize that many Americans are not without culture; they simply have a different culture from that of Bennett and Hirsch. What they really lack, for the most part, is any way of analyzing and criticizing the power of a text like the Budweiser commercial — not its power to sell beer, which is easily resisted, especially once you have tasted better beer — but its power to sell America. For the sort of analysis that I am suggesting, it is necessary to recover (as Eliot says) from the surrender to this text, and it is also necessary to have the tools of ideological criticism. Recovery, in fact, may depend upon critical analysis, which is why the analysis of video texts needs to be taught in all our schools.

Before moving on to the consideration of a more complex textual economy, we would do well to pause and consider the necessity of ideological criticism. One dimension of the conservative agenda for this country has been conspicuously anticritical. The proposals of William Bennett and E. D. Hirsch, for instance, different as they are in certain respects, are both recipes for the indoctrination of young people in certain cultural myths. The great books of past ages, in the eyes of Bennett, Hirsch, and Allan Bloom, are to be mythologized, turned into frozen monuments of Greatness in which our "cultural heritage" is embodied. This is precisely what Bloom does to Plato, for instance, turning the dialectical search for truth into a fixed recipe for "greatness of soul." The irony of this is that Plato can only die in this process. Plato's work can better be kept alive in our time by such irreverent critiques as that of Jacques Derrida, who takes Plato seriously as an opponent, which is to say, takes him dialectically. In this age of massive manipulation and disinformation, criticism is the only way we have of taking something seriously. The greatest patriots in our time will be those who explore our ideology critically, with particular attention to the gaps between mythology and practice. Above all, we must start with our most beloved icons, not the ones we profess allegiance to, but those that really have the power to move and shake us.

■ ■ ■

Reading Rhetorically

1. In small groups, discuss how you would divide Scholes's essay into three parts, offering a rationale for your choices. Be prepared to explain to the class the relationships you see among the different parts of the essay, and how they help Scholes make what you think is his larger point.

2. Locate the paragraphs where Scholes focuses on the Budweiser commercial. Using two pens or highlighters in different colors, mark the sentences that describe the commercial and those that analyze it. Do some sentences do both? What do you notice about the strategies Scholes uses to move between description and analysis?

3. Where does Scholes quote other people or draw on ideas that are not exclusively his own? What can you say about the placement of these passages and the role they play in helping Scholes make his larger point?

Inquiring Further

4. Now that you have a model for how to analyze a video text, use Scholes's approach to analyze a commercial that you find interesting. Tape the commercial so that you watch it repeatedly (you can be sure that Scholes watched that Budweiser commercial more than once), and write at least two paragraphs of detailed description and analysis. Read your paragraphs in small groups, and ask your listeners to tell you where your description and analysis is clear and persuasive, and where it could be strengthened.

5. In his conclusion, Scholes refers to conservative education reformers William Bennett, E. D. Hirsch, and Allan Bloom. Working in a small group, research one of these reformers. Be prepared to report to the class on at least three of the reformer's major ideas and the relationship the group sees between those ideas and Scholes's.

6. Scholes analyzes television advertisements, but his insights are useful for analyzing print advertisements as well. Gather ten advertisements from magazines you read, and use Scholes's strategies of analyzing the "stories" they tell about gender and race in the United States today. Share your conclusions with the class, using specific references to the advertisements as evidence.

Framing Conversations

7. Scholes's phrase "cultural reinforcement" (para. 2) is useful for considering the "work" done by various aspects of popular culture. Write an essay in which you use cultural reinforcement to examine the phenomena presented in Ann duCille's essay (p. 458) or Marguerite Helmers's essay (p. 679). Either pairing of these authors should offer a rich intersection of ideas about race, gender, and popular culture, and what they tell us about ourselves. In your essay, play the authors' ideas off against one another as you make a clear argument about the significance of your findings.

8. Scholes criticizes educational reformers who believe popular culture has no place in the school curriculum. What do you think are the positive and negative aspects of including popular culture in the K–12 curriculum? Write an essay in which you build a case for your perspective, drawing on the insights of Scholes, Mark Edmundson (p. 277), and Steven Johnson (p. 730).

9. Both Scholes and Michael Kimmel (p. 448) are interested in the ways we think about masculinity in modern culture. How do the ideas of these two writers build on one another, and what do you make of the connections you discover? Choose an example of a television commercial or a film that features men, and write an essay in which you use Scholes's and Kimmel's concepts about masculinity to help you analyze the significance you see in the visual text.

13

A World of Difference /
A Shrinking World

Who are "we" in relation to "others"?

The readings in this chapter confront the enormous and challenging question of who we are in relation to others in this rapidly shrinking — or what Thomas Friedman would call "flattening" — world. It is often hard to get our minds around the complex economic and political issues in an era of multiculturalism and globalization. Although most of us see and hear plenty of media sound bites on these topics, it is not always easy to understand how they affect us personally. Through their concrete, sometimes shocking, and often quite funny examples, the authors in this chapter demonstrate how thoroughly our daily experiences are shaped by these larger forces.

For example, Franklin Foer uses soccer as a lens through which to examine "the American culture wars," showing how we can track larger social trends through the popularity of certain sports. Malcolm Gladwell opens his piece by examining the resurgence of Hush Puppies, an example of the way ideas catch on both nationally and internationally. Kwame Anthony Appiah suggests that a debate by movie fans over *Million Dollar Baby* and *Sideways* reveals more than we might think about relational ethics, as can the foods people eat in different cultures. (Americans eat pigs, for example, but refuse to eat cats.) In other words, one place to look for evidence of our changing world, according to these writers, is in the stuff of our daily lives.

All the writers in this chapter move from concrete everyday experiences to the larger national and international trends they believe we need to see clearly in order to act ethically in the contemporary world. Jared Diamond, for example, urges us to learn from the many societies in the past that seemed to be thriving . . . often right up to the moment they collapsed. Thomas L. Friedman describes the landscape of outsourced economies, in which a telephone call to an American corporation is answered on the other side of the world. Is this a problem, an opportunity, or both? Diamond's and Friedman's books have climbed to the top of best-sellers' lists because although their answers are not simple, they are framed in ways that make it easier for us to grasp them.

The darker side of nationalism and globalism is the focus of Michael S. Kimmel's essay, "Gender, Class, and Terrorism," which asks us to consider a tragedy like 9/11 alongside the 1995 bombing of the Alfred P. Murrah Federal Building in Oklahoma City. In the context of the media's often pitting "us" against "them," Kimmel asks us to look at the many parallels between people who feel disenfranchised both in their own countries and in our rapidly shrinking global environment. What inspires so much fear in today's world? And why do so many respond with violence?

The essays here also raise issues about gender dynamics in different historical periods, the role of the media in mystifying or clarifying our understanding of the world, and the education we need to thrive in a quickly evolving world. In other words, these are essays about big ideas that have an impact on nearly everything you wear, do, eat, learn, and think. They do more than reveal the challenges of nationalism and globalization; they also suggest paths of understanding.

KWAME ANTHONY APPIAH

Moral Disagreement

Kwame Anthony Appiah grew up in Ghana and received his advanced degrees at Cambridge University in England. He is the Laurence S. Rockefeller University Professor of Philosophy and the University Center for Human Values at Princeton, where he teaches and does research in philosophy, ethics and identity, African and African-American cultural and literary studies, and the philosophical foundations of liberalism. He has published extensively on these topics in books like *Thinking It Through: An Introduction to Contemporary Philosophy* (2003) and *The Ethics of Identity* (2005). With Amy Gutmann, he cowrote *Color Conscious: The Political Morality of Race* (1996), a landmark text in the study of race in the United States. Appiah has also coedited a number of books with noted scholar Henry Louis Gates Jr., among them *Africana: Civil Rights; An A-to-Z Reference of the Movement That Changed America* (2005). In addition to these scholarly works, Appiah has published three novels; *Bu Me Bé: The Proverbs of the Akan* (2003), a collection of Asante proverbs cowritten with his mother, Peggy Appiah; and *In My Father's House: Africa in the Philosophy of Culture* (1992), a philosophical examination with autobiographical insights that received glowing reviews.

This reading is taken from a chapter in Appiah's book *Cosmopolitanism: Ethics in a World of Strangers* (2006), which explores the challenge of acting ethically in a world that is both shrinking and increasingly characterized by clashing civilizations. Appiah brings his philosophical training to bear on the impact of globalization, terrorism, and other economic and political realities that shape modern life, in order to understand what our obligations to others are in this rapidly changing environment. In this book, Appiah joins in conversation with George Lakoff, Martha Nussbaum, and other contemporary scholars who study the role of ethics in a politically charged world. Although Appiah is realistic about the challenges we face as global citizens, he is also optimistic about the human imagination and our ability to invent and adapt new ways of connecting.

If all this sounds too scholarly, too abstract to be interesting, you may be surprised by the pop culture examples and lively tone that characterize Appiah's writing. Pay attention to the way he draws ethical questions out of an imagined debate between fans of the film *Million Dollar Baby* and those who prefer *Sideways*. Appiah relies on this rhetorical strategy — moving from smaller personal examples to larger theoretical ones — repeatedly in this reading. Notice the ways he applies this strategy sometimes within sentences and other times between sentences. This is a key strategy of academic writing that you can try as well.

Notice, too, the effect of dividing this chapter into many short sections with catchy titles like "Red Peppers on Wednesdays" and "Gross Points." How do both sections and titles keep you interested and focused? Are there sections you find more compelling than others? Why? Appiah sets out to teach us "big ideas" about our moral universe, but he does so through many small examples of what it means to be cosmopolitan in today's environment.

You might test the applicability of Appiah's ideas by thinking about — and discussing with your classmates — the international news headlines on the day you read and analyze this piece. To what extent does Appiah offer tools for analyzing what unites and separates world citizens at this particular moment? What will it take for us to become "cosmopolitans"?

Through Thick and Thin

You don't need to leave home to have disagreements about questions of value. In a crowd of people leaving a movie theater, someone thinks *Million Dollar Baby* superior to *Sideways*, but her companion demurs. "How can you respect a movie that tells you that the life of a quadriplegic is so worthless that you ought to kill her if she asks you to?" In a lively discussion after a barroom brawl, some say that the bystander who intervened was courageous, others that he was reckless and should just have called the cops. In a classroom discussion of abortion, one student says that first-trimester abortions are bad for the mother and the fetus, but that they ought to be legal, if the mother chooses. Another thinks that killing a fetus isn't even as bad as killing a grown-up cat. A third claims all abortion is murder. If we are to encourage cosmopolitan engagement, moral conversation between people *across* societies, we must expect such disagreements: after all, they occur *within* societies.

But moral conflicts come in different varieties. To begin with, our vocabulary of evaluation is enormously multifarious. Some terms — "good," "ought" — are, as philosophers often put it, rather *thin*. They express approval, but their application is otherwise pretty unconstrained: good soil, good dog, good argument, good idea, good person. Knowing what the word means doesn't tell you much about what it applies to. Of course, there are certain acts that you can't imagine thinking are good. That's because you can't make sense of approving of them, though not because it's somehow built into the meaning of the word "good" that, say, snatching food from a starving child doesn't count.

Much of our language of evaluation, however, is much "thicker" than this. To apply the concept of "rudeness," for example, you have to think of the act you're criticizing as a breach of good manners or as lacking the appropriate degree of concern for the feelings of others. I say, *"Thank you,"* ironically, when you accidentally step on my foot, implying that you did it deliberately. That's rude. Thanking a person, without irony, for something that he's done for you isn't. "Courage" is a term of praise. But its meaning is more substantive than a thin term like "right" or "good": to be courageous requires that you do something that strikes us as risky or dangerous, something where you have something to lose. Opening the front door could be courageous: but only if you had agoraphobia or knew that the secret police had rung the doorbell.

Thin concepts are something like placeholders. When notions of right and wrong are actually at work, they're thickly enmeshed in the complications of particular social contexts. In that sense, as the distinguished American political theorist Michael Walzer says, morality starts out thick. It's when you're trying to find points of agreement with others, say, that you start to abstract out the thin concepts that may underlie the thick ones.[1]

Thin concepts seem to be universal; we aren't the only people who have the concepts of right and wrong, good and bad; every society, it seems, has terms that correspond to these thin concepts, too. Even thick concepts like rudeness and courage are ones that you find pretty much everywhere. But there are thicker concepts still that really are peculiar to particular societies. And the most fundamental level of disagreement occurs when one party to a discussion invokes a concept that the other simply doesn't have. This is the kind of disagreement where the struggle is not to agree but just to understand.

[1]Michael Walzer, *Thick and Thin: Moral Arguments at Home and Abroad* (Notre Dame: University of Notre Dame Press, 1994).

Family Matters

Sometimes, familiar values are intertwined with unfamiliar customs 6
and arrangements. People everywhere have ideas about your responsibility to your children, for instance. But who are your children? I grew up in
two societies that conceived of family in rather different ways. In part,
because these societies — Akan society in Ghana and the English world of
my mother's kin — have been in touch with one another for several centuries, these differences are diminishing. Still, an important difference
remains.

Consider the Akan idea of the *abusua*. This is a group of people related 7
by common ancestry, who have relations of love and obligation to one
another; the closer in time your shared ancestors, roughly speaking, the
stronger the bonds. Sounds, in short, like a family. But there is an important difference between an *abusua* and a family. For your membership in
an *abusua* depends only on who your mother is. Your father is irrelevant.
If you are a woman, then your children are in your *abusua*, and so are the
descendants of your daughters, and their daughters, on to the end of time.
Membership in the *abusua* is shared like mitochondrial DNA, passing only
through women. So I am in the same *abusua* as my sister's children but
not in the same one as my brother's children. And, since I am not related to
my father through a woman, he is not a member of my *abusua* either.

In short, the conception of the family in Akan culture is what anthro- 8
pologists call *matrilineal*. A hundred years ago, in most lives, your mother's
brother — your senior maternal uncle or *wɔfa* — would have played the
role a father would have been expected to play in England. He was responsible, with the child's mother, for making sure that his sister's children —
the word is *wɔfase* — were fed, clothed, and educated. Many married
women lived with their brothers, visiting their husbands on a regular
timetable. Of course, a man took an interest in his children, but his obligations to his children were relatively less demanding: rather like being an
English uncle, in fact.

Visitors are often somewhat surprised that the word that you would 9
most naturally use to refer to your brother or sister — which is *nua* — is
also the word for the children of your mother's *sisters*. And, in fact, people
sometimes will tell you, in Ghanaian English, that someone is "my sister,
same father, same mother," which you might have thought was a couple of
qualifications too many. (If someone tells you that a woman is his junior
mother, on the other hand, he's referring to his mother's younger sister.)

When I was a child all this was changing. More men were living with 10
their wives and children and not supporting their sisters' children. But my
father still got the school reports of his sisters' children, sent them pocket
money, discussed, with their mothers, their schooling, paid the bills at the
family house of his *abusua*. He also regularly ate with his favorite sister,
while his children and wife — that's us — ate together at home.

There are, in short, different ways of organizing family life. Which one *11*
makes sense to you will depend, in good measure, on the concepts with
which you grew up. As long as a society has a way of assigning responsibilities for the nurture of children that works and makes sense, it seems to
me, it would be odd to say that one way was the right way of doing it, and
all the others wrong. We feel, rightly, that a father who is delinquent in his
child support payments is doing something wrong. Many Asante, especially in the past, would feel the same about a delinquent *wɔfa*. Once you
understand the system, you'll be likely to agree: and it won't be because
you've given up any of your basic moral commitments. There are thin, universal values here — those of good parenting — but their expression is
highly particular, thickly enmeshed with local customs and expectations
and the facts of social arrangements.

Red Peppers on Wednesdays

But there are other local values that scarcely correspond to anything you *12*
might recognize as important. My father, for example, wouldn't eat "bush
meat," animals killed in the forest. This included venison, and, he used to
tell us, when he once ate it by accident in England, his skin broke out in a
rash the next day. Had you asked him why he wouldn't eat bush meat,
though, he wouldn't have said he didn't like it or that he was allergic to it.
He would have told you — if he thought it was any of your business — that
it was *akyiwadeɛ* for him, because he was of the clan of the Bush Cow. Ety-
mologically *akyiwadeɛ* means something like "a thing you turn your back
on," and, if you had to guess at the translation of it, you would presumably
suggest "taboo." That is, of course, a word that came into English from a
Polynesian language, where it was used to refer to a class of things that
people of certain groups strenuously avoided.

As in Polynesia, in Asante doing one of these forbidden things leaves *13*
you "polluted," and there are various remedies, ways of "cleansing" yourself. We all have experience with the sense of revulsion, and the desire to
cleanse ourselves, but that doesn't mean that we really have the concept of
akyiwadeɛ. Because to have that idea — that thick concept — you have to
think that there are things that you ought not to do because of your clan
membership, or because they are taboo to a god to whom you owe allegiance. Now, you might say that there's a rationale of sorts for a member of
the Bush Cow clan's not eating bush meat. Your clan animal is, symbolically, a relative of yours; so, for you, eating it (and its relatives) is a bit like
eating a person. And perhaps this is one rationalization that a member of
the clan might offer. But the list of *akyiwadeɛ* in traditional Asante society
far exceeds anything that you can make sense of in this sort of way. One
shrine god named Edinkra — mentioned in the 1920s by Captain Rattray,
the colonial anthropologist who first wrote extensively about Asante
traditions — had among its taboos red peppers on Wednesdays.

Now, I don't claim that you can't learn what *akyiwadeɛ* means: indeed, *14*
I hope you pretty much grasp how the word is used on the basis of what
I've told you already, and if you read the complete works of Captain Rattray, you'd know a lot more about Akan taboos, certainly enough to grasp
the concept. Nevertheless, this isn't an idea that plays any role in your
actual thinking. There are acts we avoid that we rather loosely call "taboo,"
of course: the prohibition on incest, for example. But you don't really think
incest is to be avoided because it is taboo. Your thought is exactly the other
way round: it's "taboo" because there are good reasons not to do it.

Some *akyiwadeɛ*, like the one that prohibited my father from eating *15*
venison, are specific to particular kinds of people, as is evidenced in a
proverb that makes a metaphor of the fact:

> Nnipa gu ahodoɔ mmiɛnsa, nanso obiara wɔ n'akyiwadeɛ: ɔhene,
> ɔdehyeɛ na akoa. Ɔhene akyiwadeɛ ne akyinnyeɛ, ɔdehyeɛ deɛ ne nsamu,
> na akoa deɛ ne nkyeraseɛ.
> *People fall into three kinds, but everyone has his own taboo: the ruler, the*
> *royal, and the slave. The ruler's taboo is disagreement, the royal's is disrespect,*
> *and the slave's is the revealing of origins.*

As a result, even if you were in Asante, many taboos wouldn't affect you,
since you don't belong to an Asante clan and don't have obligations to
shrine gods. But there are many things all Asantes "turn their backs on"
and would expect everyone else to as well. Given that some of them have to
do with contact with menstruating women or men who have recently had
sex, they can affect strangers, even if strangers don't act on them. Once you
know about the taboos, they can raise questions as to how you should act.
Since, for example, shaking hands with a menstruating woman is taboo to
a chief, some visitors to the Asante court have a decision to make about
whether to come to a meeting.

I have deliberately not used the word "moral" to describe these taboos. *16*
They are certainly values: they guide acts, thoughts, and feelings. They are
unlike what we would think of as moral values, however, in at least three
ways. First, they don't always apply to everybody. Only members of the
Ekuona clan have the obligation to avoid bush meat. Second, you are polluted if you break a taboo, even if you do it by accident. So, whereas with
an offense against morality, "I didn't mean to do it" counts as a substantial
defense, with taboo breaking, the reply must be, "It doesn't matter what
you meant to do. You're polluted. You need to get clean." Oedipus was no
better off for having broken the incest taboo unknowingly. A final difference between taboos and moral demands is that breaches of them pollute
mostly *you:* they aren't fundamentally about how you should treat other
people; they're about how you should keep yourself (ritually) clean.

Now, all around the world many people have believed in something *17*
like *akyiwadeɛ*, and the analogous term, *tabu* or whatever, is certainly a
powerful part of evaluative language. But — at least nowadays — while
the avoidance of taboos is still important to people, it isn't as important as

many other sorts of values. That's partly because, as I said, while breaches of taboo produce pollution, that pollution can usually be ritually cleansed. The laws of kashrut for Orthodox Jews in our country are like this, too: obedience to them is important, and so is a commitment to obeying them if you can. If you break them accidentally, however, the right response is not guilt but the appropriate ritual form of purification. Moral offenses — theft, assault, murder — on the other hand, are not expiated by purification. Now there are historical trends that help explain why a concern with *akyiwadeε* plays a smaller part in contemporary life in my hometown than it would have done when my father was growing up. One reason is that even more people now are Christian and Muslim, and these taboos are associated with earlier forms of religion. Our earlier religious ideas survive, as I've noted, even in the lives of devout believers in these global faiths. They just have less weight than they had before they were competing with Jehovah and Allah. In the old days, you had reason to fear the wrath of the gods or the ancestors if you broke taboos — that was part of why it was important to make peace with them by cleansing yourself. But these powers have less respect in the contemporary world. . . .

Another reason is that the forms of identity — the clan identities, for [18] example — with which they are often associated are just a good deal less significant than they used to be. People still mostly know their clans. And in the past, when you showed up in a strange town in another part of the Akan world, you could have sought hospitality from the local leaders of your clan. Now, however, there are hotels; travel is commoner (so the demands of clan hospitality could easily become oppressive); and clans, like the families of which they are a part, recede in importance anyway when so many people live away from the places where they were born.

Equally important, I think, most people in Kumasi know now that our [19] taboos are local: that strangers do not know what is and is not taboo and that, if they do, they have taboos of their own. So increasingly people think of taboos as "things *we* don't do." The step from "what *we* don't do" to "what we *happen* not to do" can be a small one; and then people can come to think of these practices as the sort of quaint local custom that one observes without much enthusiasm and, in the end, only when it doesn't cause too much fuss.

Gross Points

The *akyiwadeε* is, as we've seen, thickly enmeshed in all sorts of customs [20] and factual beliefs (not least the existence of irascible ancestors and shrine gods), and one response to such alien values is just to dismiss them as primitive and irrational. But if that is what they are, then the primitive and the irrational are pervasive here, too. Indeed, the affect, the sense of repugnance, that underlies *akyiwadeε* is surely universal: that's one reason it's not difficult to grasp. Many Americans eat pigs but won't eat cats. It would be hard to make the case that cats are, say, dirtier or more intelligent than pigs. And since there are societies where people *will* eat cats, we know that it is possible for human beings to eat them with pleasure and without danger. Most American meat eaters who refuse to eat cats have only the defense that the very thought of it fills them with disgust. Indeed, all of us have things that we find contact with polluting: touching them makes us feel dirty; eating them would nauseate us. We're likely to run off to wash our hands or wash out our mouths if we come into contact with them. Mostly, when we have these responses, we defend them as rational: cockroaches and rats and other people's saliva or vomit do actually carry diseases, we say; cats and dogs taste horrible. Yet these reactions are not really explained by the stories we tell. Flies carry most of the same risks as cockroaches, but usually produce less "pollution." And people are disgusted by the idea of drinking orange juice that has had a cockroach in it, even if they know that the cockroach was rigorously cleansed of all bacteria by being autoclaved in advance. They're reluctant to eat chocolate shaped like dog feces, even if they know exactly what it is.

Psychologists (notably Paul Rozin, who has conducted many experiments along these lines) think that this capacity for disgust is a fundamental human trait, one that evolved in us because distinguishing between what you will and will not eat is an important cognitive task for an omnivorous species like our own. Disgust goes with nausea, because it is a response that developed to deal with food that we should avoid. But that capacity for disgust, like all our natural capacities, can be built on by culture. Is it the *same* capacity that makes some men in many cultures feel polluted when they learn they have shaken hands with a menstruating woman? Or that makes most Americans squirm in disgust at the thought of incest? I don't think we yet know. The pervasiveness of these taboo responses does suggest, however, that they draw on something deep in human nature.[2]   21

Most people in this country, both secular and religious, think that the attitudes of some of their contemporaries to certain sexual acts — masturbation and homosexuality, for instance, or even consensual adult incest — are simply versions of taboos found in many cultures around the world. In the so-called Holiness Code, at the end of Leviticus, for example, eating animals that have died of natural causes requires you to wash yourself and your clothes, and even then you will be unclean until the evening (Leviticus 17:15–16). Priests, "the sons of Aaron," are told at Leviticus 22:5–8 that if they touch people or "any swarming thing" that is polluting, they must bathe and wait until sunset before they can eat the "sacred donations." The same chapters proscribe the consuming of blood, bodily self-mutilation (tattoos, shaving for priests, cutting gashes in one's flesh,   22

[2]See Paul Rozin, "Food Is Fundamental, Fun, Frightening, and Far-reaching," *Social Research* 66 (1999): 9–30. I am grateful to John Haidt for a discussion of these issues.

though not, of course, male circumcision), and seeing various of one's relatives naked, while prescribing detailed rules for certain kinds of sacrifice. For most modern Christians, these regulations are parts of Jewish law that Christ freed people from. But the famous proscriptions of a man's "lying with a man as with a woman" are to be found alongside these passages, along with commands to avoid incest and bestiality, which most Christians still endorse.[3]

Earlier in Leviticus, we find an extensive set of proscriptions on contact, both direct and indirect, with menstruating women and rules for cleansing oneself from that form of pollution; as well as rules that indicate that male ejaculation is polluting, so that, even after a man has bathed, he is ritually unclean until evening.[4] Like Akan traditions, these rules are embedded in metaphysical beliefs: they are repeatedly said to be laws given by God to Moses for the Israelites, and often they have religious explanations embedded in them. The prohibition on consuming blood is explained thus:

> For the life of the flesh is in the blood. And as for Me, I have given it to you on the altar to ransom your lives, for it is the blood that ransoms in exchange for life. Therefore have I said to the Israelites: no living person among you shall consume blood, nor shall the sojourner who sojourns in your midst consume blood.[5]

Leviticus should remind us that appeals to values do not come neatly parceled out according to kinds. You might think that failing to respect your parents is a bad thing, but that it's bad in a way that's different from adultery; different, too, from sex with an animal; different, again, from incest with your daughter-in-law. I confess that I do not think sex between men, even if they lie with one another "as with a woman," is bad at all. But all of these acts are proscribed in succession by the Holiness Code; in fact (in Leviticus 20:9–13) all of them are deemed worthy of death.

Among those who take them seriously, these prohibitions evoke a deep, visceral response; they're also entangled in beliefs about metaphysical or religious matters. The combination of these two features is what makes them so difficult to discuss with people who share neither the response nor the metaphysics. Yet even with values we do not take seriously, there is something to be hoped for: namely, understanding. Nor do you have to share a value to feel how it might motivate someone. We can be moved by Antigone's resolve to bury her brother's corpse, even if (unlike those Indians and Greeks that Darius scandalized) we couldn't care less about how cadavers are disposed of, and think she shouldn't really, either.

And while taboos can lead to genuine disagreements about what to do, many people readily understand that such values vary from place to place. Asante people largely accept now that others don't feel the power of our

[3]Leviticus 18:22 and 20:13.
[4]Menstruation: Leviticus 15:19–28. Male ejaculation: Leviticus 15:16–18.
[5]Leviticus 17:11–13. . . . The proscription itself is in the preceding verse.

taboos; we know that they may have their own. And, most importantly, these local values do not, of course, stop us from also recognizing, as we do, kindness, generosity, and compassion, or cruelty, stinginess, and inconsiderateness — virtues and vices that are recognized widely among human societies. So, too, scattered among the various abominations in Leviticus we come across, from time to time, appeals to values that are universal and that discipline the demands made by the taboos. Leviticus 19 commands us to leave a share of our crops for the poor, to avoid lying and dissembling, fraud, and theft; not to speak ill of the deaf or put a stumbling block in the way of the blind; not to slander our relatives. Indeed, it makes the impossibly demanding command that "you shall love your fellow man as yourself" (Leviticus 19:18). There are values here that not all of us recognize; there are many we all do.

Terms of Contention

Cosmopolitans suppose that all cultures have enough overlap in their   27
vocabulary of values to begin a conversation. But they don't suppose, like some universalists, that we could all come to agreement if only we had the same vocabulary. Despite what they say in Japan, almost every American knows what it is to be polite, a thickish concept. That doesn't mean that we can't disagree about when politeness is on display. A journalist interviews a foreign dictator, someone who is known for his abuses of human rights. She speaks deferentially, frequently calling him Your Excellency. She says, "Some people have suggested that you have political prisoners in your jails," when everybody knows that this is so. "What do you say, Your Excellency, to the accusations of torture by your secret police?" "Nonsense," he replies. "Lies made up by people who want to confuse foreigners about the progress we are making in my country." She moves on. Is this politeness? Or is it a craven abdication of the journalist's obligation to press for the truth? Can it be both? If it is politeness, is it appropriate, in these circumstances, to be polite? You can imagine such a conversation proceeding for a long while without resolution.

Politeness is a value term from the repertory of manners, which we   28
usually take to be less serious than morals. But this sort of controversy also surrounds the application of more straightforwardly ethical terms — like "brave" — and more centrally moral ones — like "cruel." Like most terms for virtues and vices, "courage" and "cruelty" are what philosophers call "open-textured": two people who both know what they mean can reasonably disagree about whether they apply in a particular case.[6] Grasping

---

[6]H. L. A. Hart introduced the idea of "open texture" to discussions of jurisprudence in *The Concept of Law* (Oxford: Clarendon Press, 1997), chap. 6. He borrowed the idea of open texture from F. Waismann, who thought open texture was an irreducible feature of language. The example of the bylaw about vehicles in the park is Hart's; see his "Positivism and the Separation of Law and Morals," *Harvard Law Review* 71 (1958): 593–629.

what the words mean doesn't give you a rule that will definitively decide whether it applies in every case that might come along. Nearly half a century ago, the philosopher of law H. L. A. Hart offered as an example of open texture, a bylaw that prohibits "vehicles" in a public park. Does it apply to a two-inch-long toy car in a child's pocket? "Vehicle" has an open texture. There are things to be said on either side. Of course, in the context of the rule, it may be clear that the idea was to stop people from driving around, disturbing the peace. Let the child bring in the toy. But doesn't that rationale suggest that a skateboard is a vehicle? There need be no reason to think that those who made the rule had any answer to this question in mind. Our language works very well in ordinary and familiar cases. Once things get interesting, even people who know the language equally well can disagree.

The open texture of our evaluative language is even more obvious. One 29 of my great-uncles once led a cavalry charge against a machine-gun emplacement, armed with a sword. Brave? Or just foolhardy? (You may have guessed that this uncle was Asante; actually, he was English, fighting against the Ottomans in the First World War. Great-Uncle Fred called his autobiography *Life's a Gamble*, so you can tell he was willing to take risks.) Aristotle argued that courage involved an *intelligent* response to danger, not just ignoring it. Perhaps, in the circumstances and given his aims, that saber charge *was* the smartest thing to do. Still, even if we got as full a story as we could ask for about the exact circumstances, you and I might end up disagreeing.

Several years ago, an international parliament of religious leaders 30 issued what they called a "universal declaration of a global ethic." The credo's exhortations had the quality of those horoscopes that seem wonderfully precise while being vague enough to suit all comers. "We must not commit any kind of sexual immorality": a fine sentiment, unless we don't agree about what counts as sexual immorality. "We must put behind us all forms of domination and abuse": but societies that, by our lights, subject women to domination and abuse are unlikely to recognize themselves in that description. They're convinced that they're protecting women's honor and chastity. "We must strive for a just social and economic order, in which everyone has an equal chance to reach full potential as a human being": a Randian will take this to be an endorsement of unfettered capitalism, as a Fabian will take it to be an endorsement of socialism.

And so it goes with our most central values. Is it cruel to kill cattle in 31 slaughterhouses where live cattle can smell the blood of the dead? Or to spank children in order to teach them how to behave? The point is not that we couldn't argue our way to one position or the other on these questions; it's only to say that when we disagree, it won't always be because one of us just doesn't understand the value that's at stake. It's because applying value terms to new cases requires judgment and discretion. Indeed, it's often part of our understanding of these terms that their applications are *meant* to be argued about. They are, to use another piece of philosopher's jargon, *essentially contestable*. For many concepts, as W. B. Gallie wrote in introducing the term, "proper use inevitably involves endless disputes about their proper use on the part of users."[7] Evaluative language, I've been insisting, aims to shape not just our acts but our thoughts and our feelings. When we describe past acts with words like "courageous" and "cowardly," "cruel" and "kind," we are shaping what people think and feel about what was done — and shaping our understanding of our moral language as well. Because that language is open-textured and essentially contestable, even people who share a moral vocabulary have plenty to fight about. . . .

■ ■ ■

Reading Rhetorically

1. Explain in your own words what Appiah means by the terms *thick* and *thin* as applied to the concept of morality, and give several examples of each category. Then explain your reasoning using examples to illustrate your ideas.

2. What is the purpose of the long list of taboos Appiah includes in "Gross Points," the section that begins on page 384? What effect do you think he hopes to have on his readers by describing the things that disgust people in different cultures? How is this strategy connected to the overall purpose of this excerpt?

3. Appiah poses many of his ideas as questions in the "Terms of Contention" section of his text (pp. 387–89). Discuss the purpose these questions serve. How might you use a similar strategy in your own writing? Draft a few questions of this sort to include in an essay you are currently composing.

Inquiring Further

4. To learn more about food taboos, search the Web for "food and taboos." You can narrow your search by country, religion, or ethnicity, if you like. Find at least three scholarly articles that seem interesting and read them closely enough to report what you learn to the rest of the class. How do Appiah's ideas help you understand your responses to what you have learned?

5. In paragraph 4, Appiah talks about the ideas of Michael Walzer, a well-known political theorist who has written about many aspects of justice in daily life. Using a Google search on Walzer's name to get you started, find and read several interviews with Walzer and/or reviews of his work to learn more about his ideas; then share your findings with your classmates. Why do you think Appiah finds Walzer so helpful in building his own argument?

6. How much do you know about matrilineal family models? Discuss what you know with your classmates, and use the library to find out more about

[7]W. B. Gallie, "Essentially Contested Concepts," *Proceedings of the Aristotelian Society* 56 (1956): 169.

where and when these social models have existed. You also might interview an anthropology professor on your campus about this topic. Share what you have learned with the class, and then discuss how matrilineal models would alter contemporary Western social practices.

Framing Conversations

7. How do Appiah's ideas about widely varying cultural concepts apply to Mary Louise Pratt's analysis of culture (p. 354)? Write an essay in which you draw on both authors' ideas and examples to take a stand on how we might understand cultural clashes and their significance. Include your own examples if you like to support your point.

8. What skills and knowledge does Appiah think contemporary world citizens ought to have? How do his ideas compare with those Héctor Tobar (p. 533) writes about? With your own ideas? Write an essay in which Appiah, Tobar, and you "converse" about what skills and knowledge world citizens ought to have, and why. Be sure to support your claims with concrete examples.

9. How do you think Appiah and Malcolm Gladwell (p. 432) would analyze each other's concepts about cultural similarities and differences? In an essay that plays these authors' ideas off one another, make an argument of your own about the significance of recognizing that there may be similarities between cultures that we sometimes fail to see, and that there may be differences between cultures that really cannot be bridged. Draw on a specific political event to support your thinking.

JARED DIAMOND

Why Do Some Societies Make Disastrous Decisions?

Jared Diamond is an evolutionary biologist who has received a MacArthur Fellowship (a "genius grant"), a Pulitzer Prize, and numerous other awards for his teaching, public lectures, research, and writing. He has held professorships in physiology and geography at the University of California, Los Angeles. Although his research includes seventeen expeditions to New Guinea and its neighboring islands to study bird evolution, most readers know Diamond from his big best-selling books on the evolution of human societies. His book on hominoid evolution, *The Third Chimpanzee: The Evolution and Future of the Human Animal* (1992), explores the way humans, who are just another large mammal, came to conquer the world. Some of the ideas in that book are developed further in a catchily titled book, *Why Is Sex Fun? The Evolution of Human Sexuality* (1997). Diamond's *Guns, Germs, and Steel: The Fates of Human Societies* (2005) earned him the Pulitzer and a wide reading public fascinated with the connections between geographic and environmental effects on countries and their ability to develop and dominate other countries politically and militarily.

In this excerpt from *Collapse: How Societies Choose to Fail or Succeed* (2004), Diamond examines ancient and modern societies that have flourished or collapsed based on their ability or inability to discern coming disasters. Whatever the cause of the disasters — overmining, overhunting, overpopulation, or the failure to recognize brewing social disintegration — learning from history, Diamond claims, is crucial to meeting the deadly challenges we face in our own time. Like the frog who sits willingly in a pan of water heating on a stove until it is boiled to death, we often fail to recognize the dangers around us, Diamond argues.

In this excerpt from a chapter in *Collapse*, readers get a glimpse of Professor Diamond interacting with his students as they ponder the "question of why societies end up destroying themselves through disastrous decisions" (para. 3). As you read, consider what it feels like as a reader to be placed in the role of student to Diamond's teacher. How is this chapter shaped like a class lecture? What are the possible strengths and shortcomings of this organization?

Diamond's claims are based on a good deal of research, and he invites us to learn more from the sources he lists in the "Further Readings" section that follows this chapter. This is a different format from citing sources in notes or in a list of references. What does it offer that differs from more traditional methods of citing sources? As you read, notice the ways Diamond distinguishes his own ideas from those of others — his use of Joseph Tainter's theories in paragraphs 3 and 4 is especially interesting — and how he uses sources to help him develop his points. Not all critics are persuaded that the connections Diamond makes are convincing, so read with an open but critical mind. If you find a number of his leaps between past and present, or between one society and another, more or less persuasive than the other connections he makes, ask yourself why.

Diamond is a contemporary writer whose popularity makes him a public intellectual with real influence on the way many people have come to think about social evolution. If you find Diamond's approach to understanding social dynamics interesting, you might want to read *Collapse* in its entirety or one of his other equally provocative books, or watch the **PBS** documentary version of *Guns, Germs, and Steel.*

E ducation is a process involving two sets of participants who supposedly play different roles: teachers who impart knowledge to students, and students who absorb knowledge from teachers. In fact, as every open-minded teacher discovers, education is also about students imparting knowledge to their teachers, by challenging the teachers' assumptions and by asking questions that the teachers hadn't previously thought of. I recently repeated that discovery when I taught a course, on how societies cope with environmental problems, to highly motivated undergraduates at my institution, the University of California at Los Angeles (UCLA). In effect, the course was a trial run-through of this book's material, at a time when I had drafted some chapters, was planning other chapters, and could still make extensive changes.

My first lecture after the class's introductory meeting was on the col- 2 lapse of Easter Island society. . . . In the class discussion after I had finished my presentation, the apparently simple question that most puzzled my students was one whose actual complexity hadn't sunk into me before: how on earth could a society make such an obviously disastrous decision as to cut down all the trees on which it depended? One of the students asked what I thought the islander who cut down the last palm tree said as he was doing it. For every other society that I treated in subsequent lectures, my students raised essentially the same question. They also asked the related question: how often did people wreak ecological damage intentionally, or at least while aware of the likely consequences? How often did people instead do it without meaning to, or out of ignorance? My students wondered whether — if there are still people left alive a hundred years from now — those people of the next century will be as astonished about our blindness today as we are about the blindness of the Easter Islanders.

This question of why societies end up destroying themselves through 3 disastrous decisions astonishes not only my UCLA undergraduates but also professional historians and archaeologists. For example, perhaps the most cited book on societal collapses is *The Collapse of Complex Societies*, by the archaeologist Joseph Tainter. In assessing competing explanations for ancient collapses, Tainter remained skeptical of even the possibility that they might have been due to depletion of environmental resources, because that outcome seemed a priori so unlikely to him. Here is his reasoning: "One supposition of this view must be that these societies sit by and watch the encroaching weakness without taking corrective actions. Here is a major difficulty. Complex societies are characterized by centralized decision-making, high information flow, great coordination of parts, formal channels of command, and pooling of resources. Much of this structure seems to have the capability, if not the designed purpose, of countering fluctuations and deficiencies in productivity. With their administrative structure, and capacity to allocate both labor and resources, dealing with adverse environmental conditions may be one of the things that complex societies do best (see, for example, Isbell [1978]). It is curious that they would collapse when faced with precisely those conditions they are equipped to circumvent. . . . As it becomes apparent to the members or administrators of a complex society that a resource base is deteriorating, it seems most reasonable to assume that some rational steps are taken toward a resolution. The alternative assumption — of idleness in the face of disaster — requires a leap of faith at which we may rightly hesitate."

That is, Tainter's reasoning suggested to him that complex societies 4 are not likely to allow themselves to collapse through failure to manage their environmental resources. Yet it is clear from all the cases discussed in this book that precisely such a failure has happened repeatedly. How did so many societies make such bad mistakes?

My UCLA undergraduates, and Joseph Tainter as well, have identified a baffling phenomenon: namely, failures of group decision-making on the part of whole societies or other groups. That problem is of course related to the problem of failures of individual decision-making. Individuals, too, make bad decisions: they enter bad marriages, they make bad investments and career choices, their businesses fail, and so on. But some additional factors enter into failures of group decision-making, such as conflicts of interest among members of the group, and group dynamics. This is obviously a complex subject to which there would not be a single answer fitting all situations. 5

What I'm going to propose instead is a road map of factors contributing to failures of group decision-making. I'll divide the factors into a fuzzily delineated sequence of four categories. First of all, a group may fail to anticipate a problem before the problem actually arrives. Second, when the problem does arrive, the group may fail to perceive it. Then, after they perceive it, they may fail even to try to solve it. Finally, they may try to solve it but may not succeed. While all this discussion of reasons for failure and societal collapses may seem depressing, the flip side is a heartening subject: namely, successful decision-making. Perhaps if we understood the reasons why groups often make bad decisions, we could use that knowledge as a checklist to guide groups to make good decisions. 6

The first stop on my road map is that groups may do disastrous things because they failed to anticipate a problem before it arrived, for any of several reasons. One is that they may have had no prior experience of such problems, and so may not have been sensitized to the possibility. 7

A prime example is the mess that British colonists created for themselves when they introduced foxes and rabbits from Britain into Australia in the 1800s. Today these rate as two of the most disastrous examples of impacts of alien species on an environment to which they were not native. . . . These introductions are all the more tragic because they were carried out intentionally at much effort, rather than resulting inadvertently from tiny seeds overlooked in transported hay, as in so many cases of establishment of noxious weeds. Foxes have proceeded to prey on and exterminate many species of native Australian mammals without evolutionary experience of foxes, while rabbits consume much of the plant fodder intended for sheep and cattle, outcompete native herbivorous mammals, and undermine the ground by their burrows. 8

With the gift of hindsight, we now view it as incredibly stupid that colonists would intentionally release into Australia two alien mammals that have caused billions of dollars in damages and expenditures to control them. We recognize today, from many other such examples, that introductions often prove disastrous in unexpected ways. That's why, when you go to Australia or the U.S. as a visitor or returning resident, one of the first 9 questions you are now asked by immigration officers is whether you are carrying any plants, seeds, or animals — to reduce the risk of their escaping and becoming established. From abundant prior experience we have now learned (often but not always) to anticipate at least the potential dangers of introducing species. But it's still difficult even for professional ecologists to predict which introductions will actually become established, which established successful introductions will prove disastrous, and why the same species establishes itself at certain sites of introduction and not at others. Hence we really shouldn't be surprised that nineteenth-century Australians, lacking the twentieth century's experience of disastrous introductions, failed to anticipate the effects of rabbits and foxes.

In this book we have encountered other examples of societies under- 10 standably failing to anticipate a problem of which they lacked prior experience. In investing heavily in walrus hunting in order to export walrus ivory to Europe, the Greenland Norse could hardly have anticipated that the Crusades would eliminate the market for walrus ivory by reopening Europe's access to Asian and African elephant ivory, or that increasing sea ice would impede ship traffic to Europe. Again, not being soil scientists, the Maya at Copán could not foresee that deforestation of the hill slopes would trigger soil erosion from the slopes into the valley bottoms.

Even prior experience is not a guarantee that a society will anticipate a 11 problem, if the experience happened so long ago as to have been forgotten. That's especially a problem for non-literate societies, which have less capacity than literate societies to preserve detailed memories of events long in the past, because of the limitations of oral transmission of information compared to writing. For instance, . . . Chaco Canyon Anasazi society survived several droughts before succumbing to a big drought in the twelfth century A.D. But the earlier droughts had occurred long before the birth of any Anasazi affected by the big drought, which would thus have been unanticipated because the Anasazi lacked writing. Similarly, the Classic Lowland Maya succumbed to a drought in the ninth century, despite their area having been affected by drought centuries earlier. . . . In that case, although the Maya did have writing, it recorded kings' deeds and astronomical events rather than weather reports, so that the drought of the third century did not help the Maya anticipate the drought of the ninth century.

In modern literate societies whose writing does discuss subjects besides 12 kings and planets, that doesn't necessarily mean that we draw on prior experience committed to writing. We, too, tend to forget things. For a year or two after the gas shortages of the 1973 Gulf oil crisis, we Americans shied away from gas-guzzling cars, but then we forgot that experience and are now embracing SUVs, despite volumes of print spilled over the 1973 events. When the city of Tucson in Arizona went through a severe drought in the 1950s, its alarmed citizens swore that they would manage their water better, but soon returned to their water-guzzling ways of building golf courses and watering their gardens.

Another reason why a society may fail to anticipate a problem involves *13* reasoning by false analogy. When we are in an unfamiliar situation, we fall back on drawing analogies with old familiar situations. That's a good way to proceed if the old and new situations are truly analogies, but it can be dangerous if they are only superficially similar. For instance, Vikings who immigrated to Iceland beginning around the year A.D. 870 arrived from Norway and Britain, which have heavy clay soils ground up by glaciers. Even if the vegetation covering those soils is cleared, the soils themselves are too heavy to be blown away. When the Viking colonists encountered in Iceland many of the same tree species already familiar to them from Norway and Britain, they were deceived by the apparent similarity of the landscape. . . . Unfortunately, Iceland's soils arose not through glacial grinding but through winds carrying light ash blown out in volcanic eruptions. Once the Vikings had cleared Iceland's forests to create pastures for their livestock, the light soil became exposed for the wind to blow out again, and much of Iceland's topsoil soon eroded away.

A tragic and famous modern example of reasoning by false analogy *14* involves French military preparations from World War II. After the horrible bloodbath of World War I, France recognized its vital need to protect itself against the possibility of another German invasion. Unfortunately, the French army staff assumed that a next war would be fought similarly to World War I, in which the Western Front between France and Germany had remained locked in static trench warfare for four years. Defensive infantry forces manning elaborate fortified trenches had been usually able to repel infantry attacks, while offensive forces had deployed the newly invented tanks only individually and just in support of attacking infantry. Hence France constructed an even more elaborate and expensive system of fortifications, the Maginot Line, to guard its eastern frontier against Germany. But the German army staff, having been defeated in World War I, recognized the need for a different strategy. It used tanks rather than infantry to spearhead its attacks, massed the tanks into separate armored divisions, bypassed the Maginot Line through forested terrain previously considered unsuitable for tanks, and thereby defeated France within a mere six weeks. In reasoning by false analogy after World War I, French generals made a common mistake: generals often plan for a coming war as if it will be like the previous war, especially if that previous war was one in which their side was victorious.

The second stop on my road map, after a society has or hasn't anticipated a *15* problem before it arrives, involves its perceiving or failing to perceive a problem that has actually arrived. There are at least three reasons for such failures, all of them common in the business world and in academia.

First, the origins of some problems are literally imperceptible. For *16* example, the nutrients responsible for soil fertility are invisible to the eye, and only in modern times did they become measurable by chemical analysis. In Australia, Mangareva, parts of the U.S. Southwest, and many other locations, most of the nutrients had already been leached out of the soil by rain before human settlement. When people arrived and began growing crops, those crops quickly exhausted the remaining nutrients, with the result that agriculture failed. Yet such nutrient-poor soils often bear lush-appearing vegetation; it's just that most of the nutrients in the ecosystem are contained in the vegetation rather than in the soil, and are removed if one cuts down the vegetation. There was no way for the first colonists of Australia and Mangareva to perceive that problem of soil nutrient exhaustion — nor for farmers in areas with salt deep in the ground (like eastern Montana and parts of Australia and Mesopotamia) to perceive incipient salinization — nor for miners of sulfide ores to perceive the toxic copper and acid dissolved in mine runoff water.

Another frequent reason for failure to perceive a problem after it has *17* arrived is distant managers, a potential issue in any large society or business. For example, the largest private landowner and timber company in Montana today is based not within that state but 400 miles away in Seattle, Washington. Not being on the scene, company executives may not realize that they have a big weed problem on their forest properties. Well-run companies avoid such surprises by periodically sending managers "into the field" to observe what is actually going on, while a tall friend of mine who was a college president regularly practiced with his school's undergraduates on their basketball courts in order to keep abreast of student thinking. The opposite of failure due to distant managers is success due to on-the-spot managers. Part of the reason why Tikopians on their tiny island, and New Guinea highlanders in their valleys, have successfully managed their resources for more than a thousand years is that everyone on the island or in the valley is familiar with the entire territory on which their society depends.

Perhaps the commonest circumstance under which societies fail to *18* perceive a problem is when it takes the form of a slow trend concealed by wide up-and-down fluctuations. The prime example in modern times is global warming. We now realize that temperatures around the world have been slowly rising in recent decades, due in large part to atmospheric changes caused by humans. However, it is not the case that the climate each year has been exactly 0.01 degree warmer than in the previous year. Instead, as we all know, climate fluctuates up and down erratically from year to year: three degrees warmer in one summer than in the previous one, then two degrees warmer the next summer, down four degrees the following summer, down another degree the next one, then up five degrees, etc. With such large and unpredictable fluctuations, it has taken a long time to discern the average upwards trend of 0.01 degree per year within that noisy signal. That's why it was only a few years ago that most professional climatologists previously skeptical of the reality of global warming became convinced. As of the time that I write these lines, President Bush of the U.S. is still not convinced of its reality, and he thinks that we need more research. The medieval Greenlanders had similar difficulties in recognizing that their climate was gradually becoming colder, and the Maya and Anasazi had trouble discerning that theirs was becoming drier.

Politicians use the term "creeping normalcy" to refer to such slow *19* trends concealed within noisy fluctuations. If the economy, schools, traffic congestion, or anything else is deteriorating only slowly, it's difficult to recognize that each successive year is on the average slightly worse than the year before, so one's baseline standard for what constitutes "normalcy" shifts gradually and imperceptibly. It may take a few decades of a long sequence of such slight year-to-year changes before people realize, with a jolt, that conditions used to be much better several decades ago, and that what is accepted as normalcy has crept downwards.

Another term related to creeping normalcy is "landscape amnesia": *20* forgetting how different the surrounding landscape looked 50 years ago, because the change from year to year has been so gradual. An example involves the melting of Montana's glaciers and snowfields caused by global warming. . . . After spending the summers of 1953 and 1956 in Montana's Big Hole Basin as a teenager, I did not return until 42 years later, in 1998, when I began visiting every year. Among my vivid teenaged memories of the Big Hole were the snow covering the distant mountaintops even in mid-summer, my resulting sense that a white band low in the sky encircled the basin, and my recollection of a weekend camping trip when two friends and I clambered up to that magical band of snow. Not having lived through the fluctuations and gradual dwindling of summer snow during the intervening 42 years, I was stunned and saddened on my return to the Big Hole in 1998 to find the band almost gone, and in 2001 and 2003 actually all melted off. When I asked my Montana resident friends about the change, they were less aware of it: they unconsciously compared each year's band (or lack thereof) with the previous few years. Creeping normalcy or landscape amnesia made it harder for them than for me to remember what conditions had been like in the 1950s. Such experiences are a major reason why people may fail to notice a developing problem, until it is too late.

I suspect that landscape amnesia provided part of the answer to my *21* UCLA students' question, "What did the Easter Islander who cut down the last palm tree say as he was doing it?" We unconsciously imagine a sudden change: one year, the island still covered with a forest of tall palm trees being used to produce wine, fruit, and timber to transport and erect statues; the next year, just a single tree left, which an islander proceeds to fell in an act of incredibly self-damaging stupidity. Much more likely, though, the changes in forest cover from year to year would have been almost undetectable: yes, this year we cut down a few trees over there, but saplings are starting to grow back again here on this abandoned garden site. Only the oldest islanders, thinking back to their childhoods decades earlier, could have recognized a difference. Their children could no more have comprehended their parents' tales of a tall forest than my 17-year-old sons today can comprehend my wife's and my tales of what Los Angeles used to be like 40 years ago. Gradually, Easter Island's trees became fewer, smaller, and less important. At the time that the last fruit-bearing adult palm tree was cut, the species had long ago ceased to be of any economic significance. That left only smaller and smaller palm saplings to clear each year, along with other bushes and treelets. No one would have noticed the falling of the last little palm sapling. By then, the memory of the valuable palm forest of centuries earlier had succumbed to landscape amnesia. Conversely, the speed with which deforestation spread over early Tokugawa Japan made it easier for its shoguns to recognize the landscape changes and the need for preemptive action.

The third stop on the road map of failure is the most frequent, the most 22 surprising, and requires the longest discussion because it assumes such a wide variety of forms. Contrary to what Joseph Tainter and almost anyone else would have expected, it turns out that societies often fail even to attempt to solve a problem once it has been perceived.

Many of the reasons for such failure fall under the heading of what 23 economists and other social scientists term "rational behavior," arising from clashes of interest between people. That is, some people may reason correctly that they can advance their own interests by behavior harmful to other people. Scientists term such behavior "rational" precisely because it employs correct reasoning, even though it may be morally reprehensible. The perpetrators know that they will often get away with their bad behavior, especially if there is no law against it or if the law isn't effectively enforced. They feel safe because the perpetrators are typically concentrated (few in number) and highly motivated by the prospect of reaping big, certain, and immediate profits, while the losses are spread over large numbers of individuals. That gives the losers little motivation to go to the hassle of fighting back, because each loser loses only a little and would receive only small, uncertain, distant profits even from successfully undoing the minority's grab. Examples include so-called perverse subsidies: the large sums of money that governments pay to support industries that might be uneconomic without the subsidies, such as many fisheries, sugar-growing in the U.S., and cotton-growing in Australia (subsidized indirectly through the government's bearing the cost of water for irrigation). The relatively few fishermen and growers lobby tenaciously for the subsidies that represent much of their income, while the losers (all the taxpayers) are less vocal because the subsidy is funded by just a small amount of money concealed in each citizen's tax bill. Measures benefiting a small minority at the expense of a large majority are especially likely to arise in certain types of democracies that bestow "swing power" on some small groups: e.g., senators from small states in the U.S. Senate, or small religious parties often holding the balance of power in Israel to a degree scarcely possible under the Dutch parliamentary system.

A frequent type of rational bad behavior is "good for me, bad for you 24 and for everybody else" — to put it bluntly, "selfish." As a simple example, most Montana fishermen fish for trout. A few fishermen who prefer to fish for a pike, a larger fish-eating fish not native to western Montana, surreptitiously and illegally introduced pike to some western Montana lakes and rivers, where they proceeded to destroy trout fishing by eating out the trout. That was good for the few pike fishermen and bad for the far greater number of trout fishermen.

An example producing more losers and higher dollar losses is that, 25 until 1971, mining companies in Montana on closing down a mine just left it with its copper, arsenic, and acid leaking out into rivers, because the state of Montana had no law requiring companies to clean up after mine closure. In 1971 the state of Montana did pass such a law, but companies discovered that they could extract the valuable ore and then just declare bankruptcy before going to the expense of cleaning up. The result has been about $500,000,000 of cleanup costs to be borne by the citizens of Montana and the U.S. Mining company CEOs had correctly perceived that the law permitted them to save money for their companies, and to advance their own interests through bonuses and high salaries, by making messes and leaving the burden to society. Innumerable other examples of such behavior in the business world could be cited, but it is not as universal as some cynics suspect. [Still] that range of outcomes results from the imperative for businesses to make money to the extent that government regulations, laws, and public attitudes permit.

One particular form of clashes of interest has become well known 26 under the name "tragedy of the commons," in turn closely related to the conflicts termed "the prisoner's dilemma" and "the logic of collective action." Consider a situation in which many consumers are harvesting a communally owned resource, such as fishermen catching fish in an area of ocean, or herders grazing their sheep on a communal pasture. If everybody overharvests the resource, it will become depleted by overfishing or overgrazing and thus decline or even disappear, and all of the consumers will suffer. It would therefore be in the common interests of all consumers to exercise restraint and not overharvest. But as long as there is no effective regulation of how much resource each consumer can harvest, then each consumer would be correct to reason, "If I don't catch that fish or let my sheep graze that grass, some other fisherman or herder will anyway, so it makes no sense for me to refrain from overfishing or overharvesting." The correct rational behavior is then to harvest before the next consumer can, even though the eventual result may be the destruction of the commons and thus harm for all consumers.

In reality, while this logic has led to many commons resources becom- 27 ing overharvested and destroyed, others have been preserved in the face of harvesting for hundreds or even thousands of years. Unhappy outcomes include the overexploitation and collapse of most major marine fisheries, and the extermination of much of the megafauna (large mammals, birds, and reptiles) on every oceanic island or continent settled by humans for the first time within the last 50,000 years. Happy outcomes include the maintenance of many local fisheries, forests, and water sources. . . . Behind these happy outcomes lie three alternative arrangements that have evolved to preserve a commons resource while still permitting a sustainable harvest.

One obvious solution is for the government or some other outside   28 force to step in, with or without the invitation of the consumers, and to enforce quotas, as the shogun and daimyo in Tokugawa Japan, Inca emperors in the Andes, and princes and wealthy landowners in sixteenth-century Germany did for logging. However, that is impractical in some situations (e.g., the open ocean) and involves excessive administrative and policing costs in other situations. A second solution is to privatize the resource, i.e., to divide it into individually owned tracts that each owner will be motivated to manage prudently in his/her own interests. That practice was applied to some village-owned forests in Tokugawa Japan. Again, though, some resources (such as migratory animals and fish) are impossible to subdivide, and the individual owners may find it even harder than a government's coast guard or police to exclude intruders.

The remaining solution to the tragedy of the commons is for the con-   29 sumers to recognize their common interests and to design, obey, and enforce prudent harvesting quotas themselves. That is likely to happen only if a whole series of conditions is met: the consumers form a homogeneous group; they have learned to trust and communicate with each other; they expect to share a common future and to pass on the resource to their heirs; they are capable of and permitted to organize and police themselves; and the boundaries of the resource and of its pool of consumers are well defined. A good example is the case . . . of Montana water rights for irrigation. While the allocation of those rights has been written into law, nowadays the ranchers mostly obey the water commissioner whom they themselves elect, and they no longer take their disputes to court for resolution. Other such examples of homogeneous groups prudently managing resources that they expect to pass to their children are the Tikopia Islanders, New Guinea highlanders, members of Indian castes, and other groups. . . . Those small groups, along with the Icelanders and the Tokugawa Japanese constituting larger groups, were further motivated to reach agreement by their effective isolation: it was obvious to the whole group that they would have to survive just on their resources for the foreseeable future. Such groups knew that they could not make the frequently heard "ISEP" excuse that is a recipe for mismanagement: "It's not my problem, it's someone else's problem."

Clashes of interest involving rational behavior are also prone to arise   30 when the principal consumer has no long-term stake in preserving the resource but society as a whole does. For example, much commercial harvesting of tropical rainforests today is carried out by international logging companies, which typically take out short-term leases on land in one country, cut down the rainforest on all their leased land in that country, and then move on to the next country. The loggers have correctly perceived that, once they have paid for their lease, their interests are best served by cutting its forest as quickly as possible, reneging on any agreements to replant, and leaving. In that way, loggers destroyed most of the lowland forests of the Malay Peninsula, then of Borneo, then of the Solomon Islands and Sumatra, now of the Philippines, and coming up soon of New Guinea, the Amazon, and the Congo Basin. What is thus good for the loggers is bad for the local people, who lose their source of forest products and suffer consequences of soil erosion and stream sedimentation. It's also bad for the host country as a whole, which loses some of its biodiversity and its foundations for sustainable forestry. The outcome of this clash of interests involving short-term leased land contrasts with a frequent outcome when the logging company owns the land, anticipates repeated harvests, and may find a long-term perspective to be in its interests (as well as in the interests of local people and the country). Chinese peasants in the 1920s recognized a similar contrast when they compared the disadvantages of being exploited by two types of warlords. It was hard to be exploited by a "stationary bandit," i.e., a locally entrenched warlord, who would at least leave peasants with enough resources to generate more plunder for that warlord in future years. Worse was to be exploited by a "roving bandit," a warlord who like a logging company with short-term leases would leave nothing for a region's peasants and just move on to plunder another region's peasants.

A further conflict of interest involving rational behavior arises when *31* the interests of the decision-making elite in power clash with the interests of the rest of society. Especially if the elite can insulate themselves from the consequences of their actions, they are likely to do things that profit themselves, regardless of whether those actions hurt everybody else. Such clashes, flagrantly personified by the dictator Trujillo in the Dominican Republic and the governing elite in Haiti, are becoming increasingly frequent in the modern U.S., where rich people tend to live within their gated compounds and to drink bottled water. For example, Enron's executives correctly calculated that they could gain huge sums of money for themselves by looting the company coffers and thereby harming all the stockholders, and that they were likely to get away with their gamble.

Throughout recorded history, actions or inactions by self-absorbed *32* kings, chiefs, and politicians have been a regular cause of societal collapses, including those of the Maya kings, Greenland Norse chiefs, and modern Rwandan politicians. . . . Barbara Tuchman devoted her book *The March of Folly* to famous historical examples of disastrous decisions, ranging from the Trojans bringing the Trojan horse within their walls, and the Renaissance popes provoking the Protestant succession, to the German decision to adopt unrestricted submarine warfare in World War I (thereby triggering America's declaration of war), and Japan's Pearl Harbor attack that similarly triggered America's declaration of war in 1941. As Tuchman put it succinctly, "Chief among the forces affecting political folly is lust for power, named by Tacitus as 'the most flagrant of all passions.'" As a result of lust for power, Easter Island chiefs and Maya kings acted so as to accelerate deforestation rather than to prevent it: their status depended on their putting up bigger statues and monuments than their rivals. They were trapped in a competitive spiral, such that any chief or king who put up smaller statues or monuments to spare the forests would have been scorned and lost his job. That's a regular problem with competitions for prestige, which are judged on a short time frame.

Conversely, failures to solve perceived problems because of conflicts of [33] interest between the elite and the masses are much less likely in societies where the elite cannot insulate themselves from the consequences of their actions. . . . The high environmental awareness of the Dutch (including their politicians) goes back to the fact that much of the population — both the politicians and the masses — lives on land lying below sea level, where only dikes stand between them and drowning, so that foolish land planning by politicians would be at their own personal peril. Similarly, New Guinea highlands big-men live in the same type of huts as everyone else, scrounge for firewood and timber in the same places as everyone else, and were thereby highly motivated to solve their society's need for sustainable forestry. . . .

All of these examples in the preceding several pages illustrate situations in [34] which a society fails to try to solve perceived problems because the maintenance of the problem is good for some people. In contrast to that so-called rational behavior, other failures to attempt to solve perceived problems involve what social scientists consider "irrational behavior": i.e., behavior that is harmful for everybody. Such irrational behavior often arises when each of us individually is torn by clashes of values: we may ignore a bad status quo because it is favored by some deeply held value to which we cling. "Persistence in error," "wooden-headedness," "refusal to draw inference from negative signs," and "mental standstill or stagnation" are among the phrases that Barbara Tuchman applies to this common human trait. Psychologists use the term "sunk-cost effect" for a related trait: we feel reluctant to abandon a policy (or to sell a stock) in which we have already invested heavily.

Religious values tend to be especially deeply held and hence frequent [35] causes of disastrous behavior. For example, much of the deforestation of Easter Island had a religious motivation: to obtain logs to transport and erect the giant stone statues that were the object of veneration. At the same time, but 9,000 miles away and in the opposite hemisphere, the Greenland Norse were pursuing their own religious values as Christians. Those values, their European identity, their conservative lifestyle in a harsh environment where most innovations would in fact fail, and their tightly communal and mutually supportive society allowed them to survive for centuries. But those admirable (and, for a long time, successful) traits also prevented them from making the drastic lifestyle changes and selective adoptions of Inuit technology that might have helped them survive for longer.

The modern world provides us with abundant secular examples of 36 admirable values to which we cling under conditions where those values no longer make sense. Australians brought from Britain a tradition of raising sheep for wool, high land values, and an identification with Britain, and thereby accomplished the feat of building a First World democracy remote from any other (except New Zealand), but are now beginning to appreciate that those values also have downsides. In modern times a reason why Montanans have been so reluctant to solve their problems caused by mining, logging, and ranching is that those three industries used to be the pillars of the Montana economy, and that they became bound up with Montana's pioneer spirit and identity. Montanans' pioneer commitment to individual freedom and self-sufficiency has similarly made them reluctant to accept their new need for government planning and for curbing individual rights. Communist China's determination not to repeat the errors of capitalism led it to scorn environmental concerns as just one more capitalist error, and thereby to saddle China with enormous environmental problems. Rwandans' ideal of large families was appropriate in traditional times of high childhood mortality, but has led to a disastrous population explosion today. It appears to me that much of the rigid opposition to environmental concerns in the First World nowadays involves values acquired early in life and never again reexamined: "the maintenance intact by rulers and policy-makers of the ideas they started with," to quote Barbara Tuchman once again.

It is painfully difficult to decide whether to abandon some of one's 37 core values when they seem to be becoming incompatible with survival. At what point do we as individuals prefer to die than to compromise and live? Millions of people in modern times have indeed faced the decision whether, to save their own life, they would be willing to betray friends or relatives, acquiesce in a vile dictatorship, live as virtual slaves, or flee their country. Nations and societies sometimes have to make similar decisions collectively.

All such decisions involve gambles, because one often can't be certain 38 that clinging to core values will be fatal, or (conversely) that abandoning them will ensure survival. In trying to carry on as Christian farmers, the Greenland Norse in effect were deciding that they were prepared to die as Christian farmers rather than live as Inuit; they lost that gamble. Among five small Eastern European countries faced with the overwhelming might of Russian armies, the Estonians and Latvians and Lithuanians surrendered their independence in 1939 without a fight, the Finns fought in 1939–40 and preserved their independence, and Hungarians fought in 1956 and lost their independence. Who among us is to say which country was wiser, and who could have predicted in advance that only the Finns would win their gamble?

Perhaps a crux of success or failure as a society is to know which 39 core values to hold on to, and which ones to discard and replace with new values, when times change. In the last 60 years the world's most power-ful countries have given up long-held cherished values previously central to their national image, while holding on to other values. Britain and France abandoned their centuries-old role as independently acting world powers; Japan abandoned its military tradition and armed forces; and Russia aban-doned its long experiment with communism. The United States has retreated substantially (but hardly completely) from its former val-ues of legalized racial discrimination, legalized homophobia, a sub-ordinate role of women, and sexual repression. Australia is now reevaluating its status as a rural farming society with British identity. Societies and indi-viduals that succeed may be those that have the courage to take those diffi-cult decisions, and that have the luck to win their gambles. The world as a whole today faces similar decisions about its environmental problems. . . .

FURTHER READINGS

Along with questions by my UCLA students, Joseph Tainter's book *The Collapses of Com-plex Societies* (Cambridge: Cambridge University Press, 1988) provided a starting point for this chapter, by stating clearly why a society's failure to solve its environmental prob-lems poses a puzzle crying out for explanation. Thomas McGovern et al. "Northern islands, human error, and environmental degradation: a view of social and ecological change in the medieval North Atlantic" (*Human Ecology* 16:225–270 (1988)) traces a sequence of reasons why the Greenland Norse failed to perceive or solve their own envi-ronmental problems. The sequence of reasons that I propose in this chapter overlaps partly with that of McGovern et al., whose model should be consulted by anyone inter-ested in pursuing this puzzle.

Elinor Ostrom and her colleagues have studied the tragedy of the commons (alias common-pool resources), using both comparative surveys and experimental games to identify the conditions under which consumers are most likely to recognize their com-mon interests and to implement an effective quota system themselves. Ostrom's books include Elinor Ostrom, *Governing the Commons: The Evolution of Institutions for Collec-tive Action* (Cambridge: Cambridge University Press, 1990) and Elinor Ostrom, Roy Gardner, and James Walker, *Rules, Games, and Common-Pool Resources* (Ann Arbor: University of Michigan Press, 1994). Her more recent articles include Elinor Ostrom, "Coping with tragedies of the commons" *Annual Reviews of Political Science* 2:493–535 (1999); Elinor Ostrom et al., "Revisiting the commons: local lessons, global challenges" *Science* 284:278–282 (1999); and Thomas Dietz, Elinor Ostrom, and Paul Stern, "The struggle to govern the commons" *Science* 302:1907–1912 (2003).

Barbara Tuchman, *The March of Folly: From Troy to Vietnam* (New York: Ballantine Books, 1984) covers disastrous decisions over exactly the time span that she names in the book's title, also reflecting en route from Troy to Vietnam on the follies of the Aztec emperor Montezuma, the fall of Christian Spain to the Moslems, England's provocation of the American Revolution, and other such self-destructive acts. Charles Mackay, *Extraordi-nary Popular Delusions and the Madness of Crowds* (New York: Barnes and Noble, 1993, reprint of the original 1852 edition) covers an even wider range of follies than does Tuch-man, including (just to name a few) the South Sea bubble in eighteenth-century England, tulip madness in seventeenth-century Holland, prophecies of the Last Judgment, the Cru-sades, witch hunting, belief in ghosts and sacred relics, dueling, and kings' decrees about hair length, beards, and mustaches. Irving Janis, *Groupthink* (Boston: Houghton Mifflin, 1983, revised 2nd ed.) explores the subtle group dynamics that contributed to the success or failure of deliberations involving recent American presidents and their advisors. Janis's case studies are of the 1961 Bay of Pigs invasion, the American army's crossing of the 38th parallel in Korea in 1950, American's non-preparation for Japan's 1941 Pearl Harbor attack, America's escalation of the Vietnam War from 1964 to 1967, the Cuban Missile Crisis of 1962, and America's adoption of the Marshall Plan in 1947.

Garrett Hardin's classic and often-cited article "The tragedy of the commons" appeared in *Science* 162:1243–1248 (1968). Mancur Olson applies the metaphor of stationary bandits and roving bandits to Chinese warlords and other extractive agents in "Dictatorship, democracy, and development" (*American Political Science Review* 87:567–576 (1993)). Sunk-cost effects are explained by Hal Arkes and Peter Ayton, "The sunk cost and Concorde effects: are humans less rational than lower animals?" (*Psychological Bulletin* 125:591–600 (1999)), and by Marco Janssen et al., "Sunk-cost effects and vulnerability to collapse in ancient societies" (*Current Anthropology* 44:722–728 (2003)).

■ ■ ■

Reading Rhetorically

1. In paragraph 3, Diamond quotes archeologist Joseph Tainter at length. How does Diamond use this quote to help set up his own point? How effective do you find this strategy? Would you use it in your own writing? Why or why not?

2. Diamond uses the metaphor of a road map to describe the way he organizes his writing. Locate and mark the places in the text where Diamond refers to the road map. How do these references to the overall organization affect your experience of reading this piece?

3. Although most of Diamond's text is not personal in nature, he does include some experiences from his own life, particularly relating to his teaching and his visits to Montana. Bracket the sections where he discusses his own experience, and take note of where they appear in the excerpt. What function does each personal reference serve in the larger purpose of the piece?

Inquiring Further

4. This text is an excerpt from Diamond's 592-page book *Collapse: How Societies Choose to Fail or Succeed*. Use your library's resources to find several reviews of this book, and read what others have said about Diamond's book and concepts. What key ideas come up in the reviews, and how do they relate to your own responses to Diamond's writing?

5. Diamond mentions the slow response to global warming in his "second stop" on the road map (para. 18). How much do you know about the perspectives on global warming? Brainstorm with your class, and then working in a small group or individually, find and read three recent scholarly articles on the topic. What have you discovered? What information is most surprising to you?

6. Choose one of Diamond's examples you would like to learn more about, and find two or three scholarly perspectives on it to develop your understanding of what happened at this moment in history. Share what you learn with your classmates, discussing where the sources you've gathered agree or disagree. What do you make of the similarities? Of the conflicts?

Framing Conversations

7. Both Diamond and Kwame Anthony Appiah (p. 378) explore cultures and their often clashing values. Write an essay in which you draw on both authors' ideas and examples in order to consider this claim by Diamond: "Perhaps a crux of success or failure as a society is to know which core values to hold on to, and which ones to discard and replace with new values, when times change" (para. 39). Test this quotation against the examples you find most compelling in each author's text, and teach your readers what you think is most important about what you discover.

8. Diamond mentions the concept of "creeping normalcy" to describe trends that develop so slowly that most people fail to recognize them (para. 19). How does this idea relate to Malcolm Gladwell's (p. 432) concept of a tipping point? Compose an essay in which you use Diamond's concept to analyze some of Gladwell's examples, and Gladwell's concept to analyze some of Diamond's examples. Build an argument about what you find useful, or not so useful, about these concepts as a way of understanding historical events and trends.

9. At the beginning of this piece, Diamond describes one of his teaching methods. How might Mark Edmundson (p. 277), bell hooks (p. 293), or Mary Louise Pratt (p. 354) respond to the approach Diamond takes in his classes? Write an essay in which you assess Diamond as a teacher from the perspective of one of these authors and from your own perspective on effective teaching. For example, you might focus on the roles of teachers in relation to students, and the relationship between power and knowledge in the classroom. You also might consider Diamond's text itself as an exercise in teaching, with his readers as his students.

■ FRANKLIN FOER ————————————————————————

From How Soccer Explains the World: An Unlikely Theory of Globalization

Franklin Foer is the editor of *The New Republic*, a magazine that covers a broad spectrum of political and cultural topics. He also has worked as a journalist, covering Congress for *U.S. News & World Report* and publishing frequently in the online journal *Slate*. And his writing has appeared in the *New York Times*, the *Washington Post*, and *Spin*. This reading is excerpted from *How Soccer Explains the World: An Unlikely Theory of Globalization* (2004), a book that brought Foer to the attention of many sports fans. Although soccer does not have the same hold on Americans that it has on people in other parts of the world, Foer makes use of soccer — "its fans, its players, and strategies" (para. 4) — to address larger issues.

Foer writes in a tradition of sports reporting that goes far beyond describing the plays and the score of a game. He is interested in the culture of sport — in this case, soccer — and how and why it has such a grip on the imaginations of fans. Other books in this tradition are John

Feinstein's *A Good Walk Spoiled: Days and Nights on the PGA Tour* (1995), and L. Jon Wertheim's *Venus Envy: A Sensational Season Inside the Women's Tennis Tour* (2001). This type of sports writing addresses not only practitioners and fans, but also a broader reading audience interested in the business and cultural influence of sports.

In this reading we reproduce the prologue and last chapter of Foer's book. In the prologue, he lays out his rationale for his "unlikely" method of using soccer as a way to examine a series of national and global dynamics. As you read, consider what he accomplishes there by proposing that "soccer — its fans, its players, and strategies" can be used "as a way of thinking about how people would identify themselves in this new era" of globalization (para. 4). How are these ideas "in conversation" with the material that follows on "How Soccer Explains the American Culture Wars?" Foer includes some autobiography in this section, humorously describing his own shameful childhood soccer career in the early 1980s, before the suburban soccer leagues became so highly organized and before the term "soccer mom" was coined to describe the necessary parental support system for this pastime. Although Foer does not use MLA style to cite sources in the text, notice the ways he includes the ideas and phrases of others to give context to the "culture war" that raged over soccer in the 1980s. How does the anxiety Foer describes here about soccer seeming "un-American" apply to current political and cultural conversations in which we Americans are encouraged to think of ourselves as different from others for this or that reason? How does Foer explain the political and cultural conflicts that soccer has come to exemplify? What solutions does he offer, if any? Finally, what does imported goat cheese (para. 29) have to do with soccer? Read on, and see if you can make other connections between soccer and globalization. As Foer demonstrates, if you can offer clear examples, any connection can be fair game.

Prologue

At about the time that I started working on this book, in the fall of 2001, the consensus on globalization changed considerably — for obvious reasons. It was no longer possible to speak so breathlessly, so messianically of the political promise of economic interdependence. And there was another problem. The world's brief experiment in interdependence didn't come close to delivering the advertised result of prosperity. This book tries to use the metaphor of soccer to address some of the nagging questions about this failure: Why have some nations remained poor, even though they had so much foreign investment coursing through them? How dangerous are the multinational corporations that the Left rails against?

This is not to dredge up the tired old Marxist criticisms of corporate capitalism — the big question of the book is less economic than cultural. The innovation of the anti-globalization left is its embrace of traditionalism: its worry that global tastes and brands will steamroll indigenous cultures. Of course, soccer isn't the same as Bach or Buddhism. But it is often more deeply felt than religion, and just as much a part of the community's fabric, a repository of traditions. During Franco's rule, the clubs Athletic Bilbao and Real Sociedad were the only venues where Basque people could express their cultural pride without winding up in jail. In English industrial towns like Coventry and Derby, soccer clubs helped glue together small cities amid oppressive dinginess.

By the logic of both its critics and proponents, the global culture should 3 have wiped away these local institutions. Indeed, traveling the world, it's hard not to be awed by the power of mega-brands like the clubs Manchester United and Real Madrid, backed by Nike and Adidas, who have cultivated support across continents, prying fans away from their old allegiances. But that homogenization turned out to be more of an exception than I had anticipated. Wandering among lunatic fans, gangster owners, and crazed Bulgarian strikers, I kept noticing the ways that globalization had failed to diminish the game's local cultures, local blood feuds, and even local corruption. In fact, I began to suspect that globalization had actually increased the power of these local entities — and not always in such a good way.

On my travels, I tried to use soccer — its fans, its players, and 4 strategies — as a way of thinking about how people would identify themselves in this new era. Would they embrace new, more globalized labels? Would people stop thinking of themselves as English and Brazilian and begin to define themselves as Europeans and Latin Americans? Or would those new identities be meaningless, with shallow roots in history? Would people revert back to older identities, like religion and tribe? If soccer is an object lesson, then perhaps religion and tribe have too much going for them.

This book has three parts. The first tries to explain the failure of global- 5 ization to erode ancient hatreds in the game's great rivalries. It is the hooligan-heavy section of the book. The second part uses soccer to address economics: the consequences of migration, the persistence of corruption, and the rise of powerful new oligarchs like Silvio Berlusconi, the president of Italy and the AC Milan club. Finally, the book uses soccer to defend the virtues of old-fashioned nationalism — a way to blunt the return of tribalism.

The story begins bleakly and grows progressively more optimistic. In 6 the end, I found it hard to be too hostile toward globalization. For all its many faults, it has brought soccer to the far corners of the world and into my life.

How Soccer Explains the American Culture Wars

I.

My soccer career began in 1982, at the age of eight. This was an entirely dif- 7 ferent moment in the history of American soccer, well before the youth game acquired its current, highly evolved infrastructure. Our teams didn't have names. We had jersey colors that we used to refer to ourselves: "Go Maroon!" Our coach, a bearded German named Gunther, would bark at us in continental nomenclature that didn't quite translate into English. Urging me to stop a ball with my upper body, he would cry out, "Use your breasts, Frankie!"

That I should end up a soccer player defied the time-tested laws of 8 sporting heredity. For generations, fathers bequeathed their sporting loves unto their sons. My father, like most men of his baby boom age, had grown up madly devoted to baseball. Why didn't my dad adhere to the practice of handing his game to his son? The answer has to do with the times and the class to which my parents belonged, by which I mean, they were children of the sixties and we lived in the yuppie confines of Upper Northwest Washington, D.C., a dense aggregation of Ivy League lawyers with aggressively liberal politics and exceptionally protective parenting styles. Nearly everyone in our family's social set signed up their children to play soccer. It was the fashionable thing to do. On Monday mornings, at school, we'd each walk around in the same cheaply made pair of white shorts with the logo of our league, Montgomery Soccer Inc.

Steering your child into soccer may have been fashionable, but it 9 wasn't a decision to be made lightly. When my father played sandlot baseball, he could walk three blocks to his neighborhood diamond. With soccer, this simply wasn't possible. At this early moment in the youth soccer boom, the city of Washington didn't have any of its own leagues. My parents would load up our silver Honda Accord and drive me to fields deep in suburban Maryland, 40-minute drives made weekly across a landscape of oversized hardware stores and newly minted real estate developments. In part, these drives would take so long because my parents would circle, hopelessly lost, through neighborhoods they had never before visited and would likely never see again.

As I later discovered, my parents made this sacrifice of their leisure 10 time because they believed that soccer could be transformational. I suffered from a painful, rather extreme case of shyness. I'm told that it extended beyond mere clinging to my mother's leg. On the sidelines at halftime, I would sit quietly on the edge of the other kids' conversations, never really interjecting myself, My parents had hoped that the game might necessitate my becoming more aggressive, a breaking through of inhibitions.

The idea that soccer could alleviate shyness was not an idiosyncratic 11 parenting theory. It tapped into the conventional wisdom among yuppie parents. Soccer's appeal lay in its opposition to the other popular sports. For children of the sixties, there was something abhorrent about enrolling kids in American football, a game where violence wasn't just incidental but inherent. They didn't want to teach the acceptability of violence, let alone subject their precious children to the risk of physical maiming. Baseball, where each batter must stand center stage four or five times a game, entailed too many stressful, potentially ego-deflating encounters. Basketball, before Larry Bird's prime, still had the taint of the ghetto.

But soccer represented something very different. It was a tabula rasa, *12* a sport onto which a generation of parents could project their values. Quickly, soccer came to represent the fundamental tenets of yuppie parenting, the spirit of *Sesame Street* and Dr. Benjamin Spock. Unlike the other sports, it would foster self-esteem, minimize the pain of competition while still teaching life lessons. Dick Wilson, the executive director of the American Youth Soccer Organization since the early seventies, described the attitude this way: "We would like to provide the child a chance to participate in a less competitive, win-oriented atmosphere. . . . We require that teams be balanced; and that teams not remain intact from year to year, that they be dissolved and totally reconstituted in the next season. This is done to preclude the adults from building their own dynasty 'win at all cost' situations."

This was typical of the thinking of a generation of post-'60s parenting *13* theories, which were an extension of the counterculture spirit — Theodor Adorno's idea that strict, emotionally stultifying homes created authoritarian, bigoted kids. But for all the talk of freedom, the sixties parenting style had a far less laissez-faire side, too. Like the 1960s consumer movement which brought American car seatbelts and airbags, the soccer movement felt like it could create a set of rules and regulations that would protect both the child's body and mind from damage. Leagues like the one I played in handed out "participation" trophies to every player, no matter how few games his (or her) team won. Other leagues had stopped posting the scores of games or keeping score altogether. Where most of the world accepts the practice of heading the ball as an essential element of the game, American soccer parents have fretted over the potential for injury to the brain. An entire industry sprouted to manufacture protective headgear, not that different-looking from a boxer's sparring helmet, to soften the blows. Even though very little medical evidence supports this fear, some youth leagues have prohibited headers altogether.

This reveals a more fundamental difference between American youth *14* soccer and the game as practiced in the rest of the world. In every other part of the world, soccer's sociology varies little: It is the province of the working class. Sure, there might be aristocrats, like Gianni Agnelli, who take an interest, and instances like Barca, where the game transcendently grips the community. But these cases are rare. The United States is even rarer: It inverts the class structure of the game. Here, aside from Latino immigrants, the professional classes follow the game most avidly and the working class couldn't give a toss about it. Surveys, done by the sporting goods manufacturers, consistently show that children of middle class and affluent families play the game disproportionately. Half the nation's soccer participants come from households earning over $50,000. That is, they come from the solid middle class and above.

Elites have never been especially well liked in postwar American *15* politics — or at least they have been easy to take swipes at. But the generation of elites that adopted soccer has been an especially ripe target. That's because they came through college in the sixties and seventies, at a time when the counterculture self-consciously turned against the stultifying conformity of what it perceived as traditional America. Even as this group shed its youthful radical politics, it kept some of its old ideals, including its resolute cosmopolitanism and suspicions of middle America, "flyover country." When they adopted soccer, it gave the impression that they had turned their backs on the American pastime. This, naturally, produced even more disdain for them — and for their sport.

Pundits have employed many devices to sum up America's cultural [16] divisions. During the 1980s, they talked about the "culture war" — the battle over textbooks, abortion, prayer in school, affirmative action, and funding of the arts. This war pitted conservative defenders of tradition and morality against liberal defenders of modernity and pluralism. More recently this debate has been described as the split between "red and blue America" — the two colors used to distinguish partisan preference in maps charting presidential election voting. But another explanatory device has yet to penetrate political science departments and the national desks of newspapers. There exists an important cleavage between the parts of the country that have adopted soccer as its pastime and the places that haven't. And this distinction lays bare an underrated source of American cultural cleavage: globalization.

II.

Other countries have greeted soccer with relative indifference. The Indian [17] subcontinent and Australia come to mind. But the United States is perhaps the only place where a loud portion of the population actively disdains the game, even campaigns against it. This anti-soccer lobby believes, in the words of USA Today's Tom Weir, "that hating soccer is more American than apple pie, driving a pickup, or spending Saturday afternoons channel surfing with the remote control." Weir exaggerates the pervasiveness of this sentiment. But the cadre of soccer haters has considerable sway. Their influence rests primarily with a legion of prestigious sportswriters and commentators, who use their column inches to fulminate against the game, especially on the occasions of World Cups.

Not just pundits buried in the C Section of the paper, but people with [18] actual power believe that soccer represents a genuine threat to the American way of life. The former Buffalo Bills quarterback Jack Kemp, one of the most influential conservatives of the 1980s, a man once mentioned in the same breath as the presidency, holds this view. In 1986, he took to the floor of the United States Congress to orate against a resolution in support of an American bid to host the World Cup. Kemp intoned, "I think it is important for all those young out there, who someday hope to play real football, where you throw it and kick it and run with it and put it in your hands, a distinction should be made that football is democratic, capitalism, whereas soccer is a European socialist [sport]."

Lovers of the game usually can't resist dismissing these critics as xeno-   *19*
phobes and reactionaries intoxicated with a sense of cultural superiority,
the sporting wing of Pat Buchanan's America First conservatism. For a
time, I believed this myself. But over the years I've met too many conservatives who violently disagree with Kemp's grafting of politics onto the
game. And I've heard too many liberals take their shots at soccer, people
who write for such publications as the *Village Voice* and couldn't be plausi-
bly grouped in the troglodyte camp of American politics. So if hatred of
soccer has nothing to do with politics, conventionally defined, why do so
many Americans feel threatened by the beautiful game?

For years, I have been collecting a file on this anti-soccer lobby. The   *20*
person whose material mounts highest in my collection is the wildly popular radio shock jock Jim Rome. Rome arrived on the national scene in the
mid-nineties and built an audience based on his self-congratulatory flout-
ing of social norms. Rome has created his own subculture that has enrap-
tured a broad swath of American males. They are united by their own
vernacular, a Walter Winchell–like form of slang that Rome calls "smack,"
derived in part from the African American street and in part from the fraternity house. An important part of this subculture entails making fun of
the people who aren't members of it. Rome can be cruelly cutting to callers
who don't pass his muster, who talk the wrong kind of smack or freeze up
on air. These putdowns form a large chunk of his programs. The topics of
his rants include such far-ranging subject matter as the quackery of chiro-
practors, cheap seafood restaurants, and, above all, soccer.

Where specific events trigger most soccer hating — a World Cup, news   *21*
of hooligan catastrophes that arrive over the wires — Rome doesn't need a
proximate cause to break into a tirade. He lets randomly rip with invec-
tive. "My son is not playing soccer. I will hand him ice skates and a shim-
mering sequined blouse before I hand him a soccer ball. Soccer is not a
sport, does not need to be on my TV, and my son will not be playing it."
In moments of honesty, he more or less admits his illogic. "If it's incredibly stupid and soccer is in any way related, then soccer must be the root
cause [of the stupidity]," he said in one segment, where he attacked the
sporting goods manufacturer Umbro for putting out a line of clothing
called Zyklon, the same name as the Auschwitz gas. (Zyklon translates
as cyclone. By his logic, the words "concentration" or "camp" should be
purged from conversational English for their Holocaust associations.) He
often inadvertently endorses some repulsive arguments. One segment
ripped into African soccer teams for deploying witch doctors. "So you can
add this to the laundry list of reasons why I hate soccer," he frothed.

Such obvious flaws make it seem he is proud of his crassness, and that   *22*
would be entirely in keeping with character. These arguments would be
more easily dismissed were they the product of a single demented individual. But far smarter minds have devolved down to Rome's level. Allen
Barra, a sportswriter for the *Wall Street Journal,* is one of these smarter
minds. Usually, Barra distinguishes himself from his colleagues by making

especially rarified, sharp arguments that follow clearly from the facts and have evidence backing his provocative claims. But on soccer, he slips from his moorings. He writes, "Yes, OK, soccer is the most 'popular' game in the world. And rice is the most 'popular' food in the world. So what? Maybe other countries can't afford football, basketball and baseball leagues: maybe if they could afford these other sports, they'd enjoy them even more."

Unlike Rome, Barra has some sense of why he flies off the handle on 23 this subject. It has to do with his resentment of the game's yuppie promoters. He argues, "Americans are such suckers when it comes to something with a European label that many who have resisted thus far would give in to trendiness and push their kids into youth soccer programs." And more than that, he worries that the soccer enthusiasts want the U.S. to "get with the rest of the world's program."

As Barra makes clear, the anti-soccer lobby really articulates the same 24 fears as Eurico Miranda and Alan Garrison, a phobia of globalization. To understand their fears, it is important to note that both Barra and Rome are proud aficionados of baseball. The United States, with its unashamedly dynamic culture, doesn't have too many deeply rooted, transgenerational traditions that it can claim as its own. Baseball is one of the few. That's one reason why the game gets so much nostalgia-drenched celebration in Kevin Costner movies and Stephen Jay Gould books.

But Major League Baseball, let's face it, has been a loser in globaliza- 25 tion. Unlike the NBA or NFL, it hasn't made the least attempt to market itself to a global audience. And the global audience has shown no hunger for the game. Because baseball has failed to master the global economy, it has been beat back by it. According to the Sporting Goods Manufacturers Association of America, the number of teens playing baseball fell 47 percent between 1987 and 2000. During that same period, youth soccer grew exponentially. By 2002, 1.3 million more kids played soccer than Little League. And the demographic profile of baseball has grown ever more lily white. It has failed to draw African Americans and attracts few Latinos who didn't grow up playing the game in the Caribbean. The change can also be registered in the ballot box that matters most. Nielsen ratings show that, in most years, a World Series can no longer draw the same number of viewers as an inconsequential Monday night game in the NFL.

It's not surprising that Americans should split like this over soccer. 26 Globalization increasingly provides the subtext for the American cultural split. This isn't to say America violently or even knowingly divides over globalization. But after September 11 opened new debates over foreign policy, two camps in American politics have clearly emerged. One camp believes in the essential tenets of the globalization religion as preached by European politicians, that national governments should defer to institutions like the UN and WTO. These tend to be people who opposed the war in Iraq. And this opinion reflects a worldview. These Americans share cultural values with Europeans — an aggressive secularism, a more relaxed set of cultural mores that tolerates gays and pot smoking — which isn't surprising, considering that these Americans have jobs and tourist interests that put them in regular contact with the other side of the Atlantic. They consider themselves to be part of a cosmopolitan culture that transcends national boundaries.

On the other side, there is a group that believes in "American excep   27
tionalism," an idea that America's history and singular form of government has given the nation a unique role to play in the world; that the U.S. should be above submitting to international laws and bodies. They view Europeans as degraded by their lax attitudes, and worry about the threat to American culture posed by secular tolerance. With so much relativism seeping into the American way of life, they fret that the country has lost the self-confidence to make basic moral judgments, to condemn evil. Soccer isn't exactly pernicious, but it's a symbol of the U.S. junking its tradition to "get with the rest of the world's program."

There are many conservatives who hate relativism, consider the   28
French wussy, and still adore soccer. But it's not a coincidence that the game has become a small touchstone in this culture war.

III.

I wish that my side, the yuppie soccer fans, were blameless victims in   29
these culture wars. But I've been around enough of America's soccer cognoscenti to know that they invite abuse. They are inveterate snobs, so snobbish, in fact, that they think nothing of turning against their comrades. According to their sneering critique, their fellow fans are dilettantes without any real understanding of the game; they are yuppies who admire soccer like a fine slab of imported goat cheese; they come from neighborhoods with spectacularly high Starbucks-per-capita, so they lack any semblance of burning working-class passion.

This self-loathing critique can be easily debunked. I've seen the coun   30
terevidence with my own eyes. In the spring of 2001, the U.S. national team played Honduras in Washington's Robert Francis Kennedy stadium. This vital World Cup qualifying match had generated the packed, exuberant stadium that the occasion deserved. Fans wore their nation's jersey. Their singing and stomping caused the steel and concrete to undulate like the Mexican wave. In a country with lesser engineering standards, it would have been time to worry about a stadium collapse. On the field, stewards scampered to pick up scattered sneakers. Fans had removed them and thrown them at the opposing goalkeeper, a small gesture of homage to the madness of Glasgow and the passion of Barcelona. They mercilessly booed the linesman, softening him up by insulting his slut of a mother. It might not have quite ascended to the atmospheric wonders of a game played by the English national team, but it wasn't far from that mark.

There is, however, an important difference between a home game in   31
London and Washington. The majority of English fans will root for England. In Washington, more or less half the stadium wore the blue-and-white Honduran jersey, and they were the ones who shouted themselves hoarse

and heaved their shoes. The American aspiration of appearing in the World Cup rested on this game. But on that day, the Washington stadium might as well have been in Tegucigalpa.

Traveling through Europe, you hear the same complaint repeated over *32* and over: Americans are so "hypernationalistic." But is there any country in the world that would tolerate such animosity to their national team in their own national capital? In England or France or Italy, this would have been cause for unleashing hooligan hell.

Nor were the American fans what you'd expect of a hegemonic power. *33* The *Washington Post* had published a message from the national soccer federation urging us to wear red shirts as a sign of support — and to clearly distinguish ourselves from the Hondurans. But most American soccer fans don't possess a red USA jersey and aren't about to go down to the sporting goods store to buy one. They do, however, own red Arsenal, Man U., and Ajax jerseys, or, in my case, an old Barcelona one, that they collected on continental travels. While we were giving a patriotic boost, we couldn't help revealing our Europhilic cosmopolitanism.

I mention this scene because many critics of globalization make *34* America the wicked villain in the tale. They portray the U.S. forcing Nike, McDonald's and *Baywatch* down the throats of the unwilling world, shredding ancient cultures for the sake of empire and cash. But that version of events skirts the obvious truth: Multinational corporations are just that, multinational; they don't represent American interests or American culture. Just as much as they have changed the tastes and economies of other countries, they have tried to change the tastes and economy of the United States. Witness the Nike and Budweiser campaigns to sell soccer here. No other country has been as subjected to the free flows of capital and labor, so constantly remade by migration, and found its national identity so constantly challenged. In short, America may be an exception, but it is not exceptionally immune to globalization. And we fight about it, whether we know it or not, just like everyone else.

■　■　■

Reading Rhetorically

1. This excerpt from Foer's book *How Soccer Explains the World: An Unlikely Theory of Globalization* includes the prologue and the final chapter. Where and how are the ideas Foer sets out in the prologue developed in the chapter about "the American culture wars"?

2. More so than many of the authors in this collection, Foer relies on his own experiences to develop his argument. Witness his description of his "soccer career" at the start of the second section. Using two different colored pens, mark along the edges of the text where Foer draws on personal experience and where he discusses his subject in other ways. What do you notice about the organization of the reading? How does using these two different approaches to his topic help Foer make his point?

3. Foer uses self-criticism to address those who disagree with him. Look for examples of this and other strategies for countering the arguments of the antisoccer contingent. Discuss with your class the effectiveness of these strategies and ways you might use them in your own writing.

Inquiring Further

4. Soccer now carries cultural interest beyond the sport: Think of the term *soccer mom* and the popularity of films like *Bend It Like Beckham.* Using your library's electronic resources, search for articles on "soccer and culture" or "soccer and politics." You might also add a specific country to your search terms. Find and read three articles that catch your interest, and then share what you learn from them with the class. Based on your reading, why do you think soccer is such a popular topic for scholars?

5. What does Foer mean by *globalization*? Brainstorm with the class about your understanding of the term, and then look up definitions to enhance that understanding. A Google search can help you reach the Web sites of reputable organizations with different perspectives. Share what you find on several of these sites with your classmates, and discuss how you can tell if a Web site is reputable.

6. Interview a soccer coach about the skills the game fosters. Choose several key points from Foer's text to paraphrase, and ask the coach to comment on them. (You could also ask two or three skilled soccer players to comment on the paraphrases.) Report the results of your interview(s) to the class. What surprised you most about the ideas that emerged in your primary research?

Framing Conversations

7. Both Foer and Michael Kimmel (p. 448) are interested in the intersection between masculinity and cultural standards and behaviors, particularly in the aftermath of September 11, 2001. Compose an essay in which you draw on both authors' ideas and your own examples as you build an argument about expectations of masculinity in an age of globalization. What do you want your readers to come away thinking about contemporary masculinity?

8. Foer describes a division between prosoccer Americans and antisoccer Americans. Kwame Anthony Appiah (p. 378) also examines the ways different cultural groups perceive themselves as opposed to others. Write an essay in which you draw on both authors' insights about how and why cultural groups tend to see themselves in terms of us versus them. Teach your readers what you think is lost and, perhaps, gained by seeing the world this way. How does each author — and how do you — suggest we can overcome or at least understand our differences?

9. Like Foer, Thomas Frank (p. 497) explores the "culture wars," but his emphasis is more political — on what Foer calls "the split between 'red and blue America'" (para. 16). How do these authors' ideas complement or contradict one another? Write an essay in which you play one author's ideas off the other's in the process of building your argument about the significance of the culture wars. How real do you think they are? Draw on your own examples to help you develop your point.

While I Was Sleeping

Thomas L. Friedman is an award-winning journalist who has written for the *New York Times* since 1981. Over the years, he has served as bureau chief in Beirut and Israel, chief economic correspondent in the Washington bureau, and chief White House correspondent. He writes "Foreign Affairs," a widely syndicated column, for which he won his third Pulitzer Prize. (The previous two were for his international reporting.) In his column, Friedman analyzes issues relating to globalization, international politics, fundamentalism, the domestic and international economy, and, since 9/11, the country's "war on terror."

Friedman is also the author of four best-selling books: *From Beirut to Jerusalem* (1989); *The Lexus and the Olive Tree: Understanding Globalization* (1999, rev. ed. 2000); *Longitudes and Attitudes: Exploring the World After September 11* (2002); and the book from which this excerpt was taken, *The World Is Flat: A Brief History of the Twenty-First Century* (2005, exp. ed. 2006). Friedman's provocative title is meant to catch us by surprise. *The World Is Flat* examines the daily realities and possible long-term effects of globalization on our economy, politics, and the way we think of our place in the world. Friedman argues that if we don't pay attention to rapidly shifting trends in technology, outsourcing, and the economy, we could find the twenty-first century passing us by. The title of this reading — "While I Was Sleeping" — suggests how easily that might happen.

Friedman claims he was "sleeping" while the world was flattening (para. 16); but he is certainly wide awake in this text. Like many well-trained journalists, he is able to grasp a complex situation and offer readers concrete examples that illustrate the many parts they must understand to understand the whole. This clarity, and Friedman's careful analysis of the significance of each situation he describes, helps readers make sense of what could otherwise be an abstract — perhaps even boring — topic. Given this risk, pay attention to your responses to the anecdotes Friedman uses to open this text. What is the effect of his moving quickly from Christopher Columbus's journal to a description of playing golf in downtown Bangalore, "India's Silicon Valley" (para. 3)? How does Friedman's strategy of introducing readers to individuals in each setting help us see global economic implications in more human terms?

Many other authors are participating in this conversation about the rapidly globalizing economy. Benjamin Barber's *Jihad vs. McWorld: How Globalism and Tribalism Are Reshaping the World* (1995; rev. ed. 1996) and Joseph Stiglitz's *Making Globalization Work* (2006) are just two of the many books that examine the relationship among technology, politics, and the economy. Increasingly, the conversation on these topics is expanding beyond scholars to citizens who want to understand the world in which they live.

Whether you come to Friedman's writing with a comfortable understanding of the economic implications of what he calls a flattening world, or with only vague ideas about the global economy, this text will help you understand the human face of the rapidly changing world workforce.

Friedman's goal is to help us understand the exciting new opportunities created by technology, as well as the potential costs. Whose jobs, whose lives, are at stake in Globalization 3.0? Friedman offers answers we need to hear.

Your Highnesses, as Catholic Christians, and princes who love and promote the holy Christian faith, and are enemies of the doctrine of Mahomet, and of all idolatry and heresy, determined to send me, Christopher Columbus, to the above-mentioned countries of India, to see the said princes, people, and territories, and to learn their disposition and the proper method of converting them to our holy faith; and furthermore directed that I should not proceed by land to the East, as is customary, but by a Westerly route, in which direction we have hitherto no certain evidence that anyone has gone.

— Entry from the journal of CHRISTOPHER COLUMBUS on his voyage of 1492

No one ever gave me directions like this on a golf course before: "Aim at *1* either Microsoft or IBM." I was standing on the first tee at the KGA Golf Club in downtown Bangalore, in southern India, when my playing partner pointed at two shiny glass-and-steel buildings off in the distance, just behind the first green. The Goldman Sachs building wasn't done yet; otherwise he could have pointed that out as well and made it a threesome. HP and Texas Instruments had their offices on the back nine, along the tenth hole. That wasn't all. The tee markers were from Epson, the printer company, and one of our caddies was wearing a hat from 3M. Outside, some of the traffic signs were also sponsored by Texas Instruments, and the Pizza Hut billboard on the way over showed a steaming pizza, under the headline "Gigabites of Taste!"

No, this definitely wasn't Kansas. It didn't even seem like India. Was *2* this the New World, the Old World, or the Next World?

I had come to Bangalore, India's Silicon Valley, on my own Columbus- *3* like journey of exploration. Columbus sailed with the *Niña*, the *Pinta*, and the *Santa María* in an effort to discover a shorter, more direct route to India by heading west, across the Atlantic, on what he presumed to be an open sea route to the East Indies — rather than going south and east around Africa, as Portuguese explorers of his day were trying to do. India and the magical Spice Islands of the East were famed at the time for their gold, pearls, gems, and silk — a source of untold riches. Finding this short-cut by sea to India, at a time when the Muslim powers of the day had blocked the overland routes from Europe, was a way for both Columbus and the Spanish monarchy to become wealthy and powerful. When Columbus set sail, he apparently assumed the Earth was round, which was why he was convinced that he could get to India by going west. He miscalculated the distance, though. He thought the Earth was a smaller sphere than it is. He also did not anticipate running into a landmass before he reached the East Indies. Nevertheless, he called the aboriginal peoples he encountered in the new world "Indians." Returning home, though, Columbus was able to tell his patrons, King Ferdinand and Queen Isabella, that although he never did find India, he could confirm that the world was indeed round.

I set out for India by going due east, via Frankfurt. I had Lufthansa 4 business class. I knew exactly which direction I was going thanks to the GPS map displayed on the screen that popped out of the armrest of my airline seat. I landed safely and on schedule. I too encountered people called Indians. I too was searching for the source of India's riches. Columbus was searching for hardware — precious metals, silk, and spices — the source of wealth in his day. I was searching for software, brainpower, complex algorithms, knowledge workers, call centers, transmission protocols, breakthroughs in optical engineering — the sources of wealth in our day. Columbus was happy to make the Indians he met his slaves, a pool of free manual labor.

I just wanted to understand why the Indians I met were taking our 5 work, why they had become such an important pool for the outsourcing of service and information technology work from America and other industrialized countries. Columbus had more than one hundred men on his three ships; I had a small crew from the Discovery Times channel that fit comfortably into two banged-up vans, with Indian drivers who drove barefoot. When I set sail, so to speak, I too assumed that the world was round, but what I encountered in the real India profoundly shook my faith in that notion. Columbus accidentally ran into America but thought he had discovered part of India. I actually found India and thought many of the people I met there were Americans. Some had actually taken American names, and others were doing great imitations of American accents at call centers and American business techniques at software labs.

Columbus reported to his king and queen that the world was round, 6 and he went down in history as the man who first made this discovery. I returned home and shared my discovery only with my wife, and only in a whisper.

"Honey," I confided, "I think the world is flat." 7

How did I come to this conclusion? I guess you could say it all started in 8 Nandan Nilekani's conference room at Infosys Technologies Limited. Infosys is one of the jewels of the Indian information technology world, and Nilekani, the company's CEO, is one of the most thoughtful and respected captains of Indian industry. I drove with the Discovery Times crew out to the Infosys campus, about forty minutes from the heart of Bangalore, to tour the facility and interview Nilekani. The Infosys campus is reached by a pockmarked road, with sacred cows, horse-drawn carts, and motorized rickshaws all jostling alongside our vans. Once you enter the gates of Infosys, though, you are in a different world. A massive resort-size swimming pool nestles amid boulders and manicured lawns, adjacent to a huge putting green. There are multiple restaurants and a fabulous health club. Glass-and-steel buildings seem to sprout up like weeds each week. In some of those buildings, Infosys employees are writing specific software programs for American or European companies; in others, they are running the back rooms of major American- and European-based multinationals — everything from computer maintenance to specific research projects to answering customer calls routed there from all over the world. Security is tight, cameras monitor the doors, and if you are working for American Express, you cannot get into the building that is managing services and research for General Electric. Young Indian engineers, men and women, walk briskly from building to building, dangling ID badges. One looked like he could do my taxes. Another looked like she could take my computer apart. And a third looked like she designed it!

After sitting for an interview, Nilekani gave our TV crew a tour of   *9* Infosys's global conferencing center — ground zero of the Indian outsourcing industry. It was a cavernous wood-paneled room that looked like a tiered classroom from an Ivy League law school. On one end was a massive wall-size screen and overhead there were cameras in the ceiling for teleconferencing. "So this is our conference room, probably the largest screen in Asia — this is forty digital screens [put together]," Nilekani explained proudly, pointing to the biggest flat-screen TV I had ever seen. Infosys, he said, can hold a virtual meeting of the key players from its entire global supply chain for any project at any time on that supersize screen. So their American designers could be on the screen speaking with their Indian software writers and their Asian manufacturers all at once. "We could be sitting here, somebody from New York, London, Boston, San Francisco, all live. And maybe the implementation is in Singapore, so the Singapore person could also be live here . . . That's globalization," said Nilekani. Above the screen there were eight clocks that pretty well summed up the Infosys workday: 24/7/365. The clocks were labeled US West, US East, GMT, India, Singapore, Hong Kong, Japan, Australia.

"Outsourcing is just one dimension of a much more fundamental   *10* thing happening today in the world," Nilekani explained. "What happened over the last [few] years is that there was a massive investment in technology, especially in the bubble era, when hundreds of millions of dollars were invested in putting broadband connectivity around the world, undersea cables, all those things." At the same time, he added, computers became cheaper and dispersed all over the world, and there was an explosion of software — e-mail, search engines like Google, and proprietary software that can chop up any piece of work and send one part to Boston, one part to Bangalore, and one part to Beijing, making it easy for anyone to do remote development. When all of these things suddenly came together around 2000, added Nilekani, they "created a platform where intellectual work, intellectual capital, could be delivered from anywhere. It could be disaggregated, delivered, distributed, produced, and put back together again — and this gave a whole new degree of freedom to the way we do work, especially work of an intellectual nature . . . And what you are seeing in Bangalore today is really the culmination of all these things coming together."

We were sitting on the couch outside of Nilekani's office, waiting for *11* the TV crew to set up its cameras. At one point, summing up the implications of all this, Nilekani uttered a phrase that rang in my ear. He said to me, "Tom, the playing field is being leveled." He meant that countries like India are now able to compete for global knowledge work as never before — and that America had better get ready for this. America was going to be challenged, but, he insisted, the challenge would be good for America because we are always at our best when we are being challenged. As I left the Infosys campus that evening and bounced along the road back to Bangalore, I kept chewing on that phrase: "The playing field is being leveled."

What Nandan is saying, I thought, is that the playing field is being flat- *12* tened . . . Flattened? Flattened? My God, he's telling me the world is flat!

Here I was in Bangalore — more than five hundred years after Colum- *13* bus sailed over the horizon, using the rudimentary navigational technologies of his day, and returned safely to prove definitively that the world was round — and one of India's smartest engineers, trained at his country's top technical institute and backed by the most modern technologies of his day, was essentially telling me that the world was *flat* — as flat as that screen on which he can host a meeting of his whole global supply chain. Even more interesting, he was citing this development as a good thing, as a new milestone in human progress and a great opportunity for India and the world — the fact that we had made our world flat!

In the back of that van, I scribbled down four words in my notebook: *14* "The world is flat." As soon as I wrote them, I realized that this was the underlying message of everything that I had seen and heard in Bangalore in two weeks of filming. The global competitive playing field was being leveled. The world was being flattened.

As I came to this realization, I was filled with both excitement and *15* dread. The journalist in me was excited at having found a framework to better understand the morning headlines and to explain what was happening in the world today. Clearly, it is now possible for more people than ever to collaborate and compete in real time with more other people on more different kinds of work from more different corners of the planet and on a more equal footing than at any previous time in the history of the world — using computers, e-mail, networks, teleconferencing, and dynamic new software. That is what Nandan was telling me. That was what I discovered on my journey to India and beyond. And that is what this book is about. When you start to think of the world as flat, a lot of things make sense in ways they did not before. But I was also excited personally, because what the flattening of the world means is that we are now connecting all the knowledge centers on the planet together into a single global network, which — if politics and terrorism do not get in the way — could usher in an amazing era of prosperity and innovation.

But contemplating the flat world also left me filled with dread, profes-   *16*
sional and personal. My personal dread derived from the obvious fact that
it's not only the software writers and computer geeks who get empowered
to collaborate on work in a flat world. It's also al-Qaeda and other terrorist
networks. The playing field is not being leveled only in ways that draw in
and superempower a whole new group of innovators. It's being leveled in a
way that draws in and superempowers a whole new group of angry, frustrated, and humiliated men and women.

Professionally, the recognition that the world was flat was unnerving   *17*
because I realized that this flattening had been taking place while I was
sleeping, and I had missed it. I wasn't really sleeping, but I was otherwise
engaged. Before 9/11, I was focused on tracking globalization and exploring the tension between the "Lexus" forces of economic integration and
the "Olive Tree" forces of identity and nationalism — hence my 1999 book,
The Lexus and the Olive Tree. But after 9/11, the olive tree wars became all-
consuming for me. I spent almost all my time traveling in the Arab and
Muslim worlds. During those years I lost the trail of globalization.

I found that trail again on my journey to Bangalore in February 2004.   *18*
Once I did, I realized that something really important had happened
while I was fixated on the olive groves of Kabul and Baghdad. Globalization had gone to a whole new level. If you put *The Lexus and the Olive
Tree* and this book together, the broad historical argument you end up with
is that that there have been three great eras of globalization. The first
lasted from 1492 — when Columbus set sail, opening trade between
the Old World and the New World — until around 1800. I would call this
era Globalization 1.0. It shrank the world from a size large to a size
medium. Globalization 1.0 was about countries and muscles. That is, in
Globalization 1.0 the key agent of change, the dynamic force driving
the process of global integration was how much brawn — how much muscle, how much horsepower, wind power, or, later, steam power — your
country had and how creatively you could deploy it. In this era, countries
and governments (often inspired by religion or imperialism or a combination of both) led the way in breaking down walls and knitting the world
together, driving global integration. In Globalization 1.0, the primary
questions were: Where does my country fit into global competition and
opportunities? How can I go global and collaborate with others through
my country?

The second great era, Globalization 2.0, lasted roughly from 1800 to   *19*
2000, interrupted by the Great Depression and World Wars I and II. This
era shrank the world from a size medium to a size small. In Globalization 2.0,
the key agent of change, the dynamic force driving global integration, was
multinational companies. These multinationals went global for markets
and labor, spearheaded first by the expansion of the Dutch and English
joint-stock companies and the Industrial Revolution. In the first half of
this era, global integration was powered by falling transportation costs,
thanks to the steam engine and the railroad, and in the second half by

falling telecommunication costs — thanks to the diffusion of the telegraph, telephones, the PC, satellites, fiber-optic cable, and the early version
of the World Wide Web. It was during this era that we really saw the birth
and maturation of a global economy, in the sense that there was enough
movement of goods and information from continent to continent for there
to be a global market, with global arbitrage in products and labor. The
dynamic forces behind this era of globalization were breakthroughs in
hardware — from steamships and railroads in the beginning to telephones
and mainframe computers toward the end. And the big questions in this
era were: Where does my company fit into the global economy? How does
it take advantage of the opportunities? How can I go global and collaborate with others through my company? *The Lexus and the Olive Tree* was
primarily about the climax of this era, an era when the walls started falling
all around the world, and integration, and the backlash to it, went to a
whole new level. But even as the walls fell, there were still a lot of barriers
to seamless global integration. Remember, when Bill Clinton was elected
president in 1992, virtually no one outside of government and the academy
had e-mail, and when I was writing *The Lexus and the Olive Tree* in 1998,
the Internet and e-commerce were just taking off.

Well, they took off — along with a lot of other things that came together   20
while I was sleeping. And that is why I argue in this book that around the
year 2000 we entered a whole new era: Globalization 3.0. Globalization 3.0
is shrinking the world from a size small to a size tiny and flattening the
playing field at the same time. And while the dynamic force in Globalization 1.0 was countries globalizing and the dynamic force in Globalization
2.0 was companies globalizing, the dynamic force in Globalization 3.0 —
the thing that gives it its unique character — is the newfound power for
individuals to collaborate and compete globally. And the lever that is
enabling individuals and groups to go global so easily and so seamlessly
is not horsepower, and not hardware, but software — all sorts of new
applications — in conjunction with the creation of a global fiber-optic network that has made us all next-door neighbors. Individuals must, and can,
now ask, Where do *I* fit into the global competition and opportunities of the
day, and how can *I*, on my own, collaborate with others globally?

But Globalization 3.0 not only differs from the previous eras in how it   21
is shrinking and flattening the world and in how it is empowering individuals. It is different in that Globalization 1.0 and 2.0 were driven primarily
by European and American individuals and businesses. Even though
China actually had the biggest economy in the world in the eighteenth century, it was Western countries, companies, and explorers who were doing
most of the globalizing and shaping of the system. But going forward, this
will be less and less true. Because it is flattening and shrinking the world,
Globalization 3.0 is going to be more and more driven not only by individuals but also by a much more diverse — non-Western, nonwhite — group
of individuals. Individuals from every corner of the flat world are being
empowered. Globalization 3.0 makes it possible for so many more people

to plug and play, and you are going to see every color of the human rainbow take part.

(While this empowerment of individuals to act globally is the most important new feature of Globalization 3.0, companies — large and small — have been newly empowered in this era as well. . . .) 22

Needless to say, I had only the vaguest appreciation of all this as I left Nandan's office that day in Bangalore. But as I sat contemplating these changes on the balcony of my hotel room that evening, I did know one thing: I wanted to drop everything and write a book that would enable me to understand how this flattening process happened and what its implications might be for countries, companies, and individuals. So I picked up the phone and called my wife, Ann, and told her, "I am going to write a book called *The World Is Flat.*" She was both amused and curious — well, maybe *more* amused than curious! Eventually, I was able to bring her around, and I hope I will be able to do the same with you, dear reader. Let me start by taking you back to the beginning of my journey to India, and other points east, and share with you some of the encounters that led me to conclude the world was no longer round — but flat. 23

Jaithirth "Jerry" Rao was one of the first people I met in Bangalore — and I hadn't been with him for more than a few minutes at the Leela Palace hotel before he told me that he could handle my tax returns and any other accounting needs I had — from Bangalore. No thanks. I demurred, I already have an accountant in Chicago. Jerry just smiled. He was too polite to say it — that he may already be my accountant, or rather my accountant's accountant, thanks to the explosion in the outsourcing of tax preparation. 24

"This is happening as we speak," said Rao, a native of Mumbai, formerly Bombay, whose Indian firm, MphasiS, has a team of Indian accountants able to do outsourced accounting work from any state in America and the federal government. "We have tied up with several small and medium-sized CPA firms in America." 25

"You mean like my accountant?" I asked. "Yes, like your accountant," said Rao with a smile. Rao's company has pioneered a work flow software program with a standardized format that makes the outsourcing of tax returns cheap and easy. The whole process starts, Jerry explained, with an accountant in the United States scanning my last year's tax returns, plus my W-2, W-4, 1099, bonuses, and stock statements — everything — into a computer server, which is physically located in California or Texas. "Now your accountant, if he is going to have your taxes done overseas, knows that you would prefer not to have your surname be known or your Social Security number known [to someone outside the country], so he can choose to suppress that information," said Rao. "The accountants in India call up all the raw information directly from the server in America [using a password], and they complete your tax returns, with you remaining anonymous. All the data stays in the U.S. to comply with privacy regulations . . . We take data protection and privacy very seriously. The accountant in 26

India can see the data on his screen, but he cannot take a download of it or print it out — our program does not allow it. The most he could do would be to try to memorize it, if he had some ill intention. The accountants are not allowed to even take a paper and pen into the room when they are working on the returns."

I was intrigued at just how advanced this form of service outsourcing had become. "We are doing several thousand returns," said Rao. What's more, "Your CPA in America need not even be in their office. They can be sitting on a beach in California and e-mail us and say, 'Jerry, you are really good at doing New York State returns, so you do Tom's returns. And Sonia, you and your team in Delhi do the Washington and Florida returns.' Sonia, by the way, is working out of her house in India, with no overhead [for the company to pay]. 'And these others, they are really complicated, so I will do them myself.' "

In 2003, some 25,000 U.S. tax returns were done in India. In 2004, the number was 100,000. In 2005, it is expected to be 400,000. In a decade, you will assume that your accountant has outsourced the basic preparation of your tax returns — if not more.

"How did you get into this?" I asked Rao.

"My friend Jeroen Tas, a Dutchman, and I were both working in California for Citigroup," Rao explained. "I was his boss and we were coming back from New York one day together on a flight and I said that I was planning to quit and he said, 'So am I.' We both said, 'Why don't we start our own business?' So in 1997–98, we put together a business plan to provide high-end Internet solutions for big companies . . . Two years ago, though, I went to a technology convention in Las Vegas and was approached by some medium-size [American] accounting firms, and they said they could not afford to set up big tax outsourcing operations to India, but the big guys could, and [the medium guys] wanted to get ahead of them. So we developed a software product called VTR — Virtual Tax Room — to enable these medium-size accounting firms to easily outsource tax returns."

These midsize firms "are getting a more level playing field, which they were denied before," said Jerry. "Suddenly they can get access to the same advantages of scale that the bigger guys always had."

Is the message to Americans, "Mama, don't let your kids grow up to be accountants"? I asked.

Not really, said Rao. "What we have done is taken the grunt work. You know what is needed to prepare a tax return? Very little creative work. This is what will move overseas."

"What will stay in America?" I asked.

"The accountant who wants to stay in business in America will be the one who focuses on designing creative complex strategies, like tax avoidance or tax sheltering, managing customer relationships," he said. "He or she will say to his clients, 'I am getting the grunt work done efficiently far away. Now let's talk about how we manage your estate and what you are going to do about your kids. Do you want to leave some money in your trusts?' It means having the quality-time discussions with clients rather than running around like chickens with their heads cut off from February to April, and often filing for extensions into August, because they have not had the quality time with clients."

Judging from an essay in the journal *Accounting Today* (June 7, 2004), 36 this does, indeed, seem to be the future. L. Gary Boomer, a CPA and CEO of Boomer Consulting in Manhattan, Kansas, wrote, "This past [tax] season produced over 100,000 [outsourced] returns and has now expanded beyond individual returns to trusts, partnerships and corporations . . . The primary reason that the industry has been able to scale up as rapidly as it has over the past three years is due to the investment that these [foreign-based] companies have made in systems, processes and training." There are about seventy thousand accounting grads in India each year, he added, many of whom go to work for local Indian firms starting at $100 a month. With the help of high-speed communications, stringent training, and standardized forms, these young Indians can fairly rapidly be converted into basic Western accountants at a fraction of the cost. Some of the Indian accounting firms even go about marketing themselves to American firms through teleconferencing and skip the travel. Concluded Boomer, "The accounting profession is currently in transformation. Those who get caught in the past and resist change will be forced deeper into commoditization. Those who can create value through leadership, relationships and creativity will transform the industry, as well as strengthen relationships with their existing clients."

What you're telling me, I said to Rao, is that no matter what your 37 profession — doctor, lawyer, architect, accountant — if you are an American, you better be good at the touchy-feely service stuff, because anything that can be digitized can be outsourced to either the smartest or the cheapest producer, or both. Rao answered, "Everyone has to focus on what exactly is their value-add."

But what if I am just an average accountant? I went to a state univer- 38 sity. I had a B+ average. Eventually I got my CPA. I work in a big accounting firm, doing a lot of standard work. I rarely meet with clients. They keep me in the back. But it is a decent living and the firm is basically happy with me. What is going to happen to me in this system?

"It is a good question," said Rao. "We must be honest about it. We are 39 in the middle of a big technological change, and when you live in a society that is at the cutting edge of that change [like America], it is hard to predict. It's easy to predict for someone living in India. In ten years we are going to be doing a lot of the stuff that is being done in America today. We can predict our future. But we are behind you. You are defining the future. America is always on the edge of the next creative wave . . . So it is difficult to look into the eyes of that accountant and say this is what is going to be. We should not trivialize that. We must deal with it and talk about it honestly . . . Any activity where we can digitize and decompose the value chain, and move the work around, will get moved around. Some people will say, 'Yes, but you can't serve me a steak.' True, but I can take the reservation for your table sitting anywhere in the world, if the restaurant does not have an operator. We can say, 'Yes, Mr. Friedman, we can give you a table by the window.' In other words, there are parts of the whole dining-out experience that we can decompose and outsource. If you go back and read the basic economics textbooks, they will tell you: Goods are traded, but services are consumed and produced in the same place. And you cannot export a haircut. But we are coming close to exporting a haircut, the appointment part. What kind of haircut do you want? Which barber do you want? All those things can and will be done by a call center far away."

As we ended our conversation, I asked Rao what he is up to next. He *40* was full of energy. He told me he'd been talking to an Israeli company that is making some big advances in compression technology to allow for easier, better transfers of CAT scans via the Internet so you can quickly get a second opinion from a doctor half a world away.

A few weeks after I spoke with Rao, the following e-mail arrived from *41* Bill Brody, the president of Johns Hopkins University, whom I had just interviewed for this book:

> Dear Tom, I am speaking at a Hopkins continuing education medical meeting for radiologists (I used to be a radiologist). . . . I came upon a very fascinating situation that I thought might interest you. I have just learned that in many small and some medium-size hospitals in the US, radiologists are outsourcing reading of CAT scans to doctors in India and Australia!!! Most of this evidently occurs at night (and maybe weekends) when the radiologists do not have sufficient staffing to provide in-hospital coverage. While some radiology groups will use teleradiology to ship images from the hospital to their home (or to Vail or Cape Cod, I suppose) so that they can interpret images and provide a diagnosis 24/7, apparently the smaller hospitals are shipping CAT scan images to radiologists abroad. The advantage is that it is day-time in Australia or India when it is nighttime here — so after-hours coverage becomes more readily done by shipping the images across the globe. Since CAT (and MRI) images are already in digital format and available on a network with a standardized protocol, it is no problem to view the images anywhere in the world. . . . I assume that the radiologists on the other end . . . must have trained in [the] US and acquired the appropriate licenses and credentials. . . . The groups abroad that provide these after-hours readings are called "Nighthawks" by the American radiologists that employ them.
> Best,
> Bill

. . . Some of the signs of flattening I encountered back home, though, had *42* nothing to do with economics. On October 3, 2004, I appeared on the CBS News Sunday morning show *Face the Nation*, hosted by veteran CBS correspondent Bob Schieffer. CBS had been in the news a lot in previous weeks because of Dan Rather's *60 Minutes* report about President George W. Bush's Air National Guard service that turned out to be based on bogus documents. After the show that Sunday, Schieffer mentioned that the oddest thing had happened to him the week before. When he walked out of the CBS studio, a young reporter was waiting for him on the sidewalk. This isn't all that unusual, because as with all the Sunday-morning shows, the major networks — CBS, NBC, ABC, CNN, and Fox — always send crews to one another's studios to grab exit interviews with the guests. But this young man, Schieffer explained, was not from a major network. He politely introduced himself as a reporter for a Web site called InDC Journal and asked whether he could ask Schieffer a few questions. Schieffer, being a polite fellow, said sure. The young man interviewed him on a device Schieffer did not recognize and then asked if he could take his picture. A picture? Schieffer noticed that the young man had no camera. He didn't need one. He turned his cell phone around and snapped Schieffer's picture.

"So I came in the next morning and looked up this Web site and there 43 was my picture and the interview and there were already three hundred comments about it," said Schieffer, who, though keenly aware of online journalism, was nevertheless taken aback at the incredibly fast, low-cost, and solo manner in which this young man had put him up in lights.

I was intrigued by this story, so I tracked down the young man from 44 InDC Journal. His name is Bill Ardolino, and he is a very thoughtful guy. I conducted my own interview with him online — how else? — and began by asking about what equipment he was using as a one-man network/newspaper.

"I used a minuscule MP3 player/digital recorder (three and a half 45 inches by two inches) to get the recording, and a separate small digital camera phone to snap his picture," said Ardolino. "Not quite as sexy as an all-in-one phone/camera/recorder (which does exist), but a statement on the ubiquity and miniaturization of technology nonetheless. I carry this equipment around D.C. at all times because, hey, you never know. What's perhaps more startling is how well Mr. Schieffer thought on his feet, after being jumped on by some stranger with interview questions. He blew me away."

Ardolino said the MP3 player cost him about $125. It is "primarily 46 designed to play music," he explained, but it also "comes prepackaged as a digital recorder that creates a WAV sound file that can be uploaded back to a computer . . . Basically, I'd say that the barrier to entry to do journalism that requires portable, ad hoc recording equipment is [now] about $100 — $200 to $300 if you add a camera, $400 to $500 for a pretty nice recorder and a pretty nice camera. [But] $200 is all that you need to get the job done."

What prompted him to become his own news network?   47

"Being an independent journalist is a hobby that sprang from my 48 frustration about biased, incomplete, selective, and/or incompetent information gathering by the mainstream media," explained Ardolino, who describes himself as a "center-right libertarian." "Independent journalism and its relative, blogging, are expressions of market forces — a need is not being met by current information sources. I started taking pictures and doing interviews of the antiwar rallies in D.C., because the media was grossly misrepresenting the nature of the groups that were organizing the gatherings — unrepentant Marxists, explicit and implicit supporters of terror, etc. I originally chose to use humor as a device, but I've since branched out. Do I have more power, power to get my message out, yes. The Schieffer interview actually brought in about twenty-five thousand visits in twenty-four hours. My peak day since I've started was fifty-five thousand when I helped break 'Rathergate.' . . . I interviewed the first forensics expert in the Dan Rather National Guard story, and he was then specifically picked up by the *Washington Post, Chicago Sun-Times, Globe, NYT,* etc., within forty-eight hours.

"The pace of information gathering and correction in the CBS fake   49 memo story was astounding," he continued. "It wasn't just that CBS News 'stonewalled' after the fact, it was arguably that they couldn't keep up with an army of dedicated fact-checkers. The speed and openness of the medium is something that runs rings around the old process . . . I'm a twenty-nine-year-old marketing manager [who] always wanted to write for a living but hated the AP style book. As überblogger Glenn Reynolds likes to say, blogs have given the people a chance to stop yelling at their TV and have a say in the process. I think that they serve as sort of a 'fifth estate' that works in conjunction with the mainstream media (often by keeping an eye on them or feeding them raw info) and potentially function as a journalism and commentary farm system that provides a new means to establish success.

"Like many facets of the topic that you're talking about in your book,   50 there are good and bad aspects of the development. The splintering of media makes for a lot of incoherence or selective cognition (look at our country's polarization), but it also decentralizes power and provides a better guarantee that the *complete* truth *is* out there . . . somewhere . . . in pieces."

On any given day one can come across any number of stories, like the   51 encounter between Bob Schieffer and Bill Ardolino, that tell you that old hierarchies are being flattened and the playing field is being leveled. As Micah L. Sifry nicely put it in *The Nation* magazine (November 22, 2004): "The era of top-down politics — where campaigns, institutions and journalism were cloistered communities powered by hard-to-amass capital — is over. Something wilder, more engaging and infinitely more satisfying to individual participants is arising alongside the old order."

I offer the Schieffer-Ardolino encounter as just one example of how   52 the flattening of the world has happened faster and changed rules, roles, and relationships more quickly than we could have imagined. And, though I know it is a cliché, I have to say it nevertheless: *You ain't seen nothin' yet.* We are entering a phase where we are going to see the digitization, virtualization, and automation of almost everything. The gains in productivity will be staggering for those countries, companies, and individuals who can absorb the new technological tools. And we are entering a phase where more people than ever before in the history of the world are going to have access to these tools — as innovators, as collaborators, and, alas, even as terrorists. You say you want a revolution? Well, the real information revolution is about to begin. I call this new phase Globalization 3.0 because it followed Globalization 2.0, but I think this new era of globalization will prove to be such a difference of degree that it will be seen, in time, as a difference in kind. That is why I introduced the idea that the world has gone from round to flat. Everywhere you turn, hierarchies are being challenged from below or transforming themselves from top-down structures into more horizontal and collaborative ones.

"Globalization is the word we came up with to describe the changing   53 relationships between governments and big businesses," said David Rothkopf, a former senior Department of Commerce official in the Clinton administration and now a private strategic consultant. "But what is going on today is a much broader, much more profound phenomenon." It is not simply about how governments, business, and people communicate, not just about how organizations interact, but is about the emergence of completely new social, political, and business models. "It is about things that impact some of the deepest, most ingrained aspects of society right down to the nature of the social contract," added Rothkopf. "What happens if the political entity in which you are located no longer corresponds to a job that takes place in cyberspace, or no longer really encompasses workers collaborating with other workers in different corners of the globe, or no longer really captures products produced in multiple places simultaneously? Who regulates the work? Who taxes it? Who should benefit from those taxes?"

If I am right about the flattening of the world, it will be remembered as   54 one of those fundamental changes — like the rise of the nation-state or the Industrial Revolution — each of which, in its day, noted Rothkopf, produced changes in the role of individuals, the role and form of governments, the way we innovated, the way we conducted business, the role of women, the way we fought wars, the way we educated ourselves, the way religion responded, the way art was expressed, the way science and research were conducted, not to mention the political labels we assigned to ourselves and to our opponents. "There are certain pivot points or watersheds in history that are greater than others because the changes they produced were so sweeping, multifaceted, and hard to predict at the time," Rothkopf said.

If the prospect of this flattening — and all of the pressures, disloca-   55 tions, and opportunities accompanying it — causes you unease about the future, you are neither alone nor wrong. Whenever civilization has gone through one of these disruptive, dislocating technological revolutions — like Gutenberg's introduction of the printing press — the whole world has changed in profound ways. But there is something about the flattening of the world that is going to be qualitatively different from other such profound changes: the speed and breadth with which it is taking hold. The introduction of printing happened over a period of decades and for a long time affected only a relatively small part of the planet. Same with the Industrial Revolution. This flattening process is happening at warp speed and directly or indirectly touching a lot more people on the planet at once. The faster and broader this transition to a new era, the more likely is the potential for disruption, as opposed to an orderly transfer of power from the old winners to the new winners.

To put it another way, the experiences of the high-tech companies in *56* the last few decades who failed to navigate the rapid changes brought about in their marketplace by these types of forces may be a warning to all the businesses, institutions, and nation-states that are now facing these inevitable, even predictable, changes but lack the leadership, flexibility, and imagination to adapt — not because they are not smart or aware, but because the speed of change is simply overwhelming them.

And that is why the great challenge for our time will be to absorb these *57* changes in ways that do not overwhelm people but also do not leave them behind. None of this will be easy. But this is our task. It is inevitable and unavoidable. It is the ambition of this book to offer a framework for how to think about it and manage it to our maximum benefit.

■　■　■

Reading Rhetorically

1. What is the effect of Friedman's decision to begin this piece with an excerpt from Christopher Columbus's journal? Why does he open his first paragraph with sentences that contrast so much in tone? What connections do you find between the content of the Columbus excerpt and Friedman's anecdote about golf course directions? Discuss the strategies Friedman uses to catch his readers' interest in paragraphs 1–6, leading up to his confiding to his wife, in paragraph 7, "I think the world is flat."

2. What does Friedman mean, exactly, by the phrase "the world is flat"? Identify several passages that help you define and understand his thinking.

3. Friedman uses a journalistic technique throughout this excerpt, including conversations between himself and his sources. Look at several of these passages closely — like the conversation with Jerry Rao that begins in paragraph 24 — and discuss the effect of including these conversations rather than simply paraphrasing them. How useful do you think this strategy would be in your own academic writing? Explain your answer.

Inquiring Further

4. This reading is an excerpt from Friedman's best-selling book *The World Is Flat: A Brief History of the Twenty-First Century.* Use your library's resources to locate reviews of the book, and read at least three of them, taking notes to share with the class. Alternatively, locate a copy of the book (most public libraries carry it, as do most campus libraries), and read

another chapter, taking notes so that you can summarize the chapter for the class.

5. What do other scholars say about the phenomenon of outsourcing? Search on "outsourcing and globalization" in an academic database — EBSCOhost, for example — to find at least three scholarly articles that interest you. (You can further narrow your search with a country's name, if you like.) Skim the articles closely enough so that you can summarize the arguments for the class in a discussion of the contemporary debate among scholars on this topic.

6. Friedman's column, "Foreign Affairs," is syndicated in many newspapers. Use your library's resources (the *New York Times* also has an online archive of his columns) to locate and skim ten of Friedman's columns to get a sense of the kinds of issues he writes about. In what ways are those issues related to the issues in this reading?

Framing Conversations

7. How do Friedman and Kwame Anthony Appiah (p. 378) conceive of the possibilities and challenges of being a global citizen? Write an essay in which you play their ideas off against one another. What skills and knowledge do you think are necessary to being a "good" global citizen?

8. How do you think Friedman's ideas about the flattening of the world apply to Michael Kimmel's ideas in "Gender, Class, and Terrorism" (p. 448)? Compose an essay in which you consider how flattening might account for some of the behaviors Kimmel describes in his essay. Be sure to quote and analyze specific passages in each text as you teach your reader what you find significant about the authors' ideas.

9. How do Friedman's ideas about globalization connect to Cynthia Selfe's argument (p. 783)? Write an essay in which you consider what each author might make of the other's argument and examples, and include your own perspective on both. What sense of the benefits and risks of globalization do these writers share? Where do they differ? Where do you stand?

■ **MALCOLM GLADWELL**

From The Tipping Point: How Little Things Can Make a Big Difference

Malcolm Gladwell is a staff writer for *The New Yorker* whose two books, *The Tipping Point: How Little Things Can Make a Big Difference* (2000) and *Blink: The Power of Thinking Without Thinking* (2005), both made the *New York Times* best sellers' list. He is known for his ability to help readers see big ideas through small, even ordinary events. For example, the concept for *Blink* — how and why people make snap judgments — came from the experiences he had when he let his tightly curled hair grow out after years of wearing it conservatively cropped. (Gladwell's heritage is mixed: His father is white; his mother, black). For the first time in his life, as his hair began to grow, he found himself regularly being pulled over by the police, and once even stopped on the street, for questioning about a crime. Although nothing of substance about him had changed, Gladwell suddenly found himself the target of some very damaging snap judgments. As an intellectual, he used his experiences to develop a rich discussion in *Blink* of "rapid cognition" — what we commonly think of as gut instinct — to sort out what might be good and what might be dangerous about this practice. The insights in the book caught the attention of the business community, and Gladwell has become a sought-after speaker at business meetings, helping managers and CEOs rethink hiring practices, risk taking, and other activities that rely in part on judgments made without full knowledge of consequences.

This reading comes from *The Tipping Point,* an examination of how small and random events can set off an "epidemic" of like events. Gladwell moves around the globe and through history for examples to help us understand mass behaviors — spikes in teen suicide or smoking, for example, or a sudden resurgence of interest in Hush Puppies. The notion of a tipping point is part of our cultural conversation now. Witness the media's fascination with how word-of-mouth campaigns suddenly take off, how blogging can influence national politics, and how other kinds of communications technology catch on and help disseminate ideas.

Gladwell calls his book the "biography of an idea" (para. 7) — a phrase you might want to mull over. The idea, Gladwell goes on to say, "is very simple. It is that the best way to understand the emergence of fashion trends, the ebb and flow of crime waves, or, for that matter, the transformation of unknown books into bestsellers, or the rise of teenage smoking . . . or any number of the other mysterious changes that mark everyday life is to think of them as epidemics. Ideas and products and messages and behaviors spread just like viruses do." As he fleshes out this unusual idea, pay attention to the connections he makes. How does he get from Hush Puppies to crime in New York City, for example? Which examples do you find most persuasive? How effectively do you think he deploys numbers to support his claims? Although he is writing for a general audience with an interest in social trends, like any well-trained scholar Gladwell incorporates the ideas of other researchers and writers and cites his sources in end notes.

Gladwell offers readers a set of tools for interpreting social trends, and his ideas might spark an interest in analyzing other epidemics through a tipping-point lens. Consider the increasing popularity of Facebook and MySpace, for example. Gladwell is a big-idea person who invites the rest of us to participate in a lively game of connect-the-dots. The fact that the dots seem at first to be as insignificant as an ugly pair of Hush Puppies is part of the unexpected pleasure of this kind of playful but rigorous thinking.

Introduction

For Hush Puppies — the classic American brushed-suede shoes with the lightweight crepe sole — the Tipping Point came somewhere between late 1994 and early 1995. The brand had been all but dead until that point. Sales were down to 30,000 pairs a year, mostly to backwoods outlets and small-town family stores. Wolverine, the company that makes Hush Puppies, was thinking of phasing out the shoes that made them famous. But then something strange happened. At a fashion shoot, two Hush Puppies executives — Owen Baxter and Geoffrey Lewis — ran into a stylist from New York who told them that the classic Hush Puppies had suddenly become hip in the clubs and bars of downtown Manhattan. "We were being told," Baxter recalls, "that there were resale shops in the Village, in Soho, where the shoes were being sold. People were going to the Ma and Pa stores, the little stores that still carried them, and buying them up." Baxter and Lewis were baffled at first. It made no sense to them that shoes that were so obviously out of fashion could make a comeback. "We were told that Isaac Mizrahi was wearing the shoes himself," Lewis says. "I think it's fair to say that at the time we had no idea who Isaac Mizrahi was."

By the fall of 1995, things began to happen in a rush. First the designer John Bartlett called. He wanted to use Hush Puppies in his spring collection. Then another Manhattan designer, Anna Sui, called, wanting shoes for her show as well. In Los Angeles, the designer Joel Fitzgerald put a twenty-five-foot inflatable basset hound — the symbol of the Hush Puppies brand — on the roof of his Hollywood store and gutted an adjoining art gallery to turn it into a Hush Puppies boutique. While he was still painting and putting up shelves, the actor Pee-wee Herman walked in and asked for a couple of pairs. "It was total word of mouth," Fitzgerald remembers.

In 1995, the company sold 430,000 pairs of the classic Hush Puppies, and the next year it sold four times that, and the year after that still more, until Hush Puppies were once again a staple of the wardrobe of the young American male. In 1996, Hush Puppies won the prize for best accessory at the Council of Fashion Designers awards dinner at Lincoln Center, and the president of the firm stood up on the stage with Calvin Klein and Donna Karan and accepted an award for an achievement that — as he would be the first to admit — his company had almost nothing to do with. Hush Puppies had suddenly exploded, and it all started with a handful of kids in the East Village and Soho.

How did that happen? Those first few kids, whoever they were, weren't deliberately trying to promote Hush Puppies. They were wearing them precisely because no one else would wear them. Then the fad spread to two fashion designers who used the shoes to peddle something else — haute couture. The shoes were an incidental touch. No one was trying to make Hush Puppies a trend. Yet, somehow, that's exactly what happened. The shoes passed a certain point in popularity and they tipped. How does a thirty-dollar pair of shoes go from a handful of downtown Manhattan hipsters and designers to every mall in America in the space of two years?

I.

There was a time, not very long ago, in the desperately poor New York City ⁵ neighborhoods of Brownsville and East New York, when the streets would turn into ghost towns at dusk. Ordinary working people wouldn't walk on the sidewalks. Children wouldn't ride their bicycles on the streets. Old folks wouldn't sit on stoops and park benches. The drug trade ran so rampant and gang warfare was so ubiquitous in that part of Brooklyn that most people would take to the safety of their apartment at nightfall. Police officers who served in Brownsville in the 1980s and early 1990s say that, in those years, as soon as the sun went down their radios exploded with chatter between beat officers and their dispatchers over every conceivable kind of violent and dangerous crime. In 1992, there were 2,154 murders in New York City and 626,182 serious crimes, with the weight of those crimes falling hardest in places like Brownsville and East New York.[1] But then something strange happened. At some mysterious and critical point, the crime rate began to turn. It tipped. Within five years, murders had dropped 64.3 percent to 770 and total crimes had fallen by almost half to 355,893. In Brownsville and East New York, the sidewalks filled up again, the bicycles came back, and old folks reappeared on the stoops. "There was a time when it wasn't uncommon to hear rapid fire, like you would hear somewhere in the jungle in Vietnam," says Inspector Edward Messadri, who commands the police precinct in Brownsville. "I don't hear the gunfire anymore."

The New York City police will tell you that what happened in New ⁶ York was that the city's policing strategies dramatically improved. Criminologists point to the decline of the crack trade and the aging of the population. Economists, meanwhile, say that the gradual improvement in the city's economy over the course of the 1990s had the effect of employing those who might otherwise have become criminals. These are the conventional explanations for the rise and fall of social problems, but in the end none is any more satisfying than the statement that kids in the East Village caused the Hush Puppies revival. The changes in the drug trade, the population, and the economy are all long-term trends, happening all over the country. They don't explain why crime plunged in New York City so much more than in other cities around the country, and they don't explain why it all happened in such an extraordinarily short time. As for the improvements made by the police, they are important too. But there is a puzzling

---

[1]For a good summary of New York City crime statistics, see: Michael Massing, "The Blue Revolution," in the *New York Review of Books*, November 19, 1998, pp. 32–34. There is another good discussion of the anomalous nature of the New York crime drop in William Bratton and William Andrews, "What We've Learned About Policing," in *City Journal*, Spring 1999, p. 25.

gap between the scale of the changes in policing and the size of the effect on places like Brownsville and East New York. After all, crime didn't just slowly ebb in New York as conditions gradually improved. It plummeted. How can a change in a handful of economic and social indices cause murder rates to fall by two-thirds in five years?

II.

The Tipping Point is the biography of an idea, and the idea is very simple. It [7] is that the best way to understand the emergence of fashion trends, the ebb and flow of crime waves, or, for that matter, the transformation of unknown books into bestsellers, or the rise of teenage smoking, or the phenomena of word of mouth, or any number of the other mysterious changes that mark everyday life is to think of them as epidemics. Ideas and products and messages and behaviors spread just like viruses do.

The rise of Hush Puppies and the fall of New York's crime rate are text- [8] book examples of epidemics in action. Although they may sound as if they don't have very much in common, they share a basic, underlying pattern. First of all, they are clear examples of contagious behavior. No one took out an advertisement and told people that the traditional Hush Puppies were cool and they should start wearing them. Those kids simply wore the shoes when they went to clubs or cafes or walked the streets of downtown New York, and in so doing exposed other people to their fashion sense. They infected them with the Hush Puppies "virus."

The crime decline in New York surely happened the same way. It [9] wasn't that some huge percentage of would-be murderers suddenly sat up in 1993 and decided not to commit any more crimes. Nor was it that the police managed magically to intervene in a huge percentage of situations that would otherwise have turned deadly. What happened is that the small number of people in the small number of situations in which the police or the new social forces had some impact started behaving very differently, and that behavior somehow spread to other would-be criminals in similar situations. Somehow a large number of people in New York got "infected" with an anti-crime virus in a short time.

The second distinguishing characteristic of these two examples is that [10] in both cases little changes had big effects. All of the possible reasons for why New York's crime rate dropped are changes that happened at the margin; they were incremental changes. The crack trade leveled off. The population got a little older. The police force got a little better. Yet the effect was dramatic. So too with Hush Puppies. How many kids are we talking about who began wearing the shoes in downtown Manhattan? Twenty? Fifty? One hundred — at the most? Yet their actions seem to have single-handedly started an international fashion trend.

Finally, both changes happened in a hurry. They didn't build steadily [11] and slowly. It is instructive to look at a chart of the crime rate in New York City from, say, the mid-1960s to the late 1990s. It looks like a giant arch. In

1965, there were 200,000 crimes in the city and from that point on the number begins a sharp rise, doubling in two years and continuing almost unbroken until it hits 650,000 crimes a year in the mid-1970s. It stays steady at that level for the next two decades, before plunging downward in 1992 as sharply as it rose thirty years earlier. Crime did not taper off. It didn't gently decelerate. It hit a certain point and jammed on the brakes.

These three characteristics — one, contagiousness; two, the fact that little causes can have big effects; and three, that change happens not gradually but at one dramatic moment — are the same three principles that define how measles moves through a grade-school classroom or the flu attacks every winter. Of the three, the third trait — the idea that epidemics can rise or fall in one dramatic moment — is the most important, because it is the principle that makes sense of the first two and that permits the greatest insight into why modern change happens the way it does. The name given to that one dramatic moment in an epidemic when everything can change all at once is the Tipping Point. . . .

Case Study: Suicide, Smoking, and the Search for the Unsticky Cigarette

Not long ago, on the South Pacific islands of Micronesia, a seventeen-year-old boy named Sima got into an argument with his father.[2] He was staying with his family at his grandfather's house when his father — a stern and demanding man — ordered him out of bed early one morning and told him to find a bamboo pole-knife to harvest breadfruit. Sima spent hours in the village, looking without success for a pole-knife, and when he returned empty-handed, his father was furious. The family would now go hungry, he told his son, waving a machete in rage. "Get out of here and go find somewhere else to live."

Sima left his grandfather's house and walked back to his home village. Along the way he ran into his fourteen-year-old brother and borrowed a pen. Two hours later, curious about where Sima had gone, his brother went looking for him. He returned to the now empty family house and peered in the window. In the middle of a dark room, hanging slack and still from a noose, was Sima. He was dead. His suicide note read:

> My life is coming to an end at this time. Now today is a day of sorrow for myself, also a day of suffering for me. But it is a day of celebration for Papa. Today Papa sent me away. Thank you for loving me so little. Sima.
>
> Give my farewell to Mama. Mama you won't have any more frustration or trouble from your boy. Much love from Sima.

[2]The story of Sima is beautifully told by the anthropologist Donald H. Rubinstein in several papers, among them: "Love and Suffering: Adolescent Socialization and Suicide in Micronesia," *Contemporary Pacific* (Spring 1995), vol. 7, no. 1, pp. 21–53.

In the early 1960s, suicide on the islands of Micronesia was almost *15* unknown. But for reasons no one quite understands, it then began to rise, steeply and dramatically, by leaps and bounds every year, until by the end of the 1980s there were more suicides per capita in Micronesia than anywhere else in the world. For males between fifteen and twenty-four, the suicide rate in the United States is about 22 per 100,000. In the islands of Micronesia the rate is about 160 per 100,000 — more than seven times higher. At that level, suicide is almost commonplace, triggered by the smallest of incidents. Sima took his own life because his father yelled at him. In the midst of the Micronesian epidemic, that was hardly unusual. Teens committed suicide on the islands because they saw their girlfriends with another boy, or because their parents refused to give them a few extra dollars for beer. One nineteen-year-old hanged himself because his parents didn't buy him a graduation gown. One seventeen-year-old hanged himself because he had been rebuked by his older brother for making too much noise. What, in Western cultures, is something rare, random, and deeply pathological, has become in Micronesia a ritual of adolescence, with its own particular rules and symbols. Virtually all suicides on the islands, in fact, are identical variations on Sima's story. The victim is almost always male. He is in his late teens, unmarried, and living at home. The precipitating event is invariably domestic: a dispute with girlfriends or parents. In three-quarters of the cases, the victim had never tried — or even threatened — suicide before. The suicide notes tend to express not depression but a kind of wounded pride and self-pity, a protest against mistreatment. The act itself typically occurs on a weekend night, usually after a bout of drinking with friends. In all but a few cases, the victim observes the same procedure, as if there were a strict, unwritten protocol about the correct way to take one's own life. He finds a remote spot or empty house. He takes a rope and makes a noose, but he does not suspend himself, as in a typical Western hanging. He ties the noose to a low branch or a window or a doorknob and leans forward, so that the weight of his body draws the noose tightly around his neck, cutting off the flow of blood to the brain. Unconsciousness follows. Death results from anoxia — the shortage of blood to the brain.

In Micronesia, the anthropologist Donald Rubinstein writes, these rit- *16* uals have become embedded in the local culture. As the number of suicides have grown, the idea has fed upon itself, infecting younger and younger boys, and transforming the act itself so that the unthinkable has somehow been rendered thinkable. According to Rubinstein, who has documented the Micronesian epidemic in a series of brilliant papers,

> suicide ideation among adolescents appears widespread in certain Micronesian communities and is popularly expressed in recent songs composed locally and aired on Micronesian radio stations, and in graffiti adorning T-shirts and high school walls. A number of young boys who attempted suicide reported that they first saw or heard about it when they were 8 or 10 years old. Their suicide attempts appear in the spirit of imitative or experimental

play. One 11-year-old boy, for example, hanged himself inside his house and when found he was already unconscious and his tongue protruding. He later explained that he wanted to "try" out hanging. He said that he did not want to die, although he knew he was risking death. Such cases of imitative suicide attempts by boys as young as five and six have been reported recently from Truk. Several cases of young adolescent suicide deaths recently in Micronesia were evidently the outcome of such experiments. Thus as suicide grows more frequent in these communities the idea itself acquires a certain familiarity if not fascination to young men, and the lethality of the act seems to be trivialized. Especially among some younger boys, the suicide acts appear to have acquired an experimental almost recreational element.[3]

There is something very chilling about this passage. Suicide isn't supposed to be trivialized like this. But the truly chilling thing about it is how familiar it all seems. Here we have a contagious epidemic of self-destruction, engaged in by youth in the spirit of experimentation, imitation, and rebellion. Here we have a mindless action that somehow, among teenagers, has become an important form of self-expression. In a strange way, the Micronesian teen suicide epidemic sounds an awful lot like the epidemic of teenage smoking in the West.

I.

Teenage smoking is one of the great, baffling phenomena of modern life. No one really knows how to fight it, or even, for that matter, what it is. The principal assumption of the anti-smoking movement has been that tobacco companies persuade teens to smoke by lying to them, by making smoking sound a lot more desirable and a lot less harmful than it really is. To address that problem, then, we've restricted and policed cigarette advertising, so it's a lot harder for tobacco companies to lie. We've raised the price of cigarettes and enforced the law against selling tobacco to minors, to try to make it much harder for teens to buy cigarettes. And we've run extensive public health campaigns on television and radio and in magazines to try to educate teens about the dangers of smoking.

It has become fairly obvious, however, that this approach isn't very effective. Why do we think, for example, that the key to fighting smoking is educating people about the risks of cigarettes? Harvard University economist W. Kip Viscusi recently asked a group of smokers to guess how many years of life, on average, smoking from the age of twenty-one onward would cost them.[4] They guessed nine years. The real answer is somewhere around six or seven. Smokers aren't smokers because they underestimate the risks of smoking. They smoke even though they overestimate the risk of smoking. At the same time, it is not clear how effective it is to have

_17_

_18_

---

[3]Donald H. Rubinstein, "Epidemic Suicide Among Micronesian Adolescents," _Social Science and Medicine_ (1983), vol. 17, p. 664.

[4]W. Kip Viscusi, _Smoking: Making the Risky Decision_ (New York: Oxford University Press, 1992), pp. 61–78.

adults tell teenagers that they shouldn't smoke. As any parent of a teenage child will tell you, the essential contrariness of adolescents suggests that the more adults inveigh against smoking and lecture teenagers about its dangers, the more teens, paradoxically, will want to try it. Sure enough, if you look at smoking trends over the past decade or so, that is exactly what has happened. The anti-smoking movement has never been louder or more prominent. Yet all signs suggest that among the young the anti-smoking message is backfiring. Between 1993 and 1997, the number of college students who smoke jumped from 22.3 percent to 28.5 percent. Between 1991 and 1997, the number of high school students who smoke jumped 32 percent. Since 1988, in fact, the total number of teen smokers in the United States has risen an extraordinary 73 percent.[5] There are few public health programs in recent years that have fallen as short of their mission as the war on smoking.

The lesson here is not that we should give up trying to fight cigarettes.   19
The point is simply that the way we have tended to think about the causes of smoking doesn't make a lot of sense. That's why the epidemic of suicide in Micronesia is so interesting and potentially relevant to the smoking problem. It gives us another way of trying to come to terms with youth smoking. What if smoking, instead of following the rational principles of the marketplace, follows the same kind of mysterious and complex social rules and rituals that govern teen suicide? If smoking really is an epidemic like Micronesian suicide, how does that change the way we ought to fight the problem?

II.

The central observation of those who study suicide is that, in some places   20
and under some circumstances, the act of one person taking his or her own life can be contagious. Suicides lead to suicides. The pioneer in this field is David Phillips, a sociologist at the University of California at San Diego, who has conducted a number of studies on suicide, each more

---

[5]These statistics on the teen smoking rise come from a number of sources, and they differ according to how "new smokers" are measured. According to a Centers for Disease Control study released in October of 1998, for example, the number of American youths — people under the age of 18 — taking up smoking as a daily habit increased from 708,000 in 1988 to 1.2 million in 1996, an increase of 73 percent. The rate at which teens became smokers also increased. In 1996, 77 out of every 1,000 nonsmoking teens picked up the habit. In 1988, the rate was 51 per 1,000. The highest rate ever recorded was 67 per 1,000 in 1977, and the lowest was 44 per 1,000 in 1983. ("New teen smokers up 73 percent": Associated Press, October 9, 1998.) It is also the case that smoking among college students — a slightly older cohort — is also on the rise. In this study by the Harvard School of Public Health — published in the *Journal of the American Medical Association*, November 18, 1998 — the statistic used was percentage of college students who had smoked at least one cigarette in the past 30 days. In 1993, the number was 22.3 percent. By 1997, it had increased to 28.5 percent.

fascinating and seemingly improbable than the last.[6] He began by making a list of all the stories about suicide that ran on the front page of the country's most prominent newspapers in the twenty-year stretch between the end of the 1940s and the end of the 1960s. Then he matched them up with suicide statistics from the same period. He wanted to know whether there was any relationship between the two. Sure enough, there was. Immediately after stories about suicides appeared, suicides in the area served by the newspaper jumped. In the case of national stories, the rate jumped nationally. (Marilyn Monroe's death was followed by a temporary 12 percent increase in the national suicide rate.) Then Phillips repeated his experiment with traffic accidents. He took front-page suicide stories from the *Los Angeles Times* and the *San Francisco Chronicle* and matched them up with traffic fatalities from the state of California. He found the same pattern. On the day after a highly publicized suicide, the number of fatalities from traffic accidents was, on average, 5.9 percent higher than expected. Two days after a suicide story, traffic deaths rose 4.1 percent. Three days after, they rose 3.1 percent, and four days after, they rose 8.1 percent. (After ten days, the traffic fatality rate was back to normal.) Phillips concluded that one of the ways in which people commit suicide is by deliberately crashing their cars, and that these people were just as susceptible to the contagious effects of a highly publicized suicide as were people killing themselves by more conventional means.

The kind of contagion Phillips is talking about isn't something rational or even necessarily conscious. It's not like a persuasive argument. It's something much more subtle than that. "When I'm waiting at a traffic light and the light is red, sometimes I wonder whether I should cross and jaywalk," he says. "Then somebody else does it and so I do too. It's a kind of imitation. I'm getting permission to act from someone else who is engaging in a deviant act. Is that a conscious decision? I can't tell. Maybe afterwards I could brood on the difference. But at the time I don't know whether any of us knows how much of our decision is conscious and how much is unconscious. Human decisions are subtle and complicated and not very well understood." In the case of suicide, Phillips argues, the decision by someone famous to take his or her own life has the same effect: it gives other people, particularly those vulnerable to suggestion because of immaturity or mental illness, permission to engage in a deviant act as well. "Suicide stories are a kind of natural advertisement for a particular response to your problems," Phillips continues. "You've got all these people

---

[6]David Phillips's first paper on suicide rates after news stories of celebrity suicides was: D. P. Phillips, "The Influence of Suggestion on Suicide: Substantive and Theoretical Implications of the Werther Effect," *American Sociological Review* (1974), vol. 39, pp. 340–354. A good summary of that paper — and the statistic about Marilyn Monroe — can be found at the beginning of his paper on traffic accidents, David P. Phillips, "Suicide, Motor Vehicle Fatalities, and the Mass Media: Evidence toward a Theory of Suggestion," *American Journal of Sociology* (1979), vol. 84, no. 5, pp. 1150–1174.

who are unhappy and have difficulty making up their minds because they are depressed. They are living with this pain. There are lots of stories advertising different kinds of responses to that. It could be that Billy Graham has a crusade going on that weekend — that's a religious response. Or it could be that somebody is advertising an escapist movie — that's another response. Suicide stories offer another kind of alternative." Phillips's permission-givers . . . — whose deaths give others "permission" to die — serve as the Tipping Points in suicide epidemics.

The fascinating thing about this permission-giving, though, is how *22* extraordinarily specific it is. In his study of motor fatalities, Phillips found a clear pattern. Stories about suicides resulted in an increase in single-car crashes where the victim was the driver. Stories about suicide-murders resulted in an increase in multiple-car crashes in which the victims included both drivers and passengers. Stories about young people committing suicide resulted in more traffic fatalities involving young people. Stories about older people committing suicide resulted in more traffic fatalities involving older people. These patterns have been demonstrated on many occasions. News coverage of a number of suicides by self-immolation in England in the late 1970s, for example, prompted 82 suicides by self-immolation over the next year.[7] The "permission" given by an initial act of suicide, in other words, isn't a general invitation to the vulnerable. It is really a highly detailed set of instructions, specific to certain people in certain situations who choose to die in certain ways. It's not a gesture. It's speech. In another study, a group of researchers in England in the 1960s analyzed 135 people who had been admitted to a central psychiatric hospital after attempting suicide. They found that the group was strongly linked socially — that many of them belonged to the same social circles. This, they concluded, was not coincidence. It testified to the very essence of what suicide is, a private language between members of a common subculture. The author's conclusion is worth quoting in full:

> Many patients who attempt suicide are drawn from a section of the community in which self-aggression is generally recognized as a means of conveying a certain kind of information. Among this group the act is viewed as comprehensible and consistent with the rest of the cultural pattern. . . . If this is true, it follows that the individual who in particular situations, usually of distress, wishes to convey information about his difficulties to others, does not have to invent a communicational medium de novo. . . . The individual within the "attempted suicide subculture" can perform an act which carries a preformed meaning; all he is required to do is invoke it. The process is essentially similar to that whereby a person uses a word in a spoken language.[8]

---

[7]V. R. Ashton and S. Donnan, "Suicide by burning as an epidemic phenomenon: An analysis of 82 deaths and inquests in England and Wales in 1978–79," *Psychological Medicine* (1981), vol. 11, pp. 735–739.

[8]Norman Kreitman, Peter Smith, and Eng-Seong Tan, "Attempted Suicide as Language: An Empirical Study," *British Journal of Psychiatry* (1970), vol. 116, pp. 465–473.

This is what is going on in Micronesia, only at a much more profound 23 level. If suicide in the West is a kind of crude language, in Micronesia it has become an incredibly expressive form of communication, rich with meaning and nuance, and expressed by the most persuasive of permission-givers. Rubinstein writes of the strange pattern of suicides on the Micronesian island of Ebeye, a community of about 6,000. Between 1955 and 1965, there wasn't a single case of suicide on the entire island. In May 1966, an eighteen-year-old boy hanged himself in his jail cell after being arrested for stealing a bicycle, but his case seemed to have little impact. Then, in November of 1966, came the death of R., the charismatic scion of one of the island's wealthiest families. R. had been seeing two women and had fathered a one-month-old child with each of them. Unable to make up his mind between them, he hanged himself in romantic despair. At his funeral, his two lovers, learning of the existence of the other for the first time, fainted on his grave.

Three days after R.'s death, there was another suicide, a twenty-two- 24 year-old male suffering from marital difficulties, bringing the suicide toll to two over a week in a community that had seen one suicide in the previous twelve years. The island's medic wrote: "After R. died, many boys dreamed about him and said that he was calling them to kill themselves." Twenty-five more suicides followed over the next twelve years, mostly in clusters of three or four over the course of a few weeks. "Several suicide victims and several who have recently attempted suicide reported having a vision in which a boat containing all the past victims circles the island with the deceased inviting the potential victims to join them," a visiting anthropologist wrote in 1975. Over and over again, the themes outlined by R. resurfaced. Here is the suicide note of M., a high school student who had one girlfriend at boarding school and one girlfriend on Ebeye, and when the first girlfriend returned home from school, two girlfriends at once — a complication defined, in the youth sub-culture of Ebeye, as grounds for taking one's own life: "Best wishes to M. and C. [the two girlfriends]. It's been nice to be with both of you." That's all he had to say, because the context for his act had already been created by R. In the Ebeye epidemic, R. was the Tipping Person, . . . the one whose experience "overwrote" the experience of those who followed him. The power of his personality and the circumstances of his death combined to make the force of his example endure years beyond his death.

III.

Does teen smoking follow this same logic? In order to find out more about 25 the reasons teenagers smoke, I gave several hundred people a questionnaire, asking them to describe their earliest experiences with cigarettes. This was not a scientific study. The sample wasn't representative of the United States. It was mostly people in their late twenties and early thirties, living in big cities. Nonetheless the answers were striking, principally because of how similar they all seemed. Smoking seemed to evoke a particular kind of childhood memory — vivid, precise, emotionally charged. One person remembers how she loved to open her grandmother's purse, where she would encounter "the soft smell of cheap Winstons and leather mixed with drugstore lipstick and cinnamon gum." Another remembers "sitting in the back seat of a Chrysler sedan, smelling the wonderful mixture of sulfur and tobacco waft out the driver's window and into my nostrils." Smoking, overwhelmingly, was associated with the same thing to nearly everyone: sophistication. This was true even of people who now hate smoking, who now think of it as a dirty and dangerous habit. The language of smoking, like the language of suicide, seems incredibly consistent. Here are two responses, both describing childhood memories:

> My mother smoked, and even though I hated it — hated the smell — she had these long tapered fingers and full, sort of crinkly lips, always with lipstick on, and when she smoked she looked so elegant and devil-may-care that there was no question that I'd smoke someday. She thought people who didn't smoke were kind of gutless. Makes you stink, makes you think, she would say, reveling in how ugly that sounded.

> My best friend Susan was Irish-English. Her parents were, in contrast to mine, youthful, indulgent, liberal. They had cocktails before dinner. Mr. O'Sullivan had a beard and wore turtlenecks. Mrs. O'Sullivan tottered around in mules, dressed slimly in black to match her jet-black hair. She wore heavy eye-makeup and was a little too tan and always, virtually always, had a dangerously long cigarette holder dangling from her manicured hands.

This is the shared language of smoking, and it is as rich and expressive as the shared language of suicide. In this epidemic, as well, there are also Tipping People, . . . permission-givers. Time and time again, the respondents to my survey described the particular individual who initiated them into smoking in precisely the same way.

> When I was around nine or ten my parents got an English au pair girl, Maggie, who came and stayed with us one summer. She was maybe twenty. She was very sexy and wore a bikini at the Campbells' pool. She was famous with the grownup men for doing handstands in her bikini. Also it was said her bikini top fell off when she dove — Mr. Carpenter would submerge whenever she jumped in. Maggie smoked, and I used to beg her to let me smoke too.

> The first kid I knew who smoked was Billy G. We became friends in fifth grade, when the major distinctions in our suburban N.J. town — jocks, heads, brains — were beginning to form. Billy was incredibly cool. He was the first kid to date girls, smoke cigarettes and pot, drink hard alcohol and listen to druggy music. I even remember sitting upstairs in his sister's bedroom — his parents were divorced (another first), and his mom was never home — separating the seeds out of some pot on the cover of a Grateful Dead album. . . . The draw for me was the badness of it, and the adult-ness, and the way it proved the idea that you could be more than one thing at once.

The first person who I remember smoking was a girl named Pam P. I met her when we were both in the 10th grade. We rode the school bus together in Great Neck, L.I., and I remember thinking she was the coolest because she lived in an apartment. (Great Neck didn't have many apartments.) Pam seemed so much older than her 15 years. We used to sit in the back of the bus and blow smoke out the window. She taught me how to inhale, how to tie a man-tailored shirt at the waist to look cool, and how to wear lipstick. She had a leather jacket. Her father was rarely home.

There is actually considerable support for this idea that there is a common personality to hard-core smokers. Hans Eysenck, the influential British psychologist, has argued that serious smokers can be separated from non-smokers along very simple personality lines. The quintessential hard-core smoker, according to Eysenck, is an extrovert, the kind of person who

> is sociable, likes parties, has many friends, needs to have people to talk to. . . . He craves excitement, takes chances, acts on the spur of the moment and is generally an impulsive individual. . . . He prefers to keep moving and doing things, tends to be aggressive and loses his temper quickly; his feelings are not kept under tight control and he is not always a reliable person.[9]

In countless studies since Eysenck's groundbreaking work, this picture of the smoking "type" has been filled out. Heavy smokers have been shown to have a much greater sex drive than nonsmokers. They are more sexually precocious; they have a greater "need" for sex, and greater attraction to the opposite sex. At age nineteen, for example, 15 percent of nonsmoking white women attending college have had sex. The same number for white female college students who do smoke is 55 percent. The statistics for men are about the same according to Eysenck.[10] They rank much higher on what psychologists call "anti-social" indexes: they tend to have greater levels of misconduct, and be more rebellious and defiant. They make snap judgments. They take more risks. The average smoking household spends 73 percent more on coffee and two to three times as much on beer as the average nonsmoking household. Interestingly, smokers also seem to be more honest about themselves than nonsmokers. As David Krogh describes it in his treatise *Smoking: The Artificial Passion*, psychologists have what they call "lie" tests in which they insert inarguable statements — "I do not always tell the truth" or "I am sometimes cold to my spouse" — and if test-takers consistently deny these statements, it is taken as evidence that they are not generally truthful. Smokers are much more truthful on these tests. "One theory," Krogh writes, "has it that their lack of deference and their surfeit of defiance combine to make them relatively indifferent to what people think of them."[11]

---

[9]H. J. Eysenck, *Smoking, Health and Personality* (New York: Basic Books, 1965), p. 80. This reference is found in David Krogh's *Smoking: The Artificial Passion*, p. 107.

[10]The statistics on smoking and sexual behavior come from: H. J. Eysenck, *Smoking, Personality and Stress* (New York: Springer-Verlag, 1991), p. 27.

[11] David Krogh, *Smoking: The Artificial Passion* (New York: W. H. Freeman, 1991).

These measures don't apply to all smokers, of course. But as general *27*
predictors of smoking behavior they are quite accurate, and the more
someone smokes, the higher the likelihood that he or she fits this profile.
"In the scientific spirit," Krogh writes, "I would invite readers to demonstrate [the smoking personality connection] to themselves by performing
the following experiment. Arrange to go to a relaxed gathering of actors,
rock musicians, or hairdressers on the one hand, or civil engineers, electri-
cians, or computer programmers on the other, and observe how much
smoking is going on. If your experience is anything like mine, the differences should be dramatic."

Here is another of the responses to my questionnaire. Can the extro- *28*
verted personality be any clearer?

> My grandfather was the only person around me when I was very little who
> smoked. He was a great Runyonesque figure, a trickster hero, who immi-
> grated from Poland when he was a boy and who worked most of his life as
> a glazier. My mother used to like to say that when she was first brought to
> dinner with him she thought he might at any moment whisk the tablecloth
> off the table, leaving the settings there, just to amuse the crowd.

The significance of the smoking personality, I think, cannot be overstated.
If you bundle all of these extroverts' traits together — defiance, sexual precocity, honesty, impulsiveness, indifference to the opinion of others, sensation seeking — you come up with an almost perfect definition of the kind
of person many adolescents are drawn to. Maggie the au pair, and Pam P.
on the school bus and Billy G. with his Grateful Dead records were
all deeply cool people. But they weren't cool because they smoked.
They smoked because they were cool. The very same character traits of
rebelliousness and impulsivity and risk-taking and indifference to the
opinion of others and precocity that made them so compelling to their
adolescent peers also make it almost inevitable that they would also
be drawn to the ultimate expression of adolescent rebellion, risk-taking,
impulsivity, indifference to others, and precocity: the cigarette. This may
seem like a simple point. But it is absolutely essential in understanding why the war on smoking has stumbled so badly. Over the past decade,
the anti-smoking movement has railed against the tobacco companies
for making smoking cool and has spent untold millions of dollars of
public money trying to convince teenagers that smoking isn't cool. But
that's not the point. Smoking was never cool. *Smokers* are cool. Smoking
epidemics begin in precisely the same way that the suicide epidemic in
Micronesia began or word-of-mouth epidemics begin or the AIDS epidemic began, because of the extraordinary influence of Pam P. and Billy G.
and Maggie and their equivalents. . . . In this epidemic, as in all others,
a very small group — a select few — are responsible for driving the
epidemic forward. . . .

■   ■   ■

Reading Rhetorically

1. This reading is taken from Gladwell's book, *The Tipping Point: How Little Things Can Make a Big Difference*. Find specific passages in the reading that help you understand the concept of a tipping point. What other examples of tipping points can you think of?

2. Gladwell first sets out each of his opening examples (Hush Puppies and the crime rate in certain New York City neighborhoods) and then draws a connection between them. What is the effect of this strategy on readers? How could you make use of this approach in your own writing?

3. This reading is excerpted from the introduction to Gladwell's book and one of the chapters, or case studies. Why does Gladwell use the term *case study*? (You may need to look up the term.) Point to specific passages in the material on teen suicide and smoking that illustrate the claims Gladwell makes in his introduction. Which examples illustrate his central argument most effectively? Why?

Inquiring Further

4. Like most of the readings in this chapter, Gladwell's is taken from a best-selling book. Use your library's resources to find three reviews of *The Tipping Point*. What aspects of the book do the reviewers praise? What do they criticize? What do you think of their evaluations based on what you have read of Gladwell's book?

5. Gladwell maintains his own Web site (gladwell.com), with information about his books, an archive of his *New Yorker* articles, and his blog. Look through the materials gathered there, particularly his recent writing. What topics seem to catch his interest? What connections do you see between these topics?

6. Ask your librarian how to find the most accurate and current online data on teen smoking (try searching on "youth smokers") in the United States or, if available, in your state. What kinds of organizations sponsor this research and these Web sites? Discuss with the class both your findings and your analysis of the purpose and legitimacy of the sites you used.

Framing Conversations

7. Both Gladwell and Jared Diamond (p. 390) explore groups of people who often behave in ways that are not healthy for them . . . and that sometimes are deadly. Write an essay in which you use both authors' ideas about human behavior as tools to analyze a case study of an unhealthy behavior of your choice. Be sure to provide clear details about the behavior to support your claims. Are there aspects of this behavior that Gladwell's and Diamond's concepts fail to explain?

8. How does Gladwell's discussion of the ways teenagers pick up on cool trends relate to Thomas Friedman's analysis of recent trends in technology (p. 417)? Write an essay in which you draw on both authors' insights to build your own argument about how and why recent technological

innovations have caught on in this age group. Develop specific examples of your own to make your point, and include your evaluation of what is positive and negative about these trends.

9. How do Gladwell's ideas about the ways teen behaviors catch on intersect with Eric Schlosser's examination of the marketing tactics used by McDonald's and Disney (p. 754)? In an essay, apply each author's analysis to a specific marketing strategy aimed at teens by either corporation. Be sure to include and analyze specific examples, and to include your thoughts on the significance of your findings.

MICHAEL S. KIMMEL

Gender, Class, and Terrorism

Michael S. Kimmel is a professor of sociology at the State University of New York at Stony Brook, and is known internationally for his research and writing on men and masculinity. He is part of a growing group of academics who have followed feminist theorists in thinking about gender as a cultural construct, distinct from biological gender. Although femininity as a concept has been researched in women's studies programs for several decades, men's studies has only recently been developed as a field, and Kimmel is among the most prominent writers contributing to this body of knowledge. Kimmel is also a spokesperson of NOMAS (the National Organization for Men Against Sexism) and describes himself as a "profeminist man," arguing that it is in men's best interest, as well as women's, to work for gender equality.

Kimmel has written many articles on the topic of men's socialization and has published several books that are considered landmark texts in masculinity studies, among them *Men Confront Pornography* (1990), *The Politics of Manhood: Profeminist Men Respond to the Mythopoetic Men's Movement (and the Mythopoetic Leaders Answer)* (1995), and *The Gender of Desire: Essays on Male Sexuality* (2005). As a sociologist, Kimmel is interested in the many aspects of everyday life that teach boys to become men who follow a certain kind of social script — one that often privileges toughness, violence, and displays of power and confidence. Kimmel is curious about the ways popular culture reinforces gender roles (the film *Fight Club*, for example) and about the short- and long-term effects tough-guy scripts have on boys and men. This is a key theme in this reading about masculinity and terrorism. For example, look at paragraph 24, where Kimmel describes Mohammed Atta, one of the pilots who crashed a plane into the World Trade Center on 9/11. Consider the impact of Atta's father urging the boy to "toughen up."

This essay, "Gender, Class, and Terrorism," appeared in the sixth edition of *Men's Lives* (2004), which Kimmel coedited with Michael A. Messner. It was originally published in a newspaper for academics, the *Chronicle of Higher Education*, in 2002. Although Kimmel does not formally cite his sources, he does build on existing research on masculinity and violence, referring to concepts by Barbara Ehrenreich, Peter Marsden, and Lothar Machtan, among others.

Before you read, you might think (and talk with your classmates) about your expectations for a piece on gender and terrorism. What focus do you expect? What examples? Consider the images of terrorists you usually see in the media and the explanations you have heard or read on the motivation of terrorists. Keep them in mind as you read. Think about Kimmel's strategy in organizing the essay as he does. What surprises do you find, and what do you make of your responses?

Like many scholars of contemporary culture, Kimmel hopes to teach us something beyond what we might read in *Newsweek* or *Time*. Although the debate he enters here — why people use terrorist tactics that are as deadly to themselves as to others — is certainly a debate we hear in the media, Kimmel uses his sociological insights about masculinity to frame the issue in new ways, to help us make connections we otherwise may not see or want to see.

■ ■ ■

The events of September 11 [2001] have sent scholars and pundits alike *1*
scrambling to make sense of those seemingly senseless acts. While most analyses have focused on the political economy of globalization or the perversion of Islamic teachings by Al Qaeda, several commentators have raised gender issues.

Some have reminded us that in our haste to lionize the heroes of the *2*
World Trade Center collapse, we ignored the many women firefighters, police officers, and rescue workers who also risked their lives. We've been asked to remember the Taliban's vicious policies toward women; indeed, even Laura Bush seems to be championing women's emancipation.

A few have asked us to consider the other side of the gender coin: men. *3*
Some have rehearsed the rather tired old formulae about masculine bloodlust or the drive for domination and conquest, with no reference to the magnificent humanity displayed by so many on September 11. In an article in *Slate*, the Rutgers anthropologist Lionel Tiger trotted out his old malebonding thesis but offered no understanding of why Al Qaeda might appeal to some men and not others. Only the journalist Barbara Ehrenreich suggests that there may be a link between the misogyny of the Taliban and the masculinity of the terrorists.

As for myself, I've been thinking lately about a letter to the editor of *4*
a small, upstate–New York newspaper, written in 1992 by an American GI after his return from service in the Gulf War. He complained that the legacy of the American middle class had been stolen by an indifferent government. The American dream, he wrote, has all but disappeared; instead, most people are struggling just to buy next week's groceries.

That letter writer was Timothy McVeigh from Lockport, N.Y. Two ⁵ years later, he blew up the Murrah federal building in Oklahoma City in what is now the second-worst act of terrorism ever committed on American soil.

What's startling to me are the ways that McVeigh's complaints were ⁶ echoed in some of the fragmentary evidence that we have seen about the terrorists of September 11, and especially in the portrait of Mohammed Atta, the suspected mastermind of the operation and the pilot of the first plane to hit the World Trade Center.

Looking at these two men through the lens of gender may shed some ⁷ light on both the method and the madness of the tragedies they wrought.

McVeigh was representative of the small legion of white supremacists — ⁸ from older organizations like the John Birch Society, the Ku Klux Klan, and the American Nazi Party, to newer neo-Nazi, racist-skinhead, white-power groups like Posse Comitatus and the White Aryan Resistance, to radical militias.

These white supremacists are mostly younger (in their early 20s), ⁹ lower-middle-class men, educated at least through high school and often beyond. They are the sons of skilled workers in industries like textiles and tobacco, the sons of the owners of small farms, shops, and grocery stores. Buffeted by global political and economic forces, the sons have inherited little of their fathers' legacies. The family farms have been lost to foreclosure, the small shops squeezed out by Wal-Marts and malls. These young men face a spiral of downward mobility and economic uncertainty. They complain that they are squeezed between the omnivorous jaws of global capital concentration and a federal bureaucracy that is at best indifferent to their plight and at worst complicit in their demise.

As one issue of *The Truth at Last*, a white-supremacist magazine, put it: ¹⁰

> Immigrants are flooding into our nation willing to work for the minimum wage (or less). Super-rich corporate executives are flying all over the world in search of cheaper and cheaper labor so that they can lay off their American employees. . . . Many young White families have no future! They are not going to receive any appreciable wage increases due to job competition from immigrants.

What they want, says one member, is to "take back what is rightfully ¹¹ ours."

Their anger often fixes on "others" — women, members of minority ¹² groups, immigrants, gay men, and lesbians — in part because those are the people with whom they compete for entry-level, minimum-wage jobs. Above them all, enjoying the view, hovers the international Jewish conspiracy.

What holds together these "paranoid politics" — antigovernment, ¹³ anti–global capital but pro–small capitalist, racist, sexist, anti-Semitic, homophobic — is a rhetoric of masculinity. These men feel emasculated by big money and big government — they call the government "the Nanny

State" — and they claim that "others" have been handed the birthright of native-born white men.

In the eyes of such downwardly mobile white men, most white American males collude in their own emasculation. They've grown soft, feminized, weak. White supremacists' Web sites abound with complaints about the "whimpering collapse of the blond male"; the "legions of sissies and weaklings, of flabby, limp-wristed, non-aggressive, non-physical, indecisive, slack-jawed, fearful males who, while still heterosexual in theory and practice, have not even a vestige of the old macho spirit."   14

American white supremacists thus offer American men the restoration of their masculinity — a manhood in which individual white men control the fruits of their own labor and are not subject to emasculation by Jewish-owned finance capital or a black- and feminist-controlled welfare state. Theirs is the militarized manhood of the heroic John Rambo, a manhood that celebrates their God-sanctioned right to band together in armed militias if anyone, or any government agency, tries to take it away from them. If the state and the economy emasculate them, and if the masculinity of the "others" is problematic, then only "real" white men can rescue America from a feminized, multicultural, androgynous melting pot.   15

Sound familiar? For the most part, the terrorists of September 11 come from the same class, and recite the same complaints, as American white supremacists.   16

Virtually all were under twenty-five, educated, lower middle class or middle class, downwardly mobile. The journalist Nasra Hassan interviewed families of Middle Eastern suicide bombers (as well as some failed bombers themselves) and found that none of them had the standard motivations ascribed to people who commit suicide, such as depression.   17

Although several of the leaders of Al Qaeda are wealthy — Osama bin Laden is a multimillionaire, and Ayman al-Zawahiri, the fifty-year-old doctor thought to be bin Laden's closest adviser, is from a fashionable suburb of Cairo — many of the hijackers were engineering students for whom job opportunities had been dwindling dramatically. (Judging from the minimal information I have found, about one-fourth of the hijackers had studied engineering.) Zacarias Moussaoui, who did not hijack one of the planes but is the first man to be formally charged in the United States for crimes related to September 11, earned a degree at London's South Bank University. Marwan al-Shehhi, the chubby, bespectacled twenty-three-year-old from the United Arab Emirates who flew the second plane into the World Trade Center, was an engineering student, while Ziad Jarrah, the twenty-six-year-old Lebanese who flew the plane that crashed in Pennsylvania, had studied aircraft design.   18

Politically, these terrorists opposed globalization and the spread of Western values; they opposed what they perceived as corrupt regimes in several Arab states (notably Saudi Arabia and Egypt), which they claimed were merely puppets of American domination. "The resulting anger is   19 naturally directed first against their rulers," writes the historian Bernard Lewis, "and then against those whom they see as keeping those rulers in power for selfish reasons."

Central to their political ideology is the recovery of manhood from the emasculating politics of globalization. The Taliban saw the Soviet invasion and westernization of Afghanistan as humiliations. Bin Laden's October 7 videotape describes the "humiliation and disgrace" that Islam has suffered "for more than eighty years." And over and over, Nasra Hassan writes, she heard the refrain: "The Israelis humiliate us. They occupy our land, and deny our history." 20

Terrorism is fueled by a fatal brew of antiglobalization politics, convoluted Islamic theology, and virulent misogyny. According to Ehrenreich, while these formerly employed or self-employed males "have lost their traditional status as farmers and breadwinners, women have been entering the market economy and gaining the marginal independence conferred by even a paltry wage." As a result, "the man who can no longer make a living, who has to depend on his wife's earnings, can watch Hollywood sexpots on pirated videos and begin to think the world has been turned upside down." 21

The Taliban's policies thus had two purposes: to remasculinize men and to refeminize women. Another journalist, Peter Marsden, has observed that those policies "could be seen as a desperate attempt to keep out that other world, and to protect Afghan women from influences that could weaken the society from within." The Taliban prohibited women from appearing in public unescorted by men, from revealing any part of their body, and from going to school or holding a job. Men were required to grow their beards, in accordance with religious images of Muhammad, yes; but also, perhaps, because wearing beards has always been associated with men's response to women's increased equality in the public sphere, since beards symbolically reaffirm biological differences between men and women, while gender equality tends to blur those differences. 22

The Taliban's policies removed women as competitors and also shored up masculinity, since they enabled men to triumph over the humiliations of globalization and their own savage, predatory, and violently sexual urges that might be unleashed in the presence of uncovered women. 23

All of these issues converged in the life of Mohammed Atta, the terrorist about whom the most has been written and conjectured. Currently, for example, there is much speculation about Atta's sexuality. Was he gay? Was he a repressed homosexual, too ashamed of his sexuality to come out? Such innuendoes are based on no more than a few circumstantial tidbits about his life. He was slim, sweet-faced, neat, meticulous, a snazzy dresser. The youngest child of an ambitious lawyer father and a pampering mother, Atta grew up shy and polite, a mama's boy. "He was so gentle," his father said. "I used to tell him, 'Toughen up, boy!'" 24

When such revelations are offered, storytellers seem to expect a reaction like "Aha! So that explains it!" (Indeed, in a new biography of Adolf Hitler, 25

The Hidden Hitler, Lothar Machtan offers exactly that sort of explanation. He argues that many of Hitler's policies — such as the killing of longtime colleague and avowed homosexual Ernst Rohm, or even the systematic persecution and execution of gay men in concentration camps — were, in fact, prompted by a desire to conceal his own homosexuality.)

But what do such accusations actually explain? Do revelations about [26] Hitler's or Atta's possible gay propensities raise troubling connections between homosexuality and mass murder? If so, then one would also have to conclude that the discovery of Shakespeare's "gay" sonnet explains the Bard's genius at explicating Hamlet's existential anguish, or that Michelangelo's sexuality is the decisive factor in his painting of God's touch in the Sistine Chapel.

Such revelations tell us little about the Holocaust or September 11. [27] They do, however, address the consequences of homophobia — both official and informal — on young men who are exploring their sexual identities. What's relevant is not the possible fact of Hitler's or Atta's gayness, but the shame and fear that surround homosexuality in societies that refuse to acknowledge sexual diversity.

Even more troubling is what such speculation leaves out. What unites [28] Atta, McVeigh, and Hitler is not their repressed sexual orientation but gender — their masculinity, their sense of masculine entitlement, and their thwarted ambitions. They accepted cultural definitions of masculinity, and needed someone to blame when they felt that they failed to measure up. (After all, being called a mama's boy, a sissy, and told to toughen up are demands for gender conformity, not matters of sexual desire.) Gender is the issue, not sexuality.

All three failed at their chosen professions. Hitler was a failed artist — [29] indeed, he failed at just about every job he ever tried except dictator. McVeigh, a business-college dropout, found his calling in the military during the Gulf War, where his exemplary service earned him commendations; but he washed out of Green Beret training — his dream job — after only two days. And Atta was the odd man out in his family. His two sisters both became doctors — one a physician and one a university professor. His father constantly reminded him that he wanted "to hear the word 'doctor' in front of his name. We told him, your sisters are doctors and their husbands are doctors and you are the man of the family."

Atta decided to become an engineer, but his degree meant little in a [30] country where thousands of college graduates were unable to find good jobs. After he failed to find employment in Egypt, he went to Hamburg, Germany, to study architecture. He was "meticulous, disciplined, and highly intelligent, an ordinary student, a quiet, friendly guy who was totally focused on his studies," according to another student in Hamburg.

But his ambitions were constantly undone. His only hope for a good [31] job in Egypt was to be hired by an international firm. He applied and was continually rejected. He found work as a draftsman — highly humiliating for someone with engineering and architectural credentials and an imperious and demanding father — for a German firm involved with razing low-income Cairo neighborhoods to provide more scenic vistas for luxury tourist hotels.

Defeated, humiliated, emasculated, a disappointment to his father 32 and a failed rival to his sisters, Atta retreated into increasingly militant Islamic theology. By the time he assumed the controls of American Airlines Flight 11, he evinced a hysteria about women. In the message he left in his abandoned rental car, he made clear what mattered to him in the end. "I don't want pregnant women or a person who is not clean to come and say good-bye to me," he wrote. "I don't want women to go to my funeral or later to my grave." Of course, Atta's body was instantly incinerated, and no burial would be likely.

The terrors of emasculation experienced by lower-middle-class men 33 all over the world will no doubt continue, as they struggle to make a place for themselves in shrinking economies and inevitably shifting cultures. They may continue to feel a seething resentment against women, whom they perceive as stealing their rightful place at the head of the table, and against the governments that displace them. Globalization feels to them like a game of musical chairs, in which, when the music stops, all the seats are handed to others by nursemaid governments.

The events of September 11, as well as of April 19, 1995 (the Oklahoma 34 City bombing), resulted from an increasingly common combination of factors — the massive male displacement that accompanies globalization, the spread of American consumerism, and the perceived corruption of local political elites — fused with a masculine sense of entitlement. Someone else — some "other" — had to be held responsible for the terrorists' downward mobility and failures, and the failure of their fathers to deliver their promised inheritance. The terrorists didn't just get mad. They got even.

Such themes were not lost on the disparate bands of young white 35 supremacists. American Aryans admired the terrorists' courage and chastised their own compatriots. "It's a disgrace that in a population of at least 150 million White/Aryan Americans, we provide so few that are willing to do the same [as the terrorists]," bemoaned Rocky Suhayda, the chairman of the American Nazi Party. "A bunch of towel head/sand niggers put our great White Movement to shame."

It is from such gendered shame that mass murderers are made.   36

■   ■   ■

Reading Rhetorically

1. What effect do you think Kimmel hopes to achieve with his comparisons of Timothy McVeigh, Mohammed Atta, and Adolf Hitler? What similarities does he mention? How are these comparisons important to Kimmel's argument?

2. Circle any words that are unfamiliar to you — perhaps *misogyny* or *emasculation*. Look them up so that you feel comfortable explaining them in your own words. Based on his vocabulary and examples, who is Kimmel's audience?

3. What role do the topics of homosexuality and homophobia play in Kimmel's argument? Find passages where he raises these topics, and discuss how he both addresses them and uses them in his own argument.

Inquiring Further

4. Kimmel has written widely on the topic of masculinity. Use one of your library's online databases to search for other articles Kimmel has written. Choose two or three to skim, taking notes on his main arguments and most interesting examples. Share your findings with the class, and discuss how Kimmel's other articles are related to this one.

5. How do other scholars describe the relationship between masculinity and terrorism? Use your library's online databases to search on "masculinity and terrorism." Make a list of the kinds of the titles you find. Choose two articles that interest you most, and read them closely enough to share key ideas and arguments with your classmates. What range of perspectives do you find on this topic? Where does Kimmel fit into this conversation?

6. Visit the Web site of the white supremacist newspaper *The Truth at Last*. Analyze the rhetoric you find there, using Kimmel's strategies to look for evidence of "paranoid politics" (para. 13) or anxiety about masculinity. Discuss as a class how your findings compare to Kimmel's.

Framing Conversations

7. How does Kimmel's approach to writing about us-versus-them cultures compare to Kwame Anthony Appiah's approach (p. 378)? Compose an essay in which you analyze the strategies each author takes, noting both similarities and differences, and specific aspects of each author's approach you find especially strong or weak. Through these comparisons, make an argument for an approach you think works best for comparing very different cultures, particularly in troubled times. Be sure to use examples to support your claims.

8. Both Kimmel and Franklin Foer (p. 406) are interested in the relationship between the expected behaviors of American men and masculine behaviors in other countries and cultures. Write an essay in which you draw on each author's insights and examples to make an argument about how and why you think we often focus on "what it means to be a man" when it comes to defining cultures. What do discussions about masculinity reveal and, perhaps, conceal? Be clear in your essay about what you think readers should know to be able to analyze discussions of masculinity.

9. Using insights drawn from Kimmel's piece and Judith Lorber's essay on gender roles (p. 617), write an essay in which you analyze the Web site of

one of the white supremacist groups Kimmel mentions in paragraph 8. (Another resource is Marguerite Helmers's analysis of gendered Web sites, which begins on page 679.) What do the images and language suggest about what is at stake and for whom? What is the significance of your findings? Be sure to quote, describe, and analyze specific details from the site in making your point.

14

"Check All the Boxes That Apply": Unstable Identities in the United States

How do we experience the daily effects of race and class assumptions?

The title of this chapter refers to any form that requires us to identify ourselves within categories set up by someone else. Do you get frustrated by this tidy bureaucratic method of documenting your identities? How accurately do those checked boxes capture the complexity of who you are, particularly in a culture in which identity categories are evolving so rapidly? The lively readings in this chapter offer new perspectives and language for exploring two complex aspects of identity in the United States: race and class. How do shifting categories affect our daily experiences as well as the assumptions — conscious or unconscious — others make about us and we make about others?

Because you have likely studied diversity at other times in your education, we took care to choose texts that add fresh and provocative thinking to the diversity conversation. For example, Ann duCille's often funny and sometimes heartbreaking analysis of toy culture reveals a good deal more than multicultural Barbie's strange heritage. By taking child's play seriously, duCille exposes children's desire to belong to a dominant culture, even when this does not serve them well. Barbara Ehrenreich takes a similar approach to studying housecleaning in an absorbing (and sometimes revolting) description of the household work many Americans prefer be done by others. Who are these "others," and why in the land of supposed equal opportunity are we obsessed with sorting people into categories? Why do we invent markers of difference that divide us even when our differences are not great?

Some of these readings invite you to think about the source of our assumptions. Thomas Frank's analysis of the political landscape of Kansas is rich with historical factoids that make the present even more fascinating. Noel Ignatiev and Héctor Tobar also contextualize the present with historical narratives in ways that we believe are startling. For example, Ignatiev asks how the Irish and Greeks became "white" in the racial categories of nineteenth-century America. And Tobar wonders if Spanish-speaking Los Angeles will become a model for the entire country. Learning how racial and ethnic categories are constantly in flux, how they are defined by the politics of the moment, helps us better understand our past and our present.

We know that discussions of race and class can be difficult, and we have very few models in popular culture of ways to make these conversations easier and more productive. But we are optimistic that these readings provide new and possibly transformative strategies. In her essay, for example, Peggy McIntosh describes her realization that as a white woman, she is racially privileged, and demonstrates how she gradually learned to pay attention to the small, everyday details that accumulate into the often poisonous, if unconscious, racial assumptions we make about ourselves and others. Her strategy is not to blame; instead she reveals the pleasure of living with eyes wide open, and practicing ways to change that will improve the lives of all Americans.

As a nation we claim to prize equality. But as McIntosh and other writers here point out, this "myth of meritocracy" is often just that — a myth. Do we really believe all Americans are born with equal opportunities to live good and successful lives? If not, how should we respond? The quirky personal examples in these readings, along with the wide-ranging research that supports these writers' arguments, offer largely optimistic perspectives on what we can gain by recognizing the divisions in our culture and envisioning these differences as opportunities, not barriers, to personal and social growth.

■ ANN duCILLE

Dyes and Dolls: Multicultural Barbie and the Merchandising of Difference

Ann duCille has served as the chair and director of the Center for African American Studies at Wesleyan University. She has written widely on black women writers and on race and popular culture, particularly in her books *The Coupling Convention: Sex, Text, and Tradition in Black Women's Fiction* (1993) and *Skin Trade* (1996), which won the Myers Center Award for the Study of Human Rights in 1997. The essay here originally appeared in the Spring 1994 issue of *differences: A Journal of Feminist Cultural Studies.*

DuCille studies literature as well as popular culture and politics. So, for example, she has written about Zora Neale Hurston and other well-known writers of the Harlem Renaissance, as well as the politics of spectacle in the

O. J. Simpson trial. When she trains her analytical eye on cultural artifacts, she considers the circumstances of their creation and the significance of consumers' responses to them. In other words, she examines the ideology of production and consumption — how we all contribute to the making of culture through the ways we produce and consume goods and ideas.

A quick look through duCille's MLA-style works cited list at the end of the essay shows that she draws on a range of academic conversations to frame her analysis of Barbie. She responds not only to scholars who write about Barbie but also to those who write about adolescent self-image, raising African American children, and various aspects of multicultural-ism and diversity. As you read duCille's essay, keep track of when and how she draws on those she calls "Barbiologists" and those whose ideas give context to her broader analysis of culture. You too are likely to find your-self moving between and among sources often as you write.

Notice also how duCille constructs sentences in which she disagrees with her sources. For example, in paragraph 22 she writes: "In spite of their own good intentions, the Hopsons, in linking play with 'beautiful' dolls to positive self-imagining, echoed Mattel's own marketing cam-paign." And watch how she applies other scholars' ideas to her own sub-ject matter. In paragraph 10, for instance, she invokes philosopher Louis Althusser this way: "In fact, I regard Barbie and similar dolls as Louis Althusser might have regarded them: as objects that do the dirty work of patriarchy and capitalism in the most insidious way — in the guise of child's play." These sentences can serve as models for agreeing or disagree-ing with other scholars in your own writing. They also can help you apply other scholars' ideas to contexts of your own devising.

Particularly in her opening paragraphs, duCille invites readers to share and identify with her personal experiences. How effectively do per-sonal experiences — her own and others' — draw you into the piece? Do they shed new light on toys you played with as a child, toys you may have forgotten all about? What about her adult reflections on toys? What do you think when you read, "This, then, is my final doll story. Groucho Marx said that he wouldn't want to belong to a club that would have him as a mem-ber. In that same vein, I am not so sure that most of us would want to buy a doll that 'looked like us'" (para. 50)?

Taking as a given culture's focus on both race and physical appear-ance, duCille ends her essay by asking, "Is Barbie bad?" Her answer: "Barbie is just a piece of plastic, but what she says about the economic base of our society — what she suggests about gender and race in our world — ain't good." How do you respond — both as a scholar and a person — to duCille's lively voice, her many questions, and the answers she supplies? Possibly more importantly, how do you respond to those questions she doesn't answer?

The white missionaries who came to Saint Aug's from New England were darling to us. They gave Bessie and me these beautiful china dolls that probably were very expensive. Those dolls were white, of course. You couldn't get a colored doll like that in those days. Well, I loved mine, just the way it was, but do you know what Bessie did?

She took an artist's palette they had also given us and sat down and mixed the paints until she came up with a shade of brown that matched her skin. Then she painted that white doll's face! None of the white missionaries ever said a word about it. Mama and Papa just smiled. (Sarah Delany)

This is my doll story (because every black journalist who writes about race gets around to it sometime). Back when I started playing with Barbie, there were no Christies (Barbie's black friend, born in 1968) or black Barbies (born in 1980, brown plastic poured into blond Barbie's mold). I had two blonds, which I bought with Christmas money from girls at school.

I cut off their hair and dressed them in African-print fabric. They lived together (polygamy, I guess) with a black G.I. Joe bartered from the Shepp boys, my downstairs neighbors. After an "incident" at school (where all of the girls looked like Barbie and none of them looked like me), I galloped down our stairs with one Barbie, her blond head hitting each spoke of the banister, thud, thud, thud. And galloped up the stairs, thud, thud, thud, until her head popped off, lost to the graveyard behind the stairwell. Then I tore off each limb, and sat on the stairs for a long time twirling the torso like a baton. (Lisa Jones)

Growing up in the 1950s, in the shadow of the second world war, it was natural for children — including little black children like my two brothers and me — to want to play war, to mimic what we heard on the radio, what we watched in black and white on our brand new floor model Motorola. In these war games, everyone wanted to be the Allied troops — the fearless, conquering white male heroes who had made the world safe for democracy, yet again, and saved us all from yellow peril. No one, of course, wanted to play the enemy — who most often was not the Germans or the Italians but the Japanese. So the enemy became or, more rightly, remained invisible, lurking in bushes we shot at with sticks we pretended were rifles and stabbed at with make-believe bayonets. "Take that," we shouted, liberally peppering our verbal assaults with racial epithets. "And that! And that!" It was all in fun — our venom and vigor. All's fair in wars of words. We understood little of what we said and nothing of how much our child's play reflected the sentiments of a nation that even in its finer, pre-war moments had not embraced as citizens its Asian immigrants or claimed as countrymen and women their American-born offspring.

However naively imitative, our diatribe was interrupted forever one summer afternoon by the angry voice of our mother, chastising us through the open window. "Stop that," she said. "Stop that this minute. It's not nice. You're talking about the Japanese. *Japanese*, do you understand? And don't let me ever hear you call them anything else." In the lecture that accompanied dinner that evening, we were made to understand not the history of Japanese-Americans, the injustice of internment, or the horror of Hiroshima, but simply that there were real people behind the names we called; that name-calling always hurts somebody, always undermines someone's humanity. Our young minds were led on the short journey from "Jap" to "nigger"; and if we were too young then to understand the origins and fine points of all such pejoratives, we were old enough to know firsthand the pain of one of them.

I cannot claim that this early experience left me free of prejudice, but it did assist me in growing up at once aware of my own status as "different" and conscious of the exclusion of others so labeled. It is important to note, however, that my sense of my own difference was affirmed and confirmed not simply by parental intervention but also by the unrelenting sameness of the tiny, almost exclusively white town in which I was raised. There in the country confines of East Bridgewater, Massachusetts, the adults who surrounded me (except for my parents) were all white, as were the teachers who taught me, the authors who thrilled me (and instilled in me a love of literature), and the neighborhood children who called me nigger one moment and friend the next. And when my brothers and I went our separate ways into properly gendered spheres, the dolls I played with — like almost everything else about my environment — were also white: Betsy Wetsy, Tiny Tears, and Patty Play Pal.

It seems remarkable to me now, as I remember these childish things long since put away, that, for all the daily reminders of my blackness, I did not take note of its absence among the rubber-skin pinkness of Betsy Wetsy, the bald-headed whiteness of Tiny Tears, and the blue-eyed blondness of Patty Play Pal. I was never tempted like Elizabeth Delany to paint the dolls I played with brown like me or to dress them in African-print fabric like Lisa Jones. (Indeed, I had no notion of such fabrics and little knowledge of the "dark continent" from which they came.) Caught up in fantasy, completely given over to the realm of make-believe, for most of my childhood I neither noticed nor cared that the dolls I played with did not look like me. The make-believe world to which I willingly surrendered more than just my disbelief was thoroughly and profoundly white. That is to say, the "me" I invented, the "I" I imagined, the Self I day-dreamed in technicolor fantasies was no more black like me than the dolls I played with. In the fifties and well into the sixties of my childhood, the black Other who was my Self, much like the enemy Other who was the foreign body of our war games, could only be imagined as faceless, far away, and utterly unfamiliar.

As suggested by my title, I am going to use the figure of multicultural Barbie to talk about the commodification of race and gender difference. I wanted to back into the present topic, however, into what I have to say about Barbie as a gendered, racialized icon of contemporary commodity culture, by reaching into the past — into the admittedly contested terrain of the personal — to evoke the ideological work of child's play. More than simple instruments of pleasure and amusement, toys and games play crucial roles in helping children determine what is valuable in and around them. Dolls in particular invite children to replicate them, to imagine themselves in their dolls' images. What does it mean, then, when little girls are given dolls to play with that in no way resemble them? What did it mean for me that I was nowhere in the toys I played with?

If the Japan and the Africa of my youth were beyond the grasp (if not the reach) of my imagination, children today are granted instant global gratification in their play — immediate, hands-on access to both Self and Other. Or so we are told by many of the leading fantasy manufacturers — Disney, Hasbro, and Mattel, in particular — whose contributions to multicultural education include such play things as Aladdin (movie, video, and dolls), G.I. Joe (male "action figures" in black and white), and Barbie (now available in a variety of colors and ethnicities). Disneyland's river ride through different nations, like Mattel's Dolls of the World Collection, instructs us that "It's a Small World After All." Those once distant lands of Africa, Asia, Australia, and even the Arctic regions of the North Pole (yes, Virginia, there is an Eskimo Barbie) are now as close to home as the local Toys R Us and F.A.O. Schwarz. And lo and behold, the inhabitants of these foreign lands — from Disney's Princess Jasmine to Mattel's Jamaican Barbie — are just like us, dye-dipped versions of archetypal white American beauty. It is not only a small world after all, but, as the Grammy award–winning theme from *Aladdin* informs us, "it's a whole new world."

Many of the major toy manufacturers have taken on a global perspective, a kind of nearsightedness that constructs this whole new world as small and cultural difference as consumable. Perhaps nowhere is this universalizing myopia more conspicuous than in the production, marketing, and consumption of Barbie dolls. By Mattel's reckoning, Barbie enjoys 100 percent brand name recognition among girls ages three to ten, ninety-six percent of whom own at least one doll, with most owning an average of eight. Five years ago, as Barbie turned thirty, *Newsweek* noted that nearly 500 million Barbies had been sold, along with 200 million G.I. Joes — "enough for every man, woman, and child in the United States and Europe" (Kantrowitz 59–60). Those figures have increased dramatically in the past five years, bringing the current world-wide Barbie population to 800 million. In 1992 alone, $1 billion worth of Barbies and accessories were sold. Last year, Barbie dolls sold at an average of one million per week, with overall sales exceeding the $1 billion all-time high set the year before. As the *Boston Globe* reported on the occasion of Barbie's thirty-fifth birthday on March 9, 1994, nearly two Barbie dolls are sold every second somewhere in the world; about fifty percent of the dolls sold are purchased here in the United States (Dembner 16).

The current Barbie boom may be in part the result of new, multiculturally oriented developments both in the dolls and in their marketing. In the fall of 1990, Mattel, Inc. announced a new marketing strategy to boost its sales: the corporation would "go ethnic" in its advertising by launching an ad campaign for the black and Hispanic versions of the already popular doll. Despite the existence of black, Asian, and Latina Barbies, prior to the fall of 1990 Mattel's print and TV ads featured only white dolls. In what *Newsweek* described as an attempt to capitalize on ethnic spending power,

Mattel began placing ads for multicultural Barbies in such Afrocentric publications as *Essence* magazine and on such Latin-oriented shows as "Pepe Plata" after market research revealed that most black and Hispanic consumers were unaware of the company's ethnic dolls. This targeted advertising was a smart move, according to the industry analysts cited by *Newsweek*, because "Hispanics buy about $170 billion worth of goods each year, [and] blacks spend even more." Indeed, sales of black Barbie dolls reportedly doubled in the year following this new ethnically-oriented ad campaign.[1] But determined to present itself as politically correct as well as financially savvy, Mattel was quick to point out that ethnic audiences, who are now able to purchase dolls who look like them, also have profited from the corporation's new marketing priorities. Barbie is a role model for all of her owners, according to product manager Deborah Mitchell, herself an African American. "Barbie allows little girls to dream," she asserted — to which the *Newsweek* reporter added (seemingly without irony): "now, ethnic Barbie lovers will be able to dream in their own image" (Berkwitz 48).

Dream in their own image? The *Newsweek* columnist inadvertently put his finger on precisely what is so troubling to many parents, feminist scholars, and cultural critics about Barbie and dolls like her. Such toys invite, inspire, and even demand a potentially damaging process not simply of imagining but of interpellation. When little girls fantasize themselves into the conspicuous consumption, glamour, perfection, and, some have argued, anorexia of Barbie's world, it is rarely, if ever, "in their own image that they dream."[2] Regardless of what color dyes the dolls are dipped in or what costumes they are adorned with, the image they present is of the same mythically thin, long-legged, luxuriously-haired, buxom beauty. And while Mattel and other toy manufacturers may claim to have the best interests of ethnic audiences in mind in peddling their integrated wares, one does not have to be a cynic to suggest that profit remains the motivating factor behind this merchandising of difference.[3]

---

[1]Mattel introduced the Shani doll — a black, Barbie-like doll — in 1991, which also may have contributed to the rise in sales, particularly since the company engaged the services of a PR firm that specializes in targeting ethnic audiences.

[2]Of course, the notion of "dreaming in one's own image" is always problematic since dreams, by definition, engage something other than the "real."

[3]Olmec Toys, a black-owned company headed by an African American woman named Yla Eason, markets a line of black and Latina Barbie-like dolls called the Imani Collection. Billed on their boxes as "African American Princess" and "Latin American Fantasy," these dolls are also presented as having been designed with the self images of black children in mind. "We've got one thing in mind with all our products," the blurbs on the Imani boxes read: "let's build self-esteem. Our children gain a sense of self importance through toys. So we make them look like them." Given their obvious resemblance to Barbie dolls — their long, straight hair and pencil-thin plastic bodies — Imani dolls look no more "like them," like "real" black children, than their prototype. Eason, who we are told was devastated by her son's announcement that he couldn't be a superhero because he wasn't white, may indeed want to give black children toys to play with that "look like them." Yet, in order to compete in a market long dominated by Mattel and Hasbro, her company, it seems, has little choice but to conform to the Barbie mold.

Far from simply playing with the sixty or so dolls I have acquired in *10*
the past year, then, I take them very seriously. In fact, I regard Barbie and
similar dolls as Louis Althusser might have regarded them: as objects that
do the dirty work of patriarchy and capitalism in the most insidious
way — in the guise of child's play. But, as feminists have protested almost
from the moment she hit the market, Barbie is not simply a child's toy or
just a teenage fashion doll; she is an icon — perhaps *the* icon — of true
white womanhood and femininity, a symbol of the far from innocent ideological stuff of which the (Miss) American dream and other mystiques of
race and gender are made.

Invented by Ruth Handler, one of the founders of Mattel, and named *11*
after her daughter, Barbie dolls have been a very real force in the toy market since Mattel first introduced them at the American Toy Fair in 1959. In
fact, despite the skepticism of toy store buyers — who at the time were primarily men — the first shipment of a half million dolls and a million costumes sold out immediately (Larcen A7). The first Barbies, which were
modeled after a sexy German doll and comic strip character named Lilli,
were all white, but in 1967 Mattel premiered a black version of the doll
called "Colored Francie." "Colored Francie," like white "Francie Fairchild"
introduced the year before, was supposed to be Barbie's "MODern" younger
cousin. As a white doll modeled and marketed in the image of Hollywood's
Gidget, white Francie had been an international sensation, but Colored
Francie was not destined to duplicate her prototype's success. Although
the "black is beautiful" theme of both the civil rights and black power
movements may have suggested a ready market for a beautiful black doll,
Colored Francie in fact did not sell well.

Evelyn Burkhalter, owner, operator, and curator of the Barbie Hall of *12*
Fame in Palo Alto, California — home to 16,000 Barbie dolls — attributes
Colored Francie's commercial failure to the racial climate of the times. Doll
purchasing patterns, it seems, reflected the same resistance to integration
that was felt elsewhere in the nation. In her implied family ties to white Barbie, Colored Francie suggested more than simple integration. She implied
miscegenation: a make-believe mixing of races that may have jeopardized
the doll's real market value. Cynthia Roberts, author of *Barbie: Thirty Years of
America's Doll* (1989), maintains that Colored Francie flopped because of her
straight hair and Caucasian features (44), which seemingly were less acceptable then than now. No doubt Mattel's decision to call its first black Barbie
"Colored Francie" also contributed to the doll's demise. The use of the outmoded, even racist term "colored" in the midst of civil rights and black power
activism suggested that while Francie might be "MODern," Mattel was still
in the dark(y) ages. In any case, neither black nor white audiences bought
the idea of Barbie's colored relations, and Mattel promptly took the doll off
the market, replacing her with a black doll called Christie in 1968.

While a number of other black dolls appeared throughout the late six- *13*
ties and seventies — including the Julia doll, modeled after the TV character
played by black singer and actress Diahann Carroll — it was not until 1980

that Mattel introduced black dolls that were called Barbie like their white counterparts. Today, Barbie dolls come in a virtual rainbow coalition of colors, races, ethnicities, and nationalities — most of which look remarkably like the prototypical white Barbie, modified only by a dash of color and a change of costume. It is these would-be multicultural "dolls of the world" — Jamaican Barbie, Nigerian and Kenyan Barbie, Malaysian Barbie, Chinese Barbie, Mexican, Spanish, and Brazilian Barbie, et cetera, et cetera, et cetera — that interest me. For me these dolls are at once a symbol and a symptom of what multiculturalism has become at the hands of contemporary commodity culture: an easy and immensely profitable way off the hook of Eurocentrism that gives us the face of cultural diversity without the particulars of racial difference.

If I could line up across the page the ninety "different" colors, cultures, and other incarnations in which Barbie currently exists, the fact of her unrelenting sameness (or at least similarity) would become immediately apparent. Even two dolls might do the trick: "My First Barbie" in white and "My First Barbie" in black, for example, or white "Western Fun Barbie" and black "Western Fun Barbie." Except for their dye jobs, the dolls are identical: the same body, size, shape, and apparel. Or perhaps I should say *nearly* identical because in some instances — with black and Asian dolls in particular — coloring and other subtle changes (stereotypically slanted eyes in the Asian dolls, thicker lips in the black dolls) suggest differently coded facial features.

In other instances, when Barbie moves across cultural as opposed to racial lines, it is costume rather than color that distinguishes one ethnic group or nation from another. Nigeria and Jamaica, for instance, are represented by the same basic brown body, dolled-up in different native garbs — or Mattel's interpretation thereof.[4] With other costume changes, this generic black body becomes Western Fun Barbie or Marine Barbie or Desert Storm Barbie, and even Presidential Candidate Barbie, who, by the way, comes with a Nancy Reagan–red taking-care-of-business suit as well as a red, white, and blue inaugural ball gown. Much the same is true of the generic Asian doll — sometimes called Kira — who reappears in a variety of different dress-defined ethnicities. In other words, where Barbie is concerned, clothes not only make the woman, they mark the racial and/or cultural difference.

Such difference is marked as well by the cultural history and language lessons that accompany each doll in Mattel's international collection. The back of Jamaican Barbie's box tells us, for example, *"How-you-du* (Hello) from the land of Jamaica, a tropical paradise known for its exotic fruit,

---

[4]After many calls to the Jamaican Embassy in Washington, D.C., and to various cultural organizations in Jamaica, I have determined that Jamaican Barbie's costume — a floor-length granny-style dress with apron and headrag — bears some resemblance to what is considered the island's traditional folk costume. I am still left wondering about the decision-making process, however: why the doll representing Jamaica is figured as a maid, while the doll representing Great Britain, for example, is presented as a lady — a blonde, blue-eyed Barbie doll dressed in a fancy riding habit with boots and hat.

sugar cane, breathtaking beaches, and reggae beat!" The box goes on to explain that most Jamaicans have ancestors from Africa. Therefore, "even though our official language is English, we speak patois, a kind of '*Jamaica Talk*,' filled with English and African words." The lesson ends with a brief glossary (eight words) and a few more examples of this "Jamaica Talk," complete with translations: "*A hope yu wi come-a Jamaica!* (I hope you will come to Jamaica!)" and "*Teck care a yusself, mi fren!* (Take care of yourself, my friend!)" A nice idea, I suppose, but for me these quick-and-dirty ethnographies only enhance the extent to which these would-be multicultural dolls treat race and ethnic difference like collectibles, contributing more to commodity culture than to the intercultural awareness they claim to inspire.

Is the current fascination with the black or colored body — especially *17* the female body — a contemporary version of the primitivism of the 1920s? Is multiculturalism to postmodernism what primitivism was to modernism? It was while on my way to a round table discussion on precisely this question that I bought my first black Barbie dolls in March of 1993. As carbon copies of an already problematic original, these colorized Mattel toys seemed to me the perfect tools with which to illustrate the point I wanted to make about the collapse of multiculturalism into an easy pluralism that simply adds what it constructs as the Other without upsetting the fundamental precepts and paradigms of Western culture or, in the case of Mattel, without changing the mold.

Not entirely immune to such critiques, Mattel sought expert advice *18* from black parents and early childhood specialists in the development and marketing of its newest line of black Barbie dolls. Chief among the expert witnesses was clinical psychologist Darlene Powell Hopson, who coauthored with her husband Derek S. Hopson a study of racism and child development entitled *Different and Wonderful: Raising Black Children in a Race-Conscious Society* (1990). As part of their research for the book, the Hopsons repeated a ground-breaking study conducted by black psychologists Kenneth and Mamie Clark in the 1940s.

The Clarks used black and white dolls to demonstrate the negative *19* effects of racism and segregation on black children. When given a choice between a white doll and a black doll, nearly 70 percent of the black children in the study chose the white doll. The Clarks' findings became an important factor in *Brown v. the Board of Education* in 1954. More recently, some scholars have called into question not necessarily the Clarks' findings but their interpretation: the assumption that, in the realm of make-believe, a black child's choosing a white doll necessarily reflects a negative self concept.[5] For the Hopsons, however, the Clarks' research remains

---

[5]See among others Morris Rosenberg's books *Conceiving the Self* (1979) and *Society and the Adolescent Self-Image* (1989) and William E. Cross's *Shades of Black: Diversity in African American Identity* (1991), all of which challenge the Clarks' findings. Cross argues, for example, that the Clarks confounded or conflated two different issues: attitude toward race in general and attitude toward the self in particular. How one feels about race is not necessarily an index of one's self-esteem.

compelling. In 1985 they repeated the Clarks' doll test and found that an alarming 65 percent of the black children in their sample chose a white doll over a black one. Moreover, 76 percent of the children interviewed said that the black dolls "looked bad" to them (Hopson xix).

In addition to the clinical uses they make of dolls in their experiments, 20 the Hopsons also give considerable attention to what they call "doll play" in their book, specifically mentioning Barbie. "If your daughter likes 'Barbie' dolls, by all means get her Barbie," they advise black parents. "But also choose Black characters from the Barbie world. *You do not want your child to grow up thinking that only White dolls, and by extension White people, are attractive and nice*" (Hopsons 127, emphasis original). (Note that "Barbie," unmodified in the preceding passage, seems to mean *white* Barbie dolls.) The Hopsons suggest that parents should not only provide their children with black and other ethnic dolls but that they should get involved in their children's doll play. "Help them dress and groom the dolls while you compliment them both," they advise, offering the following suggested routine: "'This is a beautiful doll. It looks just like you. Look at her hair. It's just like yours. Did you know your nose is as pretty as your doll's?'" (119). They also suggest that parents use "complimentary words such as *lovely, pretty, or nice* so that [the] child will learn to associate them with his or her own image" (124).

Certainly it is important to help children feel good about themselves. 21 One might argue, however, that the "just like you" simile and the beautiful doll imagery so central to these suggestions for what the Hopsons call positive play run the risk of transmitting to the child a colorized version of the same old beauty myth. Like Barbie dolls themselves, they make beauty — and by implication worth — a matter of physical characteristics.

In spite of their own good intentions, the Hopsons, in linking play 22 with "beautiful" dolls to positive self-imagining, echoed Mattel's own marketing campaign. It is not surprising, then, that the Hopsons' findings and the interventional strategies they designed for using dolls to instill ethnic pride caught the attention of Mattel. In 1990 Darlene Hopson was asked to consult with the corporation's product manager Deborah Mitchell and designer Kitty Black-Perkins — both African Americans — in the development of a new line of "realistically sculpted" black fashion dolls. Hopson agreed and about a year later Shani and her friends Asha and Nichelle became the newest members of Barbie's ever-expanding family.

Shani means "marvelous" in Swahili, according to the dolls' press kit. 23 But as *Village Voice* columnist Lisa Jones has noted, the name has other meanings as well: "startling, a wonder, a novelty" (36). My own research indicates that while Shani is a Swahili female name meaning marvelous, the Kiswahili word "shani" translates as "an adventure, something unusual" (Stewart 120). So it seems that Mattel's new play thing is not just marvelous, too marvelous for words, but, as her name also suggests, she is difference incarnate — a novelty, a new enterprise or, perhaps, as the black female Other so often is, an exotic. Mattel, it seems to me, both plays up and plays on what it presents as the doll's exotic black-is-beautiful difference. As the back of her package reads:

> Shani means marvelous in the Swahili language . . . and marvelous she is! With her friends Asha and Nichelle, Shani brings to life the special style and beauty of the African American woman.
>
> Each one is beautiful in her own way, with her own lovely skin shade and unique facial features. Each has a different hair color and texture, perfect for braiding, twisting and creating fabulous hair styles! Their clothes, too, reflect the vivid colors and ethnic accents that showcase their *exotic looks* and fashion flair!
>
> Shani, Asha and Nichelle invite you into their glamorous world to share the fun and excitement of being a top model. Imagine appearing on magazine covers, starring in fashion shows, and going to Hollywood parties as you, Shani, Asha and Nichelle live your dreams of beauty and success, *loving every marvelous minute!* (emphasis added)

While these words attempt to convey a message of black pride — after the fashion of the Hopsons' recommendations for positive play — that message is clearly tied to bountiful hair, lavish and exotic clothes, and other outward and visible signs not of brains but of beauty, wealth, and success. Shani may be a top fashion model, but don't look for her (or, if Mattel's own oft-articulated theory of Barbie as role model holds, yourself or your child) at M.I.T.

Like any other proud, well-to-do parents of a debutante, Mattel gave [24] Shani her own coming out party at the International Toy Fair in February of 1991. This gala event included a tribute to black designers and an appearance by En Vogue singing the Negro National Anthem, "Lift Every Voice and Sing!" — evidently the song of choice of the doll Mattel describes as "tomorrow's African American woman." Also making their debuts were Shani's friends Asha and Nichelle, notable for the different hues in which their black plastic skin comes — an innovation due in part to Darlene Hopson's influence. Shani, the signature doll of the line, is what we call in the culture "brown-skinned"; Asha is honey-colored (some would say "high-yella"); and Nichelle is deep mahogany. Their male friend Jamal, added in 1992, completes the collection.

For the un(make-)believing, the three-to-one ratio of the Shani quartet — [25] three black females to one black male — may be the most realistic thing about these dolls. In the eyes and the advertising of Mattel, however, Shani and her friends are the most authentic black female thing the mainstream toy market has yet produced. "Tomorrow's African American woman" (an appellation which, as Lisa Jones has noted, both riffs and one-ups *Essence's* "Today's Black Woman") has broader hips, fuller lips, and a broader nose, according to product manager Deborah Mitchell. Principal designer Kitty Black-Perkins, who has dressed black Barbies since their birth in 1980, adds that the Shani dolls are also distinguished by their unique, culturally-specific clothes in "spice tones, [and] ethnic fabrics," rather than "fantasy colors like pink or lavender" (qtd. in Jones 36) — evidently the colors of the faint of skin.

The notion that fuller lips, broader noses, wider hips, and higher 26
derrières somehow make the Shani dolls more realistically African American raises many difficult questions about authenticity, truth, and the ever-
problematic categories of the real and the symbolic, the typical and the
stereotypical. Just what are we saying when we claim that a doll does or
does not "look black"? How does black look? What would it take to make a
doll look authentically African American? What preconceived, prescriptive
ideals of legitimate blackness are inscribed in such claims of authenticity?
How can doll manufacturers or any other image makers — the film industry, for example — attend to cultural, racial, and phenotypical differences
without merely engaging the same simplistic big-lips/broad-hips stereotypes that make so many of us — blacks in particular — grit our (pearly
white) teeth? What would it take to produce a line of dolls that more fully
reflects the wide variety of sizes, shapes, colors, hair styles, occupations,
abilities, and disabilities that African Americans — like all people — come
in? In other words: what price difference?

If such specificity — such ethnic "authenticity" — were possible to 27
achieve in a doll, its purchase price, I suspect, would be much higher than
a profit-driven corporation like Mattel would be willing to pay. Let me
again invoke Shani to prove my point. On the one hand, Mattel was concerned enough about producing an ethnically correct black doll to seek the
advice of black image specialists such as Darlene Hopson in the development and marketing of the Shani line. Ultimately, however, the company
was not willing to follow the advice of such experts where doing so would
cost the corporation more than the price of additional dyes and ethnic
fabrics.

For example, Hopson reportedly argued not just for gradations in skin 28
tones in the Shani dolls but also for variations in body type and lengths
and styles of hair — for an Afro here or an asymmetrical cut there. But,
while Mattel acknowledged both the legitimacy and the ubiquity of such
arguments, profit motive mediated against the very realism the corporation set out to achieve in these dolls. "To be truly realistic, one [Shani
doll] should have shorter hair," Deborah Mitchell confessed to Lisa Jones.
"But little girls of all races love hair play. We added more texture. But
we can't change the fact that long, combable hair is still a key seller"
(Jones 36).

Mitchell, of course, has a point. It is after all the taste of consumers 29
that is inscribed in Barbie's long, combable hair. In the process of my own
archival research — poking around in the dusty aisles of Toys R Us — I
encountered a black teenage girl in search, like me, of the latest black Barbie. During the impromptu interview that ensued, my subject confessed to
me in gory, graphic details the many Barbie murders and mutilations she
had committed over the years. "It's the hair," she said emphatically several
times. "The hair, that hair; I want it. I want it." Her words recalled my own
torturous childhood struggles with the straightening combs, curling irons,
and relaxers that bi-weekly transformed my wooly, "just like a sponge"

kinks into what the white kids at school marveled at as my "Cleopatra [read straight] hair." During one of those bi-weekly sessions with my mother and the straightening comb, I was foolish enough to say out loud what I had wished for a long time: that I had straight hair like the white girls at school. I still remember my mother's hurt, her sense of her daughter's racial heresy. Mitchell and Mattel indeed have a point. The difficult truth may just be that part of Shani's and black Barbie's attraction for little black girls in particular is the escape from their own often shorter, harder-to-comb hair that these dolls' lengthy straight locks represent.

Barbie's svelte figure, like her long combable hair, became Shani's *30* body type as well. And here too marketability seems to have overruled professed attempts to capture the "unique facial features" and the "special style and beauty of the African American people." Even the reported subtle changes that are supposed to signify Shani's black difference — her much-remarked broader hips and elevated buttocks, for example — are little more than optical illusions, according to anthropologists Jacqueline Urla and Alan Swedlund of the University of Massachusetts at Amherst. Urla and Swedlund, who have been studying the anthropometry — the body measurements — of Barbie for some time, argue that, while Shani's hips may appear to be wider, they are actually smaller in both circumference and breadth than those of other Barbie dolls. It is essential, after all, that all the dolls be able to share the same clothes, thus making any dramatic alterations in body type unlikely. The effect of a higher buttocks is achieved, Urla and Swedlund maintain, by changing the angle of the doll's back. In other words, the Shani doll's buttocks may appear stereotypically higher, but she is not really dimensionally different from all the other eleven-and-a-half inch fashion dolls.

Lisa Jones concludes her *Village Voice* article on Barbie by noting that *31* the women behind Shani — black women like Hopson and Mitchell — want the doll to be more than just a Barbie in blackface. While Hopson, in particular, certainly hoped for — shall I say — *different* difference she nevertheless maintains that the Shani dolls demonstrate "social consciousness on Mattel's part" (Jones 36). British fashion designer and Barbie aficionado extraordinaire BillyBoy made a similar point in praising Mattel for integrating Barbie's family with first Colored Francie and then Christie in the late 1960s (BillyBoy 82). After nearly thirty years, I think we can forgive Mattel its Colored Francie faux pas and perhaps even applaud the attempt. But if Shani (who came out in a new scantily clad Soul Train edition in 1993) stands as Mattel's best effort to "go ethnic," as it were — to corner the contemporary mainstream market in "realistically sculpted" black dolls that "bring to life" the "special style and beauty of the African-American people" — she stands on shaky ground.

And yet it may not be fair to single out Mattel as an example of what *32* seems to be a national if not international phenomenon. Racial difference, like ethnic Barbie, is a hot commodity, and it isn't only Mattel who is making money. In the words of David Rieff, a contributing editor of *Harper's Magazine:*

> Everything is commodifiable, even Afrocentrism (there is money being made on all the Kinte [sic] cloth and Kwanza [sic] paraphernalia that are the rage among certain segments of the black community, and not only the black community), bilingualism (currently the hottest growth market in publishing is Spanish-language children's books), and the other "multicultural" tendencies in American society that conservatives fear so desperately.

Rieff goes so far as to call this newly globalized consumer economy multiculturalism's silent partner. I want to be careful in expressing my own concerns about the relationship between multiculturalism and the conspicuous consumption of difference, however, lest my critique appear complicit with that of the conservatives to whom Rieff refers, who fear the possibilities of a truly transformative social, cultural, and economic order, which I in fact would welcome.

All cultural commodities are not created equal. It seems to me that 33 however profitable their production may be for the publishing industry, Spanish-language children's books serve a useful, educational function for their target audiences. On the other hand, even taking into account the argument that black girls need black dolls to play with, I have a difficult time locating the redeeming social value in Mattel's little plastic women, even — or perhaps especially — when they are tinted brown and decorated in Kente cloth and Kufi hats, as the new Soul Train Shani dolls are. And while I am certain that hordes of black consumers are grateful for the black haircare products and cosmetics marketed by mainstream corporations such as Clairol, Revlon, and Mary Kay, I am less convinced that J. C. Penney's target audience will really find much cultural enlightenment in the Kente cloth potholders, napkin rings, and dish towels that the store is currently marketing as "expressions of cultural pride."

In *Fashion Influences*, a catalog clearly intended to cater to what it 34 takes to be the tastes of black audiences, J. C. Penney advertises an assortment of housewares, ethnic artifacts, and exclusive designer fashions with "Afrocentric flair." Such specialty items as triple-woven cotton throws, which sell for $50 each, are available in four culturally edifying patterns: 01 Kwanzaa; 02 Kente; 03 Martin Luther King; and 04 Malcolm X. For another $40, customers can complement their Kwanzaa-patterned throw with a Kwanzaa needlepoint pillow. (For the not quite multiculturally literate shopper, Penney's provides a cultural history lesson: "Kwanzaa means 'first fruits of the harvest' in Swahili," the catalog informs. "Created in 1966, Kwanzaa is a seven-day celebration synthesizing elements from many African harvest festivals.") And just so consumers know precisely how politically correct their Penney's purchases are, many of the catalog descriptions inform shoppers that these Afrocentric items are made in the U.S.A. The Ivory Coast Table Linens, for example, are billed as an "exuberantly colored interpretation of authentic African woven cloth . . . Made in the U.S.A." The Kente-cloth pillows are made in the U.S.A. of fabric imported from Africa, but the MLK and Malcolm X throws are just plain made in the U.S.A. In other words, for not-so-modest prices, culturally and socially conscious American consumers can look for the union label as they shop for these and other interpretations-of-authentic-African-inspired-made-in-America goods.

Thus it is that from custom-designed bedroom coordinates inspired 35 by mud cloth from Mali in West Africa to an embroidered metallic caftan or "Uwe (pronounced yoo-way, meaning dress)" inspired by "garments worn by the royal court on special occasions," what J. C. Penney is trading in and trading on in this blaxploitation catalog is cultural difference and, if you will, mis-spent racial pride. Although I doubt that Penney's cares who buys its Kufi hats, black-on-black dishware, and "In Search of Identity" games, it is also clear that the company does not waste such catalogs on just any body. I, for example, have been a loyal Penney's catalog shopper for years; I receive the annual seasonal catalogs, as well as special fliers advertising queen-size fashions. I only happened upon Penney's blaxploitation catalog recently, however, when it was mailed not to me — faithful shopper — nor to my home but to the Center for African American Studies at Wesleyan University. While my shopping history identified me as larger-sized, there was evidently nothing about my purchasing pattern that identified me as black. Penney's marketing division seems to have assumed — quite cleverly, I think — that a Center for African American Studies would be a likely place to find middle-class, culturally-conscious black consumers who might actually be able to afford the high-priced items in its Afrocentric catalog. (What a miscalculation in that last regard.)

I suspect that such catalogs are mailed not only to black studies depart- 36 ments but also to black beauty parlors (indeed I found a similar catalog from Spiegel at the shop where I get my hair cut) and black churches, where there is sure to be a ready-made market for the Sunday-go-to-meetin' hats, high-heel shoes, and church-lady suits "with an Afrocentric flair" that fill their pages. Just to bring this discussion full circle, let me note that six Black Barbie dolls are available through this special catalog — Black Desert Storm Barbie and Ken and Soul Train Shani and her three friends Asha, Nichelle, and Jamal. Army Barbie and Ken are dressed in "authentic desert fatigues with authentic insignias for enlisted personnel," and the Shani dolls are decked out in "cool hip-hop fashions inspired by the hot T.V. dance show." But don't let these patriotic, all-American girls and boys fool you; they are all imported from Malaysia.

The Body Politic(s) of Barbie

Barbie's body is a consumer object itself, a vehicle for the display of clothing and the spectacular trappings of a wealthy teenage fantasy life. Her extraordinary body exists not simply as an example of the fetishized female form typical of those offered up to the male gaze, but as a commodity vehicle itself whose form seduces the beholder and sells accessories, the real source of corporate profit. Like Lay's chips, no one can buy just one outfit for the doll. Barbie is the late capitalist girl incarnate. (McCombie)

In focusing thus far on the merchandising of racial, perhaps more so than gender, difference, I do not mean to imply that racial and gender identities are divisible, even in dolls. Nor, in observing that most if not all of Mattel's "dolls of the world" look remarkably like what the company calls the "traditional, blond, blue-eyed Barbie," do I mean to suggest that the seemingly endless recapitulation of the white prototype is the only way in which these dolls are problematic. In fact, the most alarming thing about Barbie may well be the extent to which she functions as what M. G. Lord calls a teaching tool for femininity, whatever her race or ethnicity. Lord, the author of *Forever Barbie: The Unauthorized Biography of a Real Doll*, due out later this year, describes Barbie as a "space-age fertility icon. She looks like a modern woman, but she's a very primitive totem of female power" (qtd. in Dembner 1). 37

Barbie has long had the eye and ire of feminists, who, for the most part, have reviled her as another manifestation of the damaging myths of female beauty and the feminine body that patriarchy perpetuates through such vehicles as popular and commodity culture. A counter narrative also exists, however, one in which Barbie is not an empty-headed, material girl bimbo, for whom math class is tough, but a feminist heroine, who has been first in war (a soldier who served in the Gulf, she has worn the colors of her country as well as the United Colors of Benetton), first in peace (she held her own summit in 1990 and she's a long-time friend of UNICEF, who "loves all the children of the world"), and always first in the hearts of her country (Americans buy her at the rate of one doll every second). While time does not allow me to reiterate or to assess here all the known critiques and defenses of Barbie, I do want to discuss briefly some of the gender ideals that I think are encoded in and transmitted by this larger-than-life little woman and what Barbie's escalating popularity says about contemporary American culture. 38

In *Touching Liberty: Abolition, Feminism, and the Politics of the Body* (1993), Karen Sanchez-Eppler argues that all dolls are intended to teach little girls about domesticity (133). If such tutelage is Barbie's not so secret mission, her methodology is far more complex and contradictory than that of the Betsy Wetsy and Tiny Tears baby dolls I played with thirty-five years ago. Those dolls invoked and evoked the maternal, as they and the baby bottles and diapers with which they were packaged invited us to nestle, nurse, and nurture. Barbie's curvaceous, big-busted, almost fully female body, on the other hand, summons not the maternal but the sexual, not the nurturant mother but the sensuous woman. As Mel McCombie has argued, rather than rehearsing parenting, as a baby doll does, Barbie's adult body encourages children to dress and redress a fashion doll that 39 yields lessons about sexuality, consumption, and teenage life (3). Put another way, we might say that Barbie is literally and figuratively a titillating toy.

Bodacious as they may be, however, Barbie's firm plastic breasts have no nipples — nothing that might offend, nothing that might suggest her own pleasure. And if her protruding plastic mounds signify a simmering sensuality, what are we to make of her missing genitalia? McCombie suggests that Barbie's genital ambiguity can be read as an "homage to 'good taste'" and as a "reflection of the regnant mores for teenage girls — to be both sexy and adult yet remain virginal" (4). I agree that her body invites such readings, but it also seems to me that there is nothing ambiguous about Barbie's crotch. It's missing in inaction. While male dolls like Ken and Jamal have bumps "down there" and in some instances simulated underwear etched into the plastic, most Barbies come neither with drawers nor with even a hint of anything that needs covering, even as "it" is already covered or erased. As an icon of idealized femininity, then, Barbie is locked into a never-never land in which she must be always already sexual without the possibility of sex. Conspicuously sensual on top but definitively nonsexual below, her plastic body indeed has inscribed within it the very contradictory, whore/madonna messages with which patriarchy taunts and even traumatizes young women in particular. `40`

This kind of speculation about Barbie's breasts has led the doll's creator, Ruth Handler, to chide adults for their nasty minds. "In my opinion people make too much of breasts," Handler has complained. "They are just part of the body" (qtd. in BillyBoy 20). Mrs. Handler has a point (or maybe two). I feel more than just a little ridiculous myself as I sit here contemplating the body parts and sex life of a piece of plastic. What is fascinating, however, what I think is worth studying, what both invites and resists theorizing, is not the lump of molded plastic that is Barbie, but the imaginary life that is not — that is *our* invention. Barbie as a cultural artifact may be able to tell us more about ourselves and our society — more about society's attitudes toward its women — than anything we might say about the doll her- or, rather, *itself.* `41`

In the nineteenth century, Alexis de Tocqueville and others argued that you could judge the character, quality, and degree of advancement of a civilization by the status and treatment of its women. What is the status of women in soon to be twenty-first-century America, and can Barbie serve as a barometer for measuring that status? Barbie, it seems to me, is a key player in the process of socialization — of engendering and racialization — that begins in infancy and is furthered by almost everything about our society, including the books children read, the toys they play with, and the cartoons they watch on television. `42`

While changing channels one Saturday morning, I happened upon a cartoon, just a glimpse of which impelled me to watch on. At the point that I tuned in, a big, gray, menacingly male bulldog was barking furiously `43` at a pretty, petite, light-colored cat, who simply batted her long lashes, meowed coquettishly, and rubbed her tiny feline body against his huge canine leg in response. The more the dog barked and growled, the softer the cat meowed, using her slinky feline body and her feminine wiles to win the dog over. Her strategy worked; before my eyes — and, I imagine, the eyes of millions of children — the ferocious beast was transformed into a lovesick puppy dog, who followed the cat everywhere, repeatedly saving her from all manner of evil and danger. Time and time again, the bulldog rescued the helpless, accident-prone pussy from falling girders, oncoming traffic, and other hazards to which she, in her innocent frailty, was entirely oblivious. By the end, the once ferocious bulldog was completely domesticated, as his no longer menacing body became a kind of bed for the cat to nestle in.

There are, of course, a number of ways to read the gender and racial politics of this cartoon. I suppose that the same thought process that theorizes Barbie as a feminist heroine for whom men are mere accessories might claim the kitty cat, too, as a kind of feminist feline, who uses her feminine wiles to get her way. What resonates for me in the cartoon, however, are its beauty and the beast, light/dark, good/evil, female/male, race and gender codes: light, bright, cat-like femininity tames menacing black male bestiality. Make no mistake, however; it is not wit that wins out over barbarism but a mindless, can't-take-care-of-herself femininity. 44

Interestingly enough, these are the kinds of messages of which fairy tales and children's stories are often made. White knights rescue fair damsels in distress from dark, forbidding evils of one kind or another. As Darlene and Derek Hopson argue: "Some of the most blatant and simplistic representations of white as good and black as evil are found in children's literature," where evil black witches and good white fairies — heroes in white and villains in black — abound (121). 45

What Barbie dolls, cartoons like the one outlined above, and even the seemingly innocent fairy tales we read to our children seem to me to have in common are the mythologies of race and gender that are encoded in them. Jacqueline Urla and Alan Swedlund maintain that Barbie's body type constructs the bodies of other women as deviant and perpetuates an impossible standard of beauty. Attempting to live up to the Barbie ideal, others argue, fosters eating and shopping disorders in teenage girls — nightmares instead of dreams. BillyBoy, one of Barbie's most ardent supporters, defends his heroine against such charges by insisting that there is nothing abnormal about the proportions of Barbie's body. Rather, he asserts, "she has the ideal that Western culture has insisted upon since the 1920s: long legs, long arms, small waist, high round bosom, and long neck" (22). The irony is that BillyBoy may be right. "Unrealistic" or not, Barbie's weight and measurements (which if proportionate to those of a woman 5'6" tall would be something like 110 pounds and a top-heavy 39–18–33) are not much different from those of the beauty queens to 46 whom Bert Parks used to sing "Here she is, Miss America. Here she is, our ideal."[6] If Barbie is a monster, she is our monster, our ideal.

"But is Barbie bad?" Someone asked me the other day if a black doll that looks like a white doll isn't better than no black doll at all. I must admit that I have no ready answer for this and a number of other questions posed by my own critique. Although, as I acknowledged in the beginning, the dolls I played with as a child were white, I still remember the first time I saw a black doll. To me, she was the most beautiful thing I had ever seen; I wanted her desperately, and I was never again satisfied with white Betsy Wetsy and blonde, blue-eyed Patty Play Pal. She was something else, something *Other*, like me, and that, I imagine, was the source of her charm and my desire.

If I did not consciously note my own absence in the toys I played with, that absence, I suspect, had a profound effect on me nevertheless. We have only to read Toni Morrison's chilling tale *The Bluest Eye* to see the effect of the white beauty myth on the black child. And while they were by no means as dire for me as for Morrison's character Pecola Breedlove, I was not exempt from the consequences of growing up black in a white world that barely acknowledged my existence. I grew up believing I was ugly: my kinky hair, my big hips, the gap between my teeth. I have spent half my life smiling with my hand over my mouth to hide that gap, a habit I only began to get over in graduate school when a couple of Nigerian men told me that in their culture, where my body type is prized much more than Barbie's, such gaps are a sign of great beauty. I wonder what it would have meant for me as a child to see a black doll — or any doll — with big hips and a gap between her two front teeth.

Today, for $24.99, Mattel reaches halfway around the world and gives little girls — black like me — Nigerian Barbies to play with. Through the wonders of plastic, dyes, and mass production, the company brings into the homes of African American children a Nigeria that I as a young child did not even know existed. The problem is that Mattel's Nigeria does not exist either. The would-be ethnic dolls of the world Mattel sells, like their "traditional, blond, blue-eyed" all-American girl prototype, have no gaps, no big ears, no chubby thighs or other "imperfections." For a modest price, I can dream myself into Barbie's perfect world, so long as I dream myself in her image. It may be a small world, a whole new world, but there is still no place for me as *me* in it.

This, then, is my final doll story. Groucho Marx said that he wouldn't want to belong to a club that would have him as a member. In that same vein, I am not so sure that most of us would want to buy a doll that "looked

---

[6]In response to criticism from feminists in particular, the Miss America Pageant has attempted to transform itself from a beauty contest to a talent competition, whose real aim is to give college scholarships to smart, talented women (who just happen to look good in bathing suits and evening gowns). As part of its effort to appear more concerned with a woman's IQ than with her bra size, the pageant did away with its long-standing practice of broadcasting the chest, waist, and hip measurements, as well as the height and weight, of each contestant.

like us." Indeed, efforts to produce and market such truer-to-life dolls have not met with much commercial success. Cultural critics like me can throw theoretical stones at her all we want, but part of Barbie's infinite appeal is her very perfection, the extent to which she is both product and purveyor of the dominant white Western ideal of beauty.

And what of black beauty? If Colored Francie failed thirty years ago in part because of her Caucasian features, what are we to make of the current popularity and commercial success of Black Barbie and Shani, straight hair and all? Have we progressed to a point where "difference" makes no difference? Or have we regressed to such a degree that "difference" is only conceivable as similarity — as a mediated text that no matter what its dye job ultimately must be readable as white. Listen to our language: we "*tolerate* difference"; we practice "racial tolerance." Through the compound fractures of interpellation and universalization, the Other is reproduced not in her own image but in ours. If we have gotten away from "Us" and "Them," it may be only because Them R Us. 51

Is Barbie bad? Barbie is just a piece of plastic, but what she says about the economic base of our society — what she suggests about gender and race in our world — ain't good. 52

NOTE

I am particularly pleased to be publishing this essay in differences, *since its genesis was at a roundtable discussion on multiculturalism and postmodernism, sponsored by the Pembroke Center for Teaching and Research on Women at Brown University, in March of 1993. I wish to thank the many friends and colleagues who have encouraged this project, especially Indira Karamcheti and her four-year-old daughter Gita, who introduced me to the miniature Barbies that come with McDonald's "Happy Meals," and Erness Brody, who, with her daughter Jennifer Brody, is a veteran collector of vintage dolls. I owe a special debt to fellow "Barbiologists" M. G. Lord, Mel McCombie, Jacqueline Urla, and Eric Swedlund, who have so generously shared their research, and to Darlene Powell Hopson for talking with me about her work with Mattel. I wish to acknowledge as well the work of Erica Rand, an art historian at Bates College, who is also working on Barbie.*

WORKS CITED

Berkwitz, David N. "Finally, Barbie Doll Ads Go Ethnic." *Newsweek* 13 Aug. 1990: 48.

BillyBoy. *Barbie: Her Life and Times.* New York: Crown, 1987.

Cross, William E., Jr. *Shades of Black: Diversity in African American Identity.* Philadelphia: Temple UP, 1991.

Delany, Sarah, and Delany, A. Elizabeth. *Having Our Say: The Delany Sisters' First 100 Years.* New York: Kodansha, 1993.

Dembner, Alice. "Thirty-five and Still a Doll." *Boston Globe* 9 Mar. 1994: 1+.

Jones, Lisa. "A Doll Is Born." *Village Voice* 26 Mar. 1991: 36.

Kantrowitz, Barbara. "Hot Date: Barbie and G.I. Joe." *Newsweek* 20 Feb. 1989: 59–60.

Hopson, Darlene Powell and Derek S. *Different and Wonderful: Raising Black Children in a Race-Conscious Society.* New York: Simon, 1990.

Larcen, Donna. "Barbie Bond Doesn't Diminish with Age." *Hartford Courant* 17 Aug. 1993: A6–7.

Lord, M. G. *Forever Barbie: The Unauthorized Biography of a Real Doll.* New York: Morrow, 1994.

McCombie, Mel. "Barbie: Toys Are Us." Unpublished essay.

Morrison, Toni. *The Bluest Eye.* New York: Washington Square, 1970.

Rieff, David. "Multiculturalism's Silent Partner." *Harper's* Aug. 1993: 62–72.

Roberts, Cynthia. *Barbie: Thirty Years of America's Doll.* Chicago: Contemporary, 1989.

Rosenberg, Morris. *Conceiving the Self.* New York: Basic, 1979.

——— . *Society and the Adolescent Self-Image.* Middletown: Wesleyan UP, 1989.

Sanchez-Eppler, Karen. *Touching Liberty: Abolition, Feminism, and the Politics of the Body.* Berkeley: U of California P, 1993.

Stewart, Julia. *African Names.* New York: Carol, 1993.

Urla, Jacqueline, and Alan Swedlund. "The Anthropometry of Barbie: Unsettling Ideals of the Feminine in Popular Culture." *Deviant Bodies.* Ed. Jennifer Terry and Jacqueline Urla. Bloomington: Indiana UP, [1995].

Reading Rhetorically

1. List the key words and phrases duCille uses to make her point, along with your own explanation of these terms. What does she mean by "the commodification of race and gender difference" (para. 5) or the idea that Barbie is a "cultural artifact" (para. 41), for example?

2. Find three passages where duCille uses a specific doll as an example to illustrate her larger argument. What phrases does she use to move between her detailed descriptions of the dolls, and their packaging, and her analysis of those details? How persuasive do you find her claims based on the evidence in the three passages? Explain your answer.

3. Locate and mark sentences throughout duCille's essay where she signposts — saying what she is doing in the essay and why. For example, in paragraph 5 she writes: "As suggested by my title, I am going to use the figure of multicultural Barbie to talk about the commodification of race and gender difference." How does her use of signposts change as the essay progresses? How does this affect your reading of the essay?

Inquiring Further

4. Visit a toy store and make a list of toys that fall into gendered or racial categories. Use duCille's insights to analyze the appearance and packaging of these toys. For example, does the language on the packaging seem to target a specific audience? How are dolls marketed differently from action figures? Do your observations confirm or contradict duCille's claims? Explain your answer.

5. Use duCille's strategy of analyzing dolls to analyze another cultural commodity in which race and gender overlap. For example, you might examine the marketing of different television or film personalities, or sports figures. How well do duCille's strategies transfer to other media? What conclusions can you draw?

6. DuCille is one of many writers who are interested in the significance of children's popular culture. Using your library's resources, find three other pieces on the cultural importance of children's toys, video games, cartoons, or the like. Where does duCille's voice fit into the larger conversation on children's popular culture?

7. Although duCille concentrates on Barbie as a cultural icon of race and gender, she also is interested in the way race and gender themes are played out in visual media, like the cartoon she describes in paragraph 43. Henry Giroux explores similar territory in his analysis of Disney movies (p. 567). Write an essay in which you place duCille and Giroux in conversation about the role of race, gender, and marketing in an animated children's film, using as your example a film Giroux does not analyze in his essay. What conclusions can you draw?

8. DuCille examines the relationship between American capitalism and culture and the appeal (and fear) of the "exotic other," as does Cynthia Selfe in the section of her essay titled "Narrative #1: The 'Global Village' and the 'Electronic Colony'" (pp. 786–90). Kwame Anthony Appiah (p. 378) similarly explores the desire and anxiety that can arise when we try to cross cultures. How do these writers' ideas complement or contradict one another? Write an essay in which you consider duCille's arguments and those of either Selfe or Appiah on this topic. You might focus on the examples each author includes and the nature of the analysis. What do you want to teach your readers about the ideas raised in the two texts you've chosen?

9. DuCille's emphasis on women's bodies and the marketplace intersects with the concerns of two other writers in our book, Jean Kilbourne (p. 592) and Judith Lorber (p. 617). Write an essay in which you use these three writers' ideas as a means of extending and developing an analysis of a product (and perhaps its advertising) that relies on gender — feminine or masculine — for its marketing.

BARBARA EHRENREICH

Maid to Order: The Politics of Other Women's Work

Barbara Ehrenreich is one of the best-known journalists publishing social commentary in the United States today. She earned a PhD in cell biology, but has a voracious appetite for learning and writing about topics far beyond science. She has published and lectured on the state of health care, the history of women as healers, the anxieties of the middle class, women's advice manuals, the sex-work industry, politics, women's participation in the torture at Abu Ghraib, and the history of dancing, to name just a few of the topics she's addressed. In addition to the many books she has written, cowritten, and edited, she writes prolifically for newspapers and magazines, including the *New York Times Magazine, The Washington Post Magazine, The Atlantic, The Nation,* and *The New Republic.* She has also taught writing at the Graduate School of Journalism at the University of California, Berkeley.

This essay, "Maid to Order: The Politics of Other Women's Work," appeared in *Harper's* in 2000 and generated so much mail the magazine designed a separate section to publish it. Another version of the essay appears in her best-selling book *Nickel and Dimed: On (Not) Getting By in America* (2001), which has become a popular choice for university and city one-book reading programs, in which many people read and gather to discuss the same text. Part of the appeal of *Nickel and Dimed,* and of this essay, is that to research the lives of working-class Americans struggling to make ends meet, Ehrenreich actually went under cover, getting hired and working as a waitress, hotel maid, Wal-Mart employee, nursing home aide, and housecleaner, struggling to live only on the wages she earned. The result, as you will see in her experiences with The Maids International, is autobiographical journalism with a twist: She is reporting, simply describing and analyzing the physical, intellectual, and emotional experience of low-wage work; but she is also acting — never revealing herself as a journalist to her coworkers on each job.

The title of this piece tells us something about Ehrenreich and her intended readers: This is a portrait of "other women's" labor. Ehrenreich is writing for those who might not have thought much about low-wage work. In paragraph 2, for example, she gives readers a detailed view from the hands-and-knees perspective of a housecleaner scrubbing the floor, where "you find elaborate dust structures held together by a scaffolding of dog hair; dried bits of pasta glued to the floor by their sauce; the congealed remains of gravies, jellies, contraceptive creams, vomit, and urine." She also reveals the invisibility of these workers, helping readers understand the class structures that leave some work — and therefore some workers — out of sight and out of mind.

Although much of this essay is autobiographical, Ehrenreich puts her experience in context with research on the politics of housework, statistics about the housecleaning industry, mention of forced labor, and a global perspective on who does what kind of work, for whom, and for what wages.

As you read, notice your responses to different passages. What do you find most compelling? Why? Do Ehrenreich's rich descriptions of the very dirty work of cleaning surprise you? Or do they seem all too familiar? The statistics and scholarly references may open new perspectives for you; or they may confirm and clarify what you already suspected. Ehrenreich has constructed a story we cannot resist. Her objective: to help us see the world from her two perspectives — as a maid scrubbing on her knees and as a scholar at the keyboard, plenty angry about what she has learned.

In line with growing class polarization, the classic posture of submission is making a stealthy comeback. "We scrub your floors the old-fashioned way," boasts the brochure from Merry Maids, the largest of the residential-cleaning services that have sprung up in the last two decades, "on our hands and knees." This is not a posture that independent "cleaning ladies" willingly assume — preferring, like most people who clean their own homes, the sponge mop wielded from a standing position. In her comprehensive 1999 guide to homemaking, *Home Comforts,* Cheryl Mendelson warns: "Never ask hired housecleaners to clean your floors on their hands and knees; the request is likely to be regarded as degrading." But in a society in which 40 percent of the wealth is owned by 1 percent of households while the bottom 20 percent reports negative assets, the degradation of others is readily purchased. Kneepads entered American political discourse as a tool of the sexually subservient, but employees of Merry Maids, The Maids International, and other corporate cleaning services spend hours every day on these kinky devices, wiping up the drippings of the affluent.

I spent three weeks in September 1999 as an employee of The Maids International in Portland, Maine, cleaning, along with my fellow team members, approximately sixty houses containing a total of about 250 scrubbable floors — bathrooms, kitchens, and entryways requiring the hands-and-knees treatment. It's a different world down there below knee level, one that few adults voluntarily enter. Here you find elaborate dust structures held together by a scaffolding of dog hair; dried bits of pasta glued to the floor by their sauce; the congealed remains of gravies, jellies, contraceptive creams, vomit, and urine. Sometimes, too, you encounter some fragment of a human being: a child's legs, stamping by in disgust because the maids are still present when he gets home from school; more commonly, the Joan & David–clad feet and electrolyzed calves of the female homeowner. Look up and you may find this person staring at you, arms folded, in anticipation of an overlooked stain. In rare instances she may try to help in some vague, symbolic way, by moving the cockatoo's cage, for example, or apologizing for the leaves shed by a miniature indoor tree. Mostly, though, she will not see you at all and may even sit down with her mail at a table in the very room you are cleaning, where she would remain completely unaware of your existence unless you were to crawl under that table and start gnawing away at her ankles.

Housework, as you may recall from the feminist theories of the Sixties and Seventies, was supposed to be the great equalizer of women. Whatever else women did — jobs, school, child care — we also did housework, and if there were some women who hired others to do it for them, they seemed too privileged and rare to include in the theoretical calculus. All women were workers, and the home was their workplace — unpaid and unsupervised, to be sure, but a workplace no less than the offices and factories men repaired to every morning. If men thought of the home as a site of leisure and recreation — a "haven in a heartless world" — this was to ignore the invisible female proletariat that kept it cozy and humming. We were on the march now, or so we imagined, united against a society that devalued our labor even as it waxed mawkish over "the family" and "the home." Shoulder to shoulder and arm in arm, women were finally getting up off the floor.

In the most eye-catching elaboration of the home-as-workplace theme, *4* Marxist feminists Maria Rosa Dallacosta and Selma James proposed in 1972 that the home was in fact an economically productive and significant workplace, an extension of the actual factory, since housework served to "reproduce the labor power" of others, particularly men. The male worker would hardly be in shape to punch in for his shift, after all, if some woman had not fed him, laundered his clothes, and cared for the children who were his contribution to the next generation of workers. If the home was a quasi-industrial workplace staffed by women for the ultimate benefit of the capitalists, then it followed that "wages for housework" was the obvious demand.

But when most American feminists, Marxist or otherwise, asked the *5* Marxist question *cui bono?* they tended to come up with a far simpler answer — men. If women were the domestic proletariat, then men made up the class of domestic exploiters, free to lounge while their mates scrubbed. In consciousness-raising groups, we railed against husbands and boyfriends who refused to pick up after themselves, who were unaware of housework at all, unless of course it hadn't been done. The "dropped socks," left by a man for a woman to gather up and launder, joined lipstick and spike heels as emblems of gender oppression. And if, somewhere, a man had actually dropped sock in the calm expectation that his wife would retrieve it, it was a sock heard round the world. Wherever second-wave feminism took root, battles broke out between lovers and spouses over sticky countertops, piled-up laundry, and whose turn it was to do the dishes.

The radical new idea was that housework was not only a relationship *6* between a woman and a dust bunny or an unmade bed; it also defined a relationship between human beings, typically husbands and wives. This represented a marked departure from the more conservative Betty Friedan, who, in *The Feminine Mystique,* had never thought to enter the male sex into the equation, as either part of the housework problem or part of an eventual solution. She raged against a society that consigned its educated women to what she saw as essentially janitorial chores, beneath "the abilities of a woman of average or normal human intelligence," and, according to unidentified studies she cited, "peculiarly suited to the capacities of feeble-minded girls." But men are virtually exempt from housework in *The Feminine Mystique* — why drag them down too? At one point she even disparages a "Mrs. G.," who "somehow couldn't get her housework done before her husband came home at night and was so tired then that he had to do it." Educated women would just have to become more efficient so that housework could no longer "expand to fill the time available."

Or they could hire other women to do it — an option approved by *7* Friedan in *The Feminine Mystique* as well as by the National Organization for Women, which she had helped launch. At the 1973 congressional hearings on whether to extend the Fair Labor Standards Act to household workers, NOW testified on the affirmative side, arguing that improved wages and working conditions would attract more women to the field, and offering the seemingly self-contradictory prediction that "the demand for household help inside the home will continue to increase as more women seek occupations outside the home." One NOW member added, on a personal note: "Like many young women today, I am in school in order to develop a rewarding career for myself. I also have a home to run and can fully conceive of the need for household help as my free time at home becomes more and more restricted. Women know [that] housework is dirty, tedious work, and they are willing to pay to have it done. . . ." On the aspirations of the women paid to do it, assuming that at least some of them were bright enough to entertain a few, neither Friedan nor these members of NOW had, at the time, a word to say.

So the insight that distinguished the more radical, post-Friedan cohort 8 of feminists was that when we talk about housework, we are really talking, yet again, about power. Housework was not degrading because it was manual labor as Friedan thought, but because it was embedded in degrading relationships and inevitably served to reinforce them. To make a mess that another person will have to deal with — the dropped socks, the toothpaste sprayed on the bathroom mirror, the dirty dishes left from a late-night snack — is to exert domination in one of its more silent and intimate forms. One person's arrogance — or indifference, or hurry — becomes another person's occasion for toil. And when the person who is cleaned up after is consistently male, while the person who cleans up is consistently female, you have a formula for reproducing male domination from one generation to the next.

Hence the feminist perception of housework as one more way by which 9 men exploit women or, more neutrally stated, as "a symbolic enactment of gender relations." An early German women's liberation cartoon depicted a woman scrubbing on her hands and knees while her husband, apparently excited by this pose, approaches from behind, unzipping his fly. Hence, too, the second-wave feminists' revulsion at the hiring of maids, especially when they were women of color: At a feminist conference I attended in 1980, poet Audre Lorde chose to insult the all-too-white audience by accusing them of being present only because they had black housekeepers to look after their children at home. She had the wrong crowd; most of the assembled radical feminists would no sooner have employed a black maid than they would have attached Confederate flag stickers to the rear windows of their cars. But accusations like hers, repeated in countless conferences and meetings, reinforced our rejection of the servant option. There already were at least two able-bodied adults in the average home — a man and a woman — and the hope was that, after a few initial skirmishes, they would learn to share the housework graciously.

A couple of decades later, however, the average household still falls far 10 short of that goal. True, women do less housework than they did before the feminist revolution and the rise of the two-income family: down from an average of 30 hours per week in 1965 to 17.5 hours in 1995, according to a July 1999 study by the University of Maryland. Some of that decline reflects a relaxation of standards rather than a redistribution of chores; women still do two-thirds of whatever housework — including bill paying, pet care, tidying, and lawn care — gets done. The inequity is sharpest for the most despised of household chores, cleaning: In the thirty years between 1965 and 1995, men increased the time they spent scrubbing, vacuuming, and sweeping by 240 percent — all the way up to 1.7 hours per week — while women decreased their cleaning time by only 7 percent, to 6.7 hours per week. The averages conceal a variety of arrangements, of course, from minutely negotiated sharing to the most clichéd division of labor, as described by one woman to the *Washington Post:* "I take care of the inside, he takes care of the outside." But perhaps the most disturbing finding is that almost the entire increase in male participation took place between the 1970s and the mid-1980s. Fifteen years after the apparent cessation of hostilities, it is probably not too soon to announce the score: In the "chore wars" of the Seventies and Eighties, women gained a little ground, but overall, and after a few strategic concessions, men won.

Enter then, the cleaning lady as *dea ex machina*, restoring tranquility ₁₁ as well as order to the home. Marriage counselors recommend her as an alternative to squabbling, as do many within the cleaning industry itself. A Chicago cleaning woman quotes one of her clients as saying that if she gives up the service, "my husband and I will be divorced in six months." When the trend toward hiring out was just beginning to take off, in 1988, the owner of a Merry Maids franchise in Arlington, Massachusetts, told the *Christian Science Monitor*, "I kid some women. I say, 'We even save marriages. In this new eighties period you expect more from the male partner, but very often you don't get the cooperation you would like to have. The alternative is to pay somebody to come in. . . .'" Another Merry Maids franchise owner has learned to capitalize more directly on housework-related spats; he closes between 30 and 35 percent of his sales by making follow-up calls Saturday mornings, which is "prime time for arguing over the fact that the house is a mess." The micro-defeat of feminism in the household opened a new door for women, only this time it was the servants' entrance.

In 1999, somewhere between 14 and 18 percent of households employed ₁₂ an outsider to do the cleaning, and the numbers have been rising dramatically. Mediamark Research reports a 53 percent increase, between 1995 and 1999, in the number of households using a hired cleaner or service once a month or more, and Maritz Marketing finds that 30 percent of the people who hired help in 1999 did so for the first time that year. Among my middle-class, professional women friends and acquaintances, including some who made important contributions to the early feminist analysis of housework, the employment of a maid is now nearly universal. This sudden emergence of a servant class is consistent with what some economists have called the "Brazilianization" of the American economy: We are dividing along the lines of traditional Latin American societies — into a tiny overclass and a huge underclass, with the latter available to perform intimate household services for the former. Or, to put it another way, the home, or at least the affluent home, is finally becoming what radical feminists in the Seventies only imagined it was — a true "workplace" for women and a tiny, though increasingly visible, part of the capitalist economy. And the question is: As the home becomes a workplace for someone else, is it still a place where you would want to live?

Strangely, or perhaps not so strangely at all, no one talks about the "politics of housework" anymore. The demand for "wages for housework" has sunk to the status of a curio, along with the consciousness-raising groups in which women once rallied support in their struggles with messy men. In the academy, according to the feminist sociologists I interviewed, housework has lost much of its former cachet — in part, I suspect, because fewer sociologists actually do it. Most Americans, over 80 percent, still clean their homes, but the minority who do not include a sizable fraction of the nation's opinion-makers and culture producers — professors, writers, editors, politicians, talking heads, and celebrities of all sorts. In their homes, the politics of housework is becoming a politics not only of gender but of race and class — and these are subjects that the opinion-making elite, if not most Americans, generally prefer to avoid. 13

Even the number of paid houseworkers is hard to pin down. The Census Bureau reports that there were 549,000 domestic workers in 1998, up 9 percent since 1996, but this may be a considerable underestimate, since so much of the servant economy is still underground. In 1995, two years after Zoe Baird lost her chance to be attorney general for paying her undocumented nanny off the books, the *Los Angeles Times* reported that fewer than 10 percent of those Americans who paid a housecleaner reported those payments to the IRS. Sociologist Mary Romero, one of the few academics who retain an active interest in housework and the women who do it for pay, offers an example of how severe the undercounting can be: The 1980 Census found only 1,063 "private household workers" in El Paso, Texas, though the city estimated their numbers at 13,400 and local bus drivers estimated that half of the 28,300 daily bus trips were taken by maids going to and from work. The honesty of employers has increased since the Baird scandal, but most experts believe that household workers remain, in large part, uncounted and invisible to the larger economy. 14

One thing you can say with certainty about the population of household workers is that they are disproportionately women of color: "lower" kinds of people for a "lower" kind of work. Of the "private household cleaners and servants" it managed to locate in 1998, the Bureau of Labor Statistics reports that 36.8 percent were Hispanic, 15.8 percent black, and 2.7 percent "other." Certainly the association between housecleaning and minority status is well established in the psyches of the white employing class. When my daughter, Rosa, was introduced to the wealthy father of a Harvard classmate, he ventured that she must have been named for a favorite maid. And Audre Lorde can perhaps be forgiven for her intemperate accusation at the 15 feminist conference mentioned above when we consider an experience she had in 1967: "I wheel my two-year-old daughter in a shopping cart through a supermarket . . . and a little white girl riding past in her mother's cart calls out excitedly, 'Oh look, Mommy, a baby maid.' " But the composition of the household workforce is hardly fixed and has changed with the life chances of the different ethnic groups. In the late nineteenth century, Irish and German immigrants served the northern upper and middle classes, then left for the factories as soon as they could. Black women replaced them, accounting for 60 percent of all domestics in the 1940s, and dominated the field until other occupations began to open up to them. Similarly, West Coast maids were disproportionately Japanese American until that group, too, found more congenial options. Today, the color of the hand that pushes the sponge varies from region to region: Chicanas in the Southwest, Caribbeans in New York, native Hawaiians in Hawaii, whites, many of recent rural extraction, in Maine.

The great majority — though again, no one knows exact numbers — 16 of paid housekeepers are freelancers, or "independents," who find their clients through agencies or networks of already employed friends and relatives. To my acquaintances in the employing class, the freelance housekeeper seems to be a fairly privileged and prosperous type of worker, a veritable aristocrat of labor — sometimes paid $15 an hour or more and usually said to be viewed as a friend or even treated as "one of the family." But the shifting ethnic composition of the workforce tells another story: This is a kind of work that many have been trapped in — by racism, imperfect English skills, immigration status, or lack of education — but few have happily chosen. Interviews with independent maids collected by Romero and by sociologist Judith Rollins, who herself worked as a maid in the Boston area in the early Eighties, confirm that the work is undesirable to those who perform it. Even when the pay is deemed acceptable, the hours may be long and unpredictable; there are usually no health benefits, no job security, and, if the employer has failed to pay Social Security taxes (in some cases because the maid herself prefers to be paid off the books), no retirement benefits. And the pay is often far from acceptable. The BLS found full-time "private household cleaners and servants" earning a median annual income of $12,220 in 1998, which is $1,092 below the poverty level for a family of three. Recall that in 1993 Zoe Baird paid her undocumented household workers about $5 an hour out of her earnings of $507,000 a year.

At the most lurid extreme there is slavery. A few cases of forced labor 17 pop up in the press every year, most recently — in some nightmare version of globalization — of undocumented women held in servitude by high-ranking staff members of the United Nations, the World Bank, and the International Monetary Fund. Consider the suit brought by Elizabeth Senghor, a Senegalese woman who alleged that she was forced to work fourteen-hour days for her employers in Manhattan, without any regular pay, and was given no accommodations beyond a pull-out bed in her employers' living room. Hers is not a particularly startling instance of domestic slavery; no beatings or sexual assaults were charged, and Ms. Senghor was apparently fed. What gives this case a certain rueful poignancy is that her employer, former U.N. employee Marie Angelique Savane, is one of Senegal's leading women's rights advocates and had told the *Christian Science Monitor* in 1986 about her efforts to get the Senegalese to "realize that being a woman can mean other things than simply having children, taking care of the house."

Mostly, though, independent maids — and sometimes the women who *18* employ them — complain about the peculiar intimacy of the employer-employee relationship. Domestic service is an occupation that predates the refreshing impersonality of capitalism by several thousand years, conditions of work being still largely defined by the idiosyncrasies of the employers. Some of them seek friendship and even what their maids describe as "therapy," though they are usually quick to redraw the lines once the maid is perceived as overstepping. Others demand deference bordering on servility, while a growing fraction of the nouveau riche is simply out of control. In August 1999, the *New York Times* reported on the growing problem of dinner parties being disrupted by hostesses screaming at their help. To the verbal abuse add published reports of sexual and physical assaults — a young teenage boy, for example, kicking a live-in nanny for refusing to make sandwiches for him and his friends after school.

But for better or worse, capitalist rationality is finally making some head- *19* way into this weird preindustrial backwater. Corporate cleaning services now control 25 to 30 percent of the $1.4 billion housecleaning business, and perhaps their greatest innovation has been to abolish the mistress-maid relationship, with all its quirks and dependencies. The customer hires the service, not the maid, who has been replaced anyway by a team of two to four uniformed people, only one of whom — the team leader — is usually authorized to speak to the customer about the work at hand. The maids' wages, their Social Security taxes, their green cards, backaches, and child-care problems — all these are the sole concern of the company, meaning the local franchise owner. If there are complaints on either side, they are addressed to the franchise owner; the customer and the actual workers need never interact. Since the franchise owner is usually a middle-class white person, cleaning services are the ideal solution for anyone still sensitive enough to find the traditional employer-maid relationship morally vexing.

In a 1997 article about Merry Maids, *Franchise Times* reported tersely *20* that the "category is booming, [the] niche is hot, too, as Americans look to outsource work even at home." Not all cleaning services do well, and there is a high rate of failure among informal, mom-and-pop services. The "boom" is concentrated among the national and international chains — outfits like Merry Maids, Molly Maids, Mini Maids, Maid Brigade, and The Maids International — all named, curiously enough, to highlight the more antique aspects of the industry, though the "maid" may occasionally be male. Merry Maids claimed to be growing at 15 to 20 percent a year in 1996, and spokesmen for both Molly Maids and The Maids International told me that their firms' sales are growing by 25 percent a year; local franchisers are equally bullish. Dan Libby, my boss at The Maids, confided to me that he could double his business overnight if only he could find enough reliable employees. To this end, The Maids offers a week's paid vacation, health insurance after ninety days, and a free breakfast every morning consisting — at least where I worked — of coffee, doughnuts, bagels, and bananas. Some franchises have dealt with the tight labor market by participating in welfare-to-work projects that not only funnel employees to them but often subsidize their paychecks with public money, at least for the first few months of work (which doesn't mean the newly minted maid earns more, only that the company has to pay her less). The Merry Maids franchise in the city where I worked is conveniently located a block away from the city's welfare office.

Among the women I worked with at The Maids, only one said she had 21 previously worked as an independent, and she professed to be pleased with her new status as a cleaning-service employee. She no longer needed a car to get her from house to house and could take a day off — unpaid of course — to stay home with a sick child without risking the loss of a customer. I myself could see the advantage of not having to deal directly with the customers, who were sometimes at home while we worked and eager to make use of their supervisory skills: Criticisms of our methods, and demands that we perform unscheduled tasks, could simply be referred to the franchise owner.

But there are inevitable losses for the workers as any industry moves 22 from the entrepreneurial to the industrial phase, probably most strikingly, in this case, in the matter of pay. At Merry Maids, I was promised $200 for a forty-hour week, the manager hastening to add that "you can't calculate it in dollars per hour" since the forty hours include all the time spent traveling from house to house — up to five houses a day — which is unpaid. The Maids International, with its straightforward starting rate of $6.63 an hour, seemed preferable, though this rate was conditional on perfect attendance. Miss one day and your wage dropped to $6 an hour for two weeks, a rule that weighed particularly heavily on those who had young children. In addition, I soon learned that management had ways of shaving off nearly an hour's worth of wages a day. We were told to arrive at 7:30 in the morning, but our billable hours began only after we had been teamed up, given our list of houses for the day, and packed off in the company car at about 8:00 A.M. At the end of the day, we were no longer paid from the moment we left the car, though as much as fifteen minutes of work — refilling cleaning-fluid bottles, etc. — remained to be done. So for a standard nine-hour day, the actual pay amounted to about $6.10 an hour, unless you were still being punished for an absence, in which case it came out to $5.50 an hour.

Nor are cleaning-service employees likely to receive any of the perks or 23
tips familiar to independents — free lunches and coffee, cast-off clothing,
or a Christmas gift of cash. When I asked, only one of my coworkers could
recall ever receiving a tip, and that was a voucher for a free meal at a
downtown restaurant owned by a customer. The customers of cleaning
services are probably no stingier than the employers of independents; they
just don't know their cleaning people and probably wouldn't even recognize them on the street. Plus, customers probably assume that the fee they
pay the service — $25 per person-hour in the case of The Maids franchise I
worked for — goes largely to the workers who do the actual cleaning.

But the most interesting feature of the cleaning-service chains, at least 24
from an abstract, historical perspective, is that they are finally transforming the home into a fully capitalist-style workplace, and in ways that the
old wages-for-housework advocates could never have imagined. A house is
an innately difficult workplace to control, especially a house with ten or
more rooms like so many of those we cleaned; workers may remain out of
one another's sight for as much as an hour at a time. For independents, the
ungovernable nature of the home-as-workplace means a certain amount of
autonomy. They can take breaks (though this is probably ill-advised if the
homeowner is on the premises); they can ease the monotony by listening
to the radio or TV while they work. But cleaning services lay down rules
meant to enforce a factorylike — or even conventlike — discipline on their
far-flung employees. At The Maids, there were no breaks except for a daily
ten-minute stop at a convenience store for coffee or "lunch" — meaning
something like a slice of pizza. Otherwise, the time spent driving between
houses was considered our "break" and the only chance to eat, drink, or
(although this was also officially forbidden) smoke a cigarette. When the
houses were spaced well apart, I could eat my sandwich in one sitting; otherwise it would have to be divided into as many as three separate, hasty
snacks.

Within a customer's house, nothing was to touch our lips at all, not 25
even water — a rule that, on hot days, I sometimes broke by drinking from
a bathroom faucet. TVs and radios were off-limits, and we were never,
ever, to curse out loud, even in an ostensibly deserted house. There might
be a homeowner secreted in some locked room, we were told, ear pressed
to the door, or, more likely, a tape recorder or video camera running. At the
time, I dismissed this as a scare story, but I have since come across ads for
devices like the Tech-7 "incredible coin-sized camera" designed to "get a
visual record of your babysitter's actions" and "watch employees to prevent theft." It was the threat or rumor of hidden recording devices that
provided the final capitalist-industrial touch — supervision.

What makes the work most factorylike, though, is the intense Tay- 26
lorization imposed by the companies. An independent, or a person cleaning his or her own home, chooses where she will start and, within each
room, probably tackles the most egregious dirt first. Or she may plan her
work more or less ergonomically, first doing whatever can be done from a

standing position and then squatting or crouching to reach the lower levels. But with the special "systems" devised by the cleaning services and imparted to employees via training videos, there are no such decisions to make. In The Maids' "healthy touch" system, which is similar to what I saw of the Merry Maids' system on the training tape I was shown during my interview, all cleaning is divided into four task areas — dusting, vacuuming, kitchens, and bathrooms — which are in turn divided among the team members. For each task area other than vacuuming, there is a bucket containing rags and the appropriate cleaning fluids, so the biggest decision an employee has to make is which fluid and scrubbing instrument to deploy on which kind of surface; almost everything else has been choreographed in advance. When vacuuming, you begin with the master bedroom; when dusting, with the first room off of the kitchen; then you move through the rooms going left to right. When entering each room, you proceed from left to right and top to bottom, and the same with each surface — top to bottom, left to right. Deviations are subject to rebuke, as I discovered when a team leader caught me moving my arm from right to left, then left to right, while wiping Windex over a French door.

It's not easy for anyone with extensive cleaning experience — and I 27 include myself in this category — to accept this loss of autonomy. But I came to love the system: First, because if you hadn't always been traveling rigorously from left to right it would have been easy to lose your way in some of the larger houses and omit or redo a room. Second, some of the houses were already clean when we started, at least by any normal standards, thanks probably to a housekeeper who kept things up between our visits; but the absence of visible dirt did not mean there was less work to do, for no surface could ever be neglected, so it was important to have "the system" to remind you of where you had been and what you had already "cleaned." No doubt the biggest advantage of the system, though, is that it helps you achieve the speed demanded by the company, which allots only so many minutes per house. After a week or two on the job, I found myself moving robotlike from surface to surface, grateful to have been relieved of the thinking process.

The irony, which I was often exhausted enough to derive a certain 28 malicious satisfaction from, is that "the system" is not very sanitary. When I saw the training videos on "Kitchens" and "Bathrooms," I was at first baffled, and it took me several minutes to realize why: There is no water, or almost no water, involved. I had been taught to clean by my mother, a compulsive housekeeper who employed water so hot you needed rubber gloves to get into it and in such Niagaralike quantities that most microbes were probably crushed by the force of it before the soap suds had a chance to rupture their cell walls. But germs are never mentioned in the videos provided by The Maids. Our antagonists existed entirely in the visible world — soap scum, dust, counter crud, dog hair, stains, and smears — and were attacked by damp rag or, in hardcore cases, by a scouring pad. We scrubbed only to remove impurities that might be detectable to a customer by hand or by eye; otherwise our only job was to wipe. Nothing was ever said, in the videos or in person, about the possibility of transporting bacteria, by rag or by hand, from bathroom to kitchen or even from one house to the next. Instead, it is the "cosmetic touches" that the videos emphasize and to which my trainer continually directed my eye. Fluff out all throw pillows and arrange them symmetrically. Brighten up stainless steel sinks with baby oil. Leave all spice jars, shampoos, etc., with their labels facing outward. Comb out the fringes of Persian carpets with a pick. Use the vacuum to create a special, fernlike pattern in the carpets. The loose ends of toilet paper and paper towel rolls have to be given a special fold. Finally, the house is sprayed with the service's signature air freshener — a cloying floral scent in our case, "baby fresh" in the case of the Mini Maids.

When I described the "methods" employed to housecleaning expert 29 Cheryl Mendelson, she was incredulous. A rag moistened with disinfectant will not get a countertop clean, she told me, because most disinfectants are inactivated by contact with organic matter — i.e., dirt — so their effectiveness declines with each swipe of the rag. What you need is a detergent and hot water, followed by a rinse. As for floors, she judged the amount of water we used — one half of a small bucket — to be grossly inadequate, and, in fact, the water I wiped around on floors was often an unsavory gray. I also ran The Maids' cleaning methods by Don Aslett, author of numerous books on cleaning techniques and self-styled "number one cleaner in America." He was hesitant to criticize The Maids directly, perhaps because he is, or told me he is, a frequent speaker at conventions of cleaning-service franchise holders, but he did tell me how he would clean a countertop: First, spray it thoroughly with an all-purpose cleaner, then let it sit for three to four minutes of "kill time," and finally wipe it dry with a clean cloth. Merely wiping the surface with a damp cloth, he said, just spreads the dirt around. But the point at The Maids, apparently, is not to clean so much as it is to create the appearance of having been cleaned, not to sanitize but to create a kind of stage setting for family life. And the stage setting Americans seem to prefer is sterile only in the metaphorical sense, like a motel room or the fake interiors in which soap operas and sitcoms take place.

But even ritual work takes its toll on those assigned to perform it. 30 Turnover is dizzyingly high in the cleaning-service industry, and not only because of the usual challenges that confront the working poor — childcare problems, unreliable transportation, evictions, and prior health problems. As my long-winded interviewer at Merry Maids warned me, and my coworkers at The Maids confirmed, this is a physically punishing occupation, something to tide you over for a few months, not year after year. The hands-and-knees posture damages knees, with or without pads; vacuuming strains the back; constant wiping and scrubbing invite repetitive stress injuries even in the very young. In my three weeks as a maid, I suffered nothing more than a persistent muscle spasm in the right forearm, but the damage would have been far worse if I'd had to go home every day to my own housework and children, as most of my coworkers did, instead of returning to my motel and indulging in a daily after-work regimen of ice packs and stretches. Chores that seem effortless at home, even almost recreational when undertaken at will for twenty minutes or so at a time, quickly turn nasty when performed hour after hour, with few or no breaks and under relentless time pressure.

So far, the independent, entrepreneurial housecleaner is holding her   *31* own, but there are reasons to think that corporate cleaning services will eventually dominate the industry. New users often prefer the impersonal, standardized service offered by the chains, and, in a fast-growing industry, new users make up a sizable chunk of the total clientele. Government regulation also favors the corporate chains, whose spokesmen speak gratefully of the "Zoe Baird effect," referring to customers' worries about being caught paying an independent off the books. But the future of housecleaning may depend on the entry of even bigger players into the industry. Merry Maids, the largest of the chains, has the advantage of being a unit within the $6.4 billion ServiceMaster conglomerate, which includes such related businesses as TruGreen-ChemLawn, Terminix, Rescue Rooter, and Furniture Medic. Swisher International, best known as an industrial toilet-cleaning service, operates Swisher Maids in Georgia and North Carolina, and Sears may be feeling its way into the business. If large multinational firms establish a foothold in the industry, mobile professionals will be able to find the same branded and standardized product wherever they relocate. For the actual workers, the change will, in all likelihood, mean a more standardized and speeded-up approach to the work — less freedom of motion and fewer chances to pause.

The trend toward outsourcing the work of the home seems, at the moment,   *32* unstoppable. Two hundred years ago women often manufactured soap, candles, cloth, and clothing in their own homes, and the complaints of some women at the turn of the twentieth century that they had been "robbed by the removal of creative work" from the home sound pointlessly reactionary today. Not only have the skilled crafts, like sewing and cooking from scratch, left the home but many of the "white collar" tasks are on their way out, too. For a fee, new firms such as the San Francisco–based Les Concierges and Cross It Off Your List in Manhattan will pick up dry cleaning, baby-sit pets, buy groceries, deliver dinner, even do the Christmas shopping. With other firms and individuals offering to buy your clothes, organize your financial files, straighten out your closets, and wait around in your home for the plumber to show up, why would anyone want to hold on to the toilet cleaning?

Absent a major souring of the economy, there is every reason to think   *33* that Americans will become increasingly reliant on paid housekeepers and that this reliance will extend ever further down into the middle class. For one thing, the "time bind" on working parents shows no sign of loosening; people are willing to work longer hours at the office to pay for the people — housecleaners and baby-sitters — who are filling in for them at home. Children, once a handy source of household help, are now off at soccer practice or SAT prep classes; grandmother has relocated to a warmer climate or taken up a second career. Furthermore, despite the fact that people spend less time at home than ever, the square footage of new homes swelled by 33 percent between 1975 and 1998, to include "family rooms," home entertainment rooms, home offices, bedrooms, and often bathrooms for each family member. By the third quarter of 1999, 17 percent of new homes were larger than 3,000 square feet, which is usually considered the size threshold for household help, or the point at which a house becomes unmanageable to the people who live in it.

One more trend impels people to hire outside help, according to cleaning experts such as Aslett and Mendelson: Fewer Americans know how to clean or even to "straighten up." I hear this from professional women defending their decision to hire a maid: "I'm just not very good at it myself" or "I wouldn't really know where to begin." Since most of us learn to clean from our parents (usually our mothers), any diminution of cleaning skills is transmitted from one generation to another, like a gene that can, in the appropriate environment, turn out to be disabling or lethal. Upper-middle-class children raised in the servant economy of the Nineties are bound to grow up as domestically incompetent as their parents and no less dependent on people to clean up after them. Mendelson sees this as a metaphysical loss, a "matter of no longer being physically centered in your environment." Having cleaned the rooms of many overly privileged teenagers in my stint with The Maids, I think the problem is a little more urgent than that. The American overclass is raising a generation of young people who will, without constant assistance, suffocate in their own detritus. 34

If there are moral losses, too, as Americans increasingly rely on paid household help, no one has been tactless enough to raise them. Almost everything we buy, after all, is the product of some other person's suffering and miserably underpaid labor. I clean my own house (though — full disclosure — I recently hired someone else to ready it for a short-term tenant), but I can hardly claim purity in any other area of consumption. I buy my jeans at the Gap, which is reputed to subcontract to sweatshops. I tend to favor decorative objects no doubt ripped off, by their purveyors, from scantily paid Third World craftspersons. Like everyone else, I eat salad greens just picked by migrant farm workers, some of them possibly children. And so on. We can try to minimize the pain that goes into feeding, clothing, and otherwise provisioning ourselves — by observing boycotts, checking for a union label, etc. — but there is no way to avoid it altogether without living in the wilderness on berries. Why should housework, among all the goods and services we consume, arouse any special angst? 35

And it does, as I have found in conversations with liberal-minded employers of maids, perhaps because we all sense that there are ways in which housework is different from other products and services. First, in its inevitable proximity to the activities that compose "private" life. The home that becomes a workplace for other people remains a home, even when 36 that workplace has been minutely regulated by the corporate cleaning chains. Someone who has no qualms about purchasing rugs woven by child slaves in India or coffee picked by impoverished peasants in Guatemala might still hesitate to tell dinner guests that, surprisingly enough, his or her lovely home doubles as a sweatshop during the day. You can eschew the chain cleaning services of course, hire an independent cleaner at a generous hourly wage, and even encourage, at least in spirit, the unionization of the housecleaning industry. But this does not change the fact that someone is working in your home at a job she would almost certainly never have chosen for herself — if she'd had a college education, for example, or a little better luck along the way — and the place where she works, however enthusiastically or resentfully, is the same as the place where you sleep.

It is also the place where your children are raised, and what they learn [37] pretty quickly is that some people are less worthy than others. Even better wages and working conditions won't erase the hierarchy between an employer and his or her domestic help, because the help is usually there only because the employer has "something better" to do with her time, as one report on the growth of cleaning services puts it, not noticing the obvious implication that the cleaning person herself has nothing better to do with her time. In a merely middle-class home, the message may be reinforced by a warning to the children that that's what they'll end up doing if they don't try harder in school. Housework, as radical feminists once proposed, defines a human relationship and, when unequally divided among social groups, reinforces preexisting inequalities. Dirt, in other words, tends to attach to the people who remove it — "garbagemen" and "cleaning ladies." Or, as cleaning entrepreneur Don Aslett told me with some bitterness — and this is a successful man, chairman of the board of an industrial cleaning service and frequent television guest — "The whole mentality out there is that if you clean, you're a scumball."

One of the "better" things employers of maids often want to do with [38] their time is, of course, spend it with their children. But an underlying problem with post-nineteenth-century child-raising, as Deirdre English and I argued in our book *For Her Own Good* years ago, is precisely that it is unmoored in any kind of purposeful pursuit. Once "parenting" meant instructing the children in necessary chores; today it's more likely to center on one-sided conversations beginning with "So how was school today?" No one wants to put the kids to work again weeding and stitching; but in the void that is the modern home, relationships with children are often strained. A little "low-quality time" spent washing dishes or folding clothes together can provide a comfortable space for confidences — and give a child the dignity of knowing that he or she is a participant in, and not just the product of, the work of the home.

There is another lesson the servant economy teaches its beneficiaries [39] and, most troublingly, the children among them. To be cleaned up after is to achieve a certain magical weightlessness and immateriality. Almost everyone complains about violent video games, but paid housecleaning has the same consequence-abolishing effect: You blast the villain into a mist of blood droplets and move right along; you drop the socks knowing they will eventually levitate, laundered and folded, back to their normal dwelling place. The result is a kind of virtual existence, in which the trail of litter that follows you seems to evaporate all by itself. Spill syrup on the floor and the cleaning person will scrub it off when she comes on Wednesday. Leave the *Wall Street Journal* scattered around your airplane seat and the flight attendants will deal with it after you've deplaned. Spray toxins into the atmosphere from your factory's smokestacks and they will be filtered out eventually by the lungs of the breathing public. A servant economy breeds callousness and solipsism in the served, and it does so all the more effectively when the service is performed close up and routinely in the place where they live and reproduce.

Individual situations vary, of course, in ways that elude blanket 40 judgment. Some people — the elderly and disabled, parents of new babies, asthmatics who require an allergen-free environment — may well need help performing what nursing-home staff call the "ADLs," or activities of daily living, and no shame should be attached to their dependency. In a more generous social order, housekeeping services would be subsidized for those who have health-related reasons to need them — a measure that would generate a surfeit of new jobs for the low-skilled people who now clean the homes of the affluent. And in a less gender-divided social order, husbands and boyfriends would more readily do their share of the chores.

However we resolve the issue in our individual homes, the moral chal- 41 lenge is, put simply, to make work visible again: not only the scrubbing and vacuuming but all the hoeing, stacking, hammering, drilling, bending, and lifting that goes into creating and maintaining a livable habitat. In an ever more economically unequal culture, where so many of the affluent devote their lives to such ghostly pursuits as stock-trading, image-making, and opinion-polling, real work — in the old-fashioned sense of labor that engages hand as well as eye, that tires the body and directly alters the physical world — tends to vanish from sight. The feminists of my generation tried to bring some of it into the light of day, but, like busy professional women fleeing the house in the morning, they left the project unfinished, the debate broken off in midsentence, noble intentions unfulfilled. Sooner or later, someone else will have to finish the job.

■   ■   ■

Reading Rhetorically

1. What significance do you see in the title of this piece — "Maid to Order: The Politics of Other Women's Work"? Look at the phrases on each side of the colon, and discuss what each might mean. What do they suggest about the assumptions Ehrenreich is making about her audience? What can you say about those assumptions?

2. What role does personal experience play in Ehrenreich's argument? Pointing to specific examples, explain what you think are the possible positive and negative aspects of her using personal experience to build her case. What is she arguing, exactly?

3. Mark all the different places where Ehrenreich uses statistics in her essay. Which statistics stand out to you as particularly surprising? Which are most persuasive? Least persuasive? Discuss your responses with your classmates.

Inquiring Further

4. A version of this piece is in Ehrenreich's *Nickel and Dimed: On (Not) Getting By in America*. In other chapters, she describes waitressing in Florida and working at Wal-Mart in Minnesota. She also includes opening and concluding chapters on her rationale for the book and her research methods, and the conclusions she draws after experiencing survival on low wages. Look up the book and choose another chapter to read and report on to the rest of the class. What themes emerge in other chapters that are similar to or different from those in the chapter we include here?

5. In paragraph 4, Ehrenreich mentions Maria Rosa Dallacosta and Selma James, "Marxist feminists" who took on housework as a political issue in the early 1970s. What have other critics said about housework since the early 1970s? Working in small groups in your library, search for books and articles on housework from one of the following decades: the 1970s, the 1980s, the 1990s, the 2000s to date. Each group should try to find at least four books, chapters from books, or articles and be ready to report back to the rest of the class. What were the issues in each decade? As a class, how do you see the conversation about housework changing (or not changing)? What significance do you see in your findings?

6. Gather some of your own statistics on gender and housework to place in the context of Ehrenreich's. You might survey your classmates or design a short survey to conduct with a broader group to learn how many hours most families spend on housework a week, how chores break down along gender lines, the division of household labor students envision for their future households, or other questions you come up with. Analyze your results, and discuss your findings with the class.

Framing Conversations

7. Ehrenreich points out that "when we talk about housework, we are really talking, yet again, about power" (para. 8). Judith Lorber's essay in this book (p. 617) analyzes gendered assumptions and power dynamics, as does Peggy McIntosh's essay (p. 520), which also takes up class and race power relations. Write an essay in which you use the work of these three writers to help you argue about what you can and cannot tell about gender, class, and race power dynamics in the United States by focusing on housework. Where do you and these writers agree and disagree, and why?

8. Both Ehrenreich and Eric Schlosser (p. 754) explore the power dynamics of American businesses and workplaces. What does each writer have to say about the relationship among employer, employee, and profit margins? What insights from each writer might you apply to the other writer's text, and with what results? Where do you stand in relation to these ideas? Using ideas and examples from the two essays, write an argument about the need to change or maintain current American business practices.

9. Like Ehrenreich, Mark Edmundson (p. 277) is interested in the consumer culture's emphasis on appearance over substance. Although these writers take up different settings — Ehrenreich focuses on the home as a space where we consume goods and services, while Edmundson focuses on college as a place increasingly organized around consumer expectations — they both examine what they see as problems in America's consumer culture. Write an essay in which you place these writers and yourself in conversation with one another to explore and draw conclusions about the American consumer culture. How do the three of you understand the strengths and weaknesses of that culture? What changes would you make? What is at stake and for whom if things stay the same or change?

■ THOMAS FRANK

The Two Nations

Thomas Frank writes analyses of popular culture meant to be accessible to a general audience. He is the editor of *The Baffler*, a journal he began producing while still a student at the University of Virginia. The magazine was a response to critiques of mass culture written in what Frank describes as a "baffling" style — pretentious and deliberately obscure. By contrast, *The Baffler* uses journalistic language informed by scholarly research to explore topics like the media's popularization of poker, recent twists in the political landscape, and the artsy reinvention of downtown areas. In addition to the many articles he has written for publications like *Harper's* and *The New York Review of Books*, Frank is the author of *The Conquest of Cool: Business Culture, Counterculture, and the Rise of Hip Consumerism* (1997) and *One Market Under God: Extreme Capitalism, Market Populism, and the End of Economic Democracy* (2000). This essay is a chapter in Frank's best-selling book *What's the Matter with Kansas? How Conservatives Won the Heart of America* (2004), which drew enormous attention for its analysis of how both conservatives and liberals stereotype each other, in the process further dividing the country.

Although Frank seems to lean left in this piece, he is an equal-opportunity critic, taking conservatives and liberals to task as he puzzles through the implications of seeing the United States as a collection of red (conservative) and blue (liberal) states. Kansas serves as the book's test case because this traditionally liberal, populist state has swung to the right in recent national elections. Frank is interested in how conservatives have "won the heart of America," as the book's subtitle claims, and why liberals seem to have failed to respond to the needs and wants of many working-class

Americans. Although he often is praised for bringing into focus the economic and social class differences that tend to be ignored in political analyses, Frank has been criticized for failing to take into consideration racial issues, including the concerns of some working-class whites who many believe fueled the backlash against 1970s liberalism in the 1980s, bringing Ronald Reagan to power.

Frank is less interested in taking sides in the red-versus-blue debate than he is in the significance of the media's production of this divide. He also is curious about the "purple" areas, shared concerns that might bring citizens together if issues were framed in different language. As you read, test your own responses to the many media stereotypes Frank lays out — the latte liberals and NASCAR fan conservatives, for example. In his text and meticulously detailed footnotes, Frank cites a long list of red-state/blue-state debates that have appeared in books, newspapers, and magazines. He also adds context to his argument by analyzing voting patterns in recent national elections. In particular, notice his criticism of David Brooks, one of the people he holds responsible for popularizing this media-invented divide. Pay attention to the ways Frank uses other writers' ideas to challenge the mythologies of both conservatives and liberals in political discourse.

Frank's writing is lively, a function of several writing strategies. Notice his frequent use of rhetorical questions like "What characterizes the good people of Red America?" (para. 17). He also loves to quote and unpack the meaning of political catchphrases. Pay attention to his analysis of terms from the 1890s in paragraph 26, as well as his fascination with contemporary political language, like the quotation from an anti–Howard Dean television commercial that claimed Dean should "take his tax-hiking, government-expanding, latte-drinking, sushi-eating, Volvo-driving, *New York Times*–reading, body-piercing, Hollywood-loving, left-wing freak show back to Vermont, where it belongs" (see footnote, para. 11).

Wherever you find yourself on the red-blue political spectrum, Frank's provocative questions may give you new insight into the current political climate and where we go from here.

I n the backlash imagination, America is always in a state of quasi–civil   *1*
war: on one side are the unpretentious millions of authentic Americans; on the other stand the bookish, all-powerful liberals who run the country but are contemptuous of the tastes and beliefs of the people who inhabit it. When the chairman of the Republican National Committee in 1992 announced to a national TV audience, "We are America" and "those other people are not," he was merely giving new and more blunt expression to a decades-old formula. Newt Gingrich's famous description of Democrats as "the enemy of normal Americans" was just one more winning iteration of this well-worn theme.

The current installment of this fantasy is the story of "the two Americas,"   *2*
the symbolic division of the country that, after the presidential election of 2000, captivated not only backlashers but a sizable chunk of the pundit class. The idea found its inspiration in the map of the electoral results that

year: there were those vast stretches of inland "red" space (the networks all used red to designate Republican victories) where people voted for George W. Bush, and those tiny little "blue" coastal areas where people lived in big cities and voted for Al Gore. On the face of it there was nothing really remarkable about these red and blue blocs, especially since in terms of the popular vote the contest was essentially a tie.

Still, many commentators divined in the 2000 map a baleful cultural 3 cleavage, a looming crisis over identity and values. "This nation has rarely appeared more divided than it does right now," moaned David Broder, the *Washington Post's* pundit-in-chief, in a story published a few days after the election. The two regions were more than mere voting blocs; they were complete sociological profiles, two different Americas at loggerheads with each other.

And these pundits knew — before election night was over and just by 4 looking at the map — what those two Americas represented. Indeed, the explanation was ready to go before the election even happened.[1] The great dream of conservatives ever since the thirties has been a working-class movement that for once takes *their* side of the issues, that votes Republican and reverses the achievements of working-class movements of the past. In the starkly divided red/blue map of 2000 they thought they saw it being realized: the old Democratic regions of the South and the Great Plains were on their team now, solid masses of uninterrupted red, while the Democrats were restricted to the old-line, blueblood states of the Northeast, along with the hedonist left coast.*

I do not want to minimize the change that this represents. Certain 5 parts of the Midwest were once so reliably leftist that the historian Walter Prescott Webb, in his classic 1931 history of the region, pointed to its persistent radicalism as one of the "Mysteries of the Great Plains." Today the mystery is only heightened; it seems inconceivable that the Midwest was ever thought of as a "radical" place, as anything but the land of the bland, the easy snoozing flyover. Readers in the thirties, on the other hand, would have known instantly what Webb was talking about, since so many of the great political upheavals of their part of the twentieth century were launched from the territory west of the Ohio River. The region as they knew it was what gave the country Socialists like Eugene Debs, fiery progressives like Robert La Follette, and practical unionists like Walter Reuther; it spawned the anarchist IWW and the coldly calculating UAW; and it was periodically convulsed in gargantuan and often bloody industrial disputes. They might even have known that there were once Socialist newspapers in Kansas and Socialist voters in Oklahoma and Socialist mayors in Milwaukee, and that there were radical farmers across the region forever enlisting

---

[1]The red-state/blue-state narrative drew heavily on *One Nation, Two Cultures*, a culture-warring book brought forth in 1999 by the neoconservative doyenne Gertrude Himmelfarb, wife of Irving Kristol and mom of Bill Kristol, editor of the *Weekly Standard.*

*The handful of midwestern states that also went Democratic did not fit easily into this scheme, and so were rarely taken into account by commentators.

in militant agrarian organizations with names like the Farmers' Alliance, or the Farmer-Labor Party, or the Non-Partisan League, or the Farm Holiday Association. And they would surely have been aware that Social Security, the basic element of the liberal welfare state, was largely a product of the midwestern mind.

Almost all of these associations have evaporated today. That the region's character has been altered so thoroughly — that so much of the Midwest now regards the welfare state as an alien imposition; that we have trouble even believing there was a time when progressives were described with adjectives like *fiery*, rather than *snooty* or *bossy* or *wimpy* — has to stand as one of the great reversals of American history.

So when the electoral map of 2000 is compared to that of 1896 — the year of the showdown between the "great commoner," William Jennings Bryan, and the voice of business, William McKinley — a remarkable inversion is indeed evident. Bryan was a Nebraskan, a leftist, and a fundamentalist Christian, an almost unimaginable combination today, and in 1896 he swept most of the country outside the Northeast and upper Midwest, which stood rock-solid for industrial capitalism. George W. Bush's advisers love to compare their man to McKinley,[2] and armed with the electoral map of 2000 the president's fans are able to envisage the great contest of 1896 refought with optimal results: the politics of McKinley chosen by the Middle America of Bryan.

From this one piece of evidence, the electoral map, the pundits simply veered off into authoritative-sounding cultural proclamation. Just by looking at the map, they reasoned, we could easily tell that George W. Bush was the choice of the plain people, the grassroots Americans who inhabited the place we know as the "heartland," a region of humility, guilelessness, and, above all, stout yeoman *righteousness*. The Democrats, on the other hand, were the party of the elite. Just by looking at the map we could see that liberals were sophisticated, wealthy, and materialistic. While the big cities blued themselves shamelessly, the *land* knew what it was about and went Republican, by a margin in square miles of four to one.[3]

---

[2]See, for example, David Frum's account of the Bush White House, *The Right Man* (New York: Random House, 2003), p. 36, or the story by James Harding in the *Financial Times* for May 20, 2003. In the latter, the Bush strategist Karl Rove was reported to be reading a biography of McKinley and speaks of the Republican Party winning a grand realignment just as McKinley did.

[3]I am referring here to the county-by-county results, in square miles. Bush won the votes of counties occupying 2,427,039 square miles, while Gore only took the votes of 580,134 square miles.

You think this is so obviously irrelevant no one in their right mind would ever bring it up? Think again. An article that appeared on *National Review Online* a year after the election used this fact to show that Bush's vote was more "representative of the diversity of the nation" than Gore's: "A look at the county-by-county map of the United States following the 2000 vote shows only small islands (mostly on the coasts) of Gore Blue amid a wide sea of Bush Red. In all, Bush won majorities in areas representing more than 2.4 million square miles, while Gore was able to garner winning margins in only 580,000."

The attraction of such a scheme for conservatives was powerful and *9*
obvious.[4] The red-state narrative brought majoritarian legitimacy to a president who had actually lost the popular vote. It also allowed conservatives
to present their views as the philosophy of a region that Americans — even
sophisticated urban ones — traditionally venerate as the repository of
national virtue, a place of plain speaking and straight shooting.

The red-state/blue-state divide also helped conservatives perform one *10*
of their dearest rhetorical maneuvers, which we will call the *latte libel:* the
suggestion that liberals are identifiable by their tastes and consumer preferences and that these tastes and preferences reveal the essential arrogance
and foreignness of liberalism. While a more straightforward discussion of
politics might begin by considering the economic interests that each party
serves, the latte libel insists that such interests are irrelevant. Instead it's the
places that people live and the things that they drink, eat, and drive that are
the critical factors, the clues that bring us to the truth. In particular, the
things that *liberals* are said to drink, eat, and drive: the Volvos, the imported
cheese, and above all, the lattes.*

The red-state/blue-state idea appeared to many in the media to be a *11*
scientific validation of this familiar stereotype, and before long it was a
standard element of the media's pop-sociology repertoire. The "two Americas" idea became a hook for all manner of local think pieces (blue Minnesota is only separated by one thin street from red Minnesota, but my,
how different those two Minnesotas are); it provided an easy tool for contextualizing the small stories (red Americans love a certain stage show in
Vegas, but blue Americans don't) or for spinning the big stories (John
Walker Lindh, the American who fought for the Taliban, was from California and therefore a reflection of blue-state values); and it justified countless *USA Today*–style contemplations of who we Americans really are,
meaning mainly investigations of the burning usual — what we Americans
like to listen to, watch on TV, or buy at the supermarket.

---

[4]The "two Americas" was, for the most part, a pop narrative generated by conservatives. As far as I have been able to determine, there were only a few attempts to define the
red-state/blue-state divide in a liberal manner, the most notable being Paul Krugman's
effort to stand the narrative on its head by depicting red Americans as freeloaders, living
off the tax money (i.e., farm subsidies) of wealthy blue America. Needless to say, this
viewpoint was not widely embraced, even though, by the definitions of the "two Americas" narrative, blue-state people are supposed to dominate the nation's media and constantly to distort the news to depict themselves in a favorable light.

*The state of Vermont is a favorite target of the latte libel. In his best-selling *Bobos
in Paradise*, David Brooks ridicules the city of Burlington in that state as the prototypical
"latte town," a city where "Beverly Hills income levels" meet a Scandinavian-style social
consciousness. In a TV commercial aired in early 2004 by the conservative Club for
Growth, onetime Democratic presidential candidate Howard Dean, the former governor
of Vermont, is reviled by two supposedly average people who advise him to "take his tax-
hiking, government-expanding, latte-drinking, sushi-eating, Volvo-driving, *New York
Times*–reading, body-piercing, Hollywood-loving, left-wing freak show back to Vermont,
where it belongs."

Red America, these stories typically imply,[5] is a mysterious place   *12*
whose thoughts and values are essentially foreign to society's masters. Like
the "Other America" of the sixties or the "Forgotten Men" of the thirties, its
vast stretches are tragically ignored by the dominant class — that is, the
people who write the sitcoms and screenplays and the stories in glossy
magazines, all of whom, according to the conservative commentator
Michael Barone, simply "can't imagine living in such places." Which is
particularly unfair of them, impudent even, because Red America is in fact
the *real* America, the part of the country where reside, as a column in the
Canadian *National Post* put it, "the original values of America's founding."

And since many of the pundits who were hailing the virtues of the red   *13*
states — pundits, remember, who were conservatives and who supported
George W. Bush — actually, physically lived in blue states that went for
Gore, the rules of this idiotic game allowed them to present the latte libel
in the elevated language of the confession. David Brooks, who has since
made a career out of projecting the liberal stereotype onto the map, took
to the pages of *The Atlantic* magazine to admit on behalf of *everyone who
lives in a blue zone* that they are all snobs, toffs, wusses, ignoramuses, and
utterly out of touch with the authentic life of the people.

> We in the coastal metro Blue areas read more books and attend more plays
> than the people in the Red heartland. We're more sophisticated and
> cosmopolitan — just ask us about our alumni trips to China or Provence, or
> our interest in Buddhism. But don't ask us, please, what life in Red America
> is like. We don't know. We don't know who Tim LaHaye and Jerry B. Jenkins
> are. . . . We don't know what James Dobson says on his radio program, which
> is listened to by millions. We don't know about Reba and Travis. . . . Very few
> of us know what goes on in Branson, Missouri, even though it has seven mil-
> lion visitors a year, or could name even five NASCAR drivers. . . . We don't
> know how to shoot or clean a rifle. We can't tell a military officer's rank by

---

[5]My roundup of the red-state/blue-state literature incorporated the following, listed
in chronological order: David Broder, "Burying the Hatchet," *Washington Post*, November 10, 2000; Robert Tracinski, "Rural Individualists," *National Post*, November 30,
2000; Matt Bai, "Red Zone vs. Blue Zone," *Newsweek*, January 1, 2001; Newt Gingrich,
"Two Americas," *Chief Executive*, February 1, 2001; John Podhoretz, "The Two Americas:
Ironic Us, Simple Them," *New York Post*, March 13, 2001; Michael Barone, "The 49 Per-
cent Nation," *National Journal*, June 9, 2001; Andrew Sullivan, "Lizzie Crashes into
America's Class War," *Sunday Times* (London), July 29, 2001; David Brooks, "One
Nation, Slightly Divisible," *The Atlantic*, December 2001; "Sons of Liberty," *Wall Street
Journal*, December 7, 2001; James Poniewozik, "The NASCAR of News," *Time*,
February 11, 2002; Jill Lawrence, "Values, Votes, Points of View Separate Towns," *USA
Today*, February 18, 2002; Blake Hurst, "The Plains vs. the Atlantic," *The American Enter-
prise*, March 1, 2002; Ronald A. Buel, "Winning Over Oregon," *Portland Oregonian*,
March 17, 2002; Paul Krugman, "Those Farm Subsidy Blues: Blame It on the Red
States," *Milwaukee Journal-Sentinel*, May 9, 2002; Doug Saunders, "Caught in the Cross-
fire of the 'Two Americas,'" *Toronto Globe and Mail*, October 12, 2002; Roy Huntington,
"The Insider," *American Handgunner*, January–February 2003; Steve Berg, "The Red and
the Blue," *Minneapolis Star Tribune*, February 9, 2003.

looking at his insignia. We don't know what soy beans look like when they're growing in a field.[6]

One is tempted to dismiss Brooks's grand generalizations by rattling off the many ways in which he gets it wrong: by pointing out that the top three soybean producers — Illinois, Iowa, and Minnesota — were in fact blue states; or by listing the many military bases located on the coasts; or by noting that when it came time to build a NASCAR track in Kansas, the county that won the honor was one of only two in the state that went for Gore. Average per capita income in that same lonely blue county, I might as well add, is $16,000, which places it well below Kansas and national averages, and far below what would be required for the putting on of elitist or cosmopolitan airs of any kind.[7]

[6]Disingenuously adopting the voice of the hated liberal Other is a not-uncommon rhetorical device among conservative commentators. In 2002 it was used by Peggy Noonan, who claimed to speak for the spirit of just-departed Minnesota Democrat Paul Wellstone in order to scold Wellstone's still-living supporters.

In Brooks's case, though, the device proved just a bit too tricky for his readers. Conservatives across the country apparently believed that Brooks meant it about being "more sophisticated and cosmopolitan" than people in the red states, and they raced to their keyboards to complain. A Missouri farmer named Blake Hurst was even moved to write a three-thousand-word article for *The American Enterprise* magazine flogging Brooks for his elitist blue-state pretensions and, bizarrely, taking Brooks's many passages of straightforward praise for red America as concessions wrung from a dedicated foe. These passages Hurst then proceeded to expand upon (that's right, we *are* more humble than you), effectively making his article a mirror image of Brooks's own.

Ordinarily it would be an embarrassing mistake for a magazine to publish an essay based on a misunderstanding that a sixth-grader should have been able to catch, but instead Hurst's article was celebrated widely among right-wingers on the Internet as a thundering riposte to Brooks, who was now (despite his years of contributions to conservative publications) thought to be a liberal-elitist devil-figure. Hurst's essay was reprinted on the *Wall Street Journal Online* and numerous farm publications, incidentally helping to validate one of the stereotypes that both he and Brooks had set out to dismiss: that Middle Americans are dopes.

Among the many who misunderstood Brooks's use of the second person, the most amusing response came from Phil Brennan, a conservative of the old school, who took to the right-wing Web site NewsMax.com to charge Brooks with "insufferable elitism as displayed in his look at an America neither he nor his fellow snobs pretend to understand." Brennan went on to find confirmation in Brooks's article of a rather curious theory of the decline of journalism. In the old days, he tells us, journalists "were a manly sort, utterly devoted to heterosexual activity, who fully understood who and what they were. And their reporting reflected that. And because of that self-knowledge there wasn't an elitist among them." http://www.newsmax.com/archives/articles/2002/2/20/15555.shtml.

[7]I am referring to Wyandotte County, where Kansas City, Kansas, is found. It went for Gore by 67 percent to 29 percent. *Kansas Statistical Abstract 2001*, Thelma Helyar, ed. (Lawrence, Kans.: Policy Research Institute, 2002). Income statistics are from 1999 and can be found on p. 320, election results on p. 180. Wyandotte does produce some of the best barbecue in America, but call someone there a "bobo" or an "elitist," and you'd be asking for a fight.

Since the Republican–NASCAR connection figures so prominently in contemporary populist fantasies, it is worth pointing out that conservative Republicans are by no

It's pretty much a waste of time, however, to catalog the contradic- 15
tions[8] and tautologies[9] and huge, honking errors[10] blowing round in a
media flurry like this. The tools being used are the blunt instruments of
propaganda, not the precise metrics of sociology. Yet, as with all successful
propaganda, the narrative does contain a grain of truth: we all know that
there *are* many aspects of American life that are off the culture industry's
radar; that vast reaches of the country *have* gone from being liberal if not
radical to being stoutly conservative; and that there *is* a small segment of
the "cosmopolitan" upper middle class that considers itself socially
enlightened, that knows nothing of the fine points of hayseediana, that
likes lattes, and that opted for Gore.

---

means universal fans of NASCAR. Indeed, the populist conservatives of Kansas vigorously opposed the construction of the Kansas Speedway on the grounds that it was corporate welfare, which it may well have been. (Some of them don't like Branson either,
but we'll have to save that for another book.) John Altevogt, a newspaper columnist who
was for a time the chairman of the Wyandotte County Republican Party, has even written that he and his neighbors "do not consider NASCAR a 'good corporate neighbor' ";
indeed, they "consider it to be little more than a nuisance and a giant eyesore." *Metro
Voice News* (Kansas City), March 5, 2001.

[8]Consider the snowmobile dilemma: As in one of those "You might be a redneck
if . . ." books, David Brooks insists in the above-mentioned *Atlantic* article that one can
trace the red-state/blue-state divide by determining whether a person does outdoor
activities with motors (the good old American way) or without (the pretentious blue-
state way): "We [blue-state people] cross-country ski; they snowmobile." And yet in
Newsweek's take on the blue/red divide, a "town elder" from red America can be heard
railing against people who drive snowmobiles for precisely the opposite reason: snowmobiles signal big-city contempt for the "small-town values" of Bush country!

How are the bold sociologists of politics to resolve this vexing matter of the snowmobile? What does snowmobiling truly signify? Populism or elitism? Conservatism or
liberalism? Arrogance or humility? Perhaps the answer lies not in a yes-snowmobile or a
no-snowmobile verdict but in a more subtle parsing of the snowmobile signifier, one
that takes into consideration the long-simmering feud between the rival snowmobile
brands — a feud that is of paramount importance in certain reaches of the Upper Midwest (even ranking above the various NASCAR controversies) but with which Brooks is
probably unfamiliar because he is such a "sophisticated" blue-state dude.

To wit: The Polaris is a distinctly Republican brand of snowmobile, humble yet
martial in its red, white, and blue color scheme. Democrats, on the other hand, do their
proud prowling on Arctic Cats, a brand of snowmobile that has taken as its colors the
show-off and suggestively third-worldish combination of green, purple, and black.

[9]In the selection printed above, Brooks tosses off a few names from the conservative political world as though they were uncontroversial folk heroes out in the hinter-
land, akin to country music stars or favorite cartoonists. But the real reason liberals
don't know much about James Dobson or Tim LaHaye is not because they are out of
touch with America but because both of these men are far-right ideologues. Those who
listen to Dobson's radio program or buy LaHaye's novels, suffused as they are in Bircher-
style conspiracy theory, tend to be people who agree with them, people who are conservatives, people who voted for Bush in 2000.

[10]Brooks asserts at one point in his *Atlantic* essay that "upscale areas everywhere"
went for Gore in 2000. While the phenomenon of well-to-do Democrats is interesting
and worth considering, as a blanket statement about the rich — or, by extension, about
corporate America, the system that made them rich — this is not even close to correct.

But the "two nations" commentators showed no interest in examining 16 the mysterious inversion of American politics in any systematic way. Their aim was simply to bolster the stereotypes using whatever tools were at hand: to cast the Democrats as the party of a wealthy, pampered, arrogant elite that lives as far as it can from real Americans; and to represent Republicanism as the faith of the hardworking common people of the heartland, an expression of their unpretentious, all-American ways just like country music and NASCAR. At this pursuit they largely succeeded. By 2003 the conservative claim to the Midwest was so uncontested that Fox News launched a talk show dealing in culture-war outrage that was called, simply, *Heartland*.

What characterizes the good people of Red America? Reading through 17 the "two Americas" literature is a little like watching a series of Frank Capra one-reelers explaining the principles of some turbocharged Boy Scout Law:

A red-stater is humble. In fact, humility is, according to reigning jour- 18 nalistic myth, the signature quality of Red America, just as it was one of the central themes of George W. Bush's presidential campaign. "In Red America the self is small," teaches David Brooks. "People declare in a million ways, 'I am normal.'" As evidence of this modesty, Brooks refers to the plain clothing that he saw residents wearing in a county in Pennsylvania that voted for Bush, and in particular to the unremarkable brand names he spotted on the locals' caps. The caps clearly indicate that the people of Red

---

Bush was in fact the hands-down choice of corporate America: according to the Center for Responsive Politics, Bush raised more in donations than Gore in each of ten industrial sectors; the only sector in which Gore came out ahead was "labor." In fact, Bush raised so much money from wealthy contributors (more than any other candidate in history, a record that he then broke in 2003), he established a special (and notorious) organization for them: the Pioneers.

Nor is Brooks's statement valid even within its limited parameters. When he says "upscale areas everywhere" voted for Gore, he gives Chicago's North Shore as an example of what he means. In fact, Lake Forest, the definitive and the richest North Shore burb, chose the Republican, as it always does, by a whopping 70 percent. (According to the official election results of Lake County, Illinois.) Winnetka and Kenilworth, the other North Shore suburbs known for their being "upscale," went for Bush by 59 percent and 64 percent respectively. (According to the official election results of Cook County, Illinois.)

And there were obviously dozens of other "upscale areas" where Bush prevailed handily: Morris, Somerset, and Hunterdon Counties, New Jersey; Fairfax County, Virginia (suburban D.C.); Cobb County, Georgia (suburban Atlanta); DuPage County, Illinois (more of suburban Chicago); Chester County, Pennsylvania (suburban Philadelphia); and Orange County, California (the veritable symbol of upscale suburbia), to name but a few. Or, keeping within the parameters of this book, there's Mission Hills, Kansas, by far the wealthiest town in the state, which chose Bush over Gore by 71 percent to 25 percent. Johnson County, Kansas, the most upscale county in the state, also gave Bush a lopsided victory, choosing him over Gore by 60 percent to 36 percent. (According to the official election results of the State of Kansas.)

America enjoy trusting and untroubled relationships with Wal-Mart and McDonald's; ipso facto they are humble.

John Podhoretz, a former speechwriter for Bush the Elder, finds the   *19* same noble simplicity beneath every adjusto-cap. "Bush Red is a simpler place," he concludes, after watching people at play in Las Vegas; it's a land "where people mourn the death of NASCAR champion Dale Earnhardt, root lustily for their teams, go to church, and find comfort in old-fashioned verities."

When the red-staters themselves get into the act, composing lists   *20* of their own virtues, things get bad fast. How "humble" can you be when you're writing a three-thousand-word essay claiming that all the known virtues of democracy are sitting right there with you at the word processor? This problem comes into blinding focus in a much-reprinted red-state blast by the Missouri farmer Blake Hurst that was originally published in *The American Enterprise* magazine. He and his fellow Bush voters, Hurst stepped forward to tell the world, were *humble, humble, humble, humble!*

> Most Red Americans can't deconstruct post-modern literature, give proper orders to a nanny, pick out a cabernet with aftertones of licorice, or quote prices from the Abercrombie and Fitch catalog. But we can raise great children, wire our own houses, make beautiful and delicious creations with our own two hands, talk casually and comfortably about God, repair a small engine, recognize a good maple sugar tree, tell you the histories of our towns and the hopes of our neighbors, shoot a gun and run a chainsaw without fear, calculate the bearing load of a roof, grow our own asparagus . . .

And so on.

On the blue side of the great virtue divide, Brooks reports, "the self is   *21* more commonly large." This species of American can be easily identified in the field by their constant witty showing off: *They think they are so damn smart.* Podhoretz, a former Republican speechwriter, remember, admits that "we" blue-staters "cannot live without irony," by which he means mocking everything that crosses our path, because "we" foolishly believe that "ideological and moral confusion are signs of a higher consciousness." Brooks, who has elsewhere ascribed the decline of the Democratic Party to its snobbery,[11] mocks blue-staters for eating at fancy restaurants and shopping in small, pretentious stores instead of at Wal-Mart, retailer to real America. He actually finds a poll in which 43 percent of liberals confess that they "like to show off," which he then tops with another poll in which 75 percent of liberals describe themselves as "intellectuals." Such

---

[11]In *The New York Times* for October 21, 2003, Brooks writes that of all the Democrats then vying for their party's presidential nomination, John Edwards offers the most "persuasive theory" of Democratic decline: "that the Democrats' besetting sin over the past few decades has been snobbery."

admissions, in this company, are tantamount to calling yourself a mind-twisting communist.

Which was, according to that Canadian columnist, precisely what lib- 22
erals were, as one could plainly see from the famous electoral map. While humble red-state people had been minding their own business over the years, "intellectuals educated at European universities" were lapping up the poisonous teachings of Karl Marx, then returning to "dominate our universities," where they "have condemned America's values and indoctrinated generations of students in their collectivist ideals." Thus the reason that liberals rallied to Al Gore was the opportunity to advance "collectivism." (Podhoretz, for his part, claims liberals liked Gore because he was so witty!)

A red-stater, meanwhile, *is reverent.* As we were repeatedly reminded 23
after the election, red-state people have a better relationship with God than the rest of us. They go to church regularly. They are "observant, tradition-minded, moralistic," in Michael Barone's formulation. Liberals of the coasts, meanwhile, are said to be "unobservant, liberation-minded, relativistic."

But don't worry; *a red-stater is courteous, kind, cheerful.* They may 24
be religious, but they aren't at all pushy about it. The people David Brooks encountered in that one county in Pennsylvania declined to discuss abortion with him, from which he concludes that "potentially controversial subjects are often played down" throughout Red America. Even the preachers he met there are careful to respect the views of others. These fine people "don't like public scolds." They are easygoing believers, not interested in taking you on in a culture war. Don't be frightened.

A red-stater is loyal. This is the part of the country that fills the army's 25
ranks and defends the flag against all comers. While the European-minded know-it-alls of blue land waited only a short time after 9/11 to commence blaming America for the tragedy, the story goes, sturdy red-staters stepped forward unhesitatingly to serve their country one more time. For Blake Hurst of Missouri, this special relationship with the military is both a matter of pride ("Red America is never redder than on our bloodiest battlefields") and a grievance — you know, the usual one, the one you saw in *Rambo,* the one where all the cowards of the coasts stab the men of red land in the back during the Vietnam War.

But above all, *a red-stater is a regular, down-home working stiff,* 26
whereas a blue-stater is always some sort of pretentious paper shuffler. The idea that the United States is "two nations" defined by social rank was first articulated by the labor movement and the historical left. The agrarian radicals of the 1890s used the "two nations" image to distinguish between "producers" and "parasites," or simply "the robbers and the robbed," as Sockless Jerry Simpson, the leftist congressman from Kansas, liked to put it. The radical novelist John Dos Passos used the phrase to describe his disillusionment with capitalist America in the twenties, while the Democratic

presidential candidate John Edwards has recently made a point of reviving the term in its original meaning.[12] For the most part, however, the way the "two Americas" image is used these days, it incorporates all the disillusionment, all the resentment, but none of the leftism. "Rural America is pissed," a small-town Pennsylvania man told a reporter from *Newsweek* in 2001. Explaining why he and his neighbors voted for George Bush, he said: "These people are tired of moral decay. They're tired of everything being wonderful on Wall Street and terrible on Main Street." Let me repeat that: they're voting *Republican* in order to *get even with Wall Street.*

This is not yet the place to try to sort out the tangled reasoning that   *27* leads a hardworking citizen of an impoverished town to conclude that voting for George W. Bush is a way to strike a blow against big business, but it is important to remind ourselves of the context. During the decade that was then ending, the grand idea that had made the pundits gawk and the airwaves sing had been the coming of a New Economy, a free-market millennium in which physical work was as obsolete as the sundial. It was the age of the "knowledge worker," we were told, the heroic entrepreneur who was building a "weightless" economy out of "thin air." Blue-collar workers, meanwhile, were the ones who "didn't get it," fast-fading relics of an outmoded and all-too-material past. Certain celebrated capitalist thinkers even declared, at the height of the boom, that blue collars and white collars had swapped moral positions, with workers now the "parasites" freeloading on the Olympian labors of management.[13]

The red-state/blue-state literature simply corrected this most egregious   *28* excess of the previous decade, rediscovering the nobility of the average worker and reasserting the original definitions of *parasite* and *producer.*[14]

---

[12]Richard Hofstadter's thoughts on the Populist language of the "two nations" is particularly compelling given the current circumstances. See *The Age of Reform: From Bryan to F.D.R.* (New York: Knopf, 1955), chap. 2. The quote from Jerry Simpson can be found on p. 64.

Dos Passos's famous "two nations" passage can be found in *The Big Money*, the third volume of the *U.S.A.* trilogy (New York: Harcourt, Brace and Company, 1937), pp. 462–3:

> all right we are two nations
> America our nation has been beaten by strangers who have bought the laws and fenced off the meadows and cut down the woods for pulp and turned our pleasant cities into slums and sweated the wealth out of our people and when they want to they hire the executioner to throw the switch.

[13]"The people who lift 'things' (the . . . RAPIDLY . . . declining fraction) are the new parasites living off the carpal-tunnel syndrome of the computer programmers' perpetually strained keyboard hands," screeched Tom Peters in 1997. (*The Circle of Innovation: You Can't Shrink Your Way to Greatness* [New York: Knopf, 1997], p. 8.) He wasn't alone. "The rich, the former leisure class, are becoming the new overworked," declared *Wired* magazine in its January 1998 issue. "And those who used to be considered the working class are becoming the new leisure class."

[14]This is not the first time conservatives have rediscovered the virtues of a conservative working class after a period of overheated reverence for the creative white-collar

What was novel was that it did so in the service of the very same free-market policies that characterized the hallucinatory nineties. The actors had put away their laptops and donned overalls, but the play remained the same.

Consider, in this connection, the "two nations" story that appeared in *American Handgunner*, which tells us how the 9/11 terrorist attack brought home the truth to one "self-described 'Blue' American in New York City." As she stood "alongside other New York 'intellectuals'" watching the construction workers and firefighters do their job, she realized that

> those tired men and women passing in trucks make it all happen. They are the ones who do the actual work of running the country. They cause the electricity to flow, the schools to be built, the criminals to be arrested and society to run seamlessly. She realized, with a blazingly bright lightbulb of awareness flashing in her mind, she didn't know how to change a tire, grow tomatoes, or where electricity comes from.

This deracinated white-collar worker cast her mind back over her "power lunches" and other pretentious doings and suddenly understood that "she had no real skills." No lightbulb flashes to remind her that the rescue and construction workers were *also* from a blue state and probably voted for Gore. Instead, we are told, she has become a humbler person, a red-stater in attitude if not in place of residence. The tale then ends with an exhortation to get out there and vote.

Blake Hurst, the Missouri farmer who is so proud of being humble, also chimes in on this theme, pointing out in *The American Enterprise* that "the work we [red-staters] do can be measured in bushels, pounds, shingles nailed, and bricks laid, rather than in the fussy judgments that make up office employee reviews." But there's something fishy about Hurst's claim to the mantle of workerist righteousness, something beyond the immediate fishiness of a magazine ordinarily given to assailing unions and saluting the Dow now printing such a fervent celebration of blue-collar life. Just being familiar with the physical world shouldn't automatically make you a member of the beaten-down producer class any more than does living in a state that voted for George W. Bush. Indeed, elsewhere Hurst describes himself not as a simple farmer but as the co-owner of a family business overseeing the labors of a number of employees, employees to whom, he confides, he and his family "don't pay high wages." Hurst has even written an essay on that timeless lament of the boss, the unbelievable laziness of workers today.[15] This man may live in the sticks, but he is about as much a blue-collar toiler as is Al Gore himself.

---

type. As Barbara Ehrenreich points out in chap. 3 of *Fear of Falling: The Inner Life of the Middle Class* (New York: HarperCollins, 1990), the same thing happened at the tail end of the sixties, the decade that introduced so many of the business-revolutionary fantasies that came to flower in the New Economy nineties.

[15]See Blake Hurst, "In Real Life," *The American Enterprise*, November–December 1999.

Perhaps that is why Hurst is so certain that, while there is obviously a   *31*
work-related divide between the two Americas — separating them into
Hurst's humble, producer America and the liberals' conceited, parasite
America — it isn't the scary divide that Dos Passos wrote about, the sort of
divide between workers and bosses that might cause problems for readers
of *The American Enterprise.* "Class-consciousness isn't a problem in Red
America," he assures them; people are "perfectly happy to be slightly overweight [and] a little underpaid."

David Brooks goes even further, concluding from his fieldwork in Red   *32*
America that the standard notion of class is flawed. Thinking about class in
terms of a hierarchy, where some people occupy more exalted positions than
others, he writes, is "Marxist" and presumably illegitimate. The correct
model, he suggests, is a high school cafeteria, segmented into self-chosen
taste clusters like "nerds, jocks, punks, bikers, techies, druggies, God Squad-
ders," and so on. "The jocks knew there would always be nerds, and the
nerds knew there would always be jocks," he writes. "That's just the way life
is." We choose where we want to sit and whom we want to mimic and what
class we want to belong to the same way we choose hairstyles or TV shows
or extracurricular activities. We're all free agents in this noncoercive class
system, and Brooks eventually concludes that worrying about the problems
faced by workers is yet another deluded affectation of the blue-state rich.[16]

As a description of the way society works, this is preposterous. Even   *33*
by high school, most of us know that we won't be able to choose our station in life the way we choose a soda pop or even the way we choose our
friends. But as a clue into the deepest predilections of the backlash mind,
Brooks's scheme is a revelation.[17]

What divides Americans is *authenticity,* not something hard and ugly   *34*
like economics. While liberals commit endless acts of hubris, sucking down
lattes, driving ostentatious European cars, and trying to reform the world,
the humble people of the red states go about their unpretentious business,
eating down-home foods, vacationing in the Ozarks, whistling while they

---

[16]Brooks's inventive explanation for the red-staters' complete comfort with free-
market capitalism is that they don't know need or envy. "Where they live," he writes,
"they can afford just about anything that is for sale." On the other hand, blue-state
people are reminded constantly that there are people higher than they on the social lad-
der, simply because of the spatial dynamics of the city. Evidently, there are no other
grounds for disgruntlement at all, which leads to the clear conclusion that no one would
ever complain about free-market capitalism — that many of the revolutions and wars
and social welfare schemes of the last century could have been avoided — if only the
rich would hide themselves better.

[17]Indeed, Brooks himself seems undecided as to whether the cafeteria metaphor
describes reality or describes conservative ideas about reality. In his 2001 red/blue story
in the *Atlantic Monthly,* which is quoted here, the cafeteria metaphor is presented as an
objective observation about American life. This cafeteria business is just the way life is.
Brooks repeats the argument on the *New York Times* op-ed page on January 12, 2003,
only now as something that "most Americans" agree with and understand instinctively.

work, feeling comfortable about who they are, and knowing they are secure under the watch of George W. Bush, a man they love as one of their own.

■ ■ ■

Reading Rhetorically

1. We claim in the headnote to this reading that Frank is an "equal-opportunity critic, taking both conservatives and liberals to task." Do you agree? Point to specific words and phrases in this reading where he critiques those on the left and those on the right. Where do his own political leanings come through? What effect might Frank's own politics have on the way he casts his argument? What is his central argument in this reading?

2. Who is Frank's audience? Given the language and examples he uses, what assumptions does he make about his readers? Point to specific phrases to help you explain your points.

3. Where and why does Frank offer historical background information? How does this information help him make his larger point?

Inquiring Further

4. Brainstorm with your peers about the stereotypes associated with red states and blue states. Where do these stereotypes come from? How accurate do you think they are? Be sure to offer evidence for your claims.

5. Working in pairs or small groups, interview two political science professors on your campus about the voting patterns in your state and local area. Be prepared to paraphrase some of Frank's points about the demographics of Republican and Democratic voters, and ask the professors for their analysis of Frank's ideas. Then, in class, discuss the responses you receive.

6. What have other political analysts said about the concept of two nations (divided by economic class, culture, etc.)? Using your library's electronic resources, look up the arguments about two nations or two Americas made by some of the people Frank mentions — David Brooks, Michael Barone, John Edwards — and those he does not. (Internet searches of "two Americas" or "two nations" yield many hits.) Share with your classmates the range of perspectives you find.

Framing Conversations

7. What does it mean to be one nation or two? Place Frank's ideas in conversation with Jonathan Kozol's (p. 308) or Héctor Tobar's (p. 533) in an essay in which you explore the meaning of America as one nation. What do "we" share as a nation of differences? Given what you have read in these texts, what do you think ultimately unites and/or divides "us"?

8. Frank's analysis of red and blue states includes impressions about economic class divisions and the belief systems that often go along with those class divisions. Drawing on the ideas about economic class in this text and in Barbara Ehrenreich's text (p. 479), write an essay in which you consider the role economic class plays in the ways Americans see themselves.

9. Many of the ideas Frank explores about red and blue states contain assumptions about gender roles. Write an essay in which you use strategies of analyzing gender from Judith Lorber's (p. 617) and Deborah Tannen's (p. 654) texts to examine the role gender plays in the political dynamics Frank describes. What significance do you see in your findings?

NOEL IGNATIEV

Immigrants and Whites

Noel Ignatiev worked for twenty years in factories and mills before pursuing a PhD in history. He has taught at Harvard University and the Massachusetts College of Art, and is best known for writing about whiteness as a concept. Until fairly recently, those who studied race focused on people of color; but Ignatiev is part of a widening group of intellectuals working in the new field of whiteness studies, scholars who argue that whiteness is just as much an invention of historical circumstance as any other category of race.

The title of his book, *How the Irish Became White* (1995), reveals a great deal about Ignatiev's belief that race changes with historical and cultural beliefs, that it is not fixed in our biology. The story of the Irish in the United States, after all, is one of persecution and prejudice: The Irish were seen as second-class citizens through much of the nineteenth century. The "Irish Need Not Apply" signs that hung in workplaces were an example of the blatant prejudice the Irish faced because they did not count as white within the cultural hierarchy of the time. As waves of newer immigrants swelled the population of the United States in the late 1800s, however, the Irish gradually were accepted as white — though their skin color certainly had not changed. This example is one of many Ignatiev cites to help readers understand how much of our concept of race is both social and cultural, which means it can be reimagined, in the process making America a truly democratic nation.

Ignatiev also has made his scholarly mark with the journal *Race Traitor*, which he edits with John Garvey. The journal's first issue, in 1992, carried the slogan "Treason to whiteness is loyalty to humanity." This provocative statement is sometimes interpreted by critics as racist in its own way, but Ignatiev argues that he is urging readers to think beyond race. He asks us to question our notion that race is biological and to recognize that racial categories are constructed by culture, mostly to uphold inequities and perceived differences. The fact that our ideas about race change over time is proof, he suggests, of his claim.

The reading reprinted here first appeared in *Race Traitor* in 1996. Pay particular attention to the opening paragraphs, in which Ignatiev lays the groundwork for his argument in historical anecdotes and in theories about race as a category. Ignatiev includes many voices from the past to illustrate how Americans' thinking about race in the context of U.S. immigration has changed. Which examples most catch your eye as a reader, and why? Consider your own family history as you read. Have racial categories defined your ancestors and yourself? In what ways? With what effects?

Ignatiev draws on the research of other scholars to help make his point, as you can see in his in-text citations and his footnotes. In addition to the research on race in the United States, however, Ignatiev also uses fiction to demonstrate his argument. Notice, for example, his references to Mark Twain's *Pudd'nhead Wilson* (para. 7) and the excerpt from Flannery O'Connor's short story "The Displaced Person" (para. 8). What effect do these references to fiction have in an essay about a politically charged topic? What kinds of truth can fiction tell us?

You might find it interesting to look up the racial breakdown in the most recent U.S. census and keep those statistics in mind as you consider the implications of Ignatiev's argument. Why do we count people by race at all? What do racial categories tell us — and what don't they tell us — about what it means to be American? Through his writing, Ignatiev hopes to raise questions that readers will respond to personally, politically, and with the curiosity of scholars.

A t the turn of the century an investigator into conditions in the steel *1* industry, seeking employment on a blast furnace, was informed that "only Hunkies[1] work on those jobs, they're too damn dirty and too damn hot for a 'white' man." Around the same time, a West Coast construction boss was asked, "You don't call an Italian a white man?" "No, sir," came the reply, "an Italian is a dago." Odd though this usage may seem today, it was at one time fairly common. According to one historian, "in all sections native-born and northern European laborers called themselves 'white men' to distinguish themselves from the southern Europeans they worked beside."[2] I have even heard of a time when it was said in the Pacific Northwest logging industry that no whites worked in these woods, just a bunch of Swedes.

Eventually, as we know, Europeans of all national origins were *2* accepted as "whites"; only rarely and in certain parts of the country is it any longer possible to hear the Jew or the Italian referred to as not white. The outcome is usually hailed as a mighty accomplishment of democratic assimilation. In this essay, I shall argue two points: first, that the racial status of the immigrants, far from being the natural outcome of a spontaneous process, grew out of choices made by the immigrants themselves and those receiving them; second, that it was in fact deeply tragic, because to the extent the immigrants became "white" they abandoned the possibility of becoming fully American. Finally, I shall speculate a bit on the future.

The general practice in the social sciences is to view race as a natural *3* category. A representative example of this approach is the book by Richard

[1]"Hunkies" is a pejorative term for Bohemian laborers, derived from the slang "Bohunk." [Editors' note]

[2]David Brody, *Steelworkers in America: The Non-Union Era* (New York, 1969), 120; John Higham, *Strangers in the Land: Patterns of American Nativism 1860–1925* (New York, 1963), 66, 173.

Sennett and Jonathan Cobb, *The Hidden Injuries of Class* (New York, 1973). The authors declare the subject of their study to be the "white working class." As well-trained sociologists, they are careful to specify what they mean by "working class," but they do not find it necessary to define "white." *Of course everybody knows* what is "white." However, for some, including this writer, the inquiry becomes most necessary just at the point Sennett and Cobb take for granted.

It is beyond the scope of this essay to review the work showing the origins in the seventeenth century of "white" as a social category. The term came into common usage only in the latter part of the century, that is, after people from Africa and people from Europe had been living together for seven decades on the North American mainland.

In an April 1984 essay in *Essence*, "On Being 'White' . . . And Other Lies," James Baldwin wrote that "No one was white before he/she came to America." Once here, Europeans became white "by deciding they were white. . . . White men — from Norway, for example, where they were Norwegians — became white: by slaughtering the cattle, poisoning the wells, torching the houses, massacring Native Americans, raping Black women."

Now it is some time since settlers from Norway have slaughtered any cattle, poisoned any wells, or massacred any Indians, and few Americans of any ethnic background take a direct hand in the denial of equality to people of color; yet the white race still exists as a social category. If it is not an inherited curse, whiteness must be reproduced in each generation. Although Sennett and Cobb treat it as a natural classification, they recount a story that reveals some of how it is re-created. One of the characters in their book is a man they call Ricca Kartides, who came to America from Greece, worked as a building janitor, and, after a few years, "*bought property in a nearby suburb of Boston*" (emphasis added).

What social forces, what history framed the fearful symmetry of Mr. Kartides's choice of location? Was that the turning point in his metamorphosis from a Greek immigrant into a white man? What alternative paths were open to him? How would his life, and his children's lives, have been different had he pursued them? There is a great deal of history subsumed (and lost) in the casual use of the term "white." Even in the narrowest terms, "white" is not a self-evident category. Barbara J. Fields recounts the apocryphal story of an American journalist who once asked Papa Doc Duvalier what portion of the Haitian people was white. Duvalier answered unhesitatingly, "Ninety-eight percent." The puzzled reporter asked Duvalier how he defined white. "How do you define black in your country?" asked Duvalier in turn. When the answer came back that in the U.S. anyone with any discernible African ancestry was considered black, Duvalier replied, "Well, that's the way we define white in my country."[3] Along the same lines, every character in Mark Twain's novel *Pudd'nhead Wilson*, black and white, is of predominantly European descent.

---

[3]"Ideology and Race in American History," in J. Morgan Kousser and James M. McPherson, *Region, Race and Reconstruction* (New York, 1982).

If whiteness is a historical product, then it must be transmitted. Like all knowledge, white consciousness does not come easily. In one case in a small town in Louisiana at the beginning of the [twentieth] century, five Sicilian storekeepers were lynched for violating the white man's code: they had dealt mainly with black people and associated with them on equal terms.[4] In her short story "The Displaced Person," Flannery O'Connor describes how the immigrant is taught to be white. The story takes place shortly after World War II. A Polish immigrant comes to labor on a small southern farm. Among the other laborers are two black men. After he has been on the farm for a while, the Pole arranges to pay a fee to one of the black men to marry his cousin, who is in a DP camp in Europe, in order for her to gain residence in the U.S. When the farm owner, a traditional southern white lady, learns of the deal, she is horrified and undertakes to explain to the Pole the facts of life in America.

> "Mr. Guizac," she said, beginning slowly and then speaking faster until she ended breathless in the middle of a word, "that nigger cannot have a white wife from Europe. You can't talk to a nigger that way. You'll excite him and besides it can't be done. Maybe it can be done in Poland but it can't be done here . . ."
>
> "She no care black," he said. "She in camp three year."
>
> Mrs. McIntyre felt a peculiar weakness behind her knees. "Mr. Guizac," she said, "I don't want to have to speak to you about this again. If I do, you'll have to find another place yourself. Do you understand?"

The story ends tragically as a consequence of the Pole's failure to learn what is expected of him in America.

In what relation, then, does whiteness stand to Americanism? If adoption by the immigrant of prevailing racial attitudes is the key to adjusting successfully to the new country, does it then follow that to become white is to become American? The opposite is closer to the truth: for immigrants from Europe (and elsewhere, to the extent they have a choice), the adoption of a white identity is the most serious barrier to becoming fully American. (From a *political* standpoint the degree of cultural assimilation is largely irrelevant. The two least culturally assimilated groups in the country are the Amish of Lancaster County — the so-called Pennsylvania Dutch — and the Hasidic Jews; yet both enjoy all the rights of whites.)

Like Cuba, like Brazil, like other places in the New World in which slavery was important historically, the United States is an Afro-American country. In the first place, persons of African descent constituted a large portion of the population throughout the formative period (how large no one can say, but probably around one-fifth for most of the first two centuries). Second, people from Africa have been here longer than most of the immigrant groups, longer in fact than all groups except for the Indians, the "Spanish" of the Southwest (themselves a mixture of Spaniards, Africans, and Indians), and the descendants of early English settlers (who

[4]Higham, *Patterns*, 169.

by now also include an African strain). Above all, the experience of people from Africa in the New World represents the distillation of the American experience, and this concentration of history finds its expression in the psychology, culture, and national character of the American people.

What is the distinctive element of the American experience? It is the   *11* shock of being torn from a familiar place and hurled into a new environment, compelled to develop a way of life and culture from the materials at hand. And who more embodies that experience, is more the essential product of that experience, than the descendants of the people from Africa who visited these shores together with the first European explorers (and perhaps earlier, as recent researches have suggested), and whose first settlers were landed here a year before the Mayflower?

In *The Omni-Americans* (New York, 1970), Albert Murray discusses   *12* the American national character. He draws upon Constance Rourke, who saw the American as a composite, part Yankee, part backwoodsman (himself an adaptation of the Indian), and part Negro. "Something in the nature of each," wrote Rourke,

> induced an irresistible response. Each had been a wanderer over the lands, the Negro a forced and unwilling wanderer. Each in a fashion of his own had broken bonds, the Yankee in the initial revolt against the parent civilization, the backwoodsman in revolt against all civilization, the Negro in a revolt which was cryptic and submerged but which nonetheless made a perceptible outline.[5]

"It is all too true," writes Murray, "that Negroes unlike the Yankee and   *13* the backwoodsman were slaves. . . . But it is also true — and as things have turned out even more significant — that they were slaves who *were living in the presence of more human freedom and individual opportunity than they or anybody else had ever seen before.*" Later he writes:

> The slaves who absconded to fight for the British during the Revolutionary War were no less inspired by *American* ideas than those who fought for the colonies: the liberation that the white people wanted from the British the black people wanted from white people. As for the tactics of the fugitive slaves, the Underground Railroad was not only an innovation, it was also an extension of the American quest for democracy brought to its highest level of epic heroism.

American culture, he argues, is *"incontestably mulatto."*

> After all, such is the process by which Americans are made that immigrants, for instance, need trace their roots no further back in either time or space than Ellis Island. *By the very act of arrival*, they emerge from the bottomless depths and enter the same stream of American tradition as those who landed

---

[5]*American Humor: A Study of National Character* (New York, 1931), 98.

at Plymouth. In the very act of making their way through customs, they begin the process of becoming, as Constance Rourke would put it, part Yankee, part backwoodsman and Indian — and part Negro!

It is very generous of Murray, as a descendant of old American stock, to welcome the newcomers so unreservedly. But what if their discovery, as he puts it, of the "social, political, and economic value in white skin" leads them to "become color-poisoned bigots"?

Their development into Americans is arrested. Like certain insects 14 that, under unfavorable conditions, do not complete their metamorphosis and remain indefinitely at the larval stage, they halt their growth at whiteness.

John Langston Gwaltney wrote, in *Drylongso: A Self-Portrait of Black* 15 *America* (New York, 1980), "The notion that black culture is some kind of backwater or tributary of an American 'mainstream' is well established in much popular as well as standard social science literature. To the prudent black American masses, however, core black culture *is* the mainstream." At issue is not, as many would have it, the degree to which black people have or have not been assimilated into the mainstream of American culture. Black people have never shown any reluctance to borrow from others when they thought it to their advantage. They adopted the English language — and transformed it. They adopted the Christian religion — and transformed it. They adopted the twelve-tone musical scale — and did things with it that Bach never dreamed of. In recent years they have adopted the game of basketball — and placed their own distinctive stamp on the style of play. And they have adopted spaghetti, okra, refried beans, noodle pudding, liver dumplings, and corned beef, and modified them and made them a part of ordinary "drylongso" cuisine.

It is not black people who have been prevented from drawing upon the 16 full variety of experience that has gone into making up America. Rather, it is those who, in maddened pursuit of the white whale, have cut themselves off from human society, on sea and on land, and locked themselves in a "masoned walled-town of exclusiveness."

All this is not to deny that whites in America have borrowed from 17 black people. But they have done so shamefacedly, unwilling to acknowledge the sources of their appropriations, and the result has generally been inferior. The outstanding example of this process was Elvis Presley, who was anticipated by Sam Phillips's remark, "If I can find a white man who sings like a Negro, I'll make a million dollars." Other examples are Colonel Sanders's chicken and Bo Derek's braids. There are exceptions: Peggy Lee comes immediately to mind.

Can the stone be rolled back? If race, like class, is "something which in 18 fact happens (and can be shown to have happened) in human relationships" — to borrow the words of E. P. Thompson — then can it be made to unhappen? Can the white race be dissolved? Can "white" people cease to be?

I cite here two details which point to the possibility of the sort of mass   *19*
shifts in popular consciousness that would be necessary to dissolve the
white race. The first is the sudden and near-unanimous shift by Afro-
Americans in the 1960s from the self-designation "Negro" to "black" or
"Black." (Among prominent holdouts are Ralph Ellison and the Negro
Ensemble Company.) The shift involved more than a preference for one
term over another; although its precise implications were and still are
unclear, and although much of its substance has disappeared or been
reduced to mere symbol, there seems little doubt that the initial impulse
for the change was a new view among black people of their relation to official society. "Black" stood in opposition to "white."

The second detail I cite is an apparently trivial incident I happened to   *20*
witness. At Inland Steel Company's Indiana Harbor Works in East
Chicago, there used to be a shuttle-bus system that operated at shift-
change time, picking up workers at the main gate and delivering them to
the various mills within the plant, as much as a mile away. One morning,
as the bus began to pull away from the gate, I saw, from my passenger's
seat, a man running to catch it. He was in his early twenties, apparently
white, and was dressed in the regulation steelworker's garb — steel-toed
shoes, fire-resistant green jacket and pants, hard hat — underneath which
could be seen shoulder-length hair, in the fashion of the time, the early
1970s. The driver pulled away and, as he did so, said over his shoulder, "I
would have stopped for him if he'd had short hair."

That small incident brought home to me with great force some of the   *21*
meaning of the revolution in style that swept so-called white youth in
those years. At the time, many young people were breaking with the values
that had guided their parents. In areas as seemingly unrelated as clothing
and hair styles, musical tastes, attitudes toward a war, norms of sexual
conduct, use of drugs, and feelings about racial prejudice, young people
were creating a special community, which became known as the counterculture. In particular, long hair for males became the visible token of their
identification with it. It was a badge of membership in a brotherhood cast
out from official society — *exactly the function of color for Afro-Americans.*
As that incident with the bus driver reveals, and as anyone who lived
through those years can testify, it was perceived that way by participants
and onlookers alike.

Granted that only a minority of eligible youth ever identified fully with   *22*
the counterculture, that the commitment of most participants to it was not
very deep, that few in it were aware of all its implications, that the whole
movement did not last very long, and that its symbols were quickly taken
up and marketed by official society — nevertheless, it contained the elements of a mass break with the conformity that preserves the white race.

Normally the discussion of immigrant assimilation is framed by   *23*
efforts to estimate how much of the immigrants' traditional culture they
lose in becoming American. Far more significant, however, than the choice

between the old and the new is the choice between two identities which are both new to them: white and American.

NOTE

This article, written in the spring of 1987, appeared in *Konch*, Vol. 1, No. 1 (Winter 1990) in a slightly different version, under the title "'Whiteness' and American Character."

■ ■ ■

Reading Rhetorically

1. Locate and mark sentences throughout Ignatiev's text where he signposts, telling us what he's doing in the essay and why. How do the signposts help you understand his larger point in the essay?

2. How does Ignatiev use questions to develop his essay? Find and underline the questions he asks, and discuss the effect of his posing his ideas as questions. How would these moments in the essay be different without the questions? What conclusions can you draw about how questions can be used to develop an argument?

3. Explain the relationship between the final two examples (in paragraphs 19 and 20) and Ignatiev's larger point.

Inquiring Further

4. Other scholars also have explored whiteness as a complex category of inquiry. Using your library's resources, locate and skim three other articles on whiteness, taking notes so you can share your findings. Discuss the relationship you see between Ignatiev's ideas and the ideas in the three articles. What is the most interesting new idea you have learned?

5. What information can you find on the shift in popular use from the term *Negro* to the term *black*? (You might begin your search at http://www.encyclopedia.com/, and then follow up on ideas and texts mentioned there.) How do the ideas you read about connect with the points Ignatiev makes?

6. What do you already know about the treatment of the Irish in nineteenth-century America? Read about Ignatiev's book *How the Irish Became White*. (You might begin with online book reviews.) Then discuss as a class how the Irish experience of shifting racial categories sheds light on "Immigrants and Whites."

Framing Conversations

7. Ignatiev and Peggy McIntosh (p. 520) both explore aspects of whiteness. How do their ideas work in conversation with one another? Use your analysis of these authors' examples and ideas in an essay in which you consider the significance of the whiteness category.

8. What is at stake in the practice of assimilation in American culture? Write an essay in which you use points from both Ignatiev and Héctor Tobar (p. 533) to explore what is lost and gained in the act of assimilation. Include your analysis of two or three of each author's examples, drawing on examples of your own to analyze as well if you like.

9. How does the concept of transculturation as explained by Mary Louise Pratt (p. 354) help you analyze the dynamics of immigration and assimilation in the examples Ignatiev includes in his text? Write an essay in which you use transculturation as a lens through which to analyze Ignatiev's examples. Do Ignatiev's examples reveal weaknesses in Pratt's explanation of transculturation? Explain your answer. What conclusions can you draw?

PEGGY McINTOSH

White Privilege and Male Privilege: A Personal Account of Coming to See Correspondences Through Work in Women's Studies

Peggy McIntosh is associate director of the Wellesley Centers for Women on the campus of Wellesley College. She is also the founder and codirector of the National SEED Project on Inclusive Curriculum. (SEED stands for Seeking Educational Equity and Diversity.) She taught at Harvard University, Trinity College in Washington, D.C., and the University of Durham in England before taking on her position as a senior research scientist and administrator at Wellesley. McIntosh has written extensively on multicultural and gender-equitable curricula and is a sought-after lecturer on these topics. The ideas in this very influential essay are drawn from conference presentations in 1986 and 1987, and were published as a working paper in 1988 and reprinted in the Winter 1990 issue of *Independent School*.

When McIntosh initially spoke out about white privilege, she was among the first scholars to examine whiteness as a racial category. Along with writers like Noel Ignatiev (p. 512), McIntosh came to see that race in the United States had come to mean skin color, that European Americans had become an "invisible norm" against which other racial groups often were measured. In this article, McIntosh traces her own shift from simply seeing nonwhites as disadvantaged to seeing her own whiteness as an unearned privilege. As she describes early in the essay, it was not until she analyzed her frustration with male colleagues who failed to see themselves as unfairly advantaged that she made the connection about "interlocking" hierarchies in U.S. society:

> I think whites are carefully taught not to recognize white privilege,
> as males are taught not to recognize male privilege. So I have begun
> in an untutored way to ask what it is like to have white privilege. . . .

> I have come to see white privilege as an invisible package of unearned assets that I can count on cashing in each day, but about which I was "meant" to remain oblivious. White privilege is like an invisible weightless knapsack of special provisions, assurances, tools, maps, guides, codebooks, passports, visas, clothes, compass, emergency gear, and blank checks. (paras. 3–4)

One of McIntosh's key contributions to the discussion of race in the United States is this insight that whether or not whites want to see themselves as having "an unearned entitlement" (para. 22), they partake in a long list of social advantages stemming from the concept that "whites are taught to think of their lives as morally neutral, normative, and average, and also ideal, so that when we work to benefit others, this is seen as work that will allow 'them' to be more like 'us'" (para. 10). Her aim is not to make readers feel guilty; instead, she urges readers to become aware of their unearned privileges and ask, "Having described it, what will I do to lessen or end it?" (para. 7).

McIntosh claims that this piece is "a partial record of my personal observations and not a scholarly analysis" (para. 3); but this is academic writing. McIntosh places her insights into the context of other writers' ideas, citing some sources in the footnotes and describing others that have influenced her (for example, see paragraph 13). Perhaps the most striking feature of this essay, rare in scholarly writing, is the long personal list in the middle of the piece in which she details the unearned advantages she experiences in her daily life. A common assignment is to have students develop their own version of this list. (You will find just such an invitation in the questions following the reading.) This strategy of connecting everyday experiences — no matter how ordinary — to larger systems of power enables readers to see with new eyes the advantages that can come from social class, nationality, educational status, gender, sexuality, nationality, or able-bodied status. In other words, McIntosh's approach is one we might all use to analyze different aspects of our daily lives.

In her final paragraph, McIntosh leaves readers with a provocative question: "What will we do with such knowledge?" In this piece, McIntosh takes risks, revealing her previous ignorance and her slow learning process; in so doing, she invites readers to take similar risks and to begin learning too.

Through work to bring materials and perspectives from Women's Studies into the rest of the curriculum, I have often noticed men's unwillingness to grant that they are overprivileged in the curriculum, even though they may grant that women are disadvantaged. Denials that amount to taboos surround the subject of advantages that men gain from women's disadvantages. These denials protect male privilege from being fully recognized, acknowledged, lessened, or ended.

Thinking through unacknowledged male privilege as a phenomenon 2
with a life of its own, I realized that since hierarchies in our society are
interlocking, there was most likely a phenomenon of white privilege that
was similarly denied and protected, but alive and real in its effects. As a
white person, I realized I had been taught about racism as something that
puts others at a disadvantage, but had been taught not to see one of its
corollary aspects, white privilege, which puts me at an advantage.

I think whites are carefully taught not to recognize white privilege, as 3
males are taught not to recognize male privilege. So I have begun in an
untutored way to ask what it is like to have white privilege. This paper is a
partial record of my personal observations and not a scholarly analysis. It
is based on my daily experiences within my particular circumstances.

I have come to see white privilege as an invisible package of unearned 4
assets that I can count on cashing in each day, but about which I was
"meant" to remain oblivious. White privilege is like an invisible weightless
knapsack of special provisions, assurances, tools, maps, guides, codebooks, passports, visas, clothes, compass, emergency gear, and blank
checks.

Since I have had trouble facing white privilege, and describing its 5
results in my life, I saw parallels here with men's reluctance to acknowledge male privilege. Only rarely will a man go beyond acknowledging that
women are disadvantaged to acknowledging that men have unearned
advantage, or that unearned privilege has not been good for men's development as human beings, or for society's development, or that privilege
systems might ever be challenged and *changed*.

I will review here several types or layers of denial that I see at work 6
protecting, and preventing awareness about, entrenched male privilege.
Then I will draw parallels, from my own experience, with the denials that
veil the facts of white privilege. Finally, I will list forty-six ordinary and
daily ways in which I experience having white privilege, by contrast with
my African American colleagues in the same building. This list is not
intended to be generalizable. Others can make their own lists from within
their own life circumstances.

Writing this paper has been difficult, despite warm receptions for the 7
talks on which it is based.[1] For describing white privilege makes one newly
accountable. As we in Women's Studies work reveal male privilege and ask
men to give up some of their power, so one who writes about having white
privilege must ask, "Having described it, what will I do to lessen or end it?"

The denial of men's overprivileged state takes many forms in discus- 8
sions of curriculum change work. Some claim that men must be central
in the curriculum because they have done most of what is important or

---

[1]This paper was presented at the Virginia Women's Studies Association conference in
Richmond in April, 1986, and the American Educational Research Association conference
in Boston in October, 1986, and discussed with two groups of participants in the Dodge
seminars for Secondary School Teachers in New York and Boston in the spring of 1987.

distinctive in life or in civilization. Some recognize sexism in the curriculum but deny that it makes male students seem unduly important in life. Others agree that certain *individual* thinkers are male oriented but deny that there is any *systemic* tendency in disciplinary frameworks or epistemology to overempower men as a group. Those men who do grant that male privilege takes institutionalized and embedded forms are still likely to deny that male hegemony has opened doors for them personally. Virtually all men deny that male overreward alone can explain men's centrality in all the inner sanctums of our most powerful institutions. Moreover, those few who will acknowledge that male privilege systems have overempowered them usually end up doubting that we could dismantle these privilege systems. They may say they will work to improve women's status, in the society or in the university, but they can't or won't support the idea of lessening men's. In curricular terms, this is the point at which they say that they regret they cannot use any of the interesting new scholarship on women because the syllabus is full. When the talk turns to giving men less cultural room, even the most thoughtful and fair-minded of the men I know will tend to reflect, or fall back on, conservative assumptions about the inevitability of present gender relations and distributions of power, calling on precedent or sociobiology and psychobiology to demonstrate that male domination is natural and follows inevitably from evolutionary pressures. Others resort to arguments from "experience" or religion or social responsibility or wishing and dreaming.

After I realized, through faculty development work in Women's Studies, the extent to which men work from a base of unacknowledged privilege, I understood that much of their oppressiveness was unconscious. Then I remembered the frequent charges from women of color that white women whom they encounter are oppressive. I began to understand why we are justly seen as oppressive, even when we don't see ourselves that way. At the very least, obliviousness of one's privileged state can make a person or group irritating to be with. I began to count the ways in which I enjoy unearned skin privilege and have been conditioned into oblivion about its existence, unable to see that it put me "ahead" in any way, or put my people ahead, overrewarding us and yet also paradoxically damaging us, or that it could or should be changed. 9

My schooling gave me no training in seeing myself as an oppressor, as an unfairly advantaged person, or as a participant in a damaged culture. I was taught to see myself as an individual whose moral state depended on her individual moral will. At school, we are not taught about slavery in any depth; we are not taught to see slaveholders as damaged people. Slaves were seen as the only group at risk of being dehumanized. My schooling followed the pattern which Elizabeth Minnich has pointed out: Whites are taught to think of their lives as morally neutral, normative, and average, and also ideal, so that when we work to benefit others, this is seen as work that will allow "them" to be more like "us." I think many of us know how obnoxious this attitude can be in men. 10

After frustration with men who would not recognize male privilege, *11* I decided to try to work on myself at least by identifying some of the daily effects of white privilege in my life. It is crude work, at this stage, but I will give here a list of special circumstances and conditions I experience that I did not earn but that I have been made to feel are mine by birth, by citizenship, and by virtue of being a conscientious law-abiding "normal" person of goodwill. I have chosen those conditions that I think in my case *attach somewhat more to skin-color privilege* than to class, religion, ethnic status, or geographical location, though these other privileging factors are intricately intertwined. As far as I can see, my Afro-American co-workers, friends, and acquaintances with whom I come into daily or frequent contact in this particular time, place, and line of work cannot count on most of these conditions.

1. I can, if I wish, arrange to be in the company of people of my race most of the time.

2. I can avoid spending time with people whom I was trained to mistrust and who have learned to mistrust my kind or me.

3. If I should need to move, I can be pretty sure of renting or purchasing housing in an area which I can afford and in which I would want to live.

4. I can be reasonably sure that my neighbors in such a location will be neutral or pleasant to me.

5. I can go shopping alone most of the time, fairly well assured that I will not be followed or harassed by store detectives.

6. I can turn on the television or open to the front page of the paper and see people of my race widely and positively represented.

7. When I am told about our national heritage or about "civilization," I am shown that people of my color made it what it is.

8. I can be sure that my children will be given curricular materials that testify to the existence of their race.

9. If I want to, I can be pretty sure of finding a publisher for this piece on white privilege.

10. I can be fairly sure of having my voice heard in a group in which I am the only member of my race.

11. I can be casual about whether or not to listen to another woman's voice in a group in which she is the only member of her race.

12. I can go into a book shop and count on finding the writing of my race represented, into a supermarket and find the staple foods that fit with my cultural traditions, into a hairdresser's shop and find someone who can deal with my hair.

13. Whether I use checks, credit cards, or cash, I can count on my skin color not to work against the appearance that I am financially reliable.

14. I could arrange to protect our young children most of the time from people who might not like them.

15. I did not have to educate our children to be aware of systemic racism for their own daily physical protection.

16. I can be pretty sure that my children's teachers and employers will tolerate them if they fit school and workplace norms; my chief worries about them do not concern others' attitudes toward their race.

17. I can talk with my mouth full and not have people put this down to my color.

18. I can swear, or dress in secondhand clothes, or not answer letters, without having people attribute these choices to the bad morals, the poverty, or the illiteracy of my race.

19. I can speak in public to a powerful male group without putting my race on trial.

20. I can do well in a challenging situation without being called a credit to my race.

21. I am never asked to speak for all the people of my racial group.

22. I can remain oblivious to the language and customs of persons of color who constitute the world's majority without feeling in my culture any penalty for such oblivion.

23. I can criticize our government and talk about how much I fear its policies and behavior without being seen as a cultural outsider.

24. I can be reasonably sure that if I ask to talk to "the person in charge," I will be facing a person of my race.

25. If a traffic cop pulls me over or if the IRS audits my tax return, I can be sure I haven't been singled out because of my race.

26. I can easily buy posters, postcards, picture books, greeting cards, dolls, toys, and children's magazines featuring people of my race.

27. I can go home from most meetings of organizations I belong to feeling somewhat tied in, rather than isolated, out of place, outnumbered, unheard, held at a distance, or feared.

28. I can be pretty sure that an argument with a colleague of another race is more likely to jeopardize her chances for advancement than to jeopardize mine.

29. I can be fairly sure that if I argue for the promotion of a person of another race, or a program centering on race, this is not likely to cost me heavily within my present setting, even if my colleagues disagree with me.

30. If I declare there is a racial issue at hand, or there isn't a racial issue at hand, my race will lend me more credibility for either position than a person of color will have.

31. I can choose to ignore developments in minority writing and minority activist programs, or disparage them, or learn from them, but in any case, I can find ways to be more or less protected from negative consequences of any of these choices.

32. My culture gives me little fear about ignoring the perspectives and powers of people of other races.

33. I am not made acutely aware that my shape, bearing, or body odor will be taken as a reflection on my race.

34. I can worry about racism without being seen as self-interested or self-seeking.

35. I can take a job with an affirmative action employer without having my co-workers on the job suspect that I got it because of my race.

36. If my day, week, or year is going badly, I need not ask of each negative episode or situation whether it has racial overtones.

37. I can be pretty sure of finding people who would be willing to talk with me and advise me about my next steps, professionally.

38. I can think over many options, social, political, imaginative, or professional, without asking whether a person of my race would be accepted or allowed to do what I want to do.

39. I can be late to a meeting without having the lateness reflect on my race.

40. I can choose public accommodation without fearing that people of my race cannot get in or will be mistreated in the places I have chosen.

41. I can be sure that if I need legal or medical help, my race will not work against me.

42. I can arrange my activities so that I will never have to experience feelings of rejection owing to my race.

43. If I have low credibility as a leader, I can be sure that my race is not the problem.

44. I can easily find academic courses and institutions that give attention only to people of my race.

45. I can expect figurative language and imagery in all of the arts to testify to experiences of my race.

46. I can choose blemish cover or bandages in "flesh" color and have them more or less match my skin.

I repeatedly forgot each of the realizations on this list until I wrote it down. For me, white privilege has turned out to be an elusive and fugitive subject. The pressure to avoid it is great, for in facing it I must give up the myth of meritocracy. If these things are true, this is not such a free country; one's life is not what one makes it; many doors open for certain people through no virtues of their own. These perceptions mean also that my moral condition is not what I had been led to believe. The appearance of being a good citizen rather than a troublemaker comes in large part from having all sorts of doors open automatically because of my color.

A further paralysis of nerve comes from literary silence protecting privilege. My clearest memories of finding such analysis are in Lillian Smith's unparalleled *Killers of the Dream* and Margaret Andersen's review of Karen and Mamie Fields's *Lemon Swamp*. Smith, for example, wrote about walking toward black children on the street and knowing they would step into the gutter; Andersen contrasted the pleasure that she, as a white child, took on summer driving trips to the south with Karen Fields's memories of driving in a closed car stocked with all necessities lest, in stopping, her black family should suffer "insult, or worse." Adrienne Rich also recognizes and writes about daily experiences of privilege, but in my observation, white women's writing in this area is far more often on systemic racism than on our daily lives as light-skinned women.[2]

In unpacking this invisible knapsack of white privilege, I have listed conditions of daily experience that I once took for granted, as neutral, normal, and universally available to everybody, just as I once thought of a male-focused curriculum as the neutral or accurate account that can speak for all. Nor did I think of any of these perquisites as bad for the holder. I now think that we need a more finely differentiated taxonomy of privilege, for some of these varieties are only what one would want for everyone in a just society, and others give license to be ignorant, oblivious, arrogant, and destructive. Before proposing some more finely tuned categorization, I will make some observations about the general effects of these conditions on my life and expectations.

In this potpourri of examples, some privileges make me feel at home in the world. Others allow me to escape penalties or dangers that others suffer. Through some, I escape fear, anxiety, insult, injury, or a sense of not being welcome, not being real. Some keep me from having to hide, to be in disguise, to feel sick or crazy, to negotiate each transaction from the position of being an outsider or, within my group, a person who is suspected of having too close links with a dominant culture. Most keep me from having to be angry.

I see a pattern running through the matrix of white privilege, a pattern of assumptions that were passed on to me as a white person. There was one main piece of cultural turf; it was my own turf, and I was among those who could control the turf. I could measure up to the cultural standards and take advantage of the many options I saw around me to make what the culture would call a success of my life. *My skin color was an asset for any move I was educated to want to make.* I could think of myself as "belonging" in major ways and of making social systems work for me. I could

---

[2]Andersen, Margaret, "Race and the Social Science Curriculum: A Teaching and Learning Discussion." *Radical Teacher*, November, 1984, pp. 17–20. Smith, Lillian, *Killers of the Dream*, New York: W. W. Norton, 1949.

freely disparage, fear, neglect, or be oblivious to anything outside of the dominant cultural forms. Being of the main culture, I could also criticize it fairly freely. My life was reflected back to me frequently enough so that I felt, with regard to my race, if not to my sex, like one of the real people.

Whether through the curriculum or in the newspaper, the television, [17] the economic system, or the general look of people in the streets, I received daily signals and indications that my people counted and that others *either didn't exist or must be trying, not very successfully, to be like people of my race.* I was given cultural permission not to hear voices of people of other races or a tepid cultural tolerance for hearing or acting on such voices. I was also raised not to suffer seriously from anything that darker-skinned people might say about my group, "protected," though perhaps I should more accurately say *prohibited,* through the habits of my economic class and social group, from living in racially mixed groups or being reflective about interactions between people of differing races.

In proportion as my racial group was being made confident, comfort- [18] able, and oblivious, other groups were likely being made unconfident, uncomfortable, and alienated. Whiteness protected me from many kinds of hostility, distress, and violence, which I was being subtly trained to visit in turn upon people of color.

For this reason, the word "privilege" now seems to me misleading. Its [19] connotations are too positive to fit the conditions and behaviors which "privilege systems" produce. We usually think of privilege as being a favored state, whether earned, or conferred by birth or luck. School gradu-ates are reminded they are privileged and urged to use their (enviable) assets well. The word "privilege" carries the connotation of being some-thing everyone must want. Yet some of the conditions I have described here work to systematically overempower certain groups. Such privilege simply *confers dominance,* gives permission to control, because of one's race or sex. The kind of privilege that gives license to some people to be, at best, thoughtless and, at worst, murderous should not continue to be referred to as a desirable attribute. Such "privilege" may be widely desired without being in any way beneficial to the whole society.

Moreover, though "privilege" may confer power, it does not confer [20] moral strength. Those who do not depend on conferred dominance have traits and qualities that may never develop in those who do. Just as Women's Studies courses indicate that women survive their political circumstances to lead lives that hold the human race together, so "underprivileged" people of color who are the world's majority have survived their oppression and lived survivors' lives from which the white global minority can and must learn. In some groups, those dominated have actually become strong through *not* having all of these unearned advantages, and this gives them a great deal to teach the others. Members of so-called privileged groups can seem foolish, ridiculous, infantile, or dangerous by contrast.

I want, then, to distinguish between earned strength and unearned [21] power conferred systemically. Power from unearned privilege can look like strength when it is, in fact, permission to escape or to dominate. But not all of the privileges on my list are inevitably damaging. Some, like the expectation that neighbors will be decent to you, or that your race will not count against you in court, should be the norm in a just society and should be considered as the entitlement of everyone. Others, like the privilege not to listen to less powerful people, distort the humanity of the holders as well as the ignored groups. Still others, like finding one's staple foods everywhere, may be a function of being a member of a numerical majority in the population. Others have to do with not having to labor under pervasive negative stereotyping and mythology.

We might at least start by distinguishing between positive advantages that we can work to spread, to the point where they are not advantages at all but simply part of the normal civic and social fabric, and negative types of advantage that unless rejected will always reinforce our present hierarchies. For example, the positive "privilege" of belonging, the feeling that one belongs within the human circle, as Native Americans say, fosters development and should not be seen as privilege for a few. It is, let us say, an entitlement that none of us should have to earn; ideally it is an *unearned entitlement*. At present, since only a few have it, it is an *unearned advantage* for them. The negative "privilege" that gave me cultural permission not to take darker-skinned Others seriously can be seen as arbitrarily conferred dominance and should not be desirable for anyone. This paper results from a process of coming to see that some of the power that I originally saw as attendant on being a human being in the United States consisted in *unearned advantage* and *conferred dominance*, as well as other kinds of special circumstances not universally taken for granted. 22

In writing this paper I have also realized that white identity and status (as well as class identity and status) give me considerable power to choose whether to broach this subject and its trouble. I can pretty well decide whether to disappear and avoid and not listen and escape the dislike I may engender in other people through this essay, or interrupt, answer, interpret, preach, correct, criticize, and control to some extent what goes on in reaction to it. Being white, I am given considerable power to escape many kinds of danger or penalty as well as to choose which risks I want to take. 23

There is an analogy here, once again with Women's Studies. Our male colleagues do not have a great deal to lose in supporting Women's Studies, but they do not have a great deal to lose if they oppose it either. They simply have the power to decide whether to commit themselves to more equitable distributions of power. They will probably feel few penalties whatever choice they make; they do not seem, in any obvious short-term sense, the ones at risk, though they are, we are all at risk because of the behaviors that have been rewarded in them. 24

Through Women's Studies work I have met very few men who are truly distressed about systemic, unearned male advantage and conferred dominance. And so one question for me and others like me is whether we will be like them, or whether we will get truly distressed, even outraged, about 25 unearned race advantage and conferred dominance and if so, what we will do to lessen them. In any case, we need to do more work in identifying how they actually affect our daily lives. We need more down-to-earth writing by people about these taboo subjects. We need more understanding of the ways in which white "privilege" damages white people, for these are not the same ways in which it damages the victimized. Skewed white psyches are an inseparable part of the picture, though I do not want to confuse the kinds of damage done to the holders of special assets and to those who suffer the deficits. Many, perhaps most, of our white students in the United States think that racism doesn't affect them because they are not people of color; they do not see "whiteness" as a racial identity. Many men likewise think that Women's Studies does not bear on their own existences because they are not female; they do not see themselves as having gendered identities. Insisting on the universal "effects" of "privilege" systems, then, becomes one of our chief tasks, and being more explicit about the *particular* effects in particular contexts is another. Men need to join us in this work.

In addition, since race and sex are not the only advantaging systems at 26 work, we need to similarly examine the daily experience of having age advantage, or ethnic advantage, or physical ability, or advantage related to nationality, religion, or sexual orientation. Professor Marnie Evans suggested to me that in many ways the list I made also applies directly to heterosexual privilege. This is a still more taboo subject than race privilege: the daily ways in which heterosexual privilege makes some persons comfortable or powerful, providing supports, assets, approvals, and rewards to those who live or expect to live in heterosexual pairs. Unpacking that content is still more difficult, owing to the deeper imbeddedness of heterosexual advantage and dominance and stricter taboos surrounding these.

But to start such an analysis I would put this observation from my 27 own experience: The fact that I live under the same roof with a man triggers all kinds of societal assumptions about my worth, politics, life, and value and triggers a host of unearned advantages and powers. After recasting many elements from the original list I would add further observations like these:

1. My children do not have to answer questions about why I live with my partner (my husband).

2. I have no difficulty finding neighborhoods where people approve of our household.

3. Our children are given texts and classes that implicitly support our kind of family unit and do not turn them against my choice of domestic partnership.

4. I can travel alone or with my husband without expecting embarrassment or hostility in those who deal with us.

5. Most people I meet will see my marital arrangements as an asset to my life or as a favorable comment on my likability, my competence, or my mental health.

6. I can talk about the social events of a weekend without fearing most listeners' reactions.

7. I will feel welcomed and "normal" in the usual walks of public life, institutional and social.

8. In many contexts, I am seen as "all right" in daily work on women because I do not live chiefly with women.

Difficulties and dangers surrounding the tasks of finding parallels are 28 many. Since racism, sexism, and heterosexism are not the same, the advantages associated with them should not be seen as the same. In addition, it is hard to isolate aspects of unearned advantage that derive chiefly from social class, economic class, race, religion, region, sex, or ethnic identity. The oppressions are both distinct and interlocking, as the Combahee River Collective statement of 1977 continues to remind us eloquently.[3]

One factor seems clear about all of the interlocking oppressions. They 29 take both active forms that we can see and embedded forms that members of the dominant group are taught not to see. In my class and place, I did not see myself as racist because I was taught to recognize racism only in individual acts of meanness by members of my group, never in invisible systems conferring racial dominance on my group from birth. Likewise, we are taught to think that sexism or heterosexism is carried on only through intentional, individual acts of discrimination, meanness, or cruelty, rather than in invisible systems conferring unsought dominance on certain groups. Disapproving of the systems won't be enough to change them. I was taught to think that racism could end if white individuals changed their attitudes; many men think sexism can be ended by individual changes in daily behavior toward women. But a man's sex provides advantage for him whether or not he approves of the way in which dominance has been conferred on his group. A "white" skin in the United States opens many doors for whites whether or not we approve of the way dominance has been conferred on us. Individual acts can palliate, but cannot end, these problems. To redesign social systems, we need first to acknowledge their colossal unseen dimensions. The silences and denials surrounding privilege are the key political tool here. They keep the thinking about equality or equity incomplete, protecting unearned advantage and conferred dominance by making these taboo subjects. Most talk by whites about equal opportunity seems to me now to be about equal opportunity to try to get into a position of dominance while denying that *systems* of dominance exist.

Obliviousness about white advantage, like obliviousness about male 30 advantage, is kept strongly inculturated in the United States so as to maintain the myth of meritocracy, the myth that democratic choice is equally

---

[3]"A Black Feminist Statement," The Combahee River Collective, pp. 13–22 in G. Hull, P. Scott, B. Smith, Eds., *All the Women Are White, All the Blacks Are Men, But Some of Us Are Brave: Black Women's Studies*, Old Westbury, NY: The Feminist Press, 1982.

available to all. Keeping most people unaware that freedom of confident action is there for just a small number of people props up those in power and serves to keep power in the hands of the same groups that have most of it already. Though systemic change takes many decades, there are pressing questions for me and I imagine for some others like me if we raise our daily consciousness on the perquisites of being light-skinned. What will we do with such knowledge? As we know from watching men, it is an open question whether we will choose to use unearned advantage to weaken invisible privilege systems and whether we will use any of our arbitrarily awarded power to try to reconstruct power systems on a broader base.

■   ■   ■

Reading Rhetorically

1. Why do you think McIntosh uses her experiences in women's studies to frame an essay that focuses on white privilege? She opens this piece with a reference to women's studies; where else in the essay does she return to women's studies, and why? Discuss the effect you think her choice of this frame has on different kinds of readers, and suggest alternative ways she might have framed this same argument.

2. If, as McIntosh claims, her list "is not intended to be generalizable" (para. 6), what is the effect of the long list McIntosh includes in this essay as she unpacks her "invisible knapsack of while privilege" (para. 14)? Does her list of heterosexual privilege serve the same function? What items on her lists stand out to you? Why?

3. Explain in your own words the distinction McIntosh makes in paragraph 21 between "earned strength" and "unearned power." What specific examples of these does she urge readers to work against, and how? What do you think of her suggestions and strategies for change?

Inquiring Further

4. Make your own list of at least ten unearned privileges you have based on your race, class, education, gender, sexuality, nationality, or religion. Using McIntosh's categories — "positive advantages that we can work to spread" or "negative types of advantage that unless rejected will always reinforce our present hierarchies" (para. 22) — mark each entry P (positive) or N (negative). Share your list with a small group of classmates, and discuss your findings and strategies for change.

5. Near the end of her essay, in paragraph 28, McIntosh mentions the Combahee River Collective statement of 1977 as an important resource for her argument. Using the information in footnote 3 as a starting point, find the document and skim it enough to summarize it and explain how it shapes McIntosh's essay. Discuss with your classmates how the Combahee River Collective statement could be updated to fit current cultural dynamics.

6. McIntosh asserts that "those who do not depend on conferred dominance have traits and qualities that may never develop in those who do" and that sometimes "those dominated have actually become strong through *not* having all of these unearned advantages, and this gives them a great deal to teach the others" (para. 20). In small groups, brainstorm to come up with historical or current examples of each of these claims. Share your group's ideas with the rest of the class.

Framing Conversations

7. McIntosh, like some other writers in this book, is interested in what she calls "the myth of meritocracy" (para. 30) in the United States. Write an essay in which you explore the significance of this idea in this essay and the essays by Jonathan Kozol (p. 308) and Héctor Tobar (below). How does each author understand the lack of equal opportunity in the United States? What solutions does each author offer? Placing yourself in this conversation of ideas, explain your own perspective on this problem and possible solutions.

8. Both McIntosh and Noel Ignatiev (p. 512) are interested in looking more closely at whiteness and how it works in the contemporary United States. How do McIntosh's and Ignatiev's ideas build on one another? Where are they in conflict, if at all? Write an essay in which you place insights from these two readings in conversation with one another and your own ideas to argue for what you think is most important to understand about whiteness as a racial concept. What changes do these writers — and you — call for? Why?

9. How does McIntosh's analysis of unearned power help explain the gender, class, and race dynamics explored in essays by bell hooks (p. 293) and Barbara Ehrenreich (p. 479)? Write an essay in which you use McIntosh's ideas to analyze some of the examples and anecdotes in hooks's and Ehrenreich's essays. What would these writers agree and disagree on? What conclusions can you draw from your findings?

◼ HÉCTOR TOBAR

From Americanismo: City of Peasants

Héctor Tobar is a journalist who has worked for the *Los Angeles Times* as bureau chief in Buenos Aires and Mexico City. He shared the 1992 Pulitzer Prize for the *Times's* coverage of the LA riots. He is the son of Guatemalan immigrants, and was raised and educated in southern California, where he studied Latin American history and later earned a master of fine arts in creative writing. In addition to his award-winning journalism, he has published a novel, *The Tattooed Soldier* (1998). Although most of Tobar's writing is nonfiction, he has been praised for his lively writing style, which borrows descriptive and storytelling techniques from fiction writing.

This piece is taken from the first chapter in *Translation Nation: Defining a New American Identity in the Spanish-Speaking United States* (2005), which brings together Tobar's travel reflections on what he calls the new "Latin Republic of the United States." The essay delves into the richness of Spanish-speaking Los Angeles as a city that exemplifies both the challenges and the possibilities of immigration. Tobar illuminates the differences between the Los Angeles of his immigrant father's young manhood and the city today, in which there are "roughly equal" numbers of Spanish speakers and English-only speakers (para. 8). Although Tobar is interested in detailing the physical and psychic landscape of the city, it is not his only focus. He argues that "today Los Angeles and California are quietly exporting their people and their way of life eastward across the continent. The city is the starting point of a new identity that is at once Latin American and — though it may not be immediately apparent — intertwined with North American traditions, with Jeffersonian ideals and the civic culture molded in the United States over the past two centuries" (para. 9). To examine the inner workings of Los Angeles, then, is to peek through the window of the nation's future.

As you read, notice that Tobar mixes his own childhood experiences with those of other figures from history, most notably the Argentine-born twentieth-century revolutionary Che Guevara. Keep track of the places where Tobar moves between his own story and Guevara's. What does Tobar gain by threading this famous — even mythic — person's life into his own? Is there a larger-than-life figure from history who serves a similar role in your family?

Tobar's text is clearly influenced by the ideas of others. He draws on writers from the past and present to illustrate his claims about the city of Los Angeles in his references to Jeffersonian ideals, Samuel Huntington, Octavio Paz, and others. Pay attention to the ways he uses these sources to develop what is in part an autobiographical story. Paragraph 6 is a good example of Tobar's strategy of moving between the personal and the scholarly, between the past and the present, and between his own experiences and those of Che Guevara.

With Latinos the fastest-growing minority in the United States, consider the significance of Tobar's claim that Los Angeles tells us something about the future of the country as a whole. What will this new "translation nation" look like? Tobar has some answers . . . but even more questions.

Los Angeles, California

Long before I understood what the word "revolution" meant, when I was a five-year-old boy growing up in the seamier half of Hollywood, California, I knew the face of Che Guevara. In the same way that other boys believed in Santa Claus and the Tooth Fairy, I knew that Che, with his Christ-like martyr's gaze and mane of wavy black hair, had come to help the poor and to make things right in the world. In real life, he was a knot of contradictions too complex to explain to a kindergartner: he was a poet who carried a gun, a dreamer known for his ruthlessness, generous to his friends and intransigent with both allies and enemies. He was a Robespierre in olive drab, who wanted to bring socialism to the Americas. But to me, behind that beard, underneath that black beret and its red star, there was a benevolent savior. Plenty of other people around me believed the same thing: it was the late 1960s, and my father, like most men in their twenties, was an idealist. My mother, his slightly younger wife, was too. Like Che, they were ambitious romantics, although neither one could appreciate this quality in the other.

"Che died for us," my father would say. "He went into the hills and fought as a guerrilla." I was small enough then that I didn't understand the difference between a guerrilla and a gorilla. I imagined a man jumping about the jungle, in imitation of an ape, ambushing the purveyors of evil.

My parents had brought Che with them when they left Guatemala in 1962. He came in their luggage, a spirit of adventure tucked in between their layers of clothes, next to the English dictionary my father brought along, the devotional cards of saints my mother depended on to protect her and her unborn baby. Like my parents, Che was a risk taker, a man with an impulsive streak.[1] As a teenager, he would not hesitate to accept an outrageous dare, like walking on an irrigation pipe suspended over an impossibly deep gorge. A similar impetuousness had placed the young couple who would become my parents in the back of a delivery truck one spring afternoon in 1962, slipping off their clothes just long enough to conceive me while a driving rainstorm beat on the roof of the truck. A few weeks later they were pregnant and married and planning to run away to California. They arrived the week of the Cuban missile crisis, on a Pan American Airways flight that dropped them off at Los Angeles International Airport. Stepping for the first time into the California sunshine, they were greeted by the striking image of the airport's new Theme Building, a structure suspended between two giant arches suggesting the orbits of atoms, the coming "Space Age." My parents, a pair of young adults with a baby on the way, would soon embrace that uniquely California élan that wove together modernity and an incipient rebelliousness. In this new land of cat-eye sunglasses, my mother quickly learned to beehive her hair and to channel the allure of wool dresses that rose suggestively toward her kneecap. She outfitted my father in argyle sweaters no Guatemalan had ever worn before. Che was the most chic thing they had of their own to add to this American stew of coolness. Long before his face started popping up all over California — carried aloft on placards at Los Angeles City College rallies and on dorm room walls in Berkeley — he had been a hero to my father.

---

[1]I was able to fill in the details of Ernesto "Che" Guevara's life thanks to Jon Lee Anderson's seminal biography, *Che Guevara: A Revolutionary Life.*

"El Che was from Argentina, but he fought in Cuba, and he lived in   4
Guatemala too," my father would say, which would lead me later to ponder
a map of the world, wondering how a man could travel such great dis-
tances swinging from tree branches, across mountains and jungles.

One of the first secrets I ever kept from my father was that I admired   5
Maury Wills, the shortstop of the Dodgers, and Jerry West of the Lakers as
much as, if not more than, El Che. For me the United States was a land
ruled by sports heroes and astronauts, where arenas were filled with cheering crowds, and rockets zoomed into space with fiery ascents that caused
hundreds of necks to crane upward and mouths to open in awe. I had
never seen Che on my television, like my other heroes, who sank baskets
from the half-court line and sent baseballs over the fence at the brand new
Dodger Stadium, or who walked on the moon as fuzzy silhouettes. I was
becoming an American, another species, different from all my ancestors.
My mother and father would become Americans too, taking the oath as
U.S. citizens within a decade of their arrival, even while believing and
telling any Spanish-speaking person they met that they were still *guatemal-
tecos*. My father, I see now, embraced Che as an antidote to the lure of
American culture, to its overwhelming power to amaze and intimidate,
especially back then in the 1960s, when America gleamed and dazzled like
the chrome bumpers and tail fins of the Fords and Chevrolets he longed to
own. To prove he had not become a total *gringo*, my father became a more
devout Guevarista, an armchair rebel with a single, loyal follower — me.

An especially self-confident brand of American identity had reached   6
its apex in the United States, the Anglo-Saxon Protestant worldview celebrated by writers like Samuel Huntington, a civic religion whose holy trinity was the Protestant work ethic, individualism, and an obsession with
orderliness in all matters, public and private. Back then, an immigrant like
my father needed to be stubborn to keep the person he had been before
from being washed out in the laundry. It took work to hold on to the idea
that you could be an outsider. "Never forget where you came from," my
parents told me, but this was not an easy command to follow, since I was
an only child, cut off from all my grandparents, my uncles and aunts, and
my cousins by thousands of miles, and by a cultural and language gap that
seemed to grow wider every year. Well into the 1970s, I could still count
the number of Guatemalans I knew in Los Angeles on one hand. Che stood
for the beliefs my family had left behind, a symbol of our Latin American
identity during the long years we lived as cultural pioneers, a lonely crew
of *chapines* (as Guatemalans call themselves) planting a flag with Che's
face on the thirty-fourth parallel of North America.

Everything is different in California today. In the decades since my   7
family arrived in Los Angeles, several accidents of geopolitics and macro-
economics brought millions of people like us to the United States, all to
experience a similar kind of attraction and repulsion to American culture,
all to remake the idea of themselves and their community with icons like
Che, or the mustachioed Mexican revolutionary Emiliano Zapata, or, more

recently, the hooded Subcomandante Marcos, who led the Mayan Indian uprising in Chiapas. We have come in so many numbers to California, America's most populous state, filling its cities and towns with our flags and pictures of our heroes, our language, our parades, and our prejudices, and so many other things that are uniquely ours, that even the notion of what it means to be an "American" has begun to change completely. You can see this transformation most dramatically in my hometown, where the Stars and Stripes still flies over the government buildings of the Civic Center downtown, an island of English-speaking culture encircled north, south, east, and west by a sprawl of *latinidad*, Latinness. Billboards for Mexican deejays in excessive Stetsons loom over the thoroughfares, and the Virgin of Guadalupe, the patron saint of Mexico, is posted outside countless liquor stores as a sentinel against graffiti and armed robbery. If you go to the flat plain of South Los Angeles on a Saturday night and stand under the milky light of the streetlamps, or visit the arroyos of Echo Park on a Saturday afternoon, you can close your eyes and feel the rural provinces of Mexico and Central America come to life in the acoustic universe that surrounds you, in the voices and the music of the people who live there.

In the most recent census, the number of Spanish speakers in the city 8 of Los Angeles (1,422,316) was roughly equal to those who spoke only English (1,438,573). The city's top-rated newscast is the Spanish Univision *noticiero*, and the city parks are beginning to resemble the exhausted public spaces of Mexico City. In 1995 Los Angeles County parents registered the name José most often on birth certificates for baby boys. At Griffith Park, where I played as a child, the city Department of Parks and Recreation has placed enormous boulders in the center of the lawns to discourage the most popular municipal pastime, the playing of soccer, a sport unknown in the California of my childhood. Che is stencil-painted across the city more than ever, almost always staring back with the dreamy eyes of his most famous portrait, from a 1960 photograph taken at a funeral in Havana. Four decades removed from that time and place, it is an image ever more stylized, a sort of George Washington in negative image, a Latin icon from the founding of an altogether different republic, staring back at his progeny not from the dollar bill but from countless printed T-shirts, posters, and postcards. Che is the "founding father" symbol of the anti-WASP republic, a nation that embraces informality, excess in emotion, the dissembling force of rebellion, and the idea of strength in collectivity.

Today Los Angeles and California are quietly exporting their people 9 and their way of life eastward across the continent. The city is the starting point of a new identity that is at once Latin American and — though it may not be immediately apparent — intertwined with North American traditions, with Jeffersonian ideals and the civic culture molded in the United States over the past two centuries. Los Angeles is to the twenty-first-century United States what New York City was to the twentieth. It is the crucible where a new national culture is being molded, where its permutations and contradictions can be seen most clearly. Once upon a time it could be said that every American city had a little bit of Ellis Island in it, or even a bit of Little Italy or the Bronx or Harlem. Something similar is happening in the twenty-first century, in which each new day sees another Spanish-speaking Angeleno set off on Interstates 5, 10, 15 from the overcrowded metropolises of our state to the greener pastures of places like Pasco, Washington, or Fayetteville, Arkansas, or even New York City itself, and in so doing helps bring a bit of Los Angeles to those places too.

In the United States and the Los Angeles I knew as a child, there was   *10* only one way to become American, the method perfected in New York and other Eastern cities. Most immigrant families stuck to the formula, the one people had followed on a path to Americanness for a century. They stopped speaking Spanish — or Italian, or Armenian, or Greek — and instead embarrassed themselves in front of their children by trying to wrap their Mediterranean or Latin American mouths around English. Their children would retain only a handful of phrases from the mother tongue, and would know the culture of the Old Country primarily as a collection of recipes and swear words and maybe from the occasional visit of a grandparent who arrived in the United States as a sort of time traveler, stumbling about the apartment or the cul-de-sac in an old fedora, like my grandfather did when he came to visit us. When they had enough money they tried to enroll their children in tennis lessons, or Little League, or any other American institution that would let them get a foot in the door.

About halfway into the twentieth century, the Mexican writer Octavio   *11* Paz had wandered into a Los Angeles similar to the one my parents encountered on their arrival, the Los Angeles of the Pax Americana at its apex. In *The Labyrinth of Solitude*, his seminal treatise on Mexican identity, Paz describes the latent Mexican feel of the city then, a faint but discernible "delight in decorations, carelessness and pomp, negligence, passion and reserve."[2] The city's Mexicanness "floats, never quite existing, never quite vanishing." Of the people of Mexican origin he encountered in Los Angeles he wrote, "They have lived in the city for many years wearing the same clothes as the other inhabitants, and they feel ashamed of their origin. . . . They act like persons who are wearing disguises, who are afraid of a stranger's look because it could strip them and leave them stark naked."

Unbeknownst to Octavio Paz, inside those withdrawn Angelenos there   *12* was a garrulous, self-confident Latin city waiting to be born. My father became a pioneer of this new city when he decreed that I would always speak to him in Spanish. At school, and in the Hollywood alleyways and side streets where I played with my friends, I did math, joked, and whined in English, but at home my father fought back against the Anglo-Saxon linguistic torrent with a steady stream of *castellano*: to this day he is

---

[2]The passages from *The Labyrinth of Solitude* by Octavio Paz are from the 1985 Grove Press edition (Lysander Kemp, Yara Milos, and Rachel Phillips, translators).

always *papá*. At the same time, he would have been deeply upset if I didn't learn English, then as now the language of commerce and government. My undeniably accent-free English, with its native-speaker intonations and fluency in the peculiar vowel sounds no native Spanish-speaker can ever quite master, was in a sense a measure of his family's achievement. He admired American institutions, and his favorite class at Los Angeles City College was U.S. history, with its crimson-bound textbook, which he passed down to me as a kind of heirloom, telling me to pay particular attention to the chapters on the Civil War. My father was ambivalent about the United States, and in that, too, he was a pioneer: his ambivalence about WASP culture never faded, never surrendered to acceptance. He made learning English his own obsession too, taking night-school classes and making himself fluent enough to write business letters, but he also went to political meetings and seethed in Spanish about *imperialismo* in group discussions led by a Guatemalan leftist whose circle of would-be rebels later contemplated hijacking a plane to Cuba — it was a bit of a fad in those days. My father told me that Che had fought to free Cuba and that he was fighting for us too, for Guatemala, where our extended family lived under a blue sky and puffy tropical clouds I got to see every Christmas vacation. If we wanted to hear Che's voice, we could take our shortwave radio, string up a copper wire over our duplex apartment, and grab his words from the atmosphere. My father marked the frequency for Radio Habana Cuba on the glass face of the receiver with a piece of cellophane tape and a marker, a blue line that ran parallel to another one for TGW, Radio Nacional de Guatemala, a much weaker signal that came in only on certain summer evenings when he and my mother would sit and listen to the sound of the Guatelinda marimba orchestra force its way through layers of static into our living room. I remember that music vividly, because it usually led my mother to quiet tears whenever she heard it. As for Che, to this day I can't tell you what his voice sounded like.

My father spoke to me about El Che in that earnest and gentle tone 13 adults have when they speak to children about things like God and history. We are part of a bigger world, his voice said, full of beauty and horrors, where brave and smart men battle the forces of ignorance and darkness. Our history and our future cannot be contained within borders. This message, I believe, is essentially the same one communicated to new generations of Californians. Today, all of California, Latino and non-Latino, is increasingly immersed in the collective, cross-border narrative of its 11 million inhabitants of Latin American descent. In my own household, these stories have their starting point in my grandparents' villages, in places with names like Huehuetenango and Rincón Tigre ("Tiger's Corner"), and in a cluster of adobe buildings with plaster skins, set amidst the banana plantations of the United Fruit Company.

I grew up believing it was my destiny to advance this essentially Latin 14 American story into new, northern territories. In the Los Angeles of today, however, the narrative traffic goes in two directions. It is not just the story of the peasant whose children follow the North Star to the California oasis of orange groves, rationality, and good wages; the story also flows southward, back down to the birthplace of the passionate, the chaotic, and the spiritual. If you grow up Latino in Los Angeles, you feel the pull of the south, of its pop singers, its revolutions, and its fads. If you can, you go to the south, in body or in mind. The frightened Mexican-Americans of Octavio Paz's day are a fading anachronism, because people feel free to dress, think, speak, or plan their futures thinking of the south.

I can remember standing and looking to the south — literally and figuratively — one day at about the turn of the millennium in the East Los Angeles neighborhood of City Terrace. I was standing on the deck of the family home of my *comadre*, which is what you call your child's godmother. The very fact that I was using such a term, "code-switching" it into my English (as a linguist would say), was itself a step backward in what should have been a steady march forward into North American assimilation. *"Hola, comadre,* how's it going? Such a long time, *qué no?"* My *comadre* María Cabildo and her husband Manuel Bernal, who was also my *compadre,* had invited a group of friends over for their annual New Year's Day tamale brunch, which we celebrated on a patio overlooking the Eastside on one of those rare days of crystalline skies that winter brings us in Southern California. In the distance you could see the Art Moderne tower of the seventy-five-year-old Sears building on Olympic Boulevard sticking up from the flat urban plain, and splashes of green palm fronds amid the gray and earth-toned cityscape of naked jacarandas and dormant maple trees, and stubby apartment buildings and warehouses. We filled the conversation with our southern obsessions. Our friend Evangeline Ordaz had been to Chiapas as a human-rights monitor, encountering Mexican soldiers and Mayan rebels outfitted with antique rifles; she had also met the famous guerrilla leader known as Subcomandante Marcos. María's brother Miguel talked about his work for the Mexico City investigative magazine *Proceso*; in recent days he had come under threat from the murderous Tijuana drug cartel. This was a conversation, like most others in the still small circles of the Latino Los Angeles upper middle class, that began in English and drifted frequently into Spanish, a language we speak with widely varying degrees of fluency. Another visitor told us the story of a recent visit to his family's Mexican village, a place deep in the dry valleys and windswept high plains made famous in the work of the writer Juan Rulfo. Our friend had wandered into the town square to find a man tied up on an enormous cross, hanging in the air with a crown of thorns on his head and just three nails short of an actual crucifixion.

"What are you doing up there?" he asked.

"I am showing my devotion to Jesus!"

"You should get down before you get a sunburn!"

We listened to this story and for a moment we were lost in the strangeness and wonder of it — a familiar sensation, because all of us have been to the places where such stories are born. Los Angeles is filled with people like us, people who have Latin American villages and peasants hovering around their lives. There are *campesinos* in our dreams, on our lawns cutting the grass, in the pickup trucks next to us on the freeway, in the picture frames on the walls of our living rooms. The peasants in the pictures might come from the age of the Mexican Revolution, or they might be twenty-first-century *campesinos* in villages connected to California by bus lines and extended family relationships. We can go down below María's family home and hear roosters crowing at sunrise from backyard chicken coops. In the newer Mexican suburbs of Watts and Compton, we can find stalks of corn growing in the front yards, a crop from the old country seemingly about to burst from its cage of wire fencing to populate all the other lawns, and a reminder to all that the gardener or the mechanic inside was once a *campesino*, and perhaps still longs to be one.

The peasant who looms over my own family is my late paternal grand- 20 father, Francisco Tobar, a *campesino* from a province of rural Guatemala called Zacapa, notorious for producing men with a penchant for settling their differences with unsharpened machetes. Here an old rail line runs past the broad-leaved banana trees, and the train station where my grandparents first met is a forgotten, crumbling ruin marked GUALAN. My grandmother bore two of Francisco's children in Gualán and then left him, running away to Guatemala City with her oldest son. One morning she returned on the inbound steam train from the capital, kidnapped her younger son (my father), and escaped on the outbound train. They moved into an orphanage in downtown Guatemala City, where my grandmother was the cook for dozens of street urchins. Coincidentally, Che Guevara arrived in Guatemala City at about the same time, with just $3 in his pocket after having ridden his motorcycle and hitching car, bus, and boat rides to Chile, Peru, Panama, and other destinations. Guatemala City was a much smaller city then, and it is not beyond the realm of possibility that their paths crossed, Ernesto the revolutionary-to-be encountering Héctor Efraín the father-to-be in the doorway of the orphanage. I can imagine my father, then a scrawny boy of twelve or so, exchanging glances with the bohemian Argentine then in his mid-twenties, a clean-shaven man not yet sprouting the stubble that would become his famous beard, his hair short and nowhere near his collar.

Che went into hiding when Guatemala's leftist government was over- 21 thrown in a 1954 coup d'état, then took refuge in the Argentine embassy and prepared his escape to Mexico City, where he would meet Fidel Castro and board a small overcrowded boat with rebels headed for Cuba. My father, then thirteen years old, hid underneath his bed in the orphanage as bombs from American fighter planes exploded throughout the city. He would grow into a gangly teenager and meet my mother in the crowd drawn to the scene of a neighborhood car crash. After the drama of a shotgun wedding, they headed to California, where I was born a few months later at Los Angeles County General Hospital. In those days, few working people in Guatemala had telephones in their homes, and the news of my birth was communicated southward via the mail. In a similar fashion, the details of the family happenings from Guatemala arrived to us in Hollywood in envelopes with blue and red borders marked "Special Delivery." "They write that European-style seven over there," the mailman would say. My mother in turn gave him letters bound for Guatemala filled with snapshots of our visit to Sea World and the San Diego Zoo, or the bulbous used Chevrolet we had purchased, pictures that announced, "We have arrived in California."

These days the traffic in letters, cash, and gifts between Los Angeles   22
and Latin America feeds an air freight industry whose final link is the motorcycle courier puttering up to the door of your relatives' home in a rural *pueblo* or an urban *colonia* neighborhood. The couriers deliver envelopes with pictures like the one I saw a young man posing for not long ago near the Harbor Freeway, across from the Financial District at the beginning of that neighborhood of tenements called Pico-Union. This man with skin the color of moist soil put his hands on his hips and smiled as he stood on one of the few spots in Los Angeles where you can line up the sky-scrapers behind you for a Manhattanesque shot. The towers glowed in green and amber in the twilight. He had found a spot that said, "I am in the big city, I am at the center of everything." He is showing the family back home the new man he has become. This is what it means to be an immi-grant. You undertake an adventure that is itself a process of reinvention. You send home the picture with a letter that tells the story of your tribula-tions in the new land. The snapshot is proof of your triumph and your transformation, and the act of placing it in the mail is a communion with the people back home and a celebration of the possible. Your letter home says: This is what *we* can become.

Ernesto Guevara sent letters home to Buenos Aires after he left,   23
famously, on his motorcycle. Each bit of news was increasingly more fan-tastic and improbable. *I have seen Machu Picchu. . . . I have climbed to the crater of a volcano covered in snow. . . . I am leading a rebel army. . . .* One day his adventures and his wandering ended in the mountains of southern Bolivia, where at thirty-nine he became a corpse displayed to the local vil-lagers, his long locks of matted hair splayed across a table, his eyes still open. Sometime after Che died I learned my first acronym: CIA, which my father pronounced in Spanish as *see-ya*, the same as *silla*, which means "chair." My father had learned about the chair at Los Angeles City College. The chair, he told me in Spanish, had dropped the bombs he had heard exploding in Guatemala City, and the chair had killed Che, too — whether this news caused me to cry or feel whatever fleeting sense of mourning a small boy can conjure, I don't remember. The next year, 1968, I started kindergarten at Ulysses S. Grant Elementary. My father told me to conquer the alphabet and arithmetic as a prelude to the battles of my adulthood. I was picked best student in my class, which meant I got to carry the Stars and Stripes in the school parade.

I can remember standing at the blacktop of my school, the flagpole   24
anchored to my belt, a nylon Old Glory catching the breeze. Being the

youngest kid, I stood at the front, a line of progressively taller children behind me, boys and girls of various brown and peach hues, redheaded girls from the Midwest, curly-headed boys from Armenia, and some Filipinos and Mexicans too, the peculiar cultural kaleidoscope of East Hollywood then, each boy or girl carrying his or her own nylon Old Glory. We probably looked like all the other patriotic schoolchildren you see in documentaries of "silent majority" America in 1968, that year of the Tet Offensive in Vietnam and the Democratic Convention in Chicago. Each year, I studied harder and brought home new triumphs. I learned very quickly that being a good and studious *guatemalteco*, dedicated to honoring the memory of El Che, also happened to make me a good "American" in a traditional, Norman Rockwell sense of the word. I studied the map of the United States that was in every classroom, and memorized all its state capitals. When my father brought home his government textbook from night school, I pored over the charts of how a bill becomes a law and the simple logic of the lines that linked boxes representing the House of Representatives, the Senate, and the Supreme Court. My sixth-grade teacher, a square-jawed Texan named Mr. Simmons, had us recite the Gettysburg Address for the school assembly that was to be our farewell to elementary school. He picked me to lead the class, and for a week I memorized those 270 words of Lincoln's that are like a civic prayer to democracy and its foundation in sacrifice, to "a new nation: conceived in liberty, and dedicated to the proposition that all men are created equal." On the afternoon of the assembly, we stood under a bank of hot lights, on a stage of polished hardwood, transforming Lincoln's words into a chorus song, until we got to the part that begins "the world will little note, nor long remember," at which point I suddenly didn't remember, and our speech turned into an incomprehensible mumble.

When I was five years old, when I was ten, even when I was a fifteen- 25 year-old going to high school in the suburbs, I never saw any contradiction in the set of beliefs that swirled around me: that I should conduct my life according to the principles of equality and national honor of Che, who said America was an imperialist dragon feeding upon the entrails of the poor countries of the globe; and that I could also believe, as my father repeated again and again, that I lived in one of the freest territories on the face of the earth, an egalitarian democracy where I might become a congressman or some other kind of important person, simply by being the best student in the class. "You will be taller than me," my father told me, more than once, as I grew up into an average-sized American kid, two inches taller than my father and unusually tall for a *guatemalteco*. "Just like I was taller than my father. And your son, when you have one, will be taller than you. In this country, people grow taller than they do in Guatemala."

Probably most sons and daughters of immigrants heard that speech in 26 1960s Los Angeles. The future was being born here, and even a skeptical Guatemalan like my father could be swept away in the feverish optimism and sense of limitless growth. We flocked to Disneyland to fly on the

Rocket to the Moon ride and to stroll through the Monsanto House of the Future in Tomorrowland, a playground celebrating our own Space Age ambition as Californians and Americans. My mother wanted to embrace this modernism but also feared being consumed by it, so she prayed to St. Martin, San Martín de Porres in Spanish, to protect her against the evils that she feared came from too much future — ambition, coldness, godlessness. St. Martín was a seventeenth-century Peruvian friar, the mulatto son of a slave and a nobleman, and in our apartment he was also a four-inch-tall statue on the windowsill, a black man in a monk's robes holding a broom with a small dog at his feet. Proof of his powers was to be found in the events surrounding my birth and the miraculous intervention of a black stranger, Booker Wade. He knocked at the door of my parents' apartment offering my mother a ride to the hospital. He drove her to one emergency room in his convertible, and then a second one after she got turned down for lack of money and immigration papers. My mother said I owed my safe entry into this world to San Martín, who had sent his brother Booker to help us.

Eight years later, at about the time my parents were getting divorced, 27 they took me to see an oracle in South-Central Los Angeles. Today, this moment is part family legend, part hazy memory: I remember only the dusty curtain that covered the doorway into the fortune-teller's room, and the smell of wet cement. My father tells me the oracle picked me out from the crowd of people waiting to see her: "Bring *that* boy to me." She stared at me for a bit before declaring, "This boy has a huge aura." Then she added, in a phrase that would resonate inside my head for the rest of my life, "This boy is going to help a lot of people one day."

Every time I came home with an A, every time I asked my parents 28 about Che or Martin Luther King, every time a teacher sent home a note suggesting I might be "gifted," my father recounted that story. *This boy is going to help a lot of people one day.* Many years later, when I reached my mid-twenties and a somewhat delayed onset of full-blown adulthood, I would feel the burden of that prophecy and slip into a depression. But when I was still a child the prophecy only fed a strange kind of prepubescent ambition: a rampant desire to be the first to memorize all the multiplication tables, to read more books than any of my classmates, and to feed more American history into my brain. I imagined it was all a prelude to a future in which I would honor Che's memory, repay St. Martin for the ride to the hospital, *and* fulfill the prophecy of the oracle of South-Central Los Angeles.

Thus did the rational world of Yankee democracy become intertwined 29 in my young mind with the antirational universe of Catholic saints, of ointments and murmured prayers. When I was young, I thought this world was mine alone, but now I see that the Latino supernatural hovers over most of the city. Los Angeles is roughly divided, in cultural and spiritual terms, by the multilaned byway called La Cienega Boulevard, a slight Anglicization of *la ciénaga*, "the swamp." Drive west across La Cienega and you are in the half of the city whose state of mind is exported to the rest of the world as the spirit of Los Angeles. Over there, mystique is something created by makeup artists and special-effects gurus, experts in the craft that is Los Angeles's best-known contribution to global culture. But on my side of the city we are ruled by the baroque, by angels who cure the sick, who relieve the suffering of wives with wayward husbands, and who sometimes take the souls of innocent children. My side of the metropolis is a round-the-clock Mass. The leaders of official, English-speaking Los Angeles might still try, as they have for more than two hundred years, to encourage the city's Spanish-speaking residents to shuffle along in good Protestant, moneymaking order, but they are working against the tide of history. They zone a corner of city territory for a business park, and then a Mexican woman passes one day and looks up at the office building that has risen there. She sees that the mirror glass of one of its windows has warped in such a way that the sunlight that shines on it is refracted into a swirl of primary colors, into the very image of the Virgin of Guadalupe. She tells all her friends and neighbors. Soon there are vast crowds of believers gathered in the building's parking lot, and police to keep the crowds in order, and English-speaking television crews to broadcast news of the crowds to English-speaking viewers: here we have hundreds of people with a strange and foreign faith, who see the pious face of a Mexican saint in the window of this nondescript office building. "Can you see it? *La virgen santísima.* Our mother. She is there."

Angelenos learned long ago that the Latin city in their midst is 30 inescapable, and have come to terms with its permanence. Other cities and towns across the continent have undergone the same pattern of response to the creeping advance of Latinization: denial, anger, acceptance. In between those stages, or maybe after, comes curiosity. These days, it is an oft-repeated ritual of American journalism for the local newspaper to send one of its reporters down into Latin America so that its readers can better understand the brown-skinned people who have come to live among them. Over the years I have read such stories in newspapers from the Louisville (Kentucky) *Courier-Journal* to the Portland *Oregonian* and the *Press Herald* of Portland, Maine.[3] "Oregon is more than just a name on the map to the 1,200 residents of San Juan Mixtepec," the *Oregonian* discovered when it went to Oaxaca, and the *Courier-Journal* tagged along with a tobacco farmer who visited the town in Nayarit where his field hands were born. The *Press-Herald* sent its correspondent to La Democracia, Guatemala, to tell the full story of a group of men who died working in Maine's North Woods. California newspapers are the pioneers of this form,

[3]The newspaper stories and column quoted in this chapter include: "Kentucky Ties Help Mexican Town," from the series "Una Vida Nueva — A New Life," Lexington, Kentucky, *Courier-Journal*, March 30, 2003; George Rede, "A World Away," Portland *Oregonian*, February 13, 1994; Josie Huang, "Pain and Desperation," Portland, Maine, *Press-Herald*, December 8, 2002; and Steve Lopez, "Finding L.A. Roots in the Dust of Mexico," *Los Angeles Times*, June 16, 2004.

which continues to be a staple. As I write these words, I read in the *Los Angeles Times* a columnist's description of his journey to a farm outside Mexico City in search of the long-lost brother of a woman from central Los Angeles, a single mother with a poignant story of separation and loss. "I was expecting you," the brother told the columnist, Steve Lopez, when Lopez found him; the brother had dreamed recently that a stranger would bring him news of his sister. The columnist and the brother talked as they walked through cornfields and past agave cactus plants. "Here on a mountain in Mexico," Lopez wrote, "I could feel the pulse of hearts split between two countries, and believed I had begun to know Los Angeles."

I made my first Mexico pilgrimage when I was twenty. I was also playing at Che, hoping that a faraway adventure in deepest Latin America would give me a raison d'être, and I reached the same destination he did — Mexico City. I stood before the murals Diego Rivera had painted at the National Palace, where portraits of centuries of presidents, rebels, and poets are crowded into a single composition, and decided immediately that this was the metropolis I should live in; I had arrived at a place explicitly connected to Latin American history. I hung out at Café La Habana in downtown Mexico City, the restaurant where Che and Fidel Castro had plotted their landing in Cuba. I sipped café con leche and ordered big bowls of the house specialty, cream of asparagus soup, delivered by indifferent waitresses who seemed to have no idea they were treading on hallowed ground. I walked through old neighborhoods of quaint plazas with gazebos whose platforms were decorated with Spanish tile, where trees and grass struggled to survive in the carbon-laced air. I stayed there just long enough for it to begin to feel like home and to simultaneously realize it could never be home.

"What *are* you?" the more inquisitive *mexicanos* I met would ask. "What do you consider yourself?" I didn't fit into the categories into which you placed brown-skinned people in Mexico: I was a U.S-born young man with Mayan features who carried himself with a vaguely American air of entitlement and spoke a fluent but strange variant of Spanish. Much is made in Mexico of its multiethnic blend of Spanish and indigenous cultures, the *mestizaje*, or mixing, celebrated in the paintings of Siqueiros and Rivera. But when it comes to the simpler notions of national identity, Mexico is a very homogeneous place. To say "I am *mexicano*" implies an identifiable set of beliefs and customs; love for the tricolor flag, reverence for early-twentieth-century revolutionary icons like Pancho Villa, and shared grievances with respect to the United States. When I responded to the question *What are you*? with a perplexed knotting of my brow, my *mexicano* acquaintances would elaborate with "Are you *norteamericano*? Are you Guatemalan?" When I told them I was both, a "citizen of the Americas," this left them unsatisfied. Clearly, I had to be one or the other.

Eventually, I decided that Los Angeles was my *tierra*, as a *mexicano* would say, my land, a landscape seared into my memory the same way the banana leaves and the river in Gualán were seared into my father's: the green flesh of the succulents, the soot-covered urban palms, playing street baseball and bouncing line drives off parked cars; the scent of ash on fall days when brush fires burn on distant mountains. I went back home and got a job writing for my hometown newspaper, and began to explore how a new city was being fashioned on that familiar landscape. . . .

■ ■ ■

Reading Rhetorically

1. How does Tobar use personal stories to build his larger point? Mark the personal-story passages in the reading, and discuss both their placement and the function they serve for readers.

2. What do you think Tobar's title — "Americanismo: City of Peasants" — means? Locate specific passages in the text to help you explain the significance of the title.

3. Why does Tobar spend so much time on the facts of Che Guevara's life in this essay? What relationships can you find between Guevara's story and the story of Tobar's family?

Inquiring Further

4. Tobar mentions Samuel Huntington in paragraph 6 of the reading. Look up Huntington's book *Who Are We? The Challenges to America's National Identity* (2004) to find out more about Huntington's perspective on immigration. How does it compare with Tobar's? As a class, discuss each writer's three most compelling points about immigration.

5. Take a few minutes to look through a U.S. Census Bureau publication titled "The Hispanic Population" (http://www.census.gov/prod/2001pubs/ c2kbr01-3.pdf), which explains the terminology used in the U.S. Census (and how it has evolved) and charts the changes in the Hispanic/Latino population in the United States between 1990 and 2000. Locate information for your state on the chart to see how the trend in your state compares with the national trend. If you like, you can find more recent estimates of the Hispanic/Latino population on the Census Bureau's main site (http:www.census.gov/). What do you find that is interesting or surprising?

6. Use your library's online resources to find biographical information about Che Guevara. Identify at least three facts about Guevara's life that Tobar does not mention, and discuss how these facts extend or complicate the picture of Guevara that Tobar paints in this essay.

Framing Conversations

7. Write an essay in which you use Tobar's text as a test case for Noel Ignatiev's claim that "to the extent . . . immigrants became 'white' they abandoned the possibility of becoming fully American" (p. 513, para. 2). Does Tobar's text confirm or refute Ignatiev's claim? Cite specific examples in your argument.

8. In what ways are the issues Tobar explores similar to and different from the issues Jonathan Kozol writes about in "Still Separate, Still Unequal" (p. 308)? Write an essay on the intersections of the two texts and the significance of your findings.

9. Both Tobar and Kwame Anthony Appiah (p. 378) are interested in the implications of the fact that our identities are less and less tied to a single nation. Drawing on ideas you find in Tobar's and Appiah's arguments and examples, write an essay in which you teach your readers what you find most significant about this changing sense of identity. Feel free to draw on examples of your own to help build your point.

15

Acting "Naturally":
The Practices of Gender

*How do we learn to think and behave
as gendered people?*

W e inhabit a culture that differentiates boys from girls in a million tiny but significant ways. The readings in this chapter invite you to look both inward and outward at the myriad ways we assign and "do" gender, and the many ways popular culture nudges us toward an often quite narrow sense of ourselves as men or women.

These authors would argue that gender is not innate, that gender categories are invented by culture, and invented differently in different cultures and at different moments in history. Making this argument is not always easy: Gender categories and traits seem to be the product of biology, though they are anything but. As Judith Lorber explains:

> Talking about gender for most people is the equivalent of fish talking about water. Gender is so much the routine ground of everyday activities that questioning its taken-for-granted assumptions and presuppositions is like thinking about whether the sun will come up.

Lorber's description of the way we habitually scrutinize clothing to discern the gender of babies may lead you to ask why we feel compelled to sort even infants into gender categories. Moving along the human-development timeline, Karin A. Martin's detailed portrait of gender dynamics in preschools is by turns funny and painful — and, above all, familiar. (This piece in particular may trigger some interesting memories from your early childhood.) As adults, you may be surprised to learn from Deborah Tannen, a leading theorist on gender and communications, how the fine shades of difference between men's and women's conversations can affect success and failure in the workplace.

Some of the writers in this chapter turn their magnifying glass on the extreme, and often dangerous, gender practices that have taken shape through popular culture. Jean Kilbourne's analysis of often poisonous advertising images, for example, reveals the ways stereotypical gender assumptions can harm both women and men.

Henry A. Giroux's close reading of Disney's animated films demonstrates how even films with strong female protagonists — films like *Mulan* and *Pocahontas* — often reinforce stereotypes about gender and race . . . and get away with it. Shari L. Dworkin and Michael A. Messner's analysis of another pastime, sports, overturns expectations about women's increasing participation in the sports culture and what that participation might mean.

All these readings offer new perspectives on gendered behaviors that may surprise and even transform you.

■ SHARI L. DWORKIN AND MICHAEL A. MESSNER

Just Do . . . What? Sport, Bodies, Gender

Shari L. Dworkin holds graduate degrees in sociology and gender studies, and biostatistics. She is a professor at Columbia University in behavioral medicine and also a research scientist focusing on HIV issues. Her interdisciplinary scholarship examines both domestic and international issues relating to sociology, gender and sexuality, and global and public health. Dworkin's coauthor, Michael A. Messner, is a professor of sociology and gender studies at the University of Southern California. Messner has published many books and articles on gender as a social construct, and is well known for his research on understandings of masculinity. His interests include gender and sport, the culture of coaching, and gender and political imagery (including an analysis of the media coverage of California governor Arnold Schwarzenegger). This essay, "Just Do . . . What? Sport, Bodies, Gender," appeared in the book *Revisioning Gender* edited by Myra Marx Ferree, Judith Lorber, and Beth B. Hess (1998).

In this essay, the authors use the *Chicago Manual of Style* to cite sources. The long list of references at the end of the reading show the number of academics participating in the conversation about gender and sport culture. Look over the list of titles to get a better sense of the kinds of issues fueling this conversation, from "vandalized vanity" to "throwing like a girl." Dworkin and Messner's essay builds on the work of these many different scholars who have examined the ways our notions of masculinity and femininity are tested, exhibited, and reinforced through participating in and watching sports. They are also interested in the important roles race and economic class play in the American sport culture.

As you read, pay attention to the many ways Dworkin and Messner give context to their points. The discussion of Title IX (paras. 5–7), for example, offers legal context. (Do you know what Title IX is? If not, this essay will explain it.) Also adding context are discussions of the media coverage of an incident at the 1996 Olympics (para. 10) and of the burgeoning business of corporate sponsorship of athletes and athletic events (paras. 12–18). The authors look at many specific examples of sporting events, images, and commercials to draw out the larger significance of sport culture to our shifting understanding of what it means to look and act masculine or feminine. Anyone who has spent time in a coed weight room knows that there is something interesting going on in relation to gender and working out: Men tend to focus on building muscle, while women, anxious about looking "too muscular," tend to focus on firming up. What is at the heart of our physical goals and our anxieties about how we look and how we want to see ourselves as athletes?

You should be able to add more recent examples of celebrity athletes to the examples in this selection. Consider how those examples confirm or test the limits of the arguments Dworkin and Messner make. Take particular care to read their conclusion closely. What's the big deal about athletics, anyway? These authors hope to make us see that by looking at sports through the lens of gender, we can learn a great deal about how flexible or rigid our ideas about gender really are.

Athletic Men: Paying the Price

When we disentangle the historical and contemporary relationship *1* between sport and men's power, we must recognize the distinction between sport as a cultural practice that constructs dominant belief systems and the individual experience of sport as an athletic career. Clearly, for at least the past 100 years, the dominant cultural meanings surrounding athletic masculinity have served mostly to stabilize hegemonic masculinity in the face of challenges by women, working-class men, men of color, and immigrants (Crosset 1990; Kimmel 1990). However, the experience of male athletes is often fraught with contradiction and paradox. Although many male athletes may dream of being the next Michael Jordan, very few ever actually make a living playing sports (Messner 1992). Even for extremely successful male athletes, the rigor of attaining and maintaining athletic stardom often comes at the cost of emotional and interpersonal development (Connell 1990). And although athletic masculinity symbolizes an image of physical health and sexual virility, athletes commonly develop alienated relationships with their bodies, learning to relate to them like machines, tools, or even weapons to be "used up" to get a job done. As a result, many athletes and former athletes suffer from permanent injuries, poor health, and low life expectancy (Sabo 1994; White, Young, and McTeer 1995). In particular, it is disproportionately young men from poor socioeconomic and racial/ethnic backgrounds who pay these costs.

To put it simply, young men from race- or class-subordinated back- *2* grounds disproportionately seek status, respect, empowerment, and upward mobility through athletic careers. Most of them do not make it to the mythical "top," but this majority is mostly invisible to the general public. Instead, those very few who do make it into the limelight — especially those in sports like football or boxing, that reward the most extreme possibilities of large, powerful, and violent male bodies — serve as public symbols of exemplary masculinity, with whom all men can identify *as men*, as separate and superior to women (Messner 1988, 1992). While serving to differentiate "men" from "women" symbolically, top male athletes — especially African American men in violent sports — are simultaneously available to be used by men as cultural symbols of differences among them. African American male athletes — for instance, boxer Mike Tyson — have become icons of an atavistic masculinity, in comparison to whom White middle-class men can construct themselves as kinder, gentler "new men" (Messner 1993a). This imagery of Black men includes a package of sexual potency and muscular power wrapped in danger. Just as African American males have been used in the past to symbolize fears of a "primitive" sexuality unleashed (Hoch 1979; Davis 1981), Americans are increasingly obsessed with documenting the sexual misbehaviors of Black male athletes (Messner 1993b).

Men's sport, then, constructs masculinities in complex and contra- *3* dictory ways. At a time in history when physical strength is of less and less practical significance in workplaces, especially in the professional and managerial jobs of most White, college-educated men, African American, poor, and working-class men have increasingly "taken over" the sports to which they have access. But having played sports is of little or no practical use to most of these young men once their athletic careers have ended. Athletic skills rarely transfer over into nonsports careers. The significance of successful African American male athletes in the current gender order is *not* that they challenge dominant social meanings or power relations. To the contrary, they serve to stabilize ideas of natural difference and hierarchy between women and men *and* among men of different social classes and races.

We can draw two conclusions from this brief discussion of men's sports. *4* First, although we can see African American men's struggles to achieve success and respect through sport as a collective response to class and racial constraints, this agency operates largely to *reproduce* — rather than to *resist* or challenge — current race, class, and gender relations of power. Put another way, Black men's agency in sport is a key element in the current hegemony of the race, class, and gender order. As in the past, men at the bottom of the stratification system achieve limited upward mobility by providing entertainment and vicarious thrills for those more advantaged. Second, we can see by looking at men's sports that *simply* employing a "gender lens" to analyze sport critically is limiting, even dangerous. The current literature supports the claim that men's sport does continue to empower "men," but for the most part, it is not the men who are doing the playing who are being empowered. Clearly, when we speak of "sport and empowerment" for men, we need to ask, Which men? These two points — that "agency" is not necessarily synonymous with "resistance," and that we need to be very cautious about employing a simplistic gender lens to speak categorically about "men and sport" — will inform our examination of women's current movement into sports.

Sex Equity for "Women in Sport"

Since the passage of Title IX of the Education Act Amendments, adopted *5* by Congress in 1972, girls' and women's sports in the United States have changed in dramatic, but paradoxical, ways. On the one hand, there is no denying the rapid movement toward equity in the number of female participants and programs for women and girls (Cahn 1994; Carpenter 1993). For example, in 1971, only 294,015 U.S. girls, compared with 3,666,917 boys, participated in interscholastic high school sports. By 1996, the number of girls participating had risen to 2,240,000, compared with 3,554,429 boys (Acosta and Carpenter 1996). Opportunities for women to play intercollegiate sports have also continued to rise. In 1978, right before the date for mandatory compliance with Title IX, colleges and universities offered an average of 5.61 women's sports per school. By 1988, the average had risen to 7.31 sports per school, and it continued to rise to an all-time high of 7.53 in 1996 (Acosta and Carpenter 1996). These numerical increases in opportunities to participate in such a masculine-structured institution as school sports prove the effectiveness of organizing politically and legally around the concept "woman." Indeed, the relative success of this post–Title IX liberal strategy of gender equity in sport was premised on the deployment of separate "male" and "female" sports.

On the one hand, at least within the confines of liberalism, a "strategic essentialism" that successfully deploys the category "woman" can result in moves toward greater distributive justice. And in this case, we can see that there are benefits that result when girls' and women's participation in sports increases. Research suggests that girls who play interscholastic sports tend to have higher self-esteem and greater self-confidence, more positive feelings about body image, lower school dropout rates, and lower levels of unwanted pregnancies than girls who do not play sports (Sabo and Women's Sports Foundation 1988; President's Council on Physical Fitness and Sports 1997). And it is likely that boys who play with, or watch, competent and powerful female athletes will develop a broader and more respectful view of women's physical capabilities than did earlier generations of boys and men (Messner and Sabo 1994).

Yet, Title IX has not yet yielded anything close to equity for girls and women within sports — more boys and men still play sports; they still have far more opportunities, from the peewee level through professional sports; and girls and women often have to struggle for access to uniforms, travel money, practice facilities, and scholarships that boys and men routinely take for granted (Lopiano 1993; Women's Sports Foundation 1997). But the dramatic movement of girls and women into sport — and the continued legal basis for challenges to inequities that are provided by Title IX precedents — makes sport an impressive example of a previously almost entirely masculine terrain that is now gender contested. The very existence of skilled and strong women athletes demanding recognition and equal access to resources is a destabilizing tendency in the current gender order.

On the other hand, there are obvious limits in the liberal quest for gender equity in sport. First, as the popularity, opportunities, and funding for women's sports have risen, the leadership positions have markedly shifted away from women to men. For example, in 1972 more than 90 percent of women's college teams had women coaches. By 1996, the proportion had dropped to 47.7 percent. Similarly, in 1972 more than 90 percent of women's college programs were headed by women athletic directors. By 1996, the figure had dropped to 18.5 percent (Acosta and Carpenter 1996). Radical critics of sport have argued that this shift toward men's control of girl and women athletes is but one indicator of the limits and dangers of a gender-blind model of equity that uncritically adopts the men's "military model" of sport (Nelson 1991). To be sure, this shift to men coaches was heroically resisted throughout the 1970s by many women coaches and athletic administrators behind the banner of the Association for Intercollegiate Athletics for Women (AIAW). The AIAW attempted to defend the idea that women's sports should be controlled by women, and should reflect the values of health, cooperation, and participation, rather than the values of cutthroat competition and star systems that dominated men's sports. But as the economic power of the National Collegiate Athletic Association (NCAA) (and its linkages with television) rapidly brought women's college sports under its aegis, "the AIAW faded quickly from the scene, closing down operations in 1982 and conceding final defeat in 1984 when it lost an antitrust suit against the NCAA" (Cahn 1994:257). Locally, most women's athletic departments were folded into male athletic departments, and the hiring of coaches for women's sports was placed in the hands of male athletic directors.

As women's sports has become controlled by men, it increasingly reflects the most valued characteristics of men's sports: "hierarchy, competitiveness and aggression" (Hall 1996:91). In the most "feminine" sports, men coaches are simultaneously demanding the aggressiveness of adult men athletes and the submissiveness of little girls — a most complex gender message! A poignant example of these dangers can be seen in women's gymnastics and ice-skating, where very young girls, typically coached mostly by men coaches who are often abusive, learn to practice with painful injuries and often develop severe eating disorders in order to keep their bodies "small, thin and prepubescent" (Ryan 1995:103).

Most people who followed media coverage of the 1996 Olympics still hold the image in their minds of a grinning coach Bela Karolyi cradling gymnast Kerri Strug in his arms, her leg in a brace, after she had courageously vaulted with a painful injury, and thus appeared to secure a gold medal for the U.S. team. Strug's deed resulted in a great deal of flag-waving and in numerous endorsement contracts for her, and it was lauded by the media as an act of bravery that symbolized the "arrival" of women's sports. But it can also be seen as an example of the limits and contradictions of the uncritical adoption of the dominant values of men's sports. The image of Karolyi's cradling the much smaller body of the young, injured Strug, so often replayed on television and prominently positioned in print coverage of the Olympics, illustrates two important points. First, the sports media today continue to frame women athletes ambivalently, symbolically denying them their power (Duncan and Hasbrook 1988). After all, it was not Strug's moment of triumphant power as she exploded off the vault, or even her difficult and painful landing on her injured leg that the media etched in all of our memories; instead, it was the aftermath of the actual athletic moment that the media seized upon. Here, an infantilized and vulnerable Strug appeared anything but powerful. It is unlikely that the sports media would frame a male athlete in a similar situation the same way. The second point that this popular image illustrates is that today, young girl and women athletes' bodies are in the literal and symbolic hands of men coaches. As Ryan's powerful book *Little Girls in Pretty Boxes* (1995) illustrates, Karolyi is seen by many as the most egregious in a system of men coaches who systematically submit aspiring young girl athletes to verbal, psychological, and physical abuse. The physical and psychological carnage that results from this professionalized system, whose main aim is to produce gold medalists for the United States every four years, is staggering. Recent discussions of exploitation, sexual harassment, and sexual abuse of young female athletes — especially those competing in the more "feminine" sports, such as swimming and gymnastics — by male coaches add another frightening dimension to this picture (Nelson 1994; Tomlinson and Yorganci 1997).

In short, as girls and women push for equity in sport, they are moving — often uncritically — into a hierarchical system that has as its main goal to produce winners, champions, and profits. Although increased participation for girls and women apparently has its benefits at the lower levels, as the incentives mount for girl and women athletes to professionalize, they increasingly face many of the same limitations and dangers (in addition to some others, such as sexual harassment and rape) as those experienced by highly competitive men.   *11*

"If You Let Me Play . . ."

In recent years, corporate America has begun to awaken to the vast and lucrative potential markets that might be developed within and subsidiary to women's sports. The 1996 Olympics and its aftermath saw unprecedented amounts of money spent on television and magazine ads featuring women athletes. Two new professional women's basketball leagues were begun in 1996 and 1997, and one of them, the Women's National Basketball Association (WNBA), began with a substantial television contract — a factor that today is the best predictor of financial success in pro sports. Although many see these developments as merely the next step in the successful accomplishment of gender equity for women in sport, we argue that the increasingly corporate context of this trend calls for special critical scrutiny.   *12*

In recent years, athletic footwear advertisements by Reebok and Nike have exemplified the ways that corporations have made themselves champions of women's athletic participation. In the early 1990s, Reebok was first to seize the lion's share of the female athletic shoe market. But by the mid-1990s, Nike had made great gains with a highly successful advertising campaign that positioned the corporation as the champion of girls' and women's rights inside and outside of sports. One influential TV spot included images of athletically active girls and women, with the voice-over saying things like, "If you let me play, I'll be less likely to drop out of school," and "If you let me play, I'll be better able to say no to unwanted sexual activity." These ads made use of the research findings from such organizations as the Women's Sports Foundation, documenting the positive, healthy, and empowering aspects of athletic participation for girls. Couching this information in the language of individual empowerment, Nike sold it to girls and women in the form of athletic shoes.   *13*

To be sure, the power of these commercials lies partly in the fact that they almost never mentioned shoes or even the Nike name. The message is that individual girls will be happier, healthier, and more in charge of their   *14* lives if we "let them play." The Nike "swoosh" logo is subtly displayed in the corner of the ads so that the viewer knows who is the source of these liberating ideas. It is through this kind of campaign that Nike has positioned itself as what Cole and Hribar (1995) call a "celebrity feminist," a corporate liberal entity that has successfully appropriated and co-opted the language of individual empowerment underlying the dominant discourse of opportunity for girls and women in sports. Aspiring athletes are then encouraged by slick advertising campaigns to identify their own individual empowerment — in essence, *their relationship to feminism* — with that of the corporate entity that acts as a celebrity feminist. If "feminist identity" can be displayed most readily through the wearing of the Nike logo on shoes and other athletic apparel, then displaying the Nike "swoosh" on one's body becomes a statement to the world that one is an independent, empowered individual — a successful young woman of the nineties.

There are fundamental limitations to this kind of "empowerment." If *15* radical feminists are correct in claiming that patriarchy reproduces itself largely through men's ability to dominate and exploit women's bodies, we might suggest a corollary: Corporations have found peace and profit with liberal feminism by co-opting a genuine quest by women for bodily agency and empowerment and channeling it toward a goal of physical achievement severely limited by its consumerist context. The kind of collective women's agency that emphasizes the building of institutions such as rape crisis centers, domestic violence shelters, and community women's athletic leagues is a *resistant agency* through which women have empowered themselves to fight against and change the institutions that oppress them. In contrast, individual women's agency expressed as identification with corporate consumerism is a *reproductive agency* that firmly situates women's actions and bodies within the structural gender order that oppresses them.

In addition, Nike's commitment to women's liberation is contradicted *16* by its own corporate practices. In 1996, when it posted its largest profits, and its CEO Phillip Knight's stock was estimated to be worth $5 billion, the mostly women Indonesian workers who manufactured the shoes were paid about $2.25 a day. Workers who attempted to organize for higher pay and better working conditions were fired (Take Action for Girls 1996). Meanwhile, U.S. women's eager consumption of corporate celebrity feminism makes it almost impossible for them to see, much less to act upon, the exploitation of women workers halfway around the globe. In fact, it is likely that the kinds of individual "empowerment" that can be purchased through consumerism seriously reduce women's abilities even to identify their collective interests in changing institutions here within the United States.

Liberal feminism in sport has come full circle: A universalized concept *17* of "women" was strategically deployed to push — with some impressive but limited success — for equal opportunities for women in sport. As these successes mounted, a key ideological support for hegemonic masculinity — the naturalized equation of male bodies with athletic ability and physical strength — was destabilized. But corporations have recently seized upon the individualist impulse of female empowerment that underlies liberal feminism, and have sold it back to women as an ideology and bodily practice that largely precludes any actual mobilizing around the collective concept of "women." Individual women are now implored by Nike to "Just do it" — just like the men "do it." Undoubtedly, many women strongly approve of, and feel good about, the Nike ads. But Nike's individualized and depoliticized "feminism" ignores how individuals who "do it" with Nike are implicated in an international system of racial, gender, and class exploitation of women workers in less developed nations.

Just as we argued in our discussion of the limits of sports for raising the status of working-class and African American men, here, too, gender analysis alone is not enough. It is not just muscular, or athletic, or "fit" bodies that must be considered in women's liberation — it is also laboring bodies as well. In fact, as we will argue next, a danger in contemporary reductionist understandings of empowerment as being synonymous with the development of one's body is that concentrating on toning muscles can easily transfer energies — especially those of women privileged by class and race — away from collective organizing to change institutions that disadvantage all women, but especially those who are poor, working-class, and racially disadvantaged. [18]

Women and Muscles

In addition to the ever-increasing numbers of women who compete in high school and college sport, more and more women today engage in fitness activities, lift weights, and enjoy the power of carrying musculature. Much of the new emphasis and popularity of fitness and muscular development among women has emerged outside of organized sport. New bodily ideals can be said to have broadened from thin and slim to tight and toned, with an "allowance" for "substantial weight and bulk" (Bordo 1993:191). By some standards, today's more muscular woman can be viewed as embodying agency, power, and independence in a way that exemplifies resistance to patriarchal ideals. However, just as within sport, women's bodily agency in fitness activities can be contradictory. Is this bodily agency resistant and/or empowering, or is the fit, muscled ideal simply the latest bodily requirement for women, a form of "self-surveillance and obedience" in service to patriarchal capitalism (Bartky 1988)? [19]

Some feminists argue that when women exercise their agency to develop bodily mobility and muscular power, these activities are self-affirming for women and antithetical to patriarchal definitions of women as passive, docile, and weak (MacKinnon 1987; Nelson 1991; Young 1990). By fighting for access to participation in sport and fitness, women have created an empowering arena where the meaning of gender is being contested and renegotiated, and where active rejections of dominant notions of femininity may be forged (e.g., Bolin 1992b; Gilroy 1989; Guthrie and Castelnuovo 1992; [20]

Kane and Lenskyj 1998; Lenskyj 1987; McDermott 1996; Theberge 1987). Other feminists, however, offer compelling counterarguments. First, there is the question as to whether bodily "empowerment" is merely a modern version of the "docile body," the intensely limiting and oppressive bodily management and scrutiny with which women learn to be complicit (Bordo 1993). For some women (especially those who are White, middle-class, and married heterosexuals) this complicit agency might result in more work on top of their already stifling "second shift" (Hochschild 1989) — a "third shift" that consists of long doses of effort invested in conforming to the latest touted bodily "requirement." It is these women, whose daily lives in families and careers might leave them feeling less than empowered, who would then respond to advertisements that encourage them to participate in sport and fitness in order to feel a sense of empowerment through their bodies. Couched in the logic of individualism and the Protestant work ethic, it seems that a woman need only enact her free will and "just do it" in order to "have it all." But "doing it" the corporate individualist way involves a radical turning inward of agency toward the goal of transformation of one's own body, in contrast to a turning outward to mobilize for collective political purposes, with the goal of transforming social institutions. Clearly, despite its uplifting tone and seemingly patriotic commitment to American women, corporate slogans such as Nike's beg several questions, such as: Just do *what*? And *for whom*?

Just as the cult of true womanhood excluded numerous women from its *21* "ideal" in the early nineteenth century, a similar conceptual vacuum arises here. After all, the dominant fitness industry message very likely "has no relevance to the majority of working-class women, or to Black women, or those from other ethnic minorities" (Hargreaves 1994:161). Bordo (1993) might disagree as she argues for the power of such messages to "normalize" across different races, classes, and sexualities. However, rather than being prematurely celebratory of bodily agency across categories of women, it may be argued that these newest images are fully compatible with the current "needs" of patriarchal capitalism for (especially and increasingly middle-class) women to be both active laborers and consumers (Bartky 1988).

Just as images of physically powerful and financially successful African *22* American men ultimately did not challenge, but instead continued to construct a stratified race, class, and gender order, current images of athletic women appear to represent a broadening of the definitional boundaries of what Connell (1987) calls "emphasized femininity" to include more muscular development. But the resistant possibilities in images of athletic women are largely contained by the continued strong assertion of (and commercial rewards for) retaining a link between heterosexual attractiveness and body image. For instance, many lauded Olympic track star Florence Griffith-Joyner's muscularity as a challenge to the dominant image of femininity and to images of men as physically superior. However, Griffith-Joyner's muscularity existed alongside "rapier-like" nails, flowing hair, and spectacular outfits, which ultimately situated her body and its markings firmly within a commercialized modernization of heterosexual femininity (Messner forthcoming). Now more than ever, the commodification of women's bodies may mean that when women "just do it," they are "just doing" 1990s "heterosexy" femininity. In the media, these bodies are not unambiguously resistant images of powerful women, but rather an ambivalent framing or subtle trivialization or sexualization of women's bodies that undermines their muscles and their athletic accomplishments (Duncan and Hasbrook 1988; Messner, Duncan, and Wachs 1996; Kane 1995; Kane and Lenskyj 1998). Female bodybuilders in particular illustrate these gender ambiguities. Research demonstrates that women can and do press and contest the limits of emphasized femininity. However, their agency is contained by the structure, rules, and ideologies of women's bodybuilding. For instance, Bolin (1992a, 1992b) found that the increasing size of the woman bodybuilder "beast" is acceptable only if "tamed" by "beauty." Female bodybuilders have faced penalties from judges for being too muscular, and they are rewarded for appearing with painted fingernails, dyed and highlighted hair, and breast implants. In short, their muscle size and body comportment is expected to be made consistent with emphasized femininity.

Researchers who study women's participation in fitness activities find *23* the same tendency to adhere to emphasized femininity as is shown by women athletes and bodybuilders. They tend to avoid lifting weights "too much" for fear of being "too big." Instead, they engage in long doses of cardiovascular work, which is thought to emphasize tone and leanness (Dworkin forthcoming; Markula 1996). Just as women in male-dominated occupations often hit a glass ceiling that halts their professional advancement, there appears to be a glass ceiling on women's musculature that constrains the development of women's muscular strength. Defined according to the latest commodified eroticization of heterosexual femininity, most women (with differences by race, class, sexuality, age) remain acutely aware of how much muscle is "allowed," how much is "still" attractive.

Conclusion

Through an examination of gender, bodies, and sport, we have made three *24* main points . . . that may illuminate more general attempts to understand and change the current gender order. First, although sport has been an arena for contesting the status quo by men of color and by White women and women of color, the positive results have been individual rather than collective. A few star athletes have become celebrities, but their popularity has not raised the overall status of disadvantaged men and women (although it may have upgraded the physical potentiality of middle-class White women). Second, whatever sport has accomplished in terms of equity, women's and men's sports are still segregated, and men's sports are still dominant in commercial value and in the media. Third, rather than breaking down conventional concepts of masculinity and femininity, organized sport has overblown the cultural hegemony of heterosexualized, aggressive, violent, heavily muscled male athletes and heterosexualized, flirtatious, moderately muscled female athletes who are accomplished and competitive but expected to be submissive to the control of men coaches and managers.

The link in all these outcomes is that organized sport is a commercial 25 activity first and foremost. Organized sport is financially underwritten by corporations that sell shoes and clothing to a public looking for vicarious thrills and personal "fitness." The corporations capitalize on the celebrity of star athletes, who use individual achievements to make more money, rather than to help upgrade the communities from which they have come. Their endorsements sell individual achievement and conventional beauty and sexuality as well as Nikes and Reeboks. A further negative consequence to the upbeat message of "Just do it" is that many of the appurtenances of sport and fitness are produced by the labor of poorly paid, malnourished, and probably physically unfit women workers.

Does this mean that women's agency in sports and other physical activ- 26 ities is a dead end that should be abandoned by feminist activists? Absolutely not. We think that sport is like any other institution: We cannot abandon it, nor can we escape from it. Instead, we must struggle within it. When liberal reforms such as Title IX are fought for and won, the results — though not revolutionary — are often positive changes in individual lives. And these changes shift the context for current and future struggles over control of resources and over ideologies and symbols that support inequalities. But we think feminists need to fight on two fronts in the battle for equity in sports. On the one hand, we must continue to push for equal opportunities for girls and women in sports. On the other hand, although the research points to benefits for girls and women who play sports at the lower levels, many of the girls and women who are professionalized into corporate sports can expect — just as most of their men counterparts in corporate sports can — to pay emotional and physical costs.

But in challenging women's uncritical adoption of the dominant values 27 of corporate sport, we must be cautious not to fall into the same trap as have past activists for girls' and women's sports. In the 1920s and 1930s, in the wake of two decades of burgeoning athleticism by girls and women, medical leaders and physical educators responded with what now appear to be hysterical fears that vigorous physical activity for girls and women carried enormous physical and psychological dangers (Cahn 1994). The result of these fears was the institutionalization of an "adapted model" (i.e., "tamed down" sports for women) that served to ghettoize women's sports, leaving the hegemonic masculinity of men's sports virtually unchallenged for the next forty years. Given this history, today's advocates of women's sports walk a perilous tightrope: They must assert the positive value of vigorous physical activity and muscular strength for girls and women while simultaneously criticizing the unhealthy aspects of men's sports. A key to the accomplishment of this task must involve the development of a critical analysis of the dominant assumptions, beliefs, and practices of *men's* sports

(Thompson 1988; Messner and Sabo 1994). In addition, we need to continue to explore feminist alternatives, for women and for men, to the "military model," with its emphasis on heroism, "playing through pain," and winning at all costs (Birrell and Richter 1987; Nelson 1991; Theberge 1985).

The activist fight for women and girls as a group will not be helped by [28] simplistic scholarship that acts as a cheering section for numerical increases in women's athletic participation, or for the increasing visibility of women's athletics in televised ads. Nor will a simple "gender lens" that views sports uncritically in terms of undifferentiated and falsely universalized categories of "men" and "women" take us very far in framing questions and analyzing data. Different groups of men and of women disproportionately benefit from and pay the costs of the current social organization of sports. We need an analytic framework that appreciates the importance of class, racial, and sexual differences among both men and women while retaining the feminist impulse that places the need to empower the disadvantaged in the foreground.

Data from empirical observation of sports demonstrate the absence of [29] absolute categorical differences between "men" and "women" — instead, there is a "continuum of performance" that, when acknowledged, can radically deconstruct dichotomous sex categories (Kane 1995). Obscuring this continuum are the social processes through which sport constructs and naturalizes differences and inequality between "men" and "women." Does this observation lead us down the path of radical deconstruction? We think the discussion in this chapter [of *Revisioning Gender* (1998)] demonstrates just the opposite. The current poststructuralist preoccupation with deconstructing binary categories like "men and women" (e.g., Butler 1990; Sedgewick 1990) has produced new discourses and practices that disrupt and fracture these binaries (Lorber 1996). Yet simply deconstructing our *discourse* about binary categories does not necessarily challenge the material basis of master categories to which subordinate categories of people stand in binary opposition: the capitalist class, men, heterosexuals, Whites. In fact, quite the contrary may be true (Stein and Plummer 1994). As many feminists have pointed out, although it is certainly true that every woman is somewhat uniquely situated, a radical deconstruction of the concept "woman" could lead to an individualism that denies similarity of experience, thus leading to depoliticized subjects. We would argue that it is currently corporations such as Nike that are in the forefront of the widespread development of this sort of depoliticized individualist "empowerment" among women. Radical deconstruction, therefore, is very much in the interests of the most powerful institutions in our world, as it leaves us feeling (at best) individually "empowered," so long as we are able to continue to consume the right products, while making it unlikely we will identify common interests with others in challenging institutions.

Rather than a shift toward radical deconstruction, the research on [30] gender, bodies, and sport suggests that it is essential to retain and build upon the concept of social structure, with its attendant emphasis on the importance of people's shared positions within social institutions (Duncan 1993; Messner 1992). Such a materialist analysis reveals how differential access to resources and opportunities and the varieties of structured constraints shape the contexts in which people think, interact, and construct political practices and discourse. A critical analysis of gender within a materialist, structural analysis of institutions entails a reassertion of the crucial importance (though not necessarily the primacy) of social class. Interestingly, as recent intellectual trends have taken many scholars away from the study of institutions toward a preoccupation with individuals, bodies, and difference, the literature has highlighted race, gender, and sexual identities in new and important ways, but social class has too often dropped out of the analysis. As we have demonstrated, discussions of the possibilities and limits of women's agency in gender equity struggles in sports, the co-optation of feminism by Nike's "celebrity feminism," and the current encouragement of physical fitness for middle-class women all need to be examined within the context of distributive justice. We also need a clear analysis of the position of women and men as workers in organized sports; as marketable celebrities; as workers in sweatshops making sport shoes, clothing, and equipment; and as consumers of these products and symbols. This analysis must be informed by feminist theories of the intersections of race, class, and gender (e.g., Baca Zinn and Dill 1996). Politically, this work can inform an alliance politics that is grounded simultaneously in a structural analysis of power and a recognition of differences and inequalities between and among women and men.

REFERENCES

Acosta, R. Vivian, and Linda Jean Carpenter. 1996. "Women in Intercollegiate Sport: A Longitudinal Study — Nineteen Year Update, 1977–1996." Brooklyn, NY: Department of Physical Education, Brooklyn College.
Baca Zinn, Maxine, and Bonnie Thornton Dill. 1996. "Theorizing Difference from Multiracial Feminism." *Feminist Studies* 22:321–31.
Bartky, Sandra L. 1988. "Foucault, Femininity, and the Modernization of Patriarchal Power." In *Feminism and Foucault: Reflections on Resistance*, edited by I. Diamond and L. Quinby. Boston: Northeastern University Press.
Birrell, Susan, and Diana M. Richter. 1987. "Is a Diamond Forever? Feminist Transformations of Sport." *Women's Studies International Forum* 10:395–409.
Bolin, Anne. 1992a. "Flex Appeal, Food, and Fat: Competitive Bodybuilding, Gender, and Diet." *Play and Culture* 5:378–400.
———. 1992b. "Vandalized Vanity: Feminine Physique Betrayed and Portrayed." Pp. 79–90 in *Tattoo, Torture, Mutilation, and Adornment: The Denaturalization of the Body in Culture and Text*, edited by Frances E. Mascia-Lees and Patricia Sharpe. Albany: State University of New York Press.
Bordo, Susan. 1993. *Unbearable Weight: Feminism, Western Culture, and the Body.* Berkeley: University of California Press.
Butler, Judith. 1990. *Gender Trouble: Feminism and the Subversion of Identity.* New York: Routledge.
Cahn, Susan K. 1994. *Coming On Strong: Gender and Sexuality in Twentieth Century Women's Sport.* New York: Free Press.

Carpenter, Linda Jean. 1993. "Letters Home: My Life with Title IX." Pp. 79–94 in *Women in Sport: Issues and Controversies*, edited by Greta L. Cohen. Newbury Park, CA: Sage.

Cole, Cheryl L., and Amy Hribar. 1995. "Celebrity Feminism: Nike Style Post-Fordism, Transcendence, and Consumer Power." *Sociology of Sport Journal* 12:347–69.

Connell, R. W. 1987. *Gender and Power.* Stanford, CA: Stanford University Press.

———. 1990. "An Iron Man: The Body and Some Contradictions of Hegemonic Masculinity." Pp. 83–95 in *Sport, Men and the Gender Order: Critical Feminist Perspectives*, edited by Michael A. Messner and Donald F. Sabo. Champaign, IL: Human Kinetics.

Crosset, Todd W. 1990. "Masculinity, Sexuality and the Development of Early Modern Sport." Pp. 45–54 in *Sport, Men and the Gender Order: Critical Feminist Perspectives*, edited by Michael A. Messner and Donald F. Sabo. Champaign, IL: Human Kinetics.

Davis, Angela Y. 1981. *Women, Race, and Class.* New York: Random House.

Duncan, Margaret Carlisle. 1993. "Beyond Analyses of Sport Media Texts: An Argument for Formal Analyses of Institutional Structures." *Sociology of Sport Journal* 10:353–72.

Duncan, Margaret Carlisle, and Cynthia A. Hasbrook. 1988. "Denial of Power in Televised Women's Sports." *Sociology of Sport Journal* 5:1–21.

Dworkin, Shari L. [2003]. "A Woman's Place Is in the . . . Cardiovascular Room? Gender Relations, the Body, and the Gym." In *Athletic Intruders*, edited by Anne Bolin and Jane Granskog. Albany: State University of New York Press.

Gilroy, S. 1989. "The Embody-ment of Power: Gender and Physical Activity." *Leisure Studies* 8:163–71.

Guthrie, Sharon R., and Shirley Castelnuovo. 1992. "Elite Women Bodybuilders: Model of Resistance or Compliance?" *Play and Culture* 5:378–400.

Hall, M. Ann. 1996. *Feminism and Sporting Bodies: Essays on Theory and Practice.* Champaign, IL: Human Kinetics.

Hargreaves, Jennifer. 1994. *Sporting Females: Critical Issues in the History and Sociology of Women's Sport.* New York: Routledge.

Hoch, Paul. 1979. *White Hero, Black Beast: Racism, Sexism and the Mask of Masculinity.* London: Pluto.

Hochschild, Arlie R. 1989. *The Second Shift.* New York: Avon.

Kane, Mary Jo. 1995. "Resistance/Transformation of the Oppositional Binary: Exposing Sport as a Continuum." *Journal of Sport and Social Issues* 19:191–218.

Kane, Mary Jo, and Helen Lenskyj. 1998. "Media Treatment of Female Athletes: Issues of Gender and Sexualities." In *MediaSport: Cultural Sensibilities and Sport in the Media Age*, edited by Lawrence A. Wenner. London: Routledge.

Kimmel, Michael S. 1990. "Baseball and the Reconstitution of American Masculinity, 1880–1920." Pp. 55–66 in *Sport, Men and the Gender Order: Critical Feminist Perspectives*, edited by Michael A. Messner and Donald F. Sabo. Champaign, IL: Human Kinetics.

Lenskyj, Helen. 1987. "Female Sexuality and Women's Sport." *Women's Studies International Forum* 4:381–86.

Lopiano, Donna A. 1993. "Political Analysis: Gender Equity Strategies for the Future." Pp. 104–16 in *Women in Sport: Issues and Controversies*, edited by Greta L. Cohen. Newbury Park, CA: Sage.

Lorber, Judith. 1996. "Beyond the Binaries: Depolarizing the Categories of Sex, Sexuality, and Gender." *Sociological Inquiry* 66:143–59.

MacKinnon, Catharine A. 1987. *Feminism Unmodified: Discourses on Life and Law.* Cambridge, MA: Harvard University Press.

Markula, Pirkko. 1996. "Firm but Shapely, Fit but Sexy, Strong but Thin: The Postmodern Aerobicizing Female Bodies." *Sociology of Sport Journal* 12:424–53.

McDermott, Lisa. 1996. "Towards a Feminist Understanding of Physicality within the Context of Women's Physically Active and Sporting Lives." *Sociology of Sport Journal* 13:12–30.

Messner, Michael A. 1988. "Sports and Male Domination: The Female Athlete as Contested Ideological Terrain." *Sociology of Sport Journal* 5:197–211.

———. 1992. *Power at Play: Sports and the Problem of Masculinity.* Boston: Beacon.

———. 1993a. " 'Changing Men' and Feminist Politics in the United States." *Theory and Society* 22:723–37.

———. 1993b. "White Men Misbehaving: Feminism, Afrocentrism, and the Promise of a Critical Standpoint." *Journal of Sport and Social Issues* 16:136–44.

———. Forthcoming. "Theorizing Gendered Bodies: Beyond the Subject/Object Dichotomy." In *Exercising Power: The Making and Remaking of the Body,* edited by Cheryl L. Cole, John Loy, and Michael A. Messner. Albany: State University of New York Press.

Messner, Michael A., Margaret Carlisle Duncan, and Faye Linda Wachs. 1996. "The Gender of Audience-Building: Televised Coverage of Men's and Women's NCAA Basketball." *Sociological Inquiry* 66:422–39.

Messner, Michael A., and Donald F. Sabo. 1990. "Towards a Critical Feminist Reappraisal of Sport, Men and the Gender Order." In *Sport, Men and the Gender Order: Critical Feminist Perspectives,* edited by Michael A. Messner and Donald F. Sabo. Champaign, IL: Human Kinetics.

———. 1994. *Sex, Violence and Power in Sports: Rethinking Masculinity.* Freedom, CA: Crossing Press.

Nelson, Mariah Burton. 1991. *Are We Winning Yet? How Women Are Changing Sports and Sports Are Changing Women.* New York: Random House.

———. 1994. *The Stronger Women Get, the More Men Love Football: Sexism and the American Culture of Sports.* New York: Avon.

President's Council on Physical Fitness and Sports. 1997. "Physical Activity and Sport in the Lives of Girls." Washington, DC: President's Council on Physical Fitness and Sports.

Ryan, Joan. 1995. *Little Girls in Pretty Boxes: The Making and Breaking of Elite Gymnasts and Figure Skaters.* New York: Warner.

Sabo, Donald F. 1994. "Pigskin, Patriarchy, and Pain." Pp. 82–88 in *Sex, Violence and Power in Sports: Rethinking Masculinity,* by Michael A. Messner and Donald F. Sabo. Freedom, CA: Crossing Press.

Sabo, Donald F., and Women's Sports Foundation. 1988. *The Wilson Report: Moms, Dads, Daughters and Sports.* East Meadow, NY: Women's Sports Foundation.

Sedgewick, Eve K. 1990. *Epistemology of the Closet.* Berkeley: University of California Press.

Stein, Arlene, and Ken Plummer. 1994. " 'I Can't Even Think Straight': Queer Theory and the Missing Sexual Revolution in Sociology." *Sociological Theory* 12:178–87.

Take Action for Girls. 1996. "The Two Faces of Nike." *Take Action for Girls Newsletter* 1 (November):2.

Theberge, Nancy. 1985. "Toward a Feminist Alternative to Sport as a Male Preserve." *Quest* 37:193–202.

———. 1987. "Sport and Women's Empowerment." *Women's Studies International Forum* 10:387–93.

Thompson, Shona M. 1988. "Challenging the Hegemony: New Zealand Women's Opposition to Rugby and the Reproduction of Capitalist Patriarchy." *International Review of the Sociology of Sport* 23:205–12.

Tomlinson, Alan, and Ilkay Yorganci. 1997. "Male Coach/Female Athlete Relations: Gender and Power Relations in Competitive Sport." *Journal of Sport and Social Issues* 21:134–55.

White, Philip G., Kevin Young, and William G. McTeer. 1995. "Sport, Masculinity, and the Injured Body." Pp. 158–82 in *Men's Health and Illness: Gender, Power, and the Body,* edited by Donald F. Sabo and Frederick Gordon. Thousand Oaks, CA: Sage.

Women's Sports Foundation. 1997. *The Women's Sports Foundation Gender Equity Report Card: A Survey of Athletic Opportunity in American Higher Education.* East Meadow, NY: Women's Sports Foundation.

Young, Iris M. 1990. *Throwing Like a Girl and Other Essays in Feminist Philosophy and Social Theory.* Bloomington: Indiana University Press.

■ ■ ■

Reading Rhetorically

1. Locate and mark sentences throughout Dworkin and Messner's essay where they use signposts, saying explicitly what they are doing and why. What role does signposting play in helping you understand their argument? What conclusions can you draw about how you might use signposting in your own writing?

2. What do the authors mean by "hegemonic masculinity" (para. 1)? Using a dictionary and the context of the article (see para. 17, in particular), explain in your own words — and with your own examples — what the phrase means. How is this concept important to the argument the authors make about sport culture?

3. Like many authors in this collection, Dworkin and Messner divide their essay into sections. Summarize the purpose of each section, and point to a key sentence or two in each section that best expresses its purpose. In class discuss how each section contributes to the larger argument the authors are making. What tips can you draw from your discussion about effective ways to organize complex essays of your own?

Inquiring Further

4. What do you know about Title IX? Use your library's online research tools to find the exact wording of the law. What is the relationship between Title IX and sports? Interview one or two coaches — perhaps one female and one male coach — about the impact of Title IX on high school and college athletics. Alternatively, use the library to locate different perspectives on this topic. Share your findings with the class.

5. What evidence can you find in recent popular magazines of Dworkin and Messner's claims about the representation of male and female athletes? Working individually or in a small group, analyze the images in five sports or health magazines aimed at male readers, and five magazines aimed at female readers. To what extent do the images there confirm Dworkin and Messner's claims, extend them, or contradict them? What conclusions can you draw?

6. Dworkin and Messner refer to feminism and feminist ideas frequently throughout this essay. As a class, generate a list of definitions for these terms. Then, using your library's online research tools, look for other definitions. Share your findings with the class. What was the most surprising or interesting definition you discovered?

Framing Conversations

7. Like Dworkin and Messner, Franklin Foer (p. 406) is interested in what sports offer those who participate in them, both on and off the field. Drawing on and analyzing the ideas of these writers, compose an essay in which you make an argument about what participation in sports offers (and, perhaps, fails to offer). Be sure to provide evidence for your claims.

8. Although Dworkin and Messner focus on women's experiences with athletics, they do offer some interesting insights into the ways in which masculinity and athleticism are closely related. Write an essay in which you

explore and develop your ideas about the relationship between assumptions about masculinity and athleticism by drawing on Dworkin and Messner's ideas and on Judith Lorber's thoughts about the ways we "do gender," particularly masculinity (p. 617). Offer examples to support your claims as you teach your readers what you think is most important about this topic.

9. In paragraph 10, Dworkin and Messner analyze the image of gymnast Kerri Strug in the arms of her coach to illustrate their point about women's bodies and athletics. Jean Kilbourne (p. 592) is similarly interested in what images of bodies tell us about our assumptions about gender. Write an essay in which you draw on these authors' strategies of visual analysis to analyze a series of images of female or male athletes (perhaps those you collected for question 5 above). Given these images, what conclusions can you draw about the relationship between gender and sports? What is the significance of your findings?

■ HENRY A. GIROUX ────────────────

Children's Culture and Disney's Animated Films

Henry A. Giroux is a professor of education and cultural studies. After teaching high school history in Rhode Island, he earned his doctorate in 1977 and has since taught at several universities, including Miami University in Ohio and Penn State University. He currently holds the Global Television Network Chair in Communication Studies at McMaster University in Ontario, Canada. He has written more than 150 articles and nearly 40 books on aspects of culture, including the aftermath of Hurricane Katrina, basketball, channel surfing, and the politics of modern education. (Like bell hooks, whose work is also in this book, Giroux has been deeply influenced by Brazilian educational theorist Paulo Freire.) This selection, "Children's Culture and Disney's Animated Films," is a chapter from his book *The Mouse That Roared: Disney and the End of Innocence* (1999).

Giroux is one of many scholars who are interested in how popular culture shapes our understandings of gender, race, and nationality (to name just a few identity categories) in ways we may not notice because the messages are packaged as entertainment — in stories, songs, and images. Disney's animated films, in particular, are the subject of much cultural scholarship, and Giroux draws on ideas from a number of academic writers, including Eric Smoodin, Jon Wiener, David Kunzle, and Jack Zipes. A glance at the footnotes shows a long list of books and articles that analyze the vast influence of the Walt Disney Company, from films to marketing campaigns.

Giroux argues that beyond simply entertaining us, Disney films function as "teaching machines" (para. 2), educating children in ways we might find surprising. He is particularly concerned that the films make stereotypes about race and gender seem like fantasy and fun. Giroux finds evidence for his claims in the racism in *Aladdin* (see if you agree with his analysis of that film's song lyrics, which begins in paragraph 41) and the representation of clashing cultures in *Pocahontas*, which may represent

Native Americans in a positive light but "bleaches colonialism of its genocidal legacy" (para. 35). Although the title characters in *The Little Mermaid*
and *Mulan* seem at first to be unconventionally strong and brave, Giroux
argues that the plot pushes both female protagonists from strength to
dependence, as their adventure stories turn into conventional love stories.

Giroux contextualizes his analysis of Disney films with critics who
look more broadly at contemporary culture, such as Mark Crispin Miller,
who researches what he calls the "national entertainment state" (quoted in
paragraph 56), in which public policy is often shaped by the myth making
of popular culture. Disney's product placements and tie-ins also catch
Giroux's eye as part of a more general trend of marketing to children, and
another one of the ways the films teach young viewers — in this case, to
become a certain kind of American consumer.

As you read, think back to your own responses to Disney's animated
films — both as a child and as an adult. Can you come up with examples
from these films that confirm or refute Giroux's analysis? Part of Giroux's
call to action is for educators, for parents — for anyone reading his
essay — to become more conscious, and conscientious, viewers. In this
essay, Giroux raises questions you could ask of any film or other storytelling medium that captures public interest.

Animation as a form of historical memory has entered real space. After all,
any space or film that uses manipulated, interactive imagery must be called,
by definition, a form of animation; and we are increasingly being submerged
in life as a video game, even while our political crises deepen, and our class
difference widens. . . . We act out stories inside cartoons now.

— Norman M. Klein, *7 Minutes: The Life and
Death of the American Animated Cartoon*

As a single father of three young boys, I found myself somewhat reluc-   *1*
tantly being introduced to the world of Hollywood animated films and,
in particular, to those produced by Disney. Before becoming an observer
of this form of children's culture, I accepted the largely unquestioned
assumption that animated films stimulate imagination and fantasy, create
a feeling of innocence and healthy adventure, and in general are "good" for
kids. In other words, such films appeared to be wholesome vehicles of
amusement, a highly regarded source of fun and joy for children.

However, within a very short period of time, it became clear to me that   *2*
these films do more than entertain.[1] Needless to say, animated films operate on many registers, but one of the most persuasive is the role they play

---

[1]For a critical engagement of commercialization, popular culture, and children's
culture, see Marsha Kinder, *Playing with Power in Movies, Television, and Video Games*
(Berkeley: University of California Press, 1991); Doug Kellner, *Media Culture* (New York:
Routledge, 1995); David Buckingham and Julian Sefton-Green, *Cultural Studies Goes to
School* (Washington, D.C.: Taylor and Francis, 1994).

as the new "teaching machines." I soon found that for my children, and I suspect for many others, these films possess at least as much cultural authority and legitimacy for teaching roles, values, and ideals as more traditional sites of learning, such as the public schools, religious institutions, and the family. Disney films combine enchantment and innocence in narrating stories that help children understand who they are, what societies are about, and what it means to construct a world of play and fantasy in an adult environment. The authority of such films, in part, stems from their unique form of representation and their ever-growing presence. But such authority is also produced and secured within a media apparatus equipped with dazzling technology, sound effects, and imagery packaged as entertainment, spin-off commercial products, and "huggable" stories.

The significance of Disney's animated films as a site of learning is heightened by the widespread recognition that schools and other public sites are increasingly beset by a crisis of vision, purpose, and motivation. The mass media, especially the world of Hollywood films, constructs a dreamlike world of security, coherence, and childhood innocence in which kids find a place to situate themselves in their emotional lives. Unlike the often hard, joyless reality of schooling, children's films provide a high-tech visual space in which adventure and pleasure meet in a fantasy world of possibilities and a commercial sphere of consumerism and commodification. The educational relevance of animated films became especially clear to me as my kids experienced the vast entertainment and teaching machine embodied by Disney. Increasingly, as I watched a number of Disney films first in the movie theater and then on video, I became aware of how necessary it was to move beyond treating these films as transparent entertainment and to question the diverse messages that constitute Disney's conservative view of the world. *3*

Trademarking Innocence

Kids learn from Disney films, so maybe it's time parents and educators paid closer attention to what these films are saying. I realize that this is heresy, especially at a time when kids are being subjected to increasing violence in Hollywood blockbusters, video games, and other commercial forms of entertainment. But while Disney films do not promote the violence that has become central to many other forms of popular and mass culture, they do carry cultural and social messages that need to be scrutinized. After all, "the happiest place on earth" has traditionally gained its popularity in part through its trademark image of innocence, which has largely protected it from the interrogation of critics. *4*

Left-wing criticism of Disney is often ignored by the popular press. Yet the recent charge by conservative Southern Baptists that Disney films promote a seditious, anti-Christian ideology received enormous publicity in the mainstream media. The reason is that such criticism appears so extreme as to be comical and, therefore, safe for the media to cover. The *5* more liberal critiques often ignore entirely the racist, sexist, and antide-mocratic ethos that permeates Disney films. For instance, the *New York Times* critic Michiko Kakutani argues that if anything is wrong with Dis-ney's animated films it is that the characters of late are too preachy and promote "wholesome messages" that "only an ogre or bigot could hate."[2] One can't help wondering what is wholesome about Disney's overt racism toward Arabs displayed in *Aladdin,* the retrograde gender roles at work in *The Little Mermaid* and *Beauty and the Beast,* and the undisguised celebra-tion of antidemocratic governments and racism (remember the hyenas, who sounded like poor blacks and Hispanics?) evident in *The Lion King.* (I discuss these films in detail later in this chapter.)

There is more at work here than a successful public relations campaign intent on promoting Disney's claim to goodness and morality. There is also the reality of a powerful economic and political empire, which in 1997 made more than $22.5 billion in revenues from all of its divisions.[3] Disney is more than a corporate giant; it is also a cultural institution that fiercely protects its legendary status as purveyor of innocence and moral virtue.

Quick to mobilize its legal representatives, public relations spokesper-sons, and professional cultural critics to safeguard the borders of its "magic kingdom," Disney has aggressively prosecuted violations of its copyrights and has a reputation for bullying authors who use the Disney archives but refuse to allow Disney censors to approve their manuscripts before they are actually published.[4] For example, in its zeal to protect its image and extend its profits, Disney has threatened legal action against three South Florida day care centers for using Disney cartoon characters on their exterior walls.

---

[2]Michiko Kakutani, "This Mouse Once Roared," *New York Times Magazine,* January 4, 1998, p. 8. Compare Kakutani's analysis with Matt Roth, "A Short History of Disney-Fascism," *Jump Cut,* no. 40 (1996), pp. 15–20.

[3]Michael D. Eisner, "Letter to Shareholders," *The Walt Disney Company 1997 Annual Report* (Burbank, Calif.: Walt Disney Company, 1997), p. 2.

[4]There is a growing list of authors who have been pressured by Disney either through its refusal to allow copyrighted materials to be used or through its influence on publishers. Examples can be found in Jon Wiener, "In the Belly of the Mouse: The Dys-peptic Disney Archives," *Lingua Franca* (July/August 1994), pp. 69–72. Also Jon Wiener, "Murdered Ink," *Nation,* May 31, 1993, pp. 743–50. One typical example occurred with a book in which one of my own essays on Disney appears. While editing a book critical of Disney, Elizabeth Bell, Lynda Haas, and Laura Sells requested permission from Disney executives to use the Disney archives. In response, the editors received a letter from one of Disney's legal assistants asking to approve the book. The editors declined, and Disney forbade the use of its name in the title of the book and threatened to sue if the Disney name was used. Indiana University Press argued that it did not have the resources to fight Disney, so the title of the book was changed from *Doing Disney* to *From Mouse to Mermaid.* In another instance, Routledge publishers omitted an essay by David Kunzle on the imperialist messages in Disney's foreign comics in a book entitled *Disney Dis-course.* Thinking that Disney would not provide permission for the use of illustrations from the Disney archives, Routledge decided they could not publish the essay. Dis-couraged, Kunzle said, "I've given up. I'm not doing any more work on Disney. I don't think any university press would take the risk. The problem is not the likelihood of Dis-ney winning in court, it's the threat of having to bear the cost of fighting them." Wiener, "In the Belly of the Mouse," p. 72.

In this instance, Disney's role as an aggressive defender of conservative family values was undermined through its aggressive endorsement of property rights. While Disney's reputation as an undisputed moral authority on American values has taken a beating in the last few years, the power of Disney's mythological status cannot be underestimated.

Disney's image as an icon of American culture is consistently rein- 8 forced through the penetration of the Disney empire into every aspect of social life. Disney's $22 billion empire shapes children's experiences through box office movies, home videos, theme parks, hotels, sports teams, retail stores, classroom instructional films, compact discs, radio programs, television shows, internet servers, and family restaurants.[5] Through the use of public visual space, Disney's network of power relations promotes the construction of an all-encompassing world of enchantment allegedly free from ideology, politics, and power.[6] At the same time, Disney goes to great lengths to boost its civic image. Defining itself as a vehicle for education and civic responsibility, Disney has sponsored teacher of the year awards, provided Doer and Dreamer scholarships, and offered financial aid, internships, and other learning opportunities to disadvantaged urban youth through educational and work programs, such as its ice-skating program called Goals. Intent on defining itself as a purveyor of ideas rather than commodities, Disney is aggressively developing its image as a public service industry.[7] For example, Disney has become a partner in a public school venture in Celebration, Florida. No longer content to spread its values through media entertainment and theme parks, Disney has now inserted itself into the growing lucrative market of the public school system.

What is interesting here is that Disney no longer simply dispenses 9 the fantasies through which childhood innocence and adventure are produced, experienced, and affirmed. Disney now provides prototypes for families, schools, and communities. From the seedy urban haunts of New York City to the spatial monuments of consumption-shaping Florida, Disney is

[5]This figure comes from Michael Meyer et al., "Of Mice and Men," *Newsweek*, September 5, 1994, p. 41.

[6]The mutually determining relationship of culture and economic power is captured in Sharon Zukin, *Landscapes of Power: From Detroit to Disney World* (Berkeley: University of California Press, 1991), p. 221:

> The domestication of fantasy in visual consumption is inseparable from centralized structures of economic power. Just as the earlier power of the state illuminated public space — the streets — by artificial lamplight, so the economic power of CBS, Sony, and the Disney Company illuminates private space at home by electronic images. With the means of production so concentrated and the means of consumption so diffused, communication of these images becomes a way of controlling both knowledge and imagination, a form of corporate social control over technology and symbolic expressions of power.

[7]For a listing of public service programs that Disney has initiated, see Jennifer J. Laabs, "Disney Helps Keep Kids in School," *Personnel Journal* (November 1992), pp. 58–68.

refiguring the social and cultural landscape while spreading its corporate ideology through the inventions of its imagineers. Disney transformed large sections of West Forty-second Street in New York City into an advertisement for a cleaned-up Disney version of America. It has also created the town of Celebration, Florida, designed after the "main streets of small-town America and reminiscent of Norman Rockwell images."[8] What Disney leaves out of its upbeat promotional literature is the rather tenuous notion of democracy that informs its view of municipal government, since Celebration is "premised upon citizens not having control over the people who plan for them and administer the policies of the city."[9]

But Disney does more than provide prototypes for upscale communi- 10 ties; it also makes a claim on the future through its nostalgic view of the past. The French theorist Jean Baudrillard provides an interesting theoretical twist on the scope and power of Disney's influence, arguing that Disneyland is more "real" than fantasy because it now provides the image on which America constructs itself. For Baudrillard, Disneyland functions as a "deterrent" designed to "rejuvenate in reverse the fiction of the real." "Disneyland is there to conceal the fact that it is the 'real' country, all of 'real' America, which is Disneyland (just as prisons are there to conceal the fact that it is the social in its entirety, in its banal omnipresence, which is carceral). Disneyland is presented as imaginary in order to make us believe that the rest is real, when in fact all of Los Angeles and the America surrounding it are no longer real but of the order of the hyperreal and of simulation."[10] Examples of the Disnification of America abound. For instance, the Houston airport modeled its monorail after the one at Disneyland. New housing developments throughout America appropriate a piece of nostalgia by imitating the Victorian architecture of Disneyland's Main Street, USA. Moreover, throughout America, shopping malls imitate Disney's approach to retailing so "that shopping takes place in themed environments."[11] It seems that the real policy makers are not in Washington, D.C., but in California, and they call themselves the Disney imagineers. The boundaries between entertainment, education, and commercialization collapse through Disney's sheer reach into everyday life. The scope of the Disney empire reveals both shrewd business practices and a sharp eye for providing dreams and products through forms of popular culture in which kids are willing to materially and emotionally invest.

Popular audiences tend to reject any link between ideology and 11 the prolific entertainment world of Disney. And yet Disney's pretense of

[8]Disney executives, quoted in Mark Walsh, "Disney Holds Up School as Model for Next Century," *Education Week* 39 (1994), p. 1.

[9]Tom Vanderbilt, "Mickey Mouse Goes to Town(s)," *Nation*, August 28/September 4, 1995, p. 199.

[10]Jean Baudrillard, *Simulations* (New York: Semiotext(e), 1983), p. 25. Also see Baudrillard, "Consumer Society," in Mark Poster, ed., *Jean Baudrillard: Selected Works* (Stanford: Stanford University Press, 1988), pp. 29–56.

[11]Alan Bryman, *Disney and His Worlds* (New York: Routledge, 1995), p. 26.

innocence appears to some critics as little more than a promotional mask that covers its aggressive marketing techniques and its influence in educating children to become active consumers. Eric Smoodin, editor of *Disney Discourse*, a book critical of Disney's role in American culture, argues that "Disney constructs childhood so as to make it entirely compatible with consumerism."[12] Even more disturbing is the widespread belief that Disney's "innocence" renders it unaccountable for the way it shapes children's sense of reality: its sanitized notions of identity, difference, and history in the seemingly apolitical cultural universe of the "magic kingdom." Jon Wiener argues that Disneyland's version of Main Street America harks back to an "image of small towns characterized by cheerful commerce, with barbershop quartets and ice cream sundaes and glorious parades." For Wiener, this view not only fictionalizes and trivializes the real Main Streets of the turn of the century, it also appropriates the past to legitimate a portrayal of a world "without tenements or poverty or urban class conflict. . . . It's a native white Protestant dream of a world without blacks or immigrants."[13]

Critiquing Disney Films

Some of Disney's animated films produced since 1989 are important because   *12*
they have received enormous praise from the dominant press and have achieved blockbuster status.[14] For many children, they represent an entrance into the world of Disney. Moreover, the financial success and popularity of these films, rivaling many adult films, do not engender the critical analyses that adult films usually do. In short, critics and audiences are more willing to suspend critical judgment about children's films. Animated fantasy and entertainment films appear to fall outside of the world of values, meaning, and knowledge often associated with documentaries, art films, and even wide-circulation adult films. Elizabeth Bell, Lynda Haas, and Laura Sells capture this sentiment: "Disney audiences . . . legal institutions, film theorists, cultural critics, and popular audiences all guard the borders of Disney film as 'off limits' to the critical enterprise, constructing Disney as a metonym for 'America' — clean, decent, industrious — 'the happiest place on earth.'"[15]

---

[12]Eric Smoodin, "How to Read Walt Disney," in Smoodin, ed., *Disney Discourse: Producing the Magic Kingdom* (New York: Routledge, 1994), p. 18.

[13]Jon Wiener, "Tall Tales and True," *Nation*, January 31, 1994, p. 134.

[14]Disney's animated film *The Lion King* may be the most financially successful film ever made. Disney's animated films released since 1990 are all among the ten top-grossing films. *The Lion King* ranked first, with $253.5 million; *Aladdin* ranked second, with $217.4 million; and *Beauty and the Beast* ranked seventh, grossing $145.9 million. See Thomas King, "Creative but Unpolished Top Executive for Hire," *Wall Street Journal*, August 26, 1994, p. B1.

[15]Elizabeth Bell, Lynda Haas, and Laura Sells, "Walt's in the Movies," in Bell, Haas, and Sells, eds., *From Mouse to Mermaid* (Bloomington: Indiana University Press, 1995), p. 3.

Given the influence that the Disney ideology has on children, it is *13* imperative for parents, teachers, and other adults to understand how such films influence the values of the children who view them. As a producer of children's culture, Disney should not be given an easy pardon because it is defined as a citadel of fun and good cheer. On the contrary, as one of the primary institutions constructing childhood culture in the United States, Disney warrants healthy suspicion and critical debate. Such a debate should not be limited to the home but should be centered in schools and other public sites of learning.

It is important not to address Disney's animated films by simply con- *14* demning Disney as an ideological reactionary corporation promoting a conservative world view under the guise of entertainment. It is equally important not to celebrate Disney as the animated version of Mr. Rogers, doing nothing more than providing joy and happiness to children all over the world.[16] Disney does both. Disney does offer children visual stimulation and joy: dramatic thunderstorms, kaleidoscopic musical numbers, and the transformation of real life into wondrous spectacles. Disney's films offer children opportunities to locate themselves in a world that resonates with their desires and interests. Pleasure is one of the defining principles of what Disney produces, and children are both its subjects and objects. Hence, Disney's animated films have to be interrogated and mined as an important site for the production of children's culture. At the same time, these films are often filled with contradictory messages. Disney's influence and power must be situated within the broader understanding of the company's role as a corporate giant intent on spreading the conservative and commercial values that erode civil society while proclaiming to restructure it.

The role that Disney plays in shaping individual identities and in con- *15* trolling the fields of social meaning through which children negotiate the world is far more complex than simple reactionary politics. If educators and other cultural workers are to include the culture of children as an important site of contestation and struggle, then it is imperative to analyze how Disney's animated films influence the way America's cultural landscape is imagined. Disney's scripted view of childhood and society needs to be engaged and challenged as "a historically specific matter of social analysis and intervention."[17] This is particularly important since Disney's

[16]The celebrations of Walt Disney are too numerous to mention in detail, but an early example is Bob Thomas, *Walt Disney: An American Original* (New York: Simon and Schuster, 1976). Thomas's book followed on the heels of a scathing attack on Disney by Richard Schickel, *The Disney Version* (New York: Simon and Schuster, 1968). A more recent version of the no-holds-barred critique of Disney is Carl Hiassen, *Team Rodent: How Disney Devours the World* (New York: Ballantine, 1998). The more moderate position is Steven Watts, *The Magic Kingdom* (New York: Houghton Mifflin, 1997). Schickel's book is one of the best critiques of Disney.

[17]Barbara Foley, "Subversion and Oppositionality in the Academy," in Maria-Regina Kecht, ed., *Pedagogy Is Politics: Literary Theory and Critical Teaching* (Urbana: University of Illinois Press, 1992), p. 79. See also Roger I. Simon, "Forms of Insurgency in the Production of Popular Memories," in Henry A. Giroux and Peter McLaren, eds., *Between Borders: Pedagogy and the Politics of Cultural Studies* (New York: Routledge, 1994).

animated films provoke and inform children's imaginations, desires, roles and dreams while simultaneously sedimenting affect and meaning.

The wide distribution and popular appeal of Disney's animated films *16* provide diverse audiences the opportunity for critical viewing. Critically analyzing how Disney films work to construct meaning, induce pleasure, and reproduce ideologically loaded fantasies is not meant as mere film criticism. Like any educational institution, Disney's view of the world needs to be discussed in terms of how it narrates children's culture and how it can be held accountable for what it does as a significant cultural public sphere — a space in which ideas, values, audiences, markets, and opinions create different publics and social formations. Of course, Disney's self-proclaimed innocence, inflexibility in dealing with social criticism, and paranoid attitude are now legendary and provide more reason that Disney be both challenged and engaged critically. Moreover, as a multibillion-dollar company, Disney's corporate and cultural influence is too enormous and far-reaching to allow it to define itself exclusively within the imaginary discourse of innocence, civic pride, and entertainment.[18]

The question of whether Disney's animated films are good for kids has *17* no easy answer and resists simple analysis within the traditional and allegedly nonideological registers of fun and entertainment. Disney's most recent films — *The Little Mermaid* (1989), *Beauty and the Beast* (1991), *Aladdin* (1992), *The Lion King* (1994), *Pocahontas* (1995), *The Hunchback of Notre Dame* (1996), *Hercules* (1997), and *Mulan* (1998) — provide ample opportunity to address how Disney constructs a culture of joy and innocence for children out of the intersection of entertainment, advocacy, pleasure, and consumerism.[19] All of these films have been high-profile releases catering to massive audiences. Moreover, their commercial success is not limited to box-office profits. Successfully connecting consumption and moviegoing, Disney's animated films provide a "marketplace of culture," a launching pad for products and merchandise, including videocassettes,

---

[18]A number of authors address Disney's imagined landscape as a place of economic and cultural power. See, for example, Zukin, *Landscapes of Power;* Michael Sorkin, "Disney World: The Power of Facade/the Facade of Power," in Sorkin, ed., *Variations on a Theme Park* (New York: Noonday, 1992); and see the especially impressive Stephen M. Fjellman, *Vinyl Leaves: Walt Disney World and America* (Boulder, Colo.: Westview, 1992).

[19]In his brilliant book, Norman M. Klein argues that Disney constructed his expanded cartoons as a form of animated consumer memory. As Klein puts it, "The atmospheric lighting of Disney epic cartoons is very similar to the reverie of shopping, to shopping arcades, even to the permanent dusk of a room illuminated by television. It takes us more to the expanded shopping mall than a planned suburb, to a civilization based on consumer memories more than urban (or suburban) locations. . . . Disney showed us how to stop thinking of a city as residential or commercial, but rather as airbrushed streets in our mind's eye, a shopper's nonscape. If we can make a city remind us of animated consumer memory, it removes the alienation of changing cities, and replaces it with a cloud of imaginary store windows." *7 Minutes: The Life and Death of the American Animated Cartoon* (London: Verso, 1993, reprinted in 1998), p. 144.

sound-track albums, children's clothing, furniture, stuffed toys, and new theme park rides.[20]

For example, *The Little Mermaid* and *Beauty and the Beast* videocassettes have combined sales of over 34 million. *Aladdin* has earned more than "$1 billion from box-office income, video sales and such ancillary baubles as Princess Jasmine dresses and Genie cookie jars"[21] and as a video interactive game sold more than 3 million copies in 1993. Similar sales are expected for the video and interactive game version of the film *The Lion King*, which had grossed $253.5 million in profits by August 24, 1994.[22] In fact, the first few weeks after *The Lion King* videocassette was released, it had sales of more than 20 million, and Disney's stock soared by $2.25 a share based on first-week revenues of $350 million. Jessica J. Reiff, an analyst at Oppenheimer and Company, says that "the movie will represent $1 billion in profits for Disney over two or three years."[23]

At the launching of *The Hunchback of Notre Dame*, Disney Records shipped 2 million sing-along home videos and seven *Hunchback* audio products, including the soundtrack CD and cassette and a toddler-targeted *My First Read-Along*. Tie-in promotions for the film included Burger King, Payless Shoes, Nestle, and Mattel.[24] While *The Hunchback of Notre Dame* did not fare well at the box office, generating a disappointing $99 million in North American revenue, it is expected, according to *Adweek* magazine, "to generate $500 million in profit (not just revenues), after the other revenue streams are taken into account."[25] Similarly, Disney characters such as Mickey Mouse, Snow White, Jasmine, Aladdin, and Pocahontas have become prototypes for toys, logos, games, and rides that fill department stores all over the world. Disney theme parks, which made more than $4 billion in revenues in 1997, produced a sizable portion of their profits through the merchandising of toys based on characters from the animated films.

The Lion King has been one of Disney's biggest commercial successes and provided a model for marketing its future animated films, including

[20]The term "marketplace of culture" comes from Richard de Cordova, "The Mickey in Macy's Window: Childhood Consumerism and Disney Animation," in Eric Smoodin, ed., *Disney Discourse*, p. 209. Disney was one of the first companies to tie the selling of toys to the consuming of movies. Challenging the assumption that toy consumption was limited to seasonal sales, Disney actively created Mickey Mouse Clubs, advertised its toys in storefront windows, and linked its movies directly to the distribution of children's toys.

[21]Richard Corliss, "The Mouse That Roars," *Time*, June 20, 1994, p. 59.

[22]Richard Turner, "Walt Disney Presents: Forward to the Future," *Wall Street Journal*, August 26, 1994, p. B1.

[23][Cited in] Sallie Hofmeister, "In the Realm of Marketing, the 'Lion King' Rules," *New York Times*, July 12, 1994, p. D1.

[24]Moira McCormick, "'Hunchback' Soundtrack Tie-Ins Abound," *Billboard*, May 25, 1996, p. 10.

[25]Robert W. McChesney, *Corporate Media and the Threat to Democracy* (New York: Seven Stories Press, 1997), pp. 20–21.

Mulan and *Hercules* (with its blatant commercial built into the movie itself). *The Lion King* produced a staggering $1 billion in merchandising profits in 1994 alone — the year of its release — not to mention the profits made from spin-off products.[26] For example, when *The Lion King* was first released, Disney shipped out more than 3 million copies of the sound track. Disney's culture of commercialism is big business and the toys modeled after Disney's animated films provide goods for the more than 365 Disney Stores worldwide. "The merchandise — Mermaid dolls, Aladdin undies, and collectibles like a sculpture of Bambi's Field Mouse — account for a stunning 20 percent of Disney's operating income."[27]

One of Disney's biggest promotion campaigns began with the summer 1995 release of *Pocahontas*. A record lineup of tie-in merchandise included *Pocahontas* stuffed animals, sheets, pillowcases, toothbrushes, games, moccasins, and more than forty "picture and activity books."[28] A consortium of corporations spent an estimated $125 million on cross-marketing *Pocahontas*. Two well-known examples include Burger King, which was converted into an advertisement for the film and gave away an estimated 50 million Pocahontas figurines, and the Mattel Corporation, which marketed more than fifty different dolls and toys.

But Disney's attempt to turn children into consumers and to make commodification a defining principle of children's culture should not suggest a parallel vulgarity in its aesthetic experiments with popular forms of representation. Disney has shown enormous inventiveness in its attempts to reconstruct the very grounds on which popular culture is defined and shaped. For example, by defining popular culture as a hybridized sphere that combines genres and forms and that often collapses the boundary between high and low culture, Disney has pushed against aesthetic form and cultural legitimacy. When *Fantasia* appeared in the 1930s, it drew the wrath of music critics, who, holding to an elite view of classical music, were outraged that the musical score drew from the canon of high culture. By combining high and low culture, Disney opened up new cultural possibilities for artists and audiences alike. Moreover, as sites of entertainment, Disney's films work because they put both children and adults in touch with joy and adventure. They present themselves as places to experience pleasure, even when we have to buy it. And yet Disney's brilliant use of aesthetic forms, musical scores, and inviting characters can only be read in light of the broader conceptions of reality shaped by these films within a wider system of dominant representations about gender roles, race, and agency that are endlessly repeated in the visual worlds of television, Hollywood film, and videocassettes.

[26]For a summation of the merchandising avalanche that accompanied the movie theater version of *The Lion King*, see Hofmeister, "In the Realm of Marketing."

[27]Karen Schoemer, "An Endless Stream of Magic and Moola," *Newsweek*, September 5, 1994, p. 47.

[28]Tom McNichol, "Pushing 'Pocahontas,'" *USA Weekend*, June 9–11, 1995, p. 4.

A number of the films mentioned draw upon the talents of songwriters   23
Howard Ashman and Alan Menken, whose skillful arrangements provide
the emotional glue of the animation experience. The rousing calypso number "Under the Sea" in *The Little Mermaid*, and "Be Our Guest," the Busby
Berkeley–inspired musical sequence in *Beauty and the Beast*, are indicative
of the musical talent at work in Disney's animated film. Fantasy abounds,
as Disney's animated films produce a host of exotic and stereotypical villains, heroes, and heroines. The Beast's enchanted castle in *Beauty and the
Beast* becomes magical as household objects are transformed into dancing
teacups and silverware and a talking teapot. And yet tied to the magical
fantasy and lighthearted musical scores are stereotypes characteristic of
Disney's view of childhood culture.

For example, Ursula, the large, oozing, black and purple squid in *The*   24
Little Mermaid, gushes with evil and irony, and the heroine and mermaid,
Ariel, appears as a cross between a typical rebellious teenager and a Southern California fashion model. Disney's representations of evil women and
good women appear to have been fashioned in the editorial office of *Vogue*.
The wolflike monster in *Beauty and the Beast* evokes a combination of
terror and gentleness. Scar, in *The Lion King*, is a suave feline who master-
fully portrays evil and betrayal. Disney's evocation of war and battle in
Mulan is expansive and provocative. The animated objects and animals
in these films are of the highest artistic standards, but they do not exist in
an ideology-free zone. They are tied to larger narratives about freedom,
rites of passage, intolerance, choice, greed, and the brutalities of male
chauvinism.

Enchantment comes at a high price, however, if the audience is meant   25
to suspend judgment of the films' ideological messages. Even though these
messages can be read from a variety of viewpoints, the assumptions that
structure these films restrict the number of cultural meanings that can be
brought to bear on these films, especially when the intended audience is
mostly children. The role of the critic of Disney's animated films, however,
is not to assign them a particular ideological reading but to analyze the
themes and assumptions that inform these films, both within and outside
of the dominant institutional and ideological formations. Such analyses
allow educators and others to understand how such films can become sites
of contestation, translation, and exchange.

And beyond merely recognizing the plurality of readings such films   26
might foster, there is also the pedagogical task of provoking audiences to
reflect upon the ways in which Disney's themes function as part of a
broader public discourse, privileging some definitions or interpretations
over others. The conservative values that Disney films promote assume
such force because of the context in which they are situated and because
they resonate so powerfully with dominant perceptions and meanings.
Pedagogically, this suggests the need for educators, parents, and others to
analyze critically how the privileged dominant readings of Disney's animated films generate and affirm particular pleasures, desires, and subject

positions that define for children specific notions of agency and its possibilities in society.

Contexts mold interpretations; but political, economic, and ideological contexts also produce the texts to be read. The focus on films must be supplemented with an analysis of the institutional practices and social structures that work to shape such texts. Such analysis should suggest pedagogical strategies for understanding how dominant regimes of power limit the range of views that children might bring to reading Disney's animated films. By making the relationship between power and knowledge visible, while simultaneously referencing what is often taken for granted, teachers and critics can analyze Disney's animated films pedagogically so that students and others can read such films within, against, and outside of the dominant codes that inform them. *27*

There is a double pedagogical movement here. First, there is the need to read Disney's films in relation to their articulation with other dominant texts in order to assess their similarities in legitimating particular ideologies. Second, there is the need to use Disney's thematization of America and America's thematization of Disney as referents to make visible — and to disrupt — dominant codings and to do so in a space that invites dialogue, debate, and alternative readings. For instance, one major pedagogical challenge is to assess how dominant ideas that are repeated over time in these films and that are reinforced through other popular cultural texts can be taken as referents for engaging children in defining themselves within such representations. The task here is to provide readings of such films to serve as pedagogical referents.[29] By providing a theoretical referent for engaging Disney films, it becomes possible to explore pedagogically how we both construct and defend the readings we actually bring to such films, providing an opportunity to expand the dialogue regarding what Disney's films mean while simultaneously challenging the assumptions underlying dominant readings of these films. Taking a position on Disney's films should not degenerate into a doctrinaire reading or legitimate a form of political or pedagogical indoctrination with children or anybody else. Rather, such an approach should address how any reading of these films is ideological and should be engaged in terms of the context, the content, and the values and social relations it endorses. Moreover, engaging such readings politically and ideologically provides the pedagogical basis for making the films problematic and, thus, open to dialogue, rather than treating them uncritically, as mere entertainment. *28*

[29]Tony Bennett touches on this issue through an explication of the concept of reading formation. He argues, "The concept of reading formation is an attempt to think of context as a set of discursive and inter-textual determinations, operating on material and institutional supports, which bear in upon a text not just externally, from the outside in, but internally, shaping it — in the historically concrete forms in which it is available as a text-to-be-read — from the inside out." "Texts in History: The Determinations of Readings and Their Texts," in Derek Atridge et al., eds., *Poststructuralism and the Question of History* (Cambridge: Cambridge University Press, 1987), p. 72.

What Children Learn from Disney

The construction of gender identity for girls and women represents one of   *29*
the most controversial issues in Disney's animated films.[30] In both *The Little
Mermaid* and *The Lion King*, the female characters are constructed within
narrowly defined gender roles. All of the female characters in these films are
ultimately subordinate to males and define their power and desire almost
exclusively in terms of dominant male narratives. For instance, modeled
after a slightly anorexic Barbie doll, Ariel, the mermaid in *The Little Mermaid*, at first glance appears to be engaged in a struggle against parental
control, motivated by the desire to explore the human world and willing to
take a risk in defining the subject and object of her desires. But, in the end,
the struggle to gain independence from her father, Triton, and the desperate
striving that motivates her dissolve when Ariel makes a Mephistophelian
pact with the sea witch, Ursula. In this trade, Ariel gives away her voice to
gain a pair of legs so that she can pursue the handsome prince, Eric.

Although girls might be delighted by Ariel's teenage rebelliousness,   *30*
they are strongly positioned to believe, in the end, that desire, choice, and,
empowerment are closely linked to catching and loving a handsome man.
Bonnie Leadbeater and Gloria Lodato Wilson explore the pedagogical
message at work in the film: "The 20th-century innocent and appealing
video presents a high-spirited role for adolescent girls, but an ultimately
subservient role for adult women. Disney's 'Little Mermaid' has been granted
her wish to be part of the new world of men, but she is still flipping her fins
and is not going too far. She stands to explore the world of men. She
exhibits her new-found sexual desires. But the sexual ordering of women's
roles is unchanged."[31] Ariel becomes a metaphor for the traditional housewife in the making. When Ursula tells Ariel that taking away her voice is
not so bad because men don't like women who talk, the message is drama-
tized when the prince attempts to bestow the kiss of true love on Ariel even
though she has never spoken to him. Within this rigid narrative, womanhood offers Ariel the reward of marrying the right man for renouncing her
former life under the sea. It is a cultural model for the universe of female
choices in Disney's world view.

The rigid gender roles in *The Little Mermaid* are not isolated instances   *31*
in Disney's filmic universe; on the contrary, Disney's negative stereotypes
about women and girls gain force through the way in which similar messages are consistently circulated and reproduced, to varying degrees, in
many of Disney's animated films. For example, in *Aladdin* the issue of
agency and power is centered primarily on the role of the young street

---

[30]Critiques of Disney's portrayal of girls and women can be found in Bell, Haas, and
Sells, eds., *From Mouse to Mermaid*; Susan White, "Split Skins: Female Agency and Bod-
ily Mutilation in *The Little Mermaid*," in Jim Collins, Hilary Radner, and Ava Preacher
Collins, eds., *Film Theory Goes to the Movies* (New York: Routledge, 1993), pp. 182–95.

[31]Bonnie J. Leadbeater and Gloria Lodato Wilson, "Flipping Their Fins for a Place
to Stand: 19th- and 20th-Century Mermaids," *Youth and Society* 27:4 (1993), pp. 466–86.

tramp, Aladdin. Jasmine, the princess he falls in love with, is simply an object of his immediate desire as well as a social stepping-stone. Jasmine's life is almost completely defined by men, and, in the end, her happiness is ensured by Aladdin, who is finally given permission to marry her.

Disney's gender theme becomes a bit more complicated in *Beauty and* 32 *the Beast, Pocahontas,* and *Mulan.* Belle, the heroine of *Beauty and the Beast,* is portrayed as an independent woman stuck in a provincial village in eighteenth-century France. Seen as odd because she always has her nose in a book, she is pursued by Gaston, the ultimate vain, macho male typical of Hollywood films of the 1980s. To Belle's credit, she rejects him, but in the end she gives her love to the Beast, who holds her captive in the hope that she will fall in love with him and break the evil spell cast upon him as a young man. Belle not only falls in love with the Beast, she "civilizes" him by instructing him on how to eat properly, control his temper, and dance. Belle becomes a model of etiquette and style as she turns this narcissistic, muscle-bound tyrant into a "new" man, one who is sensitive, caring, and loving. Some critics have labeled Belle a Disney feminist because she rejects and vilifies Gaston, the ultimate macho man.

Less obviously, *Beauty and the Beast* also can be read as a rejection of 33 hypermasculinity and a struggle between the sensibilities of Gaston and the reformed sexist, the Beast. In this reading, Belle is less the focus of the film than a prop or "mechanism for solving the Beast's dilemma."[32] Whatever subversive qualities Belle personifies in the film, they seem to dissolve when focused on humbling male vanity. In the end, Belle simply becomes another woman whose life is valued for solving a man's problems.

Disney's next femme fatale, Pocahontas, appears to both challenge 34 and reproduce some of these stereotypes. Rather than a young adolescent, Pocahontas is made over historically to resemble a shapely, contemporary, high-fashion supermodel. Bright, courageous, literate, and politically progressive, she is a far cry from the traditional negative stereotypes of Native Americans portrayed in Hollywood films. But Pocahontas's character, like that of many of Disney's female protagonists, is drawn primarily in relation to the men who surround her. Initially, her identity is defined in resistance to her father's attempts to marry her off to one of the bravest warriors in the tribe. But her coming-of-age identity crisis is largely defined by her love affair with John Smith, a blond colonist who looks like he belongs in a Southern California pinup magazine of male surfers. Pocahontas's character is drawn primarily through her struggle to save John Smith from being executed by her father. Pocahontas exudes a kind of soppy romanticism that not only saves John Smith's life but also convinces the crew of the British ship to rebel against its greedy captain and return to England.

Of course, this is a Hollywood rewrite of history that bleaches colo- 35 nialism of its genocidal legacy. No mention is made of the fact that John

---

[32]Susan Jefford, *Hard Bodies: Hollywood Masculinity in the Reagan Era* (New Brunswick: Rutgers University Press, 1994), p. 150.

Smith's countrymen would ultimately ruin Pocahontas's land, bring disease, death, and poverty to her people, and eventually destroy their religion, economic livelihood, and way of life. In the Disney version of history, colonialism never happened, and the meeting between the old and new worlds is simply fodder for another "love conquers all" narrative. One wonders how this film would have been viewed by the public if it had been about a Jewish woman who falls in love with a blond Aryan Nazi while ignoring any references to the Holocaust.

The issue of female subordination returns with a vengeance in *The Lion King*. All of the rulers of the kingdom are men, reinforcing the assumption that independence and leadership are tied to patriarchal entitlement and high social standing. The dependency that the beloved lion king, Mufasa, engenders in the women of Pride Rock is unaltered after his death, when the evil Scar assumes control of the kingdom. Lacking any sense of outrage, independence, or resistance, the women felines hang around to do Scar's bidding.

The gender stereotyping is somewhat modified in *Mulan*. The lead character of the same name is presented as a bold female warrior who challenges traditional stereotypes of young women. But for all of her independence, in the end, the film is, as the film critic Janet Maslin points out, "still enough of a fairy tale to need a Mr. Right."[33] Mulan may be an independent, strong-willed young woman, but the ultimate payoff for her bravery comes in the form of catching the handsome son of a general. And if the point is missed, when the heroine's grandmother first sees the young man as he enters Mulan's house, she affirms what she (the audience?) sees as Mulan's real victory, which is catching a man, and yells out: "Sign me up for the next war!" And there is another disturbing side to Mulan as an alleged strong woman. Rather than aligning herself against the patriarchal celebration of war, violence, and militarism, Mulan becomes a cross-dresser who proves that when it comes to war she can perform as well as any male. By embracing a masculine view of war, Mulan cancels out any rupturing of traditional gender roles. She simply becomes one of the boys. But lest the fantasy be taken too far, Disney reminds us at the conclusion of the film that Mulan is still just a girl in search of a man, and as in so many other Disney animated films, Mulan becomes an exoticized version of the All-American girl who manages to catch the most handsome boy on the block, square jaw and all.

Given Disney's purported obsession with family values, especially as a consuming unit, it is curious that, with the exception of *Mulan*, there are no strong mothers or fathers in these films.[34] Not only are powerful mothers absent, but with the exception of the fathers of Pocahontas and Mulan, all of the father figures are portrayed as weak or stupid. Only the mermaid

[33]Janet Maslin, "Disney Turns to a Warrior of the East in 'Mulan.'" *New York Times*, June 19, 1998, p. B10.

[34]I thank Valerie Janesick for this insight.

has a domineering father. Jasmine's father is outwitted by his aides, and Belle's father is an airhead.

Jack Zipes, a leading theorist on fairy tales, claims that Disney's animated films reproduce "a type of gender stereotyping . . . that has an adverse effect on children, in contrast to what parents think. . . . Parents think they're essentially harmless — and they're not harmless."[35] *39*

Racial stereotyping is another major issue in Disney films. There is a long history of racism associated with Disney, tracing back to *Song of the South*, released in 1946, and *The Jungle Book*, which appeared in 1967.[36] Moreover, racist representations of Native Americans as violent "redskins" were featured in Frontierland in the 1950s.[37] In addition, the main restaurant in Frontierland featured an actor representing the former slave Aunt Jemima, who would sign autographs for the tourists outside of her "Pancake House." Eventually, the exhibits and the Native Americans running them were eliminated by Disney executives because the "Indian" canoe guides wanted to unionize. They were displaced by robotic dancing bears. Complaints from civil rights groups got rid of the degrading Aunt Jemima spectacle.[38] *40*

One of the most controversial examples of racist stereotyping facing the Disney publicity machine occurred with the release of *Aladdin* in 1992, although such stereotyping reappeared in full force in 1994 with the release of *The Lion King*. *Aladdin* is a particularly important example because it was a high-profile release, the winner of two Academy Awards, and one of the most successful Disney films ever produced. The film's opening song, "Arabian Nights," begins its depiction of Arab culture with a decidedly racist tone. The lyrics of the offending stanza state: "Oh I come from a land / From a faraway place / Where the caravan camels roam. / Where they cut off your ear / If they don't like your face. / It's barbaric, but hey, it's home." A politics of identity and place associated with Arab culture magnified popular stereotypes already primed by the media through its portrayal of the Gulf War. Such a racist representation is furthered by a host of grotesque, violent, and cruel supporting characters. *41*

Yousef Salem, a former spokesperson for the South Bay Islamic Association, characterized the film in the following way: "All of the bad guys have beards and large, bulbous noses, sinister eyes and heavy accents, and they're wielding swords constantly. Aladdin doesn't have a big nose; he has a small nose. He doesn't have a beard or a turban. He doesn't have an accent. What makes him nice is they've given him this American character. . . . I have a daughter who says she's ashamed to call herself an Arab, *42*

[35]June Casagrande, "The Disney Agenda," *Creative Loafing*, March 17–23, 1994, pp. 6–7.

[36]Upon its release in 1946, *Song of the South* was condemned by the National Association for the Advancement of Colored People for its racist representations.

[37]For a historical context in which to understand Frontierland, see Fjellman, *Vinyl Leaves*.

[38]These racist episodes are highlighted in Wiener, "Tall Tales and True."

and it's because of things like this."[39] Jack Shaheen, a professor of broadcast journalism at Southern Illinois University, Edwardsville, along with the radio personality Casey Kasem, mobilized a public relations campaign protesting the anti-Arab themes in *Aladdin*. At first, Disney executives ignored the protest, but responding to the rising tide of public outrage agreed to change one line of the stanza in the subsequent videocassette and worldwide film release. Disney did not change the lyrics on its popular CD release of *Aladdin*.[40]

Disney executives were not unaware of the racist implications of the lyrics when they were first proposed. Howard Ashman, who wrote the title song, submitted an alternative set of lyrics when he delivered the original lines. The alternative lyrics, "Where it's flat and immense / And the heat is intense" eventually replaced the original verse, "Where they cut off your ear / If they don't like your face." Though the new lyrics appeared in the videocassette release of *Aladdin*, the line "It's barbaric, but hey, it's home" was not altered. More important, the mispronunciation of Arab names in the film, the racial coding of accents, and the use of nonsensical scrawl as a substitute for an actual written Arabic language were not removed.[41]   *43*

Racism in Disney's animated films is also evident in racially coded language and accents. For example, *Aladdin* portrays the "bad" Arabs with thick, foreign accents, while the Anglicized Jasmine and Aladdin speak in standard American English. A hint of the racism that informs this depiction is provided by Peter Schneider, president of feature animation at Disney at the time, who points out that Aladdin was modeled after Tom Cruise.   *44*

Racially coded representations and language are also evident in *The Lion King*. Scar, the icon of evil, is darker than the good lions. Moreover, racially coded language is evident, as the members of the royal family speak with posh British accents while Shenzi and Banzai, the despicable hyena storm troopers, speak with the voices of Whoopi Goldberg and Cheech Marin in the jive accents of a decidedly urban black or Hispanic youth. Disney falls back upon the same racial formula in *Mulan*. Not far removed from the Amos 'n' Andy crows in *Dumbo* is the racialized low-comedy figure of Mushu, a tiny red dragon with a black voice (Eddie Murphy). Mushu is a servile and boastful clown who seems unsuited to a mythic fable about China. He is the stereotype of the craven, backward, Southern, chitlin-circuit character that appears to feed the popular racist imagination. Racially coded language can also be found in an early version of *The Three Little Pigs*, in *Song of the South*, and in *The Jungle Book*.[42]   *45*

---

[39]Richard Scheinin, "Angry over 'Aladdin,'" *Washington Post*, January 10, 1993, p. G5.

[40]Howard Green, a Disney spokesperson, dismissed the charges of racism as irrelevant, claiming that such criticisms were coming from a small minority and that "most people were happy" with the film. Scheinin, "Angry over 'Aladdin.'"

[41]Jack Shaheen, "Animated Racism," *Cineaste* 20:1 (1993), p. 49.

[42]Susan Miller and Greg Rode, "The Movie You See, the Movie You Don't: How Disney Do's That Old Time Derision," in Bell, Haas, and Sells, *From Mouse to Mermaid*.

These films produce representations and codes through which children are taught that characters who do not bear the imprint of white, middle-class ethnicity are culturally deviant, inferior, unintelligent, and a threat.

The racism in these films is defined by both the presence of racist representations and the absence of complex representations of African Americans and other people of color. At the same time, whiteness is universalized through the privileged representation of middle-class social relations, values, and linguistic practices. Moreover, the representational rendering of history, progress, and Western culture bears a colonial legacy that seems perfectly captured by Edward Said's notion of orientalism — a particular form of Western imperialism that shapes dominant thinking about the Orient — and its dependency on new images of centrality and sanctioned narratives.[43] Cultural differences are expressed through a "natural" racial hierarchy, which is antithetical to a viable democratic society. There is nothing innocent in what kids learn about race as portrayed in the "magical world" of Disney. Even in a film such as *Pocahontas,* in which cultural differences are portrayed more positively, there is the suggestion in the end that racial identities must remain separate. *Pocahontas* is one of the few love stories in Disney's animated series in which the lovers do not live together happily ever after. It is also one of the few love stories that brings lovers from different races together.

Another feature common to many of Disney's recent animated films is the celebration of antidemocratic social relations. Nature and the animal kingdom provide the mechanism for presenting and legitimating caste, royalty, and structural inequality as part of the natural order. The seemingly benign presentation of celluloid dramas, in which men rule, strict discipline is imposed through social hierarchies, and leadership is a function of one's social status, suggests a yearning for a return to a more rigidly stratified society, one modeled after the British monarchy of the eighteenth and nineteenth centuries. In Disney's animated films, "harmony is bought at the price of domination. . . . No power or authority is implied except for the natural ordering mechanisms" of nature.[44] For children, the messages suggest that social problems such as the history of racism, the genocide of Native Americans, the prevalence of sexism, and the crisis of democracy are simply willed through the laws of nature.

Conclusion

Given the corporate reach, cultural influence, and political power that Disney exercises over multiple levels of children's culture, Disney's animated films should be neither ignored nor censored by those who dismiss the

[43]Edward Said, *Culture and Imperialism* (New York: Knopf, 1993).
[44]Susan Willis, "Fantasia: Walt Disney's Los Angeles Suite," *Diacritics* 17 (Summer 1987), pp. 83–96.

conservative ideologies they produce and circulate. There are a number of issues to be addressed regarding the forging of a pedagogy and a politics responsive to Disney's shaping of children's culture. Below, I suggest how cultural workers, educators, and parents might critically engage Disney's influence in shaping the "symbolic environment into which our children are born and in which we all live out our lives."[45]

First, it is crucial that the realm of popular culture that Disney increasingly invades to teach values and to sell goods to children be taken seriously as a site of learning and contestation. This means, at the very least, that those cultural texts that dominate children's culture, including Disney's animated films, should be incorporated into school curricula as objects of social knowledge and critical analysis. This would entail a reconsideration of what counts as useful knowledge and offer theoretical suggestions for addressing the ways in which popular media aimed at shaping children's culture are implicated in power/knowledge relationships. This is not simply a call for making media literacy a part of what kids gain from school (as crucial as such a pedagogy is)[46] but a reconsideration of what counts as school knowledge. In simple terms, this means making popular culture an essential object of social analysis in schools.

Second, parents, community groups, educators, and other concerned individuals must be attentive to the diverse messages in Disney films in order both to criticize them when necessary and, more important, to reclaim them for more productive ends. At the very least, we must be attentive to the processes whereby meanings are produced in these films and how they work to secure particular forms of authority and social relations. At stake pedagogically is the issue of paying "close attention to the ways in which [such films] invite (or indeed seek to prevent) particular meanings and pleasures."[47] In fact, Disney's films appear to assign, quite unapologetically, rigid roles to women and people of color. Similarly, such films generally produce a narrow view of family values coupled with a nostalgic and conservative view of history that should be challenged and transformed. Educators need to take seriously Disney's attempt to shape collective memory, particularly when such attempts are unabashedly defined by one of Disney's imagineers in the following terms: "What we create is a sort of 'Disney realism,' sort of Utopian in nature, where we carefully program out all the negative, unwanted elements and program in the positive

[45]George Gerbner, Larry Gross, Michael Borgan, and Nancy Signorielli, "Growing Up with Television: The Cultivation Perspective," in Jennings Bryant and Dolf Zillmann, eds., *Media Effects: Advances in Theory and Research* (Hillsdale, N.J.: Erlbaum 1995), p. 17.

[46]See, for instance, Andrew Hart, ed., *Teaching the Media: International Perspectives* (Hillsdale, N.J.: Erlbaum, 1998).

[47]David Buckingham, "Conclusion: Re-Reading Audiences," in David Buckingham, ed., *Reading Audiences: Young People and the Media* (Manchester, U.K.: Manchester University Press, 1993), p. 211.

elements."[48] Disney's rendering of entertainment and spectacle, whether expressed in Frontierland, Main Street, USA, or its video and film productions, is not merely an edited, sanitary, and nostalgic view of history, one that is free of poverty, class differences, and urban decay. Disney's writing of public memory also aggressively constructs a monolithic notion of national identity that treats subordinate groups as either exotic or irrelevant to American history, simultaneously marketing cultural differences within "histories that corporations can live with."[49] Disney's version of U.S. history is not innocent, nor can it be dismissed as simply entertainment.

Disney's celluloid view of children's culture often works to strip the *51* past, present, and future of diverse narratives and multiple possibilities, a rendering that needs to be revealed as a historically specific and politically constructed cultural "landscape of power." Rustom Bharacuha argues that "the consumption of . . . images . . . can be subverted through a particular use in which we are compelled to think through images rather than respond to them with a hallucinatory delight."[50] The images that pervade Disney's production of children's culture, along with their claim to public memory, need to be challenged and rewritten, "moved about in different ways," and read differently as part of the script of democratic empowerment.[51] It is within the drama of animated storytelling that children are often positioned pedagogically to learn what subject positions are open to them and what positions are not. Hence, the struggle over children's culture should be considered as part of a struggle over the related discourses of citizenship, national identity, and democracy itself.

Third, if Disney's films are to be viewed as more than narratives of fan- *52* tasy and escape, becoming sites of reclamation and imagination that affirm rather than deny the long-standing relationship between entertainment and pedagogy, it is important to consider how we might insert the political and pedagogical back into the discourse of entertainment. In part, this points to analyzing how entertainment can be addressed as a subject of intellectual engagement rather than as a series of sights and sounds that wash over us. This suggests a pedagogical approach to popular culture that asks how a politics of the popular works to mobilize desire, stimulate imagination, and produce forms of identification that can become objects of dialogue and critical investigation. At one level, this suggests addressing the utopian possibilities in which children often find representations of their hopes and dreams. But it also suggests recognizing

[48]Cited in Zukin, *Landscapes of Power,* p. 222. While this quotation refers to Disney's view of its theme parks, it is an ideological view of history that shapes all of Disney's cultural productions. For a comment on how this view affects Disney's rendering of adult films, see Henry A. Giroux, *Disturbing Pleasures: Learning Popular Culture* (New York: Routledge, 1994), esp. pp. 25–45.

[49]Fjellman, *Vinyl Leaves,* p. 400.

[50]Rustom Bharacuha, "Around Ayodhya: Aberrations, Enigmas, and Moments of Violence," *Third Text,* no. 24 (Autumn 1993), p. 51.

[51]Bennett, "Texts in History," p. 80.

the pedagogical importance of what kids bring with them to the classroom (or to any other site of learning) as crucial both to decentering power in the classroom and to expanding the possibility of teaching students multiple literacies, as part of a broader strategy of teaching them to read the world critically.

We must pay attention to how these Disney films and visual media 53 are used and understood differently by different kids. We must talk to children about these films so we can better understand how kids identify with them and what issues they raise, developing a language of pleasure and criticism. This suggests that we develop new ways of critically understanding and reading electronically produced visual media. Teaching and learning the culture of the book is no longer the staple of what it means to be literate.

Children learn from exposure to popular cultural forms, which pro- 54 vide a new cultural register of what it means to be literate. This suggests a cultural pedagogy, rooted in cultural practices, that utilizes students' knowledge and experience of popular cultural forms. Students should be taught to critically analyze the messages produced by the electronically mediated popular culture, but they must also be able to master the skills and technology to produce these forms, making their own films, videos, and music. Thus a cultural pedagogy also requires more resources for schools and other sites of learning, providing the conditions for students and others to become the subject, not simply the object, of pedagogical work. Asserting their role as cultural producers is crucial if students are to become attentive to the workings of power, solidarity, and difference.

Fourth, Disney's reach into the spheres of economics, consumption, 55 and culture suggest that we analyze Disney within a broad and complex range of relations of power. Eric Smoodin argues that the American public needs to "gain a new sense of Disney's importance, because of the manner in which his work in film and television is connected to other projects in urban planning, ecological politics, product merchandising, United States domestic and global policy formation, technological innovation, and constructions of national character."[52] This suggests undertaking analyses of Disney that connect, rather than separate, the various social and cultural formations in which the company engages. Clearly, such a dialectical practice not only provides a more theoretically accurate understanding of the reach and influence of Disney's power but also contributes to forms of analysis that discount the notion that Disney is primarily about the pedagogy of entertainment.

Questions of ownership, control, and public participation in deciding 56 how cultural resources are used should become a central issue in addressing the world of Disney and other corporate conglomerates that shape cultural policy. The control, production, and distribution of such films should

---

[52]Smoodin, "How to Read Walt Disney," pp. 4–5.

be analyzed as part of a wider circuit of power. In this context, Disney's influence in the shaping of children's culture cannot be reduced to critically interpreting the ideas and values Disney promotes. Any viable analysis of Disney must also confront the institutional and political power Disney exercises through its massive control over diverse sectors of what Mark Crispin Miller calls the "national entertainment state."[53] The availability, influence, and cultural power of Disney's children's films demand that they become part of a broader political discourse regarding who makes cultural policy. Issues regarding how and what children learn could be addressed through public debates about how the distribution and control of cultural and economic resources ensure that children are exposed to alternative narratives about themselves and the larger society.

When the issue of children's culture is taken up by — and shaped in — the public schools, it is assumed that this is a matter of public policy and intervention. But when children's culture is shaped in the commercial sphere, the discourse of public intervention gets lost in abstract appeals to the imperatives of the market and free speech. Free speech is only as good as the democratic framework that makes possible the extension of its benefits to all individuals, groups, and public spheres. Treating Disney as part of a media sphere that needs to be democratized and held accountable for the ways in which it wields power and manufactures social identities needs to be part of the discourse of pedagogical analysis and public policy intervention. This type of analysis and intervention is perfectly suited for cultural theorists and community activists willing to employ an interdisciplinary approach to such an undertaking, to address popular culture as an object of serious analysis, to make the pedagogical a defining principle of such work, and to insert the political into the center of such projects.[54]

This suggests that cultural workers need to readdress a politics of representation and the discourse of political economy, treating their varied interrelations as a form of cultural work that rejects the material/cultural divide. The result would be an understanding of how such modalities inform each other within different contexts and across national boundaries. It is particularly important for cultural workers to understand how Disney films work as teaching machines within and across public cultures and social formations. Within this type of analysis, the messages, emotional investments, and ideologies produced by Disney can be traced through the circuits of power that both legitimate and insert "the culture of the Magic Kingdom" into multiple and overlapping public spheres. Disney films need to be analyzed not only for what they say but also for how they are apprehended by audiences within their national and international

[53]Mark Crispin Miller, "Free the Media," *Nation*, June 3, 1996, pp. 9–15.

[54]For an example of such an analysis, see Stanley Aronowitz, *Roll Over Beethoven* (Middletown: Wesleyan University Press, 1993); Giroux, *Disturbing Pleasures*.

contexts. That is, cultural workers need to study these films intertextually and from a transnational perspective. Disney is not ignorant of different contexts; on the contrary, its power, in part, rests with its ability to address different contexts and to be read differently in different transnational formations. Disney engenders what Inderpal Grewa and Caren Kaplan call "scattered hegemonies."[55] It is precisely by addressing how these hegemonies operate in particular spaces of power, specific localities — in different transnational locations — that we will be able to understand the agendas and the politics at work.

The defeat in 1995 of Disney's proposed 3,000-acre theme park in *59* Virginia suggests that Disney can be challenged and held accountable for the so-called Disnification of American culture. In this instance, a coalition of historians, community activists, educators, and other concerned groups mobilized against the land developers supporting the project, wrote articles against Disney's trivializing of history and its implications for the park, and aroused public opinion enough to generate an enormous amount of adverse criticism against the Disney project. What was initially viewed as merely a project for bringing a Disney version of fun and entertainment to hallowed Civil War grounds in historic Virginia was translated by opposition groups into a cultural struggle. And Disney lost.

What the Virginia cultural civil war suggests is that, although it is *60* indisputable that Disney provides both children and adults with entertainment and pleasure, Disney's public responsibility does not end there. Rather than being viewed as a commercial venture innocently distributing pleasure to young people, the Disney empire must be seen as a pedagogical and policy-making enterprise actively engaged in the cultural landscaping of national identity and the "schooling" of the minds of young children. This is not to suggest that there is something sinister behind what Disney does. It points only to the need to address the role of fantasy, desire, and innocence in securing particular ideological interests, legitimating specific social relations, and making a claim on the meaning of public memory. Disney needs to be held accountable, which will require that parents, educators, and others challenge and disrupt both the institutional power and the images, representations, and values offered by Disney's teaching machine.

[55]Inderpal Grewal and Caren Kaplan, "Introduction: Transnational Feminist Practices and Questions of Postmodernity," in Inderpal Grewal and Caren Kaplan, eds., *Scattered Hegemonies* (Minneapolis: University of Minnesota Press, 1994).

■   ■   ■

Reading Rhetorically

1. What claims does Giroux make in the opening paragraphs of his essay? After you've read the whole essay carefully, return to his introduction and discuss how effectively he supports his claims there with evidence throughout the essay.

2. How does Giroux anticipate and respond to those who might disagree with him? Locate and mark specific passages where you see him responding to opposing perspectives. What strategies does he use? How successful do you think he is? What suggestions can you make for strengthening this aspect of his writing? What conclusions can you draw about how best to address counterarguments in your own writing?

3. Giroux refers often to the ideological messages in Disney films. For instance, in paragraph 25 he states:

> The role of the critic of Disney's animated films, however, is not to assign them a particular ideological reading but to analyze the themes and assumptions that inform these films, both within and outside of the dominant institutional and ideological formations. Such analyses allow educators and others to understand how such films can become sites of contestation, translation, and exchange.

What does he mean? In particular, what is he saying about ideology? Be sure to use a dictionary to look up any unfamiliar words, and be ready to explain the meaning of these sentences, which are central to Giroux's approach to analyzing films, in your own words.

Inquiring Further

4. What have other scholars said about Disney's animated films? Use your library's online resources to locate scholarly articles. You might start with search terms like "Disney and gender" or "Disney and race"; but try other combinations of topics that interest you too. Many search engines — for example, Academic Search Premier (located within EBSCOhost) — allow you to narrow your search to scholarly journals. Share with your class five entries from your searches that you find particularly interesting. How do Giroux's ideas compare to the analyses of Disney films you found?

5. Working on your own or in a small group, write a Giroux-style analysis of an animated children's film that is not discussed in this essay. Consider the representation of gender and race, the role of love narratives, the nature of the ending (Is it "happy"?), and the lessons the plot and characterizations teach viewers. Be sure to offer specific details from the film to support your claims. Present your analysis to the class, and discuss your findings.

6. Choose a recent Disney animated film — one not discussed in Giroux's essay — and research its product tie-ins. How do those products reveal Disney's assumptions about the film's audience? Present your findings to the class.

Framing Conversations

7. Giroux refers to animated films as "teaching machines" (para. 2). Use this concept as a tool to write an essay in which you explore children's toys (drawing on Ann duCille's text, p. 458) or video games (drawing on Henry

Jenkins's text, p. 700) as teaching machines. What exactly is being taught, and with what possible effects? What is machinelike about the ways we interact with these cultural objects?

8. Giroux describes Disney as "an icon of American culture" (para. 8): "Disney is more than a corporate giant; it is also a cultural institution that fiercely protects its legendary status as purveyor of innocence and moral virtue" (para. 6). Eric Schlosser (p. 754) is also interested in the way corporations like Disney and McDonald's impact our culture. Write an essay in which you place Giroux's and Schlosser's ideas in conversation with your own to argue the significance of these corporate giants of American culture. Use examples from the texts, adding examples of your own, if you like, to strengthen your point.

9. Giroux's analysis of Disney's animated films includes a look at the often-negative stereotypes of certain races. Ann duCille (p. 458) is also interested in the way products marketed to children can perpetuate racial stereotypes. Drawing on insights from both Giroux and duCille, write an essay in which you analyze the racial representations in a specific children's film or line of children's toys. Use the authors' concepts to help you determine the significance of your findings.

■ JEAN KILBOURNE

"Two Ways a Woman Can Get Hurt": Advertising and Violence

Jean Kilbourne, EdD, is an award-winning author and educator who is best known for her lively campus lectures on the effects of media images on young people. Her academic interest stems from personal experience. Although Kilbourne was a superb student when she came of age in the 1960s, she found she was rewarded more for her looks than her intelligence. Later, after she began working in journalism and education, she noticed the absurd arguments that advertisements often made, many of them insulting to women's intelligence and self-esteem. Once she found her personal and professional interests intersecting, Kilbourne began collecting and analyzing advertisements, eventually shaping them into a lecture series and then a film titled *Killing Us Softly: Advertising's Image of Women* (1979). This film, its two subsequent versions, and other films Kilbourne has produced on anorexia and on tobacco and alcohol addiction, are taught frequently in college classes today. Kilbourne also has published many articles and several books on these topics, including the book from which this essay is excerpted, *Deadly Persuasion: Why Women and Girls Must Fight the Addictive Power of Advertising* (1999).

The first thing you may notice about Kilbourne's essay is that it is filled with advertising images. Before you read, flip through the essay to see if you can get a sense of Kilbourne's argument simply from the advertisements she includes. As you read, hold these images in your head, testing them against Kilbourne's interpretation of them, and also against the information she includes from other scholars about violence in our culture (particularly sexualized violence) and the power of the media. Kilbourne is an important voice among the many media critics who have discussed the ways advertising images normalize — and even make appealing — sexual and violent situations that most often threaten women and children. As you read, pay close attention to the connections Kilbourne makes between the media and social problems. Note the passages you find most and least convincing, and ask yourself why. Getting in the habit of evaluating evidence this way will help you immeasurably when you decide on the kinds of evidence you want to include in your own writing.

Kilbourne is a scholar writing for a general audience. Although she bases her analysis on research by well-regarded scholars, including experts in the fields of anthropology, addiction, gendered violence, and media criticism, she also cites newspaper reports of crimes and trends she finds so dangerous. She uses the words "deadly" and "addictive" in her title to describe the allure of advertising images that create a climate for many unhealthy behaviors. In the rest of her book, she develops this thread at greater length, noting the ways gender stereotypes play into tobacco and alcohol advertising. "Addiction," then, has multiple meanings for Kilbourne.

Kilbourne is sometimes criticized for being too selective in her choice of images and evidence, and too narrow in her analysis. Throughout the essay, you will hear her addressing her critics, anticipating claims that she's simply reading too much into the images or taking advertising too seriously. Often she provides more than one interpretation of an image, for example, saying about the subject of one advertisement, "I suppose this could be a woman awaiting her lover, but it could as easily be a girl being preyed upon" (para. 33). She also uses the strategy of inviting readers to imagine the reversal of an image to make her point. That's what she is doing in paragraphs 26 and 27, when she suggests reversing the genders of the actors in a Diet Pepsi commercial. She wants her readers to think about why it's often deemed harmless fun for young boys to make sexually suggestive comments about an adult woman, but inappropriate and even frightening when young girls show sexual interest in a man.

Given our visually rich media culture, you are likely to find many familiar ideas and images in Kilbourne's essay, and you also are likely to find yourself strongly agreeing or disagreeing — or perhaps both — with her as she builds her case about the "deadly" power of the advertising industry. Even if you do not agree with her on every point, Kilbourne's strategy of considering the role advertising plays in making dangerous behaviors seem normal and even appealing is one all consumers can adopt to help make sense of marketing claims and popular culture.

(Heartbreaker)   (Soap and water shave)

Skintimate® Shave Gel Ultra Protection formula contains
75% moisturizers, including vitamin E, to protect your
legs from nicks, cuts and razor burn. So while guys may
continue to be a pain, shaving most definitely won't.

SKINTIMATE®SHAVE GEL
LOVE YOUR LEGS

Sex in advertising is more about disconnection and distance than connection and closeness. It is also more often about power than passion, about violence than violins. The main goal, as in pornography, is usually power over another, either by the physical dominance or preferred status of men or what is seen as the exploitative power of female beauty and female sexuality. Men conquer and women ensnare, always with the essential aid of a product. The woman is rewarded for her sexuality by the man's wealth, as in an ad for Cigarette boats in which the woman says, while lying in a man's embrace clearly after sex, "Does this mean I get a ride in your Cigarette?"

Sex in advertising is pornographic because it dehumanizes and objectifies people, especially women, and because it fetishizes products, imbues them with an erotic charge — which dooms us to disappointment since products never can fulfill our sexual desires or meet our emotional needs. The poses and postures of advertising are often borrowed from pornography, as are many of the themes, such as bondage, sadomasochism, and the sexual exploitation of children. When a

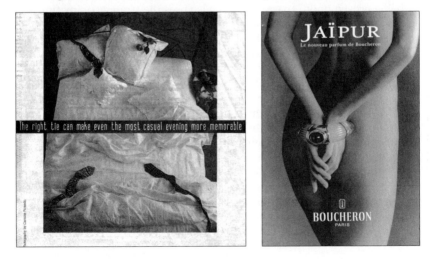

beer ad uses the image of a man licking the high-heeled boot of a woman clad in leather, when bondage is used to sell neckties in *The New York Times*, perfume in *The New Yorker*, and watches on city buses, and when a college magazine promotes an S&M Ball, pornography can be considered mainstream.

Most of us know all this by now and I suppose some consider it kinky 3 good fun. Pornography is more dangerously mainstream when its glorification of rape and violence shows up in mass media, in films and television shows, in comedy and music videos, and in advertising. Male violence is subtly encouraged by ads that encourage men to be forceful and dominant, and to value sexual intimacy more than emotional intimacy. "Do you want to be the one she tells her deep, dark secrets to?" asks a three-page ad for men's cologne. "Or do you want to be her deep, dark secret?" The last page advises men, "Don't be such a good boy." There are two identical women looking adoringly at the man in the ad, but he isn't looking at either one of them. Just what is the deep, dark secret? That he's sleeping with both of them? Clearly the way to get beautiful women is to ignore them, perhaps mistreat them.

"Two ways a woman can get hurt," says an ad for shaving gel, featuring a razor and a photo of a handsome man. My first thought is that the man is a batterer or date rapist, but the ad informs us that he is merely a "heartbreaker." The gel will protect the woman so that "while guys may continue to be a pain, shaving most definitely won't." Desirable men are painful — heartbreakers at best.

Wouldn't it be wonderful if, realizing the importance of relationships in 5 all of our lives, we could seek to learn relational skills from women and to help men develop these strengths in themselves? In fact, we so often do the opposite. The popular culture usually trivializes these abilities in women, mocks men who have real intimacy with women (it is almost always married men in ads and cartoons who are jerks), and idealizes a template for relation-

ships between men and women that is a recipe for disaster: a template that views sex as more important than anything else, that ridicules men who are not in control of their women (who are "pussy-whipped"), and that disparages fidelity and commitment (except, of course, to brand names).

Indeed the very worst kind of 6 man for a woman to be in an intimate relationship with, often a truly dangerous man, is the one considered most sexy and desirable in the popular culture. And the men capable of real intimacy (the ones we tell our deep, dark secrets to) constantly have their very masculinity impugned. Advertising

often encourages women to be attracted to hostile and indifferent men while encouraging boys to become these men. This is especially dangerous for those of us who have suffered from "condemned isolation" in childhood: like heat-seeking missiles, we rush inevitably to mutual destruction.

Men are also encouraged to never take no for an answer. Ad after ad 7 implies that girls and women don't really mean "no" when they say it, that women are only teasing when they resist men's advances. "NO" says an ad showing a man leaning over a woman against a wall. Is she screaming or laughing? Oh, it's an ad for deodorant and the second word, in very small print, is "sweat." Sometimes it's "all in good fun," as in the ad for Possession shirts and shorts featuring a man ripping the clothes off a woman who seems to be having a good time.

And sometimes it is more sinister. A perfume ad running in several 8 teen magazines features a very young woman, with eyes blackened by makeup or perhaps something else, and the copy, "Apply generously to your neck so he can smell the scent as you shake your head 'no.'" In other words, he'll understand that you don't really mean it and he can respond to the scent like any other animal.

Sometimes there seems to be no question but that a man should force a 9 woman to have sex. A chilling newspaper ad for a bar in Georgetown features a closeup of a cocktail and the headline, "If your date won't listen to reason, try a Velvet Hammer." A vodka ad pictures a wolf hiding in a flock of sheep, a hideous grin on its face. We all know what wolves do to sheep. A campaign for Bacardi Black rum features shadowy figures almost obliterated by darkness and captions such as "Some people embrace the night because the rules of the day do not apply." What it doesn't say is that people who are above the rules do enormous harm to other people, as well as to themselves.

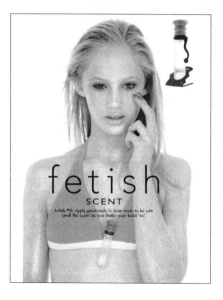

Sip exotic cocktails, dine and dance to Swing Era music at Georgetown's top nightspot. 1232 36th St., NW. Reservation call 342-0009. Free valet parking. Jackets required.

These ads are particu- *10* larly troublesome, given that between one-third and three-quarters of all cases of sexual assault involve alcohol consumption by the perpetrator, the victim, or both.[1] "Make strangers your friends, and your friends a lot stranger," says one of the ads in a Cuervo campaign that uses colorful cartoon beasts and emphasizes heavy drinking. This ad is especially disturbing when we consider the role of alcohol in date rape, as is another ad in the series that says, "The night began with a bottle of Cuervo and ended with a vow of silence." Over half of all reported rapes on college campuses occur when either the victim or the assailant has been drinking.[2] Alcohol's role has different meaning for men and women, however. If a man is drunk when he commits a rape, he is considered less responsible. If a woman is drunk (or has had a drink or two or simply met the man in a bar), she is considered more responsible.

In general, females are still held responsible and hold each other *11* responsible when sex goes wrong — when they become pregnant or are the victims of rape and sexual assault or cause a scandal. Constantly exhorted to be sexy and attractive, they discover when assaulted that that very sexiness is evidence of their guilt, their lack of "innocence." Sometimes the ads play on this by "warning" women of what might happen if they use the product. "Wear it but beware it," says a perfume ad. Beware what exactly? Victoria's Secret tempts young women with blatantly sexual ads promising that their lingerie will make them irresistible. Yet when a young woman accused William Kennedy Smith of raping her, the fact that she wore Victoria's Secret panties was used against her as an indication of her immorality. A jury acquitted Smith, whose alleged history of violence against women was not permitted to be introduced at trial.

It is sadly not surprising that the jury was composed mostly of *12* women. Women are especially cruel judges of other women's sexual behavior, mostly because we are so desperate to believe we are in control of what happens to us. It is too frightening to face the fact that male violence against women is irrational and commonplace. It is reassuring to believe that we can avoid it by being good girls, avoiding dark places, staying out of bars, dressing "innocently." An ad featuring two young women talking intimately at a coffee shop says, "Carla and Rachel considered themselves

[1]Wilsnack, Plaud, Wilsnack, and Klassen, 1997, 262.
[2]Abbey, Ross, and McDuffie, 1991. Also Martin, 1992, 230–37.

open-minded and non-judgmental people. Although they did agree Brenda was a tramp." These terrible judgments from other women are an important part of what keeps all women in line.

If indifference in a man is sexy, then violence is sometimes downright *13* erotic. Not surprisingly, this attitude too shows up in advertising. "Push my buttons," says a young woman, "I'm looking for a man who can totally floor me." Her vulnerability is underscored by the fact that she is in an elevator, often a dangerous place for women. She is young, she is submissive (her eyes are downcast), she is in a dangerous place, and she is dressed provocatively. And she is literally asking for it.

"Wear it out and make it scream," *14* says a jeans ad portraying a man sliding his hands under a woman's transparent blouse. This could be a seduction, but it could as easily be an attack. Although the ad that ran in the Czech version of *Elle* portraying three men attacking a woman seems unambiguous, the terrifying image is being used to sell jeans *to women*. So someone must think that women would find this image compelling or attractive. Why would we? Perhaps it is simply designed to get our attention, by shocking us and by arousing unconscious anxiety. Or perhaps the intent is more subtle and it is

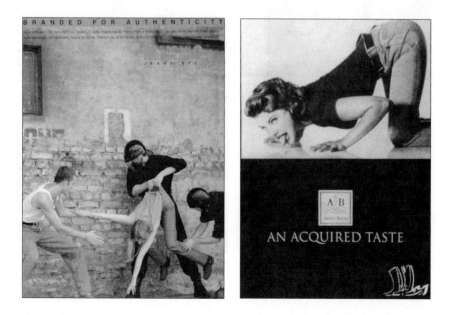

designed to play into the fantasies of domination and even rape that some women use in order to maintain an illusion of being in control (we are the ones having the fantasies, after all, we are the directors).

A camera ad features a woman's torso wrapped in plastic, her hands   *15* tied behind her back. A smiling woman in a lipstick ad has a padlocked chain around her neck. An ad for MTV shows a vulnerable young woman,

her breasts exposed, and the simple copy "Bitch." A perfume ad features a man shadowboxing with what seems to be a woman.

Sometimes women are shown dead or in the   *16* process of being killed. "Great hair never dies," says an ad featuring a female corpse lying on a bed, her breasts exposed. An ad in the Italian version of *Vogue* shows a man aiming a gun at a nude woman wrapped in plastic, a leather briefcase covering her face. And an ad for Bitch skateboards, for God's sake, shows a cartoon version of a similar scene, this time clearly targeting young people. We believe we are not affected by these images, but most of us experience visceral shock when we pay conscious attention to them. Could they be any less shocking to us on an unconscious level?

Most of us become numb to these images, just as we become numb to   *17* the daily litany in the news of women being raped, battered, and killed.

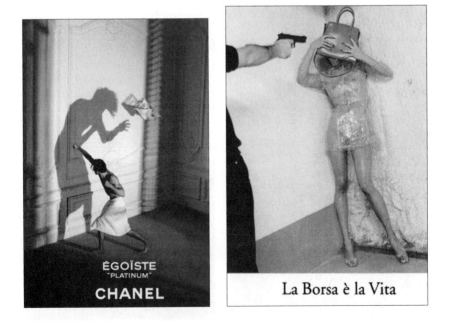

According to former surgeon general Antonia Novello, battery is the single greatest cause of injury to women in America, more common than automobile accidents, muggings, and stranger rapes combined, and more than one-third of women slain in this country die at the hands of husbands or boyfriends.[3] Throughout the world, the biggest problem for most women is simply surviving at home. The Global Report on Women's Human Rights concluded that "domestic violence is a leading cause of female injury in almost every country in the world and is typically ignored by the state or only erratically punished."[4] Although usually numb to these facts on a conscious level, most women live in a state of subliminal terror, a state that, according to Mary Daly,

keeps us divided both from each other and from our most passionate, powerful, and creative selves.[5]

Ads don't directly cause violence, of course. But the violent images contribute to the state of terror. And objectification and disconnection create a climate in which there is widespread and increasing violence. Turning a human being into a thing, an object, is almost always the first step toward justifying violence against that person. It is very difficult, perhaps impossible, to be violent to someone we think of as an equal, someone we have empathy with, but it is very easy to abuse a thing. We see this with racism, with homophobia. The person becomes an object and violence is inevitable. This step is already taken with women. The violence, the abuse, is partly the chilling but logical result of the objectification. 18

An editorial in *Advertising Age* suggests that even some advertisers are concerned about this: "Clearly it's time to wipe out sexism in beer ads; for the brewers and their agencies to wake up and join the rest of America in realizing that sexism, sexual harassment, and the cultural portrayal of women in advertising are inextricably linked."[6] Alas, this editorial was written in 1991 and nothing has changed. 19

It is this link with violence that makes the objectification of women a more serious issue than the objectification of men. Our economic system constantly requires the development of new markets. Not surprisingly, men's bodies are the latest territory to be exploited. Although we are growing more used to it, in the beginning the male sex object came as a surprise. In 1994 a "gender bender" television commercial in which a bevy of women office 20

[3]Novello, 1991. Also Blumenthal, 1995.
[4]Wright, 1995, A2.
[5]Weil, 1999, 21.
[6]Brewers can help fight sexism, 1991, 28.

workers gather to watch a construction worker doff his shirt to quaff a Diet Coke led to so much hoopla that you'd have thought women were mugging men on Madison Avenue.[7]

There is no question that men are used as sex objects in ads now as [21] never before. We often see nude women with fully clothed men in ads (as in art), but the reverse was unheard of, until recently. These days some ads do feature clothed and often aggressive women with nude men. And women sometimes blatantly objectify men, as in the Metroliner ad that says, " 'She's reading Nietzsche,' Harris noted to himself as he walked towards the cafe car for a glass of cabernet. And as he passed her seat, Maureen looked up from her book and thought, 'Nice buns.' "

Although these ads are often funny, it is never a good thing for human [22] beings to be objectified. However, there is

a world of difference between the objectification of men and that of women. The most important difference is that there is no danger for most men, whereas objectified women are always at risk. In the Diet Coke ad, for instance, the women are physically separated from the shirtless man. He is the one in control. His body is powerful, not passive. Imagine a true role reversal of this ad: A group of businessmen gather to leer at a beautiful woman worker on her break, who removes her shirt before drinking her Diet Coke. This scene would be frightening, not funny, as the Diet Coke ad is. And why is the Diet Coke ad funny? Because we know it doesn't describe any truth. However, the ads featuring images of male violence against women do describe a truth, a truth we are all aware of, on one level or another.

When power is unequal, when one group is oppressed and discrimi- [23] nated against *as a group,* when there is a context of systemic and historical oppression, stereotypes and prejudice have different weight and meaning. As Anna Quindlen said, writing about "reverse racism": "Hatred by the powerful, the majority, has a different weight — and often very different effects — than hatred by the powerless, the minority."[8] When men objectify women, they do so in a cultural context in which women are constantly objectified and in which there are consequences — from economic discrimination to violence — to that objectification.

For men, though, there are no such consequences. Men's bodies are [24] not routinely judged and invaded. Men are not likely to be raped, harassed,

[7]Kilbourne, 1994, F13.
[8]Quindlen, 1992, E17.

or beaten (that is to say, men presumed to be heterosexual are not, and very few men are abused in these ways by women). How many men are frightened to be alone with a woman in an elevator? How many men cross the street when a group of women approach? Jackson Katz, who writes and lectures on male violence, often begins his workshops by asking men to describe the things they do every day to protect themselves from sexual assault. The men are surprised, puzzled, sometimes amused by the question. The women understand the question easily and have no trouble at all coming up with a list of responses. We don't list our full names in the phone directory or on our mailboxes, we try not to be alone after dark, we carry our keys in our hands when we approach our cars, we always look in the back seat before we get in, we are wary of elevators and doorways and bushes, we carry pepper sprays, whistles, Mace.

Nonetheless, the rate of sexual assault in the United States is the 25 highest of any industrialized nation in the world.[9] According to a 1998 study by the federal government, one in five of us has been the victim of rape or attempted rape, most often before our seventeenth birthday.[10] And more than half of us have been physically assaulted, most often by the men we live with. In fact, three of four women in the study who responded that they had been raped or assaulted as adults said the perpetrator was a current or former husband, a cohabiting partner, or a date. The article reporting the results of this study was buried on page twenty-three of my local newspaper, while the front page dealt with a long story about the New England Patriots football team.

A few summers ago, a Diet Pepsi commercial featured Cindy Crawford 26 being ogled by two boys (they seemed to be about twelve years old) as she got out of her car and bought a Pepsi from a machine. The boys made very suggestive comments, which in the end turned out to be about the Pepsi's can rather than Ms. Crawford's. There was no outcry: the boys' behavior was acceptable and ordinary enough for a soft-drink commercial.

Again, let us imagine the reverse: a sexy man gets out of a car in the 27 countryside and two preteen girls make suggestive comments, seemingly about his body, especially his buns. We would fear for them and rightly so. But the boys already have the right to ogle, to view women's bodies as property to be looked at, commented on, touched, perhaps eventually hit and raped. The boys have also learned that men ogle primarily to impress other men (and to affirm their heterosexuality). If anyone is in potential danger in this ad, it is the woman (regardless of the age of the boys). Men are not seen as *property* in this way by women. Indeed if a woman does whistle at a man or touches his body or even makes direct eye contact, it is still *she* who is at risk and the man who has the power.

[9]Blumenthal, 1995, 2.
[10]Tjaden and Thoennes, 1998.

"I always lower my eyes to see if a man is worth following," says the   28
woman in an ad for men's pants. Although the ad is offensive to everyone, the
woman is endangering only herself.

"Where women are women and men are roadkill," says an ad for   29
motorcycle clothing featuring an angry-looking African-American woman.

Women are sometimes hostile and
angry in ads these days, especially
women of color who are often seen
as angrier and more threatening than
white women. But, regardless of color,
we all know that women are far more
likely than men to end up as roadkill — and, when it happens, they are
blamed for being on the road in the
first place.

Even little girls are sometimes held   30
responsible for the violence against
them. In 1990 a male Canadian judge
accused a three-year-old girl of being
"sexually aggressive" and suspended
the sentence of her molester, who was
then free to return to his job of babysitter.[11] The deeply held belief that all
women, regardless of age, are really
temptresses in disguise, nymphets, sexually insatiable and seductive, conveniently transfers all blame and responsibility onto women.

All women are vulnerable in a culture in which there is such wide-   31
spread objectification of women's bodies, such glorification of disconnection,
so much violence against women, and such blaming of the victim. When

everything and everyone is sexualized, it is
the powerless who are most at risk. Young
girls, of course, are especially vulnerable.
In the past twenty years or so, there have
been several trends in fashion and advertising that could be seen as cultural reactions to the women's movement, as
perhaps unconscious fear of female
power. One has been the obsession with
thinness. Another has been an increase in
images of violence against women. Most
disturbing has been the increasing sexualization of children, especially girls.
Sometimes the little girl is made up and
seductively posed. Sometimes the language is suggestive. "Very cherry," says the

[11]Two men and a baby, 1990, 10.

ad featuring a sexy little African-American girl who is wearing a dress with cherries all over it. A shocking ad in a gun magazine features a smiling little girl, a toddler, in a bathing suit that is tugged up suggestively in the rear.[12] The copy beneath the photo says, "short BUTTS from FLEMING FIREARMS." Other times girls are juxtaposed with grown women, as in the ad for underpants that says "You already know the feeling."

This is not only an American phenomenon. A growing national obsession in Japan with schoolgirls dressed in uniforms is called "Loli-con," after Lolita.[13] In Tokyo hundreds of "image clubs" allow Japanese men to act out their fantasies with make-believe schoolgirls. A magazine called *V-Club* featuring pictures of naked elementary-school girls competes with another called *Anatomical Illustrations of Junior High School Girls.* Masao Miyamoto, a male psychiatrist, suggests that Japanese men are turning to girls because they feel threatened by the growing sophistication of older women.[14]

In recent years, this sexualization of little girls has become even more disturbing as hints of violence enter the picture. A three-page ad for Prada clothing features a girl or very young woman with a barely pubescent body, clothed in what seem to be cotton panties and perhaps a training bra, viewed through a partially opened door. She seems surprised, startled, worried, as if she's heard a strange sound or glimpsed someone watching her. I suppose this could be a woman awaiting her lover, but it could as easily be a girl being preyed upon.

[12]Herbert, 1999, WK 17.
[13]Schoolgirls as sex toys, 1997, 2E.
[14]*Ibid.*

The 1996 murder of six-year-old Jon-Benet Ramsey was a gold mine for the media, combining as it did child pornography and violence. In November of 1997 *Advertising Age* reported in an article entitled "JonBenet keeps hold on magazines" that the child had been on five magazine covers in October, "enough to capture the Cover Story lead for the month. The pre-adolescent beauty queen, found slain in her home last Christmas, garnered 6.5 points. The case earned a *triple play* [italics mine] on the *National Enquirer*, and one-time appearances on *People* and *Star*."[15] Imagine describing a six-year-old child as "pre-adolescent."

Sometimes the models in ads are children, other times they just look like children. Kate Moss was twenty when she said of herself, "I look twelve."[16] She epitomized the vacant, hollow-cheeked look known as "heroin chic" that was popular in the mid-nineties. She also often looked vulnerable, abused, and exploited. In one ad she is nude in the corner of a huge sofa, cringing as if braced for an impending sexual assault. In

[15]Johnson, 1997, 42.
[16]Leo, 1994, 27.

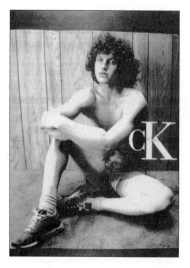

another, she is lying nude on her stomach, pliant, available, androgynous enough to appeal to all kinds of pedophiles. In a music video she is dead and bound to a chair while Johnny Cash sings "Delia's Gone."

It is not surprising that Kate Moss 36 models for Calvin Klein, the fashion designer who specializes in breaking taboos and thereby getting himself public outrage, media coverage, and more bang for his buck. In 1995 he brought the federal government down on himself by running a campaign that may have crossed the line into child pornography.[17] Very young models (and others who just seemed young) were featured in lascivious print ads and in television commercials designed to mimic child porn. The models were awkward, self-conscious. In one commercial, a boy stands in what seems to be a finished basement. A male voiceover tells him he has a great body and asks him to take off his shirt. The boy seems embarrassed but he complies. There was a great deal of protest, which brought the issue into national consciousness but which also gave Klein the publicity and free media coverage he was looking for. He pulled the ads but, at the same time, projected that his jeans sales would almost double from $115 million to $220 million that year, partly because of the free publicity but also because the controversy made his critics seem like prudes and thus positioned Klein as the daring rebel, a very appealing image to the majority of his customers.

[17]Sloan, 1996, 27.

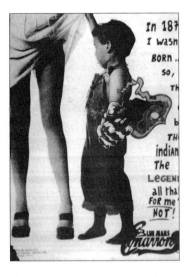

Having learned from this, in 1999 *37* Klein launched a very brief advertising campaign featuring very little children frolicking in their underpants, which included a controversial billboard in Times Square.[18] Although in some ways this campaign was less offensive than the earlier one and might have gone unnoticed had the ads come from a department store catalog rather than from Calvin Klein, there was the expected protest and Klein quickly withdrew the ads, again getting a windfall of media coverage. In my opinion, the real obscenity of this campaign is the whole idea of people buying designer underwear for their little ones, especially in a country in which at least one in five children doesn't have enough to eat.

Although boys are sometimes sexualized in an overt way, they are *38* more often portrayed as sexually precocious, as in the Pepsi commercial featuring the young boys ogling Cindy Crawford or the jeans ad portraying a very little boy looking up a woman's skirt. It may seem that I am reading too much into this ad, but imagine if the genders were reversed. We would fear for a little girl who was unzipping a man's fly in an ad (and we would be shocked, I would hope). Boys are vulnerable to sexual abuse too, but cultural attitudes make it difficult to take this seriously. As a result, boys are less likely to report abuse and to get treatment.

Many boys grow up feeling that they are unmanly if they are not *39* always "ready for action," capable of and interested in sex with any woman who is available. Advertising doesn't cause this attitude, of course, but it contributes to it. A Levi Strauss commercial that ran in Asia features the shock of a schoolboy who discovers that the seductive young woman who has slipped a note into the jeans of an older student is his teacher. And an ad for BIC pens pictures a young boy wearing X-ray glasses while ogling the derriere of an older woman. Again, these ads would be unthinkable if the genders were reversed. It is increasingly difficult in such a toxic environment to see children, boys or girls, as *children.*

In the past few years there has been a proliferation of sexually *40* grotesque toys for boys, such as a Spider Man female action figure whose exaggerated breasts have antennae coming out of them and a female Spawn figure with carved skulls for breasts. Meantime even children have easy access to pornography in video games and on the World Wide Web,

---

[18]Associated Press, 1999, February 18.

which includes explicit photographs of women having intercourse with groups of men, with dogs, donkeys, horses, and snakes; photographs of women being raped and tortured; some of these women made up to look like little girls.

It is hard for girls not to learn self-hatred in an environment in which there is such widespread and open contempt for women and girls. In 1997 a company called Senate distributed clothing with inside labels that included, in addition to the usual cleaning instructions, the line "Destroy all girls."[19] A Senate staffer explained that he thought it was "kind of cool." Given all this, it's not surprising that when boys and girls were asked in a recent study to write an essay on what it would be like to be the other gender, many boys wrote they would rather be dead. Girls had no trouble writing essays about activities, power, freedom, but boys were often stuck, could think of nothing. *41*

It is also not surprising that, in such an environment, sexual harassment is considered normal and ordinary. According to an article in the journal *Eating Disorders:* *42*

> In our work with young women, we have heard countless accounts of this contempt being expressed by their male peers: the girls who do not want to walk down a certain hallway in their high school because they are afraid of being publicly rated on a scale of one to ten; the girls who are subjected to barking, grunting and mooing calls and labels of "dogs, cows or pigs" when they pass by groups of male students; those who are teased about not measuring up to buxom, bikini-clad [models]; and the girls who are grabbed, pinched, groped and fondled as they try to make their way through the school corridors.
>
> Harassing words do not slide harmlessly away as the taunting sounds dissipate. . . . They are slowly absorbed into the child's identity and developing sense of self, becoming an essential part of whom she sees herself to be.

[19]Wire and *Times* staff reports, 1997, D1.

Harassment involves the use of words as weapons to inflict pain and assert power. Harassing words are meant to instill fear, heighten bodily discomfort, and diminish the sense of self.[20]

It is probably difficult for those of us who are older to understand how   43
devastating and cruel and pervasive this harassment is, how different from the "teasing" some of us might remember from our own childhoods (not that that didn't hurt and do damage as well). A 1993 report by the American Association of University Women found that 76 percent of female students in grades eight to eleven and 56 percent of male students said they had been sexually harassed in school.[21] One high-school junior described a year of torment at her vocational school: "The boys call me slut, bitch. They call me a 10-timer, because they say I go with 10 guys at the same time. I put up with it because I have no choice. The teachers say it's because the boys think I'm pretty."[22]

High school and junior high school have always been hell for those   44
who were different in any way (gay teens have no doubt suffered the most, although "overweight" girls are a close second), but the harassment is more extreme and more physical these days. Many young men feel they have the right to judge and touch young women and the women often feel they have no choice but to submit. One young woman recalled that "the guys at school routinely swiped their hands across girls' legs to patrol their shaving prowess and then taunt them if they were slacking off. If I were running late, I'd protect myself by faux shaving — just doing the strip between the bottom of my jeans and the top of my cotton socks."[23]

Sexual battery, as well as inappropriate sexual gesturing, touching,   45
and fondling, is increasing not only in high schools but in elementary and middle schools as well.[24] There are reports of sexual assaults by students on other students as young as eight. A fifth-grade boy in Georgia repeatedly touched the breasts and genitals of one of his fellow students while saying, "I want to get in bed with you" and "I want to feel your boobs."[25] Authorities did nothing, although the girl complained and her grades fell. When her parents found a suicide note she had written, they took the board of education to court.

A high-school senior in an affluent suburban school in the Boston area   46
said she has been dragged by her arms so boys could look up her skirt and that boys have rested their heads on her chest while making lewd comments.[26] Another student in the same school was pinned down on a lunch

[20]Larkin, Rice, and Russell, 1996, 5–26.
[21]Daley and Vigue, 1999, A12.
[22]Hart, 1998, A12.
[23]Mackler, 1998, 56.
[24]Daley and Vigue, 1999, A1, A12.
[25]Shin, 1999, 32.
[26]Daley and Vigue, 1999, A12.

table while a boy simulated sex on top of her. Neither student reported any of the incidents, for fear of being ostracized by their peers. In another school in the Boston area, a sixteen-year-old girl, who had been digitally raped by a classmate, committed suicide.[27]

According to Nan Stein, a researcher at Wellesley College: *47*

> Schools may in fact be training grounds for the insidious cycle of domestic violence. . . . The school's hidden curriculum teaches young women to suffer abuse privately, that resistance is futile. When they witness harassment of others and fail to respond, they absorb a different kind of powerlessness — that they are incapable of standing up to injustice or acting in solidarity with their peers. Similarly, in schools boys receive permission, even training, to become batterers through the practice of sexual harassment.[28]

This pervasive harassment of and contempt for girls and women con-   *48* stitute a kind of abuse. We know that addictions for women are rooted in trauma, that girls who are sexually abused are far more likely to become addicted to one substance or another. I contend that all girls growing up in this culture are sexually abused — abused by the pornographic images of female sexuality that surround them from birth, abused by all the violence against women and girls, and abused by the constant harassment and threat of violence. Abuse is a continuum, of course, and I am by no means implying that cultural abuse is as terrible as literally being raped and assaulted. However, it hurts, it does damage, and it sets girls up for addictions and self-destructive behavior. Many girls turn to food, alcohol, cigarettes, and other drugs in a misguided attempt to cope.

As Marian Sandmaier said in *The Invisible Alcoholics: Women and*   *49* *Alcohol Abuse in America*, "In a culture that cuts off women from many of their own possibilities before they barely have had a chance to sense them, that pain belongs to all women. Outlets for coping may vary widely, and may be more or less addictive, more or less self-destructive. But at some level, all women know what it is to lack access to their own power, to live with a piece of themselves unclaimed."[29]

Today, every girl is endangered, not just those who have been physically   *50* and sexually abused. If girls from supportive homes with positive role models are at risk, imagine then how vulnerable are the girls who have been violated. No wonder they so often go under for good — ending up in abusive marriages, in prison, on the streets. And those who do are almost always in the grip of one addiction or another. More than half of women in prison are addicts and most are there for crimes directly related to their addiction.[30]

[27]Vigue and Abraham, 1999, B6.
[28]Stein, 1993, 316–17.
[29]Sandmaier, 1980, xviii.
[30]Snell, 1991.

Many who are there for murder killed men who had been battering them for years. Almost all of the women who are homeless or in prisons and mental institutions are the victims of male violence.

Male violence exists within the same cultural and sociopolitical con-   51 text that contributes to addiction. Both can be fully understood only within this context, way beyond individual psychology and family dynamics. It is a context of systemic violence and oppression, including racism, classism, heterosexism, weightism, and ageism, as well as sexism, all of which are traumatizing in and of themselves. Advertising is only one part of this cultural context, but it is an important part and thus is a part of what traumatizes.

All right, you might think, these ads are shocking. They are probably   52 not good for us. But just what is the relationship of all these sexist and violent ads to addiction? Am I blaming advertisers for everything now? No. But I do contend that ads that contribute to a climate of disconnection also contribute to addiction. Ads that objectify women and sexualize children also play a role in the victimization of women and girls that often leads to addiction. When women are shown in positions of powerlessness, submission, and subjugation, the message to men is clear: women are always available as the targets of aggression and violence, women are inferior to men and thus deserve to be dominated, and women exist to fulfill the needs of men.

There is a further connection between images that legitimize male   53 domination of females and addiction. In his classic essay "The Cybernetics of Self" Gregory Bateson describes the fundamental belief of Western culture that we can dominate, control, and have power over almost every aspect of our experience.[31] We can get rid of pain, we can dominate people who threaten us, we can win in any interaction, we can be invulnerable. Bateson theorizes that this belief is fundamentally erroneous and leads to addiction, which he sees as a disordered attempt to get to a more "correct" state of mind, one in which we permit dependency, vulnerability, and mutuality. Bateson argues that we have no culturally sanctioned, non-addictive way to achieve this state.

Claudia Bepko takes Bateson's theory further by arguing that the stage   54 is set for addiction by the overriding belief system maintaining that men have power and women are the objects of that power.[32] This assumption is as erroneous as is the assumption that we can control our emotions. But our entire culture is predicated on this illusion of male dominance, and our institutions are set up in ways that perpetuate it. According to Bepko, being socialized in an erroneous belief system leads to addiction because incongruity may arise between what one believes and how one actually feels. A man who feels he must be dominant but who actually feels vulnerable might use an addictive substance to lessen his feeling of vulnerability

[31]Bateson, 1972.
[32]Bepko, 1989.

or to enhance his sense of dominance. A woman forced to show dependence who really feels powerful might use a drug or other substance either to enhance or disqualify the impulse to be powerful (as the old Jefferson Airplane song says, "One pill makes you larger and one pill makes you small"). Thus gender-role socialization both shapes and is continually challenged by addictive behavior.

Bepko describes what she calls "the yin and yang of addiction." Both 55 men and women become addicted and suffer, but their individual addictions arise from their different positions in the world and have different effects. Men operate within a context in which both autonomy and entitlement to be taken care of are assumed; women within a context in which both dependency on a man and emotional and physical nurturing and caretaking are assumed. The contradictions in these prescriptions obviously create a bind: the male is independent but taken care of and the woman is dependent but the caretaker. Addiction is one response to the pain created by these contradictions.

Although the critical issues are dependency and control, these have 56 radically different meanings and outcomes for women and men. Since money, sexuality, size, strength, and competitive work convey power and status for men, gambling, sexual addictions, and work addiction tend to be predominantly male forms of compulsive behavior (although women are catching up as gender roles change). Women are still socialized to be physically and emotionally nurturing, so eating disorders, obsessive shopping or cleaning, self-mutilation, and compulsive behavior in relationships are common female forms of addictive behavior, as is prescription drug abuse, which reflects the cultural belief that women's emotions need to be subdued and controlled. A man is more likely to engage in addictive behavior that involves having power over others, whereas a woman's attempt at control is often focused on her own body.

It would be foolish to suggest that advertising is *the cause* of violence 57 against women — or of alcoholism or eating disorders or any other major problem. These problems are complex and have many contributing factors. There is no doubt that flagrant sexism and sex role stereotyping abound in all forms of the media. There is abundant information about this. It is far more difficult to document the effects of these stereotypes and images on the individuals and institutions exposed to them because, as I've said, it is difficult to separate media effects from other aspects of the socialization process and almost impossible to find a comparison group (just about everyone in America has been exposed to massive doses of advertising).

But, at the very least, advertising helps to create a climate in which 58 certain attitudes and values flourish, such as the attitude that women are valuable only as objects of men's desire, that real men are always sexually aggressive, that violence is erotic, and that women who are the victims of sexual assault "asked for it." These attitudes have especially terrible consequences for women abused as children, most of whom grow up feeling like objects and believing they are responsible for their own abuse. These are the very women who are likely to mutilate and starve themselves, to smoke, to become addicted to alcohol and other drugs. As Judith Herman wrote in her classic book *Father-Daughter Incest:*

> These women alone suffered the consequences of their psychological impairment. Almost always, their anger and disappointment were expressed in self-destructive action: in unwanted pregnancies, in submission to rape and beatings, in addiction to alcohol and drugs, in attempted suicide.
> . . . Consumed with rage, they nevertheless rarely caused trouble to anyone but themselves. In their own flesh, they bore repeated punishment for the crimes committed against them in their childhood.[33]

Addictions are not incidental in the lives of women. Most often they are caused by (or at least related to) disturbances in relationships in childhood, often violent disturbances. They are fueled by a culture that sexualizes children, objectifies, trivializes, and silences women, disparages our interest in and skill at relating, and constantly threatens us with violence. Feeling isolated and disconnected, a girl or a woman reaches out to a substance to numb her pain, to be sure, but also to end her isolation, to relate, to connect. She reaches for alcohol or other drugs, she reaches for cigarettes, she reaches for men who don't love her, or she reaches for food. The advertisers are ready for her.

[33]Herman and Hirschman, 1981, 107–8.

BIBLIOGRAPHY

Abbey, A., Ross, L., and McDuffie, D. (1991). Alcohol's role in sexual assault. In Watson, R., ed. *Addictive behaviors in women.* Totowa, NJ: Humana Press.

Associated Press (1999, February 18). Calvin Klein retreats on ad. *Boston Globe,* A7.

Bateson, G. (1972). The cybernetics of self. In *Steps to an ecology of mind.* New York: Chandler Publishing.

Bepko, C. (1989). Disorders of power: women and addiction in the family. In McGoldrick, M., Anderson, C. M., and Walsh, F., eds. (1989). *Women in families: a framework for family therapy.* New York: W. W. Norton, 406–26.

Blumenthal, S. J. (1995, July). *Violence against women.* Washington, DC: Department of Health and Human Services.

Brewers can help fight sexism (1991, October 28). *Advertising Age,* 28.

Daley, B., and Vigue, D. I. (1999, February 4). Sex harassment increasing amid students, officials say. *Boston Globe,* A1, A12.

Hart, J. (1998, June 8). Northampton confronts a crime, cruelty. *Boston Globe,* A1, A12.

Herbert, B. (1999, May 2). America's littlest shooters. *New York Times,* WK17.

Herman, J. L., and Hirschman, L. (1981). *Father-daughter incest.* Cambridge, MA: Harvard University Press.

Johnson, J. A. (1997, November 10). JonBenet keeps hold on magazines. *Advertising Age,* 42.

Kilbourne, J. (1994, May 15). 'Gender bender' ads: same old sexism. *New York Times,* F13.

Larkin, J., Rice, C., and Russell, V. (1996, Spring). Slipping through the cracks: sexual harassment. *Eating Disorders: The Journal of Treatment and Prevention*, vol. 4, no. 1, 5–26.

Leo, J. (1994, June 13). Selling the woman-child. *U.S. News and World Report*, 27.

Mackler, C. (1998). Memoirs of a (sorta) ex-shaver. In Edut, O., ed. (1998). *Adios, Barbie*. Seattle, WA: Seal Press, 55–61.

Martin, S. (1992). The epidemiology of alcohol-related interpersonal violence. *Alcohol, Health and Research World*, vol. 16, no. 3, 230–37.

Novello, A. (1991, October 18). Quoted by Associated Press, AMA to fight wife-beating. *St. Louis Post Dispatch*, 1, 15.

Quindlen, A. (1992, June 28). All of these you are. *New York Times*, E17.

Sandmaier, M. (1980). *The invisible alcoholics: Women and alcohol abuse in America*. New York: McGraw-Hill.

Schoolgirls as sex toys. *New York Times* (1997, April 16), 2E.

Shin, A. (1999, April/May). Testing Title IX. *Ms.*, 32.

Sloan, P. (1996, July 8). Underwear ads caught in bind over sex appeal. *Advertising Age*, 27.

Snell, T. L. (1991). *Women in prison*. Washington, DC: U.S. Department of Justice.

Stein, N. (1993). No laughing matter: Sexual harassment in K-12 schools. In Buchwald, E., Fletcher, P. R., and Roth, M. (1993). *Transforming a rape culture*. Minneapolis, MN: Milkweed Editions, 311–31.

Tjaden, R., and Thoennes, N. (1998, November). *Prevalence, incidence, and consequences of violence against women: Findings from the National Violence Against Women Survey*. Washington, DC: U.S. Department of Justice.

Two men and a baby (1990, July/August). *Ms.*, 10.

Vigue, D. I., and Abraham, Y. (1999, February 7). Harassment a daily course for students. *Boston Globe*, B1, B6.

Weil, L. (1999, March). Leaps of faith. *Women's Review of Books*, 21.

Wilsnack, S. C., Plaud, J. J., Wilsnack, R. W., and Klassen, A. D. (1997). Sexuality, gender, and alcohol use. In Wilsnack, R. W., and Wilsnack, S. C., eds. *Gender and alcohol: Individual and social perspectives*. New Brunswick, NJ: Rutgers Center of Alcohol Studies, 262.

Wire and *Times* Staff Reports (1997, May 20). Orange County skate firm's 'destroy all girls' tags won't wash. *Los Angeles Times*, D1.

Wright, R. (1995, September 10). Brutality defines the lives of women around the world. *Boston Globe*, A2.

■   ■   ■

Reading Rhetorically

1. How does Kilbourne define pornography in this essay? According to Kilbourne, what distinguishes pornography from other forms of sexual expression? Cite specific sentences in Kilbourne's essay to answer these questions.

2. Kilbourne spends much of the essay explaining why she finds certain advertisements harmful to women, but she also hints at the damage they do to men. Locate those passages, and, in class, discuss how you could develop her argument that men also are harmed by advertising. How would the essay be different if she had included more material on men?

3. Kilbourne's essay includes many of the images she analyzes. Which of her analyses of these images do you find most and least persuasive, and why? Be sure to refer to specific details in the images and the text as you make

your points. What conclusions can you draw about analyzing images for your own writing?

Inquiring Further

4. This piece is a chapter from Kilbourne's book *Deadly Persuasion*. Kilbourne has written extensively on the topic of advertising and addictive behaviors, as you can see in a visit to her Web site (www.jeankilbourne.com). Spend some time looking through the materials on the site or through one of her books or videos (many college libraries carry her videos), and report to the class three interesting facts you've learned through your research.

5. How typical are the advertisements Kilbourne examines in her essay? Look through five popular magazines aimed at women or aimed at men, and, using Kilbourne's methods, analyze the ads you find. How many ads illustrate her point, and how many seem to offer alternative representations of gender that might be healthier for both women and men? What do you notice about the advertised products and the assumptions the advertisers make about the desires and expectations of the target audience? What conclusions can you draw?

6. Kilbourne includes in her essay a number of statistics about violence against women. Using an online search engine, gather recent statistics about gender-related violence on your campus and in your town. Share your findings, and your thoughts about those findings, with the class.

Framing Conversations

7. Like Kilbourne, Cynthia Selfe (p. 783) is interested in the ways advertisements reveal our beliefs and fears about gender, race, power, and national identity. Drawing on the insights and analytical strategies of both authors, write an essay in which you analyze a series of five to eight advertisements that are related in some way. Include in your analysis what each writer might say about the ads, in addition to your own insights. Build your analyses of the advertisements around a central point you would like to teach your readers about the significance of the ads.

8. Kilbourne argues that negative images, behaviors, and name-calling have become a "normal" part of gender role socialization. How do these ideas compare to Judith Lorber's (p. 617) concepts of the ways we "do gender" so that these roles feel natural to us? Write an essay in which you play these authors' ideas off against one another in your own evaluation of the negative and positive aspects of contemporary gender role socialization. Provide specific examples to support your point.

9. Both Kilbourne and Michael Kimmel (p. 448) explore the ways violence and masculinity are often connected. Using both authors' ideas, write an essay in which you analyze an example of popular culture that features masculinity — for example, a film or a series of ads featuring men. How do these authors' ideas help you analyze your example? What additional or alternative ideas can you bring to your analysis? Given your analysis of the example, organize your essay around a larger point you would like to make about masculinity.

"Night to His Day":
The Social Construction of Gender

Judith Lorber is an internationally renowned scholar and one of the most widely read gender theorists writing today. She is a professor emerita of sociology and women's studies at Brooklyn College and the Graduate School, City University of New York. She has won numerous awards for her research on feminism and sociology, including the American Sociological Association's Jessie Bernard Award for her lifetime contributions to the field. Her interest in the intersection of scientific and medical knowledge and in changing conceptions of gender is evident in the titles of her books *Women Physicians: Careers, Status and Power* (1984) and *Gender and the Social Construction of Illness* (1997; 2nd ed., 2002). She is also a leading feminist theorist, and her acclaimed book *Gender Inequality: Feminist Theories and Politics* is currently in its third edition (2005). This essay is reprinted from her book *Paradoxes of Gender* (1994).

Lorber is an important voice in the scholarly conversation about the social construction of gender, the learned (versus genetic) social and cultural behaviors that shape our notions of masculinity and femininity. Her opening sentence in this piece highlights the difficulty of this analysis: "Talking about gender for most people is the equivalent of fish talking about water." In other words, gender assumptions are so much a part of our daily lives that we rarely think about them; they just are. "Gender is so pervasive that in our society we assume it is bred into our genes," but in fact it is "constantly created and re-created out of human interaction" (para. 1). That interaction can be as mundane as how we dress, who opens doors for whom, or how we sit, gesture, and speak. Like other gender theorists, Lorber's goal is to help make visible the way all of us "do gender" so that we can analyze the process. The notion of gender as something we do rather than something we are, which she takes from sociologists Candace West and Don Zimmerman, helps us understand how our behaviors reinforce categories of masculinity and femininity whether or not we are aware of their doing so.

The title of this essay, "Night to His Day," refers to the way men and women have come to be seen in our culture as opposites: If men are considered strong, women must be weak; if men are competitive, women must be cooperative. Most of us know that these simplistic categories do not describe any of us fully — which is why culture has come up with category-breaking terms like *tomboy*. Lorber is eager for us to learn that many other cultures conceive of gender categories differently. (Did you know there are cultures with more than two genders? See paragraph 8 for more information.) She also points out that gendered behaviors vary over time, so that something considered masculine in one century might not be thought so in the next. Lorber points to parenting practices to demonstrate how quickly gender standards can change: "Seeing men taking care of small children in public is increasingly common" (para. 2). (That said, our culture still sees mothers as primary parents, as images in any parenting magazine reveal at a glance.)

Lorber builds her argument about the social construction of gender with historical examples (like the gender-bending actors in Shakespeare's age) as well as recent examples (like the anecdote at the end of the piece about the dance at West Point that led to a change in the dress code there). Although many of Lorber's illustrations are drawn from daily life, she also uses language that may challenge most readers, so keep a dictionary handy for looking up unfamiliar words. As you read, pay attention to the author's decision to divide this essay into sections, and consider how each section contributes to her larger point.

Read with an open mind, and consider how our culture might be different if women and men were not held to specific standards of femininity and masculinity, but were simply allowed to develop as people. The implications of that, Lorber argues, could well be revolutionary.

Talking about gender for most people is the equivalent of fish talking *1* about water. Gender is so much the routine ground of everyday activities that questioning its taken-for-granted assumptions and presuppositions is like thinking about whether the sun will come up.[1] Gender is so pervasive that in our society we assume it is bred into our genes. Most people find it hard to believe that gender is constantly created and re-created out of human interaction, out of social life, and is the texture and order of that social life. Yet gender, like culture, is a human production that depends on everyone constantly "doing gender" (West and Zimmerman 1987).

And everyone "does gender" without thinking about it. Today, on the *2* subway, I saw a well-dressed man with a year-old child in a stroller. Yesterday, on a bus, I saw a man with a tiny baby in a carrier on his chest. Seeing men taking care of small children in public is increasingly common — at least in New York City. But both men were quite obviously stared at — and smiled at, approvingly. Everyone was doing gender — the men who were changing the role of fathers and the other passengers, who were applauding them silently. But there was more gendering going on that probably fewer people noticed. The baby was wearing a white crocheted cap and white clothes. You couldn't tell if it was a boy or a girl. The child in the stroller was wearing a dark blue T-shirt and dark print pants. As they started to leave the train, the father put a Yankee baseball cap on the child's head. Ah, a boy, I thought. Then I noticed the gleam of tiny earrings in the child's ears, and as they got off, I saw the little flowered sneakers and lace-trimmed socks. Not a boy after all. Gender done.

Gender is such a familiar part of daily life that it usually takes a delib- *3*

---

[1] Gender is, in Erving Goffman's words, an aspect of *Felicity's Condition:* "any arrangement which leads us to judge an individual's . . . acts not to be a manifestation of strangeness. Behind *Felicity's Condition* is our sense of what it is to be sane" (1983, 27). Also see Bem 1993; Frye 1983, 17–40; Goffman 1977.

erate disruption of our expectations of how women and men are supposed to act to pay attention to how it is produced. Gender signs and signals are so ubiquitous that we usually fail to note them — unless they are missing or ambiguous. Then we are uncomfortable until we have successfully placed the other person in a gender status; otherwise, we feel socially dislocated. In our society, in addition to man and woman, the status can be *transvestite* (a person who dresses in opposite gender clothes) and *transsexual* (a person who has had sex-change surgery). Transvestites and transsexuals carefully construct their gender status by dressing, speaking, walking, gesturing in the ways prescribed for women or men — whichever they want to be taken for — and so does any "normal" person.

For the individual, gender construction starts with assignment to a sex 4 category on the basis of what the genitalia look like at birth.[2] Then babies are dressed or adorned in a way that displays the category because parents don't want to be constantly asked whether their baby is a girl or a boy. A sex category becomes a gender status through naming, dress, and the use of other gender markers. Once a child's gender is evident, others treat those in one gender differently from those in the other, and the children respond to the different treatment by feeling different and behaving differently. As soon as they can talk, they start to refer to themselves as members of their gender. Sex doesn't come into play again until puberty, but by that time, sexual feelings and desires and practices have been shaped by gendered norms and expectations. Adolescent boys and girls approach and avoid each other in an elaborately scripted and gendered mating dance. Parenting is gendered, with different expectations for mothers and for fathers, and people of different genders work at different kinds of jobs. The work adults do as mothers and fathers and as low-level workers and high-level bosses, shapes women's and men's life experiences, and these experiences produce different feelings, consciousness, relationships, skills — ways of being that we call feminine or masculine.[3] All of these processes constitute the social construction of gender.

Gendered roles change — today fathers are taking care of little children, 5 girls and boys are wearing unisex clothing and getting the same education, women and men are working at the same jobs. Although many traditional social groups are quite strict about maintaining gender differences, in other social groups they seem to be blurring. Then why the one-year-old's earrings? Why is it still so important to mark a child as a girl or a boy, to make sure she is not taken for a boy or he for a girl? What would happen if they were? They would, quite literally, have changed places in their social world.

To explain why gendering is done from birth, constantly and by every- 6 one, we have to look not only at the way individuals experience gender but at gender as a social institution. As a social institution, gender is one of the

---

[2]In cases of ambiguity in countries with modern medicine, surgery is usually performed to make the genitalia more clearly male or female.

[3]See Butler 1990 for an analysis of how doing gender *is* gender identity.

major ways that human beings organize their lives. Human society depends on a predictable division of labor, a designated allocation of scarce goods, assigned responsibility for children and others who cannot care for themselves, common values and their systematic transmission to new members, legitimate leadership, music, art, stories, games, and other symbolic productions. One way of choosing people for the different tasks of society is on the basis of their talents, motivations, and competence — their demonstrated achievements. The other way is on the basis of gender, race, ethnicity — ascribed membership in a category of people. Although societies vary in the extent to which they use one or the other of these ways of allocating people to work and to carry out other responsibilities, every society uses gender and age grades. Every society classifies people as "girl and boy children," "girls and boys ready to be married," and "fully adult women and men," constructs similarities among them and differences between them, and assigns them to different roles and responsibilities. Personality characteristics, feelings, motivations, and ambitions flow from these different life experiences so that the members of these different groups become different kinds of people. The process of gendering and its outcome are legitimated by religion, law, science, and the society's entire set of values. . . .

Western society's values legitimate gendering by claiming that it all 7 comes from physiology — female and male procreative differences. But gender and sex are not equivalent, and gender as a social construction does not flow automatically from genitalia and reproductive organs, the main physiological differences of females and males. In the construction of ascribed social statuses, physiological differences such as sex, stage of development, color of skin, and size are crude markers. They are not the source of the social statuses of gender, age, grade, and race. Social statuses are carefully constructed through prescribed processes of teaching, learning, emulation, and enforcement. Whatever genes, hormones, and biological evolution contribute to human social institutions is materially as well as qualitatively transformed by social practices. Every social institution has a material base, but culture and social practices transform that base into something with qualitatively different patterns and constraints. The economy is much more than producing food and goods and distributing them to eaters and users; family and kinship are not the equivalent of having sex and procreating; morals and religions cannot be equated with the fears and ecstasies of the brain; language goes far beyond the sounds produced by tongue and larynx. No one eats "money" or "credit"; the concepts of "god" and "angels" are the subjects of theological disquisitions; not only words but objects, such as their flag, "speak" to the citizens of a country.

Similarly, gender cannot be equated with biological and physiological 8 differences between human females and males. The building blocks of gender are *socially constructed statuses*. Western societies have only two genders, "man" and "woman." Some societies have three genders — men, women, and *berdaches* or *hijras* or *xaniths*. Berdaches, hijras, and xaniths are biological males who behave, dress, work, and are treated in most respects as social women; they are therefore not men, nor are they female women; they are, in our language, "male women."[4] There are African and American Indian societies that have a gender status called *manly hearted women* — biological females who work, marry, and parent as men; their social status is "female men" (Amadiume 1987; Blackwood 1984). They do not have to behave or dress as men to have the social responsibilities and prerogatives of husbands and fathers; what makes them men is enough wealth to buy a wife.

Modern Western societies' *transsexuals* and *transvestites* are the near- *9* est equivalent of these crossover genders, but they are not institutionalized as third genders (Bolin 1987). Transsexuals are biological males and females who have sex-change operations to alter their genitalia. They do so in order to bring their physical anatomy in congruence with the way they want to live and with their own sense of gender identity. They do not become a third gender; they change genders. Transvestites are males who live as women and females who live as men but do not intend to have sex-change surgery. Their dress, appearance, and mannerisms fall within the range of what is expected from members of the opposite gender, so that they "pass." They also change genders, sometimes temporarily, some for most of their lives. Transvestite women have fought in wars as men soldiers as recently as the nineteenth century; some married women, and others went back to being women and married men once the war was over.[5] Some were discovered when their wounds were treated; others not until they died. In order to work as a jazz musician, a man's occupation, Billy Tipton, a woman, lived most of her life as a man. She died recently at seventy-four, leaving a wife and three adopted sons for whom she was husband and father, and musicians with whom she had played and traveled, for whom she was "one of the boys" (*New York Times* 1989).[6] There have been many other such occurrences of women passing as men to do more prestigious or lucrative men's work (Matthaei 1982, 192–93).[7]

Genders, therefore, are not attached to a biological substratum. Gen- *10* der boundaries are breachable, and individual and socially organized shifts from one gender to another call attention to "cultural, social, or aesthetic dissonances" (Garber 1992, 16). These odd or deviant or third genders show us what we ordinarily take for granted — that people have to learn to be women and men. Men who cross-dress for performances or for

[4]On the hijras of India, see Nanda 1990; on the xaniths of Oman, Wikan 1982, 168–86; on the American Indian berdaches, W. L. Williams 1986. Other societies that have similar institutionalized third-gender men are the Koniag of Alaska, the Tanala of Madagascar, the Mesakin of Nuba, and the Chukchee of Siberia (Wikan 1982, 170).

[5]Durova 1989; Freeman and Bond 1992; Wheelwright 1989.

[6]Gender segregation of work in popular music still has not changed very much, according to Groce and Cooper 1990, despite considerable androgyny in some very popular figures. See Garber 1992 on the androgyny. She discusses Tipton on pp. 67–70.

[7]In the nineteenth century, not only did these women get men's wages, but they also "had male privileges and could do all manner of things other women could not: open a bank account, write checks, own property, go anywhere unaccompanied, vote in elections" (Faderman 1991, 44).

pleasure often learn from women's magazines how to "do femininity" convincingly (Garber 1992, 41–51). Because transvestism is direct evidence of how gender is constructed, Marjorie Garber claims it has "extraordinary power . . . to disrupt, expose, and challenge, putting in question the very notion of the 'original' and of stable identity" (1992, 16).

Gender Bending

It is difficult to see how gender is constructed because we take it for granted *11* that it's all biology, or hormones, or human nature. The differences between women and men seem to be self-evident, and we think they would occur no matter what society did. But in actuality, human females and males are physiologically more similar in appearance than are the two sexes of many species of animals and are more alike than different in traits and behavior (Epstein 1988). Without the deliberate use of gendered clothing, hairstyles, jewelry, and cosmetics, women and men would look far more alike.[8] Even societies that do not cover women's breasts have gender-identifying clothing, scarification, jewelry, and hairstyles.

The ease with which many transvestite women pass as men and trans- *12* vestite men as women is corroborated by the common gender misidentification in Westernized societies of people in jeans, T-shirts, and sneakers. Men with long hair may be addressed as "miss," and women with short hair are often taken for men unless they offset the potential ambiguity with deliberate gender markers (Devor 1987, 1989). Jan Morris, in *Conundrum*, an autobiographical account of events just before and just after a sex-change operation, described how easy it was to shift back and forth from being a man to being a woman when testing how it would feel to change gender status. During this time, Morris still had a penis and wore more or less unisex clothing; the context alone made the man and the woman:

> Sometimes the arena of my ambivalence was uncomfortably small. At the Travellers' Club, for example, I was obviously known as a man of sorts — women were only allowed on the premises at all during a few hours of the day, and even then were hidden away as far as possible in lesser rooms or alcoves. But I had another club, only a few hundred yards away, where I was known only as a woman, and often I went directly from one to the other, imperceptibly changing roles on the way — "Cheerio, sir," the porter would say at one club, and "Hello, madam," the porter would greet me at the other. (1975, 132)

Gender shifts are actually a common phenomenon in public roles as *13* well. Queen Elizabeth II of England bore children, but when she went to

---

[8]When unisex clothing and men wearing long hair came into vogue in the United States in the mid-1960s, beards and mustaches for men also came into style again as gender identifications.

Saudi Arabia on a state visit, she was considered an honorary man so that she could confer and dine with the men who were heads of a state that forbids unrelated men and women to have face-to-unveiled-face contact. In contemporary Egypt, lower-class women who run restaurants or shops dress in men's clothing and engage in unfeminine aggressive behavior, and middle-class educated women of professional or managerial status can take positions of authority (Rugh 1986, 131). In these situations, there is an important status change: These women are treated by the others in the situation as if they are men. From their own point of view, they are still women. From the social perspective, however, they are men.[9]

In many cultures, gender bending is prevalent in theater or dance — *14* the Japanese kabuki are men actors who play both women and men; in Shakespeare's theater company, there were no actresses. Juliet and Lady Macbeth were played by boys. Shakespeare's comedies are full of witty comments on gender shifts. Women characters frequently masquerade as young men, and other women characters fall in love with them; the boys playing these masquerading women, meanwhile, are acting out pining for the love of men characters.[10] . . .

But despite the ease with which gender boundaries can be traversed in *15* work, in social relationship, and in cultural productions, gender statuses remain. Transvestites and transsexuals do not challenge the social construction of gender. Their goal is to be feminine women and masculine men (Kando 1973). Those who do not want to change their anatomy but do want to change their gender behavior fare less well in establishing their social identity.

Paradoxically, then, bending gender rules and passing between genders *16* does not erode but rather preserves gender boundaries. In societies with only two genders, the gender dichotomy is not disturbed by transvestites, because others feel that a transvestite is only transitorily ambiguous — is "really a man or woman underneath." After sex-change surgery, transsexuals end up in a conventional gender status — a "man" or a "woman" with the appropriate genitals (Eichler 1989). When women dress as men for business reasons, they are indicating that in that situation, they want to be treated the way men are treated; when they dress as women, they want to be treated as women:

> By their male dress, female entrepreneurs signal their desire to suspend the expectations of accepted feminine conduct without losing respect and reputation. By wearing what is "unattractive" they signify that they are not intending to display their physical charms while engaging in public activity. Their loud,

[9]For other accounts of women being treated as men in Islamic countries, as well as accounts of women and men cross-dressing in these countries, see Garber 1992, 304–52.

[10]Dollimore 1986; Garber 1992, 32–40; Greenblatt 1987, 66–93; Howard 1988. For Renaissance accounts of sexual relations with women and men of ambiguous sex, see Laqueur 1990, 134–39. For modern accounts of women passing as men that other women find sexually attractive, see Devor 1989, 136–37; Wheelwright 1989, 53–59.

aggressive banter contrasts with the modest demeanor that attracts men. . . .
Overt signalling of a suspension of the rules preserves normal conduct from
eroding expectations. (Rugh 1986, 131)

For Individuals, Gender Means Sameness

Although the possible combinations of genitalia, body shapes, clothing, *17*
mannerisms, sexuality, and roles could produce infinite varieties in human
beings, the social institution of gender depends on the production and
maintenance of a limited number of gender statuses and of making the
members of these statuses similar to each other. Individuals are born
sexed but not gendered, and they have to be taught to be masculine or feminine.[11] As Simone de Beauvoir said: "One is not born, but rather becomes,
a woman . . . ; it is civilization as a whole that produces this creature . . .
which is described as feminine" (1952, 267).

Children learn to walk, talk, and gesture the way their social group *18*
says girls and boys should. Ray Birdwhistell, in his analysis of body
motion as human communication, calls these learned gender displays *tertiary* sex characteristics and argues that they are needed to distinguish
genders because humans are a weakly dimorphic species — their only sex
markers are genitalia (1970, 39–46). Clothing, paradoxically, often hides
the sex but displays the gender.

In early childhood, humans develop gendered personality structures *19*
and sexual orientations through their interactions with parents of the
same and opposite gender. As adolescents, they conduct their sexual
behavior according to gendered scripts. Schools, parents, peers, and the
mass media guide young people into gendered work and family roles.
As adults, they take on a gendered social status in their society's stratification system. Gender is thus both ascribed and achieved (West and Zimmerman 1987).

The achievement of gender was most dramatically revealed in a case *20*
of an accidental transsexual — a baby boy whose penis was destroyed in
the course of a botched circumcision when he was seven months old
(Money and Ehrhardt 1972, 118–23). The child's sex category was changed
to "female," and a vagina was surgically constructed when the child was
seventeen months old. The parents were advised that they could successfully raise the child, one of identical twins, as a girl. Physicians assured
them that the child was too young to have formed a gender identity. Children's sense of which gender they belong to usually develops around the

---

[11]For an account of how a potential man-to-woman transsexual learned to be feminine, see Garfinkel 1967, 116–85, 285–88. For a gloss on this account that points out how,
throughout his encounters with Agnes, Garfinkel failed to see how he himself was constructing his own masculinity, see Rogers 1992.

age of three, at the time that they start to group objects and recognize that the people around them also fit into categories big, little; pink-skinned, brown-skinned; boys, girls. Three has also been the age when children's appearance is ritually gendered, usually by cutting a boy's hair or dressing him in distinctively masculine clothing. In Victorian times, English boys wore dresses up to the age of three, when they were put into short pants (Garber 1992, 1–2).

The parents of the accidental transsexual bent over backward to femi- *21* nize the child — and succeeded. Frilly dresses, hair ribbons, and jewelry created a pride in looks, neatness, and "daintiness." More significant, the child's dominance was also feminized:

> The girl had many tomboyish traits, such as abundant physical energy, a high level of activity, stubbornness, and being often the dominant one in a girls' group. Her mother tried to modify her tomboyishness: " . . . I teach her to be more polite and quiet. I always wanted those virtues. I never did manage, but I'm going to try to manage them — to my daughter — to be more quiet and ladylike." From the beginning the girl had been the dominant twin. By the age of three, her dominance over her brother was, as her mother described it, that of a mother hen. The boy in turn took up for his sister, if anyone threatened her. (Money and Ehrhardt 1972, 122)

This child was not a tomboy because of male genes or hormones; according to her mother, she herself had also been a tomboy. What the mother had learned poorly while growing up as a "natural" female she insisted that her physically reconstructed son-daughter learn well. For both mother and child, the social construction of gender overrode any possibly inborn traits.

People go along with the imposition of gender norms because the *22* weight of morality as well as immediate social pressure enforces them. Consider how many instructions for properly gendered behavior are packed into this mother's admonition to her daughter: "This is how to hem a dress when you see the hem coming down and so to prevent yourself from looking like the slut I know you are so bent on becoming" (Kincaid 1978).

Gender norms are inscribed in the way people move, gesture, and even *23* eat. In one African society, men were supposed to eat with their "whole mouth, wholeheartedly, and not, like women, just with the lips, that is half-heartedly, with reservation and restraint" (Bourdieu [1980] 1990, 70). Men and women in this society learned to walk in ways that proclaimed their different positions in the society:

> The manly man . . . stands up straight into the face of the person he approaches, or wishes to welcome. Ever on the alert, because ever threat-ened, he misses nothing of what happens around him. . . . Conversely, a well brought-up woman . . . is expected to walk with a slight stoop, avoiding every

misplaced movement of her body, her head or her arms, looking down, keeping her eyes on the spot where she will next put her foot, especially if she happens to have to walk past the men's assembly. (70)

Many cultures go beyond clothing, gestures, and demeanor in gender-   24
ing children. They inscribe gender directly into bodies. In traditional Chinese society, mothers bound their daughters' feet into three-inch stumps to enhance their sexual attractiveness. Jewish fathers circumcise their infant sons to show their covenant with God. Women in African societies remove the clitoris of prepubescent girls, scrape their labia, and make the lips grow together to preserve their chastity and ensure their marriageability. In Western societies, women augment their breast size with silicone and reconstruct their faces with cosmetic surgery to conform to cultural ideals of feminine beauty. . . .

Most parents create a gendered world for their newborn by naming,   25
birth announcements, and dress. Children's relationships with same-gendered and different-gendered caretakers structure their self-identifications and personalities. Through cognitive development, children extract and apply to their own actions the appropriate behavior for those who belong in their own gender, as well as race, religion, ethnic group, and social class, rejecting what is not appropriate. If their social categories are highly valued, they value themselves highly; if their social categories are low status, they lose self-esteem (Chodorow 1974). Many feminist parents who want to raise androgynous children soon lose their children to the pull of gendered norms (Gordon 1990, 87–90). My son attended a carefully nonsexist elementary school, which didn't even have girls' and boys' bathrooms. When he was seven or eight years old, I attended a class play about "squares" and "circles" and their need for each other and noticed that all the girl squares and circles wore makeup, but none of the boy squares and circles did. I asked the teacher about it after the play, and she said, "Bobby said he was not going to wear makeup, and he is a powerful child, so none of the boys would either." In a long discussion about conformity, my son confronted me with the question of who the conformists were, the boys who followed their leader or the girls who listened to the woman teacher. In actuality, they both were, because they both followed same-gender leaders and acted in gender-appropriate ways. (Actors may wear makeup, but real boys don't.)

For human beings there is no essential femaleness or maleness, femi-   26
ninity or masculinity, womanhood or manhood, but once gender is ascribed, the social order constructs and holds individuals to strongly gendered norms and expectations. Individuals may vary on many of the components of gender and may shift genders temporarily or permanently, but they must fit into the limited number of gender statuses their society recognizes. In the process, they re-create their society's version of women and men: "If we do gender appropriately, we simultaneously sustain, reproduce, and render legitimate the institutional arrangements. . . . If we fail

to do gender appropriately, we as individuals — not the institutional arrangements — may be called to account (for our character, motives, and predispositions)" (West and Zimmerman 1987, 146).

The gendered practices of everyday life reproduce a society's view of 27 how women and men should act (Bourdieu [1980] 1990). Gendered social arrangements are justified by religion and cultural productions and backed by law, but the most powerful means of sustaining the moral hegemony of the dominant gender ideology is that the process is made invisible; any possible alternatives are virtually unthinkable (Foucault 1972; Gramsci 1971).[12]

For Society, Gender Means Difference

The pervasiveness of gender as a way of structuring social life demands that 28 gender statuses be clearly differentiated. Varied talents, sexual preferences, identities, personalities, interests, and ways of interacting fragment the individual's bodily and social experiences. Nonetheless, these are organized in Western cultures into two and only two socially and legally recognized gender statuses, "man" and "woman."[13] In the social construction of gender, it does not matter what men and women actually do; it does not even matter if they do exactly the same thing. The social institution of gender insists only that what they do is *perceived* as different.

If men and women are doing the same tasks, they are usually spatially 29 segregated to maintain gender separation, and often the tasks are given different job titles as well, such as executive secretary and administrative assistant (Reskin 1988). If the differences between women and men begin to blur, society's "sameness taboo" goes into action (Rubin 1975, 178). At a rock and roll dance at West Point in 1976, the year women were admitted to the prestigious military academy for the first time, the school's administrators "were reportedly perturbed by the sight of mirror-image couples dancing in short hair and dress gray trousers," and a rule was established that women cadets could dance at these events only if they wore skirts (Barkalow and Raab 1990, 53).[14] Women recruits in the U.S. Marine Corps are required to wear makeup — at a minimum, lipstick and eye shadow — and they have to take classes in makeup, hair care, poise, and etiquette. This feminization is part of a deliberate policy of making them clearly distinguishable from men Marines. Christine Williams quotes a twenty-five-year-old woman drill instructor as saying: "A lot of the recruits who come

[12]The concepts of moral hegemony, the effects of everyday activities (praxis) on thought and personality, and the necessity of consciousness of these processes before political change can occur are all based on Marx's analysis of class relations.

[13]Other societies recognize more than two categories, but usually no more than three or four (Jacobs and Roberts 1989).

[14]Carol Barkalow's book has a photograph of eleven first-year West Pointers in a math class, who are dressed in regulation pants, shirts, and sweaters, with short haircuts. The caption challenges the reader to locate the only woman in the room.

here don't wear makeup; they're tomboyish or athletic. A lot of them have the preconceived idea that going into the military means they can still be a tomboy. They don't realize that you are a *Woman* Marine" (1989, 76–77).[15]

If gender differences were genetic, physiological, or hormonal, gender *30* bending and gender ambiguity would occur only in hermaphrodites, who are born with chromosomes and genitalia that are not clearly female or male. Since gender differences are socially constructed, all men and all women can enact the behavior of the other, because they know the other's social script: " 'Man' and 'woman' are at once empty and overflowing categories. Empty because they have no ultimate, transcendental meaning. Overflowing because even when they appear to be fixed, they still contain within them alternative, denied, or suppressed definitions" (Scott 1988, 49). Nonetheless, though individuals may be able to shift gender statuses, the gender boundaries have to hold, or the whole gendered social order will come crashing down.

Paradoxically, it is the social importance of gender statuses and their *31* external markers — clothing, mannerisms, and spatial segregation — that makes gender bending or gender crossing possible — or even necessary. The social viability of differentiated gender statuses produces the need or desire to shift statuses. Without gender differentiation, transvestism and transsexuality would be meaningless. You couldn't dress in the opposite gender's clothing if all clothing were unisex. There would be no need to reconstruct genitalia to match identity if interests and life-styles were not gendered. There would be no need for women to pass as men to do certain kinds of work if jobs were not typed as "women's work" and "men's work." Women would not have to dress as men in public life in order to give orders or aggressively bargain with customers.

Gender boundaries are preserved when transsexuals create congru- *32* ous autobiographies of always having felt like what they are now. The transvestite's story also "recuperates social and sexual norms" (Garber 1992, 69). In the transvestite's normalized narrative, he or she "is 'compelled' by social and economic forces to disguise himself or herself in order to get a job, escape repression, or gain artistic or political 'freedom' " (Garber 1992, 70). The "true identity," when revealed, causes amazement over how easily and successfully the person passed as a member of the opposite gender, not a suspicion that gender itself is something of a put-on. . . .

---

[15]The taboo on males and females looking alike reflects the U.S. military's homophobia (Bérubé 1989). If you can't tell those with a penis from those with a vagina, how are you going to determine whether their sexual interest is heterosexual or homosexual unless you watch them having sexual relations?

BIBLIOGRAPHY

Amadiume, Ifi. 1987. *Male daughters, female husbands: Gender and sex in an African society*. London: Zed Books.

Barkalow, Carol, with Andrea Raab. 1990. *In the men's house*. New York: Poseidon Press.

Bem, Sandra Lipsitz. 1993. *The lenses of gender: Transforming the debate on sexual inequality*. New Haven: Yale University Press.

Bérubé, Allan. 1989. Marching to a different drummer: Gay and lesbian GIs in World War II. In *Hidden from history: Reclaiming the gay and lesbian past*, edited by Martin Bauml Duberman, Martha Vicinus, and George Chauncy, Jr. New York: New American Library.

Birdwhistell, Ray L. 1970. *Kinesics and context: Essays on body motion communication*. Philadelphia: University of Pennsylvania Press.

Blackwood, Evelyn. 1984. Sexuality and gender in certain Native American tribes: The case of cross-gender females. *Signs: Journal of Women in Culture and Society* 10:27–42.

Bolin, Anne. 1987. Transsexualism and the limits of traditional analysis. *American Behavioral Scientist* 31:41–65.

Bourdieu, Pierre. [1980] 1990. *The logic of practice*. Stanford, Calif.: Stanford University Press.

Butler, Judith. 1990. *Gender trouble: Feminism and the subversion of identity*. New York and London: Routledge.

Chodorow, Nancy. 1974. Family structure and feminine personality. In *Woman, culture and society*, edited by Michelle Zimbalist Rosaldo and Louise Lamphere. Stanford, Calif.: Stanford University Press.

De Beauvoir, Simone. 1953. *The second sex*, translated by H. M. Parshley. New York: Knopf.

Devor, Holly. 1987. Gender blending females: Women and sometimes men. *American Behavioral Scientist* 31: 12–40.

———. 1989. *Gender blending: Confronting the limits of duality*. Bloomington: Indiana University Press.

Dollimore, Jonathan. 1986. Subjectivity, sexuality, and transgression: The Jacobean connection. *Renaissance Drama*, n.s. 17:53–81.

Durova, Nadezhda. 1989. *The cavalry maiden: Journals of a Russian officer in the Napoleonic Wars*, translated by Mary Fleming Zirin. Bloomington: Indiana University Press.

Eichler, Margrit. 1989. Sex change operations: The last bulwark of the double standard. In *Feminist frontiers II*, edited by Laurel Richardson and Verta Taylor. New York: Random House.

Epstein, Cynthia Fuchs. 1988. *Deceptive distinctions: Sex, gender and the social order*. New Haven: Yale University Press.

Faderman, Lillian. 1991. *Odd girls and twilight lovers: A history of lesbian life in twentieth-century America*. New York: Columbia University Press.

Foucault, Michel. 1972. *The archeology of knowledge and the discourse on language*, translated by A. M. Sheridan Smith. New York: Pantheon.

Freeman, Lucy, and Alma Halbert Bond. 1992. *America's first woman warrior: The courage of Deborah Sampson*. New York: Paragon.

Frye, Marilyn. 1983. *The politics of reality: Essays in feminist theory*. Trumansburg, N.Y.: Crossing Press.

Garber, Marjorie. 1992. *Vested interests: Cross-dressing and cultural anxiety*. New York and London: Routledge.

Garfinkel, Harold. 1967. *Studies in ethnomethodology*. Englewood Cliffs, N.J.: Prentice-Hall.

Goffman, Erving. 1977. The arrangement between the sexes. *Theory and Society* 4:301–33.

———. 1983. Felicity's condition. *American Journal of Sociology* 89:1–53.

Gordon, Tuula. 1990. *Feminist mothers*. New York: New York University Press.

Gramsci, Antonio. 1971. *Selections from the prison notebooks,* translated and edited by Quintin Hoare and Geoffrey Nowell Smith. New York: International Publishers.

Greenblatt, Stephen. 1987. *Shakespearean negotiations: The circulation of social energy in Renaissance England.* Berkeley: University of California Press.

Groce, Stephen B., and Margaret Cooper. 1990. Just me and the boys? Women in local-level rock and roll. *Gender & Society* 4:220–29.

Howard, Jean E. 1988. Crossdressing, the theater, and gender struggle in early modern England. *Shakespeare Quarterly* 39:418–41.

Jacobs, Sue-Ellen, and Christine Roberts. 1989. Sex, sexuality, gender, and gender variance. In *Gender and anthropology,* edited by Sandra Morgen. Washington, D.C.: American Anthropological Association.

Kando, Thomas. 1973. *Sex change: The achievement of gender identity among feminized transsexuals.* Springfield, Ill.: Charles C Thomas.

Kincaid, Jamaica. 1978. Girl. *The New Yorker,* 26 June.

Laqueur, Thomas. 1990. *Making sex: Body and gender from the Greeks to Freud.* Cambridge, Mass.: Harvard University Press.

Matthaei, Julie A. 1982. *An economic history of women's work in America.* New York: Schocken.

Money, John, and Anke A. Ehrhardt. 1972. *Man & woman, boy & girl.* Baltimore, Md.: Johns Hopkins University Press.

Morris, Jan. 1975. *Conundrum.* New York: Signet.

Nanda, Serena. 1990. *Neither man nor woman: The hijiras of India.* Belmont, Calif.: Wadsworth.

New York Times. 1989. Musician's death at 74 reveals he was a woman. 2 February.

Reskin, Barbara F. 1988. Bringing the men back in: Sex differentiation and the devaluation of women's work. *Gender & Society* 2:58–81.

Rogers, Mary F. 1992. They were all passing: Agnes, Garfinkel, and company. *Gender & Society* 6: 169–91.

Rubin, Gayle. 1975. The traffic in women: Notes on the political economy of sex. In *Toward an anthropology of women,* edited by Rayna R[app] Reiter. New York: Monthly Review Press.

Rugh, Andrea B. 1986. *Reveal and conceal: Dress in contemporary Egypt.* Syracuse, N.Y.: Syracuse University Press.

Scott, Joan Wallach. 1988. *Gender and the politics of history.* New York: Columbia University Press.

West, Candace, and Don Zimmerman. 1987. Doing gender. *Gender & Society* 1:125–51.

Wheelwright, Julie. 1989. *Amazons and military maids: Women who cross-dressed in pursuit of life, liberty and happiness.* London: Pandora Press.

Wikan, Unni. 1982. *Behind the veil in Arabia: Women in Oman.* Baltimore, Md.: Johns Hopkins University Press.

Williams, Christine L. 1989. *Gender differences at work: Women and men in nontraditional occupations.* Berkeley: University of California Press.

Williams, Walter L. 1986. *The spirit and the flesh: Sexual diversity in American Indian culture.* Boston: Beacon Press.

■   ■   ■

Reading Rhetorically

1. Explain in your own words what Lorber means by the subtitle of the piece, "The Social Construction of Gender." According to Lorber, how is *gender* different from a *sex category*?

2. Lorber divides her essay into several sections. Discuss how each section contributes to her larger argument. You might try to locate a thesis statement in each section as a way to begin your discussion.

3. Lorber includes many examples in her essay. Which examples do you find most and least persuasive, and why? What conclusions can you draw about how to use examples effectively in your own writing?

Inquiring Further

4. Lorber claims that "gendering is done from birth, constantly and by everyone" (para. 6). Test this claim by analyzing ten birth announcements for baby boys and girls. How do the colors, images, and language on the cards assert the differences between genders? What assumptions do the cards make about baby boys and girls? Discuss the significance of your findings.

5. How is gendering "done" on your campus? Spend an hour observing your peers at the student center or a recreational facility. Take notes on specific types of behavior — body language, gestures, dress, topics of conversation, and conversational styles, for example. What can you conclude about the ways masculinity and femininity are done differently? What behaviors seem to cross gender? Discuss your observations in relation to Lorber's claims.

6. Why do you think so many of Lorber's examples focus on parenting strategies and patterns? Interview three sets of parents on the division of labor in their parenting and how that decision was made. Alternatively, use your library's online resources to research parenting, comparing the information you find on being a mother with the information on being a father. What conclusions can you draw?

Framing Conversations

7. Both Lorber and Deborah Tannen (p. 654) are interested in the ways we "do gender," and the larger social implications of gendered behaviors. Write an essay in which you place Lorber's and Tannen's insights in conversation with one another in order to make an argument about what you find most interesting about gendered behaviors and social power. Include examples from your own experience if they help you make your point.

8. How do Lorber's ideas about gender help you understand sport culture? Write an essay in which you use Lorber's ideas to analyze the arguments about sports in the texts by Franklin Foer (p. 406) and Shari Dworkin and Michael Messner (p. 551). Focus on the ideas you feel are most important for your readers to understand about your findings. If you like, include and analyze examples from your own experience with sports (in gym class, in pickup games in your neighborhood or at school, or in organized sports).

9. How can Lorber's gender analysis be applied to children's films or video games? Drawing on Lorber's ideas and those of either Henry Giroux (p. 567) or Henry Jenkins (p. 700), write an essay in which you analyze a specific children's film or video game with gender as a main component of your analysis. Be sure to explain to your readers the significance of your findings.

Becoming a Gendered Body:
Practices of Preschools

Karin A. Martin is a professor of sociology at the University of Michigan, where she teaches courses on childhood and adolescence, feminist theory, and sociological research methods. Much of her work focuses on the ways cultural norms are learned and reinforced through physical movement and practices, from childhood game-playing to young women's appearance routines. She has published many articles on these topics as well as a book, *Puberty, Sexuality, and the Self: Boys and Girls at Adolescence* (1996).

This essay first appeared in the *American Sociological Review* in 1998. As Martin notes in the first paragraph, although many social scientists acknowledge cultural influences on women's bodies, few have examined how these influences begin in childhood. So, Martin asks, "How do adult gendered bodies become gendered, if they are not naturally so?" (para. 6). She sets out to help us understand how "the gendering of children's bodies makes gender differences feel and appear natural, which allows for . . . bodily differences to emerge throughout [the] life course" (para. 6). In other words, she studies the everyday interactions that teach girls to act like girls and boys to act like boys. She does not argue that teachers intentionally train girls and boys to move or walk or throw differently, but she shows, through observations, that gender patterns are reinforced from early childhood.

One look at Martin's references reveals the large number of sources she draws on to enrich her argument. She is in conversation with sociologists, gender theorists, and a range of educational specialists. The concept of schools having a hidden curriculum is not original to her: Notice all the names she cites parenthetically when she introduces the idea in paragraph 7. But Martin includes gender in her analysis of the subjects schools teach that are not in the lesson books. (Consider, for example, how much of early schooling is about learning to stand in line, to sit quietly, and to raise your hand before you speak.) Schools teach children to behave in myriad ways; Martin argues that it also teaches children to behave as "young ladies" and "young gentlemen" in strikingly contrasting ways.

In addition to her scholarly research, Martin's data come from primary research, her observations and analyses of the behaviors of real children in school. Pay particular attention to the section on data and method, where she describes the strengths and the potential problems of doing these kinds of "semi-structured field observations" (para. 9). Notice how in the body of this essay, Martin moves between the voices of other scholars, her own data, and her analysis of those data. Because Martin includes fairly lengthy excerpts from the notes she made while observing preschool children, you may want to do some of your own analysis of these notes. What do you think is going on in the many interactions she and her research assistant describe in detail, and why? Can you think of interpretations Martin does not?

> This essay may spur you to think about your own preschool experiences. Did your preschool have a hidden gender curriculum? Martin seeks to persuade us that when teachers tell children to behave, those children may be learning more than we imagined.

■ ■ ■

Social science research about bodies often focuses on women's bodies, particularly the parts of women's bodies that are most explicitly different from men's — their reproductive capacities and sexuality (E. Martin 1987; K. Martin 1996; but see Connell 1987, 1995). Men and women in the United States also hold and move their bodies differently (Birdwhistell 1970; Henley 1977; Young 1990); these differences are sometimes related to sexuality (Haug 1987) and sometimes not. On the whole, men and women sit, stand, gesture, walk, and throw differently. Generally, women's bodies are confined, their movements restricted. For example, women take smaller steps than men, sit in closed positions (arms and legs crossed across the body), take up less physical space than men, do not step, twist, or throw from the shoulder when throwing a ball, and are generally tentative when using their bodies (Birdwhistell 1970; Henley 1977; Young 1990). Some of these differences, particularly differences in motor skills (e.g., jumping, running, throwing) are seen in early childhood (Thomas and French 1985). Of course, within gender, we may find individual differences, differences based on race, class, and sexuality, and differences based on size and shape of body. Yet, on average, men and women move differently.

Such differences may seem trivial in the large scheme of gender inequality. However, theoretical work by social scientists and feminists suggests that these differences may be consequential. Bodies are (unfinished) resources (Shilling 1993:103) that must be "trained, manipulated, cajoled, coaxed, organized and in general disciplined" (Turner 1992:15). We use our bodies to construct our means of living, to take care of each other, to pleasure each other. According to Turner, ". . . social life depends upon the successful presenting, monitoring and interpreting of bodies" (p. 15). Similarly, according to Foucault (1979), controlled and disciplined bodies do more than regulate the individual body. A disciplined body creates a context for social relations. Gendered (along with "raced" and "classed") bodies create particular contexts for social relations as they signal, manage, and negotiate information about power and status. Gender relations depend on the successful gender presentation, monitoring, and interpretation of bodies (West and Zimmerman 1987). Bodies that clearly delineate gender status facilitate the maintenance of the gender hierarchy.

Our bodies are also one *site* of gender. Much postmodern feminist work (Butler 1990, 1993) suggests that gender is a performance. Microsociological work (West and Zimmerman 1987) suggests that gender is something that is "done." These two concepts, "gender performance" and "doing gender," are similar — both suggest that managed, adorned, fashioned, properly comported, and moving bodies establish gender and gender relations.

Other feminist theorists (Connell 1987, 1995; Young 1990) argue that 4 gender rests not only on the surface of the body, in performance and doing, but becomes *embodied* — becomes deeply part of who we are physically and psychologically. According to Connell, gender becomes embedded in body postures, musculature, and tensions in our bodies.

> The social definition of men as holders of power is translated not only into mental body-images and fantasies, but into muscle tensions, posture, the feel and texture of the body. This is one of the main ways in which the power of men becomes naturalized. . . . (Connell 1987:85)

Connell (1995) suggests that masculine gender is partly a feel to one's 5 body and that bodies are often a source of power for men. Young (1990), however, argues that bodies serve the opposite purpose for women — women's bodies are often sources of anxiety and tentativeness. She suggests that women's lack of confidence and agency are embodied and stem from an inability to move confidently in space, to take up space, to use one's body to its fullest extent. Young (1990) suggests "that the general lack of confidence that we [women] frequently have about our cognitive or leadership abilities is traceable in part to an original doubt of our body's capacity" (p. 156). Thus, these theorists suggest that gender differences in minute bodily behaviors like gesture, stance, posture, step, and throwing are significant to our understanding of gendered selves and gender inequality. This feminist theory, however, focuses on adult bodies.

Theories of the body need gendering, and feminist theories of gen- 6 dered bodies need "childrening" or accounts of development. How do adult gendered bodies become gendered, if they are not naturally so? Scholars run the risk of continuing to view gendered bodies as natural if they ignore the processes that produce gendered adult bodies. Gendering of the body in childhood is the foundation on which further gendering of the body occurs throughout the life course. The gendering of children's bodies makes gender differences feel and appear natural, which allows for such bodily differences to emerge throughout that life course.

I suggest that the hidden school curriculum of disciplining the body is 7 gendered and contributes to the embodiment of gender in childhood, making gendered bodies appear and feel natural. Sociologists of education have demonstrated that schools have hidden curriculums (Giroux and Purpel 1983; Jackson 1968). Hidden curriculums are covert lessons that schools teach, and they are often a means of social control. These curriculums include teaching about work differentially by class (Anyon 1980; Bowles and Gintis 1976; Carnoy and Levin 1985), political socialization (Wasburn 1986), and training in obedience and docility (Giroux and

Purpel 1983). More recently, some theorists and researchers have examined the curriculum that disciplines the body (Carere 1987; Foucault 1979; McLaren 1986). This curriculum demands the practice of bodily control in congruence with the goals of the school as an institution. It reworks the students from the outside in on the presumption that to shape the body is to shape the mind (Carere 1987). In such a curriculum teachers constantly monitor kids' bodily movements, comportment, and practices. Kids begin their day running wildly about the school grounds. Then this hidden curriculum funnels the kids into line, through the hallways, quietly into a classroom, sitting upright at their desks, focused at the front of the room, "ready to learn" (Carere 1987; McLaren 1986). According to Carere (1987), this curriculum of disciplining the body serves the curriculums that seek to shape the mind and renders children physically ready for cognitive learning.

I suggest that this hidden curriculum that controls children's bodily 8 practices serves also to turn kids who are similar in bodily comportment, movement, and practice into girls and boys, children whose bodily practices are different. Schools are not the only producers of these differences. While the process ordinarily begins in the family, the schools' hidden curriculum further facilitates and encourages the construction of bodily differences between the genders and makes these physical differences appear and feel natural. Finally, this curriculum may be more or less hidden depending on the particular preschool and particular teachers. Some schools and teachers may see teaching children to behave like "young ladies" and "young gentlemen" as an explicit part of their curriculums.

Data and Method

The data for this study come from extensive and detailed semi-structured 9 field observations of five preschool classrooms of three-to five-year-olds in a midwestern city. Four of the classrooms were part of a preschool (Preschool A) located close to the campus of a large university. A few of the kids were children of faculty members, more were children of staff and administrators, and many were not associated with the university. Many of the kids who attended Preschool A attended part-time. Although teachers at this school paid some attention to issues of race and gender equity, issues of diversity were not as large a part of the curriculum as they are at some preschools (Jordan and Cowan 1995; Van Ausdale and Feagin 1996). The fifth classroom was located at Preschool B, a preschool run by a Catholic church in the same city as Preschool A. The kids who attended Preschool B were children of young working professionals, many of whom lived in the vicinity of the preschool. These children attended preschool "full-time" — five days a week for most of the day. . . .

A total of 112 children and fourteen different teachers (five head *10* teachers and nine aides) were observed in these classrooms. All teachers were female. . . .

A research assistant and I observed in these classrooms about three *11* times a week for eight months. Our observations were as unobtrusive as possible, and we interacted little with the kids. . . . We observed girls and boys for equal amounts of time, and we heeded Thorne's (1993) caution about the "big man bias" in field research and were careful not to observe only the most active, outgoing, "popular" kids. . . .

Results

Children's bodies are disciplined by schools. Children are physically *12* active, and institutions like schools impose disciplinary controls that regulate children's bodies and prepare children for the larger social world. While this disciplinary control produces docile bodies (Foucault 1979), it also produces gendered bodies. As these disciplinary practices operate in different contexts, some bodies become more docile than others. I examine how the following practices contribute to a gendering of children's bodies in preschool: the effects of dressing-up or bodily adornment, the gendered nature of formal and relaxed behaviors, how the different restrictions on girls' and boys' voices limit their physicality, how teachers instruct girls' and boys' bodies, and the gendering of physical interactions between children and teachers and among the children themselves.

Bodily Adornment: Dressing Up

Perhaps the most explicit way that children's bodies become gendered is *13* through their clothes and other bodily adornments. Here I discuss how parents gender their children through their clothes, how children's dress-up play experiments with making bodies feminine and masculine, and how this play, when it is gender normative, shapes girls' and boys' bodies differently, constraining girls' physicality.

Dressing Up (1). The clothes that parents send kids to preschool in *14* shape children's experiences of their bodies in gendered ways. Clothes, particularly their color, signify a child's gender; gender in preschool is in fact color-coded. On average, about 61 percent of the girls wore pink clothing each day. Boys were more likely to wear primary colors, black, fluorescent green, and orange. Boys never wore pink.

> The teacher is asking each kid during circle (the part of the day that includes formal instruction by the teacher while the children sit in a circle) what their favorite color is. Adam says black. Bill says "every color that's not pink." (Five-year-olds)

Fourteen percent of three-year-old girls wore dresses each day com-   *15*
pared to 32 percent of five-year-old girls. Wearing a dress limited girls'
physicality in preschool. However, it is not only the dress itself, but knowledge about how to behave in a dress that is restrictive. Many girls already
knew that some behaviors were not allowed in a dress. This knowledge
probably comes from the families who dress their girls in dresses.

> Vicki, wearing leggings and a dress-like shirt, is leaning over the desk to look
> into a "tunnel" that some other kids have built. As she leans, her dress/shirt
> rides up exposing her back. Jennifer (another child) walks by Vicki and as she
> does she pulls Vicki's shirt back over her bare skin and gives it a pat to keep it in
> place. It looks very much like something one's mother might do. (Five-year-olds)
>   Four girls are sitting at a table — Cathy, Kim, Danielle, and Jesse. They
> are cutting play money out of paper. Cathy and Danielle have on overalls and
> Kim and Jesse have on dresses. Cathy puts her feet up on the table and crosses
> her legs at the ankle; she leans back in her chair and continues cutting her
> money. Danielle imitates her. They look at each other and laugh. They put
> their shoulders back, posturing, having fun with this new way of sitting. Kim
> and Jesse continue to cut and laugh with them, but do not put their feet up.
> (Five-year-olds)

Dresses are restrictive in other ways as well. They often are worn with   *16*
tights that are experienced as uncomfortable and constraining. I observed
girls constantly pulling at and rearranging their tights, trying to untwist
them or pull them up. Because of their discomfort, girls spent much time
attuned to and arranging their clothing and/or their bodies.

Dresses also can be lifted up, an embarrassing thing for five-year-   *17*
olds if done purposely by another child. We witnessed this on only one
occasion — a boy pulled up the hem of a girl's skirt. The girl protested and
the teacher told him to stop and that was the end of it. Teachers, however,
lifted up girls' dresses frequently — to see if a child was dressed warmly
enough, while reading a book about dresses, to see if a child was wet. Usually this was done without asking the child and was more management of
the child rather than an interaction with her. Teachers were much more
likely to manage girls and their clothing this way — rearranging their
clothes, tucking in their shirts, fixing a ponytail gone astray. Such management often puts girls' bodies under the control of another and calls girls'
attentions to their appearances and bodily adornments.

Dressing Up (2). Kids like to *play* dress-up in preschool, and all the   *18*
classrooms had a dress-up corner with a variety of clothes, shoes, pocketbooks, scarves, and hats for dressing up. Classrooms tended to have more
women's clothes than men's, but there were some of both, as well as some
gender-neutral clothes — capes, hats, and vests that were not clearly for
men or women — and some items that were clearly costumes, such as
masks of cats and dogs and clip-on tails. Girls tended to play dress-up
more than boys — over one-half of dressing up was done by girls. Gender
differences in the amount of time spent playing dress-up seemed to

increase from age three to age five. We only observed the five-year-old boys dressing up or using clothes or costumes in their play three times, whereas three-year-old boys dressed up almost weekly. Five-year-old boys also did not dress up elaborately, but used one piece of clothing to animate their play. Once Phil wore large, man's winter ski gloves when he played monster. Holding up his now large, chiseled looking hands, he stomped around the classroom making monster sounds. On another occasion Brian, a child new to the classroom who attended only two days a week, walked around by himself for a long time carrying a silver pocketbook and hovering first at the edges of girls' play and then at the edges of boys' play. On the third occasion, Sam used ballet slippers to animate his play in circle.

When kids dressed up, they played at being a variety of things from 19 kitty cats and puppies to monsters and superheroes to "fancy ladies." Some of this play was not explicitly gendered. For example, one day in November I observed three girls wearing "turkey hats" they had made. They spent a long time gobbling at each other and playing at being turkeys, but there was nothing explicitly gendered about their play. However, this kind of adornment was not the most frequent type. Children often seemed to experiment with both genders when they played dress-up. The three-year-olds tended to be more experimental in their gender dress-up than the five-year-olds, perhaps because teachers encouraged it more at this age.

> Everett and Juan are playing dress-up. Both have on "dresses" made out of material that is wrapped around them like a toga or sarong. Everett has a pocketbook and a camera over his shoulder and Juan has a pair of play binoculars on a strap over his. Everett has a scarf around his head and cape on. Juan has on big, green sunglasses. Pam (teacher) tells them, "You guys look great! Go look in the mirror." They shuffle over to the full-length mirror and look at themselves and grin, and make adjustments to their costumes. (Three-year-olds)

The five-year-old children tended to dress-up more gender normatively. Girls in particular played at being adult women.

> Frances is playing dress-up. She is walking in red shoes and carrying a pocketbook. She and two other girls, Jen and Rachel, spend between five and ten minutes looking at and talking about the guinea pigs. Then they go back to dress-up. Frances and Rachel practice walking in adult women's shoes. Their body movements are not a perfect imitation of an adult woman's walk in high heels, yet it does look like an attempt to imitate such a walk. Jen and Rachel go back to the guinea pigs, and Frances, now by herself, is turning a sheer, frilly lavender shirt around and around and around trying to figure out how to put it on. She gets it on and looks at herself in the mirror. She adds a sheer pink and lavender scarf and pink shoes. Looks in the mirror again. She walks, twisting her body — shoulders, hips, shoulders, hips — not quite a (stereotypic) feminine walk, but close. Walking in big shoes makes her take little bitty steps, like walking in heels. She shuffles in the too big shoes out into the middle of the classroom and stops by a teacher. Laura (a teacher) says, "Don't you look fancy, all pink and purple." Frances smiles up at her and walks off,

not twisting so much this time. She goes back to the mirror and adds a red scarf. She looks in the mirror and is holding her arms across her chest to hold the scarf on (she can't tie it) and she is holding it with her chin too. She shuffles to block area where Jen is and then takes the clothes off and puts them back in the dress-up area. (Five-year-olds)

I observed not only the children who dressed up, but the reaction of those around them to their dress. This aspect proved to be one of the most interesting parts of kids' dress-up play. Children interpreted each others' bodily adornments as gendered, even when other interpretations were plausible. For instance, one day just before Halloween, Kim dressed up and was "scary" because she was dressed as a woman:

> Kim has worn a denim skirt and tights to school today. Now she is trying to pull on a ballerina costume — pink and ruffly — over her clothes. She has a hard time getting it on. It's tight and wrinkled up and twisted when she gets it on. Her own clothes are bunched up under it. Then she puts on a mask — a woman's face. The mask material itself is a clear plastic so that skin shows through, but is sculpted to have a very Anglo nose and high cheek bones. It also has thin eyebrows, blue eye shadow, blush, and lipstick on it. The mask is bigger than Kim's face and head. Kim looks at herself in the mirror and spends the rest of the play time with this costume on. Intermittently she picks up a plastic pumpkin since it is Halloween season and carries that around too. Kim walks around the classroom for a long time and then runs through the block area wearing this costume. Jason yells, "Ugh! There's a woman!" He and the other boys playing blocks shriek and scatter about the block area. Kim runs back to the dress-up area as they yell. Then throughout the afternoon she walks and skips through the center of the classroom, and every time she comes near the block boys one of them yells, "Ugh, there's the woman again!" The teacher even picks up on this and says to Kim twice, "Woman, slow down." (Five-year-olds)

The boys' shrieks indicated that Kim was scary, and this scariness is linked in their comments about her being a woman. It seems equally plausible that they could have interpreted her scary dress as a "trick-or-treater," given that it was close to Halloween and she was carrying a plastic pumpkin that kids collect candy in, or that they might have labeled her a dancer or ballerina because she was wearing a tutu. Rather, her scary dress-up was coded for her by others as "woman."

Other types of responses to girls dressing up also seemed to gender their bodies and to constrain them. For example, on two occasions I saw a teacher tie the arms of girls' dress-up shirts together so that the girls could not move their arms. They did this in fun, of course, and untied them as soon as the girls wanted them to, but I never witnessed this constraining of boys' bodies in play.

Thus, how parents gender children's bodies through dressing them and the ways children experiment with bodily adornments by dressing up make girls' and boys' bodies different and seem different to those around them. Adorning a body often genders it explicitly — signifies that it is a feminine or masculine body. Adornments also make girls' movements smaller, leading girls to take up less space with their bodies and disallowing some types of movements.

Formal and Relaxed Behaviors

Describing adults, Goffman (1959) defines front stage and backstage 23 behavior:

> The backstage language consists of reciprocal first-naming, co-operative decision making, profanity, open sexual remarks, elaborate gripping, smoking, rough informal dress, "sloppy" sitting and standing posture, use of dialect or substandard speech, mumbling and shouting, playful aggressivity and "kidding," inconsiderateness for the other in minor but potentially symbolic acts, minor physical self-involvements such as humming, whistling, chewing, nibbling, belching, and flatulence. The front stage behavior language can be taken as the absence (and in some sense the opposite) of this. (p. 128)

Thus, one might not expect much front stage or formal behavior in 24 preschool, and often, especially during parents' drop-off and pick-up time, this was the case. But a given region of social life may sometimes be a backstage and sometimes a front stage. I identified several behaviors that were expected by the teachers, required by the institution, or that would be required in many institutional settings, as formal behavior. Raising one's hand, sitting "on your bottom" (not on your knees, not squatting, not lying down, not standing) during circle, covering one's nose and mouth when coughing or sneezing, or sitting upright in a chair are all formal behaviors of preschools, schools, and to some extent the larger social world. Crawling on the floor, yelling, lying down during teachers' presentations, and running through the classroom are examples of relaxed behaviors that are not allowed in preschool, schools, work settings, and many institutions of the larger social world (Henley 1977). Not all behaviors fell into one of these classifications. When kids were actively engaged in playing at the water table, for example, much of their behavior was not clearly formal or relaxed. I coded as formal and relaxed behaviors those behaviors that would be seen as such if done by adults (or children in many cases) in other social institutions for which children are being prepared.

In the classrooms in this study, boys were allowed and encouraged to 25 pursue relaxed behaviors in a variety of ways that girls were not. Girls were more likely to be encouraged to pursue more formal behaviors. Eighty-two percent of all formal behaviors observed in these classrooms were done by girls, and only 18 percent by boys. However, 80 percent of the behaviors coded as relaxed were boys' behaviors.

These observations do not tell us *why* boys do more relaxed behaviors 26 and girls do more formal behaviors. Certainly many parents and others would argue that boys are more predisposed to sloppy postures, crawling on the floor, and so on. However, my observations suggest that teachers help construct this gender difference in bodily behaviors. Teachers were more likely to reprimand girls for relaxed bodily movements and comportment. Sadker and Sadker (1994) found a similar result with respect to hand-raising for answering teachers' questions — if hand-raising is considered a formal behavior and calling out a relaxed behavior, they find that boys are more likely to call out without raising their hands and demand attention:

> Sometimes what they [boys] say has little or nothing to do with the teacher's questions. Whether male comments are insightful or irrelevant, teachers respond to them. However, when girls call out, there is a fascinating occurrence: Suddenly the teacher remembers the rule about raising your hand before you talk. (Sadker and Sadker 1994:43)

This gendered dynamic of hand-raising exists even in preschool, although our field notes do not provide enough systematic recording of hand-raising to fully assess it. However, such a dynamic applies to many bodily movements and comportment:

> The kids are sitting with their legs folded in a circle listening to Jane (the teacher) talk about dinosaurs. ("Circle" is the most formal part of their preschool education each day and is like sitting in class.) Sam has the ballet slippers on his hands and is clapping them together really loudly. He stops and does a half-somersault backward out of the circle and stays that way with his legs in the air. Jane says nothing and continues talking about dinosaurs. Sue, who is sitting next to Sam, pushes his leg out of her way. Sam sits up and is now busy trying to put the ballet shoes on over his sneakers, and he is looking at the other kids and laughing, trying to get a reaction. He is clearly not paying attention to Jane's dinosaur story and is distracting the other kids. Sam takes the shoes and claps them together again. Jane leans over and tells him to give her the shoes. Sam does, and then lies down all stretched out on the floor, arms over his head, legs apart. Adam is also lying down now, and Keith is on Sara's (the teacher's aide) lap. Rachel takes her sweater off and folds it up. The other children are focused on the teacher. After about five minutes, Jane tells Sam "I'm going to ask you to sit up." (She doesn't say anything to Adam.) But he doesn't move. Jane ignores Sam and Adam and continues with the lesson. Rachel now lies down on her back. After about ten seconds Jane says, "Sit up, Rachel." Rachel sits up and listens to what kind of painting the class will do today. (Five-year-olds)

Sam's behavior had to be more disruptive, extensive, and informal than Rachel's for the teacher to instruct him and his bodily movements to be quieter and for him to comport his body properly for circle. Note that the boys who were relaxed but not disruptive were not instructed to sit properly. It was also common for a teacher to tell a boy to stop some bodily behavior and for the boy to ignore the request and the teacher not to enforce her instructions, although she frequently repeated them.

The gendering of body movements, comportment, and acquisitions of   28
space also happens in more subtle ways. For example, often when there
was "free" time, boys spent much more time in child-structured activities
than did girls. In one classroom of five-year-olds, boys' "free" time was usually spent building with blocks, climbing on blocks, or crawling on the
blocks or on the floor as they worked to build with the blocks whereas girls
spent much of their free time sitting at tables cutting things out of paper,
drawing, sorting small pieces of blocks into categories, reading stories,
and so on. Compared to boys, girls rarely crawled on the floor (except
when they played kitty cats). Girls and boys did share some activities. For
example, painting and reading were frequently shared, and the three-year-
olds often played at fishing from a play bridge together. Following is a list
from my field notes of the most common activities boys and girls did during the child-structured activity periods of the day during two randomly
picked weeks of observing:

> Boys   played blocks (floor), played at the water table (standing and splash-
> ing), played superhero (running around and in play house), played
> with the car garage (floor), painted at the easel (standing).
>
> Girls   played dolls (sitting in chairs and walking around), played dress-up
> (standing), coloring (sitting at tables), read stories (sitting on the
> couch), cut out pictures (sitting at tables).

Children sorted themselves into these activities and also were sorted   29
(or not unsorted) by teachers. For example, teachers rarely told the three
boys that always played with the blocks that they had to choose a different
activity that day. Teachers also encouraged girls to sit at tables by suggesting table activities for them — in a sense giving them less "free" time or
structuring their time more.

> It's the end of circle, and Susan (teacher) tells the kids that today they can
> paint their dinosaur eggs if they want to. There is a table set up with paints
> and brushes for those who want to do that. The kids listen and then scatter
> to their usual activities. Several boys are playing blocks, two boys are at the
> water table. Several girls are looking at the hamsters in their cage and
> talking about them, two girls are sitting and stringing plastic beads. Susan
> says across the classroom, "I need some painters, Joy, Amy, Kendall?"
> The girls leave the hamster cage and go to the painting table. Susan pulls
> out a chair so Joy can sit down. She tells them about the painting project.
> (Five-year-olds)

These girls spent much of the afternoon enjoying themselves painting
their eggs. Simon and Jack joined them temporarily, but then went back to
activities that were not teacher-structured.

Events like these that happen on a regular basis over an extended   30
period of early childhood serve to gender children's bodies — boys come
to take up more room with their bodies, to sit in more open positions, and

to feel freer to do what they wish with their bodies, even in relatively formal settings. Henley (1977) finds that among adults, men generally are more relaxed than women in their demeanor and women tend to have tenser postures. The looseness of body-focused functions (e.g., belching) is also more open to men than to women. In other words, men are more likely to engage in relaxed demeanors, postures, and behaviors. These data suggest that this gendering of bodies into more formal and more relaxed movements, postures, and comportment is (at least partially) constructed in early childhood by institutions like preschools.

Controlling Voice

Speaking (or yelling as is often the case with kids) is a bodily experience 31 that involves mouth, throat, chest, diaphragm, and facial expression. Thorne (1993) writes that an elementary school teacher once told her that kids "reminded her of bumblebees, an apt image of swarms, speed, and constant motion" (p. 15). Missing from this metaphor is the buzz of the bumblebees, as a constant hum of voices comes from children's play and activities. Kids' play that is giggly, loud, or whispery makes it clear that voice is part of their bodily experiences.

Voice is an aspect of bodily experience that teachers and schools are 32 interested in disciplining. Quiet appears to be required for learning in classrooms. Teaching appropriate levels of voice, noise, and sound disciplines children's bodies and prepares them "from the inside" to learn the school's curriculums and to participate in other social institutions.

The disciplining of children's voices is gendered. I found that girls were 33 told to be quiet or to repeat a request in a quieter, "nicer" voice about three times more often than were boys. This finding is particularly interesting because boys' play was frequently much noisier. However, when boys were noisy, they were also often doing other behaviors the teacher did not allow, and perhaps the teachers focused less on voice because they were more concerned with stopping behaviors like throwing or running.

Additionally, when boys were told to "quiet down" they were told in 34 large groups, rarely as individuals. When they were being loud and were told to be quiet, boys were often in the process of enacting what Jordan and Cowan (1995) call warrior narratives:

> A group of three boys is playing with wooden doll figures. The dolls are jumping off block towers, crashing into each other. Kevin declares loudly, "I'm the grown-up." Keith replies, "I'm the police." They knock the figures into each other and push each other away. Phil grabs a figure from Keith. Keith picks up two more and bats one with the other toward Phil. Now all three boys are crashing the figures into each other, making them dive off towers. They're having high fun. Two more boys join the group. There are now five boys playing with the wooden dolls and the blocks. They're breaking block buildings; things are crashing; they're grabbing each other's figures and yelling loudly.

Some are yelling "fire, fire" as their figures jump off the block tower. The room is very noisy. (Five-year-olds)

Girls as individuals and in groups were frequently told to lower their voices. Later that same afternoon:

During snack time the teacher asks the kids to tell her what they like best in the snack mix. Hillary says, "Marshmallows!" loudly, vigorously, and with a swing of her arm. The teacher turns to her and says, "I'm going to ask you to say that quietly," and Hillary repeats in a softer voice. (Five-year-olds)

These two observations represent a prominent pattern in the data. The 35 boys playing with the wooden figures were allowed to express their fun and enthusiasm loudly whereas Hillary could not loudly express her love of marshmallows. Girls' voices are disciplined to be softer and in many ways less physical — toning down their voices tones down their physicality. Hillary emphasized "marshmallows" with a large swinging gesture of her arm the first time she answered the teacher's question, but after the teacher asked her to say it quietly she made no gestures when answering. Incidents like these that are repeated often in different contexts restrict girls' physicality.

It could be argued that context rather than gender explains the differ- 36 ence in how much noise is allowed in these situations. Teachers may expect more formal behavior from children sitting at the snack table than they do during semistructured activities. However, even during free play girls were frequently told to quiet down:

Nancy, Susan, and Amy are jumping in little jumps, from the balls of their feet, almost like skipping rope without the rope. Their mouths are open and they're making a humming sound, looking at each other and giggling. Two of them keep sticking their tongues out. They seem to be having great fun. The teacher's aide sitting on the floor in front of them turns around and says, "Shhh, find something else to play. Why don't you play Simon Says?" All three girls stop initially. Then Amy jumps a few more times, but without making the noise. (Five-year-olds)

By limiting the girls' voices, the teacher also limits the girls' jumping and their fun. The girls learn that their bodies are supposed to be quiet, small, and physically constrained. Although the girls did not take the teacher's suggestion to play Simon Says (a game where bodies can be moved only quietly at the order of another), they turn to play that explores quietness yet tries to maintain some of the fun they were having:

Nancy, Susan, and Amy begin sorting a pile of little-bitty pieces of puzzles, soft blocks, Legos, and so on into categories to "help" the teacher who told them to be quiet and to clean up. The three of them and the teacher are stand-ing around a single small desk sorting these pieces. (Meanwhile several boys are playing blocks and their play is spread all over the middle of the room.) The teacher turns her attention to some other children. The girls continue sorting and then begin giggling to each other. As they do, they cover their mouths. This becomes a game as one imitates the other. Susan says something nonsensical that is supposed to be funny, and then she "hee-hees" while covering her mouth and looks at Nancy, to whom she has said it, who covers her mouth and "hee-hees" back. They begin putting their hands/fingers cupped over their mouths and whispering in each others' ears and then giggling quietly. They are intermittently sorting the pieces and playing the whispering game. (Five-year-olds)

Thus, the girls took the instruction to be quiet and turned it into a 37 game. This new game made their behaviors smaller, using hands and mouths rather than legs, feet, and whole bodies. Whispering became their fun, instead of jumping and humming. Besides requiring quiet, this whispering game also was gendered in another way: The girls' behavior seemed to mimic stereotypical female gossiping. They whispered in twos and looked at the third girl as they did it and then changed roles. Perhaps the instruction to be quiet, combined with the female role of "helping," led the girls to one of their understandings of female quietness — gossip — a type of feminine quietness that is perhaps most fun.

Finally, by limiting voice teachers limit one of girls' mechanisms for 38 resisting others' mistreatment of them. Frequently, when a girl had a dispute with another child, teachers would ask the girl to quiet down and solve the problem nicely. Teachers also asked boys to solve problems by talking, but they usually did so only with intense disputes and the instruction to talk things out never carried the instruction to talk *quietly.*

Keith is persistently threatening to knock over the building that Amy built. He is running around her with a "flying" toy horse that comes dangerously close to her building each time. She finally says, "Stop it!" in a loud voice. The teacher comes over and asks, "How do we say that, Amy?" Amy looks at Keith and says more softly, "Stop trying to knock it over." The teacher tells Keith to find some place else to play. (Five-year-olds)

Cheryl and Julie are playing at the sand table. Cheryl says to the teacher loudly, "Julie took mine away!" The teacher tells her to say it more quietly. Cheryl repeats it less loudly. The teacher tells her, "Say it a little quieter." Cheryl says it quieter, and the teacher says to Julie, "Please don't take that away from her." (Three-year-olds)

We know that women are reluctant to use their voices to protect themselves from a variety of dangers. The above observations suggest that the denial of women's voices begins at least as early as preschool, and that restricting voice usually restricts movement as well.

Finally, there were occasions when the quietness requirement did not 39 restrict girls' bodies. One class of three-year-olds included two Asian girls, Diane and Sue, who did not speak English. Teachers tended to talk about them and over them but rarely to them. Although these girls said little to other children and were generally quiet, they were what I term body instigators. They got attention and played with other children in more bodily ways than most girls. For example, Sue developed a game with another girl that was a sort of musical chairs. They'd race from one chair to another to see who could sit down first. Sue initiated this game by trying to squeeze into a chair with the other girl. Also, for example,

> Diane starts peeking into the play cardboard house that is full of boys and one girl. She looks like she wants to go in, but the door is blocked and the house is crowded. She then goes around to the side of the house and stands with her back to it and starts bumping it with her butt. Because the house is cardboard, it buckles and moves as she does it. The teacher tells her, "Stop — no." Diane stops and then starts doing it again but more lightly. All the boys come out of the house and ask her what she's doing. Matt gets right in her face and the teacher tells him, "Tell her no." He does, but all the other boys have moved on to other activities, so she and Matt go in the house together. (Three-year-olds)

Thus, Diane and Sue's lack of voice in this English-speaking classroom led to greater physicality. There may be other ways that context (e.g., in one's neighborhood instead of school) and race, ethnicity, and class shape gender and voice that cannot be determined from these data (Goodwin 1990).

Bodily Instructions

Teachers give a lot of instructions to kids about what to do with their bodies. Of the explicit bodily instructions recorded 65 percent were directed to boys, 26 percent to girls, and the remaining 9 percent were directed to mixed groups. These numbers suggest that boys' bodies are being disciplined more than girls. However, there is more to this story — the types of instructions that teachers give and children's responses to them are also gendered.   *40*

First, boys obeyed teachers' bodily instructions about one-half of the time (48 percent), while girls obeyed about 80 percent of the time. Boys may receive more instructions from teachers because they are less likely to follow instructions and thus are told repeatedly. Frequently I witnessed a teacher telling a boy or group of boys to stop doing something — usually running or throwing things — and the teacher repeated these instructions several times in the course of the session before (if ever) taking further action. Teachers usually did not have to repeat instructions to girls — girls either stopped on their own with the first instruction, or because the teacher forced them to stop right then. Serbin (1983) finds that boys receive a higher proportion of teachers' ". . . loud reprimands, audible to the entire group. Such patterns of response, intended as punishment, have been repeatedly demonstrated to reinforce aggression and other forms of disruptive behavior" (p. 29).   *41*

Second, teachers' instructions directed to boys' bodies were less substantive than those directed to girls. That is, teachers' instructions to boys were usually to stop doing something, to end a bodily behavior with little   *42* suggestion for other behaviors they might do. Teachers rarely told boys to change a bodily behavior. A list of teachers' instructions to boys includes: stop throwing, stop jumping, stop clapping, stop splashing, no pushing, don't cry, blocks are not for bopping, don't run, don't climb on that. Fifty-seven percent of the instructions that teachers gave boys about their physical behaviors were of this undirected type, compared with 15 percent of their instructions to girls. In other words, teachers' instructions to girls generally were more substantive and more directive, telling girls to do a bodily behavior rather than to stop one. Teachers' instructions to girls suggested that they alter their behaviors. A list of instructions to girls includes: talk to her, don't yell, sit here, pick that up, be careful, be gentle, give it to me, put it down there. Girls may have received fewer bodily instructions than did boys, but they received more directive ones. This gender difference leaves boys a larger range of possibilities of what they might choose to do with their bodies once they have stopped a behavior, whereas girls were directed toward a defined set of options.

Physical Interaction Between Teachers and Children

Teachers also physically directed kids. For example, teachers often held 43 kids to make them stop running, tapped them to make them turn around and pay attention, or turned their faces toward them so that they would listen to verbal instructions. One-fourth of all physical contacts between teachers and children was to control children's physicality in some way, and 94 percent of such contacts were directed at boys.

Physical interaction between teachers and children was coded into 44 three catagories: positive, negative, or neutral. Physical interaction was coded as positive if it was comforting, helpful, playful, or gentle. It was coded as negative if it was disciplining, assertive (not gentle), restraining, or clearly unwanted by the child (e.g., the child pulled away). Physical interaction was coded as neutral if it seemed to have little content (e.g., shoulders touching during circle, legs touching while a teacher gave a group of kids directions for a project). About one-half of the time, when teachers touched boys or girls, it was positive. For example, the teacher and child might have bodily contact as she tied a shoe, wiped away tears, or tickled a child, or if a child took the teacher's hand or got on her lap. For girls, the remaining physical interactions included 15 percent that were disciplining or instructing the body and about one-third that were neutral (e.g., leaning over the teacher's arm while looking at a book). For boys, these figures were reversed: Only 4 percent of their physical interactions with teachers were neutral in content, and 35 percent were negative and usually included explicit disciplining and instructing of the body.

This disciplining of boys' bodies took a particular form. Teachers usu- 45 ally attempted to restrain or remove boys who had "gone too far" in their play or who had done something that could harm another child:

> Irving goes up to Jack, who is playing dress-up, and puts his arms up, makes a monster face and says, "Aaarhhh!" Jack looks startled. Irving runs and jumps in front of Jack again and says "Aaaarrhh!" again. Marie (teacher) comes from behind Irving and holds him by the shoulders and arms from behind. She bends over him and says, "Calm down." He pulls forward, and eventually she lets him go. He runs up to Jack again and growls. Marie says, "He doesn't want you to do that." (Three-year-olds)

As Serbin (1983) suggests, frequent loud reprimands of boys may increase their disruptive behavior; more frequent physical disciplining interactions between teachers and boys may do so as well. Because boys more frequently than girls experienced interactions in which their bodies were physically restrained or disciplined by an adult who had more power and was angry, they may be more likely than girls to associate physical interaction with struggle and anger, and thus may be more likely to be aggressive or disruptive.

Physical Interaction Among Children

Thorne (1993) demonstrates that children participate in the construction of gender differences among themselves. The preschool brings together large groups of children who engage in interactions in which they cooperate with the hidden curriculum and discipline each others' bodies in gendered ways, but they also engage in interactions in which they resist this curriculum.

Girls and boys teach their same-sex peers about their bodies and physicality. Children in these observations were much more likely to imitate the physical behavior of a same-sex peer than a cross-sex peer. Children also encourage others to imitate them. Some gendered physicality develops in this way. For example, I observed one boy encouraging other boys to "take up more space" in the same way he was.

> James (one of the most active boys in the class) is walking all over the blocks that Joe, George, and Paul have built into a road. Then he starts spinning around with his arms stretched out on either side of him. He has a plastic toy cow in one hand [and] is yelling, "Moo." He spins through half of the classroom, other children ducking under his arms or walking around him when he comes near them. Suddenly he drops the cow and still spinning, starts shouting, "I'm a tomato! I'm a tomato!" The three boys who were playing blocks look at him and laugh. James says, "I'm a tomato!" again, and Joe says, "There's the tomato." Joe, George, and Paul continue working on their block road. James then picks up a block and lobs it in their direction and then keeps spinning throughout this half of the classroom saying he's a tomato. Joe and George look up when the block lands near them and then they get up and imitate James. Now three boys are spinning throughout much of the room, shouting that they are tomatoes. The other children in the class are trying to go about their play without getting hit by a tomato. (Five-year-olds)

The within-gender physicality of three-year-old girls and boys was *48* more similar than it was among the five-year-olds. Among the three-year-old girls there was more rough-and-tumble play, more physical fighting and arguing among girls than there was among the five-year-old girls.

> During clean up, Emily and Sara argue over putting away some rope. They both pull on the ends of the rope until the teacher comes over and separates them. Emily walks around the classroom then, not cleaning anything up. She sings to herself, does a twirl, and gets in line for snack. Sara is behind her in line. Emily pushes Sara. Sara yells, "Aaahh," and hits Emily and pushes her. The teacher takes both of them out of line and talks to them about getting along and being nice to each other. (Three-year-olds)
>
> Shelly and Ann have masks on. One is a kitty and one is a doggy. They're crawling around on the floor, and they begin play wrestling — kitties and doggies fight. The teacher says to them, "Are you ok?" They stop, lift up their masks, and look worried. The teacher says, "Oh, are you wrestling? It's ok, I just wanted to make sure everyone was ok." The girls nod; they're ok. Then, they put their masks back on and crawl on the floor some more. They do not resume wrestling. (Three-year-olds)

From lessons like these, girls have learned by age five that their play with each other should not be "too rough." The physical engagement of girls with each other at age five had little rough-and-tumble play:

> Two girls are playing with the dishes and siting at a table. Keisha touches Alice under the chin, tickles her almost, then makes her eat something pretend, then touches the corners of her mouth, telling her to smile. (Five-year-olds)

I do not mean to suggest that girls' physical engagement with each *49* other is the opposite of boys' or that all of boys' physical contacts were rough and tumble. Boys, especially in pairs, hugged, gently guided, or helped each other climb or jump. But often, especially in groups of three or more and especially among the five-year-olds, boys' physical engagement was highly active, "rough," and frequent. Boys experienced these contacts as great fun and not as hostile or negative in any way. . . .

The physical engagement of boys and girls *with each other* differed *50* from same-sex physical engagement. Because girls' and boys' play is semi-segregated, collisions (literal and figurative) in play happen at the borders of these gender-segregated groups (Maccoby 1988; Thorne 1993). As Thorne (1993) demonstrates, not all borderwork is negative — 40 percent of the physical interactions observed between girls and boys were positive or neutral.

> Ned runs over to Veronica, hipchecks her and says "Can I be your friend?" and she says "Yes." Ned walks away and kicks the blocks again three to four times. (Five-year-olds)

However, cross-gender interactions were more likely to be negative than same-sex interactions. In fact, physical interactions among children were twice as likely to be a negative interaction if they were between a girl and boy than if they were among same-gender peers. Approximately 30 percent of the interactions among girls and among boys were negative (hostile, angry, controlling, hurtful), whereas 60 percent of mixed-gender physical interactions were negative. Sixty percent of 113 boy-girl physical interactions were initiated by boys, 39 percent were initiated by girls, and only 1 percent of these interactions were mutually initiated.

At the borders of semi-segregated play there are physical interactions *51* about turf and toy ownership:

> Sylvia throws play money on the floor from her play pocketbook. Jon grabs it up. She wrestles him for it and pries it from his hands. In doing this she forces him onto the floor so that he's hunched forward on his knees. She gets behind him and sandwiches him on the floor as she grabs his hands and gets the money loose. Then, two minutes later, she's giving money to kids, and she gives Jon some, but apparently not enough. He gets right close to her face, inches away and loudly tells her that he wants more. He scrunches up his face, puts his arms straight down by his sides and makes fists. She steps back; he steps up close again to her face. She turns away. (Five-year-olds)

Negative interactions occur when there are "invasions" or interruptions of play among children of one gender by children of another:

> Courtney is sitting on the floor with the girls who are playing "kitties." The girls have on their dress-up clothes and dress-up shoes. Phil puts on big winter gloves and then jumps in the middle of the girls on the floor. He lands on their shoes. Courtney pushes him away and then pulls her legs and clothes and stuff closer to her. She takes up less space and is sitting in a tight ball on the floor. Phil yells, "No! Aaarrhh." Julie says, "It's not nice to yell." (Five-year-olds)

As Thorne (1993) suggests, kids create, shape, and police the borders of gender. I suggest that they do so physically. In this way, they not only sustain gender segregation, but also maintain a sense that girls and boys are physically different, that their bodies are capable of doing certain kinds of things. This sense of physical differences may make all gender differences feel and appear natural.

Conclusion

Children also sometimes resist their bodies being gendered. For example, *52* three-year-old boys dressed up in women's clothes sometimes. Five-year-old girls played with a relaxed comportment that is normatively (hegemonically) masculine when they sat with their feet up on the desk and their chairs tipped backward. In one classroom when boys were at the height of their loud activity — running and throwing toys and blocks — girls took the opportunity to be loud too as the teachers were paying less attention to them and trying to get the boys to settle down. In individual interactions as well, girls were likely to be loud and physically assertive if a boy was being unusually so:

> José is making a plastic toy horse fly around the room, and the boys playing with the blocks are quite loud and rambunctious. José flies the toy horse right in front of Jessica's face and then zooms around her and straight toward her again. Jessica holds up her hand and waves it at him yelling, "Aaaarrrh." José flies the horse in another direction. (Five-year-olds)

These instances of resistance suggest that gendered physicalities are not natural, nor are they easily and straightforwardly acquired. This research demonstrates the many ways that practices in institutions like preschools facilitate children's acquisition of gendered physicalities.

Men and women and girls and boys fill social space with their bodies 53 in different ways. Our everyday movements, postures, and gestures are gendered. These bodily differences enhance the seeming naturalness of sexual and reproductive differences that then construct inequality between men and women (Butler 1990). As MacKinnon (1987) notes, "Differences are inequality's post hoc excuse . . ." (p. 8). In other words, these differences create a context for social relations in which differences confirm inequalities of power.

This research suggests one way that bodies are gendered and physical 54 differences are constructed through social institutions and their practices. Because this gendering occurs at an early age, the seeming naturalness of such differences is further underscored. In preschool, bodies become gendered in ways that are so subtle and taken-for-granted that they come to feel and appear natural. Preschool, however, is presumably just the tip of the iceberg in the gendering of children's bodies. Families, formal schooling, and other institutions (like churches, hospitals, and workplaces) gender children's physicality as well.

Many feminist sociologists (West and Zimmerman 1987) and other 55 feminist scholars (Butler 1990, 1993) have examined how the seeming naturalness of gender differences underlies gender inequality. They have also theorized that there are no meaningful natural differences (Butler 1990, 1993). However, how gender differences come to feel and appear natural in the first place has been a missing piece of the puzzle.

Sociological theories of the body that describe the regulation, disci- 56 plining, and managing that social institutions do to bodies have neglected the gendered nature of these processes (Foucault 1979; Shilling 1993; Turner 1984). These data suggest that a significant part of disciplining the body consists of gendering it, even in subtle, micro, everyday ways that make gender appear natural. It is in this sense that the preschool as an institution genders children's bodies. Feminist theories about the body (Bordo 1993; Connell 1995; Young 1990), on the other hand, tend to focus on the adult gendered body and fail to consider how the body becomes gendered. This neglect may accentuate gender differences and make them seem natural. This research provides but one account of how bodies become gendered. Other accounts of how the bodies of children and adults are gendered (and raced, classed, and sexualized) are needed in various social contexts across the life course.

REFERENCES

Anyon, Jean. 1980. Social class and the hidden curriculum of work. *Journal of Education* 162:67–92.

Birdwhistell, Ray. 1970. *Kinesics and contexts.* Philadelphia: University of Pennsylvania Press.

Bordo, Susan. 1993. *Unbearable weight.* Berkeley: University of California Press.

Bowles, Samuel, and Herbert Gintis. 1976. *Schooling in capitalist America.* New York: Basic Books.

Butler, Judith. 1990. *Gender trouble.* New York: Routledge.

———. 1993. *Bodies that matter.* New York: Routledge.

Butterfield, Stephen, and E. Michael Loovis. 1993. Influence of age, sex, balance, and sport participation on development of throwing by children in grades K–8. *Perceptual and Motor Skills* 76:459–64.

Carere, Sharon. 1987. Lifeworld of restricted behavior. *Sociological Studies of Child Development* 2:105–38.

Carnoy, Martin, and Henry Levin. 1985. *Schooling and work in the democratic state.* Stanford: Stanford University Press.

Connell, R. W. 1987. *Gender and power.* Stanford: Stanford University Press.

———. 1995. *Masculinities.* Berkeley: University of California Press.

Foucault, Michel. 1979. *Discipline and punish: The birth of the prison.* New York: Vintage Books.

Giroux, Henry, and David Purpel. 1983. *The hidden curriculum and moral education.* Berkeley: McCutchan.

Goffman, Erving. 1959. *The presentation of self in everyday life.* Garden City, NY: Doubleday.

Goodwin, Marjorie Harness. 1990. *He-said-she-said: Talk as social organization among black children.* Bloomington: Indiana University Press.

Haug, Frigga. 1987. *Female sexualization: A collective work of memory.* London: Verso.

Henley, Nancy. 1977. *Body politics.* New York: Simon and Schuster.

Jackson, Philip W. 1968. *Life in classrooms.* New York: Holt, Rinehart, and Winston.

Jordan, Ellen, and Angela Cowan. 1995. Warrior narratives in the kindergarten classroom: Renegotiating the social contract. *Gender and Society* 9:727–43.

Maccoby, Eleanor. 1988. Gender as a social category. *Developmental Psychology* 24:755–65.

MacKinnon, Catharine. 1987. *Feminism unmodified.* Cambridge, MA: Harvard University Press.

Martin, Emily. 1987. *The woman in the body.* Boston: Beacon Press.

Martin, Karin. 1996. *Puberty, sexuality, and the self: Boys and girls at adolescence.* New York: Routledge.

McLaren, Peter. 1986. *Schooling as a ritual performance: Towards a political economy of educational symbols and gestures.* London: Routledge and Kegan Paul.

Plimpton, Carol E., and Celia Regimbal. 1992. Differences in motor proficiency according to gender and race. *Perceptual and Motor Skills* 74:399–402.

Sadker, Myra, and David Sadker. 1994. *Failing at fairness: How America's schools cheat girls.* New York: Charles Scribner and Sons.

Serbin, Lisa. 1983. The hidden curriculum: Academic consequences of teacher expectations. In *Sex differentiation and schooling,* edited by M. Marland. London: Heinemann Educational Books.

Shilling, Chris. 1993. *The body and social theory.* London: Sage.

Smoll, Frank, and Robert Schutz. 1990. Quantifying gender differences in physical performance: A developmental perspective. *Developmental Psychology* 26:360–69.

Suransky, Valerie Polakow. 1982. *The erosion of childhood.* Chicago: University of Chicago Press.

Thorne, Barrie. 1993. *Gender play: Girls and boys in school.* New Brunswick, NJ: Rutgers University Press.

Thomas, Jerry, and Karen French, 1985. Gender differences across age in motor performance: A meta-analysis. *Psychological Bulletin* 98:260–82.

Turner, Bryan S. 1984. *The body and society: Explorations in social theory.* New York: Basil Blackwell.

———. 1992. *Regulating bodies: Essays in medical sociology.* London: Routledge.

Van Ausdale, Debra, and Joe R. Feagin. 1996. Using racial and ethnic concepts: The critical case of very young children. *American Sociological Review* 61:779–93.

Wasburn, Philo C. 1986. The political role of the American school. *Theory and Research in Social Education* 14:51–65.

West, Candace, and Don Zimmerman. 1987. Doing gender. *Gender and Society* 1:127–51.

Young, Iris. 1990. *Throwing like a girl.* Bloomington: Indiana University Press.

■ ■ ■

Reading Rhetorically

1. Martin's essay contains original data gathered for this study. Locate places in the essay where she describes how and why she and her research assistant gathered data through observation. What advantages and limitations do you see in the method? What suggestions might you make for adjusting the method, and how do you think that would affect the outcome of the study?

2. Explain in your own words what Martin means by the "hidden school curriculum" (para. 7) she found in preschools. What evidence do you find most and least compelling in her support of this concept? Point to specific examples, and explain your thinking.

3. Martin includes both qualitative data (information and interactions recorded and described in language) and quantitative data (information and interactions recorded in numbers). Using two different-color pens, mark the qualitative data and the quantitative data. What different insights do you gain from each kind of data?

Inquiring Further

4. Educators take many different positions on the ways traditional classrooms favor boys or girls. Using your library's research tools, find at least three articles with different perspectives on this issue. (You might begin with general search terms like "American education and boys" and "American education and girls.") Discuss with your classmates the issues and perspectives that you discover in your research, and your thoughts on both.

5. Spend at least half an hour observing a group of children playing with adults nearby (perhaps at a playground or in a play area at a mall). Using Martin's strategies, pay close attention to the ways the children move (and how their clothes affect their movements), vocalize, and interact — and the ways the adults interact with them. How do your informal findings

compare with Martin's? How do you account for similarities or differences? Share your findings and ideas with the class.

6. Look through the references at the end of Martin's essay. Choose an article that looks interesting to you, and locate it through your library. Skim the article, noting both the main argument and the portion Martin draws on in this essay. What conclusions can you draw about why and how Martin uses this author's ideas to develop her own argument?

Framing Conversations

7. The hidden curriculum is a concept that could apply outside the classroom as well. Drawing on ideas in the essays by Henry Giroux on animated films (p. 567) or Henry Jenkins on video games (p. 700), write an essay in which you apply the concept of the hidden curriculum to children's popular culture. Be sure to explain both what you think the hidden curriculum is and how you see it being taught. What conclusions can you draw?

8. According to Martin, gender becomes *"embodied — becomes deeply part of who we are physically and psychologically"* (para. 4). How does this concept of gender connect to Judith Lorber's (p. 617) ideas about the process by which gender comes to seem natural to us? Write an essay in which you draw on the ideas of both Martin and Lorber to make an argument about what you think is most significant about the ways we learn gender and gender roles, and the short- and long-term implications of that learning process.

9. One focus of Martin's analysis of behaviors in preschools is the way children interact vocally with one another and their teachers. Deborah Tannen focuses on this interaction exclusively in "Talking Up Close" (below). Write an essay in which you use both Martin's and Tannen's ideas to analyze a verbal exchange in a film or television show. (You will need to quote these interactions accurately to analyze them in your essay.) How do these authors help you interpret the role and implications of gender behaviors in the vocal interaction you are writing about?

■ **DEBORAH TANNEN** ─────────────────────────────────

Talking Up Close: Status and Connection

Deborah Tannen, a professor of linguistics at Georgetown University, is well known by both scholars and general readers who are interested in the ways people communicate. As a linguistic researcher, Tannen is curious about the relationship between the speech patterns we develop as a result of our socialization and the ways we are heard and misheard in the classroom, the workplace, our homes, and our culture. Tannen's book *You Just Don't Understand: Women and Men in Conversation* (1990) was on the *New York Times* best-sellers' list for nearly four years, and was one of the books that popularized interest in gender and different communication styles.

(Another is John Gray's *Men Are from Mars, Women Are from Venus* [1993].) Her books have made best-sellers' lists in several other countries as well — an indication that her research topic has broad appeal to people everywhere who want to understand and improve communication dynamics in their lives. The subject has become increasingly important as effective communication has become essential to success in most aspects of our personal and professional lives. Tannen's analysis of the discussion styles that are rewarded in schools and politics, *The Argument Culture: Stopping America's War of Words* (1999), includes eye-opening examples from non-Western societies that demonstrate alternatives to the aggressive speech tactics sometimes expected in American classrooms, and the shouting matches that often develop between political commentators on news and opinion shows. Tannen also has written about communication styles within families in her award-winning books *I Only Say This Because I Love You: Talking to Your Parents, Partner, Sibs, and Kids When You're All Adults* (2001) and *You're Wearing That? Understanding Mothers and Daughters in Conversation* (2006). This selection is taken from a chapter in her book *Talking from 9 to 5: How Women's and Men's Conversational Styles Affect Who Gets Heard, Who Gets Credit, and What Gets Done at Work* (1994).

Because of her interest in the ways real people speak to one another, you will notice that Tannen includes many examples of conversations — some quite lengthy — in her writing. She opens the essay with several snapshots of verbal exchanges between women and men to lead up to the problem she poses: How do two people — in particular, two differently gendered people — come away from the same event with such different understandings of what happened? Before you read this piece, take a moment to consider a conversation you've had in which the gender of the other person seems to play a role in a misunderstanding. Then, as you read Tannen's piece, consider how her insights help explain that misunderstanding.

Tannen's writing style is influenced by journalism: Although her ideas are complex, she states them in short, punchy sentences. She also moves smoothly between very accessible conversational examples and the scholarly sources she uses to interpret those exchanges. Notice how she makes these shifts when she introduces the research of anthropologists, for example, in paragraph 10 or the sociolinguistic research in paragraph 20. Tannen is a scholar who is able to combine an approachable writing style with academic rigor. And for context she draws on the insights of both popular and academic writers. She is interested in bringing many voices into this conversation about conversation.

Critics sometimes complain that Tannen's examples are too selective, that she generalizes claims from too little evidence. But she also has many admirers among academics, book award committees, and the millions of readers who purchase her books. It's difficult to be neutral about Tannen's work because she forces us to question the ways we interact with others, and this feels very personal — as it should. This selection focuses on linguistic dynamics in the workplace, but you may find that her insights will make you think about conversations you have had in almost every part of your life.

A woman and a man were talking about the manager of a large division *1*
of their company. The woman was saying that this manager had connections in many of the company's departments, so she was successful at
fulfilling her agenda. "What you mean," the man offered, "is that she has
clout." "Not really," the woman clarified. "I mean she's built relationships
with people that she can call on when she needs to get around rules or
hurry things up." "That's what I said," the man retorted. "She's been there
long enough to develop clout." "No," the woman objected, becoming irritated. "I'm not talking about clout. I'm talking about relationships." "But
what it comes down to," the man retorted, equally irritated, "is clout. She
can make things happen."

In a sense, this is the kind of conversation I wrote about in *You Just* *2*
Don't Understand, where I showed that women and men often walk away
from the same conversation having seen different aspects of it. In this conversation, the man was focused on status — who's in the one-up position,
and who's one-down? (Having "clout" means being one-up, so you can get
others to do what you want.) The woman is focusing on connection: The
person they are talking about can get things done because she has "built
relationships," established connections to others. But there is a danger in
this formulation. It can be taken to imply that status and connection are
parallel and mutually exclusive. They aren't. They are two different dynamics of interaction — dynamics that dovetail and often entail each other.
The manager being discussed in this example did have clout, which
resulted in part from the relationships she had built up.

Competing for status can be a means of establishing connection, which *3*
is more or less what happens in sports and in boys' social groups. People can
also compete for connection, which is more or less what happens in popularity contests, and in girls' social groups, according to sociologists and
anthropologists who have studied them.[1] Rather than thinking of status and
connection as mutually exclusive opposites, to understand the dynamics of
talking at work we have to explore the ways they are intertwined.

A woman was at home when her husband arrived and announced that *4*
his arch rival had invited him to contribute a chapter to a book. The
woman remarked on how nice it was that the rival was initiating a rapprochement by including her husband in his book. He responded that she
had got it wrong: By taking the position of editor, the one in control, and

---

[1]Some researchers who have written about this are Donna Eder, Penelope Eckert
("Cooperative Competition in Adolescent 'Girl Talk' "), Daniel Maltz and Ruth Borker,
and Eleanor Maccoby. Sociologist Donna Eder, for example, in her article "Serious and
Playful Disputes: Variation in Conflict Talk Among Female Adolescents," shows that
some of the junior high school girls in her study who came from working- or lower-class
backgrounds engaged in a kind of ritual insulting that was competitive in the sense that
they tried to top each other's insults but was not a means to maintain or subvert status
hierarchies, as was the boys' characteristic use of ritual insults.

casting him as merely a contributor, the rival was actually trying to solidify his dominance, "get me under his thumb." He thought she was naive. She thought he was paranoid.

Whose interpretation was right? The answer is, both. But they were 5 focusing on different aspects of the relationship. She was asking herself how close or distant the two people would be as a result of the transaction and concluded it would bring them closer. He was asking who would be in control and concluded that he would be in a one-down position. I don't know what the editor of the collection had in mind; to determine that, I'd have to know how he would react if their roles were reversed. But regardless of what the editor thought, inviting someone to contribute to a book you are editing could be seen as either an exercise of power or an invitation to rapprochement. In that sense, it is ambiguous. Even more, it has elements of both; it "means" both at the same time. The linguistic term for meaning more than one thing at the same time is "polysemy" (pronounced pul-LIH-sih-mee), from *poly*, Greek for "many," and *semy*, Greek for "meaning").[2] Using this term, the invitation was "polysemous" (pul-LIH-sih-mus).

The same double meaning explains my surprise when a man born and 6 raised in Europe expressed his annoyance at what he called Americans' obsession with knowing everyone's roots, expressed in their continually asking others where they are from and where their parents were born. He said it is an attempt to get power over you by pinning you down. I was surprised because to me asking someone's background is a means of establishing connection, finding a point of reference from which to select topics of conversation and discover areas of shared experience. In fact, it can be either or both. (I suspect this practice is more common in the Northeast, where this man lives, than in the Midwest, South, and West, where such questions are less common and can even be considered rude.)

If you have a friend who repeatedly picks up the check when you dine 7 together, is she being generous and sharing her wealth, or is she trying to flaunt her money and remind you that she has more of it than you do? Although the intention may be kindness, her repeated generosity may make you feel bad by reminding you that she has more money. It also can establish a sense of obligation and therefore feel like control. Many people feel that if a man pays for a woman's meal or theater ticket, then the evening becomes a date, and she owes him something in exchange. (This quid pro quo was made explicit in a 1963 guide to behavior for young women which cautioned, "Remember . . . that the evening is costing him a sizable amount, and that it's up to you to see that he's enjoying every minute.")[3]

---

[2]Although she does not use this term, linguist Sally McConnell-Ginet makes a similar observation about intonation.

[3]Judith Unger Scott, *The Art of Being a Girl*. New York: Grosset & Dunlap, p. 177. Thanks to Shari Kendall for calling this to my attention.

Both of you are caught in the web of the ambiguity of status and connection. Even if you believe your friend's motive was purely generous, you may still feel denigrated by her generosity because the fact that she can act on this impulse is evidence that she has more money than you. Both interpretations exist at once: connection — she is paying to be nice — and status — her generosity reminds you that she is richer and makes you feel obligated. That is why offering to pick up the check is not just ambiguous but polysemous: It means both at once.

The double meaning of generosity explains an observation that initially surprised me: Greta Paules, an anthropologist who wrote a book about the culture of waitressing called *Dishing It Out,* found that waitresses in a restaurant chain were offended not only by tips that were too small, but also by tips that were too large. They felt that a customer leaving an unusually large tip was implying that the amount of money left was insignificant to the tipper but significant to the waitress. And this they found insulting. . . . 8

Dominance Hierarchies and Networks of Alliances

In order to grasp how inextricably intertwined are the dynamics of status on one hand and connection on the other, it is illuminating to consider primate behavior. The point is not to equate human and animal behavior, but rather that the behavior of primates provides insight into the dovetailing of dominance hierarchies and networks of alliances. 9

In a book entitled *How Monkeys See the World,* Dorothy Cheney and Robert Seyfarth show that both male and female monkeys have dominance hierarchies, and that negotiating their position in the hierarchy is a matter of forging and monitoring alliances. Females, for example, inherit their rank from their mothers, but in many monkey populations, high-ranking females have larger families, so one reason for treating a high-ranking female with respect is the fear that her family members will come to her aid if she is angered. High-ranking females also have more friends: They are better at forming alliances with monkeys outside their own families, which is easy for them to do since other females prefer to form alliances with those of high rank. The role of alliances in maintaining rank is dramatic: Although a female's rank rarely shifted, in the cases where it did, a high-ranking female had lost her allies to predators or disease. 10

Just as dominance is based in part on alliances, so alliances cannot be forged without competition. Grooming each other is the monkeys' primary means of establishing bonds, but competition arises for grooming partners, since monkeys prefer to share the pleasure of grooming with others of high rank. 11

Competition for alliances is a dynamic pervasive in girls' friendships, as the research of sociologist Donna Eder and of anthropologist Penelope 12

Eckert has shown. Eder, for example, presents a conversation in which sixth-grade girls are fighting about whether or not one of the friends was combing another girl's hair:

TAMI: Why were you combing Peggy's hair yesterday?
HEIDI: I didn't.
TAMI: Yes, you were!
HEIDI: I was not.
TAMI: You were feathering it back.
HEIDI: I was not.
TAMI: You were *too*.
HEIDI: I was *not*. You can go ask Peggy. [Peggy walks by.] Peggy, was I combing your hair yesterday? [Peggy shakes her head no.]
TAMI: Whose hair were you combing?
HEIDI: I wasn't combing anybody's hair.
TAMI: Who was combing Peggy's hair?
HEIDI: I don't know.[4]

The argument about hair combing was clearly a dispute about alliances: who is closer friends with whom.

The ability to maintain alliances helped Jay Leno gain the position he *13* wanted as successor to Johnny Carson on NBC's *Tonight* show, according to the book *The Late Shift* by Bill Carter. This is how a reviewer summarized Carter's analysis:

Mr. Leno played an inside game, building friendly relationships with NBC executives, local affiliates (whose support was crucial) and advertisers. He was the guy everyone liked, and he was always willing to help out with a free promotional spot, a few minutes of stand-up at an affiliates meeting, an interview with the local press. So when Mr. Carson announced his retirement, Mr. Leno stood, if you will, as the machine candidate. Along with his title as Mr. Carson's permanent guest host and his considerable skills as a stand-up comic, he had an influential booster club of television insiders.[5]

Even if you are not looking for a promotion, having social contacts *14* with many people means that when you need them, the channels of communication to them are open. If you see them at lunch, you can ask for information or present your view of a situation in an informal way. If you have had lunch with them in the past, and your relationship is friendly, you can call them directly (knowing they will take your call) and ask for what you need or what you want to know.

---

[4]The excerpt of girls arguing comes from Donna Eder, "Serious and Playful Disputes," pp. 70–71. See also Penelope Eckert, "Cooperative Competition in Adolescent 'Girl Talk.'"

[5]The review of *The Late Shift: Letterman, Leno and the Network Battle for the Night* by Bill Carter was written by Jay Rosen and appeared under the heading "How Letterman (and CBS) Won," *The New York Times*, February 22, 1994, p. C20.

I saw one woman, highly placed in her organization, who brimmed *15* with this form of friendliness. She regularly organized lunches at work and dinners at her home with many of the executives at and above her level, including the company president. When a problem arose involving their departments, it was easy for her to call them up and resolve it quickly, one-on-one. It seemed to me that this was simply an extension of her naturally sociable temperament, but it served her well on the job. A similar kind of camaraderie can be established through playing golf, a phenomenon well enough recognized in corporations that, according to an anecdote reported to me, a rising young star, identified for advancement, was sent for a weeklong stint at golf school in California at the company's expense.

In other words, hierarchies and alliances, status and connection, are *16* intertwined and inextricable. In trying to understand the dynamics of interaction, we must see these two forces as inseparable, each one implying the other.

Hierarchy Has Taken a Bad Rap

For Americans, "hierarchy" usually has negative connotations. But all *17* human relations are more or less hierarchical and also involve connection. The American sense that hierarchy is bad may result from our democratic ideology by which "all men are created equal." Yet most people would agree that a mother-child relationship is, at least potentially, a lovely thing. Would one therefore want to insist that it is not hierarchical? Does the mother's superior status and power over her child undercut their closeness? Realizing the hierarchical nature of the mother-child bond is particularly ironic, since much of what is written about women — especially if it is attempting to romanticize them — focuses on women's ability to bear children and attendant "nurturing" qualities. Yet nothing is more hierarchical than motherhood, and "nurturing" frames the nurturer as more capable, more competent — in a word, one-up. Imposing discipline is an inevitable part of nurturing, though American culture has tended to separate them, associating discipline with the father and nurturing with the mother, regardless of who actually does either or both in particular families.

In a classic work on Japanese psychology, Takeo Doi points out that *18* the Japanese regard the mother-child relationship as the prototype for all others, including the one between superiors and subordinates in the workplace, so the notion of hierarchy has a positive connotation for them. According to linguists Ron and Suzanne Wong Scollon, the same is true for Chinese. The Japanese, like the Chinese and members of many other cultures of the world, are most comfortable in hierarchically ordered groups or relationships. What is uncomfortable is not knowing your place in the hierarchy, and hence not knowing how to speak or how to behave. A person who is oblivious to hierarchy would be regarded not as morally superior but as a social misfit. In this schema, knowing one's place in a hierarchical network is a prerequisite for being human — with equal emphasis on "network" and "hierarchy."

Americans tend to assume that hierarchy precludes closeness, so 19 employers and employees cannot "really" be friends, and if they do become friends, complications arise that must be worked out. I myself was inclined to assume that hierarchy is distancing, so that taking a one-up position is synonymous with pushing someone away. But the Japanese perspective made me rethink that assumption.

Sociolinguist Suwako Watanabe compared how American and Japanese 20 students spoke in group discussions with others of the same background. She concluded that the Americans in her study saw themselves as individuals participating in a joint activity, whereas the Japanese students saw themselves as members of a group united by hierarchy. When I first read Watanabe's words, I was caught up short: How could hierarchy unite? But her study, and a little thought, made clear that feeling you are in your rightful place in a hierarchy can feel as safe and close as being in your family — a quintessentially hierarchical institution.

Part of the reason Americans feel hierarchy is negative is that we tend 21 to think of its benefits as flowing one way only: The person in the superior position has the right to tell a subordinate what to do, and the person in the subordinate position has to obey. In this spirit, if someone says he is being treated like a child, he is sure to be heard as registering a complaint, synonymous with saying he is being humiliated. In fact, Murray Bookchin argues, in a book entitled *Remaking Society,* that hierarchy is the source of society's ills.

But in the minds of Japanese, Chinese, Javanese, and members of 22 many other world cultures, there are obligations as well as privileges that go along with both the superior and the subordinate roles. After all, parents have to do a great deal for their children, just as surely as they have power over them. And it is awareness of the privileges associated with the child's role that gives the term "dependence" a positive rather than negative connotation in these cultures. The English title of Takeo Doi's book, *The Anatomy of Dependence,* about what he regards as the key theme in Japanese character, *amae,* sounds to American ears slightly embarrassing if not downright insulting. The positive connotations of the word "dependence" in Asian culture, however, come through in the following statement that Ron Scollon tells me one of his Chinese students in Hong Kong wrote in a paper: "Parents generally give more freedom to their daughters than to sons to have dependent behaviors, for example, touching, crying, and seeking help."

In our assumption that equality is good and hierarchy is bad, Americans 23 tend to regard the sibling relationship as the ultimate in reciprocity. Such statements as "We're like sisters" or "He's like a brother to me" are usually understood as references to closeness, not hierarchy. It is as if to say, "We're so close, there are no power games between us." And yet anyone who has had a flesh-and-blood sibling knows that age differences resulting from birth order are the ultimate in hierarchy: Older siblings can both protect and torment younger ones, who, in return, idolize or resent them or both. And none of this means that they cannot be close.

Anthropology provides many examples of cultural contexts in which   24
hierarchical relationships are seen as close and mutually, not unilaterally, empowering. For example, anthropologist William Beeman shows that Iranians often struggle to "get the lower hand." Taking the lower-status position evokes a cultural schema by which the higher-status person is obligated to offer protection, so "getting the lower hand" is a way of getting someone to do things for you — exactly our notion of power. It's a game of one-downmanship. Anthropologist Judith Irvine describes a similar process among the Wolof of Africa as "self-lowering." A Wolof noble may try to grab the lower position to forestall requests for gifts.

Yet another such culture is described by anthropologist Clare Wol-   25
fowitz: the Javanese community in Suriname. Wolfowitz explains that a style of speech called "respect/deference" is experienced not as subservience but as an assertion of claims. It is typified by the grandchild-grandparent relationship, one that is both very unequal and very close. (Equality, in contrast, is associated with relatively distant relationships that are formed in the public sphere rather than in the family.)

It's All in the Family

The relationships that form a backdrop to office relations are illumi-   26
nated by this sampling of cultural perspectives. Although Americans do not tend to think of office relations in terms of the mother-child relationship as explicitly as do the Japanese, nonetheless family relations are probably the model through which we understand all others. If you remind co-workers of members of their family, it can have either a positive or a negative impact. Indeed, the implications of reminding people of members of their family can be complex, as complex as family relationships themselves.

I could see the positive effects of associations with family members   27
when I asked a man who was very highly placed in his organization why he was particularly interested in making sure that women got a fair shake in his organization. He said it was because he had two daughters. "When I saw them coming up at their jobs," he said, "I realized they weren't playing on a level playing field."

Individuals may benefit from reminding others of family members,   28
and such reminders need not follow gender lines. A physician experienced first negative and then positive effects of reminding a supervisor of his

son. She recalled her experience as the only woman in her internship program:

> I remember walking down the hall with a very, very, very powerful patriarchal domineering physician who told his patients what and where to do. And I had been on his service, as they call it, for about three weeks, and he was a bombastic kind of an individual, and we were walking down the hall, and suddenly he turned to me, and his — he was infuriated. He was angry. And he looked at me and he said, "What I wanna know is why my son can't be like you."

Eventually, this professor became her ardent supporter. As she put it, "He thought I was the world."

This woman also described how at first she was physically tested, put   *29* through more physical trials than her male counterparts. She was, she recalled,

> challenged — could I stand up longer than anybody else in the surgical assist? Could I be on o.b. call just a little bit longer than anybody else? . . . I would go down to look at my scrub, in surgery, and I would start at 8:00, and I would get the long cases. So that very frequently I wouldn't get the lunch break. And it was — it was subtle. I mean, nobody really — but sometimes guys would look at it and say, "Gosh, you know you're really getting the longest cases."

I asked her if this had been a sort of hazing ritual, and she answered:

> I think that it started out as a hazing, but then what happened was you know you can turn a weakness into a strength. What happened was, I did so well that then some of the men — older men became very paternalistic. And then they wanted to give me the good cases. . . . Nobody had — I mean it wasn't written on paper, but there was a point at which you passed and from then on, it was no question that I became a favorite child.

According to this physician's account, her being female drew attention to herself in first a negative but then a positive way. The word "paternalistic" suggests the fatherlike aspect of a superior watching out for a subordinate. Indeed, the superior who compared her with his son came to think she was "the world" just as a favorite child is "the world" to a doting parent. The phrase "bringing up" a younger colleague, commonly used in business, also suggests parenting.

If younger colleagues can remind older ones of their children, older   *30* colleagues, especially bosses, can remind younger ones of their parents. I heard references to this in a positive spirit — the senior being seen as protective and helpful — as well as a negative one, by which the senior may be seen as, in the words of one manager, "arbitrary and unreinforcing, like my father." Gender, again, is not necessarily a determining factor here. A graduate student who got into a conflict with a woman supervising professor said that the professor "reminded her of her father, a high-school football coach who wanted [her] to excel at sports but couldn't show any pleasure when she did."[6]

A parentlike stance can be projected in many ways, including choice *31* of metaphors. An executive was recruiting a high-level manager for a directorship. After explaining that the new position would entail far more responsibility for the candidate than his current one, he assured him, "Don't worry; I'll put limits around you so you can't hurt yourself." The metaphor he chose suggested a parent baby-proofing a house or setting the baby up in a playpen. . . .

Who Calls the Chats?

In the course of a workday, talk shifts continually between work and social *32* topics, and these shifts too can reflect and negotiate status relations. Charlotte Linde noticed in her study of police helicopter crews that when the immediate demands of work subside, the crew may engage in social chat, which will stop if work requirements intrude. And she found that the switch from work talk to social talk was more often initiated by the pilot, who functioned as a superior in command. For example, if it was quiet, the pilot might begin free conversation by noticing the view ("This reservoir or lake or whatever looks pretty"), returning to a previous topic ("So you gonna, uh, look for another car or try to get that one fixed?"), or commenting on the mission just completed ("That guy was kinda calm and cool for havin' just ripped down somebody").[7]

This is exactly the pattern that sociolinguist Janice Hornyak noticed in *33* a study of talk in an all-female office at an accounting firm.[8] As the women in the office shifted between work and personal talk, the shift was always initiated by the highest-ranking person in the room, the office manager. If she was busy, nobody else began telling personal stories or chatting. But if the office manager was ready to take a break and chat, the others followed suit. No one worried about whether the office temp had work to do or not, or whether her work required concentration that would be interrupted by social banter.

In this way, hierarchies are reflected, reinforced, and created through- *34* out a workday, in even the most automatic and casual conversation.

---

[6]The example of a graduate student whose supervising professor reminded her of her football-coach father comes from an article entitled "A Most Dangerous Method," by Margaret Talbot, *Lingua Franca*, January/February 1994, p. 33.

[7]Linde's examples of the pilot beginning free conversation, and her comments on them, appear in her articles "Who's in Charge Here?" and "Linguistic Consequences of Complex Social Structures: Rank and Task in Police Helicopter Discourse."

[8]I have taken Janice Hornyak's observations from her dissertation proposal.

"What Are You Going to Do About It?"

Talk intended to create connection always runs the risk of offending co- 35
workers who have different styles, but the risks are even greater in hierarchical relationships. Complaining about situations at work may be
perceived as creating connections — "We're in this together" — among
people at the same rank, but it can be taken as a literal complaint — and
therefore either a request for action or an implicit criticism — when
addressed to a boss.

A fire chief who listened to a lecture I gave was interested in my point 36
that some people engage in complaining to create rapport. He recalled
a woman who worked for him who was aghast when he acted on a
complaint she had made. "I was just sounding off," she said. "I didn't want
you to *do* anything." But the more he thought about it, the more convinced he was that he had no choice but to act when a subordinate told
him about a problem. After all, he said, that is his job; he could be
faulted for negligence if he didn't take action to solve a problem reported
to him.

Applied linguist Lena Gavruseva analyzed a conversation in which 37
this double meaning of complaining was key. The conversation took place
between John, the editor of a small local newspaper, and Dan, a young
writer who had recently been hired. In the middle of a friendly chat, John
mentioned that another writer at the paper had just gotten a new computer and added, "You just have that little shitburner of an XT." He then
asked, "How is your computer?" Taking his cue from John, Dan matched
his boss's tone and replied, "It sucks." But John took this as a literal complaint and began a line of insistent questioning about what was wrong
with the computer. The conversation went like this:

> JOHN: How is your computer?
> DAN: It sucks. I mean —
> JOHN: Why?
> DAN: I — 'Cause it doesn't —
> JOHN: Why, it's slow?
> DAN: No, it's not that. It's just like there are all sorts of keys that don't work and
> stuff.
> JOHN: What do you mean keys that don't work?
> DAN: Like the caps lock doesn't work.
> JOHN: It can — You want it to?
> DAN: No, it doesn't.
> JOHN: You want it to?
> DAN: Okay.
> JOHN: All right. What else would you like?
> DAN: um, I don't know. It was just sort of —
> JOHN: No no no, come on.
> DAN: Like I can't turn it off because —

JOHN: You would like — you'd like to be able to turn it off? Why? 'Cause it both-
     ers you?

DAN: And it's — it's frozen up on me like three times.

JOHN: Yeah?

DAN: Yeah.

JOHN: Like is there a pattern?

DAN: No, I mean maybe there is, I haven't noticed it. I — I don't know. It hasn't
     done it for about a week or so, so don't worry. I'm just griping. I've never —
     I've got no particular complaints because it — all I need to — I'm not — I'm
     not one of these, I'm not a computer junkie, so I don't really care.

JOHN: So if you want your caps-lock key to work, there's no problem. I can come
     in and do that.

DAN: No, I don't really need a caps lock.

JOHN: It'll take me twenty-five seconds.

Dan had interpreted John's profanity (his reference to Dan's "shitburner of
an XT") as an invitation to engage in friendly complaining, a ritual of camaraderie. But John took it literally as a complaint, and perhaps even a criticism of him as boss for providing inadequate equipment. It is also possible
that John's response was an automatic impulse to put Dan back in his
place, because his use of profanity ("It sucks") in describing his computer's
failings might have struck John as impudent. In the companies where I
observed, the general pattern was that the higher a man's rank, the more
likely he would curse.

Humor to the Rescue

Gavruseva, who interviewed both speakers, shows that Dan was getting   *38*
increasingly uncomfortable with the line of questioning, but something
snapped when John said he could fix the caps lock on Dan's computer
in twenty-five seconds. At that point in the conversation, which had been
proceeding very quickly, with many of the turns coming fast on the heels
(or stepping on the toes) of the one before, there was a two-and-a-half second pause — a very long silence in a fast-paced conversation. Then Dan
said:

DAN: I'd like to s — Okay, I challenge you to do it. I think it's broken.

Dan then repeated the challenge, making it more formal and therefore less
serious:

DAN: I challenge you, John Ryan.

Dan was using the cover of humor to talk back to his boss, redressing the
power imbalance that had been taking shape.

John joined in on the joke, responding in the exaggerated, mock-tough ³⁹
voice of a radio-play gangster:

> JOHN: Yes, the John Ryan challenge? [2-second pause] You are a fool if you think
> you can challenge *me*, Mr. Computer!

John agreed to make fun of his own self-assurance with regard to fixing
the computer. Humor was used to smooth over the mounting tension and
restore the balance of power that had been threatened when Dan had
begun to feel that he was being "shown up" and put "on the spot" (as he
expressed it to Gavruseva).

Joining in Small Talk

What happened next is interesting.⁹ After another two-and-a-half-second ⁴⁰
pause, Dan turned the conversation to another topic. Knowing that John
had recently been sick, Dan inquired about his health:

> DAN: How are you feeling today, John?
> JOHN: What's that?
> DAN: How are you feeling? Are you still —
> JOHN: um, Actually my guts started grinding, and I thought, "Hey, it's back," but
> I had like a heavy night last night. I mean I went to bed at six and only came
> out to like piss and drink water, and eat a can of tuna fish. I mean it was bad.
> I get a gastrointestinal thing at both ends. It was — it was spewing. It was
> violent.
> DAN: [laughing] Not simultaneously. Please tell me no.
> JOHN: No no no, but it was intense. And it made me so glad that there was no
> girlfriend around, nobody could take care of me. There's only one fucking
> thing I hate, it's being sick and somebody wants to take care of me.

Asking John how he felt served not only to change the topic but to focus on
an area in which John was not heroic and full of mastery but rather vulnerable. By giving so many details about his intestinal ailments, John
agreed to the realignment. When he added how glad he was that there was
no girlfriend around trying to take care of him, and did so using language
few men would use in front of women, he realigned himself with Dan, setting them apart from hypothetical women. Although editor and newly
hired young writer were not the same rank, they were both men and could
bond on that basis.¹⁰

---

⁹Gavruseva's analysis did not extend to this part of the exchange. The following is
my interpretation of the conversation she taped and transcribed.

¹⁰Gavruseva pointed out to me, though, that John is still presenting himself as
someone who does not need help, which still positions him as one-up.

This example shows how small talk can be used to restore a balance of *41* power, but it also strikes me as a conversation that would be unlikely to take place between two women. That does not mean, however, that women's small talk might not also serve the purpose of restoring balance. The following example shows how a very different kind of small talk was used by women to mask (and reinforce) power differences and to include an intruder in a conversation.

The conversation took place in the office where Janice Hornyak was *42* working as a temp while recording talk as part of her research. The three women in the office were taking a break from work, listening to one of them telling a personal story, when a fourth woman, June, arrived with the day's mail. A clerical worker in her early twenties, June did not have high status in this organization. Tina, who had been telling the story, stopped midstream, but found another way to make June feel welcome. Calling out in high-pitched voices, drawn-out vowels, and singsong intonation, she and Heather complimented June on her clothes:

> JUNE: Hii.
> TINA: Hey! Ah, we gotta see this getup. Come on in.
> HEATHER: C'mere, June!
> TINA: She — she — she's — uh, that's cute.
> HEATHER: Love that beautiful blouse!
> JANICE: Hey, high fashion today.
> TINA: Cool.
> JUNE: Hi. I had the blouse /?/ and didn't know what to wear it with. And I just took the tag off and /?/ said /?/ I'm gonna wear it with a vest.
> TINA: And that hair too.
> JANICE: Oh, that's neat.
> HEATHER: Is that your Mom's?
> [Tina laughs.]
> JUNE: No I got this from uh /?/
> TINA: What is it?
> JUNE: /It's from/ Stylo.
> TINA: I've heard of it.
> JUNE: The one in Trader Plaza that has all that wild stuff.
> HEATHER: What'd you do to your hair?
> JUNE: Added /?/. Judith said, "You just are bored, you have to do something."
> [All laugh.]

Just as John extended a friendly hand to Dan by including him in "boy talk" replete with graphic details about being sick and grumbling about how irritating women's ministrations can be to a man in that state, Heather, Tina, and Janice extended a friendly hand to June by including her in "girl talk" about clothing and hairstyle. These two different types of small talk are fairly similar in overall function — establishing rapport — yet are quite different in tone. They are also fairly typical of other instances of small talk among men as compared to women in the range of companies where I observed.

These small-talk episodes are an essential element in keeping the interactional wheels turning at work. But speakers' relative rank never stops influencing how they all talk, even when it is not in focus. Tina was the head of the office and, in fact, the owner's daughter. So it is not coincidental that she was the one who initiated the talk about June's clothes, and she and Heather, the next in rank, who used the most exaggerated, singsong intonation in admiring them. It seems unlikely that June herself, when walking into the office to deliver mail, would have called out to Tina or Heather and initiated an extended interchange about their clothes and hair, and it does not seem surprising that throughout the interchange, both June (the mail clerk) and Janice (the office temp) spoke in relatively low-key tones. *43*

It Looks Different from Up (or Down) Here

Let's return to the conversation about the computer with a broken caps-lock key. Lena Gavruseva's analysis allows us to see how Dan and John's different positions in the hierarchy altered their perceptions of the conversation. Gavruseva asked Dan why he continued to complain about his computer if he didn't really care whether or not it was fixed. He said he had to play along so as not to "rebuff" his boss. This miscommunication led to another. John interpreted Dan's way of talking as evidence of his personality rather than his reaction to John. He felt that Dan really wanted the computer fixed but was too wishy-washy to make a demand in a more assertive way. *44*

Like many people in the superior position, John was unaware of the impact of his own status and power on a subordinate. This can be equally true for those with relatively authoritarian styles and those who foster an atmosphere of equality. There is little that people in power can do to assure subordinates to ignore their power, since their gatekeeping role cannot be revoked. A person in a superior position who extends the olive branch of equality is in a position to yank it back. *45*

I saw this happen some years ago, following a lecture I had delivered. I was taken to dinner by several managers at the nonprofit organization that had invited me to speak, together with the organization's president, who was hosting the dinner. When we were seated at the restaurant, the president made a grand gesture and invited everyone to order drinks before dinner, saying, "Let's live it up; I'll take care of it." But when one of the managers began perusing the wine list to order wine with dinner, the president rebuked him: "Hey, c'mon, don't try to take advantage — the budget isn't that big!" The manager was left feeling foolish and out of line, *46* reminded that he did not hold the purse strings, even though he would not have thought to suggest wine had it not been for the president's suggestion that they order drinks.

Anything that is done in an organization in which some people have 47 power over others can be affected by that hierarchy. It might make sense to express concerns to a superior who can offer help and encouragement, but any expression of insecurity can become the basis for holding you back, not giving you a particular assignment at a later date. In fact, the repercussions of a chance remark can get magnified into an ineradicable stain, as someone I will call Anthony discovered.

Anthony had been assigned to a task together with Justin, whose 48 working style was so different from his own that it was driving him crazy. Anthony was the kind of person who liked to be prepared well in advance, but Justin was a last-minute type who never had his part ready until the night before the deadline. Not wanting to bad-mouth Justin, Anthony asked not to be assigned to work with Justin again by saying he preferred to work alone. Though he was accommodated in this, he got a reputation for being a loner, not a team player, and found himself passed over not only for team assignments but also for promotion. The gesture of connection — trying to put a positive face on his request not to work with a particular co-worker — was passed through a status filter by which he was negatively evaluated when promotion decisions were made.

Much of the power associated with higher rank resides in the gate- 49 keeping aspect of the superior's role. In addition to helping or teaching, a boss has the right — and often the obligation — to determine the future of subordinates' careers. This intertwining of status and connection is nowhere more apparent than in teaching, which requires both helping and gatekeeping. Teachers help students learn, but at the end of the term they assign grades, and in some situations decide or help decide who can advance to the next level or remain in the school. Students may later be dependent on teachers for letters of recommendation even after they've left the program. So whenever students ask teachers questions, in addition to getting information, they are giving impressions of their ability. If a student asks for help, the teacher may comply but also conclude that the student doesn't know as much as other students who do not seem to need help.

The same double vision can blur the role of "coach" in a business 50 environment, where a higher-ranked employee is assigned to guide a newer one. Insofar as the coach has the ear of those who make decisions about promotion, or has a voice in those decisions, the helping aspect of the coaching role is complicated by gatekeeping overtones. Having the power to pass judgment on someone's work and convey that judgment upward can become a filter through which all "helping" utterances are passed, so that suggestions for improvement can be heard as criticism. Moreover, taking the role of teacher in itself positions the coach as one-up.

"Don't Talk While I'm Interrupting"

Status and connection are inextricably intertwined in some linguistic *51* strategies that most people feel they instinctively understand, including interruption.

It's almost a truism that interrupting others is a way of dominating *52* them. It is rare to find an article on gender and language that does not make this claim. Tellingly, however, linguists Deborah James and Sandra Clarke reviewed all the research they could find on gender and interruption and did not find a clear pattern of males interrupting females. Especially surprising was their conclusion that the studies that investigated how much interruption took place in all-female as compared to all-male conversations actually found more interruption, not less, in all-female groups. James and Clarke note that in order to understand this pattern, it is necessary to ask what the speakers are *doing* when they talk over other speakers. Does the interruption show support for the other speaker, or does it contradict or change the topic? Overlapping talk can be a way of exerting status or establishing connection. (I prefer to use the term "overlap" to avoid the interpretation — and accusation — implicit in the term "interruption.")

Some speakers consider talking along with another to be a show *53* of enthusiastic participation in the conversation, creating connections; others assume that only one voice should be heard at a time, so for them any overlap is an interruption, an attempt to wrest the floor, a power play. The result of this difference is that enthusiastic listeners who talk along to establish rapport can be perceived by others as interrupting — and are furthermore blamed for bad intentions: trying to "dominate" the conversation.

The key to whether an overlap (something neutral) becomes an inter- *54* ruption (something negative) depends on whether or not there is symmetry, or balance. If one speaker repeatedly overlaps and another repeatedly gives way, the resulting communication is unbalanced, and the effect (though not necessarily the intent) is domination. But if both speakers avoid overlap, or if both speakers overlap each other and win out equally, there is symmetry and no domination, regardless of speakers' intentions. The very engagement in a symmetrical struggle for the floor can be experienced as creating rapport, in the spirit of ritual opposition analogous to sports. Further, an imbalance can result from differences in the purpose for which overlap is used. If one speaker chimes in to show support, and the other cuts in to take the floor, the floor-taking overlapper will tend to dominate by determining the topics and expressing more ideas and opinions.

To know whether an overlap is an interruption, you must consider the *55* context (for example, cooperative overlapping is more likely to occur in casual conversation among friends than in a job interview), speakers' habitual styles (overlaps are more likely not to be interruptions among those with a style I call "high-involvement"), and the interaction of their styles (an interruption is more likely to result between speakers whose styles differ with regard to pausing and overlap). This is not to say that one cannot use interruption to dominate a conversation or a person, but only that overlap is not always intended as an interruption and an attempt to dominate.

"Cat Got Your Tongue?"

Silence has been seen as evidence of powerlessness, and doing most of the 56
talking can seem synonymous with dominating. Researchers have counted numbers of words spoken, or timed how long people have talked, to demonstrate that men talk more than women and thereby dominate interactions.[11] Undoubtedly, there is truth to this observation in some settings. But the association of volubility with dominance does not hold for all people, all settings, and all cultures. Silence can also be the privilege of a higher-ranking person, and even an instrument of power. Imagine, for example, an interrogation in which the interrogator does little of the talking but holds much of the power.

The potential double meaning of talking a lot or a little or even 57
remaining silent is highlighted in Margaret Mead's analysis of "end linkage," a concept developed jointly by Mead, Gregory Bateson, and Geoffrey Gorer. Universal and biologically constructed relationships, such as parent-child, are linked to different behaviors in different cultures. One of the paradigm examples is the apportionment of spectatorship and exhibitionism — that is, the question of who performs and who watches silently. In middle-class American culture, children, who are obviously the weaker party in the constellation, are expected to exhibit while their more powerful parents are spectators. Consider, for example, American children who are encouraged (or forced) to demonstrate for guests how well they can recite the alphabet or play the piano. In contrast, in middle- and upper-class British culture, exhibition is associated with the parental role and spectatorship with children, who are expected to be seen and not heard.

Amusingly, according to Cheney and Seyfarth, the assumption that 58
higher-ranking individuals vocalize more holds for at least some monkeys in some settings:

[11]See Deborah James and Janice Drakich for a summary of research comparing women and men with regard to who talks more. ["Understanding Gender Differences in Amount of Talk," in *Gender and Conversational Interaction*, edited by Deborah Tannen. New York and Oxford: Oxford University Press. 281–312.]

In Amboseli, high-ranking female vervets are usually (but by no means always) more active and aggressive participants in intergroup encounters than low-ranking females, and they also give more *wrr* calls.[12]

For people in a work setting, it is often the case that the higher-ranking 59 people talk more, but not always. At a meeting, the high-ranking person may dominate discussion, or may sit silently, taking it all in and keeping the others guessing about the impression they are making. In one company, I observed a man who influenced the direction a meeting took even though he spoke little. The fact that he was British may well have played a role in how little he spoke. It was sometimes hard for him to find a way into American conversations, which were faster-paced than those he was used to.[13] Indeed, one day when I was shadowing him, he conducted a telephone conversation with a compatriot back in England on the speaker phone, so I could listen in. The slow pace and long pauses that characterized their conversation surprised me. I frequently thought that pauses I heard were pre-closings, indicating that the conversation was winding down, but it kept on going. When the call ended, I asked his impression of the interchange, and he said it had been very comfortable, just the right pace for a pleasant conversation. Hearing those nice long pauses, I could easily see why he would have a hard time getting the floor in American conversations that leave no gap for him to step into.

This example shows that the amount people talk can result from style 60 differences rather than their individual intentions. Pacing and pausing is an element of conversation that differs greatly depending on regional, cultural, and subcultural background. When you talk to others who leave longer pauses than you expect, you become uncomfortable and start speaking to fill in the pauses, with the result that you do all the talking — and blame them for not doing their part. When you talk to others who leave shorter pauses than you expect, then they start speaking to fill what they perceive as comfortable silence, and you end up not getting a word in edgewise — and blame them for hogging the floor.

Yet another apparent sign of power is the question of who raises the 61 topics that get discussed. This too can result from style differences, since whoever speaks first tends to set the topic. A speaker who thinks the other

---

[12]The quotation comes from Cheney and Seyfarth, p. 66. The authors define a *wrr* call as "a loud, relatively long, trilling call given by females and juveniles when they spot another group" (p. 65).

[13]Yet I should note that at least one British colleague told me he finds American speech slow but inexorable. It turned out that he had in mind some particular Midwesterners whom he knew. Because of the range of styles in both the United States and the United Kingdom, I want to stress that I am not suggesting that all Britons speak more slowly than all Americans, but only that this individual Briton had a sense of conversational rhythm that differed from his American co-workers', and this made it hard for him to find the right moment to enter a conversation.

has no more to say on a given topic may try to keep the conversation afloat by raising another topic. But a speaker who was intending to say more and had simply paused for breath will feel that the floor was taken away and the topic aggressively switched. This could also occur if one speaker is overlapping cooperatively, as explained in the previous section, but is perceived to be interrupting. In other words, any style difference that results in an interruption can also result in two speakers polarizing into a voluble one and a taciturn one, and in the apparent interrupter controlling choice of topics. Yet again, the impression of dominance might result from style differences.[14] . . .

"Is It You or Me?"

Again and again, when I have explained two different ways of saying or doing the same thing, I am asked, "Which way is best?" or "Which way is right?" We are all in pursuit of the right way of speaking, like the holy grail. But there is no one right way, any more than there is a holy grail — at least not one we can hope to find. Most important, and most frustrating, the "true" intention or motive of any utterance cannot be determined merely by considering the linguistic strategy used.   *62*

Intentions and effects are not identical. When people have differing conversational styles, the effect of what they say may be very different from their intention. And anything that happens between two people is the result of both their actions. Sociolinguists talk about this by saying that all interaction is "a joint production." The double meaning of status and connection makes every utterance potentially ambiguous and even polysemous (meaning many things at once).   *63*

When we think we have made ourselves clear, or think we understand what someone else has said, we feel safe in the conviction that we know what words mean. When someone insists those words meant something else, we can feel like Alice trying to talk to Humpty-Dumpty, who isn't fazed by her protest that "glory doesn't mean a nice knock-down argument" but claims with aplomb, "When I use a word it means what I want it to mean, neither more nor less." If others get to make up their own rules for what words mean, the earth starts slipping beneath our feet. One of the sources of that slippage is the ambiguity and polysemy of status and connection — the fact that the same linguistic means can reflect and create one or the other or both. Understanding this makes it easier to   *64*

---

[14]In their book *Narrative, Literacy, and Face in Interethnic Communication*, Ron and Suzanne Scollon show how these dynamics operate between Athabaskan Indians and Anglos in Alaska. The Scollons and I have discussed them so much that I surely owe to them some of my understanding of these phenomena.

understand the logic behind others' apparently willful misinterpretations and makes the earth feel a little more firm beneath our feet.

■ ■ ■

Reading Rhetorically

1. What important ideas does Tannen capture in the terms *status* and *connection*? Explain the terms in your own words, and discuss how Tannen develops the significance of the terms in each section of her essay.

2. Tannen includes and analyzes fairly long conversations in her text to help make her point. Choose two examples and analyses of conversations, and evaluate their effectiveness in helping Tannen make her argument. What makes each example more or less successful as evidence? What suggestions can you make for improving the effectiveness of this kind of evidence?

3. Look closely at Tannen's final section, "Is It You or Me?" (p. 674). How and why does she refer to the conversation between Alice and Humpty Dumpty here? What key ideas does she reinforce in this conclusion?

Inquiring Further

4. Study the patterns of conversation in your classes. Over the course of a week, keep track of the gender of those who speak in your classes as well as how they speak. Use Tannen's strategy of noticing small talk, silences, interruptions, and other linguistic habits. Does Tannen's essay help you interpret the significance of the patterns you find? Do your observations point to any shortcomings in Tannen's argument? Explain your answers.

5. Reread Tannen's essay, placing a box around the names of those Tannen quotes or draws ideas from. What kinds of experts does she seem to rely on? What significance do you see in her choices? Choose one of these experts, look that person up in your library or on the Internet, and read more of her or his writing. Does this broader context help you understand how the writer's ideas serve Tannen's purpose in this essay?

6. Tannen introduces dominance hierarchies early in the essay (p. 658). Follow up on her reference to hierarchies in other cultures using your library's research tools to find two articles on social hierarchies in Japanese, Chinese, Javanese, or other cultures. How do the ideas you read there fit into the claims Tannen makes in this reading?

Framing Conversations

7. How do Tannen's insights about alliances and competition apply to similar ideas discussed by Franklin Foer (p. 406) and Michael Kimmel (p. 448)? Write an essay in which you draw on Tannen's ideas and examples and those of either Foer or Kimmel to develop your own argument about the ways alliances and competition work to further — or hinder — our goals.

8. Tannen's text could be seen as a follow-up to the linguistic analysis of preschoolers in Karin Martin's text (p. 632). In what ways are the observations each author makes similar and different, and to what do you attribute these similarities and differences? Write an essay in which you explore these questions and explain the significance of your findings.

9. How do Tannen's analyses of linguistic interactions shed light on patterns of female and male speech behavior in the classroom? Write an essay in which you compare Tannen's ideas and Judith Lorber's (p. 617) theories about the ways we "do gender," and apply those ideas to speaking in class. Feel free to draw on your own experiences or observations as you develop your argument about the significance of classroom speech patterns.

16

Indoctrination or Revolution?
Technologies of Popular Culture

*How does popular culture reinforce or unsettle
social standards?*

Who among us can resist a premise like that of Steven Johnson's title, *Everything Bad Is Good for You*? Johnson, like the other authors in this chapter, believes that popular culture, far from being too "lite" to take seriously, is the very ground we should be exploring carefully if we wish to make sense of our lives today. These writers discover meanings that may surprise you in the many pastimes, entertainments, and guilty pleasures that tempt us every day. When scholars study "fun" — video games and movies and Happy Meals, to name just a few of the bad-for-us pleasures analyzed in these texts — we learn how every cultural artifact, no matter how seemingly insignificant, carries meaning that shapes our lives in often quite significant ways.

Johnson argues that today's games make children smarter. For Henry Jenkins, video games serve another purpose as well: offering children whose play spaces are limited the freedom to explore and grow in a virtual world.

Children are also the focus of the texts by Eric Schlosser and Elizabeth Teare. Both examine marketing campaigns targeted at youngsters, and they are not particularly pleased with what they see. Schlosser's selection is from his best-selling book, *Fast Food Nation: The Dark Side of the American Meal*. It is an analysis of how Ray Kroc, the founder of McDonald's, borrowed from Walt Disney to market fast food with toys, in the process fostering a taste in children for very specific forms of popular culture. Elizabeth Teare sees a similar appeal to young consumers in the Harry Potter phenomenon. She finds the marketing strategies for the books and the films in conflict with the author's and publisher's professed ethical standards. She even finds tension between the books themselves and those standards. After all, she points out, Harry's "first act on learning he is a wizard is to go shopping for a wand."

Other authors in this chapter look more closely at technology. Marguerite Helmers examines Web sites honoring the memory of Princess Diana. Although some might call these sites "fluff" (or worse), Helmers's analysis suggests there is a lot we might learn about power and authorship in the relatively new realm of cyberspace. By contrast, Cynthia L. Selfe questions the wonderful world of technology proclaimed in the advertisements she discusses in her essay. Despite the potential of technology to change the world, she insists that it does not rid us of the fears and prejudices that ultimately bind us to the status quo.

The readings in this chapter acknowledge the possibilities of technology and popular culture, but they also help us understand that the past is always with us in our concerns for the present and hopes for the future. Whether you see pop culture today as the end of culture as we knew it, the same old stuff, or something entirely new — or perhaps all three — these readings point to the significance of our pastimes.

■ MARGUERITE HELMERS

Media, Discourse, and the Public Sphere: Electronic Memorials to Diana, Princess of Wales

Marguerite Helmers is a professor of English at the University of Wisconsin Oshkosh, where she teaches rhetoric, composition, and visual literacy. She is the author of *Writing Students: Composition, Testimonials, and Representations of Students* (1994), which examines the way writing instructors interpret both their students and their students' writing, and *The Elements of Visual Analysis* (2005). Helmers is also the editor of *Intertexts: Reading Pedagogy in College Writing Classrooms* (2002) and coeditor with Charles A. Hill of *Defining Visual Rhetorics* (2004). She has published articles in *College English*, the *Journal of Advanced Composition,* and the electronic journals *Kairos* and *Enculturation*. Helmers is part of a widening circle of scholars writing and theorizing about visual literacy — in particular, how we make sense of screen images.

This essay on electronic memorials to Princess Diana appeared in March 2001 in *College English*, a journal for professors of literature and composition. In this piece, Helmers plunges us into the large community of Diana fans who have developed elaborate Web sites commemorating different aspects of the princess's life and death. Before you read the essay, spend a few minutes on a general Internet search for "Princess Diana and web ring" to gather your own first impressions of the images, sounds, and language that characterize these sites. Take notes of similarities and differences you see, the range of sites, and the kinds of interaction they invite from visitors.

Most of you are likely familiar with Web sites like these; you may even have built one or more sites of your own, making decisions about color, music, text, and graphics, as well as links to other sites. As you read Helmers's essay, test your personal experience as a reader and perhaps writer or designer of Web sites against her claims about the ways authorship and arguments work uniquely in these Internet formats. In this essay, Helmers quotes both scholars and the authors of the Web sites whose sentences are sometimes filled with grammatical and other kinds of errors. Consider the effect of this wide range of voices on the larger point Helmers makes about an increasingly democratic form of authorship. Do you find yourself agreeing with Helmers's analysis of the sites she describes? Or, based on your own experience as a Web author or reader, do you see aspects she misses?

Although the subject of Helmers's essay is in the realm of popular culture, this is clearly a scholarly essay: She uses complex words and she cites many scholars in her detailed footnotes and long list of works cited. As an accomplished academic writer, she is also an expert at signposting, guiding readers through the essay to help them see both her larger point and important connections. Mark these sentences as you read, to help you keep track of the ways the parts of this rich essay fit together.

> You may well have more extensive experience writing and reading in cyberspace than many of the scholars theorizing on this topic. Bring your Internet insights to bear on this essay that asks us to take writing on the Web seriously enough to make sense of its implications.

The aristocrat Diana Frances Spencer (1961–1997) was unknown to Americans before she married the Prince of Wales, Queen Elizabeth's son Charles, in 1982. The highly publicized wedding was called a "fairy tale." Lady Diana arrived at St. Paul's Cathedral in London in a golden coach. Her dress was a Victorian fantasy, yards of ivory silk billowing over crinolines. Charles wore ceremonial military regalia. The wedding catapulted her into international stardom. In the ensuing years, Diana became a mother to the future king, William, and his brother, Harry, but following admissions of adultery by Diana and Charles, the Prince and Princess separated in 1992 and their divorce was granted August 28, 1996. One year later, on August 31, 1997, Diana was killed in a car crash in Paris.

The public life of Diana Spencer was bound at two ends by spectacle: her marriage and her funeral. Her marriage into the Royal Family of England made her into a celebrity, a princess who would be queen, and in the intervening seventeen years until her death, she lived a life in front of print and visual media as a humanitarian and fabulously coifed jet-setter. Her funeral attracted hundreds of mourners to London and was watched by millions on worldwide television. Because of the spectacular nature of her presentation to the public, Diana accrued a public sphere about her presence, one that crossed class and national lines. The events of her life were eagerly watched and anticipated by an audience who initiated a partially fictional discourse about an ontological Diana who eventually became "Diana" as character and icon.[1] The ordinary person's experience of characters and events is mediated by electronic technology, which forms a "popular memory." In a society of technological complexity, the difference between what is real or an "immediate" experience and what is simulation is increasingly difficult to delineate, yet publics depend on an event or a sequence of events to coalesce. The highly mediated life of Diana kept her public — her "constituency of the rejected" (as her brother called them)[2] — duly supplied with new activities, traumas, and fashions. Richard Johnson points out that this possibility for narrative was an essential

---

[1]In the essay "Diana between Two Deaths," Adrian Kear surrounds the name Diana in quotation marks when he wants "to distinguish between the ontological Diana (the woman who lived the life) and her ghostly hauntological counterpart (the 'Diana' of phantasmatic investment and imaginary construction)" (180, n. 3). I am not convinced that such a stark difference can be made, since Diana in life was the subject of so many diverse representations that her presence was always already fictionalized.

[2]Thanks to John Schilb for making this observation at his talk, "It's the (Brad) Pitts" (July 16, 1999, Writing Program Administration summer conference, Purdue University).

element in the relationship of the people to the "People's Princess." Significant others in our lives, whether "real" or mediated icons, are embedded in narratives, fictionalized, and ascribed characteristics that derive more or less from observed phenomena and more or less from our own desire to ratify our sense of self:

> It is often argued that there was a surplus of "fantasy" in people's relationships with her, fantasies heightened by media representation. Yet fantasy accompanies all our relationships: we idealize, install as "good objects," the living and the dead, our companions and our public hero/ines. (Johnson 18)

Fantasies are something like schema, formulaic plot outlines awaiting the detail that will gratify readers. Thus, Diana was appealing to many because she was able to portray "Princess" and, later, "victim," formulas which are both familiar and pacific to certain elements of the public sphere. In his book on fantasy and media, Lacanian critic Slavoj Zizek adds that, in modern life, the fictionalization of the real is a mass-mediated phenomenon that captures and creates public fantasies: "Fantasies are increasingly immediately externalized in the public symbolic space; the sphere of intimacy is more and more directly socialized" (164). Personal reverie is immediately published for public consumption. Writerly texts, fragmented and unfinished, are exhibited for immediate inspection.

In its deployment of popular narrative forms, the Diana story illustrates the connection between discourse and the public sphere. In every time, ordinary people have recorded their responses to historical events. A war, a plague, the funeral procession of a queen, the assassination of a president, all have been marked in the diaries or letters of citizens who are not moneyed, not tutored in formal schools, or not noble, and these records find their way into authorized histories. The elements of fairy tale ascribed to Diana's life — the fact that she, like Cinderella, was an obscure country girl from a worthy background chosen to marry the prince of the realm — and the relationship between Diana and the British monarchy have been popular subjects for analysis in English studies since her death, spawning three collections, a fourth in progress, and two special editions of British scholarly journals.[3] Christine Geraghty comments, "Like all fairy-tales, this story ended with a wedding, with the kiss on the balcony" (70). However, none of the critics has examined the ways in which members of the public sphere utilized these myths of health, power,

---

[3]These collections are Mandy Merck, editor, *After Diana: Irreverent Elegies*; Adrian Kear and Deborah Lynn Steinberg, editors, *Mourning Diana: Nation, Culture and the Performance of Grief*; Tony Walter, editor, *The Mourning for Diana*. A new collection has recently been announced, with a publisher yet unnamed. *Theory and Event* 1.4, the special issue on the death of Diana, was published in 1997 and may be accessed through Project Muse, http://muse.jhu.edu/journals/tge/. The Spring 1998 issue of the British journal *Screen* (39.1) included a special debate on the death of Diana (67–84). *Time* magazine featured a memorial issue to Diana on September 15, 1997 (150.11) that included essays by Joyce Carol Oates and Martin Amis.

and beauty to construct and publish their own narratives. Her death inspired many who perhaps would not typically publish to publish memorials, tributes, and commentary on the World Wide Web, which at one time hosted hundreds of continuously maintained web sites devoted to the memory of Diana. Many of these sites are organized formally as "web rings" through the auspices of webring.com. The electronic memorials linked by web rings form a significant archive of popular response to the death of a noble and a celebrity. They have been authored and published on the web by "common" users, writers outside formal publishing structures, and, overall, the site authors identify themselves as women. In this essay, I provide something of a thick description of the way in which people are writing and using the Internet in everyday life, with a special emphasis on the way in which this writing brings them into a public sphere, or, as Todd Gitlin describes it, a "sphericule," reflecting the division of the American public into the abundances of the information age: specialized interest groups, bits and bytes, cable television channels, and mega-stores (170).

The electronic memorials dedicated to Diana indicate a conscious decision to find "a place in history," to witness, to provide testimony (Merck 7). While many agreed that the writings and drawings left by mourners at the palace gates were "an extraordinary testament to the power of Diana as an icon" (Gilroy), they were surprised that the mediated life of Diana would provoke creative and collective actions on the part of her fans. After all, notes Paul Gilroy, "mass culture and its star system" are conventionally thought to engender passivity.

"Notably absent from the sites is the egoism that drives most web pages," comments thesite.com's Ali Hossaini. "However you may feel about the media coverage" of the Princess's death, "these web sites give the event a whole different cast. For the first time in history, ordinary people have been able to create their own media *and* put it on par with the big outlets." Hossaini believes the pages attest to "the growth of a truly global online community." The copious amount of writing on the web sites, the care taken to arrange the sites into narratives of the Princess's life and achievements, even the reinvention of the poetic form of the elegy in poems written by the site authors, indicate that the memorials exist as far more than hysteric outpourings in response to mass media frenzy. Diana is a heuristic prompting writing that is historical, biographical, and autobiographical. If, as William J. Spurlin claims, an icon is "that legible grid onto which our fantasies, desires and aspirations are projected" (156), Diana is the signifier or punctum that prompted that articulation of emotions and beliefs. Diana became the locus around which stories were organized, stories that recorded the emotions of the public at her death.

Belonging to a web ring is free. Of all the users of the World Wide Web, anyone can post a page that memorializes the Princess, but pages seeking to be linked to the virtual community of web rings need to be reviewed or "queued" to be accepted into one or all of the seven primary web rings:[4] *England's Rose Memorial Webring* (hosting 101 individual memorials), *The Princess Diana Memorial WebRing* (hosting 562 sites), *The Princess Sleeps* (hosting 36), *The True Spirit of Diana* (hosting 35 individual memorials), *Lady Diana — Princess of Wales* (totaling 47 sites), *In Memory of Princess Diana* (hosting 564 individual memorials), and *In Memory of an Angel* (hosting 65 memorials). Many sites have evocative titles such as *A Holiday Season with the Princess*, *Flowers for the Princess*, *The Queen of Hearts*, *A Single Carnation*, *Tears Flow Across Nations*, *The Realm of Lady Moonlight*, and *The Sweetest Garden: Diana as Mother and Wife*. Pages added to the Diana web rings must conform to particular guidelines that define the expectations of the audience. For example, the following warning comes from the *England's Rose Memorial Webring*. Here, as in all subsequent quotations from sites, I have not altered punctuation, spelling, or grammar:

> Sites about her life, her family, her charities, etc. are acceptable.
>
> It must depict the Princess in a respectable manner (ie: no vulgar or obscene jokes, etc.)
>
> NOT contain any adult material

The creators of the web sites are taking on the significant task of writers, aware of audience in a way that few first-year writing students are, creating their own rules for content, discourse, and document design. Heather Guck, author of a site-content explanation that demonstrates her own desire to read carefully, is attuned to image, document design, and text:

> Since I cannot monitor every site listed, every second of the day . . . I cannot vowge for any of the following links IN ANY WAY except — I did try to go through and pick out the nasty ones that laughed at di or people who were glad that she was dead. I tried to find nice sites with tributes or condolences.

Rhetorically, then, at the level of selection, the pages overtly construct a particular cleansed image of Diana. To link through the sites as a user is to encounter a continuous display of a uniform Diana image: fairy-tale princess, caring humanitarian, and woman searching for love. An inventory of the content of the pages includes most of the following as common features: pictures of the princess, personal expressions of grief by the site designer, an electronic condolence book with expressions of grief by others, the lyrics to Elton John's "Candle in the Wind," Earl Charles Spencer's funeral oration, condolence poetry written by the owner of the site, an abbreviated life story of Diana (perhaps with pictures of Diana as a young girl), and links to "Althorp On-line," an official virtual tour of the hereditary Spencer estate where Diana is buried. Many of the pages are composed

---

[4]These titles are taken from a site inventory conducted in July 1999. My earlier estimates of the number of sites included in web rings totaled close to two thousand in December 1997.

in diary form, a single page with dated entries marking the site owner's immediate reaction to the death of Diana. Sites can be accessed 300 to 500 times per month, although activity peaks at certain days of the year. August and September (marking the anniversary of Diana's death and funeral) and July 1 (marking Diana's birthday). As an example of their popularity, one counter recorded that I was the 11,000th visitor to the site in July 1999.

If cultural literacy means coming to terms with the texts that confront 8 us in daily life, these memorial home pages are just such texts. The personal home page itself is a popular form of expression in the late twentieth century; it is quick to produce and relatively inexpensive to maintain. Because "rhetorical strategies" may be "hidden in the texts of everyday experience," as Barry Brummett and Detine Bowers contend (117), it is not only "great" works of literature that invite readers to join them in making meaning. To cite the oft-quoted observation of Raymond Williams, "culture is ordinary"; thus, what better subject for rhetorical and semiotic analysis by students and critics in English studies than she who was the "mirror of the ordinary" (as Martin Amis referred to her), Princess Diana?

Diana Remembered Through Hypermedia

Linda Barlow, author of *Diana, A Candle in the Dark*, constructs her web 9 tribute as a long two-columned document. The left-hand column contains a description of the purpose of the site ("to post . . . feelings about her death") and hypertext links to Diana-related web presences ("RealAudio of Earl Spencer's Eulogy and Elton John's Song"). By August 1999, Barlow had become an associate of Amazon.com in order to sell books about the life and death of Diana through her site. The body of the page, to the right of the running column of links, consists of Barlow's personal reactions to Diana's death. She dates her entries August 31 (the date of death), September 3, September 5, and September 6 (the date of the funeral). Each entry contains a title, signifying a step beyond a personal entry into a public world of storytelling, for the section titles function like the chapters of a book, summing up the action; "The World Mourns Princess Diana," "What's Wrong with the Windsors?," "The Royal Family Responds to the People," and "A Funeral Fit for a Queen."

Barlow's site is something of a gift to Diana and Diana's followers. She 10 subtitles her site "From One Woman to Another." The transactive nature of her title indicates the desire for, if not the actual awareness of, an audience for her text. Her first entry, describing the significance of Diana for her and other women, concludes with a personal request directed at this audience:

> Please, if you're feeling a need to express your thoughts and feelings about
> the loss of this dearly beloved woman, please leve your own peronal message

about what Diana meant to you. Maybe by sharing we can all help each
other . . .

The heightened eloquence of the first diary entry — its use of words such
as *heartbreaking, elegant, beautiful, glamour, adored, embraced* — suggests
a sadness that is genuinely seeking for language to express itself. At the
same time, it is clear from her plea to a readership that she does not see
herself expressing an exclusively personal grief, nor does she envision herself as being *singularly* touched by grief: she is a woman among women
with shared concerns.

After a few days, Barlow's entries turn to anger, which is, as Peter *11*
Sacks points out in his study of English elegy, a traditional progression for
the elegiac text. By September 3, she engages in an "outbreak of vengeful
anger" (Sacks 2) and is prepared to vilify the Queen and Prince Charles for
their lack of communication with the public about their *own* feelings, a
type of disclosure which is denied by royal protocol. Despite not knowing
Diana personally, Barlow has been willing not only to speak, but to write
and develop an elaborate tribute available for global viewing. Yet, as she
points out, those who knew Diana the best were silent ("What's Wrong
with the Windsors?"). Privileging confessional discourse, demanding that
private emotions be articulated for the public, she asks, "Do they care?"

Barlow's diary entry for the day of the funeral is hyperlinked within *12*
the text, with links pointing to photographs from ABC and CNN online
sites devoted to the "magnificent service" and "solemn procession" of the
funeral. By September 6, then, Barlow has undertaken a significant shift in
her relationship to her text. She acts as media commentator, standing in
for Tom Brokaw and Barbara Walters in order to record and describe the
chronology of events to her Internet community. Opening the September 6
entry is a summative paragraph that sets the context and significance for
the day, "Her funeral was witnessed by thousands of people in the Abbey
itself, and by millions watching on television around the world." The following three paragraphs of the entry move chronologically to witness the
events, from "[b]efore the service," to "[i]n Westminster Abbey," and "[a]fter
the funeral service."

Shauna Brunette, creator of the tribute *A Compassionate Queen of* *13*
Hearts, similarly divides her single-page site into dated entries. Unlike
Barlow, who links to an outside world of news and media reports, Brunette
uses her site as a personal space to "[vent] her own anger and concern,"
although she is aware that she is unleashing these emotions for a readership. Beginning with a short comment that seems to challenge any of her
would-be critics, "Is it, in heav'n, a crime to love too well?" (cited as the
work of "Pope Alexander [1688–1744]"), she initially speaks through her
own silence, employing the emotionally charged medium of song and reproducing the lyrics to "Candle in the Wind" in its entirety. Inventing an audience for her eulogy, she issues condolences to Princes William and Harry,
to the "family," and "the Royal family." Then she begins a long reactionary

commentary that particularly finds fault with "the photographers that were so ruthlessly following" Diana to cause her death. This commentary stands out because of one paragraph, in which Brunette implicates herself in Diana's death, a full identification and placement within the public sphere that has come to embody the private:

> I came to my senses and really thought about it. The fact is I feel somewhat guilty myself. I have purchased trash magazines before and because of that I contributed to this tragic event. In my own defense I have never purchased any tabloid about Princess Diana, but I have bought a lot of magazines about her. Maybe some of the photos in those magazines were taken by the same photographers that killed her.
>
> I am human and I am curious. I want to know about people, their lives, their happiness, heartaches, and how they overcome diversity. But I do not want to know these things if it means that someone must loose their lives in the process. I have the right to know, but they have the right to privacy and safety. Privacy and safety outweigh my rights of being nosey.

Brunette's identification of her inquiring mind with "The Crash" seem to bear out what Diane Rubenstein identifies as an obsession with "wound culture," the titillation that arises from the horrifying spectacle of death, the fascination with orgies of blood and tissue. Like Barlow, Brunette also reveals that she was angry for a time, until she could turn that anger against herself in a pathological connection to the deceased. The movement seems to signal that, if Brunette could not know Diana personally in real life, she could settle for an illicit, and ultimately very personal, connection of murderer and victim. Even so, Brunette's self-derision is also a repetition of a generally expressed, popular sense that "we" in the public sphere killed Diana, as Mandy Merck puts it, "our public avarice for spectacle spurring on the paparazzi" (Merck 7).

Despite this rather funereal characterization of the text of only two of *14* several hundred web memorials, it is clear that visitors to the sites are probably not looking for interpretive commentary, since the texts are so formulaic and the restrictions on the site do not promote alternative viewpoints (recall, in Heather Guck's words, that the sites must be "nice"). They are seeking photographs and visual stimulation that will cover the absence of Diana with the presence of her image. As Judith Williamson has commented about the aftermath of Diana's death: "it was, at first, hard to believe not only because of its suddenness, but because the absence of someone whose image had been so present in our culture seemed a contradiction in terms" (25). What one is likely to notice first is the particular visual appeal of the pages. Pictures of Diana are, of course, most prevalent and thus appeal to readers' pleasure principle while also arguing for a homogeneous vision of Diana. As Craig Stroupe recently pointed out, web-based communication requires readers to be adept in decoding visual and verbal material. Addressing his remarks to teachers of language and literature, Stroupe argues that writers and readers must come to recognize that "verbal expertise [is] only one among many forms of literacy and professional/ rhetorical authority" (608). This necessity appears to be an assumption that the writers of the Diana memorials have already instantiated, for they adeptly reverse the hierarchy of text to photograph. Pages are "announced" in a familiar manner, featuring photographs of Diana (which we recognize from the cover of tabloids), while making the personal text secondary. Visitors to web memorials often must scroll down pages to access any original text, and text is punctuated by additional photographs.

The electronic memorials communicate "sentiment" and share a design *15* aesthetic that borrows from the Victorian sentimental style, what Harriet Beecher Stowe in 1897 called "Pink and White Tyranny" (Douglas 8). Common designs are roses, angels, candles, and shades of pink. Brunette runs a gentle pattern of Victorian cherubs holding roses down the left column of her page; her text is in pink. Barlow uses a large, repeating, pink-toned image of Diana as her background and her section titles are in red. Jennifer Gardner selected a rippled cream satin background for her site, *In Loving Memory,* which, without a doubt, evokes a casket lining.

The closest genre relative to these web pages is the Hallmark sympa- *16* thy card, whose design hearkens back to the nineteenth-century American Sunday School movement.[5] Best known for encouraging the development of religious material culture, the Sunday School movement also led women to compose consolation literature such as obituary poems, memoirs, and magazine articles, what Ann Douglas refers to as "lachrymose verse" (8). Hallmark sympathy cards feature sentimental verse and floral designs; many are colored in tones of pink or mauve. Of the six that I randomly selected at a major distributor in my area, the sentiments illustrated the structure of feeling between the sender and the recipient, such as "Our thoughts are with you" or "With our sympathy," echoing Barlow's transactional gift "from one woman to another." One card in particular, "In the loss of your mother," is almost identical in visual design to a web memorial. This card uses a textured cover of deep dusty rose embossed with a faint gold ripple; a window opens from the rose to a (reproduced) background of a heavily knotted silk rose lying against natural-color linen or raw silk. Its evocation of postwar 1940s formal wear recalls the one-hundred-year-old Queen Mother's wardrobe. An unattributed quotation on the rose page reads, "They know the deepest sorrow who have known the dearest joy." The use of the quotation is indicative of the Diana memorials as well, which liberally employ quotations from Shakespeare and Spenser on their pages, as well as a host of other allusions to popular song, such as

---

[5]In the 1995 book *Material Christianity: Religion and Popular Culture in America,* Colleen McDannell points out the widespread (and medieval) belief that "not everyone can approach God through the intellect . . . The uneducated, women, and children were particularly responsive to sacred images, objects, and spaces" (9). Thus, Protestant marketers began to disseminate devotional items of "taste" to the American public in the early years of the twentieth century.

"Stairway to Heaven." Many reprint the lyrics of "Candle in the Wind" as their homage. Lines from Spenser's *The Faerie Queene* adorn the icon for the web ring *The Princess Sleeps*:

> For all that the faire is, she is by nature good,
> that is a sign to know the gentle blood.

Certainly, with a scanner or point-and-click technology through the browser the pictures of Diana become readily available; however, technology does not explain the decision to repeat the same images over hundreds of pages. John Fiske's assertion that "[F]an collections tend to be of cheap, mass-produced objects, and stress quantity and all-inclusiveness over quality or exclusivity" (45) is not an adequate explanation in this case. The repetition and reproduction are most likely indicative of the need for visitors' comfort and familiarity in a hypermedia environment that depends on reappearance as a design and content trope. One explanation is that, like epic storytelling, the pages' repetition helps to affirm a reality that extends beyond individual experience. *17*

Second, in words and pictures, there is an emphasis on Princess Diana's physical beauty. Each page contains at least one photograph of the Princess on the page and many make use of the "photo tribute." Although the pages reproduce many of the same photographs, the methods of presentation vary with the vision of each site designer and their construction — or vision — of Diana. For example, "Net Angel's" (also known as "Net Girl") memorial opens with a montage: six colorful pictures of the chic Diana in hats and jewels and five grainy black and white cameos of Diana as a child. The juxtaposition of the ages of Diana seem to echo the placement of private photographs into a family scrapbook. Subsequent photographs show Diana with her children and in casual clothes. Net Angel's Diana is the mother and friend. Author "Marvelicious" uses white text against a black background to evoke the elegant Diana. Along the left edge of the site is a continuously repeating vertical banner with a sepia-toned photograph of Diana in dangling diamond earrings and off-the-shoulder black dress. White roses surround her title, *Goodbye England's Rose*. She chooses to frame her pictures of Diana in colorful electronic photo frames of red, green, blue, and pink, which gives her site the air of a mantel or étagère filled with family photographs. The most prominent in her collection is a wedding photograph of the Prince and Princess. Bill Sperry Jr.'s *Memorial for Lady Diana Frances Spencer* employs the Princess's favorite color, purple, as a background to eight pictures of Diana as a child. An animated image of Diana dances slowly from left to right across the screen to the computerized MIDI voicings of "Candle in the Wind." Similarly, the "Remembering Gallery" designed by Nicholas Paulin employs classic black-and-white photography framed in four "galleries." *18*

Ironically, while the authors make liberal use of images of Princess Diana, they decry tabloid photojournalism. For example, Net Angel, author of *Forever Young: A Tribute to Diana, Princess of Wales*, includes a petition on her site titled "I remember Princess Diana: A Petition to the World," the *19* purpose of which is to copyright photographs: "Do you believe that you should own the copyright to all pictures taken of you, regardless of who took them or where they were taken?" Ironically, in order to emphasize her point that we should never forget in whose name we ban tabloid photojournalism, she uses pictures of Diana. Like other writers, Net Angel's rationale for developing her web site involves a complex and contradictory blend of spectatorship (she followed the events of Diana's life), knowledge (she felt as if she was "getting to know Diana"), emotion (she enjoins readers to keep Diana "in our hearts"), and consumerism (noting that a monetary fund will keep Diana's legacy alive):

> After spending many years of my life following the events in her life and in a way getting to know Diana (I am proud to say that I have never purchased a tabloid in my life), it is my opinion that Diana would not have wanted us to grieve over her for too long. She will live on forever in her two very handsome boys, who will continue her sort of special magic in the British monarchy. She will live on forever in the memorial fund, that was set up in her name, and in that way she will continue her heroic deeds. She will live on forever in our memories of her beauty, charm, dedication, and love — as long as we cherish those memories. She will live on forever as long as we keep her in our hearts, where she will always reign as queen. (Net Angel)

As elegies, the web sites can be experienced "as a work" in Peter [20] Sacks's words, "both in the commonly accepted meaning of a product and in the more dynamic sense of the working through of an impulse of experience — the sense that underlies Freud's phrase 'the work of mourning'" (1), which underscores how language reacts to a sense of loss by seeking to cover it with the imperfect medium of language itself. Connecting the web sites further to elegy are the spontaneous tribute poems that underscore the memory work of photographs and personal testimony. In fact, several sites advertise themselves as sites of commemorative poetry; commemorative poetry has also appeared in small-press publications such as *Remembering Diana* and William Heyen's collection *Diana, Charles, and the Queen*.[6] As an illustration, the "Ode to Diana, a sonnet" by Jennifer Gardner is typical of the imagery, sentiment, meter, and rhyme scheme of the poems. Graphically, many of the poems are centered on the screen, giving them a prominence within the memorial web pages and distinguishing them as having a different status from other text. In the following, taken from Jennifer Gardner's web site, spelling, punctuation, and word and line spacing have not been altered from the original:

> She was for us to see once more,
> moving slowly to her home.

---

[6]Rick Blalock and K. Thomas Oglesby edited *Remembering Diana: The People's Tribute to Their Princess*, a collection of verses of sympathy, notes of regret, and Earl Spencer's eulogy. Many of William Heyen's poems were written prior to the death of Diana, although the collection of his works, *Diana, Charles, and the Queen*, was published after her death (in 1998).

> In life she loved both rich and poor.
> Her poor Princes, now alone.
> In life her hands touched sick and old.
> Her eyes saw all our pain
> But now her folded hands are cold.
> Her eyes, closed against her fame.
> Now the world weeps all around
> for prey, hunted to the kill.
> Diana's voice of soft sweet sound
> muted as her body's still.
> Folded hands and sealed eyes,
> to us, Diana never dies.

The "Ode to Diana" makes use of the same meter as the Hallmark sym- 21
pathy card titled "The Rose Beyond the Wall" and parts of "Candle in the
Wind." Of 86 words in the poem, 74 are monosyllabic. The single metaphor,
"prey, hunted to the kill" is borrowed from Earl Spencer's funeral oration,
in which he compared the irony of the classical naming of Diana, the god-
dess of the hunt, now hunted to her death. The Hallmark card, "The Rose
Beyond the Wall" uses a six-stanza, rhymed quatrain to convey its sorrow.
The card notes that this rhymed evocation is "from writings of A. L. Frink,"
the attribution lending a kind of literary authority to the poem, distinguishing it from other cards penned in Hallmark studios. In simple meter,
the poem tells the story of a rose that grew alongside a stone wall, "Near
shady wall a rose once grew." It pushes its way through a crack in the stones
and now blooms on the other side. Although the (absent) addressee — in
this case, the recipient of the card, the one suffering grief — cannot see it,
he or she should realize that the rose is still there, visible in another space.
Like the rose of Hallmark, images of England's Rose Diana gaze out at her
audience in the virtual public sphere of electronic memorials, a presence
never quite erased from memory.

Appended to every memorial web site is an electronic condolence 22
book. If the condolences in the memorial books at the palace are similar to
those left at Harrod's or posted to the web, they are directed to Diana herself. She is an absent other, not really gone. Many of the entries address the
Princess, employing the vocative, in the first person directed to Diana, as
in the following comment, "Princess Diana, Many Will miss you." The letters (in the epistolary tradition) attempt to connect she who is absent to
the writer. Browsing the books reveals, if the postings are to be believed,
entries from Angola, India, Australia, and the Philippines. Entries from
English-speaking countries are usually in a written format that indicates
that the writers are not skilled in writing or not familiar with conventions
of written prose. For example, this post by Tammy (identified as from the
United States) features a dropped *s* sending ("year"), a missing preposition
("of"), and sentence boundary problems:

Name: Tammy . . .

Time: 1999-01-10 06:54:41

COMMENTS: I THINK PRINCESS DIANA WAS ONE THOSE KIND THAT ONLY HAPPENS
EVERY ONCE IN A MILLION YEAR WHERE A PERSON JUST HAVE A SPECIAL "MAGIC" THAT
GIVES PEOPLE ALL WALKS OF LIFE A WARM FEELING OF HAPPINESS AS WELL AS MAKING
ANY INDIVIDUALS SICK OR HEALTHY, POOR OR RICH, THAT HE OR SHE IS SPECIAL TO HER
HEART — EVEN IF IT'S JUST FOR A MINUTE FROM HER GLANCE OR TOUCH. SHE'S NOT
PERFECT AND SHE DOES HAVE MANY FAULTS BUT AT LEAST SHE IS REAL, NOT MAKE
BELIEVE LIKE SOME OF HER IN-LAWS WHO COWARDLY HIDE BEHIND A TITLE AND SOME
SORRY EXCUSES SUCH AS "WE ARE ROYALS, IT'S THE TRADITION, AND IT'S OUR WORLD
AND EVERYONE REVOLVES AROUND IT" ATTITUDE. BAH-HUM-BUG! GET WITH THE CUR-
RENT TIMES ROYALS! THANK GOD I'M NOT A ROYAL. . . . I WOULDN'T WANT TO BE ASSO-
CIATED WITH A FAMILY SUCH AS THEIRS EVEN WITH ALL THE NICE "FRINGE BENEFITS"
THAT COME WITH BEING A "ROYAL". YUCK!

The condolence books extend the work of mourning performed at the
gates of Buckingham Palace, offering ordinary citizens the opportunity to
react to a media-mediated event. These desires to connect with history are
present still in the shrine to Dodi Fayed and Diana at the base of the
"Egyptian elevator" in Harrod's Department Store, London. In itself, the
memorial erected by Dodi's father Mohamed al Fayed is a work of fictionalization, joining Diana and Dodi in a symbolic marriage. Their photographs are circled by two golden rings, entwined at the center and graced
by a golden dove. Here, as at other physical and virtual sites, one finds the
same penned offerings to the dead, such as the one I reproduce here:

> Diana & Dodi,
> You've gone from our lives but you'll never be forgotten
> You're both missed and are thought of everyday.
> Rest in Peace as I'm sure that you now will.
>   Della
>   Marlborough, WILTS XXX

This brief tribute, on a piece of lined notepaper, employs the mode of
direct address to Diana that is prevalent in tributes to her. It contains the
curious gesture of including a return address, as if Diana might write back.
Considering the devotional aspects of the sites and the inevitable comparison of the mother Diana to the holy Mother Mary who hears our prayers,
this compositional gesture may not be so unusual after all.

Memory Work in the Electronic Public Sphere

Roland Barthes made the famous declaration that the age of photography   23
corresponds with the "explosion of the private into the public" (98). There
is almost no better life to illustrate his claim than the life of Diana, the
woman hunted to death by the paparazzi. If Diana created a virtual, mediated public sphere, what forms of discourse and rhetorical strategies are
deployed in this public sphere? Various popular forms of narrative construction that derive from television and mass-cultural print media reap-
pear in the web pages.

Adrian Kear and Deborah Lynn Steinberg identify two phases in 24
mourning Diana. The first was the actual death and the coverage of events
by the media; the second was the commentary on Diana's death that
emerged from the coverage. This second level was metacommentary, commentary *about* the coverage, and interpretation of the consequences of
Diana's death. As Kear and Steinberg point out, the coverage and commentary immediately created a group of fictionalized "Dianas," both royal
and ordinary (2).

> Diana's status as a tragic figure was formed in a fusion of modern and anachro-
> nistic tragic forms. She inhabited both the "elevated" status of royal Protago-
> nist (that quality central to Aristotle's understanding of the power of tragedy
> as deriving from the representation of the terrifying and pitiable end that
> befalls even the best of men [sic]) and the ubiquitous "ordinariness" of the
> "anti-hero" of modern tragedy whose terrible/pitiful existence could connect
> with any of us. . . . (Kear and Steinberg 10)

Kear and Steinberg argue that the "prosaic manner of the death of Diana, in
itself no more than an ordinary, everyday incident, nonetheless set in play a
series of extraordinary spectacular *Diana effects*" (3, emphasis in text). In
the words of a colleague, Diana died an undignified death, an unsuitable
death for a royal. Having glided safely through landmines in Angola, she
died on her way to spend the night with her boyfriend, driven to a hotel by a
drunken security guard. Nonetheless, to her fans around the world, "It
seemed that without the restriction of the living referent, these industries of
reverence, revenance and remembrance were no longer held back by the
demands of ontological presence" (3). Thus, almost simultaneously with her
death, Diana became a manipulable, plural icon, a figure capable of
embroidery and invention. Kear and Steinberg refer to the icon Diana as an
"open text," able to "sustain a variety of identifications" (8). In particular,
her popular image could be deployed in a variety of representational situations: to illustrate princess, royalty, fashion icon, mother, mourning, nation,
and social consciousness.

It is clear that writers and readers identified with the fairy-tale princess 25
who also had a failed marriage and bulimia. Many influential fiction writers, historians, and critics weighed in with Diana commentary and analysis at one time or another, such as Jan Morris, Martin Amis, Joyce Carol
Oates, Judith Williamson, and Camille Paglia. The failed marriage exemplified the trope of woman scorned that is familiar from both classic literature and popular television. The tropes used to describe Diana, however,
are selective, neglecting the childish behavior and the spiteful attacks that
are part of the iconoclastic — "not nice" — Diana record. Sally Bedell
Smith reports the spiteful comments that Diana made about her sister-in-
law Sarah Ferguson, records comments on Diana's multiple insecurities,
self-mutilation, and wild eating binges from several different friends of
Diana, and ultimately concludes that Diana suffered from "borderline personality disorder" (363). Even the subtitle of Smith's biography — *Portrait
of a Troubled Princess* — signals the extent to which Smith attempts to

demystify the myths constructing Diana as People's Princess, humanitarian, and angel.

Yet all the myths, dissenting or sympathetic, serve to reify Diana as a representative character. In general, the web sites place the greatest emphasis on Diana's character as human being, which, because of the absence of personal knowledge, is constructed from textual accounts. Twenty years ago, Rosalind Coward argued that it was only possible to know the royal family through impersonal accounts and thus "The Royals" were as fictional as any soap opera. To a greater extent than any of her royal counterparts, however, Diana was embedded in common story forms, such as the romance of her marriage and the tragedy of her death, stories which serve to embed her character as a passive entity caught in an unforgiving plot. The plot development depends on the audience's recognition of the story form in order to make meaning, a meaning that is by this time given. Diana is always already "good." Finally, the unique possibilities of hypermedia allow document design to underscore character, plot, and emotional attitude toward audience through the use of color, animation, music, and photograph.

Diana serves as a representative character because she was the child of divorce who was divorced herself. As Jon Simons writes, she was an "empty signifier" because she was all things: "Cinderella, the anorexic girl, the betrayed wife, the divorcee, the single mother, the girl about town, the rock-'n'roll princess, the nurturer, the victim, the strong woman, the besieged star, the adoring mother." While American women are beset by the struggle for the perfect California *Baywatch* body, she, too, expressed the same struggle through her admission of bulimia. Diana, like the women who watched and idolized her, admitted to being a product of the media, actively following accounts of herself in the press (cf. Smith). Women, believing they are destined to marry for love, find life much as Diana did, "cruelly awakened to the world of hurt, betrayal and humiliation," no longer a fairy tale (Oates). Diana may be a punctum for composition, but she is also a character in a traditional literary sense. She can be analyzed and emplotted precisely because people did not know her personally. She was always shot through by representations that made her manipulable. This very quality of exploitability provided direction for those who followed her story. Whether she was encoded as "humanitarian" or "bulimic," she was a representative character, one who exemplified all the contradictory aspects of "achievement, success, failure, genius, struggle, triumph" (Baty 8). As S. Paige Baty argues, representative characters "exist at the intersection of cultural production and consumption, circulating in specific times and places where they are made to mediate values to a given community" (9).[7] In the media, "actors and events become typified into

___

[7]Among these icons are John F. Kennedy, Ronald Reagan, Martin Luther King, O. J. Simpson, Elvis Presley, and Marilyn Monroe. Baty draws the term "representative character" from Ralph Waldo Emerson, describing it as "a cultural figure through whom the character of political life is articulated" (8).

more general codes," as in the stock figures of fairy tales and the story, forms are more "generic" or familiar and thus "resonate with the society's culture" (Alexander and Jacobs 31):

> [M]edia texts provide a certain flow of cultural material from producers to audiences, who in turn use them in their lifeworld settings to construct a meaningful world and to maintain a common cultural framework through which intersubjectivity becomes possible, even among those who may never come into contact with one another. (Alexander and Jacobs 27)

Thus, mass media provides citizens with common stories, shared cultural memory, and mandatory rituals. The web memorials position viewers as members of a temporal, yet temporary, public sphere that shares the awareness of the media event. Yet the memorials have no discourse of their own but borrow liberally from traditional forms, even if those forms are themselves less the products of dominant culture than of popular media.

The plot structure of the romance most closely resembles the emplot- 28 ment of electronic Diana memorials, which revel in the fairy-tale wedding of the Princess to the Prince on July 26, 1982, and repeatedly invoke the words "charmed" and "fairy tale" to express her life. Indeed, as Scott Wilson notes, "the media not only told her story, it wrote and re-wrote that story according to a variety of familiar genres: fairy tale, romance, soap opera, morality play, tragedy" to the extent that Diana's life was romanticized and aestheticized "even in her dying moments." Significantly, the myths of Diana drew forth elements of British legend and literature. A particular concern was given to the "care of the myth." Like the boat that becomes the Lady of Shallot's bier, Diana was borne from Westminster to her burial site on an island in a small lake at the family home Althorp, north of London, itself metamorphosed into King Arthur's mysterious and misty sepulcher.

The pastiche of form, style, and allusion are common to popular forms 29 of romance, which take greater care to emphasize the connection between characters than to exemplify historical veracity. Geraghty points out that soap opera was a main form of narrative by which the Diana story was written and understood, especially among women. Soap-opera forms selected "emotion, empathy, and talk" as the primary forms of discourse that exemplified not only the authors' own desires, but, as one web author called it, "the true spirit of Diana." But values drawn from soap opera, among other sources, also set the dominant terms of popular mourning:

> What is striking . . . is the dominance of soap opera values in the way that people spoke about Diana's death. Talk about private feelings — the staple of soap opera — was valued as the best way of expressing grief, and, indeed as a sign of grief itself. (Geraghty 73)

Diana herself was, in life, speechless and inarticulate, requiring professional writers and drama coaches to aid her in her public appearances. It was her body that was the news, Geraghty notes. And that body, once absent, provided the blank slate upon which the stories of the ordinary person could be written. The stories had more than a private function, however. Just as the testimony of the common person is valued in television programs such as *The Jerry Springer Show* and *Oprah*, stories accrue a public function. Kear and Steinberg call this a type "of testimony in which collective identity or shared experience is both referenced and invented" (9).

Jennifer Gardner's three dated diary entries on her web site *In Loving* 30 *Memory* exemplify the progression to personal discourse. She begins with an entry dated August 30, 1997, that mimics the factual form of news broadcasts and other forms of public discourse, announcing, sound-bite style, "Princess Diana is dead." She chronicles the news reports that announced that Diana was "gravely injured," detailing her own attempts to reason through the process of death. Finally, she notes, "I died too." At that moment in her diary entry the emphasis shifts from the protagonist "Diana" to the narrator "Jenny."

> My body just froze, stiffened like a corpse, my face grew cold — not knowing what expression to make — if any at all.

Gardner posts two more journal entries on this site, dated August 31 and September 2. In both, Diana is the punctum — the occasion for writing — not the main actor. On August 31, Gardner mentions the death of her kitten, drops in the names of dead friends (or relatives, or members of her community — the references are unclear), and notes that "Sarah" (her friend? her sister?) is also mourning. Death is the subject of this entry; Diana is merely another object of Death's attention, another name to add to the list. By September 2, Gardner offers a brief commentary on the meaning of Diana and then slips into a long reverie on her own life. She comments that "the devastating feeling of emptiness is all around," causing her to "deal with" the tragedy by putting "a lot of my (very few) tangible thoughts into my Diana webpage memorial."

> . . . outside of the computer and an occasional episode of Sisters and Designing Woman, there isn't really much I've taken part in lately.

She thinks about the wedding she is scheduled to attend over the weekend. She wonders about getting back together with "Todd," who left a message on her answering machine. She wonders if she is too vulnerable.

Electronic memorials to Diana illustrate some of the ways that writing 31 and document design can cover an ontological absence with the material presence of text. Although the web memorials are derivative, employing popular forms of story and not literary in the traditional sense of exemplifying an individual genius at work, they are useful documents for English studies because they demonstrate the powerful instantiation of story and character forms in daily life.

Throughout this essay, I have privileged the idea of story and image 32 while deferring a discussion of the web sites as memorials. Acts of official commemoration have traditionally been associated with commending

civic or military achievement and not conferring lasting testimony to popular icons. Of course, popular memorials are often articulated through the
commercial, such as Elvis Presley's former home Graceland, now a
museum with several gift shops attached. Even Diana's own tomb has been
enhanced by a museum of her clothes (representing the absent body) for
viewers wishing to pay the entrance fee.

A glance at the statuary around public buildings and public parks may   33
serve as illustration: the statues of conqueror on horseback are legion. In
Britain and America, the two cultures that form the axes of this discussion,
official memorials to acts of military bravery abound: from significant
statements such as the Vietnam Veterans Memorial in Washington, D.C., to
the lonely stone spires inscribed with names of World War I casualties in
country towns across England. Samuel Hynes's *Soldiers' Tale,* an eloquent
study of the effect of twentieth-century wars on ordinary citizens, points
out that whereas dead foot soldiers prior to the twentieth century were
buried in mass graves, the families of the middle-class foot soldiers who
fought in World War I were instrumental in demanding individual recognition and commemoration for their sons. The atrocities of World War II
marked such a dramatic shift in sensibility that it became impossible to
remember war without remembering the voices of the victims. The Holocaust Museum in Washington, D.C., is particularly significant in this regard
because it recognizes the sacrifices of common people who were the victims of military action by naming them, by including personal objects such
as shoes and photographs, by offering testimony. Thus, a gradual progression of remembrance has occurred in just over a century, a movement into
the personal and the textual from impersonal, nationalistic beginnings.

In contrast to this very personal act of remembering, impromptu   34
memorials are devoted to the memory of those who most of the observers
did not know. Teddy bears, photographs, notes on scraps of paper torn from
small notebooks, even combs and hair ribbons have been reported as serving a commemorative function at sites such as Oklahoma City's bombed
Murrah Federal Building and Buckingham Palace following Diana's death.

Unlike the permanent, physical structures of memorials in our culture,   35
the electronic memorials are not ratified by any high cultural tradition. As
textual, literary artifacts, they are not sufficiently complex in theme or language to merit study. Their appropriation of popularized cultural forms
brings them easily into the tabloid genre of discourse and presentation,
"just another return of the real within wound culture," as Diane Rubenstein
puts it:

> one more atrocity exhibit allied with abject art's oedipal insolence and infan-
> tile regression and congruent with the pop fascination with OJ, Jon Benet
> Ramsay, Ennis Cosby as well as all other instances of violated subjecthood
> (Oklahoma, bombing victims, victims of serial killers, and random acts of
> urban violence such as the Empire State Building shootings).

The spectacle of Diana's funeral, part ritual, part Hollywood, is one such
performance. The web memorials are another. As written composition,

they cover loss and absence. Diana gave these writers the ultimate gift, the gift of death, allowing their voices to speak. They reinvent Diana as mother and friend, as a kind and gentle human being. Forgotten are the episodes of colonic irrigation and "Squidgy Tapes" of Diana speaking sweet nothings over the phone during her affair with James Gilbey. The sites defy any contradictory opinions, any dissent. Thus, they *create* memory through repeated performances. In the preface to his analysis of cultural performance, Joseph Roach makes an important point about the necessity of ritual for public memory:

> The social processes of memory and forgetting, familiarly known as culture, may be carried out by a variety of performance events, from stage plays to sacred rites, from carnivals to the invisible rituals of everyday life. To perform in this sense means to bring forth, to make manifest, and to transmit. To perform also means, though often more secretly, to reinvent. (xi)

Electronic memorials may be a new genre of textual and visual construc- 36 tion, yet they rely on the texts of everyday life. Electronic memorials may be embedded in a culture of reproduction, but the reproduction is overtly fantasized in inventive ways. Authors are constructing new genres with rules for organization, content, language, and design. The memorials provide evidence of how people read, placing themselves into popular story forms as protagonists, often constructing a fictional Diana who is their friend and their advocate. The extent to which they come to identify with their own performance is evident again in their sense that they are implicated in her death.

Hypermedia is essential in the development and deployment of remem- 37 brance for it offers the immediate sense of audience and community. Thus, electronic memorials to Diana, Princess of Wales, are not the static texts of official commemoration, but active participants in the making of meaning in our culture.

WORKS CITED

Alexander, Jeffrey C., and Ronald N. Jacobs. "Mass Communication, Ritual and Civil Society." *Media, Ritual and Identity.* Ed. Tamar Liebes and James Curran. New York: Routledge, 1998. 23–41.

Amis, Martin. "The Mirror of Ourselves." *Time Online.* 15 September 1997. 29 June 1998 <http://www.pathfinder.com/time/magazine/1997/dom/970915/princess.the_mirror_of_.html>.

Barlow, Linda. *Diana, A Candle in the Dark.* 26 December 1997 <http://www.monash.com/diana.html>.

Barthes, Roland. *Camera Lucida: Reflections on Photography.* Trans. Richard Howard. New York: Hill and Wang, 1981.

Baty, S. Paige. *American Monroe: The Making of a Body Politic.* Berkeley: U of California P, 1995.

Blalock, Rick, and K. Thomas Oglesby, eds. *Remembering Diana: The People's Tribute to Their Princess.* Los Angeles: Milligan, 1998.

Brummett, Barry, and Detine Bowers. "Subject Positions as a Site of Rhetorical Struggle: Representing African Americans." *At the Intersection: Cultural Studies and Rhetorical Studies.* Ed. Thomas Rostek. New York: Guilford, 1999. 117–136.

Brunette, Shauna. *A Compassionate Queen of Hearts.* 9 December 1997 <http://members.tripod.com/~ladystarla/4/diana2.html>.

Coward, Rosalind. "The Royals." *Female Desires: How They Are Sought, Bought, and Packaged.* New York: Grove Weidenfeld, 1984. 161–171.

Douglas, Ann. *The Feminization of American Culture.* Garden City, NY: Anchor/Doubleday, 1988.

Fiske, John. "The Cultural Economy of Fandom." *The Adoring Audience: Fan Culture and Popular Media.* Ed. Lisa A. Lewis. New York: Routledge, 1992. 30–49.

Gardner, Jennifer. *In Loving Memory.* 23 July 1999 <http://pages.prodigy.com/JGardner/di.htm>.

Geraghty, Christine. "Story." *Screen* 39.1 (1998): 70–73.

Gilroy, Paul. "Elton's Crooning, England's Dreaming." *Theory and Event* 1.4 (1997): 7 pars. <http://muse.jhu.edu/journals/theory_&_event/v001/1.4gilroy.html>.

Gitlin, Todd. "Public Sphere or Public Sphericules?" *Media, Ritual and Identity.* Ed. Tamar Liebes and James Curran. New York: Routledge, 1999.

Guck, Heather. *Tributes to Diana — Princess of Wales On the Web.* 5 February 1999 <http://www.frontiernet.net/~guck/ntrib07.html>.

Heyen, William. *Diana, Charles, and the Queen.* Rochester: BOA Editions, 1998.

Hossaini, Ali. *Tribute to a Princess.* 4 September 1997. 9 July 1999 <http://www.zdnet.com/zdtv/thesite/0097w1/life/life846_090497.html>.

Hynes, Samuel Lynn. *The Soldier's Tale: Bearing Witness to Modern War.* New York: Lane, 1997.

Johnson, Richard. "Exemplary Differences: Mourning (and Not Mourning) a Princess." *Mourning Diana: Nation, Culture and the Performance of Grief.* Ed. Adrian Kear and Deborah Lynn Steinberg. New York: Routledge, 1999. 15–39.

Kear, Adrian. "Diana Between Two Deaths: Spectral Ethics and the Time of Mourning." *Mourning Diana: Nation, Culture and the Performance of Grief.* Ed. Adrian Kear and Deborah Lynn Steinberg. New York: Routledge, 1999. 169–186.

Kear, Adrian, and Deborah Steinberg. "Ghost Writing." *Mourning Diana: Nation, Culture and the Performance of Grief.* Ed. Adrian Kear and Deborah Lynn Steinberg. New York: Routledge, 1999. 1–14.

Marvelicious. *Goodbye England's Rose.* 28 June 1998 <http://www.marvelcreations.com/diana.html>.

McDannell, Colleen. *Material Christianity: Religion and Popular Culture in America.* New Haven: Yale UP, 1995.

Merck, Mandy, ed. *After Diana: Irreverent Elegies.* New York: Verso, 1998.

Net Angel. *Forever Young: A Tribute to Diana, Princess of Wales, 1961–1997.* 28 June 1998 <http://pages.prodigy.com/Diana/>.

Oates, Joyce Carol. "The Love She Searched For." *Time Online.* 15 September 1997. 29 June 1998 <http://www.pathfinder.com/time/magazine/1997/dom/970915/princess.the_love_she.htm>.

Paulin, Nicholas. "Remembering, 1961–1997." *The Death of a Fairy Tale Princess.* 28 June 1998 <http://www.geocities.com/RainForest/Vines/1009/remember.htm>.

Roach, Joseph. *Cities of the Dead: Circum-Atlantic Performance.* New York: Columbia UP, 1996.

Rubenstein, Diane. "'That's the Way the Mercedes Benz': Di, Wound Culture and Fatal Fetishism." *Theory and Event* 1.4 (1997): 8 pars. <http://muse.jhu.edu/journals/theory_&_event/v001/1.4rubenstein.html>.

Sacks, Peter M. *The British Elegy: Studies in the Genre from Spenser to Yeats.* Baltimore: Johns Hopkins UP, 1985.

Simons, Jon. "The Dialectics of Diana as Empty Signifier." *Theory and Event* 1.4 (1997): 15 pars. <http://muse.jhu.edu/journals/theory_&_event/v001/1.4simons.html>.

Smith, Sally Bedell. *Diana in Search of Herself: Portrait of a Troubled Princess.* New York: Random House, 1999.

Sperry, Bill, Jr. *Memorial for Lady Diana Frances Spencer.* 23 July 1999 <http://www.goldengatecountry.com/dilast.htm>.

Spurlin, William J. "I'd Rather Be the Princess Than the Queen! Mourning Diana as a Gay Icon." *Mourning Diana: Nation, Culture and the Performance of Grief.* Ed. Adrian Kear and Deborah Lynn Steinberg. New York: Routledge, 1999. 155–168.

Stroupe, Craig. "Visualizing English: Recognizing the Hybrid Literacy of Visual and Verbal Authorship on the Web." *College English* 62.5 (2000): 607–632.

Walter, Tony, Ed. *The Mourning for Diana.* Oxford and New York: Berg, 1999.

Williamson, Judith. "A Glimpse of the Void." *After Diana: Irreverent Elegies.* Ed. Mandy Merck. New York: Verso, 1998, 25–28.

Wilson, Scott. "The Indestructible Beauty of Suffering: Diana and the Metaphor of Global Consumption." *Theory and Event* 1.4 (1997): 22 pars. <http://muse.jhu.edu/journals/theory_&_event/v001/1.4wilson.html>.

Zizek, Slavoj. *The Plague of Fantasies.* London: Verso, 1997.

■ ■ ■

Reading Rhetorically

1. Throughout her essay, Helmers signposts, saying explicitly what she is doing in the essay and why. Locate and underline all the signposts you find in this essay, and, in class, discuss the relationship you see between these signposts and Helmers's central argument. What is the central argument of the essay? Where do you find it?

2. In paragraph 5, Helmers claims that "Diana is a heuristic prompting writing that is historical, biographical, and autobiographical." Look up the word *heuristic*, and then figure out the meaning of this sentence. How does it relate to Helmers's goal in this essay?

3. How effective do you find the evidence that Helmers presents in this essay? Locate two places where Helmers quotes from Web sites. Underline sentences where she frames these examples with her own argument, and evaluate how persuasive you find the connections she makes between the specific language of her examples and her larger point. What is the effect of Helmers's decision to leave the grammatical and spelling errors in these examples?

Inquiring Further

4. Helmers did her research for this article between 1997 and 1999, and the sites she examines no longer exist. However, there are many current sites devoted to memorializing Diana. A basic Internet search for "Princess Diana memorial Web sites" will bring up many possibilities. Choose a few to examine closely. How well are Helmers's claims supported by the material you find? Present to the class specific examples of visual and written material on the sites that confirm, extend, or contradict Helmers's argument. What conclusions can you draw?

5. Using Helmers's analytical strategy as your model, examine the cultural narratives you find in the electronic memorials to another celebrity who has recently died. What contradictory images and stories appear? What public functions do the sites serve? Share your findings with the class.

6. Locate one of the sources from Helmers's extensive list of works cited and read it. Prepare a short presentation for your class on how Helmers uses

the information in the source to develop her argument. How effectively do you think she uses the information? Teach your classmates one or two ideas from the source that Helmers doesn't use but that apply to discussions your class has had about this or other readings.

Framing Conversations

7. Both Helmers and Henry Jenkins (below) are fascinated by the potential and limitations of cyberspace. In particular, they focus on the way technological spaces reinforce gender roles — or, instead, unsettle such roles by raising questions, or opening new possibilities. Write an essay in which you draw on both authors' ideas about cyberspace as a place to experiment with authorship, fantasies, and game playing. According to each author, what are the possibilities and problems of cyberspace? Include your own perspective in this conversation.

8. Like Helmers, Cynthia Selfe (p. 783) finds meaning in the visual aspect of technology — in the images that appear on Web sites and in advertisements for technological products. Write an essay in which you draw on both authors' insights about the ways traditional images take on new meaning in technological contexts. How do images contribute to the ways technology reinforces old ideas and produces new ideas? What stories do these images tell about our hopes and fears? To support your argument, you can draw on the images described in Helmers's and Selfe's works as well as images from Web sites or advertisements you find on your own.

9. Helmers defends her interest in memorial Web sites by claiming that the sites make an important contribution to cultural knowledge: "If cultural literacy means coming to terms with the texts that confront us in daily life, these memorial home pages are just such texts" (para. 8). Mark Edmundson (p. 277) and Mary Louise Pratt (p. 354) also are interested in what "counts" as knowledge and how the analysis of nonscholarly texts (movies, baseball cards, Web sites) might be part of becoming culturally literate. Write an essay in which you stake out your own position in this debate, drawing on the insights of these three authors. What are the implications for education if we believe that analyzing nonscholarly texts is important, or not important, to becoming an educated person?

■ HENRY JENKINS

"Complete Freedom of Movement": Video Games as Gendered Play Spaces

Henry Jenkins is a professor of humanities and the director of the MIT Comparative Media Studies Program. He publishes frequently on a diverse range of media topics, from *World Wide Wrestling* and *Star Trek* fandom, to comic books and computer game culture . . . to name just a few. He is the author and editor of ten books, including *Textual Poachers: Television Fans and Participatory Culture* (1992), *The Children's Culture Reader* (1998), and *Hop on Pop: The Politics and Pleasures of Popular Culture* (2003). Jenkins approaches the study of popular culture from the perspective of both academic and fan. In fact, he calls his topical blog "Confessions of an Aca-Fan," an aca-fan being someone who enjoys and participates in the popular media he or she analyzes as a scholar. His newer books, *Convergence Culture: Where Old and New Media Collide, The Wow Climax: Tracing the Emotional Impact of Popular Culture,* and *Fans, Bloggers, and Gamers: Exploring Participatory Culture* were all published in 2006, which gives you a sense of how prolific he is. He describes himself as a workaholic but notes that he loves media studies so much that his work feels like play. Reviewers of his writing tend to agree that Jenkins's ideas are rigorous and well grounded in research, and his prose is so lively and engaging that it is clear he is having a wonderful time thinking through the significance of topics like gaming culture, the audience response to *American Idol,* and blogging.

Because of his expertise in gender and video game culture, Jenkins was asked to testify before the U.S. Senate Commerce Committee after the Columbine High School shootings. He has argued for more media literacy in schools and frequently speaks to the press on topics relating to children's media, particularly online games and other kinds of cyberinteraction. Visit his Web site (http://henryjenkins.org/) for a sense of his interests and his playful approach to those interests.

This essay appeared in *From Barbie to Mortal Kombat: Gender and Computer Games* (1998) which Jenkins coedited with Justine Cassell. Jenkins's subject here is the way computer culture has become yet one more gendered space — that is, with few exceptions, computer games simply reinforce cultural stereotypes about things boys like to do versus things girls like to do. He examines what he calls the "cultural geography of video game spaces" (para. 9), looking at the gender-divided history of child's play and the ways digital culture has maintained that division despite the potential to offer many alternatives. But Jenkins refuses to "blame video games for problems they do not cause" (para. 12). As he points out, "video games did not make backyard play spaces disappear; rather, they offer children some way to respond to domestic confinement" (para. 12).

As an academic, Jenkins grounds his analysis of digital games in a lot of research. Flip to the end of the essay, and you will see the long list of scholars whose ideas undergird Jenkins's own. As you read, notice how he uses these authors to help "unpack," or explain, the details in the computer games he analyzes. Notice too how he uses these authors to make observations he would not be able to make without their ideas.

It may be impossible to read this essay without thinking about all the computer games you have played. Don't resist the urge! Instead, keep your gaming experiences in mind, and use them to give context to — and perhaps test the limits of — Jenkins's ideas about the pluses and minuses of digital culture and how it often falls short of what is possible.

A Tale of Two Childhoods

Sometimes, I feel nostalgic for the spaces of my boyhood, growing up in   *1*
suburban Atlanta in the 1960s. My big grassy front yard sloped sharply
downward into a ditch where we could float boats on a rainy day. Beyond,
there was a pine forest where my brother and I could toss pine cones like
grenades or snap sticks together like swords. In the backyard, there was a
patch of grass where we could wrestle or play kickball and a treehouse,
which sometimes bore a pirate flag and at other times, the Stars and Bars
of the Confederacy. Out beyond our own yard, there was a bamboo forest
where we could play Tarzan, and vacant lots, construction sites, sloping
streets, and a neighboring farm (the last vestige of a rural area turned
suburban).

Between my house and the school, there was another forest, which,   *2*
for the full length of my youth, remained undeveloped. A friend and I would
survey this land, claiming it for our imaginary kingdoms of Jungleloca and
Freedonia. We felt a proprietorship over that space, even though others
used it for schoolyard fisticuffs, smoking cigarettes, or playing kissing games.
When we were there, we rarely encountered adults, though when we did, it
usually spelled trouble. We would come home from these secret places,
covered with Georgia red mud.

Of course, we spent many afternoons at home, watching old horror   *3*
movies or action-adventure series reruns, and our mothers would fuss at
us to go outside. Often, something we had seen on television would inspire
our play, stalking through the woods like Lon Chaney Jr.'s Wolfman or
"socking" and "powing" each other under the influence of *Batman*.

Today, each time I visit my parents, I am shocked to see that most of   *4*
those "sacred" places are now occupied by concrete, bricks, or asphalt.
They managed to get a whole subdivision out of Jungleloca and Freedonia!

My son, Henry, now 16, has never had a backyard.   *5*

He has grown up in various apartment complexes, surrounded by   *6*
asphalt parking lots with, perhaps, a small grass buffer from the street.
Children were prohibited by apartment policy from playing on the grass or
from racing their tricycles in the basements or from doing much of anything else that might make noise, annoy the non-childbearing population,
cause damage to the facilities, or put themselves at risk. There was, usually, a city park some blocks away that we could go to on outings a few
times a week and where we could watch him play. Henry could claim no
physical space as his own, except his toy-strewn room, and he rarely got
outside earshot. Once or twice, when I became exasperated by my son's
constant presence around the house, I would forget all this and tell him he
should go outside and play. He would look at me with confusion and ask
"Where?"

But, he did have video games which took him across lakes of fire,   *7*
through cities in the clouds, along dark and gloomy back streets, and into

dazzling neon-lit Asian marketplaces. Video games constitute virtual play spaces which allow home-bound children like my son to extend their reach, to explore, manipulate, and interact with a more diverse range of imaginary places than constitute the often drab, predictable, and overly familiar spaces of their everyday lives. Keith Feinstein (1997), President of the Video Game Conservatory, argues that video games preserve many aspects of traditional play spaces and culture that motivate children to

> learn about the environment that they find themselves living in. Video games present the opportunity to explore and discover, as well as to combat others of comparable skill (whether they be human or electronic) and to struggle with them in a form that is similar to children wrestling, or scrambling for the same ball — they are nearly matched, they aren't going to really do much damage, yet it feels like an all-important fight for that child at that given moment. "Space Invaders" gives us visceral thrill and poses mental/physical challenges similar to a schoolyard game of dodge-ball (or any of the hundreds of related kids' games). Video games play with us, a never tiring playmate.

Feinstein's comment embraces some classical conceptions of play (such as spatial exploration and identity formation), suggesting that video game play isn't fundamentally different from backyard play. To facilitate such immersive play, to achieve an appropriate level of "holding power" that enables children to transcend their immediate environments, video game spaces require concreteness and vividness. The push in the video game industry for more than a decade has been toward the development of more graphically complex, more visually engaging, more three-dimensionally rendered spaces, and toward quicker, more sophisticated, more flexible interactions with those spaces. Video games tempt the player to play longer, putting more and more quarters into the arcade machine (or providing "play value" for those who've bought the game) by unveiling ever more spectacular "microworlds," the revelation of a new level the reward for having survived and mastered the previous environment (Fuller and Jenkins 1995).

Video games advertise themselves as taking us places very different [8] from where we live:

> Say hello to life in the fast lane. "Sonic R" for Sega Saturn is a full-on, pedal-to-the-metal hi-speed dash through five 3D courses, each rendered in full 360 degree panoramas. . . . You'll be flossing bug guts out of your teeth for weeks. ("Sonic R" 1998)

> Take a dip in these sub-infested waters for a spot of nuclear fishin' . . . Don't worry. You'll know you're in too deep when the water pressure caves your head in. ("Critical Depth" 1998)

> Hack your way through a savage world or head straight for the arena. . . . Complete freedom of movement. ("Die by the Sword" 1998)

> Strap in and throttle up as you whip through the most realistic and immersive powerboat racing game ever made. Jump over roadways, and through passing convoys, or speed between oil tankers, before they close off the track and turn your boat to splinters. Find a shortcut and take the lead, or better yet, secure

your victory and force your opponent into a river barge at 200 miles per hour. ("VR Sports" 1998)

Who wouldn't want to trade in the confinement of your room for the immersion promised by today's video games? Watch children playing these games, their bodies bobbing and swaying to the on-screen action, and it's clear they are *there* — in the fantasy world, battling it out with the orcs and goblins, pushing their airplanes past the sound barrier, or splashing their way through the waves in their speed boats. Perhaps my son finds in his video games what I found in the woods behind the school, on my bike whizzing down the hills of the suburban back streets, or settled into my treehouse during a thunder storm with a good adventure novel — intensity of experience, escape from adult regulation; in short, "complete freedom of movement."

This essay will offer a cultural geography of video game spaces, one   *9* which uses traditional children's play and children's literature as points of comparison to the digital worlds contemporary children inhabit. Specifically, I examine the "fit" between video games and traditional boy culture and review several different models for creating virtual play spaces for girls. So much of the research on gender and games takes boy's fascination with these games as a given. As we attempt to offer video games for girls, we need to better understand what draws boys to video games and whether our daughters should feel that same attraction.

Video games are often blamed for the listlessness or hyperactivity of   *10* our children, yet sociologists find these same behavioral problems occurring among all children raised in highly restrictive and confined physical environments (Booth and Johnson 1975; van Staden 1984). Social reformers sometimes speak of children choosing to play video games rather than playing outside, when, in many cases, no such choice is available. More and more Americans live in urban or semi-urban neighborhoods. Fewer of us own our homes and more of us live in apartment complexes. Fewer adults have chosen to have children and our society has become increasingly hostile to the presence of children. In many places, "no children" policies severely restrict where parents can live. Parents, for a variety of reasons, are frightened to have their children on the streets, and place them under "protective custody." "Latch key" children return from school and lock themselves in their apartments (Kincheloe 1997).

In the nineteenth century, children living along the frontier or on   *11* America's farms enjoyed free range over a space often square miles or more. Elliot West (1992) describes boys of nine or ten going camping alone for days on end, returning when they were needed to do chores around the house. The early twentieth century saw the development of urban playgrounds in the midst of city streets, responding to a growing sense of children's diminishing access to space and an increased awareness of issues of child welfare (Cavallo 1991), but autobiographies of the period stress the availability of vacant lots and back alleys that children could claim as their own play environments. Sociologists writing about the suburban America of my boyhood found that children enjoyed a play terrain of one to five blocks of spacious backyards and relatively safe subdivision streets (Hart 1979). Today, at the end of the twentieth century, many of our children have access to the one to five rooms inside their apartments. Video game technologies expand the space of their imagination.

Let me be clear — I am not arguing that video games are as good for   *12* kids as the physical spaces of backyard play culture. As a father, I wish that my son could come home covered in mud or with scraped knees rather than carpet burns. However, we sometimes blame video games for problems they do not cause — perhaps because of our own discomfort with these technologies, which were not part of our childhood. When politicians like Senator Joseph Liberman, Democrat of Connecticut, target video game violence, perhaps it is to distract attention from the material conditions that give rise to a culture of domestic violence, the economic policies that make it harder for most of us to own homes, and the development practices that pave over the old grasslands and forests. Video games did not make backyard play spaces disappear; rather, they offer children some way to respond to domestic confinement.

Moving Beyond "Home Base": Why Physical Spaces Matter

The psychological and social functions of playing outside are as significant   *13* as the impact of "sunshine and good exercise" upon our physical well-being. Roger Hart's *Children's Experience of Place* (1979), for example, stresses the importance of children's manipulations and explorations of their physical environment to their development of self-confidence and autonomy. Our physical surroundings are "relatively simple and relatively stable" compared to the "overwhelmingly complex and ever shifting" relations between people, and thus, they form core resources for identity formation. The unstructured spaces, the playforts and treehouses, children create for themselves in the cracks, gullies, back alleys, and vacant lots of the adult world constitute what Robin C. Moore (1986) calls "childhood's domain" or William Van Vliet (1983) has labeled as a "fourth environment," outside the adult-structured spaces of home, school, and playground. These informal, often temporary play spaces are where free and unstructured play occurs. Such spaces surface most often on the lists children make of "special" or "important" places in their lives. M.H. Matthews (1992) stresses the "topophilia," the heightened sense of belonging and ownership, children develop as they map their fantasies of empowerment and escape onto their neighborhoods. Frederick Donaldson (1970) proposed two different classifications of these spaces — home base, the world which is secure and familiar, and home region, an area undergoing active exploration, a space under the process of being colonized by the child. Moore (1986) writes:

> One of the clearest expressions of the benefits of continuity in the urban land-
> scape was the way in which children used it as an outdoor gymnasium. As I
> walked along a Mill Hill street with Paul, he continually went darting ahead,
> leapfrogging over concrete bollards, hopping between paving slabs, balancing
> along the curbside. In each study area, certain kids seemed to dance through
> their surroundings on the look out for microfeatures with which to test their
> bodies. . . . Not only did he [David, another boy in the study], like Paul, jump
> over gaps between things, go "tightrope walking" along the tops of walls,
> leapfrogging objects on sight, but at one point he went "mountain climbing"
> up a roughly built, nine-foot wall that had many serendipitously placed toe
> and handholds. (p. 72)

These discoveries arise from children's active exploration of and spontaneous engagement with their physical surroundings. Children in the same
neighborhoods may have fundamentally different relations to the spaces
they share, cutting their own paths, giving their own names to features of
their environment. These spaces are far more important, many researchers
conclude, than playgrounds, which can only be used in sanctioned ways,
since the "wild spaces" allow many more opportunities for children to
modify their physical environment.

Children's access to spaces are structured around gender differences. 14
Observing the use of space within 1970s suburban America, Hart (1979)
found that boys enjoyed far greater mobility and range than girls of the
same age and class background. In the course of an afternoon's play, a typical ten-to-twelve-year-old boy might travel a distance of 2,452 yards, while
the average ten-to-twelve-year-old girl might only travel 959 yards. For the
most part, girls expanded their geographic range only to take on responsibilities and perform chores for the family, while parents often turned a
blind eye to a boy's movements into prohibited spaces. The boys Hart
(1979) observed were more likely to move beyond their homes in search of
"rivers, forts and treehouses, woods, ballfields, hills, lawns, sliding places,
and climbing trees," while girls were more like to seek commercially developed spaces, such as stores or shopping malls. Girls were less likely than
boys to physically alter their play environment, to dam creeks or build
forts. Such gender differences in mobility, access, and control over physical space increased as children grew older. As C. Ward (1977) notes:

> Whenever we discuss the part the environment plays in the lives of children,
> we are really talking about boys. As a stereotype, the child in the city is a boy.
> Girls are far less visible. . . . The reader can verify this by standing in a city
> street at any time of day and counting the children seen. The majority will be
> boys. (p. 152)

One study found that parents were more likely to describe boys as being
"outdoors" children and girls as "indoor" children (Newson and Newson
1976). Another 1975 study (Rheingold and Cook), which inventoried the
contents of children's bedrooms, found boys more likely to possess a range

of vehicles and sports equipment designed to encourage outside play, while the girls' rooms were stocked with dolls, doll clothes, and other domestic objects. Parents of girls were more likely to express worries about the dangers their children face on the streets and to structure girls' time for productive household activities or educational play (Matthews 1992).

Historically, girl culture formed under closer maternal supervision 15 and girls' toys were designed to foster female-specific skills and competencies and prepare girls for their future domestic responsibilities as wives and mothers. The doll's central place in girlhood reflected maternal desires to encourage daughters to sew; the doll's china head and hands fostered delicate gestures and movements (Formanek-Brunnel 1998). However, these skills were not acquired without some resistance. Nineteenth-century girls were apparently as willing as today's girls to mistreat their dolls, by cutting their hair or by driving nails into their bodies.

If cultural geographers are right when they argue that children's abil- 16 ity to explore and modify their environments plays a large role in their growing sense of mastery, freedom, and self-confidence, then the restrictions placed on girls' play have a crippling effect. Conversely, this research would suggest that children's declining access to play space would have a more dramatic impact on the culture of young boys, since girls already faced domestic confinement.

Putting Boy Culture Back in the Home

> Clods were handy and the air was full of them in a twinkling. They raged around Sid like a hail storm; and before Aunt Polly could collect her surprised faculties and sally to the rescue, six or seven clods had taken personal effect, and Tom was over the fence and gone. . . . He presently got safely beyond the reach of capture and punishment, and hasted toward the public square of the village, where two "military" companies of boys had met for conflict, according to previous appointment. Tom was the general of one of these armies, Joe Harper (a bosom friend) general of the other. . . . Tom's army won a great victory, after a long and hard-fought battle. Then the dead were counted, prisoners exchanged, the terms of the next disagreement agreed upon, and the day for the necessary battle appointed; after which the armies fell into line and marched away, and Tom turned homeward alone. (pp. 19–20)
>
> — MARK TWAIN, *Adventures of Tom Sawyer* (1876)

What E. Anthony Rotundo (1994) calls "boy culture" resulted from the 17 growing separation of the male public sphere and the female private sphere in the wake of the industrial revolution. Boys were cut off from the work life of their fathers and left under the care of their mothers. According to Rotundo, boys escaped from the home into the outdoor play space, freeing them to participate in a semi-autonomous "boy culture" that cast itself in opposition to maternal culture:

> Where women's sphere offered kindness, morality, nurture and a gentle spirit, the boys' world countered with energy, self-assertion, noise, and a frequent

resort to violence. The physical explosiveness and the willingness to inflict pain contrasted so sharply with the values of the home that they suggest a dialogue in actions between the values of the two spheres — as if a boy's aggressive impulses, so relentlessly opposed at home, sought extreme forms of release outside it; then, with stricken consciences, the boys came home for further lessons in self-restraint. (p. 37)

The boys transgressed maternal prohibitions to prove they weren't "mama's boys." Rotundo argues that this break with the mother was a necessary step toward autonomous manhood. One of the many tragedies of our gendered division of labor may be the ways that it links misogyny — an aggressive fighting back against the mother — with the process of developing self-reliance. Contrary to the Freudian concept of the oedipal complex (which focuses on boys' struggles with their all-powerful fathers as the site of identity formation), becoming an adult male often means struggling with (and in many cases, actively repudiating) maternal culture. Fathers, on the other hand, offered little guidance to their sons, who, Rotundo argues, acquired masculine skills and values from other boys. By contrast, girls' play culture was often "interdependent" with the realm of their mother's domestic activities, insuring a smoother transition into anticipated adult roles, but allowing less autonomy.

What happens when the physical spaces of nineteenth-century boy [18] culture are displaced by the virtual spaces of contemporary video games? Cultural geographers have long argued that television is a poor substitute for backyard play, despite its potential to present children with a greater diversity of spaces than can be found in their immediate surroundings, precisely because it is a spectatorial rather than a participatory medium. Moore (1986), however, leaves open the prospect that a more interactive digital medium might serve *some* of the same developmental functions as backyard play. A child playing a video game, searching for the path around obstacles, or looking for an advantage over imaginary opponents, engages in many of the same "mapping" activities as children searching for affordances in their real-world environments. Rotundo's core claims about nineteenth-century boy culture hold true for the "video game culture" of contemporary boyhood. This congruence may help us to account for the enormous popularity of these games with young boys. This fit should not be surprising when we consider that the current game genres reflect intuitive choices by men who grew up in the 1960s and 1970s, when suburban boy culture still reigned.

The following are some points of comparison between traditional boy [19] culture and contemporary game culture:

1. Nineteenth-century boy culture was characterized by its independ- [20] ence from the realm of both mothers and fathers. It was a space where boys could develop autonomy and self-confidence.

Video game culture also carves out a cultural realm for modern-day [21] children separate from the space of their parents. They often play the games in their rooms and guard their space against parental intrusion. Parents often express a distaste for the games' pulpy plots and lurid images. As writers like Jon Katz (1997) and Don Tapscott (1997) note, children's relative comfort with digital media is itself a generational marker, with adults often unable to comprehend the movement and colored shapes of the video screen. Here, however, the loss of spatial mobility is acutely felt — the "bookworm," the boy who spent all of his time in his room reading, had a "mama's boy" reputation in the old boy culture. Modern-day boys have had to accommodate their domestic confinement with their definitions of masculinity, perhaps accounting, in part, for the hypermasculine and hyperviolent content of the games themselves. The game player has a fundamentally different image than the "bookworm."

2. In nineteenth-century boy culture, youngsters gained recognition 22 from their peers for their daring, often proven through stunts (such as swinging on vines, climbing trees, or leaping from rocks as they crossed streams) or through pranks (such as stealing apples or doing mischief aimed at adults).

In video game culture, children gain recognition for their daring as 23 demonstrated in the virtual worlds of the game, overcoming obstacles, beating bosses, and mastering levels. Nineteenth-century boys' trespasses on neighbors' property or confrontations with hostile shopkeepers are mirrored by the visual vocabulary of the video games, which often pit smaller protagonists against the might and menace of much larger rivals. Much as cultural geographers describe the boys' physical movements beyond their home bases into developing home territories, the video games allow boys to gradually develop their mastery over the entire digital terrain, securing their future access to spaces by passing goal posts or finding warp zones.

3. The central virtues of the nineteenth-century boy culture were mas- 24 tery and self-control. The boys set tasks and goals for themselves that required discipline in order to complete. Through this process of setting and meeting challenges, they acquired the virtues of manhood.

The central virtues of video game culture are mastery (over the techni- 25 cal skills required by the games) and self-control (manual dexterity). Putting in the long hours of repetition and failure necessary to master a game also requires discipline and the ability to meet and surpass self-imposed goals. Most contemporary video games are ruthlessly goal-driven. Boys will often play the games, struggling to master a challenging level, well past the point of physical and emotional exhaustion. Children are not so much "addicted" to video games as they are unwilling to quit before they have met their goals, and the games seem to always set new goal posts, inviting us to best "just one more level." One of the limitations of the contemporary video game is that it provides only prestructured forms of interactivity, and in that sense, video games are more like playgrounds and city parks rather than wild spaces. For the most part, video game players can only exploit built-in affordances and preprogrammed pathways.

"Secret codes," "Easter Eggs," and "warp zones" function in digital space like secret paths do in physical space and are eagerly sought by gamers who want to go places and see things others can't find.

4. The nineteenth-century boy culture was hierarchical, with a member's status dependent on competitive activity, direct confrontation, and physical challenges. The boy fought for a place in the gang's inner circle, hoping to win admiration and respect. 26

Video game culture can also be hierarchical, with a member gaining status by being able to complete a game or log a big score. Video game masters move from house to house to demonstrate their technical competency and to teach others how to "beat" particularly challenging levels. The video arcade becomes a proving ground for contemporary masculinity, while many games are designed for the arcade, demanding a constant turnover of coins for play and intensifying the action into roughly two-minute increments. Often, single-player games generate digital rivals who may challenge players to beat their speeds or battle them for dominance. 27

5. Nineteenth-century boy culture was sometimes brutally violent and physically aggressive; children hurt each other or got hurt trying to prove their mastery and daring. 28

Video game culture displaces this physical violence into a symbolic realm. Rather than beating each other up behind the school, boys combat imaginary characters, finding a potentially safer outlet for their aggressive feelings. We forget how violent previous boy culture was. Rotundo (1994) writes: 29

> The prevailing ethos of the boys' world not only supported the expression of impulses such as dominance and aggression (which had evident social uses), but also allowed the release of hostile, violent feelings (whose social uses were less evident). By allowing free passage to so many angry or destructive emotions, boy culture sanctioned a good deal of intentional cruelty, like the physical torture of animals and the emotional violence of bullying. . . . If at times boys acted like a hostile pack of wolves that preyed on its own kind as well as on other species, they behaved at other times like a litter of playful pups who enjoy romping, wrestling and testing new skills. (p. 45)

Even feelings of fondness and friendship were expressed through physical means, including greeting each other with showers of brickbats and offal. Such a culture is as violent as the world depicted in contemporary video games, which have the virtue of allowing growing boys to express their aggression and rambunctiousness through indirect, rather than direct, means.

6. Nineteenth-century boy culture expressed itself through scatological humor. Such bodily images (of sweat, spit, snot, shit, and blood) reflected the boys' growing awareness of their bodies and signified their rejection of maternal constraints. 30

Video game culture has often been criticized for its dependence upon 31
similar kinds of scatological images, with the blood and gore of games like
"Mortal Kombat" (with its "end moves" of dismemberment and decapitation), providing some of the most oft-cited evidence in campaigns to
reform video game content (Kinder 1996). Arguably, these images serve
the same functions for modern boys as for their nineteenth-century
counterparts — allowing an exploration of what it's like to live in our bodies and an expression of distance from maternal regulations. Like the earlier "boy culture," this scatological imagery sometimes assumes overtly
misogynistic form, directed against women as a civilizing or controlling
force, staged toward women's bodies as a site of physical difference and as
the objects of desire or distaste. Some early games, such as "Super
Metroid," rewarded player competence by forcing female characters to
strip down to their underwear if the boys beat a certain score.

7. Nineteenth-century boy culture depended on various forms of role- 32
playing, often imitating the activities of adult males. Rotundo (1994) notes
the popularity of games of settlers and Indians during an age when the frontier had only recently been closed, casting boys sometimes as their settler
ancestors and other times as "savages." Such play mapped the competitive
and combative boy-culture ethos onto the adult realm, thus exaggerating
the place of warfare in adult male lives. Through such play, children tested
alternative social roles, examined adult ideologies, and developed a firmer
sense of their own abilities and identities.

Video game culture depends heavily on fantasy role-playing, with dif- 33
ferent genres of games allowing children to imagine themselves in alternative social roles or situations. Most games, however, provide images of
heroic action more appropriate for the rugged individualism of nineteenth-century American culture than for the contemporary information-and-service economy. Boys play at being crime fighters, race-car drivers, and
fighter pilots, not at holding down desk jobs. This gap between the excitement of boyhood play and the alienation of adult labor may explain why
video game imagery seems so hyperbolic from an adult vantage point.
Rotundo (1994) notes, however, that there was always some gap between
boys and adult males:

> Boy culture emphasized exuberant spontaneity; it allowed free rein to aggressive impulses and reveled in physical prowess and assertion. Boy culture was a
> world of play, a social space where one evaded the duties and restrictions of
> adult society. . . . Men were quiet and sober, for theirs was a life of serious business. They had families to support, reputations to earn, responsibilities to
> meet. Their world was based on work, not play, and their survival in it depended
> on patient planning, not spontaneous impulse. To prosper, then, a man had to
> delay gratification and restrain desire. Of course, he also needed to be aggressive and competitive, and he needed an instinct for self-advancement. But he
> had to channel those assertive impulses in ways that were suitable to the abstract
> battles and complex issues of middle-class men's work. (p. 55)

Today, the boys are using the same technologies as their fathers, even if they are using them to pursue different fantasies.

8. In nineteenth-century boy culture, play activities were seen as opportunities for social interactions and bonding. Boys formed strong ties that were the basis for adult affiliations, for participation in men's civic clubs and fraternities, and for business partnerships. 34

The track record of contemporary video game culture providing a basis for similar social networking is more mixed. In some cases, the games constitute both play space and playmates, reflecting the physical isolation of contemporary children from each other. In other cases, the games provide the basis for social interactions at home, at school, and at the video arcades. Children talk about the games together, over the telephone or, now, over the Internet, as well as in person, on the playground, or at the school cafeteria. Boys compare notes, map strategies, share tips, and show off their skills, and this exchange of video game lore provides the basis for more complex social relations. Again, video games don't isolate children, but they fail, at the present time, to provide the technological basis for overcoming other social and cultural factors, such as working parents who are unable to bring children to each other's houses and enlarged school districts that make it harder to get together. 35

Far from a "corruption" of the culture of childhood, video games show strong continuities with the boyhood play fondly remembered by previous generations. There is a significant difference, however. The nineteenth-century "boy culture" enjoyed such freedom and autonomy precisely because the activities were staged within a larger expanse of space, because boys could occupy an environment largely unsupervised by adults. Nineteenth-century boys sought indirect means of breaking with their mothers by escaping to spaces that were outside their control and engaging in secret activities the boys knew would have met parental disapproval. The mothers, on the other hand, rarely had to confront the nature of this "boy culture" and often didn't even know that it existed. The video game culture, on the other hand, occurs in plain sight, in the middle of the family living room, or at best, in the children's rooms. Mothers come face to face with the messy process by which western culture turns boys into men. The games and their content become the focus of open antagonism and the subject of tremendous guilt and anxiety. Sega's Lee McEnany [1998] acknowledges that the overwhelming majority of complaints game companies receive come from mothers, and Ellen Seiter (1996) has noted that this statistic reflects the increased pressure placed on mothers to supervise and police children's relations to popular culture. Current attempts to police video game content reflect a long history of attempts to shape and regulate children's play culture, starting with the playground movements of progressive America and the organization of social groups for boys, 36 such as the Boy Scouts and Little League, which tempered the more rough-and-tumble qualities of boy culture and channeled them into games, sports, and other adult-approved pastimes.

Many of us might wish to foster a boy culture that allowed the expression 37 of affection or the display of empowerment through nonviolent channels, that disentangled the development of personal autonomy from the fostering of misogyny, and that encouraged boys to develop a more nurturing, less domineering attitude to their social and natural environments. These goals are worth pursuing. We can't simply adopt a "boys will be boys" attitude. However, one wonders about the consequences of such a policing action in a world that no longer offers "wild" outdoor spaces as a safety valve for boys to escape parental control. Perhaps our sons — and daughters — need an unpoliced space for social experimentation, a space where they can vent their frustrations and imagine alternative adult roles free of inhibiting parental pressure. The problem, of course, is that unlike the nineteenth-century boy culture, the video game culture is not a world children construct for themselves but rather a world made by adult companies and sold to children. There is no way that we can escape adult intervention in shaping children's play environments as long as those environments are built and sold rather than discovered and appropriated. As parents, we are thus implicated in our children's choice of play environments, whether we wish to be or not, and we need to be conducting a dialogue with our children about the qualities and values exhibited by these game worlds. One model would be for adults and children to collaborate in the design and development of video game spaces, in the process developing a conversation about the nature and meanings of the worlds being produced. Another approach (Cassell [1998]) would be to create tools to allow children to construct their own play spaces and then give them the freedom to do what they want. Right now, parents are rightly apprehensive about a play space that is outside their own control and that is shaped according to adult specifications but without their direct input.

One of the most disturbing aspects of the boy culture is its gender seg- 38 regation. The nineteenth-century boy culture played an essential role in preparing boys for entry into their future professional roles and responsibilities; some of that same training has also become essential for girls at a time when more and more women are working outside the home. The motivating force behind the "girls' game" movement is the idea that girls, no less than boys, need computers at an early age if they are going to be adequately prepared to get "good jobs for good wages" (Jenkins and Cassell [1998]). Characteristically, the girls' game movement has involved the transposition of traditional feminine play cultures into the digital realm. However, in doing so, we run the risk of preserving, rather than transforming, those aspects of traditional "girl culture" which kept women restricted to the domestic sphere while denying them the spatial exploration and mastery associated with boy culture. Girls, no less than boys, need to develop an exploratory mindset, a habit of seeking unknown spaces as opposed to settling placidly into the domestic sphere.

Gendered Games/Gendered Books: Toward a Cultural Geography of Imaginary Spaces

These debates about gendered play and commercial entertainment are not new, repeating (and in a curious way, reversing) the emergence of a gender-specific set of literary genres for children in the nineteenth century. As Elizabeth Segel (1986) notes, the earliest writers of children's books were mostly women, who saw the genre as "the exercise of feminine moral 'influence'" upon children's developing minds, and who created a literature that was undifferentiated according to gender but "domestic in setting, heavily didactic and morally or spiritually uplifting" (p. 171). In other words, the earliest children's books were "girls' books" in everything but name, which isn't surprising at a time novel reading was still heavily associated with women. The "boys' book" emerged, in the mid-nineteenth century, as "men of action," industrialists and adventurers, wrote fictions intended to counter boys' restlessness and apathy towards traditional children's literature. The introduction of boys' books reflected a desire to get boys to read. Boy-book fantasies of action and adventure reflected the qualities of their pre-existing play culture, fantasies centering around "the escape from domesticity and from the female domination of the domestic world" (Segel 1986, p. 171). If the girls' game movement has involved the rethinking of video game genres (which initially emerged in a male-dominated space) in order to make digital media more attractive to girls (and thus to encourage the development of computational skills), the boys' book movement sought to remake reading (which initially emerged in a female-dominated space) to respond to male needs (and thus to encourage literacy). In both cases, the goal seems to have been to construct fantasies that reflect the gender-specific nature of children's play and thus to motivate those left out of the desirable cultural practices to get more involved. In this next section, I will consider the continuity that exists between gender/genre configurations in children's literature and in the digital games marketplace.

Adventure Islands: Boy Space

> Alex looked around him. There was no place to seek cover. He was too weak to run, even if there was. His gaze returned to the stallion, fascinated by a creature so wild and so near. Here was the wildest of all wild animals — he had fought for everything he had ever needed, for food, for leadership, for life itself; it was his nature to kill or be killed. The horse reared again; then he snorted and plunged straight for the boy. (p. 27)
>
> — Walter Farley, *The Black Stallion* (1941)

The space of the boy book is the space of adventure, risk-taking and danger, of a wild and untamed nature that must be mastered if one is to survive. The space of the boy book offers "no place to seek cover," and thus encourages fight-or-flight responses. In some cases, most notably in the works of Mark Twain, the boy books represented a nostalgic documentation of nineteenth-century "boy culture," its spaces, its activities, and its values. In other cases, as in the succession of pulp adventure stories that form the background of the boys' game genres, the narratives offered us a larger-than-life enactment of those values, staged in exotic rather than backyard spaces, involving broader movements through space and amplifying horseplay and risk-taking into scenarios of actual combat and conquest. Writers of boys' books found an easy fit between the ideologies of American "manifest destiny" and British colonialism and the adventure stories boys preferred to read, which often took the form of quests, journeys, or adventures into untamed and uncharted regions of the world — into the frontier of the American west (or in the twentieth century, the "final frontier" of Mars and beyond), into the exotic realms of Africa, Asia, and South America. The protagonists were boys or boy-like adult males, who had none of the professional responsibilities and domestic commitments associated with adults. The heroes sought adventure by running away from home to join the circus (*Toby Tyler*), to sign up as cabin boy on a ship (*Treasure Island*), or to seek freedom by rafting down the river (*Huckleberry Finn*). They confronted a hostile and untamed environment (as when *The Jungle Book*'s Mowgli must battle "tooth and claw" with the tiger, Sheer Khan, or as when Jack London's protagonists faced the frozen wind of the Yukon). They were shipwrecked on islands, explored caves, searched for buried treasure, plunged harpoons into slick-skinned whales, or set out alone across the desert, the bush, or the jungle. They survived through their wits, their physical mastery, and their ability to use violent force. Each chapter offered a sensational set piece — an ambush by wild Indians, an encounter with a coiled cobra, a landslide, a stampede, or a sea battle — that placed the protagonist at risk and tested his skills and courage. The persistent images of blood-and-guts combat and cliffhanging risks compelled boys to keep reading, making their blood race with promises of thrills and more thrills. This rapid pace allowed little room for moral and emotional introspection. In turn, such stories provided fantasies that boys could enact upon their own environments. Rotundo (1994) describes nineteenth-century boys playing pirates, settlers and Indians, or Roman warriors, roles drawn from boys' books.

The conventions of the nineteenth- and early-twentieth-century boys' adventure story provided the basis for the current video game genres. The most successful console game series, such as Capcom's "Mega Man" or Nintendo's "Super Mario Brothers" games, combine the iconography of multiple boys' book genres. Their protagonists struggle across an astonishingly eclectic range of landscapes — deserts, frozen wastelands, tropical rain forests, urban undergrounds — and encounter resistance from strange hybrids (who manage to be animal, machine, and savage all rolled into one). The scroll games have built into them the constant construction of frontiers — home regions — that the boy player must struggle to master and push beyond, moving deeper and deeper into uncharted space. Action is relentless. The protagonist shoots fireballs, ducks and charges, slugs it out, rolls, jumps, and dashes across the treacherous terrain, never certain what lurks around the corner. If you stand still, you die. Everything you encounter is potentially hostile, so shoot to kill. Errors in judgment result in the character's death and require starting all over again. Each screen overflows with dangers; each landscape is riddled with pitfalls and booby traps. One screen may require you to leap from precipice to precipice, barely missing falling into the deep chasms below. Another may require you to swing by vines across the treetops, or spelunk through an underground passageway, all the while fighting it out with the alien hordes. The games' levels and worlds reflect the set-piece structure of the earlier boys' books. Boys get to make lots of noise on adventure island, with the soundtrack full of pulsing music, shouts, groans, zaps, and bomb blasts. Everything is streamlined: the plots and characters are reduced to genre archetypes, immediately familiar to the boy gamers, and defined more through their capacity for actions than anything else. The "adventure island" is the archetypal space of both the boys' books and the boys' games — an isolated world far removed from domestic space or adult supervision, an untamed world for people who refuse to bow before the pressures of the civilizing process, a never-never-land where you seek your fortune. The "adventure island," in short, is a world that fully embodies the boy culture and its ethos.

Secret Gardens: Girl Space

> If it was the key to the closed garden, and she could find out where the door was, she could perhaps open it and see what was inside the walls, and what had happened to the old rose-trees. It was because it had been shut up so long that she wanted to see it. It seemed as if it must be different from other places and that something strange must have happened to it during ten years. Besides that, if she liked it she could go into it every day and shut the door behind her, and she could make up some play of her own and play it quite alone, because nobody would ever know where she was, but would think the door was still locked and the key buried in the earth. (p. 71)
>
> — FRANCES HODGSON BURNETT, *The Secret Garden* (1911)

Girl space is a space of secrets and romance, a space of one's own in a world that offers girls far too little room to explore. Ironically, "girl books" often open with fantasies of being alone and then require the female protagonist to sacrifice her private space in order to make room for others' needs. Genres aimed specifically at girls were slower to evolve, often emerging through imitation of the gothics and romances preferred by adult women readers and retaining a strong aura of instruction and self-improvement. As Segel (1986) writes:

> The liberation of nineteenth-century boys into the book world of sailors and pirates, forest and battles, left their sisters behind in the world of

childhood — that is, the world of home and family. When publishers and writers saw the commercial possibilities of books for girls, it is interesting that they did not provide comparable escape reading for them (that came later, with the pulp series books) but instead developed books designed to persuade the young reader to accept the confinement and self-sacrifice inherent in the doctrine of feminine influence. This was accomplished by depicting the rewards of submission and the sacred joys of serving as "the angel of the house." (pp. 171–172)

If the boys' book protagonist escapes all domestic responsibilities, the girls' book heroine learned to temper her impulsiveness and to accept family and domestic obligations (*Little Women, Anne of Green Gables*) or sought to be a healing influence on a family suffering from tragedy and loss (*Rebecca of Sunnybrook Farm*). Segel (1986) finds the most striking difference between the two genre traditions in the books' settings: "the domestic confinement of one book as against the extended voyage to exotic lands in the other" (p. 173). Avoiding the purple prose of the boys' books, the girls' books describe naturalistic environments, similar to the realm of readers' daily experience. The female protagonists take emotional, but rarely physical, risks. The tone is more apt to be confessional than confrontational.

Traditional girls' books, such as *The Secret Garden*, do encourage some   43 forms of spatial exploration, an exploration of the hidden passages of unfamiliar houses or the rediscovery and cultivation of a deserted rose garden. Norman N. Holland and Leona F. Sherman (1986) emphasize the role of spatial exploration in the gothic tradition, a "maiden-plus-habitation" formula whose influence is strongly felt in *The Secret Garden*. In such stories, the exploration of space leads to the uncovering of secrets, clues, and symptoms that shed light on characters' motivations. Hidden rooms often contain repressed memories and, sometimes, entombed relatives. The castle, Holland and Sherman (1986) note, "can threaten, resist, love or confine, but in all these actions, it stands as a total environment" (p. 220) that the female protagonist can never fully escape. Holland and Sherman claim that gothic romances fulfill a fantasy of unearthing secrets about the adult world, casting the reader in a position of powerlessness and daring her to overcome her fears and confront the truth. Such a fantasy space is, of course, consistent with what we have already learned about girls' domestic confinement and greater responsibilities to their families.

Purple Moon's "Secret Paths in the Forest" fully embodies the juvenile   44 gothic tradition — while significantly enlarging the space open for girls to explore. Purple Moon removes the walls around the garden, turning it into woodlands. Producer Brenda Laurel has emphasized girls' fascination with secrets, a fascination that readily translates into a puzzle game structure, though "Secret Paths" pushes further than existing games to give these "secrets" social and psychological resonance. Based on her focus-group interviews, Laurel initially sought to design a "magic garden," a series of "romanticized natural environments" responsive to "girls' highly touted nurturing desires, their fondness for animals." She wanted to create a place "where girls could explore, meet, and take care of creatures, design and grow magical or fantastical plants" (personal correspondence, 1997). What she found was that the girls did not feel magical animals would need their nurturing, and in fact, many of the girls wanted the animals to mother them. The girls in Laurel's study, however, were drawn to the idea of the secret garden or hidden forest as a "girls only" place for solitude and introspection. Laurel explains:

> Girls' first response to the place was that they would want to go there alone, to be peaceful and perhaps read or daydream. They might take a best friend, but they would never take an adult or a boy. They thought that the garden/forest would be a place where they could find out things that would be important to them, and a place where they might meet a wise or magical person. Altogether their fantasies were about respite and looking within as opposed to frolicsome play. (personal correspondence, 1997)

The spaces in Purple Moon's game are quiet, contemplative places, rendered in naturalistic detail but with the soft focus and warm glow of an impressionistic watercolor.

The world of "Secret Paths" explodes with subtle and inviting colors — *45* the colors of a forest on a summer afternoon, of spring flowers and autumn leaves and shifting patterns of light, of rippling water and moonlit skies, of sand and earth. The soundtrack is equally dense and engaging, as the natural world whispers to us in the rustle of the undergrowth or sings to us in the sounds of the wind and the calls of birds. The spaces of "Secret Paths" are full of life, as lizards slither from rock to rock, or field mice dart for cover, yet even animals which might be frightening in other contexts (coyotes, foxes, owls) seem eager to reveal their secrets to our explorers. Jessie, one of the game's protagonists, expresses a fear of the "creepy" nighttime woods, but the game makes the animals seem tame and the forest safe, even in the dead of night. The game's puzzles reward careful exploration and observation. At one point, we must cautiously approach a timid fawn if we wish to be granted the magic jewels that are the tokens of our quest. The guidebook urges us to be "unhurried and gentle" with the "easily startled" deer.

Our goal is less to master nature than to understand how we might live *46* in harmony with it. We learn to mimic its patterns, to observe the notes (produced by singing cactus) that make a lizard's head bob with approval and then to copy them ourselves, to position spiders on a web so that they may harmonize rather than create discord. And, in some cases, we are rewarded for feeding and caring for the animals. In *The Secret Garden* (1911), Mary Lennox is led by a robin to the branches that mask the entrance to the forgotten rose garden:

> Mary had stepped close to the robin, and suddenly the gusts of wind swung aside some loose ivy trails, and more suddenly still she jumped toward it and caught it in her hand. This she did because she had seen something under it — a round knob which had been covered by the leaves hanging over it. . . . The robin kept singing and twittering away and tilting his head on one side, as if he were as excited as she was. (p. 80)

Such animal guides abound in "Secret Paths": the cursor is shaped like a ladybug during our explorations and like a butterfly when we want to venture beyond the current screen. Animals show us the way, if we only take the time to look and listen.

Unlike twitch-and-shoot boys' games, "Secret Paths" encourages us to 47 stroke and caress the screen with our cursor, clicking only when we know where secret treasures might be hidden. A magic book tells us:

> As I patiently traveled along [through the paths], I found that everything was enchanted! The trees, flowers and animals, the sun, sky and stars — all had magical properties! The more closely I listened and the more carefully I explored, the more was revealed to me.

Nature's rhythms are gradual and recurring, a continual process of birth, growth, and transformation. Laurel explains:

> We made the "game" intentionally slow — a girl can move down the paths at whatever pace, stop and play with puzzles or stones, or hang out in the tree house with or without the other characters. I think that this slowness is really a kind of refuge for the girls. The game is much slower than television, for example. One of the issues that girls have raised with us in our most recent survey of their concerns is the problem of feeling too busy. I think that "Secret Paths" provides an antidote to that feeling from the surprising source of the computer. (personal correspondence, 1997)

Frances Hodgson Burnett's secret garden is a place of healing, and the 48 book links Mary's restoration of the forgotten rose garden with her repairing a family torn apart by tragedy, restoring a sickly boy to health, and coming to grips with her mother's death:

> So long as Mistress Mary's mind was full of disagreeable thoughts about her dislikes and sour opinions of people and her determination not to be pleased by or interested in anything, she was a yellow-faced, sickly, bored and wretched child. . . . When her mind gradually filled itself with robins, and moorland cottages crowded with children . . . with springtime and with secret gardens coming alive day by day . . . there was no room for the disagreeable thoughts which affected her liver and her digestion and made her yellow and tired. (p. 294)

Purple Moon's "Secret Paths" has also been designed as a healing place, where girls are encouraged to "explore with your heart" and answer their emotional dilemmas. As the magical book explains, "You will never be alone here, for this is a place where girls come to share and to seek help from one another." At the game's opening, we draw together a group of female friends in the treehouse, where each confesses her secrets and tells of her worries and sufferings. Miko speaks of the pressure to always be the best and the alienation she feels from the other children; Dana recounts her rage over losing a soccer championship; Minn describes her humiliation because her immigrant grandmother has refused to assimilate new-world customs. Some of them have lost parents, others face scary situations or emotional slights that cripple their confidence. Their answers lie along the secret paths through the forest, where the adventurers can find hidden magical stones that embody social, psychological, or emotional strengths. Along the way, the girls' secrets are literally embedded within the landscape, so that clicking on our environment may call forth memories or confessions. If we are successful in finding all of the hidden stones, they magically form a necklace that, when given to the right girl, allows us to hear a comforting or clarifying story. Such narratives teach girls how to find emotional resources within themselves and how to observe and respond to others' often unarticulated needs. Solving puzzles in the physical environment helps us to address problems in our social environment. "Secret Paths" is what Brenda Laurel calls a "friendship adventure," allowing young girls to rehearse their coping skills and try alternative social strategies.

The Play Town: Another Space for Girls?

> Harriet was trying to explain to Sport how to play Town. "See, first you make up the name of the town. Then you write down the names of all the people who live in it. . . . Then when you know who lives there, you make up what they do. For instance, Mr. Charles Hanley runs the filling station on the corner. . . ." Harriet got very businesslike. She stood up, then got on her knees in the soft September mud so she could lean over the little valley made between the two big roots of the tree. She referred to her notebook every now and then, but for the most part she stared intently at the mossy lowlands which made her town. (pp. 3–5)
>
> — LOUISE FITZHUGH, *Harriet, the Spy* (1964)

Harriet, the Spy opens with a description of another form of spatial play for girls — Harriet's "town," a "microworld" she maps onto the familiar contours of her own backyard and uses to think through the complex social relations she observes in her community. Harriet controls the inhabitants of this town, shaping their actions to her desires: "In this town, everybody goes to bed at nine-thirty" (p. 4). Not unlike a soap opera, her stories depend on juxtapositions of radically different forms of human experience: "Now, this night, as Mr. Hanley is just about to close up, a long, big old black car drives up and in it there are all these men with guns. . . . At this same minute Mrs. Harrison's baby is born" (p. 6). Her fascination with mapping and controlling the physical space of the town makes her game a pre-digital prototype for "Sim City" and other simulation games. However, compared to Harriet's vivid interest in the distinct personalities and particular experiences of her townspeople, "Sim City" seems alienated and abstract. "Sim City" 's classifications of land use into residential, commercial, and industrial push us well beyond the scale of everyday life and in so doing, strips the landscape of its potential as a stage for children's fantasies. "Sim City" offers us another form of power — the power to "play God," to design our physical environment, to sculpt the landscape or call down natural disasters (Friedman 1995), but not the power to imaginatively transform our social environment. "Sim City" embraces stock themes from boys' play, such as building forts, shaping earth with toy trucks, or damming creeks, playing them out on a much larger scale. For Harriet, the mapping of the space was only the first step in preparing the ground for a rich saga of life and death, joy and sorrow, and those are the elements that are totally lacking in most simulation games.

As Fitzhugh's novel continues, Harriet's interests shift from the imagi- 50 nary events of her simulated town and into real-world spaces. She "spies" on people's private social interactions, staging more and more "daring" investigations, trying to understand what motivates adult behavior, and writing in her notebook her interpretations of adult lives. Harriet's adventures take her well beyond the constricted space of her own home. She breaks and enters houses and takes rides on dumbwaiters, sneaks through back alleys and peeps into windows. She barely avoids getting caught. Harriet's adventures occur in public space (not the private space of the secret garden), a populated environment (not the natural worlds visited in "Secret Paths"). Yet, her adventures are not so much direct struggles with opposing forces (as might be found in a boys' book adventure) as covert operations to ferret out knowledge of social relations.

The games of Theresa Duncan ("Chop Suey," "Smarty," "Zero Zero") 51 offer a digital version of Harriet's "Town." Players can explore suburban and urban spaces and pry into bedroom closets in search of the extraordinary dimensions of ordinary life. Duncan [1998] cites *Harriet, the Spy* as an influence, hoping that her games will grant young girls "a sense of inquisitiveness and wonder." "Chop Suey" and "Smarty" take place in small Midwestern towns, a working-class world of diners, hardware stores, and beauty parlors. "Zero Zero" draws us further from home — into fin de siècle Paris, a world of bakeries, wax museums, and catacombs. These spaces are rendered in a distinctive style somewhere between the primitiveness of Grandma Moses and the colorful postmodernism of *Pee-Wee's Playhouse.* Far removed from the romantic imagery of "Secret Paths," these worlds overflow with city sounds — the clopping of horse hooves on cobblestones, barking dogs, clanging church bells in "Zero Zero" — and the narrator seems fascinated with the smokestacks and signs which clutter this man-made environment. As the narrator in "Zero Zero" rhapsodizes, "smoke curled black and feathery like a horse's tail from a thousand chimney pots" in this world "before popsicles and paperbacks." While the social order has been tamed, posing few dangers, Duncan has not rid these worlds of their more disreputable elements. The guy in the candy shop in "Chop Suey" has covered his body with tattoos. The Frenchmen in "Zero Zero" are suitably bored, ill-tempered, and insulting; even flowers hurl abuse at us. The man in the antlered hat sings rowdy songs about "bones" and "guts" when we visit the catacombs, and the women puff on cigarettes, wear too much make-up, flash their cleavage, and hint about illicit rendezvous. Duncan [1998] suggests:

> There's a sense of bittersweet experience in "Chop Suey," where not everyone has had a perfect life but they're all happy people. Vera has three ex-husbands

all named Bob. . . . Vera has problems, but she's also filled with love. And she's just a very vibrant, alive person, and that's why she fascinates the little girls.

Duncan rejects our tendency to "project this fantasy of purity and innocence onto children," suggesting that all this "niceness" deprives children of "the richness of their lives" and does not help them come to grips with their "complicated feelings" towards the people in their lives.

Duncan's protagonists, June Bug ("Chop Suey") and Pinkee LeBrun 52 ("Zero Zero"), are smart, curious girls, who want to know more than they have been told. Daring Pinkee scampers along the roofs of Paris and pops down chimneys or steps boldly through the doors of shops, questioning adults about their visions for the new century. Yet she is also interested in smaller, more intimate questions, such as the identity of the secret admirer who writes love poems to Bon Bon, the singer at the Follies. Clues unearthed in one location may shed light on mysteries posed elsewhere, allowing Duncan to suggest something of the "interconnectedness" of life within a close community. Often, as in *Harriet*, the goal is less to evaluate these people than to understand what makes them tick. In that sense, the game fosters the character-centered reading practices which Segel (1986) associates with the girls' book genres, reading practices that thrive on gossip and speculation.

Duncan's games have no great plot to propel them. Duncan [1998] said, 53 "'Chop Suey' works the way that real life does: all these things happen to you, but there's no magical event, like there is sometimes in books, that transforms you." Lazy curiosity invites us to explore the contents of each shop, to flip through the fashion magazines in Bon Bon's dressing room, to view the early trick films playing at Cinema Egypt, or to watch the cheeses in the window of Quel Fromage that are, for reasons of their own, staging the major turning points of the French Revolution. (She also cites inspiration from the more surreal adventures of *Alice in Wonderland*.) The interfaces are flexible, allowing us to visit any location when we want without having to fight our way through levels or work past puzzling obstacles. "Zero Zero" and Duncan's other games take particular pleasure in anarchistic imagery, in ways we can disrupt and destabilize the environment, showering the baker's angry faces with white clouds of flour, ripping off the table cloths, or shaking up soda bottles so they will spurt their corks. Often, there is something vaguely naughty about the game activities, as when a visit to Poire the fashion designer has us matching different pairs of underwear. In that sense, Duncan's stories preserve the mischievous and sometimes antisocial character of Harriet's antics and the transformative humor of Lewis Carroll, encouraging the young gamers to take more risks and to try things that might not ordinarily meet their parents' approval. Pinkee's first act as a baby is to rip the pink ribbons from her hair! Duncan likes her characters free and "unladylike."

In keeping with the pedagogic legacy of the girls' book tradition, "Zero 54 Zero" promises us an introduction to French history, culture, and language, and "Smarty" a mixture of "spelling and spells, math and Martians, grammar and glamour," but Duncan's approach is sassy and irreverent. The waxwork of Louis XIV sticks out its tongue at us, while Joan D'Arc is rendered in marshmallow, altogether better suited for toasting. The breads and cakes in the bakery are shaped like the faces of French philosophers and spout incomprehensible arguments. Pinkee's quest for knowledge about the coming century cannot be reduced to an approved curriculum, but rather expresses an unrestrained fascination with the stories, good, bad, happy or sad, that people tell each other about their lives.

Harriet, the Spy is ambivalent about its protagonist's escapades: her 55 misadventures clearly excite the book's female readers, but the character herself is socially ostracized and disciplined, forced to more appropriately channel her creativity and curiosity. Pinkee suffers no such punishment, ending up the game watching the fireworks that mark the change of the centuries and taking pleasure in the knowledge that she will be a central part of the changes that are coming: "tonight belongs to Bon Bon but the future belongs to Pinkee."

Conclusion: Toward a Gender-Neutral Play Space?

Brenda Laurel and Theresa Duncan offer two very different conceptions of 56 a digital play space for girls — one pastoral, the other urban; one based on the ideal of living in harmony with nature, the other based on an anarchistic pleasure in disrupting the order of everyday life and making the familiar "strange." Yet, in many ways, the two games embrace remarkably similar ideals — play spaces for girls that adopt a slower pace, are less filled with dangers, invite gradual investigation and discovery, foster an awareness of social relations and a search for secrets, and center around emotional relations between characters. Both allow the exploration of physical environments but are really about the interior worlds of feelings and fears. Laurel and Duncan make an important contribution when they propose new and different models for how digital media may be used. The current capabilities of our video and computer game technologies reflect the priorities of an earlier generation of game makers and their conception of the boys' market. Their assumptions about what kinds of digital play spaces were desirable defined how the bytes would be allocated, valuing rapid response time over the memory necessary to construct more complex and compelling characters. Laurel and Duncan shift the focus — giving priority to character relations and "friendship adventures." In doing so, they are expanding what computers can do and what roles they can play in our lives.

On the other hand, in our desire to open digital technologies as an 57 alternative play space for girls, we must guard against simply duplicating in the new medium the gender-specific genres of children's literature. The segregation of children's reading into boy- and girl-book genres, Segel

(1986) argues, encouraged the development of gender-specific reading strategies — with boys reading for plot and girls reading for character relationship. Such differences, Segel suggests, taught children to replicate the separation between a male public sphere of risk-taking and a female domestic sphere of care-taking. As Segel (1986) notes, the classification of children's literature into boys' books and girls' books "extracted a heavy cost in feminine self-esteem," restricting girls' imaginative experience to what adults perceived as its "proper place." Boys developed a sense of autonomy and mastery both from their reading and from their play. Girls learned to fetter their imaginations, just as they restricted their movements into real-world spaces. At the same time, this genre division also limited boys' psychological and emotional development, insuring a focus on goal-oriented, utilitarian, and violent plots. Too much interest in social and emotional life was a vulnerability in a world where competition left little room to be "led by your heart." We need to design digital play spaces that allow girls to do more than stitch doll clothes, mother nature, or heal their friends' hurts, and boys to do more than battle barbarian hordes.

Segel's analysis of "gender and childhood reading" suggests two ways 58 of moving beyond the gender segregation of our virtual landscape. First, as Segel (1986) suggests, the designation of books for boys and girls did not preclude (though certainly discouraged) reading across gender lines: "Though girls when they reached 'that certain age' could be prevented from joining boys' games and lively exploits, it was harder to keep them from accompanying their brothers on vicarious adventures through the reading of boys' books" (p. 175). Reading boys' books gave girls (admittedly limited) access to the boy culture and its values. Segel finds evidence of such gender-crossing in the nineteenth century, though girls were actively discouraged from reading boys' books because their contents were thought too lurid and unwholesome. At other times, educational authorities encouraged the assignment of boys' books in public schools, since girls could read and enjoy them, while there was much greater stigma attached to boys reading girls' books. The growing visibility of the "quake girls," female gamers who compete in traditional male fighting and action/adventure games (Jenkins and Cassell [1998]), suggests that there has always been a healthy degree of "crossover" interest in the games market and that many girls enjoy "playing with power." Girls may compete more directly and aggressively with boys in the video game arena than would ever have been possible in the real world of backyard play, since differences in physical size, strength, and agility are irrelevant. And they can return from combat without the ripped clothes or black eyes that told parents they had done something "unladylike." Unfortunately, much as girls who read boys' books were likely to encounter the misogynistic themes that mark boys' fantasies of separation from their mothers, girls who play boys' games find the games' constructions of female sexuality and power are designed to gratify preadolescent males, not to empower girls. Girl gamers are aggressively campaigning to have their tastes and interests factored into the development of action games.

We need to open up more space for girls to join — or play alongside —   *59*
the traditional boy culture down by the river, in the old vacant lot, within the
bamboo forest. Girls need to learn how to explore "unsafe" and "unfriendly"
spaces, and to experience the "complete freedom of movement" promised
by the boys' games, if not all the time, then at least some of the time, to
help them develop the self-confidence and competitiveness demanded of
professional women. They also need to learn how, in the words of a contemporary bestseller, to "run with the wolves" and not just follow the but-
terflies along the Secret Paths. Girls need to be able to play games where
Barbie gets to kick some butt.

However, this focus on creating action games for girls still represents   *60*
only part of the answer, for as Segel (1986) notes, the gender segregation of
children's literature was almost as damaging for boys as it was for girls: "In
a society where many men and women are alienated from members of the
other sex, one wonders whether males might be more comfortable with
and understanding of women's needs and perspectives if they had imaginatively shared female experiences through books, beginning in childhood"
(p. 183). Boys may need to play in secret gardens or toy towns just as much
as girls need to explore adventure islands. In the literary realm, Segel points
to books such as *Little House on the Prairie* and *A Wrinkle in Time* that fuse
the boy and girl genres, rewarding both a traditionally masculine interest in
plot action and a traditionally feminine interest in character relations.

Sega Saturn's "Nights into Dreams" represents a similar fusion of the   *61*
boys' and girls' game genres. Much as in "Secret Paths," our movement
through the game space is framed as an attempt to resolve the characters'
emotional problems. In the frame stories that open the game, we enter the
mindscape of the two protagonists as they toss and turn in their sleep.
Claris, the female protagonist, hopes to gain recognition on the stage as a
singer, but has nightmares of being rejected and ridiculed. Elliot, the male
character, has fantasies of scoring big on the basketball court, yet fears
being bullied by bigger and more aggressive players. They run away from
their problems, only to find themselves in Nightopia, where they must save
the dream world from the evil schemes of Wileman the Wicked and his mon-
strous minions. In the dreamworld, both Claris and Elliot may assume the
identity of Nights, an androgynous harlequin figure who can fly through
the air, transcending all the problems below. The game requires players to
gather glowing orbs that represent different forms of energy needed to
confront Claris's and Elliot's problems — purity (white), wisdom (green),
hope (yellow), intelligence (blue), and bravery (red) — a structure that
recalls the magic stones in "Secret Paths in the Forest."

The tone of this game is aptly captured by one Internet game critic,   *62*
Big Mitch: "The whole experience of "Nights" is in soaring, tumbling, and
free-wheeling through colorful landscapes, swooping here and there, and
just losing yourself in the moment. This is not a game you set out to win;
the fun is in the journey rather than the destination." Big Mitch's response
suggests a recognition of the fundamentally different qualities of this

game — its focus on psychological issues as much as on action and conflict, its fascination with aimless exploration rather than goal-driven narrative, its movement between a realistic world of everyday problems and a fantasy realm of great adventure, and its mixture of the speed and mobility associated with the boys' platform games with the lush natural landscapes and the sculpted soundtracks associated with the girls' games. Spring Valley is a sparkling world of rainbows and waterfalls and Emerald Green forests. Other levels allow us to splash through cascading fountains or sail past icy mountains and frozen wonderlands, or bounce on pillows and off the walls of the surreal Soft Museum, or swim through aquatic tunnels. The game's 3D design allows an exhilarating freedom of movement, enhanced by design features, such as wind resistance, that give players a stronger than average sense of embodiment. "Nights into Dreams" retains some dangerous and risky elements that are associated with the boys' games. There are spooky places, including nightmare worlds full of day-glo serpents and winged beasties, and enemies we must battle, yet there is also a sense of unconstrained adventure and the experience of floating through the clouds. Our primary enemy is time, the alarm clock that will awaken us from our dreams. Even when we confront monsters, they don't fire on us; we must simply avoid flying directly into their sharp teeth. When we lose "Nights" magical, gender-bending garb, we turn back into boys and girls and must hoof it as pedestrians across the rugged terrain below, a situation that makes it far less likely we will achieve our goals. To be gendered is to be constrained; to escape gender is to escape gravity and to fly above it all.

Sociologist Barrie Thorne (1993) has discussed the forms of "borderwork," which occurs when boys and girls occupy the same play spaces: "The spatial separation of boys and girls [on the same playground] constitutes a kind of boundary, perhaps felt most strongly by individuals who want to join an activity controlled by the other gender" (pp. 64–65). Boys and girls are brought together in the same space, but they repeatedly enact the separation and opposition between the two play cultures. In real-world play, this "borderwork" takes the form of chases and contests on the one hand and "cooties" or other pollution taboos on the other. When "borderwork" occurs, gender distinctions become extremely rigid and nothing passes between the two spheres. Something similar occurs in many of the books Segel identifies as gender neutral — male and female reading interests coexist, side by side, like children sharing a playground, and yet they remain resolutely separate, and the writers, if anything, exaggerate gender differences in order to proclaim their dual address. Wendy and the "lost boys" both travel to Never-Never-Land, but Wendy plays house and the "lost boys" play Indians or pirates. The "little house" and the "prairie" exist side by side in Laura Wilder's novels, but the mother remains trapped inside the house, while Pa ventures into the frontier. The moments when the line between the little house and the prairie are crossed, such as a scene in which a native American penetrates into Ma Wilder's parlor, become moments of intense anxiety. Only Laura can follow her pa across the threshold of the little house and onto the prairie, and her adventurous spirit is often presented as an unfeminine trait she is likely to outgrow as she gets older.

As we develop digital play spaces for boys and girls, we need to make 64 sure this same pattern isn't repeated, that we do not create blue and pink ghettos. On the one hand, the opening sequences of "Nights into Dreams," which frame Elliot and Claris as possessing fundamentally different dreams (sports for boys and musical performance for girls, graffiti-laden inner-city basketball courts for boys and pastoral gardens for girls), perform this kind of borderwork, defining the proper place for each gender. On the other hand, the androgynous "Nights" embodies a fantasy of transcending gender and thus achieving the freedom and mobility to fly above it all. To win the game, the player must become *both* the male and the female protagonists, and they must join forces for the final level. The penalty for failure in this world is to be trapped on the ground and fixed into a single gender.

Thorne finds that aggressive "borderwork" is more likely to occur when 65 children are forced together by adults than when they find themselves interacting more spontaneously, more likely to occur in prestructured institutional settings like the schoolyard than in the informal settings of the subdivisions and apartment complexes. All of this suggests that our fantasy of designing games that will provide common play spaces for girls and boys may be illusive and as full of its own complications and challenges as creating a "girls only" space or encouraging girls to venture into traditional male turf. We are not yet sure what such a gender-neutral space will look like. Creating such a space would mean redesigning not only the nature of computer games but also the nature of society. The danger may be that in such a space, gender differences are going to be more acutely felt, as boys and girls will be repelled from each other rather than drawn together. There are reasons why this is a place where neither the feminist entrepreneurs nor the makers of boys' games are ready to go, yet as the girls' market is secured, the challenge must be to find a way to move beyond our existing categories and to once again invent new kinds of virtual play spaces.

REFERENCES

Booth, A., and Johnson, D. 1975. "The Effect of Crowding on Child Health and Development." *American Behavioral Scientist* 18: 736–749.

Burnett, F. H. 1911. *The Secret Garden.* New York: HarperCollins.

[Cassell, J. 1998. "Storytelling as the Nexus of Change in the Relationship Between Gender and Technology: A Feminist Approach to Software Design." In J. Cassell and H. Jenkins, eds., *From Barbie to Mortal Kombat: Gender and Computer Games.* Cambridge, Mass.: MIT Press.]

Cavallo, D. 1981. *Muscles and Morals: Organized Playgrounds and Urban Reform, 1880–1920.* Philadelphia: University of Pennsylvania Press.

"Critical Depth." 1998. Advertisement, *Next Generation*, January.

"Die by the Sword." 1998. Advertisement, *Next Generation*, January.

Donaldson, F. 1970. "The Child in the City." University of Washington, mimeograph, cited in M. H. Matthews 1992, *Making Sense of Place: Children's Understanding of Large-Scale Environments.* Hertfordshire: Barnes and Noble.

Farley, W. 1941. *The Black Stallion.* New York: Random House.

Feinstein, K., and Kent, S. 1997. "Towards a Definition of 'Videogames.'" http://www .videotopia.com/errata1.htm.

Fitzhugh, L. 1964. *Harriet, the Spy.* New York: Harper & Row.

Formanek-Brunnel, M. 1996. "The Politics of Dollhood in Nineteenth-Century America." In H. Jenkins, ed., *The Children's Culture Reader.* New York: New York University Press.

Friedman, T. 1995. "Making Sense of Software: Computer Games and Interactive Textuality." In S. G. Jones, ed., *Cybersociety: Computer-Mediated Communication and Community.* Thousand Oaks, Calif.: Sage Publications.

Fuller, M., and Jenkins, H. 1995. "Nintendo and New World Travel Writing: A Dialogue." In S. G. Jones, ed., *Cybersociety: Computer-Mediated Communication and Community.* Thousand Oaks, Calif.: Sage Publications.

Hart, R. 1979. *Children's Experience of Place.* New York: John Wiley and Sons.

Holland, N. N., and Sherman, L. F. 1986. "Gothic Possibilities." In E. A. Flynn and P. P. Schweickart, eds., *Gender and Reading: Essays on Readers, Texts and Contexts.* Baltimore: Johns Hopkins University Press.

["An Interview with Lee McEnany Caraher (Sega)." 1998. In J. Cassell and H. Jenkins, eds., *From Barbie to Mortal Kombat: Gender and Computer Games.* Cambridge, Mass.: MIT Press.]

["Interviews with Theresa Duncan and Monica Gesue (Chop Suey)." 1998. In J. Cassell and H. Jenkins, eds., *From Barbie to Mortal Kombat: Gender and Computer Games.* Cambridge, Mass.: MIT Press.]

Jenkins, H., and Cassell, J. [1998]. "Chess for Girls? The Gender Politics of the Girls Game Movement." [In J. Cassell and H. Jenkins, eds., *From Barbie to Mortal Kombat: Gender and Computer Games.* Cambridge, Mass.: MIT Press.]

Katz, J. 1997. *Virtuous Reality.* New York: Random House.

Kinchloe, J. L. 1997. "*Home Alone* and 'Bad to the Bone': The Advent of a Postmodern Childhood." In S. R. Steinberg and J. L. Kincheloe, eds., *Kinder-Culture: The Corporate Construction of Childhood.* New York: Westview.

Kinder, M. 1996. "Contextualizing Video Game Violence: From 'Teenage Mutant Ninja Turtles 1' to 'Mortal Kombat 2.'" In P. M. Greenfield and R. R. Cocking, eds., *Interacting with Video.* Norwood: Ablex Publishing.

Matthews, M. H. 1992. *Making Sense of Place: Children's Understanding of Large-Scale Environments.* Hertfordshire: Barnes and Noble.

Moore, R. C. 1986. *Childhood's Domain: Play and Place in Child Development.* London: Croom Helm.

Newson, J., and Newson, E. 1976. *Seven Years Old in the Home Environment.* London: Allen and Unwin.

Rheingold, H. L., and Cook, K. V. 1975. "The Content of Boys' and Girls' Rooms as an Index of Parents' Behavior." *Child Development* 46: 459–463.

Rotundo, E. A. 1994. *American Manhood: Transformations in Masculinity from the Revolution to the Modern Era.* New York: Basic.

Searles, H. 1959. *The Non-Human Development in Normal Development and Schizophrenia.* New York: International Universities Press.

Segel, E. 1986. "'As the Twig Is Bent . . .': Gender and Childhood Reading." In E. A. Flynn and P. P. Schweickart, eds., *Gender and Reading: Essays on Readers, Texts and Contexts.* Baltimore: Johns Hopkins University Press.

Seitzer, E. 1996. Transcript of Expert Panel Meeting, Sega of America Gatekeeper Program. Los Angeles, June 21.

"Sonic R." 1998. Advertisement, *Next Generation,* January.

Tapscott, D. 1997. *Growing Up Digital: The Rise of the Net Generation.* New York: McGraw Hill.

Thorne, B. 1993. *Gender Play: Girls and Boys in School.* New Brunswick: Rutgers University Press.

van Staden, J. F. 1984. "Urban Early Adolescents, Crowding and the Neighbourhood Experience: A Preliminary Investigation." *Journal of Environmental Psychology* 4: 97–118.

Van Vliet, W. 1983. "Exploring the Fourth Environment: An Examination of the Home Range of City and Suburban Teenagers." *Environment and Behavior* 15: 567–588.

"VR Sports." 1998. Advertisement, *Next Generation,* January.

Ward, C. 1977. *The Child in the City.* London: Architectural Press.

West, E. 1992. "Children on the Plains Frontier." In E. West and P. Petrik, eds., *Small Worlds: Children and Adolescents in America, 1850–1950.* Lawrence: The University Press of Kansas. pp. 26–41.

Reading Rhetorically

1. Why do you think Jenkins chooses to open his essay with a personal experience? What are the benefits of this writing strategy? The risks? Do benefits and risks change depending on who his readers are? In the opening section of the essay, "A Tale of Two Childhoods," underline the sentences that connect Jenkins's personal experience to his larger topic. What can you conclude about how to use personal experiences effectively in your own academic writing?

2. Jenkins divides his essay into distinct sections with headings. Make a list of the different headings, and summarize — aloud or in a few sentences on paper — the key ideas in each section. How does each section contribute to Jenkins's overall argument?

3. Underline the sentences throughout Jenkins's essay that clearly state or restate his thesis, or main argument. What purpose does each statement or restatement serve? How can you apply your insights about Jenkins's strategy of using thesis statements to your own writing?

Inquiring Further

4. Using your library's resources, find and read three scholarly articles on video games to get a better sense of the academic conversation about video game culture. What seem to be the interests and concerns of these scholars? Where do their interests overlap with Jenkins's? How do his ideas respond to their concerns? Compare your findings with those of your classmates.

5. Use Jenkins's insights to analyze a video game he does not mention. For example, how do Jenkins's concepts of boy culture and girl space apply to the video game you've chosen? How might the concept of borderwork (para. 62), which Jenkins draws from sociologist Barrie Thorne, apply to this game? How does this video game reinforce or break down the "existing categories" of gender that Jenkins discusses at the end of his essay?

6. How would you apply Jenkins's ideas about the gendering of video games to contemporary movies? Consider the ways movies for children and

teenagers are marketed to boys or girls — or both. Choose three movies you know fairly well and analyze them. How do the concepts of boy culture, girl space, and borderwork apply to the movies? What conclusions can you draw about popular culture aimed at children?

Framing Conversations

7. Like Jenkins, Steven Johnson (below) argues that there are positive aspects to video game culture despite the many claims to the contrary. Drawing on both authors' ideas, write an essay in which you carefully consider their examples and claims, and then draw your own conclusions about the positive and negative aspects of video games. In making your own argument, include your evaluation of each writer's evidence and any holes you perceive in his argument.

8. Although Jenkins's interest is in computer technology, he recognizes that traditional stories shape the narratives of today's video games. Cynthia Selfe (p. 783) and Elizabeth Teare (p. 800) also show how new technology draws on "old-fashioned" images and stories — but in different ways and with different results. Write an essay in which you consider the influence of "old" ideas on "new" ones and develop an argument about what is positive and/or negative about the use of the past in the context of the technological present. Draw on the three authors' works and other examples you find of technology's "borrowing" images or stories from the past.

9. Shari L. Dworkin and Michael A. Messner (p. 551) share Jenkins's interest in the ways physical play contributes to our sense of ourselves as feminine or masculine. Drawing on the history laid out in both essays, as well as on the writers' sense of the future, write an essay in which you consider how online activity is similar to and different from physical activity in the construction of gender roles. Make an argument about the significance of your insights. Do you think your understanding of borderwork can help you develop your ideas? Explain your answer.

■ STEVEN JOHNSON ————————————————

From Everything Bad Is Good for You: How Today's Popular Culture Is Actually Making Us Smarter

Steven Johnson writes about science and culture. In 1995, he cofounded *Feed*, a leading Web magazine on technology, culture, and politics, which earned him a spot on *Newsweek*'s list of the "50 People Who Matter Most on the Internet" that year. His book *Interface Culture: How New Technology Transforms the Way We Create and Communicate* (1997) is considered one of the most important early texts to explain the impact of cybertechnology on human perception and communication, a subject he returned to in *Emergence: The Connected Lives of Ants, Brains, Cities, and Software* (2001).

Johnson became more widely known with the publication of his best-selling book *Everything Bad Is Good for You: How Today's Popular Culture Is Actually Making Us Smarter* (2005), in which he defends the value of computer games. More recently, Johnson has turned his interest in the interaction of science and social dynamics to the study of the mid-nineteenth-century cholera outbreak in London, the deadliest in the city's history, in *The Ghost Map: The Story of London's Most Terrifying Epidemic — and How It Changed Science, Cities, and the Modern World* (2006). The objectives that connect all of Johnson's research and writing are discovering how experts think about issues and then teaching general readers to understand the implications of that thinking.

This reading is excerpted from Johnson's book *Everything Bad Is Good for You*. You will immediately grasp Johnson's interest in sailing against the current. He opens with two wittily juxtaposed epigraphs, and then, in the first two paragraphs, asks readers to stand with him against those who claim the sky is falling, arguing that "the weather has never been better. It just takes a new kind of barometer to tell the difference" (para. 2).

The pages that follow are Johnson's barometer. As you read his analysis of the virtues of pop culture pastimes, consider the games you found most absorbing as a child. Do you agree with Johnson about the kinds of skills those games taught you? What about the time you spend today on technological recreation? Are you wasting time or getting smarter?

Because Johnson is writing for a general audience, he does not use scholarly citation, but he does refer explicitly to the ideas of others in the course of building his argument and in his informed and detailed notes. As you read, notice the many kinds of experts he refers to, and how he deploys their ideas to serve his larger purpose. Keep track, too, of the nonscholarly sources he uses (television shows and a Dungeons & Dragons manual are two examples). How effectively do they persuade you as a reader?

Leisure studies — research on the ways we spend our free time — is a rich area of study. The question driving Johnson's analysis here about the purposes games serve is part of this ongoing conversation. What work does our play accomplish? Johnson has answers that may surprise you.

■ ■ ■

SCIENTIST A: Has he asked for anything special?
SCIENTIST B: Yes, why, for breakfast . . . he requested something called "wheat germ, organic honey, and tiger's milk."
SCIENTIST A: Oh, yes. Those were the charmed substances that some years ago were felt to contain life-preserving properties.
SCIENTIST B: You mean there was no deep fat? No steak or cream pies or . . . hot fudge?
SCIENTIST A: Those were thought to be unhealthy. . . .

— from WOODY ALLEN's *Sleeper*

Ours is an age besotted with graphic entertainments. And in an increasingly infantilized society, whose moral philosophy is reducible to a celebration of "choice," adults are decreasingly distinguishable from children in their absorption in entertainments and the kinds of entertainments they are absorbed in — video games, computer games, hand-held games, movies on their computers and so on. This is progress: more sophisticated delivery of stupidity.

— George Will[1]

This book is an old-fashioned work of persuasion that ultimately aims *1* to convince you of one thing: that popular culture has, on average, grown more complex and intellectually challenging over the past thirty years. Where most commentators assume a race to the bottom and a dumbing down — "an increasingly infantilized society," in George Will's words — I see a progressive story: mass culture growing more sophisticated, demanding more cognitive engagement with each passing year. Think of it as a kind of positive brainwashing: the popular media steadily, but almost imperceptibly, making our minds sharper, as we soak in entertainment usually dismissed as so much lowbrow fluff. I call this upward trend the Sleeper Curve, after the classic sequence from Woody Allen's mock sci-fi film, where a team of scientists from 2173 are astounded that twentieth-century society failed to grasp the nutritional merits of cream pies and hot fudge.

I hope for many of you the argument here will resonate with a feeling *2* you've had in the past, even if you may have suppressed it at the time — a feeling that the popular culture isn't locked in a spiral dive of deteriorating standards. Next time you hear someone complaining about violent TV mobsters, or accidental onscreen nudity, or the inanity of reality programming, or the dull stares of the Nintendo addicts, you should think of the Sleeper Curve rising steadily beneath all that superficial chaos. The sky is not falling. In many ways, the weather has never been better. It just takes a new kind of barometer to tell the difference.

Introduction: The Sleeper Curve

Every childhood has its talismans, the sacred objects that look innocuous *3* enough to the outside world, but that trigger an onslaught of vivid memories when the grown child confronts them. For me, it's a sheaf of xeroxed numbers that my father brought home from his law firm when I was nine. These pages didn't seem, at first glance, like the sort of thing that would send a grade-schooler into rapture. From a distance you might have guessed that they were payroll reports, until you got close enough to notice that the names were familiar ones, even famous: Catfish Hunter, Pete Rose, Vida Blue. Baseball names, stranded in a sea of random numbers.

---

[1]George Will, "Reality Television: Oxymoron." http://www.townhall.com/columnists/georgewill/gw20010621.shtml.

Those pages my dad brought home were part of a game, though it was 4 a game unlike any I had ever played. It was a baseball simulation called APBA, short for American Professional Baseball Association. APBA was a game of dice and data. A company in Lancaster, Pennsylvania, had analyzed the preceding season's statistics and created a collection of cards, one for each player who had played more than a dozen games that year. The cards contained a cryptic grid of digits that captured numerically each player's aptitudes on the baseball diamond: the sluggers and the strikeout prone, the control artists and the speed demons. In the simplest sense, APBA was a way of playing baseball with cards, or at least pretending to be a baseball *manager*: you'd pick out a lineup, decide on your starting pitchers, choose when to bunt and when to steal.

APBA sounds entertaining enough at that level of generality — what 5 kid wouldn't want to manage a sports team? — but actually playing the game was a more complicated affair. On the simplest level, the game followed this basic sequence: you picked your players, decided on a strategy, rolled a few dice, and then consulted a "lookup chart" to figure out what happened — a strikeout, or a home run, a grounder to third.

But it was never quite that simple with APBA. You could play against a 6 human opponent, or manage both teams yourself, and the decisions made for the opposing team transformed the variables in subtle but crucial ways. At the beginning of each game — and anytime you made a substitution — you had to add up all the fielding ratings for each player in your lineup. Certain performance results would change if your team was unusually adept with the glove, while teams that were less talented defensively would generate more errors. There were completely different charts depending on the number of runners on base: if you had a man on third, you consulted the "Runner on Third" chart. Certain performance numbers came with different results, depending on the quality of the pitcher: if you were facing a "grade A" pitcher, according to the data on his card, you'd get a strikeout, while a "grade C" pitcher would generate a single to right field. And that was just scratching the surface of the game's complexity. Here's the full entry for "Pitching" on the main "Bases Empty" chart:

> The hitting numbers under which lines appear may be altered according to the grade of the pitcher against whom the team is batting. Always observe the grade of the pitcher and look for possible changes of those numbers which are underlined. "No Change" always refers back to the D, or left, column and always means a base hit. Against Grade D pitchers there is never any change — the left hand column only is used. When a pitcher is withdrawn from the game make a note of the grade of the pitcher who relieves him. If his grade is different, a different column must be referred to when the underlined numbers come up. Certain players may have the numbers 7, 8, and/or 11 in the second columns of their cards. When any of these numbers is found in the second column of a player card, it is not subject to normal grade changes. Always use the left (Grade D) column in these cases, no matter what the pitcher's grade is. Occasionally, pitchers may have A & C or A & B ratings. Always consider these pitchers as Grade A pitchers unless the A column happens to be a

base hit. Then use the C or B column, as the case may be, for the final play result.

Got that? They might as well be the tax form instructions you'd hap- 7
pily pay an accountant to decipher. Reading these words now, I have to slow myself down just to follow the syntax, but my ten-year-old self had so thoroughly internalized this arcana that I played hundreds of APBA games without having to consult the fine print. *An 11 in the second column on the batter's card? Obviously,* obviously *that means ignore the normal grade changes for the pitcher. It'd be crazy not to!*

The creators of APBA devised such an elaborate system for under- 8
standable reasons: they were pushing the limits of the dice-and-cards genre to accommodate the statistical complexity of baseball. This mathematical intricacy was not limited to baseball simulations, of course. Comparable games existed for most popular sports: basketball sims that let you call a zone defense or toss a last-minute three-point Hail Mary before the clock ran out; boxing games that let you replay Ali/Foreman without the rope-a-dope strategy. British football fans played games like Soccerboss and Wembley that let you manage entire franchises, trading players and maintaining the financial health of the virtual organization. A host of dice-based military simulations re-created historical battles or entire world wars with painstaking fidelity.

Perhaps most famously, players of Dungeons & Dragons and its many 9
imitators built elaborate fantasy narratives — all by rolling twenty-sided dice and consulting bewildering charts that accounted for a staggering number of variables.[2] The three primary manuals for playing the game were more than five hundred pages long, with hundreds of lookup charts that players consulted as though they were reading from scripture. (By comparison, consulting the APBA charts was like reading the back of a cereal box.) Here's the *Player's Handbook* describing the process by which a sample character is created:

> Monte wants to create a new character. He rolls four six-sided dice (4d6) and gets 5, 4, 4, and 1. Ignoring the lowest die, he records the result on scratch paper, 13. He does this five more times and gets these six scores: 13, 10, 15,

---

[2]"Dungeons and Dragons was not a way out of the mainstream, as some parents feared and other kids suspected, but a way back into the realm of story-telling. This was what my friends and I were doing: creating narratives to make sense of feeling socially marginal. We were writing stories, grand in scope, with heroes, villains, and the entire zoology of mythical creatures. Even sports, the arch-nemesis of role-playing games, is a splendid tale of adventure and glory. Though my friends and I were not always athletically inclined, we found agility in the characters we created. We fought, flew through the air, shot arrows out of the park, and scored points by slaying the dragon and disabling the trap. Our influence is now everywhere. My generation of gamers — whose youths were spent holed up in paneled wood basements crafting identities, mythologies, and geographies with a few lead figurines — are the filmmakers, computer programmers, writers, DJs, and musicians of today." Peter Bebergal, "How 'Dungeons' Changed the World," *The Boston Globe*, November 15, 2004.

12, 8, and 14. Monte decides to play a strong, tough Dwarven fighter. Now he assigns his rolls to abilities. Strength gets the highest score, 15. His character has a +2 Strength bonus that will serve him well in combat. Constitution gets the next highest score, 14. The Dwarf's +2 Constitution racial ability adjustment [see Table 2-1: Racial Ability Adjustments, pg. 12] improves his Constitution score to 16, for a +3 bonus. . . . Monte has two bonus-range scores left (13 and 12) plus an average score (10). Dexterity gets the 13 (+1 bonus).

And that's merely defining the basic faculties for a character. Once you released your Dwarven fighter into the world, the calculations involved in determining the effects of his actions — attacking a specific creature with a specific weapon under specific circumstances with a specific squad of comrades fighting alongside you — would leave most kids weeping if you put the same charts on a math quiz.

Which gets to the ultimate question of why a ten-year-old found any of 10 this *fun*. For me, the embarrassing truth of the matter is that I did ultimately grow frustrated with my baseball simulation, but not for the reasons you might expect. It wasn't that arcane language wore me down, or that I grew tired of switching columns on the Bases Empty chart, or that I decided that six hours was too long to spend alone in my room on a Saturday afternoon in July.

No, I moved on from APBA because it wasn't realistic enough. 11

My list of complaints grew as my experience with APBA deepened. 12 Playing hundreds of simulated games revealed the blind spots and strange skews of the simulation. APBA neglected the importance of whether your players were left-handed or right-handed, crucial to the strategy of baseball. The fielding talents of individual players were largely ignored. The vital decision to throw different kinds of pitches — sliders and curveballs and sinkers — was entirely absent. The game took no notice of *where* the games were being played: you couldn't simulate the vulnerable left-field fence in Fenway Park, so tempting to right-handed hitters, or the swirling winds of San Francisco's old Candlestick Park. And while APBA included historic teams, there was no way to factor in historical changes in the game when playing teams from different eras against each other.

And so over the next three years, I embarked on a long journey through 13 the surprisingly populated world of dice-baseball simulations, ordering them from ads printed in the back of the *Sporting News* and Street and Smith's annual baseball guide. I dabbled with Strat-o-Matic, the most popular of the baseball sims; I sampled Statis Pro Baseball from Avalon Hill, maker of the then-popular Diplomacy board game; I toyed with one title called Time Travel baseball that specialized in drafting fantasy teams from a pool of historic players. I lost several months to a game called Extra Innings that bypassed cards and boards altogether; it didn't even come packaged in a box — just an oversized envelope stuffed with pages and pages of data. You rolled six separate dice to complete a play, sometimes consulting five or six separate pages to determine what had happened.

Eventually, like some kind of crazed addict searching for an ever-purer *14*
high, I found myself designing my own simulations, building entire games
from scratch. I borrowed a twenty-sided die from my Dungeons & Dragons
set — the math was far easier to do with twenty sides than it was with six.
I scrawled out my play charts on yellow legal pads, and translated the last
season's statistics into my own home-brewed player cards. For some
people, I suppose, thinking of youthful baseball games conjures up the
smell of leather gloves and fresh-cut grass. For me, what comes to mind is
the statistical purity of the twenty-sided die.

This story, I freely admit, used to have a self-congratulatory moral to *15*
it. As a grownup, I would tell new friends about my fifth-grade days building elaborate simulations in my room, and on the surface I'd make a joke
about how uncool I was back then, huddled alone with my twenty-sided
dice while the other kids roamed outside playing capture the flag or, God
forbid, *real* baseball. But the latent message of my story was clear: I was
some kind of statistical prodigy, building simulated worlds out of legal
pads and probability charts.

But I no longer think that my experience was all that unusual. I suspect *16*
millions of people from my generation probably have comparable stories to
tell: if not of sports simulations then of Dungeons & Dragons, or the geopolitical strategy of games like Diplomacy, a kind of chess superimposed onto
actual history. More important, in the quarter century that has passed since
I first began exploring those xeroxed APBA pages, what once felt like a mav-
erick obsession has become a thoroughly mainstream pursuit.

This book is, ultimately, the story of how the kind of thinking that I was *17*
doing on my bedroom floor became an everyday component of mass entertainment. It's the story of how systems analysis, probability theory, pattern
recognition, and — amazingly enough — old-fashioned *patience* became
indispensable tools for anyone trying to make sense of modern pop culture. Because the truth is my solitary obsession with modeling complex
simulations is now ordinary behavior for most consumers of digital age
entertainment. This kind of education is not happening in classrooms or
museums; it's happening in living rooms and basements, on PCs and television screens. This is the Sleeper Curve: The most debased forms of mass
diversion — video games and violent television dramas and juvenile
sitcoms — turn out to be nutritional after all. For decades, we've worked
under the assumption that mass culture follows a steadily declining path
toward lowest-common-denominator standards, presumably because the
"masses" want dumb, simple pleasures and big media companies want to
give the masses what they want. But in fact, the exact opposite is happening: the culture is getting more intellectually demanding, not less.

Most of the time, criticism that takes pop culture seriously involves *18*
performing some kind of symbolic analysis, decoding the work to demonstrate the way it represents some other aspect of society. You can see this
symbolic approach at work in academic cultural studies programs analyzing the ways in which pop forms expressed the struggle of various disenfranchised groups: gays and lesbians, people of color, women, the third world.

You can see it at work in the "zeitgeist" criticism featured in media sections of newspapers and newsweeklies, where the critic establishes a symbolic relationship between the work and some spirit of the age: yuppie self-indulgence, say, or post-9/11 anxiety.

The approach followed in this book is more systemic than symbolic, 19 more about causal relationships than metaphors. It is closer, in a sense, to physics than to poetry. My argument for the existence of the Sleeper Curve comes out of an assumption that the landscape of popular culture involves the clash of competing forces: the neurological appetites of the brain, the economics of the culture industry, changing technological platforms. The specific ways in which those forces collide play a determining role in the type of popular culture we ultimately consume. The work of the critic, in this instance, is to diagram those forces, not decode them.

Sometimes, for the sake of argument, I find it helpful to imagine culture 20 as a kind of man-made weather system.[3] Float a mass of warm, humid air over cold ocean water, and you'll create an environment in which fog will thrive. The fog doesn't appear because it somehow symbolically reenacts the clash of warm air and cool water. Fog arrives instead as an emergent effect of that particular system and its internal dynamics. The same goes with popular culture: certain kinds of environments encourage cognitive complexity; others discourage complexity. The cultural object — the film or the video game — is not a metaphor for that system; it's more like an output or a result.

The forces at work in these systems operate on multiple levels: under- 21 lying changes in technology that enable new kinds of entertainment; new forms of online communications that cultivate audience commentary about works of pop culture; changes in the economics of the culture industry

---

[3]To be sure, television shows and video games are not water molecules; they come into the world thanks to the passions and talents of individual humans. *Hill Street Blues* needed its Steven Bochco, *SimCity* its Will Wright. These biographical explanations are not without value, but they are only part of the story. (And of course they are already ubiquitous in the mass media's coverage of themselves, in magazine profiles and newspaper reviews.) But when you're trying to explain macro trends in the history of culture, auteur theory gets you only so far. If Steven Bochco hadn't been around to invent the multithreaded serious drama, someone else would have come along to do it: the economic and technological conditions were too ripe for such an opportunity to be missed.

"Economic and technological conditions" sounds like the neo-Marxist-school cultural materialists, translating each artifact back to the "ultimately determining instance" of material history. But while the cultural materialists did important work in shedding the biographical limits of aesthetic criticism — relating works to their historical moment, and not the vicissitudes of individual genius — they remained too dependent on the symbolic architecture of ideological critique. The work of culture connected to the "economic and technological conditions" the way a mask conveys the face beneath it: representing some common features while distorting others. History churns out a steady progression of new social and technological relations, and culture floats above that world, translating its anxieties and contradictions into a code that, more often than not, makes that experiential turmoil more tolerable to the people living through it. For the kind of criticism at work in this book, on the other hand, the cultural work doesn't attempt to resolve symbolically the contradictions unleashed by historical change. The cultural work is the residue of historical change, not an imagined resolution to it.

that encourage repeat viewing; and deep-seated appetites in the human brain that seek out reward and intellectual challenge. To understand those forces we'll need to draw upon disciplines that don't usually interact with one another: economics, narrative theory, social network analysis, neuroscience.

This is a story of trends, not absolutes. I do not believe that most of   22
today's pop culture is made up of masterpieces that will someday be taught alongside Joyce and Chaucer in college survey courses. The television shows and video games and movies that we'll look at in the coming pages are not, for the most part, Great Works of Art. But they are more complex and nuanced than the shows and games that preceded them. While the Sleeper Curve maps *average* changes across the pop cultural landscape — and not just the complexity of single works — I have focused on a handful of representative examples in the interest of clarity. . . .

I believe that the Sleeper Curve is the single most important new force   23
altering the mental development of young people today, and I believe it is largely a force for good: enhancing our cognitive faculties, not dumbing them down. And yet you almost never hear this story in popular accounts of today's media. Instead, you hear dire stories of addiction, violence, mindless escapism.[4] "All across the political spectrum," television legend Steve Allen writes in a *Wall Street Journal* op-ed, "thoughtful observers are appalled by what passes for TV entertainment these days. No one can claim that the warning cries are simply the exaggerations of conservative spoil-sports or fundamentalist preachers. . . . The sleaze and classless garbage on TV in recent years exceeds the boundaries of what has traditionally been referred to as Going Too Far."[5] The influential Parents Television Council argues: "The entertainment industry has pushed the content envelope too far; television and films filled with sex, violence, and profanity send strong negative messages to the youth of America — messages that will desensitize them and make for a far more disenfranchised society as these youths grow into

---

[4]Consider this representative sample of the Trash TV mentality:

"It isn't just nags or fanatics who are disturbed by the harsh new face of TV programming in the late 1990s. Here's what the *New York Times* had to say in an April 1998 front-page story: 'Like a child acting outrageously naughty to see how far he can push his parents, mainstream television this season is flaunting the most vulgar and explicit sex, language, and behavior that it has ever sent into American homes.' A banner headline in the *Wall Street Journal* warned not long ago . . . 'It's 8 p.m. Your Kids Are Watching Sex on TV.' U.S. News summarized the trends this way: 'To hell with kids — that must be the motto of the new fall TV season. . . . The family hour is gone. . . . The story of the fall line-up is the rise of sex. Will the networks ever wise up?'

"A wide spectrum of Americans are appalled by what passes for TV entertainment these days. A 1998 poll by the Kaiser Family Foundation found that fully two-thirds of all parents say they are concerned 'a great deal' about what their children are now exposed to on television. Their biggest complaint is sexual content, followed closely by violence, and then crude language." Karl Zinsmeister, "How Today's Trash Television Harms America," *American Enterprise*, March 1999.

[5]Steve Allen, "That's Entertainment?" *The Wall Street Journal*, November 13, 1998.

adults."[6] And then there's syndicated columnist Suzanne Fields: "The television sitcom is emblematic of our culture; parents, no matter what their degree of education, have abandoned the simplest standard of shame. Their children literally 'do not know better.' The drip, drip, drip of the popular culture dulls our senses. An open society with high technology exposes increasing numbers of adults and children to the lowest common denomination of sex and violence."[7] You could fill an encyclopedia volume with all the kindred essays published in the past decade.

Exceptions to this dire assessment exist, but they are of the rule-proving variety. You'll see the occasional grudging acknowledgments of minor silver linings: an article will suggest that video games enhance visual memory skills, or a critic will hail *The West Wing* as the rare flowering of thoughtful programming in the junkyard of prime-time television. But the dominant motif is one of decline and atrophy: we're a nation of reality program addicts and Nintendo freaks. Lost in that account is the most interesting trend of all: that the popular culture has been growing increasingly complex over the past few decades, exercising our minds in powerful new ways.

24

But to see the virtue in this form of positive brainwashing, we need to begin by doing away with the tyranny of the morality play. When most op-ed writers and talk show hosts discuss the social value of media, when they address the question of whether today's media is or isn't good for us, the underlying assumption is that entertainment improves us when it carries a healthy message. Shows that promote smoking or gratuitous violence are bad for us, while those that thunder against teen pregnancy or intolerance have a positive role in society. Judged by that morality play standard, the story of popular culture over the past fifty years — if not five hundred — is a story of steady decline: the morals of the stories have grown darker and more ambiguous, and the anti-heroes have multiplied.

25

The usual counterargument here is that what media has lost in moral clarity it has gained in realism. The real world doesn't come in nicely packaged public service announcements, and we're better off with entertainment that reflects that fallen state with all its ethical ambiguity. I happen to be sympathetic to that argument, but it's not the one I want to make here. I think there is another way to assess the social virtue of pop culture, one that looks at media as a kind of cognitive workout, not as a series of life lessons. Those dice baseball games I immersed myself in didn't contain anything resembling moral instruction, but they nonetheless gave me a set of cognitive tools that I continue to rely on, nearly thirty years later. There may indeed be more "negative messages" in the mediasphere today, as the Parents Television Council believes. But that's not the only way to evaluate

26

---

[6]Parents Television Council. (The passage was found in the past at the Council's website, http://www.parentstv.org/.)

[7]Suzanne Fields, "Janet and a Shameless Culture," *The Washington Times*, February 2, 2004.

whether our television shows or video games are having a positive impact. Just as important — if not *more* important — is the kind of thinking you have to do to make sense of a cultural experience. That is where the Sleeper Curve becomes visible. Today's popular culture may not be showing us the righteous path. But it is making us smarter.

Games

You can't get much more conventional than the conventional wisdom that   27
kids today would be better off spending more time reading books, and less time zoning out in front of their video games. The latest edition of *Dr. Spock* — "revised and fully expanded for a new century" as the cover reports — has this to say of video games: "The best that can be said of them is that they may help promote eye-hand coordination in children. The worst that can be said is that they sanction, and even promote aggression and violent responses to conflict. But what can be said with much greater certainty is this: most computer games are a colossal waste of time." But where reading is concerned, the advice is quite different: "I suggest you begin to foster in your children a love of reading and the printed word from the start. . . . What is important is that your child be an avid reader."[8]

In the middle of 2004, the National Endowment for the Arts released a   28
study that showed that reading for pleasure had declined steadily among all major American demographic groups. The writer Andrew Solomon analyzed the consequences of this shift: "People who read for pleasure are many times more likely than those who don't to visit museums and attend musical performances, almost three times as likely to perform volunteer and charity work, and almost twice a likely to attend sporting events. Readers, in other words, are active, while nonreaders — more than half the population — have settled into apathy. There is a basic social divide between those for whom life is an accrual of fresh experience and knowledge, and those for whom maturity is a process of mental atrophy. The shift toward the latter category is frightening."[9]

The intellectual nourishment of reading books is so deeply ingrained   29
in our assumptions that it's hard to contemplate a different viewpoint. But as McLuhan famously observed, the problem with judging new cultural

---

[8]Benjamin Spock and Steven J. Parker, *Dr. Spock's Baby and Child Care* (New York: Pocket Books, 1998), p. 625.

[9]Andrew Solomon, "The Closing of the American Book," *The New York Times*, July 10, 2004. Solomon is a thoughtful and eloquent writer, but this essay by him contains a string of bizarre assertions, none of them supported by facts or common sense. Consider this passage: "My last book was about depression, and the question I am most frequently asked is why depression is on the rise. I talk about the loneliness that comes of spending the day with a TV or a computer or video screen. Conversely, literary reading is an entry into dialogue; a book can be a friend, talking not at you, but to you." Begin with the fact that most video games contain genuine dialogue, where your character must interact with other onscreen characters, in contrast to books, in which the "dialogue" between

systems on their own terms is that the presence of the recent past inevitably colors your vision of the emerging form, highlighting the flaws and imperfections. Games have historically suffered from this syndrome, largely because they have been contrasted with the older conventions of reading. To get around these prejudices, try this thought experiment. Imagine an alternate world identical to ours save one techno-historical change: video games were invented and popularized *before* books. In this parallel universe, kids have been playing games for centuries — and then these page-bound texts come along and suddenly they're all the rage. What would the teachers, and the parents, and the cultural authorities have to say about this frenzy of reading? I suspect it would sound something like this:

> Reading books chronically understimulates the senses. Unlike the longstanding tradition of gameplaying — which engages the child in a vivid, three-dimensional world filled with moving images and musical soundscapes, navigated and controlled with complex muscular movements — books are simply a barren string of words on the page. Only a small portion of the brain devoted to processing written language is activated during reading, while games engage the full range of the sensory and motor cortices.
>
> Books are also tragically isolating. While games have for many years engaged the young in complex social relationships with their peers, building and exploring worlds together, books force the child to sequester him- or herself in a quiet space, shut off from interaction with other children. These new "libraries" that have arisen in recent years to facilitate reading activities are a frightening sight: dozens of young children, normally so vivacious and socially interactive, sitting alone in cubicles, reading silently, oblivious to their peers.
>
> Many children enjoy reading books, of course, and no doubt some of the flights of fancy conveyed by reading have their escapist merits. But for a sizable percentage of the population, books are downright discriminatory. The reading craze of recent years cruelly taunts the 10 million Americans who suffer from dyslexia — a condition that didn't even exist as a condition until printed text came along to stigmatize its sufferers.
>
> But perhaps the most dangerous property of these books is the fact that they follow a fixed linear path. You can't control their narratives in any fashion — you simply sit back and have the story dictated to you. For those of us raised on interactive narratives, this property may seem astonishing. Why would anyone want to embark on an adventure utterly choreographed by another person? But today's generation embarks on such adventures millions of times a day. This risks instilling a general passivity in our children, making them feel as though they're powerless to change their circumstances. Reading is not an active, participatory process; it's a submissive one. The book readers of the younger generation are learning to "follow the plot" instead of learning to lead.

---

reader and text is purely metaphorical. When you factor in the reality that most games are played in social contexts — together with friends in shared physical space, or over network connections — you get the sense that Solomon hasn't spent any time with the game form he lambastes. So that by the time he asserts, "Reading is harder than watching television or playing video games," you have to ask: Which video game, exactly, is he talking about? Certainly, reading *Ulysses* is harder than playing *PacMan*, but is reading Stephen King harder than playing *Zelda* or *SimCity*? Hardly.

It should probably go without saying, but it probably goes better with 30 saying, that I don't agree with this argument. But neither is it exactly right to say that its contentions are untrue. The argument relies on a kind of amplified selectivity: it foregrounds certain isolated properties of books, and then projects worst-case scenarios based on these properties and their potential effects on the "younger generation." But it doesn't bring up any of the clear benefits of reading: the complexity of argument and story-telling offered by the book form; the stretching of the imagination trig-gered by reading words on a page; the shared experience you get when everyone is reading the same story.

A comparable sleight of hand is at work anytime you hear someone 31 bemoaning today's video game obsessions and their stupefying effects on tomorrow's generations. Games are not novels, and the ways in which they harbor novelistic aspirations are invariably the least interesting thing about them. You can judge games by the criteria designed to evaluate nov-els: Are the characters believable? Is the dialogue complex? But inevitably, the games will come up wanting. Games are good at novelistic storytelling the way Michael Jordan was good at playing baseball. Both could probably make a living at it, but their world-class talents lie elsewhere.

Before we get to those talents, let me say a few words about the virtues 32 of reading books. For the record, I think those virtues are immense ones — and not just because I make a living writing books. We should all encourage our kids to read more, to develop a comfort with and an appetite for reading. But even the most avid reader in this culture is invariably going to spend his or her time with other media — with games, television, movies, or the Inter-net. And these other forms of culture have intellectual or cognitive virtues in their own right — different from, but comparable to, the rewards of reading.

What are the rewards of reading, exactly? Broadly speaking, they fall 33 into two categories: the information conveyed by the book, and the mental work you have to do to process and store that information. Think of this as the difference between acquiring information and exercising the mind. When we encourage kids to read for pleasure, we're generally doing so because of the mental exercise involved. In Andrew Solomon's words: "[Reading] requires effort, concentration, attention. In exchange, it offers the stimulus to and the fruit of thought and feeling." Spock says: "Unlike most amusements, reading is an activity requiring active participation. We must do the reading ourselves — actively scan the letters, make sense of the words, and follow the thread of the story." Most tributes to the mental benefits of reading also invoke the power of imagination; reading books forces you to concoct entire worlds in your head, rather than simply ingest a series of prepackaged images. And then there is the slightly circular — though undoubtedly true — argument for the long-term career benefits: being an avid reader is good for you because the educational system and the job market put a high premium on reading skills.

To summarize, the cognitive benefits of reading involve these faculties: 34 effort, concentration, attention, the ability to make sense of words, to follow narrative threads, to sculpt imagined worlds out of mere sentences on the page. Those benefits are themselves amplified by the fact that society places a substantial emphasis on precisely this set of skills.

The very fact that I am presenting this argument to you in the form of 35 a book and not a television drama or a video game should make it clear that I believe the printed word remains the most powerful vehicle for conveying complicated information — though the *electronic* word is starting to give printed books a run for their money. The argument that follows is centered squarely on the side of mental exercise — and not content. I aim to persuade you of two things:

1. By almost all the standards we use to measure reading's cognitive benefits — attention, memory, following threads, and so on — the nonliterary popular culture has been steadily growing more challenging over the past thirty years.

2. Increasingly, the nonliterary popular culture is honing *different* mental skills that are just as important as the ones exercised by reading books.

Despite the warnings of Dr. Spock, the most powerful examples of both 36 these trends are found in the world of video games. Over the past few years, you may have noticed the appearance of a certain type of story about gaming culture in mainstream newspapers and periodicals. The message of that story ultimately reduces down to: Playing video games may not actually be a *complete* waste of time. Invariably these stories point to some new study focused on a minor side effect of gameplaying — often manual dexterity or visual memory — and explain that heavy gamers show improved skills compared to non-gamers.[10] (The other common let's-take-games-seriously

---

[10]I don't dwell on the manual dexterity question here, but it's worth noting how the control systems for these games have grown strikingly more complex over the past decade or so. Compare the original *Legend of Zelda* (July 1987), on the original NES, to the current *Zelda*, on the GameCube (March 2003). In sixteen years, games have changed as follows:

THEN	Now
Controller	*Controller*
4 direction buttons	2 joysticks + 4 direction buttons
2 action buttons	7 action buttons
Each button has a single function.	Each combo of buttons has a unique function.
Perspective	*Perspective*
Static overhead view	Dynamic player-controlled "camera" view
You always have complete vision.	Your vision is limited. You must control it.
The game is "flat" (two-dimensional).	The game is "virtual" (three-dimensional).
Gameplay	*Gameplay*
Movement is in one of four directions.	Movement is in any direction, including up and down.
Fighting: 2 buttons	Fighting: More than 10 different button combos. Requires accurate timing and coordination.
Objects: Press a single button.	Objects: Assign a button, learn unique controls to use each object. Requires timing, training.

story is financial, usually pointing to the fact that the gaming industry now pulls in more money than Hollywood.)

Now, I have no doubt that playing today's games does in fact improve 37 your visual intelligence and your manual dexterity, but the virtues of gaming run far deeper than hand-eye coordination. When I read these ostensibly positive accounts of video games, they strike me as the equivalent of writing a story about the merits of the great novels and focusing on how reading them can improve your spelling. It's true enough, I suppose, but it doesn't do justice to the rich, textured experience of novel reading. There's a comparable blindness at work in the way games have been covered to date. For all the discussion of gaming culture that you see, the actual experience of playing games has been strangely misrepresented. We hear a lot about the content of games: the carnage and drive-by killings and adolescent fantasies. But we rarely hear accurate descriptions about what it actually *feels like* to spend time in these virtual worlds. I worry about the experiential gap between people who have immersed themselves in games, and people who have only heard secondhand reports, because the gap makes it difficult to discuss the meaning of games in a coherent way. It reminds me of the way the social critic Jane Jacobs felt about the thriving urban neighborhoods she documented in the sixties: "People who know well such animated city streets will know how it is. People who do not will always have it a little wrong in their heads — like the old prints of rhinoceroses made from travelers' descriptions of the rhinoceroses."

So what does the rhinoceros actually look like?[11] The first and last 38 thing that should be said about the experience of playing today's video games, the thing you almost never hear in the mainstream coverage, is that games are fiendishly, sometimes maddeningly, *hard.*

The dirty little secret of gaming is how much time you spend not hav- 39 ing fun. You may be frustrated; you may be confused or disoriented; you

---

[11]Henry Jenkins has painted perhaps the most accurate picture of the rhinoceros of pop culture over the past decade: "Often, our response to popular culture is shaped by a hunger for simple answers and quick actions. It is important to take the time to understand the complexity of contemporary culture. We need to learn how to be safe, critical and creative users of media. We need to evaluate the information and entertainment we consume. We need to understand the emotional investments we make in media content. And perhaps most importantly, we need to learn not to treat differences in taste as mental pathologies or social problems. We need to think, talk, and listen. When we tell students that popular culture has no place in classroom discussions, we are signaling to them that what they learn in school has little to do with the things that matter to them at home. When we avoid discussing popular culture at the dinner table, we may be suggesting we have no interest in things that are important to our children. When we tell our parents that they wouldn't understand our music or our fashion choices, we are cutting them off from an important part of who we are and what we value. We do not need to share each other's passions. But we do need to respect and understand them." "Encouraging Conversations About Popular Culture and Media Convergence: An Outreach Program for Parents, Students, and Teachers, March–May 2000." http://web.mit.edu/21fms/www/faculty/henry3/resourceguide.html.

may be stuck. When you put the game down and move back into the real world, you may find yourself mentally working through the problem you've been wrestling with, as though you were worrying a loose tooth. If this is mindless escapism, it's a strangely masochistic version. Who wants to escape to a world that irritates you 90 percent of the time?

Consider the story of Troy Stolle, a construction site worker from Indi-   40 anapolis profiled by the technology critic Julian Dibbell. When he's not performing his day job as a carpenter building wooden molds, Stolle lives in the virtual world of *Ultima Online*, the fantasy-themed game that allows you to create a character — sometimes called an avatar — and interact with thousands of other avatars controlled by other humans, connected to the game over the Net. (Imagine a version of Dungeons & Dragons where you're playing with thousands of strangers from all over the world, and you'll get the idea.) *Ultima* and related games like *EverQuest* have famously developed vibrant simulated economies that have begun to leak out into the real world. You can buy a magic sword or a plot of land — entirely made of digital code, mind you — for hundreds of dollars on eBay. But earning these goods the old-fashioned within-the-gameworld way takes time — a lot of time. Dibbell describes the ordeal Stolle had to go through to have his avatar, named Nils Hansen, purchase a new house in the *Ultima* world:

> Stolle had had to come up with the money for the deed. To get the money, he had to sell his old house. To get that house in the first place, he had to spend hours crafting virtual swords and plate mail to sell to a steady clientele of about three dozen fellow players. To attract and keep that clientele, he had to bring Nils Hansen's blacksmithing skills up to Grandmaster. To reach that level, Stolle spent six months doing nothing but smithing: He clicked on hillsides to mine ore, headed to a forge to click the ore into ingots, clicked again to turn the ingots into weapons and armor, and then headed back to the hills to start all over again, each time raising Nils' skill level some tiny fraction of a percentage point, inching him closer to the distant goal of 100 points and the illustrious title of Grandmaster Blacksmith.
>
> Take a moment now to pause, step back, and consider just what was going on here: Every day, month after month, a man was coming home from a full day of bone-jarringly repetitive work with hammer and nails to put in a full night of finger-numbingly repetitive work with "hammer" and "anvil" — and paying $9.95 per month for the privilege. Ask Stolle to make sense of this, and he has a ready answer: "Well, it's not work if you enjoy it." Which, of course, begs the question: Why would anyone enjoy it?[12]

Why? Anyone who has spent more than a few hours trying to complete   41 a game knows the feeling: you get to a point where there's a sequence of tasks you know you have to complete to proceed further into the world, but the tasks themselves are more like chores than entertainment, something you *have* to do, not something you want to do: building roads and

[12]Julian Dibbell, "The Unreal-Estate Boom," *Wired*, January 2003.

laying power lines, retreating through a tunnel sequence to find an object you've left behind, conversing with characters when you've already memorized their lines. And yet a large part of the population performing these tasks every day is composed of precisely the demographic group most averse to doing chores. If you practically have to lock kids in their room to get them to do their math homework, and threaten to ground them to get them to take out the trash, then why are they willing to spend six months smithing in *Ultima*? You'll often hear video games included on the list of the debased instant gratifications that abound in our culture, right up there with raunchy music videos and fast food. But compared to most forms of popular entertainment, games turn out to be all about *delayed* gratification — sometimes so long delayed that you wonder if the gratification is ever going to show.

The clearest measure of the cognitive challenges posed by modern   42 games is the sheer size of the cottage industry devoted to publishing game guides, sometimes called walk-throughs, that give you detailed, step-by-step explanations of how to complete the game that is currently torturing you. During my twenties, I'd wager that I spent somewhere shockingly close to a thousand dollars buying assorted cheat sheets, maps, help books, and phone support to assist my usually futile attempt to complete a video game. My relationship to these reference texts is intimately bound up with my memory of each game, so that the *Myst* sequel *Riven* brings to mind those hours on the automated phone support line, listening to a recorded voice explain that the lever has to be rotated 270 degrees before the blue pipe will connect with the transom, while the playful *Banjo-Kazooie* conjures up a cheery atlas of vibrant level maps, like a child's book where the story has been replaced with linear instruction sets: jump twice on the mushroom, then grab the gold medallion in the moat. Admitting just how much money I spent on these guides sounds like a cry for help, I know, but the great, looming racks of these game guides at most software stores are clear evidence that I am not alone in this habit. The guidebook for the controversial hit game *Grand Theft Auto* alone has sold more than 1.6 million copies.

Think about the existence of these guides in the context of other forms   43 of popular entertainment. There are plenty of supplementary texts that accompany Hollywood movies or Billboard chart-toppers: celebrity profiles, lyrics sheets, reviews, fan sites, commentary tracks on DVDs. These texts can widen your understanding of a film or an album, but you'll almost never find yourself *needing* one. People don't walk into theaters with guidebooks that they consult via flashlight during the film. But they regularly rely on these guides when playing a game. The closest cultural form to the game guide is the august tradition of CliffsNotes marketed as readers' supplements to the Great Books. There's nothing puzzling about the existence of CliffsNotes: we accept both the fact that the Great Books are complicated, and the fact that millions of young people are forced more or less against their will to at least pretend to read them. Ergo: a thriving market for CliffsNotes. Game guides, however, confound our expectations: because we're not used to accepting the complexity of gaming culture, and because nobody's forcing the kids to master these games.

The need for such guides is a relatively new development: you didn't 44 need ten pages to explain the *PacMan* system, but two hundred pages barely does justice to an expanding universe like *EverQuest* or *Ultima*. You need them because the complexity of these worlds can be overwhelming: you're stuck in the middle of a level, with all the various exits locked and no sign of a key. Or the password for the control room you thought you found two hours ago turns out not to work. Or the worst case: you're wandering aimlessly through hallways, like those famous tracking shots from *The Shining*, and you've got no real idea what you're supposed to be doing next.

This aimlessness, of course, is the price of interactivity. You're more in 45 control of the narrative now, but your supply of information about the narrative — whom you should talk to next, where that mysterious package has been hidden — is only partial, and so playing one of these games is ultimately all about filling in that information gap. When it works, it can be exhilarating, but when it doesn't — well, that's when you start shelling out the fifteen bucks for the cheat sheet. And then you find yourself hunched over the computer screen, help guide splayed open on the desk, flipping back and forth between the virtual world and the level maps, trying to find your way. After a certain point — perhaps when the level maps don't turn out to be all that helpful, or perhaps when you find yourself reading the help guides over dinner — you start saying to yourself: Remind me why this is fun?

So why does anyone bother playing these things? Why do we use the 46 word "play" to describe this torture? I'm always amazed to see what our brains are willing to tolerate to reach the next level in these games. Several years ago I found myself on a family vacation with my seven-year-old nephew, and on one rainy day I decided to introduce him to the wonders of *SimCity 2000*, the legendary city simulator that allows you to play Robert Moses to a growing virtual metropolis. For most of our session, I was controlling the game, pointing out landmarks as I scrolled around my little town. I suspect I was a somewhat condescending guide — treating the virtual world as more of a model train layout than a complex system. But he was picking up the game's inner logic nonetheless. After about an hour of tinkering, I was concentrating on trying to revive one particularly rundown manufacturing district. As I contemplated my options, my nephew piped up: "I think we need to lower our industrial tax rates." He said it as naturally, and as confidently, as he might have said, "I think we need to shoot the bad guy."

The interesting question here for me is not whether games are, on the 47 whole, more complex than most other cultural experiences targeted at kids today — I think the answer to that is an emphatic yes. The question is why kids are so eager to soak up that much information when it is delivered to them in game form. My nephew would be asleep in five seconds if you popped him down in an urban studies classroom, but somehow an hour of playing *SimCity* taught him that high tax rates in industrial areas can stifle development. That's a powerful learning experience, for reasons we'll explore in the coming pages. But let's start with the more elemental question of desire. Why does a seven-year-old soak up the intricacies of industrial economics in game form, when the same subject would send him screaming for the exits in a classroom?

The quick explanations of this mystery are not helpful. Some might *48* say it's the flashy graphics, but games have been ensnaring our attention since the days of *Pong*, which was — graphically speaking — a huge step backward compared with television or movies, not to mention reality. Others would say it's the violence and sex, and yet games like *SimCity* — and indeed most of the best-selling games of all time — have almost no violence and sex in them. Some might argue that it's the interactivity that hooks, the engagement of building your own narrative. But if active participation alone functions as a drug that entices the mind, then why isn't the supremely *passive* medium of television repellant to kids?

Why do games captivate? I believe the answer involves a deeper prop- *49* erty that most games share — a property that will be instantly familiar to anyone who has spent time in this world, but one that is also strangely absent from most outside descriptions. To appreciate this property you need to look at game culture through the lens of neuroscience. There's a logical reason to use that lens, of course: if you're trying to figure out why cocaine is addictive, you need a working model of what cocaine is, and you need a working model of how the brain functions. The same goes for the question of why games are such powerful attractors. Explaining that phenomenon without a working model of the mind tells only half the story.

. . . Cultural critics like to speculate on the cognitive changes induced *50* by new forms of media, but they rarely invoke the insights of brain science and other empirical research in backing up those claims. All too often, this has the effect of reducing their arguments to mere superstition. If you're trying to make sense of a new cultural form's effect on the way we view the world, you need to be able to describe the cultural object in some detail, and also demonstrate how that object transforms the mind that is apprehending it. In some instances, you can measure that transformation through traditional modes of intelligence testing; in some cases, you can measure changes by looking at brain activity directly, thanks to modern scanning technology; and in cases where the empirical research hasn't yet been done, you can make informed speculation based on our understanding of how the brain works.

To date, there has been very little direct research into the question of how *51* games manage to get kids to learn without realizing that they're learning. But a strong case can be made that the power of games to captivate involves their ability to tap into the brain's natural reward circuitry. Because of its central role in drug addiction, the reward circuits of the brain have been extensively studied and mapped in recent years. Two insights that have emerged from this study are pertinent to the understanding of games. First, neuroscientists have drawn a crucial distinction between the way the brain seeks out reward and the way it delivers pleasure. The body's natural painkillers, the opioids, are the brain's pure pleasure drugs, while the reward system revolves around the neurotransmitter dopamine interacting with specific receptors in a part of the brain called the nucleus accumbens.

The dopamine system is a kind of accountant: keeping track of expected 52 rewards, and sending out an alert — in the form of lowered dopamine levels — when those rewards don't arrive as promised. When the pack-a-day smoker deprives himself of his morning cigarette; when the hotshot Wall Street trader doesn't get the bonus he was planning on; when the late-night snacker opens the freezer to find someone's pilfered all the Ben & Jerry's — the disappointment and craving these people experience is triggered by lowered dopamine levels.

The neuroscientist Jaak Panksepp calls the dopamine system the 53 brain's "seeking" circuitry, propelling us to seek out new avenues for reward in our environment. Where our brain wiring is concerned, the craving instinct triggers a desire to explore. The system says, in effect: "Can't find the reward you were promised? Perhaps if you just look a little harder you'll be in luck — it's got to be around here somewhere."

How do these findings connect to games? Researchers have long sus- 54 pected that geometric games like *Tetris* have such a hypnotic hold over us (longtime *Tetris* players have vivid dreams about the game) because the game's elemental shapes activate modules in our visual system that execute low-level forms of pattern recognition — sensing parallel and perpendicular lines, for instance. These modules are churning away in the background all the time, but the simplified graphics of *Tetris* bring them front and center in our consciousness. I believe that what *Tetris* does to our visual circuitry, most video games do to the reward circuitry of the brain.

Real life is full of rewards, which is one reason why there are now so 55 many forms of addiction. You can be rewarded by love and social connection, financial success, drug abuse, shopping, chocolate, and watching your favorite team win the Super Bowl. But supermarkets and shopping malls aside, most of life goes by without the potential rewards available to you being clearly defined. You know you'd like that promotion, but it's a long way off, and right now you've got to deal with getting this memo out the door. Real-life reward usually hovers at the margins of day-to-day existence — except for the more primal rewards of eating and making love, both of which exceed video games in their addictiveness.

In the gameworld, reward is everywhere. The universe is literally teem- 56 ing with objects that deliver very clearly articulated rewards: more life, access to new levels, new equipment, new spells. Game rewards are fractal; each scale contains its own reward network, whether you're just learning to use the controller, or simply trying to solve a puzzle to raise some extra cash, or attempting to complete the game's ultimate mission. Most of the crucial work in game interface design revolves around keeping players notified of potential rewards available to them, and how much those rewards are currently needed. Just as *Tetris* streamlines the fuzzy world of visual reality to a core set of interacting shapes, most games offer a fictional world where rewards are larger, and more vivid, more clearly defined, than life.

This is true even of games that have been rightly celebrated for their open-endedness. *SimCity* is famous for not forcing the player along a preordained narrative line; you can build any kind of community you want: small farming villages, vast industrial Coketowns, high-centric edge cities or pedestrian-friendly neighborhoods. But the game has a subtle reward architecture that plays a major role in the game's addictiveness: the software withholds a trove of objects and activities until you've reached certain predefined levels, either of population, money, or popularity. You can build pretty much any kind of environment you want playing *SimCity*, but you can't build a baseball stadium until you have fifty thousand residents. Similarly, *Grand Theft Auto* allows players to drive aimlessly through a vast urban environment, creating their own narratives as they explore the space. But for all that open-endedness, the game still forces you to complete a series of pre-defined missions before you are allowed to enter new areas of the city. The very games that are supposed to be emblems of unstructured user control turn out to dangle rewards at every corner.

"Seeking" is the perfect word for the drive these designs instill in their players. You want to win the game, of course, and perhaps you want to see the game's narrative completed. In the initial stages of play, you may just be dazzled by the game's graphics. But most of the time, when you're hooked on a game, what draws you in is an elemental form of desire: the desire to *see the next thing.* You want to cross that bridge to see what the east side of the city looks like, or try out that teleportation module, or build an aquarium on the harbor. To someone who has never felt that sort of compulsion, the underlying motivation can seem a little strange: you want to build the aquarium not, in the old mountaineering expression, because it's there, but rather because it's not there, or not there *yet.* It's not there, but you know — because you've read the manual or the game guide, or because the interface is flashing it in front of your eyes — you know that if you just apply yourself, if you spend a little more time cultivating new residents and watching the annual budget, the aquarium will eventually be yours to savor.

In a sense, neuroscience has offered up a prediction here, one that games obligingly confirm. If you create a system where rewards are both clearly defined and achieved by exploring an environment, you'll find human brains drawn to those systems, even if they're made up of virtual characters and simulated sidewalks. It's not the subject matter of these games that attracts — if that were the case, you'd never see twenty-somethings following absurd rescue-the-princess storylines like the best-selling *Zelda* series on the Nintendo platform. It's the reward system that draws those players in, and keeps their famously short attention spans locked on the screen. No other form of entertainment offers that cocktail of reward and exploration: we don't "explore" movies or television or music in anything but the most figurative sense of the word. And while there are rewards to those other forms — music in fact has been shown to trigger opioid release in the brain — they don't come in the exaggerated, tantalizing packaging that video games wrap around them.

You might reasonably object at this point that I have merely demon- 60 strated that video games are the digital equivalent of crack cocaine. Crack also has a powerful hold over the human brain, thanks in part to its manipulations of the dopamine system. But that doesn't make it a good thing. If games have been unwittingly designed to lock into our brain's reward architecture, then what positive value are we getting out of that intoxication? Without that positive value the Sleeper Curve is meaningless.

Here again, you have to shed your expectations about older cultural 61 forms to make sense of the new. Game players are not soaking up moral counsel, life lessons, or rich psychological portraits. They are not having emotional experiences with their Xbox, other than the occasional adrenaline rush. The narratives they help create now rival pulp Hollywood fare, which is an accomplishment when measured against the narratives of *Pac-Man* and *Pong*, but it's still setting the bar pretty low. With the occasional exception, the actual *content* of the game is often childish or gratuitously menacing — though, again, not any more so than your average summer blockbuster. Complex social and historical simulations like *Age of Empires* or *Civilization* do dominate the game charts, and no doubt these games do impart some useful information about ancient Rome or the design of mass transit systems. But much of the roleplay inside the gaming world alternates between drive-by shooting and princess rescuing.

De-emphasizing the content of game culture shouldn't be seen as a 62 cop-out. We ignore the content of many activities that are widely considered to be good for the brain or the body. No one complains about the simplistic, militaristic plot of chess games. ("It always ends the same way!") We teach algebra to children knowing full well that the day they leave the classroom, ninety-nine percent of those kids will never again directly employ their algebraic skills. Learning algebra isn't about acquiring a specific tool; it's about building up a mental muscle that will come in handy elsewhere. You don't go to the gym because you're interested in learning how to operate a StairMaster; you go to the gym because operating a StairMaster does something laudable to your body, the benefits of which you enjoy during the many hours of the week when you're not on a StairMaster.

So it is with games. It's not *what* you're thinking about when you're 63 playing a game, it's *the way* you're thinking that matters. The distinction is not exclusive to games, of course. Here's John Dewey, in his book *Experience and Education*: "Perhaps the greatest of all pedagogical fallacies is the notion that a person learns only that particular thing he is studying at the time. Collateral learning in the way of formation of enduring attitudes, of likes and dislikes, may be and often is much more important than the spelling lesson or lesson in geography or history that is learned. For these attitudes are fundamentally what count in the future."[13]

This is precisely where we need to make our portrait of the rhinoceros *64* as accurate as possible: defining the collateral learning that goes beyond the explicit content of the experience. Start with the basics: far more than books or movies or music, games force you to make *decisions*. Novels may activate our imagination, and music may conjure up powerful emotions, but games force you to decide, to choose, to prioritize. All the intellectual benefits of gaming derive from this fundamental virtue, because learning how to think is ultimately about learning to make the right decisions: weighing evidence, analyzing situations, consulting your long-term goals, and then deciding. No other pop cultural form directly engages the brain's decision-making apparatus in the same way. From the outside, the primary activity of a gamer looks like a fury of clicking and shooting, which is why so much of the conventional wisdom about games focuses on hand-eye coordination. But if you peer inside the gamer's mind, the primary activity turns out to be another creature altogether: making decisions, some of them snap judgments, some long-term strategies.

[13]John Dewey, *Experience and Education* (London: Collier, 1963), p. 48.

■ ■ ■

Reading Rhetorically

1. How does Johnson set up his argumentative strategy in paragraphs 1 and 2 of the selection? Locate and mark the sentences that explain his very different perspective on popular culture. What effect does he hope his argument will have on his readers?

2. Johnson defines the "Sleeper Curve" in the first paragraph; he defines it again in several other passages. What different examples does he offer, and which do you find most helpful? Working on your own or in a small group, develop a few more pop culture examples that either support or refute Johnson's concept of the Sleeper Curve.

3. One of Johnson's rhetorical patterns is the use of questions. Underline all the questions you find in the selection. What purposes do these questions serve? In particular, consider where they appear in a paragraph, what they set up, and how Johnson answers them or does not answer them. How might you apply the strategy of asking questions in your own writing?

Inquiring Further

4. Using your library's resources, find and read three scholarly articles on one of the games Johnson writes about. Look for articles from a range of

perspectives and academic disciplines (for example, sociology, psychology or developmental psychology, and cultural studies). What concerns do these articles raise? How well does Johnson's argument address them? Share your findings with your classmates.

5. In paragraph 29, Johnson performs a "thought experiment": He imagines what experts would say about the dangers of reading if reading had become popular after, rather than before, video games. Working with a small group, try a similar thought experiment, developing an argument *against* something that currently is thought to be a positive educational pursuit, and *for* a pastime currently thought to be bad for us but that you believe has educational value. Each group should present its arguments, and then the class should discuss what can be learned from constructing such "unlikely" arguments. Refer to paragraph 30 for Johnson's strategies for evaluating arguments.

6. In paragraph 63, Johnson presents a central component of his argument: "It's not *what* you're thinking about when you're playing a game, it's *the way* you're thinking that matters." The relative importance of students' acquiring content over skills is a topic of debate among educators. Use your library's resources to find two scholarly articles that explore this issue, and share your findings with your classmates. Where do you stand on this issue, and why?

Framing Conversations

7. How does Henry Jenkins's term *boy culture* help explain both the appeal of and the audience for the game culture Johnson describes in his essay? What do Cynthia Selfe's insights about the marketing of technology contribute to your thoughts on the examples in Johnson's essay? Write an essay in which you analyze Johnson's examples through the concepts of gender and technology presented by Jenkins (p. 700) and Selfe (p. 783). What points can you make about Johnson's examples that he does not make? Take a stand in this conversation about how and why some pastimes (you can offer other examples) become identified with one gender.

8. Johnson argues that "everything bad is good for you"; Eric Schlosser, on the other hand, argues almost the opposite in his attack on "your trusted friends" at McDonald's (p. 754). Using the strategies these authors employ, write an essay in which you argue against the prevailing opinion that some aspect of popular culture is either "good" or "bad" for us. As Johnson and Schlosser do, be sure to offer concrete and detailed examples.

9. Like Johnson, Mary Louise Pratt (p. 354) argues the importance of seemingly insignificant knowledge — baseball trivia, for example. According to these two authors, what does this kind of knowledge offer children? Write an essay in which you evaluate the claims these two authors make about the uses of "useless" knowledge. (You will need to do an online search for one or two articles by educators who take the content side in the content-verses-skill debate.) What stand do you take in this debate? What is at stake, and for whom?

■ ERIC SCHLOSSER

Your Trusted Friends

Eric Schlosser has won numerous awards for his exposé-style journalism, which has appeared in *The Atlantic, Rolling Stone, Vanity Fair, The Nation,* and *The New Yorker,* among other magazines. He has published several best-selling books, including *Reefer Madness: Sex, Drugs, and Cheap Labor in the American Black Market* (2003) and, with Charles Wilson, *Chew on This: Everything You Don't Want to Know About Fast Food* (2006), which introduces middle school readers to the history of the fast-food industry and the agribusiness and animal-raising practices that industry fosters. *Chew on This* evolved from *Fast Food Nation: The Dark Side of the All-American Meal* (2001), from which the reading here is taken. The book has been assigned for campuswide reading at many universities, and it inspired a 2006 film version, directed by Richard Linklater and starring Greg Kinnear. Schlosser's expertise on America's food industry has made him a popular lecturer on and off campus; he also has addressed Congress about the risk to the food supply from bioterrorism.

Fast Food Nation has been compared to Upton Sinclair's book *The Jungle* (1905), which exposed the meat industry to public scrutiny. The ensuing outcry over the dangerous and unsanitary industry helped fuel the passage of the Pure Food and Drugs Act (1906) and the Meat Inspection Act (1906). Schlosser is one of a growing number of writers who focus on "sausage making" in the food industry, including Michael Pollan, whose book *The Omnivore's Dilemma: A Natural History of Four Meals* (2006) traces the sources of four meals, and Morgan Spurlock, who documented thirty days of eating at McDonald's in his film *Super Size Me* (2004). Because the food we eat is controversial, Schlosser documents his sources carefully, as you can see from the extensive footnotes. Although his writing is for a general audience, Schlosser fills his paragraphs with examples and quotations drawn from other sources. As you read, consider how this painstakingly documented research affects the credibility of his claims.

Schlosser's interest in the fast-food industry extends to the industry's marketing campaigns and their focus on children. Schlosser claims that campaigns that target children, particularly through the use of toys, reflects a "perfect synergy" (para. 47) of Walt Disney's and Ray Kroc's marketing strategies. Think back to your own childhood encounters with Happy Meals. How did the toys, the packaging, and the commercials affect your association with fast food? Do Schlosser's insights change your thinking about marketing campaigns by fast-food restaurants? If yes, how?

Like any good writer, Schlosser uses details to persuade his readers. Keep track of the images and facts you find most compelling, and consider how you might use similar strategies in your own writing. Pay attention to the way Schlosser weaves together the strands of his argument about the past and present of fast food, the intersection of dining and consumer culture, and the effects of aggressive marketing to children. Schlosser helped ignite a conversation about what we eat — and why — that is likely to continue for a long time. If you find the ideas here fascinating, there are

many other books about food-industry reform you might enjoy. This reading may introduce you to a conversation you would like to be part of, and
that could change the way you eat as well as the way you think.

■ ■ ■

Before entering the Ray A. Kroc Museum, you have to walk through *1*
McStore. Both sit on the ground floor of McDonald's corporate headquarters, located at One McDonald's Plaza in Oak Brook, Illinois. The
headquarters building has oval windows and a gray concrete façade — a
look that must have seemed space-age when the building opened three
decades ago. Now it seems stolid and drab, an architectural relic of the
Nixon era. It resembles the American embassy compounds that always
used to attract antiwar protesters, student demonstrators, flag burners.
The eighty-acre campus of Hamburger University, McDonald's managerial
training center, is a short drive from headquarters. Shuttle buses constantly go back and forth between the campus and McDonald's Plaza, fer-
rying clean-cut young men and women in khakis who've come to study for
their "Degree in Hamburgerology." The course lasts two weeks and trains a
few thousand managers, executives, and franchisees each year. Students
from out of town stay at the Hyatt on the McDonald's campus. Most of the
classes are devoted to personnel issues, teaching lessons in teamwork and
employee motivation, promoting "a common McDonald's language" and
"a common McDonald's culture." Three flagpoles stand in front of McDonald's Plaza, the heart of the hamburger empire. One flies the Stars and
Stripes, another flies the Illinois state flag, and the third flies a bright red
flag with golden arches.

You can buy bean-bag McBurglar dolls at McStore, telephones shaped *2*
like french fries, ties, clocks, key chains, golf bags and duffel bags, jewelry,
baby clothes, lunch boxes, mouse pads, leather jackets, postcards, toy
trucks, and much more, all of it bearing the stamp of McDonald's. You can
buy T-shirts decorated with a new version of the American flag. The fifty
white stars have been replaced by a pair of golden arches.

At the back of McStore, past the footsteps of Ronald McDonald sten- *3*
ciled on the floor, past the shelves of dishes and glassware, a bronze bust of
Ray Kroc marks the entrance to his museum. Kroc was the founder of the
McDonald's Corporation, and his philosophy of QSC and V — Quality,
Service, Cleanliness, and Value — still guide it. The man immortalized in
bronze is balding and middle-aged, with smooth cheeks and an intense look
in his eyes. A glass display case nearby holds plaques, awards, and letters of
praise. "One of the highlights of my sixty-first birthday celebration," President Richard Nixon wrote in 1974, "was when Tricia suggested we needed a
'break' on our drive to Palm Springs, and we turned in at McDonald's. I had
heard for years from our girls that the 'Big Mac' was really something

special, and while I've often credited Mrs. Nixon with making the best hamburgers in the world, we are both convinced that McDonald's runs a close second. . . . The next time the cook has a night off we will know where to go for fast service, cheerful hospitality — and probably one of the best food buys in America."[1] Other glass cases contain artifacts of Kroc's life, mementos of his long years of struggle and his twilight as a billionaire. The museum is small and dimly lit, displaying each object with reverence. The day I visited, the place was empty and still. It didn't feel like a traditional museum, where objects are coolly numbered, catalogued, and described. It felt more like a shrine.

Many of the exhibits at the Ray A. Kroc Museum incorporate neat *4* technological tricks. Dioramas appear and then disappear when certain buttons are pushed. The voices of Kroc's friends and coworkers — one of them identified as a McDonald's "vice president of individuality" — boom from speakers at the appropriate cue. Darkened glass cases are suddenly illuminated from within, revealing their contents. An artwork on the wall, when viewed from the left, displays an image of Ray Kroc. Viewed from the right, it shows the letters QSC and V. The museum does not have a life-size, Audio-Animatronic version of McDonald's founder telling jokes and anecdotes. But one wouldn't be out of place. An interactive exhibit called "Talk to Ray" shows video clips of Kroc appearing on the *Phil Donahue Show,* being interviewed by Tom Snyder, and chatting with Reverend Robert Schuller at the altar of Orange County's Crystal Cathedral. "Talk to Ray" permits the viewer to ask Kroc as many as thirty-six predetermined questions about various subjects; old videos of Kroc supply the answers. The exhibit wasn't working properly the day of my visit. Ray wouldn't take my questions, and so I just listened to him repeating the same speeches.

The Disneyesque tone of the museum reflects, among other things, *5* many of the similarities between the McDonald's Corporation and the Walt Disney Company. It also reflects the similar paths of the two men who founded these corporate giants. Ray Kroc and Walt Disney were both from Illinois; they were born a year apart, Disney in 1901, Kroc in 1902; they knew each other as young men, serving together in the same World War I ambulance corps; and they both fled the Midwest and settled in southern California, where they played central roles in the creation of new American industries. The film critic Richard Schickel has described Disney's powerful inner need "to order, control, and keep clean any environment he inhabited."[2] The same could easily be said about Ray Kroc, whose obsession with cleanliness and control became one of the hallmarks of his restaurant chain. Kroc cleaned the holes in his mop wringer with a toothbrush.

Kroc and Disney both dropped out of high school and later added the *6* trappings of formal education to their companies. The training school for

---

[1]Exhibit, Ray A. Kroc Museum.
[2]Schickel, *Disney Version,* p. 24.

Disney's theme-park employees was named Disneyland University. More importantly, the two men shared the same vision of America, the same optimistic faith in technology, the same conservative political views. They were charismatic figures who provided an overall corporate vision and grasped the public mood, relying on others to handle the creative and financial details. Walt Disney neither wrote nor drew the animated classics that bore his name. Ray Kroc's attempts to add new dishes to McDonald's menu — such as Kolacky, a Bohemian pastry, and the Hulaburger, a sandwich featuring grilled pineapple and cheese — were unsuccessful. Both men, however, knew how to find and motivate the right talent. While Disney was much more famous and achieved success sooner, Kroc may have been more influential. His company inspired more imitators, wielded more power over the American economy — and spawned a mascot even more famous than Mickey Mouse.[3]

Despite all their success as businessmen and entrepreneurs, as cultural figures and advocates for a particular brand of Americanism, perhaps the most significant achievement of these two men lay elsewhere. Walt Disney and Ray Kroc were masterful salesmen. They perfected the art of selling things to children. And their success led many others to aim marketing efforts at kids, turning America's youngest consumers into a demographic group that is now avidly studied, analyzed, and targeted by the world's largest corporations.

Walt and Ray

Ray Kroc took the McDonald brothers' Speedee Service System and spread it nationwide, creating a fast food empire. Although he founded a company that came to symbolize corporate America, Kroc was never a buttoned-down corporate type. He was a former jazz musician who'd played at speakeasies — and at a bordello, on at least one occasion — during Prohibition. He was a charming, funny, and indefatigable traveling salesman who endured many years of disappointment, a Willy Loman who finally managed to hit it big in his early sixties. Kroc grew up in Oak Park, Illinois, not far from Chicago. His father worked for Western Union. As a high school freshman, Ray Kroc discovered the joys of selling while employed at his uncle's soda fountain. "That was where I learned you could influence people with a smile and enthusiasm," Kroc recalled in his autobiography, *Grinding It Out*, "and sell them a sundae when what they'd come for was a cup of coffee."[4]

Over the years, Kroc sold coffee beans, sheet music, paper cups, Florida real estate, powdered instant beverages called "Malt-a-Plenty" and

---

[3]According to John Love, Ronald McDonald is the most widely recognized commercial character in the United States. Love, *Behind the Arches*, p. 222.

[4]Kroc, *Grinding It Out*, p. 17.

"Shake-a-Plenty," a gadget that could dispense whipped cream or shaving lather, square ice cream scoops, and a collapsible table-and-bench combination called "Fold-a-Nook" that retreated into the wall like a Murphy bed. The main problem with square scoops of ice cream, he found, was that they slid off the plate when you tried to eat them. Kroc used the same basic technique to sell all these things: he tailored his pitch to fit the buyer's tastes. Despite one setback after another, he kept at it, always convinced that success was just around the corner. "If you believe in it, and you believe in it hard," Kroc later told audiences, "it's impossible to fail. I don't care what it is — you can get it!"[5]

Ray Kroc was selling milk-shake mixers in 1954 when he first visited   *10* the new McDonald's Self-Service Restaurant in San Bernardino. The McDonald brothers were two of his best customers. The Multimixer unit that Kroc sold could make five milk shakes at once. He wondered why the McDonald brothers needed eight of the machines. Kroc had visited a lot of restaurant kitchens, out on the road, demonstrating the Multimixer — and had never seen anything like the McDonald's Speedee Service System. "When I saw it," he later wrote, "I felt like some latter-day Newton who'd just had an Idaho potato caromed off his skull."[6] He looked at the restaurant "through the eyes of a salesman" and envisioned putting a McDonald's at busy intersections all across the land.[7]

Richard and "Mac" McDonald were less ambitious. They were clear-   *11* ing $100,000 a year in profits from the restaurant, a huge sum in those days.[8] They already owned a big house and three Cadillacs. They didn't like to travel. They'd recently refused an offer from the Carnation Milk Company, which thought that opening more McDonald's would increase the sales of milk shakes. Nevertheless, Kroc convinced the brothers to sell him the right to franchise McDonald's nationwide. The two could stay at home, while Kroc traveled the country, making them even richer. A deal was signed. Years later Richard McDonald described his first memory of Kroc, a moment that would soon lead to the birth of the world's biggest restaurant chain: "This little fellow comes in, with a high voice, and says, 'hi.'"[9]

After finalizing the agreement with the McDonald brothers, Kroc sent a   *12* letter to Walt Disney. In 1917 the two men had both lied about their ages to join the Red Cross and see battle in Europe. A long time had clearly passed since their last conversation. "Dear Walt," the letter said. "I feel somewhat presumptuous addressing you in this way yet I feel sure you would not want me to address you any other way. My name is Ray A. Kroc. . . . I look over the Company A picture we had taken at Sound Beach, Conn., many times and recall a lot of pleasant memories." After the warm-up came the

---

[5]Voice recording, Ray A. Kroc Museum.
[6]Kroc, *Grinding It Out*, p. 71.
[7]Ibid., pp. 9–10, 72.
[8]Love, *Behind the Arches*, p. 19.
[9]Voice recording, Ray A. Kroc Museum.

pitch: "I have very recently taken over the national franchise of the McDonald's system. I would like to inquire if there may be an opportunity for a McDonald's in your Disneyland Development."[10]

Walt Disney sent Kroc a cordial reply and forwarded his proposal to an executive in charge of the theme park's concessions. Disneyland was still under construction, its opening was eagerly awaited by millions of American children, and Kroc may have had high hopes. According to one account, Disney's company asked Kroc to raise the price of McDonald's french fries from ten cents to fifteen cents; Disney would keep the extra nickel as payment for granting the concession; and the story ends with Ray Kroc refusing to gouge his loyal customers.[11] The account seems highly unlikely, a belated effort by someone at McDonald's to put the best spin on a sales pitch that went nowhere. When Disneyland opened in July of 1955 — an event that Ronald Reagan cohosted for ABC — it had food stands run by Welch's, Stouffer's, and Aunt Jemima's, but no McDonald's. Kroc was not yet in their league. His recollection of Walt Disney as a young man, briefly mentioned in *Grinding It Out*, is not entirely flattering. "He was regarded as a strange duck," Kroc wrote of Disney, "because whenever we had time off and went out on the town to chase girls, he stayed in camp drawing pictures."[12]

Whatever feelings existed between the two men, Walt Disney proved in many respects to be a role model for Ray Kroc. Disney's success had come much more quickly. At the age of twenty-one he'd left the Midwest and opened his own movie studio in Los Angeles. He was famous before turning thirty. In *The Magic Kingdom* (1997) Steven Watts describes Walt Disney's efforts to apply the techniques of mass production to Hollywood moviemaking.[13] He greatly admired Henry Ford and introduced an assembly line and a rigorous division of labor at the Disney Studio, which was soon depicted as a "fun factory."[14] Instead of drawing entire scenes, artists were given narrowly defined tasks, meticulously sketching and inking Disney characters while supervisors watched them and timed how long it took them to complete each cel. During the 1930s the production system at the studio was organized to function like that of an automobile plant. "Hundreds of young people were being trained and fitted," Disney explained, "into a machine for the manufacture of entertainment."[15]

The working conditions at Disney's factory, however, were not always fun. In 1941 hundreds of Disney animators went on strike, expressing support for the Screen Cartoonists Guild. The other major cartoon studios in

[10]Quoted in Leslie Doolittle, "McDonald's Plan Cooked Up Decades Ago," *Orlando Sentinel*, January 8, 1998.
[11]See Boas and Chain, *Big Mac*, p. 25.
[12]Kroc, *Grinding It Out*, p. 19.
[13]See Watts, *Magic Kingdom*, pp. 164–74.
[14]Ibid., p. 167.
[15]Quoted ibid., p. 170.

Hollywood had already signed agreements with the union. Disney's father was an ardent socialist, and Disney's films had long expressed a populist celebration of the common man. But Walt's response to the strike betrayed a different political sensibility. He fired employees who were sympathetic to the union, allowed private guards to rough up workers on the picket line, tried to impose a phony company union, brought in an organized crime figure from Chicago to rig a settlement, and placed a full-page ad in *Variety* that accused leaders of the Screen Cartoonists Guild of being Communists. The strike finally ended when Disney acceded to the union's demands. The experience left him feeling embittered. Convinced that Communist agents had been responsible for his troubles, Disney subsequently appeared as a friendly witness before the House Un-American Activities Committee, served as a secret informer for the FBI, and strongly supported the Hollywood blacklist. During the height of labor tension at his studio, Disney had made a speech to a group of employees, arguing that the solution to their problems rested not with a labor union, but with *a good day's work*. "Don't forget this," Disney told them, "it's the law of the universe that the strong shall survive and the weak must fall by the way, and I don't give a damn what idealistic plan is cooked up, nothing can change that."[16]

Decades later, Ray Kroc used similar language to outline his own political philosophy. Kroc's years on the road as a traveling salesman — carrying his own order forms and sample books, knocking on doors, facing each new customer alone, and having countless doors slammed in his face — no doubt influenced his view of humanity. "Look it is ridiculous to call this an industry," Kroc told a reporter in 1972, dismissing any high-minded analysis of the fast food business. "This is not. This is rat eat rat, dog eat dog. I'll kill 'em, and I'm going to kill 'em before they kill me. You're talking about the American way of survival of the fittest."[17]

While Disney backed right-wing groups and produced campaign ads for the Republican Party, Kroc remained aloof from electoral politics — with one notable exception. In 1972, Kroc gave $250,000 to President Nixon's reelection campaign, breaking the gift into smaller donations, funneling the money through various state and local Republican committees.[18] Nixon had every reason to like McDonald's, long before tasting one of its hamburgers. Kroc had never met the president; the gift did not stem from any personal friendship or fondness. That year the fast food industry was lobbying Congress and the White House to pass new legislation — known as the "McDonald's bill" — that would allow employers to pay sixteen- and seventeen-year-old kids wages 20 percent lower than the minimum wage.

[16]Quoted ibid., p. 223.

[17]Quoted in Boas and Chain, *Big Mac*, pp. 15–16.

[18]For varying interpretations of Kroc's donation, see Kroc, *Grinding It Out*, pp. 191–92; Love, *Behind the Arches*, pp. 357–59; Boas and Chain, *Big Mac*, pp. 198–206; and [Stan] Luxenberg, *Roadside Empires*: *How the Chains Franchised America* (New York: Viking, 1985), pp. 246–48.

Around the time of Kroc's $250,000 donation, McDonald's crew members earned about $1.60 an hour. The subminimum wage proposal would reduce some wages to $1.28 an hour.

The Nixon administration supported the McDonald's bill and permit- [18] ted McDonald's to raise the price of its Quarter Pounders, despite the mandatory wage and price controls restricting other fast food chains. The size and the timing of Kroc's political contribution sparked Democratic accusations of influence peddling. Outraged by the charges, Kroc later called his critics "sons of bitches."[19] The uproar left him wary of backing political candidates. Nevertheless, Kroc retained a soft spot for Calvin Coolidge, whose thoughts on hard work and self-reliance were prominently displayed at McDonald's corporate headquarters.

Better Living

Despite a passionate opposition to socialism and to any government med- [19] dling with free enterprise, Walt Disney relied on federal funds in the 1940s to keep his business afloat. The animators' strike had left the Disney Studio in a precarious financial condition. Disney began to seek government contracts — and those contracts were soon responsible for 90 percent of his studio's output.[20] During World War II, Walt Disney produced scores of military training and propaganda films, including *Food Will Win the War, High-Level Precision Bombing,* and *A Few Quick Facts About Venereal Disease.* After the war, Disney continued to work closely with top military officials and military contractors, becoming America's most popular exponent of Cold War science. For audiences living in fear of nuclear annihilation, Walt Disney became a source of reassurance, making the latest technical advances seem marvelous and exciting. His faith in the goodness of American technology was succinctly expressed by the title of a film that the Disney Studio produced for Westinghouse Electric: *The Dawn of Better Living.*

Disney's passion for science found expression in "Tomorrowland," the [20] name given to a section of his theme park and to segments of his weekly television show. Tomorrowland encompassed everything from space travel to the household appliances of the future, depicting progress as a relentless march toward greater convenience for consumers. And yet, from the very beginning, there was a dark side to this Tomorrowland. It celebrated technology without moral qualms. Some of the science it espoused later proved to be not so benign — and some of the scientists it promoted were unusual role models for the nation's children.

In the mid-1950s Wernher von Braun cohosted and helped produce a [21] series of Disney television shows on space exploration. "Man in Space" and the other Tomorrowland episodes on the topic were enormously

[19]Kroc, *Grinding It Out,* p. 191.
[20]See Watts, *Magic Kingdom,* p. 235.

popular and fueled public support for an American space program. At the time, von Braun was the U.S. Army's leading rocket scientist. He had served in the same capacity for the German army during World War II. He had been an early and enthusiastic member of the Nazi Party, as well as a major in the SS.[21] At least 20,000 slave laborers, many of them Allied prisoners of war, died at Dora-Nordhausen, the factory where von Braun's rockets were built. Less than ten years after the liberation of Dora-Nordhausen, von Braun was giving orders to Disney animators and designing a ride at Disneyland called Rocket to the Moon.[22] Heinz Haber, another key Tomorrowland adviser — and eventually the chief scientific consultant to Walt Disney Productions — spent much of World War II conducting research on high-speed, high-altitude flight for the Luftwaffe Institute for Aviation Medicine.[23] In order to assess the risks faced by German air force pilots, the institute performed experiments on hundreds of inmates at the Dachau concentration camp near Munich. The inmates who survived these experiments were usually killed and then dissected. Haber left Germany after the war and shared his knowledge of aviation

[21]For von Braun's political affiliations, the conditions at Dora-Nordhausen, and the American recruitment of Nazi scientists, I have relied on Tom Bower, *The Paperclip Conspiracy: The Hunt for Nazi Scientists* (Boston: Little, Brown, 1987); Linda Hunt, *Secret Agenda: The United States Government, Nazi Scientists, and Project Paperclip, 1945 to 1990* (New York: St. Martin's Press, 1991); Michael J. Neufeld, *The Rocket and the Reich Peenemünde and the Coming of the Ballistic Missile Era* (New York: Free Press, 1995); and Dennis Piszkiewicz, *Wernher von Braun: The Man Who Sold the Moon* (Westport, Conn.: Praeger, 1998).

[22]For a brief account of Disney and von Braun, see the chapter "Disneyland" in Piszkiewicz, *von Braun*, pp. 83–91.

[23]I stumbled upon Heinz Haber's unusual career path while doing research on another project. Haber was a protégé of Dr. Hubertus Strughold, the director of the Luftwaffe Institute for Aviation Medicine. Strughold later became chief scientist at the U.S. Air Force's Aerospace Medical Division, had a U.S. Air Force library named after him, and was hailed as "the father of U.S. space medicine." I pieced together Heinz Haber's wartime behavior from the following: Otto Gauer and Heinz Haber, "Man Under Gravity-Free Conditions," in *German Aviation Medicine, World War II*, vol. 1 (Washington, D.C.: U.S. Air Force, 1950), pp. 641–43; Henry G. Armstrong, Heinz Haber, and Hubertus Strughold, "Aero Medical Problems of Space Travel" (panel meeting, School of Aviation Medicine), *Journal of Aviation Medicine*, December 1949; "Clinical Factors: USAF Aerospace Medicine," in Mae Mills Link, *Space Medicine in Project Mercury* (NASA SP-4003, 1965); "Beginnings of Space Medicine," "Zero G," and "Multiple G," in Loyds Swenson, Jr., James M. Grimwood, and Charles C. Alexander, *This New Ocean: A History of Project Mercury* (NASA SP-4201, 1966); "History of Research in Subgravity and Zero-G at the Air Force Missile Development Center 1948–1958," in *History of Research in Space Biology and Biodynamics at the US Air Force Missile Development Center, Holloman Air Force Base, New Mexico, 1946–1958* (Historical Division, Air Force Missile Development Center, Holloman Air Force Base).

Accounts of the concentration camp experiments administered by the Luftwaffe can be found in Bower, *Paperclip Conspiracy*, pp. 214–32, and Hunt, *Secret Agenda*, pp. 78–93.

medicine with the U.S. Army Air Force. He later cohosted Disney's "Man in Space" with von Braun. When the Eisenhower administration asked Walt Disney to produce a show championing the civilian use of nuclear power, Heinz Haber was given the assignment.[24] He hosted the Disney broadcast called "Our Friend the Atom" and wrote a popular children's book with the same title, both of which made nuclear fission seem fun, instead of terrifying.[25] "Our Friend the Atom" was sponsored by General Dynamics, a manufacturer of nuclear reactors. The company also financed the atomic submarine ride at Disneyland's Tomorrowland.

The future heralded at Disneyland was one in which every aspect of American life had a corporate sponsor. Walt Disney was the most beloved children's entertainer in the country. He had unrivaled access to impressionable young minds — and other corporations, with other agendas to sell, were eager to come along for the ride. Monsanto built Disneyland's House of the Future, which was made of plastic. General Electric backed the Carousel of Progress, which featured an Audio-Animatronic housewife, standing in her futuristic kitchen, singing about "a great big beautiful tomorrow." Richfield Oil offered utopian fantasies about cars and a ride aptly named Autopia. "Here you leave Today," said the plaque at the entrance to Disneyland, "and enter the world of Yesterday, Tomorrow, and Fantasy."

At first, Disneyland offered visitors an extraordinary feeling of escape; people had never seen anything like it. The great irony, of course, is that Disney's suburban, corporate world of Tomorrow would soon become the Anaheim of Today. Within a decade of its opening, Disneyland was no longer set amid a rural idyll of orange groves, it was stuck in the middle of cheap motels, traffic jams on the Santa Ana freeway, fast food joints, and industrial parks. Walt Disney frequently slept at his small apartment above the firehouse in Disneyland's Main Street, USA. By the early 1960s, the hard realities of Today were more and more difficult to ignore, and Disney began dreaming of bigger things, of Disney World, a place even farther removed from the forces he'd helped to unleash, a fantasy that could be even more thoroughly controlled.

Among other cultural innovations, Walt Disney pioneered the marketing strategy now known as "synergy." During the 1930s, he signed licensing agreements with dozens of firms, granting them the right to use Mickey Mouse on their products and in their ads. In 1938 *Snow White* proved a turning point in film marketing: Disney had signed seventy licensing deals prior to the film's release.[26] Snow White toys, books, clothes, snacks, and records were already for sale when the film opened.

[24]See Mark Langer, "Disney's Atomic Fleet," *Animation World Magazine*, April 1998.

[25]Heinz Haber, *The Walt Disney Story of Our Friend the Atom* (New York: Simon and Schuster, 1956).

[26]See Watts, *Magic Kingdom*, pp. 161–62.

Disney later used television to achieve a degree of synergy beyond anything that anyone had previously dared. His first television broadcast, *One Hour in Wonderland* (1950), culminated in a promotion for the upcoming Disney film *Alice in Wonderland*. His first television series, *Disneyland* (1954), provided weekly updates on the construction work at his theme park. ABC, which broadcast the show, owned a large financial stake in the Anaheim venture. Disneyland's other major investor, Western Printing and Lithography, printed Disney books such as *The Walt Disney Story of Our Friend the Atom*. In the guise of televised entertainment, episodes of *Disneyland* were often thinly disguised infomercials, promoting films, books, toys, an amusement park — and, most of all, Disney himself, the living, breathing incarnation of a brand, the man who neatly tied all the other commodities together into one cheerful, friendly, patriotic idea.

Ray Kroc could only dream, during McDonald's tough early years, of 25 having such marketing tools at his disposal. He was forced to rely instead on his wits, his charisma, and his instinct for promotion. Kroc believed completely in whatever he sold and pitched McDonald's franchises with an almost religious fervor. He also knew a few things about publicity, having auditioned talent for a Chicago radio station in the 1920s and performed in nightclubs for years. Kroc hired a publicity firm led by a gag writer and a former MGM road manager to get McDonald's into the news. Children would be the new restaurant chain's target customers. The McDonald brothers had aimed for a family crowd, and now Kroc improved and refined their marketing strategy. He'd picked the right moment. America was in the middle of a baby boom; the number of children had soared in the decade after World War II. Kroc wanted to create a safe, clean, all-American place for kids. The McDonald's franchise agreement required every new restaurant to fly the Stars and Stripes. Kroc understood that how he sold food was just as important as how the food tasted. He liked to tell people that he was really in show business, not the restaurant business. Promoting McDonald's to children was a clever, pragmatic decision. "A child who loves our TV commercials," Kroc explained, "and brings her grandparents to a McDonald's gives us two more customers."[27]

The McDonald's Corporation's first mascot was Speedee, a winking 26 little chef with a hamburger for a head. The character was later renamed Archie McDonald. Speedy was the name of Alka-Seltzer's mascot, and it seemed unwise to imply any connection between the two brands. In 1960, Oscar Goldstein, a McDonald's franchisee in Washington, D.C., decided to sponsor *Bozo's Circus*, a local children's television show. Bozo's appearance at a McDonald's restaurant drew large crowds. When the local NBC station canceled *Bozo's Circus* in 1963, Goldstein hired its star — Willard Scott, later the weatherman on NBC's *Today* show — to invent a new clown who could make restaurant appearances. An ad agency designed the outfit,

[27]Kroc, *Grinding It Out*, p. 114.

Scott came up with the name Ronald McDonald, and a star was born.[28] Two years later the McDonald's Corporation introduced Ronald McDonald to the rest of the United States through a major ad campaign. But Willard Scott no longer played the part. He was deemed too overweight; McDonald's wanted someone thinner to sell its burgers, shakes, and fries.

The late-1960s expansion of the McDonald's restaurant chain coincided with declining fortunes at the Walt Disney Company. Disney was no longer alive, and his vision of America embodied just about everything that kids of the sixties were rebelling against. Although McDonald's was hardly a promoter of whole foods and psychedelia, it had the great advantage of seeming new — and there was something trippy about Ronald McDonald, his clothes, and his friends. As McDonald's mascot began to rival Mickey Mouse in name recognition, Kroc made plans to create his own Disneyland. He was a highly competitive man who liked, whenever possible, to settle the score. "If they were drowning to death," Kroc once said about his business rivals, "I would put a hose in their mouth."[29] He planned to buy 1,500 acres of land northeast of Los Angeles and build a new amusement park there. The park, tentatively called Western World, would have a cowboy theme.[30] Other McDonald's executives opposed the idea, worried that Western World would divert funds from the restaurant business and lose millions. Kroc offered to option the land with his own money, but finally listened to his close advisers and scrapped the plan. The McDonald's Corporation later considered buying Astro World in Houston. Instead of investing in a large theme park, the company pursued a more decentralized approach. It built small Playlands and McDonaldlands all over the United States.

The fantasy world of McDonaldland borrowed a good deal from Walt Disney's Magic Kingdom. Don Ament, who gave McDonaldland its distinctive look, was a former Disney set designer. Richard and Robert Sherman — who had written and composed, among other things, all the songs in Disney's *Mary Poppins,* Disneyland's "It's a Great, Big, Beautiful Tomorrow" and "It's a Small World, After All" — were enlisted for the first McDonaldland commercials. Ronald McDonald, Mayor McCheese, and the other characters in the ads made McDonald's seem like more than just another place to eat. McDonaldland — with its hamburger patch, apple pie trees, and Filet-O-Fish fountain — had one crucial thing in common with Disneyland. Almost everything in it was for sale. McDonald's soon loomed large in the imagination of toddlers, the intended audience for the ads. The restaurant chain evoked a series of pleasing images in a youngster's mind: bright colors, a playground, a toy, a clown, a drink with a straw, little pieces of food wrapped up like a present. Kroc had succeeded, like his old Red Cross comrade, at selling something intangible to children, along with their fries.

---

[28]For the story of Willard Scott and Ronald McDonald, see Love, *Behind the Arches,* pp. 218–22, 244–45.

[29]Quoted in Penny Moser, "The McDonald's Mystique," *Fortune,* July 4, 1988.

[30]For Kroc's amusement park schemes, see Love, *Behind the Arches,* pp. 411–13.

Kid Kustomers

Twenty-five years ago, only a handful of American companies directed their   29
marketing at children — Disney, McDonald's, candy makers, toy makers,
manufacturers of breakfast cereal. Today children are being targeted by
phone companies, oil companies, and automobile companies, as well as
clothing stores and restaurant chains. The explosion in children's advertising occurred during the 1980s. Many working parents, feeling guilty about
spending less time with their kids, started spending more money on them.
One marketing expert has called the 1980s "the decade of the child consumer."[31] After largely ignoring children for years, Madison Avenue began
to scrutinize and pursue them. Major ad agencies now have children's divisions, and a variety of marketing firms focus solely on kids. These groups
tend to have sweet-sounding names: Small Talk, Kid Connection, Kid2Kid,
the Gepetto Group, Just Kids, Inc. At least three industry publications —
Youth Market Alert, Selling to Kids, and *Marketing to Kids Report* — cover
the latest ad campaigns and market research. The growth in children's
advertising has been driven by efforts to increase not just current, but also
future, consumption. Hoping that nostalgic childhood memories of a brand
will lead to a lifetime of purchases, companies now plan "cradle-to-grave"
advertising strategies. They have come to believe what Ray Kroc and Walt
Disney realized long ago — a person's "brand loyalty" may begin as early as
the age of two.[32] Indeed, market research has found that children often recognize a brand logo before they can recognize their own name.[33]

The discontinued Joe Camel ad campaign, which used a hip cartoon   30
character to sell cigarettes, showed how easily children can be influenced
by the right corporate mascot. A 1991 study published in the *Journal of the
American Medical Association* found that nearly all of America's six-year-
olds could identify Joe Camel, who was just as familiar to them as Mickey
Mouse.[34] Another study found that one-third of the cigarettes illegally sold
to minors were Camels.[35] More recently, a marketing firm conducted a survey in shopping malls across the country, asking children to describe their
favorite TV ads. According to the CME KidCom Ad Traction Study II,
released at the 1999 Kids' Marketing Conference in San Antonio, Texas,
the Taco Bell commercials featuring a talking chihuahua were the most
popular fast food ads.[36] The kids in the survey also liked Pepsi and Nike
commercials, but their favorite television ad was for Budweiser.

[31]McNeal, *Kids As Customers*, p. 6.

[32]Cited in "Brand Aware," *Children's Business*, June 2000.

[33]See "Brand Consciousness," *IFF on Kids: Kid Focus*, no. 3.

[34]Paul Fischer et al., "Brand Logo Recognition by Children Aged 3 to 6 Years:
Mickey Mouse and Old Joe the Camel," *Journal of the American Medical Association*,
December 11, 1991.

[35]See Judann Dagnoli, "JAMA Lights New Fire Under Camel's Ads," *Advertising Age*,
December 16, 1991.

[36]Cited in "Market Research Ages 6–17: Talking Chihuahua Strikes Chord with
Kids," *Selling to Kids*, February 3, 1999.

The bulk of the advertising directed at children today has an immedi- 31 ate goal. "It's not just getting kids to whine," one marketer explained in *Selling to Kids*, "it's giving them a specific reason to ask for the product."[37] Years ago sociologist Vance Packard described children as "surrogate salesmen" who had to persuade other people, usually their parents, to buy what they wanted.[38] Marketers now use different terms to explain the intended response to their ads — such as "leverage," "the nudge factor," "pester power." The aim of most children's advertising is straightforward: get kids to nag their parents and nag them well.

James U. McNeal, a professor of marketing at Texas A&M University, 32 is considered America's leading authority on marketing to children. In his book *Kids As Customers* (1992), McNeal provides marketers with a thorough analysis of "children's requesting styles and appeals."[39] He classifies juvenile nagging tactics into seven major categories. A *pleading* nag is one accompanied by repetitions of words like "please" or "mom, mom, mom." A *persistent* nag involves constant requests for the coveted product and may include the phrase "I'm gonna ask just one more time." *Forceful* nags are extremely pushy and may include subtle threats, like "Well, then, I'll go and ask Dad." *Demonstrative* nags are the most high-risk, often characterized by full-blown tantrums in public places, breath-holding, tears, a refusal to leave the store. *Sugar-coated* nags promise affection in return for a purchase and may rely on seemingly heartfelt declarations like "You're the best dad in the world." *Threatening* nags are youthful forms of blackmail, vows of eternal hatred and of running away if something isn't bought. *Pity* nags claim the child will be heartbroken, teased, or socially stunted if the parent refuses to buy a certain item. "All of these appeals and styles may be used in combination," McNeal's research has discovered, "but kids tend to stick to one or two of each that prove most effective . . . for their own parents."

McNeal never advocates turning children into screaming, breath- 33 holding monsters. He has been studying "Kid Kustomers" for more than thirty years and believes in a more traditional marketing approach.[40] "The key is getting children to see a firm . . . in much the same way as [they see] mom or dad, grandma or grandpa," McNeal argues.[41] "Likewise, if a company can ally itself with universal values such as patriotism, national defense, and good health, it is likely to nurture belief in it among children."

Before trying to affect children's behavior, advertisers have to learn 34 about their tastes.[42] Today's market researchers not only conduct surveys

[37]Quoted in "Market Research: The Old Nagging Game Can Pay Off for Marketers," *Selling to Kids*, April 15, 1998.

[38]See Boas and Chain, *Big Mac*, p. 127; Vance Packard, *The Hidden Persuaders* (New York: D. McKay, 1957), pp. 158–61.

[39]McNeal, *Kids As Customers*, pp. 72–75.

[40]Ibid., p. 4.

[41]Ibid., p. 98.

[42]For a sense of the techniques now being used by marketers, see Tom McGee, "Getting Inside Kids' Heads," *American Demographics*, January 1997.

of children in shopping malls, they also organize focus groups for kids as young as two or three. They analyze children's artwork, hire children to run focus groups, stage slumber parties and then question children into the night. They send cultural anthropologists into homes, stores, fast food restaurants, and other places where kids like to gather, quietly and surreptitiously observing the behavior of prospective customers. They study the academic literature on child development, seeking insights from the work of theorists such as Erik Erikson and Jean Piaget. They study the fantasy lives of young children, then apply the findings in advertisements and product designs.

Dan S. Acuff — the president of Youth Market System Consulting and   35 the author of *What Kids Buy and Why* (1997) — stresses the importance of dream research. Studies suggest that until the age of six, roughly 80 percent of children's dreams are about animals.[43] Rounded, soft creatures like Barney, Disney's animated characters, and the Teletubbies therefore have an obvious appeal to young children. The Character Lab, a division of Youth Market System Consulting, uses a proprietary technique called Character Appeal Quadrant Analysis to help companies develop new mascots. The technique purports to create imaginary characters who perfectly fit the targeted age group's level of cognitive and neurological development.

Children's clubs have for years been considered an effective means of   36 targeting ads and collecting demographic information; the clubs appeal to a child's fundamental need for status and belonging. Disney's Mickey Mouse Club, formed in 1930, was one of the trailblazers. During the 1980s and 1990s, children's clubs proliferated, as corporations used them to solicit the names, addresses, zip codes, and personal comments of young customers. "Marketing messages sent through a club not only can be personalized," James McNeal advises, "they can be tailored for a certain age or geographical group."[44] A well-designed and well-run children's club can be extremely good for business. According to one Burger King executive, the creation of a Burger King Kids Club in 1991 increased the sales of children's meals as much as 300 percent.[45]

The Internet has become another powerful tool for assembling data   37 about children. In 1998 a federal investigation of Web sites aimed at children found that 89 percent requested personal information from kids; only 1 percent required that children obtain parental approval before supplying the information.[46] A character on the McDonald's Web site told children that Ronald McDonald was "the ultimate authority in everything."[47] The

[43]Cited in Acuff, *What Kids Buy and Why*, pp. 45–46.
[44]McNeal, *Kids As Customers*, p. 175.
[45]Cited in Karen Benezra, "Keeping Burger King on a Roll," *Brandweek*, January 15, 1996.
[46]Cited in "Children's Online Privacy Proposed Rule Issued by FTC," press release, Federal Trade Commission, April 20, 1999.
[47]Quoted in "Is Your Kid Caught Up in the Web?" *Consumer Reports*, May 1997.

site encouraged kids to send Ronald an e-mail revealing their favorite menu item at McDonald's, their favorite book, their favorite sports team — and their name.[48] Fast food Web sites no longer ask children to provide personal information without first gaining parental approval; to do so is now a violation of federal law, thanks to the Children's Online Privacy Protection Act, which took effect in April of 2000.

Despite the growing importance of the Internet, television remains the 38 primary medium for children's advertising. The effects of these TV ads have long been a subject of controversy. In 1978, the Federal Trade Commission (FTC) tried to ban all television ads directed at children seven years old or younger. Many studies had found that young children often could not tell the difference between television programming and television advertising. They also could not comprehend the real purpose of commercials and trusted that advertising claims were true. Michael Pertschuk, the head of the FTC, argued that children need to be shielded from advertising that preys upon their immaturity. "They cannot protect themselves," he said, "against adults who exploit their present-mindedness."[49]

The FTC's proposed ban was supported by the American Academy of 39 Pediatrics, the National Congress of Parents and Teachers, the Consumers Union, and the Child Welfare League, among others. But it was attacked by the National Association of Broadcasters, the Toy Manufacturers of America, and the Association of National Advertisers. The industry groups lobbied Congress to prevent any restrictions on children's ads and sued in federal court to block Pertschuk from participating in future FTC meetings on the subject. In April of 1981, three months after the inauguration of President Ronald Reagan, an FTC staff report argued that a ban on ads aimed at children would be impractical, effectively killing the proposal. "We are delighted by the FTC's reasonable recommendation," said the head of the National Association of Broadcasters.[50]

The Saturday-morning children's ads that caused angry debates 40 twenty years ago now seem almost quaint. Far from being banned, TV advertising aimed at kids is now broadcast twenty-four hours a day, closed-captioned and in stereo. Nickelodeon, the Disney Channel, the Cartoon Network, and the other children's cable networks are now responsible for about 80 percent of all television viewing by kids.[51] None of these networks existed before 1979. The typical American child now spends about twenty-one hours a week watching television — roughly one and a half months of

[48]See Matthew McAllester, "Life in Cyberspace: What's McDonald's Doing with Kids' E-mail Responses?" *Newsday*, July 20, 1997.

[49]Quoted in Linda E. Demkovich, "Pulling the Sweet Tooth of Children's TV Advertising," *National Journal*, January 7, 1978.

[50]Quoted in A. O. Sulzberger, Jr., "FTC Staff Urges End to Child-TV Ad Study," *New York Times*, April 3, 1981.

[51]Cited in Steve McClellan and Richard Tedesco, "Children's TV Market May Be Played Out," *Broadcasting & Cable*, March 1, 1999.

TV every year.[52] That does not include the time children spend in front of a screen watching videos, playing video games, or using the computer. Outside of school, the typical American child spends more time watching television than doing any other activity except sleeping.[53] During the course of a year, he or she watches more than thirty thousand TV commercials.[54] Even the nation's youngest children are watching a great deal of television. About one-quarter of American children between the ages of two and five have a TV in their room.[55]

Perfect Synergy

Although the fast food chains annually spend about $3 billion on television *41* advertising, their marketing efforts directed at children extend far beyond such conventional ads.[56] The McDonald's Corporation now operates more than eight thousand playgrounds at its restaurants in the United States.[57] Burger King has more than two thousand.[58] A manufacturer of "playlands" explains why fast food operators build these largely plastic structures: "Playlands bring in children, who bring in parents, who bring in money."[59] As American cities and towns spend less money on children's recreation, fast food restaurants have become gathering spaces for families with young children. Every month about 90 percent of American children between the ages of three and nine visit a McDonald's.[60] The seesaws, slides, and pits full of plastic balls have proven to be an effective lure. "But when it gets down to brass tacks," a *Brandweek* article on fast food notes, "the key to attracting kids is toys, toys, toys."[61]

The fast food industry has forged promotional links with the nation's *42* leading toy manufacturers, giving away simple toys with children's meals and selling more elaborate ones at a discount. The major toy crazes of recent years — including Pokémon cards, Cabbage Patch Kids, and Tamogotchis — have been abetted by fast food promotions. A successful

---

[52]Cited in "Policy Statement: Media Education," American Academy of Pediatrics, August 1999.

[53]Cited in "Policy Statement: Children, Adolescents, and Television," American Academy of Pediatrics, October 1995.

[54]Cited in Mary C. Martin, "Children's Understanding of the Intent of Advertising: A Meta-Analysis," *Journal of Public Policy & Marketing*, Fall 1997.

[55]Cited in Lisa Jennings, "Baby, Hand Me the Remote," *Scripps Howard News Service*, October 13, 1999.

[56]Interview with Lynn Fava, Competitive Media Reporting.

[57]Cited in "Fast Food and Playgrounds: A Natural Combination," promotional material, Playlandservices, Inc.

[58]Ibid.

[59]Ibid.

[60]Cited in Rod Taylor, "The Beanie Factor," *Brandweek*, June 16, 1997.

[61]Sam Bradley and Betsey Spethmann, "Subway's Kid Pack: The Ties That Sell," *Brandweek*, October 10, 1994.

promotion easily doubles or triples the weekly sales volume of children's meals. The chains often distribute numerous versions of a toy, encouraging repeat visits by small children and adult collectors who hope to obtain complete sets. In 1999 McDonald's distributed eighty different types of Furby. According to a publication called *Tomart's Price Guide to McDonald's Happy Meal Collectibles*, some fast food giveaways are now worth hundreds of dollars.[62]

Rod Taylor, a *Brandweek* columnist, called McDonald's 1997 Teenie   43
Beanie Baby giveaway one of the most successful promotions in the history of American advertising.[63] At the time McDonald's sold about 10 million Happy Meals in a typical week. Over the course of ten days in April of 1997, by including a Teenie Beanie Baby with each purchase, McDonald's sold about 100 million Happy Meals. Rarely has a marketing effort achieved such an extraordinary rate of sales among its intended consumers. Happy Meals are marketed to children between the ages of three and nine; within ten days about four Teenie Beanie Baby Happy Meals were sold for every American child in that age group. Not all of those Happy Meals were purchased for children. Many adult collectors bought Teenie Beanie Baby Happy Meals, kept the dolls, and threw away the food.

The competition for young customers has led the fast food chains to   44
form marketing alliances not just with toy companies, but with sports leagues and Hollywood studios. McDonald's has staged promotions with the National Basketball Association and the Olympics. Pizza Hut, Taco Bell, and KFC signed a three-year deal with the NCAA. Wendy's has linked with the National Hockey League. Burger King and Nickelodeon, Denny's and Major League Baseball, McDonald's and the Fox Kids Network have all formed partnerships that mix advertisements for fast food with children's entertainment. Burger King has sold chicken nuggets shaped like Teletubbies. McDonald's now has its own line of children's videos starring Ronald McDonald. *The Wacky Adventures of Ronald McDonald* is being produced by Klasky-Csupo, the company that makes *Rugrats* and *The Simpsons*. The videos feature the McDonaldland characters and sell for $3.49. "We see this as a great opportunity," a McDonald's executive said in a press release, "to create a more meaningful relationship between Ronald and kids."[64]

All of these cross-promotions have strengthened the ties between   45
Hollywood and the fast food industry. In the past few years, the major studios have started to recruit fast food executives. Susan Frank, a former director of national marketing for McDonald's, later became a marketing

[62]Meredith Williams, *Tomart's Price Guide to McDonald's Happy Meal Collectibles* (Dayton, Ohio: Tomart Publications, 1995).

[63]The story of McDonald's Teenie Beanie Baby promotion can be found in Taylor, "The Beanie Factor."

[64]Quoted in "McDonald's Launches Second Animated Video in Series Starring Ronald McDonald," press release, McDonald's Corporation, January 21, 1999.

executive at the Fox Kids Network. She now runs a new family-oriented cable network jointly owned by Hallmark Entertainment and the Jim Henson Company, creator of the Muppets. Ken Snelgrove, who for many years worked as a marketer for Burger King and McDonald's, now works at MGM. Brad Ball, a former senior vice president of marketing at McDonald's, is now the head of marketing for Warner Brothers. Not long after being hired, Ball told the *Hollywood Reporter* that there was little difference between selling films and selling hamburgers.[65] John Cywinski, the former head of marketing at Burger King, became the head of marketing for Walt Disney's film division in 1996, then left the job to work for McDonald's. Forty years after Bozo's first promotional appearance at a McDonald's, amid all the marketing deals, giveaways, and executive swaps, America's fast food culture has become indistinguishable from the popular culture of its children.

In May of 1996, the Walt Disney Company signed a ten-year global 46 marketing agreement with the McDonald's Corporation. By linking with a fast food company, a Hollywood studio typically gains anywhere from $25 million to $45 million in additional advertising for a film, often doubling its ad budget. These licensing deals are usually negotiated on a per-film basis; the 1996 agreement with Disney gave McDonald's exclusive rights to that studio's output of films and videos. Some industry observers thought Disney benefited more from the deal, gaining a steady source of marketing funds.[66] According to the terms of the agreement, Disney characters could never be depicted sitting in a McDonald's restaurant or eating any of the chain's food. In the early 1980s, the McDonald's Corporation had turned away offers to buy Disney; a decade later, McDonald's executives sounded a bit defensive about having given Disney greater control over how their joint promotions would be run.[67] "A lot of people can't get used to the fact that two big global brands with this kind of credibility can forge this kind of working relationship," a McDonald's executive told a reporter. "It's about their theme parks, their next movie, their characters, their videos. . . . It's bigger than a hamburger. It's about the integration of our two brands, long-term."[68]

The life's work of Walt Disney and Ray Kroc had come full-circle, unit- 47 ing in perfect synergy. McDonald's began to sell its hamburgers and french fries at Disney's theme parks. The ethos of McDonaldland and of Disneyland, never far apart, have finally become one. Now you can buy a Happy Meal at the Happiest Place on Earth.

[65]See T. L. Stanley, *Hollywood Reporter,* May 26, 1998.

[66]See Thomas R. King, "Mickey May Be the Big Winner in Disney-McDonald's Alliance," *Wall Street Journal,* May 24, 1996.

[67]See Monci Jo Williams, "McDonald's Refuses to Plateau," *Fortune,* November 12, 1984.

[68]Quoted in James Bates, "You Want First-Run Features with Those Fries?" *Newsday,* May 11, 1997.

The Brand Essence

The best insight into the thinking of fast food marketers comes from their *48*
own words. Confidential documents from a recent McDonald's advertising
campaign give a clear sense of how the restaurant chain views its customers. The McDonald's Corporation was facing a long list of problems.
"Sales are decreasing," one memo noted. "People are telling us Burger
King and Wendy's are doing a better job of giving . . . better food at the
best price," another warned. Consumer research indicated that future
sales in some key areas were at risk. "More customers are telling us," an
executive wrote, "that McDonald's is a big company that just wants to
sell . . . sell as much as it can." An emotional connection to McDonald's
that customers had formed "as toddlers" was now eroding. The new radio
and television advertising had to make people feel that McDonald's still
cared about them. It had to link the McDonald's of today to the one people
loved in the past. "The challenge of the campaign," wrote Ray Bergold, the
chain's top marketing executive, "is to make customers believe that
McDonald's is their 'Trusted Friend.'"

According to these documents, the marketing alliances with other *49*
brands were intended to create positive feelings about McDonald's, making consumers associate one thing they liked with another. Ads would link
the company's french fries "to the excitement and fanaticism people feel
about the NBA." The feelings of pride inspired by the Olympics would be
used in ads to help launch a new hamburger with more meat than the Big
Mac. The link with the Walt Disney Company was considered by far the
most important, designed to "enhance perceptions of Brand McDonald's."
A memo sought to explain the underlying psychology behind many visits
to McDonald's: parents took their children to McDonald's because they
"want the kids to love them . . . it makes them feel like a good parent." Purchasing something from Disney was the *"ultimate"* way to make kids
happy, but it was too expensive to do every day. The advertising needed to
capitalize on these feelings, letting parents know that "ONLY MCDONALD'S
MAKES IT EASY TO GET A BIT OF DISNEY MAGIC." The ads aimed at "minivan parents" would carry an unspoken message about taking your children to
McDonald's: "It's an easy way to feel like a good parent."

The fundamental goal of the "My McDonald's" campaign that stemmed *50*
from these proposals was to make a customer feel that McDonald's "cares
about me" and "knows about me." A corporate memo introducing the campaign explained: "The essence McDonald's is embracing is 'Trusted
Friend.' . . . 'Trusted Friend' captures all the good-will and the unique emotional connection customers have with the McDonald's experience. . . .
[Our goal is to make] customers believe McDonald's is their 'Trusted
Friend.' Note: this should be done without using the words 'Trusted
Friend.' . . . Every commercial [should be] honest. . . . Every message will
be in good taste and feel like it comes from a trusted friend." The words
"trusted friend" were never to be mentioned in the ads because doing so

might prematurely "wear out a brand essence" that could prove valuable in the future for use among different national, ethnic, and age groups. Despite McDonald's faith in its trusted friends, the opening page of this memo said in bold red letters: "ANY UNAUTHORIZED USE OR COPYING OF THIS MATERIAL MAY LEAD TO CIVIL OR CRIMINAL PROSECUTION."

McTeachers and Coke Dudes

Not satisfied with marketing to children through playgrounds, toys, car- *51* toons, movies, videos, charities, and amusement parks, through contests, sweepstakes, games, and clubs, via television, radio, magazines, and the Internet, fast food chains are now gaining access to the last advertising-free outposts of American life. In 1993 District 11 in Colorado Springs started a nationwide trend, becoming the first public school district in the United States to place ads for Burger King in its hallways and on the sides of its school buses. Like other school systems in Colorado, District 11 faced revenue shortfalls, thanks to growing enrollments and voter hostility to tax increases for education. The initial Burger King and King Sooper ad contracts were a disappointment for the district, gaining it just $37,500 a year — little more than $1 per student.[69] In 1996, school administrators decided to seek negotiating help from a professional, hiring Dan DeRose, president of DD Marketing, Inc., of Pueblo, Colorado. DeRose assembled special advertising packages for corporate sponsors. For $12,000, a company got five school-bus ads, hallway ads in all fifty-two of the district's schools, ads in their school newspapers, a stadium banner, ads over the stadium's public-address system during games, and free tickets to high school sporting events.[70]

Within a year, DeRose had nearly tripled District 11's ad revenues.[71] *52* But his greatest success was still to come. In August of 1997, DeRose brokered a ten-year deal that made Coca-Cola the district's exclusive beverage supplier, bringing the schools up to $11 million during the life of the contract (minus DD Marketing's fee). The deal also provided free use of a 1998 Chevy Cavalier to a District 11 high school senior, chosen by lottery, who had good grades and a perfect attendance record.

District 11's marketing efforts were soon imitated by other school dis- *53* tricts in Colorado, by districts in Pueblo, Fort Collins, Denver, and Cherry Creek. Administrators in Colorado Springs did not come up with the idea of using corporate sponsorship to cover shortfalls in a school district's budget. But they took it to a whole new level, packaging it, systematizing it, leading the way. Hundreds of public school districts across the United States are now adopting or considering similar arrangements. Children

---

[69]Cited in Eric Dexheimer, "Class Warfare," *Denver Westword,* February 6, 1997.
[70]Ibid.
[71]Ibid.

spend about seven hours a day, one hundred and fifty days a year, in school. Those hours have in the past been largely free of advertising, promotion, and market research — a source of frustration to many companies. Today the nation's fast food chains are marketing their products in public schools through conventional ad campaigns, classroom teaching materials, and lunchroom franchises, as well as a number of unorthodox means.

The proponents of advertising in the schools argue that it is necessary to prevent further cutbacks; opponents contend that schoolchildren are becoming a captive audience for marketers, compelled by law to attend school and then forced to look at ads as a means of paying for their own education. America's schools now loom as a potential gold mine for companies in search of young customers. "Discover your own river of revenue at the schoolhouse gates," urged a brochure at the 1997 Kids Power Marketing Conference. "Whether it's first-graders learning to read or teenagers shopping for their first car, we can guarantee an introduction of your product and your company to these students in the traditional setting of the classroom."[72]

DD Marketing, with offices in Colorado Springs and Pueblo, has emerged as perhaps the nation's foremost negotiator of ad contracts for schools. Dan DeRose began his career as the founder of the Minor League Football System, serving in the late 1980s as both a team owner and a player. In 1991, he became athletic director at the University of Southern Colorado in Pueblo. During his first year, he raised $250,000 from corporate sponsors for the school's teams. Before long he was raising millions of dollars to build campus sports facilities. He was good at getting money out of big corporations, and formed DD Marketing to use this skill on behalf of schools and nonprofits. Beverage companies and athletic shoe companies had long supported college sports programs, and during the 1980s began to put up the money for new high school scoreboards. Dan DeRose saw marketing opportunities that were still untapped. After negotiating his first Colorado Springs package deal in 1996, he went to work for the Grapevine-Colleyville School District in Texas. The district would never have sought advertising, its deputy superintendent told the *Houston Chronicle*, "if it weren't for the acute need for funds."[73] DeRose started to solicit ads not only for the district's hallways, stadiums, and buses, but also for its rooftops — so that passengers flying in or out of the nearby Dallas–Forth Worth airport could see them — and for its voice-mail systems. "You've reached Grapevine-Colleyville school district, proud partner of Dr Pepper," was a message that DeRose proposed.[74] Although some

[72]Quoted in Molnar, "Sponsored Schools and Commercialized Classrooms," p. 28.
[73]Quoted in Brian McTaggart, "Selling Our Schools," *Houston Chronicle*, August 10, 1997.
[74]Quoted in G. Chambers Williams III, "Fliers May Be Seeing Ads on Roofs of Grapevine-Colleyville Schools," *Fort Worth Star-Telegram*, March 4, 1997.

people in the district were skeptical about the wild ideas of this marketer from Colorado, DeRose negotiated a $3.4 million exclusive deal between the Grapevine-Colleyville School District and Dr Pepper in June of 1997. And Dr Pepper ads soon appeared on school rooftops.

Dan DeRose tells reporters that his work brings money to school dis-   *56* tricts that badly need it.[75] By pitting one beverage company against another in bidding wars for exclusive deals, he's raised the prices being offered to schools. "In Kansas City they were getting 67 cents a kid before," he told one reporter, "and now they're getting $27."[76] The major beverage companies do not like DeRose and prefer not to deal with him. He views their hostility as a mark of success. He doesn't think that advertising in the schools will corrupt the nation's children and has little tolerance for critics of the trend. "There are critics to penicillin," he told the *Fresno Bee.*[77] In the three years following his groundbreaking contract for School District 11 in Colorado Springs, Dan DeRose negotiated agreements for seventeen universities and sixty public school systems across the United States, everywhere from Greenville, North Carolina, to Newark, New Jersey. His 1997 deal with a school district in Derby, Kansas, included the commitment to open a Pepsi GeneratioNext Resource Center at an elementary school. Thus far, DeRose has been responsible for school and university beverage deals worth more than $200 million.[78] He typically accepts no money up front, then charges schools a commission that takes between 25 and 35 percent of the deal's total revenues.

The nation's three major beverage manufacturers are now spending   *57* large sums to increase the amount of soda that American children consume. Coca-Cola, Pepsi, and Cadbury-Schweppes (the maker of Dr Pepper) control 90.3 percent of the U.S. market, but have been hurt by declining sales in Asia.[79] Americans already drink soda at an annual rate of about fifty-six gallons per person — that's nearly six hundred twelve-ounce cans of soda per person.[80] Coca-Cola has set itself the goal of raising consumption of its products in the United States by at least 25 percent a year.[81] The adult market is stagnant; selling more soda to kids has become one of the easiest ways to meet sales projections. "Influencing elementary

[75]See "The Art of the Deal," *Food Management,* February 1998.

[76]Quoted in Constance L. Hays, "Today's Lesson: Soda Rights," *New York Times,* May 21, 1999.

[77]Quoted in Tracy Correa, "Campus Market: Corporate America Is Coming to Fresno-Area Schools with Ads That Target Children and Their Parents," *Fresno Bee,* November 9, 1998.

[78]Voice mail from Dan DeRose.

[79]Cited in G. Pascal Zachary, "Let's Play Oligopoly! Why Giants Like Having Other Giants Around," *Wall Street Journal,* March 8, 1999.

[80]Cited in Greg W. Prince, "The Year of Living Dangerously," *Beverage World,* March 15, 2000.

[81]See Dean Foust, "Man on the Spot: Nowadays Things Go Tougher at Coke," *Business Week,* May 3, 1999.

school students is very important to soft drink marketers," an article in the January 1999 issue of *Beverage Industry* explained, "because children are still establishing their tastes and habits."[82] Eight-year-olds are considered ideal customers; they have about sixty-five years of purchasing in front of them. "Entering the schools makes perfect sense," the trade journal concluded.

The fast food chains also benefit enormously when children drink 58 more soda. The chicken nuggets, hamburgers, and other main courses sold at fast food restaurants usually have the lowest profit margins. Soda has by far the highest. "We at McDonald's are thankful," a top executive once told the *New York Times*, "that people like drinks with their sandwiches."[83] Today McDonald's sells more Coca-Cola than anyone else in the world.[84] The fast food chains purchase Coca-Cola syrup for about $4.25 a gallon.[85] A medium Coke that sells for $1.29 contains roughly 9 cents' worth of syrup.[86] Buying a large Coke for $1.49 instead, as the cute girl behind the counter always suggests, will add another 3 cents' worth of syrup — and another 17 cents in pure profit for McDonald's.

"Liquid Candy," a 1999 study by the Center for Science in the Public 59 Interest, describes who is not benefiting from the beverage industry's latest marketing efforts: the nation's children. In 1978, the typical teenage boy in the United States drank about seven ounces of soda every day; today he drinks nearly three times that amount, deriving 9 percent of his daily caloric intake from soft drinks. Soda consumption among teenage girls has doubled within the same period, reaching an average of twelve ounces a day. A significant number of teenage boys are now drinking five or more cans of soda every day. Each can contains the equivalent of about ten teaspoons of sugar. Coke, Pepsi, Mountain Dew, and Dr Pepper also contain caffeine. These sodas provide empty calories and have replaced far more nutritious beverages in the American diet. Excessive soda consumption in childhood can lead to calcium deficiencies and a greater likelihood of bone fractures. Twenty years ago, teenage boys in the United States drank twice as much milk as soda; now they drink twice as much soda as milk. Soft-drink consumption has also become commonplace among American toddlers. About one-fifth of the nation's one- and two-year-olds now drink

---

[82]Kent Steinriede, "Sponsorship scorecard 1999," *Beverage Industry,* January 1999.

[83]Quoted in Ernest Holsendorph, "Keeping McDonald's Out in Front: 'Gas' Is No Problem; Chicken May Be Served," *New York Times,* December 30, 1973.

[84]Cited in "Welcome to McDonald's."

[85]According to *Business Week,* Burger King annually pays Coke $170 million for 40 million gallons of syrup. That works out to a cost of about $4.25 a gallon — or 3.3 cents an ounce. It is safe to assume that McDonald's, an even larger customer, buys its syrup at a price that is equivalent, if not lower. See Foust, "Man on the Spot."

[86]The standard soft drink ratio is one part syrup to five parts carbonated water. A small Coke at McDonald's contains about 2.6 ounces of syrup; a medium Coke, about 3.5 ounces. For the composition of soft drinks, see Lauren Curtis, "Pop Art," *Food Product Design,* January 1998.

soda. "In one of the most despicable marketing gambits," Michael Jacobson, the author of "Liquid Candy" reports, "Pepsi, Dr Pepper and Seven-Up encourage feeding soft drinks to babies by licensing their logos to a major maker of baby bottles, Munchkin Bottling, Inc." A 1997 study published in the *Journal of Dentistry for Children* found that many infants were indeed being fed soda in those bottles.[87]

The school marketing efforts of the large soda companies have not   60
gone entirely unopposed. Administrators in San Francisco and Seattle have refused to allow any advertising in their schools. "It's our responsibility to make it clear that schools are here to serve children, not commercial interests," declared a member of the San Francisco Board of Education.[88] Individual protests have occurred as well. In March of 1998, 1,200 students at Greenbrier High School in Evans, Georgia, assembled in the school parking lot, many of them wearing red and white clothing, to spell out the word "Coke." It was Coke in Education Day at the school, and a dozen Coca-Cola executives had come for the occasion. Greenbrier High was hoping for a $500 prize, which had been offered to the local high school that came up with the best marketing plan for Coca-Cola discount cards. As part of the festivities, Coke executives had lectured the students on economics and helped them bake a Coca-Cola cake. A photographer was hoisted above the parking lot by a crane, ready to record the human C-O-K-E for posterity. When the photographer started to take pictures, Mike Cameron — a Greenbrier senior, standing amid the letter *C* — suddenly revealed a T-shirt that said "Pepsi." His act of defiance soon received nationwide publicity, as did the fact that he was immediately suspended from school. The principal said Cameron could have been suspended for a week for the prank, but removed him from classes for just a day.[89] "I don't consider this a prank," Mike Cameron told the *Washington Post*. "I like to be an individual. That's the way I am."[90]

Most school advertising campaigns are more subtle than Greenbrier   61
High's Coke in Education Day. The spiraling cost of textbooks has led thousands of American school districts to use corporate-sponsored teaching materials. A 1998 study of these teaching materials by the Consumers Union found that 80 percent were biased, providing students with incomplete or slanted information that favored the sponsor's products and views. Procter & Gamble's *Decision Earth* program taught that clear-cut logging was actually good for the environment; teaching aids distributed by the Exxon Education Foundation said that fossil fuels created few environmental problems and that alternative sources of energy were too

---

[87]Cited in Jacobson, "Liquid Candy," p. 10.

[88]Quoted in Martha Groves, "Serving Kids . . . Up to Marketers," *Los Angeles Times*, July 14, 1999.

[89]See Frank Swoboda, "Pepsi Prank Fizzles at School's Coke Day," *Washington Post*, March 26, 1998.

[90]Quoted ibid.

expensive; a study guide sponsored by the American Coal Foundation dismissed fears of a greenhouse effect, claiming that "the earth could benefit rather than be harmed from increased carbon dioxide."[91] The Consumers Union found Pizza Hut's Book It! Program — which awards a free Personal Pan Pizza to children who reach targeted reading levels — to be "highly commercial." About twenty million elementary school students participated in Book It! during the 1999–2000 school year; Pizza Hut recently expanded the program to include a million preschoolers.[92]

Lifetime Learning Systems is the nation's largest marketer and producer of corporate-sponsored teaching aids. The group claims that its publications are used by more than 60 million students every year.[93] "Now you can enter the classroom through custom-made learning materials created with your specific marketing objectives in mind," Lifetime Learning said in one of its pitches to corporate sponsors.[94] "Through these materials, your product or point of view becomes the focus of discussions in the classroom," it said in another, ". . . the centerpiece in a dynamic process that generates long-term awareness and lasting attitudinal change."[95] The tax cuts that are hampering America's schools have proved to be a marketing bonanza for companies like Exxon, Pizza Hut, and McDonald's. The money that these corporations spend on their "educational" materials is fully tax-deductible. 62

The fast food chains run ads on Channel One, the commercial television network whose programming is now shown in classrooms, almost every school day, to eight million of the nation's middle, junior, and high school students — a teen audience fifty times larger than that of MTV.[96] The fast food chains place ads with Star Broadcasting, a Minnesota company that pipes Top 40 radio into school hallways, lounges, and cafeterias. And the chains now promote their food by selling school lunches, accepting a lower profit margin in order to create brand loyalty. At least twenty school districts in the United States have their own Subway franchises; an additional fifteen hundred districts have Subway delivery contracts; and nine operate Subway sandwich carts.[97] Taco Bell products are sold in about forty-five hundred school cafeterias. Pizza Hut, Domino's, and McDonald's are now selling food in the nation's schools. The American School Food Service Association estimates that about 30 percent of the public high 63

---

[91]Quoted in Consumers Union, "Captive Kids."

[92]Cited in "Pizza Hut Book It! Awards $50,000 to Elementary Schools," *PR Newswire*, June 6, 2000.

[93]See Consumers Union, "Captive Kids."

[94]Quoted in Alex Molnar, "Advertising in the Classroom," *San Diego Union-Tribune*, March 10, 1993.

[95]Quoted in Consumers Union, "Captive Kids."

[96]Cited in "Prepared Testimony of Ralph Nader Before the Senate Committee on Health, Education, Labor, and Pensions," *Federal News Service*, May 20, 1999.

[97]Cited in Diane Brockett, "School Cafeterias Selling Brand-Name Junk Food," *Education Digest*, October 1, 1998.

schools in the United States offer branded fast food.[98] Elementary schools in Fort Collins, Colorado, now serve food from Pizza Hut, McDonald's, and Subway on special lunch days. "We try to be more like the fast food places where these kids are hanging out," a Colorado school administrator told the *Denver Post*. "We want kids to think school lunch is a cool thing, the cafeteria a cool place, that we're 'with it,' that we're not institutional. . . ."[99]

The new corporate partnerships often put school officials in an awk- 64 ward position. The Coca-Cola deal that DD Marketing negotiated for Colorado Springs School District 11 was not as lucrative as it first seemed.[100] The contract specified annual sales quotas. School District 11 was obligated to sell at least seventy thousand cases of Coca-Cola products a year, within the first three years of the contract, or it would face reduced payments by Coke. During the 1997–98 school year, the district's elementary, middle, and high schools sold only twenty-one thousand cases of Coca-Cola products. Cara DeGette, the news editor of the *Colorado Springs Independent*, a weekly newspaper, obtained a memorandum sent to school principals by John Bushey, a District 11 administrator. On September 28, 1998, at the start of the new school year, Bushey warned the principals that beverage sales were falling short of projections and that as a result school revenues might be affected. Allow students to bring Coke products into the classrooms, he suggested; move Coke machines to places where they would be accessible to students all day. "Research shows that vendor purchases are closely linked to availability," Bushey wrote. "Location, location, location is the key." If the principals felt uncomfortable allowing kids to drink Coca-Cola during class, he recommended letting them drink the fruit juices, teas, and bottled waters also sold in the Coke machines. At the end of the memo, John Bushey signed his name and then identified himself as "the Coke dude."

Bushey left Colorado Springs in 2000 and moved to Florida. He is now 65 the principal of the high school in Celebration, a planned community run by The Celebration Company, a subsidiary of Disney.

NOTE

For the story of Ray Kroc, I relied mainly on his memoir, *Grinding It Out;* Max Boas and Steven Chain, *Big Mac;* and John Love, *Behind the Arches.* My visit to the Ray A. Kroc museum provided many useful insights into the man. Steven Watts's *The Magic Kingdom: Walt Disney and the American Way of Life* (Boston: Houghton Mifflin, 1997) is by far the best biography of Disney, drawing extensively upon material from the Disney archive and interviews with Disney's associates. Although I disagree with some of Watts's conclusions, his research is extraordinary. Richard Schickel's *The Disney Version: The Life, Times, Art, and Commerce of Walt Disney* (New York: Avon Books, 1968) remains provocative

[98]Cited in Dan Morse, "School Cafeterias Are Enrolling as Fast-Food Franchisees," *Wall Street Journal*, July 28, 1998.

[99]Quoted in Janet Bingham, "Corporate Curriculum: And Now a Word, Lesson, Lunch, from a Sponsor," *Denver Post*, February 22, 1998.

[100]For the story of District 11's shortfall, see Cara DeGette, "The Real Thing: Corporate Welfare Comes to the Classroom," *Colorado Springs Independent*, November 25–December 1, 1998.

and highly relevant more than three decades after its publication. Leonard Mosley's *Disney's World* (New York: Stein and Day, 1985) and Marc Eliot's *Walt Disney: Hollywood's Dark Prince* (London: Andre Deutsch, 1993) offer a counterpoint to the hagiographies sponsored by the Walt Disney Company. My view of American attitudes toward technology was greatly influenced by two books: Leo Marx's *The Machine in the Garden: Technology and the Pastoral Ideal in America* (New York: Oxford University Press, 1970) and David E. Nye's *American Technological Sublime* (Cambridge, Mass.: MIT Press, 1994).

In the growing literature on marketing to children, three books are worth mentioning for what they (often inadvertently) reveal: Dan S. Acuff with Robert H. Reiher, *What Kids Buy and Why: The Psychology of Marketing to Kids* (New York: Free Press, 1997); Gene Del Vecchio, *Creating EverCool: A Marketer's Guide to a Kid's Heart* (Gretna, La.: Pelican Publishing, 1998); and James U. McNeal, *Kids As Customers: A Handbook of Marketing to Children* (New York: Lexington Books, 1992). Some of the articles in children's marketing journals, such as *Selling to Kids* and *Entertainment Marketing Letter*, are remarkable documents for future historians. Two fine reports introduced me to the whole subject of marketing in America's schools: Consumers Union Education Services, "Captive Kids: A Report on Commercial Pressures on Kids at School," Consumers Union, 1998; and Alex Molnar, "Sponsored Schools and Commercialized Classrooms: Schoolhouse Commercializing Trends in the 1990s," Center for the Analysis of Commercialism in Education, University of Wisconsin–Milwaukee, August 1998. The Center for Science in the Public Interest has been battling for food safety and proper nutrition for more than thirty years. Michael Jacobson's report "Liquid Candy: How Soft Drinks Are Harming Americans' Health," October 1998, is another fine example of the center's work. The corporate memos from the McDonald's advertising campaign were given to me by someone who thought I'd find them "enlightening," and indeed they are.

■ ■ ■

Reading Rhetorically

1. What connections does Schlosser draw between Ray Kroc and Walt Disney? Locate several passages where Schlosser connects these men and their corporations. How do these connections help Schlosser make his central argument in this piece? What might be lost (or gained) if Schlosser had chosen to leave Disney out of this chapter?

2. What assumptions does Schlosser make about his audience and their sympathies? Mark at least four places in the essay that alert you to the kind of reader Schlosser assumes he is writing for, and be ready to explain how the wording there supports your thinking. What are the benefits and risks of targeting an audience this way?

3. How persuasive do you find Schlosser's use of sources? Mark several sources that seem particularly persuasive or unpersuasive, and explain why. Does Schlosser address counterarguments? If so, where? (In answering these questions, be sure to consider the material in the text and footnotes.)

Inquiring Further

4. What is your experience with marketing in your own K–12 education? Working in a small group, discuss the positive and negative effects of corporate-school partnerships, including incentive programs you may have participated in — like the reading program sponsored by Pizza Hut, Book It! How would Schlosser analyze the examples your group brings up, and how would you respond?

5. Working in a small group, research one discipline — for example, sociology, history, American studies, or business and marketing — for information about McDonald's. Each group should choose a different discipline. Using your library's electronic resources, find three scholarly articles within that discipline. Read and prepare a presentation for the class on the argument, evidence, and rhetorical strategies in each article. After the class has heard all the presentations, draw some conclusions about what you've learned about both McDonald's and the perspectives of these scholarly disciplines.

6. This chapter is from Schlosser's 2001 best seller, *Fast Food Nation,* which should be easy to find in your campus or public library. Locate a copy of the book, and choose another chapter to read. Discuss with a small group or the rest of the class the relationships you see between Schlosser's ideas and approach in the chapter included in this collection and the new chapter you've read.

Framing Conversations

7. Schlosser writes that in its early days, Disneyland became a model for a future "in which every aspect of American life had a corporate sponsor" (para. 22). Elizabeth Teare (p. 800) is also interested in the expanding role corporations play in our daily lives, even in a personal activity like reading books. Write an essay in which you draw on these authors' ideas to make an argument about the role corporations do play and ought to play in our lives. Consider both the positive and negative aspects of corporate sponsorship. Does the age of the consumer affect your position on this issue? If so, how? Given the current structure of American life (over-filled with expensive gadgets that both improve and complicate our lives, that offer both status and often-crippling debt), is change possible? Support your claims with examples from the texts and your own experiences.

8. Schlosser's examination of McDonald's marketing tactics is interesting to consider next to the three categories of narratives Cynthia Selfe finds in advertisements for technology (p. 783). Write an essay in which you use Selfe's categories to analyze the McDonald's advertising examples Schlosser provides. Then choose another fast-food restaurant's advertising campaign to analyze through the lenses of Schlosser's and Selfe's ideas. Offer specific examples from print or television ads or other marketing tools. In drawing your conclusion about the significance of your findings, make a clear point about the progressive and/or conservative appeals you see in these marketing tools.

9. Schlosser and Mark Edmundson (p. 277) both examine the connection between marketing and American education. Place these authors' ideas and your own in conversation on this topic. What do you find significant about the effects of marketing on education? What is at stake, and for whom, if things stay the same or change? Draw examples from your own experiences, analyzing them through the frames of these authors, to help build your argument.

■ CYNTHIA L. SELFE

Lest We Think the Revolution Is a Revolution: Images of Technology and the Nature of Change

Cynthia L. Selfe is a Humanities Distinguished Professor at The Ohio State University, where she teaches courses on technology and persuasion. She is a cofounder of Computers and Composition Press and coedits *Computers and Composition: An International Journal*. She has published many articles on the uses of computers in composition classrooms, the topic also of her book *Technology and Literacy in the Twenty-First Century: The Importance of Paying Attention* (1999). Her book *Literate Lives in the Information Age: Narratives of Literacy from the United States* (2004), co-written with Gail Hawisher, follows twenty case studies of people on the path to acquiring technological literacy (with varying degrees of success). The challenges and pleasures of technology, particularly for students, fascinate Selfe. She is a frequent guest speaker and workshop leader on college campuses, offering insights about incorporating computers into the classroom . . . often in unorthodox ways. In her own classroom, students use computers to design visual arguments, persuasive public service announcements, Web sites, and wikis.

The reading here was first published in *Passions, Pedagogies, and 21st Century Technologies* (1999), a book Selfe coedited with Gail Hawisher. Selfe clearly values collaboration. In paragraphs 2 and 3, she lists a number of researchers — some her coauthors on various articles — who "remain decidedly undecided about technology and change" (para. 3). This ambivalence signals readers that the conversation about computers and education is far from over. In this essay, Selfe introduces us to the "contradictory impulses" (para. 4) in the narratives we tell ourselves about what we find promising and terrifying about computer technology. In the first section, "Change, Technology, and the Status Quo: Some Background" (p. 784), Selfe lays out her strategy: analyzing technology advertisements to discern "contradictory impulses" and to analyze them. Although the images themselves are not reprinted here, Selfe's descriptions should allow you to see the way she sees advertisements as "snapshots" that "reveal us, as Americans, to ourselves. They are laden with cultural information, shot through with the values, ideological positions, and social understandings that comprise our shared experience" (para. 10).

As you read, notice that each of the narratives Selfe describes has both a positive and a negative version. Weigh the evidence she provides for each. What recent images from computer advertising can you think of that confirm or challenge her analysis? How have these narratives developed or changed in the years since the piece was published in 1999?

Like other writers who look to popular culture to make sense of important trends, Selfe teaches her readers how to pay attention to everyday visual arguments; she also teaches us why we should pay attention. In this age of globalization, our world is "flattening," to borrow a word from Thomas Friedman (p. 417), in large part because of technology. The stories we tell, according to Selfe, affect us personally, as American citizens and as citizens of the globe. Selfe suggests educators have an important role to play in developing productive narratives and practices of computer technology. You might extend this conversation by asking, "What role should students play?"

■ ■ ■

When English studies teachers get together to talk about technology we generally end up talking about change. It is common sense, after all to link computers with change when microprocessors, according to Moore's law, double in speed every eighteen months; when biomemory, superscalar architecture, and picoprocessors become feature stories for National Public Radio; and when media generations flash by in less time than it takes to uncrate a faculty workstation and get rid of the styrofoam packing.

And, at some level, English Departments have come to terms with technological change — we have adjusted diminishing supplies and equipment budgets to accommodate an ongoing program of purchases and upgrades, accepted computer studies as a new area of scholarly focus, integrated technology into various curricula, and modified many programs to include technology training and use (c.f., Selber, 1994; McDaniel, 1990; Schwartz, Selfe, and Sosnoski, 1994; Wahlstrom and Selfe, 1994).

Like most Americans, however, even though educators have made these adaptations, we remain decidedly undecided about technology and change. At one level, we believe in the pairing; we believe in the computer's power, and we believe strongly in the beneficial ways that technology promises to improve our lives (Bump, 1990; Delany and Landow, 1991; Snyder, 1995). At other levels, we fear the effects of technology, and the potent changes that it introduces into familiar systems (Apple, 1986; Kramarae, 1988; Hawisher and Selfe, 1993; Selfe and Selfe, 1994).

These contradictory impulses are the focus of this chapter, especially as they affect the work of English studies specialists and educators. In addition, these attitudes shade subtly into one another at multiple levels of a larger collective social experience, and they are worth exploring for that reason as well.

Change, Technology, and the Status Quo: Some Background

Because our culture subscribes to several powerful narratives that link technological progress closely with social progress, it is easy for us — for Americans, in particular — to believe that technological change leads to productive social change.

Indeed, the narratives linking technological change to social change are part of the reason that English studies teachers — like many other educators — have come to embrace computer technology so enthusiastically over the past decade.

Quite simply put, like many Americans, we hope computers can help *7* us make the world a better place in which to live. In the profession of English studies, for example, we hope computers can help make us, and the students with whom we work, more productive in the classroom and other instructional settings (Hafer, 1996; Coogan, 1995; Clark, 1995; Tornow, 1997; Sirc, 1995), more effective as communicators (Blair, 1996; Minock and Shor, 1995; Sproull and Kiesler, 1991), and more responsibly involved as literate citizens in world affairs (Schuler, 1994; Selfe, 1996; Geren, 1996).

We are not alone in these stories that we tell ourselves — indeed, they *8* are echoed for us constantly and in a variety of versions. Vice President Albert Gore (1994) has noted that the Global Information Infrastructure (GII) would increase opportunities for intercultural communication among the peoples of the world. Howard Rheingold, in *The Virtual Community* (1993), describes how computer networks can support more citizens in their efforts to communicate with government agencies, corporations, political groups, and information resources. Nicholas Negroponte, in *Being Digital* (1995), sketches a picture of electronic landscapes that provide individuals new ways of making personal contributions to public deliberations and decision making. Dale Spender, while more careful in her perspective in *Nattering on the Net* (1995), speculates on what it will take to establish new kinds of electronic forums that will support women and other groups now often left out of — or kept out of — public discussions in other venues.

This optimism about technology often masks in a peculiar way, how- *9* ever, a contrasting set of extremely potent fears. Moreover, and perhaps more importantly, an exclusive focus on the positive changes associated with technology often serves to distract educators from recognizing how existing social forces actually work to resist change in connection with technology; how they support the status quo when technology threatens to disrupt the world in any meaningful way; how our culture, and the social formations that make up this culture, react with a special kind of conservatism to technology, even as we laud the changes it promises to bring.

This chapter will attempt to illustrate the ways in which change is *10* modulated and complicated by forces of stasis by focusing attention on a series of images that come from commercial advertisements about technology. These advertisements reflect a portion of our collective American cultural imagination about technology. Like most images, they tell rich and powerful stories about the social contexts in which they are produced. Like snapshots — of weddings and graduations, of Christmas and family reunions — they reveal us, as Americans, to ourselves. They are laden with cultural information, shot through with the values, ideological positions, and social understandings that comprise our shared experience. Indeed, it is because we recognize the common cultural symbols in these snapshots so clearly, because we commonly construct meaning with and through them, because they are so loaded with social significance to us, that such images are powerful communication devices.

These are also the reasons that the ads included in this chapter can *11* reveal to us the complications of our feelings toward technology and illustrate how these feelings are played out in the shared landscapes of our lived experience.

Narrative #1: The "Global Village" and the "Electronic Colony"

One of the most popular narratives Americans tell ourselves about comput- *12* ers is that technology will help us create a global village in which the peoples of the world are all connected — communicating with one another and cooperating for the commonweal. According to this popular social narrative, the computer network that spans the globe will serve to erase meaningless geopolitical borders, eliminate racial and ethnic differences, re-establish a historical familial relationship which binds together the peoples of the world regardless of race, ethnicity, or location. As Nicholas Negroponte (1995) re-tells the story to us, "a new generation is emerging from the digital landscape free from many of the old prejudices. . . . Digital technology can be a natural force, drawing people into greater world harmony" (230) within a landscape where "we are bound to find new hope and dignity" (231).

This story, as you can imagine, is appealing at a romantic level to *13* many Americans. It is also, incidentally, quite terrifying. Becoming just another member of the tribe, just another citizen of the global village, suggests the possibility that Americans could be asked to relinquish their current privileged status in the world where, as Negroponte (1995, 230) also reminds us, twenty percent of the population currently consumes eighty percent of the resources. Being just one among many village members also suggests the possibility of losing the economic benefits that have accrued to us as citizens in one of the most highly technological nations of the world and the possibility of functioning within a new global context in which classism and racism are unacceptable because so many members of the connected human family are poor and of color.

In fact, we find ourselves, as a culture, ill equipped to cope with the *14* changes that the "global village" story necessitates, unable, even, to imagine, collectively, ways of relating to the world outside our previous historical and cultural experiences. As a result, in the advertisements included here, we revise the script of the narrative to fit within the historically determined contexts that are familiar and comfortable. In doing so, we also limit our cultural vision of the technological changes that are acceptable and possible for us as a culture.

The first series of images presented in this chapter reveals how our *15* cultural imagination deals with the radical changes that the Global Village narrative implies, by re-constituting technological change within the boundaries of these more historically and socially familiar contexts. In the Global Village narrative, for example, while we maintain the vision of linking peoples around the world, we imagine ourselves, not as simple members of this electronically constituted village, but rather as discoverers of the village, explorers of its remote corners, and even colonizers of its exotic peoples.

In the revised narrative, the global village retains its geographical *16* reach, but it becomes a world in which different cultures, different peoples, exist to be discovered, explored, marveled at — in a sense, known and claimed — by those who can design and use technology. Inhabitants of this electronic global village, in turn, become foreigners, exotics, savages, objects to study and, sometimes, to control.

This revision is a familiar imaginative context for us — we have, after *17* all, a history of experiencing the world as missionaries, as colonists, as tourists, as representatives of multinational companies. The revised story leaves no doubt about our own role — Americans are the smart ones who use technological expertise to connect the world's peoples, to supply them with technology and train them to use it. Nor does the revised story leave us in doubt about the roles of other peoples in the world — they are the recipients of technology and its benefits, those who use the technology that we control. This story is so familiar because it has happened before and in ways that Americans like to remember. We have a long and admirable history of exporting technological expertise to less fortunate neighbors — through the Lend-Lease, the Peace Corps, and the Space Program among other routes.

This re-telling or re-vising of the Global Village story — we can now *18* call it the Electronic Colonial narrative — happens very naturally within the discursive venues available to our culture — on television, in our classrooms, in books, and articles, and in corporate settings — often without anyone noticing because the elements of the revised Electronic Colonial narrative are so much more familiar and acceptable to us than were those of the original Global Village story.

The following pair of images reveals these themes (figures 1 and 2). *19* Especially fascinating in terms of this revised narrative is the use in these two ads, by Virgin Sound and Records, of the "one tribe" motto.

In the first image (figure 1) we get a glimpse of both stories we have *20* described. The text here narrates the Global Village story, "For the world to have a future, we must work together as one tribe" because "encroaching civilization, disease" and "epidemics" are threatening some of the world's people with "near extinction." Virgin, the ad tells us, has donated a portion of their profits from their CD atlas, entitled *One World,* to assist the Yanomami tribe in the Amazon Basin as they establish health care programs in their villages.

The second, revised story — the Electronic Colonial narrative — is *21* revealed most clearly in the visual image represented in the ad, the picture of the Yanomami man. In accordance with the themes of the revised narrative, the Yanomami is shown in ritual dress with feathers and face paint, presented as a wondering savage, vulnerable to the crueler effects of civilization, and obviously unaware, in a critical or informed sense, of the power of the technology being used to his benefit. He is connected to Americans as "a member of the tribe," but he also remains a world away from us — the people who are creating the CD technology and donating the money to health care projects.

The second ad (figure 2), again for Virgin Sound and Records, 22 announces two products and provides us another version of the revised Electronic Colonial story. In this story, Americans use technology to become world travelers, to learn about — and acquire knowledge of — other cultures, while remaining comfortably situated within their own living rooms and, thus, comfortably separated from the other inhabitants of the global village.

On the left side of the page, the One Tribe CD is described, in which 23 "MTV star Pip Dann takes you on a journey exploring the people and cultures of our world, from the origin of the Maori islanders to the rituals of a Tibetan monk." As the ad says, "One Tribe takes you further than you can imagine — right from your own Home." On the right side of the page, the *One World* atlas offers "a stunningly rich trek around the earth," and a "wealth of maps and information all set to a culturally rich music track." The non-Americans featured in this ad are identified as exotic, albeit inviting, co-habitants of the global village. At the top left, are representations of two youngsters, spliced together to present a bizarre tribal image; on the left margin scattered among postcards from exotic destinations and lists of foreign vocabulary words, two picturesque French men sport the requisite berets and a veiled Middle Eastern woman with mysterious eyes is portrayed.

To complement the textual representation of the Electronic Colony 24 narrative, the picture in the bottom left of this ad reveals the source of this world gaze — a white, blond woman sits in a well appointed living room that is chock full of artifacts from around the world; several big-screen viewing areas in front of her feature images of exotic peoples and far-off locations; a large computer with a world map on the screen and a globe complete the representation. Virgin provides an interesting case study of the Electronic Colonial narrative. As a company, it has roots in Great Britain, but, given its marketing and advertising targets, it has acquired a decidedly American flavor, thus joining the two countries under the potency of a single colonial gesture.

And these are the tasteful and more subtle advertisements that are 25 associated with the Electronic Colony narrative. The other end of the spectrum is represented in the next two images (figures 3 and 4).

Figure 3, entitled "Unexpected," shows an Indian woman, bone picks 26 through her nose, feathers attached to her ear, beads around her neck, nursing a baby on one breast and a monkey on the other. The ad, for a color scanner, begins with a large dollar sign. The person in the image, the message suggests, is another inhabitant of the global village, but one important to Americans only as the unexpected exotic, an image that we can use to sell a piece of technology.

The next ad (figure 4), for Polyglot International software, provides yet 27 another version of the Electronic Colony story. In this image, [we see] a male, of undefined indigenous origins, with gold teeth, a broad smile, and a Carmen Miranda kind of bonnet made up of roses and topped by either a radio antenna or a birthday candle. The ad's designers have superimposed a set of aviator's goggles over the man's eyes, and across these goggles are printed a series of 1s and 0s, denoting binary code.

In this ad, the text provides the background story for the image, "You 28 need a team of software . . . experts who can help you culturally adapt every aspect of your software for global markets. What you need for what they want." The members of the global village, the ad implies, are indeed different from Americans, and strange, but we can, given the know-how that characterizes the American free enterprise system, identify what these people are seeking in terms of desirable software and provide it to them in a language that they can understand, even with a simplistic notion of our technology products.

These four advertisements — like the travelogue images we look at in 29 *National Geographic,* like the tourist brochures we pore over in the travel agency, like the slides we view after a friend's trip abroad — are representations of exotic places and exotic peoples now available to Americans as new global markets, multiplied, as Fredric Jameson (1991) and Jean Baudrillard (1983) would say, to the point of dizzying accessibility and specificity. And it is the wondering native, the silly Indian, the veiled woman that is the object of our collective technological, cultural, and capitalist gaze. Americans, in these four ads, you'll notice, go almost unrepresented in terms of images. Instead, Americans are the canny and sophisticated minds behind the text, behind the image, behind the technology. We are the designers, the providers, the village benefactors. We are cybertourists and cybercapitalists who both understand and represent the world as a private standing reserve.

This next pair of advertisements (figures 5 and 6) from IBM entitled 30 "Solutions for a small planet" also tells the Electronic Colony story, illustrating how generous Americans can be in providing other, needier countries with useful technology, and providing the story a potent cumulative power. A small map portrayed in each ad helps to orient viewers to the particular area of the world that IBM and American influence have reached.

In the first ad (figure 5), for example, with the tone of an old master, IBM 31 provides the 3-D rendering technology needed to rebuild the Frauenkirche, a church destroyed during the allied firebombing of Dresden in 1945. The ad notes that this technology, along with the experience of talented stonemasons, allows the reconstruction to proceed, linking the power of a "21st century tool" with the imagination of "18th century craftsmanship."

In the next IBM ad, this set in South Africa, IBM helps the smiling   32
driver of a South African Breweries truck "slake the thirst of . . . far flung
customers . . . so precisely that no one's ever short a drop."

If the previous series reduces the world to a series of tourist destina-   33
tions, this pair of ads — representative of a much more extensive series of
technological "solutions for a small planet" — reduces the world's problems to a set of embarrassingly quick fixes. American technology and technological know-how, these images imply, can provide reparations for the
cultural damage caused by the firebombing of Dresden, re-create the
painstaking artistic achievement of a destroyed eighteenth-century cathedral, and serve as a corrective for decades of apartheid. These implications, of course, are not only absurd; they are humiliatingly small-minded.
Nothing can provide redress for the millions of human lives, the art, the
history, the beauty lost in Dresden; nothing can totally ameliorate the pain
and the lingering inequities of South African apartheid. As much as Americans might like to think it, technology is not the solution for all of the
world's problems — and, indeed, it might well be a contributing cause to
many of them.

Technology, in these ads, is an American tool. And what we use this   34
tool for reveals all too clearly our values as *homo faber* — the tool maker.
In these images, I'm afraid, we see reflected not those fundamental and
much needed changes we talked about pursuing earlier; not improvements
in the world situation, nor the elimination of hunger or pain or suffering
or war; not, in other words, an improved life for our fellow inhabitants in
the global village or an improved understanding of their cultures and concerns, but, rather, the all too familiar stories of how to multiply our own
markets, how to increase our own cultural profits at the expense of others,
how to take more effective advantage of need and difference whenever we
identify them, and how to reduce the cultures of other people to inexcus-
able simplifications.

Narrative #2: "Land of Equal Opportunity" and "Land of Difference"

A second favorite cultural story that we tell ourselves in connection with   35
computers and change focuses on equity, opportunity, and access — all
characteristics ascribed to the electronic landscape we have constructed
on the Internet and to computer use, in general.

This landscape, Americans like to believe, is open to everybody —   36
male and female, regardless of color, class, or connection. It is, in fact, at
some level a romantic re-creation of the American story and the American
landscape themselves — a narrative of opportunity in an exciting land
claimed from the wilderness, founded on the values of hard work and fair
play. It is a land available to all citizens who place a value on innovation,
individualism, and competition, especially when tempered by a neighborly

concern for less fortunate others that is the hallmark of our democracy. If you recognize this story, it is because it has been told so many times. It is the same story that Alexis de Tocqueville (1835) told us in *Democracy in America* and one that we've been telling ourselves ever since — in *Horatio Alger* and *Huck Finn*, in *Nancy Drew* and in episodes of "Father Knows Best."

This next series of advertisements plays on this narrative, emphasiz- 37 ing, in particular, our fascination with — and strong faith in — these tradi- tional American values; in this case, specifically as they have the enduring power to inform and temper technological innovations. The first is an ad (figure 7) for Bob, Microsoft's friendly operating system. These images are all ripe with references to the 1950s, a time when America was entering the very beginning of an accelerated push toward technological growth and innovation. Although Sputnik, launched by the Russians on the 4th of October in 1957, weighed heavily on our collective minds, the fifties were chock full of optimism. We were still fresh from our successes in World War II, invigorated by the promise of the space program, tantalized by the bright future that the new world order seemed to hold for those who were innovative and farsighted, ready to help the world realize the promise of democracy and technology through special projects like the Peace Corps.

This cultural memory is a potent one for Americans, and these ads res- 38 onate with the values that we remember as characterizing that golden time — recalling for example, the down-home, no-nonsense comfort asso- ciated with a good dog, a good pipe, a warm fire, a comfortable pair of shoes (figure 7), and the other very American comforts accruing from a good salary and hard work in a culture where effort is rewarded with capi- tal gain, regardless of race, color, creed, or class.

Indeed, we tell ourselves this clearly American tale — which I'll refer 39 to as the Land of Equal Opportunity narrative — often and in many differ- ent versions. The next two images (figures 8 and 9) also play on it, for instance.

The first, for Cisco Systems, uses a picture that could have come right 40 out of a Dick and Jane reader (figure 8). It shows another very American scene, also harkening back to the magic time of the fifties. This time, the focus is on landscape inhabited by smiling people who point to airplanes as evidence of the technological progress because these machines charac- terize what American know-how can accomplish in the land of equal opportunity when circumstances are right. The text notes, "With wide- eyed optimism, you thought technology was going to let you set informa- tion free. You were going to put power into the hands of the people." The ad goes on to explain that technology uninfluenced by traditional American values can run amuck, especially in a postmodern world characterized by "conflicting standards," "rival companies," "incompatibilities," and ineffi- cient work habits.

The second image (figure 9) tells a bit more of the Land of Equal 41 Opportunity narrative. It speaks for a piece of software by CINet called "The Ultimate Internet Tour," showing what looks like a frame from an old home movie. From a wide angle shot of a fifties suburban tract home development, we get a magnified perspective on a typical American family — three smiling kids, two smiling, upwardly-mobile parents posing in front of a spanking new, functionally designed, split-level home, with all the optimism characteristic of the Eisenhower era. The message, which urges readers to "keep up with the Joneses, the Gates and your kids," suggests that citizens of the twenty-first century can achieve the same kind of happy security and personal well being that was enjoyed by citizens of the fifties — by purchasing a software package rather than a new home.

Unfortunately, Americans have no collective imaginary context for, or   *42* historical experience of, a real global village, nor do they have any real experience with an undifferentiated land of opportunity. Our cultural experience, indeed, tells us something very different — that America is the land of opportunity only for some people. The history of slavery in this country, the history of deaf education, women's suffrage, immigration, and labor unions remind us of this fact; as do our current experiences with poverty, the differential school graduation rate for blacks and whites and Hispanics, the fact that we have never had a woman President, and the presence of border guards and the razor-wire fences over the Rio Grande. All these things remind us that opportunity is a commodity generally limited to privileged groups within this country.

Thus, the revised story in the case of these last five ads — which we   *43* can call the Land of Difference narrative — is present not in what they show, but what they fail to show. These ads are what my grandmother would call "mighty white." There is a remarkable absence in all the images of people of color, and poor people, and people who are out of work, and single-parent families, and gay couples, and foreigners. If citizens of all kinds are to have access to technology and the opportunities it provides, we do not see such a narrative imagined in the Land of Difference narrative; if technology is to improve the lives of all Americans regardless of race and class and other differences, our collective ability to envision such a world is not evident in these images.

Narrative #3: "The Un-Gendered Utopia" and "The Same Old Gendered Stuff"

A third potent narrative that Americans tell ourselves about technology   *44* and change focuses on gender — specifically, this story claims that computers and that computer-supported environments will help us create a utopic world in which gender is not a predictor of success or a constraint for interaction with the world. This narrative, the Un-Gendered Utopia story, encourages educators to see and understand computers as educational allies that can support efforts to create new kinds of educational and economic opportunities for students — regardless of gender. The potency of this narrative persists despite evidence to the contrary. It is clear, for instance, that fewer girls use computers in public secondary schools than do boys, especially in the upper grades; [that] fewer women enter the advanced fields of computer science than do males; that the computer industry continues to be a space inhabited by and controlled primarily by males. Computer games are still designed for boys; computer commercials are still aimed mainly at males; computing environments are still constructed by and for males (cf., Spender, 1995; Kramarae, 1988; Jessup, 1991). Computers, in other words, are complexly socially determined artifacts that interact with existing social formations and tendencies — including sexism, classism, and racism — to contribute to the shaping of a gendered society.

This situation, complexly overdetermined as it is within our cultural   45
context, is nowhere more visible than in gendered images of technology use — especially, but not limited to, commercial images. In these richly textured images, the elaborately woven fabric of social formations that supports the male focused computer industry is coded ideologically at numerous visual and discursive levels for consumers and users. This fabric is so tightly woven, that for many computer users and consumers, for many students in our schools, it represents what Pierre Bourdieu (1977) would term "doxa" — ideological systems of belief so consistent with popular beliefs, and therefore so invisibly potent, that they preclude the consideration of other positions altogether. At the same time, all such fabrics have gaps, lacunae, that provide the space for resistance; and this one is no exception. Indeed, it is exactly because this ideological system is so densely and consistently coded that these images provide such rich sites of analysis and strategic information. In Andrea Dworkin's (1974) words, an analysis of these images can provide us the chance to unthink current discourses about technology and to transform the dialogues we hold with ourselves about gender and computers in new and productive, heterodoxic ways.

Like the Land of Equal Opportunity narrative, the Un-Gendered   46
Utopia story can appeal at a romantic level to many Americans, while, at the same time, terrifying us on a practical level. Creating an electronic ungendered utopia means that we might have to learn how to understand people outside of the limited gender roles that we have constructed for them in this country, that we may have to abandon the ways in which we have traditionally differentiated between men's work and women's work in the marketplace, that we may have to provide men and women with equitable remuneration for comparable jobs, that we may have to learn to function within new global contexts that acknowledge women as Heads of State as well as heads of households.

In fact, we find ourselves, as a culture, ill equipped to cope with the   47
changes that this Un-Gendered Utopia narrative necessitates. We cannot, indeed, even imagine, collectively, ways of relating to gender outside the context of our familiar historical and cultural set of experiences. As a result, we revise the script of the narrative to fit more snugly within the historically determined contexts that are familiar and comfortable to us.

In doing so, however, we also limit our cultural vision of gender within technological landscapes — constraining roles and expectations and possibilities to those we have already constructed as a culture, limiting the potential for change by subscribing to a conventional framework for our imagination.

In this revision, for example, while we maintain the vision of an electronic landscape that is open to all innovative and hardworking people, regardless of their gender, we also limit the actual participation of women and men within this landscape to the more traditionally determined gender roles we have already constructed within our culture. In the revised narrative — the Same Old Gendered Stuff narrative — the new electronic landscape retains a value on innovation, hard work, and the individual contributions of people of both genders, but only as they are practiced appropriately — within the traditionally gendered contexts we have historically and culturally ratified for women and men in our culture. *48*

In such a landscape, women use technology within a clearly constrained set of appropriate settings: to enrich the lives of their family and to meet their responsibilities at home — as wife, as mother, as seductress, as lover; within a business setting, women use computers to support the work of their bosses — as secretaries, executive assistants, and loyal employees. There are, of course, exceptions to this story, as we shall see, but this narrative, as Anthony Giddens (1984, p. 22) would say, is "deeply sedimented" in habit, historically determined practices, in tradition, in our imaginations, and, thus, it exerts a strong influence on even these alternative stories. Men, in contrast, use computers at home to expand their personal horizons beyond current limits — for excitement, for challenge, to enhance their own private lives as explorers, pioneers, and builders. Within the business world, men use computers to support their historically constructed roles as bosses, leaders, decision makers. *49*

This re-telling or re-vising of the Un-Gendered Utopia story happens very naturally. A good portion of our collective imagination is constructed by history and sedimented in past experience and habit. Indeed, many of the images appearing in the next series have a distinctive "retro" look that harkens back to the fifties — for many of the same reasons as those ads telling the Land of Equal Opportunity narrative discussed earlier in this chapter. *50*

In that optimistic time, women were no longer encouraged to maintain a presence in the workplace. At the close of WWII, they were displaced from the workplace by men returning home from the European and Pacific theaters (May, 1988). Women, faced with this eventuality, became the savvy managers of the private sphere — especially when they were assisted by technological innovations. These women were urged to serve their families frozen foods and TV dinners, and to acquaint themselves with the scientific principles of eating so that they could be effective nutritional advisors to the family; they were expected as well to heed the *51* advice of Dr. Spock, take advantage of the Salk vaccine for polio, and keep abreast of advances in antibiotics and modern theories of behaviorism to become effective health advisors; and they were expected to use the newly developed and improved technologies of electric vacuum cleaners, dish-washers, washing machines, televisions, cleaning products, and station wagons to be increasingly effective housekeepers.

The fact that this previous era of technological optimism provides the 52 context for Americans' collective imagination about the current cultural project of technological expansion is both interesting and important. The results are evident in numerous advertisements about computers and women that use a retro look to link women's roles in the fifties to those in the nineties — in which each gender assumes [its] appropriate role in con-nection with technology. Men use technology to accomplish things; women benefit from technology to enhance the ease of their lives or to benefit their families.

And to understand how these traditionally gendered roles of the fifties 53 are projected directly on the technological context of the nineties, readers can focus on the living room in figure 10, where images from the television era of the fifties are overlaid by those of the computer era of the nineties. Despite this fact, however, despite the fact that families in the nineties must maintain a dual presence in the work force, despite the fact that the rising incidence of divorce at the end of this century makes single-parent fami-lies the norm rather than the exception, despite the fact that the optimism of the fifties and sixties as articulated by John Kennedy has given way to the paranoia of the nineties as expressed by Pat Buchanan — the images of gender, the narratives they tell in connection with technology, remain relatively stable, disturbingly intact except for the imposition of a com-puter keyboard — held and operated by the father — and a computer menu — admired and enjoyed by the woman and children.

And so the revised narrative — the Same Old Gendered Stuff narrative — 54 remains current. Its resonance is also demonstrated in figure 11, an adver-tisement for Reveal, and in figure 12, where we meet a thoroughly modern woman, Celeste Craig of Pontiac, Illinois. Celeste, we learn, is finally achieving her dream of "going to college by staying home." The invention of a sophisticated distance-education computer network has allowed Celeste to undertake a course of study from her home in Pontiac, Illinois, while, at the same time, continuing to fulfill her role as a single mother supporting a family, parenting her children, and maintaining a household.

The gender roles of the fifties also translate into workplace roles for 55 women in the nineties. In figure 13, for example, Irma — like a good, upscale, personal business assistant in the nineties — speaks "fluent Inter-net" much like her fifties counterpart would have spoken French. In figure 14, Fran, a fifties secretary with "just another pretty face" has been transmo-grified, into a "multi-talented" nineties cyborg/robot assistant that "makes your website look good." And finally in figure 15, which suggests only a slightly revised version of the Same Old Gendered Stuff narrative, a nineties woman-as-boss, also portrayed in sepia tones against a fifties-style restaurant banquette, remains as decidedly cool, relaxed, and elegant despite the fact that she has also required the title of "hotshot," "collector," "workhorse," and "nomad."

But the roles of parent, housewife, and secretary/boss are not the only ones open to women in the new cyberlandscape represented by the Same Old Gendered Stuff narrative. Figure 16, for example, shows an ad for Nokia monitors, and, in doing so, portrays a woman in the traditional role of "beauty." In the advertisement, a sophisticated woman draped with jewels, decked out in a chic black dress, washed in sepia tones and softened by a grainy texture gazes into a computer monitor. Although the text accompanying this image ostensibly outlines the capabilities and design of the monitor, the language itself leaves no doubt of the picture's focus or intent. As it notes, the "European passion for beauty" is quickly "winning the hearts and eyes of Americans too" by seductive means. The woman pictured in this advertisement, it should be noted, gazes longingly into a monitor, but lacks a keyboard with which she could act on the computer. 56

Finally, the 1990s retro series offers Americans the role of seductress — also a traditionally defined role for women, and one that has retained enormous strength even in cyberspace where change is expected to affect so many areas of our lives. Figure 17, representing a narcissistic seductress for Samsung, illustrates the potency of these traditionally constrained roles. 57

In these ads, we see reflected the roles that our culture can imagine women playing in relation to technology. And they are familiar roles — the seductress, the beauty, the mother — all relationships ratified by our historical experience, easily accessible to our collective imagination, and informed by traditional social values. These roles exist, and are reproduced, within a set of overdetermined social formations that makes radical change hard to imagine and even harder to enact — especially when technology is involved. 58

The revision of the Un-Gendered Utopia narrative into the Same Old Gendered Stuff narrative deals no less traditionally with men's roles, it should be noted. In connection with workplace technologies, men are allowed essentially the same tie-and-oxford-cloth look in the nineties (figure 18) as they were in the fifties (figure 19), although slight variations of this role — the impatient-and-rebellious young entrepreneur on the go sans tie (figure 20) or the successful architect-net-cruiser (figure 21) sporting a turtleneck — are also permitted. Out of the workplace (figures 22–24), men are shown to adopt the equally traditional and retrograde roles of bikers, nerds, and sex maniacs. 59

These ads, of course, are only one expression of our collective experience — and I would not want to claim that they tell a totalizing story. They do indicate, however, that it will be exceedingly difficult for Americans to imagine an electronic landscape in which individuals enjoy new kinds of opportunities to relate to each other and new kinds of opportunities to make positive changes in their lives. It takes energy and careful thinking to 60 create a landscape in which women can participate in roles other than those of seductress, beauty, or mother; and in which men don't have to be bikers or abusers or rabid techno geeks or violent sex maniacs. It is far easier and more comfortable simply to re-construct for ourselves those traditional narratives that tell the same old gender stories over and over again, and that re-create the status quo ever more clearly in their re-telling.

Confronting Revised Narratives

The images in this chapter illustrate the richly textured narrative fabrics within which computer technology and other communication technologies are situated in the American cultural scene. Our work as teachers, the curricula we fashion, the corporate and public environments our students enter as professionals, the schools that make up the educational systems — these social formations are also shaped by the same sets of culturally determined values, the same complexities, the same ambiguities, the same contexts for our imaginations.   *61*

Such a realization can serve to remind teachers that technology does not necessarily bring with it social progress, and that educators had better make sure that students recognize and understand this fact if we want them to be able to make contributions of which they can be proud. Within the English studies programs that we design and administer, and participate in, we place everyone in jeopardy if we limit our understanding of technology and change to one dimension, if we teach students only one part of this complicated picture.   *62*

A good English studies curriculum will educate students robustly and intellectually rather than narrowly or vocationally. It will recognize the importance of educating students to be critically informed technology scholars rather than simply expert technology users. Graduates of English studies programs will face an increasingly complex set of issues in the workplace and in the public sphere, and our failure to provide the intellectual tools necessary to understand and cope with these issues at multiple levels signals our own inability to lead productively as professionals and as citizens.   *63*

Finally the images can serve to remind educators that even though productive changes are hard to make — with or without technology — our responsibility to work for change, especially as educators, remains undiminished in its urgency and importance. Like Paulo Freire, we need to be optimistic enough to believe that in teaching ourselves and others to recognize the inequities that challenge humanity in our world — the ethnocentrism, racism, classism, sexism — we have begun the difficult work of addressing these problems.   *64*

WORKS CITED

Apple, Michael W. 1988. *Teachers and Texts: Political Economy of Class and Gender Relations in Education.* New York: Routledge.

Baudrillard, Jean. 1983. *Simulations*. Trans. Paul Foss, Paul Patton, and Philip Beitchman. New York: Semiotext(e).

Bump, Jerome. 1990. Radical Changes in Class Discussion Using Networked Computers. *Computers and the Humanities* 24: 49–65.

Clark, Irene. 1995. Information Literacy and the Writing Center. *Computers and Composition* 12: 203–219.

Coogan, David. 1995. Email Tutoring, a New Way to Do New Work. *Computers and Composition* 12: 171–182.

Dworkin, Andrea. 1974. *Woman Hating*. New York: E. P. Dutton.

Freire, Paulo. 1996. *Pedagogy of the Oppressed*. Rev. ed. New York: Continuum.

Geren, P. 1996. Global Communications on the World Wide Web. In *The Nearness of You*, ed. Christopher Edgar and Susan Nelson Wood. New York: Teachers and Writers Collaborative. 28–36.

Giddens, Anthony. 1984. *The Constitution of Society: Outline of the Theory of Structuration*. Berkeley, CA: U of California P.

Gore, Albert J. 1994. Remarks Prepared for Delivery at the International Telecommunication Union. Address prepared for the International Telecommunications Union. Buenos Aires.

Hafer, Gary. 1996. Computer-Assisted Illustration and Instructional Documents. *Computers and Composition* 13: 49–56.

Hawisher, Gail E. and Cynthia L. Selfe. 1993. Tradition and Change in Computer-Supported Writing Environments: A Call for Action. In *Theoretical and Critical Perspectives on Teacher Change*, ed. P. Kahaney, J. Janangelo, and L. A. M. Perry. Norwood, NJ: Ablex. 155–186.

Jameson, Fredric. 1991. *Postmodernism Or the Cultural Logic of Late Capitalism*. Durham, NC: Duke UP.

Jessup, Emily. 1991. Feminism and Computers in Composition Instruction. In *Evolving Perspectives on Computers and Composition Studies: Questions for the 1990s*, ed. Gail Hawisher and Cynthia L. Selfe. Urbana, IL: NCTE. 336–355.

Kramarae, Cheris. 1988. *Technology and Women's Voices: Keeping in Touch*. New York: Routledge and Kegan Paul.

May, Elaine Tyler. 1988. *Homeward Bound: American Families in the Cold War Era*. New York: Basic.

McDaniel, Ellen. 1990. Assessing the Professional Role of the English Department Computer Person. In *Computers and Writing: Theory, Research, Practice*, ed. Deborah Holdstein and Cynthia L. Selfe. New York: MLA. 84–94.

Minock, Mary and Francis Shor. 1995. Crisscrossing Grand Canyon: Bridging the Gaps with Computer Conferencing. *Computers and Composition* 12: 355–365.

Negroponte, Nicholas. 1995. *Being Digital*. New York: Alfred A. Knopf.

Rheingold, Howard. 1993. *The Virtual Community: Homesteading on the Electronic Frontier*. Reading, MA: Addison-Wesley.

Schwartz, Helen, Cynthia L. Selfe, and James Sosnoski. 1994. The Electronic Department. *Works and Days* 12: 261–286.

Selber, Stuart. 1994. Beyond Skill Building: Challenges Facing Technical Communication Teachers in the Computer Age. *Technical Communication Quarterly* 3: 365–390.

Selfe, Cynthia L. 1996. The Gendering of Technology: Images of Women, Men, and Technology. Paper presented at CCCC. Milwaukee, WI. March.

———. 1996. Theorizing Email for the Practice, Instruction, and Study of Literacy. *Electronic Literacies in the Workplace: Technologies of Writing*, ed. Patricia Sullivan and Jennie Dautermann. Urbana, IL and Houghton, MI: NCTE and *Computers and Composition*.

——— and Richard J. Selfe. 1994. The Politics of the Interface: Power and Its Exercise in Electronic Contact Zones. *College Composition and Communication* 45 (Dec 4): 480–504.

Sirc, Geoffrey. 1995. The Twin Worlds of Electronic Conferencing. *Computers and Composition* 12: 265–278.

Snyder, Gary. 1995. *A Place in Space*. Washington, DC: Counterpoint.

Spender, Dale. 1995. *Nattering on the Net: Women, Power, and Cyberspace*. North Melbourne: Spinifex.

Sproull, Lee and Sara Kiesler. 1991. *Connections: New Ways of Working in the Networked Organization*. Cambridge: MIT P.

Tornow, Joan. 1997. *Link/Age: Composing in the Online Classroom*. Logan, UT: Utah State UP.

Wahlstrom, Billie J. and Cynthia L. Selfe. 1994. A View from the Bridge: Piloting among the Shoals of Computer Use. *ADE Bulletin*, #109 (Winter): 35–45.

Reading Rhetorically

1. Who is Selfe's audience or audiences? What specific words and phrases support your answer? Do you feel included or excluded by the way she addresses her readers, and how does this affect your response to her argument? What specific changes, if any, would you suggest in Selfe's approach to her audience?

2. Selfe refers to advertisements that are not reproduced here, but her descriptions are quite vivid. Where do you see Selfe's argument emerging in her descriptions of these ads? Find specific examples of evaluative and guiding language that makes her descriptions work toward the purpose of her argument. Can description ever be objective? Explain your answer with examples of your own.

3. Much of Selfe's argument is based on her interpretation of advertisements. What other evidence does she offer? Where does she draw on other authors, and how does this advance her argument? How does she address counterarguments? Could she do this more persuasively? Why or why not?

Inquiring Further

4. Your instructor will divide the class into three groups, each group responsible for teaching one of Selfe's three narratives to the rest of the class. Be prepared to point to the highlights of Selfe's argument in your assigned narrative, explaining how — and how well — the examples illustrate the argument, and raising questions for discussion. Each group also should find and bring to class several advertisements that illustrate — or refute — the point Selfe makes in the assigned narrative.

5. What social effects have computers had on K–12 education in the United States? Use your library's resources to look at local or national newspapers or in scholarly journals to see what kinds of social issues arise when computer technology and education are discussed. How do your findings confirm, extend, or contradict Selfe's claims in Narrative #2? Share your findings with the class.

6. Test the claims Selfe makes in Narrative #3 in the context of your own university by investigating the dynamics between gender and computer technology. What is the ratio of men to women in computer-oriented fields of study at your school? What other statistics, evidence, and anecdotes can you gather as a class that will help you analyze Selfe's claim that "computing environments are still constructed by and for males" (para. 44)?

Framing Conversations

7. What role, if any, do you think gender plays in the impact of technology? Choose an aspect of computer technology that interests you (e.g., blogging, Facebook, online gaming), and write an essay in which you use Selfe's observations on gender in Narrative #3 and the ideas about gender and computer technology in Marguerite Helmers's essay (p. 679) to build your argument about the significance of gender and this particular aspect of computer technology. You also might choose to draw on Judith Lorber's (p. 617) theories about gendered behaviors to help you build your case.

8. Selfe argues that advertisements "tell rich and powerful stories about the social contexts in which they are produced" (para. 10). Using insights from both Selfe's text and Elizabeth Teare's essay on marketing strategies for children's books (p. 800), select and analyze ten print ads and/or television commercials with a common theme, and write an essay in which you examine the cultural story — about freedom, opportunity, diversity, and gender roles, for example — you see depicted in various ways. What is the significance of your findings?

9. How would you apply Selfe's claim in Narrative #2 — that there is a popular belief that computers can improve "equity, opportunity, and access" (para. 35) — to your college experience? How can computers be used to democratize a college classroom? What are their limits? Write an essay in which you apply Selfe's theories about computer technology to your own educational experiences to make an argument about the role computers can or ought to play in improving the democratic goals of college education. In developing your argument, draw on the ideas of at least one of the following educational reformers: Mark Edmundson (p. 277), bell hooks (p. 293), Jonathan Kozol (p. 308), James Loewen (p. 332), Mary Louise Pratt (p. 354), and Robert Scholes (p. 370).

■ **ELIZABETH TEARE**

Harry Potter and the Technology of Magic

Elizabeth Teare has taught literature at Yale (where she earned her doctorate) and the University of Dayton. Her interest lies in nineteenth-century British literature, especially the history of the novel. She has written about famous Victorian writers like William Thackeray and Matthew Arnold, and on topics like smuggling, and knaves and fools, which recur as themes in novels of the period. As this essay makes clear, Teare is also interested in children's literature. She presented a draft of this piece at the 1999 Modern Language Association convention in Chicago; it was later published in a collection edited by Lana A. Whited, *The Ivory Tower and Harry Potter: Perspectives on a Literary Phenomenon* (2002).

J. K. Rowling's Harry Potter series has spawned a rich body of criticism, as book reviewers, scholars, parents, and young readers have responded to the unprecedented success of the books and films. Teare's essay, then, is in conversation with people who hold a wide range of perspectives on what they think is very good and very bad about Harry Potter. Some critics claim the books' magical theme sends an "anti-Christian" message; others find the books exemplary for their modeling of moral and philosophical virtues. Still others, like Connie Neal in the book *What's a Christian to Do with Harry Potter?* (2001), negotiate between these two perspectives by offering insights about how Rowling's books operate in a long tradition of children's literature, the battle between good and evil. Academics like Teare have applied theories from cultural and literary criticism to the series in books that are often taught in college courses for future teachers. One example, edited by Giselle Liza Anatol, is *Reading Harry Potter: Critical Essays* (2003).

Teare's focus in this essay is on the "twenty-first-century commercial and technological culture" (para. 1) that shapes both consumerist themes in children's books and the marketing of merchandise associated with children's books and films. She places Rowling's books in the context of children's fantasy literature, from J. R. R. Tolkien's *Lord of the Rings* series to C. S. Lewis's *Chronicles of Narnia,* and more recent work by Philip Pullman, Ursula K. Le Guin, and many others. Teare notes the way Rowling pokes fun at commodity culture — through her teasing portrayal of the empty-headed celebrity author Gilderoy Lockhart, for example — but she finds the books spend as much time encouraging children to participate as consumers as they do criticizing adults who fall prey to the allure of money.

As you read, pay attention to Teare's strategy of moving between her own argument and the details of the novels themselves. To what extent do you find her argument embedded in her description of characters and plot twists? Notice in particular her analysis of Lockhart in paragraphs 15 through 17. You also might focus on the ways she draws on other writers' ideas to develop her own — citing Jack Zipes (para. 11) and Ellen Seiter (para. 14), for example. Notice, too, Teare's footnotes, in which she cites authors who focus specifically on the Harry Potter phenomenon in addition to those who write more generally about children and consumer culture.

Whether or not you are a fan of J. K. Rowling's series, you may find this essay is a useful model for ways to analyze any fiction you enjoy. Although we don't often think of novels as making arguments, Teare's point is that fiction — even fiction aimed at children — can teach readers perspectives that are significant to the larger culture. Teare doesn't try to simplify the message of Rowling's novels; instead, she argues that "the novels' uneven, interesting, and compromised depiction of children and commodity culture offers a useful arena in which such concerns can be thought about, though not satisfactorily resolved" (para. 32). As you read Teare's essay, consider how many other novels you can think of that share this contradictory relationship to consumer culture, to say nothing of contemporary bookstores themselves — with their cafés, large DVD selections, stuffed toys, and entertainment. What is the significance of this latest twist to marketing books? Teare's essay may help you begin to figure that out.

⸻

The July/August 2001 issue of *Book* lists J. K. Rowling as one of the ten *1* most influential people in publishing.[1] She shares space on this list with John Grisham and Oprah Winfrey, along with less famous but equally powerful insiders in the book industry. What these industry leaders have in common is an almost magical power to make books succeed in the marketplace, and this magic, in addition to that performed with wands, Rowling's novels appear to practice. Opening weekend sales charted like those of a blockbuster movie (not to mention the blockbuster movie itself), the reconstruction of the venerable *New York Times* bestseller lists, the creation of a new nation's worth of web sites in the territory of cyberspace, and of course the legendary inspiration of tens of millions of child readers — the Harry Potter books have transformed both the technologies of reading and the way we understand those technologies. What is it that makes these books — about a lonely boy whose first act on learning he is a wizard is to go shopping for a wand — not only an international phenomenon among children and parents and teachers but also a topic of compelling interest to literary, social, and cultural critics? I will argue that the stories the books tell, as well as the stories we're telling about them, enact both our fantasies and our fears of children's literature and publishing in the context of twenty-first-century commercial and technological culture.

The classics of children's fantasy literature are Luddite, or at best *2* ambivalent, in their attitudes toward modern commodity culture. The great example is Tolkien, whose hobbits destroy the One Ring and Sauron's industrial hell to restore Middle Earth to pastoral, precapitalist serenity (though, Tolkien acknowledges, that serenity is ultimately doomed). In C. S. Lewis's Narnia, too, the arrival of industry heralds the Fall. The same principles hold true in fantasies set in more contemporary worlds. Magic in Diana Wynne Jones and Susan Cooper and Elizabeth Goudge is natural and inborn or, if man-made, is antique, given as a gift or found. Magic cannot be bought or sold: anyone who tries to commodify it is doomed to the kind of horrible fate best portrayed by Roald Dahl. The acquisitive children who accompany Charlie through the chocolate

[1]Abramson et al., "People Who Decide What America Reads," 39.

factory all get their appropriate comeuppance; James's aunts are crushed by the giant peach when they try to exhibit it for profit.

Philip Pullman's recent *His Dark Materials* trilogy comes closest to cele-   3 brating the complicated technologies of its alternate universes. Each volume of the trilogy is named for the marvelous instrument its heroes receive or construct: *The Golden Compass, The Subtle Knife, The Amber Spyglass*. All three novels celebrate the inventive technologies Pullman's parallel universes have developed, particularly the aeronautic devices: balloons, witches' broomsticks (actually pine branches), zeppelins, "gyropters," and the extraordinary "intention craft" directed by its pilot's desires.[2] As the story develops, however, all these inventions are used for, and often destroyed in, a vividly described and bloody universal war. The Subtle Knife turns out to be draining consciousness from the universe and letting in soul-sucking specters. And paradise is a world inhabited by gentle and civilized quadrupeds whose most elaborate technologies are fishing nets and the wheel.

Ursula Le Guin has recently made explicit the opposition of children's   4 fantasy literature to commodity culture. In her new collection of stories, she not only adds to her chronicle of what she carefully notes is the "non-industrial society" of her Earthsea archipelago but also includes, in her Foreword, a powerful critique of what she calls "commodified fantasy." According to Le Guin, the "mills of capitalism" take advantage of modern "long[ing] for the unalterable . . . stability, ancient truths, immutable simplicities" of fantasy by providing readers with empty imitations. Le Guin writes, "Commodified fantasy takes no risks: it invents nothing, but imitates and trivializes. It proceeds by depriving the old stories of their intellectual and ethical complexity, turning their action to violence, their actors to dolls, and their truth-telling to sentimental platitude. Heroes brandish their swords, lasers, [and] wands, as mechanically as combine harvesters, reaping profits. . . . The passionately conceived ideas of the great storytellers are copied, stereotyped, reduced to toys, molded in bright-colored plastic, advertised, sold, broken, junked, replaceable, interchangeable."[3] The metaphor in Le Guin's last sentence is particularly powerful, evoking the world of tie-in marketing campaigns and the "bright-colored plastic" toys in McDonald's Happy Meals. In returning to Earthsea in *Tales of Earthsea* and the new novel *The Other Wind*, Le Guin argues by example for a return to the "nonindustral" practice of fantasy writing. And by implication she raises questions about the Harry Potter books, with their burgeoning industry of bright plastic tie-in merchandise. Are Rowling's novels too, as they have been published and marketed, only "commodified fantasy"?

As with the plots of the fantasy genre, so with the stories we tell our-   5 selves about their place in children's culture. The producers and consumers

---

[2]Philip Pullman, *The Golden Compass*, 218.
[3]Ursula Le Guin, *Tales of Earthsea*, 267, xiii–xiv.

of children's literature have traditionally constructed their cultural position in opposition to capitalist enterprise. Books last. They are reread. It doesn't matter that their covers get torn. Child readers, according to advocates of book culture, are better children than those who clamor for the newest video games. And publishers are better, more wholesome, than the manufacturers who flood the children's market with toys like Pokémon and participate in an interlocking system of cartoons and video games and movies and plastic toys and clothing and accessories and trading cards, all designed to encourage continued consumption in search of the rare missing card, like the golden ticket to Willy Wonka's factory.

In the last twenty years, however, this pastoral vision of children's 6 book culture has become as endangered as Tolkien's Shire. Books have lost children's attention, and therefore market share, to other media that present narrative fantasies: movies, video, and video games. Pokémon is only one of the most visible examples. But it is not only the competition. Children's publishing is itself increasingly tainted. The rise of the franchise series — Animorphs, Goosebumps, the Baby Sitters Club, even the educationally "historical" American Girl — works to create the same kind of desire for mass-produced similarity and for serial acquisition that Pokémon does. (And even Pokémon has a franchised series of books.) Increasingly, too, successful children's books are part of their own systems of tie-ins. Read the American Girls and buy the dolls, their outfits and furniture (displayed behind glass in the Chicago flagship store as if they are valuable museum artifacts), the matching doll-and-owner American Girl jackets, tickets to the American Girl revue. Nancy Drew never carried all this baggage. Disney, of course, is the merchandising master of this game.

Then Harry Potter appeared on the scene, initially offering a strong 7 counternarrative to the Disney story and allowing its publishers, particularly Bloomsbury in the United Kingdom and Scholastic in the United States, to retake the high ground and redirect the story they tell about themselves. Much of the power of the Harry Potter story is in the way it seems to resist the pressures of children's commodity culture. Account after account in the press features a parent describing the change in her child (most often it is a mother and son), who has learned to love reading by reading these books: "they took my non-reader and turned him into a reader."[4] Such stories also feature children who loudly resist Harry Potter tie-in products that might trammel their imaginations. In October 1999, when Rowling's book tour took her to Washington, D.C., the *Washington Post* featured an article about the challenges faced by parents who couldn't buy ready-made Albus Dumbledore and Hermione Granger Halloween costumes and were forced, joyfully, to help their children make their own. The same article, published well before Rowling's film and product-licensing deal with Warner Brothers, quotes a boy who perfectly embodies adult fantasies of children's contented innocence and resistance to

[4]Linton Weeks, "Sheer Sorcery."

commercial exploitation of the book. "'I don't think they should make TV shows because then when you imagine stuff from the book, then it will be much different,' says Sam Piazza, 10, of Silver Spring."[5]

Rowling's authorial biography has been pressed into service to support this noncommercial narrative. According to legend, Rowling was a single mother on the dole when she developed the Harry Potter stories, writing in cafés while her daughter napped. She has protested this account of herself as an unworldly and suffering romantic genius, but she is also quoted, on the Scholastic web site as well as in numerous articles, as saying that all she wants to do is write, whether or not she is paid: "I have always written and I know that I always will; I would be writing even if I hadn't been published."[6] The publishers have matched this story of commercial innocence with one of technological innocence. They have hardly advertised, they claim; the books are a grassroots phenomenon, built on the innocent desire and pleasure of children. Rowling has endorsed this idea, claiming "she was hard-pressed to answer the question she often asked as a child. Why? 'I suppose it's mainly word of mouth,' she offered of the books' success in the London *Guardian*. 'I think children just tell one another about it.'"[7]

Supporters of the innocence myth point to experiences like that of Politics and Prose, an independent bookstore in Washington, D.C., which cited "unprecedented interest" as the reason for a special "crowd control strategy" put in place when Rowling appeared there to sign *Harry Potter and the Prisoner of Azkaban*. Elements of the strategy include the following: "2) We will give out 500 tickets, no more than 4 per person standing in line. We are sure that Ms. Rowling will be able to sign 500 books.... 3) Ms. Rowling will start to sign at 4 P.M. and she will sign NO MORE THAN ONE BOOK FOR EACH PERSON. She will sign until 6 P.M."[8] In fact, Rowling signed nine hundred books in two hours, for admirers who had lined up as early as 8 A.M. and who "clapped and cheered as though [Rowling] were Literate Spice."[9]

Linton Weeks of the *Washington Post*, who coined this Spice Girls simile, aptly captures the conflicts that lie behind the narrative of Harry Potter's innocence and suggest the fundamental question. Are the Harry Potter books a real alternative to children's commodity culture, or are they just the most cleverly packaged part of it? Rowling's celebrity is more like that of Oprah Winfrey herself than that of Oprah's Book Club authors — it is Winfrey, after all, with whom Rowling shares space on the *Book* list. And with the flood of Harry Potter products released into the marketplace since the Warner licensing agreement, it is much more difficult to differentiate

[5]Libby Copeland, "Sew-cery: Young Fans Conjure Some Wizardly Costumes."
[6]"Meet J. K. Rowling," Scholastic Press Harry Potter Web Site.
[7]Marc Shapiro, *J. K. Rowling: The Wizard behind Harry Potter*, 83.
[8]Politics and Prose bookstore, e-mail to subscribers.
[9]Linton Weeks, "Charmed, I'm Sure."

between Harry Potter and the Powerpuff girls. The release of the movie, with its ubiquitous advertising, has blurred the distinction further.

Children's literature critic Jack Zipes has argued that "it is exactly   *11* because the success of the Harry Potter novels is so great and reflects certain troubling sociocultural trends that we must try to evaluate the phenomenon." Zipes argues that the Harry Potter books are so successful because they are so "formulaic," that they could not succeed unless they were. There is something wonderfully paradoxical about the phenomena surrounding the phenomenon of the Harry Potter books. For anything to become a phenomenon in Western society, it must become *conventional;* it must be recognized and categorized as unusual, popularly accepted, praised, or condemned, worthy of everyone's attention; it must conform to the standards of exception set by the mass media and promoted by the culture industry in general. To be phenomenal means that a person or commodity must conform to the tastes of hegemonic groups that determine what makes up a phenomenon. It is impossible to be phenomenal without conforming to conventionality.[10] Zipes admits with pleasure Rowling's wit and humor, but he resists the argument that her books are something special. Their much-touted exceptionality is in fact a sign of their entanglement in the commodified culture industry they are believed to transcend. Zipes points out that the Harry Potter books, especially in hardback, are too expensive for children to buy for themselves, so they must be purchased by reasonably well-off adults; he doubts that as many children have actually read the books as have been exposed to them. The seeming success among children of the conventional Harry Potter books is for Zipes another sign that middle-class parents are "turning [their children] into commodities" by providing them with the cultural signs, like books, that adults think signal parenting success (xi).

Zipes's skepticism about the "Harry Potter phenomenon'" is justified   *12* on several counts. The publishers and marketers of Harry Potter are of course steeped in the commercial technologies they affect to despise. They couldn't buy publicity like their celebrated lack of publicity, which has garnered them everything from Rowling's 1999 "Woman of the Year" honors from *Glamour* to raves on air and in print from George Will.[11] And the novels' publishers, especially Scholastic, have made ample use of the nonprint technologies the books are said to resist. The elaborate Scholastic web site encourages young visitors to play Harry Potter trivia games and to post entries identifying the character they most admire. To play some games, they must register their "personally identifiable information," which Scholastic in a lengthy privacy notice acknowledges the company may use "to provide parents, via e-mail or other means, with information about materials, activities, or other things that may be of interest to parents or

---

[10]Jack Zipes, *Sticks and Stones: The Troublesome Success of Children's Literature from Slovenly Peter to Harry Potter,* 172, 171, 175.

[11]"1999 Women of the Year"; George Will, "Harry Potter: A Wizard's Return."

their children, including products or services of third parties."[12] There is a page for teachers and parents, too, suggesting topics of discussion for class reading groups and home discussion. It is worth pointing out that, despite the elegant interactive design of the web page, the questions it actually poses are as inane and moralizing as those in any old-fashioned junior-high literature anthology: "In *The Prisoner of Azkaban*, when Harry has the opportunity to kill the character responsible for his parents' death, he chooses not to do it. How does that separate him once and for all from his archenemy, Voldemort?"[13] A question like this could as easily appear on a dittoed handout from the 1970s as on a flickering screen in the 2000s. Such familiarity might reconcile parents who worry about the hours their children spend at the computer — if it doesn't induce despair about the unimaginative, coercive questions children now face not only at school but in the broad "cultural pedagogy" sponsored by corporations.[14]

More problematic is the relation in which the Harry Potter books find   *13* themselves to Internet commerce. In late spring 1999, as the first U.S. volume gained popularity, eager American consumers discovered that they could order copies of the second and third volumes directly from Britain over the Internet, from Amazon.com's U.K. affiliate. Scholastic immediately moved up the publication dates of its own second and third volumes and made sure the fourth and subsequent books would be published simultaneously in the United Kingdom and the United States. Scholastic also challenged Amazon.com for violating international territorial publishing rights. Amazon has argued in return that buying a book from a British web site is legally just like Americans buying it in a British bookstore when they are visiting the country. Web sites based in Britain display, though not prominently, a warning that they can ship only one copy to a customer overseas. The Association of American Publishers is now involved, and Rowling's books are providing a test case for the role of traditional territorial rights in the age of e-commerce. In this context, it is impossible to understand the Harry Potter books solely as texts, apart from their status as commodities.

It is possible, however, to take a more optimistic point of view than   *14* Zipes's on the way the books as commodities function in children's culture. In *Sold Separately: Children and Parents in Consumer Culture*, Ellen Seiter argues that "[c]hildren are creative in their appropriation of consumer goods and media, and the meanings they make with these materials are not necessarily and not completely in line with a materialist ethos."[15] In

---

[12]"Privacy Notice," Scholastic Web Site.

[13]In "Conflict," "Harry Potter Discussion Guides," Scholastic Web Site.

[14]Shirley R. Steinberg and Joe L. Kincheloe, eds., *Kinderculture: The Corporate Construction of Childhood*, 4.

[15]Ellen Seiter, *Sold Separately: Children and Parents in Consumer Culture*, 10. Zipes cites this passage from Seiter but counters that children's "creative . . . appropriation," like that of adults, is ultimately only "a false freedom of choice, for all our choices are prescribed and dictated by market systems" (Zipes, *Sticks and Stones*, 4).

the second half of this essay, I will argue that the Harry Potter books themselves attempt to make their own "creative . . . appropriation" of the problem of "consumer goods and media" in both book culture and children's culture. When Zipes concedes that "[p]erhaps it is because the novels are a hodgepodge of . . . popular entertainments that [Rowling's] novels are so appealing," he glimpses an important part of Rowling's method. Unlike Ursula Le Guin, who turns away from "commodified fantasy," Rowling works such fantasy into her fiction. The Harry Potter books offer instructions on how to live in commodity culture, with Rowling advocating, though not always consistently or successfully, resistance to the consumerist pressures both children and adults face. Their engagement with these issues is indeed one reason the novels are "so appealing."

Rowling wittily addresses questions of contemporary book culture in *15* the books themselves, particularly in *Harry Potter and the Chamber of Secrets*. This second novel in the series features celebrity author Gilderoy Lockhart, whom we first meet at a book-signing in wizard London's largest bookstore, Flourish and Blotts. Lockhart's appearance prefigures the crowds that have grown around Rowling's. Lockhart's appeal is sexual, not innocent — most of the crowd is middle-aged witches — but the long line, newspaper photographer, and cheering crowd are recognizable from any collection of articles about Rowling or, indeed, any media celebrity.

Lockhart embodies empty celebrity. He views anything that happens *16* around him as "all publicity." Like many another dim celebrity with a rudimentary sense of his own market power, Lockhart spends hours answering fan mail and signing pictures. Rowling strikes a satiric blow against the book culture into which she has been swept as Lockhart is gradually revealed as a fraud, detested by Hogwarts faculty and students alike. His spells usually fail. His franchise of autobiographical adventures, from *Gadding with Ghouls* to *Travels with Trolls* to *A Year with the Yeti*, is faked, its heroic stories stolen from less photogenic witches and wizards. Explaining this literary theft to Harry, Lockhart invokes a doctrine of "common sense" for understanding and manipulating book culture. Lockhart's cynical sense of what makes a book valuable takes on a darker tone when he decides that Harry and Ron's knowledge of his fraud is too great a threat to his success. He attacks them magically, trying to wipe out their memories rather than help them rescue Ron's sister, Ginny, from the Chamber of Secrets. To save his reputation, Lockhart is prepared not only to destroy the boys' minds but also to abandon Ginny to certain death. Here, celebrity is villainy (*Chamber of Secrets*, 63, 297).

When Lockhart's spell backfires and he loses his own identity, the pleased *17* reader echoes the dismissive comment of Professor Minerva McGonagall: "that's got *him* out from under our feet" (*Chamber of Secrets*, 295). The pleasure of unmasking Lockhart aligns Rowling's readers with Harry himself, one of the first characters to see through Lockhart's façade. Harry's resistance to Lockhart's media obsession highlights an important theme running through all the books. His distaste for the trappings of fame thrust upon him — photo ops, groupies, journalistic puff pieces — constantly reminds the reader of his boyish modesty and good taste. Through Harry, Rowling builds into her novels the possibility of resistance to celebrity book culture, as Harry models the kind of "creative appropriation" possible for children faced with such cultures in the real world.

Another sign of Rowling's knowing use of the commodification of 18 books is the 2001 publication of two of "Harry's favorite books" in support of the U.K. charity Comic Relief, to create "a fund set up in Harry Potter's name . . . specifically to help children in need throughout the world." Both *Fantastic Beasts and Where to Find Them* and *Quidditch through the Ages* are carefully and imaginatively designed to use and comment on the conventions of twenty-first-century publishing. Both books claim to be published by wizard presses (Obscurus and Whizz Hard) "in association with" Scholastic and to be sold in both wizard and Muggle bookstores. On the back covers, below the ISBN number and UPC bar code, the price appears in both Muggle and wizard money: "$3.99 US (14 Sickles 3 Knuts)." Each "special edition" features a foreword by wizard Albus Dumbledore, famous headmaster of Hogwarts; *Quidditch through the Ages* also offers a page of endorsements by several authors the devoted Harry Potter reader will recognize. The most wittily self-referential of these blurbs comes from "Gilderoy Lockhart, author *Magical Me*," who remarks that "Mr. Whisp shows a lot of promise. If he keeps up the good work, he may well find himself sharing a photoshoot with me one of these days!" Rowling's resurrection of Lockhart gives added bite to her parody of both the form and the content of publishing's promotional ephemera.

Quidditch through the Ages claims to be a Hogwarts library book, with 19 a list of borrowers, including Harry, Ron, Hermione, and the heroic Cedric Diggory, noted in the front. *Fantastic Beasts and Where to Find Them* offers a more significant conceit: it is presented as a facsimile of Harry's own book. According to Dumbledore's foreword, "You hold in your hands a duplicate of Harry Potter's own copy of *Fantastic Beasts*, complete with his and his friends' informative notes in the margins. Although Harry seemed a trifle reluctant to allow this book to be reprinted in its present form, our friends at Comic Relief feel that his small additions will add to the entertaining tone of the book" (viii). The "small additions" include games of hangman and tic-tac-toe, Quidditch graffiti, and annotations that allude to Harry's adventures with giant spiders, dragons, merpeople, werewolves, and others. The additions are indeed "entertaining," making the reader who gets the jokes feel especially clever. They also allude again to the role of celebrity in book culture: the fact that *Fantastic Beasts* bears "Harry's signature," even as a joke, does make it more appealing (and hence valuable) to its readers, as does Rowling's signature on individual volumes of the novels themselves. The market for signed copies of the Harry Potter books is strong enough that a Virginia man was able to bilk twenty eBay auction-site buyers out of hundreds of dollars for fraudulent signed first editions. Such fraud is possible because "legitimate first-edition, first-print

Harry Potter books go for more than $3,000 on the open market," according to Matt Duffy of *Auction Watch*.[16] Rowling parodies her fans' interest in books as collectible commodities when she attaches Harry's signature to the charity books at the same time as she uses that interest to generate more money for the Comic Relief fund to which she has also attached his signature and her own.

Most critics who have weighed in on the Harry Potter phenomenon to *20* date have placed the books firmly in the Luddite tradition of children's fantasy. The September 20, 1999, cover article in *Time* concludes with a celebratory contrast between Warner Brothers' plans for "fantastical" special effects for the then upcoming movie — "Technology is now incredible," says the producer — and the "interesting" fact that the wizard world of the books "contains no technology at all. Light is provided by torches and heat by massive fireplaces. Who needs electricity when you have plenty of wizards and magic wands? . . . Technology is for Muggles, who rely on contraptions because they cannot imagine the conveniences of magic. Who wouldn't choose a wizard's life?"[17] The train to Hogwarts, powered by a "scarlet steam engine," serves as a transition from the crowds at Kings Cross to what Alison Lurie calls the "pre-industrial" world of Hogwarts, where students write on rolls of parchment with quills.[18] And full-blooded wizards who have no day-to-day contact with the nonmagical Muggle world can hardly understand — though they are often fascinated by the ingenuity of — telephones or cars or the "escapators" they've heard of in the tube stations they don't need to use.

Certainly the contrast between Harry and his Muggle relatives rein- *21* forces the distance between their commercial, technological world and his purer one. His stupid cousin Dudley Dursley, in particular, who receives stacks of video games one birthday, represents all children obsessed with acquiring and discarding the electronic toys with which his playroom is littered: "Nearly everything . . . was broken. . . . Other shelves were full of books. They were the only things in the room that looked as though they'd never been touched" (*Sorcerer's Stone*, 37–38). Dudley is clearly a nonreader, the figure against whom all children who side with Harry Potter — particularly the formerly nonreading boys to whom the series famously appeals — will set themselves. (Dudley, besides being thuggish, is fat. He clearly descends from Dahl's Augustus Gloop, whose gluttony Rowling can make even more contemptible by implicitly calling on current concern about obesity and inactivity among couch-potato kids.) The Dursleys, Dudley's parents and Harry's guardians, are the kind of materialistic adults who would riot at Toys R Us for the latest Pokémon figure for their darling boy, while giving Harry old socks or fifty-pence pieces as Christmas presents.

[16]Matt Duffy, "Alleged Harry Potter Fraud on eBay."
[17]Paul Gray, "Wild about Harry: The Exploits of a Young Wizard Have Enchanted Kids," 72.
[18]Alison Lurie, "Not for Muggles."

Harry's idol, headmaster Albus Dumbledore, stakes out the anti-Dursley 22 position most clearly when he explains to Harry his reasons for destroying the Sorcerer's Stone of the first novel's title: "As much money and life as you could want! The two things most human beings would choose above all — the trouble is, humans do have a knack of choosing precisely those things that are worst for them" (*Sorcerer's Stone*, 297). Readers who see Rowling's fantasy world as more pure than our reality can turn to such Dumbledorean paradoxes, worthy of Tolkien's Gandalf or Susan Cooper's Merriman, for evidence. The problem with such a reading, however, is that Dumbledore does not represent the majority of Rowling's wizard world. In fact, he resists its desires, turning down a nomination to be Minister of Magic. Dumbledore is considered, even by admiring students, to be "a bit mad" and "off his rocker" (*Sorcerer's Stone*, 123, 302).

The virtuous Dumbledore apart, the wizard world more generally is 23 much like ours: highly commercialized and obsessed with its technologies. Gringott's, the wizard bank, is fully international (Bill Weasley works for its branch in Egypt); it also seems to have no competition. This monopoly troubles no one in the world of the novels, perhaps because Rowling takes care to make the bank a model of integrity and capitalist morality. Over its doors is engraved a poem warning patrons (and potential thieves) that they will "pay dearly" for "the sin of greed" (*Sorcerer's Stone*, 72).

In *Harry Potter and the Goblet of Fire*, the reader learns about interna- 24 tional wizard commerce as well. The Ministry of Magic, which in the earlier books has been concerned with domestic British issues, is revealed to have important international responsibilities. Percy Weasley begins working for the Department of International Cooperation, whose concerns include an effort "to standardize cauldron thickness" (for safety reasons) and to prevent the illegal import of flying carpets (56).

The first set piece of *Goblet of Fire* is also a scene of international magi- 25 cal commerce, when the Weasley family, Hermione, and Harry attend the World Cup of Quidditch. This international sporting event, like the Triwizard Tournament that follows it, not to mention the Olympics, is in theory intended to create wholesome "ties between young witches and wizards of different nationalities." In practice, the World Cup, again like the Olympics or World Cup soccer, is a richly productive site for commercial enterprise. As they approach the stadium, Harry and his friends are besieged by commodity culture: "Salesmen were Apparating every few feet, carrying trays and pushing carts full of extraordinary merchandise." The schlocky souvenirs they "push" are irresistible to the children, who arrive at the game with "their moneybags considerably lighter." The Quidditch stadium, too, is a commercial vehicle, with a "gigantic blackboard . . . flashing advertisements across the field" (*Goblet of Fire*, 187, 93, 94). Rowling is at her most playful in creating the excesses of wizardly mass production, but the humor loses some of its force when the reader remembers that "collectible figures" like those the children buy are part of the vast array of Harry Potter merchandise now available. Though these figures, easily found in bookstore children's sections and on the same Internet sites that sell the books, do not fly or stroll, some of them cost more than one hundred dollars.

Money is always a concern and often a worry in Rowling's world, as 26 we might expect, since expensive accessories of magic — spellbooks, cauldrons, potion ingredients, wands — must be purchased before any magic can be performed. The commercial mystique of wands is especially great. Although, as A. O. Scott points out, Rowling's wands appear to be "artisanal handcrafts,"[19] that fact is used primarily to enhance their market value. Venerable wand merchant and authority Mr. Ollivander himself tells Harry that "no two Ollivander wands are alike" and that "of course, you will never get such good results with another wizard's wand" (*Sorcerer's Stone*, 82–84). Magic wands, like Muggle cars or computers, are marketed to match their buyer's personality, and settling for second-hand will make you a lesser wizard. While wizardly technologies may not look like the commodities we are used to, they are nonetheless marketed and consumed as ours are.

Rowling builds her strongest critique of the importance of money to 27 children on the story of Ron Weasley and his wand, a saga that extends through the first three volumes of the series. The Weasleys, supporting seven children on a Ministry of Magic salary, are not only poorer than most wizards but also famous for their poverty, as the wealthy and sneering Draco Malfoy constantly points out. Because of his poverty, Ron faces a series of what he perceives as humiliations — hand-me-down textbooks, hideous second-hand dress robes, the constant awareness of Harry's comparative wealth — that remind the reader how sensitive children are to the pressures of consumerism. The most important of Ron's humiliations by far is his wand.

Although Mr. Ollivander has made it clear that successful wizards 28 must have custom-fitted wands, Ron begins his Hogwarts career with his brother Charlie's worn-out wand. Worse, when that wand is damaged at the beginning of the second novel, Ron doesn't dare ask his parents for a new one. Through *Chamber of Secrets*, Ron struggles in his classes as his wand, though "patched up . . . with some borrowed Spellotape . . . seems to be damaged beyond repair. It [keeps] crackling and sparking at odd moments" and causes him disaster after disaster both in class and out (95). This wand turns out to have some value, when its tendency to backfire is what foils Lockhart's memory charm on the way to the Chamber of Secrets, but Ron cannot see or recognize that value. He gets his own wand only by luck, when his father wins the lottery at the beginning of *Prisoner of Azkaban*.

Ron's sufferings, along with the more serious anxieties of his loving, 29 courageous parents and older brothers, Fred and George, talented inventors and budding entrepreneurs with no capital, allow Rowling to comment

[19]A. O. Scott, "A Dialogue on Harry Potter."

on the difficulties faced by people who don't have enough money to provide their children with the commodities that trigger self-esteem in capitalist culture. Here, she is making a serious critique. She undermines that critique, however, when she cannot bear to deprive the Weasleys of the commodities and capital that according to Harry their niceness "deserves" (*Prisoner of Azkaban*, 9). In the third novel, Mr. Weasley wins the lottery; in the fourth, Harry himself gives Fred and George his Triwizard Tournament prize money, on the condition that they also replace Ron's embarrassing dress robes (*Goblet of Fire*, 733). Harry as hero is generous and superior to the lure of gold, in part because he has plenty already, but he is also a means for Rowling to sidestep the most painful consequences, for both adults and children, of her magical world's commodity culture.

Rowling's children are fully exposed to the temptations of commerce 30 in the magic world. They love to buy, and a visit to the local village is an occasion to stock up on nose-biting teacups, dungbombs, and "shelves upon shelves of the most succulent-looking sweets imaginable" (*Prisoner of Azkaban*, 197). (What Dudley Dursley is despised for desiring, Harry and his friends eat constantly.) One particular brand of candy, Chocolate Frogs, increases its appeal by including Famous Witch and Wizard trading cards. Although Ron has about five hundred cards, he continues constantly to consume Chocolate Frogs in his search for the rare Agrippa and Ptolemy. Though they most closely resemble baseball cards, Rowling's Witches and Wizards cannot help recalling Pokémon and the more wizardly Magic: The Gathering, as well as the Harry Potter game cards now available at bookstore checkout counters.

And the most important accoutrement of wizard childhood, the 31 broomstick, is the most like Muggle toys. The brand of broomstick one rides is a status symbol, and the best model of one year, Harry's Nimbus 2000, can be made obsolete by the next year's Nimbus 2001, acquired by arch-rival Draco Malfoy. The best broomstick, the "state-of-the-art . . . streamlined, superfine" Firebolt (this is the broom's advertising copy, provided by Rowling), is an object of awed desire, too expensive and exclusive to have a price tag. Naturally responding to this tempting display, Harry realizes he has "never wanted anything as much in his whole life" (*Prisoner of Azkaban*, 51–52). Harry disciplines this desire because "he had a very good broom already," and of course he is rewarded by receiving a Firebolt from the mysterious benefactor later revealed to be the adult who cares the most about Harry — his godfather, Sirius Black. The value of this loving gift only increases in the fourth book, when Harry uses his prized Firebolt to win the first challenge of the Triwizard Tournament. In the case of broomsticks, at least, the novels endorse the value of (high-quality, expensive) consumer goods and of the purchase of those goods as a sign of adult nurturing of children.

Like her account of celebrity book culture, Rowling's depiction of her 32 consuming children is gently satiric. Unlike the adults, however, the children in her world are not punished when they succumb to the lure of commodities. Neither, in our world, are either the children or the adults whose commodities of choice are the Harry Potter books. The adult readers, critics, and publishers concerned with the definition of culture, in particular, have found in Rowling's narratives a story that allows them both to participate in the messy world of millennial commerce and technology and to hold themselves apart from it. The novels' uneven, interesting, and compromised depiction of children and commodity culture offers a useful arena in which such concerns can be thought about, though not satisfactorily resolved.

BIBLIOGRAPHY

Abramson, Marla, Jennifer Clarson, Matthew Flamm, and Kristin Cloberdanz. "Ten People Who Decide What America Reads." *Book Magazine*, July/August 2001, 36–41.

Copeland, Libby. "Sew-cery: Young Fans Conjure Some Wizardly Costumes." *Washington Post*, October 20, 1999, Style.

Duffy, Matt. "Alleged Harry Potter Fraud on eBay." *Auction Watch Daily*, April 9, 2001. <http://www.auctionwatch.com/awdaily/dailynews/april01/1-040901.html>.

Gray, Paul. "Wild about Harry: The Exploits of a Young Wizard Have Enchanted Kids." *Time*, September 20, 1999, 66+.

Le Guin, Ursula K. *Tales of Earthsea*. New York: Harcourt, 2001.

Lurie, Alison. "Not for Muggles." *New York Review of Books*, December 16, 1999. <http://www.nybooks.com/nyrev/WWWarchdisplay.cgi?19991216006R>.

"1999 Women of the Year." *Glamour*, December 1999, 168.

Politics and Prose Bookstore. Washington, D.C. E-mail to subscribers. October 18, 1999.

Pullman, Philip. *The Golden Compass*. New York: Random House, 2000.

Rowling, J. K. *Fantastic Beasts and Where to Find Them, by Newt Scamander*. New York: Scholastic, 2001.

———. *Harry Potter and the Chamber of Secrets*. London: Bloomsbury, 1998. New York: Scholastic, 1999.

———. *Harry Potter and the Goblet of Fire*. London: Bloomsbury, 2000. New York: Scholastic, 2000.

———. *Harry Potter and the Prisoner of Azkaban*. London: Bloomsbury, 1999. New York: Scholastic, 1999.

———. *Harry Potter and the Sorcerer's Stone*. New York: Scholastic, 1998.

Scholastic Press Harry Potter Web Site. <http://www.scholastic.com/harrypotter/jkinterview.htm>.

Scott, A. O. "A Dialogue on Harry Potter." *Slate*. <http://slate.msn.com//code/BookClub.asp>.

Seiter, Ellen. *Sold Separately: Children and Parents in Consumer Culture*. New Brunswick, N.J.: Rutgers University Press, 1993.

Shapiro, Marc. *J. K. Rowling: The Wizard behind Harry Potter*. New York: St. Martin's Griffin, 2000.

Steinberg, Shirley R., and Joe L. Kincheloe, eds. *Kinderculture: The Corporate Construction of Childhood*. Boulder, Colo.: HarperCollins/Westview Press, 1997.

Weeks, Linton. "Charmed, I'm Sure." *Washington Post*, October 20, 1999, Style.

———. "Sheer Sorcery." *Washington Post*, September 9, 1999, Style.

Will, George. "Harry Potter: A Wizard's Return." *Washington Post*, July 4, 2000, Op-ed.

Zipes, Jack. "The Phenomenon of Harry Potter, or Why All the Talk?" In *Sticks and Stones: The Troublesome Success of Children's Literature from Slovenly Peter to Harry Potter*, 170–89. New York: Routledge, 2000.

■   ■   ■

Reading Rhetorically

1. Read the first paragraph of Teare's essay carefully, taking note of how she organizes her introduction to her topic and issue. What different kinds of background information does she offer her readers? What is the central question fueling her essay? Locate and underline her thesis statement. Paraphrase her thesis statement, making sure you express all the different parts of the complicated argument she promises to make in the essay. After you have read the essay once, return to reread the last two sentences of the opening paragraph. Discuss with your classmates where in her essay — and how effectively — Teare answers her own question and presents evidence for her argument.

2. What does Teare assume her readers know or may not know about the Harry Potter books? Point to specific passages that support your conclusions. Given your own experience or lack of experience with Harry Potter (through reading the books or watching the movies), discuss which parts of Teare's argument, if any, might be confusing to those who are not familiar with the series. Does Teare address this potential problem for readers? If so, how? What can you conclude from her work about the most effective ways to use a central example that might be unfamiliar to certain readers in your own writing?

3. How does Teare use other critics' ideas to advance her own argument? You might focus on the passages she quotes from author Ursula Le Guin and critic Jack Zipes. Draw a box around the passages where Teare quotes or paraphrases their ideas, and underline the passages where she connects their ideas to her own larger argument. What can you conclude about effective strategies for using other people's ideas to advance your own argument in your writing?

Inquiring Further

4. Visit Scholastic's Harry Potter Web site (http://www.scholastic.com/harrypotter/home.asp). Analyze the site with Teare's argument in mind. How does the site encourage consumer behavior? How is the site connected to the experience of reading the books? What can you conclude about the uses of a site like this for children? For Scholastic?

5. In paragraph 6, Teare argues that children's literature is "increasingly tainted" by marketing tie-ins like Pokémon books and cards and toys, and the American Girl reading series with accompanying expensive merchandise. Do you agree? (You might take a trip to your local bookstore and examine the relationship between books and toys in the children's section of the store to help you think about this question.) What are the benefits and risks to children of tying books to merchandise? Working with a small group, choose a specific reading series with marketing tie-ins, and generate a list of benefits and risks to children. Debate your choices, and draw conclusions.

6. The Harry Potter series has been both widely praised and widely criticized. Use your library's resources to find reviews of the series in newspapers, magazines, and journals. Read five reviews from different perspectives, and list the aspects of the series each reviewer praises or condemns. What

can you tell about the motivations of the reviewers? Given the reviews you've read, how do you answer the question Teare raises in paragraph 1 about why these books are "a topic of compelling interest to literary, social, and cultural critics"?

Framing Conversations

7. Teare and Henry Jenkins (p. 700) are fascinated by the appeal of fantasy to children. Write an essay in which you draw on both authors' insights about what fantasy narratives offer. How are these authors' ideas complementary? Contradictory? Building on Teare's and Jenkins's ideas and on current examples of fantasy narratives in popular culture, make an argument about what is positive and what is negative about fantasy. You also might consider how the format of the fantasy (book, film, video game) shapes its impact.

8. Teare and Steven Johnson (p. 730) are interested in the way children enjoy becoming experts at their pastimes, whether that means knowing every detail in a series of books or mastering all the stages in a video game. Write an essay in which you draw on these authors' ideas and your own insights to consider the appeal to children of expertise that adults often see as useless. How is this type of expertise positive? How is it negative? You also might draw on reviews of the Harry Potter books that address the "problem" of children becoming obsessed with a series of books, or on articles on children's game culture that address an obsession with game playing.

9. Teare's essay is primarily about the Harry Potter books, but she also examines the toy culture that has sprung up around the series. The marketing of children's toys — and the ideas that are sold to children along with the toys — is also the subject of essays by Ann duCille (p. 458) and Eric Schlosser (p. 754). Write an essay in which you evaluate these authors' arguments about toy culture, and develop an argument about the positive and/or negative aspects of that culture, drawing on specific examples from the readings and toys that are currently on the market.

Assignment Sequences

T he assignment sequences invite different kinds of inquiry from the writing exercises in the questions following each reading. Those questions ask you to consider what you have just read, paying attention to specific aspects of the text and seeking new understanding by placing each reading next to others for examination and written response. In contrast, the assignments here are *sequences,* which means they define a subject for extended inquiry and offer a series of steps through readings and writing assignments that build on one another. For example, you may write an essay in which you analyze a film about American education through the lenses of two authors in this collection. Your next essay may consider the same film in light of different readings and research that gives context to your ideas by describing the ongoing conversation on the issue you are exploring. And yet another essay in the sequence may ask you to analyze test cases, texts from your own college's promotional materials, to see how the issues raised in the film are played out in those publication.

The assignment sequences are a series of assignments. Instead of writing an essay and then moving on to a new topic, you will be writing a series of essays, each essay preparing you for the next, as you consider an issue from different perspectives and a range of sources. As you draw on various combinations of resources over a series of compositions and contribute your own research — from the library or from data you've gathered yourself — your ideas about the issues you write about will become richer and more complex. Through reading, researching, and writing, you become an academic writer in conversation with other academic writers. In addition, these assignments can help you see the world around you — from your daily life at college to a Saturday night at the movies — in unexpected and insightful ways.

As an academic writer, you will need to document your sources carefully, using the guidelines for quoting and citing sources explained in Chapter 7 of the Rhetoric. We have not included page length requirements on these assignments; your instructor will determine this, in accordance with your program's guidelines.

■ **SEQUENCE ONE: What Do Media Representations Tell Us About American Education?** [Edmundson, Giroux, Lorber, Martin, Pratt, Scholes]

These assignments address the stories we tell ourselves through the media about American education. Robert Scholes argues that we tell cultural myths — some of which flatter us, some of which reveal our anxieties — in movies and on television, in advertisements, and on Web sites. The essays in this sequence act as lenses you can use to examine representations of American education — not to label them "true" or "false," "good" or "bad," but to consider what they tell us about the pleasures, the anxieties, and maybe the dangers we see played out in schoolrooms. What does it really mean to be educated in America? These assignments ask you to begin an inquiry into this always-relevant issue.

ASSIGNMENT 1: *Educated by the Movies* [Giroux, Scholes]

This assignment asks you to interpret the way a particular film represents education and to make an argument about the film's attitudes toward American education. What issues are raised in the film, and what resolutions are offered? Who is the intended audience, and how does it shape the film's issues and point? What does the film tell us about the ways Americans see education and the classroom experience? You will need to choose scenes and images to describe and analyze in detail as you build an argument about the way education is represented in this visual text.

To help you sharpen your focus and analyze your visual text, frame your argument in terms drawn from Herry A. Giroux and Robert Scholes. Consider Giroux's belief that children's animated films are "teaching machines" and Scholes's resistance to the cultural myths perpetuated by visual narratives. Use their methods for a close analysis of particular scenes and images, and then draw your own conclusions about the issues you see in the film.

The film you choose might be one that celebrates teachers' relationships with students (*Stand and Deliver, Dangerous Minds, Dead Poets' Society,* or the Harry Potter films, for example) or depicts them in vicious or even mortal conflict (*Teaching Mrs. Tingle, The Faculty, Cheaters,* or the Harry Potter films), or somewhere in between. Choose a visual text that really interests you so you can convey that interest through an argument richly supported with details from the film. Help your readers see what you see when you apply Giroux's and Scholes's insights to your media example, and then explain why the analysis is important.

ASSIGNMENT 2: *What Does Gender Have to Do with It?*
[Lorber, Martin]

Return to the media example you used for Assignment 1, but analyze the film through the lens of gender dynamics. Drawing on Judith Lorber's and/or Karin A. Martin's claims that gender is learned, reconsider the scenes you wrote about for Assignment 1 to analyze the way the film confirms or reimagines (or both) traditional gender dynamics in educational settings. What new issues and details come into focus when you apply Lorber's or Martin's ideas to the scenes? (You also can draw on scenes you did not discuss in your previous paper.) As you write, make sure all the sources you use — the film as a primary source and Lorber or Martin as a secondary source — point your reader toward a central argument about gender dynamics and education in films.

ASSIGNMENT 3: *Broadening the Conversation* [Adding scholarly research to Assignment 1 or 2]

Develop the essay you wrote for Assignment 1 or 2 further with research in your college library. What conversations are unfolding among academic writers on the issue you focused on in that assignment? Talk with a librarian about which research tools will be most effective for finding two or three recent scholarly articles on this issue. Consider drawing not only on resources from education but also on materials from sociology, psychology, or other fields that may give you a broader understanding of the dynamics you analyzed in your essay.

The object of this assignment is not simply to add more secondary sources to your paper, but to use those sources to help you reconsider your position, and, perhaps, see significant new details in your film — maybe in the very scenes you've already analyzed. You may find you need to revise your thesis as you develop a broader understanding of the issue from your research. You also may find that you no longer want to use one or more of the readings from this collection in your final draft, that other framing concepts and examples are more useful for supporting and illustrating the argument you make in your essay.

ASSIGNMENT 4: *Imagined (Perhaps) Communities in Your College*
[Edmundson, Pratt; original research]

Analyze representations of your college on its Web site and in brochures and student catalogs through the conceptual lenses offered by Mark Edmundson and Mary Louise Pratt. How does Edmundson's argument that students expect college to be "lite entertainment," with an emphasis on recreation and enjoyable learning experiences, apply to the images and text in these materials? In particular, consider Pratt's idea of the "imagined community" (an idea she borrows from another scholar, Benedict Anderson) to examine the ways these promotional materials sell the school's social and intellectual environment.

This assignment asks you to read college materials closely, in the same way you analyzed the film, looking for visual and textual details to help you determine the arguments these promotional materials are making about education at your institution. You will need to select specific materials to analyze — perhaps a section of the college's Web site and a brochure. As you focus on specific images and texts, consider both the creators' purpose and the audience. How do Edmundson's and Pratt's insights help you see the arguments these materials make about the value of the education offered at your institution? What do they imply about the school's short-comings? What do you want to teach your readers about these materials? Be sure to offer specific examples to support your central point.

■ SEQUENCE TWO: The "I" in the "We": Exploring Tensions Between Individual and Group Identities [Ehrenreich, hooks, McIntosh, Tobar]

This sequence gives you an opportunity to reflect on the many ways individuals understand their relationship to communities, whether those communities are defined by ethnicity, social class, race, religion, or something else. The writers listed here use their personal experiences as they develop their arguments, moving between those experiences and larger arguments. This sequence gives you an opportunity to consider the issues that arise when you think about yourself in relation to your community identities. It also asks you to think about the rhetorical tactic of drawing on personal experience when making a larger argument: What are the advantages of constructing an argument this way? What are the problems? As you explore these ideas through reading, writing, and research, you may find yourself rethinking your relationship to the various groups that shape your identities; you may also rethink the role of personal experience in your writing.

ASSIGNMENT 1: Seeing a Community Through the Writer's Eye/"I"
[hooks, Tobar]

Examine the tension you see between individuals and communities in the texts by bell hooks and Héctor Tobar. Look closely at the ways both writers move between personal experiences and a larger argument. How does this rhetorical strategy shape the impact of the pieces? How do these writers depict themselves as part of their communities? How do they set themselves apart? How do their representations of themselves in the past and present affect the meaning of their texts?

Write an essay in which you choose specific passages to analyze as you consider the relationship between the individual and the community in these texts. In what ways are these writers' strategies similar? How are they different? What can you conclude about the usefulness of seeing yourself as similar to and different from your communities? How can you use this tension most effectively as a rhetorical tool for making an argument?

ASSIGNMENT 2: Focusing on the Influence of Class and Race
[Ehrenreich, McIntosh]

Reconsider Assignment 1 in light of the ideas about class and race raised by Barbara Ehrenreich or Peggy McIntosh. Both Ehrenreich and McIntosh offer readers tools to see class and race hierarchies that we are often taught to ignore in American culture. How do these tools help you see the role class and race hierarchies play in the relationship between the self and the community in hooks's and Tobar's texts?

In your essay, draw on passages from Ehrenreich or McIntosh (or both, if you find both useful) that help you think about the role of class or race (or both) in the individual and community experiences that hooks and Tobar describe. How do class and race hierarchies work in positive and negative ways? How do they strengthen or weaken the relationship between the individual and his or her community? What further ideas and conclusions can you draw about hooks's and Tobar's arguments — and the strategy of making these arguments through personal experience — when you focus on class or race?

ASSIGNMENT 3: Researching the Relationship Between Individuals and Their Communities [Adding scholarly research to Assignment 1 or 2]

Now that you have written two essays, choose one to develop further with insights drawn from scholarly research on your subject. Using your library's research databases, find two articles that enrich your understanding of the relationship between individuals and their communities. For example, you might use databases through EBSCOhost (be sure to narrow your search to peer-reviewed journals) to search on "group identity and education and race." This is just one possible search, however. Other search terms you might try are "cultural boundaries" and "ethnic groups," and you can narrow your search to the United States or to specific areas of the United States. Your librarian will be able to suggest other search strategies and other databases that might be helpful.

The purpose of your research is to find two articles that will help you develop ideas from one of your two previous essays. To this end, search for framing theories and concepts that will allow you to draw richer analysis from the details and examples in hooks's and Tobar's essays and help you think about your conclusions in new ways. You will need to be willing to rethink and rewrite your essay substantially as you return to your ideas with a fresh perspective and the new meanings you've discovered in the material. Establish a clear thesis to draw through the whole essay as you teach your reader what your research has led you to find significant about individual and group identities in these texts.

ASSIGNMENT 4: Adding Other Voices Through Original Research
[Using interviews or a focus group to develop your ideas]

In this assignment, you have the opportunity to use interviews or a focus group (see Chapter 11) to discover how others have negotiated the relationship between their individual and community identities. Look back through your previous three essays and draw out the most compelling issues and ideas from the readings and research you have done. Based on this work, decide on the form your original research should take. That is, are you more likely to obtain useful material for developing your ideas through two interviews with individuals who have experience with these issues, or through a focus group?

Be sure to make good use of the framing theories and concepts you have explored in the readings and in your research as you plan questions

for your interviews or focus group. For example, you might choose to concentrate on the role education plays in sustaining or changing the relationship between an individual and his or her group identities. Or you
might focus on the way the individual's sense of self tends to shift with
membership in a particular economic, ethnic, religious, or racial group.
These are just two examples of the many paths you might take for focusing
your inquiry and analysis through interviews or a focus group.

Whatever the focus of your original research, have a clear goal in
mind about the material you want to gather so that you will have rich data
to work with as you develop a thesis for your final essay of this sequence.
You may find that you will need to do more library research to make sense
of your findings. You also may decide to use passages in the textbook readings that you have not used before; or you may return to familiar passages
but use them in new ways.

■ SEQUENCE THREE: The Benefits and Costs of Researching Others [Ehrenreich, Kimmel, Kozol, Martin]

This sequence asks you to think carefully about the relationship researchers
establish with those they study. What seem to be the advantages and disadvantages of what is called *human subjects research*? What different kinds of data do
researchers collect? What do you, as a reader, think about the conclusions they
draw about this data? The reading, thinking, and writing in this sequence
should make you more aware of the many methods we use to gather information about one another, and help you to think carefully about the conclusions
we draw based on that information.

ASSIGNMENT 1: *Researchers in the Field* [Kozol, Martin]

Examine the texts by Jonathan Kozol and Karin A. Martin with a focus on
the methods each uses to gather information about others. How do each
of their methods — a range of observation and interview strategies —
affect the information they collect? What are the advantages of the methods used in these two texts? The disadvantages? Do the texts address the
ethical issues of human-subject research? You also might examine how
each author characterizes the relationship between him- or herself and
those being observed or interviewed. Does the researcher seem affected or
changed by the process or the material gathered? If so, how?

Write an essay that explores the complexities of researching others,
drawing on examples and ideas from Kozol's and Martin's texts. Choose a
focus for your essay that will allow you to teach your readers what you
find most significant about the complex relationship between researchers
and their human subjects.

ASSIGNMENT 2: *Questioning the "Us" versus "Them" Divide* [Ehrenreich, Kimmel]

Use the texts by Barbara Ehrenreich or Michael S. Kimmel to think further about the "us" versus "them" divide, the division between researchers
and those they study. Ehrenreich's decision to go undercover for her
research blurs the line between writer-researcher and subject. Kimmel

pushes us to think about "us" versus "them" by questioning the category "terrorist" in his analysis of the 9/11 hijackers and Timothy McVeigh. He suggests we miss a lot if we see the world only in terms of "us" and "them."

Using insights from Ehrenreich or Kimmel (or both, if you find them useful), return to your first essay and reconsider the "us" and "them" categories in Kozol's and Martin's texts. What do you see now that you didn't see before about the way these categories work in the authors' essays? What are the implications of maintaining these categories? Of dissolving them? Help your reader see fresh aspects of these texts using tools from Ehrenreich or Kimmel to explore these questions.

ASSIGNMENT 3: *Researching the Researching of Others*
[Adding research to Assignment 1 or 2]

To develop your ideas in Assignment 1 or 2 (or a combination of both), find out what other scholars are saying about the challenges of human subjects research. You might begin with a general search of EBSCOhost or JSTOR to get a sense of the current conversation on this topic. Start with the term "human subjects research"; then narrow your search to focus on your particular interest by adding the words "and ethics," or "and children," for example. Consider conducting a similar search for materials in a subject database (psychology, sociology, education) if one is available.

Select two scholarly sources that will help you reconsider and develop ideas that have emerged in your first two essays for this sequence about researching others. You may find that you need to return to the readings to make use of different passages. Or you may decide not to use one of the readings you wrote about previously, as you allow your research and thinking to move in a new direction or further down a specific path. Help your readers see what you find most compelling or problematic about the process of researching others, offering framing concepts and examples from your sources to develop and illustrate your claims.

ASSIGNMENT 4: *Adding Voices from Your Campus or Community*
[Interviewing human subjects researchers]

Interview one or two people on campus or in the community (perhaps at a medical facility) who do human subjects research. Alternatively, you might interview someone who sits on the Institutional Review Board on your campus, the group that regulates and approves human and animal subjects research. Using the strategies described in Chapter 11, develop questions for your interviewees that will help you learn more about the aspects of researching others that you find most compelling. For example, you might ask how ethical considerations shape the person's research or what challenges the researcher has faced in the process of studying other people. Or you might ask about the kinds of relationships or power dynamics that arise between a researcher and his or her subjects. Be sure to shape your questions in ways that will invite substantive responses that are pertinent to this assignment.

Contextualize your interviewees' ideas with framing concepts from the texts you have read for this sequence. Consider the ways your interviews confirm, contradict, complicate, or enrich the scholarly conversation you've discovered through your reading and research. And, as you would with any other text, be sure you are analyzing not just what your interviewees say but how they say it.

■ SEQUENCE FOUR: Visualizing Meaning: How Do Images Make Arguments? [Helmers, Jenkins, Kilbourne, Selfe]

This sequence gives you the opportunity to practice analyzing images in order to consider how visual arguments work. We are surrounded by images in our culture, so it is important to learn how to make sense of what these images tell us about what we believe and what others want us to believe. The readings in this sequence offer concrete strategies for analyzing visual arguments on Web sites and in advertisements and video games. You will have the opportunity to pursue areas of interest to you, both through your research and the test cases you analyze. Reading, researching, collecting, and writing about visual arguments will help you see the world around you with fresh — and perhaps startling — clarity.

ASSIGNMENT 1: *Analyzing Advertising* [Kilbourne, Selfe]

Consider the strategies Jean Kilbourne and Cynthia L. Selfe use to analyze advertisements, and apply their insights to three advertisements of your choice. Kilbourne and Selfe argue that images are not neutral, that like any text, they project perspectives and arguments. Reread the authors' essays to determine their most effective strategies for analyzing the images and language in advertisements. How are their strategies similar? How are they different?

Choose three visual advertisements that share a focus or theme that interests you, and, using tools drawn from Kilbourne and Selfe, write an essay about how these advertisements make their arguments. Consider the assumptions the ads make about their audience, and the ideas and associations they play on in order to sell the product. How does the language of each ad work in relation to the image? As you teach your reader how Kilbourne and Selfe help you analyze these visual arguments, be sure to offer concrete examples to illustrate your claims and to explain why a particular method of analysis is important.

ASSIGNMENT 2: *Applying a Critical Eye to the Web* [Helmers, Jenkins]

Although Marguerite Helmers and Henry Jenkins focus their analysis on the visual aspects of computer culture rather than on advertisements, their ideas about Web sites and video games will help you build on the analytical strategies you practiced in Assignment 1. Choose a Web site or video game to examine through the lens of either Helmers's or Jenkins's essay. What arguments does the Web site or video game make? Draw on your insights from your first essay to analyze the assumptions your current example makes about the gender (or other identity categories) or the values and interests of those who interact with the Web site or game. What meanings come into focus when you apply these scholars' insights to this example? How are they significant? Illustrate your claims with details from your example.

ASSIGNMENT 3: What Is the Broader Conversation About Visual Arguments? [Adding scholarly research to Assignment 1 or 2]

Develop your Assignment 1 or 2 essay through scholarly research. Which of the ideas you've read and written about concerning visual arguments spark your interest most? Building on those ideas, use your library's databases to find out what other scholars have said on your particular topic. For example, you might begin with a general database like EBSCOhost and a search on "advertising and gender" or "video games and race" — to name just two of the many possibilities. Your librarian can help you narrow your search and find the most useful database for your needs. Read broadly enough in your search results to gain a clear sense of the scholarly conversation on your issue, and select two articles that will help you further develop the ideas you have written about for this sequence.

Given the direction your essay takes, you may want to return to the examples you used in the earlier assignments, or you may decide to use fresh passages and examples to support the focus and argument in this essay. Drawing on the broader conversation you've researched and joined, what new ideas can you teach your readers?

ASSIGNMENT 4: Working with a Larger Archive [Developing your ideas with test cases]

This assignment requires you to gather test-case materials to analyze, using the readings in this sequence. So, depending on your interests, develop a collection of advertisements, video games, or Web sites to use as your data for this essay. Think carefully about what you would like to learn from this process to be sure the materials you collect will address your interest. Your instructor and classmates can also help you reflect on how best to develop a collection and how large your collection should be to answer your research question responsibly.

Draw on the theories and ideas you have read and learned in the assignments in this sequence, and apply them to your collection of test cases to help you explore the significance of your collection and address your focus in this essay. This essay is your opportunity to contribute to the scholarly conversation on how visual arguments work because you will be the expert on the collection of materials you are using for your content analysis.

▦ SEQUENCE FIVE: Reading Bodies [duCille, Dworkin and Messner, Foer, Ignatiev]

This sequence asks you to analyze bodies as cultural texts, to consider what we can learn about cultural beliefs from the ways we learn to appear, move, and act. The readings and assignments ask you to consider, from different perspectives, how our bodies display cultural values. An awareness of the arguments bodies make may allow you to analyze popular culture in a new way, as well as consider the ways your own body is capable of confirming or challenging cultural expectations.

ASSIGNMENT 1: *Plastic Bodies: How Are Our Bodies Commodities?*
[duCille, Giroux]

Read Ann duCille's analysis of multicultural Barbie dolls and Henry Giroux's argument about gender in children's films, and consider what it means that our culture places so much emphasis on buying into — or just buying — a certain kind of body and identity. Although duCille focuses on toy culture, her argument is a broader one about the kinds of bodies that "sell" in American culture. Similarly, Giroux sees children's films as "teaching machines" that sell stereotypes about gender and race hand-in-hand with popular culture.

In your own essay, use duCille's and Giroux's ideas to help you think about the significance of these cultural trends in children's entertainment. What are these authors pessimistic or optimistic about, and where do you place yourself in this conversation? These authors focus on female bodies and experience, but you certainly can choose to apply their insights to male bodies and experience. Using specific insights and analyzing examples from each text, teach your readers what you find most significant about what you've learned.

ASSIGNMENT 2: *Sporting Bodies: What Can We Learn from the Games We Play?* [Dworkin and Messner, Foer]

Reconsider the ideas you wrote about for Assignment 1 in the context of sports culture. How do our expectations of what gendered bodies should look like influence our ideas about female and male athletes? What role does money play (in the form of athletic scholarships for students, or salaries and commercial contracts for professional athletes) in demonstrating the kinds of sporting bodies our culture values?

Using concepts and examples from Shari L. Dworkin and Michael A. Messner's text and/or Franklin Foer's text, write an essay in which you address these questions. Don't leave behind the ideas you explored in your first essay; instead, think about how duCille's and Giroux's insights might apply to the sports culture. Use concrete examples to illustrate your claims. (A quick look through any sports magazine should provide you with lots of examples to analyze.) You want to anchor your ideas to the concepts you've learned and so strengthen your argument.

ASSIGNMENT 3: *What Role Does Race Play?* [Ignatiev; adding scholarly research to Assignment 1 or 2]

Return to the essays you wrote for Assignments 1 and 2, and choose one to develop in light of the role race plays in the way we "read" bodies. Noel Ignatiev's ideas about assimilation should help you think about the ways racial categories work in the United States, both asserting differences between us and shifting over time. Whichever essay you choose to develop with a focus on race, reread the texts with fresh eyes to find passages on race that might help you develop your own thinking.

In addition, investigate the broader scholarly conversation about interpreting race. Search EBSCOhost, JSTOR, or another source recommended by a librarian for an article to help you analyze the role of race in the context of your essay's focus (sports culture, "buying" bodies, remaking bodies, for example). Work with a librarian to develop search terms that will yield the best results, an article that offers you the analytical tools you need for a fresh focus.

ASSIGNMENT 4: Hearing from Your Peers [Using a focus group to develop your ideas]

Use a focus group to find out what your peers think about an issue you have written about in this sequence. (Refer to the discussion in Chapter 11 about designing and conducting an effective focus group.) Given the topics and issues you have explored in these essays, decide on a specific focus for this final paper that can be enriched with the data you collect in a focus group. Think carefully about the kinds of information you need as you choose participants for the focus group and write your questions for them. (See Chapter 11, too, for a discussion of the kinds of claims you can make based on focus-group data.) As you consider how best to analyze and contextualize the material you gather in your focus group, return to your previous essays and the readings themselves to choose the most useful tools to make sense of your findings.

▨ SEQUENCE SIX: Telling Histories: Whose Perspective Has the Final Word? [Diamond, Frank, Loewen, Pratt]

This sequence invites you to use the insights of specific scholars to explore the significance of understanding history as subjective rather than objective. How are the stories we tell about our past just as much about our understanding of ourselves and others in the present as they are about what actually happened? The readings and essay assignments here will guide you through successive stages of inquiry about the nature of history and the complexity of teaching history. What happens when we misunderstand our past? How do students and teachers make sense of different perspectives on historical events? This sequence may not lead you to final answers, but it will help you fine-tune your understanding of the uses of history.

ASSIGNMENT 1: Schooled in History: The Significance of How We Learn About the Past [Loewen, Pratt]

Teach your readers what you find most significant about the ideas of James W. Loewen and Mary Louise Pratt, who write about history and education from slightly different perspectives. As you reread their texts, imagine how each writer would analyze the concepts of the other. On which points would they agree? On which points would they disagree? Given the many ways history gets distorted, how can we ever learn the truth about the past? What solutions does each writer offer, if any?

In your own essay, construct an argument based on what you've learned from these readings about how history ought to be taught and why. If you like, you can draw on your own experiences learning history or examples from history texts you've used in school to help you build your point.

ASSIGNMENT 2: How Can We Use History to See Ourselves More Clearly? [Diamond, Frank]

Take the conclusions you drew in Assignment 1, and focus on how you think we can best use history to better understand our present-day selves. Use the work of either Jared Diamond or Thomas Frank to help you reframe your ideas. How — and why — do we often fail to learn either positive or negative lessons from history?

Return to your first essay with Diamond's or Frank's text fresh in your mind, and consider which text will be the most effective tool for pushing your thoughts in this new direction. Be sure to place this additional author in conversation with Loewen and Pratt as you develop your argument. Feel free to include other examples of learning or failing to learn from history to support your argument.

ASSIGNMENT 3: Expanding the Conversation [Including other scholarly voices]

Develop your ideas about the challenges of learning about and from history by researching what other scholars have said about a specific historic event. Explore an event you mention in Assignments 1 or 2, or use this assignment to find out more about another historical event. Start with an EBSCOhost search on the event. Your librarian can help you shape your search as well.

Find two articles that will help you build on the ideas you find most interesting in your previous essays for this sequence. Think about what you would like to teach your readers about the ways this historical event has been understood, misunderstood, taught, and learned. You might focus on the implications for students of history, or for citizens who understand or misunderstand their country's history. Whatever focus you choose, be sure to place your new articles in conversation with specific ideas from the texts you have been writing about. Make sure every paragraph of the essay points your readers toward your particular focus and argument.

ASSIGNMENT 4: What Insights Do Other History Teachers Have? [Using interviews to gain new perspectives]

Review the suggestions in Chapter 11 about constructing and conducting interviews, and then design interviews with two professors or instructors of history. (You can choose to interview teachers of any educational level, depending on your particular interests.) Decide on a specific focus for your paper that will allow you to develop ideas from your previous essays in this sequence, and build on the readings and research you have done. Think about what your interviewees can offer in terms of insights about how teaching history has changed over the years, how they think students learn best, or what misconceptions students often have — whatever best suits your focus for this essay. This is your opportunity to find out "from the horse's mouth" what it's like to teach history. So, seize the moment to learn what you would most like to learn about the perspective from the front of the history classroom. As you construct an argument about the teaching of history, add context to your interview data with the sources you've read for this sequence.

(Acknowledgments continued from p. ii)

Jared Diamond. "Why Do Some Societies Make Disastrous Decisions?" From *Collapse: How Societies Choose to Fail or Succeed* by Jared Diamond. Copyright © 2005 by Jared Diamond. Used by permission of Viking Penguin, a division of Penguin Group (USA) Inc.

Ann duCille. "Dyes and Dolls: Multicultural Barbie and the Merchandising of Difference." Originally published in *differences: A Journal of Feminist Cultural Studies*, vol. 6, no. 1 (Spring 1994). Copyright © 1994 by Ann duCille. Reprinted with permission of the author.

Shari L. Dworkin and Michael A. Messner. "Just Do . . . What? Sport, Bodies, Gender." From *Revisioning Gender*, edited by Myra Marx Feree, Judith Lorber, and Beth B. Hess. Copyright © 1999. Reprinted by permission of Sage Publications, Inc.

Mark Edmundson. "On the Uses of a Liberal Education." Copyright © 1997 by *Harper's Magazine*. All rights reserved. Reproduced from the September issue by special permission.

Barbara Ehrenreich. "Cultural Baggage." From *The New York Times Magazine*, April 5, 1992. Copyright © 1992 by Barbara Ehrenreich. Reprinted with permission. "Maid to Order: The Politics of Other Women's Work." Originally published in *Harper's Magazine*, April 2000. Copyright © 2000 by Barbara Ehrenreich. Reprinted by permission of International Creative Management.

Franklin Foer. Prologue and "How Soccer Explains the American Culture Wars." From *How Soccer Explains the World: An Unlikely Theory of Globalization* by Franklin Foer. Copyright © 2004 by Franklin Foer. Reprinted by permission of HarperCollins Publishers.

Thomas Frank. "The Two Nations" (and corresponding notes). From *What's the Matter with Kansas? How Conservatives Won the Heart of America* by Thomas Frank. Copyright © 2004 by Thomas Frank. Reprinted by permission of Henry Holt & Company, LLC.

Thomas L. Friedman. "While I Was Sleeping." Excerpts from *The World Is Flat: A Brief History of the Twenty-First Century* by Thomas L. Friedman. Copyright © 2005 by Thomas L. Friedman. Reprinted by permission of Farrar, Straus & Giroux, LLC.

Henry A. Giroux. "Children's Culture and Disney's Animated Films." From *The Mouse That Roared: Disney and the End of Innocence* by Henry A. Giroux. Copyright © 1999 by Henry A. Giroux. Reprinted by permission of Rowman and Littlefield Publishers, Inc.

Malcolm Gladwell. Introduction and "Case Study: Suicide, Smoking, and the Search for the Unsticky Cigarette." Excerpted from *The Tipping Point: How Little Things Can Make a Big Difference* by Malcolm Gladwell. Copyright © 2000 by Malcolm Gladwell. Reprinted by permission of Little, Brown and Company.

Marguerite Helmers. "Media, Discourse, and the Public Sphere: Electronic Memorials to Diana, Princess of Wales." From *College English*, vol. 63, no. 4 (March 2001). Copyright © 2001 by the National Council of Teachers of English. Reprinted and used with permission.

E. D. Hirsch Jr. "Preface to *Cultural Literacy*." From *Cultural Literacy* by E. D. Hirsch Jr. Copyright © 1987 by Houghton Mifflin Company. Reprinted by permission of Houghton Mifflin Company. All rights reserved.

bell hooks. "Teaching to Transgress" and "Engaged Pedagogy." From *Teaching to Transgress: Education as the Practice of Freedom* by bell hooks. Copyright © 1994 by bell hooks. Reproduced by permission of Routledge, a division of Taylor & Francis Group.

Myra Sadker and David Sadker. "Hidden Lessons." From *Failing at Fairness: How Our Schools Cheat Girls* from *The New York Times*. Copyright © 1994 by Myra Sadker and David Sadker. Reprinted with the permission of Scribner, an imprint of Simon & Schuster. All rights reserved.

Eric Schlosser. "Your Trusted Friends." From *Fast Food Nation: The Dark Side of the All-American Meal* by Eric Schlosser. Reprinted by permission of Houghton Mifflin Company.

Robert Scholes. "On Reading a Video Text." Excerpted from *Protocols of Reading* by Robert Scholes. Copyright © 1989 by Yale University Press. Reprinted by permission of the publisher.

Cynthia L. Selfe. "Lest We Think the Revolution Is a Revolution: Images of Technology and the Nature of Change." Originally published in *Passions, Pedagogies, and 21st Century Technologies*, edited by Gail Hawisher and Cynthia L. Selfe. Copyright © 1999 by Cynthia Selfe. Reprinted by permission of Utah State University Press.

Ronald Takaki. "Policies: Strategies and Solutions." From *Debating Diversity: Clashing Perspectives on Race and Ethnicity in America*, Third Edition, edited by Ronald Takaki. Copyright © 2002 by Oxford University Press, Inc. Reprinted with the permission of Oxford University Press, Inc.

Deborah Tannen. "Talking Up Close: Status and Connection." From *You Just Don't Understand* by Deborah Tannen, PhD. Copyright © 1990 by Deborah Tannen. Reprinted by permission of HarperCollins Publishers, Inc.

Elizabeth Teare. "Harry Potter and the Technology of Magic." From *The Ivory Tower and Harry Potter: Perspectives on a Literary Phenomenon*, edited by Lana A. Whited. Copyright © 2002 by the Curators of the University of Missouri. Reprinted by permission of the University of Missouri Press.

Héctor Tobar. "Americanismo: City of Peasants." Originally published in *Translation Nation: Defining a New American Identity in the Spanish-Speaking United States* by Héctor Tobar. Copyright © 2005 by Héctor Tobar. Reprinted by permission of William Morris Agency, LLC on behalf of the author.

Index of Authors, Titles, and Key Terms

abstract, 119
AIDS in Women: A Growing Educational Concern (student writer), 98
Americanismo: City of Peasants, 533
analysis, 12
anecdote, 217
annotate, 25
annotated bibliography, 253
Anyon, Jean
  Economic Is Political, The, 190
Appiah, Kwame Anthony
  Moral Disagreement, 378
argument, 2
Arts of the Contact Zone, 354
ask questions, 13
audience, 34
authoritative source, 55

Becoming a Gendered Body: Practices of Preschools, 632
binary thinking, 16
block quotation, 155

Children's Culture and Disney's Animated Films, 567
claim, 3, 34, 47
claim of fact, 51
claim of policy, 52
claim of value, 52

comparison, 218
"Complete Freedom of Movement": Video Games as Gendered Play Spaces, 700
concession, 56
conclusion, 181
constraint, 73
context, 89
contrast, 218
core skills, 3
counterargument, 57
critical reading, 25
critical thinking, 2
Cultural Baggage, 43

data, 216
Debating the Civil Rights Movement: The View from the Nation, 131
Debating the Civil Rights Movement: The View from the Trenches, 139
deductive argument, 182
Diamond, Jared
  Why Do Some Societies Make Disastrous Decisions?, 390
duCille, Ann
  Dyes and Dolls: Multicultural Barbie and the Merchandising of Difference, 458

Dworkin, Shari L., and Michael A.
    Messner
  Just Do . . . What? Sport, Bodies,
    Gender, 551
Dyes and Dolls: Multicultural Barbie
    and the Merchandising of Differ-
    ence, 458

Eck, Jenny (student writer)
  Nuestra Clase: Making the Class-
    room a Welcoming Place
    for English Language
    Learners, 89
Economic Is Political, The, 190
editing, 228
Edmundson, Mark
  On the Uses of a Liberal
    Education, 277
Ehrenreich, Barbara
  Cultural Baggage, 43
  Maid to Order: The Politics of Other
    Women's Work, 479
ellipsis, 155
empathy, 19
ethos, 167
Everything Bad Is Good for You:
    How Today's Popular
    Culture Is Actually Making Us
    Smarter, 730
evidence, 47
examine alternatives, 13
example, 216
expert testimony, 55

focus group, 265
Foer, Franklin
  How Soccer Explains the World: An
    Unlikely Theory of Globalization,
    406
frame, 71
Frank, Thomas
  Two Nations, The, 497
Friedman, Thomas L.
  While I Was Sleeping, 417

Gender, Class, and Terrorism, 448
genre, 35
Giroux, Henry A.
  Children's Culture and Disney's Ani-
    mated Films, 567
gist of an argument, 134
Gladwell, Malcolm
  Tipping Point: How Little Things
    Can Make a Big Difference, The,
    432

habits of mind, 2, 11
Harry Potter and the Technology of
    Magic, 800
Heath, Shirley Brice
  Protean Shapes in Literacy Events:
    Ever-Shifting Oral and Literate
    Traditions, 95
Helmers, Marguerite
  Media, Discourse, and the
    Public Sphere: Electronic
    Memorials to Diana, Princess
    of Wales, 679
Hidden Lessons, 48
Hirsch Jr., E. D.
  Preface to *Cultural Literacy*, 29
Hispanic in America: Starting
    Points, 40
hooks, bell
  Teaching to Transgress: Education
    as the Practice of Freedom,
    293
How Soccer Explains the World:
    An Unlikely Theory of Globaliza-
    tion, 406

Ignatiev, Noel
  Immigrants and Whites, 512
Immigrants and Whites, 512
index, 120
inductive argument, 182
inference, 51
inquiry, 13
interpretation, 51
interrogative introduction, 204
interview, 261
inverted-triangle introduction,
    202
irony, 177
Isasi-Díaz, Ada María
  Hispanic in America: Starting
    Points, 40
issue, 4, 16
issue-based question, 78

Jenkins, Henry
  "Complete Freedom of Movement":
    Video Games as Gendered Play
    Spaces, 700
Johnson, Steven
  Everything Bad Is Good for You:
    How Today's Popular Culture
    Is Actually Making Us
    Smarter, 730
Just Do . . . What? Sport, Bodies,
    Gender, 551

keyword, 115
Kilbourne, Jean
 "Two Ways a Woman Can Get
   Hurt": Advertising and
   Violence, 592
Kimmel, Michael S.
 Gender, Class, and Terrorism, 448
Kozol, Jonathan
 Still Separate, Still Unequal:
   America's Educational Apartheid,
   308

Land of Opportunity, The, 168
Lawson, Steven F.
 Debating the Civil Rights Move-
   ment: The View from the
   Nation, 131
Lest We Think the Revolution Is a
   Revolution: Images of Technol-
   ogy and the Nature of Change,
   783
Lies My Teacher Told Me: Everything
   Your American History Textbook
   Got Wrong, 332
Loewen, James W.
 Land of Opportunity, The, 168
 Lies My Teacher Told Me: Every-
   thing Your American History
   Textbook Got Wrong, 332
logical fallacy, 186
logos, 167
Lorber, Judith
 "Night to His Day": The Social Con-
   struction of Gender, 617

Maid to Order: The Politics of Other
   Women's Work, 479
main claim, 34
Martin, Karin A.
 Becoming a Gendered Body: Prac-
   tices of Preschools, 632
Martínez, Elizabeth
 Reinventing "America": Call for a
   New National Identity, 209
McIntosh, Peggy
 White Privilege and Male Privilege:
   A Personal Account of Coming
   to See Correspondences
   Through Work in Women's
   Studies, 520
Media, Discourse, and the Public
   Sphere: Electronic Memorials to
   Diana, Princess of Wales, 679
Memory Through Photography (early
   draft) (student writer), 235

Memory Through Photography
   (second draft) (student writer), 239
Memory Through Photography (near-
   final draft) (student writer), 243
Messner, Michael A., and Shari L.
   Dworkin
 Just Do . . . What?: Sport, Bodies,
   Gender, 551
Metheny, Ryan (student writer)
 Problems and Dangers of Assimila-
   tory Policies, The, 59
minding-the-gap introduction, 206
minor claim, 34
Moral Disagreement, 378

narrative, 203
"Night to His Day": The Social Con-
   struction of Gender, 617
No Place Like Home, 74
Nuestra Clase: Making the Classroom
   a Welcoming Place for English
   Language Learners (student
   writer), 89

observation, 13
On Reading a Video Text, 370
On the Uses of a Liberal Education,
   277
original research, 249

paradoxical introduction, 205
paraphrase, 126
pathos, 167
Payne, Charles
 Debating the Civil Rights Move-
   ment: The View from the
   Trenches, 139
peer review, 111
plagiarism, 150
Policies: Strategies and Solutions, 142
popular source, 111
Potish, Jessie (student writer)
 AIDS in Women: A Growing Educa-
   tional Concern, 98
Pratt, Mary Louise
 Arts of the Contact Zone, 354
Preacher, Brett (student writer)
 Representing Poverty in Million
   Dollar Baby, 231
Preface to Cultural Literacy, 29
premise, 181
primary source, 110, 249
Problems and Dangers of Assimilatory
   Policies, The (student writer), 59
proposal, 251

Protean Shapes in Literacy Events: Ever-Shifting Oral and Literate Traditions, 95
purpose, 33

Quindlen, Anna
   No Place Like Home, 74
quotation(s), 152

Reinventing "America": Call for a New National Identity, 209
relevance, 54
Representing Poverty in *Million Dollar Baby* (student writer), 231
Research Paper Proposal: A Case Study of One Homeless Child's Education and Lifestyle (student writer), 257
researched argument, 59
revising, 227
rhetoric, 3
rhetorical analysis, 29
Rogerian approach to argument, 58
Ronan, Mary (student writer)
   Research Paper Proposal: A Case Study of One Homeless Child's Education and Lifestyle, 257

Sadker, Myra, and David Sadker
   Hidden Lessons, 48
sarcasm, 177
Schlosser, Eric
   Your Trusted Friends, 754
scholarly source, 111
Scholes, Robert
   On Reading a Video Text, 370
secondary source, 110
Selfe, Cynthia L.
   Lest We Think the Revolution Is a Revolution: Images of Technology and the Nature of Change, 783
situation, 33
skimming, 119
source, 4
statistic, 55
Still Separate, Still Unequal: America's Educational Apartheid, 308
story, 203

summary, 130
syllogism, 182
synthesis, 138

Takaki, Ronald
   Policies: Strategies and Solutions, 142
Talking Up Close: Status and Connection, 654
Tannen, Deborah
   Talking Up Close: Status and Connection, 654
Taylor, Tasha (student writer)
   Memory Through Photography (early draft), 235
   Memory Through Photography (second draft), 239
   Memory Through Photography (near-final draft), 243
Teaching to Transgress: Education as the Practice of Freedom, 293
Teare, Elizabeth
   Harry Potter and the Technology of Magic, 800
thesis, 4, 34, 83
timeline, 256
Tipping Point: How Little Things Can Make a Big Difference, The, 432
Tobar, Héctor
   Americanismo: City of Peasants, 533
tone, 177
topic, 78
topic sentence, 213
transition word, 215
Two Nations, The, 497
"Two Ways a Woman Can Get Hurt": Advertising and Violence, 592

While I Was Sleeping, 417
White Privilege and Male Privilege: A Personal Account of Coming to See Correspondences Through Work in Women's Studies, 520
Why Do Some Societies Make Disastrous Decisions?, 390
working thesis, 84

Your Trusted Friends, 754